Simulation
Using
GPSS

Contents

3 Sampling from Probability Distributions in GPSS

4 Intermediate GPSS Modeling Concepts, Part I

List of Case Studies

Simulation
Using
GPSS

Simulation Using GPSS

Thomas J. Schriber

Professor of Management Science
The University of Michigan

John Wiley & Sons

New York   London   Sydney   Toronto

Library of Congress Cataloging in Publication Data:

Schriber, Thomas J   1935–
   Simulation Using GPSS.

   Bibliography: p.
   1. GPSS (Computer program language)   2. Digital
computer simulation.   I. Title.
QA76.73.G18S37   001.6'425   73–21896
ISBN 0–471–76310–1

Printed in the United States of America

10 9 8 7 6 5 4 3 2 1

To Ann,
in recognition of the many hours stolen from our family life for this writing task, and with thanks for her patience, understanding, and good cheer

Preface

GPSS (*General Purpose Simulation System*) is a simulation programming language used to build computer models for discrete-event simulations. This book's objective is to help the reader to acquire active mastery of GPSS. In striving for this objective, the book introduces fundamental concepts of discrete-event simulation, describes their implementation in GPSS, illustrates their application through a series of 27 GPSS case studies, and poses over 300 problems for the reader to use in testing his or her understanding of the material.

As a simulation programming language, GPSS contains special features for reproducing the dynamic behavior of systems which operate in time, and in which changes of state occur at discrete points in time. When used to model such systems, GPSS offers programming convenience, and at the same time serves as a vehicle for concept articulation. This latter point makes GPSS more than just another programming language. Indeed, GPSS is an excellent medium through which to teach and learn many concepts of discrete-event simulation in a highly pragmatic fashion.

Of its nature, discrete-event simulation presupposes a fundamental understanding of probability and statistics. The reader is expected to have had a first course in the precalculus probability, with some elementary statistics included. There are no other requirements for learning GPSS and the underlying modeling concepts which the language supports. Prior programming experience, although perhaps desirable, is not necessary. In fact, those already familiar with a procedural language (such as FORTRAN, or BASIC, or PL/I) will discover that they must set aside several key procedural ideas in coming to grips with GPSS. With or without previous knowledge of programming, the person who uses this book will be delighted to discover how easily and rapidly simulation models can be built in GPSS, once the initial learning threshhold has been crossed and the GPSS worldview has been mastered.

GPSS offers programming convenience because the GPSS simulator itself accomplishes many tasks automatically which would otherwise fall to the model builder. For example, GPSS implicitly and unobtrusively collects data describing a model's simulated behavior, then automatically prints out summaries of these data at the end of a simulation. The model builder need not supply computational statements for collecting and summarizing these data, or provide format statements indicating how the data summaries are to be displayed. Other, more imaginative things are also accomplished in the language at an implicit level. For example, GPSS maintains a simulated clock, schedules events to occur in future simulated time, causes these events to occur in the proper, time-ordered sequence, and provides a means of assigning relative priorities to be used in resolving time ties.

It is clear, then, that much of the underlying logic of discrete-event simulation is built into the GPSS simulator. Unfortunately, this language advantage becomes a *disadvantage* for the model builder who does not understand the simulator's internal logic, and yields to the temptation to use GPSS blindly. Blind use of this high-level language almost invariably results in model invalidities. These invalidities are frequently of a subtle nature, and therefore can easily go undetected. This book carefully takes these considerations into account and, as described below, follows an approach designed to produce a model builder who thoroughly understands the GPSS models which he or she creates.

The plan of the book is straightforward. Chapter 1 introduces key simulation concepts at the procedural level, in pre-GPSS fashion. In particular, Chapter 1 provides a brief introduction to the modeling of systems in which events occur at random. The essence of the chapter is a procedural model for a one-line, one-server queuing system. Developed and presented through a series of standard flow-charts, the model provides a vehicle for discussing such things as random number generators, the concept of event scheduling, the logic involved in ordering events over time, and the problem of time ties. It serves as a springboard into Chapter 2 which introduces GPSS and a basic subset of the Blocks used to construct GPSS models. The first GPSS case study in Chapter 2 is a model for the same one-line, one-server system modeled in Chapter 1. This makes it possible for the reader to compare the step-by-step, procedural approach of the first chapter with the much more highly macro approach used to model the identical system in GPSS.

Immediately after the first Chapter 2 case study, the GPSS Current and Future Events Chains are introduced, and fundamentals of the simulator's internal logic are spelled out. The internal logic is then illustrated with a numeric example which shows how the simulator does its job, step by step. This internal logic is additionally illustrated with numeric examples following the second and third GPSS case studies in Chapter 2. Experience in teaching the language has shown that discussion of the simulator's logic can be introduced at this early point with a high degree of success. Although the numeric examples are tedious, they do take much of the mystery out of GPSS for the reader. As new GPSS concepts are introduced, they are interpreted, where appropriate, in terms of the Current and Future Events Chains and the simulator's internal logic. This promotes rapid and thorough assimilation of GPSS concepts, and produces a model builder capable of using these concepts with confidence.

Whenever Operands must be supplied in Chapter 2 for the various GPSS Blocks introduced there, they are supplied directly, as constants. Furthermore, uniform distributions are used throughout the chapter, with sampling from these distributions performed implicitly by the simulator. This minimizes the detail for which the reader is responsible initially, and lets him or her focus on the philosophy of GPSS and the internal logic of the simulator.

Chapter 3 describes the GPSS random number generators, and the definition and use of Functions for sampling from both uniform and nonuniform distributions in the language. Special attention is paid to replication of exogeneous event sequences, so that alternative system configurations can be studied under otherwise-identical sets of experimental conditions. Chapter 4 then describes many of the GPSS Standard Numerical Attributes, and illustrates their use. Taken together, Chapters 3 and 4 show how to supply Operand values indirectly, through user-defined Functions and simulator-defined Standard Numerical Attributes, and how to model with nonuniform distributions. Chapter 4 also introduces the use of the Table entity for estimating the way dependent random variables are distributed.

The language elements introduced in Chapters 2, 3, and 4 rely entirely on the GPSS simulator to conduct tests and carry out computations implicitly. Chapter 5 goes on to describe and illustrate language features for incorporating explicit tests and user-defined computations into GPSS models. These features greatly extend the range of modeling which can be accomplished in the language.

In a sense, the materials in Chapters 1 through 5 constitute the introductory and intermediate treatments of GPSS. Chapters 6 and 7 cover most of the remaining key features of the language including: definition and use of Boolean Variables, the GPSS implementation of indirect addressing, the concept of modeling alternative system configurations in parallel, and the remaining three types of GPSS chains which the model builder can use directly and indirectly to build relatively more sophisticated models. Chapter 8 summarizes the several language features not otherwise given explicit treatment in the book.

GPSS exists in many dialects. The most widely used, widely available dialect, GPSS/360, is the one discussed in this book. GPSS V, which is an extension of GPSS/360, is described in Appendix A, and additional references to it are provided in Appendix B. The reader who learns GPSS/360 is learning a major subset of GPSS V. No unlearning is necessary, then, for the person who studies this book, and plans to use GPSS V for simulation modeling. In fact, after mastering the material in this book and reading Appendix A, a person needs to spend only a little time with the GPSS V user's manual to assimilate those GPSS V features not found in GPSS/360.

Both GPSS/360 and GPSS V are versions of GPSS produced by the IBM (International Business Machines) Corporation. These versions, in turn, are lineal descendants of several earlier versions of GPSS introduced by IBM. The first IBM-produced version of GPSS can be viewed, then, as a seminal language. In addition to its lineal descendants, a number of near relatives of the seminal language have been implemented by particular research and hardware-manufacturing groups outside of IBM. Important among these are NGPSS/6000 [GPSS produced for the United States Naval Air Development Command by the Norden Division of the United Aircraft Corporation, and designed for use on Control Data Corporation's 6000-series computers], GPSS/NORDEN [a time-shared version of GPSS also developed at Norden], GPSS/UCC [a version of GPSS developed by the University Computing Corporation, and available for remote-batch use], GPSSTS [a time-shared version of the language developed by the Information Network Division of Computer Sciences Corporation], GPSS-V/6000 [a GPSS V implementation developed at Northwestern University for Control Data Corporation's 6000-series computers, and licensed by Control Data for use on CYBERNET and for sale to Control Data hardware customers], and GPSS-10 [a version of GPSS recently developed at the University of Western Ontario for the PDP-10 computer]. Details of these various GPSS implementations are not discussed in this book. In most cases, however, direct study of GPSS/360 is equivalent to direct study of a major subset of these other versions. The person who has mastered the concepts in this book should be able to transfer his or her understanding of GPSS/360 to the various near relatives of the language easily.

The case studies in this book, and the materials which surround them, were developed for teaching purposes in credit courses at The University of Michigan, for in-house training programs taught at the Ford Motor Company and the Stanford Research Institute, and for total-immersion one- and two-week courses regularly taught in the Engineering Summer Conferences at The University of Michigan, and in extension at the University of California at Santa Cruz. Most of the book's contents, then, have been extensively classroom tested. The book contains twelve Appendices designed principally to provide convenient language summaries for the active model builder. Solutions to selected problems are available to instructors in a separate Solutions Manual.

When a textbook is written, there is always a question about the level of detail to provide, and the extent to which ideas should be reinforced through repetition. An author can miss his mark by being too terse, or not terse enough. My choice here has been to be highly explicit, and therefore probably not as terse as some would like. The unhappy result of this may be to make some readers a bit impatient as ideas are developed in more detail than they think is needed in their case. Hopefully, the happy result will be that through the use of this book, the majority of readers can master GPSS less painfully, and more efficiently and incisively, than might otherwise have been the case.

The book has been written with the needs in mind of those who must learn much, if not all, of the language on their own initiative. This should be a boon to those with little or no opportunity to hear formal classroom lectures on GPSS. Inclusion of so much explicit detail also means that those who teach from the book can minimize the amount of lecture time devoted to exposition of the language. Other class time can be gainfully used in discussing solutions to selected problems, in developing the concepts, philosophy, and subtleties of simulation, and in reviewing outside readings assigned to provide balance and perspective in the design, conduct, and use of simulation experiments.

It is a pleasure to thank Mary Jean Sortet, of the IBM Corporation, for contributing the comparison and contrast between GPSS/360 and GPSS V contained in Appendix A, and for providing the IBM GPSS literature summary in Appendix B; Julian Reitman, of the Norden Division of the United Aircraft Corporation, for supplying information about NGPSS/6000 and GPSS/NORDEN; Kenneth D. Weaver, of University Computing Corporation, for literature describing GPSS/UCC; Stephen J. Fierberg and James K. Lo, of the Information Network Division of Computer Sciences Corporation, for providing information about GPSSTS; Charles B. Krabek, of Control Data Corporation, for comments on GPSS-V/6000; and M. David Martin, of the University of Western Ontario, for a description of GPSS-10. Special acknowledgement goes to James O. Henriksen, a software expert at The University of Michigan's Computing Center, for innumerable informative conversations about the makeup of the GPSS simulator. These conversations have refined my understanding of GPSS considerably, and evidence themselves both directly and indirectly in many places in the book. Finally, thanks are due my students both at The University of Michigan and elsewhere, who have motivated me to attempt to articulate GPSS concepts clearly, and who have offered helpful suggestions for improving the book. Any residual oversights and errors are my responsibility.

Ann Arbor, Michigan   *Thomas J. Schriber*

Basic Concepts in Queuing Systems Modeling

1.1 Introduction

The purpose of this book is to make the reader self-sufficient in building computer simulation models of queuing systems, using the special-purpose language GPSS (General Purpose Simulation System). Nevertheless, the treatment of GPSS does not begin until Chapter 2. In anticipation of GPSS, this chapter introduces the notion of using a procedural language (such as FORTRAN, BASIC, or PL/I) to build computer models of queuing systems. This raises the question, why not start immediately with GPSS? There are two principal reasons. First, most of those who use this book to study GPSS will be familiar with at least one procedural language. The question will occur to such readers, why not simply build models of queuing systems in one of the procedural languages? This chapter will provide a somewhat detailed answer to this question. This will be done by first considering the logic required to build a computer model for a simple queuing system at the procedural level. Then, making reference to this model, the relative advantages of a special-purpose language such as GPSS will be indicated. Second, GPSS models are compact, usually containing far fewer statements than equivalent procedural models. This compactness, which is one of the advantages of the language, comes about because much of the underlying logic of systems simulation is built into GPSS. Unfortunately, such compactness

can be a *disadvantage* for the model builder if he has no understanding of the basic logic required in a simulation model. Without such understanding, there is a tendency to view GPSS in "black box" fashion, and make assumptions about the operation of GPSS models which, if unjustified, can result in model invalidity. One purpose of this chapter, then, is to introduce elements of the logic basic to building models of queuing systems. This paves the way for the later study of the internal logic of GPSS, which is considered quite carefully in this book.

For these reasons, then, a procedural model for a simple "one-line, one-server" queuing system is presented in this chapter. First, the nature of a one-line, one-server system is

1

described, and a request is made for development of a computer model which simulates the system. Basic considerations in building such a model are then introduced. Where possible, these considerations are presented and summarized through a sequence of flowcharts, or flowchart segments. These developments eventually conclude with a detailed flowchart showing an algorithm for the requested model.

The one-line, one-server model assumes the existence of a random number generator. The generator is postulated to be available as a function which, when called, returns a value drawn at random from the population uniformly distributed between .000000 and .999999, inclusive. Almost without exception, one or more random number generators are included in the library of functions available at any computer installation. One of the basic schemes used to construct such generators is briefly discussed in this chapter. This provides an opportunity to make some pertinent observations about sequences of random numbers. Furthermore, the scheme discussed is closely related to the one used in GPSS to generate random numbers. The reader consequently benefits by learning something about the internal makeup of the GPSS random-number generators.

The actual computer implementation of the one-line, one-server model is not included here. Instead, in a set of exercises the reader is asked to implement the algorithm, in a procedural language of his own choosing. It is strongly recommended that such implementation be carried out. This will bring the details of the algorithm into sharper focus, and will provide the reader with what may be his or her first direct experience with a computer model of a queuing system. This implementation can be made more demanding if the basic one-line, one-server model is modified to gather additional statistics, or to increase the complexity of the queuing system, or both. Suggestions along these lines are included in a set of exercises.

As mentioned, a principal purpose of the one-line, one-server algorithm, and the exercises based on it, is to provide a benchmark in terms of which the advantages of GPSS can be indicated. This chapter concludes by pointing out some general features of GPSS in light of the one-line, one-server model. This sets the stage for Chapter 2, and the introduction of GPSS itself.

1.2 The One-Line, One-Server Queuing System Problem

Consider an isolated system consisting of a single person who performs some sort of service on demand. The person might be the attendant at a toll booth on a turnpike, the clerk at the express checkout counter in a supermarket, the girl at a theatre ticket booth, the barber in a one-man barber shop, or the only clerk working in a tool crib. "Customers" come up to this "server" at random times, wait their turn (if necessary) for service, are served on a first-come, first-served basis, and then leave. This situation is shown schematically in Figure 1.1, in which

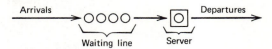

FIGURE 1.1   Illustration of a one-line, one-server queuing system

the row of circles represents waiting customers, the square represents the server, and the circle within the square represents the customer currently in service. The waiting line formed by those waiting for service is termed a queue. The configuration consisting of the server, the customer being served, and those waiting for service, is termed a queuing system.

The simple queuing system shown in Figure 1.1 is characterized by two independent random variables. The time between consecutive arrivals of customers to the system, often called "inter-arrival time," is a random variable. The time required for the server to perform a service is also a random variable. The distributions followed by these two independent random variables influence system properties of interest. Some of these system properties, which are themselves random variables, are listed below.

1. The number of customers who arrive for service during a given time span.
2. The number of customers who are able to go immediately into service when they arrive.
3. The average time customers spend in the queue.
4. The average length of the queue.
5. The maximum length of the queue.
6. The server's utilization; that is, the fraction of the time that the server spends providing service during a given time span.

System properties such as these are of special interest when economic considerations are involved. For example, if the server is a barber and if there are already "too many" waiting for a haircut when a potential customer arrives, the customer may go elsewhere for service. In this case, lost business results for the barber. Or, if the "customers" are repairmen waiting to check out tools at a tool crib, the cost of waiting vs. the cost of providing service must be considered. While they wait, repairmen are idle, even though they are on the payroll. On the other hand, decreasing the waiting time of repairmen by providing more than one tool crib clerk has the effect of decreasing the overall clerk utilization. In such circumstances, a cost tradeoff clearly exists.

It can be of interest, then, to model queuing systems even as simple as the one shown in Figure 1.1. Using a procedural approach, we will now develop the logic for a computer model which simulates the one-line, one-server queuing system. The development will proceed under the following conditions.

1. The interarrival-time random variable is assumed to be uniformly distributed and integer valued. This means, for example, that if the interarrival time is uniformly distributed between 12 and 24 minutes, inclusive, then it can take on any of the thirteen values 12, 13, 14, 15, . . . , 22, 23, and 24 with equal likelihood.

2. Like interarrival time, service time is assumed to be uniformly distributed and integer valued. For example, if service time is uniformly distributed between 12 and 20 minutes, inclusive, then it can take on any of the nine values 12, 13, 14, . . . , 18, 19, and 20 with equal likelihood.

3. A uniform random-number generator is assumed to be available. It will be postulated that the generator takes the form of a function which, when called, returns as its value a six-digit number drawn at random from the population uniformly distributed between .000000 and .999999, inclusive.

4. It will be assumed that all arriving customers remain for service, independent of the length of the queue.

5. When the simulation begins, the system will be assumed to be "empty and idle." That is, there are no customers in the queue initially, and the server is idle.

6. After the simulation has been started, it should continue until a length of simulated time provided to the model as data has been spanned. As soon as this prescribed time interval has been spanned, the simulation should be stopped. In general, then, when the simulation is stopped the server may be in the process of providing service, and there may be one or more customers in the queue.

7. As the simulation proceeds, information on the maximum queue length should be recorded. Then, when the simulation stops, this maximum queue length should be printed out. In addition, the interarrival time and service time distributions in effect, and the interval of simulated time spanned during the simulation, should be printed out.

1.3 Elements of a Solution Procedure

The problem calls for building a computer model with which to observe the behavior of a system as simulated time elapses. The interest in building such models extends beyond the simple one-line, one-server problem to a wide variety of queuing problems. As a result, a method of attack will be described in this section which can be applied in general, whenever it is proposed to use a procedural approach in modeling a queuing system.

1.3.1 Primary and Secondary Events

In queuing systems, "events" occur as a simulation proceeds. In the one-line, one-server system, such things as arrival of a customer, initiation of a service, and completion of a service, are events. When a system is to be modeled, the various events which can occur in the system must be identified, and the effect each of these events has on the state of the system must be assessed. Then the model must be taught how to allow these events to occur, and how to update the state of the system as a consequence of their occurrence. Furthermore, as events occur in simulated fashion, two logical requirements must be honored.

1. Event times (that is, the time of event occurrences) must be consistent with the independent random variables which govern system behavior.

2. Events must be caused to occur in the proper chronological sequence.

Although these two points seem obvious, the second point is worth some elaboration. Simulated time elapses as events occur in a simulation, one by one. It is natural, then, to use a "simulated clock" as part of a queuing-system model. A variable is introduced to represent this clock. The variable is then used to record what simulated time it is. Suppose now that a simulation is taking place, and consider those events which have not yet occurred, but will eventually occur. These events can only be caused to occur either "now" (at the current reading of the simulated clock), or "later" (at points in simulated time which have not yet been reached). The possibility of moving backward in time, even on a temporary basis, is ruled out. This is simply another way of saying that events must occur in the proper chronological sequence.

When systems are complicated, arranging for events to occur in the proper time sequence can be difficult. For this reason, it pays to use a methodical approach in the modeling process. A good way to begin is to divide all possible system events into two categories, termed *primary* events, and *secondary* events. By definition, a primary event is one whose time of occurrence is *scheduled in advance* of its actual occurrence. Any event which is not primary is, by definition, secondary. Secondary events, then, are not scheduled in advance. They occur when primary events do, but in "dependent" fashion, as a direct result of primary-event occurrence.

It is easy to list the various types of primary events which can occur in a given queuing system. Among the data supplied to describe the system, it is simply necessary to single out those data which are *time values*. Each independent set of time-valued data has exactly one type of primary event associated with it. For example, in the one-line, one-server system, two time-valued sets of data are given to describe the system. The first such set of data describes the distribution of customer interarrival times. "Customer arrivals" are the type of primary event associated with this first set of data. The second such set of data describes the distribution of service times. "Service completions" are the type of primary event associated with this second set of data.

Consider now what it means to say that primary events are scheduled in advance. Suppose that a simulation is being performed for the one-line, one-server system, and that a customer has just arrived "now" (at the current point in simulated time). Then, as a consequence of the arrival, the time of arrival of the *next* customer must be scheduled. This involves two steps.

1. First, a sample is drawn from the interarrival-time distribution. The sampled value can be interpreted as the amount of simulated time which will go by before the next customer arrives.

2. Then, the sampled interarrival-time value is added to a copy of the current value of the simulated clock. The sum of these two values equals the point in future time at which the next customer will arrive. In effect, the time of the next customer's arrival is "forecast" (but forecast with complete accuracy) by this computation.[1]

To illustrate scheduling an arrival event, assume that a simulation is in progress, and that a customer arrives at simulated time 21. This arrival sets up the need to schedule the next arrival. First, a sample is drawn from the interarrival-time distribution. Assume the sampled value is 18. Adding 18 to 21 results in the exact forecast that the next customer will arrive at future time 39. (Of course, appropriate steps must now be taken within the model to see to it that the next customer does indeed arrive at simulated time 39. The way this is done will become evident later.)

Figure 1.2 shows a time diagram for the numeric example just given. The time diagram shows the relationship between current time, the sampled interarrival-time value, and the future time at which the next arrival will take place. When future time 39 has been reached and this next customer has been caused to arrive, the time of arrival of *his* successor will then have to be scheduled. For the problem at

[1] Note that in a computer model, a certain fiction is involved. During a simulation of the one-line, one-server system, for example, the model "knows" (because of the concept of scheduling) when the next customer will arrive. The time of the next customer arrival is *not* known in the *real* system. Nevertheless, it is clear that in the long run, the model will be true to the real system in a statistical sense.

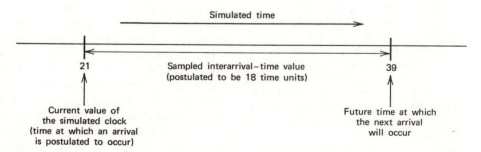

FIGURE 1.2   A time diagram illustrating the scheduling of a customer-arrival event

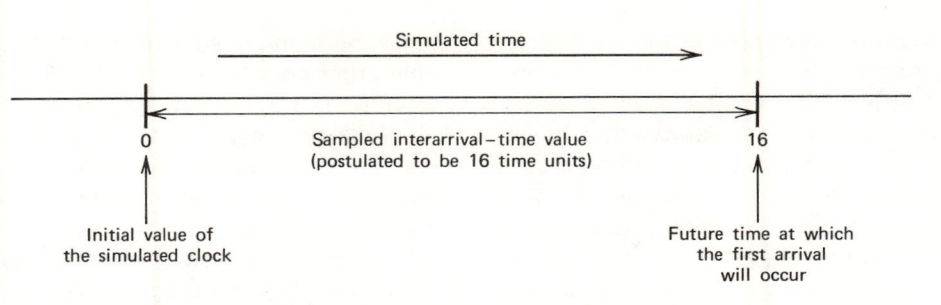

FIGURE 1.3   A time diagram illustrating the scheduling of the first customer-arrival event

hand, then, at no time is there ever more than one arrival event which has been scheduled. In short, a "bootstrapping" technique is used to establish customer arrival times. When an arrival occurs, this sets into motion the procedure for determining the time of the next arrival.

The question now comes up, what is done to arrange for arrival of the *first* customer, thereby setting the bootstrapping process into motion? The time of the first arrival must be scheduled as one of the steps taken to initialize the simulation. Assume that when a simulation begins, the simulated clock itself is initialized with a value of zero. Then, to schedule the first arrival, a sample is drawn from the interarrival-time distribution at this first clock reading. The sampled value equals the future time at which the first arrival will occur. (Because the value of the simulated clock is zero, this direct use of the sampled value is numerically equivalent to computing the time of first arrival by adding the sampled value to a copy of the simulated clock.)

Figure 1.3 shows the time diagram for a numeric example indicating how the time of the first arrival event is determined. The example assumes that in scheduling the initial arrival, a value of 16 is drawn from the interarrival-time distribution. As the time diagram shows, this simply means that the first arrival will occur at simulated time 16.

Now consider "service-completion events,"

which is the other type of primary event in the one-line, one-server system. A service-completion event is scheduled when a customer goes into service. That is, when service begins on a customer, the future time at which the service will be completed is forecast exactly, using a computation analogous to that for scheduling customer arrivals. First, a sample is drawn from the distribution of service times. The sampled value is then added to a copy of the simulated clock. The sum of these two values equals the future time at which the customer in question will come out of service.

For example, assume that a simulation is in progress, and that a customer goes into service at simulated time 56. This sets up the need to schedule a service completion. First, a sample is drawn from the service-time distribution. Assume the sampled value is 15. Adding 15 to 56 results in the exact forecast that the customer will come out of service at future time 71. (Of course, as is true with arrival events, steps must now be taken within the model to guarantee that this customer does indeed come out of service at simulated time 71. The method for doing this will be indicated later.)

Figure 1.4 shows a time diagram for the numeric example just given. The time diagram shows the relationship between current time, the sampled service-time value, and the future time at which the service completion will occur.

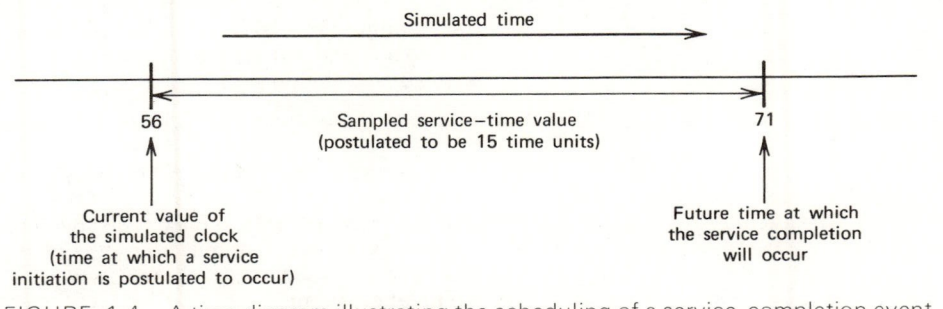

FIGURE 1.4   A time diagram illustrating the scheduling of a service-completion event

The strong analogy between Figures 1.4 and 1.2 should be evident.

When an arrival occurs, the need arises to schedule the next arrival. In contrast, it is not necessarily true that when a service completion occurs, the need arises to schedule the next service completion. Steps are taken to schedule a service completion only if (1) a service completion has just occurred, *and* there is another customer waiting to be put into service, or (2) a customer arrives and finds the server is idle, meaning the customer can go into service immediately. Note that under the conditions in (2), occurrence of a primary event makes it necessary to schedule both an arrival, and a service completion.

In general, then, when a primary event occurs, it may or may not be necessary to schedule one or more additional primary events. Scheduling requirements are dictated both by the nature of the primary event which has just occurred, and the state of the system at the time of event occurrence.

Very little has been said so far about *secondary* events, except that they depend on primary events for their occurrence. In the one-line, one-server system, "putting a customer into service" is a secondary event. This event can only take place when it is immediately preceded by a primary event. For example, when the primary event "customer arrival" occurs, and the arriving customer finds the server is idle, then the secondary event "put a customer into service" can occur. Its occurrence involves (1) changing the server's status from "idle" to "busy," and

(2) scheduling a service completion event. The only other possibility for "putting a customer into service" is for the primary event "service completion" to occur when another customer is waiting for service. In this case, putting a customer into service involves (1) removing the waiting customer from the waiting line, and (2) scheduling a service-completion event.

There is no advanced scheduling, then, of the time when a customer will be put into service. No distribution of times between putting customers into service is supplied as part of the independent data describing the properties of the one-line, one-server system. The event "put a customer into service" is therefore by definition secondary, not primary.

Table 1.1 summarizes the one-line, one-server system in terms of primary events and their consequences. The first column in the table simply lists the two primary event categories. Their corresponding consequences, which are composed both of secondary events and scheduling requirements, are included in the second column. With the exception of scheduling, the indicated consequences can be thought of as secondary events. For example, in addition to "putting a customer into service," the events "put a customer into the waiting line," and "remove a customer from the waiting line," can be thought of as secondary events.

Throughout this section, the phrase "cause an event to occur" has been used from time to time. Causing an event to occur simply requires performing the associated event logic. In this context, the second column in Table 1.1 is just

TABLE 1.1. A Summary of Primary Events and Their Consequences in the One-Line, One-Server Queuing System

Primary Event	Consequences (Secondary Events, and Scheduling)
Arrival of a customer	(1) Schedule the next arrival event. (2) Test the server's status. Is he available? *NO:* Put the customer into the waiting line. *YES:* Put the customer into service. This involves (a) changing the server's status from "idle" to "busy," and (b) scheduling the next service completion event.
Completion of a service	(1) Test the status of the waiting line. Is there a customer waiting? *NO:* Change the server's status from "busy" to "idle." *YES:* Put the customer into service. This involves (a) removing the customer from the waiting line, and (b) scheduling the next service completion event.

a summary of the event logic for the two types of primary events in the one-line, one-server system.

The event logic in Table 1.1 does not include any provisions for making statistical observations on the behavior of the system. In practice, steps for accumulating desired statistical data must be included at appropriate points within the event logic. For example, if the maximum length of the waiting line is to be determined, then the arrival-event logic must be expanded accordingly. In particular, after the secondary event "put a customer into the waiting line" occurs, the line length will have to be tested to determine if a new maximum has just been established. If it has, the record of maximum observed length will have to be updated accordingly.

1.3.2 More About the Simulated Clock

In the discussion of primary events, it was necessary to briefly introduce the idea of a simulated clock. Some of the specific properties of the simulated clock will now be described, and methods for updating the clock's value during a simulation will be explored.

When a simulation begins, the simulated clock is usually initialized with a value of zero. It is up to the analyst to decide for himself what this base value of zero corresponds to, in terms of the real time which is being simulated. For example, zero might correspond to 8 a.m. on the first simulated day, or to 1 p.m. on the first simulated day, or whatever.

In a procedural approach, the analyst usually also has the option of deciding whether to use an integer clock, or a floating-point clock. For our purposes in this chapter, an integer-valued clock will be used. (GPSS also uses an integer clock. As a result, throughout this entire book the simulated clock will be integer valued.) This is appropriate for the one-line, one-server problem at hand, because interarrival times and service times are assumed to be integer valued. This means that events can only occur at integer-valued points in simulated time. There is no need, then, for the clock to record anything but integer values.

It is also up to the analyst to decide how much time one clock unit represents. The unit of time may be 1 second, 5 seconds, 1 minute, 15 minutes, 1 hour, or whatever. Of course, when the time unit has been chosen, all time-valued data read in by the model, or otherwise built into the model, must be expressed in terms of this time unit. For example, suppose that interarrival times are uniformly distributed between 12 and 24 minutes, inclusive, and that the choice of time unit for a particular model is 1 second. Interarrival times will then have to be uniformly distributed between 720 and 1440 time units, inclusive, within the model.

In practice, the unit of simulated time must be small enough to realistically reflect the time spans which occur in the system being modeled. When modeling a computer system, for example, then perhaps the time unit cannot be larger than one microsecond, and it may have to be much smaller than that. In the one-line, one-server system of interest here, the natural choice of time unit is 1 minute. There is no need to go to a smaller unit to incorporate the supplied data into the model.

Now suppose that a simulation is in progress, and the state of the system has just been updated at the current point in simulated time. The next logical step is to "advance the clock." But to what value should the clock be advanced? There are two alternative ways to answer this question.

1. Advance the clock by exactly one time unit. Then scan the system to determine whether any events have been scheduled to occur at this new clock reading. If so, update the system by performing the logic for these events, then advance the clock again by one time unit, and so on. When testing indicates no events have been scheduled to occur at the clock's new reading, simply advance the clock immediately to its next value, etc. The logic of this approach, which uses a *fixed time-increment clock*, is summarized in Figure 1.5.

2. The second approach to clock maintenance uses a *variable time-increment clock*. In this approach, when conditions call for advancing the clock, it is advanced to the time of the "imminent event." The imminent event is the one which has been scheduled to occur at the next earliest point in simulated time. In general, then, the amount by which the clock is advanced differs from advance to advance, giving rise to the phrase "variable time-increment clock." The logic of this approach is summarized in Figure 1.6.

Comparison of Figures 1.5 and 1.6 seems to imply that the best approach to clock maintenance is to use a variable time increment, not a fixed time increment. The apparent advantage of the variable-time-increment clock seems to be that intermediate points in time when nothing has been scheduled to occur anyway are jumped over, thereby probably saving computer time.

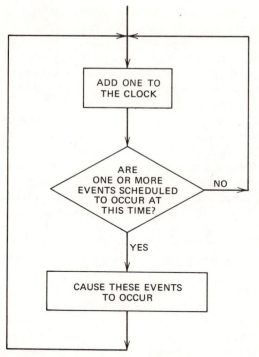

FIGURE 1.5 A flowchart fragment showing the basic logic of a fixed-time-increment clock

This apparent advantage is not necessarily always in effect, however. Whether it is or not depends on the number of primary events in the system,

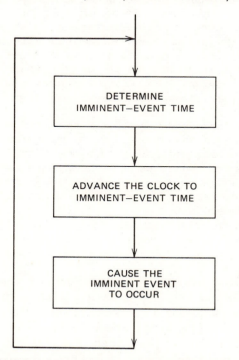

FIGURE 1.6 A flowchart fragment showing the basic logic of a variable-time-increment clock

the time spans between their occurrences, the relative efficiency of sorting methods that might be used to maintain ordered event-time lists, and so on. Discussion of these issues is not called for here.[2]

For the one-line, one-server problem at hand, a variable time-increment clock will be used. This raises the question, how can imminent-event time be determined? One way is to maintain a list of the times at which the various primary events have been scheduled to occur. When the time comes to advance the clock, the event-time list can be searched to find which event is imminent.[3] The clock can then be set to this value, and control can be routed to that segment of the model where the event in question, and its consequences, are caused to occur.

1.3.3 Stopping the Simulation

The flowchart fragments in Figures 1.5 and 1.6 do not provide any way to stop the simulation. Indeed, both of the flowchart fragments are "infinite loops" (that is, closed loops from which no means of exiting has been provided). In practice, after a certain point in simulated time has been reached, the next step usually is to stop the simulation.[4] How can this possibility be incorporated into the logic of Figure 1.6? One simple way is to introduce into the model a "pseudo" primary event called "stop simulation." One of the steps performed in initializing the model will then be the scheduling of this stop-simulation event. The time at which the simulation is to be stopped is usually supplied as data. It is an easy matter, then, to schedule this event. As the simulation proceeds, the stop-simulation

[2] In "Some Problems of Digital Systems Simulation," by R. W. Conway, B. M. Johnson, and W. L. Maxwell, *Management Science*, Vol. 6, No. 1 (October, 1959, pp. 92–110), "the problem of synchronization" is discussed, and a figure showing "regions of advantage for the two timing methods" is presented. The person interested in exploring timing methods might begin by reading this article.

[3] Alternatively, if the event-time list is kept in order of increasingly later event times, then no search is required to advance the clock. The clock can be set immediately to the event time of the event at the top of the list.

[4] Sometimes, instead of stopping the simulation *immediately* when a certain time has come, steps are simply taken at that time to *start to stop* the simulation. For example, it might be desirable to prevent entry of additional customers into the system beyond a certain time, but to continue with the simulation until the system has returned to a condition of "empty and idle." In a barber shop, for example, the door to the shop would be locked at 5 p.m., to prevent additional customers from entering; but the barber would stay on and continue working until all customers already in the shop at 5 p.m. had been served. See exercise 12 in Section 1.6.

event will eventually become the next imminent event. When this happens, the clock will be advanced to stop-simulation time, and control will be routed to that part of the model which handles the stop-simulation details.

Figure 1.7 shows a flowchart fragment which uses the idea of a stop-simulation event, and which in addition has been prepared specifically for the one-line, one-server queuing system. As suggested in the figure, each next imminent event can be any one of three: customer arrival; service completion; or "stop simulation." Testing is conducted to determine which of the three is imminent, and then control is sent to whichever part of the model implements the logic for that type of event.

1.3.4 No Scheduled Service Completion

As indicated in the discussion of the simulated clock, advancing the clock to imminent-event time requires finding the smallest entry in an event-time list. For the problem at hand, the event-time list consists of at most three entries, one each for customer arrival, service completion, and "stop simulation." There is always a customer-arrival entry in this list, because of the bootstrapping method used to simulate customer arrivals. Furthermore, the stop-simulation time entry is also always in this list, because it is placed there as one of the steps in model initialization. However, the event-time list does not always contain a meaningful "time of service completion" entry. Whenever the server is idle, no service is in progress, and no service completion has been scheduled. Two methods suggest themselves for finding imminent event time.

1. Test first to determine if the server is idle. If he is, then search a two-entry event-time list to find out if customer arrival or "stop simulation" is imminent.

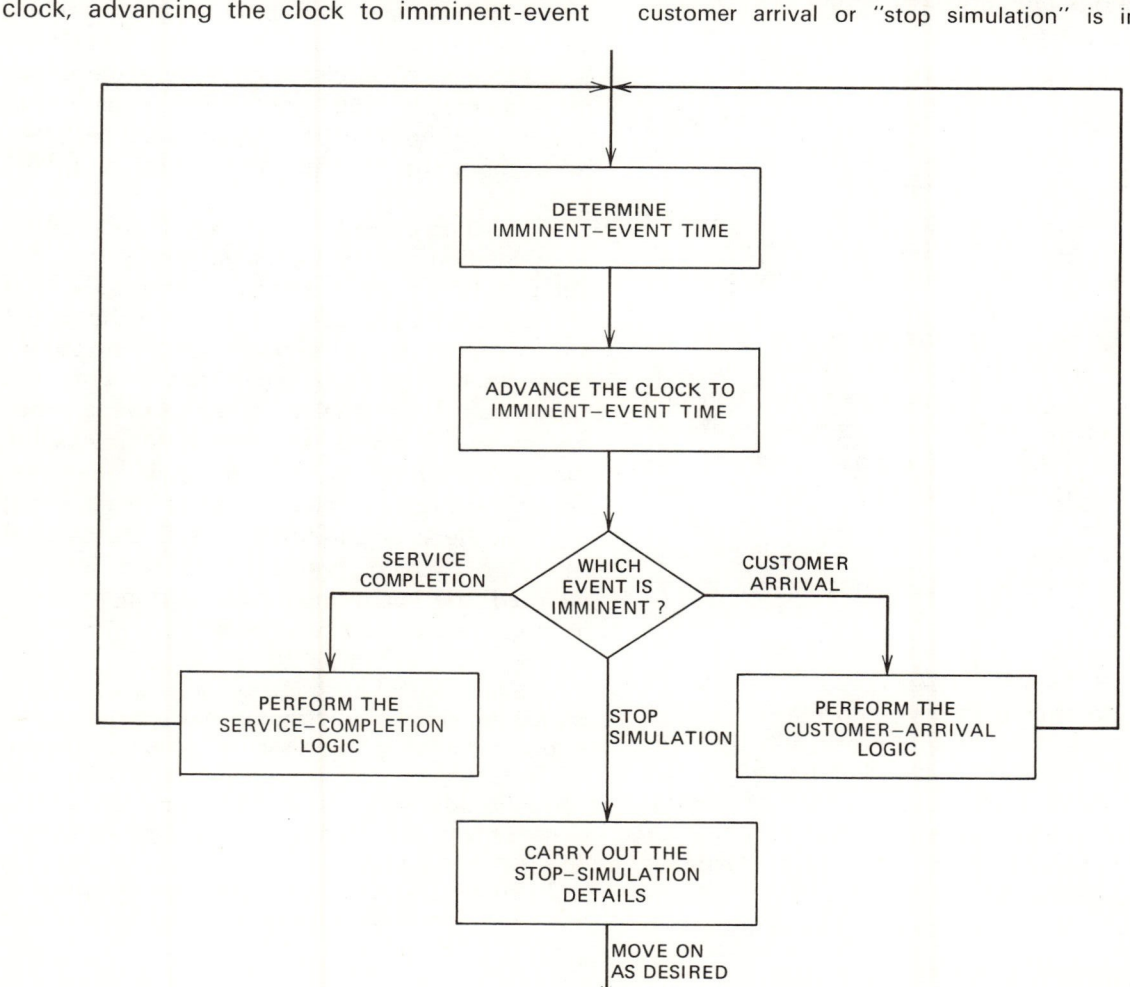

FIGURE 1.7 An expansion of the Figure 1.6 flowchart fragment customized for the one-line, one server queuing system

Otherwise, search a three-entry event-time list to find out if customer arrival, service completion, or "stop simulation" is imminent.

2. Design the logic so that, if the server is idle, "service-completion time" is given a large enough value so that "service completion" cannot possibly be the imminent event. This amounts to conditionally "poisoning" the entry for service time completion. If this is done, imminent event time can always be found by searching a three-entry event-time list, independent of whether the server is idle or busy.

The second of these methods is the least complicated for our immediate purposes, and is the one that will be used here. Under this method, what large value should be used to poison the service-completion time when no service is in progress? Any value larger than stop-simulation time will do nicely. In particular, service-completion time can be poisoned by assigning it a value one time unit larger than stop-simulation time.

1.3.5 Simultaneous Events

Nothing has yet been said about what happens in the case of time ties. Time ties come about whenever two or more events have been scheduled to occur at the same point in simulated time. Whenever this circumstance arises, the events involved are said to be simultaneous events.

Consider what happens when a time tie occurs in the one-line, one-server system. Suppose there is a tie for the next imminent event between customer arrival and service completion. Referring to the Figure 1.7 flowchart fragment, the clock is advanced to the time in question, and then the test is conducted to determine "which event is imminent?" Under the conditions hypothesized, there is not a unique answer to this question. Nevertheless, only one of the paths exiting the Figure 1.7 test box can be followed to arrive at the next step in the simulation. The path chosen will depend entirely on the way the test is constructed. Suppose we arbitrarily assume that the service-completion path is followed. Control is then routed to the corresponding model segment, and the service-completion logic is performed. One consequence of this is to increase the value of the "time of next service completion."[5] The service-completion logic does

nothing, however, to change the time of the next arrival event. The arrival will consequently be the next imminent event. Furthermore, when the clock is advanced to the time of this arrival event, there will be no real change in the clock's value. Under the time-tie hypothesis, the clock's "new" value (time of arrival) will equal the clock's "old" value (time of service completion). At the next step, when the test is conducted to determine "which type of event is imminent?", the answer will be "customer arrival," uniquely. Control will then be routed to the model segment containing the arrival event logic, that logic will be performed, and so on.

The steps just traced out reveal that, in case of time ties, the events involved in the ties are caused to occur sequentially, that is, one after the other. To put this differently, "simultaneous events take place sequentially in a simulation model." This fact can often lead to subtle modeling problems. The reason is that when time ties occur, some decision must be made about the sequence in which the simultaneous events will be performed. The sequence chosen may have important implications in terms of model validity.

In the simple one-line, one-server model under consideration, no model invalidity can come about when time ties occur. The only two primary events that can take place in the model are customer arrival and service completion.[6] When there is a tie between these events, the sequence in which the events are performed does not matter. Consider why this is true. Assume that the server is busy, the waiting line is empty, and that service completion and customer arrival occur at the same simulated time. Depending on how the "which event next?" test is constructed, the events might be caused to occur in either one of two sequences.

1. Suppose that the service-completion event is caused to occur first. Because the waiting line is empty, a consequence of service completion is that the server's status is changed from busy to idle. Then, when the arrival event is caused to occur, the arriving customer finds that he can immediately go into service. This is as it should be.

2. Now suppose that the arrival event is caused to occur first. The arriving customer finds that he cannot

---

[5] This happens either (a) because another customer is put into service, as part of the service completion logic, or (b) because there is no customer waiting to go into service, which means that the "time of next service completion" will be assigned a value equal to "stop simulation" time, plus 1.

[6] The pseudoprimary event, "stop simulation," will be ignored in the discussion in this section. Of course, it is quite possible that one of the events eventually involved in a time tie is "stop simulation." See exercise 8b in Section 1.6.

go into service, because the server is still in busy status. As a result, the customer is put into the waiting line. Next, the service completion is caused to occur. As indicated in Table 1.1, part of the service-completion logic involves checking the waiting line to determine if the now-available server can be kept in busy status. Finding the just-arrived customer in the waiting line, steps are then taken to remove him from the waiting line, and put him into service. There are consequently no problems associated with this event sequence, either.

The above analysis shows that the event sequence is inconsequential when time ties occur in the simple one-line, one-server queuing system. Nevertheless, the first sequence may be aesthetically preferable to the second. In the first sequence, the arriving customer captures the server immediately, without being put into the waiting line first. In the second sequence, the arriving customer is put into the waiting line, "temporarily." His "residence time" in the line is zero, however. In this sense, it might be argued that for all practical purposes, the second sequence doesn't really put him into the waiting line, either. (But see exercise 8a in Section 1.6.)

It is easy to change the conditions of the one-line, one-server system so that the event sequence followed in resolving time ties *does* matter. It has been implied so far that arriving customers are always willing to wait for the server, if necessary. Suppose this is not always true. In particular, suppose the next arriving customer will stay for service only if he can go into service immediately. Also suppose that his arrival time is coincident with a service completion, and that the waiting line is empty. If event sequence (1) above is followed, the arriving customer will stay for service. If event sequence (2) is followed, he will not.

The problem of simultaneous events, considered here only briefly, will come up again in later chapters of the book. In fact, several of the exercises in this chapter involve time-tie problems.

1.3.6 Sampling from Uniform Distributions of Integers

In the discussion of primary and secondary events, the phrases "draw a sample from the interarrival-time distribution" and "draw a sample from the service-time distribution" were used frequently. The need to draw values from distributions is an integral part of modeling systems characterized by randomness. The starting point in such sampling usually is some source of "uniform random numbers." More particularly, in terms of computer modeling, the starting point is usually a function (or subroutine) which, when called, returns as its value a number drawn at random from the population uniformly distributed over the interval from 0.0 to 1.0. Such a function (or subroutine) is simply referred to as a random-number generator. Whether such a generator can actually return values of 0.0 and/or 1.0, or just values between these extremes, will depend on the generator itself. Furthermore, the number of digits in each returned value will depend both on the generator and on the computer being used. This sort of information is usually supplied as part of the documentation for the generator.

In the Section 1.2 description of the one-line, one-server problem, the availability of a uniform random-number generator was assumed. It was postulated there that the generator takes the form of a function which, when called, returns a six-digit number drawn at random from the population uniformly distributed between .000000 and .999999, inclusive. For our purposes here, let us assume that the name of this random-number function is URAND.

The problem at hand involves both interarrival-time and service-time populations which are uniformly distributed and integer valued. Before considering how to use URAND to sample from such populations, we must first consider how to describe specific instances of these populations. One way would be to state the smallest and largest integer values contained in the population. For example, it might be stated that service time is uniformly distributed over the integers ranging from 12 to 20, inclusive. Note that the average value in this population is 16, and that the "distance" between this average value, and the extreme values of 12 and 20, is 4. This distance between the average and the extremes is sometimes called the "half width" of the distribution. Hence, another way to describe the population in this example would be to say that its average value is 16, and its half width is 4. Put more compactly, the service time is 16 ± 4 minutes. This latter notation, taking the general form $A \pm B$, is generally used to indicate a uniform distribution over the closed interval of integers from $A - B$ to $A + B$, where A and B are themselves integers. This is the notation which will be used throughout this book to describe these uniformly distributed integer populations.[7]

Now, it is a simple matter to draw a value at random from the population $A \pm B$. This can be done by adding to the smallest possible population value a "random fraction" of the "width" of the population. The smallest possible value is $A - B$, and the width of the population is $2B$. Furthermore, the value returned by a uniform random number generator can be thought of as a "random fraction." In terms of URAND, then, a value returned by URAND can be converted into an equivalent value drawn from the population $A \pm B$ via the *tentative* use of equation (1.1).

$$\text{Sampled Value} = (A - B) + (\text{URAND})(2B)$$

$$(1.1)$$

The understanding is that after the right-hand side of equation (1.1) has been evaluated, the fractional part of the result will be discarded (without rounding), and the integer portion of the result will be used as the sampled value. This leads to a problem, however. The sampled value would be the largest possible population value only if and when URAND returned a value of 1.0. But, by hypothesis, the largest value URAND can assume is .999999. In turn, the largest sampled value which could result by using equation (1.1) would not be $A + B$, but would be $A + B - 1$, which is unsatisfactory.

To remedy this situation, equation (1.1) can be modified somewhat, taking the form shown in equation (1.2).[8]

$$\text{Sampled Value} = (A - B) + (\text{URAND})(2B + 1)$$

$$(1.2)$$

A bit of thought shows that equation (1.2) does accomplish the objective of converting values returned by URAND into values sampled at random from the population $A \pm B$. The minimum sampled value, $A - B$, results for values of URAND ranging from .000000 up to, but not

including, $1/(2B + 1)$. These values occur with probability $1/(2B + 1)$. The next larger population value, $A - B + 1$, occurs for values of URAND ranging from $1/(2B + 1)$ up to, but not including, $2/(2B + 1)$. And so on, until finally the largest sampled value, $A + B$, results for values of URAND ranging from $(2B)/(2B + 1)$ up to, but not including, $(2B + 1)/(2B + 1)$, i.e., 1.0. Of course, these largest values also occur with probability $1/(2B + 1)$, consistent with the uniform distribution requirement.

1.4 The Logic of a Particular Random-Number Generator

The topic of random-number generation and testing is sufficiently broad and complex to be the subject of a book itself. Indeed, many researchers have devoted considerable time and effort to developing algorithms for generating random numbers, and applying statistical tests of randomness to proposed and existing generators, to assess their relative degree of goodness. As a result, a considerable literature exists in this area.

In many cases, the person whose immediate interest is to build computer models of nondeterministic systems is quite willing to take the existence of one or more good random-number generators as a given. Unfortunately, there can be considerable danger in simply using a conveniently available random-number generator, without prior critical assessment of its suitability. Not all random-number generators are good ones. Even some of those in rather widespread use fall short of being entirely satisfactory. This means that caution is in order.

No attempt will be made in this book to go into the elements of random-number generation and testing. As indicated in Section 1.2, the existence of a uniform random-number generator is to be assumed in building the procedural model for the one-line, one-server system called for in this chapter. And, throughout the remaining chapters of the book, the random-number generators built into GPSS will be used without question, on the assumption that they constitute good random-number sources. Nevertheless, against the possibility that the reader does not otherwise know how a random-number generator might be constructed, an algorithm for a particular generator will be considered in this section. The purpose here is to make the possibility of random-number generation plausible in the first place, and to point out some basic

---

[7] A *disadvantage* of this notation is that it can only be used to describe populations consisting of an *odd* number of integers. Hence, 16 ± 4 describes a population containing 9 values; 17 ± 5 describes a population containing 11 values, and so on. As it happens, however, it is especially easy in GPSS to sample from interarrival-time and service-time distributions describable with the $A \pm B$ notation. It is in anticipation of GPSS that this notation is adopted here.

[8] The largest value that a random-number generator returns in GPSS is .999999. Furthermore, an equation identical to equation (1.2) is used automatically in GPSS to sample from the population $A \pm B$. Hence, the procedure being described here is precisely the one which GPSS uses.

considerations concerning random-number sequences. In addition, because the algorithm to be explained here is highly similar to the one used in GPSS, some of the particulars of random-number generation in GPSS will be described at the end of this section.

The algorithm itself is very simple. Let us assume the objective is to generate four-digit random numbers uniformly distributed on the interval from .0000 to .9999, inclusive. To do this, the algorithm uses two positive, odd, integer numbers, each containing up to four digits. The first of these two numbers, which here will be called the "seed," never changes in value. The second of these two numbers, which here will be called the "multiplier," is subject to change in value; indeed, each time the algorithm is used to generate the next random number, the value of the multiplier is changed as a consequence.[9]

Whenever a random number is needed, the first step in the algorithm is to multiply the seed by the multiplier. This results (in general) in an eight-digit integer product. This product is then used both to supply a new value for the multiplier, in anticipation of the next use of the algorithm, and to supply the desired random number. In

particular, the rightmost four digits in the product are used as the new value assigned to the multiplier, and the middle four digits in the product are used as the desired random number (with a decimal being placed accordingly).

Now consider a numeric example for this algorithm. Suppose that a value of 5167 is chosen for the seed, and that the initial value of the multiplier is taken as 3729. The following steps are then carried out to generate the first random number.

1. Form the product of the seed and the multiplier. $5167 \times 3729 = 19267743$.
2. Assign 7743 (the rightmost four digits in the product) as the new value of the multiplier.
3. Use .2677 (the middle four digits in the product, with a decimal placed accordingly) as the desired random number.

When the second random number is generated, its value will be .0080 (the seed, 5167, times the multiplier, 7743, equals 40008081, resulting in a new multiplier of 8081, and a random number of .0080), and so on.

This numeric example is summarized and extended in Table 1.2, showing the values of the first 10 random numbers generated by the algorithm. Pointers are used in the first several rows of the table to indicate how the eight-digit product is decomposed to produce each next multiplier value, and the random number itself.

Inspection of the algorithm implied in Table 1.2 makes it clear why the random numbers it

---

[9] The terms "seed" and "multiplier" are being used here in a sense opposite to their use in the general literature. The number whose value never changes is usually called the *multiplier*; and the term *seed* usually describes the initial value given to the "other number." In the IBM literature on GPSS, however, this terminology is reversed. In the interest of compatibility with the IBM literature, the IBM terminology is being used in this book.

TABLE 1.2   A Summary of Details Involved in Generating the First 10 Random Numbers

	Multiplier Value	Eight-Digit Product*	The Resulting Random Number	
Initial multiplier	3729	19267743	.2677	
	7743	40008081	.0080	
	8081	41754527	.7545	Successive random numbers generated by the algorithm
Successive multipliers generated by the algorithm	4527	23391009	.3910	
	1009	5213503	.2135	
	3503	18100001	.1000	
	1	5167	.0051	
	5167	26697889	.6978	
	7889	40762463	.7624	
	2463	12726321	.7263	

*Formed by using an invariant seed of 5167.

generates can range from .0000 to .9999, inclusive. Values of .0000 are produced whenever the four middle digits in the eight-digit product are all zeros; and values of .9999 result whenever the four middle digits are all nines. There is no way for this algorithm, as defined, to generate a value less than .0000, or larger than .9999.

In Table 1.2, note that the sixth time the algorithm is performed, the next multiplier turns out to be 1. This brings to mind the possibility that if the next multiplier ever turned out to be exactly zero, the algorithm would fail. (From that point forward, whenever the algorithm was performed, the eight-digit product would be zero, and the random number would also always be zero.) It is precisely to guard against this possibility that both the seed and the initial multiplier must be *odd* numbers. The product of two odd numbers is itself always an odd number. Hence, the rightmost digit in the product can never be a zero, which means that the next value of the multiplier can never be zero, either.

The concept of the "reproducibility of random numbers" is evident in Table 1.2. As soon as the seed and initial multiplier have been chosen, the sequence of random numbers generated by the algorithm is completely determined. For example, when the seed is 5167 and the initial multiplier is 3729, the third random number generated will always be .7545, and so on. As a result, the random numbers which are generated are not *truly* random. They are said to be *pseudo*random.

Reproducibility of random-number sequences is not a bad thing. The property of reproducibility makes it possible to reproduce the precise sequence of independent events which occur when a simulation experiment is conducted. This means that alternative system configurations can be studied under identical sets of experimental conditions. The result is to sharpen the contrast in the behavior of the alternative configurations, and make possible relatively strong statements of the "other things being equal" type. Methods for taking advantage of pseudorandomness to reproduce experimental conditions will be considered later in the book, beginning at the end of Chapter 3.

A question raised in examining Table 1.2 is, how many times can the algorithm be performed before a previously generated multiplier appears again? After return to an earlier multiplier value, it is clear that the generator will repeat the sequence of random numbers produced earlier.

The number of random numbers produced before the sequence begins to repeat is called the *period* (or *length*) of the random number generator. In the example at hand, the maximum *feasible* period is 5000. (There are only 5000 different odd integers in the closed interval from 1 to 9999. Hence, at most only 5000 different multiplier values could occur before a previously encountered multiplier came up again.[10]) A generator with a maximum period of 5000 is almost bound to be unsatisfactory for any realistic purposes. It is easy to increase the maximum feasible period of the generator in this scheme, however. This simply requires using a seed and multiplier which contain more than four digits.

In GPSS, there are eight built-in random-number generators.[11] Whenever any one of these generators is used, it produces a value drawn at random from the population uniformly distributed between .000000 and .999999, inclusive.[12] The algorithm used to generate random numbers in GPSS is highly similar to the algorithm implied in Table 1.2. The GPSS scheme differs from the Table 1.2 scheme in only the following respect.[13]

1. In the four-digit scheme in Table 1.2, the seed and multiplier values are in the interval of odd integers from 1 to 9999, inclusive. In the GPSS scheme, the seed and multiplier values are in the interval of odd integers from 1 to 2,147,483,647, inclusive.

2. Each GPSS generator has eight seeds at its disposal. The seed values are 37,584,381, 1,909,996,635, 1,964,463,183, 1,235,671,459, 1,480,745,561, 442,596,621, 340,029,185, and 2,030,226,625. Of

---

[10]The situation is more complex than this. The only way to have the multiplier end in 5 (except perhaps initially) is to have either the seed or the initial multiplier (or both) end in 5. But then the multiplier will *always* end in 5. Hence, the maximum feasible period is not 5000, but is either 4000 or 1000, depending on the choice of values for the seed and the initial multiplier.

[11]It is often convenient to have more than one random-number generator available. This makes it possible, for example, to dedicate a private random-number sequence to each of two or more sources of randomness in a model. As we will see later, such dedication of otherwise-unused sequences can be important if the objective is to compare alternative system configurations under identical sets of experimental conditions.

[12]The value produced by a GPSS random-number generator is actually context dependent. The value is either a six-digit random number, as suggested above, or is a value drawn at random from the population of integers uniformly distributed between 000 and 999, inclusive. The contexts leading to these two different possibilities will be pointed out later.

[13]The statements made about the GPSS random-number generators in this book apply to GPSS implementations on IBM computers in the 360 and 370 series. For similar information applicable to other GPSS implementations, the pertinent documentation should be consulted.

course, per the Table 1.2 scheme, generating a random number only requires using one seed. Whenever a GPSS generator produces a random number, the particular seed used in the process is chosen at random from among the eight possiblities. Each of the eight seeds is equally likely to be the one chosen.

3. Suppose that any one of the eight GPSS generators is called upon to produce a random number. First, that generator's current multiplier value is multiplied by a randomly chosen seed. The resulting product is used for three purposes.

(a) The "rightmost half" of the product becomes the next value of the multiplier for that generator.

(b) An interior portion of the product is used as the random number (with a decimal being placed accordingly).

(c) Another interior portion of the product is used to randomly determine which of the eight seeds will be chosen the next time a random number is produced by that generator.

Uses (a) and (b) are analogous to the two uses to which the product is put in the four-digit scheme described in this section. Use (c) arises in the GPSS scheme because eight seeds are available, not just one.

4. Finally, the base 2 number system is used internally in GPSS, not the base 10 system which was conveniently adopted here for purposes of Table 1.2.

In the Table 1.2 scheme, the user can influence the sequence of random numbers generated by supplying the value for the seed, and/or the initial value for the multiplier. It is natural to wonder what options the user has, if any, for influencing the sequence of random numbers generated in GPSS. As already indicated, the eight seed values are built in. There is no option for supplying these values. Furthermore, the seed chosen when a generator is used is determined at random, based on steps performed during the *preceding* call on the generator in question. The only *logical* possibility for an option here is to let the user dictate, generator by generator, which seed will be used the *first* time a random number is produced by that generator. However, GPSS does not provide this option to the user. Each of the eight generators makes use of the first seed (i.e., the seed whose value is 37,584,381) the first time it produces a random number.

There is only one other possible way for the user to influence the GPSS random-number sequences. This is by providing, generator by generator, the initial value of the *multiplier*. The user is given this option in GPSS, but is not forced to exercise it. If the option is not exercised, each of the eight multipliers has an initial value of either

1, or 37, by default.[14, 15] If the option is exercised, the user can supply, for each generator, his choice of initial multiplier for that generator. Each choice must take the form of a positive, odd, integer number, not exceeding five digits in length.[16] For example, a user might supply initial multiplier values of 431, 99837, and 5, for the second, fifth, and sixth generators, respectively. If this were done, then the default initial multiplier value would be in effect for each of the first, third, fourth, seventh, and eighth generators.

The use of the GPSS random-number generators is considered in complete detail in Chapter 3. Use of the generators requires only a limited knowledge of the algorithm on which they are based. For this reason, except for the details just presented, the GPSS random-number algorithm will not be further commented on in this book.

1.5 A Detailed Algorithm for the Model

The various elements required for a model of the one-line, one-server system have now been introduced and discussed. The last step is to integrate these elements in a self-contained model. This will be done here first in general fashion, without including all of the step-by-step details. Then the model will be presented in more detail, as it might appear just prior to computer implementation.

The general logic for the model is shown in the Figure 1.8 flowchart, which repeats the flowchart fragment in Figure 1.7 but extends it to include startup and shutdown features. The nature of the specific details implied in Figure 1.8 has been spelled out earlier. At the READ DATA box, for example, the values to be read consist of (1) the mean and half width of the interarrival-time distribution, (2) the mean and half width of the service-time distribution, and (3) "stop

[14]The default multiplier values are all 1 in GPSS/360, Version 1. The default values are all 37 in GPSS/360, Version 2, and in GPSS V. These different versions of GPSS are discussed briefly at the beginning of Chapter 2.

[15]Note that if the default initial multiplier values are in effect, the sequence of random numbers produced by each of the eight generators will be identical. This follows because each of the eight generators makes use of the first seed the first time it produces a random number. This guarantees that each of the eight generators will use one and the same "randomly chosen" seed the second time it produces a random number, etc.

[16]As indicated under (1) in the above list, "multiplier values are in the interval of odd integers from 1 to 2,147,483,647, inclusive." Nevertheless, in supplying *initial* multiplier values, the user is subject to a five-digit restriction.

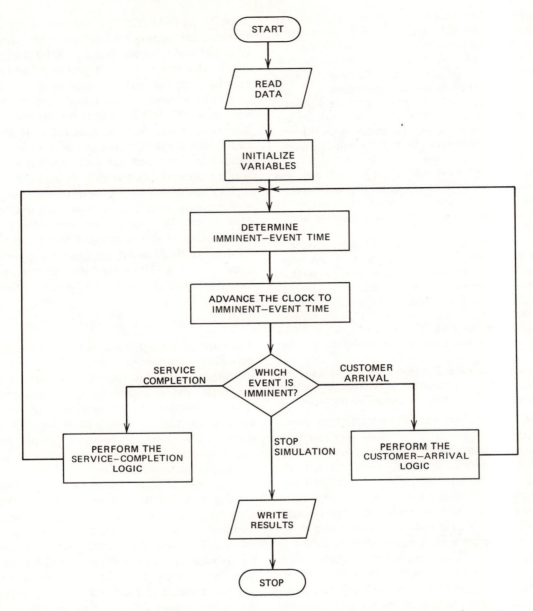

FIGURE 1.8   A flowchart for the general logic of the one-line, one-server queuing system

time," i.e., the simulated time at which the simulation is to be stopped. At the INITIALIZE VARIABLES box, such things as initializing the clock with a value of zero, setting the server's status to idle, "poisoning" the time of the next service completion, and scheduling the first arrival event, must be done. At the PERFORM THE CUSTOMER-ARRIVAL LOGIC box, the steps involved in performing the Table 1.1 arrival event logic must be spelled out, and so on.

Figure 1.9 shows a more particularized version of the Figure 1.8 flowchart. Here, names have been introduced for pertinent variables in the model, the explicit tests required as part of arrival event logic, and service completion logic, have been included, etc. Table 1.3 provides a dictionary for the variables used in Figure 1.9. Hence, IATA is the mean interarrival time, IATB is the half width of the interarrival-time distribution, CLOCK is the simulated clock, IDLE is the server's status variable, TOSC is the time of the next service completion, and so on. Each of the variables used in Figure 1.9 is of integer mode.

To avoid clutter, use has been made in Figure 1.9 of three "predefined processes," or functions, to support the logic of the model. These functions

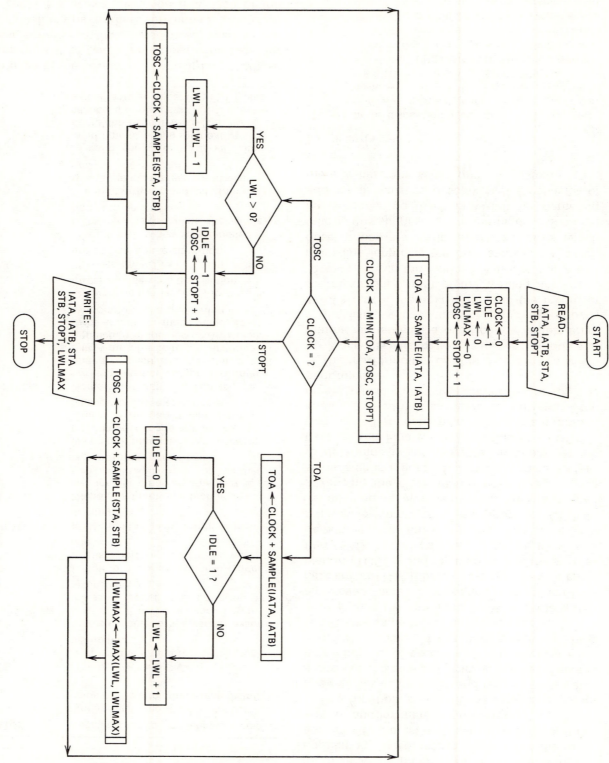

FIGURE 1.9   A particularized flowchart corresponding to the Figure 1.8 algorithm

TABLE 1.3 A Dictionary for the Variables and Functions Used in Figure 1.9

Variable	Definition
CLOCK	Variable used to simulate the clock
IATA	"Interarrival time _A_ value"; mean value of the interarrival-time distribution
IATB	"Interarrival time _B_ value"; half width of the interarrival-time distribution
IDLE	Status variable for the server; assumes a value of 1 or 0, corresponding to the server being "idle" or "busy," respectively
LWL	Length of the waiting line; number of customers currently in the waiting line
LWLMAX	Maximum observed length of the waiting line
MAX	Name of a function which accepts two integer-mode arguments, and returns an integer-mode copy of the larger of these arguments
MIN	Name of a function which accepts three integer-mode arguments, and returns an integer-mode copy of the smallest of these arguments
SAMPLE	Name of a function which accepts two integer-mode arguments, interpreted, respectively, as the mean and half width of a uniformly distributed population of integers; SAMPLE returns an integer-mode value drawn at random from the population
STA	"Service time _A_ value"; mean value of the service-time distribution
STB	"Service time _B_ value"; half width of the service-time distribution
STOPT	"Stop time"; when the simulated clock reaches this value, the simulation is to be stopped
TOA	"Time of arrival"; simulated time at which the next arrival event will occur
TOSC	"Time of service completion"; simulated time at which the next service-completion event will occur. If no service is in progress, TOSC is assigned a value equal to STOPT plus 1

are used at the several rectangular boxes whose ends consist of two vertical lines. The logic for these simple functions must be supplied by the user. Definitions for these functions are included in Table 1.3. It is understood that each of the functions returns a value in integer mode.

The function named SAMPLE accepts as its inputs the mean and half width of a uniformly distributed population of integers, and returns as its value a sample drawn at random from this population. Of course, to do its work the function SAMPLE must itself call upon another function, a random-number generator.

The function named MIN accepts a list of three values as its input, and returns as its value a copy of the smallest entry in the list. There is no guarantee, of course, that this smallest entry is unique. In case of ties, MIN simply returns a copy of the value for which the tie occurs.

In Figure 1.9, the input to MIN is the three-entry event-time list consisting of the time of the next arrival (TOA), time of the next service completion (TOSC), and the time to stop the simulation (STOPT). MIN's task in context, then, is to determine imminent-event time. The value MIN returns is immediately assigned to CLOCK. Hence, finding imminent-event time, and then advancing the clock to this time, appears as a single step in Figure 1.9. However, this step fails to determine _which_ event is imminent. At the next step in Figure 1.9, the value of CLOCK is then tested to determine which event time it equals, and control is routed to the part of the model where the corresponding event logic is performed.

The third function used in Figure 1.9 is MAX. MAX accepts a list of two values as its input, and returns as its value a copy of the largest entry in the list. As inspection of Figure 1.9 shows, MAX's task in context is to keep the record of the maximum length of the waiting line up to date. In fact, in the Figure 1.9 model, this maximum line length is the _only_ statistic for which observations are made. In the exercises which follow, it is suggested that the Figure 1.9 model be expanded to make provision for gathering additional statistics describing the behavior of the one-line, one-server queuing system.

1.6 Exercises

1. (a) In the discussion of equation (1.1), the objection was made that the sampled value can never equal $A + B$, because the largest value URAND can return is .999999. Assume for the moment that URAND returns values uniformly distributed between .000000 and 1.00000, inclusive, instead of between .000000 and .999999, inclusive. Would equation (1.1) then be suitable for sampling from the uniformly distributed population of integers $A \pm B$?

(b) In equation (1.1), the understanding is that after the right-hand side has been evaluated, the fractional part of the result will be discarded (without rounding), and the integer portion of the result will be used as the sampled value. Assume that a rounding feature is provided in equation (1.1) by including the term $+0.5$ on the right-hand side. Continuing to assume that URAND returns values uniformly distributed between .000000 and .999999, inclusive, can this modified form of equation (1.1) now be used to sample from the uniformly distributed population of integers $A \pm B$?

2. Equation (1.2) shows how a computation can be performed to convert a value returned by URAND into an equivalent value from the uniformly distributed population of integers $A \pm B$. Suppose that a population of integers is not uniformly distributed. In particular, suppose it is necessary to draw samples at random from the population distributed as shown in Table E2. In a situation like this, instead of using a *computation,* it is more likely that some sort of a table-lookup procedure would be performed to convert a value from URAND into an equivalent value from the distribution of interest. Develop an algorithm for sampling from the Table E2 distribution. Show the specific details of the algorithm in the form of a flowchart.

TABLE E2

Population Value	Relative Frequency of Occurrence
2	0.15
5	0.20
8	0.25
9	0.22
12	0.18

3. (a) Suppose that 1 is chosen as the seed for the random-number scheme summarized in Table 1.2. What will be true of the resulting sequence of random numbers generated by the scheme?
   (b) Describe the conditions under which the sequence of random numbers generated in the Table 1.2 scheme would all equal some non-zero constant.

4. Consulting one or more of the references listed in the next section, do the following.
   (a) Find and discuss at least two algorithms for random-number generators which differ from the algorithm introduced in Section 1.3.
   (b) Find and discuss at least three different tests which are applied to random-number se-

quences to determine their degree of goodness.
   (c) Find a way to convert random numbers (drawn from the population uniformly distributed on the interval from .000000 to .999999, inclusive) to a random number drawn from the normally distributed population with a mean of zero, and a standard deviation of 1.
   (d) Find a way to convert a random number drawn from the population uniformly distributed on the interval from .000000 to .999999, inclusive, into a value drawn from the exponential population with a mean of 1.

5. This question refers to random-number generators available at your computing center.
   (a) How many different random-number generators are included in the library of programs available at the computing center? From which populations do they return sampled values?
   (b) Does the generator which returns values uniformly distributed over the interval from 0.0 to 1.0 include 0.0 and/or 1.0 among the values it can return, or not? Approximately how many digits are included in the value returned by this generator? What algorithm does the generator use?
   (c) What options do you have, if any, in influencing the sequence of random numbers returned by the generator in (b)? How are these options exercised?
   (d) Suppose you want to use the generator in (b) in a computer program you propose to run at your computing center. Explain exactly how to go about doing this.
   (e) Write a simple program which fetches the first 100 values returned by the generator in (b), and prints them out, along with their mean and standard deviation. Compare the results with the mean and standard deviation of the population from which the samples were drawn.
   (f) Write a program which applies one of the tests you found in exercise 4b to the generator in (b) above. Then run the program. Having done this, what kinds of statements are you willing to make about the degree of goodness of the generator in (b)?

6. (a) Is it necessary in the Figure 1.9 model to initialize CLOCK with a value of zero?
   (b) Do you think it would be necessary in *any* queuing-systems model to explicitly assign zero as the value of the simulated clock, in the spirit of initializing the model?

7. Depending on the data, it is not inconceivable that interarrival times of zero can be realized in a

model. It may even be possible for service times of zero to occur (although it may be difficult to supply a meaningful interpretation for this if it happens).

   (a) Describe how the Figure 1.9 model behaves if a sampled interarrival time turns out to have a value of zero.

   (b) Describe how the Figure 1.9 model behaves if a sampled service time turns out to have a value of zero.

8. These questions refer to possible time-tie situations in the Figure 1.9 model.

   (a) Suppose that, when time ties occur between customer arrival and service completion, the arrival event is caused to occur first. Discuss the effect this might have on the maximum-queue-length statistic which appears in the output.

   (b) Suppose that a time tie involving the stop-simulation event occurs. Discuss the extent to which the sequence in which the tied events are performed matters, if at all.

   (c) Suppose the model has been modified so that an arriving customer chooses *not* to remain for service if he finds there is another customer in the waiting line. In addition, assume there is a customer in the waiting line, and that a time tie occurs between next customer arrival, and service completion. Discuss the effect the choice of event sequence has in determining whether the arriving customer will remain for service or not.

9. (a) In the procedural language with which you are familiar, is there a single statement equivalent to the test "CLOCK = ?" in the Figure 1.9 model? If not, show how to replace that test with equivalent logic which can be programmed in the procedural language you know.

   (b) Suppose that a simulation is being performed with the one-line, one-server model in Figure 1.9, and that a time tie occurs between arrival and service completion. In the equivalent logic you prepared for (a) above, will the arrival or the service completion be caused to occur first? How would you have to change this equivalent logic to reverse the event sequence in case of time ties?

   (c) Finding imminent-event time, and then advancing the clock to this time, appears as a single step in Figure 1.9. However, this step fails to determine *which type* of event is imminent. As a result, the value of the simulated clock must subsequently be tested to determine which event time it equals, so that control can be routed to the part of the model where the corresponding event logic is per-

formed. This sequence could be made more efficient if the *type of imminent event* were recorded when imminent-event time is found. Then, after advancing the clock, control could be routed immediately to the proper event logic. Do you think this improvement can be programmed in the procedural language with which you are familiar? If so, explain in detail how the improvement can be made.

10. (a) Show flowcharts for algorithms which accomplish the tasks performed by the functions MAX, MIN, and SAMPLE in the Figure 1.9 model.

   (b) Prepare language statements for the functions MAX, MIN, and SAMPLE, and for the Figure 1.9 model, in a procedural language of your own choosing. Then submit the resulting program for running on your computer, using the data given in Section 1.2. What maximum queue length was observed during the simulation? Can you state for certain whether the line was actually at this length for one or more simulated time units? (Hint: see exercise 8a.)

11. Modify the Figure 1.9 model so that it will collect and print out one or more of the following measures of system behavior.

   (a) The number of customers who arrive for service during the simulation.

   (b) The number of customers who are able to go immediately into service when they arrive.

   (c) The server's utilization.

   (d) The average time required for the server to perform a service. (What do you do in computing this statistic when there is a customer in service at the time the simulation stops?)

   (e) The average residence time in the queue, based on all customers who arrived for service (including those who did not have to wait at all). (What do you do in computing this statistic when there are one or more customers in the queue at the time the simulation stops?)

   (f) The average residence time in the queue, based only on those customers who did have to wait for one or more simulated time units. [The question raised in (e) also applies here.]

   (g) The average number of customers in the queue. (Hint: To gain an appreciation for the meaning of this statistic, draw a plot of queue content vs. simulated time for a hypothetical case. The plot consists of a sequence of consecutive rectangles. The average height of these rectangles equals the average number of customers in the queue.)

Carefully check the logic for the modified model.

Then implement the model on your computer, making one or more "deterministic runs" to further investigate model validity. (A "deterministic run" is one in which all randomness has been eliminated, thereby making it possible to compute correct results by hand, independent of the model itself. As a partial indication of model validity, the output produced by the model can be checked against the results known to be correct. For example, suppose that customer interarrival time is always exactly 20 time units, and that service time is always exactly 15 time units. Then, if "stop time" is 480, exactly 24 customers will arrive during the simulation, including the arrival at simulated time 480. One hundred percent of these customers will be able to go into service immediately. The server's utilization will be 0.718[+]. Average service time will be 15. Both measures of average queue-residence time will be zero, and the average number of customers in the queue will be zero. Note that this deterministic set of conditions is brought about by supplying zero as the data values for IATB and STB in the Figure 1.9 model. Not much imagination is required to make up other sets of deterministic conditions. For example, does your model produce correct output when interarrival time and service time are both exactly 20 time units? Does it produce correct output when interarrival time is exactly 20 time units, and service time is exactly 30 time units?)

12. (a) Show what changes to make in the Figure 1.9 model so that the simulation simply *starts to stop* at "stop time." That is, prevent additional customers from entering the system at this point, but have the model continue the simulation until the system has returned to a condition of "empty and idle." The output should indicate at what simulated time the simulation finally stopped. (Note that, for this modified model, the time the simulation finally stops will be a random variable.) In case of a time tie between the "start to stop" event and the next customer-arrival event, does your model let the arriving customer enter the system, or not?

(b) Carefully check the logic of the modified model. Then make a deterministic run with the model on your computer, using an interarrival time of 30, a service time of 35, and a "start to stop" time of 480. Does the simulation finally stop at the proper simulated time?

(c) Now run the model for several different sets of nondeterministic experimental conditions (i.e., different starting points for the underlying random number generator). At what simulated times do the various simulations finally stop?

13.[17] Two types of customers arrive at a one-man barber shop. Customers of the first type want only a haircut. Their interarrival time distribution is 35 ± 10 minutes. Customers of the second type want a shave as well as a haircut. Their interarrival time distribution is 60 ± 20 minutes. The barber provides service to his customers first-come, first-served. This situation can be visualized in terms of Figure E13, where circles represent customers who want only a haircut, and squares signify customers wanting both a shave and a haircut. At the time represented in Figure E13, a "haircut only" customer is in the barber's chair, while "haircut only," "shave and haircut," and "haircut only" customers are waiting, in that order, for service.

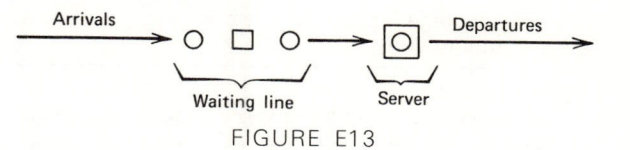

FIGURE E13

It takes the barber 18 ± 6 minutes to give a haircut. When he gives a shave, 10 ± 2 minutes are required.

Build a procedural model for this barber shop, gathering only the simple statistic "maximum length of the waiting line." (Note that, although there are two different types of customers, there is still only one waiting line.) After carefully checking your logic, investigate the model's validity by doing several deterministic simulations with the model.

14.[17] Expand the exercise 13 model so that it gathers the waiting-line statistics described under (e), (f), and (g) in exercise 11. For purposes of these statistics, do not make any distinctions as to the types of customers in the line. (This means that from the output you will know the average queue content was 0.85, for example, but you will not know what portion of the 0.85 consisted of haircut-only customers, with the rest being shave-and-haircut customers.) Investigate the validity of the modified model by making several deterministic runs with it.

15.[17] Now expand the model for exercise 14 so that it does distinguish between the two types of customers in terms of the waiting-line statistics it gathers. That is, waiting-line statistics should be *segregated* according to customer type (even though the customers themselves are not segre-

[17] In Chapter 2, Case Study 2B shows a GPSS model for the system described in exercise 13. The model automatically gathers the statistics called for in exercise 14. Then, in the discussion of the model, a method is shown for gathering both aggregated and segregated waiting-line statistics, as requested in exercise 15.

TABLE E15

	Segregated for Haircut-Only Customers	Segregated for Shave-and-Hair-cut Customers	Aggregated for Both Types of Customers
Number of customers who arrive for service	13	8	21
Number of customers who go immediately into service	1	3	4
Average residence time in the queue, including those who did not have to wait at all	15.7	6.0	12.0
Average residence time in the queue, excluding those who did not have to wait at all	17.0	9.6	14.8
Average number of customers in the queue	0.424	0.100	0.524

gated in the waiting line). In addition, as in exercise 14, the model should continue to gather a set of *aggregated* waiting line statistics, i.e., statistics in which distinctions are not made as to the types of customers in the waiting line. Information such as that shown in Table E15 might then typically appear in the output. Investigate your model's validity by doing several deterministic simulations with it.

16.[18] In a certain factory, a tool crib is manned by a single clerk. The clerk checks out tools to mechanics, who use them to repair failed machines. (The tools are too expensive, and too numerous, for each mechanic to have each tool in his tool box.) The time to process a tool request depends on the type of tool involved. Requests fall into two categories. Pertinent data are shown in Table E16.

TABLE E16

Category of Tool Request	Mechanic Inter-arrival Time (Seconds)	Service Time (Seconds)
1	420 ± 360	300 ± 90
2	360 ± 240	100 ± 30

The clerk has been serving the mechanics first-come, first-served, independent of request. This queue discipline is shown in Figure E16(a), where circles and triangles represent mechanics making requests in Category 1 and 2, respectively. In

[18] In Case Study 2C in Chapter 2, GPSS models are used to investigate the system described in exercise 16. The Case Study 2C models are not designed to reproduce the precise sequence of independent events for which the two alternative queue disciplines are compared. Later, in Case Study 3C in Chapter 3, the system is investigated again, and this time the alternative queue disciplines are compared under otherwise-identical experimental conditions.

Figure E16(a), a Category 2 request is being served, while one request in Category 1, and two in Category 2, are waiting in that order for the server.

Because failed machines are out of production, it costs 0.25¢ per second ($9 per hour) when a mechanic waits for service at the tool crib. This cost is independent of the tool to be checked out. Management believes the average number of waiting mechanics can be reduced if Category 2 requests are serviced at the tool crib before those in Category 1.[19] That is, only when no Category 2 requests are waiting is the clerk to service requests in Category 1. This queue discipline is pictured in Figure E16(b) where, in effect, the line that forms ahead of the server consists of two segments. The segment at the front of the line is of "high priority"; that at the back of the line is of "low priority." The Figure E16(b) queue discipline is said to be "first-come, first-served, within priority class."

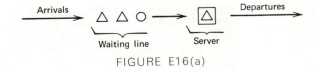

FIGURE E16(a)

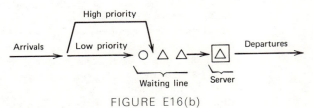

FIGURE E16(b)

[19] The average Category 2 service time is less than for Category 1. When the server chooses as his next customer the one with the smallest *average* service time requirement, a "shortest imminent operation" queue discipline is said to be in effect.

The waiting-mechanic situation in Figure E16(b) is identical to that in Figure E16(a). The server is currently working on a Category 2 request (triangle). Two other Category 2 requests are waiting; and one Category 1 request is waiting (circle). Only when the high-priority segment of the line is empty will the low-priority segment be served.

Build a procedural model for this tool-crib system, gathering only the statistic "average content of the waiting line." After carefully checking your logic, investigate the model's validity by doing several deterministic simulations with the model. Then use the model in nondeterministic mode to determine whether the proposed new queue discipline actually will reduce the average number of mechanics in the waiting line. In terms of the cost of lost production, what daily savings can be realized when priority distinctions are made? Do not include in the cost consideration the time mechanics spend in service, i.e., being served.

1.7 Selected References

The following references are offered for the person who may not otherwise have started to familiarize himself or herself with the literature in the area of discrete-event simulation. Most of these references contain additional references themselves. Far from being all inclusive, these references are suggested simply as convenient starting points for entry into the literature.

A. Textbooks Offering a Relatively Broad Treatment of Simulation Topics

(1) Emshoff, James R., and Roger L. Sisson, *Design and Use of Computer Simulation Models* (Macmillan, 1970).

(2) Fishman, George S., *Concepts and Methods in Discrete Event Digital Simulation* (Wiley-Interscience, 1973).

(3) Gordon, Geoffrey, *Systems Simulation* (Prentice-Hall, 1969).

(4) Maisel, Herbert, and Guiliano Gnugoli, *Simulation of Discrete Stochastic Systems* (Science Research Associates, 1972).

(5) Martin, Francis F., *Computer Modeling and Simulation* (John Wiley & Sons, 1968).

(6) McMillan, Claude, and Richard F. Gonzalez, *Systems Analysis: A Computer Approach to Decision Models* (Richard D. Irwin, 1973), rev. ed.

(7) Meier, Robert C., William T. Newell, and Harold L. Pazer, *Simulation in Business and Economics* (Prentice-Hall, 1968).

(8) Mize, Joe H., and J. Grady Cox, *Essentials of Simulation* (Prentice-Hall, 1968).

(9) Naylor, Thomas H., Joseph L. Balintfy, Donald S. Burdick, and Kong Chu, *Computer Simulation Techniques* (John Wiley & Sons, 1966).

(10) Naylor, Thomas H., ed., *Computer Simulation Experiments with Models of Economic Systems* (John Wiley & Sons, 1971).

(11) Reitman, Julian, *Computer Simulation Applications* (John Wiley & Sons, 1971).

(12) Schmidt, J. W., and R. E. Taylor, *Simulation and Analysis of Industrial Systems* (Richard D. Irwin, 1970).

B. Sources Devoted to Random Number Generation and Testing

(1) Chambers, R. P., "Random Number Generation," *IEE Spectrum*, Volume 4, No. 2 (February, 1967; pp. 48–56). [This article treats random-number generation and testing in introductory fashion, and includes an interesting appendix on "straight-line patterns in random-number plots."]

(2) Gorenstein, Samuel, "Testing a Random Number Generator," *Communications of the Association for Computing Machinery*, Volume 10, No. 2 (February, 1967; pp. 111–118). [This paper discusses the application of statistical tests to the first 1,000,000 numbers produced by the random-number generator used in GPSS III.]

(3) Knuth, Donald E., "Random Numbers," in *The Art of Computer Programming*, Volume 2, Chapter 3 (Addison-Wesley, 1969). [This chapter provides a definitive discussion of random-number generation.]

(4) Lewis, P. A. W., A. S. Goodman, and J. M. Miller, "A Pseudo-Random Number Generator for the System/360," *IBM Systems Journal*, Volume 8, No. 2 (1969; pp. 136–146). [This article will be of interest to anyone using random numbers on a System/360 or System/370 computer.]

(5) Reitman, Julian, *Computer Simulation Applications* (John Wiley & Sons, 1971). [Reitman's book—see also item A(11)—contains some discussion of tests of the relative goodness of the GPSS/360 random-number generators. See pages 99 to 110.]

C. Some Other Specific Sources of Interest

Bibliographies

(1) *Bibliography on Simulation*, IBM Corporation, Form Number 320-0924 (1966). [To quote from the introduction, "This bibliography represents a search and annotation of source material which appeared in over 75 journals and books, most of which were published during the years 1960 through 1964. The 948 papers, articles, and

books which are referenced in this collection are indexed by subject."]

(2) *Management Science at Work*, IBM Corporation, Form Number GC20-1741 (1971). [To quote from the Introduction, "This manual is a specially organized three-way index to almost 5,000 journal articles and conference papers which have mentioned the application of analytic methods to various business, industrial, and scientific problems." Simulation is one of the many methods included in the index.]

(3) Naylor, Thomas H., "Simulation and Gaming," Bibliography 19, *Computing Reviews*, Volume 10, No. 1 (January, 1969; pp. 61–69). [This is the most recent comprehensive bibliography devoted to simulation. This bibliography is currently (1974) being updated by Professor Naylor.]

Conference Proceedings

(4) *Proceedings of the Annual Simulation Symposiums* (Annual Simulation Symposium, P.O. Box 22573, Tampa, Florida 33622). [Entitled *Proceedings of the Sixth Annual Simulation Symposium* (March, 1973), *Proceedings of the Fifth Annual Simulation Symposium* (March, 1972), etc., and dating back to 1968, the proceedings from this annual conference each contain a variety of articles on simulation and its applications.]

(5) *Proceedings of the Winter Simulation Conferences* (AFIPS Press, Montevale, New Jersey 07645). [Recently entitled *Proceedings of the 1973 Winter Simulation Conference* (January, 1973), *Proceedings of the 1971 Winter Simulation Conference* (December, 1971), and dating back to selected papers published after the first "winter simulation conference" (December, 1967), the proceedings from these annual conferences each contain several dozen articles reflecting current thought and practice in simulation techniques and applications.]

Fundamental Concepts and Considerations

(6) Conway, Richard W., "Some Tactical Problems in Digital Simulation," *Management Science*, Volume 10, No. 8 (October, 1963; pp. 47–61).

(7) Kiviat, Philip J., "Digital Computer Simulation: Modeling Concepts," RAND Corporation Memorandum RM-5378-PR, 1967 (The RAND Corporation, Santa Monica, California 90406). [This is but one in a series of RAND Memoranda which cover a range of topics in discrete-event simulation. For more complete information, get "A Bibliography of Selected RAND Publications: Computer Simulation (SB-1042; February, 1973)" from The Rand Corporation, Publica-

tions Department, 1700 Main Street, Santa Monica, California 90406. Also note that Rand has placed subscription collections of its publications in over 270 libraries in the United States and abroad.]

Language Perspectives

(8) Kiviat, Philip J., "Digital Computer Simulation: Computer Programming Languages," RAND Corporation Memorandum RM-5883-PR, 1969 (The RAND Corporation, Santa Monica, California 90406). [This Memorandum is the basis for an appendix in item A(10) above.]

(9) Teichroew, Daniel, and John F. Lubin, "Computer Simulation: Discussion of the Technique and Comparison of Languages," *Communications of the Association for Computing Machinery*, Volume 9, No. 10 (October, 1966; pp. 723–741).

Statistical Considerations

(10) Fishman, George S., and Philip J. Kiviat, "Digital Computer Simulation: Statistical Considerations," RAND Corporation Memorandum RM-5378-PR, 1967 (The RAND Corporation, Santa Monica, California 90406). [This Memorandum was the basis for the article by Fishman and Kiviat entitled "The Statistics of Discrete-Event Simulation," *Simulation*, Volume 10, No. 4 (April, 1968; pp. 185–196).]

(11) Fishman, George S., "Digital Computer Simulation: Estimating Sample Size," RAND Corporation Memorandum RM-5866-PR, 1969 (The RAND Corporation, Santa Monica, California 90406).

(12) Fishman, George S., "Output Analysis for Queuing Simulations," Technical Report 56 (Health Services Research Program, Institution for Social and Policy Studies, Yale University, New Haven, Connecticut 06520; April, 1972).

(13) Naylor, T. H., K. Wertz, and T. H. Wonnacott, "Methods of Analyzing Data from Computer Simulation Experiments," *Communications of the Association for Computing Machinery*, Volume 10, No. 11 (November, 1967; pp. 703–710).

(14) Mihram, G. Arthur, *Simulation: Statistical Foundations and Methodology* (Academic Press, 1972).

Verification and Validation Considerations

(15) Naylor, T. H., and J. M. Finger, "Verification of Computer Simulation Models," *Management Science*, Volume 14, No. 2 (October, 1967; pp. B-92–B-106).

(16) Van Horn, Richard L., "Validation of Simulation Results," *Management Science*, Volume 17, No. 5 (January, 1971; pp. 247–258).

1.8 Epilogue

This chapter has presented some of the very fundamental concepts which apply to building procedural models of queuing systems. The chapter sections have dealt only with conceptualization, not with actual computer implementation. The chapter cannot have its intended effect unless some of the suggested computer exercises have been performed. In particular, exercises 10 (computer implementation of the Figure 1.9 model) and 11 (expansion of the Figure 1.9 model so that it gathers basic statistics of interest) should be completed. In addition, either exercise 14 or exercise 16 should be worked. If these things have been done, then (1) some of the details which arise in building procedural models of queuing systems will have come into sharp focus, (2) the straightforward but burdensome complications arising when statistics are to be gathered (exercise 11), or when simple system variations are introduced (exercises 14 and 16) will be appreciated, (3) the prospect of being able to model these situations (and much more complicated ones as well) with relative ease in GPSS will be a most welcome one, and (4) the groundwork will have been laid for coming to a careful understanding of the operation of models constructed in GPSS.

In light of the Figure 1.9 model and the exercises, here are some things it might be reasonable to expect to find among the features of a special-purpose language for modeling queuing systems.

1. Built-in random-number generators.
2. Features making it easy to sample from some of the well known distributions, such as the uniformly distributed population of integers $A \pm B$, the exponential distribution, and the normal distribution (see exercise 4c and 4d), as well as others.
3. An easily used facility for defining and sampling from empirical distributions (see exercise 2).
4. A built-in simulated clock.
5. Automatic implementation of certain logical actions, such as checking the waiting line ahead of a server when a service completion has just occurred, to determine whether another customer is waiting to be put into service.
6. Automatic clock maintenance; that is, automatic advance of the clock to the time of the next imminent event.
7. Automatic routing of control to that part of the model implementing the logic for the event which is imminent.
8. The capability of giving certain types of events higher priority than certain other types of events, so

that event sequences can be controlled when certain time ties occur.
9. Automatic gathering of statistics at the request of the model builder, so that for example the following kinds of information can be obtained with relative ease.

(a) Statistical measures of queue properties, such as the maximum number of customers in the queue, the average number of customers in the queue, the average residence time of customers in the queue, and so on.

(b) Statistical measures of the experience of various servers in the model, such as the number of times each server was used, the utilization of each server, the average time required by the server to perform a service, and so on.
10. Ability to tag various customers with different priority levels, so that a "first-come, first-served, within priority level" queue discipline is practiced automatically by servers in the model, if this is what the model builder wants (see exercise 16).
11. Provision for modeling queue disciplines other than "first-come, first-served, within priority level."
12. Automatic printing out of the various statistics describing model behavior, so that at his option, the model builder can avoid supplying such things as "write" statements, and "format" statements, as part of the model.

The above list has been deliberately constructed to provide a preview of some of the features which are part of the special-purpose language GPSS. Indeed, with the exception that it is unreasonably difficult in GPSS to sample from the exponential and normal distributions (as well as from other theoretical distributions), each feature in the above list has been implemented in GPSS. This greatly eases the task of building GPSS models of queuing systems. For example, only 12 statements are required in the GPSS model equivalent to the Figure 1.8 algorithm. None of these 12 GPSS statements involve explicit "tests"; the tests shown in Figure 1.9 are automatically performed within the GPSS model, as an understood part of the basic logic of a queuing-systems model. In addition, the 12-statement model automatically gathers and prints out a full set of statistics for the queue and server in the Figure 1.9 model, including each of the statistical measures listed in problem 11. If a procedural model fully equivalent to this 12-statement GPSS model is prepared, more than 60 statements are required. It should be clear, then, that GPSS is quite compact, in terms of the number of statements it requires. Of course, a consequence of this compactness is that many of the operational details of a GPSS model are masked from view. It is precisely for this reason that the intelligent construction of GPSS models is more subtle than appears to be the case at first glance.

We proceed now to Chapter 2, and the study of GPSS itself. The initial objective in Chapter 2 is to develop the GPSS wherewithal required to model the simple one-line, one-server queuing system. The first case study in Chapter 2, Case Study 2A, presents a GPSS model for this simple system. Immediately after this model has been presented, the elements of the internal logic of GPSS are taken up, and the operation of the Case Study 2A model is interpreted in terms of this internal logic. The pattern subsequently followed throughout the rest of the book is to interleave (1) simulation concepts, (2) their GPSS implementation, and (3) fully documented case studies which show the concepts and their GPSS implementation in meaningful contexts. Even before the end of the book is reached, the reader should be self-sufficient in the use of GPSS.

2

Basic GPSS Modeling Concepts

2.1 Some Preliminary Considerations

GPSS (<u>G</u>eneral <u>P</u>urpose <u>S</u>imulation <u>S</u>ystem) is both a language and a computer program. As a language, it has a well-defined vocabulary and grammar with which certain types of system models can be unambiguously described. As a computer program, it interprets a model described in the GPSS language, thereby making it possible to conduct experiments with the model on a computer. Without such interpretation, the computer would not be able to directly act out, or simulate, the system represented by the model. The computer program which performs this interpretation will be referred to as the "GPSS Processor," or simply as the "Processor."

There are many versions of GPSS. This is a result of historical developments dating back to the late 1950's and early 1960's. Some of the earlier versions were named GPSS, GPSS II, and GPSS III. The implementation now probably most frequently used is GPSS/360, so named because it can be used with computers in International Business Machine corporation's "System/360" (and 370) families. Even for GPSS/360, a distinction is made between Version 1 and Version 2.

GPSS/360, Version 1, became available in 1967 at no charge. Version 2 was released in late 1969 at a charge of $20 per month. Then, in late 1970, IBM made available an extension of GPSS/360, Version 2, calling it GPSS V and charging $55 per month for its use. In 1971, IBM ceased supporting GPSS/360, Versions 1 and 2.

Briefly, this means that IBM ceased maintaining and improving those GPSS Processors at that time. Finally, in early 1973, IBM withdrew Versions 1 and 2 from its program library. As a result, it is no longer possible to obtain GPSS/360, Version 1, from IBM, or to initiate rental of GPSS/360, Version 2. (Withdrawal also means that IBM will no longer accept orders for manuals or for other documentation for GPSS/360, Versions 1 and 2.) Of course, those who already have Version 1 can continue to use it, and can freely make copies of it available to others. Furthermore, as of this writing (January, 1974) those who currently rent Version 2 can continue uninterrupted rental indefinitely.

Despite these developments, it is expected that GPSS/360, Version 1, will continue to be used at least until the end of the 1970's. This projection is made for several reasons. First of all, this version is available on a widespread basis in numerous computer installations. Secondly, the fact that it is free means many colleges and universities which have System/360 or 370 computers will choose to use Version 1 as long as possible, instead of initiating rental of GPSS V. Finally, GPSS/360 is a highly useful language in its own right, and provides the model for many non-IBM GPSS implementations (see the preface for further comments).

For the above reasons, only GPSS/360 will be discussed in this book. Fortunately, there is upward compatibility among Versions 1 and 2, and GPSS V. This means that the person intending to use any of these GPSS implementations can profitably study the material presented here. Indeed, after the basic subset of GPSS introduced here has been mastered, a person will be self-sufficient in the language. That is, a person will be able to intelligently and efficiently study the documentation for other GPSS implementations, and rapidly reach proficiency in whatever implementation may be of immediate interest.

A comparison and contrast between GPSS/360, and GPSS V, is contained in Appendix A. Written by an IBM authority on GPSS, Mary Jean Sortet, this comparison and contrast is especially appropriate for those who want to rapidly determine what the pertinent extensions of GPSS V over GPSS/360 are. Those with additional interest in GPSS V should obtain detailed literature from IBM on the subject. A bibliography for IBM literature on GPSS is contained in Appendix B.

GPSS is also available in many instances to users of non-IBM hardware. For example, during 1971–1972 the Norden Division of the United Aircraft Corporation developed a form of GPSS called NGPSS/6000 for the United States Navy. As its name suggests, this form of GPSS runs on the Control Data Corporation's 6000 computer series. NGPSS/6000 is currently available to the Department of Defense and to other federal agencies. In time, it may be available to all users of Control Data 6000-series computers.

Experimentation with modified forms of GPSS actually began at the Norden Division of United Aircraft as early as 1966, under the direction of Norden's Julian Reitman. This work led to the release of GPSS/360-NORDEN in the late 1960's and early 1970's, and to GPSS/NORDEN in 1973. GPSS/NORDEN is available on a time-shared basis through National CSS (formerly National Computer Software and Systems). GPSS/NORDEN features such things as interactive use, display of output on a cathode ray tube, an overlay capability which enhances available core, an improved output editor, and facilities which promote the use of matrix-driven models.

During 1969 and 1970, Ken Weaver, working for the University Computing Corporation (UCC), in Dallas, authored an implementation of GPSS/360 for the Univac 1108 computer. Called GPSS/UCC, this version can be used on a remote-batch basis via UCC's Fastback system. GPSS/UCC is virtually identical to GPSS/360, Version 2.

There are implementations of GPSS other than GPSS/360, GPSS V, NGPSS/6000, GPSS/NORDEN, and GPSS/UCC. No attempt will be made here to comment on each of these other implementations, or even to list them all.[1]

2.2 Approach to Model-Building in GPSS

A GPSS model of a system may be expressed either as a Block Diagram, or as the punchcard equivalent of a Block Diagram. The model builder usually begins his work by constructing a Block Diagram of the system he intends to simulate. The punchcard version of the Block Diagram is then prepared and presented to the computer for implementation. Model conceptualization most often takes place at the Block Diagram level. After a Block Diagram has been developed, the process of producing its equivalent as a deck of punched cards is then straightforward and mechanical.

A Block Diagram is a collection of characteristically shaped figures (Blocks) connected by directed line segments. There is a set of more than 40 Blocks which GPSS makes available to the model builder. The shapes of these Blocks are predefined. The distinction among shapes eases the process of becoming familiar with a model by studying its Block Diagram. Of course the various shapes have no significance, *as such*, in the punchcard version of the model.

Models are built by selecting certain Blocks from the available set and arranging them in a diagram so that, at the time of model implementation, they (that is, their images) interact meaningfully with one another. The logical requirements

---

[1] The interested person can find more details about the history of GPSS, and its currently available forms, in Stanley Greenberg, *A GPSS Primer* (Wiley-Interscience, New York, 1972).

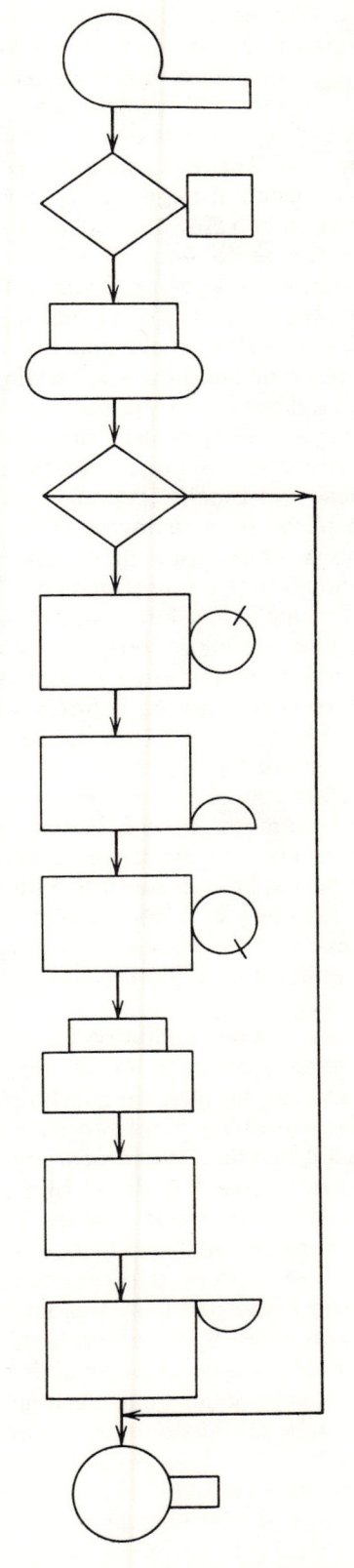

FIGURE 2.1   The silhouette of a typical GPSS Block Diagram

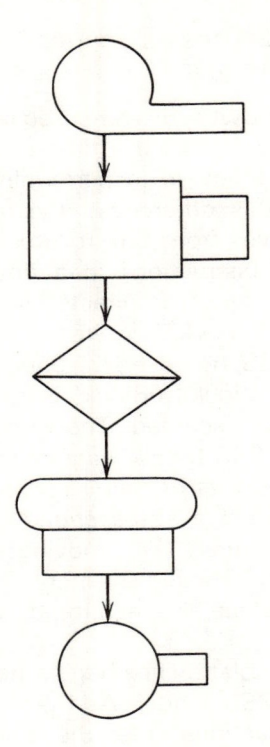

of the system being modeled dictate which Blocks are used in constructing the model. When the model is implemented, it is the interaction among the Blocks which is analogous to (simulates) the interaction of elements in the real system being modeled.

The silhouette of a typical GPSS Block Diagram is shown in Figure 2.1. Thirteen different Blocks can be identified in the figure. Several of them appear more than one time. Detailed information that would typically appear in the Blocks has been deliberately deleted. The intent here is to provide a first glimpse of a Block Diagram for the sake of perspective.

The properties of a basic subset of Blocks will be taken up in this chapter. The subset is chosen to make it possible to build complete, although relatively simple, GPSS models of systems. In succeeding chapters of the book, additional Blocks will be studied, and their use will be illustrated in context. As the model builder's Block vocabulary grows, he can build models of increasingly complicated systems. When the entire set of Blocks has been mastered, rather sophisticated models can be built in GPSS with relative ease.

2.3 Transactions: Dynamic Entities in GPSS Models

Lines with arrowheads were used in the Chapter 1 flowcharts to represent a time-ordered series of steps to be followed in performing procedures. Expressing this differently, it can be said that "control moves from box to box" (or, from instruction to instruction) in a flowchart of the Chapter 1 variety. The directed line segments in the Figure 2.1 Block Diagram also suggest movement. In GPSS, however, the concept of "control moving from Block to Block" is not entirely valid and must be discarded. The directed line segments in a GPSS Block Diagram represent paths along which *units of traffic* move. Each unit of traffic is termed a *Transaction*.[1a] Transactions, then, are dynamic (i.e., moving) entities in a GPSS model. Their movement from Block to Block takes place as execution of a GPSS model proceeds.

When a simulation first begins, no Transactions exist in a GPSS model. As the simulation proceeds, Transactions enter the model at certain times, according to the logical requirements of the system being modeled. Similarly, Transactions leave the model at certain times during the course of a simulation. In general, then, there are many Transactions in a model. Nevertheless, only one of these Transactions moves forward at a time.

After it is set into motion, a Transaction moves from Block to Block along whichever path it is in. Each Block can be thought of as a point at which a subroutine can be called. When a Transaction enters a Block, the corresponding subroutine is executed, and the Transaction then (in general) tries to move into another Block. A Transaction's forward motion is continued until any one of three possible circumstances arises:

1. The Transaction moves into a Block whose purpose is to hold it there for a prescribed length of time.
2. The Transaction moves into a Block whose purpose is to remove it from the model.
3. The Transaction *attempts* to move into the next Block in its path, but that Block refuses to let it enter. In this case, the Transaction is held in whatever Block it currently occupies. Later, it will repeat its attempt to gain entry to the next Block. As model conditions change, one of the subsequent attempts will, in general, be successful. The Transaction can then resume its movement in the model.

After a Transaction comes to rest for one of the three reasons explained, the forward motion of another Transaction in the model is initiated. (The order in which Transactions are moved will be explained in detail later.) Eventually it, too, comes to rest, and the forward motion of yet another Transaction begins. It is in this fashion that execution of a GPSS model proceeds. Recall that each successful entry of a Transaction into a Block results in a call on a subroutine. Model execution, then, consists of a series of subroutine calls which result from movement of Transactions.

Given this much information, certain inferences can now be drawn from Figure 2.1. For example, two Blocks in the figure are "sinks"; that is, the path on which they lie does not extend beyond them. These two Blocks, identical in shape, must have the purpose of removing from the model Transactions which enter them. Similarly, there are two Blocks in the figure which are "sources"; that is, no path leads into them. These Blocks must represent points at which Transactions are brought into a model. Finally, note that Figure 2.1 consists of two separate, free-standing segments. In general, a GPSS model can consist of many free-standing segments. As a simulation proceeds, activity occurs in the segment containing the currently moving Transaction. When it comes to rest, the next Transaction set into motion may happen to be in a different model segment, resulting in a switch of the action to that segment. The concept of free-standing Block Diagram segments, then, is entirely valid in GPSS.

Until now, the discussion of Transactions has been completely abstract. An attempt has been made to answer the question, "What *is* a Transaction?" But nothing has been said to answer the parallel question, "What *meaning* do Transactions have?" The "meaning" of Transactions is determined by the model builder. This is done by establishing an analogy, or correspondence, between Transactions and elements of the system being modeled. These analogies are never declared to the GPSS Processor. They exist only in the mind of the analyst who builds the model. Of course, each model must be built in a way consistent with the analogies the analyst has in mind.

Some examples of possible analogies between Transactions and elements of real systems appear in Table 2.1. In a model of a barber shop, for example, a Transaction might represent a customer. In the real system, the customer arrives at the shop, joins a waiting line, waits until his

---

[1a] Many everyday terms have specialized meanings in the context of GPSS. "Transaction", "Facility", and "Storage" are such terms and are capitalized throughout the book to emphasize their specialized use. Other terms such as Processor, Block, and Block Diagram are similarly noted.

TABLE 2.1 Examples of Possible Interpretations for Transactions

System	System Element Represented by a Transaction
Supermarket	Shopper
Highway	Car
Maintenance shop	Part
Inventory control	Demand
Barber shop	Customer

turn comes, then uses the services of the barber and leaves. The customer can clearly be thought of as a "unit of traffic" moving through the barber shop. In a GPSS model of the shop, various Blocks must be used to provide for such things as a customer's arrival (entry of a Transaction), a customer's use of the barber, a customer's departure (removal of a Transaction), and so on. Movement of a Transaction from Block to Block in the model is then analogous to movement of a customer from stage to stage in the barber shop.

These analogies between Transactions and real-system elements will be brought into sharper focus as properties of the GPSS language are unfolded.

2.4 The Simulation Clock

Time passes as various events occur in real systems. A customer arrives at a barber shop. Later, his turn comes and the barber begins to cut his hair. Still later, the haircut is finished and the customer leaves. If such events are to be represented in a simulation model, they must occur against a background of simulated time. As a consequence, the GPSS Processor automatically maintains a simulated clock.

When a simulation begins, the Processor first schedules Transaction arrivals to the extent possible. The simulated clock is then set to the earliest time that a Transaction is to enter the model. This Transaction (and others, if any, which are to enter at the same time) is then brought into the model. Then, it (or they, one by one) is moved through as many Blocks as possible. Eventually, there is nothing else which is to occur in the system at this first clock reading. The GPSS Processor then advances the clock to the time when the next event, or series of events, is scheduled to take place. These events, as represented by Transaction movement through Blocks, are then caused to occur. When there are no more Transaction movements left to perform at this second clock reading, the clock is again advanced, and so on. It is in this manner that the passage of time is simulated.

A numeric example will help explain the process just described in general terms. In a one-man barber shop, suppose the first few events on a given day are as shown in Table 2.2. As modeled in GPSS, the Processor would maintain the clock as follows. The shop is opened at the start of the simulation. Nothing is to occur until time 22.[2] The clock is therefore set to 22, and customer 1 arrives (a Transaction enters the model). Finding he does not have to wait, the customer immediately gets into the barber's chair (the Transaction moves forward, Block by Block, until it enters a Block which deliberately holds it to simulate hair-cutting time). No further events are to take place until time 29. The clock is consequently advanced to 29, and customer 2 arrives (another Transaction enters the model). This customer has to wait for the barber (the Transaction is denied permission to move into the Block whose execution simulates the act of capturing the barber). Nothing else is to happen at time 29. The Processor then moves the clock to

---

[2] As indicated in Chapter 1, the concept of event scheduling is used to determine the times at which events are to occur in a simulation. The details of event scheduling, as implemented in GPSS, will be explained later in this chapter.

TABLE 2.2 A Possible Sequence of Events in a One-Man Barber Shop

Sequence in Which the Event Occurs	The Event Itself	Real Time of Occurrence	Simulated Time of Occurrence*
1	The barber opens the shop	8:00 a.m.	0
2	Customer 1 arrives and goes into service	8:22 a.m.	22
3	Customer 2 arrives	8:29 a.m.	29
4	Customer 3 arrives	8:33 a.m.	33
5	Customer 1 is finished	8:47 a.m.	47
6	Customer 2 goes into service	8:47 a.m.	47
7	Customer 4 arrives	9:07 a.m.	67

*Expressed in minutes, relative to a base of zero at 8:A.M.

33, causes customer 3 to arrive (yet another Transaction enters the model), and so on.

It should be clear by now how intimately the reading of the simulated clock is related to the sequence of events which can, in general, occur in a simulation model. One of the advantages of GPSS is that it automatically updates the simulation clock as required by the logic described in a model. There is no need for the analyst to explicitly arrange for this clock maintenance, as was the case in the Chapter 1 example of the one-line, one-server queuing system. The precise manner in which the GPSS Processor updates the clock will be explained in due course.

There are several important features of GPSS and the GPSS clock which will now be stated, point by point.

1. The GPSS clock registers only *integer* values. This means that events can only occur at "whole" time values in GPSS models.

2. The unit of time which the clock registers is determined by the analyst. However, the time unit chosen is never declared to the Processor. It is expressed implicitly in terms of the time data built into the model. If all time data are expressed in minutes, then the minute is the implicit unit of time. Or, if all time data are in milliseconds, then the unit of time is the millisecond. The analyst is responsible for deciding the smallest time unit required to realistically reflect real-system events in his model. He must then take care to express all his time data in terms of this smallest unit.

In the Table 2.2 barber shop example, the implicit time unit is 1 minute. This means it would not be possible for a customer to arrive at, say, the forty-seventh second after 8:51 a.m. If it is necessary to have arrivals occur to the nearest second in the model, then the implicit time unit cannot be larger than 1 second.

3. GPSS is a "next event" simulator. That is, after a model has been fully updated at a given point in simulated time, the clock is advanced to the nearest time at which one or more next events are scheduled to occur. *Potential* clock readings are jumped over when no events are to take place at those times. *This means that for all practical purposes execution-time requirements are independent of the implicit time unit chosen by the analyst.*

Finally, care should be taken to distinguish between simulated time and real time. When the simulation clock is advanced to a next reading, that reading remains fixed while the model is updated. Nevertheless, *real* time passes as the updating occurs. It may require hours of real time to move models of some systems (e.g.,

computer systems) through only minutes of simulated time. On the other hand, experiments equivalent to weeks, months, or even years of simulated time can often be conducted in only seconds of real time on a computer. This ability to compress time is one of the potential advantages of experimenting with systems by simulating them on a computer.

2.5 General Details Associated with Blocks in a GPSS Block Diagram

The Figure 2.1 Block Diagram silhouette is repeated in Figure 2.2, where the general Block details have been filled in. Each Block carries with it information falling into three categories.

1. *Location*. Each Block occupies a specific Location in a Block Diagram. Strictly speaking, Locations are designated numerically. The first Block in a model occupies Location 1, the second Block occupies Location 2, and so on. Fortunately, it is not necessary for the model builder to provide Location numbers. When the GPSS Processor reads in the punchcard version of a model, it assigns the Location numbers in the order in which the cards for the various Blocks have been placed in the card deck.

It frequently happens that the analyst wants to know which Locations are occupied by certain Blocks in a model. This information may be required so the Blocks in question can be referenced from one or more other Blocks. When this need arises, it would be tedious to count Blocks to predict the Location numbers ultimately to be assigned by the GPSS Processor. Rather than counting, the analyst has the option of providing *symbolic Location names* for the Blocks of interest. When such symbolic names are used, the Processor later supplies absolute Location numbers in their place.

Symbolic names are composed of from three to five alphanumeric characters, with the restriction that the first three be alphabetic. Examples of valid and invalid symbolic Location names are shown in Table 2.3.

TABLE 2.3   Examples of Valid and Invalid Names for Block Locations

Valid	Invalid
BYPAS	BY25
BLOK1	2AND4
OUT	NO
JOE23	A2B
FLO2M	P

Normally, the analyst only assigns a symbolic name to the Location occupied by a Block when it is necessary to refer to that Block from other parts of the model.

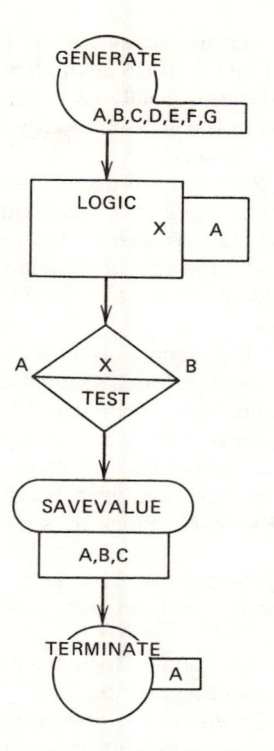

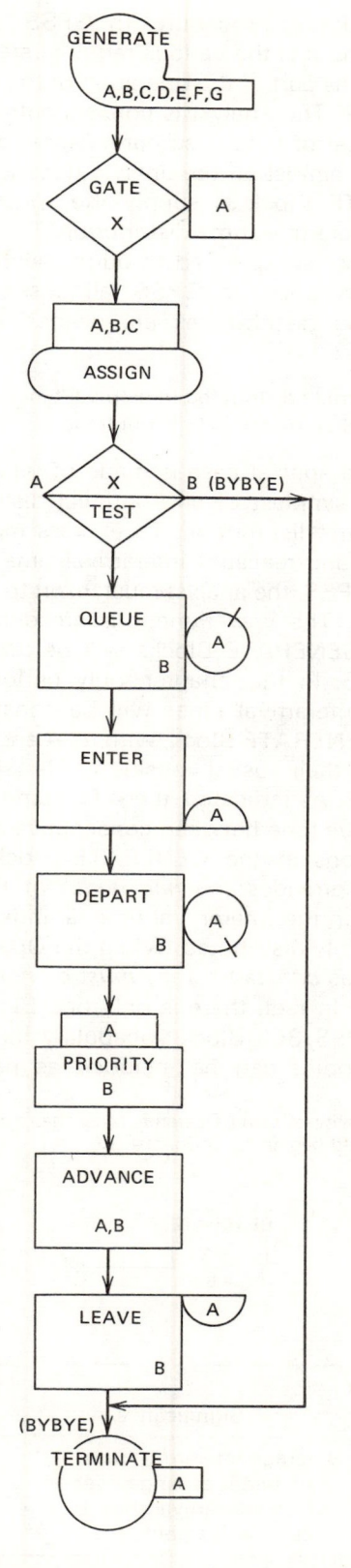

FIGURE 2.2   A repetition of Figure 2.1, with general Block details shown

In Figure 2.2, for example, the Location occupied by one of the two "TERMINATE" Blocks in the model has been symbolically named BYBYE. The Location name is written just above and to the left of the TERMINATE Block, and is enclosed in parentheses. (The parentheses are not part of the name.) Note how the Location BYBYE is referenced at another Block in the model (i.e., at the "TEST" Block). The name BYBYE is supplied at the horizontal exit from the TEST Block to indicate one of the Locations which Transactions entering the TEST Block might move to next. The other exit from the TEST Block is shown as a vertical path leading into the "QUEUE" Block. The QUEUE Block is sequential to the TEST Block. It is usually not necessary to provide Location names for Blocks which Transactions can only reach sequentially, that is, along a path leading from the preceding Block. This explains why no Location name appears with the QUEUE Block (or, for that matter, with any Blocks except the one TERMINATE Block) in Figure 2.2.

2. *Operation.* The "Operation" of a Block is a "verb" suggestive of the task the Block accomplishes. Each Block type is characterized by its own, predefined verb. The Operations GENERATE, GATE, ASSIGN, TEST, QUEUE, ENTER, DEPART, PRIORITY, ADVANCE, LEAVE, TERMINATE, LOGIC, and SAVE-VALUE all appear in Figure 2.2. When the punchcard version of a Block Diagram is prepared, each Block Operation must be specified. (In most cases, but not all, it is permissible to abbreviate the Operation word by supplying only the first four characters in the word. For example, GENERATE can be shortened to GENE, TERMINATE can be shortened to TERM, etc. The

words which *cannot* be abbreviated in this fashion are SAVEVALUE, START, and UNLINK. In any event, such abbreviations are not officially endorsed, and there is no guarantee that they will be honored in future releases of the GPSS Processor.)

Some GPSS Blocks make use of "Auxiliary Operators." An Auxiliary Operator is represented in general with the letter X. As indicated by the presence of X's in Figure 2.2, then, the use of Auxiliary Operators is involved at "GATE" Blocks, "TEST" Blocks, and "LOGIC" Blocks.

3. *Operands*. The various Blocks have Operands associated with them. A Block's Operands provide the specific information on which the Block's action is based. The Operands may be conveniently thought of as the arguments used in calls on subroutines.

The number of Operands each Block has depends on the type of Block. No Block uses more than seven Operands. Most use only one or two. The Operands are represented *in general* as A, B, C, D, E, F, and G. The Operands are shown only in this general fashion in Figure 2.2.

For some Blocks, certain Operands must always be specified, whereas others are optional. In some cases, when optional Operands are not explicitly provided, the Processor assumes default values to be in effect.

2.6 Bringing Transactions into a Model: The GENERATE Block

The GENERATE Block can be thought of as a door through which Transactions enter a model. In fact, the GENERATE Block is the Block-type referred to earlier as a "source Block." There is no limit to the number of different GENERATE Blocks a given model can contain.

Now, it is usually the analyst's intention to have Transactions come into a model at different points in time. The time between two consecutive Transaction arrivals at a given GENERATE Block is termed interarrival time. The interarrival-time concept discussed in the Chapter 1 queuing model is applicable here. In fact, the approach used in GPSS to arrange for Transaction arrivals is identical to the one taken in arranging for customer arrivals in the Chapter 1 model. That is, when a Transaction enters a model through a GENERATE Block, the Processor schedules its successor's time of arrival by sampling from an interarrival-time distribution, then adding the sampled value to a copy of the clock's current value. When that future time is reached, another Transaction is brought into the model through that GENERATE Block, and so on.

In the Chapter 1 queuing model, the analyst had to supply the logic necessary to support this scheduling procedure. In GPSS, the Processor conducts the various required steps automatically, as part of the operation of the GENERATE Block. The analyst is consequently relieved of a number of otherwise burdensome details.

In fact, almost all the analyst does in using a GENERATE Block is supply the specifications for the interarrival-time distribution. The required information is expressed through the Block's A and B Operands. In GPSS, all possible interarrival-time distributions are divided into two categories:

1. Uniformly distributed interarrival times.
2. All other interarrival distributions.

In short, a special case is made of what is perhaps the simplest of all nontrivial distributions, the uniform distribution. To express more complicated (and realistic) interarrival-time distributions in GPSS, the analyst must resort to Function definition. The way Functions are defined and used at GENERATE Blocks will be taken up in Chapter 3. In this chapter, only uniformly distributed interarrival times will be considered.

The GENERATE Block, with its A and B Operands in their usual positions, is shown in Figure 2.3. As indicated, the A Operand specifies the *average* time between consecutive arrivals of Transactions at the GENERATE Block. The B Operand provides the *half-width* of the range over which the interarrival time is understood to be uniformly distributed. When the Operands are supplied as *constants*, they *must* be *nonnegative* integers.[3] In fact, there is only one Block in the entire GPSS/360 Block vocabulary for which a decimal point can be included as part of an

[3] The possibility of using Operands other than constants will be considered beginning in Chapter 3.

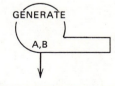

Operand	Significance	Default Value
A	Average interarrival time	Zero
B	Half-width of range over which interarrival time is uniformly distributed	Zero

FIGURE 2.3   The GENERATE Block, and its A and B Operands

Operand. In all other circumstances, *it is an error* to include decimals when expressing Block Operands.

Figure 2.4 provides a specific example of the GENERATE Block. The A and B Operands are 5 and 3, respectively. The interarrival time, then, is uniformly distributed over the range 5 ± 3, that is, over the *integers* 2, 3, 4, 5, 6, 7, and 8. Recall that the GPSS clock only registers *integer* values. For this reason, Transactions can only be brought into a model at integer-valued points in time. This explains why 5 ± 3 describes the closed interval of integers from 2 to 8, rather than the continuum of all values between 2 and 8. In this example, then, interarrival time can take on any one of seven different values. Because the values are uniformly distributed, each occurs with a relative frequency of one-seventh.

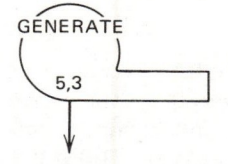

FIGURE 2.4   A GENERATE Block with specific A and B Operand values

To illustrate scheduling, suppose a Transaction arrives at the Figure 2.4 GENERATE Block at simulated time 15. After this Transaction has moved to the next Block in the model, the GPSS Processor draws a sample from the 5 ± 3 interarrival-time distribution. The sampled value is, say, 7. The Processor then schedules arrival of the next Transaction *at that GENERATE Block* at future time 15 + 7, or 22. When that Transaction appears at the GENERATE Block and moves to the next Block, the time of *its* successor's arrival will then have to be scheduled. In short, a bootstrapping technique is used to arrange for Transaction arrivals. Again, note the similarity between the approach used here, and that used to schedule customer arrivals in the one-line, one-server model in Chapter 1.

As suggested in Figure 2.3, values for the A and/or B Operands do not have to be provided explicitly at a GENERATE Block. When no values are specified, "default" values of zero are assumed by the Processor. Figure 2.5 shows an example in which the default option has been taken with the B Operand. The A Operand is 10. Because a value of zero is assumed for the B Operand, the interarrival times are uniformly distributed over the integers 10 ± 0. That is,

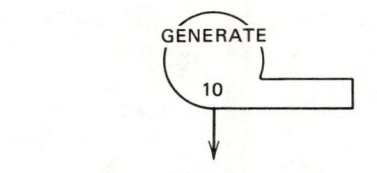

FIGURE 2.5   A GENERATE Block with no explicit B Operand

interarrival times are always exactly 10. This is an example, then, of deterministic (i.e., nonrandom) interarrival times.

Three additional GENERATE Block Operands will now be introduced and discussed. They are shown in Table 2.4. The C Operand, if used, supplies an *Offset Interval*. The Offset Interval is a *time*. In particular, it is the time when the *first* Transaction is to arrive at the GENERATE Block. After this first arrival, all subsequent arrivals follow the interarrival-time distribution provided through the A and B Operands. Put differently, the C Operand can be used by the analyst to *force* the *first* Transaction arrival to occur at whatever particular time he specifies. After that, times of arrival are generally random, per the information provided at the A and B Operands. When the C Operand is not used, *all* arrivals at that GENERATE Block take place at times governed by the A and B Operands.

TABLE 2.4   Significance of the GENERATE Block C, D, and E Operands

Operand	Significance	Default Value
C	Offset Interval	No offset in effect
D	Limit Count	Infinity
E	Priority Level	Zero

The D Operand places a limit on the total number of Transactions which can enter the model through a given GENERATE Block during a simulation. When that many arrivals have occurred, the GENERATE Block becomes inactive. If no Limit Count is specified, the GENERATE Block remains active throughout a simulation.

The E Operand states the Priority Level, or Priority Class, of each Transaction entering the model through a given GENERATE Block. For reasons to be made clear later, it is convenient to make distinctions among Transactions with respect to their relative processing priority. In total, 128 different Priority Levels are possible in a model. These Priority Levels are designated numerically as 0, 1, 2, 3, 4, . . . , 125, 126, and

127. The higher the number, the higher the priority. The lowest possible priority, then, is 0. As indicated in Table 2.4, it is this lowest priority which is assigned to Transactions entering a model through a GENERATE Block for which no explicit E Operand is provided.

Figures 2.6(a), (b), and (c) show examples of GENERATE Blocks in which values have been explicitly provided for the C, D, and E Operands in some cases. In Figure 2.6(a), the first arrival is to take place at time 10. After that, inter-arrival times vary at random over the range 3 ± 3, that is, from 0 to 6, inclusive. However, only five Transactions are to arrive in total through that GENERATE Block.

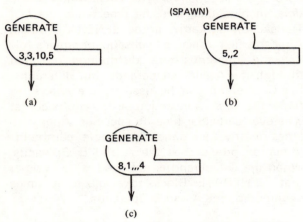

FIGURE 2.6 Additional GENERATE Block examples. (a) A GENERATE Block with Operands A through D specified. (b) A GENERATE Block with Operands A and C specified. (c) A GENERATE Block with Operands A, B, and E specified.

In Figure 2.6(b), the first arrival is to take place at time 2. After that, arrivals are to occur every five time units. That is, arrivals will occur at times 2, 7, 12, 17, 22, 27, and so on. Note the two consecutive commas which appear after the A Operand. Because nothing is entered between the two commas, there is no B Operand. The default value of zero is consequently in effect. Note that the Block Location has been given the symbolic name SPAWN.

In Figure 2.6(c), all arrivals follow the 8 ± 1 interarrival-time distribution. No Offset Interval is used. Arrivals will continue at the Block throughout the simulation, because no Limit Count has been provided. Each Transaction brought into a model through the Figure 2.6(c) GENERATE Block will have a Priority Level of 4, as specified by the E Operand. Note the three

consecutive commas between the B and E Operands. These have the effect of forcing default values for the C and D Operands.

It should already be apparent that the beginning GPSS model builder usually must look up the role of the various Block Operands in the process of constructing models. For this reason, Appendix L provides an alphabetic listing of each of the Blocks introduced in this book, and indicates what information is supplied by each Block's Operands. Turn to Appendix L now, and read about the "braces and brackets" notation used there to indicate whether Operands are required or optional. Then find the GENERATE Block in Appendix L, and note how the roles of Operands A, B, C, D, and E are described for this Block.

2.7 Exercises

1. Show a GENERATE Block at which Transactions will arrive every 7 ± 2 time units, throughout the course of a simulation. Assuming that the third arrival occurs at time 21, list the possible times at which the fourth arrival might take place. What is the probability that the fourth arrival takes place at time 30? What Priority Level will be assigned to Transactions arriving at the GENERATE Block?

2. Show a GENERATE Block at which Transactions will arrive:
   (a) Every 6 time units.
   (b) Every 6 time units, except that the first is to arrive at time 15.
   (c) Every 6 time units, but only until 10 have arrived in total.

3. Show a GENERATE Block at which Transactions will arrive every 15 ± 5 time units:
   (a) With a Priority Level of 0.
   (b) With a Priority Level of 9.

4. Interarrival times at a particular GENERATE Block are to be uniformly distributed over the integers:
   (a) 4, 5, 6, 7, and 8. Show a GENERATE Block which will have the desired effect.
   (b) 4, 5, 6, 7, 8, and 9. Can you show a GENERATE Block to accomplish this? [When Functions are discussed in Chapter 3, a method will be shown for solving this exercise.]

5. The GENERATE Block shown in Figure E5 will result in an error condition when the model in which it is used is run on the computer. Can you tell why?

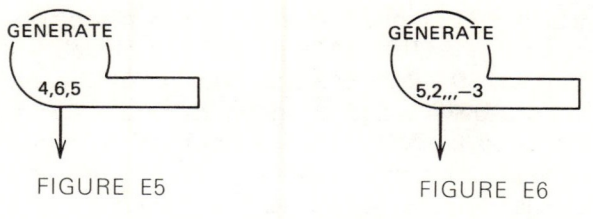

FIGURE E5

FIGURE E6

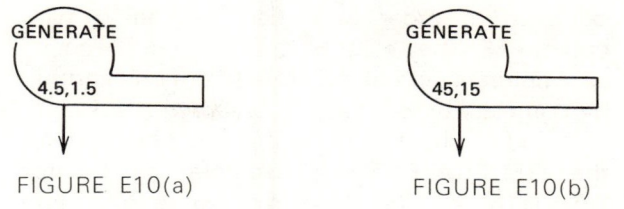

FIGURE E10(a)

FIGURE E10(b)

6. Why is the Figure E6 GENERATE Block invalid?

7. Why is the Figure E7 GENERATE Block invalid?

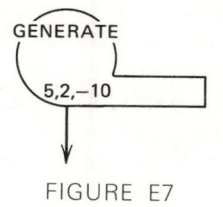

FIGURE E7

8. Figure E8(a) is valid, whereas Figure E8(b) is invalid. Explain why.

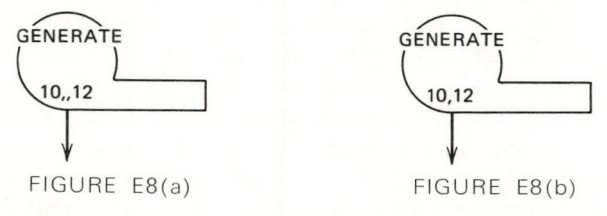

FIGURE E8(a)   FIGURE E8(b)

9. Assume that only the GENERATE Blocks shown in Figure E9 are used in a particular GPSS model, and that at time 20 no Transactions have yet been removed from the model. How many Transactions with Priority Level 0 are in the model at time 20? With Priority Level 7? With Priority Level 13?

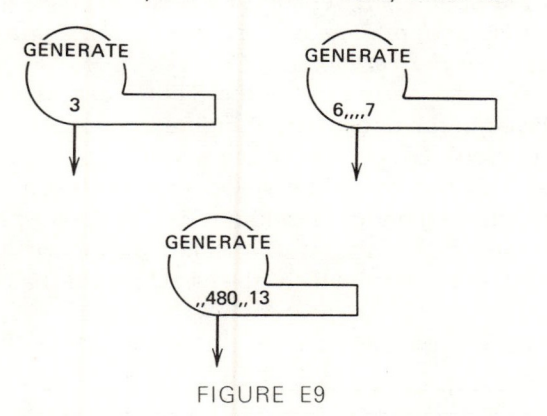

FIGURE E9

10. (a) Suppose it is an analyst's intention to have the implicit time unit in a model be 1 minute. At a particular point in the model, Transactions are to be introduced with interarrival times uniformly distributed between 3 and 6 minutes. The analyst provides the GENERATE Block shown in Figure E10(a) to produce this effect. Why is his work in error?

(b) Realizing his error, the analyst decides to make the implicit time unit be 0.1 minutes. He modifies the GENERATE Block Operands, with the result shown in Figure E10(b). How many different values can the inter-arrival-time random variable take on here?

(c) Still later, the analyst decides that he must work with a smaller implicit time unit. He chooses 1 second as the unit. Show the appearance of the Figure E10(a) GENERATE Block as modified to correspond to this smaller time unit. Now how many different interarrival times can be realized at the GENERATE Block?

11. Transactions are to arrive at a GENERATE Block every 0.6 ± 0.2 days. State what the A and B Operands should be for the GENERATE Block if the implicit time unit is to be:

(a) 0.1 days
(b) 1/5 day
(c) 0.3 hours
(d) 0.1 hours

2.8 Punchcards Corresponding to Blocks in GPSS Block Diagrams

The three types of information carried by Blocks have already been described in Section 2.5. Corresponding to this information, there are three fields laid out on the punchcard used for Block representation. The card columns making up each field are shown in Table 2.5.

TABLE 2.5   Punchcard Fields in which Block Information Is Entered

Card Columns	Block Information
2–6	Location
8–18	Operation
19–71	Operation

The symbolic Location name (if any) of a Block must be punched in consecutive columns anywhere within the field consisting of columns 2 through 6. The Block's Operation is entered in consecutive columns in the field beginning with card column 8. The Operands must be punched in order in a field beginning with column 19. They must be entered in consecutive card columns and be separated from one another by commas, *without any intervening blanks*.

A coding sheet showing punchcard images for the GENERATE Block examples in Figures 2.6(a), (b), and (c) appears in Figure 2.7.[4] Note that "explanatory comments" have been entered in Figure 2.7, beginning (arbitrarily) in column 31. The same comments could also be entered on the punchcards themselves. This is because the *first blank column* encountered in the Operands field causes the GPSS Processor to terminate its scan of that punchcard Explanatory comments can consequently be included toward the end of each punchcard for purposes of model documentation.

Note that column 1 is not part of the Location field. When an *asterisk* is entered in column 1, the Processor ignores the entire card. This provides further possibilities for documenting models with lengthy comments, and/or leaving space between distinct model segments. In this spirit, "blank cards" have been inserted between the three examples in Figure 2.7.

The first and third examples in Figure 2.7 have nothing entered in the Location field. This is consistent with the fact that, in Figures 2.6(a) and (c), the GENERATE Blocks have not been given Location names. The Figure 2.6(b) Block has been tagged with the symbolic Location name SPAWN. That name is therefore entered in columns 2 through 6 in the second Figure 2.7 example.

2.9 Removing Transactions from a Model: The TERMINATE Block

Transactions are removed from a model whenever they move into a TERMINATE Block. TERMINATE Blocks always accept Transactions

[4] Pads of GPSS coding sheets are available from IBM. The Form Number for these pads is GX20-1701.

which try to move into them. There may be any number of TERMINATE Blocks in a model.

The TERMINATE Block, with its A Operand in its usual position, is shown in Figure 2.8. As indicated, the A Operand is a *Termination Counter decrement*. That is, it is the amount by which a special counter, called the *Termination Counter*, is to be decremented each time a Transaction moves into the TERMINATE Block. When the analyst chooses not to provide a TERMINATE Block A Operand, a default value of zero is in effect. Movement of Transactions into such TERMINATE Blocks then does not decrease the value of the Termination Counter.

What is the Termination Counter? It is a computer memory location in which a positive integer value is stored at the time a simulation run is begun. As the simulation proceeds, Transactions move into TERMINATE Blocks from time to time, resulting in decrementation of this counter. *As soon as the counter has been decremented to zero (or less), the simulation stops.*

Note carefully that, although there may be many TERMINATE Blocks in a model, there is *only one* Termination Counter. It is this Termination Counter which will be decremented whenever a Transaction moves into *any* TERMINATE Block in a model.

As already indicated, the Termination Counter is supplied with its initial value at the time a simulation begins. The GPSS Processor starts the simulation when it encounters a START card in the punchcard version of a model. *It uses the A Operand on the START card as the initial value for the Termination Counter.*

The general format for the START card is displayed in the upper part of Figure 2.9. As shown, the word START is entered in the *Operation field* on the card. The A Operand, as usual, is entered beginning in column 19. The lower part of Figure 2.9 shows a specific example of a START card in which the A Operand has a value of 1.

Now consider an example in which the

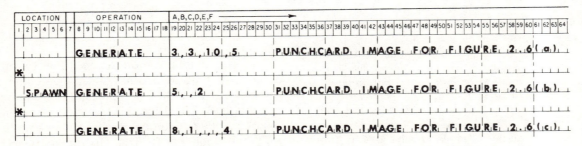

FIGURE 2.7   Punchcard images for the Blocks in Figures 2.6(a), (b), and (c)

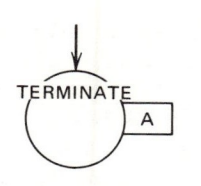

FIGURE 2.8 The TERMINATE Block and Its A Operand

TERMINATE Block and START card are used in harmony to control the duration of a simulation run. Suppose a model builder has chosen 1 minute as the implicit time unit in a model. He wants to run the model through 8 hours of simulated time, and then have it shut off. This is the approach he might use:

1. He includes in the model the two-Block segment shown in Figure 2.10.
2. At all other TERMINATE Blocks in the model, *he defaults on the A Operand.* This means that terminations occurring at those Blocks during the simulation do not cause the Termination Counter to be decremented.
3. He uses 1 as the A Operand on the START card.

The A Operand of 1 on the START card causes the Processor to give the Termination Counter an initial value of 1 when the simulation is started. As the simulation proceeds, Transaction terminations that occur from time to time at *other* TERMINATE Blocks in the model have no effect on the Termination Counter. Then, at simulated time 480, a Transaction is brought into the model through the Figure 2.10 GENERATE Block. The Transaction moves immediately into the sequential TERMINATE Block, causing the underlying TERMINATE subroutine to be executed. Because the TERMINATE Block has an A Operand of 1, 1 is consequently subtracted from the Termination Counter. This decreases the counter's value from 1 to 0. As a result, the Processor shuts off the simulation.

This use of a Termination Counter may seem like a strange way to implement run control in a model. Nevertheless, it is the *only* way to control the duration of a run in a GPSS model.

Now suppose that, to accomplish the same

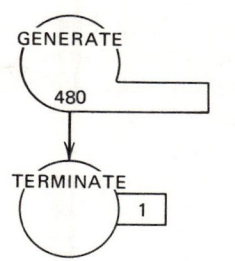

FIGURE 2.10 A two-Block segment which causes a simulation to stop at simulated time 480 (assuming two other conditions are satisfied)

objective stated in the preceding example, the analyst uses this approach:

1. He includes in the model the two-Block segment shown in Figure 2.11.
2. At all other TERMINATE Blocks in the model, he defaults on the A Operand.
3. He uses 480 as the A Operand on the START card.

Note that, at the Figure 2.11 GENERATE Block, the interarrival time is 1. That is, Transactions arrive there at times 1, 2, 3, 4, . . . , 478, 479, and 480. Upon arrival, each of these Transactions moves to the sequential TERMINATE Block, where it is removed from the model and the Termination Counter is decreased by 1. When the four hundred and eightieth Transaction moves into the Figure 2.11 TERMINATE Block, then, the Termination Counter has already been decremented to 1. The four hundred and eightieth Transaction causes it to be decreased from 1 to 0, and the simulation stops.

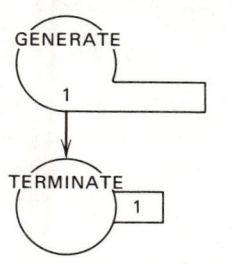

FIGURE 2.11 An alternative two-Block segment which causes a simulation to stop at simulated time 480 (assuming two other conditions are satisfied)

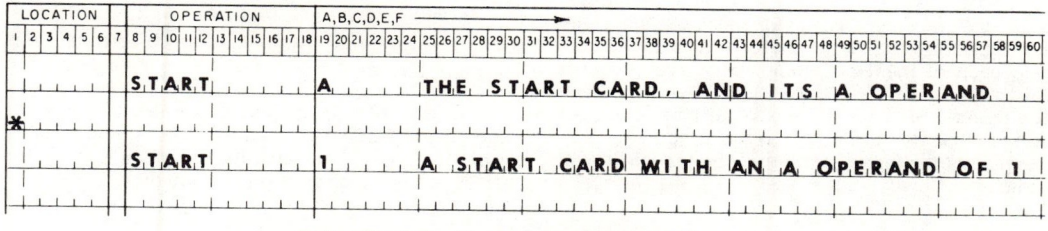

FIGURE 2.9 Format for the START card

The approach shown in the first example is preferable to the one just shown. Although both approaches are logically sound, the latter requires 480 executions of the GENERATE and TERMINATE Blocks in Figure 2.11. Of course, each Block execution consumes computer time.[5] The latter approach, then, is at least 480 times more expensive than the former.[6]

2.10 Exercises

For each of these exercises, assume that all TERMINATE Blocks other than the ones shown have default values of zero for their A Operands.

1. The two-Block segment in Figure E1 is used as a "timer" in a GPSS model. The START card has 8 entered as the A Operand. At what simulated time will the run shut off?

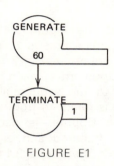

FIGURE E1

2. Suppose that the A Operand in the Figure E1 GENERATE Block is changed to 70, and that all other conditions are left the same. At what simulated time will the run shut off?

3. Suppose that the A Operand in the START card in exercise 1 is changed to 3, and that all other conditions are left the same. At what time will the GPSS Processor shut off the model? What will be the final value of the Termination Counter in this case?

---

[5] On the System/360, Model 67, each Block execution requires about 1 millisecond of computer time. This time varies, of course, depending on the type of Block in question. The 1 millisecond figure is nonetheless a convenient (and somewhat conservative) rule of thumb.

[6] In the latter approach, the GPSS Processor is forced to become a fixed time increment simulator, because the clock must take on values of 1, 2, 3, 4, . . . , 478, 479, and 480, corresponding to each of the Transaction arrival events which occur at the Figure 2.11 GENERATE Block. This very likely increases the number of times the clock must be advanced during the simulation. The resulting increase in housekeeping overhead means that the factor of 480 may be too small by a significant amount.

4. A modeler decides to use *two*, two-Block segments to control a simulation run. The two segments are shown in Figure E4. If he uses a START card with an A Operand of 25, when does the simulation shut off? Is the final value of the Termination Counter 0, or −1? Explain your answer.

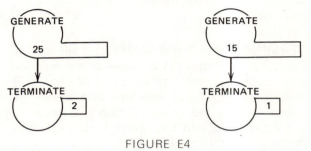

FIGURE E4

2.11 Entities to Simulate Single Servers: Facilities

Consider the concept of entities whose purpose is to perform "service upon demand." Such entities might either be people, or things. For example, these people provide service on demand:

1. A barber
2. A gas station attendant
3. A repairman
4. An insurance agent
5. A carpenter

In a similar sense, these things are designed to provide service on demand:

1. A card punch
2. A pencil
3. A parking space
4. An opera glass
5. A crane

Whether people or things, entities such as those listed above will be referred to as "servers." As understood here, servers are characterized by two properties of interest.

1. Each server can only respond to *one demand for service at a time*. If a new service demand arises when the server is already providing service, then the new demand must either (a) wait its turn for the server, or (b) go elsewhere.[7]

2. When a server has been engaged, time elapses while the service demanded is performed. This time is termed *service time*.

---

[7] There is a third possibility. If the new demand is important enough, it can *interrupt* the server at the expense of the earlier demand. This interrupt capability can be modeled in GPSS. It will be discussed in Chapter 7.

In GPSS, the term "Facility" is a synonym for "server." Just as there can be many servers at different points in a system, there can be many Facilities in a GPSS model. *Names* are given to Facilities, making it possible to distinguish among them. The names are supplied by the model builder, rather than being predefined. Names can be either *numeric*, or *symbolic*.

When Facilities are named numerically, *positive whole numbers* must be used. The largest number which is valid equals the maximum number of different Facilities allowable in a model.[8]

When Facilities are named symbolically, the same set of rules that applies for naming Block Locations must be followed. As previously discussed, symbolic names are composed of from three to five alphanumeric characters, with the restriction that the first three be alphabetic. Examples of valid and invalid names for Facilities, both numeric and symbolic, are shown in Table 2.6.

TABLE 2.6   Examples of Valid and Invalid Names for Facilities

Valid	Invalid
CRANE	IT
26	26KEY
CPU	OS
SURVR	−5
1	94528

It was pointed out in Section 2.3 that the abstract concept of "Transaction" has meaning, from the analyst's point of view, in terms of the analogies he draws between Transactions and elements in the real system being modeled. The same observation holds for Facilities. A modeler might choose, for example, to let Facility 9 represent a repairman in a maintenance system. Or, the Facility named CPU might be chosen to represent a central processing unit in a computer system, and so on. The process of drawing analogies between abstract concepts in GPSS, and their real-system equivalents, is an inherent part of modeling in the GPSS language.

[8]The maximum number of Facilities allowed in a model depends on the amount of computer storage available. For example, in GPSS/360, the normal quantity of Facilities with 64K (i.e., 64,000) bytes of memory is 35; with 128K bytes, 150; and with 256K bytes, 300. Hence, in a model run with 64K bytes of memory, no Facility number can normally exceed 35. Appendix F shows the normally available quantities of the various GPSS entities.

2.12 Engaging and Disengaging Facilities: The SEIZE and RELEASE Blocks

Suppose we want to use a server. In doing so, we go through this series of steps.

1. We wait our turn, if necessary. Of course, waiting takes place over an *interval* of time.
2. When our turn comes, we engage the server. It might also be said that we "capture," or "seize," the server. The event "seize the server" occurs at a *point* in time.
3. We hold the server in a state of capture while the service demanded is performed. The service is performed over an *interval* of time.
4. When the demanded service has been performed, we disengage the server. It might also be said that we "release" him. The event "release the server" occurs at a *point* in time.

As would be expected, this same series of steps is followed when simulating the use of a server in GPSS. The GPSS implementation of Steps (2) and (4) will now be considered. The means of providing Step (3), and the possibility of gathering statistics on the Step (1) waiting process, are then taken up in the following sections.

In GPSS, the entities which place demands on Facilities for service are *Transactions*. It is the nature of Transactions that they tend to move forward in a model, Block by Block. Suppose that, as its next activity, a Transaction is to seize a Facility (i.e., capture a server). The Transaction accomplishes this objective by moving (or *attempting* to move) into a particular Block associated with the Facility of interest. The Block has these features:

1. If the Facility is already in use, the Transaction is denied entry to the Block, i.e., it is not permitted to seize the Facility at this time, but must wait its turn. This "denial of permission" to enter a Block brings the moving Transaction temporarily to rest, as was described in Section 2.3.
2. If the Facility is not in use, the Transaction is permitted to enter the Block. Movement of a Transaction into a Block causes the underlying Block subroutine to be executed. A consequence of the subroutine execution is to change the status of the Facility from "not in use" to "in use."

The Block which has these properties is the SEIZE Block. This Block and its A Operand are shown in Figure 2.12.

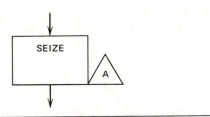

Operand	Significance	Default Result
A	The name (numeric or symbolic) of the Facility to be seized	Error

FIGURE 2.12   The SEIZE Block and Its A Operand

Just as movement of a Transaction into a SEIZE Block simulates capturing a server, movement of the same Transaction into another particular Block simulates releasing the server. The purpose of this other Block, of course, is to change the status of the previously-captured Facility from "in use" to "not in use." The Block which has this purpose is the RELEASE Block. The Block and its A Operand are shown in Figure 2.13.

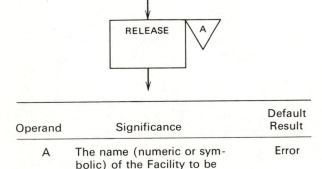

Operand	Significance	Default Result
A	The name (numeric or symbolic) of the Facility to be released	Error

FIGURE 2.13   The RELEASE Block and Its A Operand

The RELEASE Block never denies entry to a Transaction seeking to enter it. It would be illogical, however, for a Transaction to attempt to release a Facility not already in use. If such an attempt is made, the GPSS Processor outputs an error message and terminates execution of the model.[9] Furthermore, if the Transaction seek-

[9]Appendix C contains a complete list of GPSS/360 error messages.

ing to release the Facility is not the very same one which has it "in use," an error message is outputted and execution of the model stops.

It is not necessary to declare the existence of particular Facilities to the GPSS Processor before referring to them at SEIZE Blocks. The fact that they are referenced at SEIZE Blocks causes the Processor to recognize their existence. By the same token, recall that when Transactions were discussed, nothing was said about declaring their existence to the Processor before attempting to bring them into a model. In short, the Processor automatically provides Transactions and Facilities (and other GPSS entities not yet discussed) as required by the logic in a model. Whereas Transactions lead a transient existence, however, all Facilities used in a model exist throughout the course of a simulation.

When a single server is modeled, it may be important to collect information summarizing the server's experiences during the simulation. For example, answers to questions like the following are often of interest.

1. What fraction of the time was the server busy?
2. How many different times was the server captured?
3. What was the average holding time per capture of the server?

One of the nice features of the GPSS language is that answers to such questions are *automatically* provided for each Facility used in a model. These answers, or statistical summaries, are printed out by the Processor at the end of a simulation.

In concluding this section, note that the events "capture a server" and "release a server" are complementary. The latter event reverses the effect produced by the former. The SEIZE and RELEASE Blocks, then, are a complementary pair. Many other GPSS Blocks exist in comple-

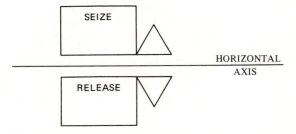

FIGURE 2.14   The SEIZE and RELEASE Blocks as mirror images

mentary pairs. One member of the pair always has the effect of undoing, or reversing, the effect of the other pair member. In most cases, the characteristic shapes of complementary Blocks are mirror images of each other with respect to a horizontal axis. This makes the shapes easier to remember. Figure 2.14 shows the SEIZE and RELEASE Blocks in a mirror-image perspective.

2.13 Providing for the Passage of Time: The ADVANCE Block

Assume that a Transaction has just moved into a SEIZE Block, thereby capturing a Facility. After executing the Block subroutine, the Processor immediately attempts to move the Transaction into the next sequential Block. There are very few restrictions on what this next Block might be. For example, it could be another SEIZE Block, referencing another Facility. This would make sense logically if it were necessary, say, to capture both a repairman *and* a particular tool before a certain type of service could be performed. If the repairman and the tool were simulated with a pair of Facilities, the Transaction would have to simultaneously hold both in a state of capture before its demand for service could be met.

Usually, though, a Transaction captures a Facility with the objective of immediately receiving service from it. As noted in Section 2.12, time passes while the service is performed. While this time is passing, the Transaction should cease its forward motion in the model. Only after the service time has elapsed should it move on into a RELEASE Block to disengage the server.

The ADVANCE Block is provided in GPSS to accomplish the task of freezing a Transaction's motion for a prescribed length of time. The prescribed length of time is usually a random variable. This is consistent with the experience that service time usually varies from one service to the next.

The information required to describe the applicable service time distribution is expressed through the ADVANCE Block's A and B Operands. The various possible service time distributions are divided into two categories:

1. Uniformly distributed service times.
2. All other service time distributions.

In short, as with the GENERATE Block, a special case is made of the uniform distribution. Ex-

pressing more complicated distributions requires the use of GPSS Functions. Because Function definition is deferred to the next chapter, only uniformly distributed service times will be considered for now.

Figure 2.15 shows the ADVANCE Block with its A and B Operands. As indicated, the A Operand supplies the average time that Transactions entering the Block are held there. The B Operand provides the half width of the range over which the holding times are uniformly distributed.

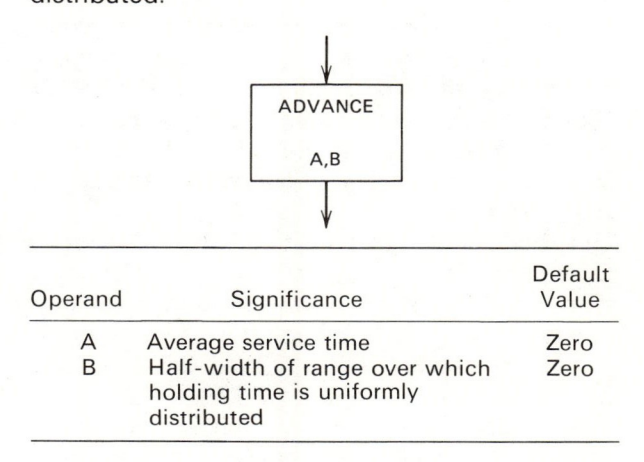

Operand	Significance	Default Value
A	Average service time	Zero
B	Half-width of range over which holding time is uniformly distributed	Zero

FIGURE 2.15   The ADVANCE Block and Its A and B Operands

Figure 2.16 shows an ADVANCE Block with A and B Operands of 30 and 5, respectively. For each Transaction moving into that Block, the range of possible holding times varies over the integers from 25 to 35, inclusive. Suppose a Transaction moves into the Block at time 134 and, executing the Block subroutine, the Processor draws a sample of 31 from the 30 ± 5 distribution. The Transaction will then be delayed at the Block until future time 134 + 31, or 165. At that time, the Processor will attempt to move it into the next sequential model Block.

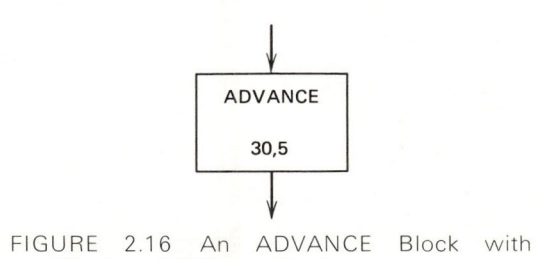

FIGURE 2.16   An ADVANCE Block with specific A and B Operand values

The ADVANCE Block never refuses entry to a Transaction. Any number of Transactions can be held there simultaneously. Whenever a Transaction moves into such a Block, the underlying subroutine is executed again and a customized holding time is computed. The newcomer, then, is in no way influenced by the presence of other Transactions in the Block.

Depending on an ADVANCE Block's A and B Operand values, it is not inconceivable that a holding time of "zero" will be computed for a Transaction when it moves into an ADVANCE Block. For example, at the Block "ADVANCE 12,12", a holding time of zero will be computed for about 4 percent of the Transactions which move into the Block. When this happens, instead of holding the Transaction in the ADVANCE Block, the Processor immediately attempts to move it into the sequential Block. There are in fact occasions when it is convenient to use the ADVANCE Block as a "dummy Block." This can be done by defaulting on the Block's Operands, thereby guaranteeing that holding time at the Block will always be zero. Situations in which this is done come up later in the book.

The classical SEIZE–ADVANCE–RELEASE pattern is shown in Figure 2.17. A Transaction moving down the indicated path eventually will capture the Facility symbolically named JOE, hold it for 16 ± 4 time units, and then release it. After the Transaction enters the RELEASE Block and that subroutine has been executed, the

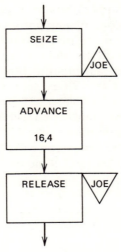

FIGURE 2.17 An example of a SEIZE–ADVANCE–RELEASE sequence

Processor will attempt to move it into the next Block in the model. Meantime, with execution of the RELEASE subroutine completed, the next Transaction intending to use the Facility named Joe will be able to capture it.

Do not form the conclusion from the Figure

2.17 example that ADVANCE Blocks can only be placed after SEIZE Blocks in a GPSS model, or that RELEASE Blocks must follow them. ADVANCE Blocks can actually be put *anyplace* in a model. Of course, the choice of their locations should be defensible on logical grounds.

2.14 When Waiting Occurs: Where and with What Privileges Transactions Wait

Suppose that a Transaction arrives at the Figure 2.17 model segment and finds that the Facility named JOE is already in a state of capture. The Transaction is denied permission, then, to move into the SEIZE Block. Two questions arise.

1. While the Transaction "waits" for the Facility, *where* does it wait?

2. If two or more Transactions are waiting for the Facility when it again becomes available, which of the waiting Transactions will be permitted to capture it next?

The answer to the first question becomes clear when it is remembered that the Transaction *is currently in some other Block*, from which it is trying to make its move into the SEIZE Block. When the SEIZE Block denies entry to this Transaction, it waits *in its current Block*. Does this mean that the effect of the Transaction having entered its current Block has not yet taken place? Not at all. Remember that, when a Transaction moves "through" a Block, the sequence of events is (1) the Block subroutine is executed as soon as the Transaction moves *into* the Block, *then* (2) the Processor attempts to move the Transaction into the next Block. It is entirely possible for a Transaction to come to rest in a Block after it has caused that Block's subroutine to be executed. *This* type of coming to rest is "involuntary"; the Transaction would prefer to keep moving forward in the model, if system conditions permitted. Contrast this with a Transaction "voluntarily" coming to rest in an ADVANCE Block.

The answer to the second question touches on the concept of *queue discipline*. The queue discipline exercised by a server is the *rule* he follows in determining whom to serve next, given that two or more demands for service await him. In our normal activities, we usually encounter "first-come, first-served" queue discipline. The person who has been waiting the longest for the server captures him next. *This is the queue discipline which is implemented by the GPSS Processor as the default case.*

Actually, the default queue discipline implemented in GPSS is slightly more flexible than "first-come, first-served." It is first-come, first-served, *within Priority Class*. It was pointed out in Section 2.6 that each Transaction has a particular priority associated with it. The Priority Level of waiting Transactions is automatically taken into account by the Processor when selecting the one which is to capture a Facility next. In a case study later in this chapter (Case Study 2C), it is shown how priority distinctions can be put to use in models, and made clear why the GPSS default queue discipline is first-come, first-served, within Priority Class.

2.15 Gathering Statistics When Waiting Occurs: The QUEUE and DEPART Blocks

GPSS provides an option for automatically gathering statistics describing the involuntary waiting which may occur from time to time at various points in a model. The first part of this section introduces the Blocks corresponding to this option, and illustrates their basic use. A seldom-used feature of these Blocks is then described. Finally, two misconceptions about the statistics-gathering process are commented on.

2.15.1 Fundamental Use of the QUEUE and DEPART Blocks

Almost by definition, queuing systems involve constrained resources. A resource is constrained when there simply isn't enough of it to always respond immediately to the demands made on it. For example, the barber in a one-man barber shop is a constrained resource. If he is already busy when the next customer arrives, then the new arrival must wait his turn. In fact, it is this very waiting which produces queues, and gives rise to the term queuing systems.

Consider our own experience when we use a constrained resource, and go through a line in the process. Three steps can be identified.

1. We join the waiting line. That is, we "queue up." Queuing up is an event which occurs at a *point* in time.
2. We wait our turn. The waiting occurs over an *interval* of time.
3. We depart the waiting line. The departure is an event which occurs at a *point* in time.

Now, it is frequently of interest to gather statistics describing key features of the waiting process implied above in Step (2). These de-scriptive statistics provide answers to questions such as these.

1. How many entries were there to the (potential) waiting line?
2. How many of these entries were actually forced to wait, in contrast with being able to capture the server immediately?
3. What was the maximum number waiting at any one time?
4. What was the average number waiting?
5. Of those who had to wait, how much time did they spend in the queue on average?

A special-purpose language designed for modeling queuing systems should provide the capability of collecting this kind of statistical information with relative ease. GPSS provides such a capability through the so-called *Queue entity*. When the model builder uses the GPSS Queue entity at points in a model where constrained resources are simulated, the GPSS Processor responds by automatically collecting statistics describing the waiting (if any) which occurs at those points.

The Queue entity is similar to the Facility entity in several general ways. As with Facilities, there can be many different Queues in a model. This is because waiting usually can occur at many different points in a system. By using a different Queue at each point of potential waiting, a separate set of statistics describing waiting-line behavior can be gathered at each individual point. Of course, to distinguish among different Queues, *names* must be supplied for them by the model builder. The naming conventions are the same as for Facilities. Names can either be numeric, or symbolic. If numeric, they must be positive integers. The largest number which is valid equals the maximum number of Queues allowable in a model.[10] If symbolic, names are composed of from three to five alphanumeric characters, with the first three being alphabetic.

As in the case of Facilities, the analyst incorporates Queues into a model by making use of a pair of complementary Blocks. The complementary Block pair for the Queue entity is used to simulate the events (1) and (3) above. When a Transaction moves into the first of these Blocks, the event "join a waiting line" is simulated. Similarly, when a Transaction moves into

---

[10]As is true with Facilities, the maximum number of Queues allowed in a model depends on the amount of computer storage available. Referring to Appendix F, it can be seen that the normal quantities of Queues are 70, 150, and 300 for 64K, 128K, and 256K bytes of memory, respectively.

the second of these Blocks, the event "depart a waiting line" is simulated. The Blocks corresponding to the "join" and "depart" events are the QUEUE and DEPART Blocks, respectively. These two Blocks are shown with their A Operand in Figure 2.18.

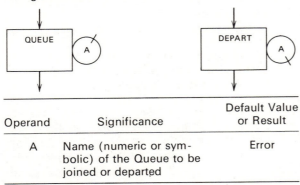

Operand	Significance	Default Value or Result
A	Name (numeric or symbolic) of the Queue to be joined or departed	Error

FIGURE 2.18 The QUEUE and DEPART Blocks, with their A Operands

As shown in Figure 2.18, the A Operand is used at the QUEUE and DEPART Blocks to indicate the name of a particular Queue. When a Transaction moves into the QUEUE Block, execution of the underlying Block subroutine causes these four things to happen.

1. The "total entry count" for the referenced Queue is increased by 1.
2. The record of the "current content" of the referenced Queue is increased by 1.
3. The Transaction is tagged with a copy of the Queue's name.
4. The Transaction is tagged with a copy of the current value of the simulated clock.

When a Transaction joins a Queue, then, tags are put on the Transaction to that effect. In this sense, information indicating that a particular Transaction is a Queue member is carried by the Transaction itself. The Transaction will cease being a Queue member only when it moves into a DEPART Block referencing the Queue in question. When this happens, and the underlying Block subroutine is executed, the Processor does the following things:

1. The record of the "current content" of the referenced Queue is decreased by 1.
2. Using the clock tag the Transaction picked up earlier at the QUEUE Block, the Processor determines whether the Transaction spent *zero* units of simulated time as a Queue member. If so, this Transaction is *by definition* a so-called "zero entry" to the Queue, and a "zero entry" counter is updated accordingly. (The manner in which zero entries can come about is explained later in this section.)

3. The Transaction's tag indicating membership in the referenced Queue is removed.

It is relatively easy, then, for the Processor to maintain information about Queues. At the end of a simulation, the Processor automatically prints out such Queue content statistics as "total entry count," "maximum content," "average content," and "current content." It also prints out several statistics involving the "average residence time in the Queue."

Consider this matter of average Queue-residence time more closely. The Processor could compute this statistic in either of two quite different ways. One way would be to compute a residence time for each Transaction only when the Transaction moves into a DEPART Block, and thereby terminates its Queue membership. This is not what the Processor does, however. Instead, independent of DEPART Block execution, the Processor keeps track of "total Queue-residence time experienced so far," summed over all past and present Queue members. At any time, then, the Processor can compute "average residence time in the Queue" by dividing the Queue's "total entry count" into "total Queue-residence time experienced so far." The *advantage* of this approach is that it takes into account those Transactions which are still Queue members at the time the computation is performed. The *disadvantage* of this approach is that it can result in a downward bias in the average residence-time statistic, because those Transactions which are still Queue members (if any) are destined to experience some remaining Queue-residence time, and this isn't taken into account in the computation.

The Processor actually computes two Queue-residence-time statistics. One of these statistics is residence time averaged over *all* Queue entries. In general, though, *some* of the Queue entries may have experienced zero residence time in the Queue, i.e., may not have had to wait at all. As a result, the Processor also computes a statistic for "average Queue-residence time, *excluding* those entries which did not have to wait at all." This explains why a Transaction is tagged with a clock copy at the QUEUE Block, and why the Processor then determines at the DEPART Block whether the Transaction was a zero entry to the Queue or not. This Transaction tagging is necessary only because of the zero entry concept.

Now consider an example of placement of

the QUEUE and DEPART Block pair in a model. Referring again to Figure 2.17, it is clear that waiting might occur with respect to use of the Facility named JOE. Suppose that statistics are to be collected for this waiting process. A Queue is introduced into the model segment by sandwiching the SEIZE Block between the QUEUE–DEPART Block pair, as shown in Figure 2.19. The symbolic name JOEQ has been given to the Queue. Subject to the previously mentioned naming rules, this choice of Queue name is of course arbitrary.

Just how does the Figure 2.19 model segment work in practice? Suppose that a Transaction moves into the model segment when the Facility JOE is not in a state of capture. The Transaction enters the QUEUE Block, and that subroutine is executed. The total entry count to the Queue is updated, the content of the Queue is increased by 1, and the Transaction is tagged with the name of the Queue, and the time of Queue entry. The Processor then immediately attempts to move the Transaction into the SEIZE Block. Because JOE is available, the attempt is successful. The SEIZE subroutine is performed, and the status of the Facility JOE is

changed from "not in use" to "in use." The Transaction then immediately moves into the DEPART Block. That subroutine is executed, and the current content of the Queue is decreased by 1, etc. Continuing its forward motion, the Transaction next moves into the ADVANCE Block. A holding time is computed by sampling from the 16 ± 4 distribution, and the Transaction temporarily comes to rest. All of this has happened at a particular reading of the simulated clock. This means that although the Transaction joined the Queue named JOEQ, it spent zero units of simulated time as a member of that Queue. In other words, the Transaction was a zero entry to the Queue. Such zero entries can occur for the simple reason that the SEIZE Block is sandwiched between the QUEUE–DEPART Block pair. All Transactions capturing the Facility must move through the QUEUE and DEPART Blocks in the process, even if the Facility is available at the time they arrive to attempt the capture.

Now suppose that while the Facility JOE is in a state of capture, another Transaction moves into the Figure 2.19 model segment. Entering the QUEUE Block, it causes the total entry count and the current content to be updated, and is tagged with the Queue name and the time of Queue entry. The Transaction then immediately tries to move into the SEIZE Block. Permission to enter is denied, however, because the Facility JOE is in use. The would-be capturer consequently comes to rest involuntarily, remaining in the QUEUE Block in this example. Later, when the current user of the Facility finishes its use, the waiting Transaction will again try to enter the SEIZE Block. This time, the attempt will be successful. Having resumed its forward motion, the new capturer will then move into the DEPART Block, decrementing the current content of the Queue by 1, etc. For the situation described, the Transaction moved into the QUEUE and DEPART Blocks at different points in simulated time. This means that a "nonzero entry" to the Queue has taken place.

The exact nature of the Queue statistics which the Processor prints out at the end of a simulation will be examined as part of the case study to be presented in Section 2.17.

2.15.2 Use of a B Operand with the QUEUE and DEPART Blocks

Although it was not mentioned above, there is an optional B Operand which can be used with the

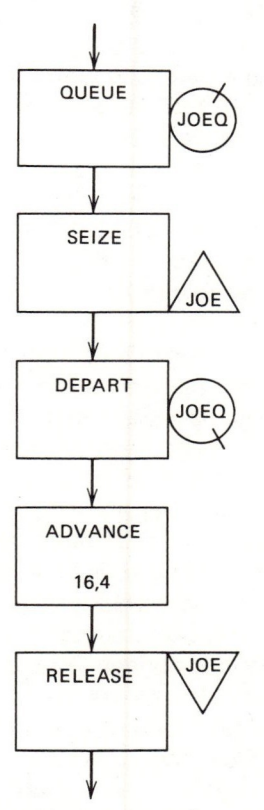

FIGURE 2.19 Repetition of the Figure 2.17 model segment with a Queue included

QUEUE and DEPART Blocks. Figure 2.20 is a repetition of Figure 2.18, except that the existence of this optional B Operand is recognized. As shown in the Figure, the B Operand indicates *the number of units by which the content of the Queue is to be modified*. In case of default,

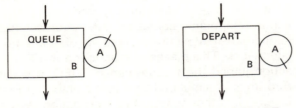

FIGURE 2.20 The QUEUE and DEPART Blocks, with their A and B Operands

Operand	Significance	Default Value or Result
A	Name (numeric or symbolic) of the Queue to be joined or departed	Error
B	Number of units by which the recorded content of the Queue is to be modified	1

the B Operand's value is understood to be 1. It is this default value which is in effect in Figure 2.19.

The role of the B Operand is best explained by reviewing what the Processor does when the QUEUE and DEPART Block subroutines are executed. These four things happen when the QUEUE subroutine is executed.

1. The "total entry count" for the referenced Queue is increased *by an amount equal to the value of the B Operand*.

2. The record of the "current content" of the referenced Queue is increased *by an amount equal to the value of the B Operand*.

3. The Transaction is tagged with a copy of the Queue's name.

4. The Transaction is tagged with a copy of the current value of the simulated clock.

Items (3) and (4) are as explained earlier. Items (1) and (2) show that the B Operand has its effect in terms of the recorded content of the Queue, indicating the amount by which the total entry count and current content are to be incremented. It should be evident, then, that if B Operand values other than 1 are used at QUEUE Blocks, a Queue's total entry count does not equal the number of Transactions which have

moved into QUEUE Blocks referencing that Queue. Similarly, a Queue's current count does not necessarily equal the number of Transactions which are tagged as being current members of the Queue. For example, when a Transaction moves into the Block "QUEUE LINE,2", both the total entry count and the current content of the Queue are increased by 2, but the number of Transactions which have become Queue members only increases by 1, and the number of Transactions which are currently Queue members only increases by 1.

Now consider what happens when the DEPART Block subroutine is executed.

1. The record of the current content of the referenced Queue is decreased *by an amount equal to the value of the B Operand*.

2. Using the clock tag the Transaction picked up earlier at the QUEUE Block, the Processor determines whether the Transaction spent zero units of simulated time as a Queue member. If the Transaction was a zero entry to the Queue, the zero entry counter is incremented *by an amount equal to the value of the DEPART Block's B Operand*.

3. The Transaction's tag indicating membership in the referenced Queue is removed.

To illustrate item (2), suppose that a Transaction moves into the Block "QUEUE QUEUP,5", and then at the same simulated time moves into the Block "DEPART QUEUP,5". By definition, the Transaction is a zero entry to the Queue. Remember, though, that the Processor maintains its Queue information with respect to units of content, not with respect to Transactions. As a result, in this example the count of zero entries to the Queue is increased by 5, not just by 1.

If QUEUE and DEPART Block B Operands other than 1 have been used in a particular case, it is clear that the Queue statistics produced by the Processor must be interpreted accordingly. When statistics such as total entry count, maximum content, average content, current content, and zero entries are printed out, it must be remembered that the reference here is not with respect to Transactions, but with respect to units of content. In summary, there is a one-to-one relationship between "Queue content" and "Transactions viewed as past and/or current Queue members" only if the B Operand at the various QUEUE and DEPART Blocks is 1 (either explicitly, or by default). Fortunately, there is rarely occasion to make use of the B Operand at QUEUE and DEPART Blocks, meaning that the one-to-one relationship is almost always in effect. In fact, in this book the occasion never arises to do anything other than default on the B Operand at QUEUE and DEPART Blocks.

2.15.3 Some Misconceptions About the Queue Entity

For the person just beginning the study of GPSS, it is quite easy to have several misconceptions about use of the Queue entity in the language. Two of the more common of these misconceptions will now be commented on.

The first misconception is to mistakenly think that the Queue entity *must* be used at each point in a model at which waiting might occur. The thinking here seems to be that "if the Queue entity is not used, then no provision has been made to allow the possibility of waiting." This is not true. Use of the Queue entity is entirely optional. When the Queue entity is used, the Processor gathers statistics on the waiting process; when it is not used, no statistics are gathered, but waiting occurs anyway if the system being modeled requires it. In Figure 2.19, for example, whether or not the SEIZE Block is sandwiched between a QUEUE–DEPART Block pair, it will be impossible for a Transaction to move into the SEIZE Block when the Facility JOE is "in use." Waiting is conditioned on the status of the Facility, then, and not on the use of the Queue entity.

On many occasions, even when waiting is known to occur at certain points in a model, the model builder chooses not to use the Queue entity at those points. If there is no plan to use the resulting statistics on a postsimulation basis, then it is better not to collect the statistics in the first place. The result is a savings in the computer time required to perform the simulation.

To illustrate this point, Figure 2.21 is intended to suggest a system in which waiting might potentially occur at up to six different locations. The model builder might want to maintain statistics on the waiting process at each of the six locations, or at none of them. Or, he may want to study the waiting process at some of the locations, but not all. He might decide to gather statistics at locations 2, 4, 5, and 6, but not at locations 1 and 3, for example. There are a number of case studies in this book in which the Queue entity is not used at points where waiting is known to occur. The fourth and fifth case studies in this chapter provide examples of this.

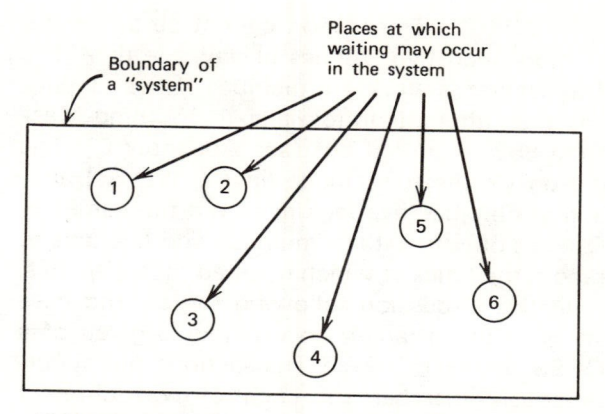

FIGURE 2.21 Six locations at which waiting might occur in a particular system

The second common misconception about the Queue entity is to mistakenly think that a Transaction is not a Queue member unless it is in a QUEUE Block. This is not true. A Transaction simply *initiates* its Queue membership by moving into a Queue Block, thereby becoming tagged with the name of the Queue, and the time of entry to the Queue. Whether or not the Transaction subsequently remains in the QUEUE Block, the Transaction's Queue membership continues until the Transaction moves into a DEPART Block referencing the Queue in question. Depending on the way the model has been built, a Transaction can, in general, do a good bit of moving around in a model between the time it leaves the QUEUE Block, and the time it moves into a corresponding DEPART Block. One of the things it might do in the meantime, for example, is join (and then perhaps depart) some other Queue in the model.

It is implied above that a Transaction can be a member of more than one Queue at a time. This is not as strange as it may seem at first. It is easy to find situations in which people are simultaneously members of two or more waiting lines. Note here that being a member of a waiting line does not necessarily require physical presence in the line. For example, consider the case of a shopper who "takes a number" when she enters a meat market. When that number is called, it will be her turn to be served. If the shopper judges that her number won't come up for a while, she might go next door to a bakery, join a waiting line there, eventually be served, and then return to the meat market to continue waiting there. As a matter of record, she has been in the meat market all the time, even though she has joined and departed another waiting line.

In GPSS, a Transaction cannot be a member of more than five Queues at any one time. If a Transaction is already a member of five Queues and then attempts to join a sixth, Warning Message 853 is printed out (see Appendix C). The reason for the five-Queue limit is that a Transaction only has five tags to record the names of Queues of which it is a member, and five tags to record the times at which it joined those Queues.

In the discussion following the second case study in this chapter, an example is given of a GPSS model in which Transactions are simultaneously members of each of two different Queues.

2.16 Documentation Standard for Case Studies

In this book, frequent use is made of case studies to illustrate pertinent features of GPSS. A consistent documentation pattern is followed in presenting these cases. These are the components of the documentation:

1. *Statement of the Problem.* This component provides a sufficiently detailed description of the problem so that a GPSS model for the system described can be built and run.

2. *Approach Taken in Building the Model.* This section attempts to explain how the task of interpreting the problem in the context of GPSS was approached. The intention is to explain the rationale behind the particular approach used. For some of the easier problems, the approach is almost trivial. For more difficult problems, this may not be true.

3. *Table of Definitions.* The importance of using analogies in building GPSS models is clear. Good model documentation includes a description of the analogies chosen by the analyst. The Table of Definitions is a listing of the various GPSS entities used in the model, with a brief explanation of their interpretation as elements in the system being modeled. The implicit time unit chosen by the analyst appears at the head of this table. Then the interpretation given to Transactions appears. After that, alphabetic order is followed for the other entities and their interpretations.

4. *The Block Diagram.* In a sense, the Block Diagram *is* the model. An unadorned Block Diagram can be difficult for someone other than the model builder to follow. For this reason, *annotations* are placed adjacent to the Blocks in the diagram. Annotations are brief comments which indicate what the Block simulates, or helps to simulate, in the system being modeled.

5. *Extended Program Listing.* As the GPSS Processor reads in the punchcard version of a model, these three steps are performed (among others).

(a) A Block Number (that is, a Location number) is assigned to each Block in the model.

(b) A Card Number is assigned to each punchcard in the deck.

(c) For each card, this information is copied to the printer.

   (i) Block Number (if the card is a Block image).

   (ii) Information punched in the Location, Operation, and Operands fields in the card, including comments, if any.

   (iii) Card Number (number of the position this card occupies in the deck).

The result is a Processor-produced listing of the original program. Actually, because numeric Block Locations and Card Numbers are included in this listing, but are not entered on the original cards themselves, this listing is better described as an "Extended Program Listing." The extended listing is included in model documentation because it implicitly answers the sometimes-asked questions, "where do the cards go?" and "exactly what definition has been used for this or that feature of the model?"

6. *Program Output.* The printout produced when the simulation is run is shown to display what the analyst receives for his efforts, and often to serve as the basis for discussion. Frequently, only "selected" output is shown. This is done to save space, and to emphasize those portions of the output which are of most interest. In some cases, rather than showing direct printout, summaries are presented.

7. *Discussion.* The discussion may involve *model logic*, *model implementation*, and *program output*.

Model Logic. When appropriate, features in the Block Diagram are discussed to relate them to facets of the problem itself, or to the particular approach taken for interpretation of the problem in a GPSS context.

Model Implementation. The punchcard version of a model contains cards corresponding to Blocks, but it also contains cards supplying other information. For example, the START card discussed in Section 2.9 must be included as part of the model implementation. There is no Block in a Block Diagram which corresponds to the START card. Similarly, other possibilities exist for including information in the card deck which does not appear directly in the Block Diagram. When the occasion demands, this information will be singled out in the Extended Program Listing and discussed.

Program Output. The program output may occasionally be evaluated in terms of the sense in which it provides an answer to the original problem. The primary purpose of the case studies, though, is to illustrate model-building in GPSS, not to develop numeric answers to problems. For this reason, discussion of program output is not particularly emphasized.

2.17 CASE STUDY 2A
A One-Line, One-Server Queuing System

(1) Statement of the Problem

The interarrival time of the customers at a one-chair barber shop is uniformly distributed over the range 18 ± 6 minutes. Service time for haircuts is 16 ± 4 minutes, uniformly distributed. Customers coming to the shop get their hair cut, first-come, first-served, then leave. Model the shop in GPSS, making provisions to collect data on the waiting line. Then run the model through 8 hours of simulated time. Interpret the output produced by the model in the context of the barber shop.

(2) Approach Taken in Building the Model

This model is easily constructed as a single sequence of Blocks, excepting the run-control component. The order in which the Blocks appear corresponds to the sequence of stages through which customers move in the real system. Customers arrive; if necessary, they wait their turn; then they engage the barber, get their hair cut, release the barber; and leave. Except for the GENERATE and TERMINATE Blocks, this sequence has already been displayed and discussed in Figure 2.19.

To control the duration of the run, a two-Block "timer segment" can be used. In Figure 2.10, a segment accomplishing the objective required here was presented and discussed, under the assumption that the implicit time unit in effect is 1 minute. That segment will be used for this model.

(3) Table of Definitions

Time unit: 1 Minute

TABLE 2A.1   Table of Definitions for Case Study 2A

GPSS Entity	Interpretation
Transactions	
Model Segment 1	Customers
Model Segment 2	A timer
Facilities	
JOE	The barber
Queues	
JOEQ	The Queue used to gather statistics on the waiting experience of customers

(4) Block Diagram

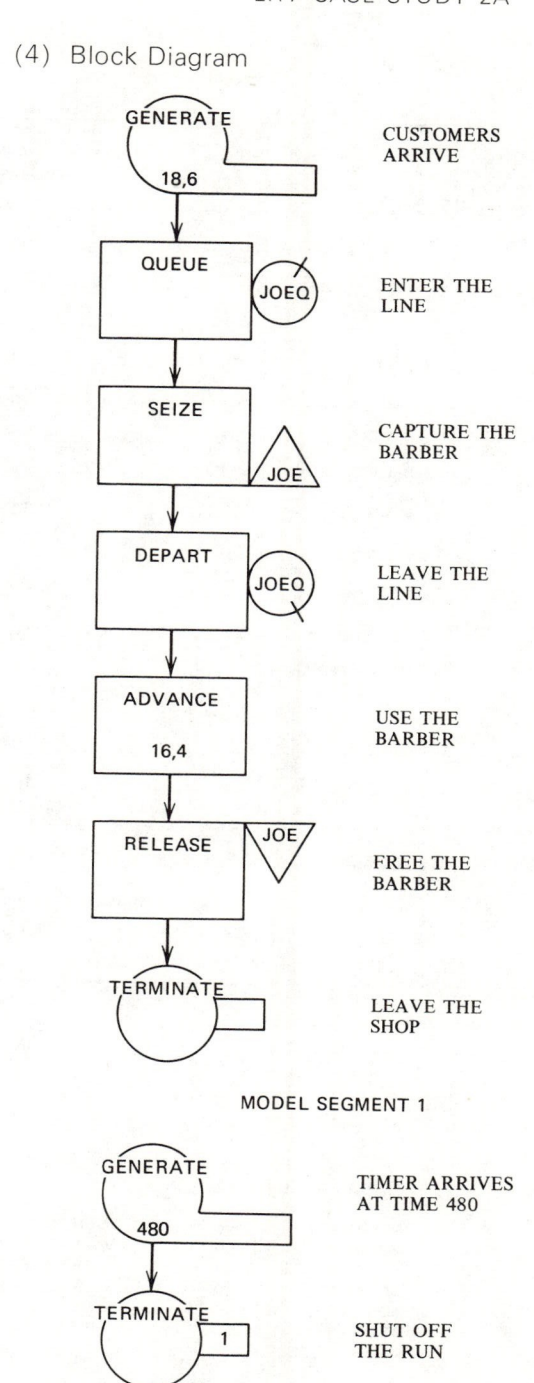

MODEL SEGMENT 1

MODEL SEGMENT 2

FIGURE 2A.1   Block Diagram for Case Study 2A

(5) Extended Program Listing

```
LOCATION | OPERATION | A,B,C,D,E,F ------->
          SIMULATE
*
*         MODEL SEGMENT 1
*
          GENERATE   18,6      CUSTOMERS ARRIVE
          QUEUE      JOEQ      ENTER THE LINE
          SEIZE      JOE       CAPTURE THE BARBER
          DEPART     JOEQ      LEAVE THE LINE
          ADVANCE    16,4      USE THE BARBER
          RELEASE    JOE       FREE THE BARBER
          TERMINATE            LEAVE THE SHOP
*
*         MODEL SEGMENT 2
*
          GENERATE   480       TIMER ARRIVES AT TIME 480
          TERMINATE  1         SHUT OFF THE RUN
*
*         CONTROL CARDS
*
          START      1         START THE RUN
          END                  RETURN CONTROL TO OPERATING SYSTEM
```

(a)

BLOCK NUMBER	*LOC	OPERATION	A,B,C,D,E,F,G	COMMENTS	CARD NUMBER
		SIMULATE			1
					2
	*				3
	*	MODEL SEGMENT 1			4
	*				5
1		GENERATE	18,6	CUSTOMERS ARRIVE	6
2		QUEUE	JOEQ	ENTER THE LINE	7
3		SEIZE	JOE	CAPTURE THE BARBER	8
4		DEPART	JOEQ	LEAVE THE LINE	9
5		ADVANCE	16,4	USE THE BARBER	10
6		RELEASE	JOE	FREE THE BARBER	11
7		TERMINATE		LEAVE THE SHOP	12
	*				13
	*	MODEL SEGMENT 2			14
	*				15
8		GENERATE	480	TIMER ARRIVES AT TIME 480	16
9		TERMINATE	1	SHUT OFF THE RUN	17
	*				18
	*	CONTROL CARDS			19
	*				20
		START	1	START THE RUN	21
		END		RETURN CONTROL TO OPERATING SYSTEM	

(b)

FIGURE 2A.2   The Case Study 2A model as submitted, and the corresponding Extended Program Listing. (a) Completed coding sheet for the punchcard version of the model. (b) Extended Program Listing produced for the model in (a)

(6) Program Output

```
*
*        MODEL SEGMENT 1                    FACILITY SYMBOLS AND CORRESPONDING NUMBERS
*
1        GENERATE    18    6
2        QUEUE        1
3        SEIZE        1                              1    JOE
4        DEPART       1
5        ADVANCE     16    4                              (b)
6        RELEASE      1
7        TERMINATE
*
*        MODEL SEGMENT 2
*
8        GENERATE   480
9        TERMINATE    1
*
*        CONTROL CARDS
*
         START        1        RELATIVE CLOCK      480  ABSOLUTE CLOCK         480
                                BLOCK COUNTS
                                BLOCK CURRENT   TOTAL   BLOCK CURRENT   TOTAL   BLOCK CURRENT   TOTAL
            (a)                   1      0        27
                                  2      1        27
                                  3      0        26
                                  4      0        26
                                  5      1        26
QUEUE SYMBOLS AND CORRESPONDING NUMBERS    6      0        25
                                  7      0        25
                                  8      0         1
                                  9      0         1
            1    JOEQ
```

1	JOEQ

(c)   (d)

FACILITY	AVERAGE UTILIZATION	NUMBER ENTRIES	AVERAGE TIME/TRAN	SEIZING TRANS. NO.	PREEMPTING TRANS. NO.
JOE	.860	26	15.884	3	

(e)

QUEUE	MAXIMUM CONTENTS	AVERAGE CONTENTS	TOTAL ENTRIES	ZERO ENTRIES	PERCENT ZEROS	AVERAGE TIME/TRANS	$AVERAGE TIME/TRANS	TABLE NUMBER	CURRENT CONTENTS
JOEQ	1	.160	27	12	44.4	2.851	5.133		1

$AVERAGE TIME/TRANS = AVERAGE TIME/TRANS EXCLUDING ZERO ENTRIES

(f)

FIGURE 2A.3 Selected Program Output for Case Study 2A. (a) Assembled model. (b) Symbol dictionary for Facilities. (c) Symbol dictionary for Queues. (d) Clock values and Block Counts. (e) Facility statistics. (f) Queue statistics

(7) Discussion

Model Logic.   In the model presented here, no provision is made for "removing customers from the barber shop" when the simulation shuts off at time 480. If the barber were to be true to the model, he would simply have to "walk out of the shop" at the end of his 8-hour day. Conversely, if the model were to be true to the barber, it would simulate locking the door after 8 hours, but the simulation would not stop until all customers already in the shop at that time had been serviced. It will eventually be seen how this latter approach can be implemented in GPSS.

Model Implementation.   The coding sheet from which the punchcard version of the model was prepared is shown in Figure 2A.2(a). The corresponding Extended Program Listing produced by the Processor appears in Figure 2A.2(b). Notice how the Processor has augmented the original information in producing the Extended Program Listing. The extensions consist of the "Block Number" and "Card Number" columns appearing at the extreme left and right, respectively, in Figure 2A.2(b). Inspection of the Block Number column shows that Block Numbers have been assigned, in sequence, to each punchcard representing a Block image. In the Card Number column, note that each card in the deck has been assigned a sequence number.

"Comments" have been used liberally to document the model. Cards 2, 3, 4, 12, 13, 14, 17, 18, and 19 in Figure 2A.2(b) are comments cards which set off the model segments, and the Control Card segment. An asterisk (*) has been entered in column 1 on each of these cards. The Block-image punchcards also carry comments in the Operands field. These comments are identical to the annotations written next to the corresponding Blocks in the Figure 2A.1 Block Diagram.

Card 1 in Figure 2A.2(b) is the SIMULATE card. If the analyst is submitting a deck to have a run made, this card usually must be the first one the Processor encounters when it inputs the deck. The card consists of the single word SIMULATE, punched in the Operation field. If the SIMULATE card is absent, the Processor checks the deck for violations of the language rules, but makes no run with the model.

As stated in Section 2.9, the Processor starts the simulation when it finds a START card in the model. A START card has been placed, then,

at the end of the model (Card 20). A "1" has been entered as the A Operand on the START card.

After a run shuts off, the computer session is not necessarily finished. Many additional options remain open to the analyst. Whether or not these options are exercised, the analyst eventually reaches the point at which all instructions for the run have been included in the deck. At this point, he puts in an END card. This card instructs the Processor to return control to the operating system. The END card appears after the START card in Figure 2A.2(b). It consists of the word END, punched in the Operation field.

The order of the cards *within a model segment* is critical, but the relative ordering of model segments within the card deck is not. For example, the timer segment could have been placed ahead of the major segment in Figure 2A.2 without having any effect on the model. If this had been done, the Extended Program Listing would appear as shown in Figure 2A.4.

Program Output.[11]   It is not evident from examining either the Block Diagram or the Extended Program Listing how any output is produced by the model. At the end of a simulation, the GPSS Processor *automatically* prints out an extensive set of information pertaining to the model. This information includes statistics for each of the various entities used, i.e., for Facilities and Queues (and other entity types not yet discussed).

Most of the output produced by running the Figure 2A.2(a) model is shown in Figure 2A.3. In part (a) of that figure is displayed the assembled model. It has four noticeable features.

1. The absolute Block Numbers assigned by the Processor appear in the assembled model. The numbers 1 through 9 in the left column in Figure 2A.3(a) are these Block Numbers.

2. Instead of appearing in consecutive columns and being separated by commas, the Operands have been printed left-justified in adjacent six-column fields, and the commas have been eliminated. (It is not immediately evident in Figure 2A.3(a) that six-column fields have been used to display the Operands.)

3. All symbolic entity names in the model have been replaced with the corresponding numeric equivalents assigned by the Processor. Hence, the A Operand of the QUEUE Block (Block 2) is 1, not "JOEQ"; the A Operand of the SEIZE Block (Block 3) is 1, not

---

[11] The total CPU time required by the simulation on an IBM 360/67 computer was 1.6 seconds. Computer time requirements for GPSS simulations are discussed in Chapter 4.

```
BLOCK                                                                        CARD
NUMBER  *LOC    OPERATION  A,B,C,D,E,F,G              COMMENTS               NUMBER
                SIMULATE                                                      1
         *                                                                    2
         *      MODEL SEGMENT 2                                               3
         *                                                                    4
1               GENERATE   480            TIMER ARRIVES AT TIME 480           5
2               TERMINATE  1              SHUT OFF THE RUN                     6
         *                                                                    7
         *      MODEL SEGMENT 1                                               8
         *                                                                    9
3               GENERATE   18,6           CUSTOMERS ARRIVE                   10
4               QUEUE      JOEQ           ENTER THE LINE                     11
5               SEIZE      JOE            CAPTURE THE BARBER                 12
6               DEPART     JOEQ           LEAVE THE LINE                     13
7               ADVANCE    16,4           USE THE BARBER                     14
8               RELEASE    JOE            FREE THE BARBER                    15
9               TERMINATE                 LEAVE THE SHOP                     16
         *                                                                   17
         *      CONTROL CARDS                                                18
         *                                                                   19
                START      1              START THE RUN                      20
                END                       RETURN CONTROL TO OPERATING SYSTEM 21
```

FIGURE 2A.4   Extended Program Listing for Case Study 2A, with Model Segments interchanged

"JOE", and so on. (In Chapter 4, the method the Processor uses to establish a correspondence between symbolically named entities and their numeric equivalents will be described.)

4. "Comments" entered on punchcard images of Blocks have been suppressed. "Pure" comments cards (that is, cards with an asterisk entered in card column 1) have not been suppressed, however. They are reproduced in their entirety in the printout of the assembled program.

Parts (b) and (c) in Figure 2A.3 show symbol dictionaries for Facilities and Queues. In the symbol dictionary for Facilities, the numeric equivalent assigned by the Processor for all symbolically named Facilities is shown. Hence, the Facility symbolically named JOE is Facility 1 in the assembled model; and the Queue symbolically named JOEQ is Queue 1. This is consistent with the A Operands for the SEIZE–RELEASE and QUEUE–DEPART Blocks in Figure 2A.3(a). If any Block Locations had been named symbolically in the model, a corresponding symbol dictionary also would have been provided in the output. Actually, if symbolic Location names have been used, the correspondence between them and Location numbers is apparent in the Extended Program Listing.

Figure 2A.3(d) shows clock values and Block Counts. As indicated in the top line of that figure, there are two clocks, the "Relative Clock" and the "Absolute Clock." The distinction between these two clocks will be explained later. For now, it is enough to note that both clocks show values of 480 in Figure 2A.3(d). This simply means that the simulation shut off at simulated time 480.

Immediately under the clock line in Figure 2A.3(d) are shown the Block Counts. This information appears in three columns, "Block Numbers" (labeled simply as BLOCK in the figure), "Current Count" (shown as CURRENT), and "Total Count" (shown as TOTAL). The Block Numbers correspond to those shown in Figure 2A.3(a). The Current Count is the count of Transactions in the corresponding Blocks at the time the simulation shut off. The Total Count is a count of the total number of Transactions which entered the corresponding Blocks during the simulation, including those that are still in the Block (if any). For example, the Total Count at Block 1 is 27, meaning that 27 Transactions entered the model through the Location 1 GENERATE Block. Similarly, the Total Count at Block 2 is 27, meaning that 27 Transactions moved into the QUEUE Block in Location 2. The Current Count at Block 2 is 1, meaning that one Transaction is still in the QUEUE Block, i.e., one customer was waiting for the barber when the model shut off. At the Block in Location 5, the ADVANCE Block, the Current Count is 1 and the Total Count is 26. That is, 26 customers have captured the barber; of the 26, one still has him captured. The Total Counts at the SEIZE and RELEASE Blocks are 26 and 25, respectively, which is consistent with the ADVANCE Block Counts.

In Figure 2A.3, parts (e) and (f) show the statistics gathered for the Facility JOE and the Queue JOEQ. The Facility statistics are shown again in Figure 2A.5, where the columns have been numbered for ease of reference. The Table appearing in the lower part of Figure 2A.5 in-

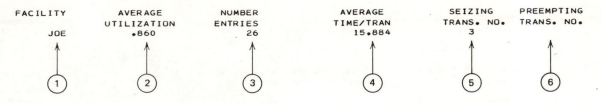

FACILITY	AVERAGE UTILIZATION	NUMBER ENTRIES	AVERAGE TIME/TRAN	SEIZING TRANS. NO.	PREEMPTING TRANS. NO.
JOE	.860	26	15.884	3	
①	②	③	④	⑤	⑥

Column	Significance	Column	Significance
1	Names (numeric and/or symbolic) of the various Facilities used in the model	5	Number of the Transaction (if any) which currently has the Facility captured. (Transaction numbers are discussed later in this chapter.)
2	Fraction of the time that the corresponding Facilities were in a state of capture during the simulation	6	Number of the Transaction (if any) which currently has the Facility preempted. (Preemption will not be explained until Chapter 7.)
3	Number of captures		
4	Average holding time per capture		

FIGURE 2A.5   Interpretation of the information shown in Figure 2A.3(e)

dicates the significance of the entries in the various columns. Similarly, in Figure 2A.6, the Queue statistics have been repeated with column numbers included. The Table at the bottom of that figure indicates the meaning of the various Queue statistics. The tables in Figures 2A.5 and 2A.6 should be studied, making reference to the output immediately above them in the process. Note these features of the information provided in those figures.

1. Joe was in use 86 percent of the time (AVERAGE UTILIZATION = .860).

2. JOE was captured 26 times (NUMBER EN-

TRIES = 26). This is consistent with the previously noted Total Count of 26 for the SEIZE Block.

3. The average holding time per capture of JOE was 15.884 minutes (AVERAGE TIME/TRAN = 15.884).

4. Transaction number 3 had JOE in a state of capture when the simulation shut off (SEIZING TRANS. NO. = 3). The fact that JOE was "in use" when the simulation shut off is consistent with the previously-noted Current Count of 1 at the ADVANCE Block. As for Transaction "numbers," they will be discussed in Section 2.21.

5. There was never more than one customer in the Queue JOEQ (MAXIMUM CONTENT = 1).

QUEUE	MAXIMUM CONTENTS	AVERAGE CONTENTS	TOTAL ENTRIES	ZERO ENTRIES	PERCENT ZEROS	AVERAGE TIME/TRANS	$AVERAGE TIME/TRANS	TABLE NUMBER	CURRENT CONTENTS
JOEQ	1	.160	27	12	44.4	2.851	5.133		1
①	②	③	④	⑤	⑥	⑦	⑧	⑨	⑩

Column	Significance	Column	Significance
1	Names (numeric and/or symbolic) of the various Queues used in the model	7	Average time that each Queue entry spent waiting in the Queue (zero entries are *included* in this average)
2	Largest value the record of Queue content ever assumed	8	Average time that each Queue entry spent waiting in the Queue (zero entries are *excluded* from this average)
3	Average value of the Queue content	9	Name (numeric and/or symbolic) of the GPSS Table in which the distribution of Queue residence time is being tabulated. (The Table concept is not discussed until Chapter 4.)
4	Total number of entries to the Queue		
5	Total number of entries to the Queue which experienced no waiting ("zero entries")		
6	Percentage of total Queue entries which experienced no waiting	10	Current value of the Queue content

FIGURE 2A.6   Interpretation of the information shown in Figure 2A.3(f)

6. The average number of customers in the waiting line was .160 (AVERAGE CONTENTS = .160).

7. The total number of entries to the waiting line was 27 (TOTAL ENTRIES = 27).

8. Included among the 27 total entries to the waiting line were 12 zero entries (ZERO ENTRIES = 12).

9. Of the total entries to the waiting line, 44.4 percent of them were zero entries (PERCENT ZEROS = 44.4).

10. The average residence time in the waiting line per entry (*including* zero entries) was 2.851 minutes (AVERAGE TIME/TRANS = 2.851).

11. The average residence time in the waiting line *per nonzero entry* was 5.133 minutes ($AVERAGE TIME/TRANS = 5.133).

12. At the time the simulation shut off, there was one Transaction in the waiting line (CURRENT CONTENTS = 1). This is consistent with the previously-noted Current Count of 1 at the QUEUE Block.

The statistical measures in Figures 2A.5 and 2A.6 are highly intuitive in meaning, then, and are almost without need of definition. This is especially true for *Facilities*. Because only one Transaction at a time can use a Facility, NUMBER ENTRIES is a direct count of the number of Transactions which captured the Facility, and AVERAGE TIME/TRAN is the average time that each capturing Transaction held the Facility. The same simple comments apply to Queue statistics *if* the B Operand at the QUEUE and DEPART Blocks is 1 (as is true by default in the Case Study 2A model). Recall from the section on Queues, however, that the Processor computes Queue statistics with respect to "units of content," *not* with respect to "Transactions." In Case Study 2A (and throughout this book), each Transaction moving through a Queue contributes exactly one unit of content. If this were not the case, the following extended interpretation would have to be applied to Queue statistics.

1. TOTAL ENTRIES is the number of "units of content" which entered the Queue. More precisely, TOTAL ENTRIES is the value of a counter initialized at zero, and incremented by an amount equal to the QUEUE Block's B Operand each time the QUEUE Block is executed. Except when the QUEUE Block's B Operand is 1, this value does not equal the total number of Transactions which became Queue members during the simulation.

2. ZERO ENTRIES is the number of "units of content" which spent zero residence time in the Queue. More precisely, ZERO ENTRIES is the value of a counter initialized at zero, and incremented by an amount equal to the DEPART Block's B Operand each time the DEPART Block is executed by a Transaction whose residence time in the Queue is zero. Except when the DEPART Block's B Operand is 1, this value does not equal the number of Transactions which became Queue members, and then experienced zero residence time in the Queue.

3. AVERAGE TIME/TRANS is the average residence time in the Queue per "unit of content." Fortunately, this value is identical to the "average Queue residence time *per Transaction*," assuming that each Transaction moving through the Queue *decrements* the "current content" by the same amount that it *incremented* the "current content" earlier. If this condition is not satisfied, then the label AVERAGE TIME/TRANS is misleading.

4. Similarly, the labels MAXIMUM CONTENTS, AVERAGE CONTENTS, PERCENT ZEROS, $AVERAGE TIME/TRANS, and CURRENT CONTENTS must all be interpreted with respect to "units of contents," and not with respect to "Transactions," except of course when QUEUE and DEPART B Operands are 1.

Another feature of both Facility and Queue statistics should be noted. If a Facility is in a state of capture when Facility statistics are printed out, there is a *downward bias* in the AVERAGE TIME/TRAN statistic. This is because AVERAGE TIME/TRAN is computed by dividing NUMBER ENTRIES into the total simulated time during which the Facility was in a state of capture. If there is a current user who is not yet done when the simulation stops, then what would have been his *entire* holding time is not taken into account in computation of the AVERAGE TIME/TRAN statistic. The same observation can be made with respect to Queues. AVERAGE TIME/TRANS is computed for Queues by dividing TOTAL ENTRIES into total Queue residence time. If the Queue has CURRENT CONTENTS when the simulation stops, then they have not yet contributed their full measure to total Queue residence time. This results in a downward bias in AVERAGE TIME/TRANS, and also in AVERAGE TIME/TRANS.

Finally, as will be explained in Section 2.21, the earliest simulated time at which Transactions can experience movement in a model is 1. This means that the content of all Queues in a model is necessarily zero during the simulated time interval from 0 to 1, all Facilities are necessarily "available" during the simulated time interval from 0 to 1, etc. Because statistics such as "average Queue content," "Facility utilization," and so on, are computed as though the simulation started at time 0, a slight bias may consequently be introduced into these statistics.

2.18 External Control Cards Required to Run GPSS Models

After the punchcard version of a GPSS model has been prepared, the resulting card deck must be placed within an appropriate control card sequence before the model can be run. These external control cards have nothing to do with the logic of the model itself. Instead, they provide information specifying the user's account number, indicating that the task to be performed requires use of the GPSS Processor, and so on. When the GPSS model has had the applicable control cards placed around it, the resulting "job" can then be submitted for a computer run.

Figure 2A.2 shows only the punchcard images (and Processor-supplied extensions) of the GPSS model for Case Study 2A; no external control card images are shown in the figure. The control cards which are appropriate for a job depend on the computer installation at which the job is to be run. For this reason, no attempt is made in this book to provide specific details about these external control cards.[12] As indicated in IBM's GPSS/360 Operator's Manual, "The individual who is responsible for the installation and maintenance of the GPSS processor at a given computing center should issue a memo to all GPSS users listing the necessary control cards required for the execution of the GPSS program at that center."[13] It is assumed here that such information has been obtained from the computing center at which the GPSS modeling is to be accomplished.

2.19 Exercises

1. (a) Using Appendix F, determine the normal maximum quantity of Transactions which can be in a model at one time. To what extent is this quantity influenced by the amount of computer memory available?

    (b) Use Appendix C to look up the meaning of each of the following error-message numbers. For each error indicated, try to show a Block or Block sequence which could give rise to the error, or otherwise discuss its significance. 30; 201; 216; 413; 415; 428; 498; 500; 505; 530; 853; 854.

    (c) Assume that the Block "QUEUE   LINE" is executed at times 32, 56, and 88 during a

simulation, and that the Block "DEPART LINE" is executed at times 70 and 77 during the same simulation. Assuming that the simulation stops at time 100, determine what values will be printed out for the following statistics for the Queue LINE: AVERAGE CONTENTS; TOTAL ENTRIES; ZERO ENTRIES; PERCENT ZEROS; AVERAGE TIME/TRANS; $AVERAGE TIME/TRANS; CURRENT CONTENTS. Why is it not necessary to know whether the Transaction departing the Queue at time 70 is the one which entered at time 32, or the one which entered at time 56?

2. (a) Using the average customer interarrival time in Figure 2A.1, determine how many customers are expected to arrive at the barber shop during a typical 8-hour day. Compare this expected number of arrivals with the actual number of arrivals indicated via the Total Count at the Location 1 GENERATE Block [see Figure 2A.3(d)].

    (b) Using the average customer interarrival time and average service time in Figure 2A.1, compute the long-run utilization of the barber in Case Study 2A. Compare this with the utilization statistics in Figure 2A.3(e).

    (c) In Figure 2A.3(e), show how to compute AVERAGE UTILIZATION, given NUMBER ENTRIES and AVERAGE TIME/TRAN, and knowing the duration of the simulation. Does your independently computed value equal 0.860 as shown in Figure 2A.3(e)?

    (d) From information available in Figure 2A.3(f), give an estimate of the probability that a customer will have to wait for the barber.

    (e) In Figure 2A.3(f), show how to compute AVERAGE CONTENTS, given TOTAL ENTRIES and AVERAGE TIME/TRANS, and knowing the duration of the simulation. Does your independently computed value equal 0.160 as shown in Figure 2A.3(f)?

    (f) In Figure 2A.3(f), show how to compute $AVERAGE TIME/TRANS, given AVERAGE TIME/TRANS, TOTAL ENTRIES, and ZERO ENTRIES. Does your independently computed value equal 5.133 as shown in Figure 2A.3(f)?

    (g) In the statistics for a Queue, would it be possible for PERCENT ZEROS to be 100.0 and MAXIMUM CONTENTS to be 1? Explain.

3. Prepare the punchcards corresponding to Figure 2A.2. Then, having determined what external control cards are necessary to run a GPSS model at your computing center, place the applicable control cards around the model and submit the resulting job for running. Compare the resulting program output with the output shown in Figure 2A.3. Are the Facility and Queue statistics in your output in agreement with the statistics in Figure 2A.3? It is

[12] The IBM GPSS/360: OS Operator's Manual [Form Number GH20-0311] gives examples of the control cards required for execution of a GPSS/360 program when running under IBM's Operating System/360.

[13] Ibid, page 8.

quite possible that the statistics will *not* be in agreement. Because of the essential randomness of interarrival times and service times, results from operation of the barber shop will vary from simulated day to simulated day. If the results *are* in exact agreement, this simply means that the underlying source of random numbers in your GPSS implementation exactly matches the random-number source used in producing the Figure 2A.3 output. (The random-number sources in GPSS will be discussed in some detail in Chapter 3.)

4. Modify the Figure 2A.2 model to correspond to a customer interarrival-time distribution of 15 ± 4 minutes. Run the resulting model for 480 minutes of simulated time. Compare the barber's utilization, number of customers entering the shop, and the number of zero entries to the waiting line with the corresponding information in Figure 2A.3. Discuss the observed differences in terms of the changed interarrival-time distribution.

5. Modify the Figure 2A.2 model under the assumption that the implicit time unit is 1 second, not 1 minute. Run the resulting model for the equivalent of an 8-hour day. Compare the barber's utilization, number of customers entering the shop, and the number of zero entries to the waiting line with the corresponding information in Figure 2A.3. Discuss any observed differences in terms of the change in the implicit time unit.

6. (a) In the Figure 2A.1 model, the number of customers served is a random variable. That is, the number of customers served will, in general, vary from 8-hour day to 8-hour day. Modify the model so that it shuts off after exactly 25 customers have been served. (Hint: As part of the modification, eliminate the two-Block timer segment.) Run the resulting model. At what times does the model shut off (what is the reading of the Relative Clock in the program output?). Note that, in the modified model, the number of customers served is strictly determined, whereas the time of model shutdown is a random variable. In the Figure 2A.1 model, the time of model shutdown is strictly determined, whereas the number of customers served is a random variable.

   (b) Show that changes to make in the Figure 2A.1 model so that it will shut off as soon as one of these two events occurs: (1) the simulation clock reaches a value of 480; or (2) exactly 25 customers have been served.

7. Mechanics arrive at a tool crib every 300 ± 250 seconds. There they check out tools for use in repairing failed machines. The clerk who works at the crib requires 280 ± 150 seconds to fill each mechanic's request for a tool.

   (a) Build a GPSS model for this situation, then run the model through 8 hours of simulated time. Suppose that, due to lost production attributable to a failed machine, it costs 0.5¢ per second (i.e., $18 per hour) to have a mechanic wait for service at the tool crib. In this sense, what is the total cost associated with the 8-hour day you simulated?

   (b) Suppose that the clerk described in (a) earns $4 per hour. The clerk can be replaced with another who earns $4.50 per hour, and who requires 280 ± 50 seconds to fill each mechanic's request for a tool. Simulate for an 8-hour day with the alternative clerk and compute the resulting cost associated with waiting mechanics. Is it better to use the first clerk or the second at the tool crib? In light of the sample size (i.e., an 8-hour day simulation) used to compare the two alternatives, how "strong" is your conclusion? What would you do to improve your degree of confidence in the conclusion that you draw?

2.20 Internal Logic of the GPSS Processor

An effort has been made in earlier sections of this chapter to provide some insight into the operation of the GPSS Processor. The insight is necessarily still very incomplete. For example, there has been considerable discussion of movement of Transactions from Block to Block. Nevertheless, the Block Diagram in Figure 2A.1 no doubt still appears to be much more *static* in nature than *dynamic*. And there are still unanswered questions, such as "when a Transaction stops moving, which other Transaction is moved next by the Processor?" and "why is the implicit queue discipline first-come, first-served, within Priority Class?" These questions can only be resolved satisfactorily by understanding the logic on which the Processor itself is based. The next several sections are devoted to considerations of this logic.

Much of the Processor's logic can be understood by considering the mechanism used to keep track of the various Transactions moving through a model. The Processor regards each Transaction as being on one of several "chains." Each Transaction on a chain may be thought of as a link in the chain. The chains are "open," not "closed," so they have a front end, and a back end. As a chain resident, then, a Transaction occupies a specific location relative to the front of the chain. A Transaction's chain location is closely involved with when it will again be that Transaction's turn to be moved forward in the model by the

Processor. The processing sequence, in turn, has strong implications for "what occurs when," when a model is run.

There are five categories of chains.

1. Current Events Chain
2. Future Events Chain
3. User Chains
4. Interrupt Chains
5. Matching Chains

As the choice of words suggest, there is only one Current and one Future Events Chain. In general, there is more than one User Chain, Interrupt Chain, and Matching Chain. Study of the role of the Current and Future Events Chains in GPSS will begin now, and will continue throughout the book. The topic of User, Interrupt, and Matching Chains will not be taken up, however, until Chapter 7.

The Current Events Chain is composed of all Transactions which are scheduled to be moved through one or more Blocks at the current instant in simulated time, *or as soon as possible*. As the italicized phrase indicates, included on the Current Events Chain are those Transactions which are experiencing a blocking condition in the model.[14] For example, a Transaction might be temporarily blocked because it is scheduled to move into a SEIZE Block, but the Facility it wants is already in a state of capture.

The Future Events Chain consists of those Transactions not scheduled to move through one or more Blocks until some future time. This condition can only result in two ways.

1. A Transaction is at an ADVANCE Block, and is not scheduled to attempt to move to the next sequential Block until a later time.
2. A Transaction has been scheduled to enter a model at some future time via a GENERATE Block.

Actually, a third situation can lead to inclusion of Transactions on the Future Events Chain, but only in a highly specialized context that need not be considered here.

Suppose now that a GPSS model is under discussion. Briefly consider the question, where *is* a particular Transaction which is in the model? Note that the answer can be given from two entirely different points of view.

[14] At the analyst's option, blocked Transactions can be removed from the Current Events Chain and put on a User Chain. This may be done to decrease model execution time, or to implement a nonstandard queue discipline, or for both of these reasons. This relatively advanced topic is discussed in Chapter 7.

1. From the Block Diagram point of view, the Transaction is in a particular Block in the model.
2. From the point of view of chains, the Transaction is on a particular chain.

That is, a Transaction is simultaneously "in a Block" and "on a chain." Whether a Block-oriented or chain-oriented answer is given to the above question depends on the context in which a Transaction is being discussed. The distinction between the two different orientations should be kept clearly in mind.

Transactions on the Future Events Chain are ordered according to their scheduled time of future movement. For example, assume the simulated clock currently reads 48. Then, a Transaction scheduled to move from an ADVANCE Block at time 54 is nearer the front of the Future Events Chain than another Transaction scheduled to move from the same (or another) ADVANCE Block at, say, time 59.

GPSS updates the model by scanning the Current Events Chain from front to back, Transaction by Transaction. As each next Transaction is encountered, the Processor "picks it up" and moves it forward along its path in the model until one of three situations is encountered:

1. The Transaction moves into an ADVANCE Block where a positive holding time is computed. When this happens, the Processor then puts the Transaction on the Future Events Chain, merging it into that chain according to the time it will attempt to move to the next sequential Block.
2. A blocking condition occurs, meaning the Transaction cannot enter the next Block in its path. When this happens, the Transaction is left by the Processor on the Current Events chain (and in its current Block). Note that the blocked Transaction may have successfully moved through several Blocks before encountering the blocking condition. The GPSS Processor will, of course, update its record of the Transaction's *Block Location in the model*.
3. The Transaction moves into a TERMINATE Block. When this happens, the Processor removes the Transaction from the model.

When a Transaction has finally stopped moving, the Processor takes one of two steps.

1. Continuing toward the back of the Current Events Chain, it picks up the next Transaction and tries to move it forward in the model.
2. Without advancing the clock, it restarts its scan of the Current Events Chain. Restarting the scan means the Processor returns to the front of the chain, picks up the first Transaction, and moves it forward in the model if possible. When *that* Transaction stops

moving, the Processor again takes one of the two steps now being described, and so on.

The scan is restarted only under very special conditions. The conditions depend on which Block subroutines were executed by the Transaction which has just stopped moving. When a Transaction moves through a SEIZE or a RELEASE Block, the scan is restarted *after that Transaction comes to rest*.[15] The rationale of the scan restart when a RELEASE Block has been executed is that previously blocked Transactions may now be able to move, because a Facility has been released. The purpose of rescanning is to process any Transactions near the front of the Current Events Chain which are in that category.

It is not immediately apparent why the Current Events Chain scan should be restarted as a result of a SEIZE Block having been executed. It is possible that elsewhere in the model, a Transaction may be experiencing a blocking condition (at a type of Block not yet introduced) because a particular server *is* available. Hence, both the capture of a server and the release of a server can, in general, have the effect of eliminating a blocking condition.

Now assume that the Transaction at the back of the Current Events Chain has just been processed. There is no "next Transaction" on that chain. (There may be other Transactions on the Current Events Chain; if so, they are toward the front of the chain, experiencing blocking conditions.) As its next step, the Processor examines the Transaction at the front of the *Future* Events Chain. It advances the simulation clock to the time that Transaction is scheduled to make its next move. That Transaction is then transferred from the Future to the Current Events Chain. Any other Transactions scheduled to make their move at the new clock reading are also transferred from the Future to the Current Events Chain. Each incoming Transaction is *merged* into the Current Events Chain *according to its Priority Level*. The higher the Priority Level, the closer to the front of the Current Events Chain is the Transaction. In case of ties, each newcomer is placed on the Current Events Chain as the last member in its Priority Class.

After the transfer of Transactions from the Future to the Current Events Chain is complete, the Processor begins its scan of the Current Events Chain anew. The basic cycle is then repeated. It is in this overall fashion that the Processor moves the model of a system forward in simulated time.

The various steps taken by the Processor, as just described, are summarized in diagrammatic form in Figures 2.22 and 2.23. Figure 2.22 shows the *Clock Update Phase*. Figure 2.23 shows the *Scan Phase*. The several paragraphs in this section should be reread, and the correspondence between Figures 2.22 and 2.23, and the prose description of the Processor's steps, should be noted.

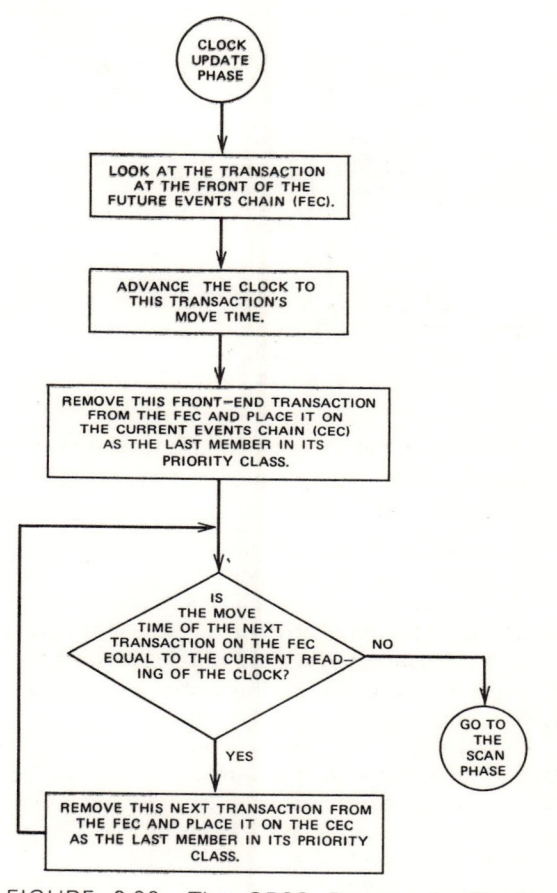

FIGURE 2.22 The GPSS Processor's Clock Update Phase

The major segments of the Processor's logic have now been described. They will be brought into sharper focus by going through the details of a numeric example, using the one-line, one-server case as the system being modeled.

2.21 A First Example of the Use of Current and Future Events Chains

An example showing how the GPSS Processor uses the Current and Future Events Chains will

---

[15] Execution of certain other Blocks not yet studied also leads to scan restarts in this fashion.

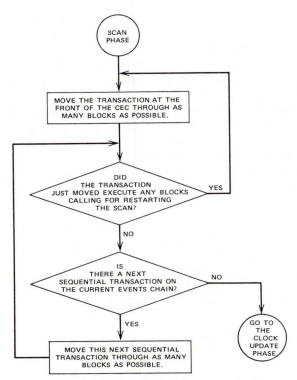

FIGURE 2.23 The GPSS Processor's Scan Phase

now be given for the one-line, one-server model in Figure 2A.1. This sequence will be followed in presenting the example.

1. A notation will be adopted for recording pertinent information about Transactions.

2. A sequence of interarrival and service times at the GENERATE and ADVANCE Blocks will be assumed.

3. A tabular display will be introduced to record the time-dependent positions Transactions occupy on the Current and Future Events Chains.

4. The steps taken by the Processor as it manipulates Transactions on the Current and Future Events Chains will be explained, showing how the Processor updates information about Transactions as they move through a model.

2.21.1 Notation for Transactions

The five pieces of information to be recorded for each Transaction are its number ("Transaction Number"), the time it is scheduled to attempt to move into a next Block ("Move Time"), the number of the Block it is currently in ("Current Block"), its "Priority Level," and the number of the next Block it will attempt to move into

("Next Block Attempted"). This information will be recorded in a five-tuple in the order indicated. The general appearance of such a five-tuple, then, takes the form shown in Figure 2.24(a). A numeric example is shown in Figure 2.24(b). The numeric example indicates that Transaction 9 will attempt at time 68 to move from Block 5 into Block 6. Transaction 9 has a Priority Level of 0.

As suggested above, the GPSS Processor assigns numbers to Transactions. The range of feasible Transaction numbers depends on how many Transactions can simultaneously exist in a model. This quantity is determined by the amount of computer memory available. At a memory level of 64K bytes, the maximum normal quantity of Transactions is 200, as shown in Appendix F. At this level, the Transaction numbers then range from 1 to 200.

Transactions belong to either one of two groups. One group is the "latent pool" of Transactions, those not currently "in existence" in a model. The other group is the "active pool" of Transactions, those which have entered the model through one or more GENERATE Blocks,[16] and have not yet been removed from the model.

Before a simulation starts, Transactions in the latent pool reside in a stack ordered by increasing Transaction number. In a 64K model, Transactions in the latent pool therefore initially form a stack in which the Transactions are ordered 1, 2, 3, 4, 5, . . . , 198, 199, 200. This stack can be thought of on a "top-to-bottom" basis. Transaction 1 is at the top of the stack, Transaction 2 is under it, and so on, until finally Transaction 200 is at the bottom of the stack.

When conditions call for scheduling the entry of a Transaction into the model, the Processor fetches the Transaction *from the top of the stack* in the latent pool. This Transaction is then brought into the model, via the Future Events Chain, by a procedure to be described below. Conversely, when model conditions call for elimination of a particular Transaction, it is removed from the model and put back into the latent pool *on the top of the stack*. The move-

[16]There is also one other type of Block through which Transactions can be brought into a model. Discussion of that Block type is deferred until Chapter 6.

[Transaction Number, Move Time, Current Block, Priority Level, Next Block Attempted]

   (a) General Form

     [9,68,5,0,6]

   (b) Numeric Example

FIGURE 2.24 Transactions information as recorded in five-tuples

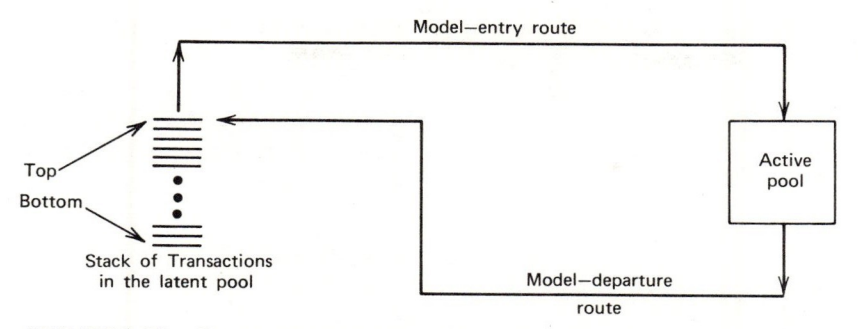

FIGURE 2.25 Transaction movement between the latent and active pools

ment of Transactions between the latent and active pools is shown in Figure 2.25.

As for Block Numbers, the steps followed by the Processor in assigning numbers to Blocks was discussed in Section 2.5. The Block Numbers are assigned in the order in which the cards for the various Block images have been placed in the card deck. For convenience, Figure 2.26 is a repetition of the Extended Program Listing in Figure 2A.2, with the Processor-assigned Block numbers shown in the leftmost column.

2.21.2 Assumed Interarrival and Service Times

Table 2.7 shows the sequence of sampled values that will be assumed to result when the GPSS Processor samples the first four times from the 18 ± 6 distribution at the Block 1 GENERATE Block.

Table 2.8 shows the sample values that will be assumed to result when the Processor samples the first three times from the 16 ± 4 distribution at the Block 5 ADVANCE Block.

2.21.3 Chain History for the Figure 2.27 Model

Figure 2.27 displays the Current and Future Events Chains for the first few clock readings when a simulation is performed with the Figure 2.26 model. Each line of information in Figure 2.27 has been given a "Line Number" (column one). This has been done so specific lines can be referred to during the discussion of the figure. The various times registered by the clock as the simulation proceeds are also shown in Figure 2.27, in the "Simulated Time" column (column two). The third column shows the Current Events Chain. The fourth column shows the Future Events Chain. Viewing a chain from left-to-right in the figure corresponds to examining it from front-to-back.

Encoding information in five-tuples, the Transactions which are chain residents are shown in Figure 2.27, occupying consecutive positions in a row in columns three and four. From time to time, a chain may have no Transactions on it.

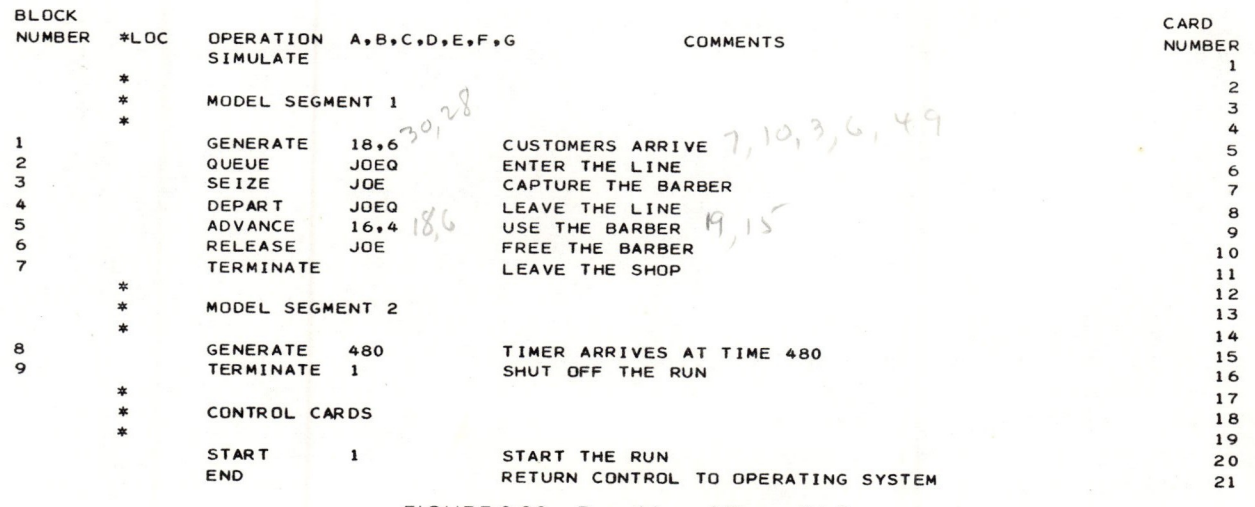

```
BLOCK
NUMBER  *LOC    OPERATION  A,B,C,D,E,F,G           COMMENTS                        CARD
                                                                                    NUMBER
                SIMULATE                                                            1
        *                                                                           2
        *       MODEL SEGMENT 1                                                     3
        *                                                                           4
1               GENERATE   18,6  30,28   CUSTOMERS ARRIVE  7,10,3,6,49             5
2               QUEUE      JOEQ          ENTER THE LINE                            6
3               SEIZE      JOE           CAPTURE THE BARBER                        7
4               DEPART     JOEQ          LEAVE THE LINE                            8
5               ADVANCE    16,4  18,6    USE THE BARBER    19,15                   9
6               RELEASE    JOE           FREE THE BARBER                           10
7               TERMINATE                LEAVE THE SHOP                            11
        *                                                                           12
        *       MODEL SEGMENT 2                                                     13
        *                                                                           14
8               GENERATE   480           TIMER ARRIVES AT TIME 480                 15
9               TERMINATE  1             SHUT OFF THE RUN                          16
        *                                                                           17
        *       CONTROL CARDS                                                       18
        *                                                                           19
                START      1             START THE RUN                             20
                END                      RETURN CONTROL TO OPERATING SYSTEM        21
```

FIGURE 2.26 Repetition of Figure 2A.2

TABLE 2.7 The Assumed Interarrival-Time Sequence Produced by Sampling at Block 1 in Figure 2.26

Number of Sample	Sampled Value
1	14
2	13
3	17
4	15

TABLE 2.8 The Assumed Holding-Time Sequence Produced by Sampling at Block 5 in Figure 2.26

Number of Sample	Sampled Value
1	18
2	12
3	14

This condition is indicated by use of the word "Empty."

Lines 1 and 2 in Figure 2.27 display chain information before and after the "Input Phase" is finished. The Processor's reading-in of the model constitutes the Input Phase. Beneath Lines 1 and 2, two lines of information are shown for each clock reading. The *first line* at any given clock value shows the chains after the most recent Clock Update Phase is finished, but before the next Scan Phase has begun. Such information, then, is the "input" to the next Scan Phase. The *second line* at the same clock value shows the chains after the next Scan Phase is finished, and just before the next Clock Update Phase is begun. This information is the "input" to the next Clock Update Phase.

Remember that between the *first and second lines* at any given clock value, the steps outlined in Figure 2.23 (Scan Phase) have been performed by the GPSS Processor. In general, many intermediate moves are made by Transactions as those steps are performed. The Figure 2.27 history does not show those intermediate moves, one-by-one. Instead, in the second line at each time frame, the result of all the intermediate moves is displayed.

Similarly, between the second line at any given clock value, and the first line at the next clock value, the steps outlined in Figure 2.22 (Clock Update Phase) have been performed by the Processor. Again, no attempt is made in Figure 2.27 to show how the chains change, step-by-

step, as the Clock Update Phase proceeds. Instead, the first line at each time frame shows the chains after the Clock Update Phase is finished.

The steps followed by the Processor to produce the chain history in Figure 2.27 will now be explained.

2.21.4 Explanation of the Figure 2.27 Chain History

Input Phase (From Line 1 to Line 2). The first thing the Processor does is input the model. *Before* this *Input Phase* begins, the Current and Future Events Chains are empty (Line 1, Figure 2.27). *During* the Input Phase, the Processor examines each card as it is read, to determine if it is a GENERATE card. When a GENERATE card is read, the Processor immediately "primes" the GENERATE Block by arranging for a Transaction arrival at that Block. To do this, the Processor must first determine a simulated time of arrival. If an Offset Interval has been supplied via the GENERATE Block's C Operand, the arrival time is set equal to the value of the C Operand. Otherwise, a sample is drawn from the interarrival-time distribution described by the GENERATE Block's A and B Operands. The time of arrival is then set equal to the sampled value. Next, the Processor fetches a Transaction from the top of the stack in the latent pool, and places it on the Future Events Chain, scheduled to enter the GENERATE Block at the arrival time in question.[17] At this point, note that the Transaction in question is simply "on its way to the model," via the Future Events Chain. It is not yet currently in any Block.

For the Figure 2.26 model, when the Block 1 GENERATE card is read during the Input Phase, a sample is drawn from the 18 ± 6 population. This first sampled value, via Table 2.7, is 14. The Processor then fetches Transaction 1 from the latent pool and places it on the Future Events Chain, scheduled to enter Block 1 at time 14.

As the Input Phase continues, the Block 8 GENERATE card is eventually read. For this Block, a deterministic interarrival time of 480 is in effect. The Processor fetches Transaction 2 from the latent pool and places it on the FEC,

[17] If the arrival-time value is *zero* (either because the value of the C operand is zero, or because a value of zero was drawn from the interarrival-time distribution), it is automatically redefined by the Processor to be 1. This means it is impossible to have Transactions arrive at GENERATE Blocks at simulated time zero. Their earliest possible time of arrival is 1.

Line Number	Simulated Time	Current Events Chain → Front of Chain	Future Events Chain → Front of Chain
1	Before Input Phase	Empty	Empty
2	After Input Phase	Empty	[1.14.NONE.0.1] [2.480.NONE.0.8]
3	14	[1.ASAP.NONE.0.1]	[2.480.NONE.0.8]
4	14	Empty	[3.27.NONE.0.1] [1.32.5.0.6] [2.480.NONE.0.8]
5	27	[3.ASAP.NONE.0.1]	[1.32.5.0.6] [2.480.NONE.0.8]
6	27	[3.ASAP.2.0.3]	[1.32.5.0.6] [4.44.NONE.0.1] [2.480.NONE.0.8]
7	32	[3.ASAP.2.0.3] [1.ASAP.5.0.6]	[4.44.NONE.0.1] [2.480.NONE.0.8]
8	32	Empty	[4.44.5.0.6] [2.480.NONE.0.8]
9	44	[4.ASAP.NONE.0.1] [3.ASAP.5.0.6]	[2.480.NONE.0.8]
10	44	Empty	[4.58.5.0.6] [1.59.NONE.0.1] [2.480.NONE.0.8]

FIGURE 2.27 Chain history for first example of the use of Current and Future Events Chains

scheduled to enter Block 8 at time 480. Because the Processor orders Transactions on the FEC according to their Move Time, Transaction 2 is put behind Transaction 1 on the Future Events Chain.

After the Block 9 TERMINATE card is read, the next card is the START card. Reading this card, the Processor determines the value of its A Operand, then places a copy of this value in the Termination Counter. For our purposes here, the Input Phase is now finished. Examination of the Future Events Chain at the conclusion of the Input Phase (Line 2, Figure 2.27) shows two Transactions on it, *one for each GENERATE Block in the model.* Transaction 1 represents the first customer, on his way to the barber shop. He will arrive at the shop at simulated time 14. The scheduled movement of Transaction 1 into Block 1 is analogous to the customer's arrival at the door of the shop. Transaction 2 is the timer, on his way to shut off the simulation. When the simulation clock eventually reaches a value of 480, the timer Transaction will arrive and, moving into the TERMINATE Block (Block 9), cause the simulation to shut off.

Note that the third entry in each of the two five-tuples at Line 2 in Figure 2.27 is "NONE." Recall that the third entry designates the number of the Location occupied by the Block which a Transaction is currently in. But Transactions 1 and 2 are not yet "in" any Block. They are simply on their way to the model. This explains why the word NONE has been used to indicate their Current Block number.

The flowchart in Figure 2.28 summarizes those features of the Input Phase which are pertinent for our purposes. The overall Input-Phase logic expressed in that flowchart should be reviewed in light of the preceding discussion.

As indicated in Figure 2.28, when the Input Phase is complete, the Processor next goes into the Clock Update Phase. After this first clock updating, the Scan Phase will be performed for the first time. Then the Clock Update Phase will be performed a second time, the Scan Phase will be a performed a second time, the Clock Update Phase will be performed a third time, and so on.

First Clock Update Phase (From Line 2 to Line 3). The Processor first sets the clock at 14, the Move Time of the Transaction (Transaction 1) at the front of the Line 2 Future Events Chain. It then transfers Transaction 1 from the

Future Events Chain to the previously empty Current Events Chain. The next Transaction (Transaction 2) on the FEC does not have a Move Time of 14. The first execution of the Clock Update Phase is therefore finished.

Note then, at Line 3 in Figure 2.27, that the Current Events Chain contains the single Transaction designated [1,ASAP,NONE,0,1]. The time entry in the five-tuple is "ASAP", for "As Soon As Possible." *All* Transactions on the CEC have ASAP as their Move Time. This is because they want to move into their next Block *now* (i.e., at the current reading of the simulated clock) or, if the Block will not now accept them, *as soon as possible.* The "Current Block" entry for this Transaction is still NONE, because the Transaction still has not become the occupant of any Block in the model. It will become a Block occupant when it is processed during the Scan Phase.

With the first Clock Update Phase complete, the first execution of the Scan Phase can now begin.

First Scan Phase (From Line 3 to Line 4). Picking up Transaction 1 from the front end of the Line 3 CEC, the Processor moves it into Block 1 (the GENERATE Block), then tests to determine whether the Transaction can move from Block 1 into the sequential Block (Block 2, the QUEUE Block). The QUEUE Block cannot refuse · entry, so the attempted move will be successful.

Now, because the Transaction can move out of its GENERATE Block, the Processor *temporarily stops moving it* and schedules the arrival of a next Transaction at that GENERATE Block. Sampling for the second time from the 18 ± 6 interarrival-time distribution, a sample value of 13 is obtained per Table 2.7. The Transaction at the top of the stack in the latent pool (Transaction 3) is fetched and placed on the Future Events Chain, scheduled to enter Block 1 at future time "now + 13," that is, at time 27. Note carefully that the sampled interarrival-time value is *added to a copy of the clock's current value* to determine the arrival time of the next Transaction.

As to the operation of GENERATE Blocks, two points should be noted here:

1. The Processor does not schedule the next arrival at a GENERATE Block until the preceding Transaction can successfully move to the next Block. If the next Block is of a type which can refuse entry

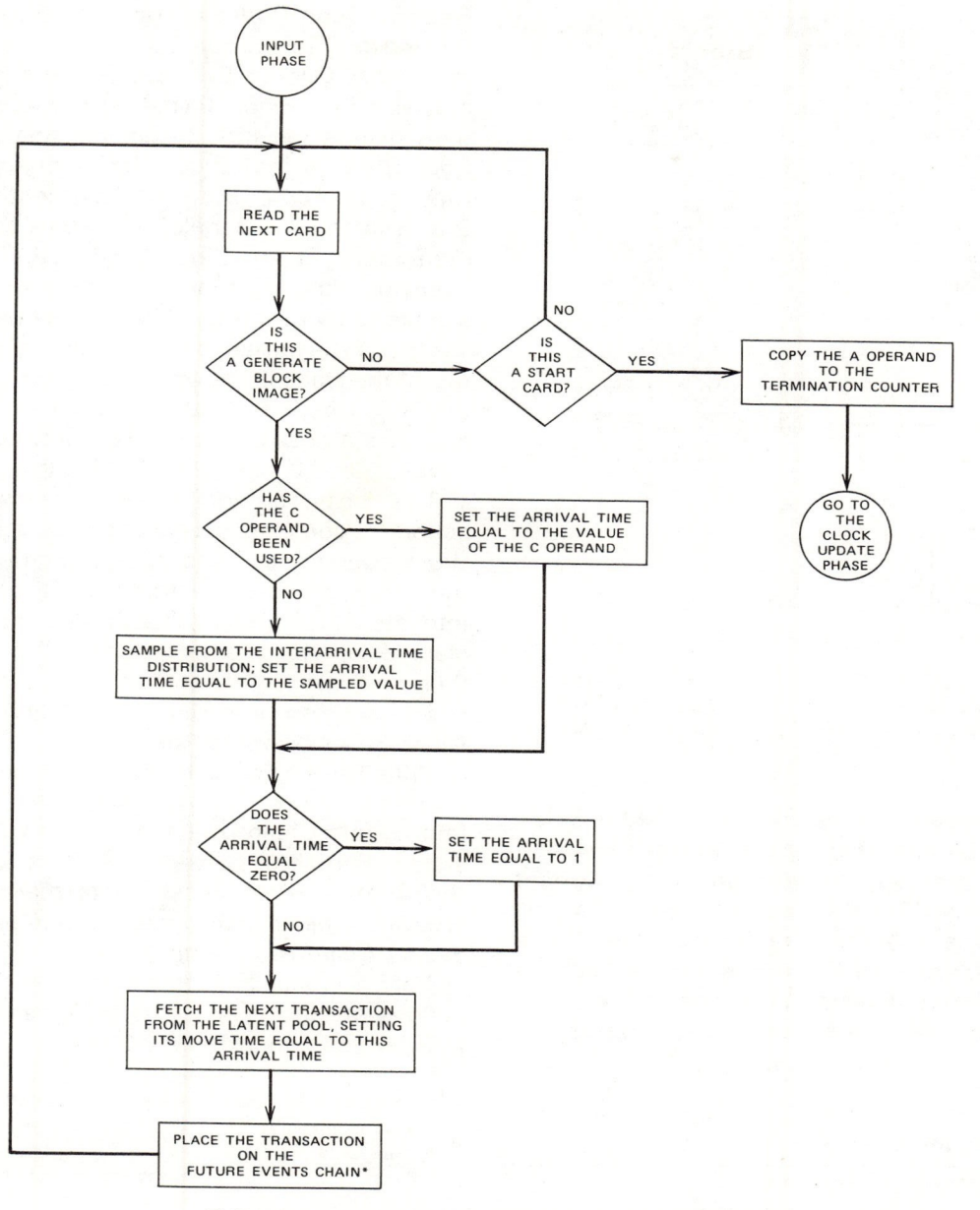

FIGURE 2.28   The GPSS Processor's Input Phase
*Scheduled to enter the model through this GENERATE Block, at the Move Time in question

(such as a SEIZE Block), the scheduling step might not take place until some time after a Transaction has arrived at the GENERATE Block.

2. The Processor *interrupts movement* of the Transaction exiting the GENERATE Block while it schedules its successor's arrival. After the scheduling is finished, the forward movement of the exiting Transaction is resumed.

Figure 2.29 illustrates these two points in the form of a flowchart. With the scheduling step completed, Transaction 1 now executes the QUEUE Block subroutine. From the QUEUE Block, the Processor then successfully moves the Transaction through the SEIZE and DEPART Blocks, and into the ADVANCE Block. At the ADVANCE Block (Block 5), a holding time is determined by sampling from the 16 ± 4 distribution. Per Table 2.8, the first sampled value is 18. Transaction 1 is therefore removed from the CEC and placed on the FEC, scheduled to move from Block 5 into Block 6 (the RELEASE Block) at future time "now + 18," that is, at time 32.

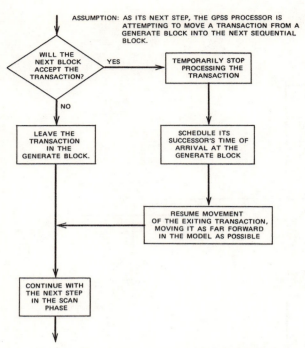

FIGURE 2.29   A flowchart segment showing the Processor's logic for moving a Transaction from a GENERATE Block, and scheduling its successor's arrival

Now, because Transaction 1 caused a SEIZE Block to be executed as part of its movement, the Processor restarts its scan of the Current Events Chain. But the chain is empty. The next step, then, is to perform the Clock Update Phase.

Before continuing, note that the Transactions on the Future Events Chain at Line 4, considered in left-to-right order, have the significance shown in Table 2.9.

TABLE 2.9   Significance of Transactions on the Future Events Chain, Line 4, Figure 2.27

Transaction Number	Significance
3	Second customer, on his way to the shop
1	First customer, having his hair cut
2	The timer Transaction

Second Clock Update Phase (From Line 4 to Line 5).   The Processor advances the clock to 27, the Move Time of the Transaction (Transaction 3) at the front of the Line 4 Future Events Chain. It then transfers Transaction 3 from the FEC to the previously empty CEC. The next Transaction on the FEC (Transaction 1) does not have a Move Time of 27. The second execution of the Clock Update Phase is therefore finished. The next Scan Phase execution can begin.

Second Scan Phase (From Line 5 to Line 6). Picking up Transaction 3 from the front end of the Line 5 Current Events Chain, the Processor moves it into Block 1 (the GENERATE Block), then determines that it can immediately move from Block 1 into Block 2. Temporarily interrupting the processing of Transaction 3, the Processor then schedules the arrival of a next Transaction at the Block 1 GENERATE Block. Corresponding to an interarrival time of 17 (third sample drawn from the 18 ± 6 distribution, per Table 2.7), Transaction 4 is fetched from the top of the stack in the latent pool and placed on the FEC, scheduled to enter Block 1 at time 44. It occupies a position on the FEC between Transactions 1 and 2, per the FEC ordering criterion.

The Processor now resumes moving Transaction 3, completing execution of the QUEUE Block subroutine. Transaction 3 then unsuccessfully attempts to move from the QUEUE Block into the SEIZE Block. The Facility JOE is in a state of capture, so entry is denied. The Processor therefore leaves Transaction 3 in the QUEUE Block and on the CEC, scheduled to enter Block 3 "As Soon As Possible."

With Transaction 3 at rest, the Processor continues to the next Transaction on the Line 5 Current Events Chain. But there is no next Transaction there. The next step, then, is to perform the Clock Update Phase. *Note that the clock is about to be advanced even though the Current Events Chain is not empty.*

Before proceeding, take note that the Transactions at Line 6 in Figure 2.27 have the significance shown in Table 2.10.

TABLE 2.10   Significance of Transactions on the Current and Future Events Chains, Line 6, Figure 2.27

Chain	Transaction Number	Significance
CEC	3	Second customer, waiting for the barber
FEC	1	First customer, having his hair cut
FEC	4	Third customer, on his way to the shop
FEC	2	The timer Transaction

Third Clock Update Phase (From Line 6 to Line 7).   The Processor advances the clock to 32, the Move Time of the Transaction (Transaction 1) at the front of the Line 6 Future Events Chain. It then transfers Transaction 1 to the

Current Events Chain, where it is merged in as the last member in its Priority Class. In the Line 7 CEC, note that Transaction 1 is *behind* Transaction 3. (Transaction 3 was already on the Current Events Chain when the third execution of the Clock Update Phase began.)

The next Transaction on the FEC (Transaction 4) does not have a Move Time of 32. The next execution of the Scan Phase can consequently begin.

At this point, consider the significance of the two Transactions on the Line 7 Current Events Chain, as indicated in Table 2.11.

TABLE 2.11   Significance of Transactions on the Current Events Chain, Line 7, Figure 2.27

Transaction Number	Significance
3	Second customer, waiting for the barber
1	First customer, just at the point of having his haircut completed

Third Scan Phase (From Line 7 to Line 8). Picking up Transaction 3 at the front end of the Line 7 CEC, the Processor fails in its attempt to move it from Block 2 into Block 3 (SEIZE). Entry to Block 3 is denied, of course, because the Facility is still engaged. Transaction 3 consequently remains in the QUEUE Block and on the CEC, still scheduled to enter Block 3 as soon as possible. Continuing to the next Line 7 CEC Transaction (Transaction 1), the Processor moves it from Block 5 into Block 6 (RELEASE), and then from Block 6 into Block 7 (TERMINATE), where it is removed from the model and returned to the top of the stack of Transactions in the latent pool.

Now, because Transaction 1 caused a RELEASE Block to be executed, the Processor restarts the scan of the Current Events Chain. Transaction 3 is picked up again, and attempts again to move from Block 2 into Block 3. This time, the attempt is successful. The SEIZE–ADVANCE–RELEASE sequence follows, and a holding time of 12 is drawn from the 16 ± 4 distribution (second sample, Table 2.8). Transaction 3 is then removed from the CEC and placed on the FEC, scheduled to move from Block 5 to Block 6 at time "now + 12," or 44. Note that, on the FEC, Transaction 3 is involved in a time tie with Transaction 4, which also has a Move Time of 44. Because Transaction 4 was *already on* the FEC, Transaction 3 is put *behind*

it. Again, whenever time ties occur on the FEC, the incoming Transaction is merged onto the chain as the last member in its Move Time category.

Now, because Transaction 3 caused a SEIZE Block to be executed, the Processor restarts its scan of the Current Events Chain. But the chain is empty. The next step, then, is to perform the Clock Update Phase.

At this point, Transactions on the Future Events Chain in Line 8 have the significance indicated in Table 2.12.

TABLE 2.12   Significance of Transactions on the Future Events Chain, Line 8, Figure 2.27

Transaction Number	Significance
3	Second customer, having his hair cut
4	Third customer, on his way to the shop
2	The timer Transaction

Fourth Clock Update Phase (From Line 8 to Line 9). The Processor advances the clock to 44, the Move Time of the Transaction (Transaction 4) at the front of the Line 8 Future Events Chain. It then transfers Transaction 4 from the FEC to the previous empty CEC. The next Transaction on the FEC (Transaction 3) also has a Move Time of 44. It, too, is transferred to the Current Events Chain, where it is put behind Transaction 4, as the last member in its Priority Class. The next Transaction on the Future Events Chain (Transaction 2) does not have a Move Time of 44. The fourth Clock Update Phase is therefore finished.

Before continuing, consider the significance of the two Transactions on the Line 9 Current Events Chain, as indicated in Table 2.13.

TABLE 2.13   Significance of Transactions on the Current Events Chain, Line 9, Figure 2.27

Transaction Number	Significance
4	Third customer, just arriving at the door to the shop
3	Second customer, just at the point of having his haircut completed

Fourth Scan Phase (From Line 9 to Line 10). Picking up Transaction 4 at the front end of the Line 9 CEC, the Processor moves it into Block 1, then determines that it can move from Block 1 into Block 2. Temporarily interrupting the processing of Transaction 4, the Processor schedules the arrival of its successor at the Block 1 GENERATE Block. Transaction 1 is fetched from the top of the stack of Transactions in the latent pool and placed on the Future Events Chain, scheduled to enter Block 1 at time "now + 15", or 59. (Per Table 2.7, the fourth sampled value from the 18 ± 6 distribution is 15.)

Note that it is Transaction 1 which is coming back into the model from the latent pool. The Transaction had previously been in the model, simulating the first customer of the day; it now comes back into play, simulating the day's *fourth* customer. Because the Processor always takes Transactions from and returns them to the top of the stack in the latent pool, it should now be clear that some Transactions may live many lives during the course of a simulation.

With its movement resumed, Transaction 4 then finds it must remain in Block 2 (QUEUE), because the SEIZE Block will not accept it. The Processor then moves the next Line 9 CEC Transaction (Transaction 3) through the RE-LEASE—TERMINATE sequence, returning it to the top of the stack in latent pool. Then, because a RELEASE Block was executed, the Processor restarts its scan of the Current Events Chain. Transaction 4 is picked up again and moved through the SEIZE and DEPART Blocks, and into the ADVANCE Block (Block 5). Per Table 2.8, the third value sampled from the 16 ± 4 distribution at the ADVANCE Block is 14. Transaction 4 is therefore removed from the Current Events Chain and placed on the Future Events Chain, scheduled to move from Block 5 to Block 6 at time 58.

Now, because a SEIZE Block was executed, the Processor restarts its scan of the Current Events Chain. But the chain is empty. The next step, then, is to execute the Clock Update Phase for the fifth time.

This completes the explanation of the chain history shown in Figure 2.27.

2.22 Comments on Simultaneous Events in a GPSS Context

In Chapter 1, the question of time ties was discussed to some extent (see Section 1.3.5, and exercises 8, 9b, and 12a, Section 1.6). As pointed out there, time ties come about whenever two or more events have been scheduled to occur at the same point in simulated time. When this cir-

cumstance arises, the events involved are said to be simultaneous events. It was also established in Chapter 1 that, in case of time ties, the events involved in the ties are caused to occur sequentially, that is, one after the other. In other words, "simultaneous events take place sequentially in a simulation model." When time ties occur, then, some decision must be made about the sequence in which the simultaneous events will be performed. If no formal decision is made in this regard, then the event sequence will simply depend on chance.

As a specific example of simultaneity of events in a GPSS context, consider the Case Study 2A model, and the corresponding chain history shown in Figure 2.27. At Line 9 in Figure 2.27, the Current Events Chain reveals that two events have been scheduled to occur at simulated time 44. The first of these events, as represented by the Transaction [4,ASAP,NONE,0,1], is arrival of a customer at the barber shop. The second of these events, as represented by the Transaction [3,ASAP,5,0,6], is completion of service on the customer currently in the barber's chair. In reality, the next customer is walking in the door just as the current customer is getting out of the barber's chair.

Now consider how this reality is simulated in Case Study 2A. In its scan of the Current Events Chain, the GPSS Processor first encounters Transaction 4. Transaction 4 consequently enters the GENERATE Block, then moves into the QUEUE Block, and comes to rest there. In effect, then, the Processor has "caused the next customer to come in the door, and join the waiting line." Then, continuing with the scan of the Current Events Chain, the Processor next encounters Transaction 3. This Transaction is moved into the RELEASE and TERMINATE Blocks, which amounts to "causing the current customer to get out of the barber's chair, and leave the shop." At this point, then, the two events "customer arrival" and "service completion" have been caused to occur. The event sequence followed was "customer arrival," and then "service completion," simply because Transaction 4 happened to be ahead of Transaction 3 on the Current Events Chain. If the relative position of these two Transactions on the CEC had been reversed, then the event sequence would have been reversed, too.

Of course, at this point the system is not completely updated at simulated time 44. Conditions now call for the event "capture the barber" to occur. Because a RELEASE Block was executed as part of the service completion event, the Processor restarts its scan of the Current Events Chain. As a result, the Processor again picks up Transaction 4, this time moving it through the SEIZE and DEPART Blocks and into the AD-VANCE Block. Hence, the capture event is caused to occur. This completes the action at simulated time 44.

It should be clear that when time ties occur in the Case Study 2A model, the sequence in which the tied events are performed depends strictly on chance. No formal control of event sequences is necessary in this simple model, thanks to the fact that the Processor restarts its scan of the CEC when a RELEASE Block has been executed. If it weren't for this fact, the model would be invalid. That is, although there would be both a waiting customer and an available barber at simulated time 44, no processing would be performed whereby the customer would capture the barber. It is due to the way the Processor has been constructed, then, that there was no problem with simultaneous occurrence of events *in this model*.

It is easy to change the conditions in the Case Study 2A model so that a problem *is* caused by the event sequence in the Figure 2.27 chain history at simulated time 44. Suppose that the arriving customer chooses to stay for service only if he can immediately capture the barber, and that the model is modified to reflect this assumption. (Note that we have not yet learned how to modify the model this way.) In this case, if the arrival event occurs before the service-completion event, the arriving customer will not stay for service; if the event sequence is reversed, however, he will stay for service. Under these circumstances, it might be important to design the model so that, in case of time ties, service completion is always caused to occur before customer arrival. It is evident that this would always be the event sequence if steps could be taken to guarantee that the "service completion" Transaction is closer to the front of the CEC than is the "customer arrival" Transaction. It has already been mentioned that the relative positions of Transactions on the CEC are determined by Priority Levels. If the "service completion" Transaction had a higher Priority Level than the "customer arrival" Transaction, the desired event sequence would be in effect. We will see later how Priority Levels can be put to good use on occasions like this to defend against potential

problems which might otherwise result from time ties.

2.23 Exercises

1. (General Questions Based on Sections 2.20 and 2.21)
   (a) What is "Move Time"?
   (b) What information is provided by the fifth entry in a "Transaction five-tuple"?
   (c) How many Current and Future Events Chains are there?
   (d) How are Transactions ordered on the Future Events Chain?
   (e) In what sense can ties occur on the Future Events Chain? When ties do occur, how are they resolved?
   (f) How are Transactions ordered on the Current Events Chain?
   (g) In what sense can ties occur on the Current Events Chain? When ties do occur, how are they resolved?
   (h) When the Clock Update Phase begins, how does the GPSS Processor determine the time of the next future event in the model?
   (i) After the simulation clock is advanced, how many Transactions are removed from the Future Events Chain and brought to the Current Events Chain?
   (j) Under what conditions is a Transaction removed from the Current Events Chain and placed back onto the Future Events Chain?
   (k) What is the distinction between the latent pool and the active pool of Transactions in a model?
   (l) How are Transactions ordered in the latent pool?
   (m) Why is it never necessary to resolve ties relative to Transaction ordering in the latent pool?
   (n) How is it possible for a Transaction to "live many lives" during the course of a simulation run?
   (o) Critically discuss this statement: "After each updating of the simulation clock, the GPSS Processor scans the Current Events Chain exactly one time, then proceeds with the next updating of the clock."
   (p) Why is it that the Current Events Chain is not necessarily empty when the Processor, as its next move, performs the Clock Update Phase?
   (q) Critically discuss this statement: "After the model Input Phase is complete, there is exactly one Transaction on the Future Events Chain for every GENERATE Block in the model."
   (r) Critically discuss this statement: "The smallest Move Time that a Transaction can ever have is 1."
   (s) Is it true that the Current Events Chain is always

empty when the Input Phase has just been completed?

2. (Specific Questions Based on the Section 2.21 Example of Chain Usage)

(a) What is the Priority Level of all Transactions in the Figure 2.26 model? Why is this Priority Level the one in effect?

(b) Will Transaction 2 ever come into play in the model as a customer at the barber shop? Why or why not?

(c) Extend Figure 2.27 to include Lines 11, 12, 13, and 14. In doing this, assume that the next interarrival time sampled at Block 1 is 16, and the next service time sampled at Block 5 is 17. Now answer these questions:

(i) What is the clock reading at lines 11 and 12?

(ii) What is the clock reading at lines 13 and 14?

(iii) What is the number of the Transaction representing the fourth customer?

(iv) How much idle time does the barber experience between finishing the third customer, and beginning work on the fourth customer?

(v) What is the number of the Transaction simulating the fifth customer?

(vi) When will the fifth customer arrive at the barber shop?

(vii) How long will the fifth customer have to wait for service, if at all?

3. Consider the model in Figure 2.26. Assume that the Block 1 and Block 5 Operands are "30,28" and "18,6," respectively, and that the first portions of the interarrival- and holding-time sequences actually realized in a particular simulation are as shown below.

Interarrival-time sequence: 7, 10, 3, 6, 49, . . .
Service-time sequence: 19, 15, . . .

Using the approach illustrated in Section 2.21, track the progress made by Transactions through the model in terms of their residence on the Current and Future Events Chains, completing the first ten lines of the chain history. Then answer these questions:

(a) What value is registered by the simulation clock at Line 10 in the chain history?

(b) What will be the number of the fourth Transaction to engage the barber?

(c) Are there ever exactly two Transactions on the Current Events Chain *after* a Scan Phase completion? What are the numbers of the two Transactions involved when and if this condition arises?

4. Referring to Figure 2.29, discuss the difference between the two Block Diagram segments in Figure E4.

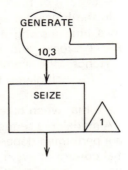

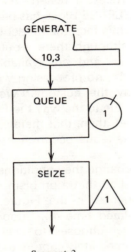

Segment 1

Segment 2

FIGURE E4

5. (a) Assume that the QUEUE–DEPART Block pair is removed from the model in Figure 2.26. Using the interarrival- and service-time sequences shown in Tables 2.7 and 2.8, state the times at which the second, third, and fourth customers of the day arrive at the barber shop. (Define "arrival at the barber shop" as movement of the customer-Transaction from the GENERATE Block to the sequential Block.)

(b) Suppose that an analyst does not want to collect Queue data for the system modeled in Figure 2.26. As (a) above demonstrates, he cannot simply remove the QUEUE–DEPART Block pair from the model, because this produces a distortion in the interarrival-time sequence he wants to be in effect. Show how he can avoid the distortion by introducing an ADVANCE Block between the GENERATE and SEIZE Blocks.

6. Consider the model in Figure E6.

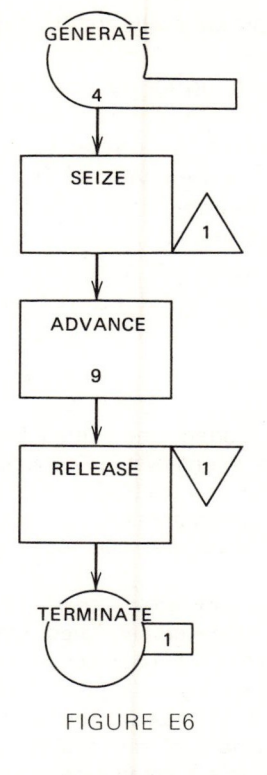

FIGURE E6

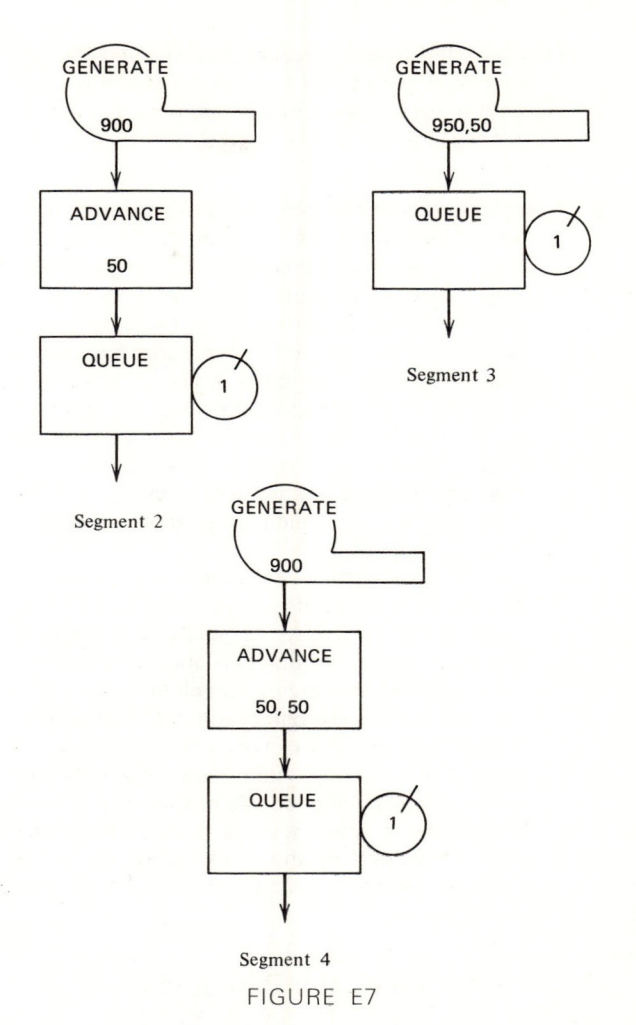

FIGURE E7

Assume that the model is run, and that 4 is entered as the A Operand on the START card.

(a) At what time does the first Transaction arrive at the GENERATE Block?
(b) At what time does its successor arrive at the GENERATE Block?
(c) At what time does its successor exit the GENERATE Block?
(d) At what time does the third Transaction arrive at the GENERATE Block?
(e) When is Facility 1 seized for the third time?
(f) How much time elapses between exiting of successive Transactions from the GENERATE Block?
(g) At what time does the simulation shut off?

7. Consider the four Block Diagram segments in Figure E7.

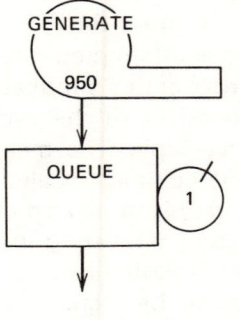

Segment 1

(a) At what times do the first three Transactions which come through Segment 1 move into the QUEUE Block?
(b) At what times do the first three Transactions which come through Segment 2 move into the QUEUE Block?
(c) What are the earliest and latest *feasible* times at which the first three Transactions which come through Segment 3 could move into the QUEUE Block?
(d) What are the earliest and latest *feasible* times at which the first three Transactions which come through Segment 4 could move into the QUEUE Block?

8. In a certain model, Transactions represent planes arriving at an airport. Upon arriving, they join the Queue STACK, which simulates planes stacked over the airport, waiting their turn to land. Planes are scheduled to arrive at the airport every 900 time units, but they may be 50 ± 50 time units late. Consecutive arrivals are independent of each other.

That is, the delay possibly experienced by an arriving plane is not to influence the arrival time of the next plane. Show a model segment simulating the planes arriving at the airport and joining the Queue.

9. This problem concerns time ties in Case Study 2A.
   (a) At simulated time 44 in Figure 2.27, there is a time tie between the events "customer arrival," and "service completion." The GPSS Processor causes the arrival event to occur ahead of the service completion event, for the simple reason that the "customer arrival" Transaction precedes the "service completion" Transaction on the Current Events Chain. *Why* are the two Transactions in question ordered in this fashion? Provide an answer in terms of the real-time sequence in which the events in question were scheduled.
   (b) In the Case Study 2A model as shown in Figure 2A.1, could it ever be true that (1) the waiting line is empty, (2) there is a time tie between service completion and customer arrival, and (3) the service completion event will be caused to occur before the customer arrival event? Explain why or why not, in detail.
   (c) Why is it that two customer arrival events can never occur simultaneously in Case Study 2A? Describe two different ways in which the problem conditions in the case study could be changed so that customer arrival time ties could occur.

2.24 Model-Produced Printouts of Current and Future Events Chains

In some treatments of GPSS, the topic of chains is deferred until quite late, or is not covered at all. It is true that a person can do a lot of modeling in GPSS without being aware of the underlying chain concepts. It is also true, unfortunately, that a person can do a lot of *invalid* modeling when the chain concepts are not taken into account. Even if the system to be modeled is only moderately complex, the analyst inevitably comes upon questions which takes the form, "what happens next in the model?" Because simultaneous events are performed sequentially in GPSS, the question of what happens next in a model can be of the utmost importance. An explanation of what happens next can always be given in terms of the chain concepts. The analyst unfamiliar with these concepts must either content himself with vague answers to the "what next" questions, or ignore the questions entirely and simply hope that the model will be

valid, or approximately valid, anyway. This is not acceptable.

Rather than ignoring chains, the analyst familiar with them will find it convenient to think in terms of them in coming to a better understanding of the behavior of his models. From time to time, he may also want to obtain a printout of the chains to reinforce his conclusions about how a particular model is operating. Chain printouts can be obtained in these several different ways.

1. When certain error conditions are encountered during a simulation, the GPSS Processor automatically prints out the Current and Future Events Chains for possible use by the analyst in "debugging" his model.
2. At the end of a simulation, the GPSS Processor will include chain printouts as part of its standard output *if 1 has been punched as the D Operand on the START card.*
3. During a simulation, chain printouts can be produced at whatever simulated times the analyst desires. This effect is only accomplished, however, when the analyst makes explicit arrangements for it in the logic of his model. The results constitute a series of snapshots of the chains as the model is moved forward in simulated time.

It is of interest now to see what chains look like when they are printed out by the GPSS Processor. Suppose the approach mentioned in (2) above is used to obtain such a printout with the Figure 2A.2 model. All that is involved is entering a 1 as the D Operand an the START card, and resubmitting the model for running. The resulting output is shown in Figures 2.30 and 2.31, where the Current and Future Events Chains are shown, respectively.

In Figures 2.30 and 2.31, columns containing the information carried in the Transaction five-tuples previously introduced in Section 2.21 have been labeled A, B, C, D, and E, for ease of identification. These columns contain "Transaction Number", "Move Time" (i.e., Block Departure Time), "Current Block", "Priority Level", and "Next Block Attempted", respectively. The left-to-right order of this information in the chain printouts is identical to the order used earlier within each five-tuple. The meaning of the information in the columns labeled A through E is summarized in tabular form as part of Figure 2.30. The other columns appearing in the Figure 2.30 and 2.31 chain printouts will not be commented on now, but will be explained at appropriate points throughout the rest of the book. (For

CURRENT EVENTS CHAIN

TRANS	BDT	BLOCK	PR	SF	NBA	SET	MARK-TIME	P1	P2	P3	P4	SI	TI	DI	CI	MC	PC	PF
4	472	2			3	4	472	0	0	0	0	1			2			
3	480	5			6	3	453	0	0	0	0	1			2			

Arrows: Ⓐ → (TRANS) Ⓑ → (BDT) Ⓒ → (BLOCK) Ⓓ → (PR) Ⓔ → (NBA)

Column	Significance
A	Transaction Number.
B	Block Departure Time (BDT); same as Move Time, i.e., time of attempted move into the next Block. On the Current Events Chain, note that the Processor does *not* use the notation "ASAP."
C	"Current Block"; number of the Block which the Transaction is in currently. On the Future Events Chain, note that the

Column	Significance
D	Priority Level (PR); "blank" entries indicate a Priority Level of 0.
E	Next Block Attempted (NBA); number of the next Block the Transaction will attempt to enter.

Processor does *not* use the notation "NONE" when a Transaction is not yet in a Block, but simply leaves the entry "blank."

FIGURE 2.30 The makeup of the Current Events Chain when the Figure 2A.2 simulation stops

FUTURE EVENTS CHAIN

TRANS	BDT	BLOCK	PR	SF	NBA	SET	MARK-TIME	P1	P2	P3	P4	SI	TI	DI	CI	MC	PC	PF
1	489				1	1	-27	0	0	0	0				4			
5	960				8	5	-1	0	0	0	0							

Arrows: Ⓐ → 5 Ⓑ → 960 Ⓒ → Ⓓ → Ⓔ → 8

FIGURE 2.31 The makeup of the Future Events Chain when the Figure 2A.2 simulation stops (Significance of Columns A, B, C, D, and E are shown in Figure 2.30)

TABLE 2.14   Interpretations for the Transactions in Figure 2.30

Transaction Number	Transaction Information As a Five-Tuple	Significance
4	[4,472,2,0,3]	Transaction 4 is a customer at the barber shop, waiting for the barber. Its "Next Block Attempted" is Block 3 (SEIZE). The barber is busy, servicing Transaction 3.
3	[3,480,5,0,6]	Transaction 3 is a customer just about to finish having his hair cut. Note that it is poised to move into Block 6 (RELEASE) at time 480, the time of model shutdown.

convenience, Appendix D provides a complete summary of the meaning of the various columns of information in GPSS chain printouts.)

The information displayed in the Figure 2.30 Current Events Chain printout is explained and interpreted in Table 2.14, in the context of Case Study 2A. The interpretations provided in the table should now be studied, keeping in mind that Figure 2.30 shows the Current Events Chain at simulated time 480, just after the simulation shut off. Note that the Figure 2.30 chain information has been reexpressed in five-tuple form in Table 2.14, as an aid in matching up the simple five-tuple notation with the equivalent information as it appears in actual chain printouts. It is evident that the chain printouts provide considerably more information than that shown in the five-tuples. It should also be noted that, in a Current Events Chain printout, the GPSS Processor does not enter "ASAP" in the "Move Time" column (the column labeled B in Figure 2.30). The entry that does appear in the column in an actual chain printout is the most recent meaningful Move Time value for the Transaction in question. The ASAP notation was simply introduced in Section 2.21 as a convenient device to assist in the explanation.

The two Transactions displayed in the Figure 2.31 Future Events Chain printout are shown in five-tuple form in Table 2.15. The table gives an interpretation for the first of these Transactions in the context of Case Study 2A. It is left as an exercise to provide an interpretation for the other Transaction. Table 2.15 should now be studied, remembering as before that Figure 2.31 shows the Future Events Chain at simulated time 480, just after the simulation shut off. Note that the Processor does not enter "NONE" in the "Current

Block" column (column C in Figure 2.31) for Transactions which have not yet moved into their GENERATE Block. Instead, the Processor leaves the column blank in these cases. Like ASAP, the notation NONE was used in Section 2.21 for convenience.

The way the analyst can get chain printouts *during* a simulation, instead of just after a simulation shuts off, will be described in Section 2.42. For the time being, it is enough to know what a chain printout looks like, and how one can be produced at the end of a run.

2.25 Exercises

1. Two events were scheduled to occur simultaneously at time 480 in the Case Study 2A model. These two events are "model shutdown" and "service completion."
   (a) Explain why it is possible to make the above statements.
   (b) Which of the two events was caused to occur first at time 480? Why was it the first event to be caused?
   (c) Was the other event caused to occur before the model shut off?
   (d) Suggest a method whereby the event sequence at time 480 could be reversed. (That is, suggest a method for forcing the "timer" to be the last Transaction processed at simulated time 480.)
   (e) If the event sequence were reversed at time 480, how many Transactions would be left on the Current Events Chain when the model shut off? Explain your answer in detail.

2. In Figure 2.31, what is the significance of Transaction 5 on the Future Events Chain? Why was that Transaction fetched from the latent pool and

TABLE 2.15   Interpretations for the Transactions in Figure 2.31

Transaction Number	Transaction Information As a Five-Tuple	Significance
1	[1,489,NONE,0,1]	Transaction 1 is the next customer on the way to the barber shop. It is scheduled to move into Block 1 (GENERATE) at time 489. It will be "9 minutes too late."
5	[5,960,NONE,0,8]	See exercise 2, Section 2.25.

placed on the Future Events Chain before the model shut off?

3. At time 480 in Case Study 2A, there is one customer waiting for the barber. Referring to Figure 2.30, state how long that customer has been waiting.

4. In Figure 2.26, modify the A and B Operands at Blocks 1, 5, and 8 to make them "30,0", "20,0", and "90,0", respectively. Then do the following.

(a) By hand, produce a chain history analogous to Figure 2.27 for the resulting model. Note that, with the timer Transaction "arriving" at time 90, only a few time frames will be required before the model shuts off.

(b) Submit the modified model for a run on the computer, punching 1 as the D Operand on the START card so that the Current and Future Events Chains will be printed out when the model shuts off.

(c) Compare the Current and Future Events Chain printout with their appearance in the last row in your hand-produced chain history. They should, of course, be in agreement with each other. If they are not, correct the hand-produced history until it agrees with that printed out by the computer.

(d) Examine the hand-produced chain history to determine for how many of the 90 simulated minutes the barber is idle. Use this information to compute his utilization (fraction of the time he is busy). Your hand-computed utilization should be in agreement with that appearing in the Facility information produced in the computer output.

2.26 CASE STUDY 2B
Extended Modeling of the One-Line One-Server Queuing System

(1) Statement of the Problem

Two types of customers arrive at a one-chair barber shop. Customers of the first type want only a haircut. Their interarrival-time distribution is 35 ± 10 minutes. Customers of the second type want a shave as well as a haircut. Their interarrival-time distribution is 60 ± 20 minutes. The barber provides service to his customers first-come, first-served. This situation can be visualized in terms of Figure 2B.1, where circles represent customers who want only a haircut, and squares signify customers wanting both a shave and a haircut. At the time represented in Figure 2B.1, a "haircut only" customer is in the barber's chair, while "haircut only," "shave and haircut," and "haircut only" customers are waiting, in that order, for service. It takes the barber 18 ± 6 minutes to give a haircut. When he gives a shave, 10 ± 2 minutes are required.

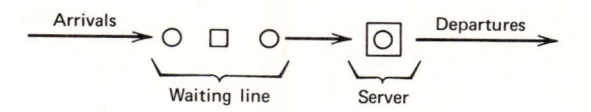

FIGURE 2B.1   First-come, first-served queue discipline, with two types of customers

Model the barber shop in GPSS, making provisions to collect data on the waiting line that forms ahead of the barber. Then run the model through 8 hours of simulated time. Interpret the output produced by the model in the context of the barber shop.

(2) Approach Taken in Building the Model

The first impulse might be to attempt to model this one-line, one-server system with a single sequence of Blocks, analogous to the Figure 2A.1 model. But then such questions would arise as "how can one GENERATE Block be used to simulate both types of arrivals?" and "how can a distinction be made as to the different service times required by haircut-only, and shave-and-haircut, customers?" The conclusion can be rapidly drawn that the wherewithal required to model this system with a single sequence of Blocks has not yet been developed.

The system is easily modeled, however, with two distinct major Block segments, or sequences. One sequence models the haircut-only customers; the other models the shave-and-haircut customers. In each of the two sequences, a QUEUE—DEPART Block pair referencing one and the same waiting line is included so that customers moving through each sequence contribute to the waiting-line statistics being gathered. And, in each of the two segments, a SEIZE—RELEASE Block pair referencing one and the same Facility is used to accomplish simulation of the barber himself. In the haircut-only segment, a single ADVANCE Block is used to simulate service time; in the shave-and-haircut segment, a pair of consecutive ADVANCE Blocks is used to simulate the time required to give a shave, and then a haircut, respectively. When approached in this fashion, then, it is relatively simple to model the system.

(3) Table of Definitions

Time Unit: 1 Minute

TABLE 2B.1   Table of Definitions for Case Study 2B

GPSS Entity	Interpretation
Transactions	
Model Segment 1	Haircut-only customers
Model Segment 2	Shave-and-haircut customers
Model Segment 3	A timer
Facilities	
JOE	The barber
Queues	
JOEQ	The Queue used to gather statistics on the combined waiting experience of both customer types

(4) Block Diagram

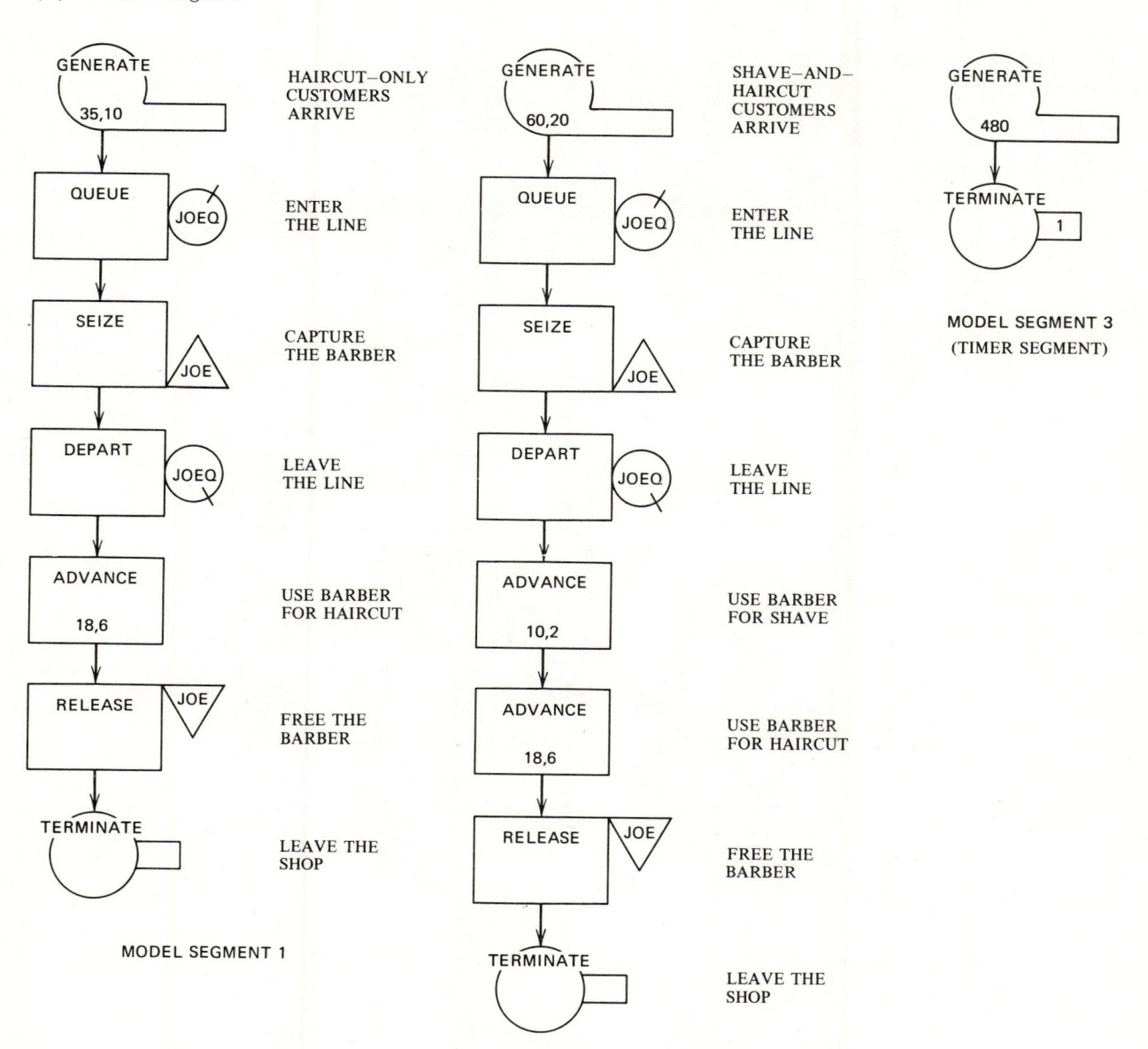

FIGURE 2B.2   Block Diagram for Case Study 2B

```
BLOCK                                                                            CARD
NUMBER   *LOC   OPERATION   A,B,C,D,E,F,G      COMMENTS                           NUMBER

                SIMULATE                                                            1
          *                                                                         2
          *     MODEL SEGMENT 1                                                     3
          *                                                                         4
   1            GENERATE    35,10    HAIRCUT-ONLY CUSTOMERS ARRIVE                   5
   2            QUEUE       JOEQ     ENTER THE LINE                                  6
   3            SEIZE       JOE      CAPTURE THE BARBER                              7
   4            DEPART      JOEQ     LEAVE THE LINE                                  8
   5            ADVANCE     18,6     USE BARBER                                      9
   6            RELEASE     JOE      FREE THE BARBER                                10
   7            TERMINATE            LEAVE THE SHOP                                 11
          *                                                                        12
          *     MODEL SEGMENT 2                                                    13
          *                                                                        14
   8            GENERATE    60,20    SHAVE-AND-HAIRCUT CUSTOMERS ARRIVE            15
   9            QUEUE       JOEQ     ENTER THE LINE                                16
  10            SEIZE       JOE      CAPTURE THE BARBER                            17
  11            DEPART      JOEQ     LEAVE THE LINE                                18
  12            ADVANCE     10,2     USE BARBER FOR SHAVE                          19
  13            ADVANCE     18,6     USE BARBER FOR HAIRCUT                        20
  14            RELEASE     JOE      FREE THE BARBER                               21
  15            TERMINATE            LEAVE THE SHOP                                22
          *                                                                        23
          *     MODEL SEGMENT 3                                                    24
          *                                                                        25
  16            GENERATE    480      TIMER ARRIVES AT TIME 480                     26
  17            TERMINATE   1        SHUT OFF THE RUN                              27
          *                                                                        28
          *     CONTROL CARDS                                                      29
          *                                                                        30
                START       1,,1     START THE RUN; GET CHAIN PRINTOUT AT END      31
                END                  RETURN CONTROL TO OPERATING SYSTEM            32
```

FIGURE 2B.3   Extended Program Listing for Case Study 2B

(a)

RELATIVE CLOCK 480   ABSOLUTE CLOCK 480

BLOCK COUNTS

BLOCK	CURRENT	TOTAL	BLOCK	CURRENT	TOTAL	BLOCK	CURRENT	TOTAL
1	0	13	11	0	8			
2	1	13	12	0	8			
3	0	12	13	1	8			
4	0	12	14	0	7			
5	0	12	15	0	7			
6	0	12	16	0	7			
7	0	12	17	0	1			
8	0	12						
9	0	8						
10	0	8						

(b)

FACILITY	AVERAGE UTILIZATION	NUMBER ENTRIES	AVERAGE TIME/TRAN	SEIZING TRANS. NO.	PREEMPTING TRANS. NO.
JOE	.897	20	21.549	1	

(c)

QUEUE	MAXIMUM CONTENTS	AVERAGE CONTENTS	TOTAL ENTRIES	ZERO ENTRIES	PERCENT ZEROS	AVERAGE TIME/TRANS	$AVERAGE TIME/TRANS	TABLE NUMBER	CURRENT CONTENTS
JOEQ	2	.524	21	4	19.0	12.000	14.823		1

$AVERAGE TIME/TRANS = AVERAGE TIME/TRANS EXCLUDING ZERO ENTRIES

(d)

CURRENT EVENTS CHAIN

TRANS	BDT	BLOCK	PR	SF	NBA	SET	MARK-TIME	P1	P2	P3	P4	SI	TI	DI	CI	MC	PC	PF
6	457	2			3	6	457	0 0	0 0	0 0	0 0	1	1	2	4			

(e)

FUTURE EVENTS CHAIN

TRANS	BDT	BLOCK	PR	SF	NBA	SET	MARK-TIME	P1	P2	P3	P4	SI	TI	DI	CI	MC	PC	PF
1	490	13			14	1	457	0...0	0...0	0...0	0...0	4		4	4			
4	502				1	4	-13											
5	504				8	5	-8											
2	960				16	2	-1											

FIGURE 2B.4   Selected Program Output for Case Study 2B. (a) Clock values and Block Counts. (b) Facility statistics. (c) Queue statistics. (d) Current Events Chain. (e) Future Events Chain.

(7) Discussion

Model Logic. The Block Diagram corresponding to the approach described above appears in Figure 2B.2. Segment 1 models the haircut-only customers. Segment 2 models the shave-and-haircut customers. Segment 3 provides the logic for the timer.

Note how Segments 1 and 2 each contain a QUEUE–DEPART Block pair referencing the same Queue (JOEQ). Also note how each of these two segments contains a SEIZE–RELEASE Block pair referencing the same Facility (JOE). The possibility of having more than one Block pair reference a given Queue or a given Facility was not previously mentioned, but there is no reason why this cannot be done. Indeed, the flexibility in allowing multiple points of reference to given GPSS entities is made evident in this example.

Program Output.[18] Statistics describing the performance of the one Facility in the model are shown in Figure 2B.4(b). These statistics represent the aggregate effect of both types of customers on the barber. Under NUMBER ENTRIES, it is seen that the barber was captured by 20 customers in total. No distinction is made as to how many of these 20 customers were of the haircut-only type, or how many were of the shave-and-haircut variety. The output also shows that the barber was busy 89.7 percent of the time, but does not distinguish between that part of his time spent serving haircut-only customers, and that part spent serving shave-and-haircut customers.

Similarly, statistics in Figure 2B.4(c) describing the behavior of the one Queue in the model are aggregate in nature. No distinctions are made between the waiting experiences of the haircut-only customers vs. those of the shave-and-haircut customers. The model simply is not designed to make these distinctions. If such distinctions are to be made, the model must be redesigned accordingly.

Assume it is important to gather Queue statistics segregated according to customer type, as well as aggregated over both types of customers. To get the segregated statistics, the Figure 2B.2 model must be extended by introducing an additional Queue in Segment 1, and

[18]The total CPU time required by the simulation on an IBM 360/67 computer was 1.8 seconds. See Chapter 4 for a discussion of computer time requirements in GPSS modeling.

an additional Queue in Segment 2. When this is done, the model will simultaneously maintain three separate sets of waiting line records.

Figure 2B.5 shows the Figure 2B.2 Block Diagram as modified to take these suggested additions into account. Additional Queues named TYPE1 and TYPE2 have been introduced in Segments 1 and 2, respectively. Note that, when a customer arrives in Segment 1, he joins the Queue JOEQ, then the Queue TYPE1, and then attempts to capture the Facility. When a capture is made, the customer then departs the Queues TYPE1 and JOEQ before service time is simulated at the ADVANCE Block. While waiting to capture, then, a haircut-only customer contributes simultaneously to the records being kept for two statistically different waiting lines. One set of records is unique to the haircut-only customer type; the other is a set maintained for all customers waiting for the Facility, independent of type. The same observations can be made for the shave-and-haircut customers simulated in model Segment 2.

It is important to realize that the *inherent logic* in the Figure 2B.5 model does not differ from that in Figure 2B.2. Logically, there is still only one line of customers waiting to capture the barber. The queue discipline exercised by the barber is still first-come, first-served. Whether the analyst chooses to maintain segregated waiting-line statistics or not is beside the point. In short, as indicated in Section 2.15, residence in a GPSS Queue is simply a matter of records.

Note in Figure 2B.3 that 1 has been entered as the D Operand in the START card. As a result, the Current and Future Events Chains were printed out by the Processor at the end of the simulation. These chains are shown in Figure 2B.4(d) and (e). Block Counts are shown in Figure 2B.4(a). The next set of exercises has several questions based on this information.

2.27 A Second Example of the Use of Current and Future Events Chains

In glancing at Figure 2B.2, it might hastily be concluded that some sort of redundancy exists with respect to the Facility JOE, or, for that matter, with respect to the Queue JOEQ. In terms of the Facility, for example, there is a tendency to ask, "how can one Facility be used at two different locations?" Questions like this apparently arise because the Facility is referenced from two pairs of SEIZE–RELEASE Blocks in the

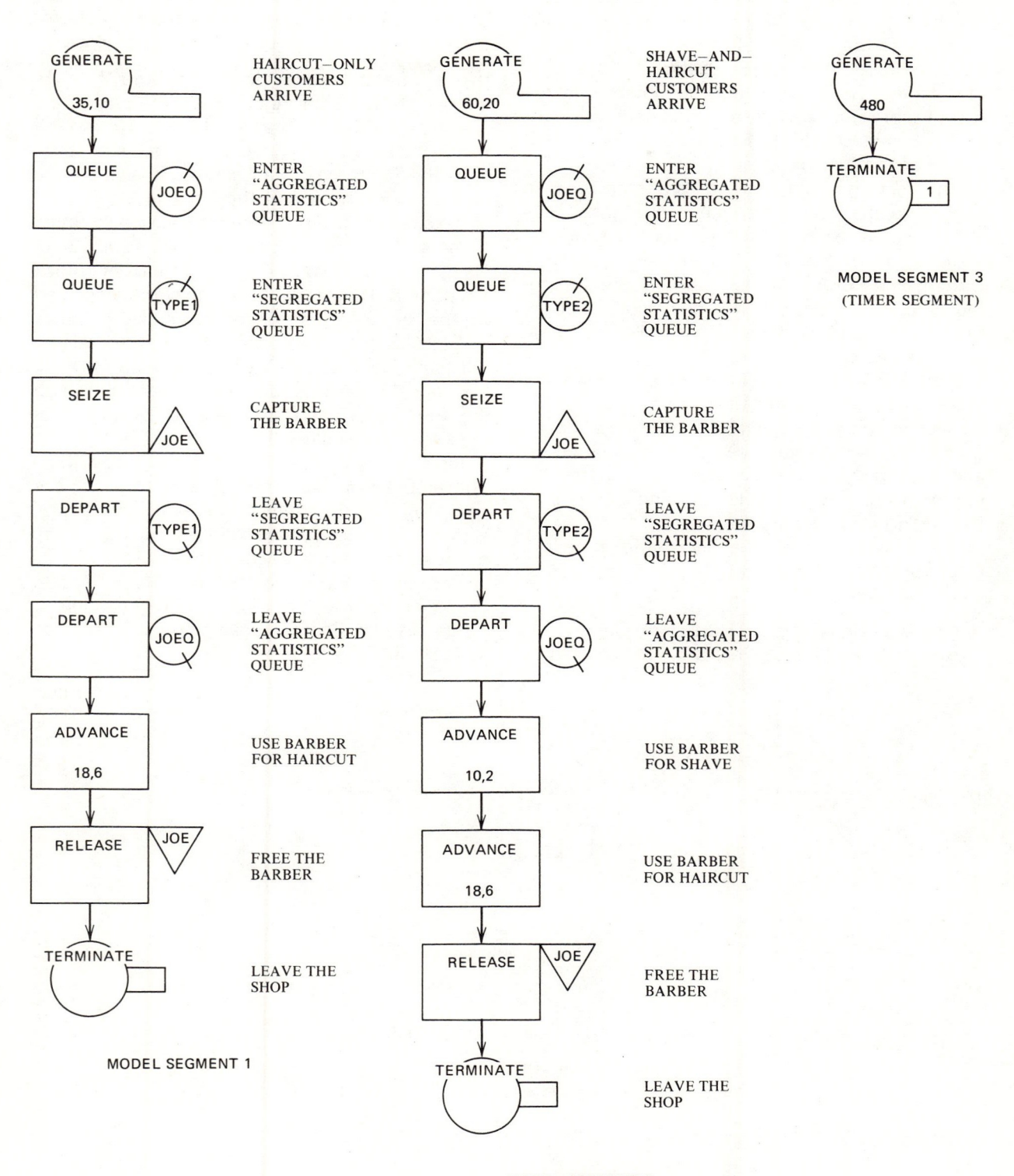

FIGURE 2B.5   Case Study 2B modeled with segregated and aggregated Queues for the two types of customers

model. The number of pairs of SEIZE–RELEASE Blocks in the model, however, is not necessarily identical to the number of servers in the system being modeled. In Case Study 2B, there is only one server. There is no reason, however, why use of that server cannot be simulated with two or more pairs of SEIZE–RELEASE Blocks in the model of the system.

The fact that there is no redundancy with respect to the Facility or Queue in Figure 2B.2 is best emphasized through a numeric example showing how the GPSS Processor uses the Current and Future Events Chains in performing the simulation. Following the plan established in Section 2.21, then, such an example will now be presented.

Figure 2.32 is a repetition of the Extended Program Listing for the Case Study 2B model. Using the Block Numbers in Figure 2.32, Table 2.16 displays the sequences of interarrival times and service times which will be assumed in effect at the various GENERATE and ADVANCE Blocks in the model.

Remembering that the five-tuple notation used to record information about Transactions takes the form

[Transaction Number, Move Time, Current Block, Priority Level, Next Block Attempted],

Figure 2.33 shows the history of Transaction residence on the Current and Future Events for the first few readings of the simulated clock.

Input Phase (From Line 1 to Line 2). As shown at Line 1 in Figure 2.33, the chains are empty when the Input Phase begins. During the Input Phase, Block Number 1 is found to be a GENERATE Block. Transaction 1 is therefore fetched from the top of the stack in latent pool and placed on the Future Events Chain, scheduled to enter Block 1 at time 44, per Table 2.16. Next, a GENERATE card is found at Block Location 8. Transaction 2 is consequently placed on the Future Events Chain, scheduled to move to Block 8 at time 41, per Table 2.16. Finally, a third and last GENERATE card is found at Block Location 16. Transaction 3 is therefore placed on the FEC, scheduled to move to Block 16 at time 480, per Table 2.9.

Line 2 in Figure 2.33 shows these three Transactions on the Future Events Chain at the completion of the Input Phase. Note that Transaction 2 preceeds Transaction 1 on the chain, because of its smaller Move Time.

Before continuing to the first Clock Update Phase, note the significance of the Line 2 Future Events Chain Transactions, as indicated in Table 2.17.

```
BLOCK                                                                      CARD
NUMBER  *LOC    OPERATION  A,B,C,D,E,F,G          COMMENTS                  NUMBER
                SIMULATE                                                   1
        *                                                                  2
        *       MODEL SEGMENT 1                                            3
        *                                                                  4
1               GENERATE   35,10      HAIRCUT-ONLY CUSTOMERS ARRIVE        5
2               QUEUE      JOEQ        ENTER THE LINE                      6
3               SEIZE      JOE         CAPTURE THE BARBER                   7
4               DEPART     JOEQ        LEAVE THE LINE                       8
5               ADVANCE    18,6        USE BARBER                          9
6               RELEASE    JOE         FREE THE BARBER                     10
7               TERMINATE              LEAVE THE SHOP                      11
        *                                                                  12
        *       MODEL SEGMENT 2                                            13
        *                                                                  14
8               GENERATE   60,20       SHAVE-AND-HAIRCUT CUSTOMERS ARRIVE  15
9               QUEUE      JOEQ        ENTER THE LINE                      16
10              SEIZE      JOE         CAPTURE THE BARBER                   17
11              DEPART     JOEQ        LEAVE THE LINE                       18
12              ADVANCE    10,2        USE BARBER FOR SHAVE                19
13              ADVANCE    18,6        USE BARBER FOR HAIRCUT              20
14              RELEASE    JOE         FREE THE BARBER                     21
15              TERMINATE              LEAVE THE SHOP                      22
        *                                                                  23
        *       MODEL SEGMENT 3                                            24
        *                                                                  25
16              GENERATE   480         TIMER ARRIVES AT TIME 480          26
17              TERMINATE  1           SHUT OFF THE RUN                    27
        *                                                                  28
        *       CONTROL CARDS                                              29
        *                                                                  30
                START      1,,,1       START THE RUN; GET CHAIN PRINTOUT AT END  31
                END                    RETURN CONTROL TO OPERATING SYSTEM  32
```

FIGURE 2.32   Repetition of Figure 2B.3

TABLE 2.16   Interarrival Times and Service Times Used for the Second Chain Example

Block Number	Block Type	System Aspect Simulated	Assumed Sequence of Interarrival Times or Service Times
1	GENERATE	Arrival of haircut-only customers	44, 28, 35, 40, . . .
5	ADVANCE	Servicing of haircut-only customers	20, 18, 22, 17, . . .
8	GENERATE	Arrival of shave-and-haircut customers	41, 72, 52, 60, . . .
12	ADVANCE	Shaving of shave-and-haircut customers	9, 11, 10, 12, . . .
13	ADVANCE	Hair-cutting of shave-and-haircut customers	14, 15, 20, 19, . . .
16	GENERATE	Timer	480

TABLE 2.17   Significance of Transactions on the Future Events Chain, Line 2, Figure 2.33

Transaction Number	Significance
2	First shave-and-haircut customer, on his way to the shop
1	First haircut-only customer, on his way to the shop
3	The timer Transaction

First Clock Update Phase (From Line 2 to Line 3). The Processor first sets the clock at 41, the Move Time of the Transaction (Transaction 2) at the front of the Line 2 Future Events Chain. It next transfers Transaction 2 to the previously empty Current Events Chain. The next Transaction (Transaction 1) on the Future Events chain does not have a Move Time of 41. The first execution of the Clock Update Phase is therefore finished.

Note at the Line 3 Current Events Chain that Transaction 2 is the first shave-and-haircut customer, just arriving at the barber shop.

First Scan Phase (From Line 3 to Line 4). Picking up Transaction 2 from the front end of the Current Events Chain at Line 3, the Processor moves it into Block 8, then begins to move it from Block 8 into Block 9. Temporarily interrupting the processing of Transaction 2, the Processor now schedules the arrival of the next Transaction at the Block 8 GENERATE Block. Corresponding to an interarrival time of 72 (second sample drawn from the 60 ± 20 distribution, per Table 2.16), Transaction 4 is fetched from the latent pool and placed on the FEC, scheduled to enter Block 8 at time 41 + 72, or 113.

The movement of Transaction 2 is then re-sumed. The Transaction moves through the QUEUE–SEIZE–DEPART–ADVANCE sequence (Blocks 9, 10, 11, and 12). At Block 12, a holding time of 9 minutes is sampled, per Table 2.16. Transaction 2 is then removed from the CEC and placed on the FEC, scheduled to enter Block 13 at time 50.

Because a SEIZE Block was executed, the Processor now restarts its scan of the Current Events Chain. But the chain is empty. The next step, then, is to perform the Clock Update Phase.

Note that at Line 4 in Figure 2.33, Transactions on the Future Events Chain have the significance indicated in Table 2.18. In particular, consider the first shave-and-haircut customer, who is now being shaved. He moved through the QUEUE–DEPART Block pair at Blocks 9 and 11 at clock reading 41, thereby counting as a zero entry to the Queue JOEQ. He captured the Facility JOE by moving into the SEIZE Block which is Block 10 in the model.

TABLE 2.18   Significance of Transactions on the Future Events Chain, Line 4, Figure 2.33

Transaction Number	Significance
1	Haircut-only customer, on his way to the shop
2	First shave-and-haircut customer, being shaved
4	Second shave-and-haircut customer, on his way to the shop
3	The timer Transaction

Second Clock Update Phase (From Line 4 to Line 5). Examining the Transaction at the front end of the FEC in Line 4, the Processor advances the clock to a value of 44. The front end FEC Transaction is then transferred to the pre-

Line Number	Simulated Time	Current Events Chain Front of Chain →	Future Events Chain Front of Chain →
1	Before Input Phase	Empty	Empty
2	After Input Phase	Empty	[2,41,NONE,0.1] [3,480,NONE,0.16]
3	41	[2,ASAP,NONE,0.8]	[1,44,NONE,0.1] [3,480,NONE,0.16]
4	41	Empty	[1,44,NONE,0.1] [2,50,12,0.13] [4,113,NONE,0.8] [3,480,NONE,0.16]
5	44	[1,ASAP,NONE,0.1]	[2,50,12,0.13] [4,113,NONE,0.8] [3,480,NONE,0.16]
6	44	[1,ASAP,2,0.3]	[2,50,12,0.13] [5,72,NONE,0.1] [4,113,NONE,0.8] [3,480,NONE,0.16]
7	50	[1,ASAP,2,0.3] [2,ASAP,12,0.13]	[5,72,NONE,0.1] [4,113,NONE,0.8] [3,480,NONE,0.16]
8	50	[1,ASAP,2,0.3]	[2,64,13,0.14] [5,72,NONE,0.1] [4,113,NONE,0.8] [3,480,NONE,0.16]
9	64	[1,ASAP,2,0.3] [2,ASAP,13,0.14]	[5,72,NONE,0.1] [4,113,NONE,0.8] [3,480,NONE,0.16]
10	64	Empty	[5,72,NONE,0.1] [1,84,5,0.6] [4,113,NONE,0.8] [3,480,NONE,0.16]

FIGURE 2.33 Chain history for second example of the use of Current and Future Events Chains

viously empty CEC. There are no other FEC-to-CEC transfers at time 44. The next Scan Phase can now begin.

Second Scan Phase (From Line 5 to Line 6). Picking up Transaction 1 from the front end of the CEC at Line 5, the Processor moves it into Block 1, then begins to move it from Block 1 into Block 2. Temporarily interrupting the processing of Transaction 1, the Processor then schedules the arrival of the next Transaction at the Block 1 GENERATE Block. Corresponding to an inter-arrival time of 28 (second sample drawn from the 35 ± 10 distribution, per Table 2.16, Transaction 5 is fetched from the latent pool and placed on the FEC, scheduled to enter Block 1 at time 44 + 28, or 72.

The Processor then resumes moving Transaction 1, completing execution of the QUEUE Block subroutine (Block 2). The Transaction is then denied entry to the SEIZE Block (Block 3). The reason, of course, is that the referenced Facility, JOE, is in a state of capture. It was captured at simulated time 41 by Transaction 2, which executed the SEIZE at that time at Block 10. The Processor consequently leaves Transaction 1 in the QUEUE Block (Block 2) and on the Current Events Chain, scheduled to SEIZE at Block 3 as soon as possible. While waiting to move into Block 3, Transaction 1 still contributes, of course, to the statistics being gathered for the Queue JOEQ. Hence, it is a member of the Queue for which Transaction 1 was a zero entry at simulated time 41, via execution of the QUEUE–DEPART pair at locations 9 and 11.

Lines 7, 8, 9, and 10 in the Figure 2.33 chain history will not be commented upon in this discussion. It should already be clear that multiple references to GPSS entities in a model pose no problems for the GPSS Processor. The essential point is that there is only one Current Events Chain, and one Future Events Chain. By using these two chains, the Processor can record a variety of system events occurring in a model. Within this framework, multiple entity references are easily accommodated. The practical consequence of this, as the Figure 2B.2 model illustrates, is to provide considerable flexibility in the model-building process.

2.28 Exercises

1. (Questions Based on Figure 2B.4, Case Study 2B)
  (a) Note that the Current Count at Block 2 is 1, from Figure 2B.4(a). What is the number of the Transaction currently in that Block?
  (b) Note that the Current Count at Block 13 is 1, from Figure 2B.4(a). What is the number of the Transaction currently in that Block?
  (c) At Figure 2B.4(c), the current content of the Queue JOEQ is indicated to be 1. What Transaction is contributing to the content of the Queue? For how many time units has it been in the Queue?
  (d) Which type of customer will next arrive at the shop, haircut-only, or shave-and-haircut?
  (e) How many of each type of customer have been *completely serviced* when the simulation shuts off?

2. (Questions Based on Figure 2.33)
  (a) At Line 7 in Figure 2.33, explain the significance of Transaction 2 on the Current Events Chain.
  (b) At Line 8, explain the significance of Transaction 2 on the Future Events Chain.
  (c) At what time does the first haircut-only customer get out of the barber's chair?
  (d) At simulated time 64, Transaction 2 is returned to the top of the stack in the latent pool of Transactions. At what simulated time will this Transaction be brought back into the model? Will it represent a haircut-only, or a shave-and-haircut customer at that time? (It may be necessary to extend the Figure 2.33 chain history to answer these questions. If this is done, note that additional time values are available in Table 2.16.)

3. (a) In Case Study 2B, assume that the *first* haircut-only customer, and the *first* shave-and-haircut customer, arrive at the barber shop simultaneously. Which of the two will be the first to capture the barber, and why? (Hint: note the relative order of the punchcards for Model Segment 1 and Model Segment 2 in the Figure 2B.3 Extended Program Listing.)
  (b) Repeat (a), only assume that the punchcards for Model Segment 2 have been placed *ahead of* the punchcards for Model Segment 1.
  (c) Assume that the barber is idle at simulated time 344, and that there is no one in the waiting line. Also assume that these two events have been scheduled to occur simultaneously at time 344.
    (i) A haircut-only customer will arrive at the shop.
    (ii) A shave-and-haircut customer will arrive at the shop.
  Under what conditions will the haircut-only customer be the first one to capture the barber? Under what conditions will the shave-and-haircut customer be the one to capture the barber?

TABLE E4

Block Number	Block Type	System Aspect Simulated	Assumed Sequence of Interarrival Times or Service Times
1	GENERATE	Arrival of haircut-only customers	31, 38, 29, 42, . . .
5	ADVANCE	Servicing of haircut-only customers	15, 19, 14, . . .
8	GENERATE	Arrival of shave-and-haircut customers	51, 32, 64, 49, . . .
12	ADVANCE	Shaving of shave-and-haircut customers	9, 11, 10, . . .
13	ADVANCE	Hair-cutting of shave-and-haircut customers	14, 17, 12, . . .
16	GENERATE	Timer	480 (deterministic)

4. Using Block Numbers from Figure 2.32, Table E4 displays sequences of interarrival times and service times assumed to be in effect initially at the various GENERATE and ADVANCE Blocks there. Using the interarrival times and service times in the table, construct a chain history similar to Figure 2.33, showing the Transactions resident on the Current and Future Events Chains through Line 10 in the history. Then answer these questions.
   (a) Which Transaction represents the first haircut-only customer of the day?
   (b) What is the clock reading at Line 10?
   (c) Where is the first haircut-only customer at the time Line 10 is reached?
   (d) Which Transaction represents the first shave-and-haircut customer of the day?
   (e) Where is the first shave-and-haircut customer at the time Line 10 is reached?
   (f) What type customer does Transaction 4 represent?

5. Prepare the punchcards corresponding to the Figure 2B.5 model and submit the model for running on the computer. Compare and contrast the outputted Queue statistics for the Queues TYPE1, TYPE2, and JOEQ.

6. Suppose that the "QUEUE TYPE1" and "QUEUE JOEQ" Blocks in Segment 1, Figure 2B.5, were interchanged. Do you think it would then be necessary to interchange the "DEPART TYPE1" and "DEPART JOEQ" Blocks in Segment 1 for the model to be valid? Discuss this situation.

7. Figure 2B.5 shows how to gather segregated and aggregated Queue statistics for the two customer types in the system. Show how to gather segregated and aggregated Facility statistics in the system. That is, show how to construct the model so that it continues to gather aggregate Facility statistics, and in addition measures the fraction of the time the barber is engaged by haircut-only customers, the fraction of the time he is engaged by shave-and-haircut customers, the average time he spends with each customer type, and so on.

8. Three types of mechanics arrive at a tool crib to check out tools. Their interarrival times and service-time requirements are shown in Table E8. Only one clerk works at the tool crib. Build a GPSS model for the tool crib, then run a simulation with the model until 16 Type 1 mechanics have received service at the crib. Design the model so that it maintains separate Queue statistics for each type of mechanic. Compare and contrast the waiting-line experiences of the three mechanic types. Also compute the expected utilization of the server and compare your result with the model-measured utilization.

TABLE E8

Type of Mechanic	Distribution of Interarrival Times (minutes)	Distribution of Service Times (minutes)
1	30 ± 10	12 ± 5
2	20 ± 8	6 ± 3
3	15 ± 5	3 ± 1

2.29 CASE STUDY 2C
Alternative Queue Disciplines in the One-Line, One-Server Queuing System

(1) Statement of the Problem

In a certain factory, a tool crib is manned by a single clerk. The clerk checks out tools to mechanics, who use them to repair failed machines. (The tools involved are too expensive, and too numerous, for each mechanic to have each tool in his tool box.) The time to process a tool request depends on the type of tool. Requests fall into two categories. Pertinent data are shown in Table 2C.1.

TABLE 2C.1   Interarrival Times and Service Time Requirements of Mechanics Using the Tool Crib in Case Study 2C

Category of Tool Request	Mechanic Inter-Arrival Time (seconds)	Service Time (seconds)
1	420 ± 360	300 ± 90
2	360 ± 240	100 ± 30

The clerk has been serving the mechanics first-come, first-served, independent of request. This queue discipline is shown in Figure 2C.1 where circles and triangles represent mechanics making requests in Category 1 and 2, respectively. In Figure 2C.1 a Category 2 request is being served, while one request in Category 1, and two in Category 2, are waiting in that order for the server.

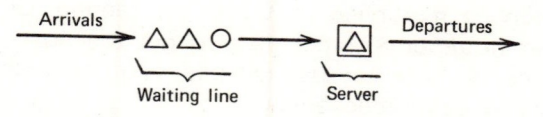

FIGURE 2C.1   First-come, first-served queue discipline, two customer types with no priority distinctions

Because failed machines are out of production, it costs 0.25¢ per second ($9 per hour) when a mechanic waits for service at the tool crib. This cost is independent of the tool to be checked out. Management believes the average number of waiting mechanics can be reduced if Category 2 requests are serviced at the tool crib before those in Category 1.[19] That is, only when no Category 2 requests are waiting is the clerk to service requests in Category 1. This queue discipline is pictured in Figure 2C.2, where, in effect, the line that forms ahead of the server consists of two segments. The segment at the front of the line is of "high priority"; that at the back of the line is of "low priority." The Figure 2C.2 queue discipline is said to be "first-come, first-served, within Priority Class."

The waiting-mechanic situation in Figure 2C.2 is identical to that in Figure 2C.1. The server is

[19]The average Category 2 service time is less than for Category 1. When the server chooses as his next customer the one with the smallest *average* service time requirement, a "shortest imminent operation" queue discipline is said to be in effect.

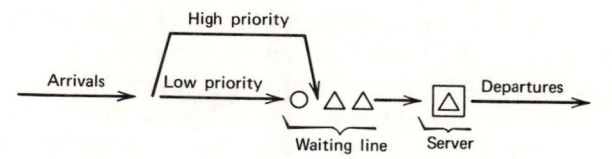

FIGURE 2C.2   First-come, first-served queue discipline, two customer types with priority distinctions

currently working on a Category 2 request (triangle). Two other Category 2 requests are waiting; and one Category 1 request is waiting (circle). Only when the high-priority segment of the line is empty will the low-priority segment be served.

Model the tool crib for each of the two queue disciplines indicated, simulating each case for an 8-hour work day. Does "first-come, first-served, within Priority Class" reduce the average number of mechanics waiting in line? In terms of the cost of lost production, what daily savings can be realized when priority distinctions are made? Do not include in the cost consideration the time mechanics spend receiving service.

(2) Approach Taken in Building the Model

The system to be modeled is very similar to that in Case Study 2B. That is, there are two different types of customers arriving at a single server. The differences are in the distributions of inter-arrival times, and service times, for the two arrival types. A further complication here, however, is that one arrival type is to have processing priority over the other type. The model can be built with an approach similar to that in Case Study 2B, then, if a method can be found to introduce this difference in processing priorities.

When entering a model, Transactions are given a Priority Level specified via their GENERATE Block's E Operand. When this was pointed out in Section 2.6, it was also stated that, "for reasons to be made clear later, it is convenient that various Transactions in a model may have distinctions made among one another with respect to their relative processing priority." In the problem at hand, just such a processing distinction is to be made.

Analogous to Case Study 2B, then, the Category 1 requests can be modeled in one segment, and Category 2 requests in another. The distinction in relative priorities is made by using a larger E Operand in the Category 2 GENERATE Block than in the Category 1 model segment. For example, Category 2 requests might enter the model through a GENERATE Block with an E Operand of 2; and Category 1 requests through a GENERATE Block with an E Operand of 1. Of course, the *absolute* Priority Levels chosen do not matter, as long as Transactions representing mechanics making Category 2 requests have a higher Priority Level than the other Transactions.

The way Priority Level influences a Transaction's processing priority is evident in terms of the Current Events Chain. Recall that, when a Transaction is transferred from the Future to the Current Events Chain, it takes a position on the Current Chain *as the last member in its Priority Class.* Furthermore, the higher the Priority Class, the closer to the front of the CEC a Transaction is. Because the GPSS Processor scans the Current Events Chain from front to back, it tries to move higher-priority Transactions forward in the model first. Later in the scan, it tries to move those with lower priorities. This means any mechanics waiting to make Category 2 requests (Priority Level 2) will be given the first opportunity to SEIZE, *then* mechanics waiting to make Category 1 requests (Priority Level 1) will have their chance to SEIZE. When the server has just become available and at least one mechanic in each category is waiting, a Category 2 mechanic will capture the server next simply because he is nearer the front of the CEC than Category 1 mechanics.

Model with No Priority Distinctions. Eliminating the priority distinctions from the model is a simple matter of having the GENERATE Block E Operands in the two major model segments be identical. The most convenient way to do this is to eliminate the E Operands from the GENERATE Blocks entirely; the result is that, by default, Category 1 and Category 2 requests have Priority Levels of zero.

The Statistic of Interest. The average number of waiting mechanics is the statistic of primary interest in this problem. This statistic is available through the AVERAGE CONTENTS of the Queue in which the mechanics wait. Because the cost of having mechanics wait is independent of their request category, it is satisfactory to use only one GPSS Queue in modeling the system. The AVERAGE CONTENTS of this Queue can then be multiplied by 0.25¢ per second, or $9 per hour, or $72 per day, to get the cost per second, hour, or day, respectively, associated with waiting mechanics.

(3) Table of Definitions

Time Unit: 1 Second

TABLE 2C.2 Table of Definitions for Case Study 2C

GPSS Entity	Interpretation
Transactions	
Model Segment 1	Mechanics making Category 1 tool requests
Model Segment 2	Mechanics making Category 2 tool requests
Model Segment 3	A timer
Facilities	
CLERK	The tool crib clerk
Queues	
LINE	The Queue used to gather statistics on the combined waiting experience of mechanics making tool requests in both categories

(4) Block Diagram

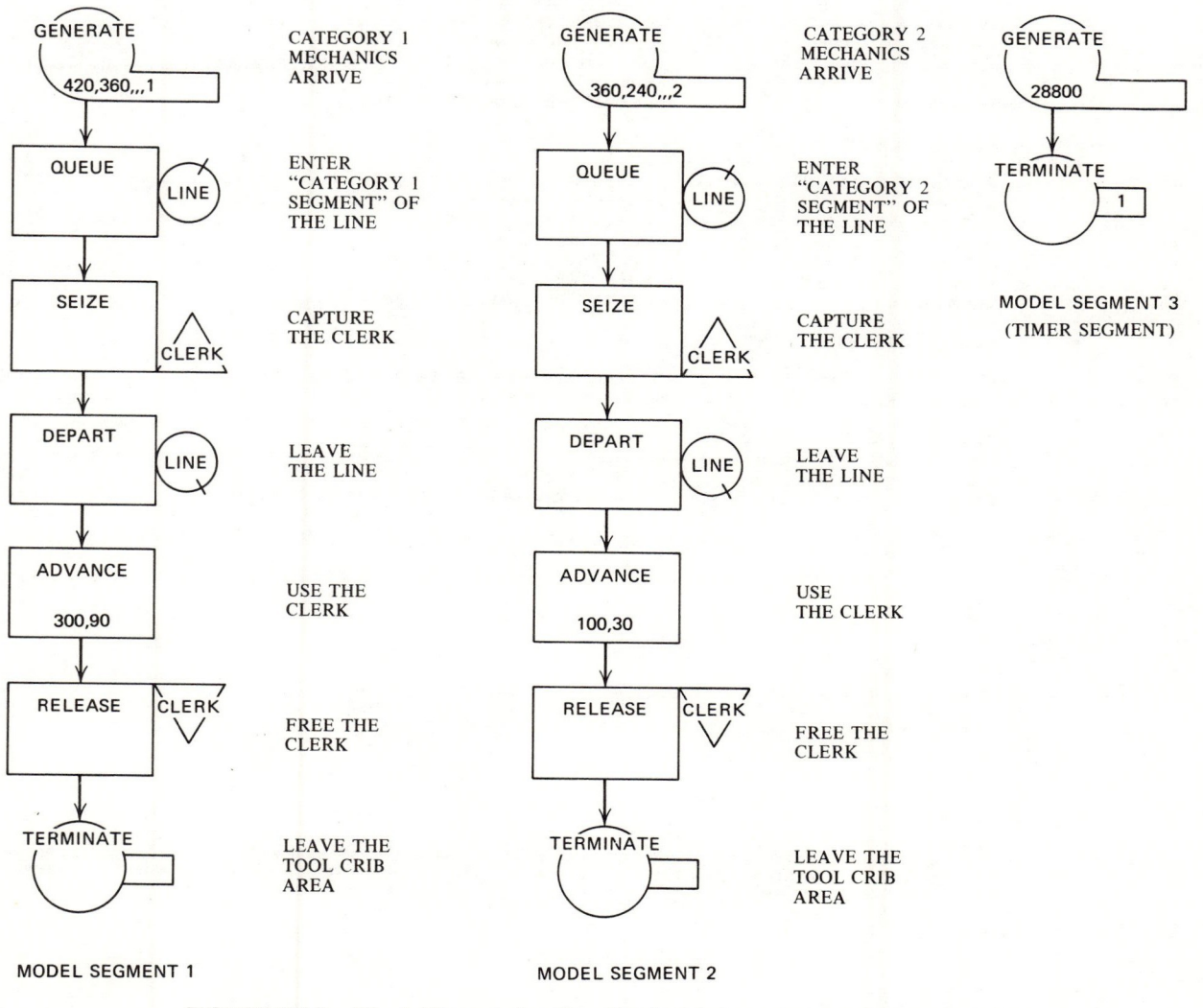

GENERATE
420,360,,,1
CATEGORY 1
MECHANICS
ARRIVE

QUEUE — LINE
ENTER
"CATEGORY 1
SEGMENT" OF
THE LINE

SEIZE — CLERK
CAPTURE
THE CLERK

DEPART — LINE
LEAVE
THE LINE

ADVANCE
300,90
USE THE
CLERK

RELEASE — CLERK
FREE THE
CLERK

TERMINATE
LEAVE THE
TOOL CRIB
AREA

MODEL SEGMENT 1

GENERATE
360,240,,,2
CATEGORY 2
MECHANICS
ARRIVE

QUEUE — LINE
ENTER
"CATEGORY 2
SEGMENT" OF
THE LINE

SEIZE — CLERK
CAPTURE
THE CLERK

DEPART — LINE
LEAVE
THE LINE

ADVANCE
100,30
USE
THE CLERK

RELEASE — CLERK
FREE THE
CLERK

TERMINATE
LEAVE THE
TOOL CRIB
AREA

MODEL SEGMENT 2

GENERATE
28800

TERMINATE
1

**MODEL SEGMENT 3
(TIMER SEGMENT)**

FIGURE 2C.3   Block Diagram for Case Study 2C (priority distinctions made)

(5) Extended Program Listings

```
BLOCK                                                                        CARD
NUMBER  *LOC   OPERATION   A,B,C,D,E,F,G              COMMENTS              NUMBER
                                                                              1
               SIMULATE                                                       2
        *                                                                     3
        *      MODEL SEGMENT 1                                                4
        *                                                                     4
1              GENERATE    420,360,,,1      CATEGORY 1 MECHANICS ARRIVE       5
2              QUEUE       LINE             ENTER "CATEGORY 1 SEGMENT" OF LINE 6
3              SEIZE       CLERK            CAPTURE THE CLERK                  7
4              DEPART      LINE             LEAVE THE LINE                     8
5              ADVANCE     300,90           USE THE CLERK                      9
6              RELEASE     CLERK            FREE THE CLERK                    10
7              TERMINATE                    LEAVE THE TOOL CRIB AREA          11
        *                                                                    12
        *      MODEL SEGMENT 2                                               13
        *                                                                    14
8              GENERATE    360,240,,,2      CATEGORY 2 MECHANICS ARRIVE       15
9              QUEUE       LINE             ENTER "CATEGORY 2 SEGMENT" OF LINE 16
10             SEIZE       CLERK            CAPTURE THE CLERK                 17
11             DEPART      LINE             LEAVE THE LINE                    18
12             ADVANCE     100,30           USE THE CLERK                     19
13             RELEASE     CLERK            FREE THE CLERK                    20
14             TERMINATE                    LEAVE THE TOOL CRIB AREA          21
        *                                                                    22
        *      MODEL SEGMENT 3                                               23
        *                                                                    24
15             GENERATE    28800            TIMER ARRIVES AFTER 8 HOURS       25
16             TERMINATE   1                SHUT OFF THE RUN                  26
        *                                                                    27
        *      CONTROL CARDS                                                 28
        *                                                                    29
               START       1                START THE RUN                    30
               END                          RETURN CONTROL TO OPERATING SYSTEM 31
```

FIGURE 2C.4   Extended Program Listing for Case Study 2C (priority distinctions made)

(6) Program Output

FACILITY	AVERAGE UTILIZATION	NUMBER ENTRIES	AVERAGE TIME/TRAN	SEIZING TRANS. NO.	PREEMPTING TRANS. NO.
CLERK	.932	140	191.878	6	

QUEUE	MAXIMUM CONTENTS	AVERAGE CONTENTS	TOTAL ENTRIES	ZERO ENTRIES	PERCENT ZEROS	AVERAGE TIME/TRANS	$AVERAGE TIME/TRANS	TABLE NUMBER	CURRENT CONTENTS
LINE	3	.770	140	20	14.2	158.500	184.916		

$AVERAGE TIME/TRANS = AVERAGE TIME/TRANS EXCLUDING ZERO ENTRIES

(a)

FACILITY	AVERAGE UTILIZATION	NUMBER ENTRIES	AVERAGE TIME/TRAN	SEIZING TRANS. NO.	PREEMPTING TRANS. NO.
CLERK	.959	142	194.605	1	

QUEUE	MAXIMUM CONTENTS	AVERAGE CONTENTS	TOTAL ENTRIES	ZERO ENTRIES	PERCENT ZEROS	AVERAGE TIME/TRANS	$AVERAGE TIME/TRANS	TABLE NUMBER	CURRENT CONTENTS
LINE	7	2.731	145	13	8.9	542.593	596.030		3

$AVERAGE TIME/TRANS = AVERAGE TIME/TRANS EXCLUDING ZERO ENTRIES

(b)

FIGURE 2C.5   Selected Program Output for Case Study 2C. (a) Output when priority distinctions are made. (b) Output when no priority distinctions are made.

(7) Discussion

Model Implementation. The model shown in Figure 2C.4 was first submitted for running. Then, the E Operands were eliminated from the GENERATE cards, and the resulting no-priority-distinction model was submitted for processing in a separate run. This approach is relatively awkward, requiring two separate runs. A method for accomplishing the processing in a single run will be described later in this chapter.

Program Output.[20]   As indicated, the Queue statistic of primary interest is the AVERAGE CONTENTS. Figure 2C.5(b) shows that the average number of waiting mechanics when no priority distinctions are made is 2.731 *for the 8-hour day simulated*. When priority distinctions are made, this average decreases to 0.770, as shown in Figure 2C.5(a). Making a priority distinction, then, has led to improved system performance in the sense that the average number of waiting mechanics has been decreased by about 70 percent. Note that this difference is based on about 140 to 145 entries to the Queue [TOTAL ENTRIES, Figure 2C.5(a) or (b)]. Due to randomness, there were five more arrivals at the tool crib during the no-priority-distinction simulation than during the priority-distinction run.

When no priority distinctions are made, the cost of waiting mechanics for the day simulated amounts to about $197 (2.731 times $72/day = $196.63). With priority distinctions in effect, the experienced cost was about $55 ($55.44). The difference in the experienced costs is then about $141 ($141.19).

Despite this difference in experienced costs, the duration of simulation used in this case study is so small that any conclusions drawn from the model output are tentative at best. After certain other features of GPSS have been introduced, this tool-crib problem will be further investigated. In Case Study 3C, additional experimentation with the tool crib suggests that the expected daily savings resulting from a priority-distinction queue discipline is about $48, meaning that the savings indicated above is quite untypical.

2.30 A Third Example of the Use of Current and Future Events Chains

In Case Study 2C, a distinction is made among the Priority Levels of Transactions in two different

segments of the model. This results in modeling a queue discipline described as "first-come, first-served, within Priority Class." Any doubts as to why this queue discipline is in effect as a consequence of controlling Transaction Priority Levels can be resolved by considering a numeric example showing how the GPSS Processor uses the Current and Future Events Chains to move the Figure 2C.4 model forward in simulated time. The initial details of such an example will now be presented.

Figure 2.34 is a repetition of the Extended Program Listing for the Case Study 2C model. Using the Block Numbers in Figure 2.34, Table 2.19 displays the sequence of interarrival times and service times which will be assumed in effect at the various GENERATE and ADVANCE Blocks in the model. Finally, Figure 2.35 shows the history of Transaction residence on the Current and Future Events Chains.

The details of Figure 2.35 will not be completely traced. Those interested can construct the chains as shown following the procedure already illustrated in the first and second chain examples. Of primary interest here are Lines 6, 8, and 10, showing the chain appearances at the completion of the Scan Phase after simulated times 403, 615, and 682, respectively. The significance of Transactions on the chains at those times will now be indicated.

The several Transactions on the chains at Line 6 have the interpretations shown in Table 2.20. In particular, Transaction 2 is waiting for the clerk, while Transactions 4 and 5 represent mechanics on their way to the tool crib.

Then, at simulated time 615, the second Category 1 mechanic (Transaction 4) arrives at the tool crib. Note that, in being transferred from the Future to the Current Events Chain, Transaction 4 has been put behind Transaction 2 on the Line 7 CEC. This is consistent with the ordering property imposed on the Current Events Chain (incoming Transactions take up the last position in their Priority Class). Transaction 4 has a Priority Level of 1, whereas that of Transaction 2 is 2. In fact, even if the Priority Level of Transaction 4 were 2, it would be behind Transaction 2. At this point, then, the difference in Priority Levels has had no effect on the operation of the model. On the Current Events Chain after the Scan Phase (Line 8), Transactions 2 and 4 are waiting for the services of the tool-crib clerk in "natural" order, based on their time of arrival at the crib.

```
BLOCK                                                                                                    CARD
NUMBER   *LOC   OPERATION  A,B,C,D,E,F,G                    COMMENTS                                     NUMBER
                SIMULATE                                                                                    1
          *                                                                                                 2
          *     MODEL SEGMENT 1                                                                             3
          *                                                                                                 4
  1             GENERATE   420,360,,,1          CATEGORY 1 MECHANICS ARRIVE                                 5
  2             QUEUE      LINE                  ENTER "CATEGORY 1 SEGMENT" OF LINE                          6
  3             SEIZE      CLERK                 CAPTURE THE CLERK                                           7
  4             DEPART     LINE                  LEAVE THE LINE                                              8
  5             ADVANCE    300,90               USE THE CLERK                                               9
  6             RELEASE    CLERK                 FREE THE CLERK                                             10
  7             TERMINATE                        LEAVE THE TOOL CRIB AREA                                   11
          *                                                                                                12
          *     MODEL SEGMENT 2                                                                            13
          *                                                                                                14
  8             GENERATE   360,240,,,2          CATEGORY 2 MECHANICS ARRIVE                                15
  9             QUEUE      LINE                  ENTER "CATEGORY 2 SEGMENT" OF LINE                         16
 10             SEIZE      CLERK                 CAPTURE THE CLERK                                          17
 11             DEPART     LINE                  LEAVE THE LINE                                             18
 12             ADVANCE    100,30               USE THE CLERK                                              19
 13             RELEASE    CLERK                 FREE THE CLERK                                             20
 14             TERMINATE                        LEAVE THE TOOL CRIB AREA                                   21
          *                                                                                                22
          *     MODEL SEGMENT 3                                                                            23
          *                                                                                                24
 15             GENERATE   28800                 TIMER ARRIVES AFTER 8 HOURS                               25
 16             TERMINATE  1                     SHUT OFF THE RUN                                           26
          *                                                                                                27
          *     CONTROL CARDS                                                                              28
          *                                                                                                29
                START      1                     START THE RUN                                             30
                END                              RETURN CONTROL TO OPERATING SYSTEM                        31
```

FIGURE 2.34   Repetition of Figure 2C.4

TABLE 2.19   Interarrival Times and Service Times Used for the Third Chain Example

Block Number	Block Type	System Aspect Simulated	Assumed Sequence Interarrival Times or Service Times
1	GENERATE	Arrival of mechanics making Category 1 requests	392, 223, 426, . . .
5	ADVANCE	Servicing of Category 1 requests	309, . . .
8	GENERATE	Arrival of mechanics making Category 2 requests	403, 279, 352, . . .
12	ADVANCE	Servicing of Category 2 requests	Not Used in Example
15	GENERATE	Timer	28800 (Deterministic)

Line Number	Simulated Time	Current Events Chain — Front of Chain →	Future Events Chain — Front of Chain →
1	BIP*	Empty	Empty
2	AIP**	Empty	[1.392.NONE.1.1] [2.403.NONE.2.8] [3.28800.NONE.0.15]
3	392	[1.ASAP.NONE.1.1]	[2.403.NONE.2.8] [3.28800.NONE.0.15]
4	392	Empty	[2.403.NONE.2.8] [4.615.NONE.1.1] [3.28800.NONE.0.15]
5	403	[2.ASAP.NONE.2.8]	[4.615.NONE.1.1] [1.701.5.1.6] [3.28800.NONE.0.15]
6	403	[2.ASAP.9.2.10]	[4.615.NONE.1.1] [5.682.NONE.2.8] [1.701.5.1.6] [3.28800.NONE.0.15]
7	615	[2.ASAP.9.2.10] [4.ASAP.2.1.3]	[5.682.NONE.2.8] [1.701.5.1.6] [3.28800.NONE.0.15]
8	615	[2.ASAP.9.2.10] [4.ASAP.2.1.3]	[5.682.NONE.2.8] [1.701.5.1.6] [6.1041.NONE.1.1] [3.28800.NONE.0.15]
9	682	[2.ASAP.9.2.10] [5.ASAP.NONE.2.8] [4.ASAP.2.1.3]	[1.701.5.1.6] [6.1041.NONE.1.1] [3.28800.NONE.0.15]
10	682	[2.ASAP.9.2.10] [5.ASAP.9.2.10] [4.ASAP.2.1.3]	[1.701.5.1.6] [7.1034.NONE.2.8] [6.1041.NONE.1.1] [3.28800.NONE.0.15]

*BIP: Before Input Phase.
**AIP: After Input Phase.

FIGURE 2.35   Chain history for the third example of the use of Current and Future Events Chains

TABLE 2.20   Significance of Transactions on the Current and Future Events
Chains, Line 6, Figure 2.35

Chain	Transaction Number	Significance
CEC	2	Mechanic waiting to make the first Category 2 request
FEC	4	Second Category 1 mechanic, on his way to the tool crib
FEC	5	Second Category 2 mechanic, on his way to the tool crib
FEC	1	First Category 1 mechanic, having his request serviced by the tool crib clerk
FEC	3	The timer Transaction

Then, in the next Clock Update Phase, the clock is advanced to 682, the time of arrival of the second Category 2 mechanic (Transaction 5). Removing Transaction 5 from the front of the Future Events Chain at Line 8, the Processor places it *between* Transactions 2 and 4 on the Current Events Chain (Line 9). In that position, it appears *ahead* of the lower-priority Transaction which was already resident on that chain, but *behind* the previous Priority Level 2 chain resident. The direct consequence of this ordering is that, eventually, Transaction 5 will capture the Facility ahead of Transaction 4, even though Transaction 4 has been waiting longer. Furthermore, if any additional Priority Level 2 Transactions are brought to the CEC before Transaction 4 has moved into Block 3 (SEIZE), they, too, will be merged ahead of it on the Current Events Chain, further delaying the time when the Facility will be made available to it.

Hence, the three elements of (1) Transaction Priority Level, (2) ordering property on the Current Events Chain, and (3) scan and rescan of the CEC from front to back, combine to make first-come, first-served, within Priority Class the default queue discipline in GPSS.

2.31 Exercises

1. In the third example of the use of Current and Future Events Chains, assume that, after the Scan Phase at time 28752, these conditions are in effect:
   1. The tool crib clerk is idle.
   2. Transaction 2 is on the Future Events Chain, representing a mechanic scheduled to arrive at the tool crib at time 28800 (shutoff time).
   3. Except for Transactions 2 and 3 (the timer), no other Transactions in the model have a Move Time of 28800 or less.

   Answer these questions.
   (a) What is the composition of the Current Events Chain?
   (b) What is the number of the Transaction at the front of the Future Events Chain?
   (c) When the model shuts off, will the tool crib clerk be idle or in a state of capture?

2. Build a model for exercise 8 of Section 2.28 (three types of arrivals at a tool crib). The server at the tool crib should use "shortest imminent operation" as a queue discipline. That is, he should serve next that request which is expected to require the smallest service time. Design the model so that it maintains separate Queue statistics for each of the three types of arrivals.

   Simulate with the model until 16 Type 1 arrivals have received service at the crib. Compare and contrast the waiting experiences of the three arrival types.

   Also compare and contrast the various waiting experiences with those determined for exercise 8, where queue discipline was first-come, first-served.

   At what simulated time does the model of exercise 2 shut off? When did the exercise 8 model shut off? How would you explain this difference?

3. In Case Study 2A, the barber works for 480 consecutive minutes, without taking a break. Show how to modify the model in that case study to include these features.
   (a) Assume that the barber shop opens at 8:30 a.m. and closes at 5:00 p.m. The barber takes a 30-minute lunch break at 12:00 noon, *or as soon thereafter as possible* (i.e., if he is at an intermediate point in working on a customer when it becomes noon, he finishes with that customer before taking the 30-minute lunch break). Customers who arrive at the shop during the

barber's break wait for him to return. What will be the barber's long-run utilization?

(b) Assume the shop opens at 8:00 a.m. and closes at 5:00 p.m. The barber takes these breaks at the indicated times, or as soon thereafter as possible.
   1. Coffee break, 10:00–10:15 a.m.
   2. Lunch break, 12:00–12:30 p.m.
   3. Coke break, 3:00–3:15 p.m.
Customers who arrive during any of the breaks choose to wait for the barber. After showing how to modify the case study 2A model to incorporate these changes, compute the barber's long-run utilization.

2.32 Routing Transactions to Nonsequential Blocks

It is occasionally of interest to divert Transactions unconditionally to some nonsequential Block in a GPSS model. This can be accomplished by using the TRANSFER Block in *unconditional transfer mode*. As used in this mode, the TRANSFER Block is shown in Figure 2.36.

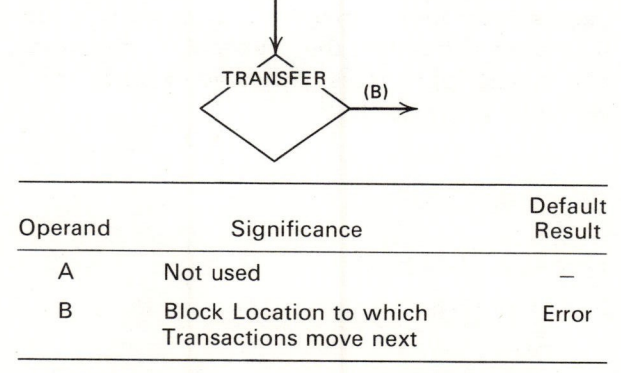

Operand	Significance	Default Result
A	Not used	—
B	Block Location to which Transactions move next	Error

FIGURE 2.36   The TRANSFER Block in Unconditional Transfer Mode

The A Operand is not employed in this TRANSFER Block usage. This means that a comma must be entered in card column 19 when the Block's punchcard image is prepared. This is suggested by the comma placed within the Block.

The B Operand names the Location occupied by the next Block the Transaction will attempt to enter. For brevity, whatever Block is in that Location will be termed the "B Block". The Block Location can be provided either symbolically or numerically. A symbolic Location name is usually the most convenient to use.

Otherwise, it is necessary for the analyst to determine the absolute Location number that will be assigned to the "B Block" by the Processor.

In Figure 2.36, parentheses have been used around the B Operand. These parentheses appear only in the Block Diagram of the model. They are not part of the B Operand, and do not appear in the punchcard image of the TRANSFER Block.

In unconditional transfer mode, the TRANSFER Block cannot refuse entry to a Transaction. When a Transaction enters the Block, it immediately tries to move into the B Block. If that Block denies entry, the Transaction is left in the TRANSFER Block and on the Current Events Chain. At each next scan of the Current Events Chain (whether due to a scan restart within the current Scan Phase, or to initiation of the next Scan Phase), an attempt is again made to move the Transaction into the B Block. Eventually, the attempt will presumably be successful.

As pointed out, the TRANSFER Block usage described above is termed "TRANSFER Block in unconditional transfer mode." There are alternative modes in which the TRANSFER Block can be used. Discussion of some of these alternatives will be taken up later.

Use of the TRANSFER Block in unconditional transfer mode is illustrated in Case Study 2D in the next section.

2.33 CASE STUDY 2D
A One-Line, One-Server Queuing System with Feedback

(1) Statement of the Problem

The manufacture of a certain line of widgets involves a relatively lengthy assembly process, followed by a short firing time in an oven. Since ovens are expensive to maintain, several assemblers share a single oven, which holds only one widget at a time. An assembler cannot begin assembling a new widget until he has removed the old one from the oven.

This is the pattern followed, then, by each assembler:

1. Assemble next widget.
2. Wait, first-come, first-served, to use the oven.
3. Use the oven.
4. Return to 1.

Time and cost studies have been conducted to provide the information in Tables 2D.1 and 2D.2, respectively.

Build a GPSS model of this manufacturing process. Use the model to determine the optimal number of assemblers to be assigned to an oven. The optimal number is understood in this con-

TABLE 2D.1   Operation Times for Case Study 2D

Operation	Time Required (minutes)
Assemble	30 ± 5
Fire	8 ± 2

TABLE 2D.2   Financial Data for Case Study 2D

Item	Cost Information
Assembler's salary	$3.75 per hour
Oven cost	$80 per 8-hour work day (independent of utilization)
Raw material	$2 per widget
Value of finished widgets	$7 per widget

text to be the one maximizing profit. Base the determination on simulations equivalent to 40 hours of simulated time. Assume there are no discontinuities within a working day, or in moving between consecutive 8-hour work days.

(2) Approach Taken in Building the Model

A good approach to use in building many GPSS models is this:

1. First, identify the *constraints* in the system to be modeled.
2. Then, make a decision about which GPSS entities to use to simulate these constraints in the model itself.

In the current problem, there are two constraints. First, there is only one oven involved. Second, there is some fixed number of assemblers who are in the system. It is natural to choose a Facility to simulate the oven. It is equally natural to let a Transaction represent an assembler. Then, even as the assemblers can be thought of as circulating through the system as they move repeatedly through the assemble–fire cycle, the Transactions can circulate through the GPSS model of the system.

In the system itself, after each assembler takes a fired widget from the oven, he goes back to begin his next assembly. In the model of the system, after a Transaction has released the Facility simulating the oven, it can be routed back via a TRANSFER Block to the ADVANCE Block where the next assembly process is simulated. As to constraining the total number of Transactions which circulate through the model, the D Operand at the GENERATE Block provides a convenient method for fixing this total number.

Ultimately, to compute the profit associated with a given number of assemblers, it will be necessary to know how many finished widgets they produced during the course of a simulation. The number of releases of the oven Facility conveniently provides this count.

(3) Table of Definitions

Time Unit: 1 Minute

TABLE 2D.3   Table of Definitions for Case Study 2D

GPSS Entity	Interpretation
Transactions	
Model Segment 1	Assemblers
Model Segment 2	The timer
Facilities	
OVEN	The oven

(4) Block Diagram

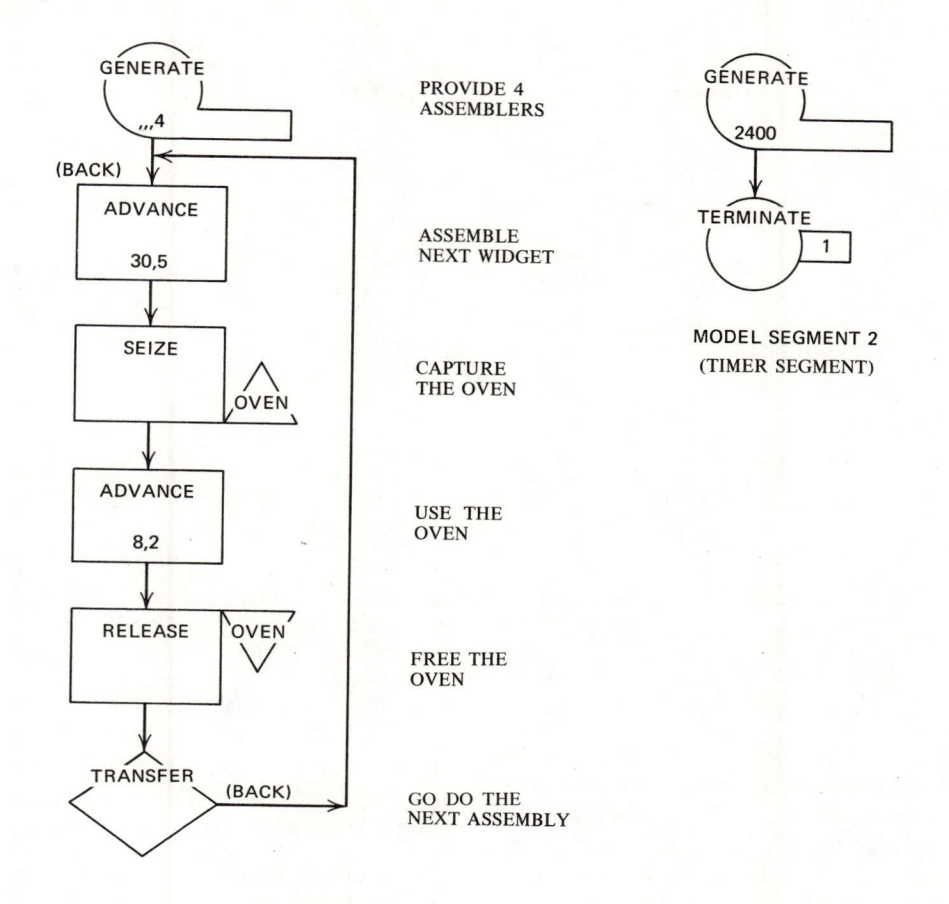

FIGURE 2D.1   Block Diagram for Case Study 2D (four assemblers used)

(5) Extended Program Listing

```
BLOCK                                                                              CARD
NUMBER   *LOC    OPERATION   A,B,C,D,E,F,G              COMMENTS                  NUMBER
                 SIMULATE                                                           1
         *                                                                          2
         *       MODEL SEGMENT 1                                                    3
         *                                                                          4
1                GENERATE    ,,,4          PROVIDE 4 ASSEMBLERS                      5
2        BACK    ADVANCE     30,5          ASSEMBLE NEXT WIDGET                      6
3                SEIZE       OVEN          CAPTURE THE OVEN                          7
4                ADVANCE     8,2           USE THE OVEN                             8
5                RELEASE     OVEN          FREE THE OVEN                            9
6                TRANSFER    ,BACK         GO DO THE NEXT ASSEMBLY                  10
         *                                                                         11
         *       MODEL SEGMENT 2                                                   12
         *                                                                         13
7                GENERATE    2400          TIMER ARRIVES AFTER 5 DAYS              14
8                TERMINATE   1             SHUT OFF THE RUN                        15
         *                                                                         16
         *       CONTROL CARDS                                                     17
         *                                                                         18
                 START       1             START THE RUN                           19
                 END                       RETURN CONTROL TO OPERATING SYSTEM      20
```

FIGURE 2D.2   Extended Program Listing for Case Study 2D (four assemblers used)

(6) Program Output

FACILITY	AVERAGE UTILIZATION	NUMBER ENTRIES	AVERAGE TIME/TRAN	SEIZING TRANS. NO.	PREEMPTING TRANS. NO.
OVEN	.785	236	7.991	5	

(a)

FACILITY	AVERAGE UTILIZATION	NUMBER ENTRIES	AVERAGE TIME/TRAN	SEIZING TRANS. NO.	PREEMPTING TRANS. NO.
OVEN	.952	280	8.160	5	

(b)

FACILITY	AVERAGE UTILIZATION	NUMBER ENTRIES	AVERAGE TIME/TRAN	SEIZING TRANS. NO.	PREEMPTING TRANS. NO.
OVEN	.988	295	8.040	1	

(c)

FIGURE 2D.3   Selected Program Output for Case Study 2D. (a) Oven statistics when four assemblers are used. (b) Oven statistics when five assemblers are used. (c) Oven statistics when six assemblers are used.

(7) Discussion

Model Logic.   This is the first model in which there has been occasion to give a symbolic name to a Block Location. In Figure 2D.1, the Location of the "ADVANCE 30,5" Block has been given the name BACK. In Figure 2D.2, this symbolic name appears in the Location Field (under the label *LOC) on the card image of the ADVANCE Block. In the Block Number column in that figure, it is seen that the symbolic location BACK is equivalent to numeric Location 2.

In Figure 2D.1, although assemblers must wait for the oven, the SEIZE Block is not sandwiched between a QUEUE—DEPART Block pair. No Queue statistics are needed for the problem as stated. As a result, no provisions are made to gather waiting-line data in the model.

Assemblers waiting to use the oven are represented by Transactions on the Current Events Chain, waiting to move into Block 3 (SEIZE) "as soon as possible." From the point of view of Block Counts, these Transactions contribute to the Current Count at Block 2 (ADVANCE). This is the case even though their computed holding time at the ADVANCE Block has already elapsed.

Model Implementation. The three assembler-to-oven ratios investigated were studied by making three separate computer runs. Only the D Operand in the Segment 1 GENERATE Block was changed from run to run, to provide for the changing assembler-to-oven ratio. In Section 2.34, a GPSS control card will be introduced which makes it possible to study a variety of assembler-to-oven ratios in sequence, with a single computer run.

Program Output.[21]   The cost of the oven for the 40-hour week simulated is $400. Each assembler earns $150 per week. The number of widgets *finished* during the 40-hour week were 235, 279, and 294 for the cases of four, five, and six assemblers, respectively. (This finished widget count excludes the widget still in the oven, if any, at the end of the simulation.) The corresponding return-after-costs for the three cases is easily computed to be $175, $245, and $170, respectively. Hence, the optimal number of assemblers per oven is 5.

This problem involves a simple tradeoff between the cost of waiting assemblers, and the cost of an idle oven. With four assemblers, assembler waiting time (not determined by the model) is relatively low, but oven utilization is also low [0.785, Figure 2D.3(a)]. With five assemblers, assembler waiting time increases, but so does oven utilization [0.952, Figure 2D.3(b)]. Hence, the salary of the additional assembler is more than offset by the increased oven utilization. With six assemblers, however,

[21]Total CPU time for the simulation on an IBM 360/67 computer was 2.0 seconds.

assembler waiting time increases even more, but the oven utilization is not affected that greatly [0.988, Figure 2D.3(c)]. The modest increase in oven utilization with six assemblers is not enough to offset the cost of the additional assembler.

2.34 GPSS Control Cards: The CLEAR Card

In Case Study 2D, having built a model for the system to be simulated, it was necessary to make a series of sequential runs with slightly modified versions of the model. The model modification involved changing the D Operand in the Segment 1 GENERATE Block. This, in turn, amounted to reconfiguring the system, in the sense that it changed the number of assemblers using a single oven. The need and desire to reconfigurate models, then make more computer runs, often arises in simulation modeling. In fact, one of the principal uses of simulation is to measure the behavior of alternative systems that might be used to accomplish a given objective.

It would clearly be convenient if the analyst, instead of submitting a series of batch jobs to perform the change-and-run steps, could have these steps performed in a single batch session. This would have the following implications.

1. After a given simulation shuts off and the system statistics have been outputted, the existing model would have to be susceptible to modification. Such modification might take one or more of the following forms.

   (a) Redefine the *Operands* in effect at one or more of the Blocks in the model, without however redefining the *types* of Blocks in question.

   (b) Redefine the types of Blocks occupying one or more Locations in the model.

   (c) Augment the model by adding one or more self-contained model segments to it.

2. After modification of the model, it would have to be made ready to run again. This would entail three things:

   (a) All model statistics would have to be set back to zero.

   (b) All Transactions that were in the model at the end of the previous simulation would have to be removed. This means that the chains would have to be emptied, with Transactions on them at the time of the last shutoff being returned to the stack in the latent pool.

   (c) The Input Phase would have to be performed again, in the sense that the Processor would have to examine the reconfigured model, looking for

GENERATE Blocks. For each GENERATE Block found, it would be necessary to schedule the first arrival of a Transaction to the modified model through that Block.

3. Finally, after reconfiguring the model and making it ready to run again, the simulation would have to be reinitiated. The Processor would have to initialize the Termination Counter, then begin execution of the Clock Update Phase, setting the simulation clock to the Move Time of the Transaction at the front of the Future Events Chain, etc.

Each of the above steps can be accomplished in GPSS. The method for carrying this out will now be described.

Suppose that, having inputted a model and come to a START card, the Processor has initiated a simulation. Eventually, the Termination Counter is decremented to zero, the simulation shuts off, and various output is produced. The model with which the simulation has just been performed is left as it was when the simulation shut off. For example, any Transactions in the model when the simulation ended are left in whichever Blocks and on whichever chains they occupied at that time. The Processor now goes to the next card in the deck to find its next instruction.[22] Assume the next card is the image of one or more Blocks *already in the existing model*. For instance, suppose that a GENERATE Block is in the model at the Location named ALPHA, and that immediately after the first START card, the analyst has placed the card "ALPHA GENERATE 15,5,,30". Finding this new definition of the Block in the Location ALPHA, the Processor *replaces* the Block previously at that Location with this newly-defined Location occupant. This means the Block at ALPHA, although still a GENERATE Block, now has A, B, C, and D Operands of 15, 5, default value (no offset), and 30, respectively. It is this ability to redefine Location occupants which makes possible the type of model modification suggested under Step 1(a) above.

It is only on rare occasions that the analyst may want to modify a model in the sense of redefining the *types* of Blocks occupying one or more Locations, or in the sense of augmenting the model by adding one or more self-contained model segments to it. Because of this, these possibilities will not be considered here. In fact, in none of the case studies in this book is such model modification ever necessary.

---

[22] In the models presented so far, the next card has always been the END card. This card instructs the Processor to return control to the operating system.

Now suppose that, after the START card, the analyst has included one or more cards which redefine the Operands of Blocks occupying selected Locations in the model. Acting upon these cards, one by one, the Processor always goes to the next card in the deck to find out what to do next. Suppose that, after the last card redefining Block Operands, a CLEAR card appears in the deck. The CLEAR card is a GPSS control card which has the effect of making the model ready to run again, as described under Step 2 above. It consists of the word CLEAR, entered in the Operation field on a punchcard. There is no Block equivalent for it. Whenever the Processor encounters a CLEAR card, it sets model statistics back to zero (including both the Relative and Absolute Clocks), puts all Transactions back on the stack in the latent pool, and performs the Input Phase (with respect to scheduling first arrivals at GENERATE Blocks) with the model in its current state of definition.

Having accomplished this, the Processor continues with the next card in the deck. Assume that the next card is a START card. This is a signal, of course, that the Processor is to perform a simulation with the model. The Processor proceeds to initialize the Termination Counter with a copy of the value of the A Operand on the START card, then goes into the Clock Update Phase, then the Scan Phase, etc. Eventually, the Termination Counter is again decremented to zero, the simulation stops, and system statistics are outputted. The Processor then returns to the deck for its next instruction, and so on.

With respect to Steps 1 through 3 above, it is natural to wonder whether Steps 1 and 2 are interchangeable, i.e., whether the CLEAR card can be placed ahead of the Block redefinitions. The CLEAR card can indeed preceed any Block redefinitions, and can even appear somewhere within a series of Block redefinitions. However, in the sense that the CLEAR card causes a part of the model Input Phase to take place, it seems more natural to place this card immediately ahead of the next START card. This is the only reason why Block redefinition and model clearing are listed above in that relative order.

Are there ever times when the CLEAR card *must* precede one or more Block redefinitions? The answer is a qualified yes. In particular, if an attempt is made to redefine a Block *which currently contains one or more Transactions*, a fatal error occurs. An error would occur, for example, in trying to redefine an ADVANCE Block whose Current Count is nonzero. Of course, it is quite possible that when a simulation stops, one or more of the various ADVANCE Blocks in a model have one or more Transactions currently in them. If any of these ADVANCE Blocks are to be redefined, then there may be no choice but to place the CLEAR card ahead of the ADVANCE Block redefinition(s).

Fortunately, there is not that much occasion to redefine *Blocks* within the context of a single batch run. (As will be seen later, it is often of interest to redefine components of a model other than Blocks.) In the case studies in this book, for example, GENERATE Blocks are the only type ever redefined between START cards. Furthermore, this is only done at times when the Current Count at the GENERATE Block in question is known to be zero. (In fact, there is no way to have a nonzero Current Count at a GENERATE Block, unless the Block following it can refuse entry to a Transaction.) With few exceptions, then, the practice in this book is to place the CLEAR card immediately ahead of the next START card.

As for GENERATE Block redefinition, there is a potential subtlety involved which is important to understand. When the Processor encounters a new definition for a GENERATE Block, it does three things.

1. It searches out the Transaction (if any) which had been scheduled to enter the model through the old GENERATE Block. (If a Limit Count had been used with the old GENERATE Block, and if a corresponding number of Transactions had already entered the model via that GENERATE Block, then there would be no scheduled arrival.)

2. The Processor then replaces the old GENERATE Block with the newly defined GENERATE Block. This means that the new set of Operand values goes into effect.

3. Finally, the Processor schedules entry of a Transaction into the model through the newly defined GENERATE Block. Use is made, of course, of the "new" Block Operands in carrying out this scheduling step.

In summary, then, the analyst should be alert to the fact that a certain amount of Transaction manipulation is immediately carried out by the Processor when a GENERATE Block is redefined. Of special importance here is the fact that in scheduling the first arrival event at the newly-defined GENERATE Block, *a random number must be obtained and used* (unless interarrival times at the new GENERATE Block are deterministic). The same statement can be made with respect to scheduling arrival events at GENERATE Blocks when a CLEAR card is acted upon. This potentially important influence of GENERATE Block redefinition and of CLEAR card use on the setting of random-number sequences will be discussed in detail, beginning at the end of Chapter 3.

Now consider an example for use of the CLEAR card. As previously indicated, the processing in Case Study 2D was performed in a series of three consecutive batch runs. With the CLEAR card, it is now possible to accomplish the same three simulations in a single batch session.

Figure 2.37(a) shows the coding sheet prepared for the corresponding job. Figure 2.37(b) displays the Extended Program Listing produced by the Processor when the job is run. Note these features of Figure 2.37(b).

1. The GENERATE Block for assemblers (Block 1) occupies the symbolic Location KEY.

2. After the first START card (Card 19), the GENERATE Block occupying the Location KEY has been redefined. Immediately after that, the Processor has printed the message, MULTIPLE DEFINITION OF SYMBOL IN ABOVE CARD. (There is no Card Number for this message, because there is no corresponding card in the job deck.) Despite this message, the Pro-

LOCATION	OPERATION	A,B,C,D,E,F
	SIMULATE	
*		
*	MODEL SEGMENT 1	
*		
KEY	GENERATE	,,,,4 PROVIDE 4 ASSEMBLERS
BACK	ADVANCE	30,5 ASSEMBLE NEXT WIDGET
	SEIZE	OVEN CAPTURE THE OVEN
	ADVANCE	8,2 USE THE OVEN
	RELEASE	OVEN FREE THE OVEN
	TRANSFER	,BACK GO DO THE NEXT ASSEMBLY
*		
*	MODEL SEGMENT 2	
*		
	GENERATE	2400 TIMER ARRIVES AFTER 5 DAYS
	TERMINATE	1 SHUT OFF THE RUN
*		
*	CONTROL CARDS AND BLOCK REDEFINITIONS	
*		
	START	1 START THE 1ST RUN
KEY	GENERATE	,,,,5 RE-CONFIGURE FOR 2ND RUN
	CLEAR	CLEAR FOR 2ND RUN
	START	1 START THE 2ND RUN
KEY	GENERATE	,,,,6 RE-CONFIGURE FOR 3RD RUN
	CLEAR	CLEAR FOR 3RD RUN
	START	1 START THE 3RD RUN
	END	RETURN CONTROL TO OPERATING SYSTEM

(a)

FIGURE 2.37 A model for simulating three alternative Case Study 2D configurations in a single batch run. (a) Completed coding sheet for the model.

```
BLOCK                                                                                    CARD
NUMBER  *LOC    OPERATION  A,B,C,D,E,F,G                COMMENTS                         NUMBER
                SIMULATE                                                                    1
        *                                                                                   2
        *       MODEL SEGMENT 1                                                             3
        *                                                                                   4
1       KEY     GENERATE   ,,,4            PROVIDE 4 ASSEMBLERS                             5
2       BACK    ADVANCE    30,5            ASSEMBLE NEXT WIDGET                             6
3               SEIZE      OVEN            CAPTURE THE OVEN                                 7
4               ADVANCE    8,2             USE THE OVEN                                     8
5               RELEASE    OVEN            FREE THE OVEN                                    9
6               TRANSFER   ,BACK           GO DO THE NEXT ASSEMBLY                         10
        *                                                                                  11
        *       MODEL SEGMENT 2                                                            12
        *                                                                                  13
7               GENERATE   2400            TIMER ARRIVES AFTER 5 DAYS                      14
8               TERMINATE  1               SHUT OFF THE RUN                                15
        *                                                                                  16
        *       CONTROL CARDS AND BLOCK OPERAND RE-DEFINITIONS                             17
        *                                                                                  18
                START      1               START THE 1ST RUN                               19
1       KEY     GENERATE   ,,,5            RE-CONFIGURE FOR 2ND RUN                        20
MULTIPLE DEFINITION OF SYMBOL IN ABOVE CARD
                CLEAR                      CLEAR FOR 2ND RUN                               21
                START      1               START THE 2ND RUN                               22
1       KEY     GENERATE   ,,,6            RE-CONFIGURE FOR 3RD RUN                        23
MULTIPLE DEFINITION OF SYMBOL IN ABOVE CARD
                CLEAR                      CLEAR FOR 3RD RUN                               24
                START      1               START THE 3RD RUN                               25
                END                        RETURN CONTROL TO OPERATING SYSTEM             26
```

(b)

FIGURE 2.37(b)   Extended Program Listing

cessor does not consider the multiple use of a Block Location name to be an error. It outputs the message only as a *warning*, in case the analyst unintentionally assigned the same Location name to two separate Blocks in the model. Following the inserted warning message comes the CLEAR card (Card 21), the next START card (Card 22), and so on.

Realize that the redefinition of the Block at Location KEY is not effective until *after* the simulation started by the first START card has been performed. The Processor first reads in the entire model, producing the Extended Program Listing. Then, after more internal processing, the simulation(s) take place. Nevertheless, it is while the model is being read, and before the simulation(s) begin, that the warning messages about multiple card definitions are produced.

Figure 2.38 shows the output resulting from the simulation with the Figure 2.37 model. The key feature of Figure 2.38 is that, for the five

FACILITY	AVERAGE UTILIZATION	NUMBER ENTRIES	AVERAGE TIME/TRAN	SEIZING TRANS. NO.	PREEMPTING TRANS. NO.
OVEN	.785	236	7.991	5	

(a)

FACILITY	AVERAGE UTILIZATION	NUMBER ENTRIES	AVERAGE TIME/TRAN	SEIZING TRANS. NO.	PREEMPTING TRANS. NO.
OVEN	.942	281	8.053	6	

(b)

FACILITY	AVERAGE UTILIZATION	NUMBER ENTRIES	AVERAGE TIME/TRAN	SEIZING TRANS. NO.	PREEMPTING TRANS. NO.
OVEN	.989	296	8.020	1	

(c)

FIGURE 2.38   Selected Program Output produced when the Figure 2.37 model was run. (a) Oven statistics when four assemblers are used. (b) Oven statistics when five assemblers are used. (c) Oven statistics when six assemblers are used.

and six assembler configurations, the results differ from those shown in Figure 2D.3(b) and (c). Why does this turn out to be the case? When three separate batch runs were used, *the random number sequence for each configuration always began at the same point*. In the case of one batch run, the random-number sequence for each next configuration *begins at whatever point it had reached by the end of the previous simulation*. It is precisely because a different sequence of random numbers is in effect that the statistics for the five and six assembler configurations differ from those shown in Case Study 2D.

It is evident, then, that the CLEAR card does not cause "the random-number sequence" to be restored to its initial state. (The sources of random numbers in GPSS will be discussed in Chapter 3.)

2.35 EXERCISES

1. In Case Study 2D, the Model Segment 1 GENER-ATE Block is "GENERATE ,,,4". The Limit Count of 4 guarantees that only four Transactions will enter the model through that Block. Because of the default values for the A and B Operands, the inter-arrival times of these Transactions is 0.
   (a) At what simulated time does the first of these four Transactions enter the model? What is the number of this Transaction?
   (b) At what simulated time does the second of these four Transactions enter the model? What is the number of this Transaction?
   (c) When the second of the four Transactions moves into the ADVANCE Block (Block 2, Figure 2D.2), is the first of the four Transactions located on the Current or the Future Events Chain?
   Hints: (i) Review Figure 2.28, which describes the operation of the GENERATE Block. (ii) At a GENERATE Block, when the interarrival time for the *successor*-Transaction is 0, the Transaction is fetched from the latent pool and is put immediately on the *Current Events Chain*, as the last member in its Priority Class. As usual, after this scheduling step, the Processor then resumes its processing of the predecessor-Transaction, moving it forward in the model until it finally comes to rest. The Processor then continues its scan of the Current Events Chain. This means that the successor-Transaction will eventually be encountered by the Processor, and will consequently be moved forward in the model at the simulated time in question.

2. The Case Study 2D model assumes that initially each of the assemblers is just in the process of beginning an assembly. Show how to modify the model for the case of four assemblers so that it reflects the following alternative initial conditions.
   (a) Three of the assemblers are just in the process of beginning an assembly; the fourth is just beginning to use the oven to fire an assembled widget.
   (b) One assembler is just about to begin an assembly; one has 10 minutes to go before he will complete an assembly; one has 3 minutes to go before he will finish using the oven; and one is waiting to use the oven.

3. Compute the return-after-costs for the Case Study 2D data shown in Figure 2.38. Is the conclusion still that five assemblers is the optimal number to use?

4. In a particular machine shop, a single machine is used to polish castings. The steps required to polish a casting are shown below, where the times required are indicated, *in minutes*, after each step.
   1. Fetch raw casting from a storage area (12 ± 3).
   2. Load raw casting on the polishing machine (10 ± 4).
   3. Carry out polishing phase 1 (80 ± 20).
   4. Reposition the casting on the machine for additional polishing (15 ± 7).
   5. Carry out polishing phase 2 (110 ± 30).
   6. Unload the finished casting from the machine (10 ± 4).
   7. Store the finished casting (12 ± 3), then return to step (1).

   The castings are too heavy to be handled by the operator of the polishing machine. He requires the services of an overhead crane to assist in the handling process. In particular, the overhead crane is needed at Steps 1, 2, 4, 6, and 7 above.

   There is only one overhead crane available. The polishing machine operator does not have the exclusive use of this crane. It is also on call to perform service at other machines in the shop. Other calls for the crane occur every 39 ± 10 minutes. The time required for the crane to service one of these other calls is 25 ± 10 minutes.

   Build a model of the system as described. Design the model to collect data about the time the polishing-machine operator spends waiting for the crane. Distinguish between time spent waiting for the crane to perform Step 4, and time spent waiting to perform Step 6. (Assume that when the crane has been captured for Step 6, it is not then released until after Step 2 has again been performed.) Also gather waiting-time information relative to other calls on the crane.

   Run the model for 400 hours of simulated time. Compare and contrast the waiting experience at the three indicated points in the model for each of these two alternative queue disciplines.
   1. First-come, first-served.

2. Polishing-machine operator has highest priority for use of the crane.

What must be true for the priority-distinction case to make a difference in the operation of the system? How likely is it that this condition will frequently be in effect?

Did you use a Facility to model the polishing machine? Why, or why not? If you did use a Facility, consider how your model would perform if the SEIZE—RELEASE Block pair were removed from it. Would your model still be true to the system as described?

5. In a particular model, the simulation begins at midnight and continues through a series of consecutive 24-hour days. Transactions are to be brought into the model *each day* of simulated time at 1 a.m., 4 a.m., 10 a.m., and 2 p.m. Whenever a Transaction enters the model, it is to be routed to a "QUEUE STACK" Block. Under the following alternative assumptions, show a Block Diagram segment which brings Transactions into the model at the proper times.
   (a) Transactions are to move into the "QUEUE STACK" Block exactly on time.
   (b) Transactions do not always enter the model exactly on time, but are subject to a delay of 10 ± 10 minutes, uniformly distributed. Any delays which do occur, however, are independent of each other. For example, the time of arrival of the "1 a.m. Transaction" on the third day in no way influences the time of arrival of the "4 a.m. Transaction" that day, or of the "1 a.m. Transaction" the next day.
   (c) Transactions are not necessarily either exactly on time or late, but may be anywhere from 10 minutes early to 20 minutes late, with the various possibilities in this range being uniformly distributed.

A possible interpretation for this situation is that Transactions simulate planes arriving at an airport. When planes arrive, they join a "stack" of planes awaiting clearance to land. Planes often do not arrive on time; hence, parts (b) and (c) are considerably more realistic than part (a).

2.36 Entities to Simulate Parallel Servers: Storages

Two or more servers often work side by side, performing a similar service. Such servers can either be people, or things. Here are some examples of two or more people in the category of side-by-side, or parallel, servers.

1. Barbers
2. Supermarket checkout girls
3. Beauty shop operators
4. Clerks at a tool crib
5. Ticket-takers at the theatre

Here are some examples of things which perform a similar service, and which might be available in quantities of two or more.

1. Tugs for berthing and deberthing ships at a harbor
2. Overhead cranes for moving heavy castings from molds to machines
3. Parking places in a parking lot
4. A supply of a particular type of spare part, sitting on a shelf
5. Card punches in a computing center

A Facility can be used in GPSS to simulate a *single* server. Two or more side-by-side servers could be simulated in a GPSS model, then, with two or more Facilities located "side by side," i.e., in parallel. Indeed, it is sometimes necessary to use parallel Facilities to model parallel servers. This is the approach usually taken when the individual servers are *heterogeneous*, that is, are characterized by different properties, such as performing service at different rates. Many times, however, parallel servers are assumed to be *homogeneous*. This means, roughly speaking, that such servers share a common set of properties. For example, the rate at which checkout girls serve customers in a supermarket may not depend on the particular checkout girl involved.

GPSS provides a special entity for simulating homogeneous parallel servers. The name "Storage" is used for this entity. The Storage entity is similar to the Facility and Queue entities in several general ways. There can be many different Storages in a model, reflecting the fact that various groups of parallel servers can be located at many different points in a system. To distinguish among different Storages, names must be supplied for them. The naming conventions are the same as for Facilities and Queues.

The number of servers which each particular Storage simulates must be defined by the model builder. In this sense, one speaks of the *capacity* of a Storage. The method for using the Storage entity, and defining Storage capacity, is described in the next section.

2.37 Using One or More Parallel Servers: The ENTER and LEAVE Blocks

The first part of this section introduces the Blocks corresponding to the Storage entity, and discusses their basic use. An option associated with these Blocks is then described. Next, the two different methods available for defining Storage capacity are explained. Finally, the key differences between a Facility, and a Storage with a capacity of 1, are indicated.

2.37.1 Fundamental Use of the ENTER and LEAVE Blocks

The approach to using one of the parallel servers simulated with a Storage is strictly analogous to that for using a single server simulated with a Facility. The entity which captures and uses a parallel server is a Transaction. In doing so, the usual chronological pattern is followed. (1) The Transaction waits its turn, if necessary. (2) Then it captures a server. (3) It holds the server in a state of capture over some interval of time. (4) Finally, it releases the server.

As in the case of Facilities, the model builder incorporates Storages into a model by making use of a pair of complementary Blocks. These Blocks are used to simulate events (2) and (4) above. When a Transaction moves into the first of these Blocks, the event "capture one of the servers in a parallel group" is simulated. Similarly, when a Transaction moves into the second of these Blocks, the event "release a parallel server" is simulated. The Blocks corresponding to the "capture" and "release" events are the ENTER and LEAVE Blocks, respectively. These two Blocks are shown with their A Operand in Figure 2.39.

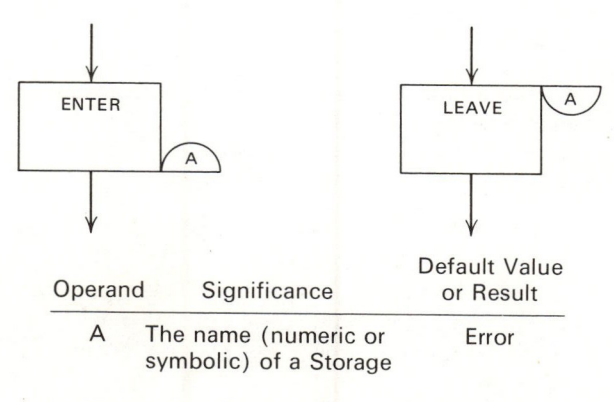

Operand	Significance	Default Value or Result
A	The name (numeric or symbolic) of a Storage	Error

FIGURE 2.39   The ENTER and LEAVE Blocks, and their A Operand

As would be expected, the A Operand is used at the ENTER and LEAVE Blocks to indicate the name of a particular Storage. When a Transaction moves into the ENTER Block, the Processor does these things.

1. The Storage's "total entry count" is increased by 1.
2. The Storage's "current content" is increased by 1.

3. The Storage's "currently available capacity" is decreased by 1.

Similarly, when a Transaction moves into a LEAVE Block, the Processor does the following things.

1. The Storage's "current content" is decreased by 1.
2. The Storage's "currently available capacity" is increased by 1.

At the end of a simulation, the Processor automatically prints out such Storage statistics as "total entry count," "average content," "current content," and "maximum content." It also prints out the "average holding time" (that is, the elapsed time, on average, between the various captures and releases).

Consider this matter of average holding time more closely. The Processor computes this statistic by keeping track of the total number of time units that various parallel servers have been in a state of capture so far. There is only one such total. It takes into account all servers being simulated with the Storage in question. This total is automatically updated whenever necessary. At any time, then, the Processor can compute average holding time by dividing the Storage's total entry count into this total. The advantage of this approach is that it takes into account those servers who are still in a state of capture at the time the computation is performed. The disadvantage of this approach is that it can result in a downward bias in the average holding-time statistic, because those servers still in a state of capture are destined to experience some remaining capture time, and this is not taken into account in the computation.

For any particular Transaction, the time that elapses while it is "in" a Storage (that is, between the time it moves through an ENTER Block, and then later moves through a LEAVE Block), is the amount of time it held one of the parallel servers in a state of capture. This means that average holding time is identical to average Transaction residence time in the Storage. Indeed, in the Storage statistics it prints out, the Processor labels the average holding-time statistic as AVERAGE TIME/TRAN.

The analogy between the way the Processor computes the AVERAGE TIME/TRANS statistic for Queues, and the AVERAGE TIME/TRAN statistic for Storages, should be evident. It should also be clear why the Processor does *not* tag a Transaction with copies of the simulated clock and the Storage name when the Transaction moves into an ENTER Block. For Storages, there is no interest in maintaining a "zero entries" counter. There is no need, then, for these Transaction tags. By the same token, there is no limit to the number of different Storages which a Transaction can be "in" at any one time.

The Storage statistics which the Processor prints out at the end of a simulation will be examined as part of the case study to be presented in Section 2.39.

The ENTER and LEAVE Blocks are of the type whose execution later causes the scan of the Current Events Chain to be restarted. Assume that one of the Blocks a Transaction moves through before finally stopping is an ENTER and/or a LEAVE Block. Then, instead of processing the sequential Transaction on the Current Events Chain as its next step, the Processor restarts the scan of the Current Events Chain.

2.37.2 Use of a B Operand with the ENTER and LEAVE Blocks

Although it was not mentioned above, there is an optional B Operand which can be used with the ENTER and LEAVE Blocks. Figure 2.40 is a repetition of Figure 2.39, except that the existence of this optional B Operand is recognized. As shown in the figure, the B Operand indicates the *number of servers* which are being captured at the ENTER Block, or being released at the LEAVE Block. In case of default, the B Operand's value is 1, which means that only one server is involved.

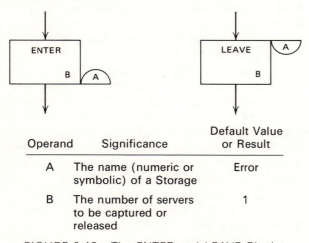

Operand	Significance	Default Value or Result
A	The name (numeric or symbolic) of a Storage	Error
B	The number of servers to be captured or released	1

FIGURE 2.40 The ENTER and LEAVE Blocks, with their A and B Operands

It is highly reasonable to allow for the possibility that a single Transaction needs to capture more than one server at the ENTER Block (and,

correspondingly, release more than one server at the LEAVE Block). For example, suppose that a Transaction simulates a ship, and a Storage simulates the tugs at a harbor. Depending on its size, a ship may need more than one tug if it is to be moved into a berth, or moved out of a berth.

GPSS uses an "all or nothing at all" approach at the ENTER Block. A Transaction does not capture servers at the ENTER Block one by one, until it has captured the number required. Instead, when a Transaction tries to move into the ENTER Block, the Processor tests to determine if the Storage's currently available capacity is greater than or equal to the B Operand value. If the test is not passed, the Transaction remains in its current Block, and will later try once again to move into the ENTER Block.

Now consider the effect of the B Operand on the statistics which the Processor maintains for a Storage. When a Transaction moves into an ENTER Block at which the B Operand is used, the Processor does these things.

1. The Storage's "total entry count" is increased by the value of the B Operand.
2. The Storage's "current content" is increased by the value of the B Operand.
3. The Storage's "currently available capacity" is decreased by the value of the B Operand.

Similarly, when the B Operand is used at the LEAVE Block, and a Transaction moves into the Block, these things are done.

1. The Storage's "current content" is decreased by the value of the B Operand.
2. The Storage's "currently available capacity" is increased by the value of the B Operand.

These things are as would be expected.

Whether or not ENTER and LEAVE Block B Operands other than 1 have been used in a particular case, it should be kept in mind that Storage statistics produced by the Processor refer to *servers*, not to Transactions. Hence, total entry count is the total number of servers captured during the simulation (some or all of them having perhaps been captured more than one time); average content is the number of servers held in a state of capture, on average; current content is the number of servers currently in a state of capture; and maximum content is the maximum number of servers who were in a state of capture at any one time. There is a one-to-one correspondence between servers and Transactions who used, or are using, those servers, only if the B Operand at the various ENTER and LEAVE Blocks is 1.

2.37.3 Capacity Definition Cards for Storages

The capacity of the various Storages in a model is defined by use of one or more *Storage capacity definition cards*. Two forms are available for these cards. The first form requires that a separate card be used for each Storage. Table 2.21 shows the card format. Like most other cards, the Storage capacity card is divided into the Location, Operation, and Operands fields. Entered in the Location field is the number or symbolic name of the Storage. The Operation field contains the word STORAGE. The A Operand specifies the capacity of the Storage. Two examples are shown in Figure 2.41, where the Storages 7 and MARY are defined to have capacities of 5 and 2, respectively.

TABLE 2.21   Format for the Card Used to Define Exactly One Storage

Punchcard Field	Information Supplied in the Field
Location	The name (numeric or symbolic) of a Storage
Operation	Literally, the word STORAGE
Operands A	The capacity of the Storage

The second form permits the analyst to define the capacity of two or more Storages with a single card. The card format is shown in Figure 2.42. As indicated, the Location field is not used. The word STORAGE is entered in the Operation field. The "basic unit" of information in the Operands field is of the form "Sname$_i$,c$_i$", where "name$_i$" is the numeric or symbolic name of the ith Storage whose capacity is being defined, and c_i is the capacity. When symbolic names are used, a dollar sign ($) must be interposed between S and the symbolic name itself. Examples of "basic units" are "S5,8", "S$TUGS,3", and "S21,5". Slashes are used to separate consecutive basic units. The first blank

column encountered by the Processor in the Operands field is interpreted as an "end of card" character. No information (except for comments) can be entered beyond card column 71. More than one of the Figure 2.42 STORAGE cards can be used, if necessary.

Figure 2.43 provides several examples of multiple Storage capacity definitions. As indicated in the first example, it is not necessary that the numbers of the Storages involved be in ascending order on the STORAGE card. The second example shows a mixture of Storages named numerically and symbolically. The third example reveals that Storages 4, 5, and 6 are each to have a capacity of 5. When Storages whose numbers form an uninterrupted sequence of integers are all to have the same capacity, the corresponding entries in the STORAGE card can be compacted to the form "$Si - Sk,c$", where i and k are the smallest and largest numbers, respectively, in the range of Storage numbers, and c is the common capacity. The fourth example in Figure 2.43 repeats the third example, making use of this compact form.

Although it is not strictly necessary, the practice in this book will be to place the Storage capacity definitions at an early point in the card deck, after the SIMULATE card but before the first card which is a Block image.

If the analysts forgets to supply a capacity definition for one or more Storages in a model, the Processor will assume a capacity of $2^{31} - 1$ (i.e., 2,147,483,647).

One possibility for reconfiguring a model, before continuing to simulate with it in the context of a single batch run, is to redefine one or more Storage capacities. This can be done by including in the card deck, after the START card for the "preceding simulation" and before the START card for the "next simulation," the new capacity definitions. The next case study illustrates this procedure (see Figure 2E.3).

It is possible for an error condition to come about when the capacity of a Storage is being redefined. In particular, an error occurs if (1) the

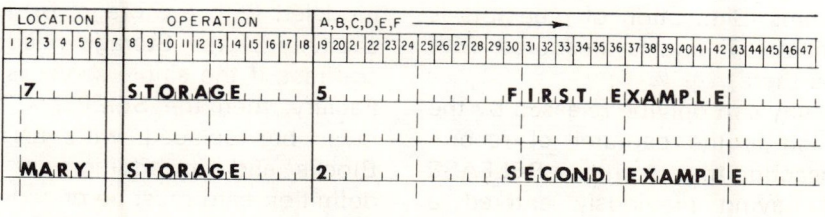

FIGURE 2.41   Examples showing use of the Table 2.21 card format

Location	Operation	Operands
Not Used	STORAGE	$Sname_1, c_1/Sname_2, c_2/ \ldots /Sname_i, c_2/ \ldots /Sname_n, c_n$

FIGURE 2.42   Format for the card used to define the capacity of one or more Storages

LOCATION	OPERATION	A,B,C,D,E,F ⟶	
	STORAGE	S5,2/S1,10/S8,6	FIRST EXAMPLE
	STORAGE	S4,5/S$TUGS,3/S$SURVS,4/S2,12	SECOND EXAMPLE
	STORAGE	S$MEN,9/S4,5/S5,5/S6,5/S3,2	THIRD EXAMPLE
	STORAGE	S$MEN,9/S4-S6,5/S3,2	FOURTH EXAMPLE

FIGURE 2.43   Examples showing use of the Figure 2.42 card format

capacity of a Storage is redefined to be *less* than what it had been previously, *and* (2) at the time of redefinition, the "current content" of the Storage *exceeds* the newly defined capacity. If the CLEAR card is used before the Storage capacity is redefined, then the "current content" of the Storage in question is set to zero, and the error cannot occur.

2.37.4 The Distinction Between a Facility, and a Storage with a Capacity of 1

It is natural to wonder what difference there is between a Facility, and a Storage with a capacity of 1. There are two differences. First of all, the server being simulated with a Facility can be *preempted*, whereas the single server being simulated with a Storage whose capacity is 1 cannot. This is easily the most important difference between Facilities and Storages. Preemption involves taking the server away from his current capturer, so the server can respond immediately to a more urgent demand for his service. Preemption is an important concept in the design of computing systems, as well as in some other systems. Simulation of preempts is discussed in Chapter 7, and is illustrated with two case studies there.

Second, a Facility can only be released by the Transaction which is the capturer of record. That is, if a Transaction tries to enter a RELEASE Block, without having previously entered a SEIZE Block referencing the Facility in question, an error condition results. In contrast, *any* Transaction can move into a LEAVE Block, without necessarily having previously moved into an ENTER Block referencing the Storage in question. An error condition occurs here only if the result is to decrement the "current content" of the referenced Storage to -1 or less.

It is difficult at this point to imagine why a model would be built in which a Transaction might "leave" a Storage without having previously "entered" it. If a Transaction ever does do this, logic usually requires that some other Transaction, in complementary fashion, "enters" that same Storage, and never "leaves" it. Otherwise, the restriction that the current content cannot become negative would eventually be violated. Although it is conceivable that the model builder might work with Storages in this counter-intuitive fashion, there is really never any compelling need to do so. The occasion to do this sort of thing never arises in this book.

In concluding, it might be noted that it is easier to replace a "single" server with two or more parallel servers if the single server is modeled with a Storage. In this case, only the capacity of the Storage need be redefined. In contrast, if the single server is simulated with a Facility, then the SEIZE and RELEASE Blocks must be replaced with ENTER and LEAVE Blocks and, in addition, a Storage capacity definition card must be provided.

2.38 One-Line, Multiple-Server Queuing Systems

Probably the most frequently occurring pattern for modeling with Storages is that shown in Figure 2.44. In addition to the ENTER–ADVANCE–LEAVE sequence in the figure, the ENTER Block has been sandwiched between a QUEUE–DEPART Block pair, to gather information about the waiting experience ahead of the ENTER Block. Of course, the QUEUE–DEPART Block pair is optional.

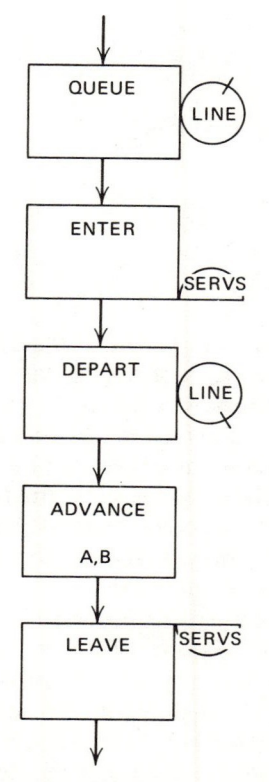

FIGURE 2.44   A frequently occurring pattern for modeling with the Storage entity

Two aspects of the queuing system modeled with the Block sequence in Figure 2.44 merit discussion. The first involves the way *a user selects a server*; the second involves the way *a server selects a user*.

Quite often, when parallel servers are involved, *a separate waiting line* forms ahead of each server. When a would-be user arrives he surveys the situation, then decides which line to join. In this sense, the user discriminates in his selection of a server. *Such discrimination is not possible when parallel servers are simulated with*

a Storage. The servers a Storage represents have no individual identity; there is consequently no way to associate a separate waiting line with each server. In essence, then, a would-be user waiting at a Storage necessarily takes the attitude, "when my turn comes, I'll go to whichever server is available." This is equivalent to having only one waiting line ahead of the parallel servers. When a would-be user arrives, he simply joins the line. After reaching the head of the line, he goes to whichever server is free next. This situation is illustrated in Figure 2.45.

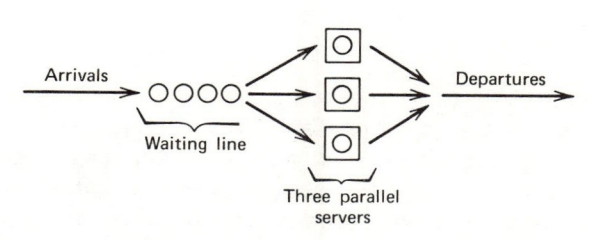

FIGURE 2.45   Illustration of a one-line, multiple-server queuing system

Interestingly enough, although the users cannot discriminate in Figure 2.44, the servers can. That is, the servers can regard the one waiting line as being segmented into "priority classes." When a server becomes available, he then selects a user by employing a "first-come, first-served, within Priority Class" queue discipline. The servers a Storage simulates practice such discrimination in GPSS automatically if the Transactions waiting for them have different Priority Levels. This is because Transactions waiting to move into the Figure 2.44 ENTER Block are arranged on the Current Events Chain in order of decreasing Priority Level. When a LEAVE Block is executed, thereby freeing one or more servers, the scan of the Current Events Chain is restarted. The available server is then captured by the highest-priority Transaction which has been waiting the longest. This situation is illustrated in Figure 2.46. As the figure suggests, would-be users do not simply go to the back of the line when they arrive; instead, they merge into the line as the last member in their Priority Class. Figure 2.46, then, is simply a repetition of Figure 2.45, except that distinctions are made among user priorities.

The one-line, multiple-server scheme is frequently used in real situations. This tends

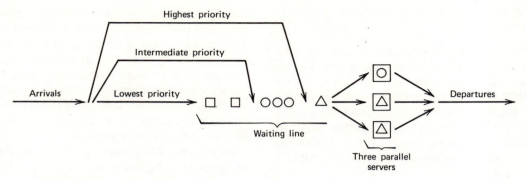

FIGURE 2.46   A one-line, multiple-server queuing system with priority distinctions

especially to be true when the items waiting for service are inanimate and, for all practical purposes, identical. This would be the case, for example, for parts moving from work station to work station on a production line. Even though the work stations might be manned by two or more people working in parallel, work would very likely be fed to them from a single line.

The one-line, multiple-server queuing system is rather frequently used, too, when those waiting for service are people, not things. It is used in some banks, for example, where it is called the "Quickline" system. A person entering such a bank, rather than selecting a teller's window and joining the line at *that* window, goes to the back of a single line which feeds *all* windows. This approach makes it impossible to get stuck behind a customer with an unusually high service time requirement (customers opening new accounts, for example, or buying and signing traveler's checks). Extreme cases of time spent waiting for service are consequently eliminated.

Quite often, when parallel servers are involved, a separate waiting line does form ahead of each server. Modeling this *multiple-line, multiple-server* queuing system is substantially more complicated than modeling the one-line, multiple-server scheme. A *queue-selection criterion* must be introduced, for example. When a new arrival comes, this criterion is then used by the arrival to determine which waiting line to join. The possibility of *line jumping* should also be allowed. When a line is moving too slowly, those toward the end of the line may choose to move to another line. Modeling multiple-line, multiple-

server queuing systems in GPSS is deferred until Chapter 4.

2.39 CASE STUDY 2E
A Problem in Production Management

(1) Statement of the Problem

In a certain garment factory, 50 sewing machines are operated 8 hours a day, 5 days a week. Each of the machines is subject to random failure. Whenever a machine fails, it is replaced with a backup machine immediately, or as soon as one becomes available. Meantime, the failed machine is sent to an in-house repair shop, where it is repaired and then assumes the status of an available backup machine.

The four stages in this closed machine cycle are shown in Figure 2E.1 for a hypothetical situation. In the figure, an open square is a machine which is either in use, or is in backup status. A crossed-out square is a machine which is either in repair, or is waiting for repair. Two machines are shown in repair, implying that there are two repairmen. In total, 59 machines are in the system shown (two in repair; two waiting for repair; 50 in production; and five available for backup purposes).

Management wants to know how many repairmen to hire for the repair shop, and how many backup machines to rent to supplement the 50 machines it owns. The objective is to minimize system costs. Wages for repairmen are $3.75 per hour, and backup machines are available on a long-term rental basis at a cost of $30 per day. The hourly cost penalty for having fewer than 50 machines in production is esti-

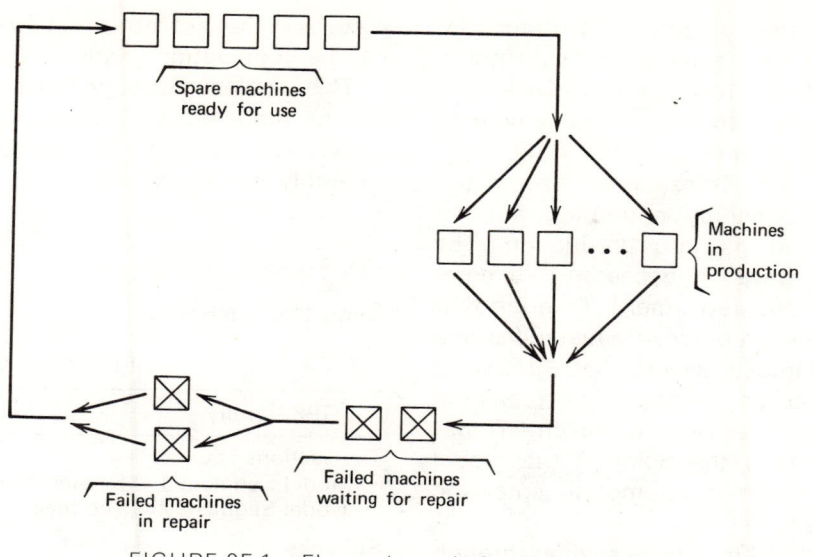

FIGURE 2E.1   Flow schematic for Case Study 2E

mated at $20 per machine. This penalty reflects lost production.

Based on past experience, the time required to repair a failed machine is 7 ± 3 hours, uniformly distributed. When a machine is put into use, its running time before failure is 157 ± 25 hours, uniformly distributed. The time required to remove a failed machine from its production station and replace it with a backup machine is negligibly small.

No distinctions are made either among repairmen, or among machines cycling through the system. That is, the distribution of repair time is independent of the particular repair man involved. And, the distribution of running time between failures is identical for both the owned and the rented machines.

The charge for rental of backup machines is independent of machine usage. For this reason, no attempt is made to maximize the number of *owned* machines in production at any given time. The implication is that a machine is taken out of production only when it fails.

Build a GPSS model for this system, then use it to investigate the cost consequences of the various "hire, rent" alternatives available to management. Use the model to determine the "hire, rent" alternative which minimizes the average daily cost of running the system.

(2) An Approach Leading to Solution

As suggested in Case Study 2D, it is oftentimes useful to approach the modeling process by first identifying the *constraints* in a system, then deciding on various GPSS entities to simulate these constraints. There are three constraints in the Figure 2D.1 system:

1. The number of repairmen.
2. The maximum number of sewing machines which are to be in production at any one time.
3. The total number of sewing machines cycling through the system.

It is convenient to choose GPSS Storages to simulate the first two constraints, and Transactions to simulate the third constraint. The reasoning behind such choices, roughly speaking, is that the repairmen and the in-production machines are stationary, occupying fixed points as suggested in Figure 2D.1. On the other hand, the sewing machines themselves are dynamic, moving from point to point as they circulate through the system.

Consider the history of a particular machine as it makes one complete cycle through the Figure 2D.1 system. Suppose that the machine is in "backup status," and that 50 machines are already in production. Then the Storage NOWON ("now on," for the number of machines now in use) is full, and the backup machine is "held in place" because it cannot enter that Storage. Eventually, the machine in backup status is given the opportunity to go into production. The Transaction simulating it determines this when, after repeated attempts to enter the Storage NOWON, an attempt is successful. Moving through the ENTER Block to ADVANCE, the Transaction then simulates running time of that machine before it fails.

Upon failure, the Transaction leaves the Storage NOWON, thereby permitting another backup machine to go into production. The Transaction then waits (if necessary) to enter the Storage MEN (for repairmen). Entering that Storage, it engages a repairman while repairtime is simulated. Eventually leaving that Storage, it frees the repairman so he can begin repair on another failed machine. Meanwhile, the Transaction cycles back to the point in the model where it again begins to attempt to enter the Storage NOWON.

The total number of machines cycling through the system equals the 50 machines owned, plus the number of machines rented for backup purposes. This number of Transactions can be created at the start of the simulation by use of the Limit Count on the GENERATE Block. The only other thing needed in the model is a timer.

Note that the Storage NOWON can really be thought of as simulating 50 sewing-machine operators. This view is consistent with the restriction that not more than 50 sewing machines can be in operation at any one time.

This problem, although inherently complicated, can be modeled with relative ease in GPSS. A FORTRAN model for the same system is considerably more involved.[23]

(3) Table of Definitions

Time Unit : 1 hour

TABLE 2E.1   Table of Definitions for Case Study 2E

GPSS Entity	Interpretation
Transactions	
Model Segment 1	Sewing machines
Model Segment 2	The timer
Storages	
MEN	The side-by-side repairmen
NOWON	The Storage whose capacity (50) is the maximum number of sewing machines ever to be in production simultaneously

[23] A FORTRAN model of this system is documented in "Three Computer Models for Probability Applications," by T. J. Schriber, *FORTRAN Applications in Business Administration*, Volume II (The University of Michigan, 1971), pp. 349–422.

(4) Block Diagram

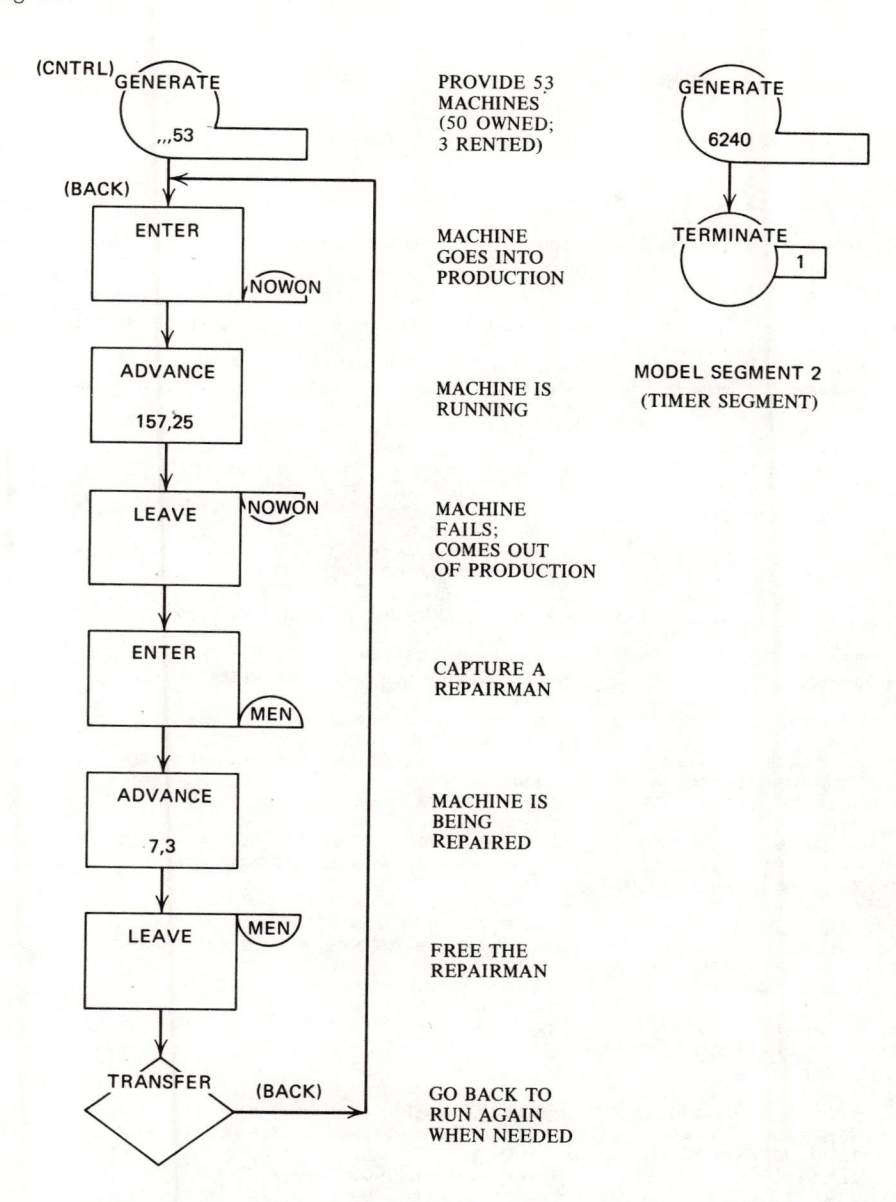

MODEL SEGMENT 1

FIGURE 2E.2   Block Diagram for Case Study 2E (four backup machines provided)

(5) Extended Program Listing

```
BLOCK                                                                      CARD
NUMBER   *LOC    OPERATION  A,B,C,D,E,F,G          COMMENTS              NUMBER
                 SIMULATE                                                   1
         *                                                                  2
         *       STORAGE CAPACITY DEFINITION(S)                             3
         *                                                                  4
                 STORAGE    S$MEN,3/S$NOWON,50      3 MEN; MAX OF 50 MACH'S RUNNING   5
         *                                                                  6
         *       MODEL SEGMENT 1                                            7
         *                                                                  8
1        CNTRL   GENERATE   ,,,53            PROVIDE 53 MACHINES (50 OWNED;  3 RENTED)   9
2        BACK    ENTER      NOWON            MACHINE GOES INTO PRODUCTION   10
3                ADVANCE    157,25           MACHINE IS RUNNING            11
4                LEAVE      NOWON            MACHINE FAILS;  COMES OUT OF PRODUCTION   12
5                ENTER      MEN              CAPTURE A REPAIRMAN           13
6                ADVANCE    7,3              MACHINE IS BEING REPAIRED     14
7                LEAVE      MEN              FREE THE REPAIRMAN            15
8                TRANSFER   ,BACK            GO BACK TO RUN AGAIN WHEN NEEDED   16
                                                                           17
         *                                                                 18
         *       MODEL SEGMENT 2                                           19
         *                                                                 20
9                GENERATE   6240             TIMER COMES AFTER 3 YEARS (40-HOUR WEEKS)   20
10               TERMINATE  1                SHUT OFF THE RUN              21
                                                                          22
         *                                                                23
         *       CONTROL CARDS, BLOCK OPERAND RE-DEFS, AND STG CAPACITY RE-DEFS   23
         *                                                                24
                 START      1                START THE 1ST RUN            25
1        CNTRL   GENERATE   ,,,54            SET RENTED MACHINES = 4 FOR 2ND RUN   26
MULTIPLE DEFINITION OF SYMBOL IN ABOVE CARD
                 CLEAR                       CLEAR FOR 2ND RUN            27
                 START      1                START THE 2ND RUN            28
1        CNTRL   GENERATE   ,,,55            SET RENTED MACHINES = 5 FOR 3RD RUN   29
MULTIPLE DEFINITION OF SYMBOL IN ABOVE CARD
                 CLEAR                       CLEAR FOR 3RD RUN            30
                 START      1                START THE 3RD RUN            31
                 STORAGE    S$MEN,4          SET REPAIRMEN HIRED = 4 FOR 4TH RUN   32
1        CNTRL   GENERATE   ,,,53            SET RENTED MACHINES = 3 FOR 4TH RUN   33
MULTIPLE DEFINITION OF SYMBOL IN ABOVE CARD
                 CLEAR                       CLEAR FOR 4TH RUN            34
                 START      1                START THE 4TH RUN            35
1        CNTRL   GENERATE   ,,,54            SET RENTED MACHINES = 4 FOR 5TH RUN   36
MULTIPLE DEFINITION OF SYMBOL IN ABOVE CARD
                 CLEAR                       CLEAR FOR 5TH RUN            37
                 START      1                START THE 5TH RUN            38
1        CNTRL   GENERATE   ,,,55            SET RENTED MACHINES = 5 FOR 6TH RUN   39
MULTIPLE DEFINITION OF SYMBOL IN ABOVE CARD
                 CLEAR                       CLEAR FOR 6TH RUN            40
                 START      1                START THE 6TH RUN            41
                 STORAGE    S$MEN,5          SET REPAIRMEN HIRED = 5 FOR 7TH RUN   42
1        CNTRL   GENERATE   ,,,53            SET RENTED MACHINES = 3 FOR 7TH RUN   43
MULTIPLE DEFINITION OF SYMBOL IN ABOVE CARD
                 CLEAR                       CLEAR FOR 7TH RUN            44
                 START      1                START THE 7TH RUN            45
1        CNTRL   GENERATE   ,,,54            SET RENTED MACHINES = 4 FOR 8TH RUN   46
MULTIPLE DEFINITION OF SYMBOL IN ABOVE CARD
                 CLEAR                       CLEAR FOR 8TH RUN            47
                 START      1                START THE 8TH RUN            48
1        CNTRL   GENERATE   ,,,55            SET RENTED MACHINES = 5 FOR 9TH RUN   49
MULTIPLE DEFINITION OF SYMBOL IN ABOVE CARD
                 CLEAR                       CLEAR FOR 9TH RUN            50
                 START      1                START THE 9TH RUN            51
                 END                         RETURN CONTROL TO OPERATING SYSTEM   52
```

FIGURE 2E.3   Extended Program Listing for Case Study 2E

(6) Program Output

STORAGE	CAPACITY	AVERAGE CONTENTS	AVERAGE UTILIZATION	ENTRIES	AVERAGE TIME/TRAN	CURRENT CONTENTS	MAXIMUM CONTENTS
MEN	3	2.185	.728	1924	7.087		3
NOWON	50	49.182	.983	1974	155.471	50	50

(a)

STORAGE	CAPACITY	AVERAGE CONTENTS	AVERAGE UTILIZATION	ENTRIES	AVERAGE TIME/TRAN	CURRENT CONTENTS	MAXIMUM CONTENTS
MEN	3	2.180	.726	1934	7.036	3	3
NOWON	50	49.486	.989	1984	155.643	50	50

(b)

STORAGE	CAPACITY	AVERAGE CONTENTS	AVERAGE UTILIZATION	ENTRIES	AVERAGE TIME/TRAN	CURRENT CONTENTS	MAXIMUM CONTENTS
MEN	3	2.184	.728	1951	6.986	3	3
NOWON	50	49.629	.992	2003	154.611	49	50

(c)

FIGURE 2E.4   Selected Program Output for Case Study 2E. (a) Storage statistics for the "three hired, three rented" configuration. (b) Storage statistics for the "three hired, four rented" configuration. (c) Storage statistics for the "three hired, five rented" configuration.

(7) Discussion

Strategy for Use of the Model. The model is to be used to estimate the hire/rent combination which minimizes the average daily cost of running the factory. Some thought should be given, then, to the way the cost is expected to behave as various hire/rent combinations are considered. For a fixed number of repairmen, average daily cost will vary with "machines rented" as shown in Figure 2E.5. With too few rented machines, costs are high because of the lost-production penalty. With too many rented machines, costs are also high because the rental fee is being paid for more backup machines than are necessary. Somewhere between these two extremes, the cost can be expected to pass through a minimum.

Similarly, for a given number of rented machines, the influence of "repairmen hired" will follow the pattern in Figure 2E.6. With too few repairmen, high costs are experienced because of the lost-production penalty. With too many repairmen, costs are high because salaries must be paid, even though the utilization of the repairmen is low. It is reasonable to expect that cost goes through a minimum between these two extremes.

A three-dimensional perspective of the situation is suggested in Figure 2E.7. Note that the mesh points in the grid laid down in the Figure 2E.7 "hired/rented" plane represent feasible (i.e., integer-valued) choices of values for the decision-variable pair. Located above each of these mesh points, in the third dimension, is the expected daily cost corresponding to that par-

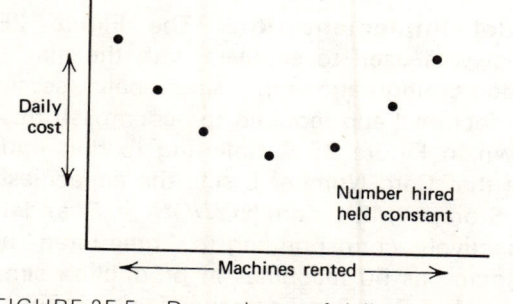

FIGURE 2E.5   Dependence of daily cost on the number of machines rented

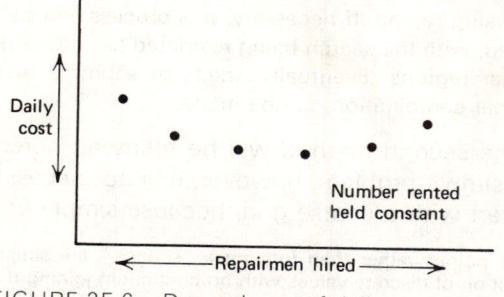

FIGURE 2E.6   Dependence of daily cost on the number of repairmen hired

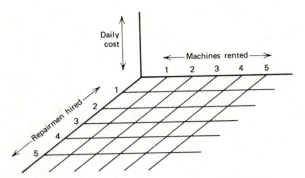

FIGURE 2E.7   A three-dimensional perspective of the daily cost surface

ticular hire/rent alternative (these points are not shown in Figure 2E.7). The collection of all such cost points forms a "cost surface" in the third dimension.[24] Figures 2E.5 and 2E.6 are then simply contours through this cost surface.

It is easy to argue that the cost surface has a single low point. The search for the optimal hire/rent combination, then, is essentially a search for this lowest point. This search might be conducted in a variety of ways. Consider two of the possibilities.

1. A "univariate searching strategy" might be employed. Briefly, this strategy involves moving through the decision-variable space from low point to low point on successive contours until all more promising directions of movement have been exhausted. Further details about this method are available elsewhere.[25] This method is especially useful if it can be conducted by interactive use of the model from a terminal, or if it is made a part of the model itself. Neither of these possibilities will be further explored here.

2. The model can be submitted for a run in which a simulation is performed for each of a series of methodically placed hire/rent combinations. A relatively coarse grid can be investigated at first, by spacing the combinations relatively far apart. Examination of the output then usually reveals which region holds promise for further investigation. In the next run, then, a simulation is performed for hire/rent combinations which are placed closer together in this smaller, promising region. If necessary, this process can be repeated, with the search being restricted to increasingly smaller regions. Eventually, then, an estimate of the optimal combination can be made.

The second method will be followed here. In this simple problem, however, it is not necessary to start with a coarse grid, because simple com-

[24]The points, rather than forming a "surface," are simply a collection of discrete values with no continuum joining them. It is nevertheless convenient to use the term "surface."
[25]For example, see the source in footnote 23.

putations make it possible to estimate approximately where the low-cost point lies. Notice first of all that the daily costs of a repairman, a backup machine, and an out-of-production machine are $30, $30, and $160, respectively. The cost due to lost production is disproportionately high, meaning that the optimal hire/rent combination will be one tending to keep lost production time low.

Now consider conditions under which there is little lost production. From the data, average machine lifetime is 157 hours, and average repair time is 7 hours. Suppose a hypothetically "ideal" system is one in which no waiting occurs. That is, in such an ideal system, failed machines never have to wait before repair begins on them; and machines coming out of repair go back into service immediately. Each machine then has an average cycle time in the system of 164 hours. Machine utilization in this ideal system is about 0.95 $[157/164 \doteq 0.95]$. If 50 machines are to be in use at all times (to eliminate lost production costs), a total of 52.6 machines must then cycle through the system $[(52.6)(0.95) = 50]$. With 50 machines in use, 2.6 machines would then be in repair. This, in turn, indicates that 2.6 repairmen would be required.

The above considerations are based on a hypothetically ideal situation. Of course, because of randomness, machines will experience some waiting, typically, at the two points where waiting can occur. Furthermore, it is not possible to rent 2.6 machines, or hire 2.6 repairmen. As a result, it seems reasonable to consider renting three or four or five backup machines, and hiring three or four or five repairmen. This suggests simulating with the nine combinations resulting from use of three, four, or five machines, and three, four, or five repairmen. As will be seen below, when the model was run with these nine configurations, the "four hired, four rented" combination produced the lowest estimate of average daily cost.

Model Implementation. The Figure 2E.2 model was used to simulate with the nine indicated configurations in a single batch session. The deck makeup required to accomplish this is shown in Figure 2E.3. Referring to that figure, note that Card Number 5 sets the capacities of the Storage MEN and NOWON at 3 and 50, respectively, corresponding to "three hired" and "as many as 50 machines in production simultaneously." Card 9 is the image of the GENERATE Block through which machine Transactions enter the model. The D Operand is 53, which corresponds to the case of three rented machines (the D Operand equals the sum of machines owned and machines rented). The GENERATE Block's Location has been symbolically named CNTRL (for "control"), so that the Block can be redefined between START cards when necessary to reflect changes in the number of rented machines. After the first START card, Cards 26, 27, and 28, respectively, reconfigure the model for the case of four rented machines, clear the model of Transactions and statistics from the first simulation, and start the simulation for the "three hired, four rented" combination. Cards 29, 30, and 31 repeat this pattern, resulting in a simulation for a "three hired, five rented" combination. Card 32 then redefines the capacity of the Storage MEN at 4. Card 33 modifies the GENERATE Block CNTRL to represent the "three rented" situation. The model is then cleared with Card 34, and Card 35 starts the simulation for the "four hired, three rented" combination. Continuing in this fashion, the remaining "hired, rented" combinations of "4,4", "4,5", "5,3", "5,4", and "5,5" are then run in that sequence.

Program Output.[26]   Figure 2E.4 shows model-outputted Storage statistics for the first three configurations studied. For each Storage, seven different pieces of information are printed out. Note these features of the information provided for the Storage named MEN in part (a) of Figure 2E.4.

1. Three parallel servers were simulated with the Storage (CAPACITY = 3).

2. On average, 2.185 of these servers were in a state of capture (AVERAGE CONTENTS = 2.185).

3. On average, these three servers were busy 72.8% of the time (AVERAGE UTILIZATION = .782).

4. The total number of times that one or another of the servers was captured was 1924 (ENTRIES = 1924).

[26] Total CPU time for the simulation on an IBM 360/67 computer was 68.2 seconds.

5. The average holding time per capture was 7.087 time units (AVERAGE TIME/TRAN = 7.087).

6. None of the servers were in a state of capture when the simulation stopped (CURRENT CONTENTS = "blank").

7. There were times during the simulation when all three of the servers were in a state of capture simultaneously (MAXIMUM CONTENTS = 3).

Scanning Figure 2E.4 from (a) to (c), note that the AVERAGE UTILIZATION of the Storage NOWON moves from 0.983 to 0.989 to 0.992. Also note that at the time of the Figure 2E.4(a) output, the factory was running at full capacity (CURRENT CONTENTS of the Storage NOWON is 50). Compare and contrast these values with the corresponding information in parts (b) and (c) of that figure.

Table 2E.2 summarizes the utilization of the Storage NOWON as a function of the nine different "hired, rented" alternatives studied with the Figure 2E.3 model. The observable trends are to be expected. For a given number of repairmen hired, utilization rises as more machines are rented. Similarly, for a given number of machines rented, utilization rises as more repairmen are hired.

TABLE 2E.2   Utilization of the Storage NOWON as a Function of Various "Hired, Rented" Combinations

Repairmen Hired	Machines Rented		
	3	4	5
3	0.983	0.989	0.992
4	0.989	0.993	0.995
5	0.991	0.993	0.997

Table 2E.3 summarizes the costs for the various hire/rent combinations investigated. In part (a), the fixed costs for salaries and machine rentals are shown. Part (b) indicates the "variable costs," which are easily computed from the utilization of the Storage NOWON, and the lost-production penalty. Part (c) displays the sum of the fixed and variable costs. Examination

TABLE 2E.3   Daily Costs for the Various "Hired, Rented" Combinations Investigated

(a) Fixed Costs ($/day)				(b) Lost Production Costs, ($/day)				(c) Total Costs, $/day			
Repairmen Hired	Machines Rented			Repairmen Hired	Machines Rented			Repairmen Hired	Machines Rented		
	3	4	5		3	4	5		3	4	5
3	180	210	240	3	136	88	64	3	316	298	304
4	210	240	270	4	88	56	40	4	298	296	310
5	240	270	300	5	72	56	24	5	312	326	324

of part (c) indicates that, based on information produced by these simulations, a "four hired, four rented" combination minimizes the overall costs. Bear in mind, however, that the utilizations in Table 2E.2 are only *estimates* of the true, long-run utilizations for the indicated hire/rent combinations. This, in turn, means the costs in part (c) of Table 2E.3 are only estimates. If the variability in the estimator is high for the sample size used, the results could be somewhat misleading. For example, it could be that the true cost associated with a "four hired, three rented" combination is lower than that for "four hired, four rented." This topic is considered further in the next section.

2.40 GPSS Control Cards: The RESET Card

Initial model conditions may vary markedly from those in effect when a state of steady operation has been reached.[27] For example, consider Case Study 2E. Under *typical* operating conditions, some of the in-production sewing machines will be nearing their time of failure, whereas others will have just recently been put into use, and so on. Hence, the "remaining running time before failure" of in-production machines will be spread at random across the range from zero (or close to it) to the maximum feasible lifetime.

At the *start* of the simulation in the Figure 2E.2 model, however, the model behaves as though all 50 machines in production *have just been turned on*. Because the lifetime distribution of each sewing machine is 157 ± 25 hours, none of these machines can fail before simulated time 132. This means that, initially, the "remaining running times" of in-production machines are very untypical. Yet, the various "hire, rent" consequences in that system should be studied only after the model reaches typical operating conditions; otherwise, misleading conclusions may be drawn from the simulation.

Consider the problem, then, of guaranteeing that the value or values of pertinent statistics are typical. The statistic of interest in Case Study 2E is utilization of the STORAGE NOWON. (As explained in the case study discussion, variable

cost in the problem depends on this statistic; variable cost, in turn, is critical in choosing the optimal operating condition.) Three approaches can be taken in estimating the typical value of this statistic.

1. Design the model so that operating conditions are typical *initially*. Then simulate with this model and begin observing the statistic immediately.
2. Run the model for such a long time that any untypical statistics gathered during the early part of the simulation are *swamped out* by the multitude of typical statistics gathered later in the simulation. That is, make the untypical observations such a small percentage of the total that their numeric influence is insignificant.
3. Follow this sequence.
   (a) Run the model until typical operating conditions have come about.
   (b) Toss out statistical observations made up to that point, without otherwise changing the state of the model.
   (c) Continue the simulation, in the process gathering statistics which are not biased by the atypical observations accumulated previously.

The first approach requires of the analyst that he (1) knows what typical operating conditions are, and (2) makes special arrangements in the model to have these conditions be in effect at the outset of the simulation. In models of complex systems, the first requirement can rarely be met. Even if it can, it may be extremely troublesome to meet the second requirement. It is left as an exercise in the next section to show how this first approach can be taken with Case Study 2E (see exercise 3, Section 2.41).

The second approach suffers from the major disadvantage that long simulations may be required before steady-state readings outweigh the early, biased observations. The cost of making long simulations with models of complex systems may be prohibitively high, making this approach undesirable.

The third approach, then, appears to be the one offering most hope. This approach can be put into perspective by comparing it to the steps involved in reconfiguring a model at intermediate points during a run, so that a series of system alternatives can be simulated with a single submit. Here are those steps.

1. Shut off the model.
2. Redefine selected Blocks in the model, redefine Storage capacities, etc.
3. "Clear" the model. Clearing the model involves

---

[27] Some systems never do reach a state of steady operation. A good example of such a system is a bank. Between opening at 9:30 a.m. and closing at 3 p.m., conditions in a bank are strongly dependent on the time of day. Discussion in this section is limited to systems in which conditions do not exhibit such time dependency.

the three things accomplished by use of a CLEAR card, namely,

(a) Set statistics back to zero.

(b) Empty the chains.

(c) Perform the Input Phase, in the sense of scheduling an arrival at each GENERATE Block in the model.

4. Restart the simulation. Restarting the simulation is accomplished by use of the START card.

Relative to the above scheme, the third approach consists exactly of Steps (1), (3a), and (4). That is, if Steps (2), (3b), and (3c) in the above scheme are not performed, the effect is one of simply tossing out statistical observations, then continuing the simulation without otherwise having changed the status of the model. We already know how to perform Steps (1) and (4). What is needed is a control card which will perform Step (3a), i.e., will set statistics back to zero but, in contrast with the CLEAR card, will *not* empty the chains and perform the Input Phase. The RESET card is the GPSS control card which has this effect. It consists of the word RESET, entered in the Operation field on a punchcard. There is no Block equivalent for it. When the Processor encounters a RESET card, it sets model statistics back to zero and then, as usual, proceeds to the next card in the deck. If the next card is a START card, the run is restarted, and accumulation of statistics during the next simulated time interval begins. With the RESET card, then, GPSS provides the analyst with a convenient tool for gathering statistics under conditions of typical model operation.

There are several statistical items which the RESET card does *not* cause to be restored to their initial values.

1. "The random-number stream" is not returned to its initial state. When the simulation is turned on again, the random-number sequence begins at whatever point it had reached by the end of the preceding simulation.

2. The *Current* Count at each Block is set equal to the number of Transactions which are at that Block. *Total* Block Counts are *all* set to zero. In the next set of Block counts produced, the Total Block Counts are then interpretable as the number of Transactions which entered the various Blocks during the most recent simulation.

3. The *Absolute Clock* is not set back to zero, even though the *Relative Clock* is. The following interpretations can consequently be given to the values of the Relative and Absolute Clocks. The Absolute Clock measures the simulated time elapsed since the model

was last cleared (or since it was first turned on if it has not been cleared). If no RESET cards have been used, the Absolute and Relative Clock readings are identical, meaning the Relative Clock provides no additional information. If the readings are not identical, the Relative Clock measures the simulated time elapsed since the model was last reset.

At the user's option, a *selective* RESET card can be used. This makes it possible to specify certain entities (for example, certain Facilities, and/or Queues, and/or Storages) for which statistics are *not* to be set back to zero as part of the resetting operation. Because use of this option in fundamental GPSS modeling is rare, its details will not be discussed in this book.

It has been implied that, if a model is run long enough, typical operating conditions will come about. The question, of course, is how long must a run be for this to happen. There are no pat answers to this question. Consequently, a frequent practice is to use the model itself, in experimental fashion, to estimate the duration of simulation required to reach steady state. The RESET card can be conveniently used for this experimentation.

As an example of such RESET card use, Figure 2.47 shows the Extended Program Listing for a job which investigates behavior of the utilization statistic for the Storage NOWON in Case Study 2E, for a "four hired, four rented" configuration. Cards 25, 26, and 27 show the typical START–RESET–START pattern corresponding to the respective steps of (1) shutting off the model, (3a) setting statistics back to zero, and (4) restarting the model, as described above. The simulation time span between resets is 1 work week (i.e., 40 hours; note that 40 is the Card 20 GENERATE Block A Operand). The number of RESET–START card pairs included in the model corresponds to a *total* simulation span of 25 work weeks. (Note that the RESET–START card pairs from Card 32 to Card 69, inclusive, have been deleted in Figure 2.47.)

Output produced from the Figure 2.47 model run is summarized in Table 2.22. Column 2 shows the utilization of the Storage NOWON experienced during the corresponding simulated week as indicated in Column 1. Column 3 shows the Storage utilization on an *accumulated* basis, as determined by simulating with the Figure 2.47 model after removing the RESET cards from it. If the second approach described earlier for attempting to reach steady state were taken ("run the model long enough to swamp

```
BLOCK                                                                              CARD
NUMBER   *LOC    OPERATION   A,B,C,D,E,F,G                COMMENTS                  NUMBER
                 SIMULATE                                                          1
         *                                                                         2
         *       STORAGE CAPACITY DEFINITION(S)                                    3
         *                                                                         4
                 STORAGE     S$MEN,4/S$NOWON,50     4 MEN; MAX OF 50 MACH'S RUNNING 5
         *                                                                         6
         *       MODEL SEGMENT 1                                                   7
         *                                                                         8
1                GENERATE    ,,,54             PROVIDE 54 MACHINES                  9
2        BACK    ENTER       NOWON             MACHINE GOES INTO PRODUCTION         10
3                ADVANCE     157,25            MACHINE IS RUNNING                   11
4                LEAVE       NOWON             MACHINE FAILS;  COMES OUT OF PRODUCTION 12
5                ENTER       MEN               CAPTURE A REPAIRMAN                  13
6                ADVANCE     7,3               MACHINE IS BEING REPAIRED            14
7                LEAVE       MEN               FREE THE REPAIRMAN                   15
8                TRANSFER    ,BACK             GO BACK TO RUN AGAIN WHEN NEEDED     16
         *                                                                         17
         *       MODEL SEGMENT 2                                                   18
         *                                                                         19
9                GENERATE    40                TIMER ARRIVES EVERY 40 HOURS         20
10               TERMINATE   1                 SHUT OFF THE RUN                     21
         *                                                                         22
         *       CONTROL CARDS                                                     23
         *                                                                         24
                 START       1                 START RUN FOR WEEK 1                 25
                 RESET                         RESET FOR WEEK 2                     26
                 START       1                 START RUN FOR WEEK 2                 27
                 RESET                         RESET FOR WEEK 3                     28
                 START       1                 START RUN FOR WEEK 3                 29
                 RESET                         RESET FOR WEEK 4                     30
                 START       1                 START RUN FOR WEEK 4                 31
                    .                              .                                 .
                    .                              .                                 .
                    .                              .                                 .
                 RESET                         RESET FOR WEEK 24                    70
                 START       1                 START RUN FOR WEEK 24                71
                 RESET                         RESET FOR WEEK 25                    72
                 START       1                 START RUN FOR WEEK 25                73
                 END                           RETURN CONTROL TO OPERATING SYSTEM  74
```

FIGURE 2.47   A model to experimentally estimate when steady state is reached

out the early, biased statistics"), observations would correspond to those in column 3. Inspection of column 2 suggests that typical operating conditions are reached after about 10 weeks of simulated time. As shown in column 3, the accumulated statistic is still far from having reached a typical value, even at the end of the twenty-fifth week. Hence, the relative economy of the "reset approach" vs. the "swamping approach" is evident in Table 2.22.

Some comment on the entries in column 2 is in order. The lifetime distribution of each sewing machine is 157 ± 25 hours. The smallest possible running time before failure is 132 hours. The model behaves as though all 50 machines in production have just been turned on at the beginning of the simulation. None of these 50 machines can fail, then, during the first 3 weeks. The utilization of the Storage NOWON should then be 1.0 at the end of each of the first 3 weeks. This is the case at the end of weeks 2 and 3, but not at the end of week 1. Why is there this aberration

in the first week's statistic? It is because, as pointed out previously, *the earliest Move Time in a model is* 1. The machines are consequently *not turned on in the model until the end of the first hour* (the Transactions are not moved into the ADVANCE Block, Block 3, until simulated time 1). But GPSS computes statistics *as though the simulation starts at time* 0. At time 40, then, the machines have only been on for 39 time units. This results in a utilization of 39 divided by 40, or 0.975. (The value 0.974 appears in the output due to truncation without rounding.)

The utilization during week 5 is also of interest. Early in week 5, many of the machines turned on at the beginning of the first week fail (that is, they fail between time 160 and 200). There are not enough backup machines available to immediately take their place, and the four repairmen require time to work on the failed machines. The result is that the number of in-production machines drops dramatically, and the utilization

TABLE 2.22   Behavior of a Critical Statistic As the Case Study 2E Model Moves from Initial Conditions Toward Steady-State Operation

Week Spanned by Time Interval	Storage Utilization During the Interval	Storage Utilization Accumulated During the Entire Simulation
1	0.974	0.974
2	1.000	0.987
3	1.000	0.991
4	0.905	0.970
5	0.632	0.902
6	0.901	0.902
7	1.000	0.916
8	0.987	0.925
9	0.984	0.932
10	0.998	0.938
11	0.999	0.944
12	0.998	0.948
13	0.986	0.951
14	0.991	0.954
15	1.000	0.957
16	1.000	0.960
17	0.975	0.961
18	1.000	0.963
19	1.000	0.965
20	0.999	0.966
21	0.988	0.968
22	0.992	0.969
23	1.000	0.970
24	0.998	0.971
25	0.991	0.972

figure falls to 0.632. It is only eventually, then, about by the end of week 10, that a consistent utilization pattern comes into effect.

The example just presented in detail illustrates use of the RESET card to estimate when a model reaches steady state operation. The next logical usage mode for the RESET card involves its use just after steady state has been reached, before the simulation is continued under the steady state conditions. In terms of Case Study 2E, for example, and conclusions reached from Table 2.22, the model would be reset after a 10-week simulation. But now another question arises. How long a run is required under steady-state conditions for the measured statistics to be typical? Even within the steady state, statistics fluctuate about their expected values. If the steady-state run is too short, certain measurements may not be typical. *A series of consecutive START cards could be used after the RESET at steady state to experimentally estimate the steady-state run required for pertinent statistics to stabilize.*

Consider the effect of having consecutive START cards in a job deck (without intermediate RESET or CLEAR cards). Suppose that, having inputted a model and come to a START card, the Processor has initiated a simulation. Eventually, the Termination Counter is decremented to zero, the simulation shuts off, and various output is produced. If the very next card the Processor encounters is another START card, the simulation is simply reinitiated. That is, the Termination Counter is initialized with the next START card's A Operand, and the Processor then goes into execution of the Clock Update Phase, etc. Of course, Transactions resident on the chains are exactly as they were at the time of the preceding shutoff. Furthermore, accumulated statistical information remains undisturbed, and is simply augmented by the continuing observations being made. In essence, then, inclusion of two or more consecutive START cards provides the analyst with *snapshots of accumulated system statistics* as a simulation proceeds. By use of consecutive START cards, a simulation is effectively composed of a series of consecutive simulations. At the end of each next simulation, system statistics are outputted, and the run then proceeds where it had left off.

Rather than performing such a START-card experiment here, it will now simply be assumed that a 20-week simulation during steady state is satisfactory for the Case Study 2E model. Figure 2.48 shows the Extended Program Listing for a job to study all combinations of three, four, and five repairmen, and three, four, and five rented machines, with the "RESET after reaching steady state" feature included. (Cards 33 through 63 have been deleted from the figure for simplicity.) Note that, after each RESET, the next START card has 2 entered as the A Operand. Hence, *two* appearances of the timer-Transaction are required before any particular steady state run shuts off. This means that the steady state simulation interval is 20 weeks, not 10. Also note how, at the conclusion of each steady state run, the model is re-configured, then cleared (with the CLEAR card), before the

START-RESET-START pattern is then repeated for the next case.

The Storage utilizations resulting when the Figure 2.48 job was run are shown in Table 2.23(a). The average daily costs corresponding to these utilizations appear in Table 2.23(b). Note that the "four hired, four rented" configuration *looks even better* now than it did in Table 2E.3. Also note that each configuration studied involved only 30 weeks of simulated time. In contrast, 156 weeks were used for each configuration in Case Study 2E. The longer simulation was required in Case Study 2E to overcome the utilization-statistic bias introduced during model startup. Of course, using the RESET card to eliminate that bias is preferable to simply simulating for a long time. The results are better defined, and execution time required for the run is substantially reduced. In

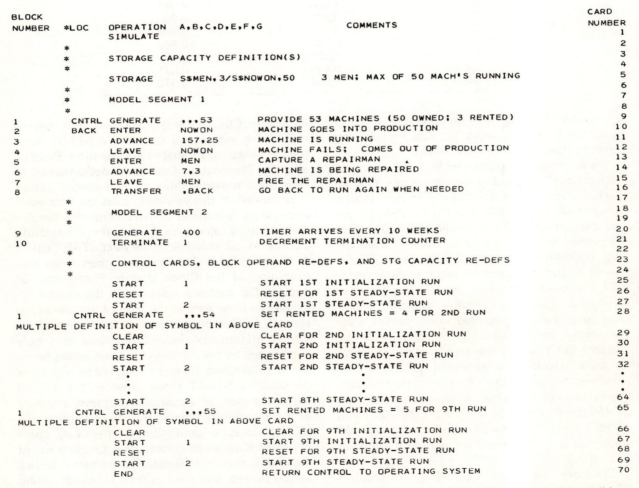

```
BLOCK                                                                                    CARD
NUMBER   *LOC    OPERATION   A,B,C,D,E,F,G              COMMENTS                          NUMBER
                 SIMULATE                                                                   1
         *                                                                                  2
         *       STORAGE CAPACITY DEFINITION(S)                                             3
         *                                                                                  4
                 STORAGE     S$MEN,3/S$NOWON,50      3 MEN; MAX OF 50 MACH'S RUNNING        5
         *                                                                                  6
         *       MODEL SEGMENT 1                                                            7
         *                                                                                  8
1        CNTRL   GENERATE    ,,,53              PROVIDE 53 MACHINES (50 OWNED; 3 RENTED)     9
2        BACK    ENTER       NOWON              MACHINE GOES INTO PRODUCTION               10
3                ADVANCE     157,25             MACHINE IS RUNNING                         11
4                LEAVE       NOWON              MACHINE FAILS;  COMES OUT OF PRODUCTION    12
5                ENTER       MEN                CAPTURE A REPAIRMAN                        13
6                ADVANCE     7,3                MACHINE IS BEING REPAIRED                  14
7                LEAVE       MEN                FREE THE REPAIRMAN                         15
8                TRANSFER    ,BACK              GO BACK TO RUN AGAIN WHEN NEEDED           16
         *                                                                                 17
         *       MODEL SEGMENT 2                                                           18
         *                                                                                 19
9                GENERATE    400                TIMER ARRIVES EVERY 10 WEEKS              20
10               TERMINATE   1                  DECREMENT TERMINATION COUNTER             21
         *                                                                                 22
         *       CONTROL CARDS, BLOCK OPERAND RE-DEFS, AND STG CAPACITY RE-DEFS           23
         *                                                                                 24
                 START       1                  START 1ST INITIALIZATION RUN              25
                 RESET                          RESET FOR 1ST STEADY-STATE RUN            26
                 START       2                  START 1ST STEADY-STATE RUN                27
1        CNTRL   GENERATE    ,,,54              SET RENTED MACHINES = 4 FOR 2ND RUN       28
MULTIPLE DEFINITION OF SYMBOL IN ABOVE CARD
                 CLEAR                          CLEAR FOR 2ND INITIALIZATION RUN          29
                 START       1                  START 2ND INITIALIZATION RUN              30
                 RESET                          RESET FOR 2ND STEADY-STATE RUN            31
                 START       2                  START 2ND STEADY-STATE RUN                32
                   .                              .                                        .
                   .                              .                                        .
                   .                              .                                        .
                 START       2                  START 8TH STEADY-STATE RUN                64
1        CNTRL   GENERATE    ,,,55              SET RENTED MACHINES = 5 FOR 9TH RUN       65
MULTIPLE DEFINITION OF SYMBOL IN ABOVE CARD
                 CLEAR                          CLEAR FOR 9TH INITIALIZATION RUN          66
                 START       1                  START 9TH INITIALIZATION RUN              67
                 RESET                          RESET FOR 9TH STEADY-STATE RUN            68
                 START       2                  START 9TH STEADY-STATE RUN                69
                 END                            RETURN CONTROL TO OPERATING SYSTEM        70
```

FIGURE 2.48   A model using RESET and CLEAR cards to investigate nine alternatives under steady state conditions

TABLE 2.23   Pertinent Results Corresponding to the Figure 2.48 Model

(a) Storage Utilizations				(b) Total Costs ($/Day)			
Repairmen	Machines Rented			Repairmen	Machines Rented		
Hired	3	4	5	Hired	3	4	5
3	0.986	0.989	0.995	3	292	298	285
4	0.989	0.995	0.995	4	298	280	310
5	0.990	0.992	0.998	5	320	334	316

this instance, the Figure 2.48 model took only about 25 percent as much computer time as the model in Case Study 2E.[28]

In summary, in addition to introducing the RESET card, this section brings out the fact that when a model has been built, the analyst's work has just begun. The analyst's next task usually requires experimenting with the model to determine (1) how long to simulate to reach steady state, and (2) how long to simulate, given that steady state has been reached. Furthermore, these "how long" determinations will generally depend on the particular statistic or statistics of interest, *and* on the model configuration in question. Case Study 2E was simple because there was only *one* statistic of interest, a Storage utilization. In addition, it was implicitly assumed that the "how long" answers determined for a "four hired, four rented" combination *are valid for all other combinations investigated*. Although that assumption is reasonably valid here, this may not be true in general. Hence, the "how long" answers may have to be determined more than one time in a given problem.

It is beyond the scope of this book to dwell in further detail on the statistical aspects of simulation. It is similarly outside the scope here to elaborate further on searching strategies which might be employed in the use of simulation models, as briefly discussed in the last section. These two important topics should be recognized, however, as a *sine qua non* of intelligent simulation.

2.41 Exercises

1. Compare and contrast the effect of using the RESET and CLEAR cards in GPSS modeling. Include a discussion of the differences, if any, in the effects of RESET and CLEAR on (a) Block Counts, (b) Relative and Absolute Clock values, and (c) the "random-number sequence."

[28]On an IBM 360/67 computer, total CPU time for the simulation with the Figure 2E.3 model was 68 seconds, whereas CPU time for the simulation with the Figure 2.48 model was 18 seconds.

2. (a) In Case Study 2E, compute the fixed costs, dollars per day, corresponding to the three-hired, three-rented configuration. Check your result against Table 2E.3(a).
   (b) In Case Study 2E, compute the lost production cost, dollars per day, from data available for the three-hired, three-rented simulation. Check your results against Table 2E.3(b).

3. As discussed at the beginning of Section 2.40, initial model conditions in Case Study 2E vary markedly from those in effect when a state of steady operation has been reached. Show how to modify the model in that case study so that operating conditions are typical *initially*. In particular, at the beginning of the simulation, the lifetime of each of the 50 in-production machines should be determined by sampling from a "remaining lifetime distribution" hypothesized to be uniformly distributed over the interval from 0 to 182 hours. Any machines subsequently put into production should have their lifetime determined by sampling from the 157 $\pm$ 25 distribution.

4. In the Case Study 2E model, "owned machines" and "rented machines" are put into use strictly on a first-come, first-served basis. When a machine is needed and there is a choice between an "owned machine" and a "rented machine," there may be some economic motivation to give preference to the "owned machine." (It may be true, for example, that rental cost is based both on the duration of rental *and* the number of hours the rented machine is actually used during that period.) Show how to modify the case study model so that owned machines are given preference in this circumstance.

5. In a particular model, the implicit time unit is 1 minute. Each 480 time units, the Termination Counter is decremented by 1. Compare and contrast the nature of the statistics printed out for the alternative Control Card sequences shown below.
   (a) START   1
       RESET
       START   1
   (b) START   1
       CLEAR
       START   1

(c) START   1
    START   1

6. In a certain model, the capacity of the Storage CARE is initially defined to be 8.
   (a) What error might result if the following control card sequence is used in the model?

```
START    1
STORAGE  S$CARE,5
CLEAR
START    1
```

   (b) Could such an error condition ever result if the STORAGE and CLEAR cards in (a) were reversed?

7. In a particular model, the implicit time unit is 1 minute. Each 240 time units, the Termination Counter is decremented by 1. Discuss the nature of the statistics printed out for the control card sequence shown in Figure E7. Include in your discussion a listing of the Relative and Absolute Clock values as they appear in the five sets of information which are printed out.

```
START    4
CLEAR
START    4
CLEAR
START    1
RESET
START    1
RESET
START    2
```
FIGURE E7

8. (a) Customers arrive at a two-man barber shop every 9 ± 4 minutes. Each of the two barbers takes 16 ± 4 minutes to provide service to a customer. Build a GPSS model to gather statistics for the line in which the customers wait. Use the model to simulate for 1 work day. Assume the barber shop opens at 9 a.m. and closes at 5 p.m. The barbers take no breaks during the day.
   (b) Modify the model for (a) to include the condition that the shop opens at 8:30 a.m. and closes at 5 p.m. Each barber takes a 30-minute lunch break at 12:00 noon, or as soon thereafter as possible (i.e., if a barber is at an intermediate point in working on a customer when it becomes noon, he finishes with the customer before taking the 30-minute lunch break). Customers who arrive at the shop during the lunch break wait for the barbers to return. What will be the long-run utilization of the barbers?

9. In Figure 2.48, the RESET card is used to zero out statistics in the Case Study 2E model, before continuing the run under steady-state conditions. Having reached steady state, a question then arises as to how much longer to run for the measured statistics of interest to be typical. The uncertainty arises because, even within steady state, statistics fluctuate about their expected values.

Show a deck for the Case Study 2E model for the "four hired, four rented" configuration in which, after resetting after a 10-week simulation, *aggregate* statistics are printed out at the end of each next week for 20 consecutive weeks. Submit the deck for running. What is your conclusion about the length of the steady-state run required to gather meaningful steady-state information? Note that, to produce the results shown in Table 2.23, it was arbitrarily assumed that a 20-week steady-state simulation for each configuration would be satisfactory.

10. In Table 2.22, the behavior of the utilization of the Storage NOWON in Case Study 2E is shown for a "four hired, four rented" configuration. It was qualitatively concluded from the information in column 2 in that table that "eventually, about by the end of week 10, a consistent utilization pattern comes into effect." This conclusion for the "four hired, four rented" configuration was then tacitly assumed to be valid for *all* configurations investigated in the Figure 2.48 job deck.

In practice, the length of run required to reach steady state may depend on the system configuration being investigated. Build and run a model to produce output similar to that shown in column 2 in Table 2.22, but for a "10 hired, 10 rented" configuration. Does the run have to be longer, shorter, or about the same as for the "four hired, four rented" configuration before a consistent utilization pattern comes about?

11. In the discussion of program output in Case Study 2C, it was pointed out that "the duration of the simulation used in this case study is so small that any conclusions drawn from the model output must be tentative at best." Construct and carry out a plan to further investigate the two alternative queue disciplines proposed in that model. As part of your plan, make use of the RESET card to estimate how long each of the two alternative models must be run for steady-state conditions to be reached. Then simulate under steady-state conditions with the objective of drawing firm conclusions about the relative merits of the two queue disciplines. Compare the resulting daily cost difference with the difference of about $141 tentatively established in Case Study 2C. As manager of the plant involved, which of the two disciplines would you have implemented at the tool crib?

12. In Case Study 2D (widget manufacture), a Transaction represents a worker cycling repeatedly through the assemble–fire–assemble–fire, etc., pattern. An *alternative*, yet equally valid, GPSS model can be built for the Case Study 2D problem by using a Storage to simulate the assemblers. In this alternative approach, a Transaction is thought of as representing the material required for a widget. Coming from the GENERATE Block as raw material, the material is transformed by assembly and firing as the corresponding Transaction moves through the model, Block by Block.

Figure E12 shows the Extended Program Listing of this alternative model. Study the model, then answer these questions.

(a) What is the interarrival time of Transactions at the main segment GENERATE Block? (Note that there are no Operands at the GENERATE Block.)

(b) At what simulated time will a Transaction first attempt to move into the ENTER Block?

(c) For the first configuration studied, how many consecutive Transactions will move into the ENTER Block at simulated time 1, before a Transaction is finally denied entry there? (See Hint 2, exercise 1, Section 2.35).

(d) What must happen in the model before the first Transaction not permitted to move into the ENTER Block is finally permitted to make that move? When will his successor then arrive at the GENERATE Block and attempt to move on in the model? What will the successor's initial experience be?

(e) Would the logic of the model be subverted if a QUEUE–DEPART Block pair were placed around the ENTER Block? Why or why not?

(f) Assume that this change is made in system conditions:

Assemblers do not operate the oven themselves. An oven attendant is provided for this purpose. As a result, as soon as an assembly is complete, the assembler can immediately begin the next assembly.

Show how to modify the Figure E12 model to incorporate this assumed change in conditions.

(g) How many different configurations will be

```
BLOCK                                                                                    CARD
NUMBER   *LOC     OPERATION  A,B,C,D,E,F,G              COMMENTS                          NUMBER
                  SIMULATE                                                                  1
         *                                                                                  2
         *        STORAGE CAPACITY DEFINITION(S)                                            3
         *                                                                                  4
                  STORAGE    S$GUYS,4      CONFIGURE FOR 4-ASSEMBLER CASE                   5
         *                                                                                  6
         *                                                                                  7
         *        MODEL SEGMENT 1                                                           8
         *                                                                                  9
  1               GENERATE                 PROVIDE UNLIMITED SOURCE OF MATERIAL            10
  2               ENTER      GUYS           ENGAGE AN ASSEMBLER                            11
  3               ADVANCE    30,5           ASSEMBLY TIME ELAPSES                          12
  4               SEIZE      OVEN           CAPTURE THE OVEN                               13
  5               ADVANCE    8,2            FIRING TIME ELAPSES                            14
  6               RELEASE    OVEN           RELEASE THE OVEN                               15
  7               LEAVE      GUYS           FREE THE ASSEMBLER                             16
  8               TERMINATE                 FINISHED WIDGET LEAVES THE SHOP                17
         *                                                                                 18
         *        MODEL SEGMENT 2                                                          19
         *                                                                                 20
  9               GENERATE   480            TIMER ARRIVES AT THE END OF EACH DAY           21
 10               TERMINATE  1              DECREMENT THE TERMINATION COUNTER BY 1         22
         *                                                                                 23
         *        CONTROL CARDS AND STORAGE CAPACITY RE-DEFINITIONS                        24
         *                                                                                 25
                  START      1              START THE 1ST INITIALIZATION RUN               26
                  RESET                     ZERO-OUT ACCUMULATED STATISTICS                27
                  START      5              START 1ST STEADY-STATE RUN                     28
                  STORAGE    S$GUYS,5       RE-CONFIGURE FOR NEXT RUN                      29
                  CLEAR                     CLEAR THE MODEL FOR THE NEXT RUN               30
                  START      1              START THE 2ND INITIALIZATION RUN              31
                  RESET                     ZERO-OUT ACCUMULATED STATISTICS                32
                  START      5              START 2ND STEADY-STATE RUN                     33
                  STORAGE    S$GUYS,6       RE-CONFIGURE FOR NEXT RUN                      34
                  CLEAR                     CLEAR THE MODEL FOR THE NEXT RUN               35
                  START      1              START 3RD INITIALIZATION RUN                   36
                  RESET                     ZERO-OUT ACCUMULATED STATISTICS                37
                  START      5              START 3RD STEADY-STATE RUN                     38
                  END                       RETURN CONTROL TO OPERATING SYSTEM            39
```

FIGURE E12

simulated when the Figure E12 job is run? Explain.

(h) How long a simulation takes place with each configuration to eliminate the bias in statistics due to startup conditions?

(i) What is the duration of the steady-state simulation for each configuration?

(j) Discuss the implications of removing the two CLEAR cards from the model.

(k) Note that, as processing of the job proceeds, the capacity of the Storage GUYS is *increased* from configuration to configuration. What problem could result if the capacity were *decreased* from configuration to configuration? Could this problem arise if the CLEAR cards were placed in the deck *ahead of* the cards redefining the capacity of the Storage?

13.[29] In Case Study 2D, it is implicitly assumed that all the widgets manufactured can be sold. The availability of only one oven as a manufacturing constraint means that, in the long run, not more than 60 widgets can be produced in an 8-hour day. (Because the firing time for each widget is 8 ± 2 minutes, an oven utilization of 1.0 would correspond to a manufacturing rate of 60 widgets per working day.)

Suppose marketing studies indicate that demand for widgets will support a manufacturing rate of 275 widgets per working day. Additional ovens are available at the indicated utilization-independent cost of $10 per hour.

Build a model which reflects the availability of more than one oven. Then use the model to determine the number of assemblers and ovens which maximizes daily profit.

In the optimal "assembler, oven" configuration, it may not be true that all of the latent demand will be satisfied. Some demand necessarily goes

[29] For a fully automated solution to this problem, see "Use of an External Optimizing Algorithm with a GPSS Model," by Robert M. Lefkowits and Thomas J. Schriber, in the *Proceedings of the 1971 Winter Simulation Conference* (AFIPS Press, Montvale, New Jersey, 1971), pp. 162–171. In that solution, GPSS is used to model the widget-manufacturing process, and FORTRAN is used to implement the univariate searching strategy (as described in Case Study 2E). The GPSS model conducts its search under the direction of the FORTRAN subroutine.

unsatisfied if the optimal configuration produces widgets at a long-run average daily rate less than 275.

On the other hand, the optimal configuration may be *capable* of producing widgets at an average daily rate greater than 275. In this event, it is not necessary to produce widgets that cannot be sold. Assemblers may "stop working early" from time to time, to avoid wasting the $2 raw material cost in the manufacture of widgets that would go unsold. Note that *it is not necessary for your model* to have assemblers "stop working early" under certain conditions. If a given configuration produces, at full capacity, 283 widgets per day, for example, you can compute "profit-after-cost" as though only exactly 275 had been made. It must be assumed, of course, that even if assemblers are occasionally told by management to stop work early, they remain on the payroll for the full 8-hour day.

14. (a) Build a model to represent the queuing system shown in Figure E14. Arrivals occur at Station 1 every 115 ± 30 seconds. The times required to perform service at Stations 1 and 2 are 335 ± 60 and 110 ± 25 seconds, respectively. Design the model to measure the waiting-line behavior ahead of Stations 1 and 2. Assume that there is unlimited space between the two stations, so that there is no maximum size beyond which waiting-line 2 entries cannot be accommodated.

Experiment with the model to determine how long a simulation must be for the average Queue contents at each of the two waiting lines to stabilize. Then run the model in the steady state to measure what the steady-state average Queue content is at the two points of waiting.

(b) Assume that, due to space limitations, the number of units in waiting-line 2 cannot exceed 1. The Station 1 servers cannot begin service on the next unit until the preceding unit has been placed in waiting line 2. Modify your model in (a) to take this constraint into account. Then use the model to measure the average and maximum Queue content at waiting line 1 under steady state conditions.

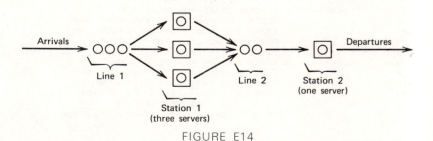

FIGURE E14

Compare the results with those obtained in (a).

(c) In part (b), suppose that the *true* utilization of the Station 1 servers is defined as the fraction of the time they spend performing service. They are not considered to be performing service when they are waiting to place the preceding unit in waiting line 2. Show how to modify part (b) so that it measures the true utilization of the Station 1 servers.

15. Ships of two types arrive at a harbor, where they unload their cargo. There are two tugs which service the harbor. Type 1 ships, which are small, require the use of only one of these tugs to dock and undock. Type 2 ships, which are larger, require the use of both tugs to dock and undock. Because of their size differences, the two ship types also unload at different berths, and have different unloading-time requirements. Appropriate data appear in Table E15.

TABLE E15

	Ship Type	
	1	2
Interarrival Time (minutes)	130 ± 30	390 ± 60
Docking Time (minutes)	30 ± 7	45 ± 12
Number of Unloading Berths Available	6	3
Unloading Time (hours)	12 ± 2	18 ± 4
Undocking Time (minutes)	20 ± 5	35 ± 10

(a) Build a model of the system, designing it to estimate the aggregate waiting time of each ship type at the harbor. Aggregate waiting time consists of time spent waiting for any reason, i.e., waiting for a berth, and/or waiting for a tug. *A ship waiting to dock is not to capture a tug until a berth is available.* (What might happen if a ship could capture a tug before a berth became available for the ship?) Furthermore, a Type 2 ship is not to capture a tug until *both* tugs are available.

Use the model to estimate the requested aggregate waiting-time statistics under conditions of steady state operation.

(b) If it costs $350 and $500 per hour, respectively, to have ships of Type 1 and 2 wait, and the cost of providing a tug is $250 per day, can addition of a third tug at the harbor be justified?

(c) Assuming the waiting-ship cost stated in (b), at what estimated berth cost per day could addition of another berth for Type 1 ships be justified? At what daily cost could addition of another berth for Type 2 ships be justified?

16. There are seven booths at a toll point on a turnpike. Each open booth can handle a car in 15 ± 3 seconds. Suppose that at 3 o'clock on a particular afternoon, there are four open booths and no cars waiting to move through the toll point. The mean hourly rate at which cars arrive at the toll point increases during the late afternoon, then decreases again early in the evening as shown in Table E16. The variation in the interarrival times for each time span is plus or minus 25 percent of the mean, and is uniformly distributed.

To compensate for the traffic increase during the rush hours, a fifth booth is opened at 4:30, and the two remaining booths are opened at 5:00.

Model this situation, then run the model to estimate the maximum and average number of cars waiting at the toll point for each of the various time spans appearing in Table E16. Do you think it would be more realistic to model this situation with a one-line, multiple-server queuing system, or a multiple-line, multiple-server system? Which of these two queuing systems does your model correspond to?

TABLE E16

Time Span	3:00–4:00	4:00–4:30	4:30–5:00
Arrival Rate (Cars/Hour)	1,000	1,250	1,600

Time Span	5:00–5:30	5:30–6:00	6:00–6:30	6:30–7:00
Arrival Rate (Cars/Hour)	2,000	1,800	1,300	1,000

2.42 Obtaining Printout During a Simulation

At the analyst's option, printouts of model statistics can be obtained *during* a simulation to supplement those produced at the end of a run. *Complete* sets of intermediate statistics are available through use of the C Operand on the START card. *Selected* sets of statistics can be obtained by making use of the PRINT Block. Details are described below.

2.42.1 The Snap Interval Option

In addition to the Termination Counter, GPSS maintains a *Snap Interval Counter*. Its initial value is specified by the START card's C Operand. When the Processor reads a START card, it initializes the Termination Counter and Snap Interval Counter with the A and C Operand values, respectively. Each time the Termination Counter is decremented during the simulation, the Snap Interval Counter (SIC) is decremented by a like amount. When the SIC has been decremented to zero, the standard model output is produced. The SIC is then automatically re-initialized to the C-Operand value, and the simulation continues. When the SIC has again been decremented to zero, the standard model output is again outputted, the SIC is again re-initialized, etc. As a result, a series of snapshots of statistical information can be obtained as a simulation proceeds.

Figure 2.49 shows two examples of START cards with the optional C Operand used. In the first example, a complete set of output is produced after the Termination Counter (and Snap Interval Counter) has been decremented by 25. The SIC is then restored to 25 in value, and the simulation continues. When the Termination Counter (and Snap Interval Counter) has been decremented by another 25, the simulation shuts off and, as usual, a complete set of output is produced.

In the second example, a complete set of statistics is outputted each time the Termination Counter (and Snap Interval Counter) is decremented by 1. By the time the simulation shuts off, five sets of output (including the one at the end of the run) have been produced. Note that an identical effect could be achieved by placing the card "START 1" in the model five consecutive times. The primary value of the Snap Interval Counter, then, is to cut down on the number of START cards otherwise required to achieve the same effect.

2.42.2 The PRINT Block

Each time a Transaction moves through a PRINT Block, the GPSS Processor outputs the standard statistical information for a specified type of entity. For example, the usual statistical information for Facilities, or Storages, or Queues can be printed out. It is also possible to be selective with respect to the particular entity members for which the information is outputted. Instead of printing the statistics for *all* the Facilities in a model, for example, it can be specified that only the information for Facility 4 is to be outputted, or for Facilities 4, 5, and 6, and so on.

The PRINT Block and its various Operands are shown in Figure 2.50. The C Operand indicates the entity class of interest. The A and B Operands specify the range of entity numbers within that class for which information is to be printed.[30] If the analyst defaults on these two Operands, the Processor prints information for all the entity members. Printing normally occurs beginning at the top of a new page. If any alphabetic character is entered as the PRINT Block's D Operand, the skip to the top of the next page does not occur.

The punchcard images corresponding to several PRINT Blocks are shown in Figure 2.51. Each time a Transaction enters the Block whose image is shown in the first example, the current statistical information for Storages 4 through 8 will be printed. It is not considered an error if one or more of the Storages in this range do not exist.

Whenever a Transaction enters the second-example Block, the Processor prints out the current statistics for Facility 5 (i.e., Facilities in

---

[30]Symbolic entity names can also be supplied for the A and/or B Operands. When this approach is used, the analyst must see to it that the Processor-assigned *numeric equivalent* of the symbolic name or names is such that the A Operand is less than or equal to the B Operand. Otherwise, an error condition will occur. Before using symbolic names for these Operands, the analyst must consequently understand how the Processor assigns numeric equivalents to symbolic entity names. This topic is taken up in Chapter 4. In general, symbolic entity names will not be used with the PRINT Block in this book.

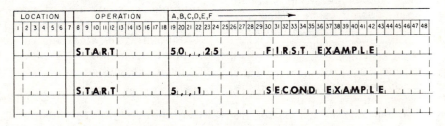

FIGURE 2.49   Examples of snap interval use

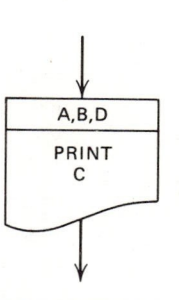

Operand	Significance	Default Value or Result
C	A mnemonic indicating the entity class of interest; F, S, and Q indicate Facilities, Storages, and Queues, respectively	Defaulting is equivalent to punching X, which indicates "fullword Savevalues" as the entity class. Savevalues will be discussed in chapter 5
A and B	The smallest and largest numbers, respectively, of entity members for which information is to be outputted	Information will be printed for all the entity members
D	Optional Operand; termed a paging indicator; if any alphabetic character is used as the D Operand, printing occurs without skipping to the top of a new page first	Printing occurs at the top of a new page

FIGURE 2.50   The PRINT Block and Its A, B, C, and D Operands

the range from "5 to 5, inclusive"). The printout takes place without skipping to the top of a new page.

A Transaction that enters the Block in the third example causes the Processor to output statistical information for *all* the Queues in a model. This is a result of defaulting on the A and B Operands. Note how commas are entered in card columns 19 and 20.

Figure 2.52 shows a complete Block Diagram segment which could be used to print out the statistics for Facilities 1, 2, and 3 in a model every 100 time units. A single Transaction circulates through the segment. The Transaction enters the segment through the GENERATE Block at time 100, and immediately prints out the Facility statistics. (It is understood that use of the Facilities is simulated in another part of the overall model.) It then goes into an ADVANCE Block for 100 time units. Exiting that Block at time 200, it unconditionally transfers back to the PRINT Block, prints out the Facility statistics

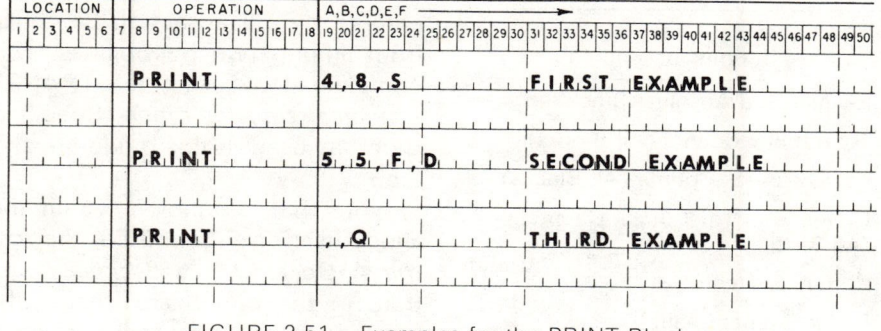

FIGURE 2.51   Examples for the PRINT Block

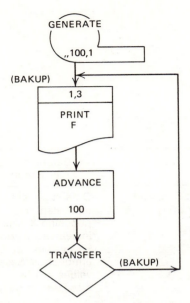

FIGURE 2.52   A self-contained Model Segment which periodically outputs statistics for selected Facilities

again, and so on. Segments like this can be appended to models to provide selected statistical output as a simulation proceeds.

The PRINT Block can also be used to output the Relative and Absolute Clock readings, Block Counts, and the Current and Future Events Chains. The PRINT Block's C Operand (i.e., field C mnemonic) for each of these possibilities is shown in Table 2.24. In each of these cases, no "range of entity members" is involved. As a result, the A and B Operands are not used. A Transaction entering the Block "PRINT ,,MOV", for example, would cause the Current Events Chain to be printed out. As another example, the Processor will print out the Relative and Absolute Clock readings each time a Transaction enters the Block "PRINT ,,C".

TABLE 2.24   Partial List of Available PRINT Block C Operands (Reproduced from Appendix E)

PRINT Block C Operand	Information Printed
C	Relative and Absolute Clock
N	Total Block Counts (All Blocks)
W	Current Block Counts (All Blocks)
B	Current and Total Block Counts (All Blocks)
MOV	Current Events Chain
FUT	Future Events Chain

Many of the additional GPSS entities not yet discussed can also be printed out with the PRINT Block. The C Operands which apply to these various possibilities are summarized in Appendix E. As further language entities are introduced, the way the PRINT Block can be used to output corresponding information will be mentioned.

The experienced user who makes use of the PRINT Block in a simulation may actually prefer suppressing the standard model output at the end of a run. This can be done by supplying NP (for No Printing) as the B Operand on the START card. Use of this option is not especially recommended when one is first gaining practice with the GPSS language.

2.43 GPSS Control Cards: The JOB Card

The analyst sometimes wants to simulate with two or more completely unrelated models in a single batch job. This can be done with use of the JOB card. When the Processor finds a JOB card in the deck, it completely erases its internal image of both the model and all associated simulations which went before the JOB card. This means that all statistics are restored to their initial status, including "the random-number sequence"; all Transactions are returned to the stack in the latent pool; and all Block images are destroyed. The Processor then acts on the next model in the deck as though it were the *first* model, or the *only* model.

The format for the JOB card is identical to that for the other control cards. The card consists simply of the word JOB, entered in the Operation field.

2.44 Random Transfer of Transactions to Either One of Two Blocks

It is sometimes of interest to have the next Block entered by a Transaction be chosen at random from among two possibilities. This can be accomplished by using the TRANSFER Block in *statistical transfer mode*. Specifications for the Block as used in this mode are shown in Figure 2.53.

Note that, as shown within the TRANSFER Block itself in Figure 2.53, *the first character in the A Operand is a decimal point*. This means that, in the punchcard image of the Block, a decimal must be entered in card column 19.

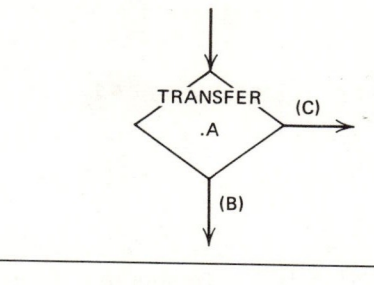

Operand	Significance	Default Value or Result
A	Fraction of the time that entering Transactions will transfer to the "C Block"	Error
B	A Block Location ("B Block")	Sequential Block
C	Another Block Location ("C Block")	Error

FIGURE 2.53   The TRANSFER Block in Statistical Transfer Mode

The rest of the A Operand is then interpreted as the fraction of the time that Transactions entering the TRANSFER Block are to randomly move next to the Block Location specified with the C Operand (i.e., the "C Block"). The rest of the time, Transactions move next to the Block at the Location specified with the B Operand (the "B Block"). Not more than three digits can be used in specifying the A Operand.

As an example, consider Figure 2.54, where the punchcard image of a TRANSFER Block operating in statistical transfer mode is shown. Transactions entering that Block will transfer about 25 percent of the time to the Block at the Location named PLAY (the "C Block"). The rest of the time (about 75 percent), they will transfer to the Block at the Location named WORK (the "B Block"). It is important to realize that each choice of a next Block is independent of the previous choices. For example, it is distinctly possible that five consecutive Transactions entering the Figure 2.54 TRANSFER Block all go to the Block at WORK as their next Block. It is only *in the long run* that about 75 percent of them will go to WORK next.

Figure 2.55 shows the punchcard image of another TRANSFER Block operating in statistical transfer mode. No "B Block" has been specified. In such a case, the "B Block" is understood to be *the sequential model Block*. Transactions entering the Figure 2.55 Block will transfer, then, about 33 percent of the time to the Block at BYPAS. The rest of the time, they will move to the sequential Block, i.e., to the Block whose image would be on the punchcard following that shown in Figure 2.55. In this sense, Transactions entering the Figure 2.51 Block are sometimes said to "fall through" to the sequential Block.

In Figure 2.55, there would be nothing wrong in naming the Location occupied by the sequential Block, then supplying this Location name as the B Operand at the TRANSFER Block itself. The B Operand default option simply spares the analyst the trouble of supplying a Location name in this situation.

In Figure 2.53, note that parentheses have been used around the B and C Operands. These parentheses appear only in the Block Diagram of the model. They are not part of the B and C Operands, and do not appear in the punched-card image of the Block.

In statistical transfer mode, the TRANSFER Block cannot refuse entry to a Transaction. When

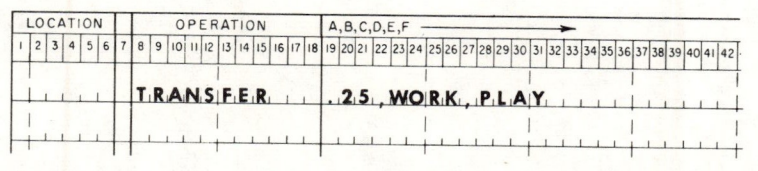

LOCATION	OPERATION	A,B,C,D,E,F ———————————➤
1 2 3 4 5 6 7	8 9 10 11 12 13 14 15 16 17 18	19 20 21 22 23 24 25 26 27 28 29 30 31 32 33 34 35 36 37 38 39 40 41 42
	T R A N S F E R	. 2 5 , W O R K , P L A Y

FIGURE 2.54   A first example for use of the TRANSFER Block in statistical transfer mode

LOCATION	OPERATION	A,B,C,D,E,F
	TRANSFER	.333,,BYPAS

FIGURE 2.55 A second example for use of the TRANSFER Block in statistical transfer mode

a Transaction enters the Block, its choice of next Block is determined once and for all. It then tries to move into that chosen Block. If that Block denies entry, the Transaction is left in the TRANSFER Block and on the Current Events Chain. At each next scan of the Current Events Chain (whether due to a scan restart within the current Scan Phase, or to initiation of the next Scan Phase), another attempt is made to move the Transaction into the previously chosen Block. Eventually, one of these attempts will presumably be successful.

Use of the TRANSFER Block in statistical transfer mode is illustrated in Case Study 2F in the next section.

2.45 CASE STUDY 2F
Inspection Station on a Production Line
(1) Statement of the Problem

Assembled television sets move through a series of testing stations in the final stage of their production. At the last of these stations, the vertical control setting on the sets is tested. If the setting is found to be functioning improperly, the offending set is routed to an adjustment station, where the setting is modified. After adjustment, the television set is sent back to the last inspection station, where the setting is again inspected. Television sets passing the final inspection phase, whether the first time or after one or more routings through the adjustment station, pass on to a packing area.

The situation described is pictured in Figure 2F.1, where circles represent television sets. Open circles are sets waiting for final inspection, whereas crossed-out circle are sets with an improper vertical control setting, and which are either being serviced at the adjustment station, or are waiting for service there.

Television sets arrive at the final inspection station from the previous station every 5.5 ± 2 minutes. Two inspectors work side-by-side at the final inspection station. The time required to inspect a set is 9 ± 3 minutes. About 85 percent of the sets pass inspection and continue on to the packing department. The other 15 percent are routed to the adjustment station, which is manned by a single worker. Adjustment of the vertical control setting requires 30 ± 10 minutes.

Design a GPSS model to simulate the operation of this segment of the production line. Use the model to estimate how much *staging space* must be provided ahead of the inspection station, and ahead of the adjustment station. Staging space is the space occupied by work (in this case, television sets) waiting for service to begin.

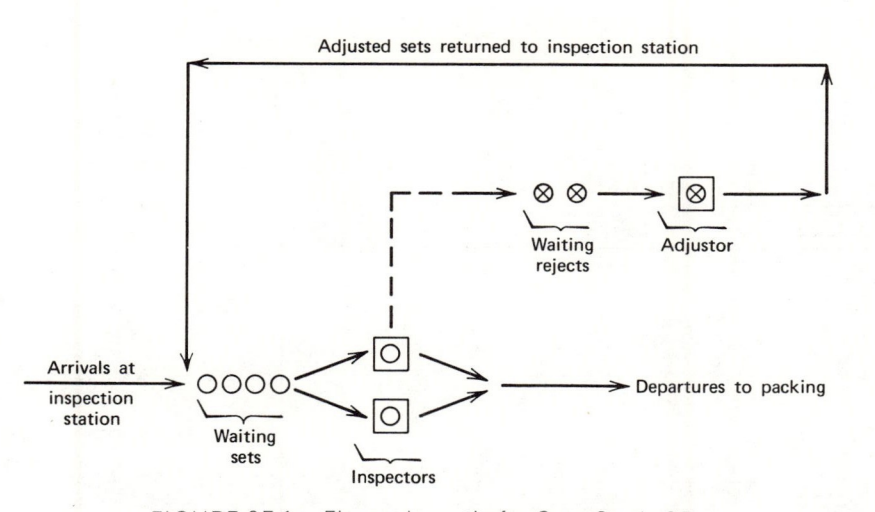

FIGURE 2F.1   Flow schematic for Case Study 2F

(2) Approach Taken in Building the Model

This model is easily constructed as a single sequence of Blocks. Television-set Transactions move through the usual QUEUE—ENTER—DEPART—ADVANCE—LEAVE sequence simulating the inspection station. From the LEAVE, they enter a TRANSFER Block in statistical transfer mode. From here, some 85 percent "fall through" to a TERMINATE Block. The remaining 15 percent take the nonsequential exit to a QUEUE—SEIZE — DEPART — ADVANCE — RELEASE sequence simulating the adjustment station. After the RELEASE, they unconditionally transfer back to the QUEUE Block associated with the inspection station. The MAXIMUM CONTENT statistic for the two Queues can be interpreted directly as the staging space required ahead of the inspection and adjustment stations, respectively.

(3) Table of Definitions

Time Unit: 0.1 Minutes

TABLE 2F.1   Table of Definitions for Case Study 2F

GPSS Entity	Interpretation
Transactions	
Model Segment 1	Television sets
Model Segment 2	A timer
Facilities	
FIXER	Adjustment station worker
Queues	
AREA1	Inspection station waiting line
AREA2	Adjustment station waiting line
Storages	
TEST	Inspection station workers

(4) Block Diagram

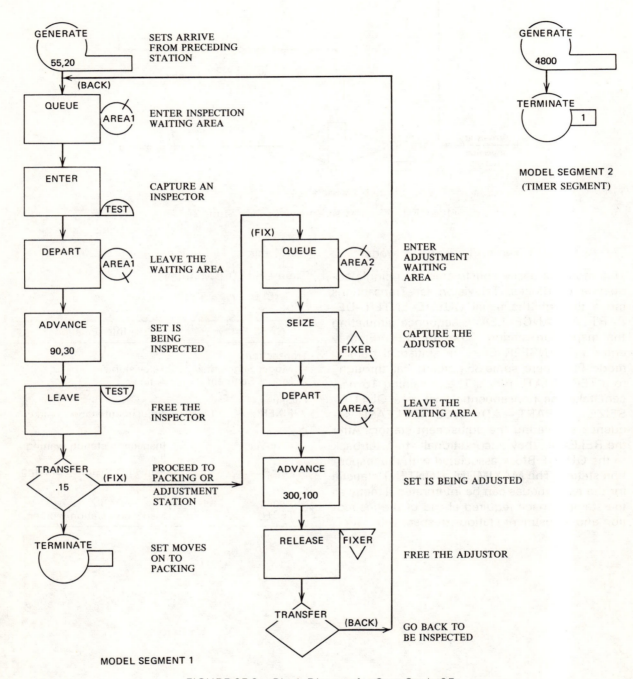

FIGURE 2F.2   Block Diagram for Case Study 2F

(5) Extended Program Listing

```
BLOCK                                                                              CARD
NUMBER  *LOC   OPERATION  A,B,C,D,E,F,G                COMMENTS                     NUMBER
               SIMULATE                                                            1
        *                                                                          2
        *      STORAGE CAPACITY DEFINITION(S)                                      3
        *                                                                          4
               STORAGE    S$TEST,2      TWO WORKERS AT LAST INSPECTION STATION     4
        *                                                                          5
        *      MODEL SEGMENT 1                                                     6
        *                                                                          7
1              GENERATE   55,20         SETS ARRIVE FROM PRECEDING STATION         8
2       BACK   QUEUE      AREA1         ENTER INSPECTION WAITING AREA              9
3              ENTER      TEST          CAPTURE AN INSPECTOR                        10
4              DEPART     AREA1         LEAVE THE WAITING AREA                      11
5              ADVANCE    90,30         SET IS BEING INSPECTED                     12
6              LEAVE      TEST          FREE THE INSPECTOR                         13
7              TRANSFER   .15,,FIX      PROCEED TO PACKING OR ADJUSTMENT STATION   14
8              TERMINATE                SET MOVES ON TO PACKING                    15
9       FIX    QUEUE      AREA2         ENTER ADJUSTMENT WAITING AREA              16
10             SEIZE      FIXER         CAPTURE THE ADJUSTOR                       17
11             DEPART     AREA2         LEAVE THE WAITING AREA                     18
12             ADVANCE    300,100       SET IS BEING ADJUSTED                      19
13             RELEASE    FIXER         FREE THE ADJUSTOR                          20
14             TRANSFER   ,BACK         GO BACK TO BE INSPECTED                    21
        *                                                                          22
        *      MODEL SEGMENT 2                                                     23
        *                                                                          24
15             GENERATE   4800          TIMER ARRIVES AT END OF EACH DAY           25
16             TERMINATE  1             PROVIDE SNAP OUTPUT OR SHUT OFF THE RUN    26
        *                                                                          27
        *      CONTROL CARDS                                                       28
        *                                                                          29
               START      5,,1          START THE RUN                              30
               END                      RETURN CONTROL TO OPERATING SYSTEM         31
                                                                                   32
```

FIGURE 2F.3   Extended Program Listing for Case Study 2F

(6) Program Output

QUEUE	MAXIMUM CONTENTS	AVERAGE CONTENTS	TOTAL ENTRIES	ZERO ENTRIES	PERCENT ZEROS	AVERAGE TIME/TRANS	$AVERAGE TIME/TRANS	TABLE NUMBER	CURRENT CONTENTS
AREA1	3	.580	101	23	22.7	27.594	35.730		2
AREA2	5	2.152	17	2	11.7	607.764	688.799		1

$AVERAGE TIME/TRANS = AVERAGE TIME/TRANS EXCLUDING ZERO ENTRIES

(a)

QUEUE	MAXIMUM CONTENTS	AVERAGE CONTENTS	TOTAL ENTRIES	ZERO ENTRIES	PERCENT ZEROS	AVERAGE TIME/TRANS	$AVERAGE TIME/TRANS	TABLE NUMBER	CURRENT CONTENTS
AREA1	3	.610	198	46	23.2	29.580	38.532		
AREA2	5	1.400	28	5	17.8	480.035	584.391		

$AVERAGE TIME/TRANS = AVERAGE TIME/TRANS EXCLUDING ZERO ENTRIES

(b)

QUEUE	MAXIMUM CONTENTS	AVERAGE CONTENTS	TOTAL ENTRIES	ZERO ENTRIES	PERCENT ZEROS	AVERAGE TIME/TRANS	$AVERAGE TIME/TRANS	TABLE NUMBER	CURRENT CONTENTS
AREA1	3	.560	296	85	28.7	27.253	38.232		1
AREA2	5	1.566	42	6	14.2	537.238	626.777		

$AVERAGE TIME/TRANS = AVERAGE TIME/TRANS EXCLUDING ZERO ENTRIES

(c)

QUEUE	MAXIMUM CONTENTS	AVERAGE CONTENTS	TOTAL ENTRIES	ZERO ENTRIES	PERCENT ZEROS	AVERAGE TIME/TRANS	$AVERAGE TIME/TRANS	TABLE NUMBER	CURRENT CONTENTS
AREA1	3	.586	393	111	28.2	28.664	39.946		
AREA2	5	1.263	53	11	20.7	457.867	577.785		1

$AVERAGE TIME/TRANS = AVERAGE TIME/TRANS EXCLUDING ZERO ENTRIES

(d)

QUEUE	MAXIMUM CONTENTS	AVERAGE CONTENTS	TOTAL ENTRIES	ZERO ENTRIES	PERCENT ZEROS	AVERAGE TIME/TRANS	$AVERAGE TIME/TRANS	TABLE NUMBER	CURRENT CONTENTS
AREA1	3	.546	493	147	29.8	26.618	37.927		
AREA2	5	1.434	70	11	15.7	491.828	583.525		2

$AVERAGE TIME/TRANS = AVERAGE TIME/TRANS EXCLUDING ZERO ENTRIES

(e)

FIGURE 2F.4   Selected Program Output for Case Study 2F. (a) Queue statistics after one day. (b) Queue statistics after two days. (c) Queue statistics after three days. (d) Queue statistics after four days. (e) Queue statistics after five days.

(7) Discussion

Model Implementation.   The model was run for five consecutive 8-hour working days, with aggregate statistics measured from the start of the simulation being printed out at the end of each day. In the Extended Program Listing in Figure 2F.3, note how this effect is accomplished with the timer-Transaction GENERATE Block (Card 26) and the START card (Card 31). Through the A and C Operands on the START card, the Termination Counter and Snap Interval Counter are initialized with values of 5 and 1, respectively. A timer-Transaction enters the model every 480 simulated minutes and immediately terminates, decrementing both of these counters by 1. For the first four timer-Trans-actions, this causes the Processor to (1) print out the standard model statistics, because the Snap Interval Counter has been decremented to zero, (2) restore the Snap Interval Counter's value to 1, and (3) continue the simulation, because the Termination Counter is not yet zero. Finally, when the fifth timer-Transaction enters the model and terminates, the simulation shuts off and the standard printout is produced for the fifth and last time.

Program Output.[31]   Referring to Figure 2F.4(e), the maximum number of television sets in the staging areas ahead of the inspection

---

[31] Total CPU time for the simulation on an IBM 360/67 computer was 4.1 seconds.

station (AREA1 Queue) and adjustment station (AREA2 Queue) did not exceed 3 and 5, respectively, for the five simulated days. These maximum contents had already been realized by the end of day 1 [Figure 2F.4(a)], suggesting that these statistics reached stable values during the simulation. In contrast, note the variation in the values of AVERAGE TIME/TRANS for the Queue AREA2 throughout the simulation.

On day 1, 17.2 percent of the television sets going through inspection were routed to the adjustment station [as shown in Figure 2F.4(a), of 101 TOTAL ENTRIES to the AREA1 Queue, 99 went through inspection and 2 are still in the Queue; of the 99 going through inspection, 17 were sent to the AREA2 Queue]. During the 5 days, Figure 2F.4(e) information reveals that 14.2 percent of the inspections resulted in sets being sent on for adjustment.

2.46 Conditional Transfer of Transactions to One of Two Blocks

When the TRANSFER Block is used in statistical transfer mode, a Transaction's choice of next Block is independent of conditions currently in effect there. If the next Block chosen denies entry, the Transaction simply waits until permission to enter is granted. In an alternative mode, the TRANSFER Block can be used to send a Transaction to *whichever one of two Blocks will first accept it*. When applied this way, the TRANSFER Block is said to be used in BOTH mode. Specifications for this mode are shown in Figure 2.56.

The A Operand is literally the word BOTH.

The B and C Operands are the names of two Block Locations in the model. A Transaction entering the TRANSFER Block in BOTH mode immediately attempts to move into the "B Block" (i.e., the Block at the Location whose name is supplied as the B Operand). If entry is denied, it then attempts to move into the "C Block." If that Block also denies entry, the Transaction is left on the Current Events Chain. From a Block-oriented point of view, the Transaction remains in the TRANSFER Block itself, where it contributes to the Current Count at that Block. At each next scan of the Current Events Chain, the Processor again attempts to move the Transaction into the B Block and, if entry is still denied there, into the C Block. Eventually, then, the Transaction moves into whichever one of the two Blocks will first accept it. Note that the B Block is tested first, then (if necessary) the C Block is tested. When both Blocks are simultaneously willing to accept the Transaction, then, it is the B Block which the Transaction enters.

As an example of BOTH mode use, assume that there are only three chairs in the waiting area of a barber shop. Customers arrive at the shop every 14 ± 5 minutes, but are willing to wait only if there is a chair for them to sit in. Otherwise, they leave and do not return later. Letting the Storage SEATS represent the seating capacity in the shop, Figure 2.57 shows a Block Diagram for a model to simulate the shop's operation. Customers entering the model first check to see if a seat is available in the waiting area. If it is, they stay; otherwise, they leave. Note that, in this example, the TRANSFER Block's "C

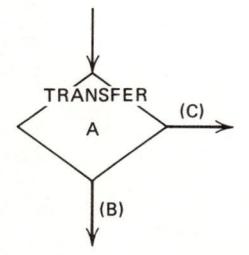

Operand	Significance	Default Value or Result
A	Literally, the word BOTH	Error
B	A Block Location ("B Block")	Sequential Block
C	Another Block Location ("C Block")	Error

FIGURE 2.56   The TRANSFER Block in BOTH Mode

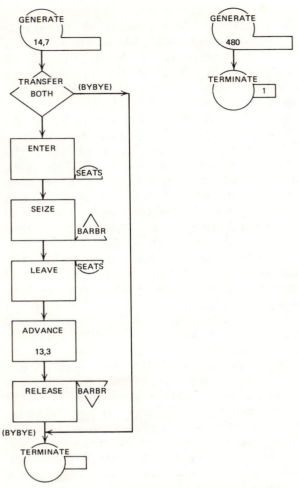

FIGURE 2.57   An example of the TRANSFER Block used in BOTH mode

Block" can never deny entry. Also note that no Location name has been given to the ENTER Block. This is a situation in which it is convenient to default on the TRANSFER Block's B Operand.

2.47 Exercises

1. In exercise 9, Section 2.41, Case Study 2E was to be run for a "four hired, four rented" configuration with resetting after a 10-week simulation, followed by collection of *aggregate* statistics at the end of each week for the next 20 weeks. Show how to do this by taking advantage of the C Operand on the START card, as contrasted with using a series of consecutive START cards in the model.

2. Show the Operands for PRINT Blocks which, when executed, will cause these printouts to occur.
   (a) Current Events Chain
   (b) Future Events Chain
   (c) Information for all the Storages in a model
   (d) Information for Facilities 3 through 7
   (e) Information for Queue 5

3. (a) Show a three-Block segment which has the same effect as the segment in Figure 2.52. Under otherwise identical conditions, which segment do you think would require less computer time, and why?
   (b) The Current Events Chain is to be printed out every 50 simulated time units, beginning at time 50. Show a self-contained Block Diagram segment which will have this effect.
   (c) Repeat (b), only assume that the printouts are to begin at time 25.

4. Critically discuss this statement: "In Case Study 2F, even if it turns out to be true that all of the entries to the Queue AREA1 are zero entries, it would be possible to have that Queue's MAXIMUM CONTENT statistic be 2."

5. In Case Study 2F, the staging space required ahead of the adjustment station depends not only on the *average* service time at the inspection and adjustment stations, but also on the amount of variation possible in this average.
   (a) Rerun the Case Study 2F model so that inspection and adjustment always require exactly 9 and 30 minutes, respectively. What is the most staging space required under these circumstances during a 5-day period?
   (b) Now rerun Case Study 2F under the assumption that inspection time is 9 ± 3 minutes, as before, whereas adjustment of the vertical control setting is now 30 ± 20 minutes. What is the most staging space required under these circumstances during a 5-day period?

6. Show how to modify the model for Case Study 2F so that not more than four television sets can simultaneously wait for service at the adjustment station. A worker at the inspection station cannot begin the next inspection until the preceding unit has been sent on to packing or has been transferred to the staging space ahead of the adjustment station. Run the resulting model and compare the behavior of the inspection station's waiting line with the behavior observed in Case Study 2F.

7. In Case Study 2F, it is unrealistically assumed that, even after it has gone through the adjustment station at least one time, the probability a television set will require further adjustment is still 0.15. Show how to modify the model in that case study under the assumption that after one or more visits to the adjustment station, the probability is only 0.03 that a set will have to be adjusted again.

The remaining exercises in this section all pertain to the

Figure 2.57 model. Except when indicated, the questions are not otherwise related to each other.

8. Assume that the barber is in a state of capture at simulated time 326, and that the Storage SEATS is full at that time. Also assume that these two events have been scheduled to occur simultaneously at time 326.
   (a) The customer who currently has the barber captured will release him.
   (b) The next customer will arrive at the shop.
   Under what conditions will the customer who is just arriving at the shop stay for service? Are there conditions under which this just-arriving customer will not stay for service, but will go BYBYE instead?

9. No explicit Queue is included in Figure 2.57. Show how to include such a Queue to gather statistics on the waiting line which forms ahead of the barber.

10. Discuss the possibility of interpreting the model-produced statistics for the Storage SEATS as applying to the waiting line which forms ahead of the barber. In light of this discussion, what additional information, if any, would be acquired by using an explicit Queue in the model as suggested in exercise 9?

11. Describe how output from the Figure 2.57 model can be used to determine how many customers "left without waiting" during the course of the simulation.

12. Show how to modify the model so there are *two* barbers who work in the shop. Service time for the first barber is still 13 ± 3 minutes. Service time for the second barber is 15 ± 4 minutes. Change the customer interarrival time to 7 ± 3 minutes, but retain the condition that customers who cannot find a chair to sit in immediately leave the shop. (Hint: use two Facilities "in parallel" to simulate the two barbers.)

13. For the conditions described in exercise 12, discuss the possibility of using a Storage with a capacity of 2 to simulate the two barbers.

14. Expand the Figure 2.57 model to include a shoeshine boy. After their haircut is finished, 25 percent of the customers *consider the possibility* of getting a shoeshine. Among them, only 20 percent are *willing to wait* for a shoeshine; if the boy is busy at the time, the others who consider getting a shine do not bother to wait. Shoeshine time is 3.5 ± 0.5 minutes.

15. Describe how output from the model in exercise 14 can be interpreted to determine how many customers considered getting a shoeshine during the simulation, but went without the shine because the boy was busy at the time.

16. Expand the Figure 2.57 model to include the condition that 40 percent of the customers leaving the shop because no chair is available come back after 15 ± 5 minutes to try again. Those who are not successful on the second try do not return.

17. Modify the Figure 2.57 model to introduce this variation on customer behavior. About 20 percent of the customers arriving at the shop remain *only if* the barber is immediately available. The others remain as long as they can at least get a seat in the waiting area.

Sampling from Probability Distributions in GPSS

3.1 Introduction

In Chapter 2, eleven GPSS Blocks were introduced and for one of them, the TRANSFER, three usage modes were described. A variety of models can be built with these eleven Blocks, as the Chapter 2 cases and exercises indicate. In the Chapter 2 models, however, all interarrival and service times were assumed to be uniformly distributed. This assumption made it possible to concentrate on relatively more important aspects of GPSS model building in that chapter. Enough is now known about GPSS, though, so that the next topic of immediate interest is the representation and use of nonuniform distributions in the language.

The analyst must use *Functions* to describe nonuniform distributions. Fortunately, this does not mean the modeling concepts developed in Chapter 2 must be discarded. After modest modification, all models built in that chapter are still valid when nonuniform interarrival and service times are in effect. The modification involves two steps.

1. Functions describing each of the pertinent nonuniform distributions must be defined.
2. At the various GENERATE and ADVANCE Blocks, the A and/or B Operands describing uniform distributions must be replaced with references to the appropriate Functions.

This chapter discusses how these steps are accomplished.

3.2 The GPSS Uniform Random-Number Generators

In general, the "source" of randomness in a simulation model is one or more functions which, when called, return a value drawn at random from a population uniformly distributed over the 0—1 interval. Recall how this was the case in Chapter 1, where a uniform random-number function was introduced and then used to sample from more general uniform populations, as well as from nonuniform distributions (see exercises 2 and 4 in Section 1.6). Drawing a value from a distribution, then, generally involves two steps.

1. First, a value is drawn from the population uniformly distributed on the 0—1 interval.
2. Then, this result is converted, or mapped, into an equivalent value from the population of interest.

143

GPSS also uses values drawn at random from the uniform 0–1 population to sample from non-uniform distributions, as well as from more general uniform populations. There are eight distinct sources of uniform random numbers in GPSS. These random-number sources are a predefined part of the Processor itself. The predefined names of these random-number generators are RN1, RN2, RN3, RN4, RN5, RN6, RN7, and RN8.

Assuming that the GPSS random-number generators are used in unmodified form, each of the eight generators returns an identical sequence of random numbers.[1] This fact is illustrated in Table 3.1, where the values of RN1 through RN8 are shown for the first ten calls on each of the random-number generators.[2] The numbers themselves in Table 3.1 are not of consequence. What is of interest is that entries across any particular row are identical. Hence, the eighth call on RN7 produces the same random value as does, say, the eighth call on RN2. Similarly, the third value returned by RN8 is identical to the third value returned by RN3, and so on.

Suppose the analyst wants to define a Function describing some particular distribution of interest. As part of this process, he must specify which one of the eight GPSS random-number generators is to be used as the starting point (i.e., as the function's *argument*) whenever a sample is drawn from the distribution of interest. Each time the analyst-defined Function is used to sample

from the particular distribution, the Processor first goes to the indicated random-number generator and determines the next value in the corresponding sequence of random numbers. The analyst-defined Function is then used to convert this "uniform random number" into an equivalent random value from the distribution of interest.

The values assumed by RN1 through RN8 are actually *context dependent*. Depending on the context in which a random-number generator is used, the value it returns falls into either one of two ranges.

1. When a random-number generator is used as a Function argument, it returns a six-digit value drawn from the population uniformly distributed on the interval between .000000 and .999999, inclusive. It is in this context that values such as those shown in Table 3.1 are returned by the random-number generators.

2. When a GPSS random-number generator is used in *any other context*, it returns a three-digit integer value drawn from the population uniformly distributed between 000 and 999, inclusive.

Throughout this chapter, and indeed throughout most of this book, the GPSS random-number generators will only be used in the context of Function arguments. In general, however, the fact that the values returned by the generators are context dependent should be kept in mind.

3.3 GPSS Sampling from Uniform Distributions at GENERATE and ADVANCE Blocks

In Chapter 2, it was implied that the GPSS Processor knows how to sample from uniform distributions. Each time a Chapter 2 model was run, it was frequently necessary to sample from uni-

[1] There is an option available whereby the random-number sequences produced by the various generators can be made to differ from one another, and/or can be made to differ from the sequence whose first ten values are shown in Table 3.1. The use of this option is described in Section 3.18.

[2] The entries in Table 3.1 were produced by GPSS/360, Version 1. Exercise 6 of Section 5.7 involves building a GPSS model which will call and display the first 10 values produced by the RN*j*, for *j* taking on values from 1 to 8.

TABLE 3.1   Values Produced by the Eight GPSS Random-Number Generators When the Generators are Used the First Ten Times

Number of the Call	Generator Called							
	RN1	RN2	RN3	RN4	RN5	RN6	RN7	RN8
1	.000573	.000573	.000573	.000573	.000573	.000573	.000573	.000573
2	.510675	.510675	.510675	.510675	.510675	.510675	.510675	.510675
3	.870337	.870337	.870337	.870337	.870337	.870337	.870337	.870337
4	.999177	.999177	.999177	.999177	.999177	.999177	.999177	.999177
5	.778871	.778871	.778871	.778871	.778871	.778871	.778871	.778871
6	.194160	.194160	.194160	.194160	.194160	.194160	.194160	.194160
7	.790719	.790719	.790719	.790719	.790719	.790719	.780719	.790719
8	.014667	.014667	.014667	.014667	.014667	.014667	.014667	.014667
9	.043340	.043340	.043340	.043340	.043340	.043340	.043340	.043340
10	.645420	.645420	.645420	.645420	.645420	.645420	.645420	.645420

form distributions with means and spreads specified by the A and B Operands at GENERATE and ADVANCE Blocks. To draw such samples, the Processor must have access to a source of random numbers uniformly distributed over the 0–1 interval. *The Processor uses RN1 as this source.*[3]

Consider how the Processor uses RN1 to sample from uniform distributions. Figure 3.1 shows the Extended Program Listing for the tool-crib model previously shown in Figure 2C.4. Suppose the Figure 3.1 model is being run. During the Input Phase, the Processor first reads the "GENERATE 420, 360" card. A sample must then be drawn from the 420 ± 360 distribution to schedule the arrival of the first Transaction at this Block. The Processor draws the sample by first calling RN1, with 0.000573 returned as the value, per Table 3.1.[4] This value is then con-

verted to 60.[5] Transaction 1 is fetched from the top of the stack in the latent pool and placed on the Future Events Chain, scheduled to move to Block 1 at time 60. Later in the Input Phase, the Processor reads the "GENERATE 360,240" card. To schedule the first arrival at that Block, RN1 is called and returns a value of 0.510675, per Table 3.1. (Note that this is the Processor's *second* call on RN1.) This value is then converted to 365. Transaction 2 is fetched from the latent pool and placed on the Future Events Chain, scheduled to move to Block 8 at time 365. Finally, at Block 15, the Processor reads the "GENERATE 28800" card. Because the inter-arrival time at this GENERATE Block is deterministic, no random number is required. Without calling RN1, the Processor immediately fetches Transaction 3 from the latent pool and

[3] The Processor also needs a random number each time it executes the TRANSFER Block in statistical transfer mode. It uses RN1 in this context, too.

[4] When RN1 is called, two 32-bit numbers are multiplied to form a 64-bit product. A subset of these 64 binary digits is then used as the next "random number." Consecutive calls on RN1 produce the sequence of random numbers shown in Table 3.1, unless the initial multiplier value is modified with use of the control card discussed in Section 3.18. As it happens, when RN1 is called to support the GENERATE and ADVANCE Block operations explained in Section 3.3, the

subset of the 64-bit product used by the Processor to form the needed random number differs from the subset used when RN1 is called in any other context. This results in values differing from those shown in Table 3.1. For simplicity, however, the Section 3.3 computations assume that the RN1 values in Table 3.1 are those used for the internal operations being described. It is the procedure explained in Section 3.3 which is important, not the numbers.

[5] As explained in Chapter 1, the value drawn from the uniform distribution $A \pm B$ is computed as the integer portion of $A - B + RN1(2B + 1)$. In this case, the value is $420 - 360 + 0.000573(720 + 1)$, or 60.4+. The integer portion is simply 60.

```
BLOCK                                                                                          CARD
NUMBER   *LOC      OPERATION   A,B,C,D,E,F,G                    COMMENTS                        NUMBER
                   SIMULATE                                                                      1
         *                                                                                       2
         *         MODEL SEGMENT 1                                                                3
         *                                                                                        4
1                  GENERATE    420,360,,,1      CATEGORY 1 MECHANICS ARRIVE                       5
2                  QUEUE       LINE             ENTER "CATEGORY 1 SEGMENT" OF LINE                6
3                  SEIZE       CLERK            CAPTURE THE CLERK                                  7
4                  DEPART      LINE             LEAVE THE LINE                                     8
5                  ADVANCE     300,90           USE THE CLERK                                      9
6                  RELEASE     CLERK            FREE THE CLERK                                     10
7                  TERMINATE                    LEAVE THE TOOL CRIB AREA                          11
         *                                                                                       12
         *         MODEL SEGMENT 2                                                               13
         *                                                                                       14
8                  GENERATE    360,240,,,2      CATEGORY 2 MECHANICS ARRIVE                       15
9                  QUEUE       LINE             ENTER "CATEGORY 2 SEGMENT" OF LINE                16
10                 SEIZE       CLERK            CAPTURE THE CLERK                                 17
11                 DEPART      LINE             LEAVE THE LINE                                    18
12                 ADVANCE     100,30           USE THE CLERK                                     19
13                 RELEASE     CLERK            FREE THE CLERK                                     20
14                 TERMINATE                    LEAVE THE TOOL CRIB AREA                          21
         *                                                                                       22
         *         MODEL SEGMENT 3                                                               23
         *                                                                                       24
15                 GENERATE    28800            TIMER ARRIVES AFTER 8 HOURS                      25
16                 TERMINATE   1                SHUT OFF THE RUN                                  26
         *                                                                                       27
         *         CONTROL CARDS                                                                 28
         *                                                                                       29
                   START       1                START THE RUN                                    30
                   END                          RETURN CONTROL TO OPERATING SYSTEM              31
```

FIGURE 3.1   Repetition of Figure 2C.4

places it on the Future Events Chain in proper fashion.

Then, with the Input Phase complete, the first Clock Update Phase begins. The clock is advanced to 60, and Transaction 1 is moved to the Current Events Chain. The scan of the CEC begins, and Transaction 1 is moved to and from its GENERATE Block. In scheduling the next arrival at that GENERATE Block, the Processor again calls RN1, with 0.870337 returned as the value. (This is the *third* call on RN1 so far.) This value is then converted to 687. Transaction 4 is fetched from the latent pool and placed on the Future Events Chain accordingly. The movement of Transaction 1 is resumed, and it enters the AD-VANCE Block (Block 5). Sampling from the 300 ± 90 distribution is consequently required. The Processor calls RN1, which returns a value of 0.999177. (This is the *fourth* call on RN1.) This value is then converted to 390. The 390 is added to a copy of the clock reading (60), producing 450. Transaction 1 is then removed from the Current Events Chain and placed on the Future Events Chain, scheduled to move to Block 6 at time 450. And so on.

Two conclusions are to be drawn from the steps traced out above.

1. A single random-number source is being referenced from multiple points in a model. In the example, RN1 is being used at two GENERATE Blocks, and at two ADVANCE Blocks. Each Block uses only a subset of the values drawn from the random-number generator. The subset used depends on the chronological order in which the various Block subroutines are executed as Transactions move into those Blocks.

2. Suppose the analyst specifies RN1 as the source of random numbers for sampling from some distribution he defines. In doing so, he may be *sharing* RN1 with the Processor. This will be true if the Processor is forced to do its own sampling from uniform distributions at one or more GENERATE and/or ADVANCE Blocks, or if it requires random numbers for the TRANSFER Block used in statistical transfer mode.

3.4 The GPSS Method for Sampling from Discrete, Nonuniform Distributions

The analyst usually wants the Processor to sample from nonuniform distributions to determine interarrival times, and service times. Some scheme must then be followed to convert a draw from the uniform 0–1 population into a draw from the nonuniform distribution of interest. The scheme followed to sample from *discrete* distributions will now be described.

A random variable is said to be *discrete* when it can take on only a finite number of different values. For example, when a die is tossed, the random variable defined as the number of points turned up can take on only the values, 1, 2, 3, 4, 5, or 6. Or, if a paycheck is known to be more than $75 but less than $80, the random variable defined as the amount of the paycheck can take on only the values 75.01, 75.02, 75.03, . . ., 79.98, and 79.99. In the first example, the random variable is discrete and integer-valued. In the second example, the random variable is also discrete, even though it is not integer-valued.

When the GPSS Processor samples from discrete distributions, it draws a random number from a uniform 0–1 source, then uses this value to perform a *table-lookup on the cumulative distribution* for the population of interest. Assume, for example, that a random variable can take on the values 2, 5, 8, 9, and 12, with corresponding relative frequencies of 0.15, 0.20, 0.25, 0.22, and 0.18. This information is shown in Table 3.2, where the values of the random variable and their relative frequencies appear in the first and second columns, respectively. The third column shows the corresponding cumulative distribution, which spans the range of values from 0 to 1. The interval within the 0–1 range corresponding to each value of the random variable is shown in column 4. For example, for a random variable value of 2, the range of cumulative values from 0.0, up to and including 0.15, is spanned. This is

TABLE 3.2   An Example of a Discrete, Integer-Valued Random Variable

Value of Random Variable	Relative Frequency	Cumulative Frequency	Portion of 0–1 Range Spanned	Interval
2	0.15	0.15	0.0 to 0.15	1
5	0.20	0.35	0.15+, to 0.35	2
8	0.25	0.60	0.35+, to 0.60	3
9	0.22	0.82	0.60+, to 0.82	4
12	0.18	1.00	0.82+, to 1.0	5

designated as Interval 1 in column 5. For a random-variable value of 5, the applicable cumulative values range from anything greater than 0.15 (that is, 0.15+) up to and including 0.35. This range is designated as Interval 2 in column 5. And so on.

Now suppose that a sample is to be drawn from the Table 3.2 distribution. First, a value is drawn from a uniform 0–1 source. Assume that the value is 0.523664. Then, by table-lookup, it is established that 0.523664 falls into Interval 3. The indicated value assumed by the random variable is consequently the third value or, in this case, 8 (third entry, column 1).

Given appropriate information about a distribution, the GPSS Processor automatically performs the table-lookup procedure when a sample must be drawn from the distribution. The information the Processor must have includes (1) the source of uniform 0–1 random numbers, (2) the values which the random variable can assume, and (3) their cumulative frequency of occurrence. The analyst supplies this information by defining a *discrete GPSS Function*. Definition of discrete GPSS Functions is described in the next section.

3.5 Defining Discrete GPSS Functions

The user must supply this information to define a discrete GPSS Function[6]:

1. A *name* must be given to the Function. The naming convention used for Facilities, Queues, and Storages also applies to Functions. Names can be numeric or symbolic. When numeric, they must be positive, whole numbers. When symbolic, names are composed of from three to five alphanumeric characters, with the restriction that the first three be alphabetic. Examples of valid and invalid names are shown in Table 3.3.

2. The Function's *argument* must be specified. The argument names the source of random numbers to be used in sampling from the distribution described by the Function. The argument will consequently be RN*j*, where *j* is 1, 2, 3, 4, 5, 6, 7, or 8. The choice of the particular random-number source is up to the user.

3. The *number of different values* that can be assumed by the discretely distributed random variable must be specified.

4. The values themselves, and their corresponding cumulative frequencies, must be provided.

TABLE 3.3   Examples of Valid and Invalid Names for Functions

Valid	Invalid
JOE	−5
7	HI
JOE23	MP2LO
SWICH	8BETA

The first three pieces of the above-indicated information are supplied on a single punchcard, which is called a *Function header card*. The format for this card is shown in Table 3.4. The Function's name is entered in the Location field, and the word FUNCTION is punched in the Operation field. The A Operand indicates the source of 0–1 random numbers to be used in evaluating the Function. The B Operand consists of the character D (for discrete), and an integer indicating how many different values the random variable can assume.

Then, the random-variable values, and their corresponding cumulative frequencies, are provided on one or more subsequent punchcards, termed *Function follower cards*. The format used for these cards is shown in Figure 3.2.[7] The "basic unit" of information on a Function follower card is X_i, Y_i, where X_i is the *i*th cumulative

[6]The normal quantities of Functions which the user can define at the 64, 128, and 256K levels are 20, 50, and 200, respectively, as indicated in Appendix F.

[7]An alternative format for the X_i, Y_i pairs is to punch them in consecutive six-column fields. When this approach is followed, no "commas" or "slashes" are used. The "comma–slash" procedure is convenient, however, and is the only one followed in this book.

TABLE 3.4   Format for the Function Header Card

Punchcard Field	Information Supplied in Field
Location	Name (numeric or symbolic) of the Function
Operation	Literally, the word FUNCTION
Operands	
A	RN*j*, where *j* = 1, 2, 3, 4, 5, 6, 7, or 8
B	D*n*, where *n* is the number of different values the random variable can assume

Card Columns	Information Entered
1 forward, but not beyond 71	$X_1, Y_1 / X_2, Y_2 / X_3, Y_3 / \ldots / X_i, Y_i / \ldots / X_n, Y_n$ where X_i and Y_i are the ith cumulative probability and the associated random-variable value, respectively, and $$X_1 < X_2 < X_3 < \ldots < X_i < \ldots < X_n$$

FIGURE 3.2   Format for Function Follower Cards

probability value, and Y_i is the corresponding value of the random variable. The first and second entries in each "basic unit" are separated by a comma. Consecutive basic units are separated by a slash. The basic units must be *ordered* so that the cumulative frequencies form a strictly ascending sequence. Basic units must be punched in consecutive card columns, beginning in column 1 and not extending beyond column 71. If necessary or convenient, two or more Function follower cards can be used. During the Input Phase, the first blank column encountered on a Function follower card causes the Processor to ignore the rest of the card. If a pair has not yet been found for each random-variable value, it is expected that additional pairs will be found on the next card, starting in column 1. Any basic unit begun on a card must be completed on that same card. The examples which follow will help clarify additional questions about formatting these cards.

A GPSS Function for sampling from the distribution described in Table 3.2 is shown in Figure 3.3. The Function has been symbolically named KATHY. RN4 has been chosen as the source of uniform 0–1 random numbers. The random variable can take on five different values. The cumulative frequencies, and the corresponding five random-variable values, are entered as five matched pairs on the next card. The cumulative values are in ascending order.

FIGURE 3.3   Example of a Function for sampling from the Table 3.2 distribution

When presenting pairs of points describing a distribution, it is optional whether decimal points are punched when the data are whole numbers. For example, the first pair in Figure 3.3 could have been punched as ".15,2.". Or, the last pair

could have been punched as "1.,12", or as "1.,12.".

The number of pairs placed on each card is optional, as long as the pairs do not extend beyond card column 71. Figure 3.4 shows an alternative way in which the Figure 3.3 example could be punched. It is usually convenient, of course, to put as many pairs as possible on each card.

FIGURE 3.4   An alternative way to define the Figure 3.3 Function

Note that the *last* pair on a card is not followed by a slash, nor is the first pair on the next card preceded by a slash. The slash is required only to separate consecutive pairs entered on the same card.

Figure 3.5 provides a graphical interpretation for the Function defined in Figure 3.3 (or in Figure 3.4). The Function consists of a series of horizontal steps. The filled-in circles at the right of each step mark the locations of the Function-defining ordered pairs of points. Each step terminates at the right in one of these circles, with the corresponding argument value being *included* in the step. For example, the first step covers values up to and including 0.15. The second step then begins with values of 0.15 + (i.e., 0.150001), and continues for values up to and including 0.35. And so on. In summary, the interior steps in Figure 3.5 are "closed" on the right, but "open" on the left.

The leftmost and rightmost steps in Figure 3.5 differ somewhat from the interior steps. Instead of being "open" on the left, the leftmost step is "closed" on the left. That is, an RN4 value of 0.000000 is included in the step. And, strictly

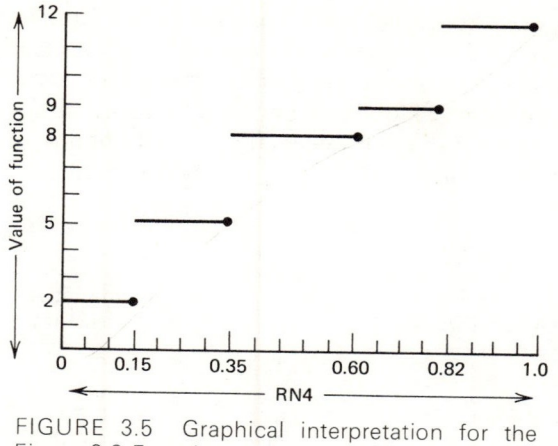

FIGURE 3.5 Graphical interpretation for the Figure 3.3 Function

speaking, instead of being "closed" on the right, the rightmost step is "open" on the right. This is because RN4 cannot assume a value of 1.0. The rightmost step then ranges from .82 + to 1.0 −, that is, from 0.820001 to 0.999999, inclusive.

The fact that the steps in discrete GPSS Functions are closed on the right means that, strictly speaking, the distribution described by the Function KATHY differs very slightly from the Table 3.2 distribution it is supposed to describe. The slight discrepancy arises with respect to the leftmost and the rightmost steps in the Function. For example, consider the leftmost step in Figure 3.5. A value of 2 results for the Function whenever the value of RN4 is anywhere between .000000 and .150000, inclusive. RN4 values in this range occur 15.0001 percent of the time, in the long run. The Table 3.2 information indicates that a value of 2 should result 15 percent of the time. With respect to the value 2, then, there is a slight inaccuracy in the Function, on the order of one part in 150,000. There is a similar inaccuracy in the rightmost step in the Function. However, no such inaccuracy is in effect for the interior steps. (The reader should establish the validity of these last two statements.)

How could the small inaccuracy in the Function KATHY be eliminated? One way would be to use these ordered pairs of points to define the Function: ".149999,2/.349999,5/.599999,8/ .819999,9/1,12". It would be troublesome to punch the Function follower card, however, and the benefit to be gained would hardly be worth the effort. A second possibility would be to have the steps in a discrete Function *closed* on the left, and *open* on the right. A simple change in the Processor would bring this about, but it

would not be feasible for most users to make such a change. A third possibility would be to modify the random-number generators, so that they return values on the closed interval from .000001 to 1.00000. Again, it would not be feasible for most users to make such a change. In practice, the majority of users simply live with the slight inaccuracy which has been described. Such is the case in this book. Compared to the other inaccuracies inherent in non-deterministic simulation, it is highly unlikely that the inaccuracy in question is of much importance.

Finally, consider how the GPSS Processor performs the table lookup when it evaluates a discrete Function. It uses the Function-defining ordered pairs of points in left-to-right fashion in doing the lookup. That is, the Processor tests whether the Function's argument is less than or equal to X_i, for $i = 1, 2, 3, \ldots$, where X_i is the first member of the ith Function-defining ordered pair (see Figure 3.2). As soon as the test is true, the Function returns Y_i as its value. Now the test will be true sooner, on average, if the analyst designs the Function so that X_1, X_2, X_3, and so on, are each as large as possible. (This statement assumes that the Function's argument is a random-number generator. In Chapter 4 and beyond, Function arguments other than random-number generators will be introduced and used.) This, in turn, means that computer time will be saved. In this sense, the Function KATHY in Figure 3.3 is somewhat inefficient. The Function was defined directly from the information in Table 3.2 and that information, in turn, is ordered according to increasing values of the random variable. If the information were reordered according to *decreasing* values of *relative* frequency, and the Function were then correspondingly defined, some efficiency in computer time would result. If this were done, the Function follower card for KATHY would be ".25,8/.47,9/ .67,5/.85,12/1,2". In this book, discrete Functions are not defined in this relatively efficient fashion; instead, as is true for the Function KATHY in Figure 3.3, they are usually set up so that the second members of the Function-defining ordered pairs form a strictly ascending sequence.

3.6 Using Discrete Functions at GENERATE and ADVANCE Blocks

Suppose that the distribution of interarrival times at a particular GENERATE Block in a model is nonuniform. The analyst arranges for Transaction arrivals at that GENERATE Block by taking these two steps.

1. He defines a Function describing the applicable interarrival-time distribution.

2. He uses the Function as the A Operand at the GENERATE Block and uses zero, either explicitly or by default, as the B Operand.

Then, when model conditions call for computing the next interarrival time at that GENERATE Block, the Processor determines the value of the A Operand by evaluating the indicated Function. *That value is then used directly as the next interarrival time.* This is just as though the analyst were specifying a uniform distribution at the GENERATE Block, with a *mean* equal to the value returned by the Function, and a *spread of zero* around that mean. With the spread of zero, the Function's value is used "deterministically" as the interarrival time. But because the Function's value is itself determined on a random basis, the effective interarrival times are also randomly distributed. The distribution they follow is, of course, the one defined by the Function.

The way a Function is referenced via a Block Operand depends on whether the Function's name is numeric or symbolic. When the name is *numeric*, the Function is referenced as FNj, where j is the number of the Function. When the name is *symbolic*, the Function is referenced as FN$sn, where sn is the Function's symbolic name. For example, Function 16 would be referenced as FN16. On the other hand, the Function symbolically named KATHY would be referenced as FN$KATHY. Note that a $ (dollar sign) is interposed between FN and the symbolic name itself.

An example of Function use at a GENERATE Block will now be given. Suppose that Table 3.5 shows the time between consecutive arrivals of orders at a distribution center. A Transaction is to be used to represent an order, and a GENERATE Block is to be used to arrange for arrival of these orders. First, the information in Table 3.5

is used to construct a corresponding Function. Table 3.5 is repeated and extended in Table 3.6, where cumulative frequency values are shown in column 3. Figure 3.6 shows a Function defined from the Table 3.6 information. The Function has been named TBO, for "time between orders."

TABLE 3.6   The Cumulative Distribution for the Table 3.5 Random Variable

Time Between Orders (hours)	Relative Frequency	Cumulative Frequency
2	0.10	0.10
3	0.30	0.40
4	0.40	0.80
5	0.20	1.0

LOCATION	OPERATION	A,B,C,D,E,F
TBO	FUNCTION	RN7,D4
1,2/.4,3/.8,4/1,5		

FIGURE 3.6   A Function for sampling from the Table 3.6 distribution

The seventh random-number generator has been chosen, arbitrarily, as the Function's argument. Figure 3.7 shows the GENERATE Block through which Transactions representing orders come into the model. The Function TBO has been used as the A Operand. The default has been taken on the B Operand. The interarrival-time distribution followed at the Block, then, is the one in Table 3.5.

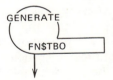

FIGURE 3.7   Use of the Figure 3.6 Function at a GENERATE Block

The procedure just described for Function use at GENERATE Blocks is equally valid for Function use at ADVANCE Blocks. For example, assume the service time at a work station in a production system follows the distribution shown in columns 1 and 2 in Table 3.7. The corresponding cumulative distribution appears in column 3 of the table. Figure 3.8 shows a Function defined from the Table 3.7 information. The Function has been named STYME, for "service time." Figure 3.9 shows the ADVANCE Block at which Transactions representing demands for service at the work station are delayed in the model, simulating the time that elapses while service is performed.

TABLE 3.5   An Example of a Discretely Distributed Interarrival-Time Random Variable

Time Between Orders (Hours)	Relative Frequency
2	0.10
3	0.30
4	0.40
5	0.20

TABLE 3.7   An Example of a Discretely Distributed Service-Time Random Variable

Service Time, Minutes	Relative Frequency	Cumulative Frequency
5	.05	.05
6	.12	.17
7	.28	.45
8	.30	.75
9	.18	.93
10	.07	1.0

LOCATION	OPERATION	A,B,C,D,E,F ──────────►
1 2 3 4 5 6 7	8 9 10 11 12 13 14 15 16 17 18	19 20 21 22 23 24 25 26 27 28 29 30 31 32 33 34 35 36
S T Y M E	F U N C T I O N	R N 3 , D 6
.05,5/	.17,6/	.45,7/ .75,8/ .93,9/ 1,10

FIGURE 3.8   A Function for sampling from the Table 3.7 distribution

Whenever a Transaction moves into the ADVANCE Block, the Function STYME is evaluated. A value is drawn from RN3, a table-lookup is performed with information given in the Function definition, and a particular value for the Function is determined. This value is then used, "plus or minus zero," as the holding time at the ADVANCE Block.

```
        │
        ▼
┌─────────────┐
│  ADVANCE    │
│             │
│  FN$STYME   │
└─────────────┘
        │
        ▼
```

FIGURE 3.9   Use of the Figure 3.8 Function at an ADVANCE Block

When Functions are used at GENERATE Blocks, the Function definitions must be placed *ahead of the GENERATE Block images* in the card deck. The reason for this is straightforward. During the Input Phase, when the Processor encounters the image of a GENERATE Block, it immediately samples from the indicated inter-arrival-time distribution while scheduling the first Transaction arrival at the Block. If the cards defining a referenced Function have not yet appeared in the deck, an error condition is assumed to be in effect. *This is the case even though the definition appears later in the deck.* As a consequence, the practice in this book is to place *all* Function definitions ahead of the first Block image. This is not necessary, strictly speaking, for Functions used at ADVANCE Blocks. Those Functions will not be needed by the Processor until sometime after the Input Phase has been completed. By that time, the Function definitions will have been encountered, as long as they appear somewhere before the START card.

3.7 CASE STUDY 3A
A Second Tour Through Case Study 2D

(1) Statement of the Problem

Case Study 2D involves a system to manufacture widgets. Assemblers working in the system move repeatedly through this cycle.

1. Assemble next widget.
2. Wait, first-come, first-served, to use the oven.
3. Use the oven.
4. Return to 1.

In Case Study 2D, the times required to assemble a widget, and use the oven, are uniformly distributed over the interval 30 ± 5 and 8 ± 2 minutes, respectively. Suppose now that, instead of being uniformly distributed, "assembly time" and "oven-use time" follow the distributions shown in Tables 3A.1 and 3A.2, respectively. These distributions have (arbitrarily) been chosen to be *symmetric*, and are centered about 30 and 8, respectively. As a result, the average assembly and oven-use times are identical to those in Case Study 2D. It is evident upon inspection, how-

TABLE 3A.1   The Distribution of Assembly Times in Case Study 3A

Assembly Time (minutes)	25	26	27	28	29	30	31	32	33	34	35
Relative Frequency	.01	.03	.05	.10	.18	.26	.18	.10	.05	.03	.01

TABLE 3A.2   The Distribution of Oven-Use Times in Case Study 3A

Oven-Use Time (minutes)	6	7	8	9	10
Relative Frequency	.05	.25	.40	.25	.05

ever, that the standard deviation of the distributions in Tables 3A.1 and 3A.2 is less than for the previously used uniform distributions.

Modify the model in Case Study 2D to take the changes in the time-distributions into account. Then use the model to simulate for a 40-hour work week, assuming there are no discontinuities within a working day, or in moving between consecutive 8-hour work days. Do this for the cases of four, five, and six assemblers. Compare and contrast the corresponding system behavior, and the number of assemblers for whom the simulated week's profit is a maximum, with the results found in Case Study 2D.

(2) Approach Taken in Building the Model

The inherent logic of the model does not differ from that in Case Study 2D. The required modi- fication of the 2D model only involves defining Functions for the distributions in Tables 3A.1 and and 3A.2, and replacing the "ADVANCE 30,5" and "ADVANCE 8,2" Block Operands with A Operands referencing the corresponding Functions, and B Operands of zero (either explicitly, or by default). Table 3A.3 repeats the information appearing in Tables 3A.1 and 3A.2 and shows the cumulative probabilities for the distributions. Figure 3A.1 shows the images of the punch-cards with which these distributions are defined through the Functions symbolically named AS-SEM and FIRE, respectively. When the Figure 3A.1 punchcards have been placed in the Case Study 2D deck, and "ADVANCE 30,5" and "ADVANCE 8,2" have been replaced with "ADVANCE FN$ASSEM" and "ADVANCE FN$FIRE", respectively, the modifications are complete.

TABLE 3A.3   Cumulative Probabilities for Assembly Time and Oven-Use Time in Case Study 3A

(a) Assembly Time			(b) Oven-Use Time		
Assembly Time (minutes)	Relative Frequency	Cumulative Frequency	Oven-Use Time (minutes)	Relative Frequency	Cumulative Frequency
25	.01	.01	6	.05	.05
26	.03	.04	7	.25	.30
27	.05	.09	8	.40	.70
28	.10	.19	9	.25	.95
29	.18	.37	10	.05	1.0
30	.26	.63			
31	.18	.81			
32	.10	.91			
33	.05	.96			
34	.03	.99			
35	.01	1.0			

FIGURE 3A.1   Function definitions for the Table 3A.1 and 3A.2 distributions

(3) Table of Definitions

Time Unit : 1 minute

TABLE 3A.4 Table of Definitions for Case Study 3A

GPSS Entity	Interpretation
Transactions	
Model Segment 1	Assemblers
Model Segment 2	The timer
Facilities	
OVEN	The oven
Functions	
ASSEM	Assembly-time distribution
FIRE	Oven-use-time distribution

(4) Block Diagram

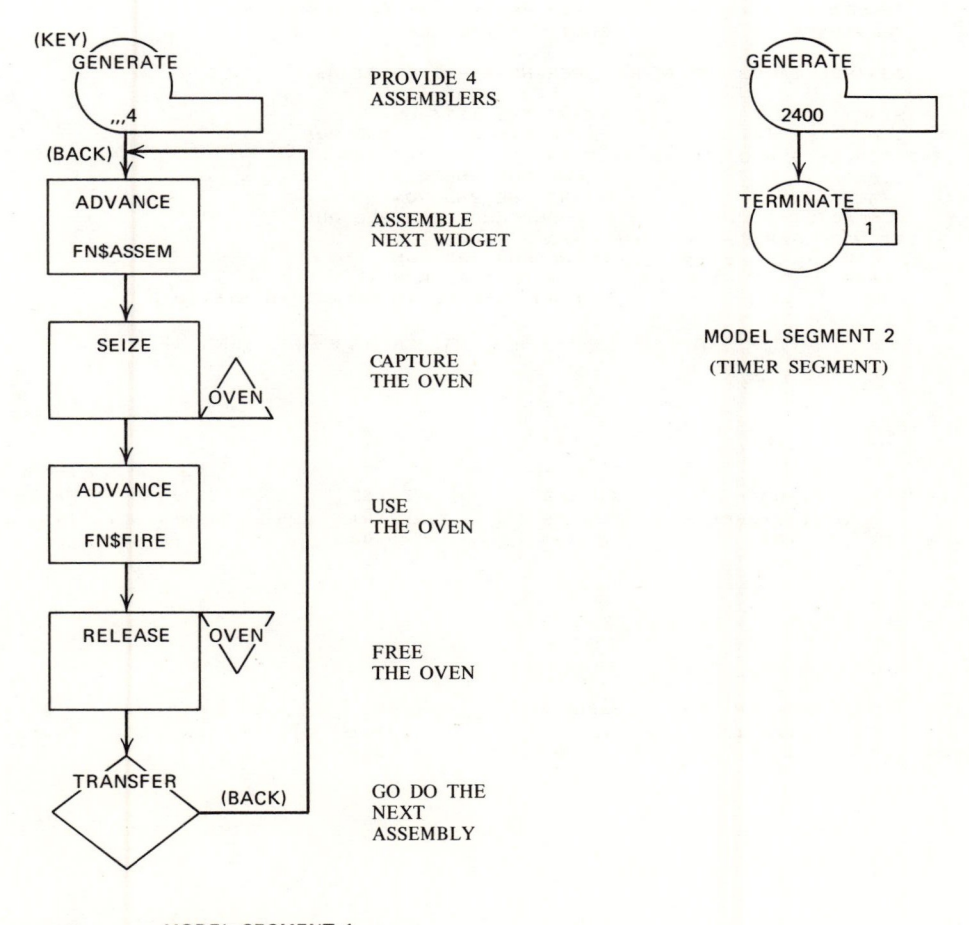

MODEL SEGMENT 1

FIGURE 3A.2   Block Diagram for Case Study 3A

(5) Extended Program Listing

```
BLOCK                                                                          CARD
NUMBER  *LOC    OPERATION  A,B,C,D,E,F,G              COMMENTS               NUMBER
                SIMULATE                                                        1
        *                                                                       2
        *       FUNCTION DEFINITION(S)                                          3
        *                                                                       4
         ASSEM  FUNCTION   RN1,D11       ASSEMBLY-TIME DISTRIBUTION             5
        .01,25/.04,26/.09,27/.19,28/.37,29/.63,30                               6
        .81,31/.91,32/.96,33/.99,34/1,35                                        7
         FIRE   FUNCTION   RN1,D5        FIRING-TIME DISTRIBUTION               8
        .05,6/.3,7/.7,8/.95,9/1,10                                             9
        *                                                                      10
        *       MODEL SEGMENT 1                                                11
        *                                                                      12
1        KEY    GENERATE   ,,,4          PROVIDE 4 ASSEMBLERS                  13
2        BACK   ADVANCE    FN$ASSEM      ASSEMBLE NEXT WIDGET                  14
3               SEIZE      OVEN          CAPTURE THE OVEN                      15
4               ADVANCE    FN$FIRE       USE THE OVEN                          16
5               RELEASE    OVEN          FREE THE OVEN                         17
6               TRANSFER   ,BACK         GO DO THE NEXT ASSEMBLY               18
        *                                                                      19
        *       MODEL SEGMENT 2                                                20
        *                                                                      21
7               GENERATE   2400          TIMER ARRIVES AFTER 5 DAYS            22
8               TERMINATE  1             SHUT OFF THE RUN                      23
        *                                                                      24
        *       CONTROL CARDS AND BLOCK OPERAND RE-DEFINITIONS                 25
        *                                                                      26
                START      1             START THE 1ST RUN                     27
1        KEY    GENERATE   ,,,5          RE-CONFIGURE FOR 2ND RUN              28
MULTIPLE DEFINITION OF SYMBOL IN ABOVE CARD
                CLEAR                    CLEAR FOR 2ND RUN                     29
                START      1             START THE 2ND RUN                     30
1        KEY    GENERATE   ,,,6          RE-CONFIGURE FOR 3RD RUN              31
MULTIPLE DEFINITION OF SYMBOL IN ABOVE CARD
                CLEAR                    CLEAR FOR 3RD RUN                     32
                START      1             START THE 3RD RUN                     33
                END                      RETURN CONTROL TO OPERATING SYSTEM    34
```

FIGURE 3A.3   Extended Program Listing for Case Study 3A

(6) Program Output

FACILITY	AVERAGE UTILIZATION	NUMBER ENTRIES	AVERAGE TIME/TRAN	SEIZING TRANS. NO.	PREEMPTING TRANS. NO.
OVEN	.812	243	8.028	4	

(a)

FACILITY	AVERAGE UTILIZATION	NUMBER ENTRIES	AVERAGE TIME/TRAN	SEIZING TRANS. NO.	PREEMPTING TRANS. NO.
OVEN	.959	291	7.914	6	

(b)

FACILITY	AVERAGE UTILIZATION	NUMBER ENTRIES	AVERAGE TIME/TRAN	SEIZING TRANS. NO.	PREEMPTING TRANS. NO.
OVEN	.988	297	7.989	6	

(c)

FIGURE 3A.4   Selected Program Output for Case Study 3A. (a) Oven statistics when four assemblers are used. (b) Oven statistics when five assemblers are used. (c) Oven statistics when six assemblers are used.

(7) Discussion

Model Implementation. As shown in Figure 3A.3, the three alternative assemblers-hired configurations were studied in a single computer run.

Program Output.[8] The oven statistics in Figure 3A.4 show that 242, 290, and 296 widgets were finished during the 40-hour week for the cases of four, five, and six assemblers, respectively. (This finished widget count excludes the widget still in the oven at the end of the simulation.) The 242, 290, and 296 figures can be compared to corresponding values of 235, 279, and 294, respectively, in Case Study 2D (Figure 2D.3). The somewhat higher rate of production resulting from the changed distributions is to be expected. The smaller standard deviations associated with assembly and oven-use times lead to relatively better synchronization between the assembly and firing steps. If there were *no* variation in these times, the system could be made to perform in perfectly synchronized fashion. For example, assume for the moment that assembly and oven-use time are exactly 30 and 8 minutes, respectively. With four assemblers, it is then possible to synchronize oven use so that all waiting is entirely eliminated. After an assembler finishes with the oven, it will be another 30 minutes before he wants it again. Meantime, the other three assemblers can each use the oven for 8 minutes, meaning it will be available when the first assembler again needs it. Under such ideal circumstances, an assembler can produce about 12.6 widgets per day [480/(30 + 8) = 12.6 +]. Four assemblers can produce about 252 widgets in a 40-hour work week. Because of randomness in the system, then, about 10 to 20 fewer widgets are produced with four assemblers each week than would be the case in a system in which all randomness had been eliminated.

Despite the changes in the time distributions, the optimal number of assemblers is still five. Return-after-costs for four, five, and six assemblers is $210, $300, and $180, respectively. The return-after-costs for five assemblers in Case Study 2D was $245. Hence, the change in time distributions has resulted in more than a 20 percent increase in profit.

[8]Total CPU time for the simulation on an IBM 360/67 computer was 4.0 seconds.

3.8 Exercises

1. (a) What are the names of the eight uniform random-number generators in GPSS?

   (b) In which three different contexts may the GPSS Processor require a source of uniform random numbers for its own purposes? Which of the eight random-number generators does the Processor use on such occasions?

   (c) Describe how the GPSS Processor samples from uniform distributions specified by using A and B Operands at GENERATE and ADVANCE Blocks.

   (d) When the Processor samples from the uniform distribution $A \pm B$, the sample value is taken to be *the integer portion* of $A - B + RN1(2B + 1)$. Why is only the integer portion used, instead of the entire value?

   (e) What is a discrete random variable? Give several examples.

   (f) Critically discuss the statement, "A discrete random variable can only assume integer values."

   (g) Describe how the GPSS Processor samples from discrete, nonuniform distributions.

   (h) What range of values can the RNj take on when used as Function arguments? What is the smallest value possible? The largest value?

   (i) What ordering property is imposed on the first members of pairs of points used in defining Functions to sample from probability distributions?

   (j) Construct a graphical interpretation of the Function defined in Figure 3.6.

   (k) Why must the definition of a Function appear in the card deck before the card image of a GENERATE Block which references that Function?

   (l) Show a GENERATE Block at which Function 3 is used as the A Operand. Default on the B Operand.

   (m) Show a GENERATE Block at which the Function SYMBL is used as the A Operand. Default on the B Operand.

   (n) Show an ADVANCE Block at which the Function JOE23 is used as the A Operand. Default on the B Operand.

   (o) For the ADVANCE Block "ADVANCE FN$CPU", why is the value returned by the Function CPU used without modification as the holding time?

   (p) When the Function TBO in Figure 3.6 is called the *first* time, what value will it return? Assume that the random-number sequence shown in Table 3.1 is in effect. What other assumption must be made before an unconditional answer can be given to the question?

   (q) When the Function STYME in Figure 3.8 is

called the *sixth* time, what value will it return? Assume that the random-number sequence shown in Table 3.1 is in effect. Is your answer conditioned on another assumption as well?

(r) How many calls are made on random-number generators when the Block "GENERATE FN$TBO,2" is executed one time? Which random-number generators are involved? (Assume that the Function TBO is the one defined in Figure 3.6.)

2. Define a discrete GPSS Function which can be used to sample from the population whose values are −3, 0, 5, 9, and 14, with probabilities 0.1, 0.05, 0.15, 0.30, and 0.40, respectively. The Function should be given the symbolic name DRAW, and should use RN7 as its argument. Could this Function meaningfully describe an interarrival-time distribution, or a service-time distribution? Why or why not?

3. The time between consecutive arrivals of ships at a harbor follows the distribution shown in Table E3.

TABLE E3

Interarrival Time (hours)	Relative Frequency
2	.06
3	.09
4	.17
5	.28
6	.24
7	.16

(a) Assuming that the implicit time unit in a GPSS model is 1 hour, define a Function named SHIPS for sampling from this distribution. Then show how the Function can be used at a GENERATE Block through which Transactions representing these ships enter a model. What source of random numbers did you specify as the Function's argument? Assuming that the sequence of random numbers in Table 3.1 is in effect, what value will your Function return the first time it is called? What value would it return on the first call if you had used one of the other sources of random numbers?

(b) Show how to redefine the Function in (a) if the implicit time unit is changed from 1 hour to 1 minute.

4. The time required to repair a failed machine is distributed as shown in Table E4.

(a) Assuming the implicit time unit in a model is 1 minute, define a Function, numbered 6, for sampling from this distribution. Then show how the Function can be used at an ADVANCE Block where Transactions representing machines are held to simulate repair time. What source of random numbers did you specify as the Function's argument?

TABLE E4

Repair Time (minutes)	Relative Frequency
10	.15
20	.20
30	.30
40	.25
50	.10

(b) Can your Function in (a) ever take on values such as 12, 15, 23, 37, and so on? If not, this means that repair times of 12, 15, 23, and 37 minutes, etc., can never occur in a model using the Function. Discuss the implications of this in terms of the extent to which such a model simulates reality.

5. Exercise 4 of Section 2.35 describes a machine shop where a single machine is used to polish castings. For convenience, the steps required to polish a casting are repeated below, where the times required are indicated, *in minutes*, after each step.

1. Fetch raw casting from a storage area (12 ± 3).
2. Load raw casting on the polishing machine (10 ± 4).
3. Carry out polishing phase 1 (80 ± 20).
4. Reposition the casting on the machine for additional polishing (15 ± 7).
5. Carry out polishing phase 2 (110 ± 30).
6. Unload the finished casting from the machine (10 ± 4).
7. Store the finished casting (12 ± 3), then return to Step (1).

(a) Suppose that instead of being uniformly distributed across the closed interval of integers from 9 to 15, the time required to fetch a raw casting from the storage area follows the distribution shown in Table E5.

TABLE E5

Time (minutes)	Relative Frequency
9	.06
10	.14
11	.27
12	.25
13	.16
14	.09
15	.03

(i) Compute the average fetch time for the distribution in Table E5, and compare it with the average value of 12 previously in effect.

(ii) Compute the standard deviation for the distribution in Table E5, and compare it with the standard deviation for the population uniformly distributed over the interval of integers 12 ± 3.

(iii) Define a discrete GPSS Function named FETCH which can be used to sample from the Table E5 distribution.

(iv) Show a graphical interpretation for the Function FETCH.

(b) Referring to Step (2), note that the time required to load a raw casting on the polishing machine is 10 ± 4 minutes. Replace this uniform distribution with any nonuniform distribution of your own choosing, retaining the restriction that loading time ranges over the integers from 6 to 14. After you have done this, carry out the assignments in (i) through (iv) of part (a) for your distribution.

(c) Now prepare a model for exercise 4 of Section 2.35, in which fetch time and load time follow the distributions in (a) and (b), respectively, whereas the distributions for Steps (3) through (7) are still uniform as previously indicated. Run the model under the conditions described in exercise 4 of Section 2.35. Has the change in the Step (1) and (2) distributions produced a noticeable change in the time the machine operator spends waiting for the overhead crane? If so, can you explain the difference in terms of the changed Step (1) and (2) distributions?

3.9 Random Variable Values: Integer vs. Noninteger

The two random variables of primary interest so far have been interarrival time and service time. Only *integer* time values are used in GPSS models, because the GPSS clock is of integer mode. When a value is drawn from a distribution of time values, then, it must eventually be treated as an integer.

Recall, for example, how the Processor samples from uniform distributions described via A and B Operands at GENERATE and ADVANCE Blocks. It uses RN1 to compute the value of the sample, then it *discards the fractional part*. Only the integer portion is retained as the result. No rounding occurs. The Processor *follows this same pro-*

cedure when using Functions to determine interarrival times and service times.

In all the Function examples used so far, the random variables have been described as assuming only integer values. This need not be the case. Consider Figure 3.10, which shows a Function that can take on noninteger values. This Function could be the A Operand at one or more GENERATE and/or ADVANCE Blocks. It is important, though, to realize what range of values will be *used* at such Blocks if this is done. In general, the values used will differ from the values taken on by the Function because only the integer portion is meaningful in GPSS as a time value.

Suppose the Figure 3.10 Function is used at the GENERATE Block shown in Figure 3.11. Table 3.8 shows the values the Function can assume, and their corresponding relative frequencies. For each assumed value, the value which will be used at the Figure 3.11 GENERATE Block is also entered in the table, in column 3. Examination of columns 2 and 3 in Table 3.8 shows that an interarrival time of 1 results 22 percent of the time, 2 occurs 24 percent of the time, 4 occurs 21 percent of the time, and 5 occurs 33 percent of the time.

As shown in Table 3.8, the fact that only the integer portion of Function values is used in a time context means that the *effective* interarrival- and service-time distributions can vary widely from those which the Functions describe. This deviation may be unacceptable. For example, if the Figure 3.10 Function describes an actual interarrival-time distribution, measured in hours, then the effective interarrival time distribution is a poor approximation to it. This problem can be remedied, of course, by *changing the implicit time unit in the model*, and *redefining the Function accordingly*. In the case of Figure 3.10, the implicit time unit could be changed from 1 hour to 0.1 hours. Then the Function MIXED could be redefined, with the second number of each ordered pair made larger by a factor of 10. The redefined Function would then take on values

FIGURE 3.10   A discrete GPSS Function which can return noninteger values

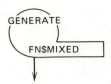

FIGURE 3.11   Use of the Figure 3.10 Function at a GENERATE Block

which could be used directly as interarrival times. There would be no need for the Processor to first discard a fractional portion.

3.10 Continuous Random Variables Viewed Discretely

In Section 3.4, it is pointed out that *discrete* random variables, by definition, take on a finite number of different values. In contrast, *continuous* random variables can take on an *infinite* number of different values. For example, the time between consecutive arrivals of customers at a ticket window can take on an infinity of values, *if one is willing to measure time with arbitrarily fine precision*. Suppose arrivals at a ticket window always occur within 15 minutes of each other. Table 3.9 shows how many different values the interarrival-time random variable can assume, depending on the precision with which time is measured. As the time unit used becomes arbitrarily small, the number of different values becomes arbitrarily large, tending toward infinity.

Strictly speaking, then, interarrival time is a continuous random variable. So is service time. So far, however, these two random variables have been treated in this book as though they are discrete, taking on a finite number of values. In fact, for our purposes, *all* random variables only take on a finite number of values *of interest*. Beyond some degree of precision, it is no longer meaningful to measure the values these random variables assume. The greatest precision required

is that which makes it possible to capture realism in a model.

It is possible, then, to sample from continuous distributions by discretizing them. After they have been discretized, they can be represented in GPSS by defining discrete Functions for them.

As an example, suppose that a particular inter-arrival time is uniformly and continuously distributed over the interval from 2 minutes, *inclusive*, to 6 minutes, *exclusive*. Measured to six digits, this means interarrival times such as 4.12274, 2.00783, and 3.57392 can be realized in practice. Because the interval is assumed to include 2 but exclude 6, the smallest and largest possible values are 2.00000 and 5.99999, respectively. If the implicit time unit in a model is 1 minute, and if *only the integer portion* of the actual six-digit interarrival time is used, then values of 2, 3, 4, and 5 will occur with equal likelihood. Table 3.10 shows the relative and cumulative frequencies for these possible values. Figure 3.12 shows a corresponding GPSS Function for the discretized random variable. The Function is named IAT, for "interarrival time." It might be noted, incidentally, that the uniform distribution of integers between 2 and 5, inclusive, *cannot* be represented by direct use of the A and B Operands at a GENERATE Block. The list "2, 3, 4, 5" contains an *even* number of entries, whereas there is always an *odd* number of entries in the list of integers described by "$A \pm B$," Where A and B are themselves integers.

3.11 Defining Continuous GPSS Functions

It is suggested in Section 3.10 that the values of continuous random variables can be discretized and used in that form in GPSS. The steps involved were easy to perform for the Table 3.10 example, but this is not always the case. In fact, it would be extremely impractical to discretize certain important random variables. For this

TABLE 3.8   Interarrival-Time Values Used at the Figure 3.11 GENERATE Block

Function Value	Relative Frequency	Corresponding Value Used	Relative Frequency of Used Values
1	.07	1 }	.22
1.9	.15	1 }	
2.6	.24	2	.24
4.3	.21	4	.21
5	.19	5 }	.33
5.6	.14	5 }	

TABLE 3.9   The Number of Different Values a Random Variable Can Assume, as a Function of the Precision with which the Values Are Measured

Time Unit Used (minutes)	Number of Different Values Between 0 (Inclusive) and 15 (Exclusive)
1.0	15
.1	150
.01	1500
.001	15000
.0001	150000
.	.
.	.
.	.

TABLE 3.10   Discretized Version of a Continuous Random Variable

Interarrival Time (minutes)	Relative Frequency	Cumulative Frequency
2	0.25	0.25
3	0.25	0.50
4	0.25	0.75
5	0.25	1.00

reason, the capability of defining *continuous Functions* is available in GPSS.

The *computational* difference between discrete and continuous GPSS Functions will now be described. Then the *definitional* difference will be indicated. Finally, several examples of elementary GPSS continuous Functions will be given.

LOCATION	OPERATION	A,B,C,D,E,F
IAT	FUNCTION	RN2,D4
.25,2/.5,3/.75,4/1,5		

FIGURE 3.12   A discrete Function corresponding to the Table 3.10 information

A continuous GPSS Function is initially evaluated in the same way as a discrete Function. When the Function is called, a number is first drawn from the random-number stream used as the Function's argument. Then, a table-lookup is performed to determine the cumulative probability interval in which the random number falls. At this point, if the Function were defined to be discrete, the second member of the corresponding pair of points would then be returned as the Function's value. In contrast, when the Function

is defined as continuous, a *linear interpolation* is performed next between the pairs of points at the ends of the cumulative probability interval. The number resulting from the interpolation is then returned as the Function's value.

From the graphical point of view, then, a discrete GPSS Function consists of a series of horizontal steps, as has been shown in Figure 3.5; a continuous GPSS Function, on the other hand, consists of a series of straight line segments connecting the pairs of points defining the Function.

A continuous GPSS Function is *defined* by using C (for "continuous"), rather than D (for "discrete"), as the first character in the B Operand on the Function header card. With this one exception, discrete and continuous GPSS Functions are defined exactly the same way.

Due to the linear interpolation feature of continuous GPSS Functions, all values *in a given cumulative-frequency interval* have an *equally likely* chance of occurring. This makes it extremely easy to sample from a continuous, *uniform* distribution in GPSS. As an example, suppose that a particular random variable is uniformly and continuously distributed over the interval from 2 to 6 −. Values of 2 are included in the interval, but values of 6 are excluded. The probability that the random variable's value is less than 2 is zero. The probability it is less than 6 is 1.0. These two cumulative probability values are used to define the continuous GPSS Function shown in Figure 3.13. A graphical interpretation of the Figure 3.13 Function is given in Figure 3.14. Note how the graph consists of a straight line connecting the two pairs of points, "0,2" and "1,6". When the Function is called, a value of RN2 is fetched, and the value is mapped into a corresponding Function value via linear interpolation. For example, if the value of RN2 is 0.650000, the value of the Function is 4.60000. This mapping of 0.65 into 4.6 is suggested graphically in Figure 3.14. When the value of RN2 is as small as possible (0.000000), the Function's value is 2. When the value of RN2 is

LOCATION	OPERATION	A,B,C,D,E,F
GOOD	FUNCTION	RN2,C2
0,2/1,6		

FIGURE 3.13   A continuous, two-point Function for sampling from a continuous, uniformly distributed population

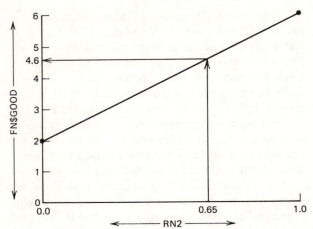

FIGURE 3.14 A graphical interpretation of the Function in Figure 3.13

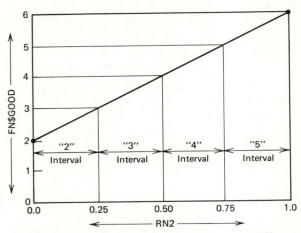

FIGURE 3.16 A graph showing the probability intervals corresponding to interarrival times of 2, 3, 4, and 5 at the Figure 3.15 GENERATE Block

as large as possible (0.999999), the Function's value is 5.99999, measured to six digits.

Now assume that the Figure 3.13 Function is used as the A Operand at a GENERATE Block, as suggested in Figure 3.15. Although the Function takes on values uniformly distributed between 2

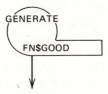

FIGURE 3.15 Use of the Figure 3.13 Function at a GENERATE Block

and 6 −, only the integer portion is used as an interarrival time. *The effective interarrival times will consequently be uniformly distributed over the integers between 2 and 5, inclusive.* The reason for this is illustrated in Figure 3.16, where the graph in Figure 3.14 has been repeated. In Figure 3.16, the various cumulative probability intervals leading to effective interarrival times of 2, 3, 4, and 5, have been marked off. The corresponding ranges of RN2 values which result in Function values with 2, 3, 4, and 5 as their integer portions are listed in Table 3.11. For example, RN2 values from 0.0 up to, but not including, 0.25 (that is, 0.25 −), lead to Function values from 2 up to, but not including, 3. The integer portion is consequently 2. This occurs 25 percent of the time, in the long run. Similarly, Function values with integer portions of 3, 4, and 5 occur about 25 percent of the time, in the long run.

It bears repeating that, although the second

pair of points used in the Function definition is "1,6", the Function can *never* return 6 as its value. RN2 is never larger than 0.999999. With this RN2 value, the returned Function value is 5.99999, measured to six digits. The largest possible integer portion of the returned value is then 5.

TABLE 3.11 A Table Listing the Precise End Points for the Various RN2 Ranges Shown Graphically in Figure 3.16

Integer Portion of Figure 3.16 Function Value	Corresponding Range of RN2 Values
2	0.0 to 0.25⁻
3	0.25 to 0.50⁻
4	0.50 to 0.75⁻
5	0.75 to 1.0⁻

The example above demonstrates how a continuous, two-point GPSS Function can be used at GENERATE and/or ADVANCE Blocks to sample from what is effectively a uniform population of integers. The utility of using this approach is not evident in the preceding example. For a better example, suppose that interarrival times are uniformly distributed between 200 and 375 seconds, *inclusive*. Figure 3.17 shows a continuous, two-point GPSS Function to sample from this population. (Note that the second member of the second pair of points is 376, not 375.) Imagine defining a *discrete* GPSS Function to accomplish this same task. A total of 176 cumulative frequencies would have to be computed, and 176 pairs of points would have to be supplied to define the Function. Furthermore, the

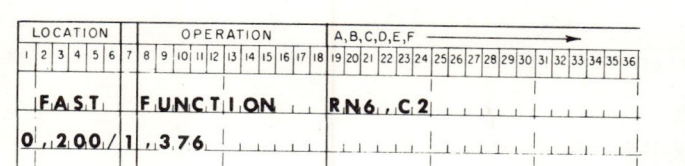

FIGURE 3.17   A continuous Function for sampling from a uniformly distributed population of integers

execution time required to do a table-lookup with the 176-point discrete Function would be much greater than that to perform a simple linear interpolation between two pairs of points. The technique demonstrated in Figure 3.17 will be appealed to later, when it will be of interest to *force the Processor to use a random-number generator other than RN1* to sample from a uniform population of integers.

3.12 Interpreting Observed Data with Continuous GPSS Functions

When a system is to be modeled, the distribution of various pertinent interarrival times and service times is usually not known initially. If the system already exists, it is possible to set up experiments to collect data with which these distributions can be estimated. These data must then be incorporated into the corresponding model of the system. This can be done by using the data to define Functions which can then be referenced from various Blocks in the model.

For example, assume that as part of a bank study, the time required for a teller to serve a customer is measured and classified within 15-second intervals.[9] The results are shown in Table 3.12. The first table entry indicates that no customer is served in fewer than 15 seconds. The second table entry indicates that 7 percent of the

[9]This example is offered without attempting to indicate why the data might have been measured in the manner described.

time, service time is 15 seconds or more, but less than 30 seconds. (The interval "from 15 to 30⁻ seconds" is understood to include 15, but exclude 30.) And so on, until finally the last table entry indicates that 8 percent of the time, service time is 75 seconds or more, but less than 90 seconds. Now suppose that these data are to be used in a model in which the implicit time unit is to be 1 second, and service times are to be represented to the nearest second. In the absence of other information, it is convenient to assume that within any of the indicated 15-second intervals, the various possible service times occur with equal likelihood. This means that the Table 3.12 data can be used to define a continuous GPSS Function representing the service-time distribution.

The definition of a continuous GPSS Function corresponding to the Table 3.12 data is shown in Figure 3.18. The first pair of points in the Function is "0.0,15", indicating the probability is zero that the service time will be less than 15 seconds. The second pair of points indicates the probability is 0.07 that the service time is less than 30 seconds. Consider the validity of this last statement. When the value of the Function's argument, RN2, is .070000 or less, the Processor interpolates linearly between service times of 15 and 30 to determine the Function's value. Of course, if RN2 equals .070000 exactly, the Function's value is 30. When the value of RN2 is .069999 or less, the linear interpolation between the first two ordered pairs in Figure 3.18 results in a Function value which is less than 30, but is greater than or equal to 15. RN2 values of .069999 or less occur 7 percent of the time, which is consistent with the Table 3.12 data. Furthermore, because all RN2 values on the closed interval from .000000 to .069999 have equally likely chances of occurring, it follows that all service times between 15 (inclusive) and 30 (exclusive) have an equal chance of being the

TABLE 3.12   A Summary of Observed Service-Time Data for a Bank Teller

Service-Time Interval	Relative Frequency with which Service Time Falls in the Interval	Cumulative Frequency
Less than 15 seconds	0.0	0.0
From 15 to 30⁻ seconds	0.07	0.07
From 30 to 45⁻ seconds	0.25	0.32
From 45 to 60⁻ seconds	0.41	0.73
From 60 to 75⁻ seconds	0.19	0.92
From 75 to 90⁻ seconds	0.08	1.0

LOCATION	OPERATION	A,B,C,D,E,F ———————————————————————▶
1 2 3 4 5 6	7 8 9 10 11 12 13 14 15 16 17 18	19 20 21 22 23 24 25 26 27 28 29 30 31 32 33 34 35 36 37 38 39 40 41 42 43 44 45 46 47 48
S E R V E	F U N C T I O N	R N 2 , C 6
0 . 0 , 1 5 /	. 0 7 , 3 0 / . . 3 2 ,	4 5 / . . 7 3 , 6 0 / . . 9 2 , . 7 5 / 1 . 0 , 9 0

FIGURE 3.18   A continuous GPSS Function constructed from the Table 3.12 data

Function's value, *given that* RN2 is .069999 or less. Similar remarks are true for the service time intervals from 30 to 45⁻ seconds, 45 to 60⁻ seconds, 60 to 75⁻ seconds, and 75 to 90⁻ seconds. Hence, the probability that the Function's value falls within any given interval agrees exactly with the Table 3.2 data, and the various values within a given interval are uniformly distributed. This overall situation is summarized in Figure 3.19, which shows a graphical interpretation of the Figure 3.18 Function.

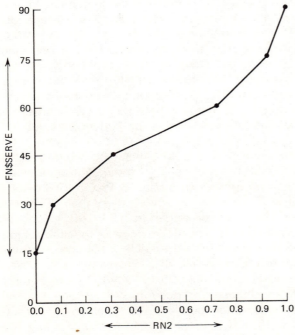

FIGURE 3.19   Graphical interpretation of the Figure 3.18 Function

The Figure 3.19 graph can be thought of as a series of straight-line segments which are being used to approximate the true, but unknown, function describing the bank teller's service-time distribution. Figure 3.20 repeats Figure 3.19, but includes a continuous curve intended to suggest what the true distribution function *might* be. The fact that the consecutive straight line segments

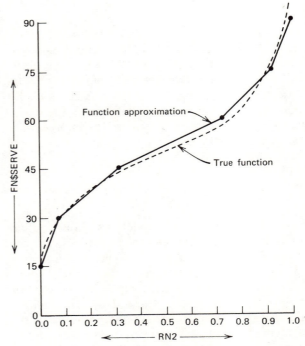

FIGURE 3.20   Graphical indication of the manner in which the Figure 3.19 Function may approximate the true (but unknown) service-time distribution

only approximate the true underlying distribution is evident in the Figure.

In this book, interarrival-time and service-time distributions will frequently be described by supplying information intended to summarize observed data, in the spirit of the preceding example. Whenever this is done, only the *random-variable values* and their corresponding *cumulative frequencies* will be stated. For example, the information in Table 3.12 would be provided as shown in Table 3.13. Whenever such information is given, the following is to be understood.

1. The random variable is continuously distributed.
2. The distribution is to be described with a continuous GPSS Function.
3. The resulting GPSS Function is an approximation to the true underlying cumulative distribution,

whatever that might be. Because of the GPSS linear interpolation feature, the true distribution is being represented with a sequence of straight-line segments.

TABLE 3.13 A Condensed Version of the Information in Table 3.12

Value of Random Variable	Cumulative Frequency
Less than 15	0.0
30	0.07
45	0.32
60	0.73
75	0.92
90	1.0

3.13 Simulation of Poisson Arrivals

When interarrival times are experimentally observed, it is sometimes found that the following conditions are satisfied.

1. The probability that an arrival occurs during a small time interval is proportional to the size of the interval.
2. The probability of two or more arrivals during a small time interval is negligibly small.
3. The interarrival times are independent of each other.

Under these conditions, analytic results can be developed which describe the distribution of the arrival *rate*. The distribution is shown in equation (3.1).

$$P_k(T) = \frac{e^{-\lambda T}(\lambda T)^k}{k!}, \quad k = 0, 1, 2, 3, \ldots \quad (3.1)$$

where $P_k(T)$ is the probability that exactly k arrivals will occur during a time interval of duration T, λ is the mean arrival rate per unit time, and e is the base of the natural logarithms. The distribution described by equation (3.1) is named after Poisson, the French mathematician credited with its development. When a "Poisson arrival process" is in effect, the arrival rates are Poisson-distributed, i.e., the rate distribution is described by equation (3.1). Similarly, the three conditions listed above and leading to the Poisson distribution are termed the "Poisson assumptions."

When a Poisson arrival process is to be simulated, it is not arrival *rates* which are of direct interest; instead, it is the corresponding *interarrival times* which must be known. This is consistent with computing the time of the next Transaction's arrival at a GENERATE Block by adding to a copy of the clock's current reading a

value drawn from an interarrival-time distribution. Equation (3.1) can be manipulated to produce the associated distribution of interarrival times.[10] The result is called the *exponential* distribution. When arrival rates are Poisson-distributed, then, the corresponding interarrival times are exponentially distributed.

The exponential distribution can be put into such a form that, given a value from a 0—1 uniform distribution, the corresponding interarrival time can be directly computed. The pertinent equation is shown as equation (3.2),

$$\text{IAT}_{\text{sample}} = (\text{IAT}_{\text{avg}})\,[\,-\log_e(1 - \text{RN}j)\,] \quad (3.2)$$

where $\text{IAT}_{\text{sample}}$ stands for the sampled interarrival-time value; IAT_{avg} is the average interarrival time in effect; $\text{RN}j$ is the name of one of the GPSS uniform random-number generators, where the choice of j, as usual, is up to the analyst; and $\log_e$ represents the natural logarithm operation. To draw a sample from the exponential distribution whose average value is IAT_{avg}, then, equation (3.2) indicates that this sequence be followed: draw a value from a 0—1 uniform distribution; compute the natural logarithm of 1 minus this random number; finally, multiply the negative of this natural logarithm by IAT_{avg}. Recalling that the values of $\text{RN}j$ range over the closed interval from .000000 to .999999, note that $\log_e(1 - \text{RN}j)$ is either 0 (for an $\text{RN}j$ value of .000000), or negative (for $\text{RN}j$ values greater than .000000). The quantity $-\log_e(1 - \text{RN}j)$ is consequently non-negative; and, because IAT_{avg} must be non-negative as well, the value of $\text{IAT}_{\text{sample}}$ computed from equation (3.2) is also non-negative.

Making use of equation (3.2) to simulate Poisson arrivals at a GENERATE Block involves two steps. First, given a value of $\text{RN}j$, $-\log_e(1 - \text{RN}j)$ must be computed. Then, this result must be multiplied by IAT_{avg}. The first step is accomplished by defining a GPSS Function having $\text{RN}j$ as its argument, and returning $-\log_e(1 - \text{RN}j)$ as its value. In algebraic programming languages such as FORTRAN, BASIC, and PL/I,

---

[10]Starting with the three Poisson assumptions, many introductory textbooks in the postcalculus probability show how to develop equation (3.1). Using the calculus, it is then an easy matter to develop equation (3.2) from equation (3.1). Furthermore, many introductory textbooks in precalculus probability show how to develop equation (3.1), using the binomial distribution as a starting point, and appealing to a limiting process. For these reasons, it seems unnecessary to repeat these developments here.

for example, a logarithm function is provided as part of the language. Given a value of RNj, the value of $-\log_e (1 - \text{RN}j)$ can be directly computed in such a language. *There is no logarithm function in GPSS*. As a result, the distribution represented by $-\log_e (1 - \text{RN}j)$ must be *approximated* with a continuous GPSS Function constructed by fitting a series of straight-line segments to the true function. An approximation suitable for this purpose has been developed by IBM. The approximation consists of a series of 23 line segments which span the range of exponential random-variable values from 0 to 8.[11] Figure 3.21 shows the true behavior of $-\log_e (1 - \text{RN}j)$, as RNj varies from 0 to 1. The 23 line segments used to approximate this true behavior are not shown in the figure, because for all practical purposes they fall directly on the true

[11] The approximation can be found in any of IBM's GPSS User Manuals or Introductory Users Manuals, as well as in Figure 3.22.

curve. Figure 3.22 shows the definition of the continuous GPSS Function composed of the 24 pairs of points used to convert values of RNj into values of $-\log_e (1 - \text{RN}j)$. The Function in Figure 3.22 has been symbolically named XPDIS, for "exponential distribution." RN1 has been arbitrarily chosen as the Function's argument.

It is pertinent to consider the degree of similarity between the Figure 3.22 Function and its theoretical counterpart. In theory, the values of $-\log_e [1 - \text{RN1}]$ can range from 0 (for an RN1 value of .000000) to infinity (for RN1 values arbitrarily close to 1.0). In practice, because the largest value of RN1 is .999999, the largest value which can be computed for $-\log_e [1 - \text{RN1}]$ is 13.8155 ($-\log_e [.000001] = 13.8155$). The Figure 3.22 Function does not even provide for this possibility, including as its last ordered pair ".9998,8". When the value of RN1 exceeds .9998, then, the Figure 3.22 Function will return a value of 8, whereas the value could be as large as 13.8155 (in practice), and could be even larger than that (in theory). However, RN1 will take on values larger than .9998 only about .0199 percent of the time. In view of the many other approximations inherent in simulation modeling, this low-frequency departure of the Figure 3.22 Function from its theoretical counterpart is acceptable in most cases.

Given that the values of FN$XPDIS are a satisfactory approximation of $-\log_e(1 - \text{RN1})$, these values must now somehow be *multiplied* by IAT$_{avg}$ so that, per equation (3.2), the interarrival times corresponding to a Poisson arrival process can be computed. A special provision is made in GPSS at the GENERATE Block to perform this multiplication automatically. When the GENERATE Block B Operand is FNj (or FN$sn), interarrival time is computed at the Block by *multiplying the value of the Function numbered j (or symbolically named sn) by the A Operand*. The integer portion of the product is

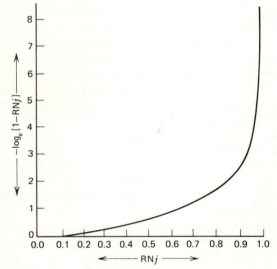

FIGURE 3.21   Graphical interpretation of the function used to sample from the exponential distribution with an expected value of 1

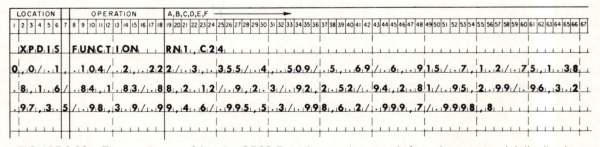

FIGURE 3.22   The continuous, 24-point GPSS Function used to sample from the exponential distribution with an expected value of 1

then used as an interarrival time. This means that a Poisson arrival process can be simulated at a GENERATE Block by doing these two things.

1. For the A Operand, use the average interarrival time.

2. For the B Operand, use FN$XPDIS, where the Function XPDIS is defined in Figure 3.22.

Suppose, for example, that at a certain point in a system arrivals occur in a Poisson stream (i.e., according to a Poisson arrival process) at an average *rate* of four arrivals every 24 hours. These arrivals are to be simulated in a model, using 1 minute as the implicit time unit. A GENERATE Block accomplishing this effect is shown in Figure 3.23. The A Operand, 360, has been determined by (1) converting the given arrival *rate* to the corresponding average interarrival time, and (2) expressing the average interarrival time in terms of the indicated implicit time unit. Hence, when four arrivals occur every 24 hours, the average time between consecutive arrivals is 6 hours, or 360 minutes. When a Transaction arrives at the Figure 3.23 GENERATE Block and moves to the next Block, the Processor will compute its successor's time of arrival by evaluating FN$XPDIS, multiplying the result by 360, and then adding the integer portion of the product to a copy of the current clock value. To evaluate the Function XPDIS, the value of RN1 must first be determined. If RN1 is, say, 0.35, then FN$XPDIS is 0.432 (halfway between .355 and .509; see the fourth and fifth pairs of points in Figure 3.22). The product of 360 and 0.432 is 155.52. The corresponding interarrival time, then, is 155.

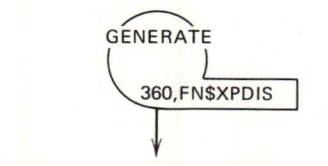

FIGURE 3.23   Example of a GENERATE Block used to simulate a Poisson arrival process

The preceding example shows that, when a Function is referenced as a GENERATE Block's B Operand, the Function's value is used as a multiplier of the A Operand. This is the first context encountered so far in which a Function's entire value, rather than just the integer portion, is used in a GPSS computation.

When a Function is used as a GENERATE Block's B Operand, the average interarrival time (A Operand) is said to be *Function-modified*. In contrast, when the B Operand is *anything other than* a Function reference, the average interarrival time is said to be *spread-modified*. Spread-modified interarrival times are always understood to be uniformly distributed over the interval of integers $A \pm B$ (i.e., the A Operand plus or minus the B Operand). Function-modified interarrival times are always understood to be the integer portion of the product of A and B (i.e., the A Operand times the value of the Function referenced with the B Operand). Strictly speaking, *any* Function can be used as a GENERATE Block B Operand. In this book, however, only the Figure 3.22 Function will be used in this context. In fact, except to simulate Poisson arrivals, there seems to be no other compelling reason to use the Function-modifier option at GENERATE Blocks.

It should be noted that the Function XPDIS can be referenced from any number of different points in a model. At one point, for example, Poisson arrivals may occur at an average rate of four every 24 hours. At another point, arrivals may occur in a Poisson stream at an average rate of three every 24 hours. The two Blocks "GENERATE 360, FN$XPDIS" and "GENERATE 480, FN$XPDIS" can be used at the corresponding points in the model to simulate the arrivals. Both GENERATE Blocks make use of the same Function, XPDIS.

One of the implications of the second Poisson assumption ("the probability of two or more arrivals during a small interval of time is negligibly small") is that two or more arrivals do not occur simultaneously. Put differently, this means that when arrivals occur in a Poisson pattern, *interarrival time is never zero*. Now, suppose Poisson arrivals are being simulated in a model at the Block "GENERATE 5, FN$XPDIS". Whenever the value of the Function XPDIS is less than one-fifth, the *product* of 5 and FN$XPDIS will be less than 1. The integer portion of the product will then be zero, *thereby violating the second Poisson assumption*. Examination of Figure 3.22 shows that FN$XPDIS will have a value less than one-fifth about 18.5 percent of the time (whenever RN1 is less than about .185, the Function's returned value is less than 0.2; the value .185 results from inverse interpolation between the points ".1, .104" and ".2, .222"). The second Poisson assumption will then frequently be violated in the model. On the other hand, suppose that in the same model, the implicit time unit is made smaller by a factor of 10. The GENERATE Block must then be changed, becoming "GENERATE 50, FN$XPDIS". For the product of 50 and FN$XPDIS to be less than 1, the value of FN$XPDIS must be less than one-fiftieth. Examination of Figure 3.22 shows that this will only occur with a probability of about 0.02, or 2 percent of the time. Violation of the second Poisson assumption to this relatively small extent may be acceptable in the model. These two examples suggest, then, that if the second Poisson assumption is not to be grossly violated, the A Operand at pertinent GENERATE Blocks *must be kept large* by choosing a correspondingly small implicit time unit. In this context, it is recommended that GENERATE Block A Operands *not be smaller than 50*.

It is of interest to note the *variation* possible in interarrival times when a Poisson arrival process is in effect. Each particular interarrival time is computed by multiplying the average by a factor that can range in value from 0 to 8. If the average is 50, for example, then realized interarrival times can vary from 0 to 400. Statistically, the variance of exponentially distributed interarrival times is the *square* of the average value. Because of the wide variation possible, large sample sizes (i.e., long simulation runs) are often required to obtain "representative" long-run results when exponential sources of randomness are present.

3.14 Exercises

1. (a) What are the three Poisson assumptions?
   (b) In words, how are the Poisson and exponential distributions related?
   (c) What is the relationship between an average arrival rate, and the corresponding average interarrival time?
   (d) Explain the difference between using a spread-modifier and a Function-modifier as the B Operand at a GENERATE Block.
   (e) What must the first two characters be in a GENERATE Block's B Operand if a Function modifier is being used?
   (f) Why is it important to have a relatively large A Operand at a GENERATE Block being used to simulate a Poisson arrival process?

2. (a) In the long run, what percentage of the time will interarrival times of zero be used at the Block "GENERATE FN$XPDIS"? (The Function XPDIS is defined in Figure 3.22.)
   (b) What is the smallest value that can be used as a GENERATE Block's A Operand if the Block is being used to simulate Poisson arrivals, and interarrival times of zero are to occur not more than 0.5 percent of the time in the long run?

3. Ships arrive at a harbor in a Poisson pattern at an average rate of four ships per week. Assuming that the implicit time unit in a GPSS model is one hour, show a GENERATE Block which can be used to simulate the arrival of these ships. What percentage of the time will the computed interarrival time turn out to be zero?

4. What interarrival times can be realized at these four GENERATE Blocks?
   (a) GENERATE   FN$IAT
   (b) GENERATE   1,FN$IAT
   (c) GENERATE   2,FN$IAT
   (d) GENERATE   FN$IAT,2
   The Function IAT is defined in Figure E4.

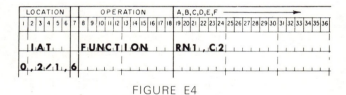

FIGURE E4

5. (a) Show how to solve exercise 4b, of Section 2.7.
   (b) Show the definition of a two-point continuous Function with which to sample from the distribution 500 ± 500.
   (c) Show the definition of a two-point continuous Function with which to sample from the integers uniformly distributed on the closed interval from 11 to 21.

6. In a certain model, the Block "GENERATE FN$IAT,,,,1" occupies the Location BETA. The argument of the Function IAT is RN2. The card sequence shown in Figure E6 appears at a certain point in the model.

```
        START      1
BETA    GENERATE   FN$IAT,,,,2
        CLEAR
        START      1
```

FIGURE E6

(a) How many random numbers will be fetched from random-number generator 2 between the time the simulation initiated with the first START card shuts off, and the time the simulation initiated with the second START card is begun? (Hint: Review the discussion of GENERATE Block redefinition, and of the CLEAR card's effect, in Section 2.34.)

(b) Would you expect the arrival time of the next

Transaction entering the model to be the same if the GENERATE and CLEAR cards were interchanged? Explain why, or why not.

3.15 Simulation of Exponentially-Distributed Holding Times

Important random variables other than interarrival times are sometimes found to be exponentially distributed. For example, the duration of telephone conversations follows the exponential distribution. So does the life of electronic-equipment components, such as transistors. The time required by a server to perform a service is also sometimes exponentially distributed. It can therefore be of interest to have the holding time at one or more ADVANCE Blocks be determined by drawing a sample from the exponential distribution.

Analogous to computation of exponentially distributed interarrival times, a particular exponentially distributed holding time, or "service time," can be computed by multiplying the average holding time by the value of $-\log_e[1 - RNj]$. This is suggested in equation (3.3), where HT_{sample} is the holding-time sample, and HT_{avg} is the average holding time:

$$HT_{sample} = (HT_{avg})\left[-\log_e(1 - RNj)\right] \quad (3.3)$$

As before, values of $-\log_e(1 - RNj)$ can be determined by use of the 24-point continuous GPSS Function defined in Figure 3.22. The Function-modifier option available via the GENERATE Block's B Operand is also available with the ADVANCE Block. That is, when the ADVANCE Block's B Operand is FNj (or FN$sn), holding time at the Block is computed by multiplying the value of the referenced Function by the Block's A Operand. The integer portion of the product is then used as the holding time. This means that exponential holding times can be simulated at an ADVANCE Block by supplying the average holding time as its A Operand, and using FN$XPDIS as its B Operand. For example, if the average service time required by a particular "exponential server" is 75 time units, the Block in Figure 3.24 can be used to simulate the server in a model.

The same remarks made concerning simulation of Poisson arrival patterns at GENERATE Blocks are in effect for simulating exponential holding times at ADVANCE Blocks. Care should be taken to distinguish between Function and

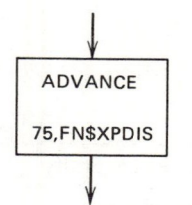

FIGURE 3.24   Example of an ADVANCE Block used to simulate an exponentially distributed holding time

spread modifiers at ADVANCE Blocks. Furthermore, the implicit time unit in a model should be sufficiently small so that when exponential holding times are to be simulated, the corresponding average holding times are no smaller than 50.

3.16 CASE STUDY 3B
Poisson Arrivals to an Exponential Server

(1) Statement of the Problem

At a one-car wash facility, it must be decided how many spaces to provide for cars waiting to use the facility. Cars arrive in a Poisson stream with an average interarrival time of 5 minutes. Car-washing time is exponentially distributed with a mean of 4 minutes. Potential customers who find no waiting space available go elsewhere to have their car washed.

Build a GPSS model for this simple system, then use the model to observe system behavior for the alternatives of one, two, and three waiting spaces. For each configuration, simulate for one 8-hour day of operation. Based· on model output, estimate the fraction of potential customers who actually remain at the car wash to be served. Compare the estimate for each configuration with the theoretically computed fraction of customers who will be served in the long run.

(2) Approach Taken in Building the Model

The model is straightforward. A Storage is used to simulate the number of waiting spaces at the car wash. When a customer-Transaction arrives at the system, it enters a TRANSFER Block operating in BOTH mode. From this Block, the customer-Transaction attempts to enter the Storage used to simulate waiting space. If entry is denied, the Transaction moves immediately to a TERMINATE Block. Based on Block Counts available in the output, it is a simple matter to compute the fraction of customers who arrived at the car wash and then remained for service, instead of immediately leaving the system.

(3) Table of Definitions

Time Unit: 0.01 Minutes

TABLE 3B.1   Table of Definitions for Case Study 3B

GPSS Entity	Interpretation
Transactions	
Model Segment 1	Customers
Model Segment 2	A timer
Facilities	
WASHR	Car-wash capability
Functions	
XPDIS	Function for sampling from the exponential distribution with a mean value of 1
Storages	
SPACE	Storage simulating the number of waiting spaces available

(4) Block Diagram

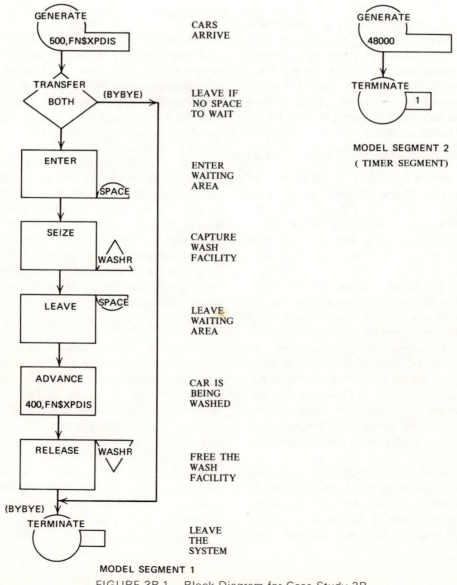

MODEL SEGMENT 1

FIGURE 3B.1   Block Diagram for Case Study 3B

(5) Extended Program Listing

```
BLOCK                                                                    CARD
NUMBER  *LOC    OPERATION  A,B,C,D,E,F,G           COMMENTS              NUMBER
                SIMULATE                                                    1
        *                                                                  2
        *       FUNCTION DEFINITION(S)                                     3
        *                                                                  4
        XPDIS   FUNCTION   RN1,C24          EXPONENTIAL DISTRIBUTION FUNCTION  5
        0,0/.1,.104/.2,.222/.3,.355/.4,.509/.5,.69/.6,.915/.7,1.2/.75,1.38   6
        .8,1.6/.84,1.83/.88,2.12/.9,2.3/.92,2.52/.94,2.81/.95,2.99/.96,3.2   7
        .97,3.5/.98,3.9/.99,4.6/.995,5.3/.998,6.2/.999,7/.9998,8             8
        *                                                                  9
        *       STORAGE CAPACITY DEFINITION(S)                            10
        *                                                                 11
                STORAGE    S$SPACE,1        ONE WAITING SPACE INITIALLY   12
        *                                                                 13
        *       MODEL SEGMENT 1                                           14
        *                                                                 15
1               GENERATE   500,FN$XPDIS     CARS ARRIVE                   16
2               TRANSFER   BOTH,,BYBYE      LEAVE IF NO SPACE TO WAIT     17
3               ENTER      SPACE            ENTER WAITING AREA            18
4               SEIZE      WASHR            CAPTURE WASH FACILITY         19
5               LEAVE      SPACE            LEAVE WAITING AREA            20
6               ADVANCE    400,FN$XPDIS     CAR IS BEING WASHED           21
7               RELEASE    WASHR            FREE THE WASH FACILITY        22
8       BYBYE   TERMINATE                   LEAVE THE SYSTEM              23
        *                                                                 24
        *       MODEL SEGMENT 2                                           25
        *                                                                 26
9               GENERATE   48000            TIMER ARRIVES AT END OF THE DAY  27
10              TERMINATE  1                SHUT OFF THE RUN              28
        *                                                                 29
        *       CONTROL CARDS AND STORAGE CAPACITY RE-DEFINITIONS         30
        *                                                                 31
                START      1                START THE 1ST RUN             32
                STORAGE    S$SPACE,2        SET WAITING SPACES = 2 FOR 2ND RUN  33
                CLEAR                       CLEAR FOR 2ND RUN             34
                START      1                START THE 2ND RUN             35
                STORAGE    S$SPACE,3        SET WAITING SPACES = 3 FOR 3RD RUN  36
                CLEAR                       CLEAR FOR 3RD RUN             37
                START      1                START THE 3RD RUN             38
                END                         RETURN CONTROL TO OPERATING SYSTEM  39
```

FIGURE 3B.2   Extended Program Listing for Case Study 3B

(6) Program Output

```
RELATIVE CLOCK       48000  ABSOLUTE CLOCK       48000
BLOCK COUNTS
BLOCK CURRENT   TOTAL   BLOCK CURRENT   TOTAL   BLOCK CURRENT
   1       0       94
   2       0       94
   3       0       62
   4       0       62
   5       0       62
   6       0       62
   7       0       62
   8       0       94
   9       0        1
  10       0        1
```

(a)

FACILITY	AVERAGE UTILIZATION	NUMBER ENTRIES	AVERAGE TIME/TRAN	SEIZING TRANS. NO.	PREEMPTING TRANS. NO.
WASHR	.674	62	522.145		

(b)

STORAGE	CAPACITY	AVERAGE CONTENTS	AVERAGE UTILIZATION	ENTRIES	AVERAGE TIME/TRAN	CURRENT CONTENTS	MAXIMUM CONTENTS
SPACE	1	.294	.294	62	227.661		1

(c)

FIGURE 3B.3   Selected Program Output for Case Study 3B (one waiting space provided). (a) Clock values and Block Counts. (b) Facility statistics. (c) Storage statistics.

TABLE 3B.2   A Summary of Program Output for Case Study 3B

Number of Waiting Spaces	Waiting Space Utilization	Number of Customers Served	Number of Customers Lost	Server Utilization	Average Service Time
1	0.294	62	32	0.674	522
2	0.233	83	15	0.670	388
3	0.272	82	9	0.660	387

(7) Discussion

Model Implementation. Note in the Table of Definitions that a time unit of 0.01 minutes is in effect. With this small implicit time unit, the average interarrival time and service time for the Poisson arrivals and the exponential server are 500 and 400, respectively. These large values insure that the method followed in sampling from the exponential distribution produces results faithful to the Poisson assumptions to a satisfactory degree.

Program Output.[12] Typical program output is shown in Figure 3B.3, for the case of one waiting space. During the simulation, 94 customers arrived at the system [Total Count, Block 1, Figure 3B.3(a)]. Of these 94, 62 remained to be served [Total Count, Block 3 (the ENTER Block)]. Hence, 32 customers were lost. Some 66 percent of the customers were served. At the time of model shutdown, no customers were in the system (all Current Counts are zero).

The Facility WASHR has an average utilization of 0.674 [Figure 3B.3(b)]. This figure can be compared with the long-run Facility utilization of 0.80 which would result in a perfectly synchronized system.

The average car-wash time for the sample of size 62 is 522 time units, or 5.22 minutes. There is considerable variation, then, between this observed value and the long-run average value of 4 minutes. On the other hand, the 94 customers who arrived at the system closely approximated the expected number of arrivals, 96.

Figure 3B.3(c) displays statistics for the Storage SPACE. Even though 34 percent of the customers found no waiting space available, utilization of the Storage is only 0.294. This fact, coupled with the large discrepancy between observed and expected Facility holding time, suggests that Poisson arrivals and/or exponential servers are characterized by a high degree of

variability, producing results which can differ markedly from those which could be realized if perfect synchronization were achieved.

Table 3B.2 shows a summary of the model output for the cases of one, two, and three waiting spaces. The observed number of lost customers is cut from 32 to 15 when two waiting spaces are available rather than just one. With three waiting spaces, only nine customers were lost.

Average Facility holding times are entered in the rightmost column in Table 3B.2. For the cases of two and three waiting spaces, these averages happen to be close to the long-run value of 400. Note that the corresponding sample sizes (number of customers served) range from 62 to 83.

Table 3B.3 compares the observed fraction of customers served with the corresponding long-run values known to be in effect. The long-run values have been computed on theoretical grounds from equation (3B.1)[13]

$$\text{Fraction Served} = 1 - \left(\frac{1 - \rho}{1 - \rho^{M+1}} \right) \rho^M$$

Where M is one larger than the number of waiting spaces, and ρ is the ratio of mean service time to mean interarrival time.

With the exception of the configuration providing one waiting space, the observed results compare reasonably well with their expected values. If the average service time in the first case had been closer to its expected value, this would have tended to increase the fraction of customers served, bringing the estimate into closer agreement with the expected value in this case.

---

[12] Total CPU time for the simulation on an IBM 360/67 computer was 3.2 seconds.

[13] For the development of this equation, see Chapter 10 in Frederick S. Hiller and Gerald J. Liberman, *Introduction to Operations Research* (Holden-Day, 1967). Exercises 3 through 6 in Section 3.17 are taken from this same chapter (Copyright © 1967 by Holden-Day, Inc.; by permission of Holden-Day, Inc.; no further reproduction or distribution is authorized without permission of Holden-Day, Inc.)

TABLE 3B.3   A Comparison Between Observed Fraction of Customers Served and the Corresponding Values Expected in the Long-Run

Number of Waiting Spaces	Fraction of Customers Served	
	Observed	Theoretical Value
1	0.660	0.738
2	0.846	0.826
3	0.902	0.861

3.17 Exercises

1. There is a particular situation in the Case Study 3B model in which the relative sequence in which simultaneous events are caused to occur can make a difference in the behavior of the model.
   (a) Identify the situation referred to. (Hint: See exercise 8, Section 2.47.)
   (b) Do you think that the two events involved might occur on a simultaneous basis frequently, or infrequently?
   (c) Suppose that the time unit in the model is changed from 0.01 minutes to 0.001 minutes. Do you think that the two events involved will now occur more or less frequently than they do when the time unit is larger?
   (d) Suppose that you know how to control the event-sequence in this case of simultaneity, so that you can force one event to occur before the other whenever the condition of simultaneity arises. (You will learn how to control the event-sequence for the Case Study 2B model in Section 4.10.) Which event would you force to occur first? Do you think there would be any philosophical implications involved in doing this? Explain in detail.

2. Consider Card 34 in the Extended Program Listing for Case Study 3B (Figure 3B.2). How many random numbers will be fetched from random-number generator 1 when this CLEAR card has its effect?

Exercises 3 through 6, like Case Study 3B, are typical of queuing systems problems for which analytic results are available. For each problem, build a GPSS model which simulates the behavior of the corresponding system, then run the model and interpret the output to provide answers (estimates) for the questions asked. Compare these estimates with the theoretical results, which are given after each problem statement.

Note that, in practice, the arrival processes in effect in these problem contexts may not be Poisson, and the service-time distributions may not be exponential. In such cases, analytic results very likely would not be available. Computer models for the systems would consequently provide useful tools with which to investigate system behavior.

It should also be noted that each analytic result given below is the *average value of a random variable*, i.e.,

describes average system behavior in the long run. The analytic results provide no indication of the extent to which short-run experience can differ from experiences averaged over a long period of time. Simulation models have the advantage of generating results which could actually take place in the short run. If enough such short-run observations are made, the *distributions* of the random variables of interest can be estimated. The method of estimating such probability distributions with GPSS models is discussed in Chapter 4.

3. It is necessary to determine how much in-process storage space to allocate to a particular work center in a new factory. Jobs would arrive at this work center according to a Poisson process with a mean rate of two per hour, and the time required to perform the necessary work has an exponential distribution with a mean of 0.4 hours. If each job would require 1 square foot of floor space while in in-process storage at the work center, how much space must be provided in order to accommodate all waiting jobs (a) 50 percent, (b) 90 percent, (c) 99 percent of the time? (*Answers:* 2, 9, and 19 square feet of floor space, respectively.)

4. Suppose that one repairman has been assigned the responsibility of maintaining three machines. For each machine, the probability distribution of the running time before a breakdown is exponential with a mean of 8 hours. The repair time also has an exponential distribution with a mean of two hours. Determine the expected number of machines that are not running. (*Answer:* 0.80)

5. A company currently has two tool cribs, each with a single clerk, in its manufacturing area. One tool crib handles only the tools for the heavy machinery, while the second one handles all other tools. However, for each crib, the arrival process is Poisson with a mean rate of 20 per hour, and the service-time distribution is exponential with a mean of 2 minutes.

Because of complaints that the mechanics coming to the tool cribs have to wait too long, the proposal has been made to combine the two tool cribs so that either clerk can handle either kind of tool as the demand arises. It is believed that the mean arrival rate to the combined two-clerk tool crib would double to 40 per hour, while the expected service time would continue to be 2 minutes.

Compare the current approach and the proposed new approach with respect to the total expected number of mechanics at the tool crib(s), and the expected waiting time (including service) for each mechanic. (*Answers:* For the current approach, there are two mechanics on average at each tool crib, and expected waiting time is 6 minutes. When the two tool cribs are combined, the total number of waiting mechanics averages 2.4, and the expected waiting time is 3.6 minutes.)

6. A particular work center in a job shop can be represented as a single-server queuing system where jobs arrive according to a Poisson process with a mean rate of 4.5 per day. Although the arriving jobs are of three distinct types, the time required to perform any of these jobs has the same exponential distribution with a mean of 0.2 working days. The practice has been to work on arriving jobs on a first-come, first-served basis. However, it is important that jobs of "type 1" do not have to wait very long, whereas this is only moderately important for jobs of "type 2," and relatively unimportant for jobs of "type 3." These three types arrive with a mean rate of 1.5, 2.0, and 1.0 per day, respectively. Since all three types have been experiencing rather long delays on the average, it has been proposed that the jobs be selected according to an appropriate priority discipline instead.

Compare the expected waiting time (including service) for each of the three types of jobs when the queue discipline is (a) first-come, first-served, and (b) first-come, first-served within priority class. (*Answers:* For the first-come, first-served queue discipline, expected waiting time is 2 days, independent of job type. When priority distinctions are made, the expected waiting times are 0.457, 1.057, and 6.2 days for jobs of type 1, 2, and 3, respectively.)

7. In exercise 5, assume that mechanic interarrival times at the two tool cribs follow the distribution shown in Table E7(a), and that service times at the cribs vary as shown in Table E7(b). Use a GPSS model to compare and contrast the "separate cribs" approach to the proposed combined operation of the cribs. Assume that the difference in service-time distributions at the two cribs is attributable to

the nature of the service demands, and not to differences between the two servers. Is the improvement resulting from the combined operation as great as the improvement found in exercise 5? Would you have expected lesser or greater improvement as a result of the changed distributions?

TABLE E7(b)

| Service Time | Relative Frequency | |
(minutes)	Tool Crib 1	Tool Crib 2
80		.03
90		.10
100	.01	.14
110	.05	.16
115	.10	.18
120	.15	.23
125	.19	.12
130	.17	.04
140	.14	
150	.12	
160	.07	

8. Modify the model in Case Study 2F under the assumption that television sets arrive at the last inspection station from the preceding station in a Poisson stream. Also assume that the inspection station workers, and the adjustment-station worker, are characterized by exponential service times. Assume that the mean interarrival time and service times from Case Study 2F are still in effect. Run the modified model, and compare the experienced staging-space requirements with those observed in the case study. Does the assumption of Poisson arrivals to exponential servers increase, or decrease, the amount of staging space required?

3.18 GPSS Control Cards: The RMULT Card

The algorithm used in GPSS to generate random numbers was explained in some detail in Section 1.4, Chapter 1. The reader should now turn to that section, and refresh his memory as to those details before continuing here.

As pointed out in Section 1.4, each of the eight GPSS random-number generators has a *multiplier* associated with it. The value of a given generator's multiplier changes each time the generator is used to produce a random number. It therefore makes sense to talk about a given multiplier's *initial* value and, after the generator has been used one or more times, about its *current* value.

In the default case, the initial value of each of the eight multipliers in the GPSS random-number

TABLE E7(a)

| Interarrival Time | Relative Frequency | |
(minutes)	Tool Crib 1	Tool Crib 2
50	.03	
100	.04	
125	.05	
150	.07	.01
160	.09	.02
170	.12	.05
175	.16	.07
180	.13	.11
185	.10	.13
190	.09	.16
200	.07	.18
210	.04	.14
235	.01	.08
260		.03
310		.02

scheme is set to 1.[14] When this default situation is in effect, all eight GPSS random-number generators produce identical sequences of random numbers. This was pointed out in Section 1.4, and is illustrated numerically in Table 3.1.

The synchronization implied in Table 3.1 is sometimes undesirable. As a result, GPSS provides a type of control card with which the current value of one or more of the eight random-number multipliers can be redefined. This type of control card can be used in a variety of ways, as summarized below.

1. It can be used in advance of the first START card, to change the default initial value of one or more multipliers before a simulation even begins.

2. It can be used between START cards, to *restore* what had been the initial multiplier values for one or more of the eight generators. The multipliers might either be restored to the default values originally assumed by the Processor, or to nondefault values which the analyst had prescribed initially.

3. It can be used between START cards to define an entirely new set of values for the multipliers.

The control card used to supply multiplier values is the RMULT card. The Location field is not used on the card. The word RMULT is entered in the Operation field. There are 8 Operands, A through H, corresponding to random-number generators 1 through 8, respectively. To redefine the current multiplier value for a given generator, it is only necessary to supply a positive, odd integer number in the corresponding Operand position on the RMULT card. The number cannot contain more than five digits. Of course, it is this number itself which will be used as the current value of the multiplier for the corresponding generator.

Figure 3.25 provides several examples for the RMULT card. The first example shows an

RMULT card which will cause all eight multipliers to be restored to their initial default values of 1. In the second example, only the multipliers for generators 2, 3, and 6 are restored to their initial default values; the other multiplier values are left undisturbed. The third example shows how the multipliers for generators 1, 2, and 4 can be defined to have current values of 453, 721, and 555, respectively.

Recall from Section 1.4 that the random number scheme in GPSS involves eight different seed values. When any of the generators is used the first time, it employs the first of these eight seeds to form a random number. In addition, the generator takes steps to determine in pseudorandom fashion which of the eight seeds will be employed the *next* time that *same* generator is used. When a random number is formed by a particular generator, then, its value will depend both on the generator's current multiplier value, and the particular seed the generator will employ. This means that to return to a previous random-number sequence, two steps must be taken. (1) The multiplier must be restored to its initial value. (2) The next time the generator is used, it must employ the first of the eight available seeds. The RMULT card accomplishes both of these steps. That is, whenever the RMULT card is used to redefine a generator's multiplier value, the Processor sets an internal pointer so that when the generator is next called to produce a random number, it will employ the first of the eight seed values in the process.

Now consider where the RMULT card should be placed in a job deck. If the analyst wants to choose a nonstandard sequence of random numbers at the beginning of a simulation, the RMULT card should be used prior to the first appearance of a GENERATE Block image. This guarantees that pertinent multipliers will be set to their nondefault values *before* the corresponding generators are used by the Processor during the Input Phase.

If certain random-number sequences are to

[14]The default multiplier values are all 1 in GPSS/360, Version 1, and are all 37 in GPSS/360, Version 2, and in GPSS V. Because GPSS/360, Version 1, has been used for all the case studies in this book, it is appropriate to assume here that the default multiplier values are all 1.

LOCATION	OPERATION	A,B,C,D,E,F ———————————————————→
	R MU LT	1,1,1,1,1,1,1,1 FIRST EXAMPLE
	R MU LT	,1,1,,,1 SECOND EXAMPLE
	R MU LT	453,721,,555 THIRD EXAMPLE

FIGURE 3.25   Examples for use of the RMULT card

be modified between simulations (that is, between START cards), and use of a CLEAR card is involved, then the RMULT card should appear prior to the CLEAR card. It was explained in Chapter 2 that, as part of the clearing operation, the Processor schedules the first Transaction arrival event at each GENERATE Block in the model. If this scheduling is to use interarrival times based on one or more new random-number generator settings, then the settings must be established before the clearing operation occurs.

Finally, care must be taken when one or more GENERATE Blocks are to be redefined between START cards, *and* one or more random-number sequences on which they depend are to be modified. As pointed out in Section 2.34, when a GENERATE Block is redefined, the Processor immediately schedules the first Transaction arrival event at the newly defined Block. If the RMULT card is placed ahead of the GENERATE Block redefinition card(s), the arrival time(s) will be based on the new random-number generator settings. Alternatively, if the RMULT card appears after the GENERATE Block redefinition(s), the arrival time(s) will be based on the "old" random number settings. The analyst must carefully consider which of these two alternatives should be used for the problem at hand. The alternative chosen will depend, in part, on whether use of a CLEAR card is also involved. This matter will be further explored in Case Study 3C, where the sequence chosen is (1) redefine GENERATE Blocks first, (2) then modify the random number settings, (3) and, finally, perform the clearing operation.

3.19 Replication of Experimental Conditions in Simulation Modeling

Experimental work in any field involves controlling as closely as possible the conditions under which experiments are performed. By deliberately changing the value of only one variable (the "independent variable"), observed changes in another variable (the "dependent variable") can be attributed exclusively to a single cause. For example, assume that variables named A, B, C, D, and E are subject to experimental control, and that A depends only on B, C, D, and E. To measure the dependence of A on B *alone*, the values of C, D, and E are held constant, then B is deliberately varied and the resulting changes in A are observed. Under the conditions described, the changes in A are due to the changes in B. In contrast, if the values of B, C, D, and E were varied simultaneously, it would be difficult and perhaps impossible to isolate B's influence on A.

These simple remarks also apply to experiments conducted with simulation models. Simulation is frequently used to compare alternative system configurations to find which one best satisfies a given objective. In this sense, the way a system is configured can be thought of as an "independent variable." By changing system configurations, the analyst is essentially changing the value of an independent variable. His goal is to observe the corresponding changes in some measure of system effectiveness. If changes in effectiveness are to be attributed exclusively to configuration changes, all other conditions under which the alternatives are investigated should be identical from experiment to experiment.

Now, each source of *randomness* in a system has a potential influence on the measure of system behavior. Important sources of randomness in GPSS models are interarrival times and service times. The analyst might think that if the A and B Operands at a given GENERATE or ADVANCE Block are the same when alternative configurations are studied, this "experimental condition" is being "controlled." This is not true. Not only is it important for pertinent interarrival- and service-time *distributions* to be the same for each configuration studied, but the *individual values* and the *sequence in which they are drawn* should ideally be duplicated for the alternative configurations tested. Otherwise, short-run patterns might influence the results in such a way that misleading conclusions are drawn.

As a case in point, consider the tool-crib system modeled in Case Study 2C. The tool crib was manned by a single clerk. Mechanics making tool requests in Category 1 arrived every 420 ± 360 seconds, each requiring 300 ± 90 seconds of the clerk's time. Category 2 requests for tools, each requiring 100 ± 30 seconds of the clerk's time, were made by mechanics arriving every 360 ± 240 seconds. The measure of system effectiveness was "average number of mechanics in the waiting line." The "independent variable" was the queue discipline used by the clerk. It was of interest to determine whether giving Category 2 mechanics a higher priority resulted in a smaller number of mechanics waiting on average, thereby reducing costs. In Case Study

2C, operation of the tool crib was simulated for an 8-hour day under both alternatives, and it was tentatively concluded that costs were significantly reduced by using a priority distinction.

For the tool-crib problem, the average number of mechanics in the waiting line depends on these *five* factors.

1. Queue discipline in effect.
2. The particular interarrival-time sequence of Category 1 mechanics.
3. The particular sequence of service times required by Category 1 mechanics.
4. The particular interarrival-time sequence of Category 2 mechanics.
5. The particular sequence of service times required by Category 2 mechanics.

The dependence of waiting time on five factors makes it difficult to interpret the results if the intention is to *isolate the influence of queue discipline*. If waiting-time differences are to be attributed solely to differences in queue discipline, then the other conditions under which the alternatives are compared should be identical.

At least three ways suggest themselves for comparing alternatives under otherwise identical conditions.

1. Devise some means for analytically modifying the simulation output to take the masking effect of "non-identical randomness" into account.
2. Make simulation runs of such extended duration that short-run patterns cancel each other out. In Case Study 2C, for example, the random variable "average number of waiting mechanics" has an expected value which depends only on the queue discipline in effect. As the duration of a simulation increases, the model's outputted estimate of this expected value tends toward the theoretical expectation.
3. Design the simulation·model so that each alternative is investigated under identical sets of conditions. In Case Study 2C, this means arranging for items (2) through (5) above to follow identical random patterns when the queue discipline is changed. This approach, then, involves "duplicating randomness" in the model by controlling the experimental conditions under which the simulation is run.

Method (3) admittedly does not eliminate the possibility that short-run patterns will produce misleading results for small sample sizes. It does sharpen the contrast among alternatives, however, and makes possible relatively strong statements of the "other things being equal" type. It is superior to method (1), because it is less demanding to duplicate randomness in a model than to take masking effects into account analytically on a postsimulation basis. Its advantage

over method (2) is that the latter may involve inordinate amounts of computer time, especially when models are large and there are many alternatives to investigate. Of course, methods (2) and (3) are not of the "either-or" type. Even when long simulation runs can be justified, it is advantageous to duplicate sources of randomness among the various alternatives.

Consider, then, how randomness can be duplicated for the two configurations studied in Case Study 2C. For convenience, the Extended Program Listing for the model with priority distinctions, as shown in Figure 2C.4, is repeated in Figure 3.26. For the model as shown, the GENERATE Blocks at Locations 1 and 8 and the ADVANCE Blocks at Locations 5 and 12 all use RN1 as their source of uniform 0–1 random numbers. (No random-number source is used at the GENERATE Block in Location 15, because a deterministic time of arrival is specified there.) In other words, the four sources of randomness "share" a single sequence of random numbers. The manner in which this sharing takes place is suggested in Table 3.14, where the first 25 calls on RN1 are listed in chronological order, and the source of the call (i.e., the Block from which the call is made) is shown both for the Figure 3.26 model ("Model 1"), and for the equivalent model with priority distinctions eliminated ("Model 2"). For the first 16 calls on RN1, the Blocks from which the corresponding calls are made match, model-by-model. Then, as indicated in Table 3.14, the seventeenth call comes from the ADVANCE Block in Location 12 in Model 1, and from the ADVANCE Block in Location 5 in Model 2. The seventeenth call is made at simulated time 1457 (as determined from information not shown in Table 3.14). In terms of the system itself, this means that at time 1457, when the tool-crib clerk completed a service, he found at least one Category 1 and one Category 2 mechanic waiting. Furthermore, the Category 1 mechanic had been waiting the longer of the two. In Model 2, the Category 1 mechanic consequently was served next. In Model 1, however, the Category 2 mechanic was given preference.

From the seventeenth call forward, the particular RN1 values used at Blocks 1, 5, 8, and 12 in Model 1 differ considerably from those used in Model 2. As pointed out in Table 3.14, for example, it is Block 5 in Model 1 which uses the twentieth value supplied by RN1, whereas Block 8 in Model 2 uses the twentieth RN1 value; and so on. In fact, it is clear that when

```
BLOCK                                                                              CARD
NUMBER  *LOC   OPERATION  A,B,C,D,E,F,G              COMMENTS                      NUMBER
               SIMULATE                                                              1
        *                                                                            2
        *      MODEL SEGMENT 1                                                        3
        *                                                                            4
1              GENERATE   420,360,,,1    CATEGORY 1 MECHANICS ARRIVE                  5
2              QUEUE      LINE           ENTER "CATEGORY 1 SEGMENT" OF LINE           6
3              SEIZE      CLERK          CAPTURE THE CLERK                            7
4              DEPART     LINE           LEAVE THE LINE                               8
5              ADVANCE    300,90         USE THE CLERK                                9
6              RELEASE    CLERK          FREE THE CLERK                              10
7              TERMINATE                 LEAVE THE TOOL CRIB AREA                    11
        *                                                                           12
        *      MODEL SEGMENT 2                                                       13
        *                                                                           14
8              GENERATE   360,240,,,2    CATEGORY 2 MECHANICS ARRIVE                 15
9              QUEUE      LINE           ENTER "CATEGORY 2 SEGMENT" OF LINE          16
10             SEIZE      CLERK          CAPTURE THE CLERK                           17
11             DEPART     LINE           LEAVE THE LINE                              18
12             ADVANCE    100,30         USE THE CLERK                               19
13             RELEASE    CLERK          FREE THE CLERK                              20
14             TERMINATE                 LEAVE THE TOOL CRIB AREA                    21
        *                                                                           22
        *      MODEL SEGMENT 3                                                       23
        *                                                                           24
15             GENERATE   28800          TIMER ARRIVES AFTER 8 HOURS                 25
16             TERMINATE  1              SHUT OFF THE RUN                            26
        *                                                                           27
        *      CONTROL CARDS                                                         28
        *                                                                           29
               START      1              START THE RUN                               30
               END                       RETURN CONTROL TO OPERATING SYSTEM         31
```

FIGURE 3.26   Repetition of Figure 2C.4

TABLE 3.14   The Source of the First 25 Calls on RN1, Depending on Which of the Two Alternative Case Study 2C Models Is Being Used

| Number of the Call | Block from Which Call is Made | |
	Model 1: with PR Distinctions	Model 2: without PR Distinctions
1	1	1
2	8	8
3	1	1
4	5	5
5	8	8
6	12	12
7	1	1
8	5	5
9	8	8
10	8	8
11	12	12
12	12	12
13	1	1
14	5	5
15	1	1
16	8	8
17	12	5
18	8	8
19	12	12
20	5	8
21	8	1
22	1	12
23	12	12
24	5	5
25	1	8

Calls With Differing Sources

the call synchronization is broken on the seventeenth call, the role played by any particular RN1 value will often differ between Models 1 and 2. With respect to calls 18 through 25 on RN1, Table 3.14 shows that the context in which the RN1 value is used differs in 50 percent of the cases. Information not shown in Table 3.14 indicates that, throughout the course of an 8-hour day, 282 and 289 calls on RN1 are made in Models 1 and 2, respectively. From call 1 through 282, the RN1 values are used in different contexts 55 percent of the time. It should be clear, then, that among the five factors on which the average number of waiting mechanics depends, no two factors are the same in both Model 1 and Model 2. The experimental investigation has not been performed under controlled conditions.

It is relatively easy to introduce controlled conditions in Case Study 2C. This simply involves taking steps to insure that each of the four sources of randomness uses its own "private" 0–1 random-number generator. Suppose, then, that Functions are defined to sample from the uniform distributions at Blocks 1, 5, 8, and 12, and that random-number generators 1, 2, 3, and 4, respectively, are specified as the Function arguments. Figure 3.27 shows the Extended Program Listing for the priority-distinction model in which this has been done. The Functions IAT1, STYM1, IAT2, and STYM2 are used at Blocks 1, 5, 8, and 12, in that order.

In Figure 3.27, note that an RMULT card (Card 5) has been employed to bring about nonidentical initial settings for the four random number generators used in the model. If the four generators had identical initial settings, an un-

```
BLOCK
NUMBER  *LOC      OPERATION   A,B,C,D,E,F,G              COMMENTS                              CARD
                  SIMULATE                                                                     NUMBER
        *                                                                                        1
        *         NON-STANDARD RANDOM NUMBER SEQUENCE INITIALIZATION(S)                          2
        *                                                                                        3
                  RMULT       511,39,7,663                                                       4
        *                                                                                        5
        *         FUNCTION DEFINITION(S)                                                          6
        *                                                                                        7
        IAT1 FUNCTION   RN1,C2       CATEGORY 1 MECHANIC INTER-ARRIVAL TIMES                      8
        0,60/1,781                                                                               9
        IAT2 FUNCTION   RN3,C2       CATEGORY 2 MECHANIC INTER-ARRIVAL TIMES                     10
        0,120/1,601                                                                             11
        STYM1 FUNCTION  RN2,C2       CATEGORY 1 MECHANIC SERVICE TIMES                           12
        0,210/1,391                                                                             13
        STYM2 FUNCTION  RN4,C2       CATEGORY 2 MECHANIC SERVICE TIMES                           14
        0,70/1,131                                                                              15
        *                                                                                       16
        *         MODEL SEGMENT 1                                                                17
        *                                                                                       18
1                 GENERATE    FN$IAT1,,,,1     CATEGORY 1 MECHANICS ARRIVE                       19
2                 QUEUE       LINE             ENTER "CATEGORY 1 SEGMENT" OF LINE                20
3                 SEIZE       CLERK            CAPTURE THE CLERK                                 21
4                 DEPART      LINE             LEAVE THE LINE                                    22
5                 ADVANCE     FN$STYM1         USE THE CLERK                                     23
6                 RELEASE     CLERK            FREE THE CLERK                                    24
7                 TERMINATE                    LEAVE THE TOOL CRIB AREA                          25
        *                                                                                       26
        *         MODEL SEGMENT 2                                                                27
        *                                                                                       28
                                                                                                29
8                 GENERATE    FN$IAT2,,,,2     CATEGORY 2 MECHANICS ARRIVE                       30
9                 QUEUE       LINE             ENTER "CATEGORY 2 SEGMENT" OF LINE                31
10                SEIZE       CLERK            CAPTURE THE CLERK                                 32
11                DEPART      LINE             LEAVE THE LINE                                    33
12                ADVANCE     FN$STYM2         USE THE CLERK                                     34
13                RELEASE     CLERK            FREE THE CLERK                                    35
14                TERMINATE                    LEAVE THE TOOL CRIB AREA                          36
        *                                                                                       37
        *         MODEL SEGMENT 3                                                                38
        *                                                                                       39
15                GENERATE    28800            TIMER ARRIVES AFTER 8 HOURS                       40
16                TERMINATE   1                SHUT OFF THE RUN                                   41
        *                                                                                       42
        *         CONTROL CARDS                                                                  43
        *                                                                                       44
                  START       1                START THE RUN                                    45
                  END                          RETURN CONTROL TO OPERATING SYSTEM               46
```

FIGURE 3.27 Extended Program Listing for the Figure 3.26 model, as modified to provide for control of experimental conditions

| QUEUE LINE | MAXIMUM CONTENTS 6 | AVERAGE CONTENTS 1.824 | TOTAL ENTRIES 148 | ZERO ENTRIES 21 | PERCENT ZEROS 14.1 | AVERAGE TIME/TRANS 354.945 | $AVERAGE TIME/TRANS 413.637 |

(a)

| QUEUE LINE | MAXIMUM CONTENTS 8 | AVERAGE CONTENTS 2.609 | TOTAL ENTRIES 148 | ZERO ENTRIES 21 | PERCENT ZEROS 14.1 | AVERAGE TIME/TRANS 507.743 | $AVERAGE TIME/TRANS 591.700 |

(b)

FIGURE 3.28   Selected output from the Figure 3.27 model and its no-priority-distinction equivalent. (a) With priority distinctions, (b) without priority distinctions

natural correlation would be in effect among the four sources of randomness. For example, under the hypothesis of identical initial settings, one and the same numeric value would result from the first call on RN1, RN2, RN3, and RN4. This means the same random number would be used to compute the time of arrival of the first Category 1 mechanic and the first Category 2 mechanic. (Similar statements could be made concerning computation of the time of arrival of the second Category 1 and Category 2 mechanics, the third Category 1 and Category 2 mechanics, etc.) This would be highly unrealistic. Similarly, the same random number would be used to compute both the time of arrival and the service time requirement of the first Category 1 mechanic. (Similar statements could be made concerning computation of the time of arrival and the service time requirement of the second Category 1 mechanic, the third Category 1 mechanic, etc. Furthermore, these statements could be extended to the first, second, etc. mechanics in Category 2.) The RMULT card has been used, then, to avoid such unrealistic correlations.

Queue statistics from the Figure 3.27 model, and its no-priority-distinction equivalent, are shown in Figure 3.28. Average queue contents with and without priority distinctions are 1.824 and 2.609, as compared with 0.770 and 2.731, respectively, in Case Study 2C. The resulting cost savings is $56.52, as compared with $141.19. What is important here is not these particular numeric differences, but the ability to say for the Figure 3.27 model and its no-priority-distinction equivalent that "on a given day, if priority distinctions had been made, a savings of thus-and-such would have been realized as compared with making no priority distinctions on the same day."

Of course, the same number of mechanic arrivals was experienced in each of the two simulations, because the interarrival-time sequences for Category 1 and Category 2 mechanics are in one-to-one correspondence between the two models. And, from CURRENT CONTENTS Queue information not shown in Figure 3.28, the tool-crib clerk in both models left five mechanics standing in line at the end of the day. In the real system, the clerk probably would not accept additional arrivals within 5 minutes of the end of the day, and/or would remain on the job beyond quitting time, if necessary, until the last service had been completed. The way such close-up conditions can be modeled in GPSS will be explained later.

There is a large discrepancy between the results produced in Case Study 2C, and those resulting from the Figure 3.27 model. Despite the replicated conditions associated with the latter output, then, the question still remains, just how much better is the priority-distinction system likely to be than the alternative *in the long run*. The case study in the next section undertakes to answer this question.

3.20 CASE STUDY 3C
A Second Tour Through Case Study 2C[15]

(1) Statement of the Problem

Modify the model shown in Figure 3.27 so that, in a single batch run, ten different days of operation will be simulated for the tool-crib problem originally described in Case Study 2C. In addition to controlling experimental conditions, arrange the model so that both the "no priority" and "priority" queue disciplines are investigated in the single run. The resulting output will provide two samples, each consisting of ten different "average Queue content" estimates for the corresponding disciplines. Compute the mean and standard deviation for each of these two samples. How much better is the priority-distinction discipline based on samples?

(5) Extended Program Listing

The Extended Program Listing appears in Figure 3C.1. For compactness, Cards 52 through 69 and 81 through 101 are not shown.

[15] Sections (2), (3), (4), and (6) are not needed in this case study, because the information they would contain has already been presented.

```
BLOCK                                                                                  CARD
NUMBER   *LOC    OPERATION  A,B,C,D,E,F,G              COMMENTS                         NUMBER
                 SIMULATE                                                                 1
         *                                                                                2
         *       NON-STANDARD RANDOM NUMBER SEQUENCE INITIALIZATIONS FOR 1ST RUN          3
         *                                                                                4
                 RMULT       511,39,7,663                                                 5
         *                                                                                6
         *       FUNCTION DEFINITION(S)                                                   7
         *                                                                                8
         IAT1    FUNCTION    RN1,C2         CATEGORY 1 MECHANIC INTER-ARRIVAL TIMES        9
         0,60/1,781                                                                      10
         IAT2    FUNCTION    RN3,C2         CATEGORY 2 MECHANIC INTER-ARRIVAL TIMES       11
         0,120/1,601                                                                     12
         STYM1   FUNCTION    RN2,C2         CATEGORY 1 MECHANIC SERVICE TIMES            13
         0,210/1,391                                                                     14
         STYM2   FUNCTION    RN4,C2         CATEGORY 2 MECHANIC SERVICE TIMES            15
         0,70/1,131                                                                      16
         *                                                                               17
         *       MODEL SEGMENT 1                                                         18
         *                                                                               19
1        TAG1    GENERATE    FN$IAT1        CATEGORY 1 MECHANICS ARRIVE                  20
2                QUEUE       LINE           ENTER BACK OF LINE                           21
3                SEIZE       CLERK          CAPTURE THE CLERK                            22
4                DEPART      LINE           LEAVE THE LINE                               23
5                ADVANCE     FN$STYM1       USE THE CLERK                                24
6                RELEASE     CLERK          FREE THE CLERK                               25
7                TERMINATE                  LEAVE THE TOOL CRIB AREA                     26
         *                                                                               27
         *       MODEL SEGMENT 2                                                         28
         *                                                                               29
8        TAG2    GENERATE    FN$IAT2        CATEGORY 2 MECHANICS ARRIVE                  30
9                QUEUE       LINE           ENTER BACK OF LINE                           31
10               SEIZE       CLERK          CAPTURE THE CLERK                            32
11               DEPART      LINE           LEAVE THE LINE                               33
12               ADVANCE     FN$STYM2       USE THE CLERK                                34
13               RELEASE     CLERK          FREE THE CLERK                               35
14               TERMINATE                  LEAVE THE TOOL CRIB AREA                     36
         *                                                                               37
         *       MODEL SEGMENT 3                                                         38
         *                                                                               39
15               GENERATE    28800          TIMER ARRIVES AFTER 8 HOURS                  40
16               TERMINATE   1              SHUT OFF THE RUN                             41
         *                                                                               42
         *       CONTROL CARDS AND BLOCK OPERAND RE-DEFINITIONS                          43
         *                                                                               44
                 START       1              START 1ST RUN                                45
                 RMULT       741,211,483,659  SET RANDOM SEQUENCES FOR 2ND RUN           46
                 CLEAR                      CLEAR FOR 2ND RUN                            47
                 START       1              START 2ND RUN                                48
                 RMULT       111,157,539,211  SET RANDOM SEQUENCES FOR 3RD RUN           49
                 CLEAR                      CLEAR FOR 3RD RUN                            50
                 START       1              START 3RD RUN                                51
                   .                            .                                         .
                   .                            .                                         .
                 RMULT       41,527,9,55    SET RANDOM SEQUENCES FOR 10TH RUN            70
                 CLEAR                      CLEAR FOR 10TH RUN                           71
                 START       1              START 10TH RUN                               72
1        TAG1    GENERATE    FN$IAT1,,,,1   RE-CONFIGURE FOR PRIORITY DIFFERENCES        73
MULTIPLE DEFINITION OF SYMBOL IN ABOVE CARD
8        TAG2    GENERATE    FN$IAT2,,,,2   RE-CONFIGURE FOR PRIORITY DIFFERENCES        74
MULTIPLE DEFINITION OF SYMBOL IN ABOVE CARD
                 RMULT       511,39,7,663   RESTORE 1ST RUN RANDOM SEQUENCES             75
                 CLEAR                      CLEAR FOR 11TH RUN                           76
                 START       1              START 11TH RUN                               77
                 RMULT       741,211,483,659  RESTORE 2ND RUN RANDOM SEQUENCES           78
                 CLEAR                      CLEAR FOR 12TH RUN                           79
                 START       1              START 12TH RUN                               80
                   .                            .                                         .
                   .                            .                                         .
                 RMULT       41,527,9,55    RESTORE 10TH RUN RANDOM SEQUENCES           102
                 CLEAR                      CLEAR FOR 20TH RUN                          103
                 START       1              START 20TH RUN                              104
                 END                        RETURN CONTROL TO OPERATING SYSTEM          105
```

FIGURE 3C.1 Extended Program Listing for Case Study 3C

(7) Discussion

Model Implementation. There are two important points to note in the Figure 3C.1 Extended Program Listing. First of all, for both of the queue disciplines being investigated, RMULT cards have been used in moving between consecutive simulated days. Secondly note the relative placement of the GENERATE, RMULT, and CLEAR cards in moving from day 10 in the no-priority case to day 1 in the priority-distinction simulation.

Before discussing the first point, recall that the need for a *first* RMULT card to provide non-identical initial settings for the four random number generators was indicated in Section 3.19. Apart from this issue, why have RMULT cards been used in moving between consecutive simulated days? For example, why has the card "RMULT 741,211,483,659" been used prior to the beginning of the second simulated day for the no-priority discipline (Card 46, Figure 3C.1), and for the priority-distinction discipline (Card 78, Figure 3C.1)? It is clear that through such use of the RMULT card, the random number settings in effect at the beginning of the second day will be the same for the two queue disciplines. But is this use of the RMULT card necessary? Why not simply leave the random number settings wherever they were at the end of the first simulated day? Wouldn't this also mean that the settings in effect at the beginning of the second day would be the same for the two queue disciplines? In this model, the answer is "no." The reason for this will now be explained.

Each day's simulation stops at the end of the eighth simulated hour. In general, then, there may still be unserved mechanics in the model when a day's simulation ends. Suppose that just before the end of the day 1 simulation, the clerk completes a service at a time when both a Category 1 and a Category 2 mechanic are in the waiting line, and the Category 1 mechanic has been in the line the longer of the two. The no-priority clerk will put the Category 1 mechanic into service next. In contrast, the priority clerk will put the Category 2 mechanic into service next. If the simulation now stops, the no-priority model will then have made one more call on RN2 (the argument for the Category 1 service-time Function) than is the case in the priority-distinction model. Similarly, the priority-distinction model will have made one more call on RN4 (the argument for the Category 2 service-time Function) than is the case in the no-priority model.

The RN2 and RN4 settings at the end of the day 1 simulation will then differ between the two models. The possibility is then ruled out for leaving the RN2 and RN4 settings "wherever they are" prior to beginning the day 2 simulation. [But see exercise 1(f) in Section 3.21.] This explains why the RMULT card is employed between consecutive simulated days to guarantee that the random number settings at the beginning of the jth day will be the same for the two queue disciplines under investigation, for $j = 2,3,4,\ldots,9$, and 10. [In Chapter 4, Case Study 4D shows how this need for an RMULT card between consecutive simulated days can be eliminated. Exercise 7(b) and (c) in Section 4.19 requests that the Chapter 4 technique be applied to Case Study 3C.]

Now consider the steps taken in the Figure 3C.1 model to move from the 10th day for the no-priority discipline, to the 1st day for the priority-distinction case. The cards involved in this transition are the two GENERATE Block redefinitions (Cards 73 and 74 in Figure 3C.1), and the RMULT and CLEAR cards (Cards 75 and 76). To restore the conditions which were in effect at the beginning of simulated day 1 for the no-priority case, care must be taken with the relative placement of these cards. For example, suppose that instead of appearing in the order shown in Figure 3C.1, Cards 73, 74, 75, and 76 had been positioned as follows:

```
        RMULT      511,39,7,663
TAG1    GENERATE   FN$IAT1,,,,1
TAG2    GENERATE   FN$IAT2,,,,2
        CLEAR
```

The RMULT card would set the random number generators at what had been their starting point for the day 1, no-priority simulation. The GENERATE Block redefinitions would then cause the Processor to eliminate the incipient arrivals at the "old" GENERATE Blocks, replacing them with freshly scheduled first arrivals at the new GENERATE Blocks. (See Section 2.34 to review what happens when a GENERATE Block is redefined.) These scheduling steps would make use of the first random number returned by each of the newly-set RN1 and RN3 sequences (to schedule arrivals at the GENERATE Blocks in Locations TAG1 and TAG2, respectively). When the CLEAR card then had its effect, these scheduled arrivals at the two GENERATE Blocks would be removed from the Future Events Chain, returned to the latent pool, and replaced with newly scheduled arrivals. This, in turn, would mean that the *second* draw from each of the newly set RN1 and RN3 sequences would be used to determine the time of the *first* arrival at the two respective GENERATE Blocks. But in day 1 for the no-priority case, it was the *first* draw from each of the RN1 and RN3 sequences which determined the time of the first arrival at these respective GENERATE Blocks. This would mean that the day 1 experimental conditions would not be identical for the alternative queue disciplines under investigation.

Based on the preceding discussion, it is left as an exercise to reason out that the relative positions of Cards 73, 74, 75, and 76 in Figure 3C.1 do produce a result whereby the *first* draw from each of the newly-set RN1 and RN3 sequences is used to schedule the first arrival at the respective GENERATE Blocks, as desired. Exercises 1(a) and (b) in Section 3.21 provide additional opportunities to think through the effect of other possible permutations of Cards 73, 74, 75, and 76.

Program Output.[16]   Table 3C.1 summarizes the information produced when the Figure 3C.1 model was run. The statistic "number of Queue entries" shows relatively little variation on a day-by-day basis. The extreme values, 141 and 154, each differ from the average value by about 4.5 percent. The situation is quite different with the statistic, "average queue content." For the "no-priority" case, the minimum and maximum values, 1.129 and 3.215, differ from the mean value by about 53 and 35 percent, respectively. The sample standard deviation, 0.833, is 35 per-

cent of the sample mean. The same observations hold for the priority-distinction case. The large day-to-day variation possible in the Queue-content statistic explains why the results for the one-day simulation in Case Study 2C, and the "controlled conditions" simulation in Section 3.18, can differ from each other to such an extent. Based on the average values in Table 3C.1, waiting costs for the "no-priority" and "priority" disciplines are about $172 and $124 per day, respectively. The daily savings for the priority-distinction case, then, is estimated at $48 from these data.

3.21 Exercises

1. Parts (a) through (e) of this exercise pertain to replication of experimental conditions in Case Study 3C.

   (a) Referring to the discussion under Model Implementation, suppose that Cards 73, 74, 75, and 76 in Figure 3C.1 were repositioned in the following sequence.

   ```
   TAG1    GENERATE    FN$IAT1,,,,1
   TAG2    GENERATE    FN$IAT2,,,,2
           CLEAR
           RMULT       511,39,7,663
   ```

   If this were done, experimental conditions on day 1 for the priority-distinction simulation would differ from those in effect on day 1 for the no-priority simulation. Explain why this statement can be made.

   (b) Now suppose that Cards 73, 74, 75, and 76 in Figure 3C.1 were repositioned as follows.

   ```
           CLEAR
           RMULT       511,39,7,663
   TAG1    GENERATE    FN$IAT1,,,,1
   TAG2    GENERATE    FN$IAT2,,,,2
   ```

[16]Total CPU time for the simulation on an IBM 360/67 computer was 8.1 seconds.

TABLE 3C.1   A Summary of Program Output for Case Study 3C

Day	Number of Queue Entries	Average Queue Content Without Distinctions	With Distinctions
1	148	2.609	1.824
2	150	3.946	2.754
3	146	2.296	1.688
4	145	1.839	1.350
5	152	3.215	2.317
6	142	1.129	0.906
7	147	2.516	1.826
8	141	1.218	0.945
9	148	2.082	1.516
10	154	3.030	2.174
Average	147.3	2.388	1.723
Standard Deviation	3.9	0.833	0.556

In this case, experimental conditions on day 1 for the priority-distinction simulation would match those in effect on day 1 for the no-priority simulation. Explain why this is true.

(c) Cards 46 (RMULT) and 47 (CLEAR) in Figure 3C.1 establish a new setting for the four random number generators, and clear the model prior to the day 2 simulation for the no-priority queue discipline, respectively. What effect would interchanging these two cards have on the day 2 simulation? If Cards 46 and 47 were interchanged, and their counterparts for the priority-distinction day 2 simulation (Cards 78 and 79) were also interchanged, would experimental conditions on day 2 be identical for the two queue disciplines under investigation? Why, or why not?

(d) In Case Study 3C, RN1 and RN3 are the arguments of the Functions IAT1 and IAT2, respectively (see Cards 9 and 11 in Figure 3C.1). Assume the model is modified to make RN1 the argument of both of these Functions. Will replicated experimental conditions be in effect if simulations are performed with the modified model? Why, or why not?

(e) Assume that the Figure 3C.1 model is modified to make RN1 the argument of the Functions IAT1 and STYM1, and to make RN3 the argument of the Functions IAT2 and STYM2. Will replicated experimental conditions be in effect if simulations are performed with this modified model? Why, or why not?

(f) The discussion under Model Implementation explains why the RN2 and RN4 settings at the end of a simulated day may depend on the queue discipline in effect. Might the RN1 and RN3 settings in effect at the end of a simulated day also depend on the queue discipline in effect? If not, discuss the possibility of defaulting on the A and C Operands of all RMULT cards in the Figure 3C.1 model (except for RMULT cards 5 and 73). Would the two queue disciplines be investigated under replicated experimental conditions if these defaults were taken?

The remaining parts of this exercise pertain to random number sequences in Case Study 3A. In that case study, the Functions ASSEM and FIRE both use RN1 as their argument (see Cards 5 and 8 in Figure 3A.2).

(g) What subset of the calls on RN1 is used to sample from the assembly-time distribution?

(h) What subset of the calls on RN1 is used to sample from the firing-time distribution?

(i) Critically discuss this statement: "If RN1 and RN2 had been used as the arguments for the Functions ASSEM and FIRE, respectively, and if these two generators had the same initial setting, the Case Study 3A model would be invalid."

2. Exercise 7 of Section 2.19 involves experimenting with two different servers to determine which one is the more economical to hire to work at a tool crib. Data on the two servers are summarized in Table E2. It costs $18 per mechanic per hour when mechanics have to wait for service at the tool crib.

Suppose that a simple 8-hour day simulation is performed with each of these servers, based on two separate runs and using GPSS/360, Version 1 (with "implicit sampling" from the interarrival- and service-time distributions at the GENERATE and ADVANCE Blocks). When this is done, Server 1 actually outperforms Server 2; that is, the average content of Server 1's waiting line is less than that of Server 2. These results are exactly the opposite of what would be expected.

TABLE E2

Server	Hourly Wage	Service Time Distribution (seconds)
1	$4.00	280 ± 150
2	$4.50	280 ± 50

(a) If you did not do so in exercise 7, Section 2.19, provide an interpretation to explain how these counter-intuitive results could come about.

(b) Discuss the possibility of replicating experimental conditions when investigating the two alternative servers.

(c) Perform simulation experiments to determine which of the two servers is indeed the more economical in the long run.

3. Exercise 5 of Section 3.17 involves a comparison of two alternative system configurations. In the spirit of Case Study 3C, show how to build appropriate GPSS models for exercise 3 of Section 3.17 in which the two alternatives are investigated under identical sets of conditions.

4. In exercise 6 of Section 3.17 two alternative queue disciplines are to be investigated. In the spirit of Case Study 3C, show how the investigation can be conducted with GPSS models which guarantee that the alternatives are compared under identical sets of conditions.

5. The alternatives under investigation in Case Study 3B are "number of waiting spaces to provide at a car wash." Devise a GPSS model to measure behavior of the system under identical circumstances when the alternatives of 1, 2, and 3 waiting spaces are investigated. By "identical circumstances" is meant that the exact time of car arrivals is to be duplicated from configuration to configuration. In addition, whether it remains for service or not, the jth arrival is to have the same randomly determined service-time requirement from configuration to configuration, for $j = 1, 2, 3, \ldots$. For example, sup-

TABLE E5

Number of Car	Latent Service Demand (minutes)	Does Car Stay for Service?		
		1-Space	2-Spaces	3-Spaces
1	8	Yes	Yes	Yes
2	5	Yes	Yes	Yes
3	6	No	Yes	Yes
4	3	No	No	Yes
5	4	Yes	Yes	Yes

pose that the first five arrivals represent the *latent* service demands shown in column 2 of Table E5. The last three columns in the table show the hypothesized behavior of these first five arrivals, depending on the configuration under investigation. Because only cars 1, 2, and 5 remain for service at the 1-space facility, the first three service times experienced there are 8, 5, and 4 minutes, in that order. Because the first three cars to arrive remain at the 2- and 3-space facilities, however, the first three service times experienced for each of those configurations are 8, 5, and 6, in that order. In short, because the 1-space Facility could not accommodate the third arrival, it lost not only the "business" but also failed to experience the demand-on-resources represented by that "business." If a given arrival did not represent the same latent service demand for each configuration, it is clear that the investigations would not be conducted under "identical circumstances."

3.22 A Quirk in the Operation of the GENERATE Block

For most GPSS Blocks, it is logically necessary that the Block Operands be evaluated when a Transaction *moves into* the Block. An exception to this is the GENERATE Block. When a Transaction enters a GENERATE Block, it is simply in the process of entering the model. There is no logical need at that time to evaluate the Block Operands. It is when a Transaction *moves out* of a GENERATE Block that its Operands must be evaluated, for the purpose of scheduling the next arrival to that Block.

Despite the above considerations, the GPSS Processor *does* evaluate a GENERATE Block's Operands when a Transaction enters the Block. The code for the Processor is written in such a way that the evaluation of Block Operands occurs whenever a Transaction enters *any* Block, including the GENERATE Block.

When a Transaction enters a GENERATE Block, it is true that the Processor immediately attempts to move it into the sequential Block. If this attempted move can be made, the Proces-

sor then pauses to schedule the successor-Transaction's arrival to the GENERATE Block. It might be thought that the scheduling step would make use of the GENERATE Block's Operand values which were determined when the predecessor-Transaction entered the Block. *But this is not what happens.* Instead, the Processor *again* evaluates the GENERATE Block's Operands to support the scheduling step. To summarize, when a Transaction moves *into* a GENERATE Block, the Block's Operands are evaluated; then, when the same Transaction moves *out of* the GENERATE Block, the Block's Operands are evaluated again.

This redundant evaluation of GENERATE Block Operands *can* have subtle implications for the analyst who is striving to control experimental conditions in simulation modeling. Whether it does depends on the form the GENERATE Block's Operands take. For example, consider the GENERATE Block in Figure 3.29. (The Block corresponds to Card 5 in Figure 3.26.) Constants are supplied as the Operand values. Hence, nothing is affected by the evaluation of these Operands. The A Operand is simply 420, the B Operand is 360, and so on. There are no subtleties here.

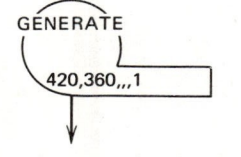

FIGURE 3.29   Example of a GENERATE Block for which redundant Operand evaluation has no subtle implications

Now consider the GENERATE Block shown in Figure 3.30. (The Block corresponds to Card 20 in Figure 3.27.) Evaluation of the A Operand requires evaluation of the Function IAT1. As defined via Cards 9 and 10 in Figure 3.27, the Function's argument is RN1. Hence, RN1 is called and the value it returns is used in the evaluation process. This means that when a

Transaction *enters* the Figure 3.30 GENERATE Block, an RN1 value is fetched to compute an A Operand value which is *never used*. When the same Transaction *leaves* the Figure 3.30 GENERATE Block, *the next RN1 value* will be fetched and used to compute the interarrival time for the Transaction's successor. In this example, then, it is only *every other value* returned by RN1 which is used to compute an "actually applied" interarrival time. The other RN1 values are essentially thrown away because of the redundant evaluation of the GENERATE Block's Operands.

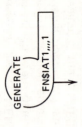

GENERATE

FN$IAT1,,,1

FIGURE 3.30   Example of a GENERATE Block for which redundant Operand evaluation has subtle implications

If experimental conditions are to be controlled in comparing alternatives, there are occasions

when the analyst must be aware of the GENERATE-Block quirk explained in this section. Knowledge of this quirk is used later in the book (in Case Study 5D, for example), to assure replication of experimental conditions when such replication might not otherwise occur.

3.23 EXERCISES

1. In light of the discussion in Section 3.22, it is true that every other value returned by a random-number generator is sometimes thrown away when a GPSS model is run. In Table 3.14, however, each call on RN1 is apparently used; none of the fetched values are thrown away. Explain why this is the case.

2. Refer to the model in Figure 3.27. Assuming that the RMULT Card (Card 5) is removed from that model, and making use of Table 3.1, state which RN1 values are used to compute interarrival times for the first 3 Transactions which enter the model through the GENERATE Block in Location 1 (see Card 20, Figure 3.27).

4
Intermediate GPSS Modeling Concepts, Part I

4.1 Introduction

In Chapter 2, constants were everywhere used to supply nondefault values for Block Operands. When constants are used like this for Block Operands, the Operand values are said to be *directly* specified. Probably the simplest (but also the least powerful) way to provide Operand values is through such *direct specification*. It is also possible to supply Operand values *indirectly*, by use of "variables" whose values are understood to be the Operand values. In Chapter 3, *indirect specification* of Operand values was introduced. Function references were provided as Block Operands in certain cases, with the understanding that the values of those Functions were to be used as Operand values. In particular, Functions were used to indirectly provide A and/or B Operand values at GENERATE and ADVANCE Blocks in Chapter 3.

Further possibilities for indirect specification of Block Operands in GPSS models will be explored in this chapter. Roughly speaking, the sources of Block Operand values to be introduced fall into two categories, *system properties* and *Transaction properties*.

System properties are values which describe the state of the system being modeled. Such quantities as "the current content of Queue 5," and "the number of times the Facility CPU has been captured," are typical system properties. Entity attributes such as these are *automatically*

185

maintained by the GPSS Processor. They are known as *Standard Numerical Attributes* (SNA's). Their values, which usually vary as a simulation proceeds, are available during a simulation. When these names are used as Block Operands, the corresponding current values are the Operand values.

Transactions also have numeric properties. One of these properties, *Priority Level*, has already been introduced, although it has not yet been used as a Block Operand. In addition to having a Priority Level, each Transaction also possesses a set of *Parameters*. A Transaction can have from 0 to 100 different Parameters. Parameters are integer valued. Their values can be assigned and modified in a model according to logic provided by the analyst when the model is built. These values can then be used to advantage in the role of Block Operands. Finally, Transactions are also endowed with a *Mark Time*. Mark Time can be thought of as a Transaction's "time of birth," or time of entry into a model. In certain contexts, Mark Time provides valuable information in assessing the relative performance of a system being modeled.

As well as discussing the use of system and Transaction properties in GPSS modeling, this chapter will introduce the Table entity. With this entity, sample values can be gathered and tabulated "automatically" during a simulation. The Table entity provides a convenient and useful method for investigating the properties of random variables with GPSS models.

4.2 Standard Numerical Attributes

During a simulation, the GPSS Processor automatically records and updates certain information about the various entities used in a model. Some of this information is then printed out at the end of the simulation run. Typical of such information are the Block Counts, Facility and Storage utilizations, average Queue-residence times, etc., that appear as part of the standard model output. Instead of only being available at the end of a run, however, many of these properties are also available *during* a run. The course of a simulation can consequently be controlled dynamically by having the model make direct use of such properties. For example, the rate at which a server works might realistically depend on the number of people waiting for service. When the length of a waiting line grows, a server might tend to work faster than otherwise. To realistically model such a situation, service time should depend on the current Queue content. If this value is available, it can be used in determining service time when each customer goes into service.

Tables 4.1, 4.2, and 4.3 show the various numeric properties of Facilities, Storages, and Queues, respectively, which can be referenced during a simulation. The properties listed in the tables are known as *Standard Numerical Attributes*, or SNA's.[1] The *name* of a Standard Numerical Attribute consists of two parts. The first part is a *family name*. It identifies both the type of entity involved (e.g., Facilities, or Storages, or Queues) and the particular information of interest (e.g., capture count of a Facility, or utilization of a Storage, or current content of a Queue). The second part identifies the *specific family member* involved (e.g., *which* Facility, or *which* Storage, or *which* Queue). In Tables 4.1, 4.2, and 4.3, the family names of the various Standard Numerical Attributes appear in capital letters in the "predefined name" column. Appended to the family name is the *number* or *symbolic name* of the specific family member involved. The number is represented in general by "j" in the tables; the symbolic name is represented by "sn."

For example, referring to the second entry in Table 4.1, FCj is the number of times the Facility numbered j has been captured during a simulation. In practice, j must be the number of a Facility in the model. FC12, for instance, is the capture count of Facility 12; FC3 is the capture count of Facility 3, and so on.

Alternatively, referring again to the second Table 4.1 entry, FC$sn is the number of times the Facility symbolically named "sn" has been captured during a simulation. FC$JOE, for instance, is the capture count of the Facility JOE; FC$KATHY is the capture count of the Facility KATHY, etc. As these examples show, a dollar sign must be inserted between the Standard Numerical Attribute's family name, and the *symbolic* name of the specific family member.

All the Standard Numerical Attributes listed in Tables 4.1, 4.2, and 4.3 are *integer-valued*. Some of the properties are inherently integer-valued, e.g., capture counts, current Queue contents, Storage entry counts, and so on. Other properties normally include a fractional part, e.g., average Storage content, average residence time in a Queue. In GPSS, only the integer part of the "complete" value is carried by the Standard Numerical Attributes as *their* value. In the case of Facility and Storage utilizations, the integer portion of the true utilizations would be zero (or at most 1) if utilizations were expressed as a decimal fraction. As a result, the Standard Numerical Attributes for Facility and Storage utilizations have values expressed in parts per thousand. For example, if a Facility has been in a state of capture 58.2 percent of the time during a simulation, then its utilization is 0.582. Expressed in parts per thousand, the utilization is 582.

Some of the definitions for the Standard

[1] There are other Standard Numerical Attributes in addition to those discussed in this section. They will be introduced in succeeding parts of the book. Appendix I contains a summary of all the Standard Numerical Attributes that are discussed in this book.

TABLE 4.1 Standard Numerical Attributes for Facilities

Predefined[a] Name	Value
Fj, or F$sn	0 if the Facility is not currently captured; 1 otherwise
FCj, or FC$sn	Number of times the Facility has been captured
FRj, or FR$sn	Facility utilization, expressed in parts per thousand
FTj, or FT$sn	Integer portion of the average Facility holding time

[a] "j" is the number of the specific family member in question; or, if the name has been chosen symbolically, "sn" is the symbolic name.

TABLE 4.2 Standard Numerical Attributes for Storages

Predefined Name	Value
Rj, or R$sn	Remaining Storage capacity
Sj, or S$sn	Current Storage content
SAj, or SA$sn	Integer portion of the average Storage content
SCj, or SC$sn	Storage entry count; each time an ENTER Block referencing the Storage is executed, SCj (or SC$sn) is incremented by the ENTER Block's B Operand; the value is never decremented
SMj, or SM$sn	Maximum Storage content; the maximum value Sj (or S$sn) has attained; not to be confused with the Storage capacity
SRj, or SR$sn	Storage utilization, expressed in parts per thousand
STj, or ST$sn	Integer portion of the average holding time; expressed relative to SCj (or SC$sn)

TABLE 4.3 Standard Numerical Attributes for Queues

Predefined Name	Value
Qj, or Q$sn	Current Queue content
QAj, or QA$sn	Integer portion of the average Queue content
QCj, or QC$sn	Queue entry count; each time a QUEUE Block referencing the Queue is executed, QCj (or QC$sn) is incremented by the QUEUE Block's B Operand; the value is never decremented
QMj, or QM$sn	Maximum Queue content; the maximum value Qj (or Q$sn) has attained
QTj, or QT$sn	Integer portion of the average residence time in the Queue, expressed relative to QCj (or QC$sn); note that QCj (or QC$sn) includes zero Queue entries, that is, entries whose residence time in the Queue was zero
QXj, or QX$sn	Integer portion of the average residence time in the Queue, expressed relative to "QCj minus QZj" (or "QC$sn minus QZ$sn"), thus excluding zero Queue entries
QZj, or QZ$sn	Zero Queue entry count; sum of Queue entries for which the residence time in the Queue was zero

Numerical Attributes listed in Tables 4.1, 4.2, and 4.3 look a bit forbidding, especially several of those for Storages and Queues. Remember that all these Standard Numerical Attributes are nothing other than the integer portion of the statistics which the GPSS Processor automatically maintains and prints out for the various Facilities, Storages, and Queues in a model. (In Section 4.5, exercises 2, 3, and 4 ask you to match up the various Standard Numerical Attributes with the statistics for Facilities, Storages, and Queues, as they appear in the output from selected Chapter 2 Case Studies.)

Like Facility statistics, Facility SNA's are straightforward. Those for Storages and Queues are also straightforward *unless* nondefault B Operands have been used with various ENTER and LEAVE or QUEUE and DEPART Blocks. Then the Storage and Queue Standard Numerical Attributes require a somewhat more careful interpretation, because they are maintained with respect to "servers" (for Storages) and "units of content" (for Queues), not with respect to Transactions. It might be useful to review the discussion of Storage and Queue statistics in Chapter 2. Storage statistics are discussed in Section 2.37, and also in Section 2.39 (as part of Case Study 2E). Queue statistics are discussed in Section 2.15, and also in Section 2.17 (as part of Case Study 2A).

Block Counts can also be referenced in a simulation as Standard Numerical Attributes. The *family names* for Current and Total Block Counts are W and N, respectively. Hence, W$BLOK1 is the number of Transactions currently at the Block in the Location BLOK1. Or, N$PATHC is the total number of Transactions which have entered the Block in the Location PATHC. The position occupied by Blocks can also be referred to numerically. For example, W17 is the Current Count at the Block in Location 17. As mentioned earlier, Block Locations are usually named symbolically; as a result, the forms W$ssn and N$ssn are most frequently used when Block Counts are included in the logic of a model.

The Relative Clock can also be used as data in a model. The name of the Relative Clock is C1. The value of the Absolute Clock is *not* available as a Standard Numerical Attribute. There is, however, a method for determining the Absolute Clock's value. The method is explained later in this chapter.

Note that Block Counts are inherently integer-valued. Also, because of the use of an integer clock in GPSS, C1 is inherently integer-valued. The random-number generators, RNj, are Standard Numerical Attributes. Functions are also Standard Numerical Attributes. The discrete and continuous Functions studied in Chapter 3 are numeric-valued. In general, the "true value" of a Function includes a fractional part. Whether this true value, or only its integer portion, is used is context-dependent.

1. When a Function is employed as the B Operand in a GENERATE or ADVANCE Block, the true value is used. (There are also two other contexts, not yet discussed, in which a Function's true value is used.)

2. In any other context, only the integer portion of a Function's true value is used.

Finally, *constants* can also be thought of as Standard Numerical Attributes in GPSS. The "family name" of a constant is K. The "specific member" is the constant itself. Hence, K3 is the constant 3; K561 is the constant 561, and so on. When constants are used in GPSS, inclusion of the K is optional. In this book the practice is to always simply write the constant itself, without prefacing it with a K.

4.3 Use of Standard Numerical Attributes

The most obvious application of Standard Numerical Attributes in a model is to use them as Block Operands. Several examples of such use are suggested in Figure 4.1. When a Transaction moves into the ENTER Block in Figure 4.1(a), for instance, it captures R3 of the parallel servers simulated with Storage 3. Because R3 is the number of *currently available* servers represented by that Storage, the Transaction consequently takes up the remaining capacity of the Storage. Or, when a Transaction moves into the Figure 4.1(b) ADVANCE Block, its holding time there equals the capture count of the Facility EMMA. And so on. These examples are out of context, and consequently do not look meaningful. They do illustrate, however, how Standard Numerical Attributes can be used as Operands in the various GPSS Blocks.

A less obvious application for Standard Numerical Attributes is to use them as *Function arguments*. The Functions introduced in Chapter 3 always had an RNj as their argument, because they were to be used in sampling from probability distributions. There is no reason, however,

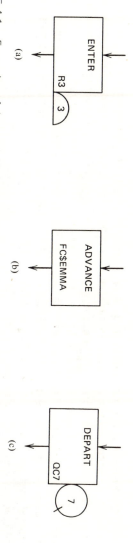

FIGURE 4.1 Examples of the use of Standard Numerical Attributes as Block Operands. (a) Use of FC$sn as a Block Operand. (b) Use of R$_j$ as a Block Operand. (c) Use of QC$_j$ as a Block Operand.

realized are restricted to being integers. This follows from the fact that Standard Numerical Attributes are integer-valued in the language.

2. When Function arguments *extend beyond the range* of values supplied in the Function definition, the Function value is taken to be that of the nearest point. In the Figure 4.2 example, the range of argument values supplied in the definition is from 5 to 15. As already indicated, for arguments less than 5 (i.e., out of range on the low side), the Function value is 1. For arguments greater than 15 (i.e., out of range on the high side), 7 would be used as the Function's value.

Functions having Standard Numerical Attributes as arguments can be either discrete or continuous. Suppose that the Figure 4.2 Function is to be continuous, rather than discrete. Definitionally, this simply involves changing the "D4" on the FUNCTION header card to "C4", as shown in Figure 4.3(a). Computationally, the

that a Function argument must be an RN$_j$. For example, consider the discrete Function defined in Figure 4.2(a). The Function's argument is the Total Count at the Block in Location MARY. When the Function is referenced during a simulation, the Total Count at the Block in that Location will be used as the value of the independent variable. The corresponding Function value will be determined in the usual manner for discrete Functions. The correspondence between argument values and Function values is shown graphically for this example in Figure 4.2(b). Argument values of 5 or less produce a Function value of 1; argument values of 8 or less, but greater than 5, produce a Function value of 2; and so on. Two considerations bear mention here.

1. When arguments other than an RN$_j$ are used in Function definitions, the argument values that can be

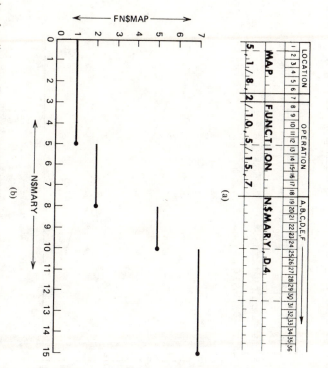

(a)

MAP. FUNCTION. N$MARY,D4.
5,1/8.,2/10.,5/15.,7

(b)

FIGURE 4.2 Example of a discrete Function with a Block Count as its argument: (a) Definition of the Function. (b) Graphical interpretation of the Function.

effect of having the Function be continuous was explained in Chapter 3. When the Function is evaluated, the interval in which the argument's value falls is first determined. Then, a linear interpolation is performed across the interval. The Function's true value, in general, will then include a fractional part. Whether the true value, or only the integer portion, will subsequently be used depends on the context in which the Function is referenced.

Figure 4.3(b) shows the graphical interpretation of the Figure 4.3(a) Function. Consecutive points have been joined with straight-line segments, indicating the linear interpolation in effect. Whenever the Function's argument is out of range, the Function's value is taken to be that of the nearest point. This situation is identical to that for discrete Functions. Whether the Figure 4.3(a) Function is defined as discrete or continuous, then, an argument of 15 or greater produces a Function value of 7. Similarly, an argument of 5 or less produces a Function value of 1.

4.4 CASE STUDY 4A
Modeling the Influence of Queue Length on Mean Service Rate

(1) Statement of the Problem

In a one-line, one-server queuing system, arrivals occur in a Poisson pattern with a mean

rate of 12 arrivals per hour. Service is performed exponentially, but the mean service time depends on the content of the waiting line ahead of the server. The dependence is shown in Table 4A.1.

Build a GPSS model of the system, then use the model to estimate the effective mean service time. If the arrival rate increases to the extent of one additional arrival per hour, will the server still be able to handle the traffic, or will the waiting line tend to become longer and longer?

TABLE 4A.1   Mean Service Time as a Function of Waiting-Line Content in Case Study 4A

Content of the Waiting Line	Mean Service Time (minutes)
0	5.5
1 or 2	5.0
3, 4, or 5	4.5
6 or more	4.0

(2) Approach Taken in Building the Model

The Block sequence used to model a one-line, one-server queuing system is already familiar, as is the method for simulating Poisson arrivals and exponential servers. The sole addition to previously developed ideas in this model is inclusion of a discrete GPSS Function using current Queue content as its argument, thereby making it possible to determine the server's mean service time in terms of waiting-line length.

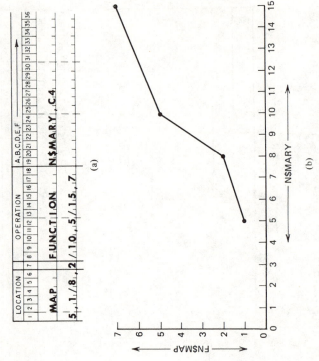

FIGURE 4.3   Example of a continuous Function with a Block Count as its argument. (a) Definition of the Function. (b) Graphical interpretation of the Function.

(3) Table of Definitions

Time Unit : 1 second

TABLE 4A.2   Table of Definitions for Case Study 4A

GPSS Entity	Interpretation
Transactions	Customers
Facilities	
SURVR	The server
Functions	
MEAN	Function relating mean service time to Queue content as shown in Table 4A.1
XPDIS	Function for sampling from the exponential distribution with a mean value of 1
Queues	
WAIT	The Queue used to maintain statistics on the condition of the waiting line

(4) Block Diagram

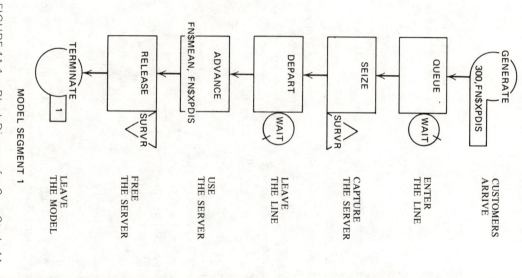

MODEL SEGMENT 1

FIGURE 4A.1   Block Diagram for Case Study 4A

(5) Extended Program Listing

```
BLOCK
NUMBER  *LOC    OPERATION   A,B,C,D,E,F,G              COMMENTS                          CARD NUMBER
                SIMULATE                                                                 1
        *                                                                                2
        *       FUNCTION DEFINITION(S)                                                   3
        *                                                                                4
        MEAN FUNCTION    Q$WAIT,D4          MEAN SERVICE TIME DISTRIBUTION               5
        0.330/2,300/5,270/6,240                                                          6
        XPDIS FUNCTION   RN1,C24            EXPONENTIAL DISTRIBUTION FUNCTION            7
        0.0/.1,.104/.2,.222/.3,.355/.4,.509/.5,.69/.6,.915/.7,1.2/.75,1.38              8
        .8,1.6/.84,1.83/.88,2.12/.9,2.3/.92,2.52/.94,2.81/.95,2.99/.96,3.2              9
        .97,3.5/.98,3.9/.99,4.6/.995,5.3/.998,6.2/.999,7/.9998,8                        10
        *                                                                                11
        *       MODEL SEGMENT 1                                                          12
        *                                                                                13
1               GENERATE    300,FN$XPDIS       CUSTOMERS ARRIVE                          14
2               QUEUE       WAIT               ENTER THE LINE                            15
3               SEIZE       SURVR              CAPTURE THE SERVER                        16
4               DEPART      WAIT               LEAVE THE LINE                            17
5               ADVANCE     FN$MEAN,FN$XPDIS   USE THE SERVER                            18
6               RELEASE     SURVR              FREE THE SERVER                           19
7               TERMINATE   1                  LEAVE THE MODEL                           20
        *                                                                                21
        *       CONTROL CARDS                                                            22
        *                                                                                23
                START       500,,100           START THE RUN                             24
                END                            RETURN CONTROL TO OPERATING SYSTEM        25
```

FIGURE 4A.2   Extended Program Listing for Case Study 4A

(6) Program Output

No program output is shown directly.

(7) Discussion

Model Implementation. In the Extended Program Listing in Figure 4A.2, note how Q$WAIT has been used as the A Operand in the Function card used to define the Function MEAN (Card Number 5). Also note that Block 5 is "ADVANCE FN$MEAN,FN$XPDIS". When a Transaction moves into the ADVANCE Block, then, the Processor evaluates the Function MEAN to determine the A Operand value in effect. This value, in turn, depends on the current Queue content. Hence, the server is sensitive to the length of the waiting line as he begins his next service.

Inspection of Card 24 shows that the START card's Snap Interval option (C Operand) has been used. "START 500,,100" causes statistical printouts to occur just after the one hundredth, two hundredth, three hundredth, four hundredth, and five hundredth completion of a service. (The model shuts off with the five hundredth service completion.) This makes it possible to trace the behavior of statistics such as mean service time as the simulation proceeds.

Program Output.[2] Tables 4A.3 and 4A.4 display selected statistics in effect just after the one hundredth, two hundredth, three hundredth,

[2] Total CPU time for the simulation on an IBM 360/67 computer was 4.8 seconds.

four hundredth, and five hundredth completion of a service, for arrival rates of 12 and 13 per hour, respectively. The information for 500 service completions in Table 4A.3 indicates that average service time is about 290 seconds, or somewhat under 5 minutes; the server is about 90 percent utilized; and there are more than four customers in the waiting line on average. About 9 percent of the customers do not have to wait for service.

In Table 4A.4, after 500 service completions the server's utilization is over 96 percent, and there have been over eight customers in the waiting line on average. Hence, changing the hourly arrival rate from 12 to 13 (an increase of about 17 percent) has almost doubled the average queue content. At the same time, the percentage of zero entries has dropped from 9 to 3.

Simple inspection of the original data shows that the server can handle the traffic when the arrival rate increases from 12 to 13 per hour. The increased rate corresponds to a mean inter-arrival time of 4.6^+ minutes. Table 4A.3 indicates that with three, four, or five customers in the waiting line, the server's mean service time is 4.5 minutes, which is just insufficient to cope with the traffic. With waiting-line content of six or more, however, the average service rate drops to 4 minutes, which more than accommodates the traffic. There is no chance, then, that the waiting line will grow without bound as the simulation proceeds.

TABLE 4A.3   A Summary of Program Output for Case Study 4A

Number of Service Completions	Facility Utilization	Average Holding Time per Capture (seconds)	Average Queue Content	Percent Zero Entries
100	0.996	313	4.6	1.9
200	0.945	296	5.0	6.4
300	0.905	291	5.3	8.7
400	0.899	284	4.5	8.9
500	0.902	292	4.3	9.2

TABLE 4A.4   A Summary of Program Output for Case Study 4A with Mean Interarrival Time Decreased from 300 to 277

Number of Service Completions	Facility Utilization	Average Holding Time per Capture (seconds)	Average Queue Content	Percent Zero Entries
100	0.999	276	12.4	0.9
200	0.993	277	11.6	0.9
300	0.989	267	10.0	1.3
400	0.955	266	7.8	3.9
500	0.964	270	8.3	3.0

4.5 Exercises

1. (a) Of what two parts do the names of Standard Numerical Attributes consist?

(b) What information is conveyed by the first part?

(c) What information is conveyed by the second part?

(d) What character stands between the first and second parts when the second part is symbolic rather than numeric?

(e) In words, what is the value of QZ14? Of SC$BOATS? Of F$ALONE?

(f) What Standard Numerical Attribute has as its value the fractional utilization of Facility 15? Of the Facility MYRNA? What Standard Numerical Attribute has as its value the current content of Queue 1 ?

(g) Discuss the difference between the fractional utilization of a Facility as it appears in standard simulation output, and as it is used as the value of a Standard Numerical Attribute.

(h) Explain the difference between QT6 and QX6. Can QX6 ever be greater than QT6? Why or why not?

(i) Explain the differences between Qj, QAj, and QM$j.

(j) Explain the difference between W$BYPAS and N$BYPAS. Would you always expect one to be at least as large as the other?

(k) What is the relationship between RBUS, SBUS, and the user-defined capacity of the Storage named BUS?

(l) What is the value of the B Operand in Figure 4.1 (b) ?

(m) What will the recorded content of Queue 7 be just after a Transaction enters the DEPART Block in Figure 4.1 (c), thereby causing that Block subroutine to be executed?

(n) What Standard Numerical Attribute has the Relative Clock as its value?

(o) What range of values can RN3 assume when it is used as a Function argument? Do these values include a fractional part?

(p) What range of values can RN3 assume when it is used in any context except as a Function argument? Do these values include a fractional part?

2. Figure E2 is a repetition of Figure 2A.5, which shows Facility statistics produced at the end of the Case Study 2A simulation.

(a) Which columns in Figure E2 correspond to the following Standard Numerical Attributes?
   (i) FC$JOE
   (ii) FR$JOE
   (iii) FT$JOE

(b) Using information shown in Figure E2, what were the values of the Standard Numerical Attributes listed under (a) when the Case Study 2A simulation shut off?

(c) What was the value of F$JOE when the Case Study 2A simulation shut off?

FACILITY	AVERAGE UTILIZATION	NUMBER ENTRIES	AVERAGE TIME/TRAN	SEIZING TRANS. NO.	PREEMPTING TRANS. NO.
JOE	.860	26	15.884	3	

FIGURE E2

QUEUE	MAXIMUM CONTENTS	AVERAGE CONTENTS	TOTAL ENTRIES	ZERO ENTRIES	PERCENT ZEROS	AVERAGE TIME/TRANS	$AVERAGE TIME/TRANS	TABLE NUMBER	CURRENT CONTENTS
JOEQ	1	.160	27	12	44.4	2.851	5.133		1

$AVERAGE TIME/TRANS = AVERAGE TIME/TRANS EXCLUDING ZERO ENTRIES

FIGURE E3

3. Figure E3 is a repetition of Figure 2A.6, which shows Queue statistics produced at the end of the Case Study 2A simulation.

(a) Which columns in Figure E3 correspond to the following Standard Numerical Attributes?

   (i) Q$JOEQ
   (ii) QA$JOEQ
   (iii) QC$JOEQ
   (iv) QM$JOEQ
   (v) QT$JOEQ
   (vi) QX$JOEQ
   (vii) QZ$JOEQ

(b) Using information shown in Figure E3, what were the values of the Standard Numerical Attributes listed under (a) when the Case Study 2A simulation shut off?

4. Figure E4 is a repetition of Figure 2E.4(a), which shows Storage statistics produced at the end of one of the Case Study 2E simulations.

STORAGE	CAPACITY	AVERAGE CONTENTS	AVERAGE UTILIZATION	ENTRIES	AVERAGE TIME/TRAN	CURRENT CONTENTS	MAXIMUM CONTENTS
MEN	3	2.185	.728	1924	7.087		3
NOWON	50	49.182	.983	1974	155.471	50	50

FIGURE E4

(a) Which columns in Figure E4 correspond to the following Standard Numerical Attributes?

   (i) S$MEN
   (ii) SA$MEN
   (iii) SC$MEN
   (iv) SM$MEN
   (v) SR$MEN
   (vi) ST$MEN

(b) Using information shown in Figure E4, what were the values of the Standard Numerical Attributes listed under (a) when the corresponding Case Study 2E simulation shut off?

(c) What was the value of R$MEN when the simulation shut off?

5. (a) At time 5, Facility 1 is captured. At time 10, it is released. Assume the Facility has not otherwise been captured.

   (i) What is F1 at time 4? at time 8? at time 12?

   (ii) What is FR1 at time 8? at time 10? at time 12?

   (iii) What is FT1 at time 8? at time 10? at time 12?

(b) At times 5 and 10, respectively, the Blocks "ENTER 4" and "LEAVE 4" are executed. Assume Storage 4 has a capacity of 3, and that no other references have been made to it.

   (i) What is SC4?
   (ii) What is SM4?
   (iii) What is SA4 at time 8? at time 12?
   (iv) What is SR4 at time 8? at time 12?
   (v) What is ST4 at time 8? at time 12?

(c) Repeat (b) when the B Operand on the indicated ENTER and LEAVE Blocks is 2.

(d) The Queue ALPHA had a content of 3 for 5 time units. In addition, it had a content of 2 for 0 time units. Assume no other entries to the Queue have occurred.

   (i) What is QC$ALPHA?
   (ii) What is QZ$ALPHA?
   (iii) What is QT$ALPHA?
   (iv) What is QX$ALPHA?
   (v) At time 10, what is QA$ALPHA? (Assume that the current Queue content at time 10 is 0.)

(e) The Queue BETA had a content of 3 for 0 time units. Assuming no other entries to the Queue have occurred, what is the value of QM$BETA?

6. The Function BOND is defined in Figure E6.

LOCATION	OPERATION	A,B,C,D,E,F
1 2 3 4 5 6 7	8 9 10 11 12 13 14 15 16 17 18	19 20 21 22 23 24 25 26 27 28 29 30 31 32 33 34 35 36
BOND	FUNCTION	SR$SHELF,D3
		200,-5/450,-1/765,12

FIGURE E6

(a) Show a graphical interpretation of the Function.

(b) What is the Function's value when SR$SHELF is 150? 450? 451? 895?

7. The Function TOUGH is defined in Figure E7.

LOCATION (1–36)	OPERATION	A,B,C,D,E,F →
TOUGH	FUNCTION	QM2,C.4
		0,0/.3,.9/.5,1.8/.8,2.0

FIGURE E7

(a) Show a graphical interpretation of the Function.

(b) What is the Function's true value when QM2 is 0? 1? 3? 4? 6? 10?

8. Define a Function whose value is to depend on the Current Count at the Block in Location PATHO as shown in Table E8. Show a graphical interpretation of the Function.

TABLE E8

Function Value	Current Count
1	0
4	1, 2, or 3
2	4 or 5
4	6
−5	7 or more

9. Define a Function whose value is to be twice the current content of the Queue ALPHA, for contents of 0, 1, 2, 3, and 4, and whose value is to be 10 otherwise. Do this two ways: (a) with a discrete, six-point Function, and (b) with a continuous, two-point Function. Show graphical interpretations for each approach.

10. Suppose that the Location occupied by the QUEUE Block in Figure 4A.1 is symbolically named HOLD. Discuss how the model in Case Study 4A would be changed, if at all, by using W$HOLD rather than Q$WAIT as the argument of the Function MEAN.

11. (a) A particular exponential server tends to work at a slower and slower rate as the 8-hour work day goes by. During the first 2 hours of the day, it takes him 12 minutes on average to perform a service. During the next 2 hours, his average service time is 15 minutes. During the fifth, sixth, and seventh hours, each service completion requires an average of 17 minutes. Service started during the eighth hour requires an average of 20 minutes for completion. Assuming that the time unit in a model is 0.1 minutes, define a discrete Function whose value is the mean time required by the server to perform a service. Then show how the Function can be used at an ADVANCE Block to simulate service time. Show a graphical interpretation for the Function.

(b) The situation described in (a) implies that the server's mean service time increases in *steps* as the day proceeds. It would be much more realistic to assume that the mean service time increases *continuously* as the day goes by. Then, instead of depending simply on the *hour* of the day, the mean service time would depend on the exact time within the hour at which service is begun. Show how to define a *continuous* Function which describes increasing service time according to this pattern: at time 0, mean service time is 12 minutes; by the end of the second hour, mean service time has increased to 15 minutes; by the end of the fourth hour, it has risen to 17 minutes; by the end of the seventh hour, it has risen to 20 minutes; and by the end of the eighth and last hour, it has risen to 25 minutes. Assume that the rise is continuous and uniform over the time intervals indicated. Also assume that the time unit is 0.1 minutes. Show a graphical interpretation for the Function you define.

4.6 Transaction Parameters

As indicated in Section 4.1, each Transaction in a GPSS model possesses a set of from 0 to 100 *Parameters*. A Transaction's Parameter set can be conveniently thought of as a collection of Standard Numerical Attributes which the Transaction owns. As a Transaction moves through a model, its Parameter values can be assigned and modified according to logic provided by the analyst. These values can then be used to advantage as Block Operands, and as Function arguments.

Some of the pertinent features of Transaction Parameters will now be considered.

1. The *number of Parameters* a Transaction has is specified via the F Operand at the GENERATE Block through which the Transaction enters a model. *The default value of the GENERATE Block F Operand is 12.* In all models shown thus far, this default value has been in effect.

2. As true with most other Standard Numerical Attributes, the *name* of a Parameter consists of two parts, a *family name* and indication of a *specific family member*. The family name is P. Specific family members are designated numerically as 1, 2, 3, 4, ..., 98, 99,

100. Hence, P22 is the name of Parameter 22 of a Transaction, P3 is the name of Parameter 3, and so on. Parameter references are written in general as Pj, where j is some integer between 1 and the number of Parameters a Transaction has. Hence, if a Transaction enters a model through a GENERATE Block with a default value for the F Operand, Pj is meaningful for it when j = 1, 2, 3, . . . , 11, or 12, but is meaningless when j = 13, 14, 15, . . . , 98, 99, or 100.

Parameters cannot be named symbolically. Hence, references such as P$YEAR, P$COLOR, and so on, are *invalid.*

3. The *values* of Parameters are *signed integers.* The maximum magnitude of a Parameter depends whether it is of the *halfword* or *fullword* type. All of a Transaction's Parameters are either of the halfword or the fullword type. The type is determined by the G Operand of the GENERATE Block. The default value of the G Operand is H (for halfword). If fullword Parameters are required, then F (for fullword) must be used as the G Operand at the corresponding GENERATE Block. Halfword Parameters can range in value from −32,768 to +32,767, inclusive (that is, from −2^{15} to +2^{15}−1). Fullword Parameters can range in value from −2,147,483,648 to +2,147,483,647, inclusive (that is, from −2^{31} to +2^{31}−1).

4. When a Transaction enters a model, the initial value of each of its Parameters is zero.

5. The *meaning* of Parameters is determined by the analyst. This is frequently done by using a numeric encoding scheme. At other times, Parameter values have direct significance. Suppose, for example, that a rent-a-car agency is being modeled, and that a Transaction is a car. The characteristics of each car might be represented as Parameter values according to the scheme shown in Table 4.4. Hence, a Transaction having P1, P2, and P3 values of 3, 1, and 1973, respectively, would represent a green Volkswagen made in 1973. The value of P3 is directly significant. The meaning of the P1 and P2 values is clear only in terms of the given encoding scheme.

6. Because Parameters are Standard Numerical Attributes, they can be used as Block Operands and Function arguments.

7. When a Parameter is used as a Block Operand or Function argument, a question arises as to *which Transaction* is involved. For example, P6 does not appear to have a unique value. After all, many different Transactions in a model may each have a Parameter

numbered 6. Data are only used, though, when Block subroutines are executed. Block subroutines, in turn, are executed only when a Transaction moves through a sequence of Blocks. When Parameter values are required as data, the values are taken from the Parameter set of the active Transaction, i.e., the Transaction currently being processed.

For example, suppose that a Function is defined as shown in Figure 4.4(a), and that a Transaction with a Parameter 5 value of 4 enters the ADVANCE Block shown in Figure 4.4(b). Execution of the Block subroutine involves evaluation of the Function AVG. This, in turn, requires finding the value of the Function's argument, P5. The P5 value of the Transaction being processed is 4. The Function's corresponding value is 8. The holding time is therefore uniformly distributed over the interval of integers 8 ± 2. The Processor now samples from this distribution, and the value drawn is used as the holding time.

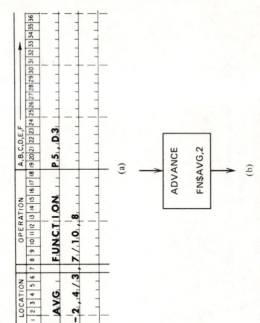

(a)

(b)

FIGURE 4.4   An example showing a Parameter used in context. (a) Definition of a Function using Parameter 5 as its argument. (b) An ADVANCE Block which uses the Function as its A Operand.

The example in Figure 4.4 shows how holding time can be made to depend on a *Transaction property.* Case Study 4A illustrated how a holding time can be made to depend on a *property of a Queue.* It should be evident that use of sys-

TABLE 4.4   A Possible Interpretation of Parameter Values in a Specific Example

Value of P1	Significance (color of car)	Value of P2	Significance (make of car)	Value of P3	Significance (model year)
1	Red	1	Volkswagen	1972	1972
2	Blue	2	Pinto	1973	1973
3	Green	3	Vega	1974	1974
4	Grey	4	Gremlin		

tem and Transaction properties as typified in these examples provides considerable flexibility in GPSS modeling. After the methods for assigning and modifying Parameter values are introduced in the next section, Case Study 4B is presented to further illustrate this flexibility.

When the Current and/or Future Events Chains are printed out, Parameter values of Transactions on those chains appear as part of the printout. The START card D Operand will be used in Case Study 4B to force a chain printout at the end of the simulation. The way Parameter values are displayed in the output will then be indicated.

4.7 Modification of Parameter Values: The ASSIGN Block

A Transaction has the value of its Parameters modified when it moves into an ASSIGN Block. This Block, and its A and B Operands, are shown in Figure 4.5. When a Transaction enters an ASSIGN Block, the B-Operand data is copied to the Parameter whose *number* is provided by the A Operand. As a result, the previous value of that Parameter is replaced by a new value. Whenever a Transaction enters the ASSIGN Block shown in Figure 4.6, for example, the value of its third Parameter becomes 25. The previous value of P3, whatever it might have been, is lost in the process.

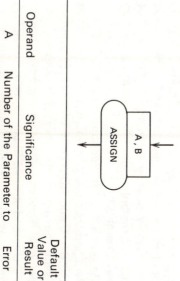

Operand	Significance	Default Value or Result
A	Number of the Parameter to be modified	Error
B	Data for be used for the modification	Error

FIGURE 4.5 The ASSIGN Block and its A and B Operands

In the Figure 4.6 example, the A and B Operands are both supplied directly, as constants. It is also possible to supply one or both of these Operands indirectly, with Standard Numerical Attributes. When a Transaction enters

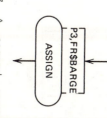

FIGURE 4.6 A first example for the ASSIGN Block

the ASSIGN Block shown in Figure 4.7, for example, the fractional utilization of the Facility BARGE will be copied to the Parameter whose number is the value of Parameter 3. If P3 has a value of 5, then the value of FR$BARGE becomes the value of P5; if P3 is 22, the value of FR$BARGE becomes the value of Parameter 22, and so on. Contrast the use of 3 and P3 as the A Operands in Figures 4.6 and 4.7, respectively.

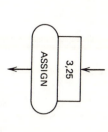

FIGURE 4.7 A second example for the ASSIGN Block

Figures 4.6 and 4.7 illustrate use of the ASSIGN Block in *replacement mode.* In this mode, the old value of a Parameter is replaced with a new value, without regard to what the old value might have been. It is also possible to use the ASSIGN Block in *increment mode,* and in *decrement mode.* In increment mode, the Parameter's new value is computed by adding the B Operand data to the old value. In decrement mode, the Parameter's new value is computed by subtracting the B Operand data from the old value. Increment and decrement mode are specified by placing a plus (+) or minus (−) sign, respectively, ahead of the comma separating the A and B Operands.

Figure 4.8 shows use of the ASSIGN Block in increment mode. When a Transaction enters the Figure 4.8 ASSIGN Block, Parameter 4 will be increased by an amount equal to the current content of Queue 5. In this example, note that the A Operand is directly specified, whereas the B Operand is indirectly specified.

Figure 4.9 shows use of the ASSIGN Block in decrement mode. When a Transaction enters

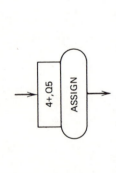

FIGURE 4.8   A third example for the ASSIGN Block

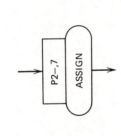

FIGURE 4.9   A fourth example for the ASSIGN Block

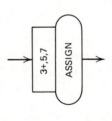

FIGURE 4.10   Example of an ASSIGN Block with which the C Operand has been used

the Figure 4.9 Block, 7 will be subtracted from the Parameter whose number is in Parameter 2. For example, if P2 is 3, a Transaction entering the Block will have 7 subtracted from Parameter 3. Or, if P2 is 2, 7 will be subtracted from Parameter 2. In Figure 4.9, the A Operand is indirectly specified, and the B Operand is directly specified.

Although not indicated in Figure 4.5, an optional C Operand can be used with the ASSIGN Block. When this is done, the C Operand supplies the *number of a Function*. The Processor performs these steps in executing the ASSIGN Block subroutine when the C Operand is used.

1. The C Operand is evaluated.
2. The Function whose number equals the C Operand's value is evaluated.
3. The Function's *entire* value is combined *multiplicatively* with the B-Operand data.
4. The *integer portion* of the product is used to replace, increment, or decrement the Parameter specified with the A Operand.

For example, assume that a Transaction enters the ASSIGN Block shown in Figure 4.10. The C Operand is directly specified as 7. Function 7 is consequently evaluated. Assume the Function's value is 1.94. This value is then multiplied by the B-Operand data, 5, producing 9.70. The integer portion of this product, 9, is then added to Parameter 3 of the entering Transaction.

The effect in Figure 4.10 would be totally different if FN7, instead of 7, had been used as the C Operand. The Processor would interpret FN7 as *indirectly specifying* the number of a Function. First, Function 7 would be evaluated. Assume as before that Function 7's value is 1.94. The Processor would take the integer portion, 1, as the number of another Function. It would then evaluate Function 1, multiply the resulting value by 5 (B-Operand data), and add the integer portion of the product to Parameter 3.

It is *invalid* to supply the *symbolic* name of a Function as the C Operand at an ASSIGN Block. The analyst is consequently forced to use numeric names in defining Functions which are to be referenced at ASSIGN Blocks via the C-Operand option.[3]

Observe that the ASSIGN Block B–C Operands stand in the same relationship to each other as the GENERATE and ADVANCE Block A–B Operands. Recall that when FNj or FNsn is used as the B Operand at a GENERATE or ADVANCE Block, the value of the Function numbered j (or symbolically named sn) is multiplied by the A-Operand data. (The format is admittedly slightly different at the ASSIGN Block, where only j, not FNj, would be used as the C Operand.)

As pointed out in Sections 3.13 and 3.15, the only significant use of Function modification at GENERATE and ADVANCE Blocks is to simulate Poisson arrivals and exponential servers, respectively. Similarly, the only important use of the C Operand at an ASSIGN Block is in sampling from the exponential distribution. For example, assume a particular exponential server requires 50 times units on average to complete a service, and that 5 is the number of the usual 24-point continuous GPSS Function for sampling from

[3] Actually, the analyst also has recourse to two alternative actions. First, he can name the pertinent Function symbolically, then *predict* the corresponding number the Processor will give it. That number can then be used at the ASSIGN Block. Alternatively, by use of the EQU control card, the analyst can *force* the Processor to make a symbolic name correspond to a given number, with the number then being used at the ASSIGN Block. Further details are given in Section 4.16.

the exponential distribution. When a Transaction enters the ASSIGN Block in Figure 4.11, a sample is drawn from the service-time distribution and stored in Parameter 9. Suppose that the Transaction eventually is to capture the exponential server in question. Holding time can then be simulated by moving the Transaction into the Block "ADVANCE P9". Service time required by the Transaction, although a random variable, would have been *predetermined* at the ASSIGN Block. This approach is of interest when it is important to control experimental conditions while simulating exponential servers. Case Study 4D in Section 4.15 makes use of such an approach.

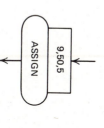

FIGURE 4.11   An example showing how an ASSIGN Block can be used to sample from the exponential distribution

4.8 CASE STUDY 4B
A Grocery Store Model

(1) Statement of the Problem

A small grocery store consists of three aisles and a single checkout counter. Shoppers arrive at the store in a Poisson pattern with a mean inter-arrival time of 75 seconds. After arriving, each customer takes a basket and *may* then go down one or more of the three aisles, selecting items for purchase as he proceeds. The probability of going down any particular aisle is shown in Table 4B.1. The time required to shop an aisle, and the number of items selected for purchase in the process, are uniformly distributed random variables. Information describing these variables, which depend on the aisle in question, is also shown in Table 4B.1.

When shopping is complete, the customers queue up first-come, first-served at the checkout counter. In this area, each customer chooses an additional 2 ± 1 "impulse items" for purchase. A customer's checkout time depends on the number of items he is buying. Checkout time is 3 seconds per item. After checking out, a customer leaves his basket at the front of the store and departs.

Build a GPSS model for the grocery store, then use the model to simulate an 8-hour day. Measure the utilization of the checkout girl, and the maximum length of the waiting line at the checkout counter. Assuming there is no limit to the number of shopping baskets, also determine the maximum number of baskets in use at any one time.

(2) Approach Taken in Building the Model

When customer-Transactions are brought into the model, they first enter the Storage CARTS, simulating the process of taking a shopping basket. No capacity-definition card is included for this Storage. The Processor consequently assumes a default capacity of 2,147,483,647, as previously explained in Chapter 2. This insures that, consistent with the problem statement, "there is no limit to the number of shopping baskets." The output can then be examined to determine the basket requirement through the statistic "MAXIMUM CONTENTS" of the Storage.

The entrance to each aisle is modeled with a TRANSFER Block operating in statistical transfer mode. A customer who decides not to shop a particular aisle moves nonsequentially from this TRANSFER Block to the equivalent TRANSFER Block placed at the entrance to the next aisle. A customer who decides to shop an aisle moves sequentially from the TRANSFER Block into an ADVANCE Block, where the time required to travel down the aisle is simulated. For each aisle, the distribution of items selected for purchase is described with a continuous, two-point GPSS Function. Moving from the aisle's ADVANCE

TABLE 4B.1   Characteristics of Shoppers in the Case Study 4B Grocery Store

Aisle	Probability of Going Down the Aisle	Time Required to Travel Down the Aisle (seconds)	Number of Items Selected During Travel
1	0.75	120 ± 60	3 ± 1
2	0.55	150 ± 30	4 ± 1
3	0.82	120 ± 45	5 ± 1

Block, a customer samples from the appropriate Function at an increment-mode ASSIGN Block, where the sampled value is added to a Parameter used to record the total number of items selected by the customer since entering the grocery store. The customer-Transaction then moves sequentially into the TRANSFER Block used to model the beginning of the next aisle.

After finishing the aisle sequence, the customer-Transaction joins the line ahead of the checkout girl. Before capturing her, selection of impulse items is simulated by referencing an appropriate Function at an ASSIGN Block. The number of these additional items is simply added to the items-total accumulated earlier. Checkout time is then determined by evaluating a Function whose argument is the Parameter containing the items-total. After checking out, the shopping basket is returned by leaving the CARTS Storage, and the customer-Transaction terminates.

In summary, model features of interest are (1) use of a Storage with no capacity definition card, (2) sampling from uniform distributions at ASSIGN Blocks, (3) increment-mode use of a Transaction Parameter, and (4) use of a Transaction Parameter as a Function's argument.

(3) Table of Definitions

Time Unit: 1 Second

TABLE 4B.2   Table of Definitions for Case Study 4B

GPSS Entity	Interpretation
Transactions	
Model Segment 1	Customers
	P1: The number of items selected for purchase
Model Segment 2	A timer
Facilities	
GIRL	The checkout girl
Functions	
AYL1, AYL2, and AYL3	Functions describing the "items selected" distributions in aisles 1, 2, and 3, respectively
COTYM	Function describing the dependence of check-out time on the number of items being purchased
IMPUL	Function describing the distribution of impulse items selected at the checkout counter
XPDIS	Function for sampling from the exponential distribution with a mean value of 1
Queues	
GIRL	The Queue used to gather statistics for the line of customers waiting to check out
Storages	
CARTS	Storage used to simulate shopping baskets

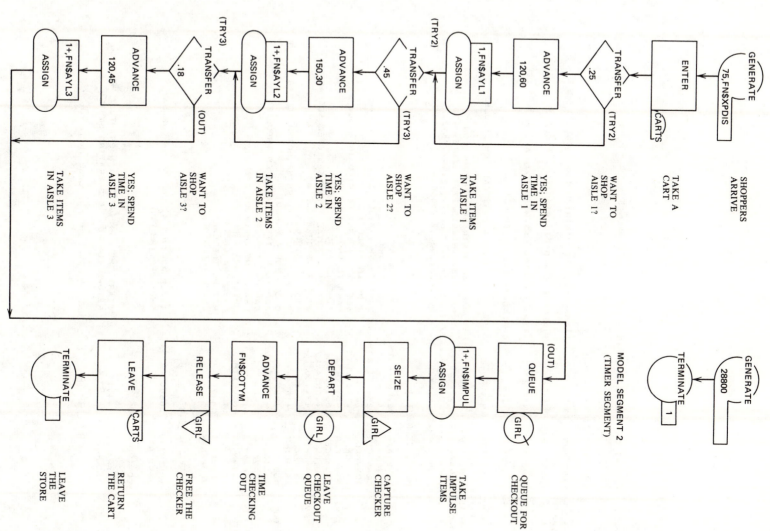

MODEL SEGMENT 1

FIGURE 4B.1   Block Diagram for Case Study 4B

(5) Extended Program Listing

```
BLOCK                                                                                    CARD
NUMBER   *LOC    OPERATION   A,B,C,D,E,F,G         COMMENTS                               NUMBER

                 SIMULATE                                                                    1
         *                                                                                   2
         *       FUNCTION DEFINITION(S)                                                      3
         *                                                                                   4
         AYL1    FUNCTION    RN1,C2        ITEMS-SELECTED DISTRIBUTION, AISLE 1              5
         0.2/1.5                                                                             6
         AYL2    FUNCTION    RN1,C2        ITEMS-SELECTED DISTRIBUTION, AISLE 2              7
         0.3/1.6                                                                             8
         AYL3    FUNCTION    RN1,C2        ITEMS-SELECTED DISTRIBUTION, AISLE 3              9
         0.4/1.7                                                                            10
         COTYM   FUNCTION    P1,C2         CHECKOUT-TIME DISTRIBUTION                       11
         1.3/18.54                                                                          12
         IMPUL   FUNCTION    RN1,C2        DISTRIBUTION OF ITEMS TAKEN ON IMPULSE           13
         0.1/1.4                                                                            14
         XPDIS   FUNCTION    RN1,C24       EXPONENTIAL DISTRIBUTION FUNCTION                15
         0.0/.1,.104/.2,.222/.3,.355/.4,.509/.5,.69/.6,.915/.7,1.2/.75,1.38                16
         .8,1.6/.84,1.83/.88,2.12/.9,2.3/.92,2.52/.94,2.81/.95,2.99/.96,3.2                17
         .97,3.5/.98,3.9/.99,4.6/.995,5.3/.998,6.2/.999,7/.9998,8                           18
         *                                                                                  19
         *       MODEL SEGMENT 1                                                            20
         *                                                                                  21

 1               GENERATE    75,FN$XPDIS   SHOPPERS ARRIVE                                  22
 2               ENTER       CARTS         TAKE A CART                                      23
 3               TRANSFER    .25,,TRY2     WANT TO SHOP AISLE 1?                            24
 4               ADVANCE     120,60        TIME IN AISLE 1                                  25
 5               ASSIGN      1,FN$AYL1     SET P1 = ITEMS SELECTED IN AISLE 1              26
 6       TRY2    TRANSFER    .45,,TRY3     WANT TO SHOP AISLE 2?                            27
 7               ADVANCE     150,30        TIME IN AISLE 2                                  28
 8               ASSIGN      1+,FN$AYL2    SET P1 = TOTAL ITEMS SELECTED SO FAR            29
 9       TRY3    TRANSFER    .18,,OUT      WANT TO SHOP AISLE 3?                            30
10               ADVANCE     120,45        TIME IN AISLE 3                                  31
11               ASSIGN      1+,FN$AYL3    SET P1 = TOTAL ITEMS SELECTED SO FAR            32
12       OUT     QUEUE       GIRL          QUEUE FOR CHECKOUT                               33
13               ASSIGN      1+,FN$IMPUL   ADD TO P1 ITEMS TAKEN ON IMPULSE                34
14               SEIZE       GIRL          CAPTURE THE CHECKER                              35
15               DEPART      GIRL          LEAVE THE CHECKOUT QUEUE                         36
16               ADVANCE     FN$COTYM      CHECK-OUT TIME                                   37
17               RELEASE     GIRL          FREE THE CHECKER                                 38
18               LEAVE       CARTS         RETURN THE CART                                  39
19               TERMINATE                 LEAVE THE STORE                                  40
         *                                                                                  41
         *       MODEL SEGMENT 2                                                            42
         *                                                                                  43
20               GENERATE    28800         TIMER ARRIVES AT END OF 8-HOUR DAY              44
21               TERMINATE   1             SHUT OFF THE RUN                                 45
         *                                                                                  46
         *       CONTROL CARDS                                                              47
         *                                                                                  48
                 START       1,,,1         START THE RUN; GET CHAIN PRINTOUT               49
                 END                        RETURN CONTROL TO OPERATING SYSTEM              50
```

FIGURE 4B.2   Extended Program Listing for Case Study 4B

(6) Program Output

FUNCTION SYMBOLS AND CORRESPONDING NUMBERS

```
1    AYL1
2    AYL2
3    AYL3
4    COTYM
5    IMPUL
6    XPDIS
```

(a)

FACILITY

FACILITY	AVERAGE UTILIZATION	NUMBER ENTRIES	AVERAGE TIME/TRAN	SEIZING TRANS. NO.	PREEMPTING TRANS. NO.
GIRL	.403	363	32.008		

(b)

QUEUE

QUEUE	MAXIMUM CONTENTS	AVERAGE CONTENTS	TOTAL ENTRIES	ZERO ENTRIES	PERCENT ZEROS	AVERAGE TIME/TRANS	$AVERAGE TIME/TRANS	TABLE NUMBER	CURRENT CONTENTS
GIRL	6	.165	363	211	58.1	13.101	31.289		3

$AVERAGE TIME/TRANS = AVERAGE TIME/TRANS EXCLUDING ZERO ENTRIES

(c)

STORAGE

STORAGE	CAPACITY	AVERAGE CONTENTS	AVERAGE UTILIZATION	ENTRIES	AVERAGE TIME/TRAN	CURRENT CONTENTS	MAXIMUM CONTENTS
CARTS	2147483647	4.027	.000	366	316.926		14

(d)

FIGURE 4B.3 Selected Program Output for Case Study 4B. (a) Function symbol table. (b) Facility statistics. (c) Queue statistics. (d) Storage statistics.

FUTURE EVENTS CHAIN																		
TRANS	BDT	BLOCK	PR	SF	NBA	SET	MARK-TIME	P1		P2	P3		P4	SI	TI	DI	CI	MC	PC	PF
16	28806	4			5	16	28632	0		0	0		0				4		
								0		0	0		0						
								0		0	0		0						
12	28830	4			5	12	28766	0		0	0		0				4		
								0		0	0		0						
								0		0	0		0						
7	28836	10			11	7	28380	8		0	0		0				4		
								0		0	0		0						
								0		0	0		0						
15	28840				1	15	-366	0		0	0		0				4		
								0		0	0		0						
								0		0	0		0						
3	57600				20	3	-1	0		0	0		0				4		
								0		0	0		0						
								0		0	0		0						

Row 1 (P1–P4)

Row 2 (P5–P8)

Row 3 (P9–P12)

FIGURE 4B.4   The makeup of the Future Events Chain at the conclusion of the Case Study 4B simulation

(7) Discussion

Program Output.[4] Figure 4B.3(a) shows the Function symbol table. The six Functions, all named symbolically in the model, have been assigned the numbers 1 through 6 by the Processor. The order in which the numbers have been assigned corresponds to the order in which the Function definitions appear in the card deck, as indicated in Figure 4B.2.

Figure 4B.3(b) indicates that utilization of the checkout girl was 0.403. Consistent with this low utilization, Queue statistics in part (c) of that figure show that less than half of the customers had to wait for service at the checkout counter. Those who had to wait were in the line about 31 seconds before being served. As many as six people were simultaneously queued up to check out.

The model was not designed to directly measure the average number of items selected for purchase. Nevertheless, average holding time at the checkout counter was about 32 seconds, indicating that about 11 items were checked out on average by each shopper. (The model uses 3 seconds per item as the deterministic checkout time.)

The Storage statistics in part (d) of Figure 4B.3 show that about four shopping baskets were in use on average, and that as many as 14 were in use simultaneously. These Storage statistics also reveal that the average customer spent about 318 seconds in the grocery store. Observe that the listed capacity of the Storage is 2,147,483,647. With this large capacity, the AVERAGE UTILIZATION correct to three decimal places is zero, even though the average Storage content was 4.

The D Operand has been used on the START card (Card 49, Figure 4B.2) to force a printout of the Current and Future Events Chains at the end of the simulation. Because no customers were waiting to check out when the simulation terminated, the Current Events Chain was empty. The Future Events Chain is shown in Figure 4B.4. The figure is primarily of interest for calling attention to the way a Transaction's Parameter values appear in a chain printout. Each Transaction in the model has 12 halfword Parameters, by default. Because only four columns are used in the chain printout to show Parameter values, three rows of numbers are required to display

[4]Total CPU time for the simulation on an IBM 360/67 computer was 5.2 seconds.

the 12 values involved. The three rows of Parameter values for the last Future Events Chain Transaction have been pointed out explicitly in Figure 4B.4. The first row contains values for P1, P2, P3, and P4; the second row for P5, P6, P7, and P8; and the third row for P9, P10, P11, and P12. Only the labels "P1," "P2," "P3," and "P4" appear above the four columns of numbers.

4.9 Exercises

1. (a) When a Transaction enters a model through the Block "GENERATE 52,FN$XPDIS,,10", how many Parameters will it have? Will the Parameters be of the halfword or fullword type?

   (b) Transactions entering a model through a particular GENERATE Block are each to have 20 fullword Parameters. The interarrival time of these Transactions is to be 42 ± 8 time units. Show a GENERATE Block which accomplishes the desired effect.

   (c) Critically discuss the statement, "−320000 is a valid Parameter value."

   (d) Critically discuss the statement, "P15 is a valid Parameter reference."

   (e) Critically discuss the statement, "P$SYMBL is a valid Parameter reference."

   (f) What is the value of each of a Transaction's Parameters when the Transaction first enters a model?

   (g) In Figure 4B.4, give interpretations for each Transaction on the Future Events Chain, and give an explanation for the indicated P1 value of each Transaction.

   (h) In Appendix C, read the description of error message 850. If an error of this type were to occur, how would you correct it?

   (i) The first Transaction entering a model through a particular GENERATE Block is to be given a value of 1 in Parameter 1. The second, third, fourth, etc. Transactions entering the model through the same GENERATE Block are to be given values of 2, 3, 4, etc., respectively, in Parameter 1. Show how this can be done.

2. Assume that the Functions ONE and TWO are defined as shown in Figure E2.

LOCATION	OPERATION	A,B,C,D,E,F
ONE	FUNCTION	P6,D3
1.10/.5,	6./,10,.15	
TWO	FUNCTION	P4,D2
1.10/.5,		
10,.1/,20,.2		

FIGURE E2

What will be the holding time when a Transaction with P4 and P6 values of 12 and 14, respectively, moves into each of the ADVANCE Blocks whose punchcard images are shown below?

(a) ADVANCE   P4
(b) ADVANCE   FN$TWO
(c) ADVANCE   P4,FN$ONE
(d) ADVANCE   P6,FN$TWO
(e) ADVANCE   FN$ONE,FN$TWO

3. Assume that the Functions ALPHA and BETA are defined as shown in Figure E3.

```
LOCATION      OPERATION           A,B,C,D,E,F
ALPHA         FUNCTION            P1,C2
0,0/10,2.0
BETA          FUNCTION            P1,C3
0,0/20,1.0/25,1.5
```

FIGURE E3

What will be the holding time when a Transaction with a P1 value of 5 moves into each of the ADVANCE Blocks whose punchcard images are shown below?

(a) ADVANCE   FN$BETA
(b) ADVANCE   FN$ALPHA,FN$BETA

4. Assume that, at a given time during the course of a simulation, the entity properties shown in Table E4(a) are in effect. Also assume that a particular Transaction has the Parameter values shown in Fig. E4(b).

TABLE E4(a)

Standard Numerical Attribute	Value
F1	0
FR1	532
R$TUGS	3
Q$LONG	8
QZ$LONG	1

TABLE E4(b)

Parameter Number	Value
1	30
2	−10
3	4
4	2
5	3

State which Parameter will have its value changed, and what the new value will be, when the Transaction moves into each of the ASSIGN Blocks whose punchcard images are shown below. (Note: assume that the ASSIGN Blocks are independent of each other.)

(a) ASSIGN   5,100
(b) ASSIGN   5−,100
(c) ASSIGN   P5,100
(d) ASSIGN   P5+,96
(e) ASSIGN   P4+,P5
(f) ASSIGN   P5+,P4
(g) ASSIGN   R$TUGS,P5
(h) ASSIGN   QZ$LONG,FR1
(i) ASSIGN   P3,F1

5. (a) Discuss the difference between the two Blocks, "ASSIGN 5−,100,3" and "ASSIGN 5−,100,FN3".

(b) Assume that FN1 has a value of 3.26, and FN3 has a value of 4.1. What value will Parameter 2 have after a Transaction enters the Blocks shown below?
  (i) ASSIGN   2,60,1
  (ii) ASSIGN   2,60,FN1

(c) Compare and contrast the Block "ASSIGN 7,1,3" and the Block "ASSIGN 7,FN3" with respect to (i) the value assigned to Parameter 7, and (ii) probable relative differences in the time required for Block execution.

6. Questions for this problem make reference to Figure 4B.2.

(a) What value does the Function COTYM return when 15 is the value of P1?

(b) Explain why the second pair of points used to define the Function COTYM is "18,54".

(c) Show what changes to make in the Function COTYM if it takes 5 seconds on average to check out an item.

(d) What is the least number of items that a shopper in the grocery store will select for purchase?

(e) For the ASSIGN Block in Location 5, discuss the possibility of using 1+, rather than 1, as the A Operand.

7. The Block Counts in the output produced when the Figure 4B.2 model was run are shown in Figure E7.

(a) Use the Block Counts to compute the fraction of customers who shopped aisle 1. Compare your results with the long-run fraction expected.

(b) Repeat (a) for aisle 2.

(c) How many shoppers were in aisles 1, 2, and 3, respectively, when the simulation shut off?

8. Show how to modify Case Study 4B to incorporate these changes.

(a) There are only 10 baskets available in the grocery store. Customers wait for baskets if none are available when they arrive at the store.

(b) There are only 10 baskets available in the store. Sixty-five percent of the customers wait for baskets if none are available when they arrive. The other 35 percent leave without shopping.

RELATIVE CLOCK 28800 BLOCK COUNTS			ABSOLUTE CLOCK 28800			28800		
BLOCK	CURRENT	TOTAL	BLOCK	CURRENT	TOTAL	BLOCK	CURRENT	TOTAL
1	0	366	11	0	306	21	0	1
2	0	366	12	0	363			
3	0	366	13	0	363			
4	2	280	14	0	363			
5	0	278	15	0	363			
6	0	364	16	0	363			
7	0	191	17	0	363			
8	0	191	18	0	363			
9	0	364	19	0	363			
10	1	307	20	0	1			

FIGURE E7

4.10 Modification of a Transaction's Priority Level: The PRIORITY Block

When a Transaction enters a model, its Priority Level is specified through the E Operand at its GENERATE Block. In all applications discussed so far, each Transaction has retained this initial Priority Level throughout its existence in the model. It is possible, however, to dynamically change a Transaction's Priority Level as a simulation proceeds. Altering a Priority Level has important implications, of course, in terms of the position a Transaction occupies when it is on the Current Events Chain. This, in turn, influences the chronological sequence in which various Transactions are moved forward in a model. Hence, the ability to dynamically change a Transaction's Priority Level can be of major consequence in GPSS modeling.

Whenever a Transaction moves into the PRIORITY Block, its Priority Level is changed. The PRIORITY Block, and its A Operand, are shown in Figure 4.12.[5] When a Transaction moves into the PRIORITY Block, the value of the A Operand is assigned as the Transaction's new Priority Level. Of course, if the "new value"

[5]There is also an optional B Operand for the PRIORITY Block. It will be discussed in Chapter 7.

happens to be identical to the "old value," no change in the Priority Level occurs.

Transactions are never denied entry to the PRIORITY Block. When such a Block is entered, this sequence of events occurs.

1. The new value of the Transaction's Priority Level is assigned.

2. The Transaction is repositioned on the Current Events Chain as the last member in its new Priority Class.

3. The Processor then continues moving the Transaction forward in the model until it comes to rest.

4. Finally, after the Transaction comes to rest, the Processor restarts its scan of the Current Events Chain. There is a reason for this. At the PRIORITY Block, the Priority Level of the Transaction may have been made smaller. The result would be to shift both the Transaction *and the point of the Current Events Chain scan* to a position toward the back of the chain. If the scan simply continued from that point, intermediate Transactions on the Current Events Chain might be bypassed in the process. Restarting the scan means that this possibility is avoided.

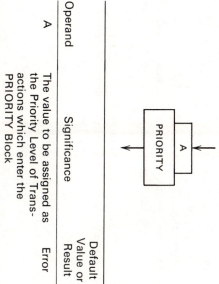

Operand	Significance	Default Value or Result
A	The value to be assigned as the Priority Level of Trans-actions which enter the PRIORITY Block	Error

FIGURE 4.12   The PRIORITY Block and its A Operand

The Priority Level of a Transaction is a Standard Numerical Attribute in GPSS. The name of the attribute is PR. The name PR in itself constitutes a complete data reference, because a Transaction only has one PR value. Whenever PR is used to indirectly specify data, the Priority Level of the *active* Transaction is used as the data.

As previously explained, PR (Priority Level) can assume integer values from 0 to 127, inclusive. Because it is a Standard Numerical Attribute, PR can be used as Block Operands, Function arguments, and so on, in the model-building process.

When the Current and/or Future Events Chains are printed out, the Priority Level of Transactions on those chains appears as part of the printout. A portion of the Figure 4B.4 Future Events Chain printout is repeated in Figure 4.13. As pointed out in the Figure, Column 4, labeled PR, contains the Priority Level information. All of the column 4 entries in Figure 4.13 are "blank," indicating that the Transactions have a Priority Level of zero.

Now consider how the PRIORITY Block can be used to control event sequences when time ties occur. Event sequences are directly determined by the relative positions occupied by Transactions on the Current Events Chain. These relative positions can be controlled through manipulation of Transaction Priority Levels. Suppose a situation arises in which two events can occur simultaneously, and it is important to control the event sequence so that one event occurs before the other. This can be done simply by giving the Transaction which is the carrier of the first event a higher Priority Level than that of the other Transaction.

Take the Case Study 3B model as a case in point. Figure 4.14(a) repeats Model Segment 1 from that case study. In the model, a car arriving at a car wash stays for service only if a waiting space is available. A problem can arise if there is a time tie between the events "next car arrival" and "service completion" *when the waiting spaces are all filled*. Under these circumstances, if the arrival event occurs first, the car-Transaction will find the Storage SPACE is full, and will immediately go BYBYE. In contrast, if the service-completion event occurs first, a waiting car-Transaction will eventually move through the "LEAVE SPACE" Block before the arriving car-Transaction is processed. This means that the arriving car will find there *is* a space in which to wait, and will elect to remain for service.

There is some motivation in the Figure 4.14(a) model, then, to have service completion occur before the arrival event occurs. Each Transaction enters the model with a default Priority Level of 0, which means that arrival events have zero priority. Suppose that a PRIORITY Block is introduced into the model to boost each Transaction's Priority Level to 1 sometime after the Transaction has arrived, but before it moves into the ADVANCE Block. Then, if a time tie occurs, the pertinent Clock Update Phase will position the service-completion Transaction ahead of the arrival-event Transaction on the Current Events Chain. During the Scan Phase that follows, the service completion will take place before the arrival event occurs, as desired.

Figure 4.14(b) shows how the model in part (a) of the figure can be modified to produce the desired boost in Priority Level. The PRIORITY Block has been placed immediately after the GENERATE Block. Of course, it could have been

FUTURE EVENTS CHAIN

TRANS	BDT	BLOCK	PR	SF	NBA	SET	MARK-TIME	P1
16	28806	4			5	16	28632	0
								0
12	28830	4			5	12	28766	0
								0
7	28836	10			11	7	28380	8
								0
15	28840				1	15	-366	0
								0
3	57600				20	3	-1	0
								0

Priority Level Information

FIGURE 4.13   Repetition of a portion of the Figure 4B.4 Future Events Chain

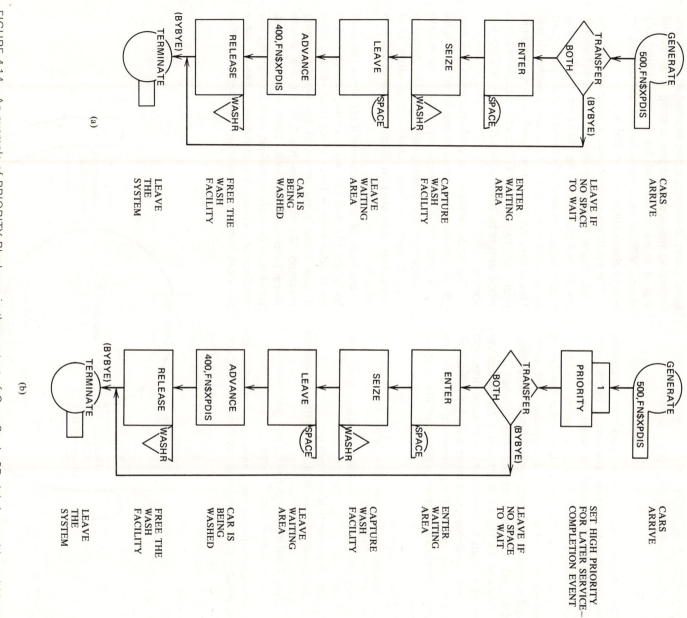

(a)

(b)

FIGURE 4.14 An example of PRIORITY Block use in the context of Case Study 3B. (a) A repetition of Model Segment 1 in Case Study 3B. (b) Model Segment 1 modified to give "service completion" priority over "customer arrival."

The PRIORITY Block finds use in a variety of contexts, not just in situations in which the analyst wants to control event sequences in case of time ties. The case study in the next section illustrates use of the PRIORITY Block in one of these other contexts.

The PRIORITY Block can also be placed in several other alternative positions with equal validity. (See exercise 2 in Section 4.12.)

4.11 CASE STUDY 4C
An Equipment Balancing Problem

(1) Statement of the Problem

After rough castings are made in a certain foundry, they must pass through a department in which finishing work is done on them. A type of machine known as a "finishing machine" is used to do the work. Only one worker is needed to operate such a machine. The work itself consists of a sequence of two processes, which are termed Process 1 and Process 2.

Assume for the moment that a rough casting has just been fetched from a storage area and has been properly positioned on a finishing machine. The steps then followed to do the finishing work are shown below, in chronological sequence.

1. Perform Process 1.
2. Reposition the casting on the machine.
3. Perform Process 2.
4. (a) Unload the finished casting from the machine.
   (b) Store the finished casting.
   (c) Fetch the next rough casting from the storage area.
   (d) Load this rough casting onto the machine.
   (e) Return to Step 1 above.

The castings are too heavy to be handled by the finishing-machine operator himself. An over-

head crane is consequently needed at each step involving movement of the casting. This means that a crane is needed for Steps (2) and (4) above. Whenever a crane is not being used for one of these steps, it is in idle state.

The relationship between a finishing machine and a crane, then, is summarized in the schematic shown in Figure 4C.1. As indicated, the finishing machine goes repeatedly through a single closed cycle consisting of the four steps listed above. The crane, on the other hand, can go through each of two distinct cycles, depending on whether it is being used for Step (2) or Step (4) above.

The times required to perform Steps (1) and (3) in the finishing process are listed in Tables 4C.1 and 4C.2, respectively. The intermediate handling of the casting in Step (2) requires 15 ± 5 minutes. The unload–store–fetch–load sequence indicated in Step (4) takes 30 ± 5 minutes.

Because of the relatively long times required by Steps (1) and (3), an overhead crane would be in idle state a large percentage of the time if one crane were provided for each finishing machine. On the other hand, if a crane serves more than one machine, there may be times when one or more machines have to wait for the services of a crane. It is of interest, then, to have the right number of machines per crane, to strike

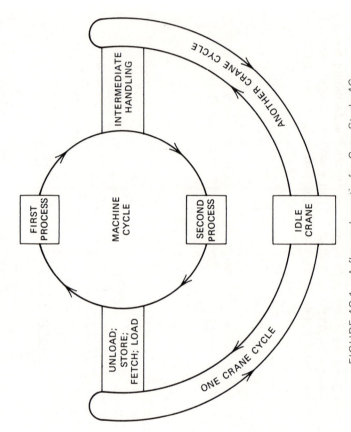

FIGURE 4C.1   A flow schematic for Case Study 4C

TABLE 4C.1   Distribution of Time Required for Process 1 in Case Study 4C

Time for Process 1 (minutes)	Cumulative Frequency
Less than 60	0.0
70	.12
80	.48
90	.83
100	1.0

TABLE 4C.2   Distribution of Time Required for Process 2 in Case Study 4C

Time for Process 2 (minutes)	Cumulative Frequency
Less than 80	0.0
90	.24
100	.73
110	1.0

a good balance in the use of these equipment resources.

Management wants a two-part study made of the finishing department. First of all, it wants to know what utilizations would result for the crane, and for the finishing machines, if the number of machines served by a single crane were three, four, five, or six. Secondly, management wants to know what the effect would be on these utilization figures if two cranes were used to serve a group of 10 machines; or if three cranes were used to serve a group of 15 machines.

Build an appropriate GPSS model to simulate the finishing department. Then use the model to provide management with utilization estimates for the various conditions indicated. For each condition, simulate for the equivalent of five 40-hour work weeks. Note that conflicts can arise over use of a crane. At any given time, one or more machines may require use of a crane for Step (2), whereas one or more other machines may require a crane for Step (4). If such conflicts arise, Step (2) is to be given priority over Step (4). Because Step (2) requires less time that Step (4), this is equivalent to using a "shortest imminent operation" queue discipline with the crane.

(2) Approach Taken in Building the Model

The two constraints in the system are the number of finishing machines, and the number of cranes. The problem statement implies that there is one operator per finishing machine. The "machine constraint" can therefore alternatively be viewed as an "operator constraint." By letting a Transaction simulate an operator, the number of operators can be controlled through the Limit Count at a GENERATE Block. These operator-Transactions can then circulate through the model, moving through the series of steps listed in the problem statement. After the last step, the operator-Transaction can then transfer back to the first step and repeat the cycle, etc.

If a Transaction simulates an operator, it is natural to use a Storage to simulate the crane constraint. (A Storage is used, instead of a Facility, because the conditions to be investigated eventually call for having more than one crane in the model.) Suppose that the Storage named CRANS simulates the crane constraint. Then, to get use of a crane, the corresponding operator-Transaction must be able to move into an "ENTER CRANS" Block, and so on. The utilization of the Storage CRANS is then equal to the crane utilization.

There is some question about what constitutes a utilized finishing machine. It can be argued that a machine is not being utilized while the store-and-fetch portion of the machine cycle is taking place. For the problem as described, however, this "nonutilization" cannot be attributed to the unavailability of a crane. In this spirit, then, a finishing machine is assumed to be nonutilized only when its operator is waiting to get a crane.

The utilization statistic for the group of finishing machines can be estimated through use of the Storage entity. Suppose that the Storage named BUSY is used for this purpose. Whenever an operator-Transaction is about to begin one of the finishing steps, it can first move into an "ENTER BUSY" Block. Whenever the next step requires use of a crane, the operator-Transaction can first move through a "LEAVE BUSY" Block, then attempt to get the crane. Later, when a crane is captured, another "ENTER BUSY" Block can be executed, and so on. The "current content" of the Storage BUSY will then equal the number of currently busy operators (which, in turn, equals the number of currently busy finishing machines). The utilization of the Storage BUSY is then a direct measure of machine utilization.

Finally, the matter of priority distinctions with respect to type of crane use must be considered. When operator-Transactions finish Process 2, and consequently need a crane, they must get in line behind any other operator-Transactions who have recently finished Process 1, and also need a crane. This relative ordering of operator-Transactions on the Current Events Chain is accomplished by making a distinction in Transaction Priority Levels. Suppose that operator-Transactions waiting to start Process 2 have a Priority Level of 1. If operator-Transactions waiting for the unload–store–fetch–load step then have a Priority Level of 0, the proper relative ordering on the Current Events Chain is guaranteed.

The Priority Level of 1 is assigned to operator-Transactions *before* they enter the ADVANCE Block to simulate the time for Process 1; then,

when they later return to the Current Events Chain after finishing Process 1, they are put down on the chain in the right position relative to their next required crane use. By the same token, the Priority Level of 0 is assigned to operator-Transactions *just before* they enter the ADVANCE Block to simulate the time for Process 2; then, when they are later returned to the Current Events Chain, they too go onto the chain in the right position relative to their next required crane use. [See Section 4.12, exercises 3a and 3b.] This means that, as operator-Transactions cycle repeatedly through the model, their Priority Level regularly alternates between 1 and 0.

(3) Table of Definitions

Time Unit: 1 Minute

TABLE 4C.3   Table of Definitions for Case Study 4C

GPSS Entity	Interpretation
Transactions	
Model Segment 1	A machine operator
Model Segment 2	A timer
Functions	
PROC1	A Function describing the distribution of time required to perform Process 1
PROC2	A Function describing the distribution of time required to perform Process 2
Storages	
CRANS	A Storage whose capacity equals the number of cranes in the finishing department
BUSY	A Storage whose capacity equals the number of machine operators

(4) Block Diagram

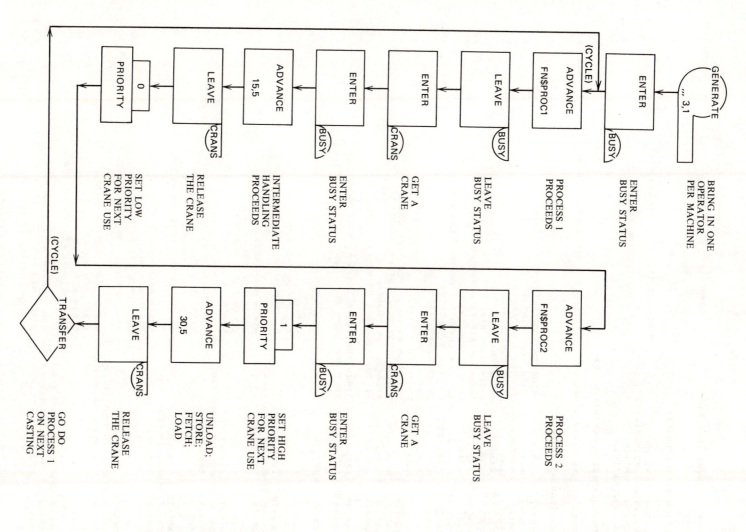

MODEL SEGMENT 1

FIGURE 4C.2   Block Diagram for Case Study 4C

(5) Extended Program Listing

BLOCK NUMBER	*LOC	OPERATION	A,B,C,D,E,F,G	COMMENTS	CARD NUMBER
		SIMULATE			1
		*			2
		*	FUNCTION DEFINITION(S)		3
		*			4
	PROC1	FUNCTION	RN1,C5	TIME REQUIRED FOR PROCESS 1	5
			0.60/.12,70/.48,80/.83,90/1,100		6
	PROC2	FUNCTION	RN1,C4	TIME REQUIRED FOR PROCESS 2	7
			0.80/.24,90/.73,100/1,110		8
		*			9
		*	STORAGE CAPACITY DEFINITION(S)		10
		*			11
		STORAGE	S$BUSY,3/S$CRANS,1	INITIALLY 3 MACHINES, 1 CRANE	12
		*			13
		*	MODEL SEGMENT 1		14
		*			15
1	BLOK1	GENERATE	,,,3,1	BRING IN 1 OPERATOR PER MACHINE	16
2		ENTER	BUSY	ENTER BUSY STATUS	17
3	CYCLE	ADVANCE	FN$PROC1	PROCESS 1 PROCEEDS	18
4		LEAVE	BUSY	LEAVE BUSY STATUS	19
5		ENTER	CRANS	GET A CRANE	20
6		ENTER	BUSY	ENTER BUSY STATUS	21
7		ADVANCE	15,5	INTERMEDIATE HANDLING PROCEEDS	22
8		LEAVE	CRANS	RELEASE THE CRANE	23
9		PRIORITY	0	SET LOW PRIORITY FOR NEXT CRANE USE	24
10		ADVANCE	FN$PROC2	PROCESS 2 PROCEEDS	25
11		LEAVE	BUSY	LEAVE BUSY STATUS	26
12		ENTER	CRANS	GET A CRANE	27
13		ENTER	BUSY	ENTER BUSY STATUS	28
14		PRIORITY	1	SET HIGH PRIORITY FOR NEXT CRANE USE	29
15		ADVANCE	30,5	UNLOAD; STORE; FETCH; LOAD	30
16		LEAVE	CRANS	RELEASE THE CRANE	31
17		TRANSFER	,CYCLE	GO DO PROCESS 1 ON NEXT CASTING	32
		*			33
18		GENERATE	12000	TIMER ARRIVES AFTER 5 40-HOUR WEEKS	34
19		TERMINATE	1	SHUT OFF THE RUN	35
		*			36
		*	CONTROL CARDS		37
		*			38
		START	1	START 1ST RUN	39
		CLEAR		CLEAR FOR 2ND RUN	40
MULTIPLE DEFINITION OF SYMBOL IN ABOVE CARD				RE-CONFIGURE FOR 4 OPERATORS	41
1	BLOK1	GENERATE	,,,4,1		
		STORAGE	S$BUSY,4	NOW 4 MACHINES, 1 CRANE	42
		START	1	START 2ND RUN	43
		CLEAR		CLEAR FOR 3RD RUN	44
MULTIPLE DEFINITION OF SYMBOL IN ABOVE CARD				RE-CONFIGURE FOR 5 OPERATORS	45
1	BLOK1	GENERATE	,,,5,1		
		STORAGE	S$BUSY,5	NOW 5 MACHINES, 1 CRANE	46
		START	1	START 3RD RUN	47
		CLEAR		CLEAR FOR 4TH RUN	48
MULTIPLE DEFINITION OF SYMBOL IN ABOVE CARD				RE-CONFIGURE FOR 6 OPERATORS	49
1	BLOK1	GENERATE	,,,6,1		
		STORAGE	S$BUSY,6	NOW 6 MACHINES, 1 CRANE	50
		START	1	START 4TH RUN	51
		CLEAR		CLEAR FOR 5TH RUN	52
MULTIPLE DEFINITION OF SYMBOL IN ABOVE CARD				RE-CONFIGURE FOR 10 OPERATORS	53
1	BLOK1	GENERATE	,,,10,1		
		STORAGE	S$BUSY,10/S$CRANS,2	NOW 10 MACHINES, 2 CRANES	54
		START	1	START 5TH RUN	55
		CLEAR		CLEAR FOR 6TH RUN	56
MULTIPLE DEFINITION OF SYMBOL IN ABOVE CARD				RE-CONFIGURE FOR 15 MACHINES	57
1	BLOK1	GENERATE	,,,15,1		
		STORAGE	S$BUSY,15/S$CRANS,3	NOW 15 MACHINES, 3 CRANES	58
		START	1	START 6TH RUN	59
		END		RETURN CONTROL TO SYSTEM	60

FIGURE 4C.3 Extended Program Listing for Case Study 4C

(6) Program Output

No program output is shown directly. Results are summarized in the next section.

(7) Discussion

Model Logic. The model assumes that initially each finishing machine has had a rough casting loaded onto it, and that Process 1 is ready to begin. When operator-Transactions come into the model, then, they immediately "enter busy status" (Block 2, Figure 4C.3), then move into an ADVANCE Block to simulate the time required by Process 1. Note that operator-Transactions come into the model with a Priority Level of 1, because their next crane use will be of the high-priority type; that is, their next crane use will be for Step (2), re-positioning the casting on the machine.

After moving out of the Process 1 ADVANCE Block (Block 3, Figure 4C.3), an operator-Transaction moves through a LEAVE–ENTER–ENTER sequence (Blocks 4, 5, and 6, Figure 4C.3). If a crane is available at the time, these moves will be made in zero simulated time, meaning that for all practical purposes, the operator did not leave busy status. On the other hand, if the operator must wait for the crane at the "ENTER CRANS" Block (Block 5), this waiting will be reflected in the utilization statistics for the Storage BUSY.

Just before moving into the Process 2 ADVANCE Block (Block 10, Figure 4C.3), an operator-Transaction moves through the "PRIORITY 0" Block to have its Priority Level stepped down in anticipation of its next crane use. The Current Events Chain position from which it later competes for this next crane use is consequently "proper"; that is, the Transaction will be behind any operator-Transactions waiting to use a crane for repositioning of the casting prior to Process 2. The Priority Level is eventually stepped up again (Block 14, Figure 4C.3) in anticipation of crane use for the high-priority repositioning step.

Program Output.[6] Utilization statistics for the simulation are summarized in Table 4C.4. These statistics are also plotted in Figure 4C.4 for conditions in which there are three, four, five, and six finishing machines per crane. As

[6] Total CPU time for the simulation on an IBM 360/67 computer was 19.3 seconds.

TABLE 4C.4 A Summary of Program Output for Case Study 4C

Machine:Crane Ratio	Machine Utilization	Crane Utilization
3:1	0.972	0.601
4:1	0.945	0.775
5:1	0.896	0.910
6:1	0.806	0.988
10:2	0.917	0.935
15:3	0.930	0.947

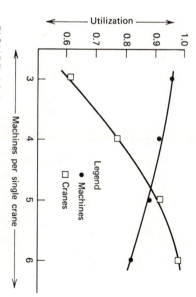

FIGURE 4C.4 A graph of selected equipment utilizations in Case Study 4C

expected, the utilizations move in directions counter to each other. A balance comes closest to being achieved for the case of five machines per crane, in the sense that the machine and crane utilizations are approximately equal for this case.

The information in Table 4C.4 shows that both the machine and crane utilizations rise as the machine:crane ratio moves from 5:1, to 10:2, to 15:3. Explanation of this phenomenon is left to the exercises [see Section 4.12, exercise 3d].

4.12 Exercises

1. (a) Explain in detail what happens when a Transaction moves into the Block "PRIORITY PR".
   (b) Critically discuss this statement: When a Transaction with a Priority Level of 3 moves into the Block "PRIORITY 3", the Block might just as well not have been there, for all practical purposes.

2. These questions are based on Figure 4.14(b).
   (a) Would the desired effect in Figure 4.14(b) have been accomplished if the "PRIORITY 1" Block had been placed between the TRANSFER Block and the ENTER Block?

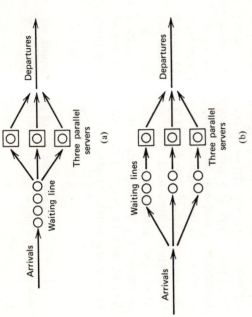

(a)

(b)

FIGURE 4.15   Alternative queuing systems involving three parallel servers. (a) One-line, multiple-server queuing system. (b) Multiple-line, multiple-server queuing system.

(b) Discuss the possibilities of having placed the PRIORITY Block between the ENTER and SEIZE, or between the SEIZE and LEAVE, or between the LEAVE and ADVANCE Blocks in Figure 4.14(b). Would the desired effect be accomplished if the PRIORITY Block were placed in any of these positions?

(c) In Figure 4.14(b), the desired effect would *not* be accomplished if the "PRIORITY 1" Block had been placed between the ADVANCE and RELEASE Blocks. Explain why, in detail.

3. These questions are based on Case Study 4C.

(a) Consider the "PRIORITY 0" Block in the case study model (Block 9, Figure 4C.3). Note that the Block appears *before* the "ADVANCE FNsPROC2" Block (Block 10). The priority distinctions required in the case study *would not* be in effect if this PRIORITY Block had been placed *after* the ADVANCE Block. Explain why, in detail.

(b) Consider the "PRIORITY 1" Block in the case study model (Block 14, Figure 4C.3). Note that the Block appears *before* the "ADVANCE 30,5" Block (Block 15). The priority distinctions required in the case study *would* still be in effect if this PRIORITY Block had been placed *after* the ADVANCE Block. Explain why, in detail.

(c) Is the Storage BUSY used in the model to simulate a system constraint? In particular, can any of the "ENTER BUSY" Blocks in the model ever refuse entry to a Transaction? Explain why or why not, in detail.

(d) Explain why the machine and crane utilizations would be expected to rise as the machine:crane ratio moves from 5:1, to 10:2, to 15:3.

4. The modeling approach used in Case Study 4C is highly analogous to that used in Case Study 2D. An alternative approach to the Case Study 2D model is shown in the model in Figure E.12, Section 2.41. Show how to build another model for the Case Study 4C problem, following the same approach as that used in the alternative to the Case Study 2D model.

4.13 Multiple-Line, Multiple-Server Queuing Systems

Figure 4.15(a) illustrates a one-line, multiple-server queuing system for the case of three parallel servers. The modeling of such a system in GPSS was discussed in Section 2.38. Recall that this involved simulating the parallel servers with a Storage, and that a single Queue was

used to gather waiting line statistics ahead of the Storage (see Figure 2.45).

Part (b) of Figure 4.15 shows a multiple-server queuing system in which a separate waiting line forms ahead of each server. The multiple-line, multiple-server queuing system arises at grocery store checkout counters, expressway toll points, bank teller windows, and so on. We have now reached the point where an elementary approach to modeling the Figure 4.15(b) system in GPSS can be introduced. The approach involves simulating each of the parallel servers with a Facility. Ahead of each Facility is a corresponding Queue. For example, suppose that Facilities 1, 2, and 3 are used to simulate the three parallel servers in Figure 4.15(b). Let the Queues ahead of the three Facilities also be numbered 1, 2, and 3, respectively. Then the multiple servers can be simulated with the Block Diagram segment shown in Figure 4.16. As suggested in the figure, Transactions moving into the Block Diagram segment select one of the three parallel branches to move through. After moving through that branch, they continue on in common in the model.

There is much repetition in each of the three parallel model segments in Figure 4.16. In fact, the Block sequences are identical in each branch. Only the A Operands at the QUEUE, SEIZE, DEPART, and RELEASE Blocks differ. If these Operands were indirectly specified as the value

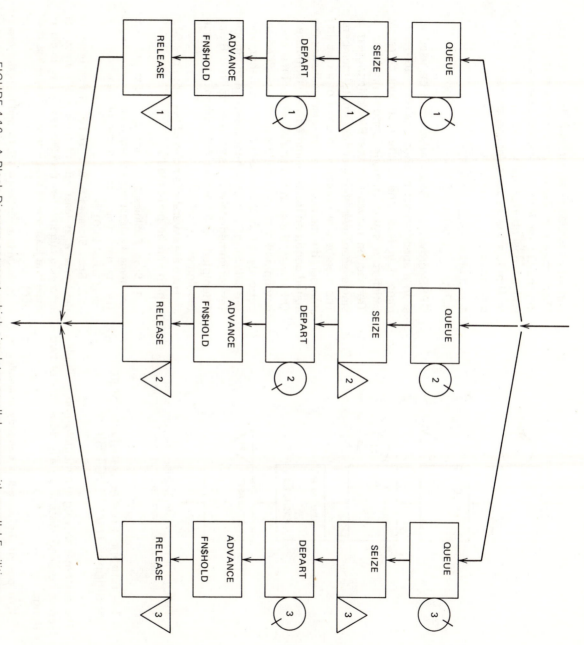

FIGURE 4.16   A Block Diagram segment which simulates parallel servers with parallel Facilities

of a Transaction Parameter, a single sequence of Blocks could be used to replace the three parallel branches.

Suppose, for example, that a Transaction "selects the number of a server" just before it reaches the Figure 4.16 model segment, and that this number is assigned as the value of Transaction Parameter 1. Figure 4.17 then shows a single Block sequence equivalent to the three Figure 4.16 parallel branches. When a Transaction with a P1 value of 1 moves through the Figure 4.17 sequence, it joins Queue 1, waits to capture Facility 1, etc. Similarly, Transactions

with P1 values of 2 or 3 join Queue 2 or 3, respectively, wait to capture Facility 2 or 3, and so on. In summary, the Figure 4.17 segment compactly accomplishes the effect of Figure 4.16. Of course, the economy of expression achieved by use of indirect specification in Figure 4.17 would be even greater if there were more than three servers in parallel.

It was assumed earlier that a Transaction "selects the number of a server" just before it reaches the Figure 4.17 (or 4.16) model segment. A method for doing this in GPSS will be discussed next.

currently available server will be introduced. Then, corresponding to (2), a means of identifying the Queue with the smallest current content will be described. Finally, use of the methods to simulate the server-selection process will be described.

4.14.1 The SELECT Block in Relational-Operator Mode

GPSS provides a Block which can be used to scan a specified set of entity members to determine if at least one of the members currently satisfies a stated numeric condition. When a Transaction moves into the Block, it triggers a single scan over the specified entity members. The members are scanned in order of increasing number. If a member is found which satisfies the stated condition the scan immediately terminates. Otherwise, the scan terminates when it has been determined that no members in the specified set currently satisfy the stated condition. Either way, the selecting Transaction moves on in the model (either immediately, or as soon as its Next Block Attempted will accept it) when the scan terminates.

Here are several examples of the types of scans which can be performed.

1. Scan Facilities 1, 2, and 3, in that order, to determine if at least one of them is not currently in use (i.e., to determine if at least one of them has an F value equal to 0).

2. Scan Storages 5, 6, 7, and 8, in that order, to determine if at least one of them has a fractional utilization currently less than 25 percent (i.e., to determine if at least one of them has an SR value less than 250).

3. Scan Queues 13, 14, 15, 16, and 17, in that order, to determine if at least one of them has an average residence time, excluding zero entries, which is currently greater than or equal to 3 (i.e., to determine if at least one of them has a QX value greater than or equal to 3).

The SELECT Block is used to conduct such scans. The Block is shown with its Auxiliary Operator and Operands in Figure 4.18. The E Operand supplies the family name of the Standard Numerical Attribute involved in the scan (such as F, SR, or QX in the above examples). The B and C Operands indicate the smallest and largest numbers, respectively, in the range of entity members subject to the scan (such as 1 and 3; 5 and 8; or 13 and 17 in the above examples). The D Operand supplies the data against which the E-Operand SNA is to be

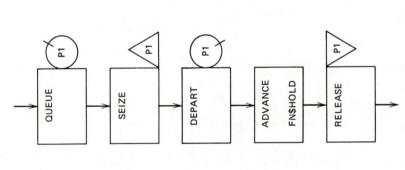

FIGURE 4.17   A single Block sequence equivalent to the three parallel branches in Figure 4.16

4.14 Finding Entities Satisfying Stated Conditions: The SELECT Block

The customer arriving at a multiple-line, multiple-server queuing system usually does one of two things.

1. If one of the servers is currently available, he captures that server.
2. If no servers are available, he joins the shortest waiting line and remains there until his turn for service comes up.

This represents the simplest possible view of the situation. Complications can easily arise. For example, even though one or more servers are free, the customer may elect to wait for a favorite server who is busy at the moment. Similarly, instead of simply joining the shortest line and waiting there, customers may jump lines when they sense there is an exceptionally long delay in their line, or that another line is moving unusually fast.

In this section, only the simplest customer behavior itemized above will be considered. First, corresponding to (1), a method of searching for a

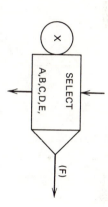

Operand	Significance	Default Value or Result
E	The family name of the Standard Numerical Attribute being investigated	Error
B and C	The smallest and largest numbers, respectively, in the set of entity members subject to the scan	
D	The data against which the E-Operand SNA is to be compared	Error
X	X is an Auxiliary Operator. It represents the *relational operator* which specifies the way in which the E-Operand SNA is to be compared to the D-Operand data. In practice, X takes one of the forms shown below.	Error

Relational Operator	Interpretation in SELECT Block Context
G	Is E greater than D?
GE	Is E greater than or equal to D?
E	Does E equal D?
NE	Does E not equal D?
LE	Is E less than or equal to D?
L	Is E less than D?

Operand	Significance	Default Value or Result
A	Number of the Parameter into which the number of an entity member currently satisfying the stated condition is to be copied	Error
F	Optional Operand: Block Location to which the selecting Transaction moves if no entity member currently satisfies the indicated condition	Selecting Transaction moves to sequential Block unconditionally

FIGURE 4.18 The SELECT Block, with its Auxiliary Operator and its A, B, C, D, E, and F Operands

compared (such as 0, 250, or 3 in the examples). The pertinent *relation* of interest between the Standard Numerical Attribute and the D-Operand data is spelled out through an *Auxiliary Operator*, represented with an X in Figure 4.18. In use, the Auxiliary Operator will be G, GE, E, NE, LE, or L to signify "greater than," "greater than or equal to," and so on.

The SELECT Block's A Operand supplies the number of a Parameter belonging to the selecting Transaction. If the scan finds an entity member which satisfies the stated condition, the number of that member is copied into the indicated Parameter. The selecting Transaction then moves sequentially from the SELECT Block.

Of course, it is quite possible that no entity member in the specified set currently satisfies the stated condition. Suppose this is the case. If the SELECT Block's optional F Operand has not been used, the value of the indicated Parameter on the selecting Transaction is set equal to zero, and the Transaction exits the SELECT Block sequentially. Alternatively, if an F Operand has been supplied for the SELECT Block and the scan was unsuccessful, the selecting Transaction exits the SELECT Block nonsequentially. The F Operand indicates the Block Location occupied by the nonsequential Block. When this nonsequential exit is taken, the value of the indicated Parameter on the selecting Transaction is not set equal to zero; instead, the SELECT Block has no effect on the Parameter's value in this case.

Figure 4.19 shows SELECT Blocks corresponding to the three scan examples given

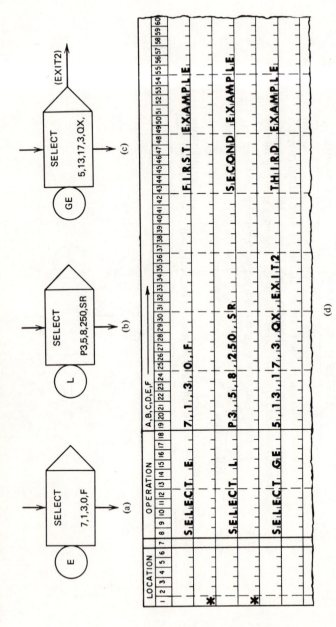

FIGURE 4.19   Examples of SELECT Block use. (a) First example. (b) Second example. (c) Third example. (d) Punchcard images for the SELECT Block examples in (a), (b), and (c).

earlier. Figure 4.19(a) shows specifications for a scan of Facilities 1, 2, and 3, in that order, to determine if one of them has an F value equal to zero. No nonsequential exit from the SELECT Block is specified. As a result, the selecting Transaction will move sequentially from the SELECT Block after the scan has been performed. In case of a successful scan, the Transaction will exit with its Parameter 7 value equal to 1, or 2, or 3, depending on which Facility was found to have its F attribute equal to zero. In case of an unsuccessful scan, the selecting Transaction will leave the SELECT Block with its Parameter 7 value equal to 0.

In the preceding example, suppose that two or all three of the Facilities have an F value equal to zero when the scan takes place. Then the number copied to Parameter 7 is that of the smallest-numbered qualifying Facility. For example, if Facilities 2 and 3 have an F value equal to zero, then the number 2 is copied to Parameter 7 of the selecting Transaction. This is a consequence of the chronological order in which the steps involved in the scan are performed.

When a Transaction moves into the Figure 4.19(b) SELECT Block, Storages 5, 6, 7, and 8 will be scanned to determine if one of them has a fractional utilization which is currently less than 250 parts per thousand. If the scan is successful, a 5, 6, 7, or 8 is placed in the Parameter whose number is the value of P3, and the selecting

Transaction continues to the sequential Block. No F Operand has been supplied at the SELECT Block. Whenever a scan is unsuccessful, then, the value of the selecting Transaction's indicated Parameter is set equal to zero, and the Transaction exits the SELECT Block sequentially.

Figure 4.19(c) shows use of the optional, non-sequential exit from the SELECT Block. When a Transaction enters that Block, Queues 13 through 17 are scanned to determine if at least one of them has a QX value greater than or equal to 3. If one of these Queues is found to satisfy this condition currently, its number is copied into Parameter 5 of the selecting Transaction, which then exits the SELECT Block sequentially. If none of these Queues satisfies the indicated condition, the selecting Transaction moves nonsequentially to the Block in the Location EXIT2, with no change having occurred in its Parameter 5 value.

Part (d) in Figure 4.19 shows the way the three SELECT Blocks in parts (a), (b), and (c) would appear on a coding sheet. Note that in each case, the Auxiliary Operator is entered in the Operation field, appearing after the corresponding Block Operation, with a single blank column separating it from the Operation word. As will be seen later, there are several other Blocks in GPSS which make use of Auxiliary Operators. When preparing punchcards for any of these Blocks, the Auxiliary Operator is punched in this fashion in the Operation field, with one blank column standing between it and the appropriate Operator word.

Finally, note the following features of the SELECT Block. First, as would be expected, the values of the A, B, C, and D Operands can be supplied either directly or indirectly. In the Figure 4.19 examples, indirect specification was only used for the A Operand in (b). Second, the condition imposed in the scan takes the form "SNA/relational-operator/D-Operand data." Hence, in Figure 4.19(b), the condition is "SR value less than 250.", *not* 250 less than SR value." Third, *all* entity members in the range described by the B and C Operands are subject to the scan. With direct use of the SELECT Block, then, it is not possible to do such things as scan for a Facility among those numbered 3, 4, 7, 10, and 12 with an F value currently equal to 0.

4.14.2 The SELECT Block in MIN or MAX Mode

The SELECT Block as just described is used in relational-operator mode to determine if any entity member in a specified set satisfies a stated numeric condition. In an alternate mode, the same Block can be used to find the set member having a minimum or maximum attribute value. This makes it possible to answer questions such as these.

1. In a set of Queues, which has the minimum current content?
2. In a set of Facilities, which has the minimum utilization?
3. In a set of Storages, which has the maximum remaining capacity?

The general form of these questions is "which entity in a given range has the minimum or maximum value of a specified attribute?" The SELECT Block can be used in MIN or MAX mode to provide the answer to such questions.

The role of the Auxiliary Operator and Operands for the SELECT Block in MIN or MAX mode is shown in Figure 4.20. The A, B, C, and E Operands have the same significance as when the SELECT Block is used in relational-operator mode. Taken together, they tell which entity attribute is of interest (E Operand), which entity members are involved (B and C Operands), and where to put the result of the search (A Operand). Because the attribute must satisfy an absolute condition, no comparative D-Operand data is needed, and the D Operand is not used. The Auxiliary Operator, instead of describing a relation, takes the form of MIN or MAX, depending on whether the entity with the minimum or maximum attribute value is sought. Finally, because *some* entity among those considered has the minimum or maximum attribute value, no optional exit can be specified for the MIN or MAX mode SELECT Block. In other words, in this mode the Block has no optional F Operand.

Figure 4.21 shows four examples of SELECT Block use in MIN and MAX mode, and provides a corresponding explanation for each Block. These examples should be studied and the role of the Block Operands should be checked. Note, in particular, that examples (c) and (d) make

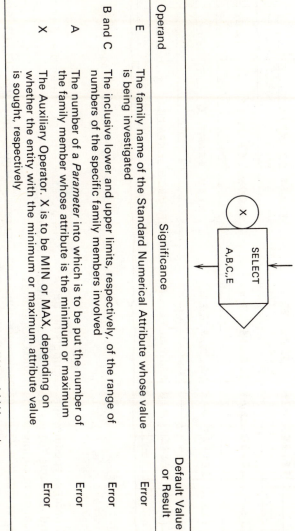

Operand	Significance	Default Value or Result
E	The family name of the Standard Numerical Attribute whose value is being investigated	Error
B and C	The inclusive lower and upper limits, respectively, of the range of numbers of the specific family members involved	
A	The number of a *Parameter* into which is to be put the number of the family member whose attribute is the minimum or maximum	Error
X	The Auxiliary Operator. X is to be MIN or MAX, depending on whether the entity with the minimum or maximum attribute value is sought, respectively	Error

FIGURE 4.20   The SELECT Block as used in MIN or MAX mode

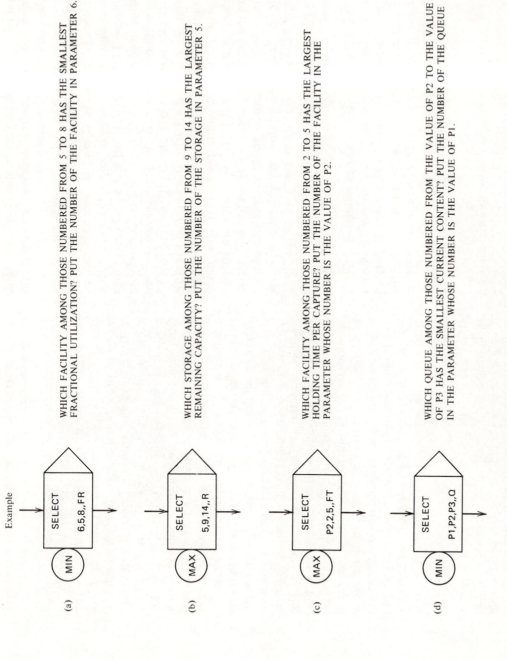

Example

(a)

```
MIN
SELECT
6,5,8,,FR
```

WHICH FACILITY AMONG THOSE NUMBERED FROM 5 TO 8 HAS THE SMALLEST FRACTIONAL UTILIZATION? PUT THE NUMBER OF THE FACILITY IN PARAMETER 6.

(b)

```
MAX
SELECT
5,9,14,,R
```

WHICH STORAGE AMONG THOSE NUMBERED FROM 9 TO 14 HAS THE LARGEST REMAINING CAPACITY? PUT THE NUMBER OF THE STORAGE IN PARAMETER 5.

(c)

```
MAX
SELECT
P2,2,5,,FT
```

WHICH FACILITY AMONG THOSE NUMBERED FROM 2 TO 5 HAS THE LARGEST HOLDING TIME PER CAPTURE? PUT THE NUMBER OF THE FACILITY IN THE PARAMETER WHOSE NUMBER IS THE VALUE OF P2.

(d)

```
MIN
SELECT
P1,P2,P3,,Q
```

WHICH QUEUE AMONG THOSE NUMBERED FROM THE VALUE OF P2 TO THE VALUE OF P3 HAS THE SMALLEST CURRENT CONTENT? PUT THE NUMBER OF THE QUEUE IN THE PARAMETER WHOSE NUMBER IS THE VALUE OF P1.

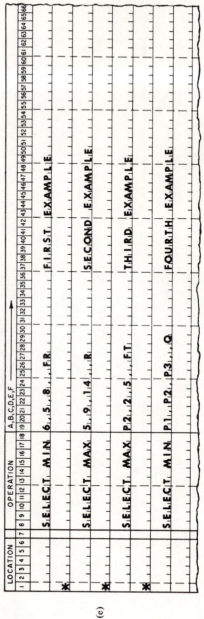

(e)

FIGURE 4.21 Examples of SELECT Block use in MIN and MAX mode. (e) Punchcard images for the SELECT Block examples in (a), (b), and (c).

use of indirect specification in supplying the A Operand. Example (d) also makes use of indirect specification in supplying the B and C Operands. Part (e) of Figure 4.21 indicates how the Blocks in parts (a) through (d) of the Figure would look on a coding sheet.

4.14.3 SELECT Block Use for the Multiple-Line Queuing System

Figure 4.22 shows how the SELECT Block can be used to support simulation of the parallel servers shown earlier in Figure 4.17. The

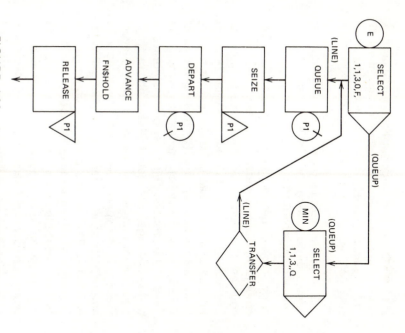

FIGURE 4.22   An example of SELECT Block use in a multiple-line queuing system

customer-Transaction first enters a SELECT Block used in relational-operator mode, where a search is conducted to find a Facility which is currently available. If such a Facility is found, the Facility number is placed in Parameter 1. The Transaction then exits sequentially to the QUEUE–SEIZE–DEPART–ADVANCE–RELEASE sequence, where use of the server is simulated. If no Facility is currently available, the Transaction exits nonsequentially from the SELECT Block, moving into the MIN-mode SELECT Block at Location QUEUP. There, the number of the shortest waiting line is placed in Parameter 1. The Transaction then transfers back to the QUEUE Block, where it becomes a member of the shortest waiting line. Hence, by use of the SELECT Block both in relational-operator and MIN mode, the simple server-selection process described earlier is easily modeled in GPSS.

4.15 CASE STUDY 4D
Comparison of Alternative Queuing Systems in a Bank

(1) Statement of the Problem

Customers arrive at a bank in a Poisson pattern at a mean rate of 200 per hour. Eight teller win-

dows are open at the bank at all times. A separate waiting line forms ahead of each teller. If a teller is free when a customer enters the bank, the customer goes immediately to that teller. Otherwise, he joins whichever waiting line is the shortest. He then remains in that line on a first-come, first-served basis until he has transacted his business, after which he leaves the bank.

The various types of business which customers transact fall into five categories. The relative frequencies of these categories, and the corresponding mean service time requirements, are shown in Table 4D.1. In each category, service time is exponentially distributed. No customer transacts business in two or more categories in a single visit to the bank.

TABLE 4D.1   Data for Business Transacted at the Bank in Case Study 4D

Category of Business	Relative Frequency	Mean Service Time (seconds)
1	.10	45
2	.19	75
3	.32	100
4	.24	150
5	.15	300

The bank's manager has noticed that the waiting lines are rather long on average. He would like to reduce the customer's typical waiting experience, but prefers not to hire one or two additional tellers to bring this about. He knows that another bank in the vicinity has introduced a "Quickline" queuing system. In such a system, customers entering the bank form a single line. Whenever a teller becomes available, the customer at the head of the line goes to that teller. The Quickline system presumably reduces waiting time by eliminating situations in which slow-moving lines form ahead of tellers who have been captured by a customer requiring a large amount of time. Because this conjecture seems reasonable, the manager decides to experiment with the Quickline system.

Build a GPSS model which gathers waiting line information for the bank's operation, both as it currently exists, and for the proposed change to Quickline. Run the model for five different 5-hour days in each case, then compare and contrast the results. Control experimental conditions so that the alternative systems are compared in as fair a manner as possible. This means that the customer interarrival-time sequence should be the same in both experiments. So should the customer service-time sequence. For example, if the twenty-first customer to arrive at the multiple-line system on the third day comes 16 minutes after the day begins, and requires 165 seconds for service, the same should be true for the twenty-first customer entering the single-line system on the third day. Finally, in case of time-ties between the events "customer arrival" and "service completion," "service completion" should be caused to occur first. (In the multiple-line system, this will have an influence on the arriving customer's choice of teller.)

(2) Approach Taken in Building the Model

The basic Block sequence for the one-line system is a familiar one. The major question that arises, then, involves arranging for control of experimental conditions. Reproducibility of the interarrival-time pattern can be guaranteed by dedicating RN1 exclusively to sampling from the interarrival-time distribution. Control of the service time pattern requires somewhat more thought. The relative order in which customers go into service will, in general, vary between the one-line and multiple-line systems. Hence, it is not possible to control the service times simply by sampling from the service time distribution *when service begins*. If this were done, for example, the twenty-first entry to the one-line system would draw the twenty-first service-time sample; in contrast, the twenty-first entry to the multiple-line system might draw, say, the eighteenth service-time sample in that model. The corresponding values would most likely differ from one another.

A simple remedy for this situation is to have each customer determine his service time *immediately upon entering the system*. Then the *j*th entering customer will draw the *j*th sample from the service-time distribution in both models, for *j* = 1, 2, 3, and so on. This predetermined service time can be stored in a Parameter of the corresponding customer-Transaction. Later, when the Transaction enters the ADVANCE Block, that Parameter can serve as the Block's A Operand. As explained in Section 4.7, the optional C Operand on the ASSIGN Block is of use in sampling from an exponential distribution. Such use of the ASSIGN Block is very convenient for this model.

Another point to consider regarding control of experimental conditions concerns the use of random-number generators in the model. Note that to determine the properties of *one* customer, *three* samples must be drawn from distributions, as summarized below.

1. A sample must be drawn from the exponential distribution to compute the customer's time of arrival.
2. A sample must be drawn from the "category of business" distribution to determine the customer's mean service time.
3. A sample must be drawn from the exponential distribution to convert the customer's mean service time into the service time he actually requires.

Now, it would be possible to dedicate a separate random-number generator to each of these sources of randomness. The disadvantages of this would be that (1) two distinct 24-point Functions would have to be defined for the exponential distribution, and (2) three of the eight GPSS random-number generators would be used in the process. This latter point is not really a disadvantage, because in this problem there are random-number generators to spare. Nevertheless, in the spirit of economy, it will now be argued that only *one* random-number generator is needed. That is, the particular chronological sequence in which samples are drawn and used makes it possible to use only one generator, and still guarantee that experimental conditions are replicated. Using 0.1 seconds as the implicit time unit, Figure 4D.1 shows the GENERATE–ASSIGN Block sequence which it is proposed to use in the models. Function 5 is the exponential distribution Function, and the Function named MEAN describes the "category of business" distribution. Both Functions use RN1 as their argument. Now consider the sequence in which RN1

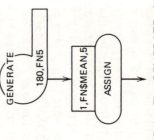

FIGURE 4D.1 The GENERATE–ASSIGN Block sequence proposed for use in the Case Study 4D models

values are called and used. Table 4D.2 displays the first part of this sequence. The first RN1 call comes from the GENERATE Block during the Input Phase; the corresponding RN1 value is used to compute the interarrival time for the first customer. Then, when this customer-Transaction later enters the GENERATE Block, the Block's Operands are evaluated by the Processor (as described in Section 3.22.) Evaluation of the B

TABLE 4D.2 Display of the Pattern in Which Calls on RN1 Are Used to Determine Customer Specifications in Case Study 4D

Number of Call on RN1	Block from Which Call is Made	Function Being Evaluated	Ultimate Use of Function's Value
1	GENERATE	5	Customer 1 interarrival time
2	GENERATE	5	"Thrown away"
3	ASSIGN	MEAN	Customer 1 service time
4	GENERATE	5	Customer 2 interarrival time
5	ASSIGN	5	Customer 1 service time
6	GENERATE	5	"Thrown away"
7	ASSIGN	MEAN	Customer 2 service time
8	GENERATE	5	Customer 3 interarrival time
9	ASSIGN	5	Customer 2 service time
10	GENERATE	5	"Thrown away"
11	ASSIGN	MEAN	Customer 3 service time
12	GENERATE	5	Customer 4 interarrival time
13	ASSIGN	5	Customer 3 service time
and so on			

Operand, FN5, leads to the second call of the simulation on RN1. Because the resulting FN5 value is never used, the RN1 value returned on this second call is described in Table 4D.2 as having been "thrown away." Next, when the Processor attempts to move this first customer-Transaction from the GENERATE Block, it evaluates the ASSIGN Block Operands as part of the process. First the B Operand, FN$MEAN, is evaluated. This forces the third call of the simulation on RN1. The ASSIGN Block's C Operand is specified directly, as the constant 5; hence, no call on RN1 is necessary to evaluate the C Operand. (It is important to make a distinction here between the value of the C Operand, which is the number of a Function, and the value of the Function itself. At this step, only the number of the Function is determined, and not the value of the Function.) Now, because the first customer-Transaction can move from the GENERATE Block, the Processor schedules the arrival of its successor. This requires evaluation of the GENERATE Block Operands, resulting in the fourth call of the simulation on RN1. Finally, after the scheduling step has been completed, movement of the first customer-Transaction is resumed. The ASSIGN Block is executed on behalf of that Transaction, resulting in the fifth call of the simulation on RN1. (To compute the first customer's service time, the value of the Function whose number is 5 is now determined; this leads to the fifth call of the simulation on RN1. The value of FN5 is then multiplied by the previously determined value of FN$MEAN, and the integer portion of the product is saved in Parameter 1 as the service-time value.) And so on.

Table 4D.2 shows the continuation of the RN1-usage pattern for Customers 2 and 3, and also indicates the determination of Customer 4's interarrival time. Note that four calls are made on RN1 per customer. Calls 1, 2, 3, and 5 are used for the first customer; calls 4, 6, 7, and 9 are used for the second customer; calls 8, 10, 11 and 13 are used for the third customer, and so on. (Customer 1's pattern is atypical; the pattern for Customers 2, 3, 4, etc. always involves using calls k, $k + 2$, $k + 3$, and $k + 5$, where $k = 4$ for customer 2, 8 for customer 3, 12 for customer 4, and so on.) If the RN1 starting point is the same on simulated day 1 in both models, the customers that day clearly will have properties which are identical in both models; similarly, if the RN1 starting point is the same on simulated day 2 in both models (but different than it was on simulated day 1), then the day 2 customers will be identical between the two models (but will differ, in general, from the day 1 customers). And so on, for each of the days in the 5-day simulation.

As the next point, consider the task of making the RN1 starting point different from simulated day to simulated day. This could be done by using the RMULT card between consecutive days. There is no need, however, to take this approach. In fact, in moving to each next day, RN1 can be left exactly where it was at the end of the preceding day. Because of the control of experimental conditions, the number of customers entering the single-line model on day 1 equals the number entering the multiple-line model on day 1. This means that the number of calls on RN1 for the day 1 simulation is the same in both models. This, in turn, guarantees that simply by leaving RN1 where it is, the RN1 starting point for day 2 will be the same in both models, and so on for days 3, 4, and 5.

Finally, there is the matter of giving the service completion event higher priority than the customer arrival event, in case of time ties. This can be done in the multiple-line system by bringing customer-Transactions into the model with a Priority Level of 0; then, anywhere between the GENERATE Block and the ADVANCE Block simulating service time, the customer-Transaction Priority Level can be boosted to 1 with the Block "PRIORITY 1". This guarantees that those Current Events Chain customer-Transactions sched-uled to cause a service completion event will be ahead of those who are just entering the model. The status of teller-Facilities and of Queue contents will consequently have been updated by the time any arriving customer-Transaction is processed.

It is interesting that no priority distinction need be made relative to simultaneous service completion and customer arrival events in the one-line model. Because there is only one Queue in that model, and because the tellers have no individual identity, it is meaningless to talk about which Queue a customer-Transaction joins, or which teller a customer-Transaction captures.

(3) Table of Definitions

TABLE 4D.3(a)   Table of Definitions for Case Study 4D: One-Line Model

GPSS Entity	Interpretation
Transactions	
Model Segment 1	Customers
	P1: Service time required by the customer
Model Segment 2	A timer
Functions	
5	Function for sampling from the exponential distribution with a mean value of 1
MEAN	Function describing the mean service time required for various categories of business
Queues	
ONE	The Queue used to gather statistics for the one waiting line in the bank
Storages	
TELRS	Storage simulating the eight bank tellers

TABLE 4D.3(b)   Table of Definitions for Case Study 4D: Multiple-Line Model

GPSS Entity	Interpretation
Transactions	
Model Segment 1	Customers
	P1: Service time required by the customer
	P2: The number of the Queue through which the customer passes, and of the teller the customer uses
Facilities	
1, 2, 3, 4, 5, 6, 7, and 8	Facilities used to simulate the 8 bank tellers
Queues	
1, 2, 3, 4, 5, 6, 7, and 8	The Queues used to gather statistics for the waiting lines ahead of tellers 1 through 8, respectively
10	The Queue used to gather aggregate waiting statistics for all customers moving through the bank

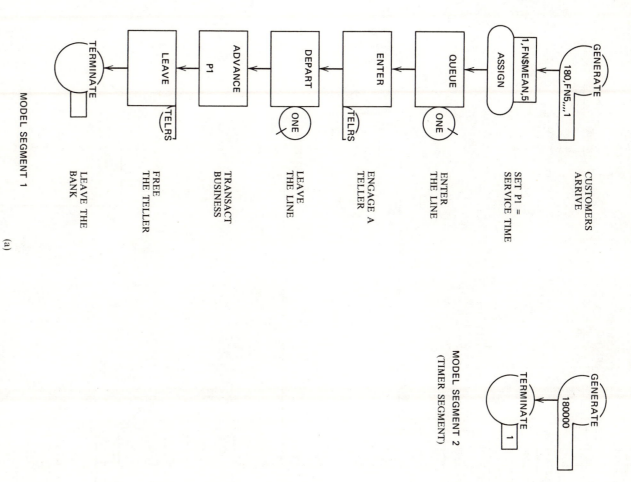

MODEL SEGMENT 1

MODEL SEGMENT 2
(TIMER SEGMENT)

(a)

FIGURE 4D.2(a)   Block Diagrams for Case Study 4D (One-line model)

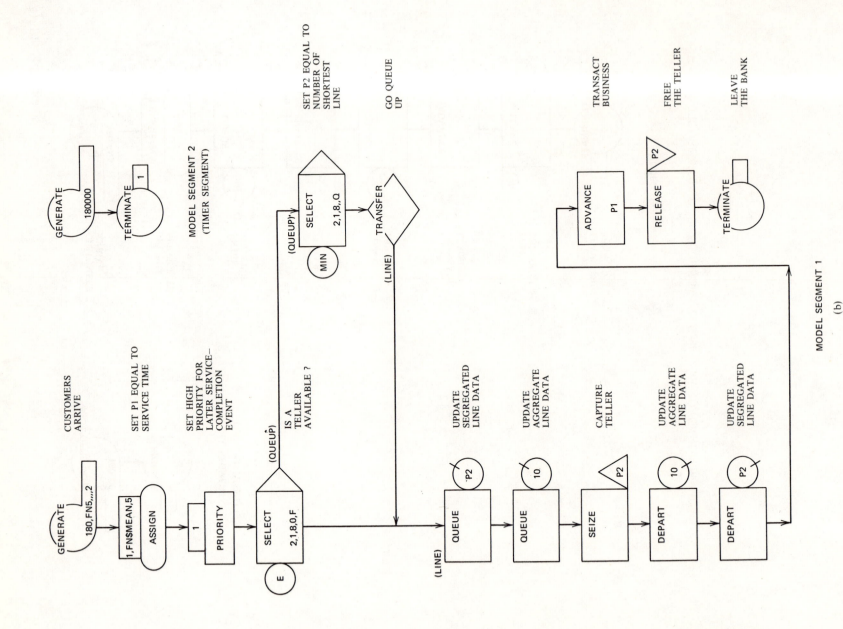

FIGURE 4D.2(b)   Block Diagrams for Case Study 4D (Multiple-line model)

(5) Extended Program Listings

(a) One-line model

```
BLOCK                                                              CARD
NUMBER  *LOC   OPERATION  A,B,C,D,E,F,G          COMMENTS         NUMBER

               SIMULATE                                             1
             *                                                      2
             * FUNCTION DEFINITION(S)                               3
             *                                                      4
         5     FUNCTION   RN1,C24   EXPONENTIAL DISTRIBUTION FUNCTION   5
0,0/.1,.104/.2,.222/.3,.355/.4,.509/.5,.69/.6,.915/.7,1.2/.75,1.38      6
.8,1.6/.84,1.83/.88,2.12/.9,2.3/.92,2.52/.94,2.81/.95,2.99/.96,3.2      7
.97,3.5/.98,3.9/.99,4.6/.995,5.3/.998,6.2/.999,7/.9998,8               8
      MEAN     FUNCTION   RN1,D5    DISTRIBUTION OF MEAN SERVICE TIME   9
.1,450/.29,750/.61,1000/.85,1500/1,3000                               10
             *                                                     11
             * STORAGE CAPACITY DEFINITION(S)                      12
             *                                                     13
               STORAGE    S$TELRS,8   PROVIDE 8 TELLERS            14
             *                                                     15
             * MODEL SEGMENT 1                                     16
             *                                                     17
  1            GENERATE   180,FN$MEAN,,1   CUSTOMERS ARRIVE        18
  2            ASSIGN     1,FN$MEAN,.5     SET P1 = SERVICE TIME   19
  3            QUEUE      ONE              ENTER THE LINE          20
  4            ENTER      TELRS            ENGAGE A TELLER         21
  5            DEPART     ONE              LEAVE THE LINE          22
  6            ADVANCE    P1               TRANSACT BUSINESS       23
  7            LEAVE      TELRS            FREE THE TELLER         24
  8            TERMINATE                   LEAVE THE BANK          25
             *                                                     26
             * MODEL SEGMENT 2                                     27
             *                                                     28
  9            GENERATE   180000   TIMER ARRIVES AFTER 5 HOURS     29
 10            TERMINATE  1        SHUT OFF THE RUN                30
             *                                                     31
             * CONTROL CARDS                                       32
             *                                                     33
               START      1        START THE RUN FOR DAY 1        34
               CLEAR               CLEAR FOR DAY 2                 35
               START      1        START THE RUN FOR DAY 2        36
               CLEAR               CLEAR FOR DAY 3                 37
               START      1        START THE RUN FOR DAY 3        38
               CLEAR               CLEAR FOR DAY 4                 39
               START      1        START THE RUN FOR DAY 4        40
               CLEAR               CLEAR FOR DAY 5                 41
               START      1        START THE RUN FOR DAY 5        42
               END                 RETURN CONTROL TO OPERATING SYSTEM  43
```

(b) Multiple-line model

```
BLOCK                                                              CARD
NUMBER  *LOC   OPERATION  A,B,C,D,E,F,G          COMMENTS         NUMBER

               SIMULATE                                             1
             *                                                      2
             * FUNCTION DEFINITION(S)                               3
             *                                                      4
         5     FUNCTION   RN1,C24   EXPONENTIAL DISTRIBUTION FUNCTION   5
0,0/.1,.104/.2,.222/.3,.355/.4,.509/.5,.69/.6,.915/.7,1.2/.75,1.38      6
.8,1.6/.84,1.83/.88,2.12/.9,2.3/.92,2.52/.94,2.81/.95,2.99/.96,3.2      7
.97,3.5/.98,3.9/.99,4.6/.995,5.3/.998,6.2/.999,7/.9998,8               8
      MEAN     FUNCTION   RN1,D5    DISTRIBUTION OF MEAN SERVICE TIME   9
.1,450/.29,750/.61,1000/.85,1500/1,3000                               10
             *                                                     11
             * MODEL SEGMENT 1                                     12
             *                                                     13
  1            GENERATE   180,FN$MEAN,,2   CUSTOMERS ARRIVE        14
  2            ASSIGN     1,FN$MEAN,.5     SET P1 = SERVICE TIME   15
  3            PRIORITY   1    SET HIGH PRIORITY FOR LATER
                               SERVICE-COMPLETION EVENT            16
  4   LINE     SELECT E   2,1,8,,F,QUEUP   IS A TELLER AVAILABLE?  17
  5            QUEUE      P2               UPDATE SEGREGATED LINE DATA  18
  6            QUEUE      10               UPDATE AGGREGATE LINE DATA   19
  7            SEIZE      P2               CAPTURE A TELLER        20
  8            DEPART     10               UPDATE AGGREGATE LINE DATA   21
  9            DEPART     P2               UPDATE SEGREGATED LINE DATA  22
 10            ADVANCE    P1               TRANSACT BUSINESS       23
 11            RELEASE    P2               FREE THE TELLER         24
 12            TERMINATE                   LEAVE THE BANK          25
 13   QUEUP    SELECT MIN 2,1,8,,Q   SET P2 = NUMBER OF SHORTEST LINE  26
 14            TRANSFER   ,LINE            GO QUEUE UP             27
             *                                                     28
             * MODEL SEGMENT 2                                     29
             *                                                     30
 15            GENERATE   180000   TIMER ARRIVES AFTER 5 HOURS     31
 16            TERMINATE  1        SHUT OFF THE RUN                32
             *                                                     33
             * CONTROL CARDS                                       34
             *                                                     35
               START      1        START THE RUN FOR DAY 1        36
               CLEAR               CLEAR FOR DAY 2                 37
               START      1        START THE RUN FOR DAY 2        38
               CLEAR               CLEAR FOR DAY 3                 39
               START      1        START THE RUN FOR DAY 3        40
               CLEAR               CLEAR FOR DAY 4                 41
               START      1        START THE RUN FOR DAY 4        42
               CLEAR               CLEAR FOR DAY 5                 43
               START      1        START THE RUN FOR DAY 5        44
               END                 RETURN CONTROL TO OPERATING SYSTEM  45
```

FIGURE 4D.3 Extended Program Listings for Case Study 4D. (a) One-line model. (b) Multiple-line model.

(6) Program Output

STORAGE	CAPACITY	AVERAGE CONTENTS	AVERAGE UTILIZATION	ENTRIES	AVERAGE TIME/TRAN	CURRENT CONTENTS	MAXIMUM CONTENTS
TELRS	8	7.515	.939	1001	1351.355	4	8

(a)

QUEUE	MAXIMUM CONTENTS	AVERAGE CONTENTS	TOTAL ENTRIES	ZERO ENTRIES	PERCENT ZEROS	AVERAGE TIME/TRANS	$AVERAGE TIME/TRANS	TABLE NUMBER	CURRENT CONTENTS
ONE	51	14.138	1001	121	12.0	2542.459	2892.047		

$AVERAGE TIME/TRANS = AVERAGE TIME/TRANS EXCLUDING ZERO ENTRIES

(b)

FACILITY	AVERAGE UTILIZATION	NUMBER ENTRIES	AVERAGE TIME/TRAN	SEIZING TRANS. NO.	PREEMPTING TRANS. NO.
1	.968	153	1139.274	50	
2	.966	116	1499.008	45	
3	.956	114	1510.280	28	
4	.943	98	1732.142	36	
5	.935	138	1220.536		
6	.925	107	1557.551		
7	.905	134	1216.500		
8	.913	141	1166.581		

(c)

QUEUE	MAXIMUM CONTENTS	AVERAGE CONTENTS	TOTAL ENTRIES	ZERO ENTRIES	PERCENT ZEROS	AVERAGE TIME/TRANS	$AVERAGE TIME/TRANS	TABLE NUMBER	CURRENT CONTENTS
1	6	2.139	153	27	17.6	2517.503	3056.968		
2	6	2.203	116	25	21.5	3418.508	4357.656		
3	6	2.075	114	19	16.6	3277.508	3933.010		
4	6	2.111	98	25	25.5	3877.846	5205.875		
5	6	1.740	138	22	15.9	2270.869	2701.551		
6	5	1.824	107	21	19.6	3069.411	3818.918		
7	5	1.615	134	26	19.4	2170.000	2692.407		
8	5	1.441	141	24	17.0	1840.453	2217.982		
10	45	15.152	1001	189	18.8	2724.756	3358.966		

$AVERAGE TIME/TRANS = AVERAGE TIME/TRANS EXCLUDING ZERO ENTRIES

(d)

FIGURE 4D.4 Selected Program Output for Case Study 4D. (a) Storage statistics (one-line model, day 1). (b) Queue statistics (one-line model, day 1). (c) Facility statistics (multiple-line model, day 1). (d) Queue statistics (multiple-line model, day 1).

(7) Discussion

Model Implementation. As suggested in the section discussing the approach taken in building the model, the 24-point continuous Function for sampling from the exponential distribution has been given a numeric name ("5") in the case study, not a symbolic name. This is because of the restriction that when the optional C Operand is used with the ASSIGN Block and its value is *directly* specified, it must be the *number* of a Function, and cannot be a Function's symbolic name.

Note that the GENERATE Block's optional F Operand has been used in the one-line and multiple-line models so that customer-Transactions in those models have exactly the 1 or 2 Parameters that they require, respectively [see Block 1 in Figures 4D.3(a) and (b)]. If the de-fault had been taken on the F Operand, customer-Transactions in both models would have had 12 halfword Parameters. The reason for economizing on the number of Transaction Parameters in this case study is explained in the next section.

Program Output.[7] Figure 4D.4 displays teller statistics and waiting line statistics produced at the end of the day 1 simulation by the one-line and multiple-line models. Pertinent waiting line information produced by the two models for the 5 simulated days is summarized in Table 4D.4. The table indicates that, for the one-line model, average waiting time for customers for the 5 days simulated was 1253 time units, or about 2.1 minutes. In the multiple-line results, average

[7]Total CPU time for the one-line simulation on an IBM 360/67 computer was 35.3 seconds. For the multiple-line simulation, it was 48.7 seconds.

TABLE 4D.4 A Summary of Program Output in Case Study 4D

	Average Queue Residence Time (tenths of seconds)[a]		Percent Zero Entries	
Day	One-Line	Multiple-Line[b]	One-Line	Multiple-Line[b]
1	2542	2724	12.0	18.8
2	900	1314	29.7	37.2
3	908	1199	34.8	44.0
4	1486	2013	21.9	28.2
5	427	666	50.1	58.7
Average	1253	1583	29.7	37.4
Standard Deviation	727	714	12.8	13.6

[a]Including zero entries
[b]Aggregate Queue

waiting time for the same 5 simulated days was 1583 time units, or about 2.6 minutes. For this experiment, there is then about a 20 percent time savings in converting from a multiple-line to a one-line system. These additional points should be noted.

1. The multiple-line model is unrealistic, because no line-switching is permitted. (The ability to incorporate the line-switching feature into queuing systems models will be discussed in Chapter 7. See exercises 19 and 20 of Section 7.11.)

2. *Average* waiting time is only one measure of customer waiting experience. In addition to its average value, other properties of the random variable "waiting time" are also important determinants of a customer's feeling about the waiting process. For example, the statistic "percentage of customers who have to wait longer than 5 minutes" may be important; and, even if the one-line and multiple-line queuing systems produce the same average waiting time, one system may be superior to the other in terms of this other measure. The models presented in this case study do not estimate the waiting-time distribution. The ability to incorporate such estimates in GPSS models is taken up at the end of this chapter.

3. Table 4D.4 indicates that the standard deviation in the day-by-day average waiting time is large, on the order of about 50 to 60 percent of the mean. This implies that, if experimental conditions were not controlled, comparison of results would be all the more difficult. For example, assume there had been no experimental control, and that the day 5 multiple-line result occurred, whereas any one of the one-line results occurred *except* that for day 5. It might then be tentatively concluded that the multiple-line system is superior. But the conclusion tentatively drawn here under controlled conditions is exactly the opposite of that.

The Table 4D.4 information shows that, for the 5 days simulated, the customers had about a 29.7 percent chance to get a teller immediately in the one-line system, and a 37.4 percent chance in the multiple-line system. This seems inconsistent with the tentative conclusion that the one-line system is superior. However, careful thought shows that the percentage zero entries in the multiple-line case *should* be higher than for the one-line system, precisely because no line-switching is permitted in the model. Reasoning this out is left as an exercise.

In Figure 4D.4(c), the teller-utilization statistics are seen to be approximately the same for each of the eight tellers in the multiple-line system. At first this might not seem likely, because when more than one of the teller-Facilities is available, the SELECT Block always selects the smallest-numbered Facility not in use. In fact, it is true that teller 8 gets business only when there are at least seven customers already in the bank. On the other hand, the Queue information in Figure 4D.4(d) indicates that the average number of people waiting for service that simulated day was over 15. (This means, then, that there were more than 23 customers in the bank that day, on average.) From this point of view, then, the utilization statistics are reasonable.

4.16 Computer Memory Considerations

When introducing Transactions, Facilities, Storages, and Queues, it was indicated that the maximum number of these entities permissible in a model depends on the amount of available computer memory. These maximum values are given in Appendix F, along with other information pertinent to computer memory considerations in GPSS. The portion of the Appendix F information applying to the GPSS entities discussed so far is repeated in Table 4.5.

Each entity has a fixed memory requirement, whether it is actually used in a model or not.

TABLE 4.5 A Tabulation of the Maximum Normal Quantities of Selected GPSS Entities, and Their Fixed and Variable Computer Memory Requirements (Reproduced from Appendix F)

Entity Type	Normally Available Quantities for Various Computer Memory Levels			Fixed Memory Requirement per Item (bytes)	Reallocation Mnemonic
	64K	128K	256K		
Transactions	200	600	1200	16[a]	XAC
Blocks	120	500	1000	12[b]	BLO
Facilities	35	150	300	28	FAC
Functions	20	50	200	32[c]	FUN
Queues	35	150	300	32	QUE
Storages	35	150	300	40	STO
COMMON (bytes)[d]	5600	14400	25600		COM

[a] Add 20 bytes of COMMON for every active Transaction, plus additional bytes for Parameters (2 bytes per halfword Parameter, 4 bytes per fullword Parameter)

[b] Add 4 bytes of COMMON for each Block using more than one Operand

[c] Add 8 bytes of COMMON for each pair of coordinates of a D type Function. Add 12 bytes of COMMON for each pair of coordinates of a C type Function

[d] COMMON is an otherwise uncommitted pool of computer memory, portions of which can be used for such purposes as storing the pairs of points used to define Functions, providing the memory needed for Transaction Parameters, and so on

These fixed requirements are shown in the second-to-last column in Table 4.5. For example, each Transaction has a fixed memory requirement of 16 bytes, each Storage has a fixed requirement of 40 bytes, and so on.

In addition, when certain items are used, *additional* memory must be committed to them. The amount of this additional memory is variable in the sense that it depends on the properties of the particular entity in question. For example, as footnote (a) to Table 4.5 indicates, each Transaction actually in a model requires another 20 bytes, plus additional bytes for its Parameter set. Blocks and Functions also have a variable memory requirement. Facilities, Storages, and Queues, however, only have fixed memory requirements.

When an entity is used, its variable memory requirement, if any, is met by using portions of otherwise uncommitted memory available in a pool called COMMON. The number of bytes of COMMON is dependent on the total available computer memory, as indicated in Table 4.5. The limitation on COMMON, coupled with its use to support entities actually being used in a model, sometimes results in the supply of COMMON becoming exhausted during a simulation. When this happens, error message 599, "LIMITS OF GPSS/360 COMMON CORE EXCEEDED," is printed out and the simulation is terminated.

Consider a typical situation which can result in the "COMMON exceeded" error message. Assume that a certain model consists only of Blocks, Facilities, Storages, and Queues. For

simplicity, ignore the amount of COMMON which the Blocks may require. As suggested in Table 4.5, the Facilities, Storages, and Queues place no demands on COMMON. Now, if each Transaction uses 12 halfword Parameters (the default case), how many Transactions can be active in the model when 64K bytes of computer memory are available? From Table 4.5, it is easy to think that the answer is 200. This is not the case, because *COMMON would be exceeded long before the two-hundredth Transaction could be brought into the model.* Footnote (a) to Table 4.5 indicates that each active Transaction with 12 halfword Parameters requires 44 bytes from COMMON $(20 + 2 \ast 12 = 44)$. Dividing 44 into 5600 (the total number of bytes in COMMON at the 64K level) shows there is only enough COMMON to support the active existence of 127 Transactions. Furthermore, this computation assumes that no COMMON is used for any other purpose. Hence, even though there can *theoretically* be 200 Transactions at the 64K level, this can only come about in practice if the analyst adjusts the number of Transaction Parameters (or takes other steps described below) so that enough COMMON is available to support this many Transactions.

It is good practice, then, to use the F-Operand on GENERATE Blocks to limit Transaction Parameters to the number actually required. This was done in Case Study 4D (see Cards 18 and 14 in Figures 4D.3(a) and (b), respectively). If the number of Transaction Parameters had not been scaled down, the Case Study 4D models would not have run at the 64K memory level. In both models, conditions arose in which COMMON would otherwise have been exceeded while trying to bring another customer into the bank (i.e., while the Processor was trying to bring another Transaction into the model).

It may be, however, that a "COMMON exceeded" condition arises even when active Transactions only carry exactly the number and size of Parameters they require. When this happens, more COMMON can be obtained simply by going to a higher K-level (assuming a higher K-level is available).[8] The disadvantage of this approach, however, is that models are more expensive to run at higher K-levels, for the simple reason that more computer memory is required to process the job.

Another way to solve the "COMMON exceeded" problem is to reallocate the use of computer memory at a given K-level. The "maximum normal quantities" shown in Table 4.5 (or, more generally, in Appendix F) are default quantities. By use of a special control card, the REALLOCATE card, the analyst can redistribute available computer memory among the various entity types within a given K-level. For example, suppose that a given model at the 64K level makes use of only 2 Storages. The fixed memory requirement of each Storage is 40 bytes, whether the Storage is being used or not. Hence, with only 2 Storages in use, 1320 bytes of memory are being wasted (40 bytes times 33 unused Storages equals 1320). If the analyst redefines the maximum number of Storages as 2, 1320 bytes are thereby freed. In the absence of other considerations, these bytes could be added to COMMON. There would then be 6920 bytes in COMMON for the model at the 64K level, an increase of almost 25 percent.

Quite apart from the constraint imposed by COMMON, a model's need for a given type of entity or entities may exceed the normally available quantities at a given K-level. When this is true, the "maximum quantity" problem can be

solved by following either approach available to solve the "COMMON exceeded" problem. If the option exists, it is possible to go to a higher K-level, although the disadvantage of increased run-cost should be kept in mind. The second approach, reallocation of the maximum quantity of entities within a given K-level, should be used before resorting to a higher K-level. In the above example, with only two Storages used in the model, 1320 bytes were freed via reallocation. These bytes could be added to COMMON. Suppose, however, that COMMON does not impose a constraint in the model in question. Instead, assume the maximum quantity of Transactions, 200, is a constraint. If it is necessary that up to 250 Transactions be in the model simultaneously, the additional 50 Transactions required can be bought with some of the 1320 bytes freed through the Storage reallocation. Because each Transaction has a fixed memory requirement of 16 bytes, the maximum quantity can be reallocated upward to 250, using 800 of the freed bytes in the process. The other 520 freed bytes might then be added to COMMON. By reallocating downward on some entities, then, it is possible to reallocate upward on other entities. In summary, considerable flexibility can be achieved through the reallocation process.

Specifications for the REALLOCATE control card are shown in Table 4.6. The Location field is not used. The word REALLOCATE is entered in the Operation field. Pairs of entries are used in the Operands field. The first entry in a pair is a mnemonic for the entity type being reallocated. The second entry is the new maximum quantity to be in effect. Mnemonics for the Table 4.5 entities are shown in the rightmost column in Table 4.5.

Examples of REALLOCATE cards appear in Figure 4.23. The A and B Operands in the first example specify that the number of Storages is to be reallocated downward to 2. As discussed above, if the model is being run in a 64K environment, 1320 bytes are freed by this reallocation. The C and D Operands in the first example specify that COMMON is to be reallocated upward to 6920 bytes. Hence, all of the bytes freed by the

[8] The K-level desired by the analyst is indicated on the exterternal control cards used in making up the job deck. See Section 2.18.

LOCATION	OPERATION	A,B,C,D,E,F
	REALLOCATE	STO,2,COM,6920 FIRST EXAMPLE
	REALLOCATE	STO,2,XAC,250,COM,6120 SECOND EXAMPLE

FIGURE 4.23   Examples for use of the REALLOCATE card

TABLE 4.6   Specifications for the REALLOCATE Control Card

Punchcard Field	Information Supplied in Field
Location	Not used
Operation	Literally, the word REALLOCATE
Operands A, C, E, etc.	Each alternate Operand is a mnemonic indicating a type of entity whose maximum normal quantity is being redefined; a partial list of mnemonics is shown in Table 4.5; a complete list appears in Appendix F
B, D, F, H, etc.	Each alternate Operand is a constant indicating the maximum normal quantity to be in effect for the entity type indicated by the preceding Operand

Storage reallocation are being added to COM-
MON.

The first example shows that, although reallocation specifications are provided pair-wise on
the REALLOCATE card, Operand pairs are *not*
separated by a slash as are pairs on Function
follower cards and Storage capacity definition
cards. Only commas are used on the REALLO-
CATE card to set apart consecutive Operands.

It is also implied in the first example that, if the
bytes freed by downward reallocation are to be
added to COMMON, this must be *explicitly* indicated through use of the COM mnemonic. It
is not to be assumed as true, then, that any freed
bytes not otherwise used by upward reallocation
are automatically added to COMMON.

In the second example, the number of Storages is reallocated downward to 2. Assuming a
64K environment, the 1320 freed bytes are then
used in part to reallocate upward to 250 Transactions (Operands C and D in the example).
This commits 800 of the freed bytes. The remaining 520 bytes are added to the 5600 otherwise available in COMMON, producing a total
of 6120 (Operands E and F in the example).

Three final observations concerning use of the
REALLOCATE card will now be made.

1. As many Operand pairs can be entered in a
REALLOCATE card as desired, as long as the pairs
do not extend beyond card column 71. More than one
REALLOCATE card can be used, if necessary or
desirable.

2. The REALLOCATE card(s), *without exception,*
must be the *first* card(s) encountered by the GPSS
Processor. It would be an error, for example, to precede
the REALLOCATE card with the SIMULATE card, or
with a GPSS comments-card (i.e., a card with an
asterisk punched in card column 1.)

3. It is recommended that the *minimum* normal
quantity specified for any entity type be 1, *not* 0.
Although 0 is *logically* a feasible minimum quantity,
a 0 specification may result in an error condition
because of the way the GPSS Processor has been
constructed.

4.17 Computer Time Requirements

Except in case-study footnotes, nothing has been
said until now about the computer time required
to run GPSS models. The time spent by the computer's central processing unit (i.e., CPU time) in
performing a simulation is important in a variety
of ways. For example, it has direct dollar consequences. CPU time might be billed at rates ranging from 15¢ to $1.00 per second, depending on
the hardware involved, and the context in which
the hardware is used.[9] Apart from cost considerations, the analyst must often estimate the *maximum* CPU time required to run a job. During the
run, if that much CPU time has been used and the
job is not yet done, the job is usually time trapped
off the system. This is to be viewed in a positive
sense; if it is established during a run that more
time is required than was estimated, this may be

[9] For example, the model in Figure 4D.3(b) used *48.7* CPU
seconds on Michigan's IBM 360/67 multiprocessing system.
Cost of the run was *$6.65.* Cost per CPU second, then, was
about 15¢ for the run. This is admittedly a coarse computation,
because Michigan's costing algorithm takes into account use
of system resources other than CPU time alone. As another
example, certain industrial users pay $1.00 per CPU second
to run GPSS in "remote batch" mode on a Univac 1108
computer. Of course, the figures of 15¢ and $1.00 cannot be
compared directly, because about 1.5 to 2.0 times as much
computation can be accomplished in 1 second on the
Univac 1108 as on the IBM 360/67. Furthermore, the code
for the Univac 1108 GPSS Processor is more efficient than
it is for the GPSS/360 Processor. Such efficiency differences
must also be factored in when comparing cost figures.

a signal that something is wrong with the logic or implementation of the model. On the other hand, when the analyst is faced with deadlines of one kind or another, it is disappointing to find that the time estimate was set unrealistically low and, even though the model was performing as expected, less than complete results are available from the run. This is especially vexing when turn-around time (i.e., the time between turning in a job, and having it ready for pickup) is hours, rather than minutes.

With one or two exceptions, the simulations discussed so far in the book have each required fewer than 10 CPU seconds.[10] This single CPU time measure is the sum of two major components. Each of the major components consists of subcomponents, as itemized in Table 4.7. As an example of the relative contribution of the subcomponents to the final CPU-time measure, Table 4.8 shows the size of the components when the Figure 4D.3(b) model was run. Execution time is usually the most significant time component, as Table 4.8 shows.

TABLE 4.7   CPU-Time Components Involved in Performing a Simulation with a GPSS Model

Major Component	Subcomponents
GPSS Processor Time	Assembly time
	Input time
	Execution time
	Output time
Operating System Time	Log on
	Load the GPSS Processor
	Unload the GPSS Processor
	Log off

TABLE 4.8   A Breakdown of CPU Time Used in the Simulation Performed with the Figure 4D.3(b) Model

Major Component or Subcomponent	CPU Time (seconds)
Assembly	0.375
Input	0.421
Execution	44.731
Output	0.648
Operating System Time	2.534
Total CPU Time:	48.709

Table 4.9 summarizes the total CPU times required to run the 13 GPSS case studies presented so far. In the Program Output section of each case

[10] All the models in this book were run on the University of Michigan's IBM 360/67 multiprocessing system.

TABLE 4.9   A Summary of the Total CPU Time Required in Each of the Case Study Simulations Presented So Far

Case Study	Total CPU Time (seconds)
2A	1.6
2B	1.8
2C	2.1
2D	2.0
2E	68.2
2F	4.1
3A	4.0
3B	3.2
3C	8.1
4A	4.8
4B	5.2
4C	19.3
4D	84.0 (both models included)

study, the practice will be continued of using a footnote to indicate the total CPU time required to perform the case study simulation.

It was indicated in a Section 2.8 footnote that those using GPSS/360 on a System 360/67 computer can estimate the CPU time required for a simulation by using "1 millisecond per Block execution" as a rule of thumb. The 1 millisecond figure is a rough approximation at best. Actual execution time depends on the types of Blocks involved, the nature of the Functions used, the number and type of blocking conditions experienced by Transactions, the number of scans and rescans of the Current Events Chain, and so on. As a test of this measure, consider again the Figure 4D.3(b) model. Using Block Counts not shown in the book, the Total Count, summed over each Block, and over each of the 5 days simulated, comes to about 66,000. This "total Total Count" can be interpreted as the number of Block executions performed. Dividing 66,000 into the 48.7 CPU seconds used, a figure of about 0.75 milliseconds per Block execution results. In this case, then, the 1 millisecond rule of thumb tends to be on the conservative side.

If it is necessary to develop a rule of thumb for another GPSS Processor and/or another hardware system, a convenient approach is to run several widely different models, then use the "total Total Count" as just illustrated to arrive at a rough approximation for estimation purposes. When such a figure is available, it is possible to forecast, albeit in crude fashion, about how much CPU time a previously untried model can be expected to consume.

In Chapter 7, some of the considerations involved in building relatively efficient GPSS models will be discussed. If CPU time is expensive or limited, designing models so that they require as little CPU time as possible is obviously a matter of some interest.

4.18 The Potential Danger of Redundancy in Naming GPSS Entities

Three possibilities have now been introduced whereby the names of entities can be supplied in the context of GPSS models.

1. Numeric names can be supplied directly. For example, at the Block "SEIZE 7","7" is supplied directly as the name of a Facility.
2. Symbolic names can be supplied directly. For example, "LINE" is directly supplied as the name of a Queue at the Block "QUEUE LINE".
3. Numeric names can be supplied indirectly. When a Transaction enters the Block "SEIZE P1", for example, the name of the Facility involved is indirectly supplied as the value of Parameter 1 of the entering Transaction.

This flexibility with respect to supplying entity names can unfortunately lead to situations in which unwanted redundancies occur. To explain what is meant by a redundancy, consider a model in which the analyst refers to one Storage with the number 1, and to another Storage with the symbolic name TUGS. Assume it is the analyst's understanding that "1" and "TUGS" are two distinct Storages in his model. Now, it was seen earlier that as part of a simulation, the Processor assigns numeric equivalents to all symbolically named entities in a model. (In fact, the Processor prints out these correspondences in the form of symbol dictionaries which are labeled BLOCK SYMBOLS AND CORRESPONDING NUMBERS, FACILITY SYMBOLS AND CORRESPONDING NUMBERS, and so on.) In the current example, depending on the way the model has been built, it is entirely possible that the Storage number assigned as the numeric equivalent of "TUGS" is "1". If this happens, then "1" and "TUGS" are the same Storage, not two distinct Storages, as the analyst had assumed. This, of course, results in a model which is logically invalid. Unfortunately, the model may not be invalid in any other sense. That is, there is no reason why the Processor will print out an error message and end the simulation just because "1" and "TUGS" are the same Storage. Such redundancies, then, can be quite insidious. It is therefore important to understand how they can arise, and how to defend against them.

In considering the redundancy question, it is necessary to know how the Processor draws correspondences between symbolic entity names, and their numeric equivalents. As the first step in performing this task, the Processor constructs a *list of numeric names*, and a separate *list of symbolic names, for each entity type* during the model Input Phase. When the Input Phase is finished, the Processor then has a list of numeric Facility names, a list of symbolic Facility names, a list of numeric Queue names, a list of symbolic Queue names, and so on, for the model. Before describing how these lists are then used to assign numeric equivalents to symbolic names, it is important to consider how the lists are constructed.

When the Processor encounters the *symbolic* name of an entity in *any* context during the model Input Phase, it places that name on the symbolic name-list for the type of entity in question. This is not true, however, for *numeric* entity names. An entity number is placed on the list of numbers for that type entity only if the number is used in the model in a *defining* context. As this statement implies, not all contexts in which entity numbers can be used are defining.

Some examples of defining and nondefining contexts for entity numbers are in order. Consider the Block "SELECT MIN 1,1,8,,Q", as used in the multiple-line model in Case Study 4D. Queues are the type of entity being referred to in the context of this Block, as signalled through the SNA "family name" Q, per the Block's E Operand. The B and C Operands on this Block have the purpose of supplying a range of Queue numbers. It is evidently the analyst's intention, then, to have Queues numbered 1 through 8 in the model. The SELECT Block, however, provides an example in which entity numbers are used in a nondefining context. That is, use of the SELECT Block itself in the model does *not* cause the Processor to add the numbers 1 through 8 to the numeric name-list for Queues, or even to add the numbers 1 and 8 to that list.

As another example, consider the multiple Storage capacity definition card. Any references to Storage numbers on such a card are nondefining. For example, when the Processor encounters the card "STORAGE S4,5/S$ALPHA,9" in a model, it puts ALPHA on the list of symbolic names for Storages, but does not put 4 on the list of numeric names for Storages. This may seem strange, but it is a fact. Although the card succeeds in defining the capacities of Storages 4 and ALPHA, respectively, as 5 and 9, and causes

ALPHA to be placed on the symbolic name-list for Storages, it does not result in the number 4 being placed on the numeric name-list for Storages.

On the other hand, the Blocks SEIZE, RE-LEASE, ENTER, LEAVE, QUEUE, and DEPART are ones in which entity numbers are used in a defining context. When the Processor encounters the cards "SEIZE 14", "ENTER 7", and "QUEUE 21", it adds the numbers 14, 7, and 21, respectively, to the numeric name-lists for Facilities, Storages, and Queues.

How is it possible to recognize which usage contexts are defining for entity numbers, and which are not? A rough rule of thumb for defining contexts is this: either the entity number must be used as the A Operand at certain Blocks (such as SEIZE, RELEASE, ENTER, LEAVE, QUEUE, and DEPART), or it must appear in the Location field of certain definition cards. Included in this latter case are Function header cards and single Storage capacity definition cards. For example, the cards "23 FUNCTION RN1,C5" and "9 STORAGE 6" constitute defining contexts for Function 23 and Storage 9, respectively. The number 23 is consequently added to the numeric name-list for Functions; and the number 9 is added to the numeric name-list for Storages, when the Processor encounters these two cards. Such a list is provided in Appendix G.

Now we come back to the problem of assigning numeric equivalents to symbolically named entities in the language. For convenience, consider the numeric and symbolic name-lists for Facilities. The Processor regards all numbers on the numeric name-list as being *unavailable* for use as the numeric equivalents of symbolic Facility names. Conversely, numbers *not* on the numeric name-list for Facilities are available for assignment as numeric equivalents. The Processor now simply assigns the available numbers to the names in the symbolic name-list for Facilities, on a one-to-one basis. That is, the smallest available number is made equivalent to the first name on the symbolic name-list; the next smallest available number is made equivalent to the second name on the symbolic name-list, and so on.

As an example, suppose that the first two columns in Figure 4.24 shows the numeric and symbolic name-lists for Facilities when the Input

Numeric Name-List	Symbolic Name-List	List of "Still Available" Numbers
5	BETA	4
2	ALPHA	6
3	GAMMA	7
1	.	8
.	.	.
.	.	35

FIGURE 4.24 The numeric name-list, the symbolic name-list and the list of "numbers still available" for Facilities in a first hypothetical situation

Phase is finished for a certain model. Entries in the numeric and symbolic name-lists appear from top-to-bottom in the table in the order in which they were added to those lists during the model Input Phase. Because they are on the numeric name-list, the numbers 5, 2, 3, and 1 are unavailable for drawing correspondences; Facilities carrying these numbers already "exist" in the model. The still-available numbers are then 4, 6, 7, 8, ..., 33, 34, and 35, as shown in column three of Figure 4.24. (It is assumed that the model is being run at the 64K level, without reallocation. As shown in Table 4.5, Facility numbers as large as 35 are allowed in these circumstances.) The smallest "still available" number, 4, is then made equivalent to the first name on the symbolic name-list, BETA. The next smallest number, 6, is made equivalent to the second name on the symbolic name-list, ALPHA, and so on. Note that although this discussion and example are in the context of Facilities, the procedure followed by the Processor is the same for Storages and Queues and for all other entity types not yet introduced in the book.

Now consider the question of what happens when entity numbers are supplied *indirectly* in a defining context. When the card "SEIZE P1" is encountered by the Processor, does it cause any numbers to be added to the numeric name-list for Facilities? No. During the Input Phase, there is no way for the Processor to know what values P1 will assume during the simulation itself. It is impossible, then, for the Processor to add any numbers to the numeric name-list when it sees the card "SEIZE P1". It is precisely at this point, and for this reason, that there is the potential for redundancy.

Probably the best way to explain how redundancy can come about is through an example. For such an example, Figure 4.25 shows the

Numeric Name-List	Symbolic Name-List	List of "Still Available" Numbers
4	DELTA	1
5	BETA	2
		3
		6
		7
		8
		.
		.
		35

FIGURE 4.25 The numeric name-list, the symbolic name-list, and the list of "still available" for Facilities in a second hypothetical situation.

numeric and symbolic name-lists for Facilities when the Input Phase is finished for a certain model being run at the 64K level, without re-allocation. Per the scheme described in the preceding example, "1" will be made the numeric equivalent of DELTA, and "2" will be made the numeric equivalent of BETA. Now suppose that the Block "SEIZE P1" is used in the model, and that the model is so designed that P1 can take on the values 1, 2, and 3 during the simulation. When P1 is 1, "SEIZE P1" is then equivalent to "SEIZE DELTA". Similarly, when P1 is 2, "SEIZE P1" is equivalent to "SEIZE BETA". In all likelihood, this is probably not what the analyst had in mind. If this was not his intention, then the model is of course invalid. The analyst's thinking probably went something like this: "I have Facilities numbered 4 and 5 in the model. Furthermore, by design, the various values P1 can assume at the "SEIZE P1" Block are 1, 2, and 3. This means that I also have Facilities numbered 1, 2, and 3 in the model. The GPSS Processor will therefore make the Facility symbols DELTA and BETA equivalent to 6 and 7." The analyst thinks, then, that there are seven different Facilities in his model, whereas there are only five.

The above discussion has centered around possible redundancies that might arise with respect to *Facilities*. Of course, the remarks made for Facilities apply to other entities as well, i.e., to Storages, Queues, and Functions, for example.

There are several ways to sidestep the potential redundancy problem.

1. All entities in a model can be named *directly*, either numerically or symbolically. The disadvantage of this approach is that the power of indirect specification is thereby lost.

2. *Symbolic* entity names can be avoided entirely. If all entity references are either numeric, or via indirect specification, the potential problem is eliminated. In this approach, the memory-aiding convenience of using symbolic names is foregone.

Case Study 4D is a case in point for this approach. In the multiple-line model, individual teller-Queues 1 through 8 were specified indirectly, through a Parameter. The number "10" was then chosen as the name of the aggregate Queue in the model. If the aggregate Queue had been named symbolically, the symbolic name would have been made equivalent to the number "1" by the Processor, and the model would have been invalid.

3. When both symbolic naming and indirect specification are used, the analyst can build his model so that, by design, the entities referenced indirectly have large numeric values. When the Processor makes symbolic names equivalent to numbers, then, the relatively smaller numbers on the "still available" list will be distinct from those that arise via indirect specification.

To illustrate this point, consider again the Case Study 4D multiple-line model. Suppose that a symbolic name had been used for the aggregate Queue in that model. Knowing the Processor would equate the symbolic name to the number 1, the numbers 2 through 9 might then have been chosen for the individual teller-Queues. It would then be convenient to let Facilities 2 through 9 be the teller-Facilities. All that would be required in the model to bring about this shift in Queue and Facility numbers would be to replace the Block "SELECT E 2,1,8,0,F,QUEUP" with "SELECT E 2,2,9,0,F,QUEUP"; and to replace the Block "SELECT MIN 2,1,8,,Q" with "SELECT MIN 2,2,9,,Q".

4. Finally, the analyst can *force* the Processor to equate symbolic names to user-selected numbers. By doing this, unwanted redundancies can be avoided. The desired relationships between symbolic names and their numeric equivalents can be specified with the Equivalence declaration card, which is explained below.

The Equivalence declaration card takes the form shown in Table 4.10. Entered in the Location field is the analyst's choice of symbolic name for an entity of interest. The Operation field contains the term EQU, for "equivalence." The A Operand is the number to which the symbolic name is to be made equivalent. Finally, the B Operand is a one-character mnemonic indicating the type of entity for which the equivalence is being declared.

Table 4.11 shows the various B Operand mnemonics in effect for the GPSS entities studied so far. Appendix H contains a complete list of Equivalence mnemonics for all the GPSS entities discussed in this book.

TABLE 4.10   Format for the Equivalence Declaration Card

Punchcard Field	Information Supplied in the Field
Location	The symbolic name of an entity
Operation	Literally, the three characters EQU
Operands	
A	The number to which the symbolic name is to be made equivalent
B	A mnemonic indicating the type of entity for which the equivalence is being declared

TABLE 4.11   A Partial List of Mnemonics for the Equivalence Declaration Card (reproduced from Appendix H)

Type of GPSS Entity	Equivalence Card Mnemonic
Facility	F
Function	Z
Queue	Q
Storage	S

LOCATION						OPERATION											A,B,C,D,E,F																		
1	2	3	4	5	6	7	8	9	10	11	12	13	14	15	16	17	18	19	20	21	22	23	24	25	26	27	28	29	30	31	32	33	34	35	36
L	I	N	E				E	Q	U									1	0	,	Q														

FIGURE 4.26   An example for use of the Equivalence declaration card

Figure 4.26 shows an example of the Equivalence declaration card. In the example, the Queue symbolically named LINE is declared to be equivalent to Queue 10. If the Figure 4.26 Equivalence declaration had been included in the multiple-line model in Case Study 4D, the Blocks "QUEUE 10" and "DEPART 10" could have been replaced with the Blocks "QUEUE LINE" and "DEPART LINE". As indicated above, *without* the Equivalence declaration, the Processor would otherwise make the symbolically named Queue LINE equivalent to Queue 1 in that model.

4.19 Exercises

1. Show SELECT Blocks to accomplish the following.

(a) Scan Queues 2 through 7 to determine if at least one of them currently has a zero-entry count of zero. If such a Queue is found, its number is to be placed in Parameter 7 of the selecting Transaction. Whether or not such a Queue is found, the selecting Transaction is to move from the SELECT Block sequentially when the scan has been completed.

(b) Scan Storages 8 through 11 to determine if at least one of them has a current content less than 3. If such a Storage is found, its number is to be placed in Parameter 1 of the selecting Transaction (which will then exit the SELECT Block sequentially). If no Storages in the indicated range currently satisfy the indicated condition, the selecting Transaction is to move nonsequentially to the Block in Location RUTE4.

(c) Scan Facilities 1 through 5 to determine if at least one of them has been captured more than ten times. Parameter 7 of the selecting Transaction contains the number of the Parameter into which to copy the number of a qualifying Facility, if such is found. If no Facility in the indicated range meets the specified condition, the selecting Transaction should move nonsequentially to the Block in the Location BYPAS when the scan has been completed.

(d) Find the Facility in the range from 4 to 9 with minimum utilization. Place the Facility number in Parameter 1.

(e) Find the Storage in the range from 2 to 3 with maximum remaining capacity. The Storage number is to be put in Parameter 3.

(f) Parameters 1 through 10 of a Transaction contain order quantities. The number of the Parameter containing the minimum order quantity is to be placed in Parameter 12 of the Transaction.

(g) Find the Queue in the range from P1 to P2 which has the minimum average residence time (including zero entries). Place the number of the Queue in Parameter 5. (All three Parameters mentioned belong to the Transaction entering the SELECT Block.)

2. Explain what happens when Transactions enter the various SELECT Blocks whose card images are shown below.

(a) SELECT E   5,3,7,5,Q,PATHA
(b) SELECT MIN P5,1,10,,FR
(c) SELECT GE   5,P1,P2,P3,SC

3. (a) Describe the two methods whereby the "normally available quantities" of GPSS entities can be increased in a model. Given a choice, which of the two methods is probably preferable, and why?

(b) At the 64K level, how many additional Storages can be "bought" if the number of Facilities is reallocated downward to 20? Show a REALLOCATE card which makes the necessary downward and upward reallocations to accomplish this. State any assumptions you may have to make.

(c) At the 64K level, how many Transactions can

be in a model if each Transaction has ten fullword Parameters? Assume that the RE-ALLOCATE card has not been used, and that no other entities in the model require memory from COMMON. (Also show a GENERATE Block through which Transactions enter a model with ten fullword Parameters.)

(d) Repeat (c), only now assume that the number of Blocks has been reallocated downward to 75, and the number of Functions to 5. Show the REALLOCATE card which accomplishes these downward reallocations, as well as the corresponding upward reallocation for COMMON.

(e) How much COMMON is required by the Function XPDIS, shown in Figure 3.22?

4. (a) Submit the model in Figure 4D.3(b) for running on your computer. Compare the total CPU time required on your system with the 48.7 seconds required on an IBM 360/67. Also compute the "total Total Count" for your simulation, and use it to compute a "millisecond per Block execution" figure.

(b) Compute "total Total Counts" and the corresponding "milliseconds per Block execution" statistics for any other three GPSS models which you have run. How much variation is there from model to model in the "milliseconds per Block execution" statistic?

5. Explain the reason why, in Case Study 4D, the percent zero entries in the multiple-line system is larger than in the one-line system.

6. In the multiple-line system, suppose that no provisions were made to force the service completion event to occur before the next arrival event in case of simultaneity. Now assume that (1) a time tie occurs between these two events, (2) each of the eight tellers is busy, (3) it is teller 4 who is about to complete a service, (4) every Queue is empty, and (5) the event-sequence happens to be in the order "arrival," followed by "service completion." Explain what happens to the arriving customer. What would happen to the arriving customer if the service completion event had occurred first?

7. (a) A common objective in Case Study 4D and Case Study 3C is to simulate for a series of different days with a given system configuration, then simulate for the same series of days with a changed system configuration. In Case Study 3C, it was necessary to use RMULT cards between consecutive simulated days to bring about replication of experimental conditions. In Case Study 4D, it was not necessary to use RMULT cards to accomplish this objective. Explain why RMULT cards were necessary in the one case study, and not in the other.

(b) Show how Chapter 4 concepts can be used to build an alternative model for Case Study 3C (see Figure 3C.1). The model should continue to use four random number generators. Except for what are now Cards 5 and 73 in Figure 3C.1, the alternative model should use no RMULT cards, but it should nonetheless be true that the two queue disciplines being studied are investigated under replicated sets of experimental conditions.

(c) Repeat (b). Use only one random number generator and no RMULT cards.

8. Figure E8 shows the sequence of different Queue references as they are encountered (via QUEUE cards) in a certain GPSS model. The references are shown in the order in which the cards appear in the model deck, from front to back.

```
QUEUE   GAMMA
QUEUE   1
QUEUE   4
QUEUE   BETA
QUEUE   3
QUEUE   6
```

FIGURE E8

To what numbers are the symbols GAMMA and BETA made equivalent?

9. Figure E9(a) shows the sequence of different Facility references in a model, in the order in which the Processor encounters them in the model deck. Figure E9(b) shows analogous information for Queues in the same model. As a Facility, what is the numeric equivalent of DELTA? As a Queue, what is the numeric equivalent of DELTA?

```
SEIZE   1            QUEUE   3
SEIZE   DELTA        QUEUE   2
SEIZE   2            QUEUE   DELTA
        (a)                  (b)
```

FIGURE E9

10. (a) Show an Equivalence definition card which makes the number 10 equivalent to the symbolic Storage name SLIPS.

(b) Describe a set of conditions under which the number 1 could be made equivalent to the Storage "TUGS," even though that was not the analyst's intention.

(c) Suggest a method for examining the output which the GPSS Processor automatically produces to find out whether redundancy has occurred in a model with respect to (i) Queues, (ii) Storages, (iii) Facilities.

11. See if you can develop or find an analytic solution for either queuing system considered in Case Study 4D. If you are successful, compare and contrast the analytic results with those produced in the case study.

12. Show how to modify the multiple-line model in Case Study 4D so that only one SELECT Block need be used. (Hint: in the case study, the customer first scans the tellers to find if one is immediately available; if not, the customer then scans the Queues to find the one with minimum content. If care is taken, the first of these SELECT Blocks can be eliminated.)

13. In Case Study 4D, suppose that service times are not exponentially distributed, but have been found to follow the distributions shown in Table E13. (Note: See Section 3.12 for an explanation of the interpretation to be given to Table E13.)

TABLE E13

Cumulative Frequency as a Function of Various Business Categories

Service Time (seconds)	1	2	3	4	5
25	0.0				
50	.10	0.0			
75	.68	.14	0.0		
100	1.0	.39	.18	0.0	
125		.72	.42	.21	
150		1.0	.58	.58	
175			.83	.79	
200			1.0	1.0	0.0
250					.09
300					.54
350					.81
400					1.0

(a) Show how to modify the models in Case Study 4D to take these service times into account. Experimental conditions should still be controlled in the same sense that they were in the case study.

(b) Assume now that the customer arrival rate increases from 200 to 240 per hour, but that a Poisson arrival process is still in effect. Simulate with the multiple-line model for the equivalent of an 8-hour day in trial-and-error fashion to determine the smallest number of tellers required if average teller utilization is to be 90 percent or greater. Before making any runs, develop an intelligent plan to follow in performing the trial-and-error investigation.

(c) Using the number of tellers determined from (b), run the Quickline version of the model. Compare and contrast system performance for the multiple-line and Quickline alternatives.

4.20 Residence Time and Transit Time as Transaction Properties

The length of time a Transaction has been in a model is its model residence time. The time that elapses while a Transaction moves between two arbitrarily designated points within a model is its transit time between the two points. There are two Standard Numerical Attributes in GPSS whose values are a Transaction's model residence time, and transit time, respectively. They will be discussed in this section.

4.20.1 Model Residence Time

Each time a Transaction enters a model, the Processor makes a record of its time of entry. The time of entry is referred to as "Mark Time." Two points should be noted carefully here.

1. A Transaction is understood to "enter" a model at the time it succeeds in *moving out of* its GENERATE Block. If a Transaction is delayed in a GENERATE Block, then, its time of model entry differs from its time of arrival at the GENERATE Block.

2. The Absolute Clock is used in determining the time of entry, not the Relative Clock. (If RESET cards are used in a model, the readings of the Absolute and the Relative Clocks may differ.)

The record of a Transaction's time of model entry is not directly available during a simulation, and therefore cannot be directly used as part of the logic in a model. In other words, there is no Standard Numerical Attribute whose value is a Transaction's Mark Time.

There is, however, a Standard Numerical Attribute which is closely related to a Transaction's time of model entry. The *name* of the Standard Numerical Attribute is M1. Its *value* is the difference between the current reading of the Absolute Clock, and the Transaction's time of model entry. Hence, M1 measures the number of time units a Transaction has been in the model. To put it differently, M1 is a Transaction's *residence time* in a model. Of course, for a given Transaction the value of M1 changes as a simulation proceeds. Just after it enters a model, a Transaction's M1 value is zero. Ten time units later, its M1 value is 10. After another 10 time units have elapsed, its M1 value is 20, and so on. For M1, the same question arises as that for Pj, and for PR. Namely, when the value of M1 is to be data, which Transaction is to be used in determining M1's value? The answer, of course, is that the M1 of the Transaction *currently being processed* is to be used.

Transaction Mark Time appears in the printout of the Current and Future Events Chain in a model. A portion of the Figure 4B.4 Future Events Chain printout is repeated in Figure 4.27. As pointed out in the figure, column 8, labeled "MARK TIME," contains the Mark Time information. The Mark Time value is not made meaningful until a Transaction succeeds in leaving its GENERATE Block. If a Transaction is delayed in its GENERATE Block, its Mark Time in the Current Events Chain is actually a negative number. This is also true of Transactions on the Future Events Chain which are "on their way" to a GENERATE Block. Inspection of Figure 4.27 shows that Transactions 15 and 3 both have negative entries in their MARK TIME column. Transaction 15 is a customer, on his way to the grocery store; Transaction 3 is the "timer," on his way to shut off the model. These values are negative for reasons which are internal to the GPSS Processor. (These Mark Time values happen to equal the negative Total Count at the GENERATE Block which is the "Next Block Attempted.")

4.20.2 Transit Time

M1 measures the time that has elapsed since a Transaction first entered a model. It is frequently of interest to know how much time elapses while a Transaction is in transit between two points *interior* to a model. Suppose the time used by a Transaction in moving between interior Points A and B is to be determined. A two-step process is involved. When the Transaction is at Point A, a record must be made of the Absolute Clock. Then, when the Transaction arrives at Point B, the difference between the value recorded at Point A, and the current value of the Absolute

Clock, must be computed. This difference is then the desired transit time. A method for accomplishing this two-step process in GPSS will now be described.

The first step involves using the GPSS MARK Block. When a Transaction enters the MARK Block, the Absolute Clock's value is copied into one of its Parameters. This is referred to as "marking the Transaction."

The MARK Block and its A Operand are shown in Figure 4.28. The A Operand specifies the number of the Parameter in which the Transaction is to be marked. The sole purpose of the MARK Block subroutine is to copy the Absolute Clock's value into the specified Parameter. By placing a MARK Block at "Point A" in the interior of a model, the first step in the two-step process consequently takes place.

When the Transaction later arrives at "Point B," the second step is to determine how much time has elapsed since the Transaction was marked. This elapsed time is the value of a Standard Numerical Attribute. The *name* of the Standard Numerical Attribute is MPj, where j is the number of the Parameter in which the Transaction was marked. To compute the *value* of MPj, the Processor subtracts the Transaction's jth Parameter value from the Absolute Clock's current reading. When the Transaction reaches "Point B," then, MPj's value *is* the transit time between Points A and B.

As pointed out earlier, there is no Standard Numerical Attribute whose value is the Absolute Clock. The MARK Block can be used, however, to sidestep any difficulties that might arise as a consequence of this. For example, assume a model requires that the value of the Absolute Clock be known when a Transaction arrives at a

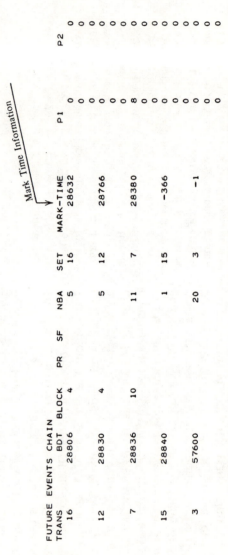

FUTURE EVENTS CHAIN

TRANS	BDT	BLOCK	PR	SF	NBA	SET	MARK-TIME	P1	P2
16	28806	4			5	16	28632	0	0
								0	0
12	28830	4			5	12	28766	0	0
								0	0
								0	0
7	28836	10			11	7	28380	8	0
								0	0
15	28840				1	15	-366	0	0
								0	0
3	57600				20	3	-1	0	0
								0	0

FIGURE 4.27   Repetition of a portion of the Figure 4B.4 Future Events Chain

Operand	Significance	Default Value or Result[a]
A	Number of the Parameter into which the Absolute Clock's value is to be copied	

[a] Defaulting *is* permitted. The result of defaulting is that the Absolute Clock's value *replaces* the Transaction's previously recorded time of model entry. This means that no Parameter is involved. Furthermore, it means that M1 no longer measures the time a Transaction has been resident in a model. Instead, it measures elapsed time since the Transaction moved into the MARK Block used in "no-A-Operand" mode. Nothing is really gained by defaulting on the A Operand. On the contrary, the record of a Transaction's time of model entry is lost. The "no-A-Operand" mode will not be further discussed or used in this book.

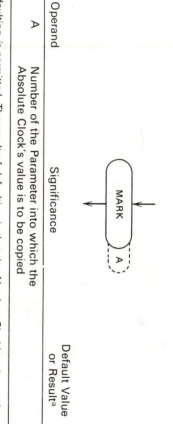

FIGURE 4.28   The MARK Block and its A Operand

certain point. If the Transaction moves into a MARK Block at that point, the value of the Parameter in which it is marked *is* the Absolute Clock's reading. If the Transaction is marked in Parameter 3, for instance, then the value of P3 is the Absolute Clock at the time of marking.

4.21 Exercises

1. (a) What is meant by a Transaction's time of entry to a model?
   (b) What is a Transaction's Mark Time?
   (c) Why is it important to distinguish between Absolute and Relative Clock time when discussing the concept of Mark Time?
   (d) When M1 is used to indirectly specify data, how does the GPSS Processor compute the value of the data?

2. (a) A Transaction enters a model at Absolute Clock time 21. At Absolute Clock time 52 it moves into the ASSIGN Block whose punchcard image is "ASSIGN 3,M1". What is the value of P3 after the ASSIGN Block subroutine has been executed?
   (b) Later, at Absolute Clock time 72, the Transaction moves into the Block "ASSIGN 5,FN$DAVID". Figure E2 shows the definition of the Function DAVID.

LOCATION	OPERATION	A,B,C,D,E,F
DAVID	FUNCTION	M1,D3
		25,5/50,10/75,15

FIGURE E2

What is the value of P5 after the ASSIGN Block subroutine has been executed?

3. (a) What task does the MARK Block subroutine accomplish? (Assume that the Block's A Operand is used.)
   (b) What does it mean when the A Operand is used?
   (c) How does the GPSS Processor compute the value of MP5?
   (d) What is the difference between M1 and MP1?
   (e) How can the value of MP7 be interpreted if P7 has a value of 0?

4. At Absolute Clock time 5, a Transaction moves into the Block "MARK 6".
   (a) After the MARK Block subroutine has been executed, what is the value of P6?
   (b) Later, at Absolute Clock time 25, the Transaction moves into the Block "ASSIGN 4,MP6". What is the value of P4 after the ASSIGN Block subroutine has been executed?
   (c) The Transaction then moves into the Block "ENTER JOE,P6". By what amount is R$JOE decreased as a result?

5. A Transaction is to capture the Facility whose number equals the current value of the Absolute Clock. Show a Block sequence which accomplishes this. (Note: although this problem may not make sense logically, it can be "solved.")

6. At a certain point in a model, Transactions must move through Queue 7. To support the model logic, the time spent by each Transaction in the Queue must be made the value of that Transaction's Parameter 5. Show a Block sequence which accomplishes this.

7. (a) Show a Block sequence through which a Transaction can move to have its Parameter-2

value set equal to 50 plus the Absolute Clock.

(b) Repeat (a), only base the problem on the Relative Clock.

4.22 Concept of the GPSS Table Entity

Suppose that a collection of numbers is produced by observing and recording the values taken on by some random variable. For example, each number in the collection might be the time required by a Transaction to move between Points *A* and *B* in a model. During a simulation, many Transactions move along the path from *A* to *B*. If the travel time of some or all of these Transactions is recorded, the result is a collection of values of the "travel-time random variable." The collection is termed a sample. The values in the sample are said to have been drawn from a random variable's population.

It is of interest to analyze the properties of the numbers in such a sample to estimate the properties of the population from whence they came. Population properties of interest include the mean, the standard deviation, and the relative frequency with which population values fall within prescribed ranges. These prescribed ranges are sometimes called *intervals*, or *frequency intervals*, or *frequency classes. Population* properties are often *estimated* by computing the corresponding properties for the *sample* drawn from the population. Given a sample, this requires performing tasks such as these.

1. Compute the sample mean.
2. Compute the sample standard deviation.
3. Count the number of sampled values which fall into each of a series of prescribed ranges.
4. Compute the percentage of values in the sample which fall into the various ranges in the series.

Such computations, although straightforward, are tedious and time consuming if done by hand. As a result, the computations have been automated in GPSS. To have them performed automatically, use must be made of the Table entity. The steps involved are described in the next section.

4.23 Defining and Using Tables: The TABLE Card and the TABULATE Block

Use of the Table entity involves two steps. First, each of the one or more Tables to be used in a model must be defined. Second, arrangements must be made to have sampled values entered,

one by one, in the various Tables of interest. The details involved are discussed below, and illustrated with an example.

4.23.1 The TABLE Card

There can be many different Tables in a model. Each Table must be defined before it can be used. A Table is defined by supplying these five pieces of information.

1. The name (numeric or symbolic) of the Table.
2. The name of the random variable whose values are to be tabulated.
3. A number known as the "first boundary point." Sampled values less than or equal to this number fall into the leftmost interval (frequency class) in the Table.
4. The width. common to all the Table intervals, excepting the leftmost (lowest) and the rightmost (highest).
5. The total number of intervals in the Table, including the lowest and the highest.

Items (3) through (5) call for some clarification. The values being tabulated can, in general, range from "minus infinity" to "plus infinity."[11] To use the Table entity, the span from minus infinity to plus infinity (i.e., the real number axis) must be divided into a series of *consecutive* intervals. The relative frequency with which tabulated values fall into each of these intervals can then be computed by the Processor. In defining a Table, items (3) through (5) indicate where the user wants the intervals to be located on the real number axis. Figure 4.29 provides a pictorial interpretation of this idea. Note that the leftmost interval consists of the values from minus infinity up to *and including* the "first boundary point." The second interval consists of values *greater than* the first boundary point, but less than *or equal to* the second boundary

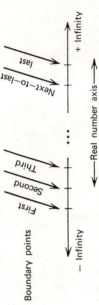

Boundary points

First   Second   Third   Next-to-last   last

... —Real number axis—

−Infinity   +Infinity

FIGURE 4.29   A pictorial interpretation of the real number axis, and its division into a series of consecutive intervals

[11] Fullword integer values in GPSS/360 range between −2,147,483,648 and +2,147,483,674, inclusive. In practical terms, then, these limiting values constitute "minus infinity" and "plus infinity," respectively.

point. All the intermediate intervals are of uniform width. Finally, the rightmost interval covers all values greater than the "last boundary point."

The five items of information are provided on a single punchcard, the Table card. Like most other cards, the Table card is divided into the Location, Operation, and Operands fields. The information entered in these fields is shown in Table 4.12.

An example of Table definition appears in Figure 4.30. In part (a) of the figure, the Table card is shown. In part (b), a pictorial interpretation of the intervals into which the real number axis is divided is given. The Table is named TYME2. The Standard Numerical Attribute being tabulated is MP3 (A Operand). The first boundary point is 10 (B Operand). The width of intermediate intervals in the Table is 5 (C Operand). This means that the second boundary point is 15 (that is, 10 + 5), the third boundary point is 20 (that is, 15 + 5), ..., and the last boundary point is 30. The real number axis is divided into a total of six consecutive intervals (D Operand). This means that, in addition to the leftmost and rightmost intervals, there are four intermediate intervals.

The values of the B, C, and D Operands on the Table card must be specified as integer constants. The B Operand can be negative; the C and D Operands, of course, must be nonnegative. Neither the boundary points nor the number of intervals can be changed as a simulation proceeds. Note that, due to the restriction that the B and C Operands must be integers, each of the boundary points in a Table is integer-valued. For that matter, all sampled values entered into a Table are also integers.

4.23.2 The TABULATE Block

Sampled values are entered into a Table one by one, as a simulation proceeds. A value is entered into a Table each time a Transaction moves into a TABULATE Block. This Block, and its A Operand, are shown in Figure 4.31. The A Operand names the Table into which a value is to be placed. A given Table can be referenced from many different TABULATE Blocks in a model, when it is logical to do so. Note that the Standard Numerical Attribute being tabulated is not specified at the TABULATE Block. It is provided only on the Table card.

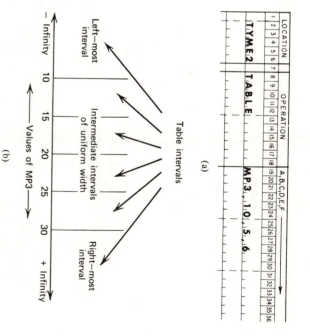

FIGURE 4.30 Definition and interpretation of a particular GPSS Table. (a) Definition of the Table. (b) Pictorial interpretation of the Table intervals.

TABLE 4.12 Specifications for the Card Used to Define a GPSS Table

Punchcard Field		Information Supplied in Field
Location		The name (numeric or symbolic) of the Table
Operation		Literally, the word TABLE
Operands	A	The name of the random variable whose values are to be entered in the Table. In particular, the A Operand will be the name of some Standard Numerical Attribute
	B	The first boundary point
	C	The width of each intermediate Table interval
	D	The total number of intervals in the Table, including the leftmost and rightmost

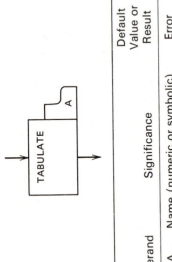

Operand	Significance	Default Value or Result
A	Name (numeric or symbolic) of the Table into which a value is to be entered	Error

FIGURE 4.31   The TABULATE Block and its A Operand

Now consider how the distribution of Transaction transit time between Points A and B in a model can be estimated. At Point A, the Transactions move through a MARK Block, where Parameter 3 (for example) is marked with a copy of the Absolute Clock's value. At Point B, the Transactions move through a TABULATE Block, where the Table TYME2 (defined in Figure 4.30) is referenced via the A Operand. By definition, the values entered in the Table TYME2 are MP3. But MP3 is the transit time of Transactions between the MARK Block, and the TABULATE Block. Each time a Transaction enters the TABULATE Block, then, another sampled value of the transit time is added to the collection of such values which are being gathered in the Table.

4.23.3 An Example of Table Use

Relative to Case Study 4B (A Grocery Store Model), suppose it is of interest to tabulate the distribution of shopper residence time in the store. Only a modest extension of the Figure 4B.2 model is required to do this. Figure 4.32 shows the Extended Program Listing for the modified model. Card 22 defines a Table, named RTIME, and having M1 as its A Operand. Card 44 is the punchcard image for a TABULATE Block which has been placed between the Blocks "LEAVE CARTS" and "TERMINATE". Just before each shopper-Transaction leaves the store, then, it passes through the TABULATE Block, and its model residence time is entered in the Table RTIME.

Figure 4.33 shows the output produced at the end of the simulation run with the Figure 4.32 model. In total, 363 shoppers had completed

their shopping at the end of the simulation ("ENTRIES IN TABLE"). The average shopper residence time was 318 seconds ("MEAN ARGUMENT" is 317.8). The standard deviation in this sample of size 363 is 121 seconds ("STANDARD DEVIATION" is 120.562). The sum of all the values entered in the Table is 115,373 ("SUM OF ARGUMENTS" is 115373.000).

Note that the label "NON-WEIGHTED" appears at the right of the SUM OF ARGUMENTS value. This label simply indicates that each sampled value placed in the Table has been used exactly one time in the computations which produced each of the various numbers displayed in the Table. In contrast to "nonweighted" Tables, it is also possible to have so-called "weighted" Tables in GPSS. This possibility will not be discussed now; it is given detailed consideration in Chapter 5.

Nine customers spent 100 seconds or less in the store ("OBSERVED FREQUENCY" is 9 for the Table interval with an UPPER LIMIT of 100). These 9 customers constituted 2.47 percent of the points in the sample ("PERCENT OF TOTAL"). The CUMULATIVE PERCENTAGE of data points falling in the interval between "minus infinity" and an UPPER LIMIT of 100 is 2.4 percent. The CUMULATIVE REMAINDER of points yet to be accounted for (because they fall into intervals further to the right in the Table) is 97.5 percent.

The entries in the rightmost two columns in Figure 4.33 provide information about the UPPER LIMIT of the corresponding frequency class, not about the entries in the frequency class. For example, the UPPER LIMIT of the leftmost frequency class is 100; this value equals 0.314 times the average Table entry ("MULTIPLE OF MEAN" is 0.314). The difference between this UPPER LIMIT of 100, and the average Table entry, is -1.806 Table standard deviations ("DEVIATION FROM MEAN" is -1.806). The same remarks hold for the other intervals.

The Table card in the Figure 4.32 model (Card 22) specifies that there are 9 Table intervals. In Figure 4.33, however, information appears for only 6 intervals. The last of these 6 intervals, which covers a range of values from 500+ to 600, contains 20 entries (OBSERVED FREQUENCY). Because none of the sampled values were larger than 600, the additional 3 Table intervals covering a range from 600+ to "infinity" were all empty. The GPSS Processor

BLOCK NUMBER	*LOC	OPERATION	A,B,C,D,E,F,G	COMMENTS	CARD NUMBER
		SIMULATE			1
	*				2
	*	FUNCTION DEFINITION(S)			3
	*				4
	AYL1	FUNCTION	RN1,C2	ITEMS-SELECTED DISTRIBUTION, AISLE 1	5
		0,.2/1,.5			6
	AYL2	FUNCTION	RN1,C2	ITEMS-SELECTED DISTRIBUTION, AISLE 2	7
		0,.3/1,.6			8
	AYL3	FUNCTION	RN1,C2	ITEMS-SELECTED DISTRIBUTION, AISLE 3	9
		0,.4/1,.7			10
	COTYM	FUNCTION	P1,C2	CHECKOUT-TIME DISTRIBUTION	11
		1,3/18,54			12
	IMPUL	FUNCTION	RN1,C2	DISTRIBUTION OF ITEMS TAKEN ON IMPULSE	13
		0,1/1,4			14
	XPDIS	FUNCTION	RN1,C24	EXPONENTIAL DISTRIBUTION FUNCTION	15
		0,0/.1,.104/.2,.222/.3,.355/.4,.509/.5,.69/.6,.915/.7,1.2/.75,1.38			16
		.8,1.6/.84,1.83/.88,2.12/.9,2.3/.92,2.52/.94,2.81/.95,2.99/.96,3.2			17
		.97,3.5/.98,3.9/.99,4.6/.995,5.3/.998,6.2/.999,7./.9998,8			18
	*				19
	*	TABLE DEFINITION(S)			20
	*				21
	RTIME	TABLE	M1,100,100,9	TABLE FOR DIST'N OF TIME SPENT IN STORE	22
	*				23
	*	MODEL SEGMENT 1			24
	*				25
1		GENERATE	75,FN$XPDIS	SHOPPERS ARRIVE	26
2		ENTER	CARTS	TAKE A CART	27
3		TRANSFER	.25,,TRY2	WANT TO SHOP AISLE 1?	28
4		ADVANCE	120,60	TIME IN AISLE 1	29
5		ASSIGN	1,FN$AYL1	SET P1 = ITEMS SELECTED IN AISLE 1	30
6	TRY2	TRANSFER	.45,,TRY3	WANT TO SHOP AISLE 2?	31
7		ADVANCE	150,30	TIME IN AISLE 2	32
8		ASSIGN	1+,FN$AYL2	SET P1 = TOTAL ITEMS SELECTED SO FAR	33
9	TRY3	TRANSFER	.18,,OUT	WANT TO SHOP AISLE 3?	34
10		ADVANCE	120,45	TIME IN AISLE 3	35
11		ASSIGN	1+,FN$AYL3	SET P1 = TOTAL ITEMS SELECTED SO FAR	36
12	OUT	QUEUE	GIRL	QUEUE FOR CHECKOUT COUNTER	37
13		ASSIGN	1+,FN$IMPUL	ADD TO P1 ITEMS TAKEN ON IMPULSE	38
14		SEIZE	GIRL	CAPTURE THE CHECKER	39
15		DEPART	GIRL	LEAVE THE CHECKOUT QUEUE	40
16		ADVANCE	FN$COTYM	CHECK-OUT TIME	41
17		RELEASE	GIRL	FREE THE CHECKER	42
18		LEAVE	CARTS	RETURN THE CART	43
19		TABULATE	RTIME	PLACE RESIDENCE TIME SAMPLE IN TABLE	44
20		TERMINATE		LEAVE THE STORE	45
	*				46
	*	MODEL SEGMENT 2			47
	*				48
21		GENERATE	28800	TIMER ARRIVES AT END OF 8-HOUR DAY	49
22		TERMINATE	1	SHUT OFF THE RUN	50
	*				51
	*	CONTROL CARDS			52
	*				53
		START	1	START THE RUN	54
		END		RETURN CONTROL TO OPERATING SYSTEM	55

FIGURE 4.32 Extended Program Listing for the Figure 4B.2 model, as modified to include tabulating the distribution of Transaction residence time in the model

TABLE RTIME

ENTRIES IN TABLE	MEAN ARGUMENT	STANDARD DEVIATION	SUM OF ARGUMENTS
363	317.831	120.562	115373.000

UPPER LIMIT	OBSERVED FREQUENCY	PER CENT OF TOTAL	CUMULATIVE PERCENTAGE	CUMULATIVE REMAINDER	MULTIPLE OF MEAN	DEVIATION FROM MEAN NON-WEIGHTED
100	9	2.47	2.4	97.5	.314	-1.806
200	59	16.25	18.7	81.2	.629	-.977
300	93	25.61	44.3	55.6	.943	-.147
400	93	25.61	69.9	30.0	1.258	.681
500	89	24.51	94.4	5.5	1.573	1.510
600	20	5.50	100.0	.0	1.887	2.340

REMAINING FREQUENCIES ARE ALL ZERO

FIGURE 4.33 Table output produced when the Figure 4.32 model was run

TABLE RTIME
ENTRIES IN TABLE 363

	MEAN ARGUMENT 317.831	STANDARD DEVIATION 120.562	SUM OF ARGUMENTS 115373.000			NON-WEIGHTED
UPPER LIMIT	OBSERVED FREQUENCY	PER CENT OF TOTAL	CUMULATIVE PERCENTAGE	CUMULATIVE REMAINDER	MULTIPLE OF MEAN	DEVIATION FROM MEAN
100	9	2.47	2.4	97.5	.314	-1.806
200	59	16.25	18.7	81.2	.629	-.977
300	93	25.61	44.3	55.6	.943	-.147
400	93	25.61	69.9	30.0	1.258	.681
500	89	24.51	94.4	5.5	1.573	1.510
OVERFLOW	20	5.50	100.0	.0		

AVERAGE VALUE OF OVERFLOW   525.84

FIGURE 4.34   An example of a GPSS Table in which "overflow" occurs

consequently suppressed printing out information for these intervals, terminating the Table with the message REMAINING FREQUENCIES ARE ALL ZERO.

When one or more sampled values do fall into the rightmost Table interval, the Processor prints the word OVERFLOW in the UPPER LIMIT column, then fills out the rest of that row with the usual information about entries in that interval. As an example of this, Figure 4.34 shows the output produced when the Figure 4.32 model was run with the D Operand on the Table card changed from 9 to 6. Although the OVERFLOW line indicates how many values fell into the rightmost interval, the analyst has no idea how large these values might have been, because the interval covers the range up to "infinity". As a result, the AVERAGE VALUE OF OVERFLOW is printed out by the Processor at the bottom of the Table. In Figure 4.34, for example, the average of the 20 values falling into the rightmost interval is 525.84.

As the estimate of a probability distribution, the information in a Table is sometimes better revealed graphically, in the form of a histogram, than it is in tabular form. Figure 4.35 shows a hand produced histogram corresponding to the Figure 4.33 Table. The horizontal line forming the "top" of each rectangular section in the histogram spans the same range of values as does the corresponding Table interval. The "height" of each rectangle is proportional to the percentage of sampled values which fall into the interval in question. For example, the leftmost rectangle in Figure 4.35 is 2.47 units high (corresponding to a relative frequency of 2.47 percent), and spans the horizontal range from 0 to 100. (The base starts at 0 in this case, not "minus infinity," because residence time cannot take on negative values.)

It is possible to have the GPSS Processor produce histograms for Tables in a model. To do so requires use of the GPSS Output Editor.

Figure 4.36 shows the histogram produced by the GPSS Processor for the Figure 4.33 Table when the Output Editor is used with the Figure 4.32 model, and appropriate specifications are provided. Actually, the Output Editor can be used to, perform a variety of services, including (1) providing analyst-supplied explanatory text and labels as part of the Processor's output, (2) selecting and printing only that statistical information which is of interest, and (3) outputting information about user-selected Standard Numerical Attributes in a graphical format, including a series of possibilities for the Table entity. Although it can be useful on occasion, the Output Editor involves a series of mechanical details and does not, in itself, contribute to or enhance the conceptual aspects of building GPSS models. For this reason, specifics of its use will not be taken up in this book. The interested reader is referred to the user's manual for the GPSS implementation he is using.

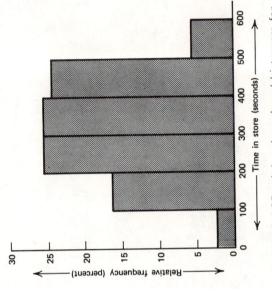

FIGURE 4.35   A hand-produced histogram for the Figure 4.33 table

HISTOGRAM FOR DISTRIBUTION OF SHOPPER RESIDENCE TIME IN A GROCERY STORE

Y AXIS: OBSERVED RELATIVE FREQUENCY, PERCENT

X AXIS: TIME IN STORE, SECONDS

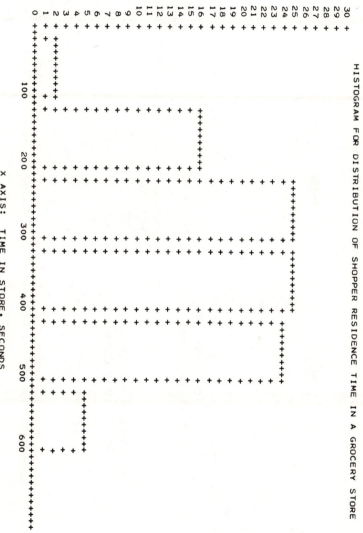

FIGURE 4.36 A histogram produced for the Figure 4.33 table with use of the GPSS Output Editor

4.24 Table Standard Numerical Attributes

Several properties of Tables are available as Standard Numerical Attributes. This means that selected Table information can be used as part of the logic of a model. The Standard Numerical Attributes, and the significance of their values, are shown in Table 4.13. The values of the Table Standard Numerical Attributes are time-dependent. TC_j, of course, is a direct count of the number of values which have been placed in the Table. As TC_j increases, the values of TB_j and TD_j generally tend to vary less than they did initially. In fact, it could be of interest to use the value of TB_j, say, to control the time span covered by a simulation. A stopping condition such as this might be imposed: "When TC_j exceeds 1,000, and a 10 percent increase in TC_j produces less than a 5 percent change in TB_j, turn off the simulation."[12]

To implement such logic in a model, it would be necessary to *test* the value of TB_j dynamically, as the simulation proceeds. The ability to construct and use such tests in GPSS models is discussed in Chapter 5.

In Section 4.2, it was emphasized that the numeric form of certain entity properties depends on whether the values appear in model output, or are used as data within the model.

TABLE 4.13 Standard Numerical Attributes for GPSS Tables

Name[a]	Value
TB_j, or TB$sn	The average value of the Table entries
TC_j, or TC$sn	The number of sampled values entered in the Table
TD_j, or TD$sn	The standard deviation of the Table entries

[a]As already indicated in the footnote to Table 4.1, "j" is the number of the particular Table in question; or, if it has been named symbolically, "sn" is its symbolic name.

[12]There would be obvious dangers in this approach. The analyst would probably also design the model to turn off if the simulated clock reached some specified large value before this other condition was yet satisfied.

This remark holds for the Table Standard Numerical Attributes as well. In the output for the Table RTIME in Figure 4.33, for example, Table mean and standard deviation appear as 317.831 and 120.562, respectively. The values of TB$RTIME and TD$RTIME, however, are 317 and 120. That is, when these two Table SNA's are used internally to indirectly specify data, only the integer portion of the true values is in effect. No such distinctions in numeric form need be made with respect to TCj (or TC$sn), because this attribute is inherently integer-valued.

4.25 Exercises

1. (a) How is the number of intermediate intervals in a Table related to the D Operand on the Table card?

(b) Show a pictorial interpretation of the Table intervals when the Table card is "JOE TABLE P3,−50,25,8".

(c) What range of values is spanned by the left-most interval in the Table JOE, as defined in (b)? What range of values is spanned by the third interval?

(d) Into which interval of the Table JOE, as defined in (b), does the value 25 fall?

(e) What is the *smallest* value that could ever be entered in the Table SOFAR, for which the Table card is "SOFAR TABLE M1,−100,50, 15"?

2. In a certain model, *two* different Tables are defined with Q$LONG used as the A Operand in the Table cards. The Table cards are shown in Figure E2.

LOCATION	OPERATION	A,B,C,D,E,F
TAB1	TABLE	Q$LONG,0,5,6
TAB2	TABLE	Q$LONG,0,1,10

FIGURE E2

One TABULATE Block is used to reference TAB1; another is used to reference TAB2. The two TABULATE Blocks are placed one after the other. Give a possible reason why the model might have been built this way. (Hint: the reason does not involve the choice of Q$LONG as the Table card A Operand.)

3. Customers may have to wait for a constrained resource at Point A in a model. Later, they may have to wait for another constrained resource at Point B. A random variable of interest in the model is "*total*" time customers spend waiting for con-strained resources." For example, if a particular customer waits 5 minutes at Point A, and another 3 minutes at Point B, then his total time spent waiting is 8 minutes. Describe how the distribution of the "total waiting time" random variable can be estimated in the model.

4. Modify the widget-manufacturing model in Case Study 2D so that it will provide estimates of the distributions of these three random variables.

1. Total *working* time per widget assembly (consists of two components: assembly time; and firing time).

2. Total clock time elapsed per widget assembly (consists of three components: assembly time; spent waiting for the oven; and firing time).

3. Assembly time.

Run the model for the case of four, five, and six assemblers, simulating for five working days for each configuration. Then do the following.

(a) The average value of the random variable in item 1, and its smallest and largest values, can easily be determined from data used in the model. Compare these known population values with the distribution *estimate* produced by the model.

(b) Using the mean value estimated by the model for the random variable in item 2, compute the number of widgets that should have been completed during each simulation. Are your computed values in agreement with the number of completed widgets as determined through Block Counts?

(c) How closely does the *estimate* of the assembly-time distribution in item 3 compare with its *known* distribution from configuration to configuration (uniform over the integers from 25 through 35, inclusive)?

5. Service time at a point in a system is exponentially distributed with a mean value of 100 time units. Devise a GPSS model to draw 1,000 samples from the service-time distribution and enter the resulting values in a Table. Print the Table after the number of entries in it is 100, 200, 300, ..., 1,000. Compare the Table mean and standard deviation, printout-by-printout, with the population mean and standard deviation, each of which is known to be 100. Which of these two statistics appears to approach its expected value the most rapidly as sample size increases? Design the Table intervals so that the relative frequency with which values fall into the range between 0+ and 20, 80+ and 100, and 140+ and 160, will be tabulated. Compare the observed relative frequencies, printout-by-printout, with the relative frequencies expected in the long run. (The long-run relative frequencies can be determined by inspecting Figure 3.22.) For which of these intervals does the estimate of relative frequency seem to converge to the known theoretical value the most rapidly? Can you explain why?

6. In a certain application, an analyst must estimate the relative frequency with which a random variable takes on values in the range between 0+ and 20, and 20+ and 40. At the same time, he must estimate the relative frequency with which the same random variable takes on values in the range between 19+ and 21, 21+ and 23, and 23+ and 25. Assuming that randomly sampled values of the random variable are contained in Parameter 2 of Transactions moving past Point A in a model, suggest a plan whereby he can obtain the necessary estimates.

7. An airline has 15 flights leaving a given base per day, each with one stewardess. The airline has a policy of keeping three reserve stewardesses on call to replace stewardesses scheduled for flights who become sick. The probability distribution for the daily number of sick stewardesses is given in Table E7. Build a GPSS model to simulate this situation for the purpose of estimating the utilization of reserve stewardesses, and the distribution of the random variable "number of flights canceled each day because no stewardess is available." Simulate for 1,000 days of operation, printing out the estimates every 100 days. By hand, compute the theoretical values of the statistics under investigation. Compare the behavior of the estimates, as a function of sample size, with their known long-run values.[13]

TABLE E7

Number Sick	Probability
0	0.20
1	0.25
2	0.20
3	0.15
4	0.10
5	0.10

8. The interarrival time of ships at a harbor which operates around the clock, 7 days a week, follows the distribution shown in Table E8. Thirty percent of the ships are of a newer type which uses high-speed unloading equipment. These ships move to Unloading Complex 1 (see Figure E8), which consists of two berths, each able to unload a ship in 1 ± 0.1 days. The older type ships move to Unloading Complex 2, which consists of six berths, each able to unload a ship in 1.5 ± 0.2 days. In order to dock, a ship must make use of a tug. There is only one tug at the harbor. Docking time is 30 ± 10 minutes. Similarly, in order to clear its berth after it has been unloaded, a ship must make use of a tug. A berth can be cleared in 15 ± 5 minutes. It is of interest to model the system to estimate the distribution of each of these two random variables: (1) total time each newer-type ship spends waiting at the harbor (note that the components of total waiting time are time spent waiting for a berth, and time spent waiting for a tug on each of two separate occasions); (2) total time each older-type ship spends waiting at the harbor.

TABLE E8

Interarrival Time (minutes)	Cumulative Frequency
Less than 125	0.0
175	0.10
225	0.22
275	0.40
325	0.55
375	0.78
425	0.90
475	1.0

(a) Using constants and/or symbolic names as the A Operands at ENTER and LEAVE Blocks, show how to build a model of the system. In this approach, you will have distinct ENTER and LEAVE Blocks for each of Unloading Complexes 1 and 2.

(b) Indirectly specifying the values of A Operands at ENTER and LEAVE Blocks, show how to build a model of the system. In this approach, a single ENTER Block and a single LEAVE Block will be used to simultaneously represent the two unloading complexes. Compare the total number of Blocks required in this approach with the number required by the approach taken in (a).

(c) By hand, compute the long run utilization of the berths in Unloading Complex 1, the berths in Unloading Complex 2, and of the tug.

(d) Use your results from (c) to estimate what reasonable steady state conditions are likely to be at the harbor. Then construct one or two self-contained model segments whose sole purpose is to bring about these steady state conditions at the start of a simulation, i.e., at simulated time 1. Design this segment, or these segments, to go along with your model from (b).

(e) Supplementing your model from (b) with your segment(s) from (d), perform experiments to determine how long a simulation must run in order to reliably estimate the average values

[13]This problem is taken, with permission, from Chapter 3 in Operations Research, Methods and Problems, by Maurice Sasieni, Arthur Yaspan, and Lawrence Friedman [Copyright © 1959 by John Wiley & Sons, Inc.; by permission of John Wiley & Sons, Inc.]

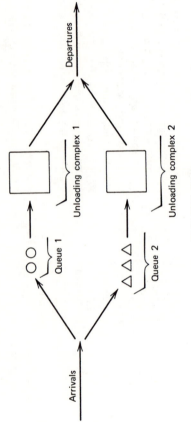

FIGURE E8

of the two "total waiting time" random variables of interest in the system.

(f) It may be of interest to reconfigure the harbor, in the sense of adding one or more additional berths in one or both of the unloading complexes, and/or adding one or more additional tugs. If alternative harbor configurations are to be compared via simulation experiments, then the comparisons will be enhanced if the model is designed so that each ship's time of arrival, unloading time, and tug-time requirements are configuration-independent.

   (i) Show how to change your model from (a) so that these various ship characteristics will be configuration-independent.

   (ii) Show how to change your model from (b) so that these various ship characteristics will be configuration-independent.

(g) Now perform experiments to provide answers to the following economic questions.

   (i) If the cost of a waiting ship is $500 per hour, at what estimated berth cost per day could addition of another berth in Unloading Complex 1 be justified?

   (ii) Repeat (i), but with respect to addition of another berth in Unloading Complex 2. To what extent do you think the answers to (i) and (ii) are independent of each other?

   (iii) If the cost of providing a tug is $250 per day, would it be more economical to have two tugs at the harbor, or just one?

9. Exercise 6, Section 3.17, requires building a model or models to compare the *average* waiting time (including service) for each of three types of jobs at a work center when the queue discipline is (1) first-come, first-served, and (2) first-come, first-served within priority class. Build and run another model or models for the work center to estimate the *distribution* of waiting time for each job type, depending on the queue discipline used. What influence does queue discipline have on such properties of the waiting time random variable as standard deviation, and the relative frequency with

which it takes on values falling within prescribed intervals? For jobs of "type 1," prepare a histogram for the waiting-time distribution when queue discipline is first-come, first-served. Then, using a different pen color, superimpose on this plot the histogram for the "job type 1" waiting-time distribution when priority distinctions are made. Discuss as many aspects of the differences in the two distributions as you can.

4.26 Additional Table Modes

There are three special modes in which Tables can be used. These modes are known as IA-mode, RT-mode, and QTABLE-mode, respectively. The modes will be discussed in this section.

4.26.1 IA-Mode Tables

Whenever a GENERATE Block is used, the distribution of interarrival times at that point in the system is required as data. Such a distribution describes one of the ways the system being modeled interfaces with its external environment. Information about these interarrival times must either be postulated, or gathered via direct measurement.

There are other interarrival time distributions which may also be important to the analyst. These distributions apply to Transactions as they arrive at points *interior* to a system. The GPSS Table entity can be conveniently used to provide estimates of such distributions as part of a simulation.

The logic of gathering data on Transaction interarrival times at a point interior to a model is straightforward. A record must be made of the Absolute Clock's value when the first Transaction arrives at the point. Later, when the second Transaction arrives, the time recorded earlier must be subtracted from the current reading of the Absolute Clock. This difference is an interarrival time. It can be entered in a GPSS Table. Then, when the next arrival occurs at the point, its interarrival time relative to its predecessor can be computed and tabled. In this fashion, the distribution of interarrival times at the point can be estimated.

Interarrival times are automatically computed and entered in GPSS Tables when they are used in a special mode, known as IA (for interarrival time) mode. If interarrival times at a point are to be the values entered in a Table, two steps must be taken.

1. The A Operand on the Table definition card must be IA. (The B, C, and D Operands have their usual significance.)

2. A TABULATE Block referencing the Table (i.e., with the Table's name as its A Operand) must be placed at the point of interest in a model.

Nothing further is required to use a Table in IA-mode.

4.26.2 RT-Mode Tables

Closely related to interarrival time is arrival rate. The analyst may want to estimate the distribution of the *rate* at which Transactions arrive at a point. There is a special Table mode with which this can be done; the mode is RT (for *rate*) mode. If arrival rates are to be tabulated, three steps must be taken.

1. RT must be entered as the A Operand on the Table definition card. (The B, C, and D Operands carry the usual information.)

2. An E Operand must be provided on the Table definition card. The E Operand is the time span relative to which the rate will be measured.

3. A TABULATE Block referencing the Table must be placed at the point of interest in the model.

Note that a rate is specified relative to some time interval. Such phrases as "cars per hour," "people every 15 minutes," and "orders every 5 days" are used to describe rates. It is necessary that the GPSS Processor know how large this time interval is to be when rate information is gathered. The user supplies this information with the E Operand on the Table definition card. The implicit time unit used in the model is understood to apply to the E Operand's value as well. If the implicit time unit is, say, 1 second, and the Table BRIAN is defined with the card "BRIAN TABLE RT,0.5,10,30", then the rate information is expressed "per 30 seconds."

The logic of gathering rate data is worth some mention. Each Table used in RT mode has a special counter associated with it. At the start of a simulation, this counter is given a value of zero. Whenever the Table is referenced at a TABULATE Block, the counter is incremented by 1. When a time interval equal to the E-Operand's value has elapsed for the first time, the value of the counter is entered in the Table, and the counter is set back to zero. The process of incrementing the counter then continues while the specified time interval is again being spanned. When the interval has been spanned the next time, the counter's value is again placed in the Table, the counter is restored to zero, and so on.

The method used by the Processor to know when it is time to enter the counter's value into an RT-mode Table should be pointed out. When the Processor encounters an RT-mode Table card during the model Input Phase, it fetches a Transaction from the top of the stack in the latent pool and places it on the top of the Future Events Chain, with its Move Time equal to the E Operand value on the Table card. When that time is reached, the Transaction is then transferred to the Current Events Chain, as would be expected. Note that this Transaction is a "dummy"; it is not scheduled to enter the model through a GENERATE Block. When the CEC scan encounters the Transaction, the corresponding counter value is placed in the Table, and the counter is restored to zero. The Table card's E Operand value is then added to a copy of the Absolute Clock, and the "dummy" Transaction is put back on the Future Events Chain, scheduled to return to the CEC at *that* next time. And so on.

The consequence of this use of a "dummy" Transaction should be kept in mind. For each RT-mode Table in a model, such a Transaction will appear on either the Future or the Current Events Chain if a chain printout is produced. The analyst should not think something is wrong when he finds such Transactions on chain listings.

4.26.3 QTABLE-Mode Tables

In Queue statistics printed out at the end of a simulation, the *average* residence time in Queues is provided.[14] Other properties concerning the distribution of Queue residence time are not automatically measured and printed out. These

[14]Actually, two measures of Queue residence time are provided in these statistics. The first, labeled AVERAGE TIME/TRANS, is based on all Queue entries. The second, labeled $AVERAGE TIME/TRANS, is based on all *non-zero* Queue entries. The discussion in this section refers exclusively to the first residence-time measure.

other properties may, however, actually be more important measures of system performance than average residence time. For example, "the percentage of the Queue entries having to wait longer than 10 minutes in the Queue" might be critical in, say, a banking application.

By using the Table entity, the analyst can easily provide logic with which to estimate the distribution of Queue residence time. The two-step sequence involved would be (1) mark Transactions in Parameter j when they enter the Queue, then (2) when they depart the Queue, move the Transactions through a TABULATE Block referencing a Table whose A Operand is MPj. Precisely the same effect can be achieved by using the Table entity in a special mode, known as QTABLE-mode. The advantages of using QTABLE-mode, instead of providing explicit logic to accomplish the same thing, are (1) there is no need to have a MARK Block at the point at which the Queue is entered, (2) there is no need to have a TABULATE Block at the point at which the Queue is departed, and (3) the execution time required is not as great.

To estimate Queue residence time distribution, all the analyst need do is provide a corresponding Table definition card in the model. Such a card differs from other Table cards in two respects.

1. The word entered in the Operation field is QTABLE, not TABLE.
2. The A Operand on the card is the *name of the Queue* for which the residence time distribution is to be gathered.

The B, C, and D Operands on the card play their accustomed role; and, as before, the Location field contains the name of the Table itself.

In Case Study 4D, the average waiting time of customers in a bank was estimated. Except for indicating the relative frequency with which the waiting time was zero, no other information was gathered in that case study about the distribution of the "waiting time random variable." Simply by adding a QTABLE card to the model, the entire distribution can now be estimated. Figure 4.37 repeats the Figure 4D.3(a) model. Extended Program Listing for the one-line queuing system,

```
BLOCK
NUMBER   *LOC     OPERATION   A,B,C,D,E,F,G          COMMENTS                              CARD
                                                                                           NUMBER
                  SIMULATE                                                                   1
          *                                                                                  2
          *       FUNCTION DEFINITION(S)                                                     3
          *                                                                                  4
          5       FUNCTION    RN1,C24         EXPONENTIAL DISTRIBUTION FUNCTION              5
          0.0/.1,.104/.2,.222/.3,.355/.4,.509/.5,.69/.6,.915/.7,1.2/.75,1.38                 6
          .8,1.6/.84,1.83/.88,2.12/.9,2.3/.92,2.52/.94,2.81/.95,2.99/.96,3.2                  7
          .97,3.5/.98,3.9/.99,4.6/.995,5.3/.998,6.2/.999,7/.9998,8                            8
          MEAN FUNCTION   RN1,D5          DISTRIBUTION OF MEAN SERVICE TIME                   9
          .1,450/.29,750/.61,1000/.85,1500/1,3000                                           10
          *                                                                                 11
          *       STORAGE CAPACITY DEFINITION(S)                                            12
          *                                                                                 13
                  STORAGE     S$TELRS,8       PROVIDE 8 TELLERS                             14
          *                                                                                 15
          *       TABLE DEFINITION(S)                                                       16
          *                                                                                 17
          INQUE   QTABLE      ONE,0,600,20    RESIDENCE TIME IN THE LINE                    18
          *                                                                                 19
          *       MODEL SEGMENT 1                                                           20
          *                                                                                 21
          1       GENERATE    180,FN5,,,,1    CUSTOMERS ARRIVE                              22
          2       ASSIGN      1,FN$MEAN,5     SET P1 = SERVICE TIME                         23
          3       QUEUE       ONE             ENTER THE LINE                                24
          4       ENTER       TELRS           ENGAGE A TELLER                               25
          5       DEPART      ONE             LEAVE THE LINE                                26
          6       ADVANCE     P1              TRANSACT BUSINESS                             27
          7       LEAVE       TELRS           FREE THE TELLER                               28
          8       TERMINATE                   LEAVE THE BANK                                29
          *                                                                                 30
          *       MODEL SEGMENT 2                                                           31
          *                                                                                 32
          9       GENERATE    180000          TIMER ARRIVES AFTER 5 HOURS                   33
          10      TERMINATE   1               SHUT OFF THE RUN                              34
          *                                                                                 35
          *       CONTROL CARDS                                                             36
          *                                                                                 37
                  START       1               START THE RUN FOR DAY 1                       38
                  END                         RETURN CONTROL TO OPERATING SYSTEM            39
```

FIGURE 4.37   Extended Program Listing for the Figure 4D.3(a) model, as modified to include tabulating the distribution of Transaction residence time in the Queue

except that now a QTABLE card has been included (Card 18), and only one day ("day 1" in Case Study 4D) will be simulated. Figure 4.38(a) shows the Queue statistics produced when the Figure 4.37 model was run.; Figure 4.38(b) shows the output for the Table, which has been symbolically named INQUE.

Following the procedure described in Section 4.18, the Processor has assigned 1 as the numeric equivalent of INQUE. In Figure 4.38(a), then, in the column labeled TABLE NUMBER, the entry "1" appears. This is an indication that Qtable Statistics are being maintained in Table 1 for the Queue symbolically named ONE. (Up until now, the TABLE NUMBER column in Queue statistics has always been blank.)

Table 4.14 shows a comparison of information taken from the Queue statistics in Figure 4.38(a), and the Qtable statistics in Figure 4.38(b). Corresponding values from the two "different" sources of information are identical. At first, this seems only natural. Normally,

though, when Queue statistics and Qtable statistics are compared, small but noticeable differences can be detected. The reason for this is that a Transaction's in-Queue residence time is not recorded in a Qtable until the Transaction moves through the DEPART Block referencing the Queue. In contrast with this, when Queue statistics are printed at the end of a run, any Transactions *still in the Queue* at that time are treated, statistically, as though their time were up in the Queue. They consequently bias the Queue statistics toward the low side; that is, their residence time in the Queue appears lower than it actually would be, if the simulation were to continue to run.

Why, then, is there an exact match in the Table 4.14 information? The reason is that when the simulation shut off, there were *no* Transactions in the Queue. [Note that the CURRENT CONTENTS column in Figure 4.38(a) is "blank."] In the more usual case, the ENTRIES IN TABLE statistic for a Qtable would be *smaller* than the

FIGURE 4.38 Selected output produced when the Figure 4.37 model was run. (a) Queue statistics. (b) Qtable statistics

QUEUE	MAXIMUM CONTENTS	AVERAGE CONTENTS	TOTAL ENTRIES	ZERO ENTRIES	PERCENT ZEROS	AVERAGE TIME/TRANS	$AVERAGE TIME/TRANS	TABLE NUMBER	CURRENT CONTENTS
ONE	51	14.138	1001	121	12.0	2542.459	2892.047	1	

$AVERAGE TIME/TRANS = AVERAGE TIME/TRANS EXCLUDING ZERO ENTRIES

(a)

TABLE ONE INQUE

ENTRIES IN TABLE	MEAN ARGUMENT	STANDARD DEVIATION	SUM OF ARGUMENTS
1001	2542.459	2158.000	2545002.000

UPPER LIMIT	OBSERVED FREQUENCY	PER CENT OF TOTAL	CUMULATIVE PERCENTAGE	CUMULATIVE REMAINDER	MULTIPLE OF MEAN	DEVIATION FROM MEAN NON-WEIGHTED
0	121	12.08	12.0	87.9	-.000	-1.178
600	125	12.48	24.5	75.4	.235	-.900
1200	97	9.69	34.2	65.7	.471	-.622
1800	112	11.18	45.4	54.5	.707	-.344
2400	99	9.89	55.3	44.6	.943	-.066
3000	86	8.59	63.9	36.0	1.179	.212
3600	50	4.99	68.9	31.0	1.415	.490
4200	71	7.09	76.0	23.9	1.651	.768
4800	62	6.19	82.2	17.7	1.887	1.046
5400	46	4.59	86.8	13.1	2.123	1.324
6000	40	3.99	90.8	9.1	2.359	1.602
6600	36	3.59	94.4	5.5	2.595	1.880
7200	30	2.99	97.4	2.5	2.831	2.158
7800	18	1.79	99.2	.7	3.067	2.436
8400	8	.79	100.0	.0	3.303	2.714

REMAINING FREQUENCIES ARE ALL ZERO

(b)

TABLE 4.14 A Comparison of Selected Queue and Qtable Statistics Appearing in Figure 4.38

	Average Time in Queue, Seconds	Standard Deviation	Percent Zero Entries
From Figure 4.38(a)	2542.459	Not Provided	12.0
From Figure 4.38(b)	2542.459	2158.000	12.08[a]

[a]The percent zero entries information is available in the Qtable as the PERCENT OF TOTAL in the Table interval with an UPPER LIMIT of 0.

TOTAL ENTRIES statistic for the corresponding Queue. This, in turn, would mean that the Queue statistics would be biased somewhat toward the low side in terms of residence-time considerations.

Although IA, RT, and QTABLE Tables are special in mode, they are Tables in every sense. In particular:

1. They appear as part of standard model output.
2. They can be outputted dynamically by use of the PRINT Block.
3. The three Table Standard Numerical Attributes apply to them.

No "special mode" Table *names* can be identical to those chosen for "normal mode" Tables in a given model. If Table 7, say, is an IA-mode Table in a model, then 7 cannot be chosen as the name of any other Table in the same model.

4.27 Exercises

1. (a) Referring to Figure 4.38(b), what percentage of the "day 1" customers had to wait more than 4 minutes in the one-line bank model?

(b) Show how to modify the multiple-line bank model in Figure 4D.3(b) to estimate the aggregate customer waiting time distribution.

(c) Rerun the Case Study 4D simulations for the one-line and multiple-line queing systems to estimate the waiting-time distributions. Use the output to compute (by hand) the mean and standard deviation of the random variable,

"percentage of customers who had to wait longer than 4 minutes." Which queuing system appears to be superior with respect to this statistic?

2. Show what changes to make in the indicated models to estimate the distributions of the indicated random variables.

(a) Case Study 2A, distribution of time between consecutive service completions.

(b) Case Study 2A, distribution of rate of service completions.

(c) Case Study 2B, time-in-service for shave-and-haircut customers.

(d) Case Study 2C, interarrival time of mechanics at the tool crib (without making distinctions as to the type of mechanic).

(e) Case Study 2E, rate of arrival of failed sewing machines at the repair facility.

(f) Case Study 2E, interarrival time of failed sewing machines at the repair facility.

(g) Case Study 2F, interarrival time of television sets at the last inspection station.

3. Develop a GPSS model which uses the Table entity to determine the distribution of the first 1,000 values produced by RN1, for 5 different initial settings of the random number generator. (The RN1 values tabulated should be three-digit integers.) The Table should consist of the intervals from 0 to 49, 50 to 99, 100 to 149, . . . , and 950 to 999. Run the model, then for each of the 5 Tables produced compare (a) the Table average, (b) the Table standard deviation, and (c) the observed frequencies for each Table interval with the corresponding theoretical expectations.

5

Intermediate
GPSS
Modeling
Concepts,
Part II

5.1 Introduction

In the GPSS modeling introduced so far, the analyst has not had to indicate *how* computations are to be performed. It has been assumed that the Processor knows how to maintain and update such things as Facility utilization, Table standard deviation, average Queue residence time, and so on. Such computations are straightforward, and it is highly appropriate that the GPSS Processor does them for the analyst, automatically. On the other hand, many computations are highly context-dependent, i.e., are peculiar to the system being modeled and the corresponding logic being implemented. The Processor cannot be designed to anticipate all of these customized situations and handle them automatically. As a result, provisions are made for the analyst to construct arithmetic expressions of his own choosing, then use them in the logic of his model. These user-defined Arithmetic Variables will be discussed in this chapter.

Furthermore, all models have been constructed thus far without the benefit of user-supplied *tests* being part of the models. Granted, a wealth of testing is required to support the logic of the models presented in the earlier chapters. But, from a Block-oriented viewpoint, this testing has taken place exclusively at SEIZE and ENTER Blocks, at the SELECT Block, and at TRANSFER Blocks in statistical mode and BOTH mode. The type of testing that takes place at these Blocks is

predefined and is relatively inflexible. Such Blocks cannot support a full range of customized decision-making. Suppose, for example, that a Transaction is to move forward in a model only if the sum of two numbers is less than or equal to the value of some other number. The ability to include such conditions in GPSS models by use of the TEST Block will be described in this chapter.

Not all tests the analyst might like to build into a model involve *numeric relationships*. It is often convenient to make model behavior depend on the *logical status* of certain entities within the GPSS language. It might be that a Transaction is not to move forward at one point in a model until some Facility elsewhere in the model has been captured. Use of the GATE Block to di-

257

rectly and efficiently model conditions such as this, which involve the logical status of selected GPSS entities, will be included in this chapter.

In none of the models presented so far has it been necessary for Transactions to be able to "talk to each other." In fact, the provision for direct communication of information between Transactions is not highly developed in the language. It is possible, though, for Transactions to communicate with each other indirectly, through a series of memory locations known as "Savevalues." These Savevalues, which are available in both a one-dimensional and a two-dimensional sense, also have a variety of other useful applications. Some of these applications will be considered through the Chapter 5 case studies.

Among the items to be taken up here, then, are Arithmetic Variables, the TEST Block, the GATE Block, and Savevalues. In addition, the GPSS Logic Switch entity will also be introduced, and possibilities for its use will be illustrated through a pair of case studies.

5.2 Arithmetic Variables

In GPSS, an Arithmetic Variable is a user-defined Standard Numerical Attribute. An Arithmetic Variable is referenced as Vj, or Vsn, where "j" is the number of the Variable if it has been named numerically, and "sn" is its symbolic name if it has been named symbolically. The *value* of an Arithmetic Variable is the value of the user-supplied arithmetic expression which defines that Variable. An arithmetic expression, in turn, is a collection of data specifications connected by arithmetic operators. In succeeding parts of this section, the discussion will focus on the arithmetic operators available in GPSS; the specification of data in arithmetic expressions; the Variable definition card; examples of Variables and the rules followed in evaluating them; and, finally, a special case of Variable definition available at the user's option.

5.2.1 The Arithmetic Operators

The arithmetic operators available in GPSS are shown in Table 5.1. The first three operators in the list are well known. The last two, integer division and modulus division, may require some elaboration.

In integer division, only the integer portion of the quotient is retained as the result of the operation. The fractional part of the quotient, if any, is discarded. For example, 17/4 equals 4. The whole quotient resulting when 17 is divided by 4 is 4.25.

TABLE 5.1   The Arithmetic Operators Available in GPSS

Symbol	Operation
+	Addition
−	Subtraction
*	Multiplication
/	Integer division
@	Modulus division

The fractional part of this whole quotient, 0.25, is discarded; the integer portion, 4, is retained as the result of the operation. Similarly, 25/3 equals 8; −21/6 equals −3; and 10/5 equals 2. As suggested by the second-to-last example, the algebraic sign carried by the result is determined by the usual laws of signs. The last example shows a case in which the result is exact, because the quotient has no fractional part.

If the value of a *divisor* in a GPSS integer-division operation turns out to be zero, the Processor sets the value of the *quotient* to zero. This proves convenient from time to time, when a divisor's value is indirectly specified, and when that value can meaningfully take on a zero value in the context of the model.

The fifth and last operator in Table 5.1, @, denotes *modulus division*. In modulus division, the *integer portion of the quotient is discarded* and the *remainder is retained* as the result of the division. For example, 13 divided by 3 is 4, with a remainder of 1. In modulus division, the 4 is discarded and the 1 is retained as the result of the division. This is usually expressed more compactly by saying that "13 modulus 3 is 1", or by writing "13 @ 3 = 1". The examples of modulus division in Figure 5.1 should be reviewed to be certain that the modulus division concept is clearly understood.

	Spoken Form	Written Form
(a)	53 modulus 26 is 1	53 @ 26 = 1
(b)	17 modulus 6 is 5	17 @ 6 = 5
(c)	3 modulus 5 is 3	3 @ 5 = 3
(d)	8 modulus 10 is 8	8 @ 10 = 8
(e)	7 modulus 7 is 0	7 @ 7 = 0
(f)	54 modulus 9 is 0	54 @ 9 = 0

FIGURE 5.1   Examples of modulus division

5:2.2 Data Specification in Arithmetic Expressions

In the expressions used to define Arithmetic Variables, data can be specified either directly, or indirectly. Data specified directly takes the form of integer constants. Data specified indirectly takes the form of Standard Numerical Attributes. All Standard Numerical Attributes which have been described can be validly used in the construction of arithmetic expressions. In fact, because they are also SNA's, the expression defining an Arithmetic Variable can include references to one or more *other* Arithmetic Variables in the model.

Consider what happens when a Function is used to indirectly provide data in an arithmetic expression. As pointed out earlier, only the integer portion of a Function's true value is used as data in most contexts. This is also true when Functions are used in constructing arithmetic expressions.

This means that *all the data involved* in an arithmetic expression are integers. When constants are used to directly specify data in such expressions, they must be integers. All the SNA's that might be used to indirectly specify data in arithmetic expressions are also integer-valued. When the operators "+, −, and *" are used to combine integer data, the results are other integers. As explained above, when the operators "/" and "@" operate on pairs of integers, integer results are also produced. In short, at each step of the way in evaluating an arithmetic expression, only integers are involved. Arithmetic Variables, then, are themselves inherently integer-valued.

5.2.3 The Variable Definition Card

An Arithmetic Variable is defined by use of a Variable definition card, sometimes simply called a Variable card. Like most other cards, the Variable card is divided into the Location, Operation, and Operands fields. The information entered in these fields is shown in Table 5.2. The name of the Variable appears in the Location field, and the word VARIABLE is entered in the Operation field. The arithmetic expression is placed in the Operands field. It must begin in card column 19 and continue in consecutive card columns, without

any intervening blanks. The first blank column encountered in the Operands field terminates the expression. The expression cannot extend beyond card column 71. Furthermore, if an expression is too long for a single card, it *cannot* be continued on a next card. In such cases, the expression must be broken up into a series of shorter expressions and defined through two or more Arithmetic Variables.

Finally, the "minus sign" can only be used in a GPSS arithmetic expression as a binary operator, and not as a unary operator. In practical terms, this means that error conditions result for a Variable definition cards which (1) contain a minus sign in card column 19, and/or (2) contain a minus sign immediately to the right of a left parenthesis.

5.2.4 Examples and Rules

Four examples of Arithmetic Variables are shown in Figure 5.2. The Variable JOE has as its value the remaining capacity of Storage 5, plus the current content of Storage 5. Of course, "remaining capacity" plus "current content" of a Storage equals its user-defined capacity. There is no Processor-supplied Standard Numerical Attribute whose value is the user-defined capacity of a Storage. As a result, this example shows how the user can construct an Arithmetic Variable having Storage capacity as its value.

The Variable PETE in Figure 5.2 is the Total Block Count at the Block in Location PATH1, modulus 10. Note that the range of values

---

TABLE 5.2 Format for the Card Used to Define an Arithmetic Variable

Punchcard Field	Information Supplied in the Field
Location	The name (numeric or symbolic) of the Arithmetic Variable
Operation	Literally, the word VARIABLE
Operands	The arithmetic expression which defines the Arithmetic Variable

---

LOCATION	OPERATION	A,B,C,D,E,F	
JOE	VARIABLE	R5+S5	FIRST EXAMPLE
PETE	VARIABLE	N$PATH1@10	SECOND EXAMPLE
MARK	VARIABLE	Q$LONG-Q5	THIRD EXAMPLE
TIM	VARIABLE	(P2-P4)/2	FOURTH EXAMPLE

FIGURE 5.2 A first set of examples of arithmetic Variables

VsPETE can assume consists of the ten integers 0, 1, 2, 3, ..., 8, and 9. This restriction on the range of values is a natural consequence of modulus division.

The Variable MARK is defined as the current content of the Queue LONG, minus the current value of Parameter 2, minus the value of Parameter 4, divided by 2. Two points are raised by the Variable TIM.

1. When Parameters indirectly specify data for Arithmetic Variables, it is the *active* Transaction whose Parameters are used. An Arithmetic Variable is only evaluated at the time a Transaction moves into a Block whose Operand values depend in some way on the Variable. It is *that* Transaction whose Parameters are used.

2. Parentheses can be used in the expressions defining Arithmetic Variables. When parentheses are used, everything within them is evaluated first, then the result is used in the rest of the expression. This is the so-called "rule of parentheses."

Now consider the set of examples of Arithmetic Variables in Figure 5.3. All three examples raise a question with respect to the *time-sequence* in which the various arithmetic operators have their effect. For example, if P5 is 5 and Q2 is 15, then VsANN might be 4 (add P5 to Q2 first, then divide by 5); or, VsANN might be 8 (divide Q2 by 5 first; then add the result to P5). The question, then, is whether one adds first, then divides; or divides first, and then adds. The "rule of precedence" resolves this question. A precedence order is imposed on the operators, with the understanding that their effect takes place in that order. Table 5.3 shows the precedence ordering for the five operators available. The rule of precedence is that, when unaltered by parentheses, the order of arithmetic operations performed within an expression is in descending order of precedence. Hence, from Table 5.3, multiplication, division, and modulus division each precede addition and subtraction in the absence of parentheses. This means that the Variable ANN in Figure 5.3 is evaluated by dividing Q2 by 5 first, then adding the result to P5.

Similarly, the Variable KATHY is evaluated by modulus-dividing RN2 by 10 first, then adding 1 to the result. Recall that, except when used as a Function argument, RNj returns a random number from the uniform distribution of integers between 000 and 999, inclusive. In the Variable KATHY, RN2@10 is consequently a random number from the uniform distribution of integers between 0 and 9, inclusive. Adding 1 to this intermediate result, VsKATHY is a random variable taking on values uniformly distributed over the closed interval of integers between 1 and 10.

In the last Figure 5.3 example, the value of VsALICE is formed by taking 5 times the PR value of the active Transaction, then subtracting from this product the remaining capacity of the Storage named TUG.

Note that the rule of precedence is conditioned on arithmetic expressions *being unaltered by parentheses*. When parentheses are used, everything within them is evaluated first, then this intermediate result is used in the rest of the expression. Of course, when evaluating expressions *within* parentheses, the rule of precedence applies. The fourth example in Figure 5.2 has already provided an example of how parentheses can be used to force subtraction to occur before division takes place.

A third set of examples of Arithmetic Variables is given in Figure 5.4. In Table 5.3, note that "*", "/", and "@" share a common precedence level. So do "+" and "−". In both of the Figure 5.4 examples, two or more operators sharing a common precedence level appear. The question then arises, in case of precedence-ties, which operations are performed first? The "tie-breaking rule" is used to answer this question. The rule states that, within precedence level, operations are performed on a left-to-right basis. The value of VsFRITZ is determined this way.

TABLE 5.3 Precedence Levels for the Arithmetic Operators in GPSS

Operator	Precedence Level
*, /, and @	Highest
+ and −	Lowest

LOCATION	OPERATION	A,B,C,D,E,F
ANN	VARIABLE	P5+Q2/5 FIRST EXAMPLE
KATHY	VARIABLE	1+RN2@10 SECOND EXAMPLE
ALICE	VARIABLE	5*P.R-R$TUG THIRD EXAMPLE

FIGURE 5.3 A second set of examples of arithmetic Variables

3. Real (i.e., floating-point) arithmetic is used in the step-by-step evaluation of the Variable-defining expression. This simply means that any fractional values which arise during intermediate parts of the computation are retained and carried throughout the entire computation. Only after the expression's final value has been determined is the fractional part eliminated, with the integer portion being retained as the value of the Real Variable.

The modulus division operator, "@," cannot be used in defining Real Variables. Furthermore, constants used in the defining expressions are still restricted to being integers. No decimal points can be used in the defining expressions. Also, the only Standard Numerical Attributes whose true values are used in evaluating Real Variables are Functions; for example, only the integer portion of Table means (TBj, or $TB\$sn$) and Table standard deviations (TDj, or $TD\$sn$) are carried in the computations leading to the value of a Real Variable. Finally, it should be noted, per (3) above, that Real Variables are *integer-valued*.

Despite the restrictions just stated, Real Variables have useful applications in GPSS modeling. Figure 5.5 shows two such applications. In the first example, the value of V$AVG is formed by summing the current contents of Queues 1, 2, and 3, then dividing by 3, then adding 1/2 to this intermediate result. As a consequence, the value of the Real Variable AVG is the integer portion of the *rounded* average current content of Queues 1 through 3. The rounding occurs because 0.5 (i.e., 1/2) is added to the true average content before the fractional portion is discarded to produce the final result. For example, suppose that Q1, Q2, and Q3 are 5, 7, and 2, respectively. Then their sum is 14. This sum, divided by 3, is 4.66666+. After 1/2 is added to this intermediate result, the true value of the expression is

---

1. Multiply 4 by PR.
2. Divide P10 by SC$FIXIT, retaining the integer portion of the quotient as the result.
3. From the Step (1) result, subtract the Step (2) result.
4. To the Step (3) result, add 2.
5. The Step (4) result is the value of V$FRITZ.

Similarly, the value of V$USCHI is found this way.

1. Divide C1 by 100, retaining the integer portion of the quotient as the result.
2. Multiply the Step (1) result by 100.
3. The Step (2) result is the value of V$USCHI.

Note that the value of V$USCHI equals C1 only if C1 is an integral multiple of 100. For example, if C1 is 400, then 400/100*100 equals 400. In like fashion, if C1 is 2700, then 2700/100*100 equals 2700. On the other hand, if C1 is 425, then 425/100*100 equals 400, *not* 425. In particular, 425/100 equals 4, not 4.25.

5.2.5 Real Variables vs. Integer Variables

The Variables discussed so far in this section are sometimes termed *Integer Variables*, because their values are computed by performing integer arithmetic on integer values. It is also possible to define *Real Variables* (i.e., floating-point Variables) in GPSS. *Definitionally*, Real Variables differ from Integer Variables only in that the word FVARIABLE, rather than VARIABLE, is entered in the Operation field on the Variable definition card. *Computationally*, the GPSS Processor determines the value of a Real Variable this way.

1. The entire value of any Functions used to indirectly specify data is used in the computation. The fractional portion, if any, is not discarded.
2. Use of the division operator, "/," does not result in the fractional portion of the quotient, if any, being discarded.

LOCATION (1–6)	OPERATION (7–18)	A,B,C,D,E,F (19–60)	
FRITZ	VARIABLE	4*PR-P10./SC$FIXIT+2	FIRST EXAMPLE
USCHI	VARIABLE	C1/100*100	SECOND EXAMPLE

FIGURE 5.4 A third set of examples of arithmetic Variables

LOCATION (1–6)	OPERATION (7–18)	A,B,C,D,E,F (19–60)	
AVG	FVARIABLE	(Q1+Q2+Q3)/3+1/2	FIRST EXAMPLE
DRAW	FVARIABLE	50*FN$XPDIS	SECOND EXAMPLE

FIGURE 5.5 Two examples of Real Variables

5.16666+. The integer portion, 5, is then the value of V$AVG. If AVG were defined as an Integer Variable, its value in this example would be 4. First of all, the sum 14, divided by 3, would be 4. Secondly, the value of 1/2 would be 0. The final result, then, would be 4 + 0, or 4. In fact, in Integer Variables, the term +1/2 and/or −1/2 in the defining expression can never contribute anything to the final value of the Variable.

Now consider the second Figure 5.5 example. Assume that FN$XPDIS is the usual 24-point continuous Function with which to sample from the exponential distribution with expected value 1. When a random sample from this distribution is multiplied by 50, the result is a random sample from the exponential population with mean 50. This Variable suggests an alternative, then, for simulating a Poisson arrival process at a GENERATE Block, or an exponential server at an ADVANCE Block. For the Variable DRAW defined in Figure 5.5, the Blocks "GENERATE 50, FN$XPDIS" and "ADVANCE V$DRAW" are fully equivalent. Similarly, the Blocks "ADVANCE 50,FN$XPDIS" and "ADVANCE V$DRAW" are equivalent.

It is instructive to consider what would happen if the Variable DRAW in Figure 5.5 were defined as an Integer Variable. Only the integer portion of FN$XPDIS would be multiplied by 50. Examination of the standard 24-point Function XPDIS reveals that about 65 percent of the time, its integer portion is 0. This means that V$DRAW would have a value of 0 about 65 percent of the time. These values could hardly be viewed as representative samples from an exponential population with mean 50.

As suggested by the examples, Real Variables and Integer Variables are referenced the same way, i.e., both types are referred to as Vj, or V$n. For this reason, they cannot have identical names in a given model. If an Integer Variable is named ZELDA, there cannot be a Real Variable in the same model which is also named ZELDA, and so on.

In the next section, the GPSS method for sampling from the normal distribution is discussed. A highly useful application of Real Variables is involved in such sampling.

5.3 Sampling from the Normal Distribution

In Section 3.13, the important *Poisson* and *exponential* random variables were introduced, their relationship to each other was indicated, and a method for simulating Poisson arrivals and exponential servers in GPSS models was developed. A similar development will now be carried out for another highly important, well-known random variable, the *normal* variable.

A normal random variable is completely described by specifying two of its properties: its *mean*, and its *standard deviation*. (In contrast, the Poisson and exponential random variables are completely described by specifying only a single property, the mean.) By definition, the *standard* normal random variable has a mean of 0, and a standard deviation of 1. A nonstandard, or *general* normal random variable is one whose mean does not equal 0, and/or whose standard deviation does not equal 1. The normal random variables of interest usually are nonstandard.

To sample from a nonstandard normal population, it is convenient first to sample from a standard normal population, then do arithmetic on the resulting value, thereby converting it to the nonstandard equivalent. The relationship between the standard sample and the nonstandard equivalent is shown in equation (5.1)

$$GNORM_{sample} = (GNORM_{stdev})(SNORM_{sample}) + GNORM_{avg} \quad (5.1)$$

where $SNORM_{sample}$ is the value drawn from the standard normal population, and $GNORM_{avg}$ and $GNORM_{stdev}$ are the average (i.e., mean) and standard deviation of the general normal random variable of interest. If a method can be found for randomly determining a value of $SNORM_{sample}$, it is a simple matter to define the right-hand side of equation (5.1) as a GPSS Arithmetic Variable. Such a Variable can then be evaluated each time another sample is required from the corresponding normal population.

As shown in any postcalculus statistics textbook, a random sample can be drawn from the standard normal population by solving equation (5.2)

$$RNj = \int_{-\infty}^{SNORM_{sample}} \frac{e^{-x^2/2}}{\sqrt{2\pi}}\, dx \quad (5.2)$$

for $SNORM_{sample}$, which appears in the equation as the upper limit of an integral. Note that RNj, on the left-hand side of equation (5.2), is a sample drawn at random from any one of the eight 0–1 uniform random-number populations in GPSS.

Equation (5.2) cannot be manipulated analytically to solve for SNORM$_{sample}$ explicitly in terms of RNj. As a result, the values of SNORM$_{sample}$ determined from equation (5.2) for various values of RNj have been tabulated.[1] Figure 5.6 displays the resulting relationship

shows the definition of the continuous GPSS Function composed of the 25 pairs of points used for the approximation.[2] The Function has been symbolically named SNORM. RN1 has been arbitrarily chosen as the Function's argument. Note that, whereas the values of SNORM$_{sample}$ satisfying equation (5.2) can range from minus infinity (for RNj values arbitrarily close to 0) to plus infinity (for RNj values arbitrarily close to 1), the values taken on by FN$SNORM defined in Figure 5.7 can only vary from −5 to +5. In view of the other inaccuracies in simulation modeling, the small discrepancies which arise in using the Figure 5.7 Function to approximate the equation (5.2) relationship are acceptable in most cases.

Suppose now that the interarrival time of orders at a warehouse is normally distributed, with a mean value of 12 hours, and a standard deviation of 2 hours. If a Transaction represents an order, and the implicit time unit in a model is 1 hour, Figure 5.8(a) shows a GENERATE Block which simulates the order-arrival process. Figure 5.8(b) shows the Variable GNORM which is used as the A Operand at the GENERATE Block. It is assumed that Figure 5.7 defines the Function SNORM. Consistent with equation (5.1), the value of the Variable GNORM is determined by drawing a sample from the standard normal population defined by the Function SNORM, multiplying this value by 2 (standard deviation of the nonstandard population), and adding 12 (mean of the nonstandard population) to the product. Each time a Transaction moves out of the Figure 5.8(a) GENERATE Block, the Processor randomly determines the value of its successor's inter-

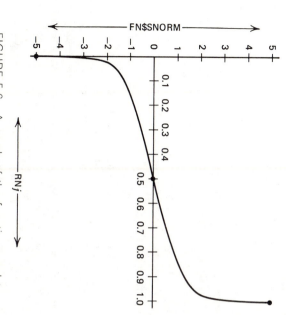

FIGURE 5.6 A graph of the function used to sample from the standard normal distribution

between RNj and SNORM$_{sample}$ in graphical form. The Figure 5.6 curve can be approximated with a continuous GPSS Function constructed by fitting a series of straight-line segments to it. An approximation suitable for this purpose has been developed by IBM. The approximation consists of a series of 24 line segments. Figure 5.7

LOCATION	OPERATION	A,B,C,D,E,F
SNORM	FUNCTION	RN1,C25

```
0,-5/.00003,-4/.00135,-3/.00621,-2.5/.02275,-2
.06681,-1.5/.11507,-1.2/.15866,-1/.21186,-.8/.27425,-.6
.34458,-.4/.42074,-.2/.5,0/.57926,.2/.65542,.4
.72575,.6/.78814,.8/.84134,1/.88493,1.2/.93319,1.5
.97725,2/.99379,2.5/.99865,3/.99997,4/1,5
```

FIGURE 5.7 A continuous 25-point GPSS Function used to sample from the standard normal distribution

[1] There are several ways to develop such a tabulation. For example, a value can be assumed for RNj. Then, by using a numerical integration technique and following a trial-and-error method, the value of SNORM$_{sample}$ for which the right-hand side of equation (5.2) equals the assumed value of RNj can be determined.

[2] The values in Figure 5.7 appear in the out-of-print IBM publication *General Purpose Systems Simulator II*, Form Number H20-6346.

(a)

LOCATION	OPERATION	A,B,C,D,E,F
GNORM	FVARIABLE	2*FN$SNORM+12

(b)

FIGURE 5.8   An example showing how to simulate normally distributed interarrival times in GPSS. (a) A GENERATE Block at which normally distributed interarrival times are simulated. (b) Definition of the Real Variable used at the GENERATE Block.

arrival time, then, in a manner faithful to the approximation of equations (5.1) and (5.2).

As another example, assume that the service time at a certain point in a model is normally distributed, and that the mean and standard deviation in effect depend on the type of service being provided. Table 5.4 shows the applicable means

TABLE 5.4   The Properties of Normally Distributed Holding Times in a Specific Example

Type of Service	Properties of Normally Distributed Service Times (minutes)	
	Mean	Standard Deviation
1	30	5
2	20	3
3	36	6

and standard deviations for the three different types of service that can be demanded. Suppose that a Transaction has its service-type recorded in Parameter 4. Figure 5.9(a) shows an AD-VANCE Block at which the service time is simulated. Figure 5.9(b) shows definitions of the Functions and the Arithmetic Variable which support the operation of the Figure 5.9(a) Block. The relationship in equation (5.2) is expressed through the Variable symbolically named SERVE in Figure 5.9(b). That Variable, in turn, calls on the Functions MEAN and STDEV to supply the

correct mean and standard deviation each time a Transaction moves into the ADVANCE Block. The Functions use the P4 value of the active Transaction as their argument.

In conclusion, three features of sampling from normal populations in GPSS should be noted.

1. The mean and standard deviation characterizing the normal population of interest are specified either directly or indirectly in a Variable definition. More than one such Variable may have to be defined, depending on the number of normal populations from which samples must be drawn in a model, and the context in which the corresponding samples are used.

2. The word FVARIABLE must be used in the Operation field of the Variable definition card when defining a Variable with which to sample from a normal distribution. Use of the word VARIABLE would mean that only the integer portion of the values drawn from the standard normal population would be carried in the subsequent computation. This, in turn, would result in unrealistic distortions in the computed non-standard values.

3. The Function SNORM defined in Figure 5.7 can return values as small as −5. If the mean of a given normal distribution is less than five standard deviations above zero, equation (5.1) shows that samples drawn from the population can consequently *be negative*. This is consistent with the fact that normally distributed values can range from minus infinity to plus infinity. In practice, however, it may be that the quantities which are postulated as being normally distributed

(a)

LOCATION	OPERATION	A,B,C,D,E,F
MEAN	FUNCTION	P4,D3
1,30/2,20/3,36		
STDEV	FUNCTION	P4,D3
1,5/2,3/3,6		
SERVE	FVARIABLE	FN$STDEV*FN$SNORM+FN$MEAN

(b)

FIGURE 5.9   An example showing how to simulate normally distributed holding times in GPSS. (a) An ADVANCE Block at which normally distributed holding times are simulated. (b) Definition of the Real Variable used at the ADVANCE Block, and of the Functions used in the Real Variable.

have meaning only when they are nonnegative. For example, negative interarrival times and negative service times are meaningless. In such contexts, then, the analyst must insure that the mean is at least five standard deviations above zero. If this condition is not satisfied, the analyst must reconsider the assumption that the random variable of interest follows a normal distribution truncated at plus and minus five standard deviations from the mean.

5.4 Exercises

1. Assuming the current value of W$RUTE6 is 7, what will be the values of the Variables named VAR1, VAR2, VAR3, and VAR4 as defined in Table E1?

TABLE E1

Location	Operation	Operands
VAR1	VARIABLE	W$RUTE6/5
VAR2	VARIABLE	W$RUTE6@5
VAR3	VARIABLE	25/W$RUTE6
VAR4	VARIABLE	W$RUTE6/25

2. How do GPSS Integer and Real Variables differ from each other? In what ways are they similar to each other?

3. Show the definition of Variables which will take on these values.
(a) The sum of the capacities of the Storages TUGS and SLIPS.
(b) The *rounded* average value of the current content of the Queues 5, 7, and LONG.
(c) A sample drawn at random from the exponential population with a mean value of 75.
(d) A sample drawn at random from the normal population with a mean of 10, and a standard deviation of 2.
(e) An integer drawn at random from the population of integers uniformly distributed between 0 and 15, inclusive.
(f) An integer drawn at random from the population of integers uniformly distributed between 1 and 15, inclusive.
(g) An integer drawn at random from the population of integers uniformly distributed between 7 and 18, inclusive.
(h) An integer drawn at random from the population of integers uniformly distributed between 1 and P2, inclusive. (Which Transaction will supply the value of P2?)

4. Define a Variable which returns a value as a function of PR according to the pattern shown in Table E4.

TABLE E4

PR	Value of Variable
1	1
2 or more	PR-1

(Which Transaction will supply the value of PR?)

5. Depending on whether its Parameter 7 value is 1, 2, 3, or 4, the holding time of a Transaction at an ADVANCE Block is to be determined by sampling from normal distributions with means and standard deviations of (20,3), (35,4), (30,4), and (25,2), respectively. Show an ADVANCE Block at which the holding time can be simulated. Also show the definitions of Variables and/or Functions needed to support operation of the ADVANCE Block.

6. (a) An analyst defines the Real Variable ALPHA with the expression (P2+P5)*0.4*R$TUG. This expression will result in an error message. Why?
(b) Show an acceptable alternative expression which produces the effect the analyst desired in (a).
(c) In an ADVANCE Block which uses a spread modifier, show how to make the spread 75 percent of the mean holding time. Assume that the mean is available as the value of Parameter 1 of Transactions which enter the ADVANCE Block.

7. The Real Variable BETA is defined with the expression 2*FN$SNORM+9, where the Function SNORM is defined in Figure 5.7. Why will an error eventually result if the Block "ADVANCE V$BETA" is included in a model? Refer to Appendix C and determine exactly which error message will result.

8. (a) The jth Transaction arriving at Point A in a model is to have j assigned as the value of its fifth Parameter, for $j = 1, 2, 3, \ldots$. Show how to accomplish this. (Caution: the Total Block Count Standard Numerical Attribute is updated *only as the last step* in execution of a Block subroutine. For example, the first Transaction to enter the Block "HERE ASSIGN 3,N$HERE" has *zero* assigned as the value of Parameter 3 because, at the time of its evaluation, a value of zero is still recorded for N$HERE. The second Transaction to enter the same Block has *one* assigned as the value of Parameter 3, and the third Transaction to enter the Block has *two* assigned as the value of Parameter 3, and so on.)
(b) The jth, $j + 10$th, $j + 20$th, etc. Transaction arriving at Point A in a model is to have j

assigned as the value of its fifth Parameter, for j = 1, 2, 3, ..., 8, 9, and 10. Show how to accomplish this.

9. Show how a single GENERATE Block can be used to bring Transactions into a model according to the specifications in exercise 5a, Section 2.35. (Hint: the sequence of interarrival times is 1, 3, 6, 4, 11, 3, 6, 4, 11, 3, 6, 4, 11, ... Construct a Function which returns the values 3, 6, 4, 11 cyclically.)

10. Explain what happens when Transactions enter the various SELECT Blocks whose card images are shown below.
(a) SELECT G 10,1,5,25,V
(b) SELECT MAX P3,P1,P2,,V
(c) SELECT NE 6,10,12,0,V,NOGO

11. In most contexts in GPSS, when data is indirectly specified via a Function, only the integer portion of the Function's value is used as the data. There are four exceptions to this. What are the four exceptions?

12. (a) Why does an error condition result when the Variable ALPHA is defined as "ALPHA VARIABLE −R$JOE+25"?
(b) If the value of P4 is 0, what is the value of the Variable BETA, defined as "BETA VARIABLE (Q1+Q2)/P4"?
(c) Why does an error condition result when the Variable GAMMA is defined as "GAMMA VARIABLE (W$BLOKA+ W$BLOKB)/(−2*P2)"?
(d) Why is the Variable DELTA in error, where the Variable is defined as "DELTA FVARIABLE ((Q$ONE+Q$TWO+Q$THREE)/3+1/2)@5"?

5.5 Savevalues: The INITIAL Card and the SAVEVALUE Block

Section 5.1 listed the "inability to compute" and the "inability to construct tests" as GPSS modeling limitations to be overcome in this chapter. The computational facility within the language has now been described. Before discussing tests, however, it is appropriate to identify several other limiting features of the models presented so far, and indicate how those limitations can be handled.

A list of the modeling restrictions implicit in the presentation until now is shown below.

1. The only way to incorporate external data into models has been by specifying it directly, as Block Operands, or by providing it as ordered pairs of points in Function definition.

2. A restriction not previously mentioned is that constants used as Block Operands cannot take up more than six columns on a punchcard. The largest possible value of a directly specified Block Operand, then, is 999999.

3. Transactions cannot directly "talk to each other," or "talk about each other." A Transaction which has just entered an ASSIGN Block, for instance, cannot have the value of some other Transaction's P5 copied into one of its Parameters. Or, at the SELECT Block in MIN mode, a Transaction cannot ask, "which one of the Transactions waiting at the Block in Location BLOK9 has the smallest P1 value?"

4. There is no direct way to have the values of Variables printed out. Their values at the end of a simulation run are not computed and outputted by the Processor; furthermore, the values of selected Variables cannot be printed out during a run by use of the PRINT Block.

Any problems these restrictions might pose can be resolved by use of a series of "permanent" memory locations whose initial values can be assigned before a simulation begins, and to and from which values can be transferred from anywhere in a model, as a simulation proceeds. These memory locations are termed *Savevalues*. They are Standard Numerical Attributes in GPSS. Unlike a Transaction's Parameter set, Priority Level, and Mark Time, which are lost when a Transaction exits a model, the Savevalues endure throughout a simulation. And, unlike such other Standard Numerical Attributes as FR_j, QC_j, S_j, etc., their values are not automatically updated by the Processor. In contrast, their values are changed only under direct control of the analyst.

Pertinent properties of Savevalues will now be discussed. Then the method of presetting their values before a simulation starts, and modifying their values as a simulation proceeds, will be described. Finally, the effect of RESET and CLEAR cards on Savevalues will be indicated.

5.5.1 Properties of Savevalues

The analyst supplies numeric and/or symbolic *names* for the Savevalues he uses. Both *halfword* and *fullword* Savevalues are available. Their respective normal maximum quantities at the 64K level are 50 and 100 (see Appendix F). At the 64K level, then, integers in the range from 1 to 50, and from 1 to 100, constitute valid numeric names for halfword and fullword Savevalues, respectively. Symbolic names are composed the usual way.

The *values* of Savevalues are *signed integers*. Halfword Savevalue values range from −32,768 to $+32{,}767$, inclusive. Fullword Savevalue values range from $-2{,}147{,}483{,}648$ to $+2{,}147{,}483{,}647$, inclusive.

The family name for halfword Savevalues is XH; and for fullword Savevalues is X. Halfword and fullword Savevalues are respectively referenced, then, as XHj (or $XH\$sn$), and Xj (or $X\$sn$). For example, XH1 refers to halfword Savevalue 1; X1 refers to fullword Savevalue 1; XH$SARAH refers to the halfword Savevalue SARAH, and so on.

As Standard Numerical Attributes, Savevalues can be used to indirectly provide data as Block Operands, and as Function and Table arguments. For example, the Table definition card "SMITH TABLE XH3,−20,5,25" might be used in a model. Each time a Transaction moved into a TABULATE Block referencing the Table SMITH, the current value of halfword Savevalue 3 would be copied into the Table. Similarly, each time a Transaction moved into the Block "ADVANCE X3,XH$SPRED", the mean holding time would be determined by sampling from the uniform distribution $X3 \pm XH\$SPRED$. Fullword Savevalue 3 would be used as the mean of the distribution, and the halfword Savevalue SPRED would be used as the spread modifier.

At the end of a simulation, all nonzero Savevalues are automatically printed out. Selected Savevalues can also be outputted during a run by use of the PRINT Block. This is accomplished by providing X, or XH, as the Block's field C mnemonic. For example, when a Transaction moves into the Block "PRINT 3,8,XH", halfword Savevalues 3 through 8 will be printed out.

5.5.2 The INITIAL Card

Normally, the GPSS Processor sets Savevalues to zero before a simulation begins. At the analyst's option, selected Savevalues can be initialized with nonzero values by use of the INITIAL card. The card takes the form shown in Figure 5.10. As indicated, the Location field is not used. The word INITIAL is entered in the Operation field. The "basic unit" of information in the Operands field is of the form "name$_i$,value$_i$," where name$_i$ is the name of the ith Savevalue being initialized, and value$_i$ is the

Location	Operation	Operands
Not Used	INITIAL	name$_1$,value$_1$/ . . . /name$_i$,value$_i$/ . . . /name$_n$,value$_n$

FIGURE 5.10 Savevalue initialization card format

initial value. Examples of "basic units" are "XH3,−450", "X$JOE,400000", and "XH49,6". Note that a "name" consists of the family name X or XH, followed by the number or symbolic name of a specific family member. The "value" entry in a basic unit can range from −32,768 to 32,767, inclusive, for halfword Savevalues, and from −2,147,483,648 to 2,147,483,647, inclusive, for fullword Savevalues.

Slashes are used to separate the "basic units" on an INITIAL card. No blanks are allowed within or between consecutive basic units. No information can be entered beyond card column 71. If there is not room enough on one card to initialize all the Savevalues of interest, more than one INITIAL card must be used.

Figure 5.11 provides several examples of the Savevalue INITIAL card. In the first example, the fullword Savevalue TIMER is initialized at one million. If it were of interest to have a "timer Transaction" appear at time 1,000,000 and turn off a model, the Block "GENERATE X$TIMER" could be used for this purpose. Note that the Block "GENERATE 1000000" is *not* acceptable, because more than six card columns are required for the A Operand. If the Processor encountered this latter GENERATE card during the Input Phase, an error message TOO MANY DIGITS IN NUMERIC CONSTANT would be printed out and the simulation would not be performed.

If one or more Savevalues are referenced as A and/or B Operands in GENERATE Blocks, and their values are to be nonzero, the INITIAL cards must appear in the card deck before the GENERATE Block images appear. The values will otherwise still be zero when the Processor encounters the GENERATE cards, and zeros will then be used in scheduling the arrival of the first Transaction at those GENERATE Blocks. It is recommended that all INITIAL cards, as well as Function definitions, Storage capacity cards, and Table cards, be placed ahead of Block images in the model.

In the second Figure 5.11 example, fullword Savevalue 3 is initialized at 25; halfword Savevalue 7 at −10; halfword Savevalue 4 at 452; and fullword Savevalue 98 at 1. This example shows that there are no restrictions on the *order*

LOCATION	OPERATION	A,B,C,D,E,F
	INITIAL	X$TIMER,1000000 FIRST EXAMPLE
	INITIAL	X3,25/XH7,-10/XH4,452/X98,1 SECOND EXAMPLE
	INITIAL	X$BETA,2/X2,3/X$ALPHA,1/X4,7 THIRD EXAMPLE
	INITIAL	XH2,3/X7,5/X8,5/X9,5/X1,-66 FOURTH EXAMPLE
	INITIAL	XH2,3/X7-X9,5/X1,-66 FIFTH EXAMPLE

FIGURE 5.11 Examples showing use of the Figure 5.10 card format

in which the Savevalues appear on the INITIAL card. It is not necessary to group the halfword or fullword Savevalues together; furthermore, it is not necessary that the numbers of the Savevalues involved be in ascending order.

The third example involves a mixture of fullword Savevalues named symbolically and numerically, indicating that such a mixture of names is allowable. The fourth example shows that fullword Savevalues 7, 8, and 9 are each to be 5 initially. When Savevalues of the same type are to have identical initial values, and the Savevalue numbers form a sequence of consecutive integers, the "basic unit" can be expressed as "$name_i - name_k$, value", where "$name_i$" and "$name_k$" are the names of the smallest and largest numbered Savevalues, respectively, and "value" is the common initial value. An alternative form for the fourth Figure 5.11 example, then, is shown in the fifth example.

In concluding the discussion of the Savevalue INITIAL card, it should be noted that the card does not provide a defining context for Savevalues named numerically. (This fact can be verified by checking Appendix G.) When the Processor encounters the INITIAL card in the third example in Figure 5.11, then, it puts BETA and ALPHA on the symbolic name-list for fullword Savevalues, but does not put 2 and 4 on the numeric name-list for fullword Savevalues. This fact could eventually lead to problems. (See exercise 2 in Section 5.7.)

5.5.3 The SAVEVALUE Block

The value of one Savevalue is modified when a Transaction moves into a SAVEVALUE Block. This Block, and its A, B, and C Operands, are shown in Figure 5.12. When a Transaction enters a SAVEVALUE Block, the B Operand data becomes the value of the Savevalue whose number,

FIGURE 5.12 The SAVEVALUE Block and its A, B, and C Operands

Operand	Significance	Default Value or Result
A	Number or symbolic name of the Savevalue to be modified	Error
B	Data to be used in the modification process	Error
C	Specifies whether the Savevalue involved is a halfword or fullword type; the character H designates a halfword type; defaulting on the C Operand implies that a fullword Savevalue is being referenced	A fullword[a] Savevalue is implied

[a]Note that the situation with respect to Savevalue types is just the opposite of that with respect to Parameter types. Savevalues are *fullword by default*; to reference halfword Savevalues, H must be entered as the SAVEVALUE Block's C Operand. On the other hand, Transaction Parameters are *halfword by default*; to obtain fullword Parameters for Transactions, F must be entered as the GENERATE Block's G Operand.

or symbolic name, is provided by the A Operand. Whenever a Transaction enters the SAVEVALUE Block shown in Figure 5.13, for example, the value of the Variable ALPHA is first computed. The result is then assigned to the fullword Savevalue whose number is in P5. The old value of the Savevalue is destroyed in the process.

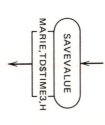

SAVEVALUE
P5,V$ALPHA

FIGURE 5.13 A first example for the SAVE-VALUE Block

A second example is shown in Figure 5.14. When a Transaction enters the SAVEVALUE Block, the standard deviation in the Table TIME3 is copied into the halfword Savevalue MARIE.

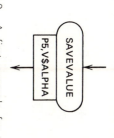

SAVEVALUE
MARIE,TD$TIME3,H

FIGURE 5.14 A second example for the SAVEVALUE Block

Like the ASSIGN Block, the SAVEVALUE Block can be used in increment mode and decrement mode, as well as in replacement mode. In increment mode, the previous value of the Savevalue is incremented by the B Operand data. In decrement mode, it is decremented by the B Operand data. Increment and decrement mode are specified by placing a plus or minus sign, respectively, ahead of the comma which separates the A and B Operands. For example, when a Transaction enters the Block "SAVEVALUE 5+,X2", the value of X5 will be increased by the amount X2. Or, when a Transaction enters the Block "SAVEVALUE DAVID—, FN$HOLD, H", the value of XH$DAVID will be decreased by the amount FN$HOLD.

LOCATION	OPERATION	A,B,C,D,E,F
CLEAR	X3,X12,X14,XH1—XH5,XH9	FIRST EXAMPLE
CLEAR	XH1—XH5,XH9,X3,X12,X14	SECOND EXAMPLE

FIGURE 5.15 Examples showing use of the selective CLEAR card

5.5.4 The Effect of RESET and CLEAR Cards on Savevalues

The values in Savevalue locations are not changed by the RESET card. Use of the CLEAR card, however, normally causes all the halfword and fullword Savevalues to be set to zero. This often proves to be inconvenient, because it may mean that an entire series of INITIAL cards must be repeated before the simulation can be started again. For this reason, there is an optional form of the CLEAR card available with which the user can specify selected Savevalues which are to be left intact. To use this so-called selective CLEAR card, all the user must do is provide in the Operands field the names of the Savevalues not to be zeroed-out when the clearing operation occurs. In contrast to the flexibilities allowed with the INITIAL card, however, the following restrictions apply to the selective CLEAR card.

1. Halfword and fullword Savevalues must be grouped on the card according to type.
2. Within each Savevalue type (i.e., halfword or fullword), the numbers of the Savevalues to be left intact must be in ascending order.

Two examples of the selective CLEAR card are shown in Figure 5.15. The first example specifies that fullword Savevalues 3, 12, and 14 and halfword Savevalues 1 through 5, and 9, are not to be set to zero when the CLEAR card has its effect. The second example is identical to the first, except that the halfword Savevalues involved are specified first, and then the fullword Savevalues are specified.

5.6 CASE STUDY 5A
A Third Tour Through Case Study 2D

(1) Statement of the Problem

Case Study 2D involved modeling a widget-manufacturing operation to determine how many assemblers should be hired to maximize profits. In the solution presented, *hand computations* based on model output were performed to determine the profit realized for each "number of assemblers" alternative investigated. Modify the

Case Study 2D solution to incorporate these features.

1. Arrange to have the average daily profit realized for each alternative be included in the model output.
2. Make the number of simulated days in effect for each simulation be a variable in the sense that it is specified through a Savevalue.
3. Investigate alternatives of 4, 5, and 6 assemblers in a single run. For each configuration, simulate for the equivalent of a 40-hour work week. Assume there are no discontinuities within a working day, or in moving between consecutive 8-hour work days.

For convenience, the description of the problem in Case Study 2D is repeated below.

The manufacture of a certain line of widgets involves a relatively lengthy assembly process, followed by a short firing time in an oven. Since ovens are expensive to maintain, several assemblers share a single oven, which holds only one widget at a time. An assembler cannot begin assembling a new widget until he has removed the old one from the oven.

This is the pattern followed by each assembler:

1. Assemble next widget.
2. Wait, first-come, first-served, to use the oven.
3. Use the oven.
4. Return to 1.

Time and cost studies have been conducted to provide the information in Tables 5A.1 and 5A.2, respectively.

(2) Approach Taken in Building the Model

In Case Study 2D, a Transaction was used to simulate an assembler. The proper number of assemblers was introduced into the model through use of the GENERATE Block Limit Count (D Operand). This value, in turn, was directly specified. In the approach taken here, the Limit Count is indirectly specified through the fullword Savevalue GUYS. This makes it possible to reconfigure the model simply by redefining the value of GUYS between consecutive runs. More importantly, the Savevalue GUYS can then also be used for the fixed-cost computations when determining the average daily profit.

The fullword Savevalue named TIMER is used as the A Operand for the GENERATE Block through which the timer Transaction enters the model. The default value of zero is in effect for the B Operand. The simulated time at which the timer enters the model, then, equals the value of X$TIMER. As explained below, the value of X$TIMER is also used in a computational role in the model, to aid in determining the average daily profit.

The average daily profit is $5 times the average number of widgets produced each day, minus the fixed daily costs. If the symbolic Location name MADE is given to the Block "RELEASE OVEN", then N$MADE is the number of widgets produced during a given simulation. If it is assumed that the implicit time unit is 1 minute, and that X$TIMER is an integral multiple of 480, then X$TIMER/480 is the number of days simulated. (Exercise 4e, Section 5.7, involves relaxing the assumption that X$TIMER is an integral multiple of 480.) Now suppose that the expression X$TIMER/480 is used to define a Variable named DAYS. Then 5*N$MADE/V$DAYS is the average daily profit before deduction of oven cost and salaries. Daily oven cost, from the statement of the problem, is $80. At $3.75 per hour, each assembler earns $30 per 8-hour day. The total daily salary, then, is 30*X$GUYS. Average daily profit is consequently the value of the expression 5*N$MADE/V$DAYS−80−30*X$GUYS. Assume this expression is used to define the Variable named PROFT (for profit). Then, when the timer Transaction enters the model, it can move through a SAVEVALUE Block, causing the average daily profit to be computed and copied into a Savevalue. When the model shuts off, this profit value will be included in the listing of Savevalues shown as part of the standard model output.

TABLE 5A.1   Operation Times for Case Study 5A

Operation	Time Required (minutes)
Assemble	30 ± 5
Fire	8 ± 2

TABLE 5A.2   Financial Data for Case Study 5A

Item	Cost Information
Assembler's salary	$3.75 per hour
Oven cost	$80 per 8-hour work day (independent of utilization)
Raw material	$2 per widget
Value of finished widgets	$7 per widget

(3) Table of Definitions

Time Unit: 1 minute

TABLE 5A.3 Table of Definitions for Case Study 5A

GPSS Entity		Interpretation
Transactions		
	Model Segment 1	Assemblers
	Model Segment 2	The timer
Facilities		
	OVEN	The oven
Savevalues		
	GUYS	The number of assemblers
	TIMER	Duration of the simulation for each alternative investigated, minutes
Variables		
	DAYS	Duration of the simulation for each alternative investigated, 8-hour days
	PROFIT	Average daily profit for the alternative being investigated, dollars

(4) Block Diagram

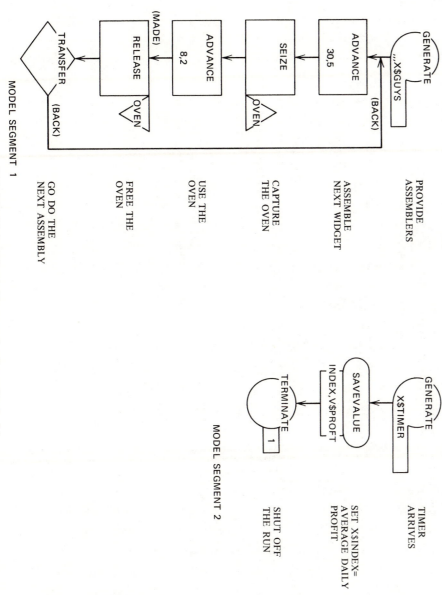

MODEL SEGMENT 1

GENERATE ...,X$GUYS   PROVIDE ASSEMBLERS

ADVANCE 30,5   ASSEMBLE NEXT WIDGET

SEIZE OVEN   CAPTURE THE OVEN

ADVANCE 8,2   USE THE OVEN

RELEASE OVEN   FREE THE OVEN

(BACK) TRANSFER ,BACK   GO DO THE NEXT ASSEMBLY

(MADE)

MODEL SEGMENT 2

GENERATE X$TIMER   TIMER ARRIVES

SAVEVALUE INDEX,V$PROFIT   SET X$INDEX= AVERAGE DAILY PROFIT

TERMINATE 1   SHUT OFF THE RUN

FIGURE 5A.1 Block Diagram for Case Study 5A

(5) Extended Program Listing

BLOCK NUMBER	*LOC	OPERATION A,B,C,D,E,F,G	COMMENTS	CARD NUMBER
		SIMULATE		1
	*			2
	*	SAVEVALUE INITIALIZATION(S)		3
	*			4
		INITIAL X$GUYS,4/X$TIMER,2400	4 ASSEMBLERS; TIMER AT 40TH HOUR	5
	*			6
	*	VARIABLE DEFINITION(S)		7
	*			8
	DAYS	VARIABLE X$TIMER/480	SIMULATION TIME IN DAYS	9
	PROFT	VARIABLE 5*N$MADE/V$DAYS-80-30*X$GUYS	AVERAGE DAILY PROFIT	10
	*			11
	*	MODEL SEGMENT 1		12
	*			13
1		GENERATE ,,,X$GUYS	PROVIDE ASSEMBLERS	14
2	BACK	ADVANCE 30,5	ASSEMBLE NEXT WIDGET	15
3		SEIZE OVEN	CAPTURE THE OVEN	16
4		ADVANCE 8,2	USE THE OVEN	17
5	MADE	RELEASE OVEN	FREE THE OVEN	18
6		TRANSFER .BACK	GO DO THE NEXT ASSEMBLY	19
	*			20
	*	MODEL SEGMENT 2		21
	*			22
7		GENERATE X$TIMER	TIMER ARRIVES	23
8		SAVEVALUE INDEX,V$PROFT	SET X$INDEX = AVERAGE DAILY PROFIT	24
9		TERMINATE 1	SHUT OFF THE RUN	25
	*			26
	*	CONTROL CARDS AND SAVEVALUE RE-INITIALIZATION(S)		27
	*			28
		START 1	START THE 1ST RUN (4 ASSEMBLERS)	29
		INITIAL X$GUYS,5	RE-CONFIGURE FOR 2ND RUN	30
		CLEAR X$GUYS,X$TIMER	SELECTIVELY CLEAR FOR 2ND RUN	31
		START 1	START THE 2ND RUN (5 ASSEMBLERS)	32
		INITIAL X$GUYS,6	RE-CONFIGURE FOR 3RD RUN	33
		CLEAR X$GUYS,X$TIMER	SELECTIVELY CLEAR FOR 3RD RUN	34
		START 1	START THE 3RD RUN (6 ASSEMBLERS)	35
		END	RETURN CONTROL TO OPERATING SYSTEM	36

FIGURE 5A.2 Extended Program Listing for Case Study 5A

(6) Program Output

FACILITY	AVERAGE UTILIZATION	NUMBER ENTRIES	AVERAGE TIME/TRAN	SEIZING TRANS. NO.	PREEMPTING TRANS. NO.
OVEN	.785	236	7.991	5	

CONTENTS OF FULLWORD SAVEVALUES (NON-ZERO)

SAVEVALUE NR.	VALUE	NR.	VALUE	NR.	VALUE	NR.	VALUE
GUYS	4	TIMER	2400	INDEX	35		

(a)

FIGURE 5A.3 Selected Program Output for Case Study 5A. (a) Facility and Savevalue information (four-assembler configuration).

FACILITY	AVERAGE UTILIZATION	NUMBER ENTRIES	AVERAGE TIME/TRAN	SEIZING TRANS. NO.	PREEMPTING TRANS. NO.
OVEN	.942	281	8.053	6	

CONTENTS OF FULLWORD SAVEVALUES (NON-ZERO)

SAVEVALUE NR.	VALUE	NR.	VALUE	NR.	VALUE	NR.	VALUE
GUYS	5	TIMER	2400	INDEX	50		

(b)

FACILITY	AVERAGE UTILIZATION	NUMBER ENTRIES	AVERAGE TIME/TRAN	SEIZING TRANS. NO.	PREEMPTING TRANS. NO.
OVEN	.989	296	8.020	1	

CONTENTS OF FULLWORD SAVEVALUES (NON-ZERO)

SAVEVALUE NR.	VALUE	NR.	VALUE	NR.	INDEX	NR.	VALUE
GUYS	6	TIMER	2400		35		50

(c)

FIGURE 5A.3 Selected Program Output for Case Study 5A. (b) Facility and Savevalue information (five-assembler configuration). (c) Facility and Savevalue information (six assembler configuration).

(7) Discussion

Model Implementation. In the Extended Program Listing in Figure 5A.2, Card 5 is the INITIAL card used to supply the fullword Savevalues GUYS and TIMER with values of 4, and 2400, respectively. This is consistent with first simulating with a four-assembler configuration, and having the timer Transaction enter the model after 40 hours (i.e., 2400 minutes) of simulated time have elapsed.

Cards 9 and 10 in Figure 5A.2 define the Variables DAYS and PROFT, respectively, as dis-

cussed earlier. Note that the Processor must evaluate the Variable DAYS as one of the steps to be performed in evaluating the Variable PROFT.

When the timer Transaction comes into the model, it enters a SAVEVALUE Block at which the value of the Variable PROFT is computed and then copied to the Savevalue named INDEX (Block 8). The timer Transaction then moves into a TERMINATE Block (Block 9), shutting off the simulation.

After the first START card (Card 29, Figure 5A.2), there is an INITIAL card which redefines the value of the Savevalue GUYS as 5. This accomplishes reconfiguring the model for the five-assembler alternative. The following card (Card 31) is then a selective CLEAR, which sets all values back to zero (with the exception of the Savevalues GUYS and TIMER), returns Transactions to the stack in the latent pool, and then schedules Transaction arrivals at the two GENERATE Blocks in the model. The START card that appears next (Card 32) causes the simulation to begin again for the newly configured model. A similar INITIAL–CLEAR–START sequence is then provided (Cards 33, 34, and 35) for the six-assembler configuration.

Program Output.[3] Facility-statistics and Savevalue values outputted by the Figure 5A.2 model are shown in Figure 5A.3. The Facility statistics for all three configurations exactly match the results produced in Section 2.34 when the CLEAR card was first introduced, then used for this same problem to study alternatives of four, five, and six assemblers sequentially (see Figures 2.37 and 2.38).

Because the Savevalues GUYS, TIMER, and INDEX were encountered by the Processor in that order in the Figure 5A.2 model, their values appear in that order in Figure 5A.3. In the Savevalue information in Figure 5A.3(a), for example, under the columns labeled NR (short for "NUMBER"), appear GUYS, TIMER, and INDEX. At the right of each NR column, in a column labeled VALUE, is entered the value of the corresponding Savevalue. Hence, GUYS has a value of 4; TIMER has a value of 2400; and INDEX has a value of 35 in Figure 5A.3(a). This means that, for the case of 4 assemblers, and based on a simulation of 2400 minutes, the average daily profit was $35. Parts (b) and (c) in Figure 5A.3 indicate average daily profits of $50 and $35 for the cases of 5 and 6 assemblers, respectively.

5.7 Exercises

1. This exercise consists of short problems for Savevalues.
   (a) Compare and contrast Savevalues with Parameters.
   (b) What is the difference between X1 and XH1?
   (c) Show an INITIAL card which initializes fullword Savevalues 3, 5, and MACRO with values

of −25, 75, and 40, respectively, and which initializes halfword Savevalues 1 through 5 with the value 100.
   (d) Show a CLEAR card which does not alter the values of halfword Savevalues 1 and 5, and fullword Savevalues 4, 5, and 6, but causes all other Savevalues to be set to zero.
   (e) Why is the Block "ADVANCE 4500000" in error? How could you avoid this error, yet accomplish the same effect?

2. (a) Referring to Appendix G, state the conditions under which additions are made to the numeric name-list for Savevalues during the model Input Phase.
   (b) Suppose that the Savevalue INITIAL card shown in the third example in Figure 5.11 is used in a particular model. Assume this is the only Savevalue INITIAL card in the model, and that it is the analyst's intention to have BETA, 2, ALPHA, and 4 be distinctly different full-word Savevalues (as the INITIAL card implies, logically).
       (i) What must be true in the model if the analyst's intention is to be fulfilled?
       (ii) Describe model conditions under which the Processor would make BETA equivalent to 2 as a fullword Savevalue.
       (iii) Describe model conditions under which the Processor would make ALPHA equivalent to 2 as a fullword Savevalue.

3. In a certain model, the Block "GENERATE X$MEAN,X$SPRED" is used. Two alternative configurations are being studied sequentially, with the understanding that the Savevalues MEAN and SPRED are to have different values for the second configuration than they do for the first. Explain the differences among the three control card sequences shown in (a), (b), and (c) below. Which sequence is correct, and why? (Suggestion: you might want to review the operation of the CLEAR card as explained in Section 2.34.)
   (a) START   1
       CLEAR
       INITIAL   X$MEAN,60/X$SPRED,30
       START   1
   (b) START   1
       CLEAR   X$MEAN,X$SPRED
       INITIAL   X$MEAN,60/X$SPRED,30
       START   1
   (c) START   1
       INITIAL   X$MEAN,60/X$SPRED,30
       CLEAR   X$MEAN,X$SPRED
       START   1

4. These exercises all pertain to Case Study 5A.
   (a) Use the Facility statistics in Figure 5A.3 to compute (by hand) the average daily profit for the cases of four, five, and six assemblers,

---

[3]Total CPU time for the simulation on an IBM 360/67 computer was 12.5 seconds.

respectively. Do your results match those appearing in the Savevalue information in Figure 5A.3?

(b) Explain how the Variable DAYS can be eliminated in the Figure 5A.2 model.

(c) Explain how to build a model for Case Study 5A which uses only the Savevalue INDEX, and does not use any other Savevalues. Show all the details involved by presenting the complete model on a coding sheet.

(d) Change the Figure 5A.2 model so that each estimate of average daily profit is based on a simulation of ten working days, not five. Make a similar change for the model you built as a solution to (c) above. How many cards had to be changed in each case? Using the number of cards changed as a measure, which model seems to be the more flexible?

(e) The Figure 5A.2 model assumes that the value of X$TIMER is an integral multiple of 480. Show how to modify the model to eliminate this assumption. The modified model should work, for example, when the value of X$TIMER is 2450. In this case, the average daily profit computation would be based on a simulated time span of five 8-hour work days, and the first 50 minutes of the sixth work day.

(f) In Case Study 5A, daily profit is a random variable. Show how to modify the Figure 5A.2 model so that the value of this random variable is entered in a GPSS Table on a day-by-day basis. The modified model should simulate with each configuration for 25 consecutive working days. Included in the output, then, will not only be the average value of the "daily profit" random variable, but an estimate of its distribution based on a sample of size 25. Clearly state all assumptions you make in modifying the model.

5. Case Study 2E involves searching for a system configuration which minimizes the average daily cost associated with a production process. The Extended Program Listing for a model which investigates nine alternative system configurations sequentially appears in Figure 2E.3. Show how to modify the Figure 2E.3 model so that the average daily-cost estimate for each configuration is included as part of the standard model output.

6. Explain what happens when Transactions enter the various SELECT Blocks whose card images are shown below.

(a) SELECT E 5,3,7,0,X
(b) SELECT E 5,3,7,0,X,RATS
(c) SELECT MIN P3,1,P2,XH
(d) SELECT MAX XH2,XH10,X12,,P

7. Suppose it is of interest to determine the first ten values of RN1 when RN1 is used in the context of a Function argument. The values are to be determined to six decimal places. Show a self-contained model segment which has the purpose of printing out these first ten values. (Hint: define a function which has RN1 as its argument, and which has the effect of multiplying RN1 by 1,000,000, thereby shifting the decimal six places to the right. Then store the result in a Savevalue.)

8. The conventional design for checkout counters at a supermarket is for several counters to operate in parallel, with a line forming at each counter. Consider a certain supermarket which has six checkout counters. A customer arriving at the checkout area either goes to an immediately available counter, or joins the waiting line at that counter for which the *sum* of waiting line length *and* the average number of items per customer in that waiting line (excluding items carried by the customer currently being checked out) is smaller than (or possibly equal to) the corresponding sum for the other waiting lines.

Show a portion of a Block Diagram with which this situation can be modeled in GPSS. Assume that a Transaction simulates a customer, and that the number of items each customer has to check out equals the value of Transaction Parameter 1. The checkout time per customer is 10 ± 5 minutes, and the implicit time unit is 1 minute.

5.8 Testing Numeric Relationships: The TEST Block

The relation between the values of two Standard Numerical Attributes can be examined by use of the TEST Block. This Block, its various Operands, and its Auxiliary Operator, are shown in Figure 5.16. The A and B Operands are the names of the two Standard Numerical Attributes involved. An SNA's are to be compared against each other. As indicated in Figure 5.16, X is to be the single letter G, E, or L (for "greater," "equal," and "less," respectively), or the pair of letters GE, NE, or LE (for "greater or equal," "not equal," and "less or equal," respectively).

The C Operand is optional. When only the A and B Operands are supplied, the test is conducted in *refusal mode*. When a Transaction attempts to enter a TEST Block used in refusal mode, entry is denied unless the answer to the question implied by the relational operator is "yes." When entry is denied, the Transaction is held at the preceding Block, where it contributes to the Current Block Count. Each time the Current Events Chain is scanned, the Transaction again attempts to gain entry to the TEST Block. Eventually, the TEST Block is successfully en-

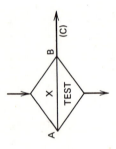

Operand	Significance	Default Value or Result
A	Name of the first Standard Numerical Attribute	Error
B	Name of the second Standard Numerical Attribute	Error
X	The Auxiliary Operator X represents the *relational operator* to be used in the test; the forms X can assume are shown below	

Relational Operator	Question Implied in TEST Block Context
G	Is A greater than B?
GE	Is A greater than or equal to B?
E	Is A equal to B?
NE	Is A not equal to B?
LE	Is A less than or equal to B?
L	Is A less than B?

Operand	Significance	Default Value or Result
C	Optional Operand; Block Location to which the testing Transaction moves if the answer to the question implied by the relational operator is "no"	The test is conducted in refusal mode when no C Operand is provided

FIGURE 5.16   The TEST Block, with its Auxiliary Operator and its A, B, and C Operands

tered because the value of one or both of the SNA's involved is presumably subject to change as the simulation proceeds. When a Transaction has gained entry to the refusal-mode TEST Block, it then attempts to move to the sequential Block, and so on.

When the TEST Block's C Operand is used, the test is conducted in *conditional transfer mode*. A Transaction which arrives at the TEST Block moves to the sequential Block if the answer to the implied question is "yes"; otherwise, it moves to the indicated nonsequential Block.[4]

[4] The TEST Block in transfer mode works *just the opposite of* conditional transfer statements in most programming languages. For example, consider the FORTRAN IV statement "IF (A .LT. B) GO TO 25". If it is *true* that A is less than B, control transfers to nonsequential statement 25; otherwise, it goes to the sequential program statement. At the TEST Block in conditional transfer mode, the Transaction transfers to the nonsequential Block when the examined condition is *false*; otherwise, it goes to the sequential Block. A convenient way to remember this is with the phrase "test true, fall through."

In conditional transfer mode, then, entry to the TEST Block is not denied. A Transaction arriving at the Block enters it immediately, and the path it is to subsequently follow is immediately determined by execution of the Block subroutine.

It is possible to have a nonzero Current Block Count at a TEST Block. This will happen for either test mode whenever the Transaction's next scheduled Block refuses to accept it. Of course, even if a Transaction does come to rest in a TEST Block, its "Next Block Attempted" has already been determined. There is no need to subsequently reexecute the TEST Block subroutine in behalf of the delayed Transaction.

Several TEST Block examples are shown in Figure 5.17. In Figure 5.17(a), the testing Transaction is to be held at the preceding Block until it is true that the contents of Queue 1 are less than or equal to those of Queue 2. In Figure 5.17(b), the testing Transaction will also move to the sequential Block if the contents of Queue 1 are less than or equal to those of Queue 2. If this condition is not satisfied, the Transaction is to move to the nonsequential Block at the Location BYPAS. In the (c) example, a Transaction is to wait until the value of its P5 exceeds the value of the Variable DELTA. Although the use of arithmetic operators is *not permitted* at the TEST Block, their use is of course allowed in defining Variables. By use of Arithmetic Variables as the A and/or B Operands, then, the values of arithmetic expressions can be examined with the TEST Block.

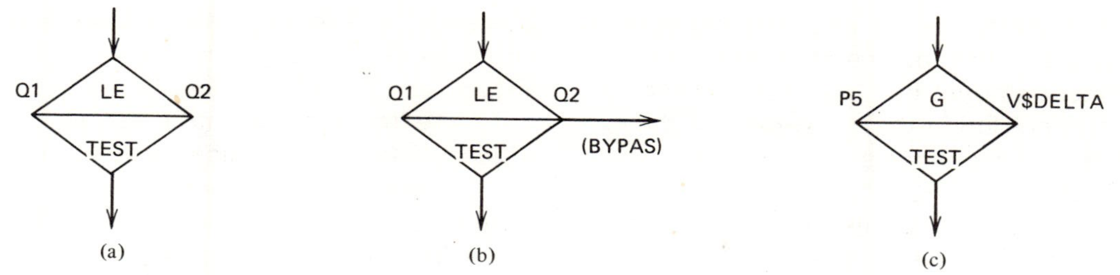

When preparing the punchcard corresponding to a TEST Block, the Auxiliary Operator is entered in the Operation field, in card column 13 (or 13 and 14). This follows the prescription given earlier for entering Auxiliary Operators in punchcards. That is, they appear in the Operation field, after the Operation itself, and separated from the Operation by a blank column.

5.9 CASE STUDY 5B
A Problem in Inventory Control

(1) Statement of the Problem

In a retail store, the daily demand for a given item is normally distributed with a mean and standard deviation of 10 and 2 units, respectively. Whenever the retailer's stock-on-hand drops to or beneath a predetermined point, called the *reorder point*, he places a stock-replenishment order with his supplier. The replenishment amount, called the *reorder quantity*, is always 100 units. The replenishment order arrives at the retail store anywhere from 6 to 10 days after placement of the order. This lapsed time between placing the replenishment order, and having it arrive at the retail store, is termed *lead time*. The lead-time distribution is shown in Table 5B.1. Demand that arises when the retailer is out-of-stock is lost; that is, customers whose demand cannot be satisfied immediately go elsewhere to transact their business.

FIGURE 5.17 Examples of TEST Block use. (a) Refusal mode. (b) Conditional transfer mode. (c) Refusal mode.

The retailer wants to know how his experience with the item will vary, depending on where he sets the reorder point. From the records summarized in Table 5B.1, he knows that lead time

TABLE 5B.1 The Distribution of Lead-Times in Case Study 5B

Lead Time (days)	Relative Frequency
6	.05
7	.25
8	.30
9	.22
10	.18

is about 8 days on average. Because average demand for the item is 10 units per day, he reasons that the reorder point must be no smaller than 80; otherwise, he would not have enough stock on hand to meet the *lead-time demand*, i.e., the demand expected to occur during the lead-time period. He reasons further that by setting the reorder point at a higher level, such as 90 or 100, the possibility that he will experience lost sales while waiting for a replenishment order to arrive decreases. On the other hand, higher reorder points mean that he is carrying more stock on average, which increases the amount of his capital tied up in stock.

Build a GPSS model for the retailer's situation. Design the model to measure the distribution of two random variables: "lost daily sales" and "number of units carried in inventory." Run the model to estimate these two distributions when the reorder quantity is 100, and the reorder point is 80, or 90, or 100. For each alternative configuration, shut off the model after a simulation of 1,000 days.

For simplicity, assume that the retailer checks his inventory level only at the end of each day's business, and then does or does not place a replenishment order. Also assume that replenishment orders always arrive after the close of a day's business; this means that none of the replenishment amount can be used to meet demand occurring during the day on which the replenishment order arrives. Also ignore any "weekend problems." Such problems arise because, in practice, the retailer may not be open for business on Saturday and/or Sunday; nevertheless, on Saturdays and Sundays, a replenishment order in transit continues to proceed toward its destination. Ignoring the weekend problem is equivalent to assuming that the retailer does business 7 days a week.

(2) Approach Taken in Building the Model

The model is composed of two separate segments. The *Demand Segment* simulates the daily demand for the item, arranges for as much of that demand to be met as possible, and enters the values of lost sales and stock-on-hand into GPSS Tables at the end of each day. The *Inventory Control Segment* maintains a watch over the stock-on-hand situation, and causes a replenishment order to be placed when stock-on-hand is at or below the reorder point *and* there is no replenishment order already en route from the supplier. These two separate segments communicate with each other through a single Savevalue, STOCK, whose value is the current stock-on-hand.

In the Demand Segment, rather than letting demand occur unit-by-unit as the day proceeds, the day's total demand is determined by a single Transaction which enters the model each day and samples from the demand distribution. This total demand, carried in Transaction Parameter 1, is then tested in conditional transfer mode against the Savevalue STOCK to determine if all the day's demand can be met. If it can, STOCK is updated, entries are made in the two tables, and the Transaction leaves the model. When the day's demand exceeds STOCK, the Transaction takes the nonsequential exit from the TEST Block and

proceeds to compute lost sales and set STOCK equal to 0. It then makes entries in the two Tables, and leaves the model.

In the Inventory Control Segment, a single office-worker Transaction is held ahead of a refusal-mode TEST Block, waiting for STOCK to drop to or beneath the reorder point. The reorder point itself is held in the Savevalue ROP (for reorder point). When the TEST Block permits passage, indicating that a replenishment order should be placed, the Transaction moves through it to an ADVANCE Block, where lead time is simulated. Moving from the ADVANCE Block after the lead time has elapsed, the office-worker updates STOCK by adding the reorder quantity to it. The reorder quantity value is held in the Savevalue ROQ (for reorder quantity). The office worker then transfers back to reestablish the watch over the stock-on-hand situation.

The Transaction in the Inventory Control Segment has a lower Priority Level than Transactions moving through the Demand Segment. This priority distinction is made to honor the problem condition that replenishment orders always arrive *after* the close of a day's business. Suppose, for example, that an order is scheduled to arrive on the fifty-first day of a simulation. The office-worker Transaction bringing in the order was put on the Future Events Chain no later than the end of the forty-fifth simulated day (minimum lead time is 6 days). With certainty, the Demand Segment Transaction was not put on the Future Events Chain until the beginning of the fiftieth day (scheduled to move into the model on the fifty-first day). The sequence of placement on the Future Chain means that, after transfer to the Current Chain, the office worker would be *ahead* of the Demand Segment Transaction if both were to have the same Priority Level. This, in turn, would mean that the replenishment order would arrive *before* the day's demand was determined, which would be a violation of the stated problem conditions. Making the Priority Level distinction reverses this situation.

(3) Table of Definitions

Time Unit : 1 Day

TABLE 5B.2   Table of Definitions for Case Study 5B

GPSS Entity	Interpretation
Transactions	
Model Segment 1	A Store Worker
	P1 : Total demand on the day in question
	P2 : Number of lost sales on the day in question
Model Segment 2	An Office Worker
Functions	
LTIME	Function describing the lead-time distribution
SNORM	Function describing the standard normal distribution
Savevalues	
ROP	Reorder point
ROQ	Reorder quantity
STOCK	Stock-on-hand
Tables	
LOSES	Table used to estimate the distribution of lost daily sales
STOCK	Table used to estimate the distribution of stock-on-hand
Variables	
DMND	Variable whose value is the total demand on the day in question
LOST	Variable whose value is the number of lost sales on the day in question

(4) Block Diagram

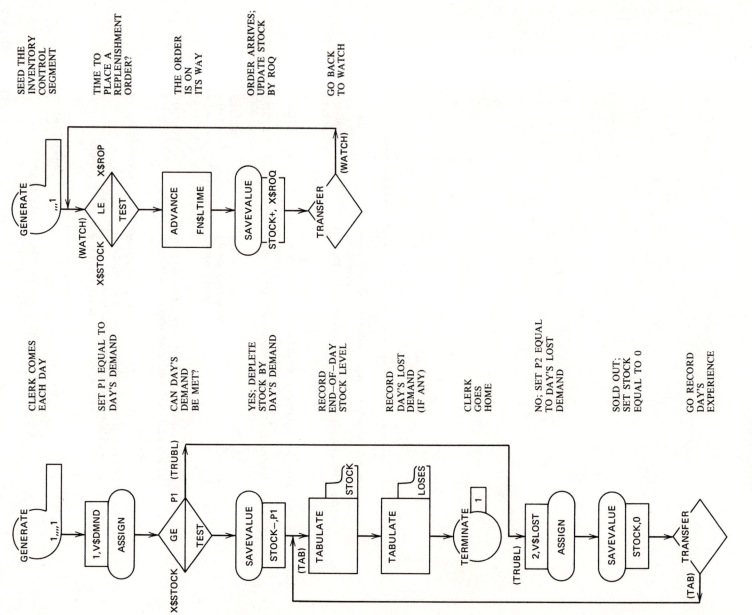

MODEL SEGMENT 1
(DEMAND SEGMENT)

FIGURE 5B.1   Block Diagram for Case Study 5B

(5) Extended Program Listing

BLOCK NUMBER	*LOC	OPERATION	A,B,C,D,E,F,G	COMMENTS	CARD NUMBER
		SIMULATE			1
		*			2
		*		NON-STANDARD RANDOM NUMBER SEQUENCE INITIALIZATION(S)	3
		*			4
		RMULT	11,33		5
		*			6
		*		FUNCTION DEFINITION(S)	7
		*			8
	LTIME	FUNCTION	RN2,D5	REPLENISHMENT ORDER LEAD-TIME DIST'N	9
			.05,6/.3,7/.6,8/.82,9/1,10		10
	SNORM	FUNCTION	RN1,C25	STANDARD NORMAL DISTRIBUTION FUNCTION	11
			0,-5/.00003,-4/.00135,-3/.00621,-2.5/.02275,-2		12
			.06681,-1.5/.11507,-1.2/.15866,-1/.21186,-.8/.27425,-.6		13
			.34458,-.4/.42074,-.2/.5,0/.57926,.2/.65542,.4		14
			.72575,.6/.78814,.8/.84134,1/.88493,1.2/.93319,1.5		15
			.97725,2/.99379,2.5/.99865,3/.99997,4/1,5		16
		*			17
		*		SAVEVALUE INITIALIZATION(S)	18
		*			19
		INITIAL	X$ROP,80	REORDER POINT = 80 FOR 1ST RUN	20
		INITIAL	X$ROQ,100	REORDER QUANTITY = 100 FOR 1ST RUN	21
		INITIAL	X$STOCK,100	INITIAL STOCK ON HAND = 100 UNITS	22
		*			23
		*		TABLE DEFINITION(S)	24
		*			25
	LOSES	TABLE	P2,0,1,17	TABLE FOR LOST DAILY SALES	26
	STOCK	TABLE	X$STOCK,0,10,12	TABLE FOR DAILY STOCK LEVEL	27
		*			28
		*		VARIABLE DEFINITION(S)	29
		*			30
	DMND	FVARIABLE	2*FN$SNORM+10	DAILY DEMAND DISTRIBUTION	31
	LOST	VARIABLE	P1-X$STOCK	DAY'S LOST SALES	32
		*			33
		*		MODEL SEGMENT 1	34
		*			35
1		GENERATE	1,,,,1	CLERK COMES EACH DAY	36
2		ASSIGN	1,V$DMND	SET P1 = DAY'S DEMAND	37
3		TEST GE	X$STOCK,P1,TRUBL	CAN DAY'S DEMAND BE MET?	38
4		SAVEVALUE	STOCK-,P1	YES; DEPLETE STOCK BY DAY'S DEMAND	39
5	TAB	TABULATE	STOCK	RECORD END-OF-DAY STOCK LEVEL	40
6		TABULATE	LOSES	RECORD DAY'S LOST DEMAND (IF ANY)	41
7		TERMINATE	1	CLERK GOES HOME	42
8	TRUBL	ASSIGN	2,V$LOST	NO; SET P2 = DAY'S LOST DEMAND	43
9		SAVEVALUE	STOCK,0	SOLD OUT; SET STOCK = 0	44
10		TRANSFER	,TAB	GO RECORD DAY'S EXPERIENCE	45
		*			46
		*		MODEL SEGMENT 2	47
		*			48
11		GENERATE	,,,1		49
12	WATCH	TEST LE	X$STOCK,X$ROP	IS IT TIME TO PLACE A REPLENISHMENT ORDER?	50
13		ADVANCE	FN$LTIME	THE ORDER IS ON ITS WAY	51
14		SAVEVALUE	STOCK+,X$ROQ	ORDER ARRIVES; ADD ROQ TO STOCK	52
15		TRANSFER	,WATCH	GO BACK TO WATCH	53
		*			54
		*		CONTROL CARDS AND SAVEVALUE RE-INITIALIZATION(S)	55
		*			56
		START	1000	START 1ST RUN (ROP = 80)	57
		RMULT	11,33	RESTORE RANDOM SEQUENCES	58
		CLEAR	X$ROQ	SELECTIVELY CLEAR FOR 2ND RUN	59
		INITIAL	X$ROP,90/X$STOCK,100	RE-CONFIGURE; SET INITIAL STOCK	60
		START	1000	START 2ND RUN (ROP = 90)	61
		RMULT	11,33	RESTORE RANDOM SEQUENCES	62
		CLEAR	X$ROQ	SELECTIVELY CLEAR FOR 3RD RUN	63
		INITIAL	X$ROP,100/X$STOCK,100	RE-CONFIGURE; SET INITIAL STOCK	64
		START	1000	START 3RD RUN (ROP = 100)	65
		END		RETURN CONTROL TO OP'ING SYSTEM	66

FIGURE 5B.2 Extended Program Listing for Case Study 5B

(6) Program Output

TABLE LOSES
ENTRIES IN TABLE 1000   MEAN ARGUMENT .516   STANDARD DEVIATION 2.015   SUM OF ARGUMENTS 517.000   NON-WEIGHTED

UPPER LIMIT	OBSERVED FREQUENCY	PER CENT OF TOTAL	CUMULATIVE PERCENTAGE	CUMULATIVE REMAINDER	MULTIPLE OF MEAN	DEVIATION FROM MEAN
0	923	92.29	92.2	7.7	-.000	-.256
1	10	.99	93.2	6.7	1.934	.239
2	2	.19	93.4	6.5	3.868	.735
3	2	.19	93.6	6.3	5.802	1.231
4	5	.49	94.1	5.8	7.736	1.727
5	5	.49	94.6	5.3	9.671	2.224
6	12	1.19	95.8	4.1	11.605	2.720
7	9	.89	96.7	3.2	13.539	3.216
8	8	.79	97.5	2.4	15.473	3.712
9	6	.59	98.1	1.8	17.408	4.208
10	8	.79	98.9	1.0	19.342	4.704
11	3	.29	99.2	.7	21.276	5.200
12	6	.59	99.8	.1	23.210	5.696
13	0	.00	99.8	.1	25.145	6.193
14	1	.09	100.0	.0	27.079	6.689

REMAINING FREQUENCIES ARE ALL ZERO

(a)

TABLE STOCK
ENTRIES IN TABLE 1000   MEAN ARGUMENT 47.815   STANDARD DEVIATION 30.875   SUM OF ARGUMENTS 47816.000   NON-WEIGHTED

UPPER LIMIT	OBSERVED FREQUENCY	PER CENT OF TOTAL	CUMULATIVE PERCENTAGE	CUMULATIVE REMAINDER	MULTIPLE OF MEAN	DEVIATION FROM MEAN
0	81	8.09	8.0	91.8	-.000	-1.548
10	75	7.49	15.5	84.3	.209	-1.224
20	94	9.39	24.9	75.0	.418	-.900
30	90	8.99	33.9	66.0	.627	-.577
40	90	8.99	42.9	57.0	.836	-.253
50	93	9.29	52.2	47.7	1.045	.070
60	95	9.49	61.7	38.2	1.254	.394
70	94	9.39	71.1	28.8	1.463	.718
80	101	10.09	81.2	18.7	1.673	1.042
90	95	9.49	90.7	9.2	1.882	1.366
100	69	6.89	97.6	2.3	2.091	1.690
OVERFLOW	23	2.29	100.0	.0		

AVERAGE VALUE OF OVERFLOW 106.86

(b)

FIGURE 5B.3   Selected Program Output for Case Study 5B (with the reorder point set equal to 80). (a) The Table for daily lost sales. (b) The Table for stock-on-hand at the end of each day.

(7) Discussion

Model Logic. In the Figure 5B.1 Block Diagram, note how the model uses one TEST Block in conditional transfer mode, and another TEST Block in refusal mode. Also note how the two model segments communicate with each other through the Savevalue STOCK.

The model is designed for duplication of experimental conditions. The two sources of randomness are daily demand and lead time. Each of the corresponding distributions is represented by a Function (Cards 9 through 16, Figure 5B.2), and each Function has its own random-number sources as an argument. With the RMULT card (Cards 5, 59, and 63 in Figure 5B.2), these random-number sources are set or reset to given starting points before the simulation begins for each different reorder point.

Program Output.[5] Figure 5B.3 shows the lost daily sales and stock-on-hand Tables produced for the simulation corresponding to a reorder point of 80. The number of entries in each Table is 1000, one for each day of the simulation. On average, 0.516 sales were lost each day (MEAN ARGUMENT in the Table LOSES). During the course of the 1000 days simulated, this amounts to 516 lost sales. On about 92 percent of the days, there were *no* lost sales (PER CENT OF TOTAL for an UPPER LIMIT of 0 in the Table LOSES). On one occasion, there were 14 lost sales in a single day.

The Figure 5B.3 Table STOCK indicates that stock-on-hand was approximately uniformly distributed between 0 and 100 units. Average stock-on-hand for the simulation on an IBM 360/67 computer was 14.3 seconds.

[5] Total CPU time for the simulation on an IBM 360/67 computer was 14.3 seconds.

on-hand was 47.8 units. About 8 percent of the time, stock-on-hand was zero at the end of the day's business, exclusive of the possibility that a replenishment order might be due in at the end of that day (PERCENT OF TOTAL for an UPPER LIMIT of 0 in the Table STOCK). On 23 of the simulated days, stock-on-hand at the end of the day exceeded 100 units.

Table 5B.3 shows a summary of the Table output for all three reorder-point alternatives investigated. The trends shown in the table are consistent with expectations. Average daily lost sales decreases as the reorder point is raised. At the same time, the average stock-on-hand increases with an increasing reorder point.

There are many more features of the inventory control problem which could be discussed. Many of these features are included in the set of exercises which follows.

5.10 Exercises

1. These exercises are designed for practice in use of the TEST BLOCK.

(a) An analyst wants a Transaction arriving at Point A in a model to move to the sequential Block if the current content of Queue 1 is less than that of Queue 2; otherwise, the Transaction is to move to the Block at RUTE7. Show the details of the TEST Block the analyst should place at Point A.

(b) Show how to hold a Transaction at Point A in a model until the remaining capacity of the Storage ALPHA exceeds the remaining capacity of the Storage BETA.

(c) When a customer arrives at a certain barber shop, he decides to wait for service only if five or less customers are already waiting for service. Otherwise, he leaves, and does not return later. Show a portion of a Block Diagram to simulate this situation. (Recall that, when a Storage is used to simulate waiting space, the TRANSFER Block can be used in BOTH mode to simulate this same situation. See Figure 2.57.)

(d) A Transaction is to be held at Point A in a model until the utilization of the Facility CRANE exceeds 50 percent. Show how this can be accomplished.

(e) Why is the Block "TEST LE Q1+Q2,Q3, BYPAS" in error? Suggest a method for eliminating the error while accomplishing the apparent purpose of the TEST Block.

(f) When a Transaction reaches Point A in a model, it is to move to the Block in Location LOC1 if Queues ONE, TWO, and THREE are all empty; otherwise, it is to move to LOC2. Show how this can be accomplished.

(g) Transactions arriving at Point A in a model choose their next Block at random. In the long run, 35 percent of them move next to the Block in Location BLOK1; the other 65 percent move next to the Block in Location BLOK2. Show a TEST Block which can be used at Point A to simulate this random selection of a next Block. (Note: the same effect can be accomplished with the TRANSFER Block in statistical transfer mode, as described in Chapter 2. *It is more efficient to use the TRANSFER Block than the TEST Block for this purpose.*)

(h) Show how a Savevalue can be used to simulate a Facility. Discuss the advantages and disadvantages of such a simulation.

(i) Show how a Savevalue can be used to simulate a Storage. Discuss the advantages and disadvantages of such a simulation.

(j) Show the Block Diagram for a self-contained model segment which has the purpose of printing out the value of the Relative Clock each time it changes.

(k) Show the Block Diagram for a self-contained model segment which has the purpose of recording the *difference* between consecutive Relative Clock values in a GPSS Table.

(l) Repeat (j) and (k), only base the problems on the value of the Absolute Clock, not the Relative Clock.

2. These exercises involve using Savevalues to simulate Queues.

(a) Discuss the possibility of using a Savevalue to simulate a Queue. Include in your discussion such things as (1) amount of computer memory saved by such a simulation, (2) probable direction of change in the CPU time requirement, and (3) change in the number of

Reorder Point	Average Daily Lost Sales	Percent of Days Stockout Occurred	Average Stock-on-Hand
80	0.516	7.7	47.8
90	0.173	3.2	55.0
100	0.005	0.4	65.0

TABLE 5B.3 A Summary of Program Output for Case Study 5B

statistics available which describe the waiting process. Can you think of one or more situations in which simulating a Queue with a Savevalue would provide an adequate representation of the Queue?

(b) Show how to use a Savevalue to simulate the Queue in your solution to exercise 1c, thereby making it possible to eliminate the QUEUE/DEPART Block pair.

(c) In Case Study 4D (the bank queuing problem), the only reason for having individual Queues ahead of each teller in the multiple-line system was to provide the "Q_j" statistic for use as the simulation proceeded. Show how to simulate the individual Queues with Savevalues in that problem, thereby eliminating the individual Queues. Do this first of all by leaving both SELECT Blocks in the solution as shown in Case Study 4D. Then do it by an alternative approach, eliminating the first of the two SELECT Blocks in the process. (See exercise 12, Section 4.19.)

3. These exercises refer to Case Study 5B.
(a) What are the numbers of the Transactions used in the Figure 5B.2 simulation?

(b) Show how Transactions in both model segments can have Priority Levels of 0, and still meet the problem condition that replenishment orders come in *after* a day's business has been concluded. Except for eliminating the GENERATE Block E Operand in the Demand segment, do *not* change any other *Blocks* in the model. The Figure 5B.2 model does *not* count replenishment orders received at the end of a day as contributing to that day's entry in the stock-on-hand Table. Show what changes to make in the model to reverse this situation.

(d) A *backorder* is said to be placed when a customer whose demand cannot be met immediately agrees to wait until the next replenishment order arrives to have his demand satisfied. Assume that each customer's demand is for exactly 1 unit of the item, and that the probability is 0.35 that a customer will be willing to backorder. Show what changes to make in the Figure 5B.2 model to incorporate these assumptions.

(e) Assume the probability a backorder will be placed depends on the number of units already on backorder, as shown in Table E3. Show

what changes to make in the Figure 5B.2 model to incorporate these backorder probabilities.

(f) In Case Study 5B, a replenishment order is placed whenever stock-on-hand is less than or equal to the reorder point, *and* no replenishment order is already en route. Show how to modify the Figure 5B.2 model so that a replenishment order is placed whenever the *sum* of stock-on-hand and replenishment orders already en route (if any) is less than or equal to the reorder point.

4. (a) There are usually three cost components in an inventory control problem: the marginal cost of placing a replenishment order; the cost of a lost sale due to stockout; and the cost of carrying inventory. In Case Study 5B, assume that the marginal cost of ordering is $10; the cost of a lost sale (because of the profit thereby lost) is $1; and the cost of carrying 1 unit of inventory for 1 year is 25 percent of the item's $10 cost. By hand, compute the average daily cost for each of the three different reorder-point policies used in Case Study 5B. Which reorder point corresponds to the lowest average daily cost? (From Block Counts not shown in the Case Study 5B program output, there were 90, 93, and 95 replenishment orders placed during the simulations for reorder points of 80, 90, and 100, respectively.)

(b) Using your computations from (a), plot the average daily cost against the reorder point. Does the cost appear to pass through a minimum? If not, use the model to experiment further until the minimum-cost reorder point corresponding to the fixed reorder quantity of 100 has been found.

(c) Show how to modify the Case Study 5B model to automate the computations requested in (a).

5. In the inventory-control problem, average daily cost usually passes through a minimum as the reorder point is varied while the reorder quantity remains fixed. This is suggested in Figure E5(a), where average daily cost is high for low reorder points (because stockout costs contribute inordinately to total costs), and is high again for high reorder points (because carrying costs contribute excessively to total costs). By the same token, average daily cost usually passes through a minimum as the reorder quantity is varied while the reorder point remains fixed, as suggested in Figure E5(b). Low reorder quantities produce high average costs, because of the frequently incurred marginal cost of ordering; and high reorder quantities result in high average costs, because of the large carrying cost component thereby incurred. In a three-dimensional setting, where average daily cost is plotted against reorder point on one axis, and reorder quantity on another, the cost can easily be visualized as passing through

TABLE E3

Number of Units Already Backordered	Backorder Probability
0–2	0.98
3–5	0.80
6–8	0.50
9–10	0.20
More than 10	0.0

a minimum. (The discussion in Case Study 2E should now be reviewed. In that problem, cost also depended on the choice of two independent decision variables, and was visualized as passing through a minimum. The univariate searching strategy was explained as a technique with which to methodically search for the low-cost point.)

In Case Study 5B, let both the reorder point *and* the reorder quantity be variable. Using the cost information given in exercise 4, experiment with the model to find the reorder-point and reorder-quantity combination for which the average daily cost is a minimum.

6. In an inventory control setting, an important random variable is lead-time demand. Lead-time demand is the total demand that occurs while lead time elapses. It is dependent on both the daily-demand distribution, and the lead-time distribution. Build a GPSS model to estimate the distribution of lead-time demand for the data given in Case Study 5B. Base the distribution estimate on a sample consisting of 1000 lead-time experiences. Use the output to estimate where the retailer should set his reorder point if the probability of stockout is to be (a) 0.05, (b) 0.10, and (c) 0.15.

7. This problem involves a scheduling-period, target-level approach to inventory control, in contrast with the reorder-point, reorder-quantity approach used in Case Study 5B.

A retailer knows from past records that the daily demand for a certain item varies randomly according to the pattern in Table E7(a). The lead

TABLE E7(a)

Quantity Demanded	Relative Frequency
0	0.30
1	0.35
2	0.13
3	0.11
4	0.07
5	0.04

time required for replenishment orders to be filled is distributed as shown in Table E7(b). When the retailer is out of stock, the probability is 0.65 that,

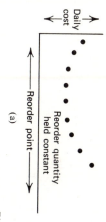

(a)

(b)

FIGURE E5

instead of backordering, a customer will go elsewhere to have his order filled.

TABLE E7(b)

Lead Time (days)	Relative Frequency
4	0.30
7	0.60
8	0.10

The retailer controls his supply of the item by placing replenishment orders at the opening of business either every Monday, or every second Monday. (The number of weeks between replenishment orders is termed the *scheduling period*.) As the lead-time data show, his replenishment order then arrives at the opening of business on a Friday, Monday, or Tuesday. He is not open for business on Saturday or Sunday.

The retailer's reorder quantity is *variable*. It is computed by subtracting the number of units of stock-on-hand from a predetermined, invariant value, called the *target level*.

The cost of placing a replenishment order is $40. Carrying cost is $1 per item per day (including weekends). The cost of a lost sale is $100.

Build a GPSS model to simulate this situation. Then use the model to determine whether the scheduling period should be 1 or 2 weeks, and what the target level should be if the objective is to minimize average weekly cost. Cost computations should be included as part of the model.

5.11 The Concept and Use of Weighted Tables

There are occasions when particular observed values of a random variable should be entered into a Table not just once, but two or more times. For example, suppose that the activities at a harbor are being modeled. Assume that whenever a ship moves into or out of a berth, the services of one or two tugs are needed, depending on the type of ship involved. If there are two tugs at the harbor and a Storage is used to simulate them, then the *average* holding time per tug capture is available in the standard output for the Storage. Suppose, however, that it is of interest to estimate the *distribution* of the random variable holding time per tug capture, and not just its average value. Values of this random variable can be sampled by recording the time of tug capture in ship-Transaction Parameter *j*, then placing the value of MP*j* in a Table when the ship releases the tug, or tugs. If the ship has had *one* tug captured during the capture–release interval, the value of MP*j* should be placed in the Table *once*. If the ship has had *two* tugs captured, however, the value of MP*j* should be placed in the Table *twice*. In effect, by using two tugs, a single ship causes two observations to be made for the random variable of interest.

In the above example, one way to have the value of MP*j* entered into a Table twice would be to have two consecutive TABULATE Blocks in the model. This would require, however, that only ship-Transactions of the two-tug type be permitted to move through the model segment in question. Furthermore, as will be seen later in this section, the number of times a given observation is to be entered into a Table is itself often random, making it literally impossible to include the right number of consecutive TABULATE Blocks in a model.

To accommodate situations like the one just described, the GPSS Processor makes an optional B Operand available for the TABULATE Block. The B Operand is termed a *weighting factor*. It indicates the *number of times* the value

being tabulated is to be entered into the corresponding Table *each time* the TABULATE Block is executed. This makes it possible to assign relatively higher weights to some observations than to others. Tables in which such weight distinctions are made are termed *weighted Tables*.

Figure 5.18 repeats the specifications for the TABULATE Block, with the role of the B Operand and indicated. Note that the default value of the B Operand is 1. Hence, if the B Operand is not used, the observed value is entered into the referenced Table just one time per TABULATE Block execution. More often than not, the analyst defaults on the TABULATE Block's B Operand, and, thereby making use of what is called an *unweighted Table*.

When a Table is weighted, the first character in the D Operand on the Table definition card must be the letter W. This is true even if the analyst enters a value of "1" for the B Operand on all the associated TABULATE Blocks. That is, whenever the TABULATE Block's B Operand is provided explicitly, instead of by default, the corresponding Table is understood to be weighted.

Figure 5.19 shows an example of a weighted Table named HTIME. The Table definition card is shown in Figure 5.19(a). Note the presence of W as the first character in the D Operand. Also note that the variable whose value is tabulated is Transaction transit time, as supported through use of Transaction Parameter 2. Whenever a Transaction moves into the Figure 5.19(b) TABULATE Block, the value of MP2 will be computed and entered in the Table HTIME a

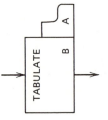

Operand	Significance	Default Value of Result
A	Name (numeric or symbolic) of the Table into which a value is to be entered	Error
B	The number of times the value is to be entered in the Table *each time* a Transaction moves into the TABULATE Block	1

FIGURE 5.18   The TABULATE Block and its A and B Operands

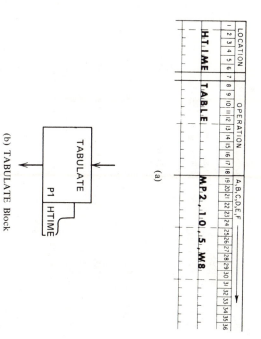

FIGURE 5.19   An example showing use of a GPSS weighted table. (a) Definition of the weighted table. (b) The TABULATE Block at which the weighted table is referenced.

number of times equal to the value of Transaction Parameter 1. If P1 has a value of 1, the value of MP2 will be placed in the Table once; if P1 has a value of 2, the value of MP2 will be placed in the Table twice; and so on. Now suppose that a Transaction simulates a ship, and that the value of Transaction Parameter 1 can be interpreted as the number of tugs that ship needs in order to move into or out of a berth. Then, if the ship-Transaction moves through the Block "MARK 2" just after capturing the required tug or tugs, and moves into the Figure 5.19(b) TABULATE Block just after releasing the tug or tugs, the result is to tabulate the distribution of the random variable "holding time per tug capture."

To further illustrate the use of weighted Tables, consider the random variables "length of a waiting line," and "residence time in a waiting line." An estimate of the *average* line length and the *average* in-line residence time is included in the standard Queue statistics provided by GPSS. Furthermore, GPSS provides Qtables to estimate the *distribution* of in-line residence time. No provisions are made in the language, however, for automatically estimating the distribution of line length. If the analyst wants such an estimate, he must provide the required logic.

Consider how one goes about estimating the distribution of line length. It is not enough simply to record the line length each time it changes, then produce an estimate from the resulting list of numbers. Instead, the time interval during which the line was at a given length must be taken into account, too. The role of the time interval is shown for a specific example in Figure 5.20, where line length is plotted vs. time in a

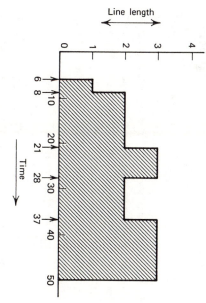

FIGURE 5.20   Fluctuations in the length of a waiting line in a hypothetical situation

hypothetical situation. As suggested in the figure, line-length observations were made over an interval of 50 time units. During this period, the line was of length 0 for 6 time units; of length 1 for 2 time units; of length 2 for 22 time units (13 time units from time 8 to time 21; then another 9 time units from time 28 to time 37); and of length 3 for 20 time units (7 time units from time 21 to time 28; then another 13 time units from time 37 to time 50). Hence, the *relative frequency* with which the line was of length 0 was 12 percent (6 time units out of 50), and so on. These ideas are summarized in Table 5.5.

TABLE 5.5   Relative Frequencies of the Various Line Lengths in Figure 5.20

Line Length	Total Time Spanned While Line was at that Length	Relative Frequency at that Length (percent)
0	6	12
1	2	4
2	22	44
3	20	40
Total:	50	

If the distribution of line length is to be estimated, one way to make the necessary observations is to record line length in a Table at each unit of time. For the Figure 5.20 example, then, a value of 0 would be placed in a Table at simulated times 1, 2, 3, 4, 5, and 6; then, a value of 1 would be recorded at simulated times 7 and 8; a value of 2 would be recorded at simulated times 9, 10, 11, etc. Such an approach would give due weight to the time through which the line was at a given length. To support the approach in GPSS, however, a Transaction would have to enter a TABULATE Block at simulated times 1, 2, 3, etc. The *strong disadvantage* of this would be to force the simulated clock to move forward in fixed increments of 1. The variable time increment feature of the GPSS clock would thereby be lost, with negative implications in terms of CPU time requirements.

A *better* approach in GPSS would be to record line length in a Table only whenever there is a net change in that length. To give due weight to the time interval spanned while the line was at a given length, the length statistic could be recorded in the Table a number of times equal to the number of time units spanned. For example, at simulated time 6 in Figure 5.20, the value 0 would be placed in a Table 6 times; at simulated time 8, the value 1 would be placed in the Table 2 times; at simulated time 21, the value 2 would be placed in the Table 13 times, and so on. By supplying the number of time units spanned as the B Operand at a TABULATE Block, this can easily be accomplished.

Unfortunately, there is a flaw in the "line-length change" approach just described. The flaw comes about because of the possibility that the *last* line length observed will not be recorded in the Table before the simulation ends. To illustrate, consider Figure 5.20. Assume that the underlying simulation corresponding to that figure ends at simulated time 50. Between times 37 and 50, the line length does not change; it remains constant at 3. Hence, if the line length is recorded in a Table only when there is a line-length change, then no entry is made in the Table at simulated time 50. One of the observations made on the line length would consequently go unrecorded.

The flaw described can be corrected by recording line length in a Table *whenever the clock changes,* instead of just when the length changes. In general, there will then be more entries made in the Table than there would be with the line-length change approach. For example, in Figure 5.20, suppose that the clock takes on consecutive values, in part, of 8, 12, 17, and 21. Then, although the line length remains constant at 2

during the time interval between 8 and 21, the value 2 would be recorded in the Table on 3 different occasions during this interval. (The value 2 would be placed in the Table 4 times at time 12; 5 times at time 17; and 4 times at time 21.) In the line-length change approach, the value 2 would simply be placed in the Table 13 times at time 21. The end results, however, would be the same. The clock change approach does have the virtue of not affecting the variable time increment feature of the GPSS simulator. Of equal importance, it has the virtue of recording all observations made on the line length, including the last.

Figure 5.21 shows the Block Diagram for a self-contained GPSS model segment which implements the clock change approach for estimating the distribution of line length for a Queue arbitrarily named ONE. A single Transaction circulates through the segment during a simulation. The Transaction enters the model at simulated time 1, then immediately saves a copy of

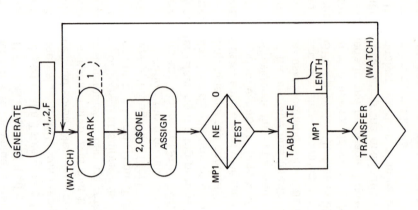

FIGURE 5.21   A self-contained Model Segment for estimating the distribution of the current content of the Queue named ONE

the Absolute Clock in Parameter 1. (Note that the Parameters are fullword; if they were half-word, and if and when the clock's value exceed-ed 32,767, an overflow error would occur at the MARK Block.) The Transaction then copies the current line length into Parameter 2. Next, the Transaction waits at a refusal-mode TEST Block until its residence time there no longer equals zero, i.e., until the clock has changed. When a clock change occurs, the Transaction enters a TABULATE Block, recording the line length pre-viously observed at the old clock time. (This re-quires that P2 be used as the A Operand on the definition card for the Table LENTH.) MP1 is used as the weighting factor at the TABULATE Block. This means that the previously-observed line length is entered in the Table once for each simulated time unit over which the clock jumped in arriving at its current value. The Transaction then goes back to update its saved copies of clock time and line length, and proceeds to wait again at the TEST Block until there is another change in the clock.

It is assumed in the Figure 5.21 model seg-ment, of course, that elsewhere in the model a Queue named ONE has been used. The fact that there are other parts to the model raises the ques-tion of Priority Levels. After the Input Phase and the first Clock Update Phase have been per-formed, the Figure 5.21 Transaction is on the Current Events Chain. Does it matter *where* the Transaction is on the Current Chain? It does indeed matter. The reason is that the Transaction makes only one line-length ob-servation per reading of the simulation clock. It is important, then, that this observation be made only *after* the model has been fully updated at each clock reading. (But see exercise 4 in Section 5.12.) Otherwise, some intermediate value of the line length might be the one observed; but this might not be the one in effect the next time the clock is incremented. The results would then not be logically sound.

The Figure 5.21 Transaction should make its line-length observation, then, just before the Processor finishes each Scan Phase prior to entering the next Clock Update Phase. This can be achieved by forcing the Transaction to be last on the Current Events Chain. In other words, the Priority Level of the Figure 5.21 Transaction must be lower than that of any other Transaction in the model. The Priority Level of the Figure 5.21

Transaction is 0. It is assumed, therefore, that all other Transactions in the rest of the model have Priority Levels of 1 or more, *with the exception of the timer-Transaction*. The timer-Transaction must also have a Priority Level of 0 when the Figure 5.21 model segment is used. Then, when the timer is finally brought to the Current Events Chain, *it* will be last on the chain. This guaran-tees that the last observation will be recorded in the line-length Table *before* the simulation shuts off at the final clock reading.

Now consider use of the Figure 5.21 model segment with the one-line queuing model pre-sented in Case Study 4D ("Comparison of Alter-native Queuing Systems in a Bank"). Figure 5.22 shows the Extended Program Listing for the one-line model originally presented in Figure 4D.2(a), but now augmented by inclusion of the Figure 5.21 segment. Figure 5.23(a) and (b) show the standard Queue statistics and the weighted Table information produced when the Figure 5.22 model was run. As indicated in the Table, the line was empty 14.82 percent of the time, was of length 5 or less (but not empty) 16.64 percent of the time, and so on.

Note in Figure 5.23(b) that two rows of num-bers appear under the labels ENTRIES IN TABLE, MEAN ARGUMENT, STANDARD DEVIATION, and SUM OF ARGUMENTS. As indicated, the first row of numbers contains those values on a NON-WEIGHTED basis. The second row shows the corresponding WEIGHTED values. The OB-SERVED FREQUENCY information, etc., in the rest of the Table is based on the weighted values.

Recall that the Table Standard Numerical At-tributes are TBj (Table average), TDj (Table standard deviation), and TCj (number of entries in the Table). As Figure 5.23(b) indicates, both a weighted and a nonweighted set of these values is maintained when a weighted Table is used. The question then naturally arises, to which of these two sets do the Table Standard Numerical Attributes apply? The answer is that the Table SNA's apply to the *nonweighted* set of values. This is unfortunate, because it is presumably the *weighted* mean, standard deviation, and number of Table entries which are of interest to the an-alyst if he is using a weighted Table in the first place. Even though the weighted values do ap-pear in the output, then, they *cannot* be accessed during the course of a simulation through use of the Table Standard Numerical Attributes.

FIGURE 5.22 Extended Program Listing for the Figure 4D.3(a) model, as supplemented by inclusion of the Figure 5.21 Model Segment

BLOCK NUMBER	*LOC	OPERATION	A,B,C,D,E,F,G	COMMENTS	CARD NUMBER
		SIMULATE			1
		*			2
		*	FUNCTION DEFINITION(S)		3
		*			4
5		FUNCTION	RN1,C24	EXPONENTIAL DISTRIBUTION FUNCTION	5
	0.0/.1,.104/.2,.222/.3,.355/.4,.509/.5,.69/.6,.915/.7,1.2/.75,1.38				6
	.8,1.6/.84,1.83/.88,2.12/.9,2.3/.92,2.52/.94,2.81/.95,2.99/.96,3.2				7
	.97,3.5/.98,3.9/.99,4.6/.995,5.3/.998,6.2/.999,7/.9998,8				8
	MEAN FUNCTION RN1,D5			DISTRIBUTION OF MEAN SERVICE TIME	9
	.1,450/.29,750/.61,1000/.85,1500/1,3000				10
		*			11
		*	STORAGE CAPACITY DEFINITION(S)		12
		*			13
		STORAGE	S$TELRS,8	PROVIDE 8 TELLERS	14
		*			15
		*	TABLE DEFINITION(S)		16
		*			17
	LENTH	TABLE	P2,0,5,W14	WEIGHTED TABLE FOR LINE LENGTH	18
		*			19
		*	MODEL SEGMENT 1		20
		*			21
1		GENERATE	180,FN5,,1,1	CUSTOMERS ARRIVE	22
2		ASSIGN	1,FN$MEAN,5	SET P1 = SERVICE TIME	23
3		QUEUE	ONE	ENTER THE LINE	24
4		ENTER	TELRS	ENGAGE A TELLER	25
5		DEPART	ONE	LEAVE THE LINE	26
6		ADVANCE	P1	TRANSACT BUSINESS	27
7		LEAVE	TELRS	FREE THE TELLER	28
8		TERMINATE		LEAVE THE BANK	29
		*			30
		*	MODEL SEGMENT 2		31
		*			32
9		GENERATE	,,,1,,2,F	SEED THE LENGTH-OBSERVATION SEGMENT	33
10	WATCH	MARK	1	SET P1 = ABSOLUTE CLOCK TIME	34
11		ASSIGN	2,Q$ONE	SET P2 = CURRENT LINE LENGTH	35
12		TEST NE	MP1,0	WAIT FOR THE CLOCK TO CHANGE	36
13		TABULATE	LENTH,MP1	RECORD LENGTH OBSERVED AT OLD CLOCK	37
		*		TIME, WEIGHTED BY THE CLOCK INCREMENT	38
14		TRANSFER	,WATCH	GO SET UP FOR THE NEXT OBSERVATION	39
		*			40
		*	MODEL SEGMENT 3		41
		*			42
15		GENERATE	180000	TIMER ARRIVES AFTER 5 HOURS	43
16		TERMINATE	1	SHUT OFF THE RUN	44
		*			45
		*	CONTROL CARDS		46
		*			47
		START	1	START THE RUN FOR DAY 1	48
		END		RETURN CONTROL TO OPERATING SYSTEM	49

(a)

FIGURE 5.23 Selected output produced when the Figure 5.22 model was run

QUEUE	MAXIMUM CONTENTS	AVERAGE CONTENTS	TOTAL ENTRIES	ZERO ENTRIES	PERCENT ZEROS	AVERAGE TIME/TRANS	$AVERAGE TIME/TRANS	TABLE NUMBER	CURRENT CONTENTS
ONE	51	14.138	1001	121	12.0	2542.459	2892.047		

$AVERAGE TIME/TRANS = AVERAGE TIME/TRANS EXCLUDING ZERO ENTRIES

TABLE LENTH	MEAN ARGUMENT	STANDARD DEVIATION	SUM OF ARGUMENTS
ENTRIES IN TABLE 1984	14.276	12.101	28324.000
179999	14.138	12.027	2545002.000

UPPER LIMIT	OBSERVED FREQUENCY	PER CENT OF TOTAL	CUMULATIVE PERCENTAGE	CUMULATIVE REMAINDER	MULTIPLE OF MEAN	DEVIATION FROM MEAN	NON-WEIGHTED / WEIGHTED
0	26690	14.82	14.8	85.1	-.000	-1.179	
5	29954	16.64	31.4	68.5	.350	-.766	
10	22976	12.76	44.2	55.7	.700	-.353	
15	25310	14.06	58.2	41.7	1.050	.059	
20	27654	15.36	73.6	26.3	1.400	.472	
25	14319	7.95	81.6	18.3	1.751	.886	
30	13297	7.38	89.0	10.9	2.101	1.299	
35	8388	4.66	93.6	6.3	2.451	1.712	
40	6277	3.48	97.1	2.8	2.801	2.125	
45	2370	1.31	98.4	1.5	3.152	2.538	
50	2372	1.31	99.7	.2	3.502	2.951	
55	392	.21	100.0	.0	3.852	3.365	

REMAINING FREQUENCIES ARE ALL ZERO

(b)

5.12 Exercises

1. Explain the difference between the two Tables whose Table cards are shown in Figure E1.

LOCATION																																				OPERATION	A,B,C,D,E,F
1	2	3	4	5	6	7	8	9	10	11	12	13	14	15	16	17	18	19	20	21	22	23	24	25	26	27	28	29	30	31	32	33	34	35	36	---	---
ONE.																																				TABLE	PR,0,5,20
TWO.																																				TABLE	PR,0,5,W20

FIGURE E1

2. Three Transactions, with P2 values of 2, 3, and 4, respectively, move through the Block "TABULATE TABL4". In the same model, two other Transactions, each with a P2 value of 5, move through the Block "TABULATE TABL4,2". Assuming no other references have been made to the Table, what are the values of TB$TABL4 and TC$TABL4 after this has happened? What must be true of the D Operand on TABL4's Table card?

3. These questions all concern Figure 5.21.

   (a) In Chapter 2, it was pointed out that the earliest simulated time at which Transactions can experience movement in a model is 1. This means that the content of all Queues in a model is necessarily zero during the simulated time interval from 0 to 1, all Facilities are necessarily "available" during the simulated time interval 0 to 1, etc. Because statistics such as average Queue content, Facility utilization, and so on, are computed as though the simulation started at time 0, a slight bias is consequently introduced into these statistics.

   In Figure 5.21, no provision is made to place a value in the Table indicating that the Queue ONE is of length zero during the simulated time interval from 0 to 1. Show how to modify the Figure 5.21 segment so that such a value will be placed in the Table. Then discuss the extent to which you think it is either fair or unfair to do this.

   (b) Suppose that the observer-Transaction in Figure 5.21 is given a Priority Level of 1. What effect would this have on the range of Priority Levels that could be assigned to other Transactions in the model?

   (c) Critically discuss this statement: "The observer-Transaction in Figure 5.21 is encountered by the GPSS Processor exactly one time during each Scan Phase."

4. The approach used in the Figure 5.21 model segment is to have the single Transaction circulating in that segment always be last on the Current Events Chain (except at the last clock reading, when the timer Transaction is placed behind it on the CEC). Show the details of an equivalent model segment in which the circulating Transaction is always the first Transaction on the Current Events Chain. Then discuss your model segment with respect to these issues.

   (a) Placement of an observation in the Table indicating that the Queue ONE is of length zero during the simulated time interval from 0 to 1.

   (b) Priority Level of the observer-Transaction.

   (c) Number of Parameters which the observer-Transaction must have.

   (d) Number of Blocks necessary in the self-contained model segment.

   (e) The number of times the observer-Transaction is likely to be encountered by the GPSS Processor during each Scan Phase.

5. Exercise 15, Section 2.41, involves a harbor used by two different types of ships. One type requires only one tug to berth or deberth; the other type requires two tugs. Show how to build a model for the problem which gathers the information originally requested in that exercise, and in addition estimates the distribution of the random variable "holding time per tug capture." Minimize the number of Blocks in the model by using indirect specification wherever possible.

6. In the standard output for Storages, the GPSS Processor includes the average value of the random variable "number of servers captured." Suppose it is of interest to estimate the distribution of this random variable. Show how this can be done for the Case Study 4D model shown in Figure 4D.2(a), where eight tellers at a bank are modeled with a Storage.

7. When parallel servers are modeled with parallel Facilities, the GPSS Processor provides no summary information about the random variable "number of servers captured." Show how the distribution of this random variable can be estimated for the Case Study 4D model shown in Figure 4D.2(b), where eight tellers at a bank are modeled with eight Facilities in parallel.

8. In exercise 15, Section 2.41, show how to estimate the distribution of the random variable "holding time per berth capture," as a function of the type of berth involved. Is it necessary to use a weighted Table in this case? Why, or why not?

9. The in-line residence-time distribution estimated by using a Qtable includes zero entries. Show how to estimate the in-line residence-time distribution when zero entries are excluded. In par-

ticular, show how to do this in the Case Study 4D model shown in Figure 4D.2(a), where a single line forms for use of parallel tellers at a bank. Is it necessary to use a weighted Table? Why, or why not?

10. In exercise 8, Section 4.25, show how to estimate the distribution of the random variable "number of ships at the harbor." Is it necessary to make use of a weighted Table? Why, or why not?

5.13 Matrix Savevalues: The MATRIX Card, the INITIAL Card, and the MSAVEVALUE Block

The Savevalues introduced in Section 5.5 are essentially linear arrays. Hence, X5 is a reference to the fifth element in a linear array consisting of fullword memory locations. Similarly, XH12 is a reference to the twelfth element in a linear array consisting of halfword memory locations. The Savevalue concept in GPSS is also valid for two-dimensional arrays, or matrices. Such Savevalues are termed Matrix Savevalues, or simply Matrices.

The method of declaring the existence of Matrices will now be discussed. Then their pertinent properties will be explained, and the method of presetting their values before a simulation starts, and modifying their values as a simulation proceeds, will be described. Finally, the effect of RESET and CLEAR cards on Matrices will be indicated.

5.13.1 The MATRIX Card

Unlike linear-array Savevalues, Matrix Save-values must have their existence declared to the GPSS Processor at the start of a simulation. This is done by providing, for each different Matrix, a MATRIX card. The card takes the form shown in Table 5.6. The Location field carries the numeric or symbolic name of the Matrix whose existence is being declared. The word MATRIX is entered in the Operation field. The A Operand is the single

TABLE 5.6 Format for the Card Used to Declare the Existence of a Matrix

Punchcard Field	Information Supplied in Field
Location	Name (numeric or symbolic) of the Matrix
Operation	Literally, the word MATRIX
Operands	
A	H or X, depending on whether the Matrix is to consist of halfword or fullword memory locations, respectively
B	A constant indicating the number of rows in the matrix
C	A constant indicating the number of columns in the matrix

character H or X, depending on whether the Matrix is to consist of halfword or fullword memory locations, respectively. The B and C Operands are constants which specify the number of rows and columns, respectively, of which the Matrix is to be composed.

Several examples of MATRIX cards are shown in Figure 5.24. In the first example, the Matrix symbolically named PHI is declared to be of the fullword type and to consist of three rows and five columns. In the second example, fullword Matrix 3 is declared to be composed of one row and ten columns. The third example shows how the halfword Matrix 5 is established as consisting of ten rows and four columns.

The MATRIX card must be placed in the deck ahead of any references to the Matrix in question.

5.13.2 Properties of Matrices

Each particular *Matrix* has a numeric or symbolic name, and consists entirely of either halfword or fullword memory locations. Each *element* in a Matrix, in turn, occupies a position in a particular row and a particular column in that Matrix. Hence,

LOCATION	OPERATION	A,B,C,D,E,F
1 2 3 4 5 6 7	8 9 10 11 12 13	14 15 16 17 18 19 20 21 22 23 24 25 26 27 28 29 30 31 32 33 34 35 36 37 38 39 40 41 42 43 44 45 46 47 48
PHI	MATRIX	X,3,5 FIRST EXAMPLE
3	MATRIX	X,1,10 SECOND EXAMPLE
5	MATRIX	H,10,4 THIRD EXAMPLE

FIGURE 5.24 Examples showing use of the Table 5.6 card format

the name of a Matrix *element* consists of these four pieces of information:

1. The Matrix type (halfword or fullword).
2. Name of the Matrix.
3. Number of the row occupied by the element (row subscript).
4. Number of the column occupied by the element (column subscript).

MH and MX are used to indicate halfword and fullword Matrix types, respectively. Immediately following the MH or MX is the number, or symbolic name, of the Matrix in question. (If a symbolic name is used, a dollar sign must be placed between the MH or MX and the symbolic name.) The row and column subscripts come last, appearing in that order, enclosed in parentheses, and separated by a comma. Hence, "MH3(2.7)" is a reference to the element in row 2, column 7, in halfword Matrix 3. "MX$JOE (4.3)" refers to the element in row 4, column 3, in the fullword Matrix symbolically named JOE. Of course, row and column subscripts can also be provided by indirect specification. For example, "MX2(P1,P2)" refers to an element in fullword Matrix 2. The element's row and column numbers are to be found in Parameters 1 and 2, respectively, of the Transaction currently being processed.

The values of Matrix elements are signed integers. The values can range between −32,768 and +32,767, inclusive, for halfword Matrices; and between −2,147,483,648 and +2,147,483,647, inclusive, for fullword Matrices.

The normal quantity of Savevalues depends on the amount of computer memory available. With 64K bytes of memory, for example, there are normally five halfword and five fullword Matrices available. Of course, the number of elements in each Matrix will depend on the way the Matrices have been dimensioned with the corresponding MATRIX cards.

As Standard Numerical Attributes, Matrix elements can be used to indirectly provide data for Block Operands, and so on. For example, each time a Transaction moves into the Block "ADVANCE MH2(1,5),P2", the mean holding time is determined by sampling from the uniform distribution MH2(1,5)±P2. The value of the element in row 1, column 5, of halfword Matrix 2 would be used as the mean of the distribution, and the value of Parameter 2 would be used as the Spread Modifier.

At the end of a simulation, all Matrices are automatically printed out. Entire Matrices can also be outputted during a run by use of the PRINT Block. This is accomplished by providing MX, or MH, as the Block's field C mnemonic. For example, when a Transaction moves into the Block "PRINT 1,3,MX", fullword Matrices 1, 2, and 3 will be printed out.

The way Matrices appear when they are printed out is illustrated in Figure 5.25. Halfword Matrix Savevalue number 2 is shown in the figure. It

MATRIX HALFWORD SAVEVALUE 2

	COL. 1	2	3	4	5
ROW 1	600	200	350	1250	0
2	650	900	1050	0	0
3	250	300	500	2500	2350

FIGURE 5.25 Example of a halfword Matrix Savevalue as it appears in output produced by the GPSS Processor

consists of 3 rows, and 5 columns. The Matrix cell in row 1, column 1, contains a value of 600; in row 1, column 2, a value of 200; and so on. Three of the cells contain values of 0.

5.13.3 The INITIAL Card

Normally, the GPSS Processor sets the value of all Matrix elements to zero before a simulation begins. At the analyst's option, selected Matrix elements can be initialized with nonzero values by use of the INITIAL card. The card takes the form shown in Figure 5.26. As indicated, the Location field is not used. The word INITIAL is entered in the Operation field. The "basic unit" of information in the Operands field is of the form "name;,value;", where name; is the name of the *i*th Matrix element being initialized, and value; is the initial value. Examples of "basic units" are "MX2(1,1),−555", "MH$ANN(5,2),77", and "MH1(2,3),20". The "value" entry in a basic unit can range from −32,768 to 32,767, inclusive, for halfword Matrix Savevalues, and from −2,147,483,648 to 2,147,483,647, inclusive, for fullword Matrix Savevalues.

Slashes are used to separate the "basic units" on an INITIAL card. No blanks are allowed within or between consecutive basic units. No information can be entered beyond card column 71. If there is not room enough on one card to ini-

Location	Operation	Operands
Not Used	INITIAL	$name_1,value_1/ \ldots /name_i,value_i/ \ldots /name_n,value_n$

FIGURE 5.26   Card format for Matrix initialization

tialize all the Matrix elements of interest, more than one INITIAL card must be used.

Figure 5.27 provides several examples of the Matrix INITIAL card. In the first example, one element in each of three different Matrices is initialized with a nonzero value. This example shows that there are no restrictions on the order in which the basic units appear on the INITIAL card. It is not necessary to group the halfword or fullword Matrices together; furthermore, it is not necessary that the numbers of the Matrices involved be in ascending order. (Note that the Location field, which is not used anyway, is not shown in Figure 5.27.)

If entries in a series of consecutive positions in a row are to be identical, a basic unit taking the form corresponding to "MX3(1,1–3),2" in the second example can be used. In this example, the Processor will assign 2 as the initial value of the three elements in row 1, columns 1, 2, and 3, in fullword Matrix 3.

Similarly, when a series of consecutive positions in a column are to have the same initial value, a basic unit like "MH2(2–5,3),–1" in the third example can be used. This unit causes the Processor to assign –1 as the initial value of the four elements in column 3, rows 2, 3, 4, and 5, in halfword Matrix 2.

Row and column ranges, as exemplified in the second and third examples, can be indicated in a single basic unit. In the fourth example, elements in the rectangular region bounded by rows 1 through 5 and columns 1 through 10 in the halfword Matrix PETE are initialized with the value 1.

Finally, it is also possible to express ranges of Matrices with the INITIAL card. In the fifth ex-

ample in Figure 5.27, elements in rows 1, 2, and 3 in column 4 of fullword Matrices 1, 2, 3, 4, and 5 are given initial values of 5.

Basic units of the type illustrated in examples two, three, four, and five can be intermixed with those of the type shown in example one.

INITIAL cards for Matrix elements which supply Operand values involving interarrival times at GENERATE Blocks should appear in the model deck ahead of the GENERATE Block images. Otherwise, arrival of the first Transaction at the corresponding GENERATE Blocks will be scheduled when the pertinent Matrix elements are still zero in value.

5.13.4 The MSAVEVALUE Block

The value of one Matrix element is modified when a Transaction moves into an MSAVEVALUE Block. This Block, and its A, B, C, D, and E Operands, are shown in Figure 5.28. When a Transaction moves into a MSAVEVALUE Block, the D Operand data becomes the value of the Matrix element occupying the "B row" and the "C column" in the "A Matrix." Because there may be both a halfword and a fullword Matrix with the same name (whether numeric or symbolic), the E Operand is provided to indicate which of the two types is involved. When the E Operand is not used, the Matrix is understood to be of the fullword type. To indicate that a halfword Matrix is being referenced, the character H must be supplied as the E Operand.

Similar to the ASSIGN and the SAVEVALUE Blocks, the MSAVEVALUE Block can be used in increment mode and decrement mode, as well

OPERATION	A,B,C,D,E,F	
INITIAL	MX5(2,4),6/MH$M1M1(1,2),10.0/MX4(5,5),–99	FIRST EXAMPLE
INITIAL	MX3(1,1–3),2	SECOND EXAMPLE
INITIAL	MH2(2–5,3),–1	THIRD EXAMPLE
INITIAL	MH$PETE(1–5,1–10),1	FOURTH EXAMPLE
INITIAL	MX1–MX5(1–3,4),5	FIFTH EXAMPLE

FIGURE 5.27   Examples showing use of the Figure 5.26 card format

as in replacement mode. In increment mode, the previous value of the Matrix element is incremented by the D Operand data. In decrement mode, it is decremented by the D Operand data. Increment and decrement mode are specified by placing a plus or minus sign, respectively, ahead of the comma which separates the A and B Operands.

5.13.5 The Effect of RESET and CLEAR Cards on Matrices

Matrix values are not changed by the RESET card. They are, however, all set to zero by the Processor when the CLEAR card is encountered. No "selective CLEAR card" option is available for Matrix Savevalues as it is for the Savevalues introduced earlier. If selected Matrix elements are to be nonzero before the next simulation starts, corresponding INITIAL cards must be placed in the deck between the CLEAR card and the next occurrence of a START card.

5.14 CASE STUDY 5C
Simulation of a Production Shop

(1) Statement of the Problem

A certain production shop is comprised of six different groups of machines. Each group consists of a certain number of machines of a given kind, as indicated in Table 5C.1. For example, group 1 consists of 14 casting units. Within any single group, the machines are identical to each other. It does not matter, then, which particular casting unit is used to perform a casting operation, or which particular shaper is used to perform a shaping operation, etc.

TABLE 5C.1   Composition of Machine-Groups in the Case Study 5C Production Shop

Group Number	Machines Kind	Machines in Group Number
1	Casting units	14
2	Lathes	5
3	Planers	4
4	Drill presses	8
5	Shapers	16
6	Polishing machines	4

Three different types of jobs move through the production shop. These job-types are designated as Type 1, Type 2, and Type 3. Each job-type requires that operations be performed at specified kinds of machines in a specified sequence. The total number and kind of machines each job-type must visit, and the corresponding visitation sequences, are shown in Table 5C.2. For example, jobs of Type 1 must visit a total of four machines. The machines themselves, listed in the sequence in which they must be visited, are casting unit, planer, lathe, and polishing machine. The table also shows the mean time required by each job-type for each operation that must be per-

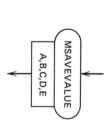

FIGURE 5.28   The MSAVEVALUE Block, and its A, B, C, D, and E Operands

Operand	Significance	Default Value or Result
A	Name (numeric or symbolic) of the Matrix in which an element is to be modified	Error
B	Row subscript	Error
C	Column subscript	Error
D	Data to be used in the modification process	Error
E	The character H indicates that the Matrix involved is of the halfword type; if a fullword Matrix is intended, the E Operand is left blank	Matrix is of the fullword type

TABLE 5C.2 Visitation Sequences and Mean Operation Times for the Three Types of Jobs in Case Study 5C

Job Type	Total Number of Machines to be Visited	Machine Visitation Sequence	Mean Operation Time (minutes)
1	4	Casting unit	125
		Planer	35
		Lathe	20
		Polishing machine	60
2	3	Shaper	105
		Drill press	90
		Lathe	65
3	5	Casting unit	235
		Shaper	250
		Drill press	50
		Planer	30
		Polishing machine	25

formed on it. For example, the casting unit operation for job-type 1 requires 125 minutes, on average. These operation times are all exponentially distributed.

Jobs arrive at the shop in a Poisson stream at a mean rate of 50 jobs per 8-hour day. Twenty-four percent of the jobs in this stream are of Type 1, 44 percent are of Type 2, and the rest are of Type 3. Whether an arriving job is of Type 1, 2, or 3 is independent of the job type of the preceding arrival.

Build a GPSS model which simulates the operation of the production shop. Run the model for the equivalent of 5 40-hour working weeks. At the end of each week, print out (1) the distribution of job residence time in the shop, as a function of job-type, and (2) the distribution of the total number of jobs in the shop, based on observations made at the end of each day during the week. Instead of aggregating the statistics, week after week, gather statistics which are segregated by week. Assume that the queue discipline used at each machine group is first-come, first-served, independent of job-type. Assume there are no discontinuities in moving between consecutive 8-hour work days.

(2) Approach Taken in Building the Model

It would be relatively simple to model the production shop by using three model segments, one for each job-type. When a job-Transaction entered the model, its job type could be determined, and the Transaction could then be routed to the appropriate model segment. There it would move through a straight sequence of Blocks, consisting of an ENTER–ADVANCE–

LEAVE combination for each machine being visited. Throughout the model, Block Operands would be specified directly, as constants.

The disadvantages in taking the approach outlined above are that (1) a relatively large number of Blocks would be required, and (2) a relatively inflexible model would result. Instead of taking such an approach here, Matrix Savevalues will be used to build a compact model. The principle part of the required model is a single ENTER–ADVANCE–LEAVE sequence. This single sequence can be used to simulate use of consecutive machines by all the job types, providing that the following provisions be made.

1. The pertinent machine group number must be supplied as the A Operand at the ENTER and LEAVE Blocks.

2. The pertinent mean operation time must be provided as the A Operand at the ADVANCE Block.

3. Each job-Transaction must move through the single ENTER–ADVANCE–LEAVE Block sequence the proper number of times (one time for each machine group to be visited).

The means for making these provision will now be considered.

As for provisions (1) and (2), the pertinent machine-group numbers can be stored in the right order in a visitation-sequence Matrix; and the pertinent mean operation times can be correspondingly stored in a mean-operation-time Matrix. At the ENTER Block, a job-Transaction then simply needs to index into the proper cell of the visitation-sequence Matrix to obtain the number of the machine group it must visit next; similarly, when a machine in the group has been captured, the job-Transaction can index into the corresponding cell in the mean-operation-time Matrix to obtain the pertinent value of the A Operand at the ADVANCE Block. Finally, with respect to provision (3), the number of machine groups a job must visit can be stored in a Parameter of the job-Transaction when it first enters the model. After each next operation has been performed, the Parameter can be decremented by 1, then tested to determine whether there are yet more operations to be performed (that is, tested to determine whether the Parameter has yet been decremented to a value of 0). If at least one additional operation is indicated, the job-Transaction can be routed back through the ENTER-ADVANCE-LEAVE sequence. Then the Parameter can be decremented and tested again, etc. The result is a highly compact model.

Consider more closely how the visitation sequence and mean operation time Matrices can be set up and used. Table 5C.3 shows the appear-

TABLE 5C.3   The "Visitation Sequence" Matrix in Case Study 5C

| Rows (Job-Types) | Columns (Number of Machine Groups Yet to be Visited J) | | | | |
	1	2	3	4	5
1	6	2	3	1	
2	2	4	5		
3	6	3	4	5	1

ance of the visitation sequence Matrix, assuming that GPSS Storages 1 through 6 are used to simulate machine groups 1 through 6, respectively. There are three rows in the Matrix, one for each job-type. There are five columns in the Matrix, corresponding to the maximum number of machine groups that any one job-type must visit. Note that the column numbers are interpretable as the number of machine groups yet to be visited by a given job. Entries in the body of the Matrix are interpreted as the numbers of the machine groups *to be visited next*. For example, as indicated in Table 5C.2, a Type 1 job must visit four machines. When it first arrives at the production shop, then, the number of machines yet to be visited is 4. In column 4, row 1 of Table 5C.3, the number of the machine group *to be visited next* (that is, to be visited "1." Machine group 1 consists of casting units (as indicated in

Table 5C.1). And, as Table 5C.2 shows, the first operation on job-type 1 is performed at a casting unit. Row 1, column 4 of the visitation sequence Matrix therefore contains the pertinent machine-group number. When the casting operation has been performed, a Type 1 job has only three machines yet to be visited. Row 1, column 3 of the visitation-sequence Matrix should consequently contain the number of the machine group to be visited next. The number in that cell is a "3." Machine group 3 consists of planers (as indicated in Table 5C.1) and, as Table 5C.2 shows, the second operation on job-type 1 is indeed performed at a planer. And so on.

As implied by the above discussion, the visitation sequence for a given job-type is read from the Table 5C.3 Matrix in *right-to-left* fashion. For example, reading from right-to-left in row 2 of the Matrix, the visitation sequence for job-type 2 is seen to be "5-4-2." (There are no column 4 and 5 entries in row 2, because job-type 2 only visits three machines in total.) Reading from Table 5C.1, the "5-4-2" pattern corresponds to "shaper; drill-press; lathe." This is consistent with the Type 2 visitation sequence as shown in Table 5C.2.

Table 5C.4 shows the mean operation time Matrix. Row and column indices have the same significance and interpretations as in Table 5C.3. Entries in the body of the matrix are mean operation times, expressed in *tenths of minutes* (the time unit used in the model). The entries in

TABLE 5C.4   The "Mean Operation Time" Matrix in Case Study 5C

| Rows (Job-Types) | Columns (Number of Machine Groups Yet to be Visited) | | | | |
	1	2	3	4	5
1	600	200	350	1250	
2	650	900	1050	2500	
3	250	300	500	2500	2350

Table 5C.4 are linked directly to given cells in Table 5C.3. For example, when job-type 1 visits machine group 1 (row 1, column 4, Table 5C.3), its mean operation time there is 1250 "tenths of minutes" (row 1, column 4, Table 5C.4). Then, when job-type 1 visits machine group 3 (row 1, column 3, Table 5C.3), its mean operation time there is 350 "tenths of minutes" (row 1, column 3, Table 5C.4). And so on.

It is a simple matter for a job-Transaction to index into the proper cell of the visitation sequence and mean operation time Matrices. Assume that when a job-Transaction enters the model, its job-type is coded in Parameter 1 as a 1, or 2, or 3. Parameter 1 can then be used as a Matrix row-index. Assume further that when a job-Transaction arrives, the number of machines it must visit (that is, "yet to be visited") is copied to Parameter 2. Parameter 2 can then be used as a Matrix column-index. When the first operation has been performed, Parameter 2 can be decremented by 1, meaning that (1) its value can be interpreted as the number of machines yet to be visited, and (2) its value can continue to be used as the appropriate Matrix column-index. Suppose that halfword-Matrix Savevalue 1 is used for the visitation sequences. Then "MH1(P1,P2)" indirectly specifies the proper current machine-group number for the scheme just described. Suppose further that halfword-Matrix Savevalue 2 is used for the mean operation times. Then, because of the cell-to-cell correspondence between the two Matrices, "MH2(P1,P2)" indirectly specifies the corresponding mean operation time.

This completes the description of the Matrix approach to the simulation. The Block Diagram and Extended Program Listing should now be studied to bring the finer details into focus.

(3) Table of Definitions

Time Unit: 0.1 Minutes

TABLE 5C.5   Table of Definitions for Case Study 5C

GPSS Entity	Interpretation
Transactions	
Model Segment 1	A job
	P1: Parameter 1 values of 1, 2, and 3 indicate jobs of Type 1, 2, and 3, respectively
	P2: Parameter 2 indicates the total number of machine groups "yet to be visited" by the job
Model Segment 2	A timer-Transaction
Functions	
GRUPS	A Function describing the total number of machine groups each job-type must visit
JTYPE	A Function describing the distribution of job-types within the stream of arriving jobs
XPDIS	Exponential distribution function
Matrix Savevalues (Halfword)	
1	Visitation sequence Matrix
2	Mean operation time Matrix
Storages	
1, 2, 3, 4, 5, 6	Storages used to simulate machine groups 1 through 6, respectively
Tables	
1, 2, 3	Tables in which the shop residence times of job-types 1, 2, and 3, respectively, are recorded
TJOBS	Table used to record the total number of jobs in the shop at the end of each day
Variables	
COUNT	A Variable whose value equals the total number of jobs in the shop

(4) Block Diagram

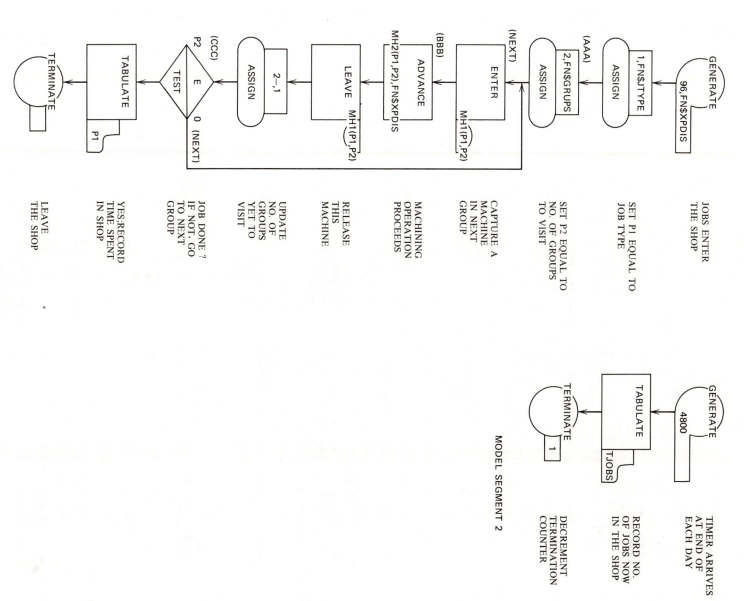

MODEL SEGMENT 1

MODEL SEGMENT 2

FIGURE 5C.1   Block Diagram for Case Study 5C

(5) Extended Program Listing

BLOCK NUMBER	*LOC	OPERATION	A,B,C,D,E,F,G	COMMENTS	CARD NUMBER
		SIMULATE			1
					2
	*	FUNCTION DEFINITION(S)			3
	*				4
	GRUPS	FUNCTION	P1,D3	NO. OF MACHINE GROUPS EACH JOB TYPE VISITS	5
		1,4/2,3/3,5			6
	JTYPE	FUNCTION	RN1,D3	DISTRIBUTION OF JOB-TYPES	7
		.24,1/.68,2/1,3			8
	XPDIS	FUNCTION	RN1,C24	EXPONENTIAL DISTRIBUTION FUNCTION	9
		0,0/.1,.104/.2,.222/.3,.355/.4,.509/.5,.69/.6,.915/.7,1.2/.75,1.38			10
		.8,1.6/.84,1.83/.88,2.12/.9,2.3/.92,2.52/.94,2.81/.95,2.99/.96,3.2			11
		.97,3.5/.98,3.9/.99,4.6/.995,5.3/.998,6.2/.999,7/.9998,8			12
					13
	*	MATRIX SAVEVALUE DECLARATION(S)/INITIALIZATION(S)			14
	*				15
1		MATRIX	H,3,5	MATRIX OF VISITATION SEQUENCES	16
		INITIAL	MH1(1,1),6/MH1(1,2),2/MH1(1,3),3/MH1(1,4),1		17
		INITIAL	MH1(2,1),2/MH1(2,2),4/MH1(2,3),5		18
		INITIAL	MH1(3,1),6/MH1(3,2),3/MH1(3,3),4/MH1(3,4),5		19
		INITIAL	MH1(3,5),1		20
	*				21
2		MATRIX	H,3,5	MATRIX OF MEAN MACHINING TIMES	22
		INITIAL	MH2(1,1),600/MH2(1,2),200/MH2(1,3),350/MH2(1,4),1250		23
		INITIAL	MH2(2,1),650/MH2(2,2),900/MH2(2,3),1050		24
		INITIAL	MH2(3,1),250/MH2(3,2),300/MH2(3,3),500/MH2(3,4),2500		25
		INITIAL	MH2(3,5),2350		26
	*				27
	*	STORAGE CAPACITY DEFINITION(S)			28
	*				29
		STORAGE	S1,14/S2,5/S3,4	PROVIDE 14, 5, AND 3 MACHINES IN	30
				GROUPS 1, 2, AND 3, RESPECTIVELY	31
	*	STORAGE	S4,8/S5,16/S6,4	PROVIDE 8, 16, AND 4 MACHINES IN	32
				GROUPS 4, 5, AND 6, RESPECTIVELY	33
	*				34
	*	TABLE DEFINITION(S)			35
	*				36
1		TABLE	M1,2400,2400,10	SHOP RESIDENCE TIME (TYPE 1 JOBS)	37
2		TABLE	M1,2400,2400,10	SHOP RESIDENCE TIME (TYPE 2 JOBS)	38
3		TABLE	M1,2400,2400,10	SHOP RESIDENCE TIME (TYPE 3 JOBS)	39
	TJOBS	TABLE	VS$COUNT,10,10,5	TOTAL JOBS IN THE SHOP	40
	*				41
	*	VARIABLE DEFINITION(S)			42
	*				43
	COUNT	VARIABLE	W$AAA+W$BBB+W$CCC	TOTAL JOBS IN THE SHOP	44
	*				45
	*	MODEL SEGMENT 1			46
	*				47
1		GENERATE	96,FN$XPDIS	JOBS ENTER THE SHOP	48
2		ASSIGN	1,FN$JTYPE	SET P1 = JOB TYPE	49
3	AAA	ASSIGN	2,FN$GRUPS	SET P2 = NO. OF GROUPS TO VISIT	50
4	NEXT	ENTER	MH1(P1,P2)	CAPTURE A MACHINE IN NEXT GROUP	51
5	BBB	ADVANCE	MH2(P1,P2),FN$XPDIS	MACHINING OPERATION PROCEEDS	52
6		LEAVE	MH1(P1,P2)	RELEASE THIS MACHINE	53
7		ASSIGN	2-,1	UPDATE NO. OF GROUPS YET TO VISIT	54
8	CCC	TEST E	P2,0,NEXT	JOB DONE? IF NOT, GO TO NEXT GROUP	55
9		TABULATE	P1	YES; RECORD TIME SPENT IN SHOP	56
10		TERMINATE		LEAVE THE SHOP	57
	*				58
	*	MODEL SEGMENT 2			59
	*				60
11		GENERATE	4800	TIMER ARRIVES AT END OF EACH DAY	61
12		TABULATE	TJOBS	RECORD NO. OF JOBS NOW IN THE SHOP	62
13		TERMINATE	1	DECREMENT TERMINATION COUNTER	63
	*				64
	*	CONTROL CARDS			65
	*				66
		START	5	START RUN FOR WEEK 1	67
		RESET		ZERO-OUT ACCUMULATED STATISTICS	68
		START	5	START RUN FOR WEEK 2	69
		RESET		ZERO-OUT ACCUMULATED STATISTICS	70
		START	5	START RUN FOR WEEK 3	71
		RESET		ZERO-OUT ACCUMULATED STATISTICS	72
		START	5	START RUN FOR WEEK 4	73
		RESET		ZERO-OUT ACCUMULATED STATISTICS	74
		START	5	START RUN FOR WEEK 5	75
		END		RETURN CONTROL TO THE SYSTEM	76

FIGURE 5C.2 Extended Program Listing for Case Study 5C

(6) Program Output

(a)

STORAGE	CAPACITY	AVERAGE CONTENTS	AVERAGE UTILIZATION	ENTRIES	AVERAGE TIME/TRAN	CURRENT CONTENTS	MAXIMUM CONTENTS
1	14	10.074	.719	136	1777.830	14	14
2	5	2.846	.569	141	484.560	3	5
3	4	1.724	.431	110	376.299	4	4
4	8	4.432	.554	150	709.166	2	8
5	16	10.657	.666	166	1540.843	16	16
6	4	1.703	.425	106	385.716	3	4

(b)

TABLE TJOBS
ENTRIES IN TABLE 5 MEAN ARGUMENT 38.799 STANDARD DEVIATION 11.625 SUM OF ARGUMENTS 194.000

UPPER LIMIT	OBSERVED FREQUENCY	PER CENT OF TOTAL	CUMULATIVE PERCENTAGE	CUMULATIVE REMAINDER	MULTIPLE OF MEAN	DEVIATION FROM MEAN	NON-WEIGHTED
10	0	.00	.0	100.0	.257	-2.477	
20	0	.00	.0	100.0	.515	-1.617	
30	2	39.99	39.9	60.0	.773	-.756	
40	1	19.99	59.9	40.0	1.030	.103	
OVERFLOW	2	39.99	100.0	.0			

AVERAGE VALUE OF OVERFLOW 50.50

(c)

MATRIX HALFWORD SAVEVALUE 1

	COL. 1	2	3	4	5
ROW 1	2	6	1	4	5
ROW 2	6	2	3	1	0
ROW 3	3	4	5	0	1

(d)

MATRIX HALFWORD SAVEVALUE 2

	COL. 1	2	3	4	5
ROW 1	600	650	900	1050	0
ROW 2	200	200	350	1250	0
ROW 3	250	300	500	2500	2350

FIGURE 5C.3 Selected Program Output for Case Study 5C. (a) Storage statistics at the end of week 1. (b) Distribution of jobs in the shop at the end of week 1, based on observations made at the end of each simulated day. (c) Visitation-sequence matrix. (d) Mean operation time matrix.

value of the Variable COUNT in the Table TJOBS. It is only every fifth day that the timer-Transaction's termination succeeds in decrement-ing the Termination Counter to 0, thereby shutting off the simulation. After the Processor then resets the model to eliminate statistics accumulated that week, the simulation for the next week is started.

Program Output.[6] Selected program output produced at the end of the first week is shown in Figure 5C.3. Output for the entire 5-week simulation is summarized in Table 5C.6. There is considerable week-by-week variation in the various statistics. The fact that the shop began in empty and idle condition initially does not appear to have had an undue influence on the Week 1 statistics. The degree of variation in the statistics is not surprising, considering the extent to which the exponential distribution is used in the model.

Model Logic. After the lengthy discussion of "approach," Model Segment 1 (Blocks 1 through 10 in Figure 5C.2) should appear brief and straightforward. One point is worth making. Note that Location names have been supplied for the ASSIGN Block (Block 3), the ADVANCE Block (Block 5), and the TEST Block (Block 8). At any given time, all job-Transactions in the model are either at this ASSIGN Block (waiting to move into the ENTER Block), or the ADVANCE Block (because they are on the Future Events Chain), or at the TEST Block (waiting to move into the ENTER Block again). Hence, the sum of the Current Counts at these three Blocks equals the total number of jobs in the shop. The Variable COUNT (Card 44, Figure 5C.2) has this sum of Current Counts as its value. It is this Variable that is evaluated at the end of each simulated day to determine how many jobs are in the shop currently.

A timer-Transaction enters Model Segment 2 at the end of each day, principally to record the

(7) Discussion

[6]Total CPU time for the simulation on an IBM 360/67 computer was 25.3 seconds.

TABLE 5C.6   Summary of Program Output for Case Study 5C

Week	Average Number of Jobs in the Shop	Average Shop Residence Time (minutes, by Job-type)		
		1	2	3
1	38.8	277	248	503
2	36.6	317	314	700
3	41.4	300	260	625
4	29.6	234	269	520
5	47.2	303	340	724

5.15 List Functions

Referring to the Function definitions in Case Study 5C (see the Extended Program Listing in Figure 5C.2), note that the Function GRUPS has two properties.

1. It is defined as discrete.
2. The first members of the Function-defining ordered pairs form an unbroken sequence of integers, beginning with 1. (For the Function GRUPS, the unbroken sequence of integers is simply 1, 2, 3.)

Whenever a Function has these two properties, it can be defined as a *list* Function. Definitionally, the B Operand of a list Function takes the form Lj, where j is the number of ordered pairs supplied to describe the Function. In every other way, list Functions are defined like discrete Functions. For example, Figure 5.29(a) shows

quired to evaluate a list Function than to evaluate its discrete Function equivalent. The reason for this is that the Processor uses the Function argument to index directly into the array of feasible Function values. Hence, no table lookup is required. Because of execution-time considerations, then, it is advantageous to use list Functions whenever possible.

If the value of a list Function's argument is found to be *out of range*, the GPSS Processor prints an error message to that effect and terminates the simulation. Compare this with what happens when a discrete Function's argument is out of range.

5.16 The LOOP Block

Blocks 7 and 8 in Figure 5C.2 are repeated diagrammatically in Figure 5.30. The purpose of this two-Block sequence is to decrement the value of Transaction Parameter 2 by 1, then test to determine if the updated value is equal to 0. If the test is true, the Transaction moves to the sequential Block. If the test is false, the Transaction is routed to the nonsequential Block in the Location NEXT.

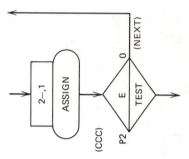

FIGURE 5.30   Repetition of part of the Figure 5C.1 Block Diagram

The decrement-and-test pattern shown in Figure 5.30 arises from time to time in a variety of GPSS modeling contexts. For this reason, a single Block is provided which performs the functions of the two Figure 5.30 Blocks. That is, a single Block which accomplishes the following steps when a Transaction moves into it.

1. The value of the indicated Parameter is decremented by 1.
2. The Parameter's updated value is tested to determine whether it equals 0.

```
LOCATION        OPERATION       A,B,C,D,E,F
GRUPS           FUNCTION        P1,D3
1,4/2,3/3,5
```
(a)

```
LOCATION        OPERATION       A,B,C,D,E,F
GRUPS           FUNCTION        P1,L3
1,4/2,3/3,5
```
(b)

FIGURE 5.29   Example of a discrete Function, and its list Function equivalent. (a) The discrete Function. (b) The equivalent list Function.

the definition of the discrete Function GRUPS, repeated from Figure 5C.2. Figure 5.29(b) shows GRUPS defined as a list Function. Except for the B Operand on the Function header card, the definitions are identical.

Computationally, less execution time is re-

3. The Transaction is routed to a nonsequential Block if the pertinent Parameter does not equal 0; otherwise, it moves to the sequential Block.

It is the LOOP Block, shown in Figure 5.31, which accomplishes these three steps. The Block's A Operand supplies the number of the so-called looping Parameter. When a Transaction enters the Block, the indicated Parameter is decremented by 1, then tested to determine if it equals 0. If it does not, the Transaction moves to the "B Block," i.e., the Block in the Location whose name appears as the LOOP Block's B Operand. When the looping Parameter equals 0,

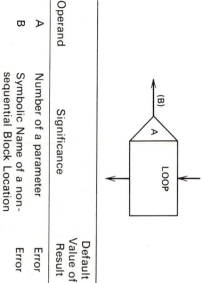

Operand	Significance	Default Value of Result
A	Number of a parameter	Error
B	Symbolic Name of a non-sequential Block Location	Error

FIGURE 5.31 The LOOP Block and its A and B Operands

the Transaction moves to the sequential Block. The LOOP Block shown in Figure 5.32, then, is equivalent to the two-Block sequence in Figure 5.30.

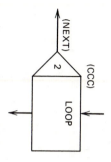

FIGURE 5.32 A LOOP Block equivalent to the two-Block sequence in Figure 5.30

The LOOP Block can only be used to count down, that is, to *decrement* a Parameter's value. Furthermore, there is no flexibility as to the size of the decrement. It is always 1. Finally, if the value of the looping Parameter is 0 or less when a Transaction *enters* the LOOP Block, an error condition is indicated and the simulation is terminated.

When the analyst uses the LOOP Block instead of supplying his own decrement-and-test logic with the ASSIGN and TEST Blocks, a savings in execution time and computer memory is realized. On the other hand, use of the LOOP Block requires that the analyst structure his thinking in terms of counting down on a looping Parameter. When loops arise, the analyst always has the alternative of explicitly supplying the logic which best serves his purposes.

5.17 Exercises

1. These exercises all refer to Case Study 5C.

(a) Explain why it was not possible in the case study to compute the number of jobs in the shop simply by taking the difference between the Total Counts at the Model Segment 1 GENERATE Block (Block 1, Figure 5C.2) and TERMINATE Block (Block 10, Figure 5C.2).

(b) Show the Block Diagram for a model to simulate the production shop, using the relatively simple approach described in the first paragraph in the "Approach Taken in Building the Model" section of the case study. How many Blocks are required? (Note that the case study model requires 13 Blocks.)

(c) Assume that the production process for jobs of Type 2 changes, so that these jobs now visit four machines, in the sequence drill press, shaper, lathe, and polishing machines. Also assume that the corresponding mean operation times are 75, 95, 60, and 10 minutes, respectively. Show what changes to make in the Figure 5C.2 Extended Program Listing to incorporate this modification into the Case Study 5C model.

(d) Using your model from (b) as a starting point, make the changes in it necessary to reflect the change in production conditions described in (c). Compare the number of *cards* that would have to be repunched for the modified model, with the number that would have to be repunched when the change in production conditions is incorporated into the Case Study 5C model.

(e) Consider the two events "a job of Type 2 arrives at the production shop," and "the casting-unit operation on a job of Type 3 comes to completion." Assume that these two events occur at the same reading of the simulation clock. The next operation for each of the two jobs is performed at the shaper machine group. Of the 16 shaping machines, assume that only 1 is available at the time.

(i) Describe the conditions under which the job of Type 2 will capture the one available shaper.

(ii) Describe the conditions under which the job of Type 3 will capture the one available shaper.

(f) In the case study model, the distribution of job residence time in the production shop, as a function of job type, is estimated via use of three Table cards and a TABULATE Block. Alternatively, Qtables could have been used to gather this same information. Show how to modify the case study model to implement this alternative approach.

(g) The case study model makes one observation per simulated day on the random variable "number of jobs in the shop." More complete information would be gathered if the value of this random variable were observed in essentially continuous fashion over time, instead of but once per simulated day. Show how to modify the case study model to accomplish this result. (Hint: make use of a weighted Table.)

2. (a) The queue discipline used in the Case Study 5C production shop is first-come, first-served. Show how to modify the model to implement a "shortest imminent operation" queue discipline at each machine group.

(b) Show what to do to the Case Study 5C model, and to your model in (a), so that the two alternative queue disciplines implemented in the models can be studied *under identical experimental conditions.*

(c) Simulate with the two models produced in (b). What influence does a "shortest imminent operation" queue discipline appear to have on the distribution of job residence time in the shop, and number of jobs in the shop?

3. Every 100 time units, the following statistics are to be gathered in a model.
(a) The utilization of the Facility JOE is to be saved in the next available column in row 1 of the Matrix DATA. (At time 100, the utilization is to be saved in row 1, column 1; at time 200, the utilization is to be saved in row 1, column 2, and so on.)
(b) The capture count of the Facility JOE is to be saved in the next available column in row 2 of the Matrix DATA.
(c) The average holding time per capture of the Facility JOE is to be saved in the next available column in row 3 of the Matrix DATA.
(d) Each of the statistics in (a), (b), and (c) is to be recorded in a Table unique to the type of statistic in question.

Show a self-contained Block Diagram segment which will gather the requested statistics. Then discuss the differences in the information available in rows 1 through 3 of the Matrix DATA, as compared with the information available in the three corresponding Tables.

4. (a) For the Function GRUPS as defined in Figure 5.29(a), what value does the Function return when P1 = -3? When P1 = 12?
(b) Repeat (a), except with respect to the Function GRUPS as defined in Figure 5.29(b).
(c) What is the meaning of Execution Error 509 in Appendix C?

5. What three conditions must be satisfied by the values a Function's argument can assume, if the Function is to be defined as being of the list type?

6. A Transaction is to cycle through a particular model segment six times, carrying a Parameter 5 value of 6 the first time through, 5 the second time through, 4 the third time through, ..., and 1 the sixth and last time through.
(a) Without using the LOOP Block, show what Blocks to place at the beginning and end of the segment to accomplish the desired effect.
(b) Repeat (a), only make use of the LOOP Block.

5.18 Entities to Simulate Control Elements: Logic Switches

Consider the concept of "entities whose purpose is to signal that a given condition exists in a system." Entities that provide such signals can usually be thought of as elements which control the sequence of events in a system. Here are some examples of system control elements.

1. The lock on a door.
2. A traffic light.
3. "Go to Next Window" sign at a bank teller's window.
4. "Lot Full" sign at a parking lot.
5. "Closed" sign in a gas station window.

In GPSS, it would be an easy matter to use Savevalues to simulate such control elements in models. For example, the Savevalue LOCK could be used to indicate whether a barber shop is open or not. X$LOCK values of 1 and 0 could be understood to mean that the shop is or is not open, respectively. As simulated by a Transaction, a customer arriving at the door of the barber shop could attempt to move through a TEST Block which tests to determine whether X$LOCK equals 1. Only if the shop is open would the customer be permitted to enter; otherwise, he would be refused entry.

Rather than forcing the analyst to use Savevalues in this fashion to simulate control elements, GPSS makes available a type of entity designed explicitly for this purpose. "Logic Switches" are the entities used to simulate control elements. Logic Switches are two-position switches. Rather than being called "on" and "off," the two different switch positions are termed "Set" and "Reset," respectively. At any given time, then, a given Logic Switch in a model is either Set or Reset. Of course, the setting of selected Logic Switches can be reversed as a simulation proceeds, to reflect changing model conditions. And Logic Switch settings can be tested and in this sense used to influence the movement of Transactions in a model.

There are at least two advantages to using Logic Switches instead of Savevalues to simulate system control elements. First of all, it is presumably more natural for the analyst to think about control elements in an "on–off" (i.e., Set–Reset) sense than in terms of the numeric encoding scheme which would be required with Savevalues. And second, the execution time required to modify and test Logic Switch settings is less than that required to perform the same actions with respect to Savevalues. Of course, Logic Switches are limited by being restricted to only two possible settings. On occasion, it might be necessary to use Savevalues to simulate more complicated control elements. A traffic light, for example, usually is in one of *three* states, red, green, or amber. These three states could be represented more easily with a Savevalue than with a Logic Switch.

The normal quantities of Logic Switches in a model with 64, 128, and 256K bytes of computer memory are 200, 400, and 1000, respectively. Like Facilities, Storages, Queues, Functions, Tables, and Savevalues, Logic Switches can be named numerically or symbolically. The usual rules hold when choosing names.

5.19 Controlling Logic Switch Settings: The INITIAL Card and the LOGIC Block

In this section, the method for presetting Logic Switch positions before a simulation begins, and reversing the positions as a simulation proceeds, will be described. Then, in Section 5.20, the Block used to test the status of Logic Switches will be introduced.

Location	Operation	Operands
Not Used	INITIAL	LSname₁/LSname₂/.../LSname_j/.../LSname_n

FIGURE 5.33 Format for the card used to put one or more Logic Switches into a Set position initially

5.19.1 The INITIAL Card

Like Savevalues, Logic Switches automatically exist in a model, whether they are used or not. Normally, the Processor puts all Logic Switches in the *Reset* position before a simulation begins. At the analyst's option, selected Logic Switches can initially be put into a Set position by use of the INITIAL card. The card takes the form shown in Figure 5.33. As indicated, the Location field is not used. The word INITIAL is entered in the Operation field. Each unit of information in the Operands field consists of LS, followed by the numeric or symbolic name of a Logic Switch whose initial position is to be Set. When symbolic names are used, a dollar sign must be interposed between LS and the symbolic name itself. Examples of possible entries in the Operands field are LS5, LS21, LS\$LOCK, and LS\$SYGNL. Slashes are used to separate consecutive units of information on an INITIAL card. The first blank column encountered by the Processor in the Operands field is interpreted as an "end of card" character. No information (except for comments) can be entered beyond card column 71. More than one INITIAL card can be used, if necessary.

Figure 5.34 provides several examples of the use of the INITIAL card. As indicated in the first example, it is not necessary that the numbers of the Logic Switches involved be in ascending order on the INITIAL card. The second example shows a mixture of Logic Switches named numerically and symbolically. The GPSS Processor establishes a correspondence between symbolic names and their numeric equivalent by the two-step procedure already described in Chapter 4 in the context of other language entities. The third example reveals that Logic Switches 8, 9, 10, and 11, among others, are initially to be in the Set position. When Logic Switches whose numbers form an uninterrupted sequence of integers are all to be Set initially, the corresponding entries on the INITIAL card can be compacted to the form "LSi–LSk", where i and k are the smallest and largest Logic-Switch numbers, respectively, in the range of switches

LOCATION	OPERATION	A,B,C,D,E,F		
	INITIAL	LS4/LS2/LS2,31/LS,50		FIRST EXAMPLE
	INITIAL	LS5/LS$MARK/LS$FLAG/LS21		SECOND EXAMPLE
	INITIAL	LS5,LS8/LS9/LS1,10/LS1,1/LS,2		THIRD EXAMPLE
	INITIAL	LS5,LS8-LS1,1/LS,2		FOURTH EXAMPLE

FIGURE 5.34 Examples showing use of the Figure 5.33 card format

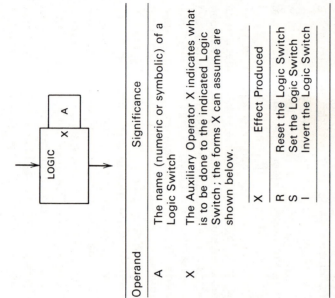

Operand	Significance
A	The name (numeric or symbolic) of a Logic Switch
X	The Auxiliary Operator X indicates what is to be done to the indicated Logic Switch; the forms X can assume are shown below.

X	Effect Produced
R	Reset the Logic Switch
S	Set the Logic Switch
I	Invert the Logic Switch

FIGURE 5.35 The LOGIC Block, with its Auxiliary Operator and its A Operand

TABLE 5.7 Various Possible Effects of the LOGIC Block

Switch Position Before Transaction Enters LOGIC Block	Auxiliary Operator Used	Switch Position After Block Subroutine is Executed
Reset	R	Reset
Set	R	Reset
Reset	S	Set
Set	S	Set
Reset	I	Set
Set	I	Reset

to be Set. The fourth example in Figure 5.34 repeats the third example, making use of this compact form.

Logic Switch settings are not affected by the RESET card. The CLEAR card causes all Logic Switches in a model to be put into the Reset position. Unlike the situation with Savevalues, *there is no* selective CLEAR card whereby certain Logic Switches can be left intact when the clearing operation takes place.

At the end of a simulation, the names of all Logic Switches *which are in a Set position* are automatically printed out. The positions of selected Logic Switches can also be outputted during a run by use of the PRINT Block. This is accomplished by providing LG as the Block's field C mnemonic. For example, when a Transaction moves into the Block "PRINT 5,10,LG", the positions of Logic Switches 5 through 10 will be printed out.

5.19.2 The LOGIC Block

The status of a Logic Switch can be changed by having a Transaction enter the LOGIC Block. This Block, and its A Operand and Auxiliary Operator, are shown in Figure 5.35. When a Transaction enters the Block, the referenced Logic Switch is put into a Reset or Set position, or Inverted, depending on whether the Auxiliary Operator is R, S, or I, respectively. Table 5.7 shows what the switch position will be after the LOGIC Block subroutine has been executed, depending both on its prior position, and the Auxiliary Operator used. The setting of a Logic Switch is changed with certainty only if the Auxiliary Operator is I. For Auxiliary Operators R and S, the referenced Logic Switch may already be in the desired position at the time a Transaction enters the LOGIC Block.

When a Transaction which has moved through a LOGIC Block finally comes to rest, the Processor restarts its scan of the Current Events

Chain. This is done because the potentially changed position of the Logic Switch may make it possible for one or more previously blocked Transactions in a model to resume their movement.

5.20 Testing the Setting of Logic Switches: The GATE Block

When the setting of a Logic Switch is tested, no numeric properties of the switch are involved. In fact, a switch has no numeric properties. This suggests that some Block other than the TEST Block must be introduced to control the flow of Transactions as a function of the Set or Reset status of Logic Switches. The Block used for this purpose is the GATE Block, which is shown in Figure 5.36 with its two Operands and Auxiliary Operator.

The GATE Block's A Operand states the name of the Logic Switch to be tested. If the name is numeric, it can be supplied directly, or indirectly. The Auxiliary Operator is a Logical Mnemonic which indicates the Logic Switch setting required for the test to be true. If the Logical Mnemonic LS is used, the TEST is true if the switch is Set; otherwise, the test is false. When LR is the Logical Mnemonic, the test is true if the switch is Reset, and is false otherwise.

The B Operand is optional. When no B Operand is used, the test is conducted in *refusal mode*. If a refusal-mode test is not true, "the

GATE is closed." When a Transaction finds the GATE closed, it is held at the Block preceding the GATE, contributing to the Current Count there. From a chain viewpoint, the blocked Transaction remains on the Current Events Chain, and an internal flag on the Transaction is turned "on" to indicate that the cause of the blockage is the status of a certain Logic Switch. Because the Transaction's flag is "on," the Transaction is said to be *scan-inactive*. This means the Processor will *not* try to move the Transaction in subsequent scans of the Current Events Chain. *This has important benefits in terms of execution time economy.*

Later in the simulation, when a LOGIC Block referencing the Logic Switch is executed *and* the result is to change the switch setting, the Processor turns the flag of the blocked Transaction (or Transactions) "off." This makes the Transaction (or Transactions) *scan-active* again. In the Current Events Chain rescan which then eventually occurs because the LOGIC Block was executed, the Processor will try to move the previously blocked Transaction (or Transactions) through the GATE. This flag-setting aspect of the Processor's internal logic, only briefly men-

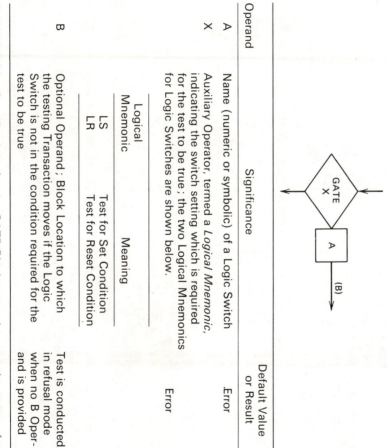

Operand	Significance	Default Value or Result
A	Name (numeric or symbolic) of a Logic Switch	Error
X	Auxiliary Operator, termed a *Logical Mnemonic*, indicating the switch setting which is required for the test to be true; the two Logical Mnemonics for Logic Switches are shown below.	Error

Logical Mnemonic	Meaning
LS	Test for Set Condition
LR	Test for Reset Condition

B	Optional Operand; Block Location to which the testing Transaction moves if the Logic Switch is not in the condition required for the test to be true	Test is conducted in refusal mode when no B Operand is provided

FIGURE 5.36   Specifications for the GATE Block as used to test the status of a Logic Switch

tioned here, will be considered in more detail in Chapter 7.

When the GATE Block's B Operand is used, testing at the GATE is conducted in *conditional transfer mode*. A Transaction which arrives at the GATE moves to the sequential Block if it is true that the Logic Switch has the indicated setting; otherwise, it moves to the nonsequential Location indicated via the B Operand.[7] In conditional transfer mode, then, entry to the GATE is not denied. A Transaction arriving at the Block enters it immediately, and the path it then will follow is determined by execution of the Block subroutine. If the first Block in that path refuses entry, the Transaction is left on the Current Events Chain, contributing to the Current Count at the GATE Block in question. Eventually, the blocking condition at the Transaction's next Block will be removed, and forward motion of the Transaction in the model will be resumed.

Examples of the GATE Block are given in Figure 5.37. In Figure 5.37 (a), the GATE is closed whenever the Logic Switch SYGNL is Reset, and is open otherwise. When the GATE is closed, Transactions must wait at the Block preceding the GATE. In Figure 5.37(b), Transactions entering the GATE move to the sequential Block next if Logic Switch 10 is Reset; otherwise, their next-Block-attempted is the one located at RUTE7 in the model.

FIGURE 5.37 Examples of the GATE Block as used to test Logic Switch status. (a) Refusal mode. (b) Conditional transfer mode.

5.21 Use of the GATE Block with Facilities and Storages

Whether a Logic Switch is Set or Reset involves a *logical* condition, not a *numeric* one. Several logical conditions associated with Facilities and Storages can also be identified. In particular, whether a Facility is in use or not, and whether a Storage is full or not, or empty or not, pertains to the logical condition of these entities. To cover these conditions, a series of Logical Mnemonics pertaining to Facilities and Storages is supplied in GPSS. With these mnemonics, the GATE Block can be used to make Transaction movement depend on the logical status of Facilities and Storages.

Logical Mnemonic	Meaning
U	Test for Facility in use
NU	Test for Facility not in use
SF	Test for Storage full
SNF	Test for Storage not full
SE	Test for Storage empty
SNE	Test for Storage not empty

FIGURE 5.38 GATE Block Logical Mnemonics for Facilities and Storages

Figure 5.38 shows the GATE Block Logical Mnemonics supplied for Facilities and Storages. Figure 5.39 shows several of these Logical Mnemonics used in a GATE Block context. (Notice the slight variation in the shape of the Block, depending on its use for Logic Switches as shown in Figure 5.37, or for Facilities or Storages as shown in Figure 5.39.) In Figure 5.39(a), Transactions are held at the Block preceding the GATE until the Storage CHANL is empty. In Figure 5.39(b), Transactions move through the GATE to the sequential Block if the Facility CRANE is not in use; otherwise, they move to the Block in Location PATH2.

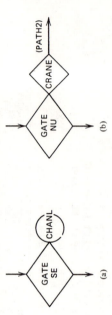

FIGURE 5.39 Examples of the GATE Block as used to test Storage and Facility status. (a) Refusal mode. (b) Conditional transfer mode.

It must be admitted that, for Facilities and Storages, the logical conditions described by the Figure 5.38 mnemonics can be evaluated by testing available *numeric* information. At the Block "TEST E S$CHANL,0", for example, a Transaction can test to determine if the Storage CHANL is empty. The effect accomplished by this TEST Block is identical to that of the GATE in Figure 5.39(a). Similarly, recalling that the

[7]Note that the GATE and TEST Blocks in conditional transfer mode are similar with respect to their true and false exits. The Transaction moves from the GATE to the nonsequential Block if it is *false* that the Logic Switch has the indicated status. Remember, "condition true, fall through."

value of the Standard Numerical Attribute F$CRANE is 0 if the Facility CRANE is not in use, the Block "TEST E F$CRANE,0,PATH2" accomplishes the same effect as the GATE in Figure 5.39(b). Why bother, then, to make Facility and Storage Logical Mnemonics available for use with the GATE Block? The reason is that, from the point of view of computer time, *GATE Blocks are more efficient than TEST Blocks.* When the analyst has a choice, then, between the GATE and TEST Blocks, *use of the GATE Block is much to be preferred.*[8]

The case study in Section 5.23 illustrates relatively straightforward use of the GATE and LOGIC Blocks in a model. Then, in Section 5.25, a more complicated situation involving use of GATE and LOGIC Blocks is presented.

[8] The specific reason why GATE Blocks are more efficient than TEST Blocks will be explained in detail in Chapter 7.

5.22 SELECT Block Use in Logical Mode

As described in Chapter 4, the SELECT Block can be used in relational-operator mode to scan a specified set of entity members in search for one which satisfies a stated *numeric* condition. It is natural to extend the use of this Block so the condition being examined can pertain to the *logical* status of entities. This makes it possible, for example, to scan a group of Logic Switches to determine if at least one of them is Set, or to scan a group of Storages to determine if at least one of them is not full, etc. The Logical Mnemonics introduced for use with the GATE Block can be used with the SELECT Block to provide these capabilities.

The SELECT Block and its specifications for use in logical mode are shown in Figure 5.40. The A, B, C, and F Operands serve the same purpose as when the SELECT Block is used in

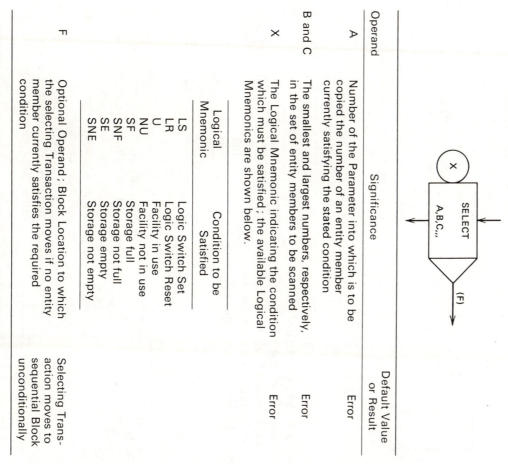

Operand	Significance	Default Value or Result
A	Number of the Parameter into which is to be copied the number of an entity member currently satisfying the stated condition	Error
B and C	The smallest and largest numbers, respectively, in the set of entity members to be scanned	Error
X	The Logical Mnemonic indicating the condition which must be satisfied; the available Logical Mnemonics are shown below.	Error

Logical Mnemonic	Condition to be Satisfied
LS	Logic Switch Set
LR	Logic Switch Reset
U	Facility in use
NU	Facility not in use
SF	Storage full
SNF	Storage not full
SE	Storage empty
SNE	Storage not empty

F	Optional Operand; Block Location to which the selecting Transaction moves if no entity member currently satisfies the required condition	Selecting Transaction moves to sequential Block unconditionally

FIGURE 5.40 Specifications for use of the SELECT Block in logical mode

relational-operator mode. As a Logical Mnemonic, the Auxiliary Operator uniquely identifies both the entity type involved, and the condition which is to be satisfied. There is no information, then, that need be supplied by the D and E Operands, and they are therefore not used.

Figure 5.41 shows two examples of SELECT Block use in logical mode. In Figure 5.41(a), Logic Switches 7 through 11 are scanned to determine if at least one of them is Set. The

Transaction is set equal to zero, and the Transaction then exits the SELECT Block sequentially.

In Figure 5.41(b), Storages 5 through 8 are scanned to determine if at least one of them is not full. If a not-filled Storage is found, its number is copied into Parameter 1 of the selecting Transaction, which then proceeds to the sequential Block. If all Storages in the range from 5 through 8 are full, Parameter 1 is left unchanged, and the selecting Transaction takes the nonsequential exit to the Block in the Location FULUP.

5.23 CASE STUDY 5D
A Gas Station Problem

(1) Statement of the Problem

The interarrival times of cars approaching a gas station with the intention of possibly stopping for service are distributed as shown in Table 5D.1. Service time for cars follows the distribution shown in Table 5D.2. A car stops for service only if the number of cars already waiting for service is less than or equal to the number of cars currently being served. (That is, a car stops only if the driver perceives that not more than one car per attendant is already waiting to be served.) Cars which do not stop go to another gas station, and therefore represent lost business.

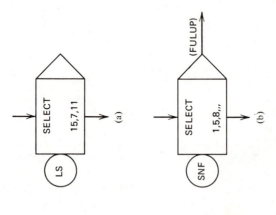

FIGURE 5.41   Examples for use of the SELECT Block in logical mode. (a) No alternate exit specified. (b) Alternate exit specified.

number of the pertinent Logic Switch is to be placed in Parameter 15 of the selecting Transaction, which then proceeds to the sequential Block. If none of the Logic Switches between 7 and 11 are Set, Parameter 15 of the selecting

TABLE 5D.1   Car Interarrival-Time Distribution for Case Study 5D

Interarrival Time (seconds)	Cumulative Frequency
Less than 0	0.0
100	.25
200	.48
300	.69
400	.81
500	.90
600	1.0

TABLE 5D.2   Service-Time Distribution for Case Study 5D

Service Time (seconds)	Cumulative Frequency
Less than 100	0.0
200	.06
300	.21
400	.48
500	.77
600	.93
700	1.0

The gas station is open from 7 a.m. until 7 p.m. The lights are turned out at 7 p.m., meaning that cars arriving later than that are not accepted for service. Any cars already waiting in line at 7 p.m. are served, however, before the attendants leave for the night.

It is estimated that the profit per car served averages $1, excluding attendants' salaries and other fixed costs. Attendants earn $2.50 per hour and are only paid for working a 12-hour day, even if they stay beyond 7 p.m. to finish service on previously waiting cars. The other fixed costs amount to $75 per day.

The station's owner wants to determine how many attendants he should hire to maximize his daily profit. Build a GPSS model simulating the operation of the station, then use the model to provide the answer. Simulate with each attendants-hired configuration for five different days. Design the model to control experimental conditions, so that the various alternatives are investigated under identical sets of circumstances. Also design the model so that, in case of a time tie between the two events completion of service on a car and arrival of another car, the service completion will be caused to occur first. This is equivalent to assuming that the driver of the arriving car can perceive that a service completion is taking place. Under some circumstances, then, when that driver would have gone elsewhere, he will choose to remain for service. Finally, if there is a time tie between the two events arrival of another car and closing up the gas station at the end of the day, the arriving car should be permitted to enter the station before the closeup takes place.

(2) Approach Taken in Building the Model

The basic structure of the model is straightforward. There are only three model segments which merit discussion. The first concerns shutting down the gas station at the end of each day; the second involves the computation of each day's profit; and the third has to do with handling the two different types of possible time ties that can occur.

Shutting down the station requires coordination between the major model segment, and the timer segment. After 12 hours of operation, no additional cars are to be allowed to enter the major model segment. This can be accomplished by placing the Block "GATE LR LOCK" immediately after the GENERATE Block through which cars arrive. When the Logic Switch LOCK is Reset, the GATE Block is open, meaning that car-Transactions can enter the model. The Logic Switch is initially Reset, by default. Then, when a timer-Transaction arrives after 12 hours, it immediately moves through a "LOGIC S LOCK" Block, thereby closing the gate in the major model segment. This prevents additional cars from entering the station.

After closing the gate, the timer-Transaction must then wait until all cars lined up for service at that time have been served. This can be accomplished with a refusal-mode TEST Block, where the timer-Transaction is forced to wait until the number of cars on which service has been completed equals the number which have stayed for service throughout the day. This is equivalent to requiring equality in the Total Counts at two appropriately chosen Blocks in the model. It is a simple matter, then, for the timer-Transaction to know when it can compute the day's profit and shut off the model.

Computation of a day's profit requires knowing how many cars were serviced that day. This statistic equals the capture count of the Storage used to simulate the station attendants. Each day's profit also depends on the number of attendants working at the station. At the end of the day's work, no attendants are in a state of capture. At that time, the number of attendants therefore equals the remaining capacity of the Storage used to simulate the attendants.

Handling possible time-ties between service completion and car arrival requires use of the PRIORITY Block. Before a car-Transaction moves into the ADVANCE Block where service time is simulated, its Priority Level can be boosted above that with which car-Transactions enter the model. In case of simultaneity between the two indicated events, then, the Transaction about to enter the LEAVE Block (thereby freeing an attendant) is closer to the front of the Current Events Chain than the Transaction simulating the just-arriving car. Service completion therefore gets higher processing priority than car-arrival.

Finally, if a time-tie occurs between car arrival and station shutdown, the arriving car is to be privileged to move into the station and be served (unless, of course, the car chooses to move on because of the number of cars already waiting). This possible time tie is resolved by giving car-Transactions a higher priority (via the E Operand at their GENERATE Block) than the timer-Transaction. At shutdown time, then, the timer-Transaction is at the back end of the Current Events Chain. If there is a car-arrival at that time, the LOCK-gate is open to that car, and is then subsequently closed by the timer-Transaction.

(3) Table of Definitions

Time Unit: 1 Second

TABLE 5D.3 Table of Definitions for Case Study 5D

GPSS Entity	Interpretation
Transactions	
Model Segment 1	A car
	P1 : The car's latent service-time requirement
Model Segment 2	A timer
Functions	
IAT	A Function describing the car interarrival-time distribution
STIME	A Function describing the car service-time distribution
Logic Switches	
LOCK	A Logic Switch simulating the "open" — "not open" condition of the gas station
Queues	
1	The Queue in which cars wait for service
Savevalues	
1	The Savevalue in which each day's profit is stored
Storages	
1	A Storage whose total capacity equals the number of attendants on duty
Variables	
NET	A Variable whose value is the day's profit after costs

(4) Block Diagram

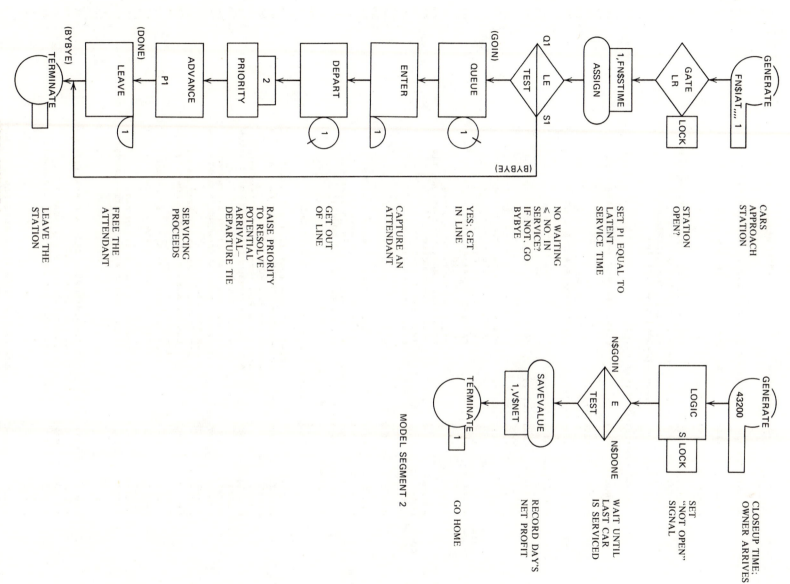

MODEL SEGMENT 1

MODEL SEGMENT 2

FIGURE 5D.1   Block Diagram for Case Study 5D

(5) Extended Program Listing

BLOCK NUMBER	*LOC	OPERATION A,B,C,D,E,F,G	COMMENTS	CARD NUMBER
		SIMULATE		1
	*			2
	*		NON-STANDARD RANDOM NUMBER SEQUENCE INITIALIZATION(S)	3
	*			4
		RMULT 111	SET RANDOM NUMBER SEQUENCE FOR 1ST RUN	5
	*			6
	*		FUNCTION DEFINITION(S)	7
	*			8
	IAT	FUNCTION RN1,C7	INTER-ARRIVAL TIME DISTRIBUTION	9
		0,0/.25,100/.48,200/.69,300/.81,400/.9,500/1,600		10
	STIME	FUNCTION RN1,C7	SERVICE TIME DISTRIBUTION	11
		0,100/.06,200/.21,300/.48,400/.77,500/.93,600/1,700		12
	*			13
	*		STORAGE CAPACITY DEFINITION(S)	14
	*			15
		STORAGE S1,1	CONFIGURE FOR 1-ATTENDANT CASE	16
	*			17
	*		DEFINE VARIABLE(S)	18
	*			19
	NET	VARIABLE SC1-75-30*R1	DAY'S PROFIT AFTER COSTS	20
	*			21
	*		MODEL SEGMENT 1	22
	*			23
1		GENERATE FN$IAT,,,,1	CARS APPROACH STATION	24
2		GATE LR LOCK	STATION OPEN?	25
3		ASSIGN 1,FN$STIME	SET P1 = LATENT SERVICE TIME	26
4		TEST LE Q1,S1,BYBYE	NO. WAITING <= NO. IN SERVICE?	27
			IF NOT, GO BYBYE	28
5	GOIN	QUEUE 1	YES; GET IN LINE	29
6		ENTER 1	CAPTURE AN ATTENDANT	30
7		DEPART 1	GET OUT OF LINE	31
8		PRIORITY 2	RAISE PRIORITY TO RESOLVE	32
			POTENTIAL ARRIVAL/DEPARTURE TIE	33
9		ADVANCE P1	SERVICING PROCEEDS	34
10	DONE	LEAVE 1	FREE THE ATTENDANT	35
11	BYBYE	TERMINATE	LEAVE THE STATION	36
	*			37
	*		MODEL SEGMENT 2	38
	*			39
12		GENERATE 43200	CLOSEUP TIME; OWNER ARRIVES	40
13		LOGIC S LOCK	SET "NOT OPEN" SIGNAL	41
14		TEST E N$GOIN,N$DONE	WAIT 'TIL LAST CAR IS SERVICED	42
15		SAVEVALUE 1,V$NET	RECORD DAY'S NET PROFIT	43
16		TERMINATE 1	GO HOME	44
	*			45
	*		CONTROL CARDS AND STORAGE CAPACITY RE-DEFINITIONS	46
	*			47
		START 1	START 1ST RUN (DAY 1; 1 ATTENDANT)	48
		RMULT 333	SET RANDOM NUMBER SEQUENCE FOR 2ND RUN	49
		CLEAR	CLEAR FOR 2ND RUN	50
		START 1	START 2ND RUN (DAY 2; 1 ATTENDANT)	51
		RMULT 555	SET RANDOM NUMBER SEQUENCE FOR 3RD RUN	52
		CLEAR	CLEAR FOR 3RD RUN	53
		START 1	START 3RD RUN (DAY 3; 1 ATTENDANT)	54
		RMULT 777	SET RANDOM NUMBER SEQUENCE FOR 4TH RUN	55
		CLEAR	CLEAR FOR 4TH RUN	56
		START 1	START 4TH RUN (DAY 4; 1 ATTENDANT)	57
		RMULT 999	SET RANDOM NUMBER SEQUENCE FOR 5TH RUN	58
		CLEAR	CLEAR FOR 5TH RUN	59
		START 1	START 5TH RUN (DAY 5; 1 ATTENDANT)	60
		RMULT 111	SET RANDOM NUMBER SEQUENCE FOR 6TH RUN	61
		CLEAR	CLEAR FOR 6TH RUN	62
		STORAGE S1,2	RE-CONFIGURE FOR 2 ATTENDANTS	63
		START 1	START 6TH RUN (DAY 1; 2 ATTENDANTS)	64
		· · ·	· · ·	· · ·
		RMULT 111	SET RANDOM NUMBER SEQUENCE FOR 11TH RUN	77
		CLEAR	CLEAR FOR 11TH RUN	78
		STORAGE S1,3	RE-CONFIGURE FOR 3 ATTENDANTS	79
		START 1	START 11TH RUN (DAY 1; 3 ATTENDANTS)	80
		· · ·	· · ·	· · ·
		RMULT 999	SET RANDOM NUMBER SEQUENCE FOR 15TH RUN	90
		CLEAR	CLEAR FOR 15TH RUN	91
		START 1	START 15TH RUN (DAY 5; 3 ATTENDANTS)	92
		END	RETURN CONTROL TO OPERATING SYSTEM	93

FIGURE 5D.2 Extended Program Listing for Case Study 5D

(6) Program Output

No program output is shown directly. Results are summarized in the next section.

(7) Discussion

Model Logic. In Figure 5D.1, note how the timer-Transaction waits for previously waiting cars to be served. The timer does its waiting at the refusal-mode TEST Block in Model Segment 2. The condition which must be satisfied for the test to be true is that N$GOIN equals N$DONE. GOIN is the Location occupied by the QUEUE Block in Model Segment 1; DONE is the Location of the LEAVE Block in that model segment. The two Total Block Counts involved are equal only when the last previously waiting car has been served and has left the model.

In the Variable NET (Card 20, Figure 5D.2), SC1 is the capture-count of Storage 1. This capture count equals the number of cars served on the day in question. Or, at an average profit of $1 per car, it is a given day's revenue. This value is reduced by $75 for non-salary overhead. The salary expense is computed as 30*R1. The "30" is the $30 per day earned by each attendant (12 hours times $2.50 per hour). R1 is the number of attendants working at the station. Strictly speaking, R1 is the remaining capacity of Storage 1; but, when the value of the Variable NET is computed, the Storage is empty, meaning R1 equals the Storage's total capacity.

In Figure 5D.2, note that a common source of random numbers, RN1, has been used as the argument for both the interarrival-time and service-time distribution Functions. [See exercise 8b, Section 5.24.] Also note that RMULT cards have been used to provide different RN1 starting points from day to day. This may seem strange at first, because in Case Study 4D ("Comparison of Alternative Queuing Systems in a Bank"), in a highly analogous modeling context, it was *not* necessary to use RMULT cards to replicate experimental conditions. In Case Study 4D, however, the timer-Transaction shut off the simulation *as soon as it arrived.* In Case Study 5D, the timer-Transaction does not in general shut off the simulation until some time *after* it has arrived. In the meantime, while the timer-Transaction waits for the station to clear, the *next* car-Transaction is on its way to the station. If this car-Transaction arrives at its GENERATE Block before the model shuts off, a value is fetched from RN1 and "thrown away"

(see Section 3.22). Whether this fetch from RN1 occurs or not clearly depends on the time of model shutdown; and shutdown time, in turn, is configuration-dependent. That is, shutdown time depends in general on the number of attendants working at the gas station. Suppose, then, that on day 3 of the simulation, for the two-attendant case, this preshutdown fetch from RN1 *does occur.* Also suppose that on day 3, for the three-attendant case, this preshutdown fetch from RN1 *does not occur.* The result is that the RN1 starting point for day 4 would differ for the two alternative configurations if RN1 were left as it is. There would then be no duplication of experimental conditions on day 4. This potential problem is easily avoided by using the RMULT card between consecutive simulated days. This insures that the RN1 starting point for each different day is configuration-independent.

Program Output.[9] Table 5D.4 summarizes the daily profit figures, in dollars, for the various runs. The two-attendant case is clearly the one

---

which maximizes daily profit. The other cases show a profit, on average, but also experienced a loss on simulated day 4. (Only 160 cars arrived at the station on day 4, whereas the numbers of cars arriving on days 1, 2, 3, and 5 were 180, 189, 190, and 194, respectively. This explains why the profit figures for day 4 are relatively low.)

5.24 Exercises

1. A certain traffic light is either red or green. When the light switches to red, it remains red for 3 minutes. When it switches to green, it remains green for 2 minutes. Using the Logic Switch LIGHT to simulate the traffic light, and interpreting Reset as green, show a self-contained

TABLE 5D.4 A Summary of Program Output for Case Study 5D

Day	Number of Attendants		
	1	2	3
1	1	36	15
2	2	50	24
3	3	46	25
4	−1	24	−5
5	2	52	29

[9]Total CPU time for the simulation on an IBM 360/67 computer was 17.6 seconds.

model segment which properly switches the light back and forth. Assume the implicit time unit is 1 second, and that at the start of the simulation, the traffic light has just turned green.

2. (a) Referring to Appendix F, show a REALLOCATE Card which reallocates the number of Logic Switches in a model downward to 100.

(b) Assuming that the model is to be run at the 64K level, extend the information in the REALLOCATE Card in (a) so that the memory freed by the downward Logic Switch reallocation is added to COMMON.

(c) Show an INITIAL card which causes the Logic Switches ALPHA, BETA, and 7 to be Set at the start of a simulation.

(d) Critically discuss this statement: "The CLEAR card has no effect on Logic Switch settings."

(e) Assuming that a Transaction has caused a LOGIC Block to be executed, what does the GPSS Processor do next after the Transaction has come to rest?

(f) What does it mean to say that a Transaction is *scan-inactive*? When a Transaction is denied entry to the Block "GATE LR 7" and has been made scan-inactive, under what conditions will it again be made scan-active?

3. Critically discuss each of the following statements.

(a) "The Current Count at a refusal-mode GATE is always zero."

(b) "If a Transaction comes to rest *in* a refusal-mode GATE Block, the next Block that Transaction will attempt to enter remains to be determined."

(c) "The Current Count at a conditional-transfer-mode GATE Block is always zero."

(d) "If a Transaction comes to rest *in* a conditional-transfer-mode GATE Block, the next Block that Transaction will attempt to enter remains to be determined."

4. For each of the following problems, show refusal-mode GATE Blocks which will be closed unless the indicated condition is true.

(a) The Logic Switch MARK is Set.
(b) Facility 9 is not in use.
(c) The Storage TUGS is empty.

5. For each of the following problems, show a conditional-transfer-mode GATE Block which will cause a Transaction to move to the nonsequential Location BYPAS unless the indicated condition is true.

(a) The Logic Switch JOE is Reset.
(b) The Facility CRANE is in use.
(c) Storage 21 is not full.

6. (a) Give a list of all conditions under which an analyst can choose between the GATE and

TEST Blocks to accomplish a desired effect. Given a choice, which of the two Block types should an analyst use, and why?

(b) Show GATE Blocks which are equivalent to each of these TEST Blocks.

(i) TEST NE R$SLIPS,0
(ii) TEST E F$CPU,1,BYPAS
(iii) TEST GE R10,1

7. (a) Show how a Logical Mnemonic can be used with a SELECT Block whose purpose is to scan Facilities 1 through 10 to determine if at least one of them is currently in use. If such a Facility is found, its number is to be copied into Parameter 12 of the selecting Transaction. Whether or not such a Facility is found, the selecting Transaction is to move from the SELECT Block sequentially when the scan has been completed.

(b) Present another solution for (a), this time using "E" instead of "U" as the SELECT Block's Auxiliary Operator.

(c) List the conditions under which an analyst can use either a Logical Mnemonic or a Relational Operator with the SELECT Block to accomplish a desired effect. Given a choice, would a Logical Mnemonic or a Relational Operator seem more "natural" to use?

(d) Show a SELECT Block which can be used to scan Logic Switches 5 through 8 to determine if at least one of them is Set. If such a Logic Switch is found, its number is to be placed in Parameter 1 of the selecting Transaction. If no Logic Switch in the indicated range is Set, the selecting Transaction should move nonsequentially to the Block in the Location SHUKS.

8. These questions pertain to Case Study 5D.

(a) Show how to replace the TEST Block in Model Segment 2 with a GATE Block. Explain why or why not the GATE Block would be a better choice than the TEST Block for use in the model.

(b) Indicate (1) which calls on RN1 are used to compute interarrival times for car-Transactions, (2) which calls on RN1 are used to determine the latent service time requirements for cars, and (3) which calls on RN1 are "thrown away." (Hint: see the "approach" section in Case Study 4D.)

(c) This series of questions pertains to the Block "TEST LE Q1,S1,BYBYE".

(i) What conditions must be in effect at the gas station before a Transaction takes the nonsequential exit from the TEST Block for the one-attendant configuration? For the two-attendant configuration? For the three-attendant configuration?

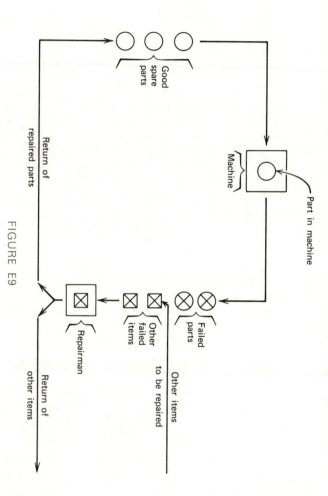

FIGURE E9

(ii) Show how to define a Variable named ITSOK so that the Block "TEST LE Q1,S1,BYBYE" can be replaced with the Block "TEST LE Q1,V$ITSOK,BYBYE", and still accomplish the same effect.

(iii) Which of the two alternative Blocks in (ii) do you think is the better Block to use, and why?

(d) Suppose that an analyst decides to replace the Block "TEST E N$GOIN,N$DONE" with the Block "TEST E Q1,0". Why would this be a mistake?

(e) Assume that the symbolic Location name GOTEM is used with the ADVANCE Block in the model. Would it then be valid to replace the Block "TEST E N$GOIN,N$DONE" with the Block "TEST E W$GOTEM,0"? Explain why or why not, in detail.

9. A certain machine uses a type of part which is subject to periodic failure. Whenever the in-use part fails, the machine must be turned off. The failed part is then removed, a good spare part is installed if available, or as soon as one becomes available, and the machine is turned on again. Failed parts can be repaired and reused.

The lifetime of a part is normally distributed, with a mean of 350 hours and a standard deviation of 70 hours. It takes 4 hours to remove a failed part from the machine. The time required to install a replacement part is 6 hours. Repair time for a failed part is normally distributed, with mean and standard deviation of 8 and 0.5 hours, respectively.

The machine operator himself is responsible for removing a failed part from the machine, and installing a replacement part in its place. There is a repairman who is responsible for repairing failed parts. The repairman's duties also include repair of items routed to him from another source. These other items arrive in a Poisson stream with a mean interarrival time of 9 hours. Their service-time requirement is 8 ± 4 hours. These other items have a higher repair priority than the failed parts used in the machine of interest.

The system is shown graphically in Figure E9. Each open circle represents either a good part in "spare" status, or a part currently in the machine. Circles with a cross in them represent parts in "failed" status. The other items which compete for the repairman's services are shown as squares with an X in them. As indicated above, and as the flow schematic suggests, these other items have a higher repair priority than the failed parts; they enter the repair queue ahead of any failed parts which may be waiting for repair.

Build a GPSS model for this machine-and-parts system, taking an approach whereby a Transaction simulates a part. The number of Transactions circulating through the machine-and-parts model segment will then equal the total number of parts which circulate through the system. Use the model to estimate the fractional utilization of the machine as a function of the number of spare parts provided. Study the system for the alternatives of providing zero, one, and two spares. Run each simulation for the equivalent of 5 years, assuming 40-hour work weeks. For each alternative, control experimental conditions partially in the sense of duplicating the competition from other items which failed parts experience at the repair facility.

10. Read the Statement of the Problem for Case Study 5E ("A Bus Stop Simulation") in the next section (Section 5.25).

(a) Before looking further at the case study, try to develop a GPSS model which simulates the events which occur at the bus stop.

(b) Now read the Approach Taken in Building the Model section in the case study. Without looking further at the case study, try to develop a GPSS model for the problem, following the approach as described.

5.25 CASE STUDY 5E
A Bus Stop Simulation

(1) Statement of the Problem

A bus is scheduled to arrive at a bus stop every 30 minutes, but it may be as much as 1.5 ± 1.5 minutes late. Whether a bus is late or not in no way depends on whether the preceding bus was late, and has no influence on whether the next bus will be late.

People arrive at the bus stop in a Poisson stream at a rate of 12 people every 30 minutes. The bus, with a capacity of 50, carries 35 ± 15 passengers when it arrives. After from three to seven of these passengers get off (uniformly distributed), as many waiting people as possible board the bus. Those unable to board after the bus is full leave the bus stop, and do not return later.

It takes 4 ± 3 seconds to unload a passenger, and 8 ± 4 seconds to load a passenger. Passengers unload one-by-one, and get aboard one-by-one. Waiting people do not begin to board until everyone intending to get off has done so. The sequence for getting aboard is first-come, first-served. Any people who arrive at the bus stop while a bus is still loading are able to get on, providing there is room for them. In case of a time tie between the events "bus is now finished loading" and "next passenger arrives," the arriving passenger is taken aboard (providing, of course, that there is room for him).

Build a GPSS model which simulates the events at the bus stop. Design the model to gather the following information.

1. Obtain waiting-line statistics for people waiting at the bus stop, including an estimate of the distribution of in-line residence time.

2. Estimate the distribution of the random variable "number of passengers per arriving bus who are unable to receive service."

Simulate with the model until 25 bus arrival-and-departures have occurred.

(2) Approach Taken in Building the Model

The model is built in two segments. Model Segment 1 simulates the passengers who arrive at the bus stop, wait for a bus, and then get on or go away mad. Model Segment 2 simulates the bus itself, including the logic whereby those on-board passengers who want to get off the bus, do so.

Model Segment 1. Each passenger-Transaction entering the model moves into the Block "QUEUE WAIT", where it remains until (1) a bus has come, and (2) it becomes *this* passenger-Transaction's turn to try to get aboard. When these conditions are in effect, a BUS-gate is opened to the passenger-Transaction. The Transaction then departs the Queue and, at a transfer-mode TEST Block, tests whether the value of the Savevalue NOWON ("now-on") is less than 50. (This Savevalue is used as a counter, to count the number of people on board the bus which is currently at the bus stop.) If there is no room left, the passenger-Transaction adds 1 to the Savevalue MAD, and then leaves the model. (The Savevalue MAD is used to count the number of people who haven't been able to get aboard the currently stopped bus.)

If there is room aboard the bus, however, the passenger-Transaction moves sequentially from the TEST Block and proceeds to close the BUS-gate. (This is done to prevent the next waiting passenger from trying to get aboard while the current passenger is boarding.) After advancing 8 ± 4 seconds, the passenger-Transaction updates the value of the Savevalue NOWON, then opens the BUS-gate for the next waiting passenger-Transaction and leaves the model.

Model Segment 2. A bus-Transaction is brought into the model every 30 minutes. It then moves into an ADVANCE Block, where delay (if any) is simulated. (The holding time at the ADVANCE Block may be 0, in which case the bus is exactly on time.) Leaving the ADVANCE Block, the bus-Transaction samples from the distribution of on-board passengers, saving the resulting value in the Savevalue NOWON. It then samples from the distribution of passengers who want to get off, saving that value in Parameter 1. Looping on Parameter 1, the bus-Transaction then lets each of these people off, simulating the corresponding time lag and updating the Savevalue NOWON in the process. After dropping out of the loop, the bus opens the BUS-gate, then waits until the last person who can board the bus has done so. Next, the bus-Transaction records in a GPSS Table the number of people not served, then resets the Savevalue MAD to 0 (in the spirit of giving this counter its initial value for the next bus). Finally, the bus-Transaction closes the BUS-gate, and leaves the model.

As an exercise, you should now attempt to construct a Block Diagram for the model as described above. Then look at the Block Diagram solution presented in Figure 5E.1, and use it as a guide to critique your own work. Given the above description, it should be quite easy for you to develop a valid solution yourself.

(3) Table of Definitions

Time Unit: 1 Second

TABLE 5E.1   Table of Definitions for Case Study 5E

GPSS Entity	Interpretation
Transactions	
Model Segment 1	A passenger
Model Segment 2	A bus
	P1: Initially, the number of people aboard the bus who want to get off; later, the number of people aboard who have yet to get off
Functions	
XPDIS	Exponential distribution function
ONBUS	A Function describing the distribution of passengers in the bus when it arrives at the bus stop
OFF	A Function describing the distribution of passengers who are getting off at the bus stop
Logic Switches	
BUS	A Logic Switch which, when Reset, indicates that these conditions are simultaneously satisfied: (1) a bus is at the stop; and (2) it is now time for the next passenger to try to get aboard
Queues	
LINE	The Queue in which people wait until the bus has come and it is their turn to try to get on.
Savevalues	
MAD	A counter used to count the number of people unable to board the bus which is currently at the bus stop
NOWON	A counter used to keep track of the number of people on the bus which is currently at the bus stop
Tables	
INQUE	The Table used to estimate the in-Queue residence time distribution
MAD	The Table used to estimate the distribution of the random variable "people not served per bus"

(4)   Block Diagram

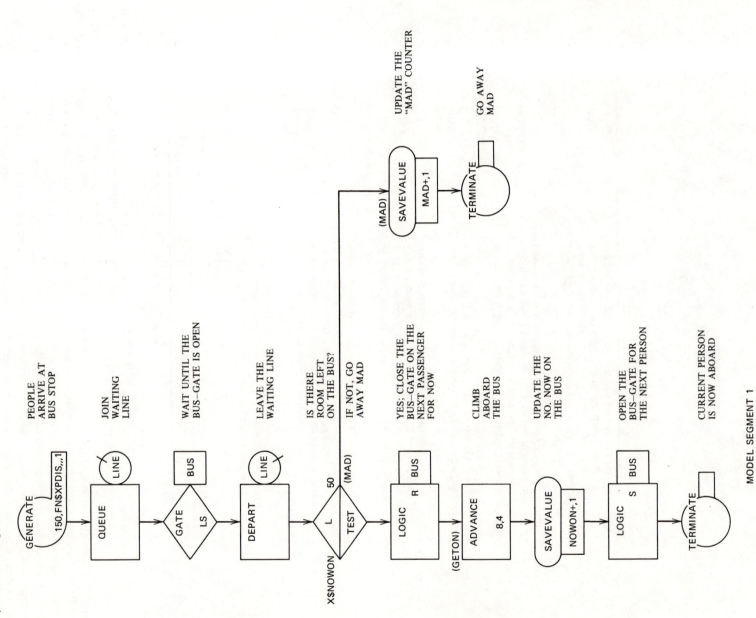

MODEL SEGMENT 1

FIGURE 5E.1   Block Diagram for Case Study 5E

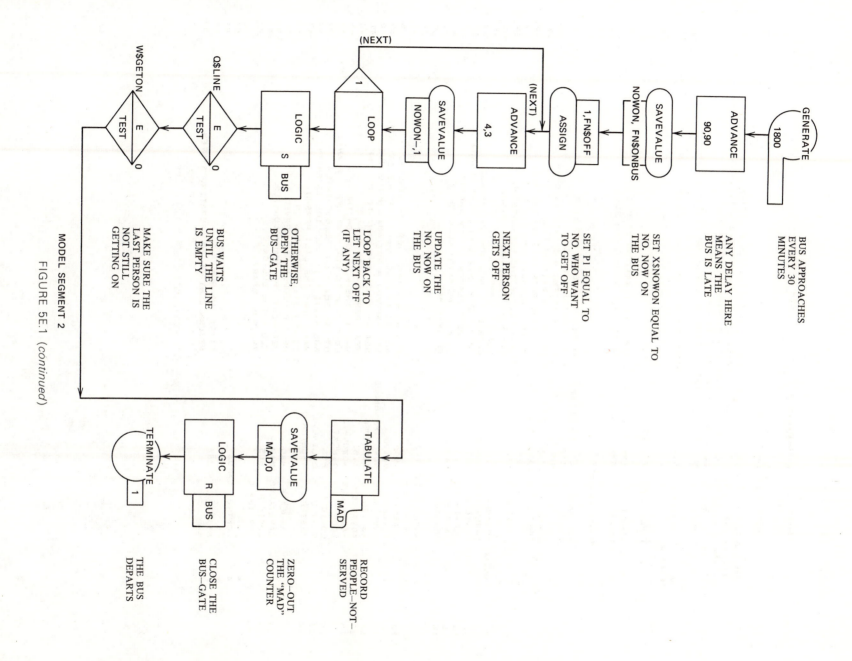

FIGURE 5E.1 (continued)

MODEL SEGMENT 2

(5) Extended Program Listing

```
BLOCK                                                                            CARD
NUMBER  *LOC    OPERATION  A,B,C,D,E,F,G              COMMENTS                   NUMBER

                SIMULATE                                                          1
        *                                                                         2
        *       FUNCTION DEFINITION(S)                                            3
        *                                                                         4
        XPDIS   FUNCTION   RN1,C24      EXPONENTIAL DISTRIBUTION FUNCTION          5
        0,0/.1,.104/.2,.222/.3,.355/.4,.509/.5,.69/.6,.915/.7,1.2/.75,1.38        6
        .8,1.6/.84,1.83/.88,2.12/.9,2.3/.92,2.52/.94,2.81/.95,2.99/.96,3.2        7
        .97,3.5/.98,3.9/.99,4.6/.995,5.3/.998,6.2/.999,7/.9998,8                  8
        ONBUS   FUNCTION   RN1,C2       DISTRIBUTION OF PEOPLE ON ARRIVING BUS     9
        0,20/1,51                                                                10
        OFF     FUNCTION   RN1,C2       DISTRIBUTION OF PEOPLE GETTING OFF BUS    11
        0,3/1,8                                                                  12
        *                                                                        13
        *       TABLE DEFINITION(S)                                              14
        *                                                                        15
        INQUE   QTABLE     LINE,300,300,7   TIME SPENT WAITING AT BUS STOP        16
        MAD     TABLE      X$MAD,0,1,10     PEOPLE NOT SERVED PER BUS             17
        *                                                                        18
        *       MODEL SEGMENT 1                                                  19
        *                                                                        20
 1              GENERATE   150,FN$XPDIS,,,1  PEOPLE ARRIVE AT BUS STOP            21
 2              QUEUE      LINE          JOIN WAITING LINE                        22
 3              GATE LS    BUS           WAIT 'TIL THE BUS-GATE IS OPEN           23
 4              DEPART     LINE          LEAVE THE WAITING LINE                   24
 5              TEST L     X$NOWON,50,MAD   IS THERE ROOM LEFT ON THE BUS?        25
                                             IF NOT, GO AWAY MAD                  26
 6              LOGIC R    BUS           YES; CLOSE THE BUS-GATE ON               27
                                             THE NEXT PASSENGER FOR NOW           28
        *                                                                        29
 7      GETON   ADVANCE    8,4           CLIMB ABOARD THE BUS                     30
 8              SAVEVALUE  NOWON+,1      UPDATE THE NO. NOW ON THE BUS            31
 9              LOGIC S    BUS           OPEN THE BUS-GATE FOR NEXT PERSON        32
10              TERMINATE                CURRENT PERSON IS NOW ABOARD            33
11      MAD     SAVEVALUE  MAD+,1        UPDATE THE "MAD" COUNTER                 34
12              TERMINATE                GO AWAY MAD                             35
        *                                                                        36
        *       MODEL SEGMENT 2                                                  37
        *                                                                        38
13              GENERATE   1800          BUS APPROACHES EVERY 30 MINUTES         39
14              ADVANCE    90,90         ANY DELAY HERE MEANS THE BUS IS LATE    40
15              SAVEVALUE  NOWON,FN$ONBUS  SET X$NOWON = NO. NOW ON THE BUS      41
16              ASSIGN     1,FN$OFF      SET P1 = NO. WHO WANT TO GET OFF        42
17      NEXT    ADVANCE    4,3           NEXT PERSON GETS OFF                    43
18              SAVEVALUE  NOWON-,1      UPDATE THE NO. NOW ON THE BUS           44
19              LOOP       1,NEXT        LOOP BACK TO LET NEXT OFF (IF ANY)      45
20              LOGIC S    BUS           OTHERWISE, OPEN THE BUS-GATE            46
21              TEST E     Q$LINE,0      BUS WAITS 'TIL THE LINE IS EMPTY        47
22              TEST E     W$GETON,0     MAKE SURE THE LAST PERSON               48
                                             IS NOT STILL GETTING ON             49
23              TABULATE   MAD           RECORD PEOPLE-NOT-SERVED                50
24              SAVEVALUE  MAD,0         ZERO-OUT THE "MAD" COUNTER              51
25              LOGIC R    BUS           CLOSE THE BUS-GATE                      52
26              TERMINATE  1             THE BUS DEPARTS                         53
        *                                                                        54
        *       CONTROL CARDS                                                    55
                START      25            START THE RUN                           56
                END                      RETURN CONTROL TO OPERATING SYSTEM      57
```

FIGURE 5E.2   Extended Program Listing for Case Study 5E

(6) Program Output

QUEUE	MAXIMUM CONTENTS	AVERAGE CONTENTS	TOTAL ENTRIES	ZERO ENTRIES	PERCENT ZEROS	AVERAGE TIME/TRANS	$AVERAGE TIME/TRANS	TABLE NUMBER	CURRENT CONTENTS
LINE	16	5.670	288	1	.3	889.919	893.020	1	

$AVERAGE TIME/TRANS = AVERAGE TIME/TRANS EXCLUDING ZERO ENTRIES

TABLE INQUE
ENTRIES IN TABLE 288 MEAN ARGUMENT 889.919 STANDARD DEVIATION 505.000 SUM OF ARGUMENTS 256297.000

UPPER LIMIT	OBSERVED FREQUENCY	PER CENT OF TOTAL	CUMULATIVE PERCENTAGE	CUMULATIVE REMAINDER	MULTIPLE OF MEAN	DEVIATION FROM MEAN NON-WEIGHTED
300	49	17.01	17.0	82.9	.337	-1.168
600	43	14.93	31.9	68.0	.674	-.574
900	61	21.18	53.1	46.8	1.011	.019
1200	41	14.23	67.3	32.6	1.348	.614
1500	50	17.36	84.7	15.2	1.685	1.208
1800	42	14.58	99.3	.6	2.022	1.802
OVERFLOW	2	.69	100.0	.0		

AVERAGE VALUE OF OVERFLOW 1846.00

(a)

(b)

TABLE MAD
ENTRIES IN TABLE 25 MEAN ARGUMENT .359 STANDARD DEVIATION .860 SUM OF ARGUMENTS 9.000

UPPER LIMIT	OBSERVED FREQUENCY	PER CENT OF TOTAL	CUMULATIVE PERCENTAGE	CUMULATIVE REMAINDER	MULTIPLE OF MEAN	DEVIATION FROM MEAN NON-WEIGHTED
0	21	83.99	83.9	16.0	-.000	-.418
1	0	.00	83.9	16.0	2.777	.744
2	3	11.99	95.9	4.0	5.555	1.906
3	1	3.99	100.0	.0	8.333	3.069

REMAINING FREQUENCIES ARE ALL ZERO

(c)

FIGURE 5E.3 Selected Program Output for Case Study 5E. (a) Queue statistics. (b) Distribution of time spent resident in the waiting line. (c) Distribution of the random variable "people not served per bus."

(7) Discussion

Model Logic. As pointed out in the problem statement, a compound condition must be true before a passenger can try to get aboard a bus. That is, there must be a bus at the bus stop, and it must be that particular passenger's turn to try to get on. Nevertheless, only *one* Logic Switch is used in the model. The setting of this switch can be controlled from either of the two model segments. In Model Segment 2, a bus-Transaction can set the Logic Switch, thereby opening the BUS-gate to indicate that a bus has arrived and loading can begin. A bus-Transaction can also reset the Logic Switch, thereby closing the BUS-gate to indicate that there is now no longer a bus at the stop. The BUS-gate does not remain open throughout the bus's stay at the stop, however. In Model Segment 1, a passenger-Transaction just beginning to board the bus can reset the switch, thereby closing the gate and forcing other passengers to wait their turn to try to get aboard. Similarly, a passenger-Transaction can set the switch, thereby opening the gate and indicating that it is now time for the next passenger in line to try to get on. Of course, the passenger-Transaction doesn't have the opportunity to do this in the first place unless a bus is at the stop. The problem logic is such, then, that a compound condition can be represented via the status of a single Logic Switch.

The logic of the problem contains a subtlety with respect to the conditions under which a bus can leave the bus stop. It is not sufficient to say that a bus can leave as soon as there are no more people in line. The reason is that nonzero time is required for a person to get aboard. Leaving the line to get aboard is consequently not the same as being aboard. Hence, in Model Segment 2, a bus-Transaction first waits at the Block "TEST E Q$LINE,0" until the line is empty. At the sequential Block, the bus-Transaction then tests to be certain that the last person is not still in the process of climbing aboard. Only when the line is empty *and* the last person is aboard are conditions right for the bus to leave the stop. (You are asked to investigate this situation further via the problems in the next section.)

Program Output.[10] Figure 5E.3(a) shows the Queue statistics for the waiting line. There were 288 entries to the line in total. (The expected value would be somewhat more than 300.) At one time, there were as many as 16 people waiting to try to get aboard a bus. One person had zero residence time in the line.

Figure 5E.3(b) shows the in-line residence-time distribution. The average wait was 889 seconds, or about 15 minutes. There were 42 passengers, however, who waited between 25 and 30 minutes. Both of these statistics are consistent with the data provided in the problem statement.

Figure 5E.3(c) displays the distribution of people not served per stopping bus. Everyone was able to get aboard the bus 21 times out of 25, or 84 percent of the time. There never was exactly one person who went away mad. On three occasions, though, there were two people who couldn't board the bus, and on one occasion three people wound up going away mad.

5.26 Exercises

All of the exercises in this section pertain to Case Study 5E.

1. (a) Why have bus-Transactions been given a lower Priority Level than passenger-Transactions?

   (b) Assume that it doesn't matter how a time tie between an about-to-depart bus and an arriving passenger is resolved, and that the analyst therefore makes no distinction in the Priority Level of bus-Transactions and passenger-Transactions. Will the case-study model be valid in this circumstance? Explain why, or why not.

   (c) It is assumed in the model that passengers get aboard the bus on a first-come, first-served basis. This is perhaps unrealistic. Show how to change the model so that the sequence in which passengers get aboard the bus is random. (Hint: it is not necessary to add any Blocks to the model to bring this about.)

   (d) Assume that there is at least one person waiting to board the bus, and that the bus-Transaction has just dropped out of the "let passengers off" loop and moved to the "TEST E Q$LINE,0" Block. Will this person start to get on during the current reading of the simulation clock? If so, explain why this is the case.

   (e) The model output indicates that one person spent zero time resident in the waiting line. Describe the conditions under which this zero-residence-time situation could result. Is it possible to say whether this person made it aboard the bus, or went away mad?

   (f) Explain why Transactions are used in the model to simulate people who want to get on the bus, whereas Transactions are *not* used to simulate passengers who want to get off the bus.

2. (a) The model would be invalid if the Block "TEST E Q$LINE,0" were removed from it. Explain why, indicating precisely how the model would behave if this Block were removed.

   (b) The model would be invalid if the Block "TEST E W$GETON,0" were removed from it. Explain why, indicating precisely how the model would behave if this Block were removed.

3. The problem unrealistically assumes that the rate at which people arrive at the bus stop is independent of time. In fact, the arrival rate very likely increases as each next scheduled stopping of a bus draws near. Develop numeric specifications for an arrival pattern of your own choosing which reflects this fact. Then show how to change the model to incorporate your arrival pattern into it. (Hint: see exercise 11b, Section 4.5.)

4. (a) The case study model can be simplified considerably if it is assumed that (1) time required to get off the bus, and (2) time required to get on the bus are both negligibly small. Show how to modify the model to reflect these assumptions.

   (b) The model can be simplified even further if it is assumed that no waiting-line statistics of any kind are required. In this case, the model would simply estimate the distribution of the random variable "people not served per bus." Show as simple a model as you can when this assumption *and* the assumptions in (a) are in effect. Try to minimize the average number of Transactions in the model in the process.

[10]Total CPU time for the simulation on an IBM 360/67 computer was 4.6 seconds.

6

Advanced GPSS Modeling Concepts, Part I

6.1 Introduction

Whereas Chapters 4 and 5 in this book deal with intermediate concepts, Chapters 6 and 7 are concerned with advanced concepts. As used here, the term "advanced" does not mean difficult. These last two chapters are advanced only in the sense that they cover most of the remaining major components of the GPSS language.

This chapter begins with the topic of Boolean Variables. These variables make it possible to take complex logical conditions into account in GPSS models. Suppose, for example, that a ship cannot move into a harbor until (1) no storm is in progress, (2) an empty berth is available, and (3) a tug can be committed to it. Boolean Variables can be used to determine whether conditions such as these are simultaneously satisfied.

Next, the BUFFER Block is considered. By using this Block, the analyst can force the GPSS Processor to restart its scan of the Current Events Chain under specified conditions. This gives the analyst somewhat more control over the sequence in which Transactions are moved during the Processor's scan of the Current Events Chain.

A secondary method for bringing Transactions into models is then studied. Through use of the SPLIT Block, a Transaction already in a model can simulate a "parent" by causing one or more additional Transactions to be fetched from the latent pool and brought into the model as its "offspring." The SPLIT Block has a

variety of uses. For example, it can be of use in connection with events whose occurrence requires that simultaneous and independent activities be set into motion. The SPLIT Block finds application in three of the five case studies in this chapter.

Another topic taken up in the chapter is that of the indirect addressing of data. *Indirect specification*, already considered in Chapters 4 and 5, involves supplying the names of "variables" (that is, Standard Numerical Attributes) whose values are the data. In this sense, the "names of the data" are used to supply data via indirect specification. *Indirect addressing* takes this idea one step further. It involves supplying data by giving the "names of the names of the data." By using indirect addressing, the analyst can build models

325

which are relatively compact, and relatively powerful. Indirect addressing is used in the last two case studies in the chapter.

This chapter also extends the Function concept in GPSS to include Functions whose values are the values of *other* Standard Numerical Attributes. These attribute-valued Functions have much in common, conceptually, with the idea of indirect addressing. In fact, because of certain limitations in the GPSS implementation of indirect addressing, attribute-valued Functions can find considerable use in the language.

In summary, then, Chapter 6 deals with Boolean Variables, the BUFFER Block, the SPLIT Block, indirect addressing, and attribute-valued Functions. In addition, Functions whose values can be interpreted as Block Locations are considered, and the possibility of modeling alternative system configurations in parallel, instead of sequentially, is introduced and illustrated through a case study.

6.2 Boolean Variables

In GPSS, a Boolean Variable is a user-defined Standard Numerical Attribute. A Boolean Variable is referenced as BVj, or BV$sn, where "$j$" is the number of the Variable if it has been named numerically, and "sn" is its symbolic name if it has been named symbolically. The *value* of a Boolean Variable is either 1 or 0, depending on whether the Boolean expression supplied by the user to define the Variable is *true* or *false*, respectively. A Boolean expression, in turn, consists of (1) references to the logical conditions of entities, or (2) logical-valued references to the numeric properties of entities, or (3) logical-valued combinations of the elements in (1) and/or (2). In succeeding parts of this section, the discussion will first focus on the construction of Boolean expressions by using elements of the type in (1), and in (2), and by combining these elements as suggested in (3). Then it will turn to the Boolean Variable definition card; examples of Boolean Variables and the rules followed in evaluating them; and, finally, the use of Boolean Variables in GPSS models.

6.2.1 Logical Operators

Logical Operators are used to reference the logical status of the so-called equipment-oriented entities in GPSS, namely Facilities, Storages, and Logic Switches. The available Logical Operators are listed in Table 6.1, with an

TABLE 6.1 The Logical Operators in GPSS

Logical Operators	Entity Condition Referenced
LS	Logic Switch Set
LR	Logic Switch Reset
FU (or F)	Facility in use
FNU	Facility not in use
SF	Storage full
SNF	Storage not full
SE	Storage empty
SNE	Storage not empty

indication of the entity condition to which they make reference.

An an element in a Boolean expression, a Logical Operator must have appended to it either the number or symbolic name of a specific member of the entity type to which it refers. As usual, if a symbolic name is used, a dollar sign must be interposed between it and the Logical Operator. Examples of Boolean expression elements constructed with Logical Operators are SNE$JANE, FNU21, and LR3. If the Storage JANE is not empty, then SNE$JANE is *true*; otherwise, it is *false*. If Facility 21 is not in use, then FNU21 is *true*; otherwise, it is *false*. Similarly, if Logic Switch 3 is Reset, then LR3 is *true*; otherwise, it is *false*. Single elements such as these constitute *simple Boolean expressions*.

The strong similarity between the Logical Operators and Logical Mnemonics should be noted. Except for Facilities, they are composed of the same character sequences. Despite the similarity in their appearance, they are used in quite different contexts. Logical Mnemonics are only used as Block Auxiliary Operators. Logical Operators are only used to construct elements in Boolean expressions.

6.2.2 Relational Operators

Relational Operators express a condition which might possibly exist between two pieces of numeric-valued data. The Relational Operators

TABLE 6.2 The Relational Operators in GPSS

Relational Operators	Condition Expressed
'G'	Greater
'GE'	Greater or Equal
'E'	Equal
'NE'	Not Equal
'LE'	Less or Equal
'L'	Less

are shown in Table 6.2, with an indication of the tentative relationship they express.

An element in a Boolean expression can be constructed by placing a Relational Operator between a pair of Standard Numerical Attributes. Examples of elements constructed this way are R$CHANL'GE'3, Q$LINE1'L'Q$LINE2, and P5'G'X$ROP. If the remaining capacity of the Storage CHANL is greater than or equal to 3, then R$CHANL'GE'3 is *true*; otherwise, it is *false*. Or, if the current content of the Queue LINE1 is less than that of the Queue LINE2, Q$LINE1'L'Q$LINE2 is *true*; otherwise, it is *false*. Finally, if P5 is greater than fullword Savevalue ROP, then P5'G'X$ROP is *true*; otherwise, it is *false*. Single elements such as these also constitute *simple Boolean expressions*.

It is evident that the Relational Operators listed in Table 6.2 strongly resemble the Auxiliary Operators available for use with the TEST Block. The same alphabetic characters are used in both instances, but as Relational Operators the characters are enclosed within single quotes.

6.2.3 Boolean Operators

Boolean data is characterized by the fact that its values, rather than being numeric, are logical. There are only two possible logical values: *true*, and *false*. Logical values are sometimes called *Boolean values*, or *truth values*.

A *Boolean Operator* stands between a pair of logical values, and produces a logical result. Such an operator can be contrasted with a Relational Operator, which stands between a pair of *numeric* values, and produces a *logical* value as a consequence. The two Boolean Operators, and the logical values they produce, depending on the logical values between which they stand, are shown in Table 6.3.

As shown by earlier examples, elements constructed with Logical Operators, and with Relational Operators, are either *true* or *false* in value, i.e., are logical-valued. As a result,

Boolean Operators can be placed between such elements. When one or more Boolean Operators are used in this fashion, a *compound Boolean expression* results. An example would be R5'G'3*LR$SYGNL. If it is true that the remaining capacity of Storage 5 is greater than 3, *and* that the Logic Switch SYGNL is Reset, then the compound Boolean expression is *true*; otherwise, the expression is *false*.

A second example of a compound Boolean expression is FNU$CPU*(SNF12+SNF$LINE). Note that two Boolean Operators are used in this case. As this example suggests, parentheses can be used to set off part of expressions within compound expressions. When this is done, the information within parentheses is evaluated first; then, the resulting value is used in the context of the overall expression. In this example, if Storage 12 is not full, or if the Storage LINE is not full, or if neither is full, then the parenthesized expression is *true*. When the parenthesized expression is *true* and, in addition, the Facility CPU is not in use, the final value of the entire expression is *true*; otherwise, it is *false*.

6.2.4 The Boolean Variable Definition Card

The format of the card used to define a Boolean Variable, shown in Table 6.4, is identical to that of an Arithmetic Variable card. The differences in card content are that the word BVARIABLE is entered in the Operation field, and the expression in the Operands field is Boolean, not arithmetic. The other features of Arithmetic

TABLE 6.3 The Boolean Operators in GPSS

Boolean Operator	Name	Result of Operation
*	And	The result is *true* when the values on both sides of the operator are *true*; otherwise, the result is *false*
+	Or	The result is *true* when either or both of the values between which the operator stands are *true*; otherwise, the result is *false*

TABLE 6.4 Format for the Card to Define a Boolean Variable

Punchcard Field	Information Supplied in the Field
Location	The name (numeric or symbolic) of the Boolean Variable
Operation	Literally, the word BVARIABLE
Operands	The Boolean expression which defines the Boolean Variable

LOCATION	OPERATION	A,B,C,D,E,F
MAIZE	BVARIABLE	SNE$JANE FIRST EXAMPLE
BLUE	BVARIABLE	R$CHAN1'GE'3 SECOND EXAMPLE
IRISH	BVARIABLE	R5'G'3*LR$SYGNL THIRD EXAMPLE

FIGURE 6.1 A first set of examples of Boolean Variables

Variable cards apply. In particular, the first blank column encountered in the Operands field terminates definition of the Boolean Variable; and expressions too long to be contained within card columns 19–71 must be broken up into a series of shorter expressions, and defined through two or more Boolean Variables.

6.2.5 Examples and Rules

Three examples of Boolean Variables are shown in Figure 6.1. Simple Boolean expressions are shown in the first and second examples. The third example shows a compound Boolean expression. These three examples were among those just discussed in the subsections on Logical Operators, Relational Operators, and Boolean Operators, respectively. Depending on whether the values of the Boolean expressions are *true* or *false*, the corresponding values of BV$MAIZE, BV$BLUE, and BV$IRISH will be 1 or 0, respectively.

For those without prior exposure to logical values and Boolean Operators, there may be some initial confusion about the way compound Boolean expressions are evaluated. As was true for Arithmetic Variables, there is a well-defined sequence of steps followed when determining the value of a Boolean expression. These steps are especially easily described in GPSS, because *arithmetic operators are not permitted in Boolean expressions.* Hence, when the symbols + and * are seen in a Boolean expression, they are known to represent Boolean Operators, and not the arithmetic operations of addition and multiplication.

These are the rules for evaluation of Boolean expressions.

1. The Logical Operators and Relational Operators share the highest precedence level. When two or more of these operators are used in a Boolean expression, their effect takes place in left-to-right order of their appearance.

2. The Boolean Operators + and * reside at the next precedence level.[1] When two or more Boolean Operators are used in a Boolean expression, their effect takes place in left-to-right order of their appearance.

3. When parentheses are used, everything within parentheses is evaluated first, using rules (1) and (2). The intermediate result thereby produced is then used in the rest of the Boolean expression.

Figure 6.2 shows several additional examples of Boolean Variables. In the first example, the Relational Operator 'GE' and the Logical Operators SE and LS first have their effect, in that order (Rule 1). Then the Boolean Operators + and * have their effect, in that order (Rule 2). For the Boolean expression to be *true*,

1. C1'GE'500 must be *true*, or SE$SPACE must be *true* (or both of these must be *true*), and

2. LS$AMBER must be *true*.

Note, then, that BV$KAPPA is *false* in any event if LS$AMBER is *false*.

In the second example in Figure 6.2, the Logical Operators FNU first operate (Rule 1).

[1]Note carefully that GPSS differs on this count from most other programming languages. In other languages, the Boolean Operators * and + usually reside at different precedence levels, with * taking precedence over +.

LOCATION	OPERATION	A,B,C,D,E,F
KAPPA	BVARIABLE	C1'GE'500+SE$SPACE*LS$AMBER FIRST EXAMPLE
ALPHA	BVARIABLE	FNU1+FNU2*FNU3+FNU4 SECOND EXAMPLE
THETA	BVARIABLE	C1'GE'500+(SE$SPACE*LS$AMBER) THIRD EXAMPLE

FIGURE 6.2 A second set of examples of Boolean Variables

Then the Boolean Operators $+$, $*$, and $+$ operate, in that sequence, from left-to-right (Rule 2). A moment's thought shows that there are 16 different true—false patterns in the Boolean expression. For eight of these patterns, FNU4 is *true*, which makes the entire expression true. Of the remaining eight patterns (the eight for which FNU4 is *false*), the expression is *true* for only three of them. These three patterns are the ones for which FNU3 is *true*, and either FNU1 or FNU2 (or both) are also *true*.

The third example repeats the first, but with parentheses introduced around part of the expression. The parentheses have been positioned to give the Boolean Operator $*$ higher precedence in the expression than the Boolean Operator $+$. For the Boolean expression to be *true*, then, either

1. C1'GE'500 must be *true*, or
2. both LS$AMBER and SE$SPACE must be *true*,

or

3. the conditions in both (1) and (2) must be satisfied.

The introduction of parentheses makes the truth conditions in the third example quite different from those in the first example.

6.2.6 Testing Boolean Variables

Because their values are either 1 or 0, the TEST Block is used to test Boolean Variables in GPSS models. Normally, one thinks of a required set of conditions as being in effect when a Boolean Variable is *true*, i.e., has a value of 1. As a consequence, Boolean Variables are usually tested to determine if their value equals 1. For example, a Transaction is held at the Block preceding "TEST E BV$ALLOK,1" until the Boolean Variable ALLOK is true. Or, a Transaction moving into the Block "TEST E BV$GREEN,1,RUTE3" continues to the sequential Block if the Boolean Variable GREEN is true, and goes to the nonsequential Location RUTE3 otherwise. Of course, there is no reason why Boolean Variables cannot be tested to determine if they are false, i.e., equal to zero. Transactions initiating such testing go to the sequential Block eventually (refusal mode) or immediately (conditional transfer mode) if the variable is false, or go immediately to the nonsequential Block (conditional transfer mode) if the variable is true.

Use of *simple* Boolean expressions (such as those in the first and second examples in Figure 6.1) is to be discouraged. A Boolean ex-pression is simple if it consists of exactly one Logical-Operator element, or of exactly one Relational-Operator element. Consider the following.

1. In the former case, the GATE Block can be used to achieve the same effect with less execution time. For example, "GATE NU CPU" is logically identical to "TEST E BV$SIMPL,1", where "SIMPL BVARIABLE FNU$CPU" defines the Boolean Variable SIMPL. As indicated previously, substantially less execution time is required with the GATE than with the TEST Block.

2. In the latter case, the TEST Block can be used to produce the desired logical effect with less execution time. For example, "TEST L Q1,Q2" is logically identical to "TEST E BV$WHY,1", where "WHY BVARIABLE Q1'L'Q2" defines the Boolean Variable WHY. The first TEST Block requires only one comparison (Q1 vs. Q2), whereas the second requires two comparisons (Q1 vs. Q2, then BV$WHY vs. 1).

6.3 CASE STUDY 6A
Oil Tanker Accommodation at a Port

A port in Africa is used to load tankers with crude oil for overwater shipment. The port has facilities for loading as many as three tankers simultaneously. The tankers, which arrive at the port every 11 ± 7 hours, are of three different types. The relative frequency of the various types, and their loading-time requirements, are shown in Table 6A.1.

There is one tug at the port. Tankers of all types require the services of this tug to move into a berth, and later to move out of a berth. Furthermore, the area experiences frequent storms, and no berthing or deberthing of a tanker can take place when a storm is in progress. When storms occur, they last 4 ± 2 hours. The time between the end of one storm, and the onset of the next, follows the exponential distribution and has a mean value of 48 hours. When a tug is available and no storm is in progress, berthing or deberthing activity takes about 1 hour. Operating experience shows that the three

TABLE 6A.1 Tanker Specifications for Case Study 6A

Type	Relative Frequency	Loading Time, Hours
1	.25	18 ± 2
2	.55	24 ± 3
3	.20	36 ± 4

berths at the port are occupied about 80 percent of the time. On average, due to delays because of storms, unavailability of a berth, or unavailability of the tug, tanker residence time at the port exceeds the mean tanker loading time by about 5 hours. This is true for each type of tanker.

A shipper is considering bidding on a contract to transport oil from the port to the United Kingdom. He has determined that five tankers of a particular type would have to be committed to this task to meet contract specifications. These tankers would require 21 ± 3 hours to load oil at the port. After loading and deberthing, they would travel to the United Kingdom, offload the oil, return to the port for reloading, etc. Their round-trip travel time, including offloading, is estimated to be 240 ± 24 hours.

Before the port authorities can commit themselves to accommodating the proposed five tankers, the effect of the additional port traffic on the in-port residence time of the current port users must be determined. Build a GPSS model to simulate the operation of the port under the proposed new commitment. Design the model to measure in-port residence time of the proposed additional tankers, as well as the three types of tankers which already use the port. Use a 1-year simulation to estimate the distributions of these residence-time random variables.

(2) Approach Taken in Building the Model

The model is composed of a major segment, and two supporting segments. In the major segment, movement of the various tankers through the port facilities is simulated. In one of the supporting segments, the five additional tankers which have been proposed are brought into the model at the beginning of the simulation, and are then routed into the major segment. In the other supporting segment, which is self-contained, the daily storm conditions are simulated. Whether it is currently storming or not is communicated to the major segment through a Logic Switch. These various segments will now be commented on in more detail.

A single Transaction circulates in the storm segment. When it first enters the segment, it moves into the Block "ADVANCE 48, FN$XPDIS", where it can be thought of as a storm which is "on its way". Leaving the ADVANCE Block, it puts the Logic Switch STORM into a Set position, indicating that a storm is now in progress. The Transaction is then held at another ADVANCE Block 4 ± 2 hours, while it storms. When the storm is over, the Logic Switch STORM is put back into a Reset position, and the Transaction transfers back to the original ADVANCE Block, thereby becoming the next storm on its way.

In the proposed-tanker initialization segment, the five tankers enter the model at the start of the simulation and are tagged by setting their P1 value to 4. (The other three tanker types will have P1 values of 1, 2, and 3.) They then enter an ADVANCE Block, where the first is held 0 hours, the second 48 hours, the third 96 hours, and so on. These staggered holding times are designed to space out the five tankers before routing them to the major model segment. The 48-hour "time between tankers" was determined from the 240-hour round-trip time in effect for each of the five tankers. After this spacing out, each tanker is assumed to have just arrived at the port (for the first time). The time-of-arrival is marked in Parameter 3, and the tanker is transferred to the major model segment.

Tanker types 1, 2, and 3 arrive at the major model segment through a GENERATE Block, are tagged in Parameter 1 with their type number, and then proceed to compete for use of the port facilities. When they are finished, they leave the model. In contrast, the five proposed tankers never leave the model. Like the other tankers, they compete in the major segment for use of the port facilities. When they leave the port, however, they are sieved out of the leaving-ship stream, and are routed to an ADVANCE Block where their round-trip time is simulated. After their round trip, their time-of-arrival back at port is marked in Parameter 3, and they proceed to compete again for use of the port facilities.

The conditions required to berth and deberth are tested in the major model segment with Boolean Variables. Three conditions must be simultaneously satisfied for berthing to occur (berth available; tug available; no storm in progress). Two conditions must be satisfied for deberthing to take place (tug available; no storm in progress). The simultaneous occurrence of these conditions is easily tested for with Boolean Variables.

Loading time for tankers at the port is determined through each Transaction's P1 value. P1 is used as the argument for a Function MEAN, which returns the proper mean loading time. P1 is also used as the argument for a Function SPRED, which returns the loading-time spread modifier. It is not possible, though, to simulate loading time at the Block "ADVANCE FN$MEAN, FN$SPRED". If this were done, the Processor would interpret the B Operand as a *Function*

modifier, and the returned value would be used as a *multiplier* of the mean. To produce the desired spread modification, each tanker-Transaction first copies the proper spread to Parameter 2. It then enters the Block "ADVANCE FN$MEAN,P2" to simulate loading time.

(3) Table of Definitions

Time Unit: 1 Hour

TABLE 6A.2   Table of Definitions for Case Study 6A

GPSS Entity	Interpretation		
Transactions			
Model Segment 1	A carrier of a potential storm		
Model Segment 2	One of the proposed tankers		
Model Segment 3	One of the tankers using the port		
	P1 : A tanker-type code		
		Value	Significance
		1	Type 1 tanker
		2	Type 2 tanker
		3	Type 3 tanker
		4	Proposed additional tanker
	P2 : Unloading-time spread, hours		
	P3 : Time of arrival at port (used only for Trans-actions simulating the proposed additional tankers)		
Model Segment 4	A times		
Facilities			
TUG	The tug		
Functions			
MEAN	Function describing mean loading time, depending on the type of tanker		
SPRED	Function describing the loading-time spread, depending on the type of tanker		
TYPE	Function describing the distribution of tankers of type 1, 2, and 3		
Logic Switches			
STORM	A Logic Switch which, when Set, indicates that a storm is in progress		
Storages			
BERTH	A Storage simulating the loading facilities at the port		
Tables			
1, 2, 3, and 4	Tables used to estimate the in-port residence-time distributions for tankers of type 1, 2, and 3, and the proposed additional tankers, respectively		
Variables (Arithmetic)			
SPACE	A Variable taking on the values 0, 48, 96, 144, and 192, in that chronological sequence; used to space out the first arrivals of the proposed additional tankers		
Variables (Boolean)			
GOIN	A Variable which is true only when the berthing conditions are satisfied		
GOOUT	A Variable which is true only when the deberthing conditions are satisfied		

(4) Block Diagrams

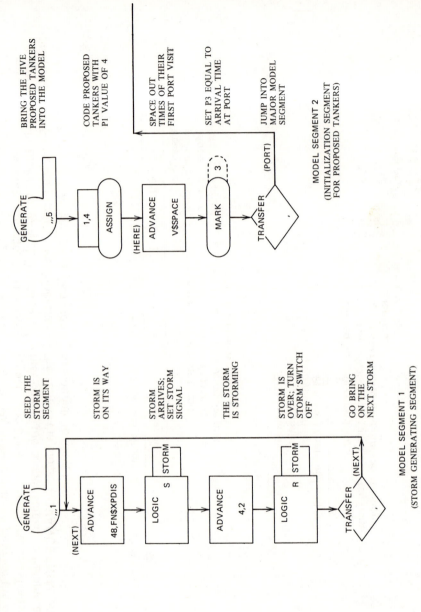

BRING THE FIVE
PROPOSED TANKERS
INTO THE MODEL

CODE PROPOSED
TANKERS WITH
P1 VALUE OF 4

SPACE OUT
TIMES OF THEIR
FIRST PORT VISIT

SET P3 EQUAL TO
ARRIVAL TIME
AT PORT

JUMP INTO
MAJOR MODEL
SEGMENT

GENERATE
,,,5

1,4
ASSIGN

(HERE)
ADVANCE
V$SPACE

MARK
3

TRANSFER
(PORT)

MODEL SEGMENT 2
(INITIALIZATION SEGMENT
FOR PROPOSED TANKERS)

SEED THE
STORM
SEGMENT

STORM IS
ON ITS WAY

STORM
ARRIVES;
SET STORM
SIGNAL

THE STORM
IS STORMING

STORM IS
OVER; TURN
STORM SWITCH
OFF

GO BRING
ON THE
NEXT STORM

GENERATE
,,,1

(NEXT)
ADVANCE
48,FN$XPDIS

LOGIC
S
STORM

ADVANCE
4,2

LOGIC
R
STORM

TRANSFER
(NEXT)

MODEL SEGMENT 1
(STORM GENERATING SEGMENT)

FIGURE 6A.1   Block Diagram for Case Study 6A

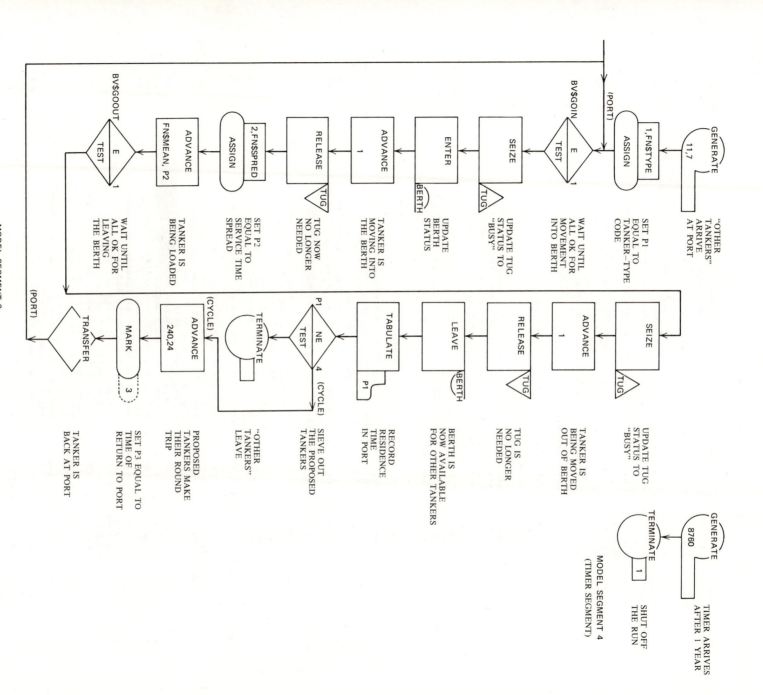

GENERATE
11,7
"OTHER TANKERS" ARRIVE AT PORT

ASSIGN
1,FN$TYPE
SET P1 EQUAL TO TANKER-TYPE CODE

(PORT)

BV$GOIN

TEST
E
1
WAIT UNTIL ALL OK FOR MOVEMENT INTO BERTH

SEIZE
TUG
UPDATE TUG STATUS TO "BUSY"

ENTER
BERTH
UPDATE BERTH STATUS

ADVANCE
1
TANKER IS MOVING INTO THE BERTH

RELEASE
TUG
TUG NOW NO LONGER NEEDED

2,FN$SPRED
SET P2 EQUAL TO SERVICE TIME SPREAD

ASSIGN
TANKER IS BEING LOADED

ADVANCE
FN$MEAN, P2

BV$GOOUT

TEST
E
1
WAIT UNTIL ALL OK FOR LEAVING THE BERTH

SEIZE
TUG
UPDATE TUG STATUS TO "BUSY"

ADVANCE
1
TANKER IS BEING MOVED OUT OF BERTH

RELEASE
TUG
TUG IS NO LONGER NEEDED

LEAVE
BERTH
BERTH IS NOW AVAILABLE FOR OTHER TANKERS

TABULATE
P1
RECORD RESIDENCE TIME IN PORT

TEST
NE
P1
4
(CYCLE)
SIEVE OUT THE PROPOSED TANKERS

TERMINATE
"OTHER TANKERS" LEAVE

ADVANCE
240,24
PROPOSED TANKERS MAKE THEIR ROUND TRIP

MARK
3
SET P3 EQUAL TO TIME OF RETURN TO PORT

(CYCLE)

TRANSFER
(PORT)
TANKER IS BACK AT PORT

MODEL SEGMENT 3
(PORT ACTIVITIES: CYCLING OF PROPOSED TANKERS)

GENERATE
8760
TIMER ARRIVES AFTER 1 YEAR

TERMINATE
1
SHUT OFF THE RUN

MODEL SEGMENT 4
(TIMER SEGMENT)

(5) Extended Program Listing

```
BLOCK                                                                                              CARD
NUMBER  *LOC    OPERATION  A,B,C,D,E,F,G              COMMENTS                                      NUMBER
                SIMULATE                                                                              1
                *                                                                                     2
                *          FUNCTION DEFINITION(S)                                                      3
                *                                                                                     4
        MEAN    FUNCTION   P1,L4                      MEAN SERVICE TIME FOR TANKER TYPE "P1"           5
                1,18/2,24/3,36/4,21                                                                    6
        SPRED   FUNCTION   P1,L4                      SERVICE TIME SPREAD FOR TANKER TYPE "P1"         7
                1,2/2,3/3,4/4,3                                                                        8
        TYPE    FUNCTION   RN1,D3                     DISTRIBUTION OF "OTHER TANKER" TYPES             9
                .25,1/.8,2/1,3                                                                        10
        XPDIS   FUNCTION   RN1,C24                    EXPONENTIAL DISTRIBUTION FUNCTION               11
                0.0/.1,.104/.2,.222/.3,.355/.4,.509/.5,.69/.6,.915/.7,1.2/.75,1.38                   12
                .8,1.6/.84,1.83/.88,2.12/.9,2.3/.92,2.52/.94,2.81/.95,2.9/.96,3.2                    13
                .97,3.5/.98,3.9/.99,4.6/.995,5.3/.998,6.2/.999,7/.9998,8                              14
                *                                                                                    15
                *          STORAGE CAPACITY DEFINITION(S)                                             16
                *                                                                                    17
                STORAGE    S$BERTH,3                  PROVIDE 3 BERTHS                                18
                *                                                                                    19
                *          TABLE DEFINITION(S)                                                        20
                *                                                                                    21
        1       TABLE      M1,20,10,9                 PORT RESIDENCE TIME, "TANKER TYPE 1"            22
        2       TABLE      M1,20,10,9                 PORT RESIDENCE TIME, "TANKER TYPE 2"            23
        3       TABLE      M1,40,10,9                 PORT RESIDENCE TIME, "TANKER TYPE 3"            24
        4       TABLE      MP3,20,10,9                PORT RESIDENCE TIME, PROPOSED TANKERS           25
                *                                                                                    26
                *          VARIABLE DEFINITION(S)                                                     27
                *                                                                                    28
        GOIN    BVARIABLE  SNF$BERTH*FNU$TUG*LR$STORM BERTH-ENTERING CONDITIONS                      29
        GOOUT   BVARIABLE  FNU$TUG*LR$STORM           BERTH-LEAVING CONDITIONS                       30
        SPACE   VARIABLE   48*N$HERE                                                                 31
                *                                                                                    32
                *          MODEL SEGMENT 1 (STORM GENERATING SEGMENT)                                 33
                *                                                                                    34
     1          GENERATE   ,,,1                       SEED THE STORM SEGMENT                          35
     2  NEXT    ADVANCE    48,FN$XPDIS                STORM IS ON ITS WAY                             36
     3          LOGIC S    STORM                      STORM ARRIVES; SET STORM SIGNAL                 37
     4          ADVANCE    4,2                        THE STORM IS STORMING                           38
     5          LOGIC R    STORM                      STORM IS OVER; TURN STORM SWITCH OFF            39
     6          TRANSFER   ,NEXT                      GO BRING ON THE NEXT STORM                      40
                *                                                                                    41
                *          MODEL SEGMENT 2 (INITIALIZATION SEGMENT FOR PROPOSED TANKERS)              42
                *                                                                                    43
     7          GENERATE   ,,,5                       BRING THE PROPOSED TANKERS INTO THE MODEL       44
     8          ASSIGN     1,4                        CODE PROPOSED TANKERS WITH P1 VALUE OF 4        45
     9  HERE    ADVANCE    V$SPACE                    SPACE OUT TIMES OF THEIR FIRST PORT VISIT       46
    10          MARK       3                          SET P3 = ARRIVAL TIME AT PORT                   47
    11          TRANSFER   ,PORT                      JUMP INTO MAJOR MODEL SEGMENT                   48
                *                                                                                    49
                *          MODEL SEGMENT 3 (PORT ACTIVITIES; CYCLING OF PROPOSED TANKERS)             50
                *                                                                                    51
    12          GENERATE   11,7                       "OTHER TANKERS" ARRIVE AT PORT                  52
    13          ASSIGN     1,FN$TYPE                  SET P1 = TANKER-TYPE CODE                       53
    14  PORT    TEST E     BV$GOIN,1                  WAIT 'TIL ALL OK FOR MOVEMENT INTO BERTH        54
    15          SEIZE      TUG                        UPDATE TUG STATUS TO "BUSY"                     55
    16          ENTER      BERTH                      UPDATE BERTH STATUS                             56
    17          ADVANCE    1                          TANKER IS BEING MOVED INTO THE BERTH            57
    18          RELEASE    TUG                        TUG NOW NO LONGER NEEDED                        58
    19          ASSIGN     2,FN$SPRED                 SET P2 = SERVICE TIME SPREAD                    59
    20          ADVANCE    FN$MEAN,P2                 TANKER IS BEING LOADED                          60
    21          TEST E     BV$GOOUT,1                 WAIT 'TIL ALL OK FOR LEAVING THE BERTH          61
    22          SEIZE      TUG                        UPDATE TUG STATUS TO "BUSY"                     62
    23          ADVANCE    1                          TANKER IS BEING MOVED OUT OF BERTH              63
    24          RELEASE    TUG                        TUG IS NO LONGER NEEDED                         64
    25          LEAVE      BERTH                      BERTH IS NOW AVAILABLE FOR OTHER TANKERS        65
    26          TABULATE   P1                         RECORD RESIDENCE TIME IN PORT                   66
    27          TEST NE    P1,4,CYCLE                 SIEVE OUT THE PROPOSED TANKERS                  67
    28          TERMINATE                             "OTHER TANKERS" LEAVE                           68
    29  CYCLE   ADVANCE    240,24                     PROPOSED TANKERS MAKE THEIR ROUND TRIP          69
    30          MARK       3                          SET P3 = TIME OF RETURN TO PORT                 70
    31          TRANSFER   ,PORT                      TANKER IS BACK AT PORT                          71
                *                                                                                    72
                *          MODEL SEGMENT 4 (TIMER SEGMENT)                                            73
                *                                                                                    74
    32          GENERATE   8760                       TIMER ARRIVES AFTER 1 YEAR                      75
    33          TERMINATE  1                          SHUT OFF THE RUN                                76
                *                                                                                    77
                *          CONTROL CARDS                                                              78
                *                                                                                    79
                START      1                          START THE RUN                                   80
                END                                   RETURN CONTROL TO OPERATING SYSTEM              81
```

FIGURE 6A.2 Extended Program Listing for Case Study 6A

(6) Program Output

TABLE 1
ENTRIES IN TABLE 193   MEAN ARGUMENT 48.704   STANDARD DEVIATION 24.937   SUM OF ARGUMENTS 9400.000

UPPER LIMIT	OBSERVED FREQUENCY	PER CENT OF TOTAL	CUMULATIVE PERCENTAGE	CUMULATIVE REMAINDER	MULTIPLE OF MEAN	DEVIATION FROM MEAN NON-WEIGHTED
20	12	6.21	6.2	93.7	.410	-1.151
30	56	29.01	35.2	64.7	.615	-.750
40	24	12.43	47.6	52.3	.821	-.349
50	19	9.84	57.5	42.4	1.026	.051
60	19	9.84	67.3	32.6	1.231	.452
70	20	10.36	77.7	22.2	1.437	.853
80	20	10.36	88.0	11.9	1.642	1.254
90	13	6.73	94.8	5.1	1.847	1.655
OVERFLOW	10	5.18	100.0	.0		

AVERAGE VALUE OF OVERFLOW 105.59

(a)

TABLE 2
ENTRIES IN TABLE 422   MEAN ARGUMENT 54.452   STANDARD DEVIATION 22.062   SUM OF ARGUMENTS 22979.000

UPPER LIMIT	OBSERVED FREQUENCY	PER CENT OF TOTAL	CUMULATIVE PERCENTAGE	CUMULATIVE REMAINDER	MULTIPLE OF MEAN	DEVIATION FROM MEAN NON-WEIGHTED
20	0	.00	.0	100.0	.367	-1.561
30	72	17.06	17.0	82.9	.550	-1.108
40	75	17.77	34.8	65.1	.734	-.655
50	61	14.45	49.2	50.7	.918	-.201
60	52	12.32	61.6	38.3	1.101	.251
70	47	11.13	72.7	27.2	1.285	.704
80	57	13.50	86.2	13.7	1.469	1.157
90	42	9.95	96.2	3.7	1.652	1.611
OVERFLOW	16	3.79	100.0	.0		

AVERAGE VALUE OF OVERFLOW 105.56

(b)

TABLE 3
ENTRIES IN TABLE 175   MEAN ARGUMENT 69.348   STANDARD DEVIATION 23.437   SUM OF ARGUMENTS 12136.000

UPPER LIMIT	OBSERVED FREQUENCY	PER CENT OF TOTAL	CUMULATIVE PERCENTAGE	CUMULATIVE REMAINDER	MULTIPLE OF MEAN	DEVIATION FROM MEAN NON-WEIGHTED
20	21	11.99	11.9	88.0	.576	-1.252
30	27	15.42	27.4	72.5	.720	-.825
40	22	12.57	39.9	60.0	.865	-.398
50	23	13.14	53.1	46.8	1.009	.027
60	31	17.71	70.8	29.1	1.153	.454
70	14	7.99	78.8	21.1	1.297	.881
80	13	7.42	86.2	13.7	1.441	1.307
90	18	10.28	96.5	3.4	1.586	1.734
OVERFLOW	6	3.42	100.0	.0		

AVERAGE VALUE OF OVERFLOW 120.33

(c)

TABLE 4
ENTRIES IN TABLE 151   MEAN ARGUMENT 50.609   STANDARD DEVIATION 23.625   SUM OF ARGUMENTS 7642.000

UPPER LIMIT	OBSERVED FREQUENCY	PER CENT OF TOTAL	CUMULATIVE PERCENTAGE	CUMULATIVE REMAINDER	MULTIPLE OF MEAN	DEVIATION FROM MEAN NON-WEIGHTED
20	1	.66	.6	99.3	.395	-1.295
30	40	26.49	27.1	72.8	.592	-.872
40	26	17.21	44.3	55.6	.790	-.449
50	17	11.25	55.6	44.3	.987	-.025
60	15	9.93	65.5	34.4	1.185	.397
70	20	13.24	78.8	21.1	1.383	.820
80	13	8.60	87.4	12.5	1.580	1.244
90	10	6.62	94.0	5.9	1.778	1.667
OVERFLOW	9	5.96	100.0	.0		

AVERAGE VALUE OF OVERFLOW 104.11

(d)

FIGURE 6A.3 Distribution of in-port residence time, Case Study 6A. (a) Type 1 tankers. (b) Type 2 tankers. (c) Type 3 tankers. (d) Proposed tankers.

(7) Discussion

Model Logic.   Notice how the spacing out of first arrivals of the proposed additional tankers is accomplished in Model Segment 2. Holding time at the spacing-out ADVANCE Block (Block 9 in Figure 6A.2) is computed through the Variable SPACE as 48*N$HERE. HERE, in turn, is the Location occupied by the ADVANCE Block itself. When the first tanker-Transaction enters the Block, N$HERE is zero, so the holding time is zero. (Remember that Block Counts are updated as the *last step* in execution of a Block's subroutine. This means that N$HERE still has a value of 0 when the product 48*N$HERE is formed.) When the second tanker-Transaction enters the Block, N$HERE is 1 (thanks to the first tanker-Transaction), so its holding time is 48. And so on. (See exercise 5a in Section 6.4.)

The ASSIGN Block in Model Segment 3 (Block 19, Figure 6A.2) is redundant to some extent. After their first visit to the harbor, Parameter 2 of the proposed additional tanker-Transactions already carries the correct value for the loading-time spread. In exercise 5b, Section 6.4, you are asked to improve on this situation, thereby eliminating a number of Block executions.

Program Output.[2]   Figure 6A.3 shows the in-port residence time Tables for the various tankers. Average in-port residence time for tanker types 1, 2, and 3 is 48.7, 54.4, and 69.3 hours, respectively (MEAN ARGUMENT in Tables 1, 2, and 3). Compared with their mean berth, load, and deberth time-totals of 20, 26, and 38 hours, respectively (assuming no delays of any kind), their delays per port visit amount to about 30 hours. The 30-hour figure can be compared with the 5-hour delays these tankers experience when they do not have to compete with the additional tankers (as indicated in the problem statement). From model output not shown, berth occupancy has jumped to about 97 percent with the additional tankers in use, as contrasted with about an 80 percent occupancy previously (as reported in the problem statement).

The proposed additional tankers spend about 2 days (50.6 hours, Table 4 in Figure 6A.3) in port on average. With no delays, their berth, load, and deberth time would amount to 23 hours on average. Hence, they experience about a 27-

[2]Total CPU time for the simulation on an IBM 360/67 computer was 21.6 seconds.

hour delay per visit to the port. Exercise 6, Section 6.4, involves further investigation of these various tanker delays.

6.4 Exercises

1. Show definitions for Boolean Variables which are true under the following conditions. Also define any Arithmetic Variables you may use as Boolean Variable components.

    (a) Queue 7 is not empty and Queue 6 is empty.

    (b) The Storage TUG is full or the Queue SHIP has a current content greater than 3.

    (c) The sum of the current contents of Queues 1 and 2 is less than the current content of Queue 3.

    (d) The Boolean Variable defined with the expression "Q1 + Q2'L'Q3" has been proposed as a solution to (c). Why will the expression result in an error condition? What would you do to eliminate the error condition?

    (e) The standard deviation in the Table LTD is less than 10 percent of the Table mean, the number of entries in the Table exceeds 250, and the Relative Clock is an integral multiple of 24.

    (f) The Queue ONE is empty, and the Queue TWO is not empty or the Storage THREE has a remaining capacity less than two.

    (g) The Logic Switch AMBER is Set, or the Storage CROSS is full, or the Savevalue RTIME is zero in value.

2. A Transaction is to move beyond a certain point in a model only if the Logic Switch BETA is Set, and the Storage MEN has a remaining capacity of 3 or more. An analyst proposes using the Block Diagram segment shown in Figure E2 to accomplish this effect. What is wrong with his approach?

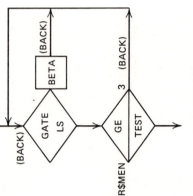

FIGURE E2

What will probably eventually happen if the corresponding model is run? What would you do to accomplish the same effect, and yet eliminate the flaw in the analyst's logic?

3. Show a Block Diagram segment delaying Trans-actions in Queue 7 until Facility 5 is not in use, Storage 3 is not full, and Logic Switch 2 is Reset.

4. A Transaction is to be sent to whichever one of the Facilities JOE and PETE is available. If both Facilities are either idle or busy, the Transaction is to go to the one whose utilization is the smaller of the two. Show a Boolean Variable and the corre-sponding TEST Block at which it can be evaluated to accomplish this routing.

5. These questions are based on Case Study 6A.

(a) Show how to simplify Model Segment 2 by eliminating the ADVANCE Block, and by changing the GENERATE Block's Operands accordingly.

(b) Show how to modify the Figure 6A.2 model to eliminate the partial redundancy represented by the presence of the ASSIGN Block in Model Segment 2 (Block 19).

(c) Through the Storage BERTH, the Figure 6A.2 model measures the fraction of the time that the berths are *occupied*. The fact that a berth is occupied, however, does not necessarily mean that it is being used to load oil onto a tanker. Show how to modify the model so that it measures the fraction of the time that the berths are actually used for oil-loading purposes.

6. In Case Study 6A, assume that the increased in-port residence time for tankers of type 1, 2, and 3 resulting from use of the port by the five additional tankers is unacceptably high. The owners of the port want estimates of the various inport residence time distributions for each of the following alternatives.

(a) The five additional tankers are given low priority at the port relative to the other type tankers. (In addition to the changed in-port residence times, to what extent does this alternative reduce the rate at which the five additional tankers can transport oil to the United Kingdom?)

(b) The additional tankers are given low priority at the port, and the number of proposed additional tankers is increased from five to six. The sixth tanker is assumed to be identical to the other five. (Besides changing in-port residence times, by how much does this alternative increase the rate at which the "six additional tankers" can transport oil to the United Kingdom?)

(c) The various tankers have equal priority at the port, but the number of loading berths is in-creased from three to four.

Make the necessary modifications to Case Study 6A to reflect these alternatives, then run the modified models to provide the requested information.

7. Show a complete GPSS Block Diagram for a model to simulate use of a single machine under the following circumstances.

(a) Jobs arrive at the machine in a Poisson stream at a mean rate of two jobs per hour.

(b) Fifty-five percent of the jobs are of Type 1; 30 percent are of Type 2; and the remaining 15 percent are of Type 3.

(c) Whether an arriving job is of Type 1, 2, or 3 is independent of the job type of the preceding arrival.

(d) Processing times for jobs of Type 1, 2, and 3 are exponentially distributed with mean values of 20, 30, and 40 minutes, respectively.

(e) The following two-part rule is used to deter-mine queue discipline at the machine.

(1) Service is provided first to jobs which have been waiting 90 minutes or longer. Within this set of jobs, the "shortest imminent operation" criterion is used.

(2) If there are no jobs which have been waiting 90 minutes or longer, the "shortest imminent operation" criterion is applied to the other jobs, if any, which are waiting for the machine.

Design the model to estimate the distribution of the random variable "time spent at the machine," as a function of job type. Time spent at the machine is the sum of waiting time, if any, and service time. The model should shut off after 100 jobs have been pro-cessed at the machine. How does your model behave when any of the several time ties possible in the system occur?

6.5 Explicitly Forcing a Restart of the Current Events Chain Scan: The BUFFER Block

It has been pointed out from time to time that under certain Scan Phase conditions, the GPSS Processor restarts its scan of the Current Events Chain. In particular, if one or more Blocks in a certain category are executed by the currently active Transaction, the Processor restarts the CEC scan after that Transaction finally comes to rest. The Blocks studied so far which have this effect are listed in Table 6.5.

SEIZE
RELEASE
ENTER
LEAVE
LOGIC
PRIORITY

Scan restarts under the above circumstances are an implicit part of the Processor's logic. That is, the analyst has no control over them. Furthermore, these implicit scan restarts do not take place until *after the active Transaction has stopped moving.* This does not happen until the active Transaction enters an ADVANCE Block (at which a nonzero holding time is computed), or a TERMINATE Block, or encounters a blocking condition.[3] In general, then, the scan is not restarted until after one or more additional Blocks have been executed by the active Transaction.

It sometimes happens that whenever a Transaction reaches a certain point in a model, the analyst wants the scan of the Current Events Chain to be restarted *immediately,* i.e., before that Transaction moves through any additional Blocks. GPSS provides a particular Block which can be used to produce exactly this effect. The Block is shown in Figure 6.3. The Block Opera-

simplicity, assume that no one person is permitted to check out more than one book at a time, and that the book a person wants is always available. To get a book, a person hands the clerk a checkout slip. The clerk then goes back into the stacks, finds the book, returns to the desk with it, and finishes the checkout procedure. If two or more people are waiting for service when the clerk again becomes available, the clerk takes each person's checkout slip and then fetches all the corresponding books at one time. The time required to locate a book or books in the stacks depends on the number of books which have to be found. The time required to pick up one or more slips, and to finish the checkout procedure after one or more books have been fetched from the stacks, is negligibly small.

Figure 6.4 shows a model for the checkout desk. Model Segment 1 simulates the customers, who arrive at the desk in a Poisson stream with a mean interarrival time of 300 seconds. Upon arrival, each customer moves into a QUEUE Block, and in general then waits there for the clerk to pick up his checkout slip (that is, waits for the SLIP-gate to be opened by the clerk). When the clerk opens the SLIP-gate (thereby simulating the act of picking up the customer's slip, or the customers' slips), the customer(s) then move into the "GATE LS SLIP" Block and wait there for the clerk to fetch the book(s) and finish the checkout procedure (that is, wait for the BOOK-gate to be opened by the clerk). When the clerk opens the BOOK-gate (thereby simulating the act of giving each customer his checked-out book), the customer(s) then move through the open gate, update the QUEUE statistics, and leave. Note that customer-Transactions have a Priority Level of 1, for reasons to be explained below.

Model Segment 2 in Figure 6.4 simulates the single clerk. In "idle" mode, the clerk waits at the Block "TEST G W\$BLOKA,0" until her services are needed. When one or more customer-Transactions are in the QUEUE Block in Model Segment 2, the clerk moves through the TEST Block, opens the SLIP-gate (by entering the Block "LOGIC S SLIP"), and moves into the BUFFER Block to let customer-Transaction(s) through the just-opened gate. Note that the clerk-Transaction has a Priority Level of 0, meaning that it occupies a position on the Current Events Chain *behind* the higher-priority cus-

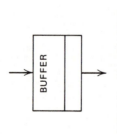

FIGURE 6.3 The BUFFER Block

tion is BUFFER. No Block Operands are involved. When a Transaction enters the BUFFER Block, the GPSS Processor ceases processing it, and immediately restarts the CEC scan. The buffering Transaction (that is, the Transaction which has entered the BUFFER Block) remains on the Current Events Chain, where it continues to occupy the position it was in when it entered the BUFFER Block. As the restarted scan proceeds, this buffering Transaction will eventually be encountered again by the Processor. At that time its forward motion in the model will be resumed.

As an example illustrating use of the BUFFER Block, consider a checkout desk at a small library which does not have an "open stack" policy (that is, which does not permit people to go into the stacks to find their own books). The checkout desk is manned by a single clerk. For

[3]Other situations not yet discussed can also bring the active Transaction to rest.

tomer-Transaction(s). By entering the BUFFER Block and thereby causing a restart of the CEC scan, the clerk-Transaction forces the GPSS Processor to process the customer-Transaction(s), moving it (them) through the SLIP-gate. After this has been done, the Processor again encounters the clerk-Transaction

on the Current Events Chain. The clerk now moves forward into the "LOGIC R SLIP" Block, closing the SLIP-gate. This must be done so any customers who arrive while the clerk is unavailable will find they must wait to have their checkout slips picked up. After closing the SLIP-gate, the clerk then fetches the book(s) (by entering the Block "ADVANCE FN$FETCH"). The time required for the fetch depends on the number of slips the clerk has, and this in turn equals W$BLOKB, i.e., the number of Transactions waiting in the Block "GATE LS SLIP". (This means that the Function FETCH, for which no definition is shown, has W$BLOKB as its argument.) When the clerk returns with the book(s), she opens the BOOK-gate (by moving into the Block "LOGIC S BOOK") and then buffers (by moving into the Block "LOGIC S BUFFER BOOK"). This forces the GPSS Processor to restart the CEC scan. The customer-Transaction(s), which had been waiting for the clerk to return from the stacks (that is, which had been delayed because of the closed BOOK-gate), now move through that gate, update Queue statistics at the DEPART Block, and leave. After this has been done, the Processor again encounters the clerk-Transaction on the Current Events Chain. The clerk now closes the BOOK-gate (by entering the Block "LOGIC R BOOK"), then transfers back to begin serving the next customer (or customers), if any, or to wait for the next customer to arrive.

The Figure 6.4 model should be studied until it is thoroughly understood. (See exercise 1, Section 6.7, for questions about the model.) In the next section, a case study is presented which involves modeling the operations at a library checkout desk. In contrast with the Figure 6.4 model, the case study allows for the possibility that more than one clerk works at the checkout desk. It also does away with the assumption that the time required to finish the checkout procedure after returning from the stacks is negligibly small. This complicates the logic required to model the checkout-completion activity.

6.6 CASE STUDY 6B
A Library Problem

(1) Statement of the Problem

Consider a library which does not have an open-stack policy. At such a library, anyone

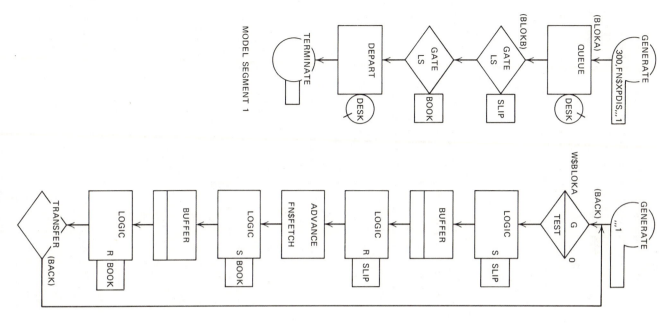

MODEL SEGMENT 1

MODEL SEGMENT 2

FIGURE 6.4 A Block Diagram illustrating BUFFER Block use

wanting a book must present a checkout slip to a clerk working behind the checkout desk. The clerk then goes into the stacks to find the book and returns to the desk with it. The rest of the checkout procedure then takes place, and the person leaves with the book.

If more than one person is waiting for service, a clerk often economizes on the time required to travel between the checkout desk and the stacks by picking up checkout slips from more than one waiting person. Because the number of books a clerk can conveniently carry is limited, however, the number of slips a clerk is willing to pick up at any one time is also limited.

Build a GPSS model to simulate the book-checkout procedure at a library under the following conditions.

1. People who want to check out books arrive at the desk in a Poisson stream at a mean rate of 30 people per hour.

2. Each person wants to check out exactly one book. Furthermore, the book wanted is always available.

3. The number of clerks who work at the checkout desk is to be a variable in the model.

4. Whenever a clerk becomes available, the clerk is willing to pick up checkout slips from as many as four people at a time (if that many are waiting for service).

5. These times are in effect.
(a) The time required to pick up checkout slips is negligibly small.
(b) A one-way trip between the checkout desk and the stacks requires 1 ± 0.5 minutes.
(c) The time required to find one, two, three, or four books is normally distributed with mean values of 3, 6, 9, and 12 minutes, respectively, and with a standard deviation equal to 20 percent of the mean.
(d) When the clerk returns from the stacks, the time required to complete the rest of the checkout procedure is 2 ± 1 minutes per person.

6. Checkout slips are picked up on a first-come, first-served basis. After a clerk returns from the stacks, the rest of the checkout procedure is also completed on a first-come, first-served basis.

7. If two or more clerks are idle when a customer arrives at the checkout desk, the clerk who has been idle the longest is the one who serves the customer.

8. If two or more people are waiting for service when two or more clerks become available, the clerks do not divide the work evenly among themselves. Instead, one clerk takes as many slips as possible (but not more than four); then, if there are still people with slips to be picked up, the next clerk takes as many slips as possible, and so on.

The model should estimate the distribution of the random variables "time spent by each person at the checkout desk," and "number of slips a clerk picks up." The utilization of the clerks should also be measured. Gather the requested information for the alternatives of three, four, and five clerks working at the checkout desk. For each alternative, run the simulation until 100 people have been completely served.

(2) Approach Taken in Building the Model

In relation to the simplified library model in Figure 6.4, there are five special considerations which must be taken into account in the more complicated case-study setting.

1. A means must be found to prevent a clerk from picking up slips from more than four customers at a time. (This contrasts with the Figure 6.4 model, in which the clerk picks up the slips from all waiting customers, no matter how many there are.)

2. Each clerk must have some way to know how many checkout slips she has when she goes into the stacks. (This information is needed to sample from the fetch-time distribution. It is also used later by the clerk to determine how many customers to hand checked-out books to when she returns from the stacks.) The Figure 6.4 method of using the Current Count at a Block cannot be repeated in the case study, because in general some customers will be waiting for the first clerk to return from the stacks, others will be waiting (at the same Block) for the second clerk to return from the stacks, and so on.

3. Because there is more than one clerk working at the desk, customers must be able to identify the clerk who picks up their slip, so that they can later know when that clerk has returned from the stacks, and has completed their checkout procedure.

4. Because there may be several different customers waiting for several different clerks to return from the stacks with books, clerks must be able to identify the customers whose books they have. Clerks can then signal to the right people that the checkout procedure has been completed for them.

5. Any one clerk completes the checkout procedure for only one customer at a time. Customers consequently are only able to leave the desk one at a time. (This contrasts with the Figure 6.4 model, in which the checkout procedure was finished simultaneously for each customer for whom the clerk had a checkout slip.)

The method used to handle each of these considerations is discussed below.

Consideration 1: Limiting the number of slips a clerk picks up. When model conditions call for slip-pickup to occur, the clerk opens the SLIP-gate. The clerk then buffers, causing the GPSS Processor to restart the Current Events Chain scan. When a high-priority customer-Transaction is processed, it moves through the open gate and enters a SAVEVALUE Block, incrementing a Savevalue by 1. (The clerk-Transaction zeroed-out the Savevalue just before opening the SLIP-gate. The Savevalue consequently counts the number of slips the clerk is picking up.) The customer-Transaction then moves into a TEST Block, where a Boolean Variable is evaluated to determine if it is true either that (1) the clerk now has picked up four slips, or (2) there are no more customers waiting for slip-pickup. If the Boolean Variable is true, the customer-Transaction itself closes the SLIP-gate; otherwise, the customer bypasses the LOGIC Block used to close the gate. In either event, the customer-Transaction then stops at another gate (corresponding to the BOOK-gate in the Figure 6.4 model), where it will wait until the clerk eventually returns from the stacks and finishes the checkout procedure. Meantime, continuing with the CEC scan, the GPSS Processor either lets more customer-Transactions through the SLIP-gate (if it is still open), or leaves them blocked at the SLIP-gate (if it has already been closed by a preceding customer-Transaction).

In the Figure 6.4 model, it was the clerk-Transaction which closed the SLIP-gate. This contrasts, then, with the case study model, in which it is a customer-Transaction which closes the SLIP-gate.

Consideration 2: Knowing how many slips a clerk has. As indicated in the discussion of Consideration 1, a count of the number of slips a clerk is picking up is maintained by the clerk-Transaction in a Savevalue. When the clerk-Transaction moves from its BUFFER Block, it enters an ASSIGN Block, copying this Savevalue to Parameter 2. This is all that is involved in arranging for the clerk to know how many slips she has picked up.

Consideration 3: Providing the clerks with individual identity. When each clerk-Transaction initially enters the model, it moves into an ASSIGN Block where its Parameter 1 is set equal to 1, or 2, or 3, etc., depending on whether it is the first clerk, the second clerk, or the third clerk, etc. This means that clerk-Transactions differ from each other via their P1 value.

To tell customers who is serving them, a clerk-Transaction begins service by entering the Block "SAVEVALUE CLERK,P1", thereby copying the clerk's identification number to the Savevalue CLERK. The clerk-Transaction then opens the SLIP-gate and buffers. After a customer-Transaction moves through the gate during the subsequent rescan, it enters the Block "ASSIGN 1,X$CLERK", thereby copying the clerk's number into Parameter 1. Hence, each customer-Transaction knows, through its Parameter 1 value, which clerk-Transaction is the one providing it with service.

Now consider the portion of the model which corresponds logically to the BOOK-gate in the Figure 6.4 model. Only one BOOK-gate was needed in Figure 6.4, because only one clerk worked at the desk. In the present model, the equivalent of a BOOK-gate is needed for *each* clerk. Because customer-Transactions waiting for a book have the clerk's identification number coded as their P1 value, the single Block "GATE LS P1" can serve as a BOOK-gate for *each* clerk. The number of gates involved equals the number of different values that Parameter 1 of customer-Transactions can assume. This, in turn, equals the number of clerks who work at the checkout desk.

For example, consider a customer-Transaction whose P1 value is 2. This means that clerk 2 is fetching the customer's book. When clerk 2 is ready to hand the book to the customer, it can indicate this by putting Logic Switch 2 into a Set position. This has the effect of opening the gate to the customer-Transaction, which will now find it can move through the Block "GATE LS P1". From the point of view of customer-Transactions with P1 values of 1, or 3, or 4, and so on, the gate continues to be closed (unless, of course, their clerk returns from the stacks and opens the gate for them).

Consideration 4: Enabling the clerks to identify their customers. It is an easy matter for a clerk to identify her customers, because those customers carry the clerk's number as their P1 value. Remember that a clerk-Transaction *also* carries the clerk's identification number as its P1 value. When the clerk-Transaction finishes a checkout, then, it can signal this by moving into the Block "LOGIC S P1", thereby opening its BOOK-gate (that is, setting the Logic Switch whose number equals its P1 value). The clerk-Transaction then buffers, letting the GPSS Processor try to move each of the customer-Transactions forward in the model. To qualify for movement through the Block "GATE LS P1", a customer-Transaction must have the proper clerk-number as its P1 value. Only a customer being served by the clerk in question is able to move through the gate.

Consideration 5: Completing only one checkout procedure at a time.

When a clerk-Transaction returns from the stacks, it enters an ADVANCE Block, where the time required to finish a single customer's checkout procedure elapses. The clerk-Transaction then opens its BOOK-gate and buffers to let the Processor move the now-finished customer-Transaction through the gate. The customer-Transaction itself then enters a "LOGIC R P1" Block, thereby closing the gate behind itself. This prevents other customer-Transactions (if any) who are being served by the same clerk from also moving through that clerk's BOOK-gate. (They can't logically move through the gate yet, because their checkout procedure hasn't yet been

finished.) The customer-Transaction then tabulates its time spent at the checkout desk, and leaves the model. As the scan proceeds, the buffering clerk-Transaction is again encountered. Moving from the BUFFER Block, the clerk next enters a LOOP Block to determine if one or more customers are still waiting for her to finish their checkout procedure. If so, the clerk goes back to the ADVANCE Block to simulate the time required for the next checkout completion; otherwise, the clerk transfers back to determine if one or more customers are currently waiting for slip-pickup, and so on.

In the Figure 6.4 model, it was the clerk-Transaction which closed the BOOK-gate. This contrasts, then, with the case study model, in which it is a customer-Transaction which closes the BOOK-gate belonging to its clerk.

The Block Diagram in Figure 6B.1 should now be studied. The remarks just made should then be reread, making frequent reference to the Block Diagram in the process. It should be realized that the Figure 6B.1 model, although it may seem complicated at first, is simply a logical extension of the Figure 6.4 model.

(3) Table of Definitions

Time Unit : 1 Second

TABLE 6B.1   Table of Definitions for Case Study 6B

GPSS Entity	Interpretation
Transactions	
Model Segment 1	A customer at the checkout desk
	P1 : Identification number of the clerk serving that customer
Model Segment 2	A clerk working at the checkout desk
	P1 : The clerk's identification number
	P2 : Initially, the number of slips the clerk has picked up ; later, the number of customers for whom the clerk has yet to complete the checkout procedure
Functions	
SNORM	Standard normal distribution function
XPDIS	Exponential distribution function
Logic Switches	
1, 2, 3, ...	Logic Switches associated with clerks 1, 2, 3, etc. ; each clerk uses her Logic Switch to signal to her customers, one by one, that the customer's book is now ready. Each customer correspondingly tests his clerk's Logic Switch to determine when his book is now ready.
SLIP	Logic Switch used by a clerk to signal that slip pick-up is about to begin ; each clerk uses one and the same Logic Switch for this purpose
Savevalues	
CLERK	Fullword Savevalue used as a channel to com-municate a clerk's identification number to the customers whose slips the clerk is picking up
COUNT	Fullword Savevalue used to count the number of slips a clerk has picked up so far during the current slip-pickup phase
Storages	
BUSY	Storage used to measure clerk utilization
Tables	
DELAY	Table used to estimate the distribution of time customers spend at the checkout counter
SLIPS	Table used to estimate the distribution of the number of slips a clerk picks up

(4) Block Diagram

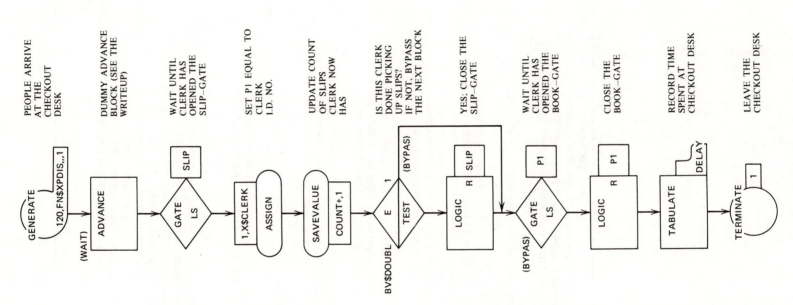

MODEL SEGMENT 1

FIGURE 6B.1   Block Diagram for Case Study 6B

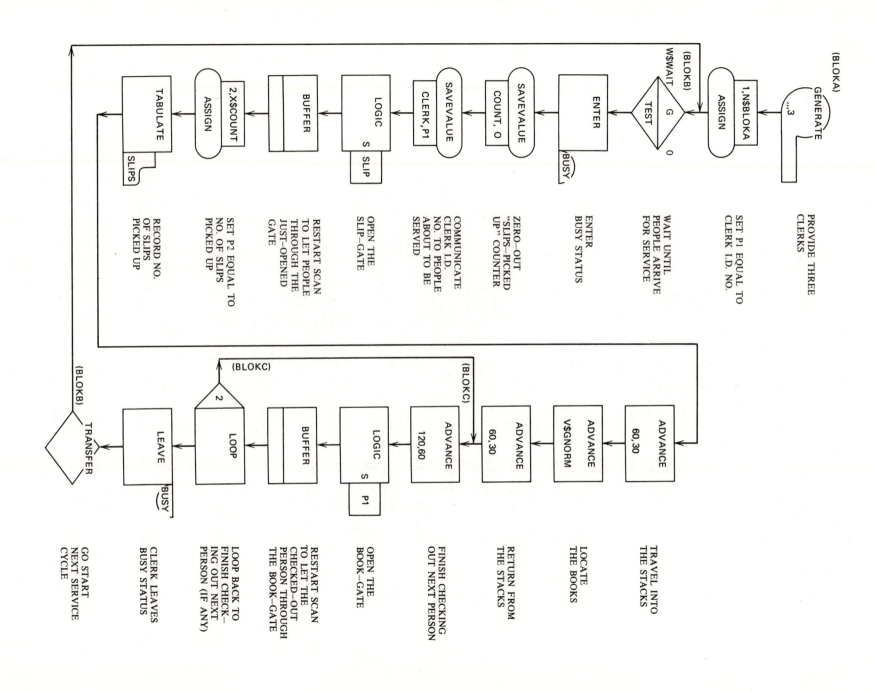

(BLOKA)

GENERATE ,,,3 — PROVIDE THREE CLERKS

ASSIGN 1,N$BLOKA — SET P1 EQUAL TO CLERK I.D. NO.

(BLOKB)
TEST G W$WAIT 0 — WAIT UNTIL PEOPLE ARRIVE FOR SERVICE

ENTER BUSY — ENTER BUSY STATUS

SAVEVALUE COUNT, 0 — ZERO—OUT "SLIPS—PICKED UP" COUNTER

SAVEVALUE CLERK,P1 — COMMUNICATE CLERK I.D. NO. TO PEOPLE ABOUT TO BE SERVED

LOGIC S SLIP — OPEN THE SLIP—GATE

BUFFER — RESTART SCAN TO LET PEOPLE THROUGH THE JUST—OPENED GATE

ASSIGN 2,X$COUNT — SET P2 EQUAL TO NO. OF SLIPS PICKED UP

TABULATE SLIPS — RECORD NO. OF SLIPS PICKED UP

(BLOKC)

ADVANCE 60,30 — TRAVEL INTO THE STACKS

ADVANCE V$GNORM — LOCATE THE BOOKS

ADVANCE 60,30 — RETURN FROM THE STACKS

ADVANCE 120,60 — FINISH CHECKING OUT NEXT PERSON

LOGIC S P1 — OPEN THE BOOK—GATE

BUFFER — RESTART SCAN TO LET THE CHECKED—OUT PERSON THROUGH THE BOOK—GATE

LOOP 2 — LOOP BACK TO FINISH CHECK—ING OUT NEXT PERSON (IF ANY)

LEAVE BUSY — CLERK LEAVES BUSY STATUS

(BLOKB)
TRANSFER — GO START NEXT SERVICE CYCLE

(BLOKC)

(5) Extended Program Listing

```
BLOCK                                                                                                   CARD
NUMBER  *LOC    OPERATION   A,B,C,D,E,F,G           COMMENTS                                             NUMBER
                SIMULATE                                                                                   1
        *                                                                                                  2
        *       EQUIVALENCE DEFINITION(S)                                                                  3
        *                                                                                                  4
        SLIP    EQU         10,L                    "SLIP" AND 10 ARE THE SAME LOGIC SWITCH                5
        *                                                                                                  6
        *       FUNCTION DEFINITION(S)                                                                     7
        *                                                                                                  8
        SNORM   FUNCTION    RN1,C25                 STANDARD NORMAL DISTRIBUTION FUNCTION                  9
        0,-5/.00003,-4/.00135,-3/.00621,-2.5/.02275,-2                                                    10
        .0668,-1.5/.11507,-1.2/.15866,-1/.21186,-.8/.27425,-.6                                            11
        .34458,-.4/.42074,-.2/.5,0/.57926,.2/.65542,.4                                                    12
        .72575,.6/.7881,.8/.84134,1/.88493,1.2/.93319,1.5                                                 13
        .9772,2/.99379,2.5/.99865,3/.99997,4/1,5                                                          14
        XPDIS   FUNCTION    RN1,C24                 EXPONENTIAL DISTRIBUTION FUNCTION                     15
        0,0/.1,.104/.2,.222/.3,.355/.4,.509/.5,.69/.6,.915/.7,1.2/.75,1.38                                16
        .8,1.6/.84,1.83/.88,2.12/.9,2.3/.92,2.52/.94,2.81/.95,2.99/.96,3.2                                17
        .97,3.5/.98,3.9/.99,4.6/.995,5.3/.998,6.2/.999,7/.9998,8                                          18
        *                                                                                                 19
        *       STORAGE CAPACITY DEFINITION(S)                                                            20
        *                                                                                                 21
                STORAGE     S$BUSY,3                SET STORAGE CAPACITY FOR 3-CLERK RUN                  22
        *                                                                                                 23
        *       TABLE DEFINITION(S)                                                                       24
        *                                                                                                 25
        DELAY   TABLE       M1,360,60,26            TIME SPENT AT CHECKOUT DESK                           26
        SLIPS   TABLE       X$COUNT,1,1,5           NUMBER OF SLIPS PICKED UP                             27
        *                                                                                                 28
        *       VARIABLE DEFINITION(S)                                                                    29
        *                                                                                                 30
        DOUBL   BVARIABLE   X$COUNT'E'4+W$WAIT'E'0                                                        31
        GNORM   FVARIABLE   (FN$SNORM/5+1)*180*P2                                                         32
        *                                                                                                 33
        *       MODEL SEGMENT 1                                                                           34
        *                                                                                                 35
  1             GENERATE    120,FN$XPDIS,,,1        PEOPLE ARRIVE AT CHECKOUT DESK                        36
  2             ADVANCE                             DUMMY ADVANCE BLOCK (SEE THE WRITEUP)                 37
  3     WAIT    GATE LS     SLIP                    WAIT 'TIL CLERK HAS                                   38
                                                    OPENED "SLIP-PICKUP" GATE                             39
  4             ASSIGN      1,X$CLERK               SET P1 = CLERK I.D. NO.                               40
  5             SAVEVALUE   COUNT+,1                UPDATE COUNT OF SLIPS CLERK NOW HAS                   41
  6             TEST E      BV$DOUBL,1,BYPAS        IS THIS CLERK DONE PICKING UP SLIPS?                  42
                                                    IF NOT, BYPASS THE NEXT BLOCK                         43
  7             LOGIC R     SLIP                    YES; CLOSE THE "SLIP-PICKUP" GATE                     44
  8     BYPAS   GATE LS     P1                      WAIT 'TIL CLERK HAS OPENED                            45
                                                    "CHECKOUT-FINISHED" GATE                             46
  9             LOGIC R     P1                      CLOSE "CHECKOUT-FINISHED" GATE                        47
 10             TABULATE    DELAY                   RECORD TIME SPENT AT CHECKOUT DESK                    48
 11             TERMINATE   1                       LEAVE THE CHECKOUT DESK                               49
        *                                                                                                 50
        *       MODEL SEGMENT 2                                                                           51
        *                                                                                                 52
 12     BLOKA   GENERATE    ,,,3                    PROVIDE 3 CLERKS                                      53
 13     BLOKB   ASSIGN      1,N$BLOKA               SET P1 = CLERK I.D. NO.                              54
 14             TEST G      W$WAIT,0                ANYONE WAITING FOR SLIP-PICKUP?                       55
 15             ENTER       BUSY                    YES; ENTER BUSY STATUS                                56
 16             SAVEVALUE   COUNT,0                 ZERO-OUT "SLIPS-PICKED-UP" COUNTER                    57
 17             SAVEVALUE   CLERK,P1                COMMUNICATE CLERK I.D. NO. TO                         58
                                                    PEOPLE ABOUT TO BE SERVED                             59
 18             LOGIC S     SLIP                    OPEN SLIP-PICKUP GATE                                 60
 19             BUFFER                              RE-START SCAN TO LET PEOPLE THROUGH                   61
                                                    THE JUST-OPENED GATE                                  62
 20             ASSIGN      2,X$COUNT               SET P2 = NO. OF SLIPS PICKED UP                      63
 21             TABULATE    SLIPS                   RECORD NO. OF SLIPS PICKED UP                         64
 22             ADVANCE     60,30                   TRAVEL INTO THE STACKS                                65
 23             ADVANCE     V$GNORM                 LOCATE THE BOOKS                                      66
 24             ADVANCE     60,30                   RETURN FROM THE STACKS                                67
 25     BLOKC   ADVANCE     120,60                  FINISH CHECKING OUT NEXT PERSON                       68
 26             LOGIC S     P1                      OPEN "CHECKOUT-FINISHED" GATE                         69
 27             BUFFER                              RE-START SCAN TO LET THIS NEXT                        70
                                                    PERSON THROUGH THE JUST-OPENED GATE                   71
 28             LOOP        2,BLOKC                 LOOP BACK TO FINISH CHECKING OUT                      72
                                                    NEXT PERSON (IF ANY)                                  73
 29             LEAVE       BUSY                    OTHERWISE, CLERK LEAVES BUSY STATUS                   74
 30             TRANSFER    ,BLOKB                  GO START NEXT SERVICE CYCLE                           75
        *                                                                                                 76
        *       CONTROL CARDS, BLOCK OPERAND RE-DEFS, AND STG CAPACITY RE-DEFS                            77
        *                                                                                                 78
                START       100                     START THE 3-CLERK RUN                                 79
                CLEAR                               CLEAR FOR THE 4-CLERK RUN                             80
 12     BLOKA   GENERATE    ,,,4                    RE-CONFIGURE FOR THE 4-CLERK RUN                      81
MULTIPLE DEFINITION OF SYMBOL IN ABOVE CARD
                STORAGE     S$BUSY,4                SET STORAGE CAPACITY FOR 4-CLERK RUN                  82
                START       100                     START THE 4-CLERK RUN                                 83
                CLEAR                               CLEAR FOR THE 5-CLERK RUN                             84
 12     BLOKA   GENERATE    ,,,5                    RE-CONFIGURE FOR THE 5-CLERK RUN                      85
MULTIPLE DEFINITION OF SYMBOL IN ABOVE CARD
                STORAGE     S$BUSY,5                SET STORAGE CAPACITY FOR 5-CLERK RUN                  86
                START       100                     START THE 5-CLERK RUN                                 87
                END                                 RETURN CONTROL TO OPERATING SYSTEM                    88
```

FIGURE 6B.2   Extended Program Listing for Case Study 6B

(6) Program Output

TABLE DELAY
ENTRIES IN TABLE 100   MEAN ARGUMENT 1065.659   STANDARD DEVIATION 484.000   SUM OF ARGUMENTS 106566.000

UPPER LIMIT	OBSERVED FREQUENCY	PER CENT OF TOTAL	CUMULATIVE PERCENTAGE	CUMULATIVE REMAINDER	MULTIPLE OF MEAN	DEVIATION FROM MEAN NON-WEIGHTED
360	2	1.99	1.9	98.0	.337	-1.457
420	7	6.99	8.9	91.0	.394	-1.334
480	6	5.99	14.9	85.0	.450	-1.210
540	10	9.99	24.9	75.0	.506	-1.086
600	2	1.99	26.9	73.0	.563	-.962
660	6	5.99	32.9	67.0	.619	-.838
720	1	.99	33.9	66.0	.675	-.714
780	1	.99	34.9	65.0	.731	-.590
840	0	.00	34.9	65.0	.788	-.466
900	2	1.99	36.9	63.0	.844	-.342
960	1	.99	37.9	62.0	.900	-.218
1020	3	2.99	40.9	59.0	.957	-.094
1080	3	2.99	43.9	56.0	1.013	.029
1140	6	5.99	49.9	50.0	1.069	.153
1200	8	7.99	57.9	42.0	1.126	.277
1260	5	4.99	62.9	37.0	1.182	.401
1320	4	3.99	66.9	33.0	1.238	.525
1380	4	3.99	70.9	29.0	1.294	.649
1440	5	4.99	75.9	24.0	1.351	.773
1500	7	6.99	82.9	17.0	1.407	.897
1560	1	.99	83.9	16.0	1.463	1.021
1620	5	4.99	88.9	11.0	1.520	1.145
1680	0	.00	88.9	11.0	1.576	1.269
1740	1	.99	89.9	10.0	1.632	1.393
1800	3	2.99	92.9	7.0	1.689	1.517
OVERFLOW	7	6.99	100.0	.0		

AVERAGE VALUE OF OVERFLOW 1965.00

REMAINING FREQUENCIES ARE ALL ZERO

(a)

TABLE SLIPS
ENTRIES IN TABLE 53   MEAN ARGUMENT 1.943   STANDARD DEVIATION 1.261   SUM OF ARGUMENTS 103.000

UPPER LIMIT	OBSERVED FREQUENCY	PER CENT OF TOTAL	CUMULATIVE PERCENTAGE	CUMULATIVE REMAINDER	MULTIPLE OF MEAN	DEVIATION FROM MEAN NON-WEIGHTED
1	32	60.37	60.3	39.6	.514	-.747
2	3	5.66	66.0	33.9	1.029	-.044
3	7	13.20	79.2	20.7	1.543	.837
4	11	20.75	100.0	.0	2.058	1.630

REMAINING FREQUENCIES ARE ALL ZERO

(b)

FIGURE 6B.3 Selected Program Output for Case Study 6B. (a) Distribution of time spent by customers at the checkout desk (three-clerk case). (b) Distribution of the number of slips a clerk picks up (three-clerk case).

(7) Discussion

Model Logic. Among other things, the model is to estimate the distribution of customer residence time at the checkout desk. One way to do this is to have customer-Transactions tabulate their M1 value just prior to leaving the model. Another way would be to use a Qtable, which would require moving customer-Transactions through a QUEUE Block when they arrive, and through a DEPART Block when they leave. The former approach has been taken in the model presented here.

There is no reason, then, to have a QUEUE–DEPART Block in the model. Note, however, that in Model Segment 1 of the Figure 6.4 model, there was a QUEUE–DEPART Block pair; furthermore, the count of Transactions waiting at the QUEUE Block indicated the number of customer-Transactions waiting for slip-pickup. To meet the need for this count in the case study model, a dummy ADVANCE Block is used in Model Segment 1. Placed immediately after the customer-Transaction's GENERATE Block, the ADVANCE Block has two purposes: (1) it lets customer-Transactions move out of the GENERATE Block immediately, thereby avoiding any distortion in the interarrival time pattern; (2) like the Figure 6.4 QUEUE Block, it is a Block whose Current Count equals the number of customer-Transactions waiting for service. Defaults are taken on the ADVANCE Block's A and B Operands; this means customer-Transactions are delayed at the Block only if the SLIP-gate which follows is closed. (See exercise 2a, Section 6.7.)

Note the method used to number the clerk-Transactions serially in Parameter 1. A Location name is given to their GENERATE Block. At the sequential Block, the Total Count at that GENERATE Block is assigned as the value of Parameter 1. As the clerk-Transactions enter the model through the GENERATE Block, one by one, the Total Count at that Block progressively takes on the values 1, 2, 3, etc. The Total Count is therefore a convenient "counter" to use in tagging clerk-Transactions with the identification numbers 1, 2, 3, etc.

Model condition (6) in the problem description states that a clerk is to pick up slips on a first-come, first-served basis. Later, the clerk is also to give checked-out books to customers in the order in which their slips were picked up. No special steps need be taken to insure these first-come, first-served properties; they occur as a natural consequence of the automatic front-to-back ordering of customer-Transactions on the Current Events Chain. (See exercise 2c, Section 6.7.)

Model condition (7) states that the clerk who has been idle the longest is the one who is to respond to the next demand for service. Again, no special steps need be taken to insure that this logic is followed. Transactions representing idle clerks are naturally arranged from front to back on the Current Events Chain in an order corresponding to increasingly later times of becoming idle. When a customer arrives, the clerk at the front of this group is the one who opens the BOOK-gate and continues on to serve the customer.

Model condition (8) states that when a clerk begins service, she takes up to four slips even if there is another available clerk who does not have any slips. This condition also comes about naturally, because of the way the GPSS Processor works. When a clerk-Transaction opens the SLIP-gate and then buffers, as many customer-Transactions as possible (but not more than four) move through the SLIP-gate before the GPSS Processor again encounters the clerk-Transaction in the scan. If there are one or more other idle clerk-Transactions, they are behind the "active" clerk on the Current Events Chain. They are not even looked at by the Processor in the CEC scan until after the first clerk is traveling to the stacks with up to four checkout-slips in hand.

Model Implementation. Logic Switches 1, 2, 3, etc. are used as the BOOK-gates for clerks

numbered 1, 2, 3, etc. These Logic Switch numbers are specified indirectly everywhere in the model, through the Parameter 1 value of both clerk and customer Transactions. If there is to be a Logic Switch symbolically named SLIP, then, care must be taken to see that the Processor does not give the symbol SLIP a numeric equivalent of 1. This is insured in the model through use of an Equivalence declaration (Card 5, Figure 6B.2). The symbolic Logic Switch SLIP is declared to have a numeric equivalent of 10, thereby avoiding what would otherwise be a redundancy between SLIP and the Logic Switch used by clerk 1 to control movement of his customer-Transactions.

Program Output.[4]   Figure 6B.3 shows Selected Program Output corresponding to the case of three clerks working at the checkout desk. Part (a) of the figure contains the estimate of the distribution of time customers spend at the checkout desk. The average time for the 100 customers is about 1065 seconds, or 17 minutes. This figure can be compared with the minimum *expected* checkout time, which is 6 minutes. (The minimum expected time corresponds to a customer being served immediately. The 6-minute expected time arises via 1 minute travel time into the stacks, 2 minutes to locate the book, 1 minute travel time back from the stacks, and 2 minutes to finish the checkout procedure.) Note that, corresponding to an UPPER LIMIT of 360 (seconds) in the Table DELAY, 2 customers out of 100 actually spent 6 minutes or less at the checkout desk. On the other hand, the information for an UPPER LIMIT of 1500 (seconds) in the Table indicates that 17 percent of the customers   (CUMULATIVE   REMAINDER = 17.0) were at the checkout desk longer than 25 minutes. In fact, in the OVERFLOW line, it is seen that seven customers were at the checkout desk longer than 30 minutes.

Part (b) of Figure 6B.3 shows the estimate of the distribution of number of slips picked up by a clerk. The average number of slips picked up was 1.94. About 60 percent of the time, a clerk picked up only one slip. On 11 occasions, a clerk picked up four slips.

Table 6B.2 summarizes the results for the three cases run. The trends shown in the table are consistent with intuition. Note that increasing the number of clerks by 66 percent

[4]Total CPU time for the simulation on an IBM 360/67 computer was 6.8 seconds.

TABLE 6B.2 A Summary of Program Output for Selected Results Produced in Case Study 6B

Number of Clerks	Customer Time at Checkout Desk (seconds)	Number of Slips Picked Up	Clerk Utilization
3	1065	1.94	0.938
4	667	1.32	0.745
5	532	1.14	0.673

(that is, from three to five) decreases the average customer waiting time by 50 percent (that is, from 1065 to 532 seconds). With five clerks, the customers are receiving reasonably good service. They wait only 532 seconds, whereas their minimum long-run waiting time under perfect conditions would be 6 minutes, or 360 seconds.

6.7 Exercises

1. These questions all pertain to the simplified library model shown in Figure 6.4.

(a) What position on the Current Events Chain is always occupied by the clerk-Transaction?

(b) Suppose that the next customer arrives at the checkout desk at the same time the clerk is picking up a slip from another customer. Will the clerk also pick up the slip of the just-arriving customer before going into the stacks?

(c) Discuss in detail the way the Figure 6.4 model will behave if the clerk and customers have the same Priority Level.

(d) Identify the two different ways in which customer-Transactions can encounter blocking conditions in Model Segment 1. Indicate which Block the customer-Transactions occupy while they are encountering the first and second of these blocking conditions, respectively.

(e) Describe two different sets of circumstances under which a customer-Transaction is blocked through a nonzero span of simulated time only once as it moves through Model Segment 1.

(f) It is usually the custom in this book to have customers check out of their Queue (i.e., move through a DEPART Block) at the time their service is *initiated*. In the Figure 6.4 model, however, customers do not check out of the Queue until their service has been *completed*. How would you interpret the Queue statistics which would be provided if a simulation were performed with the Figure 6.4 model? How would you reposition the DEPART Block in the model if customers are to check out of the Queue when service is initiated?

(g) Show how a Facility can be incorporated into Model Segment 2 to measure the utilization of the clerk. If such a Facility were provided in the model, how would you interpret the Facility statistics NUMBER ENTRIES and AVERAGE TIME/TRAN?

(h) Could the Block "TEST G WsBLOKA,0" be replaced with the Block "TEST G QsDESK,0" in Model Segment 1? Explain why, or why not. Would such a replacement be valid if two or more clerks worked at the checkout desk?

(i) Assume that an analyst wants to modify the Figure 6.4 model to simulate a situation in which two clerks work at the checkout desk. To bring this about, he replaces the Model Segment 2 GENERATE Block with the Block "GENERATE ,,,2". Will this have the desired effect? Explain why, or why not, in detail.

(j) Describe how the Figure 6.4 model would behave if the two BUFFER Blocks were eliminated from Model Segment 2.

(k) Show what changes to make in the Figure 6.4 model if it is assumed that the clerk is never willing to pick up more than one checkout slip at a time, even though more than one customer may be waiting for service.

2. These questions all pertain to Case Study 6B.

(a) In Model Segment 1, a dummy ADVANCE Block is used, in part, as a counter. The Current Count at the Block is interpretable as the number of customers waiting for slip-pickup. Show how the ADVANCE Block can be eliminated by introducing a Savevalue as a counter for the number of customers waiting for slip-pickup. From the points of view of (i) computer memory, and (ii) CPU time requirements, indicate whether the Savevalue approach is preferable to the dummy AD-VANCE Block approach.

(b) Describe how the Figure 6B.1 model would behave if the two BUFFER Blocks were eliminated from Model Segment 2.

(c) It is probably unrealistic to assume that a clerk hands books to customers in the order in which those customers handed pickup-slips to the clerk. More likely than not, the queue discipline practiced by a clerk in completing the checkout procedure, and handing back books, is random. That is, the clerk randomly selects one of the books she has as the book she will finish checking out next. Show what change to make in the Figure 6B.2 model under the assumption that a clerk practices random queue discipline when completing the check-out procedure after returning from the stacks.

3. Show how the BUFFER Block can be used to eliminate one of the two TEST Blocks in Model Segment 2 of Case Study 5E.

4. Consider the self-contained model segment whose Block Diagram is shown in Figure E4. Assume that in the model which includes this self-contained segment, all other Transactions have Priority Levels of 1 or more. Explain what effect the Figure E4 segment has in the model.

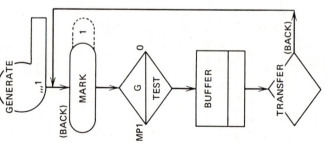

FIGURE E4

show how to build the model each of the two following ways.

(a) As is the case in the Figure 6.4 model, assume that customers do not depart the Queue until their service has been completed.

(b) Assume that customers depart the Queue at the time their service is initiated (see exercise 1f). Discuss the interpretation of the Facility statistics provided by your model(s). Also describe the way your model or models behave if there is a time tie between arrival and service-completion events.

6.8 Propagation of Transactions: The SPLIT Block

The *primary* method for bringing Transactions into a model is to use one or more GENERATE Blocks. There is also a *secondary* method for bringing Transactions into a model. The method requires use of the SPLIT Block. Whenever a Transaction already in a model moves into a SPLIT Block, one or more additional Trans-actions enter the model as a consequence of the execution of the SPLIT Block subroutine. Hence, Transactions have the capability of propagating themselves.

The SPLIT Block, and its A and B Operands, are shown in Figure 6.5.[a] It is convenient to think of the Transaction entering the SPLIT Block as the "parent." The additional Trans-actions brought into the model are termed the "offspring." When a parent moves into the SPLIT Block, the A Operand's value is the

[a]Two additional, optional SPLIT Block Operands will be introduced in Section 6.17.

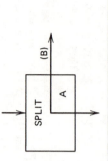

Operand	Significance	Default Value or Result
A	The number of additional Transactions to be brought into the model	Error
B	Name of the Block Location to which these additional Transactions are to be sent	Error

FIGURE 6.5 The SPLIT Block and its A and B Operands

5. Case Study 2A (a one-man barber shop) and Figure 6.4 (a library checkout desk manned by a single clerk) both present models for a one-line, one-server queuing system. The Case Study 2A model is the simpler of the two. The complication in the system modeled in Figure 6.4 is that when the server initiates a new service cycle, she immediately puts into service *all* customers who happen to be awaiting service at the time. Note that in both models, Transactions are used to simulate custom-ers. In Case Study 2A, however, a *Facility* is used to simulate the single server, whereas in the Figure 6.4 model, a *Transaction* simulates the single server.

Show how to build an alternative GPSS model for the system modeled in Figure 6.4, taking an ap-proach in which Transactions are used to simulate customers, but no Transaction is used to simulate the server. Your model should gather Facility statistics for the server, and Queue statistics for the customers. With respect to the Queue statistics,

number of offspring to be brought into the model as a result. These offspring are identical to the parent in most respects.

1. Their Priority Level is the same.
2. They have the same number of Parameters; the Parameter type (i.e., halfword or fullword) is identical to that of the parent; and the Parameter values are identical to those of the parent.
3. Their Mark Time is identical to that of the parent.

The offspring, however, are *different* Transactions. In particular, the *Transaction number* of each offspring differs from that of the parent, and from that of the other offspring.

When the parent leaves the SPLIT Block, it moves unconditionally to the sequential Block. The offspring, however, are routed to the Block in the Location whose name is used as the SPLIT Block's B Operand. This is normally a non-sequential Block.[5] It is possible, though to send the offspring to the sequential Block, along with the parent. To do this, a symbolic Location name is given to the sequential Block, and this name is specified as the SPLIT Block's B Operand.

Consider the operation of the SPLIT Block from the point of view of chains. First of all, the SPLIT Block cannot deny entry to a Transaction. When the parent enters the Block, its processing is temporarily delayed while all the offspring are fetched from the latent pool and brought into the model. The offspring are fetched one by one. Each next offspring is put immediately on the Current Events Chain, as the last member in its Priority Class. When all offspring have been placed on the CEC in this fashion, the processing of the parent is resumed. Later, as the scan of the Current Events Chain continues, the offspring Transactions are encountered by the Processor. Each of the offspring is then picked up, in turn, and moved as far forward in the model as possible, in the usual fashion.

For the SPLIT Block, the Standard Numerical Attributes Wj (Current Block Count) and Nj (Total Block Count) are incremented by 1 for the parent *and for each offspring Transaction* when the Block subroutine is executed. The Current Block Count is decremented by 1 each time any one of these Transactions succeeds in moving from the SPLIT Block to another Block. If the parent or any offspring are denied entry to their next intended Block, they are held at the SPLIT, where they continue to contribute to the Current Block Count.

Case Study 6C illustrates use of the SPLIT Block in context.

6.9 CASE STUDY 6C
A Spare Parts Problem

(1) Statement of the Problem

A certain machine uses a type of part which is subject to periodic failure. Whenever the in-use part fails, the machine must be turned off. The failed part is then removed, a good spare part is installed if available, or as soon as one becomes available, and the machine is turned on again. Failed parts can be repaired and reused.

The lifetime of a part is normally distributed, with a mean of 350 hours and a standard deviation of 70 hours. It takes 4 hours to remove a failed part from the machine. The time required to install a replacement part is 6 hours. Repair time for a failed part is normally distributed, with mean and standard deviation of 8 and 0.5 hours, respectively.

The machine operator himself is responsible for removing a failed part from the machine, and installing a replacement part in its place. There is a repairman who is responsible for repairing failed parts. The repairman's duties also include repair of items routed to him from another source. These other items arrive in a Poisson stream with a mean interarrival time of 9 hours. Their service-time requirement is 8 ± 4 hours. These other items have a higher repair priority than the failed parts used in the machine of interest.

The system is shown graphically in Figure 6C.1. Each open circle represents either a good part in "spare" status, or a part currently in the machine. Circles with a cross in them represent parts in "failed" status. The other items which compete for the repairman's services are shown as squares with a cross in them. As indicated above, and as the flow schematic suggests, these other items have a higher repair priority than the failed parts; they enter the repair queue ahead of any failed parts which may be waiting for repair.

Build a GPSS model for this machine-and-parts system, then use the model to estimate the fractional utilization of the machine as a function of the number of spare parts provided in the

[5] Actually, the SPLIT Block's B Operand is evaluated separately, offspring-by-offspring. Hence, it is possible to make the Block to which an offspring is sent be a function of the offspring itself. This possibility is discussed in Section 6.17.

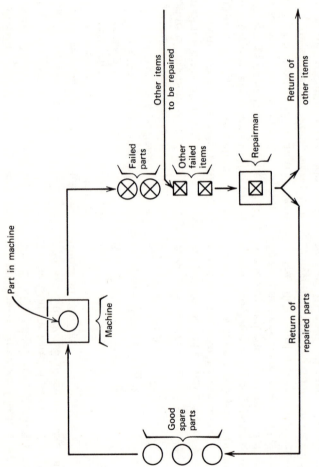

FIGURE 6C.1   Flow schematic for Case Study 6C

system. Study the system under the alternative assumptions that zero, one, and two spare parts are provided. Run each simulation for the equivalent of 5 years, assuming 40-hour work weeks. For each alternative, control experimental conditions partially in the sense of duplicating the competition from other items which failed parts experience at the repair facility.

(2) Approach Taken in Building the Model

Model Segment 1: The Supply of Parts, and the Machine. It was indicated in Chapter 2 that a useful modeling approach is to first identify system constraints, then decide which GPSS entities to use to simulate these constraints. In the present problem, the only constraint (except for the single repairman) is the number of spare parts in the system. Because these parts can be thought of as moving, as suggested in Figure 6C.1, it would be natural to let a Transaction simulate a part. Using the GENERATE Block's Limit Count feature, the required number of Transactions could then be brought into the model at the start of the simulation, and so on. In fact, this spare parts problem was stated earlier in the book, as exercise 9, Section 5.24; it was suggested there that a solution be developed via the approach of letting a Transaction simulate a part.

In contrast with the suggestion in exercise 9, Section 5.24, the approach used in this case

study will be to interpret a Transaction as the machine operator. A Savevalue will be used to keep track of the number of spare parts in the system. More specifically, a Savevalue will be used as a counter, to maintain a record of the number of good spares there are currently. When the machine operator needs a spare, then, he can check for a spare by testing the counter. By testing in refusal mode, the operator-Transaction will be forced to wait until there is an available spare part. The operator takes a spare simply by decrementing the Savevalue-counter. Similarly, when a failed part has been repaired, the count of good spares is updated simply by incrementing the Savevalue-counter.

The machine itself is simulated with a Facility. The operator-Transaction turns the machine on by capturing the Facility, and turns it off by releasing it. Hence, the Facility's utilization equals the machine's utilization. Use of a Facility to simulate the machine consequently provides a convenient method for measuring the requested utilization statistic.

At first glance, it might seem that only one operator-Transaction would be required in the model segment simulating the supply of parts and the machine. This is true when there are no failed parts in the system. After an in-use part has failed and been removed from the machine, however, two independent event-sequences take place in the system. First of all, the failed part must be routed to the repair facility. At the same time, the supply of spares must be checked to determine if a spare is available; then the spare must be installed, the machine must be turned back on, etc. Because these independent event-sequences should proceed simultaneously, they cannot be handled by a single operator-Transaction. As a result, as soon as the failed part has been removed from the machine, the operator moves into a SPLIT Block, thereby calling in a coworker (that is, bringing an off-spring-Transaction into the model). The co-worker checks for a good spare, installs it in the machine, and then turns on the machine, essentially taking over as the machine operator. Meantime, the original operator (that is, the parent Transaction) takes the failed part to the repair facility, etc. When the repair has been completed, the original operator records this fact by incrementing the Savevalue-counter. He then terminates, having surrendered the role of machine operator to the coworker.

Model Segment 2: The Repair Facility. The repairman is simulated with the Facility FIXER. In Model Segment 1, an operator-Transaction puts a failed part into repair by capturing this Facility. He must compete, however, with other items for use of the Facility. This other use is simulated in a separate, self-contained model segment (Model Segment 2). In this segment, Transactions simulating the other items enter the model with a high priority, wait to use the repairman and, after this use, leave the model. The separate segment, then, is straightforward.

(3) Table of Definitions

Time Unit: 0.1 Hours

TABLE 6C.1 Table of Definitions for Case Study 6C

GPSS Entity	Interpretation
Transactions	
Model Segment 1	A "machine operator"
Model Segment 2	An "other item"
Model Segment 3	A timer-Transaction
Facilities	
MAC	The machine whose utilization is being estimated
FIXER	The repairman
Functions	
SNORM	Standard normal distribution function
XPDIS	Exponential distribution function
Savevalues	
1	Counter used to record the number of good spares currently available
Variables	
1	Variable describing the normally distributed lifetime of the machine
FIX	Variable describing the normally distributed repair time for the type of part used by the machine

(4) Block Diagram

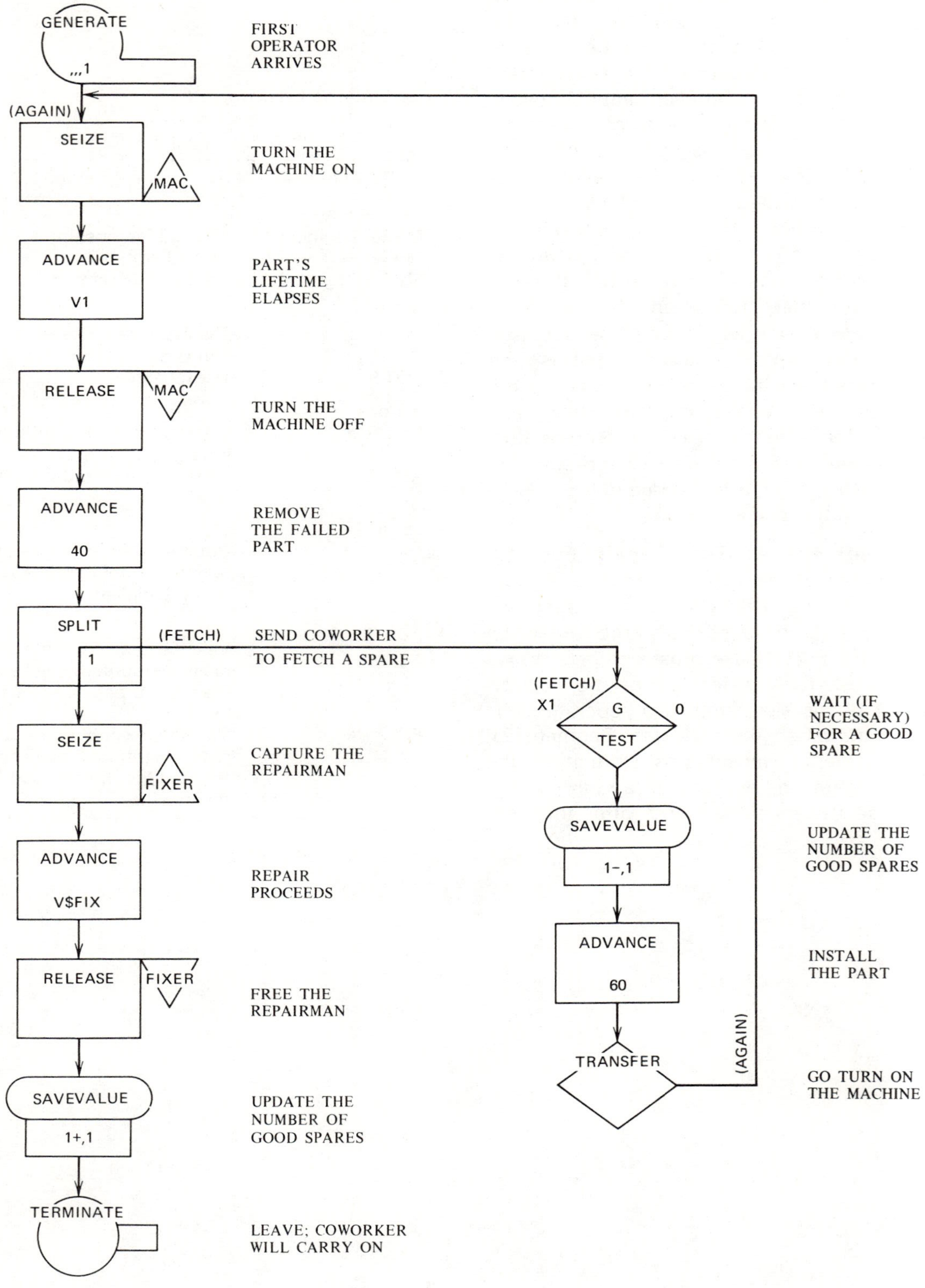

MODEL SEGMENT 1

FIGURE 6C.2 Block Diagram for Case Study 6C

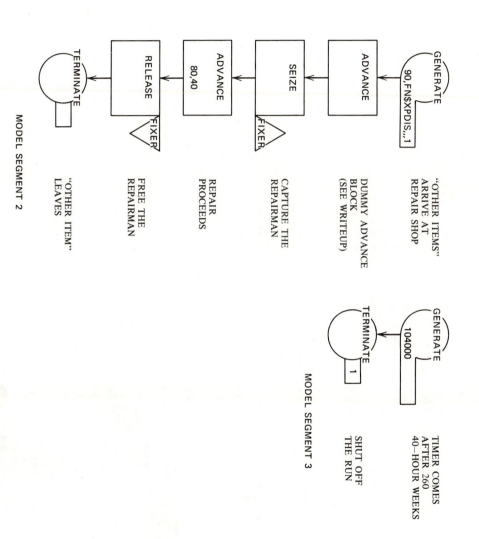

MODEL SEGMENT 2

GENERATE
90,FN$XPDIS,,,1
"OTHER ITEMS"
ARRIVE AT
REPAIR SHOP

ADVANCE
DUMMY ADVANCE
BLOCK
(SEE WRITEUP)

SEIZE
FIXER
CAPTURE THE
REPAIRMAN

ADVANCE
80,40
REPAIR
PROCEEDS

RELEASE
FIXER
FREE THE
REPAIRMAN

TERMINATE
"OTHER ITEM"
LEAVES

MODEL SEGMENT 3

GENERATE
104000
TIMER COMES
AFTER 260
40–HOUR WEEKS

TERMINATE
1
SHUT OFF
THE RUN

(5) Extended Program Listings

BLOCK NUMBER	*LOC	OPERATION A,B,C,D,E,F,G	COMMENTS	CARD NUMBER
		SIMULATE		1
		*		2
		*	NON-STANDARD RANDOM NUMBER SEQUENCE INITIALIZATION(S)	3
		*		4
		RMULT 121,,17	SET RANDOM SEQUENCES FOR 1ST RUN	5
		*		6
		*	FUNCTION DEFINITION(S)	7
		*		8
	SNORM	FUNCTION RN2,C25	STANDARD NORMAL DISTRIBUTION FUNCTION	9
		0,-5/.00003,-4/.00135,-3/.00621,-2.5/.02275,-2		10
		.06681,-1.5/.11507,-1/.15866,-.8/.21186,-.8/.27425,-.6		11
		.34458,-.4/.42074,-.2/.5,0/.57926,.2/.65542,.4		12
		.72575,.6/.78814,.8/.84134,1/.88493,1.2/.93319,1.5		13
		.97725,2/.99379,2.5/.99865,3/.99997,4/1,5		14
	XPDIS	FUNCTION RN3,C24	EXPONENTIAL DISTRIBUTION FUNCTION	15
		0,0/.1,.104/.2,.222/.3,.355/.4,.509/.5,.69/.6,.915/.7,1.2/.75,1.38		16
		.8,1.6/.84,1.83/.88,2.12/.9,2.3/.92,2.52/.94,2.81/.95,2.99/.96,3.2		17
		.97,3.5/.98,3.9/.99,4.6/.995,5.3/.998,6.2/.999,7/.9998,8		18
		*		19
		*	VARIABLE DEFINITION(S)	20
		*		21
	1	FVARIABLE 700*FN$SNORM+3500	LIFETIME FOR THE TYPE OF PART	22
	FIX	FVARIABLE 5*FN$SNORM+80	REPAIR TIME FOR THE TYPE OF PART	23
		*		24
		*	MODEL SEGMENT 1	25
		*		26
1		GENERATE ,,,1	FIRST WORKER ARRIVES	27
2	AGAIN	SEIZE MAC	TURN THE MACHINE ON	28
3		ADVANCE V1	PART'S LIFETIME ELAPSES	29
4		RELEASE MAC	TURN THE MACHINE OFF	30
5		ADVANCE 40	REMOVE THE FAILED PART	31
6		SPLIT 1,FETCH	SEND CO-WORKER TO FETCH A SPARE	32
7		SEIZE FIXER	CAPTURE THE REPAIRMAN	33
8		ADVANCE V$FIX	REPAIR PROCEEDS	34
9		RELEASE FIXER	FREE THE REPAIRMAN	35
10		SAVEVALUE 1+,1	UPDATE THE NUMBER OF GOOD SPARES	36
11		TERMINATE	LEAVE; CO-WORKER WILL CARRY ON	37
12	FETCH	TEST G X1,0	WAIT (IF NECESSARY) FOR A GOOD SPARE	38
13		SAVEVALUE 1-,1	UPDATE THE NUMBER OF GOOD SPARES	39
14		ADVANCE 60	INSTALL THE PART	40
15		TRANSFER ,AGAIN	GO TURN ON THE MACHINE	41
		*		42
		*	MODEL SEGMENT 2	43
		*		44
16		GENERATE 90,FN$XPDIS,,,1	"OTHER ITEMS" ARRIVE AT REPAIR SHOP	45
17		ADVANCE	DUMMY ADVANCE BLOCK (SEE WRITEUP)	46
18		SEIZE FIXER	CAPTURE THE REPAIRMAN	47
19		ADVANCE 80,40	REPAIR PROCEEDS	48
20		RELEASE FIXER	FREE THE REPAIRMAN	49
21		TERMINATE	"OTHER ITEM" LEAVES	50
		*		51
		*	MODEL SEGMENT 3	52
		*		53
22		GENERATE 104000	TIMER COMES AFTER 260 40-HOUR WEEKS	54
23		TERMINATE 1	SHUT OFF THE RUN	55
		*		56
		*	CONTROL CARDS AND STORAGE CAPACITY RE-DEFINITIONS	57
		*		58
		START 1	START 1ST RUN (0 SPARES PROVIDED)	59
		RMULT 121,,17	RESTORE RANDOM SEQUENCES FOR 2ND RUN	60
		CLEAR	CLEAR FOR THE 2ND RUN	61
		INITIAL X1,1	RE-CONFIGURE FOR 2ND RUN	62
		START 1	START 2ND RUN (1 SPARE PROVIDED)	63
		RMULT 121,,17	RESTORE RANDOM SEQUENCES FOR 3ND RUN	64
		CLEAR	CLEAR FOR THE 3RD RUN	65
		INITIAL X1,2	RE-CONFIGURE FOR 3RD RUN	66
		START 1	START 3RD RUN (2 SPARES PROVIDED)	67
		END	RETURN CONTROL TO OPERATING SYSTEM	68

FIGURE 6C.3 Extended Program Listing for Case Study 6C

(6) Program Output

No program output is shown directly. Results are summarized in the next section.

(7) Discussion

Model Logic. It is assumed initially that a part is installed in the machine, and the machine is ready to turn on. Hence, when an operator-Transaction first enters the model (through Block 1, Figure 6C.3), it immediately turns on the SEIZE Block in Location 2, Figure 6C.3). Note, then, that the total number of parts in the system equals the initial value of Savevalue 1, *plus* 1 (the part initially in the machine). In the first configuration, the total number of parts in the system is exactly 1. (By default, Savevalue 1 has a value of 0 in the first configuration.)

In Model Segment 1, note that the Facility MAC does not impose a constraint. That is, whenever an operator-Transaction wants to capture the Facility (by seizing at Block 2, Figure 6C.3), the capture can always occur. It is the refusal-mode TEST Block (Block 12, Figure 6C.3) where the spare-parts constraint is simulated in the model.

In Model Segment 2, the Block following the GENERATE is an ADVANCE with no Operands specified (Block 17, Figure 6C.3). Because of the implied zero holding time, this dummy ADVANCE Block does not delay other items entering the model through the preceding GENERATE Block; on the other hand, its presence guarantees that whenever another item arrives, it can move immediately from the GENERATE Block, causing the Processor to schedule arrival of the next other item. If the dummy ADVANCE Block were not included, the interarrival-time pattern of other items could be distorted, as discussed in Chapter 2. Recall that a dummy ADVANCE Block was also used in Case Study 6B under approximately the same set of circumstances.

The problem statement indicates that experimental conditions are to be controlled partially, in the sense of duplicating the competition from other items at the repair facility. This has been done by dedicating random-number generators 3 and 1 to simulation of other item interarrival times and repair times, respectively. The RMULT card is used to set these two generators at given starting points for each alternative configuration (see Cards 5, 60, and 64 in Figure 6C.3).

Program Output.[6] Table 6C.2 summarizes the program output. When there is only 1 part in the system (i.e., when there are zero spares), machine utilization is about 70 percent. This utilization increases to about 91 percent when one spare is provided, and about 96 percent when two spares are provided. (See exercise 3a, Section 6.10.)

TABLE 6C.2 A Summary of Program Output for Case Study 6C

Number of Spares in the System	Machine Utilization	Repairman Utilization
0	0.705	0.880
1	0.912	0.882
2	0.958	0.887

6.10 Exercises

1. Whenever a Transaction reaches Point A in a model, another Transaction is to enter the model 15 ± 7 time units later, moving to the Block at THERE when it arrives. Show how this can be accomplished.

2. A particular model includes the Block "GENERATE 10,3". Show how a SPLIT and ADVANCE Block combination can be used to replace this GENERATE Block in the model.

3. These exercises all refer to Case Study 6C.
   (a) Compute the maximum long-run machine utilization that can be realized for the case study machine-and-parts system under the following circumstances.
     (i) No spares are provided.
     (ii) One spare is provided.
     (iii) Two spares are provided.
   (b) The RMULT cards used in the case study are all of the form "RMULT 121,,17". Was it necessary to set random-number generators 1 and 3 at different starting points? Explain.
   (c) When no spares are provided in Case Study 6C, the coworker Transaction encounters a blocking condition when it first reaches the Block "TEST G X1,0". The Transaction is consequently left on the Current Events Chain. Meanwhile, the original operator-Transaction is (eventually) placed on the Future Events Chain, where it remains while simulating re-

---

[6]Total CPU time for the simulation on an IBM 360/67 computer was 19.1 seconds.

pair of the failed part. When this original operator is later returned to the Current Events Chain, it is merged into the chain *behind* the coworker, who is still waiting for a part to become available. In the subsequent scan of the Current Events Chain, the spare is not then made available (i.e., the original operator does not execute the Block "SAVEVALUE 1+,1") until *after* the coworker has unsuccessfully tried to move through the TEST Block. It might appear, then, that the model does not behave logically, because the coworker has found that "there are no spares available," at the clock instant in question. Do you conclude from this that the logic of the model is invalid? Explain why, or why not.

(d) Assume that when failed parts reach the repair facility, repair always begins on them *immediately*. That is, assume that for all practical purposes, there is no limit to the number of repairmen at the repair facility. Show what changes to make in the Figure 6C.2 Block Diagram to incorporate this assumption into the model.

(e) In the case study, Savevalue 1 is used as a *counter* to maintain a record of the number of spares currently available for use. A TEST Block is used to insure that at least one spare is currently available before installation of that part begins. Show how the TEST Block and the two SAVEVALUE Blocks in the model can be eliminated by making appropriate use of the GPSS Storage entity. (Hint: interpret the remaining capacity of a Storage as the number of spares currently available.) Note that the Storage statistics available in the output can be interpreted to provide information about the spare parts situation during the simulation. Compare and contrast this information with the lack of corresponding information provided in the output when the Savevalue entity is used.

(f) No information is available from the case study about the distribution of the random variable "number of spares currently available." Show what changes to make in the case-study model so that an estimate of the distribution of this random variable will be included in the output.

4. Case Study 2E involves a system in which a group of machines operate in parallel, with each machine subject to periodic failure. In the spirit of Case Study 6C, show how to use the SPLIT Block in building a model for that system.

5. If you have not yet developed a solution for exercise 9, Section 5.24, for the Transaction-interpretation described there, do so now. Compare and contrast your model with that shown in Case Study 6C.

6. Experimental conditions in Case Study 6C are controlled partially in the sense of duplicating the competitive conditions which failed parts encounter at the repair facility. Develop a model which *completely* reproduces experimental conditions in the simulation. In particular, the sequence of lifetimes of parts installed in the machine should be the same from configuration to configuration. Similarly, the sequence of failed-part repair times should be the same from configuration to configuration. Build the model under the alternative assumptions given in (a) and (b) below.

(a) Do not give the parts individual identity. For example, if the lifetime of the second part to be installed is 354 hours, then this should be true for the case of zero spares (when the second part to be installed is the part which failed most recently), and for the case of one spare (when the second part to be installed is *not* the part which failed most recently, but is a different part, even though it is a part of the same *type*).

(b) Give the parts individual identity. In this sense, the lifetime (or repair time) a part experiences depends both on *which one* of the several distinct parts it is, and *which time* it is that the particular part is being put into service.

(c) With respect to the system being modeled (and not with respect to the modeling process itself), discuss the practical differences between the approaches described in (a) and (b). Which approach do you think is more realistic, and why?

7. For the Case Study 6C system, define average hourly cost as the sum of downtime costs for the machine, and waiting costs for other items at the repair facility. Assume it costs \$25 per hour to have the machine out of production, and that the cost of having other items wait at the repair facility is \$5 per hour per item. Use the Case Study 6C model, or a variation of it, to determine which of the following queue disciplines at the repair facility minimizes the average hourly cost.

(a) Other items have higher priority than failed parts.

(b) No priority distinctions are made.

(c) Failed parts have higher priority than other items.

8. In Case Study 6C, assume that there are *three* machines in the system, instead of only one. The three machines are identical to each other; in particular, each of them uses the same type of part. Hence, the machines can and do share the spare parts in the system. For example, at a given time, a particular part may be in use in one of the machines. At a later time, the same part (after failure and repair) may be in use in another one of the machines, and so on. Each of the machines has its own operator, however, and is independent of

the other two machines, except in the sense of part-sharing.

Show the GPSS Block Diagram for a model of the system for each of the following Transaction-interpretations.

(a) As in Case Study 6C, let a Transaction simulate a machine operator.

(b) As in exercise 9, Section 5.24, let a Transaction simulate a part.

Design each model to estimate the utilization of the three machines, *treated as a group*, as a function of the number of spare parts in the system.

6.11 Indirect Addressing: The GPSS Implementation

Thus far, numeric values have been supplied in all GPSS models either through *direct specification*, as constants, or through *indirect specification*, by use of Standard Numerical Attributes. Whenever Standard Numerical Attributes have been used, the number of the associated entity has been supplied *as a constant*.[7] Hence, Q5 is the current content of waiting line number 5; R20 is the remaining capacity of Storage 20, and so on. Such data references do not depend on any properties of the Transaction currently being processed. For example, whenever a Transaction enters the TEST Block in Figure 6.6, it is always waiting line number 5 whose current content is used in the test. The test in no way depends on which particular Transaction is doing the testing.

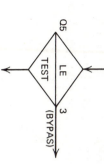

FIGURE 6.6 An example in which Block Operand values are independent of properties of the currently active Transaction

In some modeling contexts, when the value of a Standard Numerical Attribute is to be used as data, it is convenient to have the number of the entity involved depend on a property of the Transaction which triggers the data reference. In particular, it may be useful to have the entity's number *be the value of a Transaction Parameter*. This makes it possible, for example, to use single

[7]Alternatively, the symbolic name of the particular entity involved has been supplied. The discussion in this section does not pertain to symbolically named entities, however.

Blocks in GPSS models to implement the following types of logic.

1. At a TEST Block, test the current content of the Queue whose number is the value of the testing Transaction's sixth Parameter.

2. In sampling from a distribution, use the random number generator whose number is the P10 value of the Transaction currently being processed.

3. In evaluating an Arithmetic Variable, use the content of the fullword Savevalue whose number is the P3 value of the Transaction currently being processed.

In terms of an algebraic programming language such as FORTRAN, BASIC, or PL/I, the data references described above could be implemented by using P6, P10, and P3, respectively, as *subscripts*. "Q(P6)" would then have as its value the content of the Queue whose number is the value of Parameter 6; "RN(P10)" would be the value of the random number generator whose number is the value of P10; and "X(P3)" would be the value of the fullword Savevalue whose number is to be found in Parameter 3. In each of these situations, an entity index number is supplied *indirectly*, through a Transaction's Parameter. Note that a twofold level of indirection is involved here: first, a Parameter is used to indirectly provide an entity number; then, a numeric property of the entity with that number is used as the data. This approach to supplying data is known as *indirect addressing*.

Indirect addressing is available in GPSS. The *notation* used to represent indirect addressing does *not* take the form "Q(P6)," etc., however. Parentheses are not used; and, because *only the value of a Transaction's Parameter* can supply an entity number indirectly, the letter P is not used either. Instead, indirect addressing is indicated by interposing an asterisk between the family name of the SNA involved, and the number of the pertinent Parameter.[8] Hence, Q*6 has as its value the content of the Queue whose number is the value of Parameter 6; RN*10 is the name of a value returned by the random-number generator whose number is the value of P10; and X*3 is the value

[8]In a sense, the asterisk is being used as a synonym for "P," meaning Parameter. It is *invalid*, however, to write "QP6," or "RNP10," or "XP3," for example. In *indirect addressing*, the asterisk *must* be used in place of the "P." On the other hand, for *indirect specification*, the asterisk *may* be used rather than the "P." For example, an acceptable alternative for the Block "SEIZE P4" would be "SEIZE *4". In much of the IBM literature on GPSS, *j is used to indirectly specify data, rather than Pj, where j is any legal Parameter number. Rather than following this practice in this book, however, the asterisk is used only to indicate indirect addressing, or the arithmetic operation of multiplication, or the Boolean operator "and".

of the fullword Savevalue whose number is to be found in Parameter 3.

Precisely because a twofold level of indirection is involved, indirect addressing can be confusing at first. This is especially true when the number of a *Parameter* is indirectly supplied through some *other Parameter*. For example, P*7 is the value of the Parameter whose number is to be found in Parameter 7. If P7 is 5 and P5 is 3, then the value of P*7 is 3.

For a simple example of the power of indirect addressing, suppose that the utilization of the least-utilized Facility among those numbered from 2 to 6, inclusive, is to be entered in the Table ALPHA. Figure 6.7(a) shows a two-Block sequence which accomplishes this effect. When a Transaction enters the SELECT Block, the number of the minimum-utilization Facility is placed in Parameter 1. The Transaction then moves into the TABULATE Block, causing the minimum-utilization value to be entered in the Table ALPHA. Figure 6.7(b) shows the definition of the Table. As indicated by the Table card's A Operand, the value to be tabulated is FR*1. But FR*1 is the fractional utilization of the Facility whose number is in Parameter 1 of the Transaction at the TABULATE Block. The desired result is therefore achieved.

For another example of indirect addressing, assume that the holding time of a Transaction at an ADVANCE Block is to equal the value of a sample drawn from the population uniformly dis-

tributed between 10 and 20, inclusive. The random-number generator to be used for the sampling is to depend on the value of the advancing Transaction's fifth Parameter. When P5 is 1, RN1 is to be used; when P5 is 2, RN2 is to be used; when P5 is 3, RN3 is to be used, and so on. Figure 6.8(a) shows the ADVANCE Block at which the holding time is simulated. Figure 6.8(b)

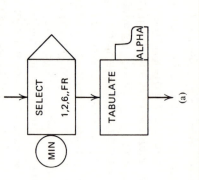

LOCATION	OPERATION	A,B,C,D,E,F
HOLD	FUNCTION	RN*5,,C2
0,,10,,1,20		

(a) ADVANCE FN$HOLD

(b)

FIGURE 6.8 A second example of indirect addressing. (a) Block Diagram segment. (b) Definition of the Function HOLD.

shows the definition of the Function HOLD, used as the A Operand at the ADVANCE Block. The Function's argument (A Operand on the Function header card) is RN*5. Hence, when a Transaction moves into the ADVANCE Block, its holding time depends on the random-number returned by RNj, where j is the Transaction's P5 value (see exercise 10, section 6.12).

The exercises in the next section provide practice in the use of indirect addressing.

6.12 Exercises

1. (a) Discuss the difference between Q5 and Q*5.
   (b) Discuss the difference between P20 and P*20.

2. (a) The values of Parameters 6 and 21 of a certain Transaction are −18 and 6, respectively. What is the value of P*21?
   (b) Suppose that the value of Parameter 5 is 5. What is the value of P*5?

3. (a) A Transaction is to record in the Table named BETA the current content of the Queue whose number is the value of the Transaction's seventh Parameter. Show the specifications for the TABULATE Block and the Table definition card.
   (b) Repeat (a), only assume that the number of

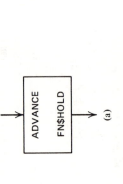

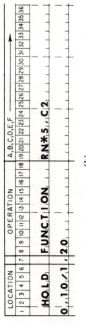

(a) SELECT MIN 1,2,6,,FR → TABULATE ALPHA

LOCATION	OPERATION	A,B,C,D,E,F
ALPHA	TABLE	FR*1,,100,,100,,1,1

(b)

FIGURE 6.7 A first example of indirect addressing. (a) Block Diagram segment. (b) Definition of the Table ALPHA.

the Queue is found in halfword Savevalue 7, not in Transaction Parameter 7.

4. Why is it that RNj is meaningful only for integer values of j from 1 to 8, inclusive, whereas RN*j can be meaningful for integer values of j from 1 to 100?

5. (a) A Transaction moves through the Block "LEAVE P7,S*7". What is the remaining capacity of the pertinent Storage just after this has happened?

(b) A Transaction moves through the Block "ENTER P10,R*10". What is the remaining capacity of the pertinent Storage just after this has happened?

6. (a) The holding time of a Transaction at an ADVANCE Block is to equal the minimum value found in fullword Savevalues 1 through 10. Show a SELECT–ADVANCE Block sequence which accomplishes this.

(b) The values of Parameters 1 through 5 of a certain Transaction are 0, 5, 6, 2, and 1, respectively. When the Transaction moves into the Block "SELECT MAX P3,P*2,P*4,,P", what value is assigned to which one of its Parameters?

(c) A Transaction is to become a member of whichever Queue in the range from 1 through 10 has the minimum current content. Show a Block sequence through which the Transaction can move to bring about the desired effect.

7. Fullword Savevalues 1 through 4 have the values 3, 0, 7, and 1, respectively. Parameters 1 through 4 of a certain Transaction have the values 4, 1, 2, and 2, respectively. State which Savevalue and/or Parameter values are changed when the Transaction moves through any one of the Block sequences shown in Figure E7, and indicate what values are in effect after the changes take place.

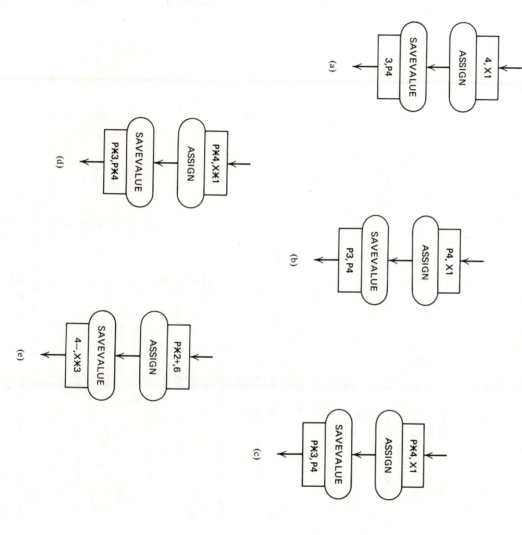

(a)

(b)

(c)

(d)

(e)

FIGURE E7

8. Without using indirect addressing, show an alternative method for accomplishing what takes place when a Transaction moves through the Block sequence shown in Figure 6.7.

9. Without using indirect addressing, show an alternative method for accomplishing what takes place when a Transaction moves through the Block sequence shown in Figure 6.8.

10. As indicated in Chapter 3, the range of values taken on by the eight uniform random-number generators in GPSS is context-dependent, as summarized below.

(a) When used as Function arguments, the random values are uniformly distributed on the closed interval between 0.000000 and 0.999999.

(b) When used in any other context, the random values are uniformly distributed on the closed interval of integers between 000 and 999.

This statement about context-dependency is valid whether the random-number generators are referenced via indirect specification (as RNj, where $j = 1, 2, 3, \ldots, 7,$ or 8), or via indirect addressing (as RN*j, where $j = 1, 2, 3, \ldots, 98,$ 99, or 100). Subsequent to IBM's March, 1973, decommitment to the GPSS/360 Processor, it was unfortunately discovered that because of an error in the GPSS/360 code, *indirectly addressed* random-number generators used as *Function arguments* take on integer values between 000 and 999, inclusive. The argument of such a Function is then almost always out of range on the high side, i.e., is almost always 1 or greater. With this error in effect, the Function then almost always returns its *largest* possible value. Devise and run a GPSS model to determine if the indicated error exists in your GPSS Processor. If your Processor is in error, have the appropriate person in your computing center put a fix on it.

11. (a) Rows 1 through 10 in fullword Matrix 3 are to be assigned values returned by the GPSS random-number generators when they are used in the first context described in exercise 10. Values returned by RNj, $j = 1, 2, 3, \ldots, 8,$ are to be stored in columns $1, 2, 3, \ldots, 8,$ respectively, of the Matrix. Show a Block Diagram segment which accomplishes this. Make the segment as compact as possible by using indirect addressing and looping. Run your model, and compare the entries in Matrix 3 with those shown in Table 3.1 in Chapter 3. (Hint: see exercise 7, Section 5.7.)

(b) Repeat part (a), only under the assumption that the random number generators are used in the second context described in exercise 10.

12. In early versions of GPSS, there were no SELECT Blocks. Assuming for the moment that there still are no SELECT Blocks, show a Block Diagram segment which has an effect equivalent to the segment shown in Figure E12. (The Block Diagram segment shown is a repetition of the segment in Figure 4.22.) Do this each of two different ways, as indicated below.

(a) Do not use the LOOP Block in your segment.

(b) Use the LOOP Block in your segment.

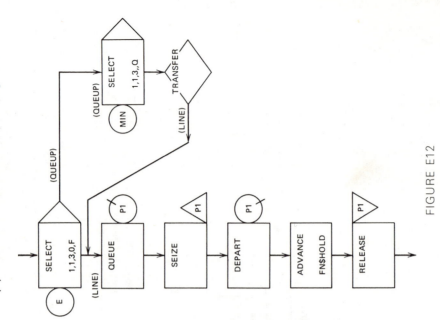

FIGURE E12

6.13 Attribute-Valued Functions

The three types of GPSS Functions which have been introduced so far are discrete, continuous, and list Functions. When these Functions are defined, *constants* are supplied as both the first *and* second members of the Function-defining ordered pairs of points. This means that each different value that such a Function can return is *directly specified* in the Function definition. (Of course, continuous Functions can also return values from the piecewise linear continuum which the Function definition describes.)

It is also possible to define *attribute-valued* Functions in GPSS. As in the case of discrete, continuous, and list Functions, the first member of each ordered pair of points used to define such a Function is a constant. In contrast, however, the second member of each ordered pair is a GPSS *Standard Numerical Attribute*. This means that each different value the Function can return is *indirectly specified* in the Function definition.

When an attribute-valued Function is defined, E is used as the first B-Operand character in the Function header card. Except for this, and the fact that Standard Numerical Attributes are used in the defining pairs of points, attribute-valued Functions are defined and used the same way as discrete, continuous, and list Functions.

An example of an attribute-valued Function is shown in Figure 6.9. The Function, named

LOCATION	OPERATION	A,B,C,D,E,F
GETUT	FUNCTION	P7,E4
		9,FR5/10,FR3/11,FR12/12,FR7

FIGURE 6.9 A first example of an attribute-valued Function

GETUT, has Parameter 7 as its argument. The Function returns as its value the fractional utilization of some Facility. For Parameter 7 values of 9, 10, 11, and 12, the Function's value is the fractional utilization of Facility 5, 3, 12, and 7, respectively.

For out-of-range arguments, the GPSS Processor treats attribute-valued Functions the same way it treats discrete Functions. For the Function GETUT, for example, if the value of P7 is less than 9, FR5 is returned as the Function's value; or, if P7's value exceeds 12, FR7 is returned as the value of the Function.

Figure 6.10 shows a second example of an attributed-valued Function. The Function's argument is random-number generator 5. The Function's name is SWICH. When the Function is called, its value equals the value of some other Function. The other Function is chosen with equal likelihood from the three Functions named JOE, PETE, and JIM.

LOCATION	OPERATION	A,B,C,D,E,F
SWICH	FUNCTION	RN5,E3
		.333,FN$JOE/.667,FN$PETE/1,FN$JIM

FIGURE 6.10 A second example of an attribute-valued Function

In Figure 6.11, an attribute-valued Function is shown which has a Savevalue as its argument. If X$CAROL has a value of 21 or less, the Function takes on the value of the Variable named RED; if X$CAROL is 22, 23, 24, or 25, the Function's value is XH35; and so on. This example shows that the second member of the Function-defining ordered pairs need not all be the same type of Standard Numerical Attribute. It also shows that one or more of the second members *can* be constants. In the example, for X$CAROL values of 26, or 27, the Function's value is simply 10.

Now consider attribute-valued Functions for which the first members of the Function-defining ordered pairs form the sequence of integers 1, 2, 3, etc. In such circumstances, attribute-valued Functions can be declared to be of the list type. List, attribute-valued Functions are defined by using M as the first B-Operand character in the Function header card. Nothing is gained *conceptually* by defining attribute-valued Functions to be of the list type, but increased speed of Function evaluation does result. And, as is the case with the list Functions introduced earlier, an error results during execution if the Function's argument is found to be out of range.

Figure 6.12(a) shows an example of an at-

LOCATION	OPERATION	A,B,C,D,E,F
MIXED	FUNCTION	X$CAROL,E4
		21,V$RED/25,XH35/27,10/36,Q$QUICK

FIGURE 6.11 A third example of an attribute-valued Function

LOCATION	OPERATION	A,B,C,D,E,F
POINT	FUNCTION	P2,E5
		1,V1/2,P2/3,X7/4,Q4/5,-99

(a)

LOCATION	OPERATION	A,B,C,D,E,F
POINT	FUNCTION	P2,M5
		1,V1/2,P2/3,X7/4,Q4/5,-99

(b)

FIGURE 6.12 An example of an attribute-valued Function, and its list Function equivalent. (a) The attribute-valued Function. (b) The equivalent list Function.

tribute-valued Function whose ordered-pair first-members are 1, 2, 3, 4, and 5. Figure 6.12(b) shows the same Function, defined as being of the list type. The only difference between the two definitions is that M, instead of E, is used as the B-Operand's first character in Figure 6.12(b).

Case Study 6D, presented in the next section, illustrates use of an attribute-valued Function in context.

6.14 CASE STUDY 6D
A Second Tour Through Case Study 6C

(1) Statement of the Problem

Case Study 6D deals with a single machine that uses a single type of part which is subject to periodic failure. Let that type of part be designated as a Type-A part. Assume now that the same machine also uses another type of part, designated as a Type-B part. Like Type-A parts, Type-B parts are subject to periodic failure. Whenever the Type-A or Type-B part in use in the machine fails, the machine must be turned off. The failed part is then removed, a good spare is installed if available, or as soon as one becomes available, and the machine is turned on again. Like Type-A parts, Type-B parts can be repaired and then reused.

When the machine is running, the "remaining lifetime before failure" of each installed part is decreasing. Suppose, for example, that the machine is turned on when the installed Type-A and Type-B parts have 330 and 415 running hours remaining, respectively, before failure. Then, when the machine is turned off 330 hours later because the Type-A part has failed, only 85 running hours remain for the Type-B part before it will fail.

The lifetime of Type-B parts is normally distributed, with mean and standard deviation of 450 and 90 hours, respectively. It takes 4 hours to remove a failed Type-B part from the machine, and 6 hours to install a replacement part of that type. The time required to repair a Type-B part follows the distribution given in Table 6D.1.

Except for the added feature of Type-B parts, the conditions under which the machine operates are identical to those described in Case Study 6C. In particular, (1) Type-A parts have the properties already described in Case Study 6C, and (2) there is only one repairman. The repairman fixes Type-A and Type-B parts on a first-come, first-served basis. In addition, he continues to repair

other items, which have a higher repair priority than parts of Type-A and Type-B. The situation is summarized in Figure 6D.1, where circles represent spare parts, and the letter A or B within a circle indicates whether the part is of Type-A or Type-B. A cross through a circle indicates that the corresponding part is in a failed state.

Build a GPSS model for this machine-and-parts system, then use the model to estimate the fractional utilization of the machine as a function of the number of Type-A and Type-B spare parts in the system. Study the system for each combination in which 0, or 1, or 2 spares of each type are provided. Run each simulation for the equivalent of 5 years, assuming 40-hour work weeks. For each alternative, control experimental conditions partially in the sense of duplicating the competition from other items which failed parts experience at the repair facility.

(2) Approach Taken in Building the Model

Model Segment 1: The Supply of Parts, and the Machine. As in Case Study 6C, a Transaction simulates a machine operator. It is assumed initially that a Type-A and a Type-B part have just been installed, so the machine is ready to turn on. When the operator enters the model, he samples from the lifetime distributions for parts of Type-A and B, saving the sampled values in Parameters 1 and 2, respectively. At the Block "SELECT MIN 3,1,2,,P", the number of the minimum-value Parameter is then copied into Parameter 3. (The P3 value is consequently 1 if the Type-A part fails next, and 2 if the Type-B part fails next.) After capturing the Facility MAC (thereby simulating turning on the machine), the operator-Transaction moves into the Block "ADVANCE P*3". If the value of P3 is 1, the holding time at the ADVANCE Block is P1; or, if the value of P3 is 2, the holding time is P2. That is, through indirect addressing, the operator-Transaction is held at the ADVANCE Block until the part with the shortest lifetime has failed.

TABLE 6D.1   Distribution of Repair Times for a Type-B Part in Case Study 6D

Repair Time (hours)	Cumulative Frequency
Less than 5	0.0
6	0.22
7	0.57
8	0.83
9	1.0

Exiting the ADVANCE Block, the operator turns off the machine (by releasing the Facility), then updates the remaining lifetime of the non-failed part (by subtracting from the Parameter whose number is *not* in Parameter 3, the value of the Parameter whose number *is* in Parameter 3). The failed part is then removed (note that removal time is identical for Type-A and Type-B parts). The operator then calls in a coworker, sending him to fetch a spare of the proper type.

Savevalues 1 and 2 are used to record the currently available number of good spares of Type-A and Type-B, respectively. The coworker automatically knows which type of part is needed, via his Parameter 3 value (which is identical to that of the offspring-Transaction's parent). He can test for part availability, then, via indirect addressing at the Block "TEST G X*3,0". After he has eventually installed the replacement part, he must then sample from the proper lifetime distribution to determine the lifetime of this part. If Variables 1 and 2 describe the lifetime distributions of part-types A and B, respectively, this can be done at the Block "ASSIGN P3,V*3". (The number of the Parameter receiving the lifetime value is indirectly specified, via P3; and the number of the Variable describing the proper lifetime

distribution is indirectly addressed, via V*3.) As in Case Study 6C, the coworker then continues on, essentially taking over as the machine operator.

Meantime, the original operator (that is, the parent Transaction) takes the failed part to the repair facility. The repair-time distribution from which to sample is either normal (if the failed part is a Type-A), or empirical (if the failed part is Type-B). Hence, either a Variable or a Function must be evaluated to simulate repair time, depending on whether the operator-Transaction's P3 value is 1 (for Type-A) or 2 (for Type-B), respectively. By defining an attribute-valued Function whose argument is P3, then, it is a simple matter to reference the proper repair time distribution. When repair has been completed, the original operator-Transaction increments the Savevalue whose number is in its Parameter 3 and then terminates, having surrendered the role of machine operator to the coworker.

Model Segments 2 and 3: The Repair Facility, and the Timer Segment. Model Segments 2 and 3 in Case Study 6C can be used without change in Case Study 6D.

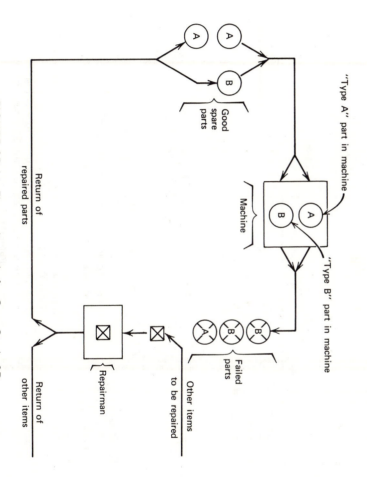

FIGURE 6D.1   Flow schematic for Case Study 6D

(3) Table of Definitions

Time Unit: 0.1 Hours

TYPE 6D.2   Table of Definitions for Case Study 6D

GPSS Entity	Interpretation
Transactions	
Model Segment 1	A machine operator
	P1: Remaining lifetime of the installed Type-A part
	P2: Remaining lifetime of the installed Type-B part
	P3: Number of that Parameter (among Parameters 1 and 2) whose value is the smallest
Model Segment 2	An other item
Model Segment 3	A timer-Transaction
Facilities	
MAC	The machine whose utilization is being estimated
FIXER	The repairman
Functions	
BFIX	Function describing the repair-time distribution of a Type-B part
FLIP	Function whose value is the number of that Parameter (among Parameters 1 and 2) whose number is *not* in Parameter 3
POINT	An attribute-valued Function whose value is a sample from the repair time distribution of a Type-A or a Type-B part, depending on the value of the Function's argument
SNORM	Standard normal distribution function
XPDIS	Exponential distribution function
Savevalues	
1, 2	Counters used to record the number of currently available good spares of Type A and Type B, respectively
Variables	
1, 2	Variables describing the normally distributed lifetimes of Type-A and Type-B parts, respectively
AFIX	Variable describing the normally distributed repair time for Type-A parts

(4) Block Diagram

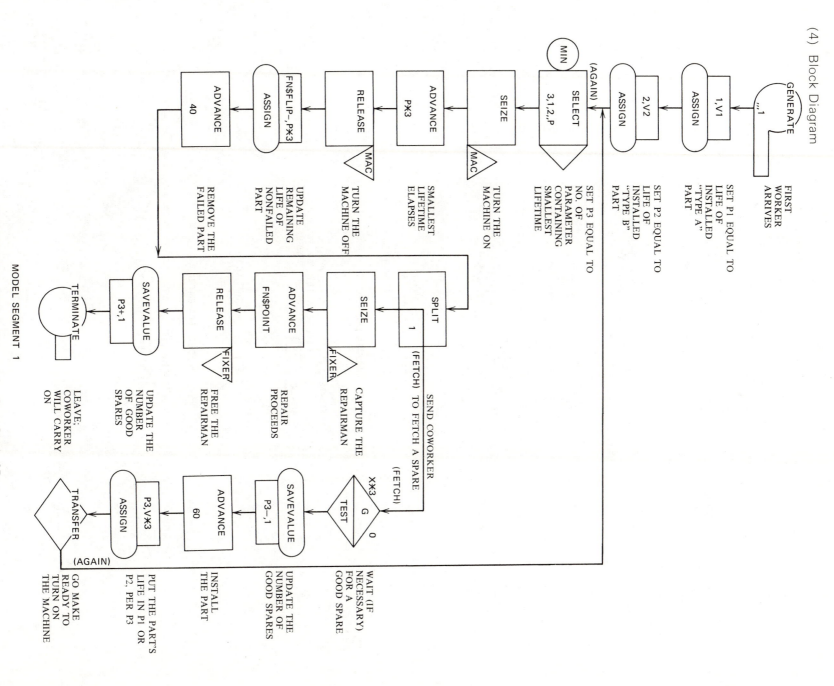

MODEL SEGMENT 1

FIGURE 6D.2   Block Diagram for Case Study 6D

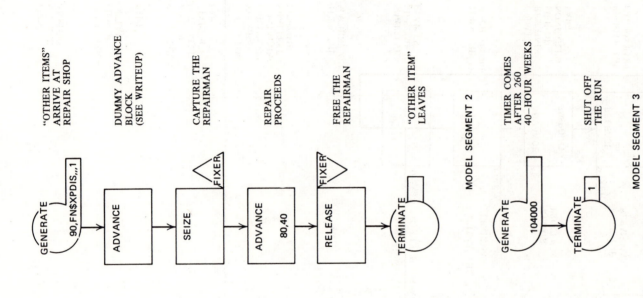

GENERATE 90,FN$XPDIS,,,1 — "OTHER ITEMS" ARRIVE AT REPAIR SHOP

ADVANCE — DUMMY ADVANCE BLOCK (SEE WRITEUP)

SEIZE FIXER — CAPTURE THE REPAIRMAN

ADVANCE 80,40 — REPAIR PROCEEDS

RELEASE FIXER — FREE THE REPAIRMAN

TERMINATE — "OTHER ITEM" LEAVES

MODEL SEGMENT 2

GENERATE 104000 — TIMER COMES AFTER 260 40-HOUR WEEKS

TERMINATE 1 — SHUT OFF THE RUN

MODEL SEGMENT 3

FIGURE 6D.2 (Continued)

(5) Extended Program Listing

BLOCK NUMBER	*LOC	OPERATION A,B,C,D,E,F,G	COMMENTS	CARD NUMBER
		SIMULATE		1
		*		2
		*	RANDOM NUMBER SEQUENCE INITIALIZATION(S)	3
		*		4
		RMULT 121,,17	SET RANDOM SEQUENCES FOR 1ST RUN	5
		*		6
		*	FUNCTION DEFINITION(S)	7
		*		8
	BFIX	FUNCTION RN2,C5	REPAIR TIME FOR A "TYPE B" PART	9
		0.50/.22,60/.57,70/.83,80/1,90		10
	FLIP	FUNCTION P3,L2	NUMBER OF "LARGEST-LIFETIME" PARAMETER	11
		1,2/2,1		12
	POINT	FUNCTION P3,M2	POINTER FOR REPAIR TIME DISTRIBUTION	13
		1,V$AFIX/2,FN$BFIX		14
	SNORM	FUNCTION RN2,C25	STANDARD NORMAL DISTRIBUTION FUNCTION	15
		0,-5/.00003,-4/.00135,-3/.00621,-2.5/.02275,-2		16
		.06681,-1.5/.11507,-1/.15866,-1/.21186,-.8/.27425,-.6		17
		.34458,-.4/.42074,-.2/.5,0/.57926,.2/.65542,.4		18
		.72575,.6/.78814,.8/.84134,1/.88493,1.2/.93319,1.5		19
		.97725,2/.99379,2.5/.99865,3/.99997,4/1,5		20
	XPDIS	FUNCTION RN3,C24	EXPONENTIAL DISTRIBUTION FUNCTION	21
		0,0/.1,.104/.2,.222/.3,.355/.4,.509/.5,.69/.6,.915/.7,1.2/.75,1.38		22
		.8,1.6/.84,1.83/.88,2.12/.9,2.3/.92,2.52/.94,2.81/.95,2.99/.96,3.2		23
		.97,3.5/.98,3.9/.99,4.6/.995,5.3/.998,6.2/.999,7/.9998,8		24
		*		25
		*	VARIABLE DEFINITION(S)	26
		*		27
	1	FVARIABLE 700*FN$SNORM+3500	LIFETIME OF A "TYPE A" PART	28
	2	FVARIABLE 900*FN$SNORM+4500	LIFETIME OF A "TYPE B" PART	29
	AFIX	FVARIABLE 5*FN$SNORM+80	REPAIR TIME FOR A "TYPE A" PART	30
		*		31
		*	MODEL SEGMENT 1	32
		*		33
1		GENERATE ,,,1	FIRST WORKER ARRIVES	34
2		ASSIGN 1,V1	SET P1 = LIFE OF	35
		*	INSTALLED "TYPE A" PART	36
3		ASSIGN 2,V2	SET P2 = LIFE OF	37
		*	INSTALLED "TYPE B" PART	38
4	AGAIN	SELECT MIN 3,1,2,,P	SET P3 = NO. OF PARAMETER	39
		*	CONTAINING SMALLEST LIFETIME	40
5		SEIZE MAC	TURN THE MACHINE ON	41
6		ADVANCE P*3	SMALLEST LIFETIME ELAPSES	42
7		RELEASE MAC	TURN THE MACHINE OFF	43
8		ASSIGN FN$FLIP-,P*3	UPDATE REMAINING LIFE	44
		*	OF NON-FAILED PART	45
9		ADVANCE 40	REMOVE THE FAILED PART	46
10		SPLIT 1,FETCH	SEND CO-WORKER TO FETCH A SPARE	47
11		SEIZE FIXER	CAPTURE THE REPAIRMAN	48
12		ADVANCE FN$POINT	REPAIR PROCEEDS	49
13		RELEASE FIXER	FREE THE REPAIRMAN	50
14		SAVEVALUE P3+,1	UPDATE THE NUMBER OF GOOD SPARES	51
15		TERMINATE	LEAVE; CO-WORKER WILL CARRY ON	52
16	FETCH	TEST G X*3,0	WAIT (IF NECESSARY) FOR A GOOD SPARE	53
17		SAVEVALUE P3-,1	UPDATE THE NUMBER OF GOOD SPARES	54

FIGURE 6D.3   Extended Program Listing for Case Study 6D

BLOCK NUMBER	*LOC	OPERATION	A,B,C,D,E,F,G	COMMENTS	CARD NUMBER
18		ADVANCE	60	INSTALL THE PART	55
19		ASSIGN	P3,V*3		56
20		TRANSFER	.AGAIN	GO MAKE READY TO TURN ON THE MACHINE	57
	*				58
	*			MODEL SEGMENT 2	59
	*				60
21		GENERATE	90,FN$XPDIS,,,1	"OTHER ITEMS" ARRIVE AT REPAIR SHOP	61
22		ADVANCE		DUMMY ADVANCE BLOCK	62
23		SEIZE	FIXER	CAPTURE THE REPAIRMAN	63
24		ADVANCE	80,40	REPAIR PROCEEDS	64
25		RELEASE	FIXER	FREE THE REPAIRMAN	65
26		TERMINATE		"OTHER ITEM" LEAVES	66
	*				67
	*			MODEL SEGMENT 3	68
	*				69
27		GENERATE	104000	TIMER COMES AFTER 260 40-HOUR WEEKS	70
28		TERMINATE	1	SHUT OFF THE RUN	71
	*				72
	*			CONTROL CARDS AND STORAGE CAPACITY RE-DEFINITIONS	73
	*				74
		START	1	START 1ST RUN (0 "A", 0 "B" SPARES)	75
		RMULT	121,,17	RESTORE RANDOM SEQUENCES FOR 2ND RUN	76
		CLEAR		CLEAR FOR 2ND RUN	77
		INITIAL	X2,1	RE-CONFIGURE FOR 2ND RUN	78
		START	1	START 2ND RUN (0 "A", 1 "B" SPARES)	79
		RMULT	121,,17	RESTORE RANDOM SEQUENCES FOR 3RD RUN	80
		CLEAR		CLEAR FOR 3RD RUN	81
		INITIAL	X2,2	RE-CONFIGURE FOR 3RD RUN	82
		START	1	START 3RD RUN (0 "A", 2 "B" SPARES)	83
		RMULT	121,,17	RESTORE RANDOM SEQUENCES FOR 4TH RUN	84
		CLEAR		CLEAR FOR 4TH RUN	85
		INITIAL	X1,1	RE-CONFIGURE FOR 4TH RUN	86
		START	1	START 4TH RUN (1 "A", 0 "B" SPARES)	87
		RMULT	121,,17	RESTORE RANDOM SEQUENCES FOR 5TH RUN	88
		CLEAR		CLEAR FOR 5TH RUN	89
		INITIAL	X1,1/X2,1	RE-CONFIGURE FOR 5TH RUN	90
		START	1	START 5TH RUN (1 "A", 1 "B" SPARES)	91
		RMULT	121,,17	RESTORE RANDOM SEQUENCES FOR 6TH RUN	92
		CLEAR		CLEAR FOR 6TH RUN	93
		INITIAL	X1,1/X2,2	RE-CONFIGURE FOR 6TH RUN	94
		START	1	START 6TH RUN (1 "A", 2 "B" SPARES)	95
		RMULT	121,,17	RESTORE RANDOM SEQUENCES FOR 7TH RUN	96
		CLEAR		CLEAR FOR 7TH RUN	97
		INITIAL	X1,2	RE-CONFIGURE FOR 7TH RUN	98
		START	1	START 7TH RUN (2 "A", 0 "B" SPARES)	99
		RMULT	121,,17	RESTORE RANDOM SEQUENCES FOR 8TH RUN	100
		CLEAR		CLEAR FOR 8TH RUN	101
		INITIAL	X1,2/X2,1	RE-CONFIGURE FOR 8TH RUN	102
		START	1	START 8TH RUN (2 "A", 1 "B" SPARES)	103
		RMULT	121,,17	RESTORE RANDOM SEQUENCES FOR 9TH RUN	104
		CLEAR		CLEAR FOR 9TH RUN	105
		INITIAL	X1,2/X2,2	RE-CONFIGURE FOR 9TH RUN	106
		START	1	START 9TH RUN (2 "A", 2 "B" SPARES)	107
		END		RETURN CONTROL TO OPERATING SYSTEM	108

FIGURE 6D.3 (Continued)

(6) Program Output

No output is shown directly. Results are summarized in the next section.

(7) Discussion

Model Logic. The Model Logic remarks made for Case Study 6C apply in reasonably direct fashion to Case Study 6D, and should be reviewed. Note especially the system conditions assumed in effect initially; the point in the model at which the parts constraint is simulated; and the method used to partially control experimental conditions.

Model Implementation. The "(Type-A, Type-B)" spare-parts combinations were studied in the sequence (0,0), (0,1), (0,2); (1,0), (1,1), (1,2); and (2,0), (2,1), (2,2). The (0,0) combination, of course, does not require use of the Savevalue INITIAL card, because Savevalues 1 and 2 have values of 0 by default. For subsequent combinations, after clearing the model, the Savevalue INITIAL card is used to set the number of spares at the right level prior to each next run. The "RMULT–CLEAR–INITIAL–START" pattern is evident in the control card section (see Cards 76 through 107 in Figure 6D.2). As a result of each CLEAR card, Savevalues 1 and 2 have their values set back to 0. For combinations in which one Savevalue is to have a value of 0, the following INITIAL card then only has to set the value of the *other* Savevalue.

Program Output.[9] Table 6D.3 summarizes the program output. Corresponding to zero Type-A spares in the system, row 1 in the table shows how machine utilization increases as the number of Type-B spares increases from 0, to 1, to 2. It is interesting to note that with no Type-A and two Type-B spares, the utilization of 74.2 percent exceeds the 70.5 percent utilization achieved in Case Study 6C (Table 6C.2) for no Type-A spares (and, in effect, no Type-B parts-constraint). The relative magnitudes of the 74.2 percent and 70.5 percent estimates are the reverse of what they would be in terms of expected values.

Inspection of rows 2 and 3 in Table 6D.3 reveals the increasing-utilization pattern which is to be expected. The 90.8 percent utilization for one Type-A and two Type-B spares is less than the 91.2 percent estimate for one Type-A spare in Case Study 6C; similarly, the 94.5 percent utiliza-

[9] Total CPU time for the simulation on an IBM 360/67 computer was 55.9 seconds.

TABLE 6D.3 A Summary of Machine Utilizations Resulting from the Case Study 6D Simulations

Number of Type-A Spares in the System	Number of Type-B Spares in the System		
	0	1	2
0	0.609	0.686	0.742
1	0.755	0.864	0.908
2	0.714	0.906	0.945

tion for two Type-A and two Type-B spares is less than the 95.8 percent estimate for two Type-A spares in Case Study 6C. In contrast with row 1, then, the relative differences in these utilizations follow the pattern in effect for the corresponding expected values.

Column 1 in Table 6D.3 shows an unexpected decrease in machine utilization in moving from one to two Type-A spares. This decrease is inconsistent with the expected-value pattern which would be in effect. If *all* experimental conditions had been replicated in the simulations, the various inconsistencies between estimates and expected values might not arise for the large sample sizes used here. (See Exercise 6, Section 6.15.)

6.15 Exercises

1. (a) An analyst wants Transaction holding time at an ADVANCE Block to equal the smallest value contained in Parameters 1 through 5 of the advancing Transaction. Show how this can be accomplished for each of the following two alternatives.

   (i) Use indirect addressing.

   (ii) Use an attribute-valued Function.

   Which of the two alternatives do you think it would be best to use, and why?

   (b) Repeat (a), only assume that the holding time at the ADVANCE Block is to equal the smallest value contained in halfword Savevalues 1 through 5.

2. These exercises refer to Case Study 6D.

   (a) Show how to define a Variable which can be used in place of the Function FLIP (see Cards 11 and 12 in Figure 6D.3).

   (b) The case study assumes that 4 hours are required to remove a failed part, whether it is of Type A or Type B. Assume instead that removal times for Type A and Type B parts are 4 and 7 hours, respectively. Show how to modify the case study to reflect this assumption.

   (c) Now assume that the removal times for Type-A and Type-B parts are uniformly distributed over the ranges 4 ± 2 hours and 7 ± 3 hours, respectively. Show how to modify the case study to incorporate this assumption.

(d) Describe how the case study model behaves if the installed Type-A and Type-B parts fail simultaneously. Do you think that the model logic is valid under this circumstance, or not? Give the details behind your reasoning.

(e) Does it always make sense to repair failed Type-A and Type-B parts on a first-come, first-served basis? If not, explain why.

3. Without making use of indirect addressing or attribute-valued Functions, show the Block Diagram for a model which simulates the machine-and-parts system described in Case Study 6D. Continue to let a Transaction simulate a machine operator, and Savevalues 1 and 2 record the number of currently available Type A and Type B spares, respectively. How many Blocks does your model require? (Note that 28 Blocks are used in Case Study 6D.)

4. An alternative model can be built for Case Study 6D by letting some Transactions simulate Type-A parts, and other Transactions simulate Type-B parts. Show the Block Diagram for such an alternative model. Compare and contrast the resulting model with that shown in the case study, from the points of view of (a) number of Blocks required, and (b) ease of building the model.

(a) As in Case Study 6D, let a Transaction simulate a machine operator.

(b) As in exercise 4 above, let some Transactions simulate Type-A parts, others simulate Type-B parts, and yet others simulate Type-C parts. Which approach do you think lends itself most readily to ease of model building?

5. Expand the machine-and-parts system described in Case Study 6D by assuming that the machine makes use of a third type of part, designated as Type C. Let removal and installation time for a Type-C part be 4 and 6 hours, respectively; and let the repair time for a Type C part be 8 ± 4 hours. Show the GPSS Block Diagram for a model of the system for each of the following Transaction-interpretations.

6. The similarity between Case Studies 6C and 6D applies to the extent to which experimental conditions are replicated from configuration to configuration. In the spirit of exercise 6, Section 6.10, show how to develop a model which *completely* reproduces experimental conditions in the Case Study 6D simulation. Do this first of all without giving individual identity to spare parts (except, of course, in the sense of distinguishing between parts of Type A and Type B). Then build another model in which an individual identity above and beyond that of part type is given to each spare part. Simulate with one or both of the resulting models,

producing a utilization table similar to Table 6D.3. Does the complete reproduction of experimental conditions eliminate the inconsistencies in the Table 6D.3 utilization estimates (as discussed under Program Output in Case Study 6D)?

7. The manager of a large fleet of taxi cabs has collected data on the frequency and cause of cab breakdowns. A breakdown is classified as occurring in one of four cab subsystems, described as "Mechanical—Motor," "Mechanical—Nonmotor," "Electrical," and "Other." The mileage-between-failures for each of these four systems is uniformly distributed over the ranges $20{,}000 \pm 8{,}000$ miles; $12{,}000 \pm 6{,}000$ miles; $25{,}000 \pm 10{,}000$ miles; and $15{,}000 \pm 5{,}000$ miles, respectively.

The cost of calling in a cab to inspect it completely and restore all four systems to their original condition is $100; the cost of repairing a failure (including lost revenue because of unscheduled removal of the cab from service) is $200; and the cost of repairing a failure and restoring all systems to their original condition at the same time is $275. Use simulation to determine which of the following maintenance policies has the smallest cost.

(a) Drive each cab until it fails, then restore only the system which failed.

(b) Drive each cab until it fails, then restore all systems to their original condition.

(c) Call in each cab every 10,000 miles for inspection. Restore each system to its original condition at that time. If a failure occurs before the scheduled call-in time, repair the failed system and restore the other systems to their original condition. Then keep the cab in use for another 10,000 miles before performing the next inspection (unless a breakdown occurs before the cab has been driven another 10,000 miles).

(d) Follow the policy outlined for (c), only experiment to find the optimal frequency of call-in. That is, instead of using 10,000 miles as the call-in criterion, determine whether a call-in figure of 12,000 miles, or 8,000 miles, or whatever, results in the lowest cost for this policy.

6.16 Functions Whose Values are Block Locations

A number of GPSS Blocks have certain Block Operands whose values are interpreted as the Location of other Blocks in a model. When a Transaction enters an unconditional-mode TRANSFER Block, for example, the Block's B Operand indicates the Location of the next Block the Transaction is to enter. Similarly, the TEST Block's C Operand (if used), the GATE Block's B Operand (if used), the SELECT Block's F

Operand (if used), the LOOP Block's B Operand, and the BOTH-mode and statistical-transfer-mode TRANSFER Block's B and C Operands all have the purpose of supplying Block Location information.

In all examples and case studies presented so far, symbolic Location names have always been supplied for these "Block-Location Operands." Strictly speaking, however, it is possible to use any GPSS Standard Numerical Attribute for these Operands. For instance, the unconditional-mode TRANSFER Block "TRANSFER ,V$POINT" could be used in a model. When a Transaction entered the Block, the Variable named POINT would be evaluated, and the Transaction would be routed to the Block whose Location number equals the Variable's value. Of course, it would be the analyst's responsibility to see to it that this would make sense logically. If there were no Block whose Location number equals the Variable's value, for example, an execution error would result.

At first glance, the possibility of being able to use a Standard Numerical Attribute in any meaningful sense as a Block-Location Operand would seem remote. It happens, however, that symbolic Location names can be used as the second member of the ordered pairs used to define *discrete* GPSS Functions. As a consequence, certain properly defined *Functions* can be put to good and meaningful use as Block-Location Operands. As an example, suppose that ALPHA, BETA, GAMMA, and DELTA are used as Location names in a particular model. Also suppose that the Function named ROUTE is defined as shown in Figure 6.13. Note that P1 has been chosen as the Func-

LOCATION	OPERATION	A,B,C,D,E,F
1 2 3 4 5 6	7 8 9 10 11 12 13 14 15 16 17 18	19 20 21 22 23 24 25 26 27 28 29 30 31 32 33 34 35 36
ROUTE	FUNCTION	P1,D4
2,ALPHA/3,BETA/4,GAMMA/5,DELTA		

FIGURE 6.13 A discrete Function whose values are Block Locations

tion's argument. Assume that Transactions arriving at Point A is a model are to be routed next to ALPHA, BETA, GAMMA, or DELTA, depending on whether their Parameter 1 value is 2, 3, 4, or 5, respectively. Figure 6.14 shows how an unconditional-mode TRANSFER Block can be used in the model at Point A to accomplish this routing. When a Transaction moves into the TRANSFER Block, the Function ROUTE is eval-

uated, and the returned value is interpreted as the number of the Block to which the Transaction is to move next.

When the GPSS Processor encounters a Function such as that shown in Figure 6.13, it assumes that the symbols used to define the Function are the Location names of Blocks in the model. This guarantees that no confusion results if one or more symbols are used in two or more different contexts in a model. For example, suppose that ALPHA is the symbolic name of a Facility, as well as the symbolic name of a Block Location. Assume that ALPHA has a value of 3 as a Facility, and a value of 37 as a Block Location. Because of the Location-names-only understanding, the value of ALPHA in the Figure 6.13 Function ROUTE is then taken to be 37, not 3.

When a Function returns values meaningful as Block Locations, there is no restriction that the Function argument be a Transaction Parameter. Any of the Standard Numerical Attributes can be used as Function arguments in this context. In this sense, these Functions are the same as any other discrete GPSS Function. Similarly, if the first members of the Function-defining ordered pairs form the sequence of integers 1, 2, 3, etc., then the Functions can be defined to be of the list type, instead of the discrete type.

The next section introduces the possibility of using a Function of the Figure 6.13 variety with the SPLIT Block.

6.17 The SPLIT Block Serialization Option

When a Transaction enters a SPLIT Block, it propagates itself by bringing offspring Transactions into the model. The number of offspring is indicated with the SPLIT Block's A Operand. The B Operand is the Location to which the offspring are routed, whereas the parent moves to the sequential Block. For the SPLIT Block as introduced in Section 6.8, the parent and its offspring are identical with respect to their Mark Time (i.e., time of model entry), Priority Level, Parameter

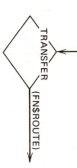

FIGURE 6.14 An example of a Function used as the B Operand at an unconditional-mode TRANSFER Block

type (i.e., halfword or fullword), and Parameter values (the parent's Parameter values are copied to each offspring). Parent and offspring differ only in that they have different Transaction numbers. But because a Transaction's number cannot be made an explicit part of modeling logic, the analyst cannot use it to make distinctions among the parent and/or its offspring.

There are times when a distinction must be made among parent and offspring Transactions. For this reason, a *serialization option* is provided with the SPLIT Block. The option is invoked by making use of an optional C Operand available with the Block. When this C Operand is used, it is understood to supply the *number of a Parameter* in which the parent and each of its offspring will be numbered serially. To clarify this, let j be the value of the C Operand, and v be the value of the parent-Transaction's jth Parameter when it enters the SPLIT Block. Then, upon leaving the SPLIT Block, the parent and its offspring have Pj values as shown in Table 6.5. The parent-Transaction has had its Pj value incremented by 1. The Pj

Now consider the possibility of having the offspring Transactions routed from the SPLIT Block to *different* Blocks in the model. The SPLIT Block's B Operand supplies Block Location information for these offspring. When the SPLIT Block is executed, the B Operand is evaluated not just once, but is evaluated repeatedly, *offspring-by-offspring*. Hence, each offspring's next Block can be made to depend on properties of the offspring-Transactions themselves. Of course, the properties of the offspring are identical, unless the SPLIT Block's serialization option has been used. In this case, the offspring have nonidentical serialization Parameter values. This fact can be made use of in routing the offspring to different next Blocks in the model.

As an example, suppose that a Transaction with a Parameter 5 value of 0 enters the SPLIT Block shown in Figure 6.15(a). The three offspring-Transactions brought into the model then have Parameter 5 values of 2, 3, and 4, respectively. They are routed, one by one, to the Block whose Location number is the value of the Function named SWICH. The Function, whose definition appears in Figure 6.15(b), has Parameter 5 as its argument. Hence, the first, second, and third offspring Transactions move to the Blocks in Locations BLOKA, BLOKB, and BLOKC, respectively.

The SPLIT Block also has an optional D Operand. When used, it indicates the number of Parameters each offspring is to have. If an offspring has more Parameters than its parent, the surplus Parameters are assigned initial values of

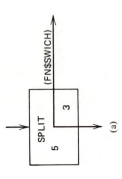

(a)

LOCATION	OPERATION	A,B,C,D,E,F
SWICH	FUNCTION	P5,D3
	2,,BLOKA/3,,BLOKB/4,,BLOKC	

(b)

FIGURE 6.15 An example showing how offspring Transactions can be routed from a SPLIT Block to a variety of "next Blocks". (a) The SPLIT Block. (b) The Function Switch.

TABLE 6.5 Values of the "Serialization Parameter" of the Parent and Its Offspring When the SPLIT Block's Optional C Operand Is Used

Transaction	Pj Value
Parent	v + 1
First offspring	v + 2
Second offspring	v + 3
Third offspring	v + 4
and so on	

value of the first offspring-Transaction equals the parent's updated Pj value, plus 1. The Pj value of the second offspring equals the parent's updated Pj value, plus 2, and so on.

For a numeric example, suppose that a Transaction with a P7 value of 0 enters the Block "SPLIT 3,RUTE9,7". Then three offspring will be brought into the model and routed to the Block at RUTE9. The parent and its offspring are to be numbered serially in Parameter 7. This means that when the parent leaves the SPLIT Block with a P7 value of 1 ("0 + 1"), and the first, second, and third offspring have P7 values of 2, 3, and 4, respectively. From a chain-oriented point of view, the first, second, and third offspring are distinguished from each other by being placed in that relative order on the Current Events Chain when they are fetched from the top of the stack in the latent Transaction pool, one by one, and brought into the model.

zero. When an offspring has fewer Parameters than the parent, the parent's Parameter values are copied to the offspring only to the extent possible. In such a case, the parent has surplus Parameters for which there are no correspondents in the offspring.

In conclusion, the SPLIT Block and its various properties are summarized in Figure 6.16.

Operand	Significance	Default Value or Result
A	The number of offspring-Transactions to be brought into the model	Error
B	Block Location to which the offspring are to be routed	Error
C	Number of the serialization Parameter	No serialization occurs
D	Number of Parameters each offspring is to have	Each offspring has the same number of Parameters as the parent

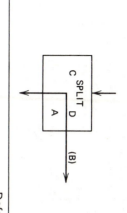

FIGURE 6.16 The SPLIT Block, and its A, B, C, and D Operands

6.18 Modeling Alternative System Configurations in Parallel

The procedure used so far to investigate alternative system configurations has been to simulate with the alternatives *sequentially*. A typical example of this is provided in Case Study 5D, the gas station problem. A simulation was run for the case of one gas-station attendant; then, by clearing the model and redefining the capacity of the attendant-Storage, a simulation was run for a two-attendant configuration, and then similarly for the three-attendant case. By use of the RMULT card, experimental conditions were also replicated in that case study. Hence, the alternatives were compared in as fair a fashion as possible.

In contrast with the sequential approach, it is also possible to investigate various system configurations *in parallel*. For the gas station prob-

lem, the spirit of the parallel approach is to build the model as though N gas stations were simultaneously operating in N locations. In the interest of replicating experimental conditions, the N locations should be identical to each other. That is, each location should be subject to the same customer interarrival-time sequence, and the same customer service-time sequence. For example, if cars arrive at the one-attendant station at 8:03, 8:08, and 8:10 a.m., with associated service-time requirements of 10, 7, and 13 minutes, respectively, then an identical stream of cars should also arrive at the two- and three-attendant stations if one-, two-, and three-attendant configurations are being investigated in parallel.

By making use of the SPLIT Block and indirect addressing, it can be a relatively simple matter to model alternative system configurations in parallel. To illustrate in terms of the gas station example, when a single car-Transaction arrives at the group of parallel stations, it can be viewed as a master car. At an ASSIGN Block, it can sample from the service-time distribution, saving the result in a Parameter. It can then SPLIT, producing exactly enough additional Transactions so that, between the parent and its carbon-copy offspring, there is now one car for each of the parallel gas stations. These cars are identical both in terms of their time of arrival and their latent service-time requirement, which has already been stored in a Parameter. Furthermore, if the serialization option is used at the SPLIT Block, the value of the serialization Parameter can be used as a numeric code indicating the station for which each Transaction represents a car. By using this Parameter for indirect specification, a single sequence of GPSS Blocks can then simultaneously simulate all the parallel stations.

The combination of indirect specification, indirect addressing, and a compact Block Diagram sometimes makes parallel modeling of alternatives difficult to envision at first. In fact, for very complicated models, the analyst may prefer studying alternatives sequentially. There are typically not as many details to keep in mind in the sequential approach. This, in turn, lessens the chance of building invalid models. On the other hand, for reasons to be made clear in the next section, the computer time required to experiment with alternatives in parallel is often less than required to do equivalent experimentation sequentially. This tends to offset the conceptual complications in the parallel approach.

The spirit and methodology of parallel modeling is brought into sharper focus in the next section, where the details of modeling the gas station problem in parallel are presented as a case study.

6.19 CASE STUDY 6E
A Second Tour Through Case Study 5D

(1) Statement of the Problem

In Case Study 5D, the problem was to determine how many attendants should be hired at a gas station to satisfy the objective of maximizing daily profit. The alternatives of hiring one, or two, or three attendants were investigated in that case study on a sequential basis, under otherwise-identical experimental conditions. It was shown that by hiring two attendants, the average daily profit at the gas station could be maximized.

Build another model for the Case Study 5D problem, simulating the various alternatives in parallel, instead of sequentially. Do this in as compact a fashion as possible by taking full advantage of indirect specification and indirect addressing. The alternatives should be investigated under experimental conditions identical to those used in Case Study 5D.

Compare the number of Block executions performed in the parallel simulation with the number performed in the sequential investigation. How much more economical of CPU time is the parallel approach in this instance?

(2) An Approach Leading to Solution

The approach used in building the parallel model has already been roughed out in Section 6.18. Here is a summary of the main features of the approach.

1. Use a single GENERATE Block to feed car-Transactions to the group of gas stations operating in parallel. View each Transaction which enters the model through this GENERATE Block as being a master car.

2. Have each master car sample from the service-time distribution at an ASSIGN Block, saving the sampled value in a Parameter.

3. Now move each master car-Transaction through a SPLIT Block, thereby bringing two offspring-Transactions into the model. There are now three cars, one for each of the three alternative gas-station configurations. These cars are identical to each other in terms of (a) their time of arrival, and (b) their service-time requirement, as previously saved in the master car's Parameter (and subsequently copied to each offspring at the SPLIT Block). In this sense, the conditions which each car imposes on each gas-station alternative are identical.

4. Finally, use the serialization option at the SPLIT Block. This means that in the serialization Parameter, the parent-car and its two offspring-cars will have values of 1, 2, and 3, respectively (assuming the parent's serialization Parameter had an initial value of 0). Let the parent be the car arriving at the one-attendant station, and the two offsprings be the cars arriving at the two- and three-attendant stations. Beyond the SPLIT Block, let this cluster of three car-Transactions move through a common Block-sequence. By taking advantage of the Transactions' distinct serialization-Parameter values, use indirect specification and indirect addressing so that this Block sequence models all three gas station alternatives.

(3) Table of Definitions

Time Unit: 1 Second

TABLE 6E.1 Table of Definitions for Case Study 6E

GPSS Entity	Interpretation
Transactions Model Segment 1	A car P1: The car's latent service-time requirement P2: A code number indicating whether the car is using the one-, two-, or three-attendant gas-station configuration; P2 values of 1, 2, and 3 correspond to the one-, two-, and three-attendant configurations, respectively
Model Segment 2	A timer
Functions IAT	A Function describing the interarrival-time distribution
STIME	A Function describing the service-time distribution
Logic Switches LOCK	A Logic Switch simulating the "open"–"not open" condition of the gas stations
Queues 1, 2, 3	The waiting lines in which cars wait for service at stations with one, two, and three attendants, respectively
Savevalues 1, 2, 3	Savevalues in which are stored the realized daily profit for the one-, two-, and three-attendant con-figurations, respectively.
Storages 1, 2, 3	Storages whose capacities are 1, 2, and 3, respectively, corresponding to the alternatives of one, two, and three gas-station attendants
Variables NET	A Variable whose value is the day's profit after costs; through indirect addressing, the one Variable applies to each of the three alternative configurations

(4) Block Diagram

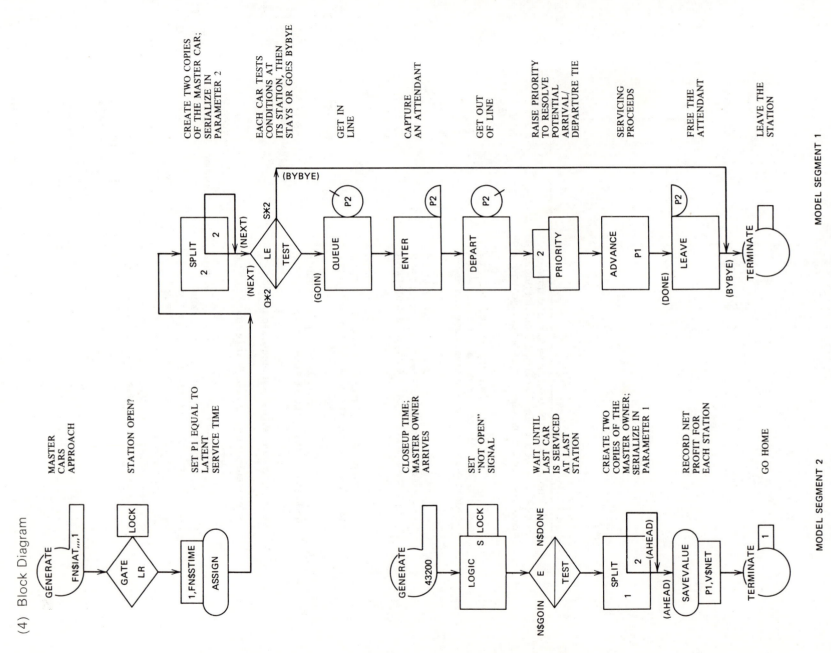

FIGURE 6E.1   Block Diagram for Case Study 6E

(5) Extended Program Listing

BLOCK NUMBER	*LOC	OPERATION	A,B,C,D,E,F,G	COMMENTS	CARD NUMBER
		SIMULATE			1
		*			2
		*			3
		*		RANDOM NUMBER SEQUENCE INITIALIZATION(S)	4
		*			5
		RMULT	111	SET RANDOM NUMBER SEQUENCE FOR 1ST RUN	6
		*			7
		*		FUNCTION DEFINITION(S)	8
		*			9
	IAT	FUNCTION	RN1,C7	INTER-ARRIVAL TIME DISTRIBUTION	10
			0,0/.25,100/.48,200/.69,300/.81,400/.9,500/1,600		11
	STIME	FUNCTION	RN1,C7	SERVICE TIME DISTRIBUTION	12
			0,100/.06,200/.21,300/.48,400/.77,500/.93,600/1,700		13
		*			14
		*		STORAGE CAPACITY DEFINITION(S)	15
		*			16
		STORAGE	S1,1/S2,2/S3,3	CONFIGURE FOR PARALLEL CASES OF	17
				1, 2, AND 3 ATTENDANTS	18
		*			19
		*		VARIABLE DEFINITION(S)	20
		*			21
	NET	VARIABLE	5C*1-75-30*R*1	DAY'S PROFIT AFTER COSTS	22
		*			23
		*		MODEL SEGMENT 1	24
		*			25
1		GENERATE	FN$IAT,,,,1	MASTER CARS APPROACH	26
2		GATE LR	LOCK	STATIONS OPEN?	27
3		ASSIGN	1,FN$STIME	SET P1 = LATENT SERVICE TIME	28
4		SPLIT	2,NEXT,2	CREATE 2 COPIES OF THE MASTER CAR;	29
				SERIALIZE IN PARAMETER 2	30
5	NEXT	TEST LE	0*2,S*2,BYBYE	EACH CAR TESTS CONDITIONS AT ITS	31
				STATION, THEN STAYS OR GOES BYBYE	32
6		QUEUE	P2	GET IN LINE	33
7	GOIN	ENTER	P2	CAPTURE AN ATTENDANT	34
8		DEPART	P2	GET OUT OF LINE	35
9		PRIORITY	2	RAISE PRIORITY TO RESOLVE	36
				POTENTIAL ARRIVAL/DEPARTURE TIE	37
10		ADVANCE	P1	SERVICING PROCEEDS	38
11		LEAVE	P2	FREE THE ATTENDANT	39
12	BYBYE	TERMINATE		LEAVE THE STATION	40
		*			41
		*		MODEL SEGMENT 2	42
		*			43
13		GENERATE	43200	CLOSEUP TIME; MASTER OWNER ARRIVES	44
14		LOGIC S	LOCK	SET "NOT OPEN" SIGNAL	45
15		TEST E	N$GOIN,N$DONE	WAIT 'TIL LAST CAR IS	46
				SERVICED AT LAST STATION	47
16		SPLIT	2,AHEAD,1	CREATE 2 COPIES OF THE MASTER OWNER;	48
				SERIALIZE IN PARAMETER 1	49
17	AHEAD	SAVEVALUE	P1,V$NET	RECORD NET PROFIT FOR EACH STATION	50
18		TERMINATE	1	GO HOME	51
		*			52
		*		CONTROL CARDS	53
		*			54
		START	3	START 1ST RUN (DAY 1)	55
		RMULT	333	SET RANDOM NUMBER SEQUENCE FOR 2ND RUN	56
		CLEAR		CLEAR FOR 2ND RUN	57
		START	3	START 2ND RUN (DAY 2)	58
		RMULT	555	SET RANDOM NUMBER SEQUENCE FOR 3RD RUN	59
		CLEAR		CLEAR FOR 3RD RUN	60
		START	3	START 3RD RUN (DAY 3)	61
		RMULT	777	SET RANDOM NUMBER SEQUENCE FOR 4TH RUN	62
		CLEAR		CLEAR FOR 4TH RUN	63
		START	3	START 4TH RUN (DAY 4)	64
		RMULT	999	SET RANDOM NUMBER SEQUENCE FOR 5TH RUN	65
		CLEAR		CLEAR FOR 5TH RUN	66
		START	3	START 5TH RUN (DAY 5)	67
		END		RETURN CONTROL TO OPERATING SYSTEM	68

FIGURE 6E.2 Extended Program Listing for Case Study 6E

(6) Program Output

No program output is shown directly. Results are presented in the next section.

(7) Discussion

Model Logic. *Model Segment 1.* Model Segment 1 in Figure 6E.1 should be studied in light of the remarks made in the "Approach Leading to Solution" section. For purposes of comparison and contrast, Model Segment 1 in Case Study 5D ("A Gas Station Problem") should also be reviewed. Except for addition of the SPLIT Block, the same Block sequences are used in Model Segment 1 in the two case studies. The chief distinction between the two segments comes in terms of the way Block Operand values are supplied at the TEST—QUEUE—ENTER—DEPART—LEAVE Blocks. In Case Study 5D, Operands are specified directly at the QUEUE—ENTER—DEPART—LEAVE Blocks; in Case Study 6E, the corresponding Block Operands are provided via indirect specification. In Case Study 5D, the TEST Block's A and B Operands are provided via indirect specification; in Case Study 6E, the same Operands are provided via indirect addressing.

Model Segment 2. It is also useful to compare the timer-Transaction segments ("Model Segment 2") in Case Studies 5D and 6E. In the sequential investigation in Case Study 5D, each timer-Transaction only had to compute one profit statistic. In the parallel investigation in Case Study 6E, each timer-Transaction must compute three profit statistics (one for each alternative configuration). After determining that there are no more cars in any of the parallel gas stations, the single timer-Transaction in Case Study 6E calls for help in computing the profit statistics. That is, the timer splits, bringing two offspring Transactions into the model (Block 16, Figure 6E.2). By using the serialization option, the original timer and its two offspring are numbered 1, 2, and 3, respectively, in Parameter 1. Each of these three Transactions then moves through a common SAVEVALUE Block (Block 17, Figure 6E.2), where the parent computes profit for the first alternative, and the two offspring do likewise for the second and third alternatives, respectively. The profit-Variable NET (Card 22, Figure 6E.2) indirectly addresses data through Parameter 1 of whatever Transaction has just moved into the SAVEVALUE Block; hence, the profit computation is cus-

tomized, Transaction by Transaction (that is, configuration by configuration).

Control of Experimental Conditions. The problem statement calls for two-fold control of experimental conditions. First of all, each of the alternative configurations is to be subjected to identical 5-day sets of circumstances in terms of car interarrival times and their latent service time requirements. In addition, the 5-day set of circumstances is to be the same as the 5-day set used for the sequential investigations in Case Study 5D.

Neither one of these requirements poses a special problem. Through such concepts as "master car," "predetermined service time," and "splitting to produce carbon copies," exposing each configuration to identical circumstances is probably more easily visualized here than it was in Case Study 5D. Furthermore, through use of the RMULT card, it is easy to set FN1 at the same starting point for a given day in Case Study 6E as was used in Case Study 5D. Hence, in both case studies, "RMULT 111" sets the starting point for day 1, "RMULT 333" sets the starting point for day 2, and so on.

Whereas 93 punchcards are used for Case Study 5D, only 68 are needed for Case Study 6E. This is a direct consequence of parallel vs. sequential investigations. Only five RMULT cards, five CLEAR cards, and five START cards have to be used in the parallel model, vs. 15 RMULT cards, 15 CLEAR cards, and 15 START cards in the sequential model.

Program Output.[10] Table 6E.2 summarizes the daily profit, in dollars, for the various runs. Entries in the table are identical to those in the corresponding Case Study 5D table (Table 5D.4). This, of course, should be the case. At the numeric level, the experiments performed with the two case studies are identical. It is only

TABLE 6E.2 A Summary of Program Output for Case Study 6E

Day	Number of Attendants		
	1	2	3
1	1	36	15
2	2	50	24
3	3	46	25
4	−1	24	−5
5	2	52	29

[10]Total CPU time for the simulation on an IBM 360/67 computer was 14.8 seconds.

at the conceptual level, in terms of sequential vs. simultaneous experimentation, that the case studies differ.

The problem statement asks for a comparison of the number of Block executions performed in the two case studies. By summing Total Block Counts not shown here, it turns out that 24,889 and 27,728 Block executions were performed in Case Studies 6E and 5D, respectively. Hence, only about 90 percent as many Block executions were required when the investigations were conducted by using the parallel approach. This can be loosely interpreted as implying that approximately only 90 percent as much CPU time was required in Case Study 6E as in Case Study 5D. (The actual CPU times were 14.8 and 17.6 seconds in Case Studies 6E and 5D, respectively; this means that CPU time in the parallel approach was about 85 percent of that in the sequential approach. See exercise 2, Section 6.20.)

The reasons why there are fewer Block executions in the parallel approach should be evident. For example, consider the first car on the first day of each of the alternative configurations. In the sequential approach, this car's interarrival time had to be computed *three* different times (once for each configuration); similarly, its latent service-time requirement had to be computed *three* different times. By contrast, in the parallel approach, this car's interarrival time was computed just *once*; and its service time was computed just *once*. Through the process of splitting, "carbon copies" of the results from these single computations were then produced to the extent required to support the requirements of each alternative under investigation. It is clear, then, that the greater the number of alternatives under investigation, the greater the potential CPU time economy in conducting experiments in parallel, instead of sequentially.

6.20 Exercises

1. A Transaction with a Parameter 4 value of 5 moves into the SPLIT Block shown in Figure E1(a). The parent Transaction and its one offspring then proceed to the sequential ASSIGN Block, as shown. For the Function definitions indicated in Figure E.1(b), state what effect the ASSIGN Block has (a) on the parent Transaction, and (b) on the offspring Transaction.

2. The number of Block executions required by a model is only a rough measure of the total CPU time required to simulate with the model. Other important determinants of CPU time requirements are (a) the number of different readings assumed by the simulation clock, and (b) the number of blocked Transactions typically on the Current Events Chain, and therefore subject to processing at each reading of the clock. Compare and contrast Case Studies 5D and 6E with respect to these two things. Be as thorough in your comparisons as possible. For example, about how many *more* times did the GPSS Processor probably have to perform the Clock Update Phase in Case Study 5D than in Case Study 6E? On the other hand, about how many *more* blocked Transactions, on average, did the Processor probably encounter on the Current Events Chain during each Scan Phase in Case Study 6E?

3. By use of indirect specification and indirect addressing, the model in Case Study 6E has been made as compact as possible, in terms of the number of Blocks used. Such compactness, however, is not a *necessary* part of models in which alternative configurations are investigated in parallel. For example, in a *single* model, there could be a Model Segment 1 which simulates nothing but the one-attendant configuration; a Model Segment 2 which simulates nothing but the two-attendant

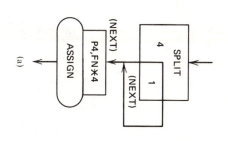

(a)

LOCATION	OPERATION	A,B,C,D,E,F
5.	FUNCTION	P4, D3
5,-1/6, 4./7, 5		
6.	FUNCTION	P4, D3
5,-3/6, -2/7, -1		
7.	FUNCTION	P4, D3
5,.12/6, 1.5/7, 1.8		

(b)

FIGURE E1

configuration; and a Model Segment 3 which simulates nothing but the three-attendant configuration. Profit computation and model-shutdown could then be handled in a Model Segment 4. Such an approach would feature (a) frequent use of direct specification, (b) a relatively large number of Blocks, and (c) use of a relatively large number of random-number generators, if experimental conditions were to be controlled.

Show the Block Diagram and required supporting details for a model which is fully equivalent to that in Case Study 6E, but which uses the brute force approach described above. Compare and contrast the model with that in Case Study 6E with respect to (a) the number of Blocks required, and (b) the number of different random-number generators required. Do you think the total number of Block executions required by the model would be closer to that in Case Study 5D, or that in Case Study 6E?

4. Consider Case Study 2D (the widget-manufacuring problem). In that case study, three alternative configurations were investigated sequentially. Show the Block Diagrams (and additional supporting details) for models which investigate the same three alternatives in parallel, using each of the following two approaches.
(a) Use the brute force approach described in exercise 3.
(b) Use the compact model approach illustrated in Case Study 6E.

Control experimental conditions in both models. This means that the assembly of the jth widget should require the same amount of time in each alternative configuration; similarly, use of the oven for the jth widget should require the same amount of time, independent of the configuration under investigation. In each of the models, the timer Transaction should also compute the profit associated with each configuration, and make these profit statistics available in the output through Savevalues.

5. Consider Case Study 2E (the garment factory problem). In that case study, nine alternative configurations were investigated sequentially. Show the Block Diagram and supporting details for a model which will simulate for the same nine configurations in parallel. Incorporate each of the following features into the model.
(a) Instead of starting the simulation with the

system idle and empty, arrange to have the initial conditions be as nearly typical as possible (see exercise 3, Section 2.41). This means that no RESET card need be used in the process of reaching steady state.
(b) Control the experimental conditions. This means that the jth sewing machine to go into use should have a lifetime which, although randomly determined, is configuration independent. Similarly, the jth sewing machine to go into repair should have a repair time which is configuration-independent.
(c) The timer Transaction should compute the cost associated with each configuration, and make these cost statistics available in the output through Savevalues.

After you have built the model, devise a plan for using it to find the optimal operating conditions for the system. Compare and contrast the strength of your conclusions, and the CPU time requirements you encounter, with the results obtained in Case Study 2E, and results obtained for the "RESET-card model" shown in Figure 2.48.

6. A drugstore wants to determine how many bundles of newspapers it should take each day from a local news company. Papers, which only come in bundles of 25, sell for ten cents each. The drugstore pays seven cents and four cents for each sold and unsold paper, respectively. (Unsold papers have some value because they are recycled by the news company to a paper manufacturer.)

Demand for the papers is believed to arise from two sources. One source consists of fairly steady customers and is uniformly distributed from 150 to 200 papers per day. The other source consists of occasional buyers whose motivation depends on the special news events of the day, if any. As a function of the type of special news events, demand from occasional buyers is distributed as shown in Table E6. Assuming that the information given above is all that the drugstore manager takes into account, determine how many bundles of papers he should take each day if his objective is to maximize profit. First conduct a preliminary numerical analysis and establish three alternative buying policies which, in your judgment, offer the most potential. Then simulate the three alternatives *in parallel.* Control experimental conditions so that the demands actually realized from day to day are identical for each alternative.

TABLE E6

		Special New Events	
	None	Type 1	Type 2	Type 3
Frequency of Occurrence	.29	.34	.25	.12
Distribution of Superimposed Demand	0	50 ± 25	100 ± 50	150 ± 60

7. The following problem is designed for practice in use of many of the GPSS concepts which have been introduced so far in the book. Depending on the approach used in building the model, the problem provides opportunity to use TEST and GATE Blocks and the SPLIT Block (including the serialization option). There is also occasion to use Logic Switches, transit times, Boolean Variables, Arithmetic Variables, Savevalues, Transaction Parameters, and the modulus division operator.

Another feature of this problem is that it utilizes the concept of *deterministic-mode simulation* as a useful tool in model validation.

An interesting objective to take while building the model is to design it in such fashion that it requires relatively small amounts of CPU time. If two or more individuals or groups model this problem independently, they can later compare and contrast their models with respect to such things as the modeling approach taken, the number of Blocks required in the various approaches, and the CPU time needed for a given simulation.

The Problem. A trucking firm has a contract with eight different stores under which it agrees to deliver packages for them within a small urban area. Packages are placed on a loading dock each day at each of the stores, at 8:00 a.m., and again at 1:00 p.m. Each store simultaneously lets the dispatching agent at the trucking firm know how many "new" packages have just been made available for delivery. (Note that, at any particular 8:00 a.m. or 1:00 p.m., there may still be "old" packages on the loading dock, which the trucking firm has not yet gotten around to picking up.) The dispatching agent consequently knows at all times exactly how many packages are waiting for pickup at each of the 8 stores.

The truck drivers work an 8-hour day. The first half of the work day is from 8 a.m. until noon. There is then a 1-hour break. The second half of the work day is from 1 p.m. until 5 p.m. If a given truck is empty when a half-day begins, the dispatcher dispatches that truck to the store with the largest number of packages on the loading dock. After arriving at the store, the trucker transfers all the packages from the loading dock to his truck, and then immediately begins to deliver the packages. The delivery continues until either (a) it is *later than* 11:30 a.m. or 4:30 p.m., or (b) all packages on the truck have been delivered. If (a) occurs first, the trucker returns to the dispatching point and knocks off until the next half-day begins. If (b) occurs first, the trucker returns to the dispatching point, reports in, gets his next assignment, proceeds to the corresponding store (unless it has now become later than 11:30 a.m. or 4:30 p.m.), etc.

If a given truck is not yet empty when a half-day begins, the trucker starts that half-day by simply continuing with the round of deliveries he failed

to complete during the preceding half-day. Condition (a) or (b) in the preceding paragraph then eventually comes about, and the trucker proceeds accordingly.

The *independent* random variables in the system are listed in Table E7(a). The *dependent* random variables of interest are listed in Table E7(b).

Build a GPSS model to study the properties of this pickup-and-delivery system. The decision variable in the model is to be the number of trucks which the trucking firm should own and operate to maximize its expected daily profit. The model should be designed to estimate the values of the dependent random variables listed in Table E7(b), which include the daily profit information. Pertinent cost information is provided below. As for the independent random variables, assume that those numbered 5, 6, 7, and 8 in Table E7(a) are negligibly small. The values of the other independent random variables are described below under two different sets of conditions. In one set, these "random" variables are assumed always to take on fixed values. In the other set, the random variables take on values determined by sampling from populations whose descriptions are given.

Cost Information. The cost of a truck is $70 per working day, including the costs of operation and maintenance, the initial investment distributed over the life of the truck, and the driver's salary.

The firm charges the stores $5 for every 15 minutes, or fraction thereof, that a truck is in use. (For example, for 63 minutes of work, the bill would be $25.) For this purpose, billing *starts* when a truck *leaves the dispatching point and starts* drives to a store. Billing *stops* as soon as the last package has been delivered, or the time comes to knock off for the current half-day, whichever occurs first. In particular, stores are *not* billed for the time a truck spends in returning to the dispatching point after its most-recently-completed delivery.

Whenever a truck returns to the dispatching point, billing takes place (for all practical purposes) for the services which have just been rendered. In determining total service time, then, the "rounding up" to the nearest 15 minutes takes place each time a truck returns to the dispatching point. In general, this means the rounding up occurs more than one time per day per store served.

To promote high-quality service from the trucking company (which otherwise might deliberately provide poor service to keep its truck utilization high), the contracts stipulate that the billing fee will be reduced whenever packages are delivered late. A package is delivered late if the delivery is not made on the same day that the package was put on the loading dock. The amount of fee reduction for late deliveries is $1 per package per day. For example, if a package is put on a loading dock on "Day 7," and is not delivered until "Day 10,"

TABLE E7(a)

Number of the Independent Random Variable	Description
1	Time required to drive from the dispatching point to a store
2	Number of "new" packages placed on the loading dock at store j and at time k, for $j = 1, 2, 3, 4, 5, 6, 7,$ and 8, and $k = 8{:}00$ a.m. and $1{:}00$ p.m. Note that there are 16 such random variables in the system
3	Time required to deliver one package, i.e., time required for the truck to drive either from the store, or from its preceding point-of-delivery, to its next point of delivery, and then offload the package
4	Time required to return to the dispatching point after the last package on the truck has been delivered
5	Time required for a store to tell the dispatcher how many packages have just been put on the loading dock at the beginning of a half-day
6	Time for the dispatcher to give a trucker his next assignment
7	Time for the trucker to transfer packages from the loading dock to his truck
8	Time the trucker spends "reporting in" at the dispatching point when he returns there, either after emptying his truck, or when knocking off until the next half-day begins

TABLE E7(b)

Dependent Random Variable	Description and/or Comments
Truck Utilization	A truck is being utilized whenever it is (a) en route to a store, or (b) making deliveries, or (c) en route back to the dispatching point
Package delivery time for store j, for $j = 1, 2, 3, 4, 5, 6, 7,$ and 8	"Package-delivery time" is defined as the time that elapses between placing a package on the loading dock, and having a truck deliver that package to its destination. Note that there are eight such random variables in the system. The *distributions* followed by each of these eight random variables are to be estimated. (These random variables are very likely not identically distributed.)
Daily Profit	The *distribution* of the random variable "daily profit, in dollars," is to be estimated. (Revenue and expense information is provided later in the problem statement.)

there is a $3 fee reduction for the store involved. Late-delivery fee reductions are not taken into account in computing a store's bill until the day on which the late delivery (or late deliveries) occur.

Specifications for Deterministic-Mode Simulations. One way to *partially* validate a simulation model is to run it in deterministic mode (i.e., without randomness in what normally would be the

sources of randomness). The resulting model output can then be compared with the known correct results, as independently computed by hand. In this spirit, after building the model run it for each of the eight different deterministic-mode data sets listed in Table E7(c). For each of the Table E7(c) data sets, simulate for three complete days of operation, printing out the values of interest at the

TABLE E7(c)

Data Set Number	Values of Independent Random Variables				Number of Trucks
	1[a]	2[b]	3[a]	4[a]	
1	15	0	15	14	4
2	15	2	15	15	4
3	15	6	15	15	4
4	15	7	15	15	4
5	15	0	15	15	8
6	15	2	15	15	8
7	15	14	15	15	8
8	15	15	15	15	8

[a] The values of independent random variables 1, 3, and 4 are expressed in minutes

[b] The values of independent random variable 2 are expressed in packages per half-day. Strictly speaking, up to 16 different values could be provided for this random variable for each data set (one "8:00 a.m." value for each of the eight stores, and one "1:00 p.m." value for each of the eight stores). For each of the deterministic data sets given here, however, a single value is assumed to apply to each of the eight stores at both 8:00 a.m. and at 1:00 p.m.

TABLE E7(d)

Data Set Number	Day 1	Day 2	Day 3
1	−$280	−$280	−$280
2	−$40	−$40	−$40
3	$280	$280	$280
4	$260	$260	$292
5	−$560	−$560	−$560
6	−$320	−$320	−$320
7	$640	$640	$640
8	$600	$536	$504

TABLE E7(e)

Store	a.m. Mean	a.m. Standard Deviation	p.m. Mean	p.m. Standard Deviation
1	5	1	7	1
2	9	1	5	1
3	11	2	8	1
4	7	1	7	1
5	12	2	6	1
6	6	1	6	1
7	8	1	9	1
8	10	2	7	1

2, 3, and 4 correspond to "slack," "no slack," and "negative slack," respectively, for a four-truck configuration. Similarly, data sets 6, 7, and 8 correspond to "slack," "no slack," and "negative slack," respectively, for an eight-truck configuration. "Slack" means that more packages were handled each day without incurring a late penalty; "no slack" means that, although all packages are delivered on the day they reach the loading dock, this would not be true if the rate of package arrival were to increase at all; "negative slack" means that the trucking firm cannot always deliver packages on the same day that they are placed on the loading dock.

Specifications for Nondeterministic-Mode Simulations. For the nondeterministic conditions, assume that independent random variables 1 and 4 take on values from the uniform populations 15 ± 5 minutes. Also assume that independent random variable 2 takes on values which are normally distributed, with the means and standard deviations shown in Table E7(e).

As for independent random variable 3, assume that the average time required to deliver a package depends on the time of day, as shown in Figure E7. Coordinates on the graph are (8,20), (9,20), (10,15), (11,12), (12,18), (1,22), (2,19), (3,15), (4,18), and (5,35). The realized time for any delivery is the average time, plus or minus 4 minutes, uniformly distributed.

end of each day. Then compare each day's profit or loss with results known to be correct, as computed independently by hand. The correct results for the 8 deterministic-mode cases are shown in Table E7(d). The Table E7(d) information should be verified through independent hand computations. (All the results except those for Data Sets 4 and 8 are relatively obvious.)

For these deterministic data, note that data sets

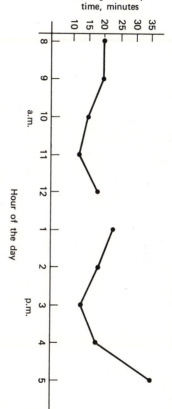

FIGURE E7

When using the model in nondeterministic mode, first determine how long a simulation is required to obtain reasonably stable estimates of the daily profit random variable. Then simulate with various values of the decision variable "number of trucks" to determine which values maximize the expected daily profit.

Hint for Efficient Debugging. For the deterministic-mode runs, consider letting a timer Transaction appear twice each day, perhaps at simulated times corresponding to 12:30 p.m. and 6:00 p.m. If this is done, and if the START card "START 6,,1,1" is used, the output will then contain Block Counts and Current and Future Events Chain printouts when the model has come to rest at the end of each half-day. The Block Count and chain information can then be used to determine where the trucks are and where any undelivered packages are at these points in time. Because the data are deterministic, it can be determined from independent reasoning where trucks and packages *should be* at these times. This makes it possible to determine whether the model appears to be performing properly; and, if it is not, the Block Count and chain information provides a basis for tracing through the model logic to pinpoint the sources of error.

Further Questions for Consideration.

(a) Did you limit your deterministic-mode runs to the eight data sets provided in Table E7(c)? These data sets do *not* cover each of the various reasonable circumstances to which your model must be able to respond, in all likelihood, in non-deterministic simulations. Compose additional deterministic data sets, covering as many distinctive circumstances as you can think of, and run your model against these data sets. (For example, will your model work for a data set for which two or more trucks are simultaneously at work delivering packages for one and the same store?)

(b) The question of what happens when there are more trucks than stores is never explicitly entertained in the problem description. In fact, the numbers of packages placed on the loading docks each half-day are such that for optimality, the trucking firm requires fewer than eight trucks. Assume the new-package rates are increased to the point that the optimal number of trucks exceeds the number of stores being served. Then it may no longer make sense always to dispatch a single truck to a given store to pick up all packages on that store's loading dock. A better dispatching criterion should be found to avoid situations in which some trucks are at work delivering many packages, whereas other trucks are in idle mode at the dispatching station. Discuss the development of a better dispatching criterion to cover such situations. Also discuss how you would go about modifying your model to implement the modified dispatching criterion you suggest.

(c) Did you build the model for study of alternative configurations sequentially, or simultaneously? The sequential approach is recommended, at least for a first cut at the model. After you have successfully modeled the problem sequentially, examine the model carefully with the thought in mind of converting it for simultaneous investigation of alternative configurations. How easy or hard do you think such a conversion would be?

(d) Discuss various ways to make the problem setting more realistic. For example, the stated conditions assume that no time is required for the dispatcher to dispatch trucks at the beginning of each half-day. Even if there is one dispatcher available for each truck driver, this assumption is somewhat unrealistic. If there is only one dispatcher and there are two or more truck drivers, the assumption becomes even more unrealistic. How important do you think it might be to improve the degree of model realism in this sense? In discussing such a question, keep in mind such things as the intended use of the model, the additional complications required in building the model, other model inaccuracies due to such things as estimates inherent in the data used, and so on.

7

Advanced GPSS Modeling Concepts, Part II

7.1 Introduction

Early in Chapter 2, these five categories of chains in GPSS were listed.

1. Current Events Chain
2. Future Events Chain
3. User Chains
4. Interrupt Chains
5. Matching Chains

The Current and Future Events Chains were then introduced, and have since been referred to repeatedly to help explain the operation of the GPSS Processor. Until now, however, there has been no discussion of User Chains, Interrupt Chains, or Matching Chains. In fact, none of these chains have been used in any of the GPSS modeling illustrated so far. In this chapter, those modeling ideas which rely on the last three chain categories will be introduced. As part of the process, User, Interrupt, and Matching Chains will be considered in some detail, and will be used in case study contexts.

User Chains are introduced first, but indirectly. Preceding their introduction, an attempt is made to motivate the idea of User Chains as a device which can promote CPU time economies in GPSS simulation, and which can also be used to model nondefault queue disciplines in the language. Then, after presenting both the concept of User Chains and many of the details surrounding their use, a series of four non-case-study examples is given to illustrate

their application. These examples give due emphasis to the importance of considering the "simultaneity of events" problem with respect to User Chains. Following these examples, a User Chain case study is presented. Finally, additional details of User Chain use are taken up, and another non-case-study example of their application is considered.

Interrupt Chains are then introduced indirectly, through the concept of Facility preemption. A Facility is said to have been preempted when one Transaction comes along and takes it away from another Transaction. Interrupt Chains enter the picture as the place where the displaced Transaction or Transactions reside, in some circumstances, while they wait for the preempter to finish with the Facility. After

TABLE 7.1 A List of Unique Blocking Conditions, and Their Remedies

Blocking Condition Number	Block(s) Producing Blocking Condition	Block Which Must be Executed to Remove Blocking Condition[a]
1	GATE LR	LOGIC R
2	GATE LS	LOGIC S
3	SEIZE / GATE NU	RELEASE
4	GATE U	SEIZE
5	GATE SNF	LEAVE
6	GATE SE	LEAVE (when result is to empty the Storage)
7	ENTER	LEAVE
8	GATE SNE	ENTER
9	GATE SF	ENTER (when result is to fill the Storage)

[a]Assuming the Logic Switch, Facility, or Storage referenced is the one responsible for the blockage.

occurs at a refusal-mode GATE, or at a SEIZE Block, or at an ENTER Block. When a Transaction is first denied permission to enter one of these Blocks, simple logic indicates that the permission will *continue to be denied* until some other particular Block in the model has been executed. For example, when a Transaction is blocked trying to "SEIZE CPU", the blocking will continue until a "RELEASE CPU" Block has been executed. Similarly, a Transaction blocked at "GATE SE DRUMS" will continue to be blocked until "LEAVE DRUMS" has been executed *and* an accompanying effect is to empty the Storage. Or, when "GATE LR SYGNL" causes blockage, it will do so until a Transaction has moved into a "LOGIC R SYGNL" Block. As these examples show, the remedies for blocking conditions such as these are uniquely determined. For this reason, such blocking conditions are said to be *unique*. Table 7.1 lists the nine unique blocking conditions associated with SEIZE, ENTER, and GATE Blocks.[1]

In contrast with the circumstances indicated in Table 7.1, no simple cause and remedy relationships always hold when blocking occurs at a TEST Block in refusal mode, or at a TRANSFER Block in BOTH mode. Conditions which produce blocking at either of these two Blocks are said to be *nonunique*.

To save execution time, the GPSS Processor makes a distinction between Transactions experiencing unique, and nonunique, blocking

[1]In addition to the nine conditions listed, there are two other unique blocking conditions which can arise. They are described later in this chapter.

appropriate discussion, the interrelated concepts of Facility preemption and Interrupt Chains are illustrated in the context of two case studies. Some additional preemption details are then described. Not all ramifications of the preemption concept and its variations are taken up in this book, but a strong enough foundation is laid to make it possible to pursue the topic further in the user's manuals for the various GPSS implementations.

Finally, Matching Chains are introduced. As with User Chains and Interrupt Chains, the idea of Matching Chains is also reached indirectly. The topic leading to Matching Chains has to do with the capability of synchronizing the movement of different Transactions in various parts of a GPSS model. There are three Blocks in GPSS which are provided to support this synchronization capability. The idea of bringing Transactions into certain degrees of synchronization requires, in general, that one or more Transactions in a model have to "wait" until one or more other Transactions reach certain prescribed points in the model. Transactions waiting for such synchronization to come about do their waiting on so-called Matching Chains. Roughly speaking, this explains the rationale for Matching Chains. After preliminary ideas and supporting details are presented, a case study and several non-case-study examples are used to illustrate use of the three synchronization Blocks. That then concludes the chapter.

7.2 More Particulars About the Current Events Chain Scan

A number of Blocks have been introduced which can conditionally refuse entry to a Transaction. The SEIZE and ENTER Blocks are in this category. So are refusal-mode TEST and GATE Blocks. When a Transaction tries to move into such a Block, and is denied entry, it is left on the Current Events Chain as a blocked Transaction. Each time the Current Chain is scanned, the Processor encounters such blocked Transactions. Inevitably, some execution time is required during the scan to determine, for each of these Transactions, whether the blocking condition is still in effect. If there are many blocked Transactions, relatively high execution times result.

For certain blocking conditions, the Processor can simplify the test it uses to determine whether a Transaction is still blocked or not. This simplification is possible for blocking which

conditions. The distinction is made by supplying each Transaction with a "Scan Status Indicator," sometimes simply termed a *Scan Indicator* (SI). A Scan Indicator is a two-setting switch. It is either "off" (that is, "Reset") or "on" (that is, "Set"). Each Transaction's Status Indicator is initially off. Then, when a Transaction first encounters a unique blocking condition, these steps are performed by the Processor.

1. The Transaction's Scan Indicator is turned on.
2. A record is made for that Transaction as to
   (a) the type of blocking condition it is encountering, and
   (b) the particular Facility, Storage, or Logic Switch responsible for the blockage.
3. The Transaction is left in its current position on the Current Events Chain.[2]

As a result of these steps, the Scan Indicator of a Transaction currently experiencing a unique blocking condition is on. Such a Transaction is said to be *scan-inactive*. When the Current Events Chain is scanned, the first thing the Processor does to a Transaction is test the setting of its SI. If the SI is on, the Processor simply leaves the scan-inactive Transaction on the Current Events Chain, and immediately proceeds to the next Transaction (if any) on the chain. It takes less time to test a Transaction's Scan Indicator than it would to actually try to move a Transaction into a Block. For this reason, the Scan Indicator concept results in execution time economies in GPSS.

Now consider how a scan-inactive Transaction is again made scan-active. Whenever one of the third-column Blocks in Table 7.1 is executed, the Processor performs these steps.

1. It turns off the Scan Indicator of each Transaction (if any) which was experiencing blocking due to the condition which has just been altered.
2. The Processor then continues to move the currently active Transaction forward in the model until it comes to rest.
3. Finally, the Processor restarts the scan of the Current Events Chain.

During the rescan of the Current Events Chain, those Transactions which have just had their SI turned off now attempt to move into the Block which had been denying them entry. All, some, or none of them may be successful, depending on the extent to which their successful movement results in restoring the blocking condition. For example, only one Transaction can successfully move into a SEIZE Block, after which other Transactions waiting to capture the given Facility find they still encounter a unique blocking condition, and have their SI's turned back on. On the other hand, if several Transactions were blocked at a "GATE LR", and movement through that Block does not have the consequence of immediately "setting" the Logic Switch again, *all* can successfully move forward. Finally, *none* may be successful if some other higher-priority Transaction, previously encountering a *nonunique* blocking condition, is now able to move forward in such a way that it restores the previous blocking condition. In any event, Transactions finding the unique blocking condition restored have their SI turned back on, so that execution time economies with respect to them are again put into effect.

The information which appears in a Current Events Chain printout includes the scan status of each Transaction on the chain. Figure 7.1 is a repetition of Figure 2.30, which shows the appearance of the Current Events Chain at the end of the Case Study 2A simulation. The scan status of the two Transactions on the chain appears in the column labeled SI, as pointed out in Figure 7.1. A "1" in the SI column indicates that the Scan Indicator is on, i.e., that the corresponding Transaction is scan-inactive. Note, then, that Transaction 4 in Figure 7.1 is scan-inactive. (The Next Block Attempted for Transaction 4 is Block 3. Referring back to Case Study 2A, it can be seen that Block 3 is a SEIZE Block. Transaction 4 is a customer waiting for the barber in the Case Study 2A model.) A blank in the SI column indicates that the Scan Indicator is off, i.e., that the corresponding Transaction is scan-active. Note, then, that Transaction 3 in Figure 7.1 is scan-active. (In the context of Case Study 2A, Transaction 3 is a customer who is just about to release the barber. Its Next Block Attempted, Block 6, is a RELEASE Block.)

The SI column also appears in printouts of the Future Events Chain. (In fact, all the various column headings are the same for both the Current and the Future Events Chains.) The Scan Indicator is really only meaningful, however, for Transactions on the Current Events

---

[2] In the IBM literature, uniquely blocked Transactions are said to be on a "delay chain" associated with the Facility, Storage, or Logic Switch in question. In this sense, a delay chain is simply a list of Transactions. In general, there are as many delay chains in a model as there are Facilities, Storages, and Logic Switches. It is important to realize that when a Transaction is on a delay chain, that same Transaction is *also resident on the Current Events Chain*. A Transaction is *not* taken off the Current Events Chain when it is put onto a delay chain.

Chain. The Scan Indicator itself is always off for each Transaction on the Future Events Chain.

As early as Chapter 2, it was indicated that under certain Scan Phase conditions, the GPSS Processor restarts the Current Events Chain scan. More light has been shed on the nature of these certain conditions in this section. Now consider the actual method used by the Processor during the Scan Phase to determine whether or not to restart the scan. The method makes use of an indicator called the *Status Change Flag* (SCF). The Status Change Flag is a two-setting switch. It is either "off" (that is, "Reset") or "on" (that is, "Set"). Whereas each Transaction has a Scan Indicator, however, *there is only one Status Change Flag in the entire model.* When a simulation begins, the Status Change Flag is off. The Processor turns the SCF on whenever one of the third-column Blocks in Table 7.1 is executed. During the scan, when a given Transaction has been moved as far as possible, the Processor tests the SCF setting as its next step. If the SCF is on, the Processor turns it off, then restarts the Current Events Chain scan. If the SCF is off, the Processor continues with the next Transaction on the Current Events Chain.

When the PRIORITY Block was introduced, it was stated that whenever the Block has been executed, the scan of the Current Events Chain is restarted after the currently active Transaction has come to rest. This simply means that execution of the PRIORITY Block also causes the Status Change Flag to be turned on. Except for the PRIORITY Block and those Blocks listed in the right column in Table 7.1, no other circumstances described so far can cause the Status Change Flag to be turned on.

That portion of the Processor's logic described in this section is summarized in flowchart form in Figure 7.2. That figure can be thought of as a somewhat refined version of the Figure 2.23 flowchart in Chapter 2, where the Processor's Scan Phase logic was first introduced. Figure 7.2 should be studied until the roles of the Scan Indicator, and the Status Change Flag, are fixed clearly in mind. Remember that a principal purpose of introducing and using these indicators in GPSS is to decrease execution time requirements whenever possible.

7.3 A Note on CPU Time Economies

It is natural to wonder how much execution-time economy is realized because of implementation of the Scan Indicator concept in GPSS. A measure of the associated economy results from study of the program for the Processor itself. The GPSS/360 Processor is written in System/360 assembler language. The question about execution time economy can consequently be phrased this way: "When a Transaction is uniquely blocked and the Processor encounters it during the Current Events Chain scan, about how many System/360 machine instruction executions are saved because its Scan Indicator is turned on?"

As might be expected, the answer to this question depends on the type of Block refusing entry to the Transaction, the way Block Operand values are supplied, and so on. Nevertheless, some insight results from considering a specific example. Suppose that a Transaction has just entered a model through the GENERATE Block shown in Figure 7.3, has moved into the QUEUE Block, and now attempts to enter the SEIZE Block. Assume that Facility 5 is in a state of capture. The attempted move then requires that 73 instructions be performed.[3] Included among these 73 instructions are 16 used to turn the Transaction's SI on, and perform other steps required to support the Scan Indicator concept. Now, whenever the Processor *subsequently* encounters this uniquely blocked Transaction on the Current Events Chain, only nine instruction-executions are required to determine that its SI is on. *With* the SI concept, then, the cost of having the Processor encounter a uniquely blocked Transaction on the Current Events Chain is nine instruction-executions.

Now suppose that the SI concept were *not* implemented in GPSS. In the Figure 7.3 example, when the Transaction first attempted to move into the SEIZE Block, only 57 instructions would be performed (57 equals 73 minus the 16 required to turn the SI on and perform the other steps required to support the Scan Indicator con-

[3]The various instruction execution counts quoted in this section apply to GPSS/360, Version 1, Modification Level 4. The code is believed to have been made more efficient for at least some of the later implementations of GPSS.

CURRENT EVENTS CHAIN

TRANS	BDT	BLOCK	PR	SF	NBA	SET	MARK-TIME	P1	P2	P3	P4	SI	TI	DI	CI	MC	PC	PF
4	472	2			3	4	472	0	0	0	0	1			1	2		
								0	0	0	0							
								0	0	0	0							
3	480	5			6	3	453	0	0	0	0					2		
								0	0	0	0							
								0	0	0	0							

Scan Indicator Information

FIGURE 7.1   Repetition of the Figure 2.30 Current Events Chain

TABLE 7.2   A Summary of the Instruction-Executions Performed When a Transaction Attempts to Enter the Figure 7.3 SEIZE Block

	With Implementation of the Scan Indicator Concept	Without Implementation of the Scan Indicator Concept
First attempt to SEIZE	73	57
Subsequent attempts to SEIZE	9	76

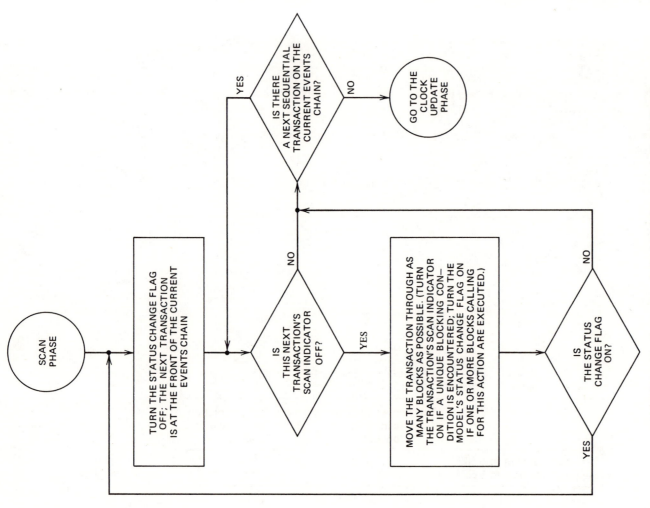

FIGURE 7.2   The logic of the GPSS Processor's Scan Phase

cept). Then, each time the Processor subsequently encountered the Transaction on the Current Events Chain, 76 instructions would be performed to determine that the Transaction is still blocked at the SEIZE Block.[4] These instruction execution counts with and without imple-

when the Transaction was first put into motion at the GENERATE Block. For *subsequent* attempts to SEIZE, the firing-up overhead is avoided when a Transaction's Scan Indicator is on. *Without* the Scan Indicator concept, however, the overhead would have to be paid again as part of each subsequent attempt to move the Transaction into the SEIZE Block. The instruction-execution count of 76, then, results from adding these 19 instruction-executions to the 57 performed in the first attempt to SEIZE.

---

[4]When the Processor encounters a Transaction during the Scan Phase, it performs these steps : (1) Test the Scan Indicator (nine instruction-executions) ; (2) if the Scan Indicator is off, "fire up" the Transaction prior to attempting to move it forward in the model (19 instruction-executions) ; (3) finally, try to move the Transaction into its next Block, etc. Note, then, the firing-up overhead of 19 instruction-executions at Step (2). This overhead was not included in the instruction count for the *first* attempt to SEIZE, because the overhead was paid

mentation of the Scan Indicator concept are summarized in Table 7.2. It is evident from inspection of the table that there is significant potential execution-time economy inherent in the concept of the Scan Indicator. Although the results in Table 7.2 pertain to a specific example, they are typical enough so that a general impression can be drawn from them.

To comment further on execution-time considerations, recall from Section 5.21 that the analyst sometimes has a choice between the GATE and TEST Blocks to implement certain types of logic. It was stated as a rule of thumb in Section 5.21 that, given a choice, the GATE Block should be used in preference to the TEST Block. The quantitative implications of choosing a GATE instead of a TEST can now be explored. For example, consider "GATE NU CPU" and its equivalent, "TEST E F$CPU,0". During the CEC scan, only nine instruction executions are required to process a Transaction waiting at the GATE to determine that its Scan Indicator is on. In contrast, 129 instructions are executed on behalf of a Transaction waiting at "TEST E F$CPU,0" (nine to determine that the Scan Indicator is off; another 19 to "fire up" the Transaction; and then another 101 for the attempted move itself). In this example, then, the TEST Block requires executing about 14 times as many instructions as the GATE.

Finally, consider the use of transfer-mode TEST Blocks under circumstances when transfer-mode GATE Blocks could be used instead. In transfer-mode usage, of course, no blockage can occur at the TEST or GATE itself, meaning that the Scan Indicator is not directly useful. As stated in Section 5.21, however, even for transfer-mode usage the GATE offers execution-time

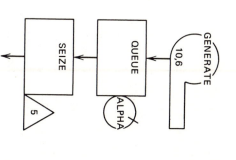

FIGURE 7.3 A GPSS Model Segment in which blocking can occur

economies over the TEST. For example, when a Transaction moves into the Block "TEST E F$CPU,0,BYPAS", the Processor performs 125 or 130 instructions in routing the Transaction to the sequential or nonsequential Block, respectively. In contrast, when a Transaction moves into the equivalent "GATE NU CPU,BYPAS" Block, 93 instructions are performed to route the Transaction to the sequential Block, and 101 to route it to the nonsequential Block. Whether the sequential or nonsequential exit is taken, then, the GATE requires only about 80 percent as much execution time in this example as the TEST.

7.4 The Concept and Utility of User Chains

When Transactions are blocked in a model, two disadvantages can arise from leaving them on the Current Events Chain.

1. The CPU time required to simulate with the model may be larger than necessary. Whether or not blocked Transactions are scan-inactive, each of them is processed at least one time at each reading of the simulation clock. It is true that the only CPU time used to process scan-inactive Transactions is that required to test their Scan Indicators. In the long run, however, this CPU time can be significant. Furthermore, if blocked Transactions are scan-active, the Processor attempts to move them into their next Block each time they are encountered in the scan, even though the logic of a given situation may make it evident (*to the analyst, not to the Processor*) that a blocking condition is still in effect. It should be clear, then, that if blocked Transactions could be made *totally inactive in a model by removing them from the Current Events Chain*, execution time economies could result.

2. The second potential disadvantage concerns queue discipline. The ordering of blocked Transactions on the Current Events Chain is determined solely by their Priority Level, and the chronological sequence in which they were placed on that chain. This is why the default queue discipline in GPSS is "first-come, first-served, within Priority Class." If some other queue discipline were to be implemented, these steps would have to be performed.

(a) Instead of leaving waiting Transactions on the Current Events Chain, they would have to be removed from that chain and put someplace else.

(b) Then, when the time came for one of them to move forward in the model (to capture a now-available server, for example), the Transaction brought from that someplace else and put back on the Current Events Chain could be selected by some criterion other than "first-come, first-served, within Priority Class."

In summary, there are two possible benefits to be realized if blocked Transactions can be removed temporarily from the Current Events Chain. The time required to simulate with a model can conceivably be decreased; and arbitrarily defined queue disciplines can be implemented.

For the reasons cited, an entity known as "User Chains" has been made a part of the GPSS language. User Chains are a "someplace else" where Transactions can be when they are in a model, but are not on the Current or Future Events Chains. Like the Current and Future Events Chains, User Chains have a front and a back. But here the similarity stops. In the case of the Current and Future Events Chains, the GPSS Processor automatically moves Transactions to and from them, and maintains a predefined ordering property for Transactions on them. In the case of User Chains, Transactions are placed on them only according to logic explicitly provided by the analyst. Furthermore, the analyst can choose from several available options to determine the position a Transaction is to occupy on a User Chain when it is placed there. In like fashion, Transactions are unlinked from User Chains and brought back into active status only according to the analyst's explicitly provided logic. The analyst can also choose from a series of options in selecting the one or more Transactions which are to be removed from a User Chain and put back onto the Current Events Chain.

Now consider the conditions under which it makes sense to put a Transaction onto a User Chain. Suppose that a Transaction wants to move into a SEIZE or ENTER Block next. If it tries to move *directly* into the Block, and is denied entry, it is doomed to remain on the Current Events Chain until the move can be made. To avoid this situation, the oncoming Transaction must "look ahead" to see whether a blocking condition currently exists at the SEIZE or ENTER Block. If there is a blocking condition, the Transaction should go directly onto the User Chain, without even directly attempting to move into the SEIZE or ENTER Block.

Consider next the circumstances under which a Transaction should be unlinked from a User Chain, and routed to a SEIZE or ENTER Block. As User Chain residents, Transactions are totally inactive. There is no way, then, that they can help themselves by checking to determine that a blocking condition now no longer exists. It is only through the action of *another Transaction,*

which is not itself on the User Chain, that a User-Chain Transaction can be brought back onto the Current Events Chain. The best way for this other Transaction to know that the blockage no longer exists is for it to be the very Transaction which had been causing the blockage. For the example of blockage at a Facility or Storage, this means the Transaction which has just moved through a corresponding RELEASE or LEAVE Block should take steps to have a waiting Transaction transferred from a User Chain to the Current Events Chain, poised to capture the just-released Facility, or enter the Storage which now has currently unused capacity.

This overall logic of User Chain use is shown schematically in Figure 7.4. Blocks in the figure have been labeled A, B, C, D, E, and F. Blocks C, D, and E suggest the basic sequence followed to simulate use of a limited resource, such as that modeled with a Facility or Storage. C, D, and E might be a SEIZE–ADVANCE–RELEASE combination, for example, or an ENTER–ADVANCE–LEAVE sequence. Block A represents the look-ahead feature of User-Chain logic, and Block B indicates the consequence which follows when the look-ahead reveals that a blocking condition exists. Block F suggests how an active Transaction which has just removed a blocking condition causes a Transaction to be unlinked from a User Chain and brought back to the Current Events Chain, scheduled to make use of the now-available resource.

As might be expected, a pair of complementary GPSS Blocks is used to accomplish the User-Chain logic shown in Figure 7.4. One of these Blocks corresponds to the "linking logic" shown at A and B in the figure. The other performs the "unlinking logic" shown at F. Use of these two Blocks will be described and illustrated in the next several sections.

User Chains have many of the same features as other GPSS entities. There can be many different User Chains in a model. Each chain can be named either numerically or symbolically, according to the usual rules. The number of different User Chains permissible depends on the amount of computer memory available to the Processor. Like Facilities, Storages, Queues, Tables, and Blocks, User Chains have a set of Standard Numerical Attributes associated with them. Furthermore, a set of User Chain statistics much like that for Queues appears as part of the standard output produced at the end of a simulation.

Like the Current and Future Events Chains,

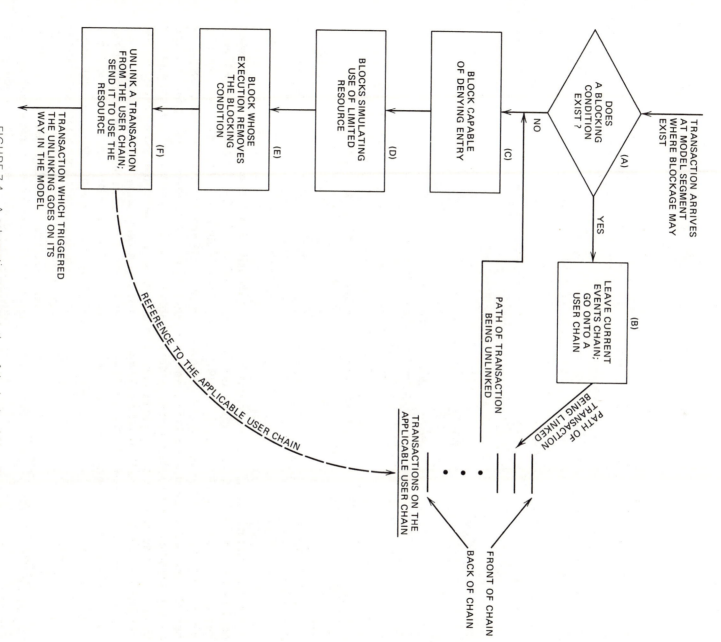

TRANSACTION ARRIVES
AT MODEL SEGMENT
WHERE BLOCKAGE MAY
EXIST

(A) DOES A BLOCKING CONDITION EXIST ?

NO

YES

(B) LEAVE CURRENT EVENTS CHAIN; GO ONTO A USER CHAIN

PATH OF TRANSACTION BEING LINKED

PATH OF TRANSACTION BEING UNLINKED

(C) BLOCK CAPABLE OF DENYING ENTRY

(D) BLOCKS SIMULATING USE OF LIMITED RESOURCE

(E) BLOCK WHOSE EXECUTION REMOVES THE BLOCKING CONDITION

(F) UNLINK A TRANSACTION FROM THE USER CHAIN; SEND IT TO USE THE RESOURCE

TRANSACTION WHICH TRIGGERED THE UNLINKING GOES ON ITS WAY IN THE MODEL

REFERENCE TO THE APPLICABLE USER CHAIN

TRANSACTIONS ON THE APPLICABLE USER CHAIN

FRONT OF CHAIN

BACK OF CHAIN

FIGURE 7.4   A schematic representation of the logic of User Chain use

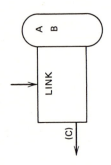

Operand	Significance		Default Value or Result
A	Name (numeric or symbolic) of a User Chain		Error
B	Specifies where the Transaction is to be placed on the User Chain; there are three possibilities.		Error
	B Operand	Indication	
	FIFO	Go on the back of the chain	
	LIFO	Go on the front of the chain	
	Pj	Merge into the chain immediately ahead of the Transaction with the next higher value of Parameter j	
C	Optional Operand; Block Location to which the Transaction moves if it is not linked onto the User Chain		Transaction is linked unconditionally onto the User Chain

FIGURE 7.5   The LINK Block and its A, B, and C Operands

nonempty User Chains are printed out by the Processor at the end of a simulation only if "1" is used as the D Operand on the START card. The PRINT Block can also be used to print out User Chains. For this purpose, the Block's A and B Operands indicate the smallest and largest numbers, respectively, of the User Chains which are to be printed out. The field C mnemonic is CHA. When a Transaction moves into the Block "PRINT 2,5,CHA", then, User Chains 2 through 5 are printed out as a result.

7.5 Transaction Movement to and from User Chains: The LINK and UNLINK Blocks

The ability to put a Transaction onto a User Chain is provided with the LINK Block. The LINK Block can be used in either one of two modes: *conditional mode*, or *unconditional mode*. A condi-

tional-mode LINK Block plays the roles of blocks A *and* B in Figure 7.4; that is, it embodies a certain "look-ahead" feature, as suggested by block A in Figure 7.4, and it has the capability of either sending a Transaction to capture an available server, or of putting a Transaction onto a User Chain if there is no available server. In contrast, an unconditional-mode LINK Block has no effective look-ahead capability; it therefore plays only the role of block B in Figure 7.4. Transactions which enter an unconditional-mode LINK Block are always put onto a User Chain as a consequence.

Because use of the LINK Block in unconditional mode is the easiest to understand, this usage mode will be discussed first. Consider Figure 7.5, which spells out the specific details associated with the LINK Block. As indicated in that figure, when no C Operand is supplied for the LINK Block, the Block is being used in unconditional-linkage mode. (In fact, if the C Operand were eliminated from the LINK Block in Figure 7.5, the path leading from the LINK Block would have to be eliminated, too.) When a Transaction moves into such a LINK Block, it is placed on the User Chain whose name is supplied by the Block's A Operand. The position an incoming Trans- action takes on the User Chain is governed by the LINK Block's B Operand. The four-character B Operands FIFO (First-In, First-Out) and LIFO (Last-In, First-Out) cause the Transaction to be placed on the back or front of the chain, respec- tively. If the B Operand is Pj, where j is some inte- ger from 1 to 100, Transactions are arranged on the User Chain in order of *increasing* Pj value.[5] Each incoming Transaction is placed ahead of those chain residents which have a higher Pj value, but behind those which have a lower Pj value. In case of ties, the incoming Transaction goes behind other residents having the same Pj value. For example, suppose that Transactions A, B, and C have P3 values of -4, 21, and 32, re- spectively, and they enter the Block "LINK HOLD,P3". Then, after the linking, Transaction A is at the front of the User Chain HOLD, B is behind it, and C is at the back of the chain. If Transaction D now enters the LINK Block and has a P3 value of 21, it is placed between Trans- actions B and C on the User Chain.

Linking is *conditional* when the LINK Block's C Operand is used. A Transaction moving into a conditional-mode LINK Block will either be placed on the User Chain, or will be routed to the "C Block," i.e., the Block in the Location whose name is supplied by the C Operand. In practice, the "C Block" often turns out to be the Block which is sequential to the LINK Block in the model. But even when this is the case, the analyst must use the C Operand on the conditional-mode LINK Block, and must attach the corresponding Location name to the sequential Block. There is no requirement, however, that the "C Block" be sequential to the LINK Block. This explains why there is a horizontal path leading from the Figure 7.5 LINK Block, instead of a vertical path.

Nothing has been said yet about what deter- mines whether a Transaction entering a condi- tional-mode LINK Block takes the C-Block exit, or is linked onto the referenced User Chain. To choose between these two possibilities, the GPSS Processor tests the setting of the referenced User Chain's *Link Indicator*. Each User Chain has its own Link Indicator. The indicator is either "on" ("Set"), or "off" ("Reset"). If the Link Indicator is off when a Transaction moves into a condi- tional-mode LINK Block, the Processor does two things.

1. It turns the Link Indicator on.
2. It does not link the Transaction onto the User Chain; instead, it routes the Transaction to the "C Block."

On the other hand, if the Link Indicator already is on when a Transaction enters a conditional-mode LINK Block, the Processor puts the Transaction onto the User Chain, and leaves the Link Indi- cator on.

As indicated earlier, the unconditional-mode LINK Block corresponds to Block B in Figure 7.4. Linking at this Block is not conditioned on the setting of the referenced User Chain's Link Indicator. In contrast, the conditional-mode LINK Block takes on the roles played by blocks A and B in Figure 7.4. The referenced User Chain's Link Indicator embodies the look-ahead feature, and can be thought of much in the sense of a green- red traffic light. When the Link Indicator is off, the traffic light is green. When a Transaction enters a conditional-mode LINK Block and finds the traffic light is green, it interprets this as a "no blockage" signal. The Transaction moves ahead in the model, but before doing so, it switches the traffic light to red (Link Indicator on) as a signal for later arrivals at the LINK Block. Conversely, if a Transaction arrives at the LINK Block and finds the traffic light is red (Link Indicator on), it in- terprets this to mean that blockage exists, and consequently goes onto the User Chain instead of moving ahead in the model.

The Link Indicator's look-ahead role cannot be fully appreciated until the Block complementary to the LINK Block has been described, and its effect on the Link Indicator's setting has been in- dicated. It might be mentioned now, however, that use of the Link Indicator for look-ahead pur- poses is extremely restricted. In fact, it is really useful as a built-in look-ahead device only when the limited resource which might offer blockage is simulated with a Facility. Most of the time, the

---

[5] Some caution is required here. In GPSS/360, when the LINK Block's B Operand is Pj, the "P" simply signals to the Processor that the linking criterion is "ordered according to the value of a Parameter." The *number* of the Parameter is *directly specified*, and is j itself. If a given LINK Block has P10 as its B Operand, then, the linking criterion is "ordered accord- ing to the value of Parameter 10," *not* "ordered according to the Parameter whose number can be found in Parameter 10." This situation has been changed in GPSS V. In GPSS V, except when the LINK Block's B Operand is LIFO or FIFO, the Operand's *value* is interpreted as the number of the Parameter on whose value the chain ordering is to be based.

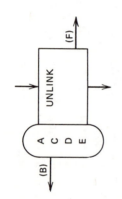

Operand	Significance	Default Value or Result
A	Name (numeric or symbolic) of a User Chain	Error
B	Block Location to which the unlinked Transaction(s) is (are) to be routed	Error
C	The number of Transactions to be unlinked (the Unlink Count); can be a constant, a Standard Numerical Attribute, or ALL	Error
D and E	Specify *which end* of the User Chain Transactions are to be taken from, per this scheme:	Transactions are unlinked from the front of the User Chain
F	Optional Operand; Block Location to which the Unlinker-Transaction moves next if *no* Transactions are unlinked	Unlinker-Transaction unconditionally moves to the sequential Block in the model

D Operand	E Operand	End Indicated
Not Used	Not Used	Front End
BACK	Not Used	Back End

FIGURE 7.6   The UNLINK Block and its A, B, C, D, E, and F Operands

analyst supplies his own look-ahead logic with a TEST or GATE Block at position A in Figure 7.4, and sends Transactions into an unconditional-mode LINK Block when the look-ahead reveals that a blocking condition exists.

The Block complementary to the LINK is the UNLINK. It is the UNLINK Block which is used at position F in Figure 7.4. The purpose of the UNLINK Block, of course, is to remove one or more Transactions from a User Chain and put them back on the Current Events Chain, so that the Processor can subsequently move them forward again in the model. By using appropriate UNLINK Block Operands, the analyst can specify *which* Transaction(s) on the User Chain qualify for unlinking. There are two possibilities here.

1. Transactions can be removed from the front or from the back of the User Chain. In this case, Transactions qualify for unlinking simply by virtue of the position they occupy on the User Chain.

2. Transactions can be removed from anywhere on the User Chain, providing that their properties satisfy analyst-specified conditions.

Only the possibilities indicated in (1) above will be described in this section. The possibilities indicated in (2) will be taken up in Section 7.12. The UNLINK Block is shown with its various Operands in Figure 7.6. In considering the Block, it is important to distinguish between the *Unlinker*-Transaction (i.e., the Transaction which moves into the UNLINK Block, thereby initiating the unlinking operation), and the *Unlinkee*-Transactions (i.e., the Transactions being unlinked). When a Transaction enters the UNLINK Block, the Processor removes from the referenced User Chain the number of Transactions specified via the C Operand (assuming this many are on the User Chain to begin with, and that they satisfy the unlinking conditions). The C Operand, which can be a constant, a Standard Numerical Attribute, or ALL, is termed the "Unlink Count." If the C Operand is ALL, then all qualifying Transactions on the referenced User Chain will be unlinked. The UNLINK Block's B Operand indicates the Location of the Block to which each of the Unlinked Transactions is to be routed. The D and E Operands are used in combination to indicate from which end of the User Chain the Unlinked Transactions are to be taken. When neither Operand is used, Transactions are unlinked from the front of the User Chain. When BACK is used as the D Operand, and the E Operand is not used, Transactions are unlinked from the back of the User Chain.

The UNLINK Block's F Operand is optional. If it is not used, the Unlinker moves unconditionally from the UNLINK Block to the sequential Block. If used, the F Operand supplies the name of the nonsequential Location to which the Unlinker moves next if no Transactions were unlinked in the attempted unlink operation.[6]

Now consider the effect of the UNLINK Block on the referenced User Chain's Link Indicator. When the User Chain is empty at the time a Transaction moves into the UNLINK Block, the Processor switches that User Chain's Link Indicator off. Using the traffic light analogy, this is equivalent to switching the traffic light from red to green. It is logical for the Unlinker to do this when it has just ceased to cause blockage at a point, and then discovers (because of the empty User Chain) that no other Transaction is currently waiting for the blockage to be removed. Later, when the next Transaction appears at the associated LINK Block, the green traffic light serves as a signal that it need not go on the User Chain. Instead, the Transaction will switch the light to red, then move ahead in the model without delay. Control of a User Chain's Link Indicator can be summarized this way.

1. The Link Indicator can be turned on (but never turned off) at the LINK Block.

2. The Link Indicator can be turned off (but never turned on) at the UNLINK Block.

Consider next a chain-oriented interpretation of the way the UNLINK Block works. When a Transaction enters the UNLINK Block, the Processor removes Transactions from the referenced User Chain, one-by-one, placing each Transaction in turn on the Current Events Chain as the last member in its Priority Class. The Processor works from the front of the User Chain toward the back, unless the D–E Operand combination is "BACK; not used," in which case it works from the back toward the front. Execution of the UNLINK Block causes the Status Change Flag to be turned on if at least one Transaction is thereby unlinked. When the UNLINK operation is complete, the Unlinker continues its forward movement in the model. This means that the Unlinked Transactions, if any, have not yet been processed. When the Unlinker finally comes to rest, the Processor tests the Status Change Flag per Figure 7.2 and, if it is on, turns it back off and restarts the scan of the Current Events Chain. This guarantees that, independent of their Priority Level, any Unlinked Transactions will be processed at the current reading of the simulation clock.

Finally, the relationship between User Chains and Block Counts should be carefully noted. When a Transaction is on a User Chain, it is not "in" any Block in the model. In particular, it is not in the LINK Block via which it was put onto the User Chain. Transactions on User Chains do not reflect themselves, then, in any fashion through Current Counts at Blocks. When a Transaction has just been unlinked from a User Chain and brought to the Current Events Chain, it would seem that it is also not yet in any Block. Conceptually, the just-unlinked Transaction has much in common with Transactions which are "on their way," to a model via a GENERATE Block into which they have not yet moved. Nevertheless, from the point of view of Current Counts, the Processor treats unlinked Transactions as though they are in the UNLINK Block whose execution caused them to be brought from the User Chain to the Current Events Chain. This fact is sometimes of importance when Current Block Counts are being interpreted. It also explains why the UNLINK Block's B Operand (i.e., the Next Block Attempted for unlinked Transactions) appears in Figure 7.6 on a path leading from the UNLINK Block. The idea here is to provide a graphic indication of the fact that unlinked Transactions do move from the User Chain via the UNLINK Block into their Next Block Attempted. In contrast, the other two paths leading from the Figure 7.6 UNLINK Block apply to the Unlinker-Transaction. One path leads to the sequential Block; the other

---

[6] For the two UNLINK Block D–E combinations in Figure 7.6, the condition "no Transactions were unlinked" can arise if and only if the referenced User Chain is empty prior to the attempted unlinking. For the other UNLINK Block D–E Operand combinations to be discussed in Section 7.12, the "no Transactions were unlinked" condition can occur even when there are Transactions on the User Chain at the time of the attempted unlinking.

leads to the nonsequential Block which is implied if the optional F Operand is used.

7.6 Basic User Chain Use with Facilities and Storages

The basic use of User Chains with Facilities and Storages is illustrated through a series of three examples in this section. First, their use with single Facilities is shown. In this situation, the User Chain Link Indicator is adequate for the required look-ahead logic. Then, their use with Storages is illustrated. Such use requires analyst-supplied look-ahead logic, and this in turn requires caution in terms of a potential simultaneity-of-events problem which can arise. Later, in Sections 7.8 and 7.12, additional examples of User Chain use will also be given.

7.6.1 User Chain Use with a Facility

The Block Diagram for the one-line, one-server queuing system modeled in Case Study 2A (one-man barber shop) is repeated in Figure 7.7, with a User Chain incorporated into it. When a customer arrives at the shop, he first updates waiting-line statistics by moving into the QUEUE Block. He then moves into the conditional-mode LINK Block. If the Link Indicator is on (traffic light red), the customer-Transaction is linked on the *back* (FIFO) of the User Chain HOLD, and the Link Indicator remains on. If the Link Indicator is found to be off (traffic light green), however, it is switched on and the customer-Transaction proceeds to the Block in location GETEM, i.e., moves into the SEIZE Block. The DEPART–ADVANCE–RELEASE sequence then follows. After the RELEASE, the customer-Transaction attempts to unlink 1 Transaction from the *front* of the User Chain HOLD, (UNLINK Block D and E Operands both blank), sending it to Block Location GETEM to capture the now-available Facility. If the attempted unlinking is unsuccessful because the User Chain is empty, the Link Indicator is switched from on to off (traffic light green) so that the next arrival, instead of linking, will move directly to SEIZE.

Note that, when the traffic light is red at the LINK Block, arriving Transactions are placed on the *back* of the User Chain (go to the back of the

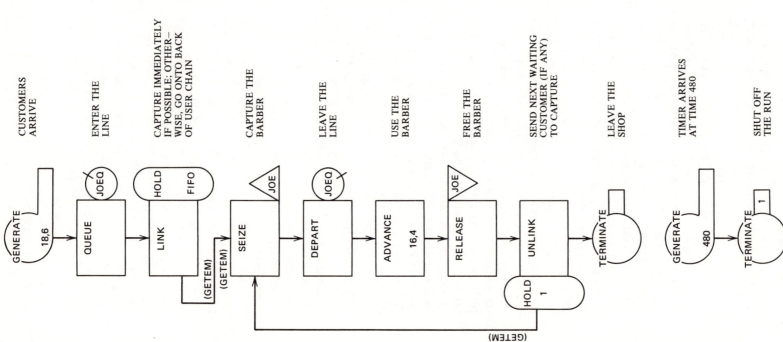

CUSTOMERS ARRIVE — GENERATE 18,6
ENTER THE LINE — QUEUE JOEQ
CAPTURE IMMEDIATELY IF POSSIBLE; OTHERWISE, GO ONTO BACK OF USER CHAIN — LINK HOLD FIFO (GETEM)
CAPTURE THE BARBER — SEIZE JOE
LEAVE THE LINE — DEPART JOEQ
USE THE BARBER — ADVANCE 16,4
FREE THE BARBER — RELEASE JOE
SEND NEXT WAITING CUSTOMER (IF ANY) TO CAPTURE — UNLINK HOLD 1 (GETEM)
LEAVE THE SHOP — TERMINATE
TIMER ARRIVES AT TIME 480 — GENERATE 480
SHUT OFF THE RUN — TERMINATE 1

FIGURE 7.7 A first example of User Chain use

line). Later, via action initiated by an Unlinker-Transaction at the UNLINK Block, they are re-moved from the *front* of the User Chain. The re-sulting queue discipline is first-come, first-served.[7]

The pattern followed by the Link Indicator in the Figure 7.7 model reveals how it serves as a built-in look-ahead device in the context of Facility use. It is initially off. The first customer-Transaction turns it on, then captures the server. While the server is being used by this first customer of the day, the Link Indicator remains on. Suppose the second customer-Transaction ar-rives while the server is still in use. Finding the Link Indicator on, the second customer goes onto the User Chain. When the first customer finishes, he unlinks the second customer and sends him to capture the barber. Meantime, because the User Chain referenced from the UNLINK Block was not empty, the Link Indicator remains on. In fact, it is on whenever *any* customer is using the barber, whether that customer (1) found the indicator off, and moved directly to capture, or (2) found the indicator on, and spent time in residence on the User Chain before eventually being sent to capture. The only way to turn the Link Indicator off is for a customer to finish with the barber when no other customers are waiting (User Chain empty). Turning the Link Indicator off in this circumstance guarantees that when the next customer does arrive, he will proceed to capture the barber immediately.

The punchcards for the Figure 7.7 model were prepared, and the model was run for one simu-lated day. The D Operand on the START card was used to force a chain printout at the end of the simulation. Figure 7.8 shows a portion of the out-put that was thereby produced. Parts (a), (b), and (c) in Figure 7.8 show the Current, Future, and User Chains, respectively. There is a single resident on the Current Events Chain, Trans-action 3; this Transaction is poised to release the Facility. The two residents on the Future Events Chain are the incipient Transaction arrivals at the two GENERATE Blocks in the model.

In Figure 7.8(c), the User Chain is described as "USER CHAIN 1". The symbolic name HOLD has been made equivalent to the number 1 by the Processor, and this numeric equivalent has been used to label the User Chain in the printout. There is one Transaction resident on the User Chain, Transaction 4. Note that the various *column/labels* for the User Chain are identical to those for the Current and Future Events Chains.

The Transaction on the User Chain is the next customer, waiting for the barber. We know this because of the problem context, but the GPSS Processor does not know this. In fact, the "des-tination" of the Transaction on the User Chain will not be known to the Processor until it is un-linked. At that time, the UNLINK Block's B Oper-and will be used by the Processor to determine the unlinked Transaction's Next Block Attempted. Note, then, that the NBA (Next Block Attempted) column in Figure 7.8(c) is blank. Also note that the entry in the BLOCK column in Figure 7.8(c) is blank. The BLOCK column indicates which Block a Transaction is currently "in." But, as ex-plained earlier, when a Transaction is on a User Chain, it is not in any Block in the model.

The BDT (Block Departure Time) column in Figure 7.8(c) shows a value of 472. Recall that a Transaction's Block Departure Time is its Move Time, i.e., is the time the Transaction is scheduled to try to move into its Next Block Attempted. As far as its future movement is concerned, the BDT entry for User Chain Transactions is meaningless. The BDT value shown in User Chain printout can

---

[7]It is sometimes *mistakenly concluded* that if the B Operand at a LINK Block is FIFO (meaning that incoming Transactions are linked onto the *back* of the User Chain), it must be specified at the associated UNLINK Block that Transactions are to be removed from the *front* of the User Chain in question; or, that if the B Operand at a LINK Block is LIFO (meaning that in-coming Transactions are linked onto the *front* of the User Chain), the associated UNLINK Block must specify that Transactions be removed from the *back* of the pertinent User Chain. This is not the case. The LINK and UNLINK Blocks are entirely independent of each other. It is the analyst's re-sponsibility to see to it that the linking and unlinking criteria interact in such a way that the overall effect makes sense in context. For example, the B Operand at a LINK Block can be FIFO, and the associated UNLINK Block can specify that Transactions are to be unlinked from the *back* of the pertinent User Chain. The resulting queue discipline, then, would be "last-come, first-served." This is precisely the same queue discipline that results if the LINK Block's B Operand is LIFO, and Transactions are unlinked from the *front* of the pertinent User Chain. Hence, there are two distinct ways to implement a "last-come, first-served" queue discipline in GPSS. (In exercise 2, Section 7.11, another way to implement "first-come, first-served" queue discipline in the Figure 7.7 model is suggested.)

CURRENT EVENTS CHAIN

TRANS	BDT	BLOCK	PR	SF	NBA	SET	MARK-TIME	P1	P2	P3	P4	SI	TI	DI	CI	MC	PC	PF
3	480	6			7	3	453	0	0	0	0					2		
								0	0	0	0							
								0	0	0	0							

(a)

FUTURE EVENTS CHAIN

TRANS	BDT	BLOCK	PR	SF	NBA	SET	MARK-TIME	P1	P2	P3	P4	SI	TI	DI	CI	MC	PC	PF
1	489				1	1	-27	0	0	0	0					4		
								0	0	0	0							
								0	0	0	0							
5	960				10	5	-1	0	0	0	0					4		
								0	0	0	0							
								0	0	0	0							

(b)

USER CHAIN   1

TRANS	BDT	BLOCK	PR	SF	NBA	SET	MARK-TIME	P1	P2	P3	P4	SI	TI	DI	CI	MC	PC	PF
4	472					4	472	0	0	0	0							
								0	0	0	0							
								0	0	0	0							

(c)

USER CHAIN	TOTAL ENTRIES	AVERAGE TIME/TRANS	CURRENT CONTENTS	AVERAGE CONTENTS	MAXIMUM CONTENTS
HOLD	18	4.277	1	.160	1

(d)

QUEUE	MAXIMUM CONTENTS	AVERAGE CONTENTS	TOTAL ENTRIES	ZERO ENTRIES	PERCENT ZEROS	AVERAGE TIME/TRANS	$AVERAGE TIME/TRANS	TABLE NUMBER	CURRENT CONTENTS
JOEQ	1	.160	27	12	44.4	2.851	5.133		1

$AVERAGE TIME/TRANS = AVERAGE TIME/TRANS EXCLUDING ZERO ENTRIES

(e)

FIGURE 7.8   Selected Program Output produced by the Figure 7.7 model at the end of the simulation. (a) Current Events Chain. (b) Future Events Chain. (c) User Chain. (d) User Chain statistics. (e) Queue statistics.

be interpreted as the time the Transaction was linked onto the User Chain.

Recall that in Chapter 2, after the Current and Future Events Chains were introduced, the Case Study 2A model was rerun, and the chains were printed out at the end of the simulation. The resulting Current and Future Events Chains were shown as Figures 2.30 and 2.31, respectively. That chain printout should now be compared with the printouts in parts (a), (b), and (c) in Figure 7.8. Of course, the Future Events Chains are identical. The Current Event Chains differ, as would be expected. In Figure 2.30, Transaction 4 is on the Current Chain, where it is uniquely blocked. (The Scan Indicator column in Figure 2.30 shows a value of 1 for Transaction 4, indicating that the Transaction is scan-inactive.) In Figure 7.8, instead of appearing on the Current Chain, Transaction 4 appears on the User Chain. This is consistent with its having been removed from the Current Chain when the "look-ahead" revealed that its path was blocked.

The statistics for the User Chain HOLD which appear in the standard output are shown in Figure 7.8(d). Figure 7.8(e) shows the statistics for the Queue JOEQ. Comparison of the two sets of statistics reveals that they are quite similar. The Queue statistics contain somewhat more information than those for the User Chain, indicating how many zero entries there were (ZERO ENTRIES), what percentage the zero entries were of the total (PERCENT ZEROS), and what the average Queue residence time was when zero entries were included (AVERAGE TIME/TRANS).

At first, it might be thought that there are no zero entries to User Chains because, "if blockage does not exist, Transactions bypass the chain and move directly forward in the model." User Chains can experience zero entries, however. That is, it is possible for some Transactions to have zero residence time on a User Chain. This will happen, for example, in the Figure 7.7 model when the following conditions are true.

1. The Facility is in use.
2. No Transaction is waiting to capture the Facility.
3. There is a time tie between the two events completion of service, and arrival of the next customer.
4. The event-sequence is arrival, followed by service completion.

In the scan of the Current Events Chain at the simulated time in question, then, the arriving customer-Transaction is processed first, per (4) above. Finding the User Chain's Link Indicator on,

the Processor puts this Transaction on the User Chain. The releasing Transaction is then processed. After moving through the RELEASE Block, it unlinks the just-arrived Transaction from the User Chain and sends it to capture the Facility. Hence, although the just-arrived Transaction was made a User Chain resident, its residence time on the chain was zero. It contributes, then, to the User Chain TOTAL ENTRIES statistic. And, from the Queue's point of view, it contributes to the ZERO ENTRIES statistic.

The phenomenon just described explains why there were 18 TOTAL ENTRIES to the User Chain in Figure 7.8(d), but only 15 nonzero entries to the Queue in Figure 7.8(e). Three of the User Chain entries were apparently of the "zero residence time" type. Note that this phenomenon also makes interpretation of the AVERAGE TIME/TRANS statistic for User Chains somewhat subtle. It would be easy to draw the false conclusion for the Figure 7.7 model that $AVERAGE TIME/TRANS in the Queue should equal the AVERAGE TIME/TRANS statistic for the User Chain. $AVERAGE TIME/TRANS measures the waiting time *only of those who had to wait*, however; in contrast, the AVERAGE TIME/TRANS value for User Chains can, in general, include Transactions which did not actually have to wait. The three "zero residence time" entries to the User Chain explains why AVERAGE TIME/TRANS is only 4.277 time units in Figure 7.8(d), whereas $AVERAGE TIME/TRANS is 5.1333 time units in Figure 7.8(e).

User Chain statistics and Queue statistics, although similar, differ from each other, then, in these three major ways.

1. Zero-entry information is provided for Queues.
2. The AVERAGE TIME/TRANS User Chain statistic requires careful interpretation.
3. The distribution of Queue residence time is easily estimated with use of the QTABLE card, whereas nothing analogous to the QTABLE card is available for User Chains.

7.6.2 More About the Link Indicator

Consider use of the LINK-UNLINK Block pair in connection with *any* segment of a GPSS Block Diagram. Figure 7.9 illustrates this situation where, for generality, the particular Blocks occupying the Block Diagram segment in question are not shown, but for specificity the LINK-UNLINK Block Operands are shown. Assume that Transactions can gain entry to the segment only by moving through the conditional-mode

7.6 BASIC USER CHAIN USE 403

tually arrives at the LINK Block, it moves immediately into the segment, causing the Link Indicator to be turned back on in the process, etc. etc.

The ideas just expressed really only repeat what was said about the Link Indicator when it was introduced in Section 7.5. Repeating the ideas in the context of Figure 7.9, however, leads directly to the two following conclusions.

Conclusion 1. When a User Chain is used in connection with a *Facility*, the SEIZE–RELEASE Block pair is *not really needed*, *unless* the analyst requires the statistics which the Facility entity provides. After all, use of a SEIZE–RELEASE Block pair has two effects.

1. It guarantees that there will *never be more than one Transaction at a time* in transit between the pair of Blocks (assuming, of course, that alternative methods of getting between the pair of Blocks are not used in the model).

2. It causes the GPSS Processor to maintain certain statistics about the use of the Facility.

But Effect (1) is exactly the effect that the Link Indicator has when a conditional-mode LINK Block is used. Consequently, if Effect (2) is not needed, the SEIZE–RELEASE Block pair can be eliminated. For example, Figure 7.10

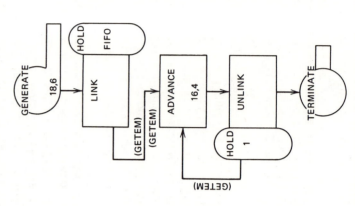

FIGURE 7.10 A Model Segment which simulates a single server without using a SEIZE–RELEASE Block pair

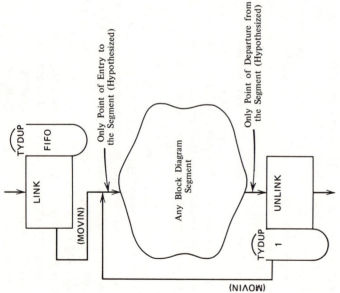

FIGURE 7.9 Use of a User Chain with an arbitrary Block Diagram segment

LINK Block in the figure, and that they can exit the segment only by moving through the UNLINK Block. *There can then never be more than one Transaction in the encircled Block Diagram segment at a time.*

This last statement can be made as a direct consequence of the properties of the User Chain's Link Indicator. The reasoning goes like this. When the simulation starts, the encircled segment is empty. Furthermore, the Link Indicator is off. When the first Transaction arrives at the LINK Block, it therefore moves immediately to the Block in the Location MOVIN, thereby entering the segment. (MOVIN is assumed to be the Location of the first Block in the encircled segment.) While the first Transaction is in the segment, then, any other arrivals at the LINK Block are put on the User Chain. When the first Transaction eventually leaves the segment via the UNLINK Block, it removes exactly one Transaction from the User Chain, routing it into the segment. Hence, the segment-exiting Transaction replaces itself in the segment with another Transaction. This replacement pattern is in effect as long as there is at least one Transaction on the User Chain when the UNLINK Block is executed. If the User Chain is *empty* when the UNLINK Block is executed, the result is that the Link Indicator gets turned off. This means that when another Transaction even-

repeats Figure 7.7, with the SEIZE–RELEASE Block pair eliminated. The QUEUE–DEPART Block pair has also been eliminated, on the hypothesis that the User Chain statistics are sufficient measures of waiting line behavior for the application at hand. The Block sequence "LINK–ADVANCE–UNLINK" in Figure 7.10 may seem a bit strange at first, but it nonetheless validly simulates a single server under the conditions stated here.

Conclusion 2. When the User Chain's Link Indicator is relied upon to supply look-ahead logic, it is *extremely inflexible*. In fact, because a consequence of its use is to let only "one Transaction at a time" in the model segment between the LINK and UNLINK Blocks, the Link Indicator is really only of value when the constrained resource being simulated between the LINK–UNLINK Blocks is a *Facility* (or a unit-capacity constraint). For example, suppose the constrained resource is being simulated with a *Storage* whose capacity is *two*. This means that up to two Transactions at a time should be permitted to be in transit between the LINK–UNLINK Block pair. Because this effect cannot be achieved with the Link Indicator, the analyst *must supply his own look-ahead logic* to determine whether an arriving Transaction can move into the model segment, or must be put onto the User Chain. The next subsection goes into further detail about use of a User Chain with the Storage entity.

7.6.3 User Chain Use with a Storage

Suppose that in the Figure 7.7 barber shop, customer interarrival time decreases to 6 ± 2 minutes and, to offset this heavier traffic pattern, two more barbers are hired. Figure 7.11 shows the Block Diagram for a model of the shop under these circumstances. Discussion of the model will be broken into two parts. First, the "GATE–ENTER–LINK" Block arrangement will be commented upon. Then the reason for placing the PRIORITY Block between the GENERATE and GATE Blocks will be explained.

As indicated under Conclusion 2 in the preceding subsection, the analyst must supply his own look-ahead logic when a User Chain is used in conjunction with a Storage. The GATE Block in Figure 7.11 provides this required look-ahead logic. When a customer-Transaction moves into the "GATE SNF 1" Block, a test is conducted to determine whether at least one barber is currently available, i.e., to determine whether the Storage used to simulate the three barbers is not full. If the "Storage Not Full" condition is true, the customer-Transaction moves sequentially through the gate and captures a barber. If the "Storage Not Full" condition is false, the customer-Transaction exits the gate nonsequentially and moves into the LINK Block. No C Operand is provided with the LINK Block, with the result that Transactions entering it are unconditionally placed on the User Chain. Transactions enter the LINK Block, however, only on the condition that the Storage is full. Via use of the GATE Block, then, the "unconditional" linking of Transactions is conditional after all.

Of course, even when the LINK Block is used in unconditional mode, the referenced User Chain continues to have a Link Indicator. Unless it already was on, it is turned on whenever a Transaction is put on the User Chain. It is likewise turned off whenever the User Chain is found to be empty at the time it is referenced from an UNLINK Block. This Link Indicator maintenance makes it possible to reference a given User Chain with both unconditional *and* conditional-mode LINK Blocks in the context of a single model.

Now consider why the "PRIORITY 1" Block has been placed between the GENERATE and GATE Blocks in the Figure 7.11 model. As might be expected, the PRIORITY Block has been used to defend against invalid logic which could come about if a certain simultaneity-of-events situation were to arise. Suppose that the following conditions are true at a given point in simulated time.

1. All three barbers are captured.
2. At least one Transaction is waiting on the User Chain.
3. One of the in-service customers is just leaving.
4. The next customer is just arriving.
5. The leaving Transaction is ahead of the arriving Transaction on the Current Events Chain.

When the leaving Transaction is processed, it first moves into the LEAVE Block, thereby changing the condition "Storage Not Full" from false to true. This leaving Transaction then moves into the UNLINK Block, causing the Transaction at the front of the User Chain to be moved to the Current Events Chain. Because of its earlier movement through the PRIORITY Block, the unlinked Transaction has a Priority

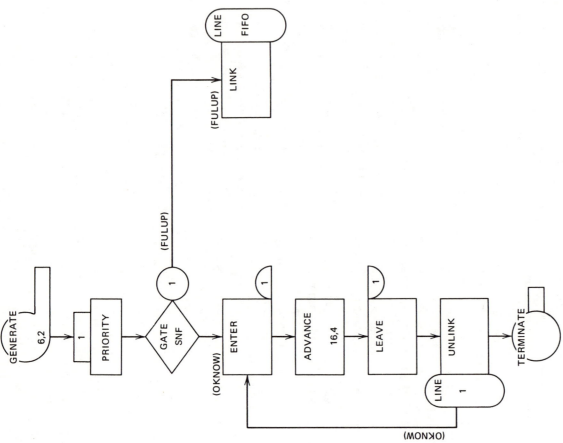

FIGURE 7.11   A second example of User Chain use

Level of 1. It is therefore placed on the Current Events Chain *ahead of* the arriving customer-Transaction, which has a Priority Level of 0. After the leaving Transaction has terminated, the Processor restarts the CEC scan. It first processes the just-unlinked customer-Transaction, moving it into the ENTER–ADVANCE sequence. Execution of the ENTER Block results in the condition "Storage Not Full" being made false again. When the arriving customer-Transaction is processed later in the scan, it therefore moves non-sequentially from the GATE Block to the LINK Block, and is put on the User Chain. The previously waiting customer has captured the barber, which is as it should be.

It is easy to see how the logic of the model would be subverted if the PRIORITY Block were removed from the model, and the conditions described above came about. The *unlinked* Transaction would be put on the Current Events Chain *behind* the just-arriving customer-Transaction. When the arriving Transaction reached the GATE Block, the "Storage Not Full" condition would be *true*. The "newcomer" would therefore capture the barber. When the just-unlinked Transaction eventually tried to move into the ENTER Block, entry would be denied. This previously waiting Transaction would have missed its chance. Furthermore, its subsequent waiting would take place on the Current Events Chain, not on the User Chain.

Note that the potential problem of simultaneity

did *not* have to be defended against when the Link Indicator provided the look-ahead logic in Figure 7.7. Explaining why this is the case is left as an exercise.

Unfortunately, the potential problem of simultaneity can arise in *any* context in which the analyst employs User Chains, and supplies his own look-ahead logic. In this book, whenever the potential problem can arise, the PRIORITY Block will be used to solve the problem. The reason for the presence of the PRIORITY Block will not be reexplained in these cases, except when the situation is complicated enough to call for further comments.

7.6.4 An Alternative for Handling the Simultaneity Problem

In the Figure 7.11 model, it was convenient to place the PRIORITY Block between the GENERATE and GATE Blocks. But this was largely because the modeling context used as an example was completely self-contained. It is not normally true that a Transaction approaches a Storage from a GENERATE Block. More often than not, the approach is made from some preceding nontrivial model segment. The question then arises, how is one to handle the problem of simultaneity in this circumstance? The purpose of this section is to suggest an alternative which can be used under more complicated circumstances.

Figure 7.12 shows the suggested alternative in the form of a Block Diagram segment corresponding to use of the Figure 7.11 Storage. It is assumed that all Transactions move into the segment with a common Priority Level, whatever that may be. The defense against the simultaneity problem takes the form of the PRIORITY–BUFFER sequence placed between the ADVANCE and LEAVE Blocks.

Consider how the PRIORITY–BUFFER combination works to eliminate the simultaneity problem. Assume that the conditions required for the simultaneity problem are in effect, as follows.

1. All three barbers are captured.
2. At least one Transaction is waiting on the User Chain.
3. One of the in-service customers is just leaving.
4. The next customer is just arriving.
5. The leaving Transaction is ahead of the arriving Transaction on the Current Events Chain.

Now, when the leaving Transaction is processed, it immediately moves into the PRIORITY Block, where its "old" Priority Level is reassigned as its "new" Priority Level. This produces no change

in Priority Level, but it *does* cause the Processor to reposition the Transaction on the Current Events Chain as the last member in its "new" Priority Class. This means that the leaving Transaction is now *behind* the arriving Transaction [which reverses condition (5) stated above]. The leaving Transaction then moves into the BUFFER Block, forcing the Processor to restart its CEC scan. As the reinitiated scan proceeds, the arriving Transaction is (eventually) encountered, finds the condition "Storage Not Full" is false (the leaving Transaction has not yet executed the LEAVE Block), and therefore transfers nonsequentially to the User Chain. Later in the scan, the Processor resumes the forward movement of the leaving Transaction,

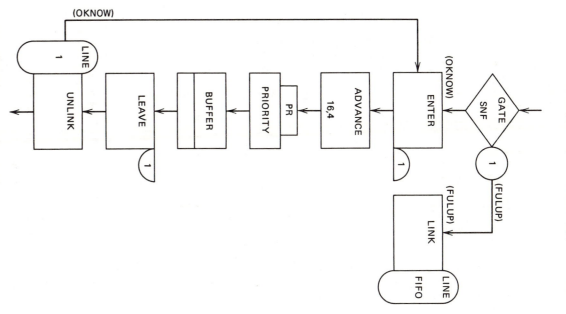

FIGURE 7.12 An alternative method for handling the potential time-tie problem in the Figure 7.11 model.

moving it through the LEAVE Block to the UNLINK Block. The Transaction at the front of the User Chain is then transferred to the Current Events Chain, and enters the Storage when the scan is restarted (execution of the LEAVE Block caused the Status Change Flag to be turned on; execution of the UNLINK Block then caused it to be turned on again, redundantly).

It should be clear what would happen under the stated conditions if the PRIORITY–BUFFER Blocks were *not* in the model. The leaving Transaction would be processed first, making the condition "Storage Not Full" true. The unlinked Transaction would be put on the Current Events Chain *behind* the arriving Transaction, since they are postulated to have the same Priority Level. The arriving Transaction would then enter the Storage, thereby capturing the server who had been intended for the unlinked Transaction. By the time the unlinked Transaction was processed, there would be no room left for it in the Storage. In short, the logic of the model would be invalid.

7.7 The PRIORITY Block BUFFER Option

The model in Figure 7.12 illustrates a situation in which a PRIORITY–BUFFER Block sequence arises. The sequence is shown in general in Figure 7.13, where the PRIORITY Block's A Operand is simply shown as "A". When a Transaction moves through this sequence, the Processor (1) repositions the Transaction on the Current Events Chain as the last member in its new Priority Class, and (2) restarts the scan of the Current Events Chain.

It is possible to achieve the effect of the Figure 7.13 Block sequence by using the so-

called BUFFER option with the PRIORITY Block. Use of this option simply requires that the word BUFFER be supplied as the PRIORITY Block's B Operand. Figure 7.14 shows a PRIORITY Block which uses the BUFFER option. The single Block in Figure 7.14, then, is exactly equivalent to the two-Block sequence shown in Figure 7.13.

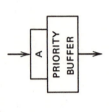

FIGURE 7.14 A PRIORITY Block which uses the BUFFER option

7.8 More Examples of User Chain Use

Two more examples of User Chain use with Facilities are given in this section. The first example illustrates application of User Chains with two Facilities operating in parallel. The second example shows how the "shortest imminent operation" queue discipline is simulated with use of Parameter-mode linking at the LINK Block.

7.8.1 User Chain Use with Two Parallel Facilities

Suppose that two barbers work in a barber shop. Service time for the first and second of these barbers is 13 ± 3 and 15 ± 4 minutes, respectively. Customers arrive at the shop every 7 ± 3 minutes. Figure 7.15 shows how a User Chain can be incorporated into a model of the barber shop. When a customer-Transaction arrives at the shop, it moves (through the PRIORITY Block) into the TEST Block shown in Figure 7.15(a). There, it evaluates the Boolean Variable CHECK, as defined in Figure 7.15(b), to determine whether either one or both of the barbers are available. If a barber is free, the customer-Transaction proceeds to the TRANSFER Block in BOTH mode, from whence it is routed to a SEIZE Block not currently denying entry. If both barbers are busy, it is routed from the transfer-mode TEST Block to the unconditional-mode LINK Block. There is linked onto the back of the User Chain LONG.

Whenever a customer-Transaction releases a barber, it causes another waiting customer to be unlinked from the User Chain and routed

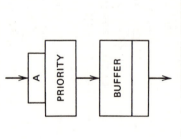

FIGURE 7.13 A PRIORITY–BUFFER Block sequence

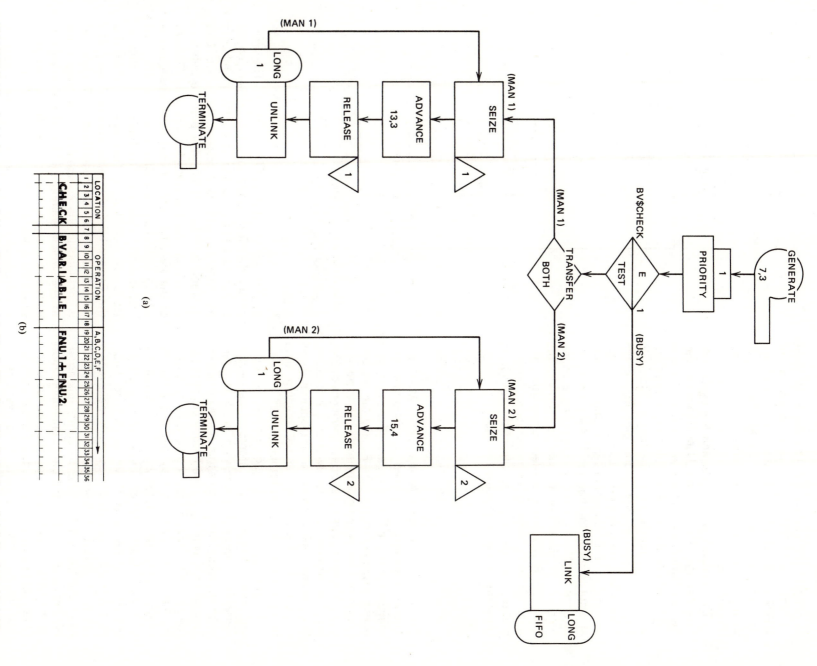

FIGURE 7.15   A third example of User Chain use. (a) Block Diagram. (b) Definition of the Boolean Variable CHECK.

directly to the pertinent SEIZE Block. Because of the "PRIORITY 1" Block following the GENERATE Block, the unlinked customer-Transaction is assured of being the one to capture the just-released barber under all circumstances.

This example is one in which the execution-time savings resulting from User Chain use can be substantial. In contrast with Figure 7.7 and 7.11, where the potential blocking conditions are both unique, the TRANSFER Block in Figure 7.15 offers nonunique blocking. If the User Chain were not used, each delayed Transaction on the Current Events Chain would attempt to move through the TRANSFER Block at each CEC scan, thereby consuming a telling amount of time. For the model shown, the TRANSFER Block is executed successfully one time by each arriving customer who finds a barber immediately available. No attempt is otherwise made to execute the Block.

7.8.2 User Chain Use for "Shortest Imminent Operation" Queue Discipline

Consider this problem. At the Facility MAC, the queue discipline practiced is "shortest imminent operation." This means that the Transaction expected to hold the Facility the shortest length of time is the one permitted to capture it next. In case of ties for shortest imminent operation, the ties are to be resolved on a first-come, first-served basis. When a Transaction does capture the Facility, its actual holding time follows the exponential distribution.

Assuming that a Transaction's expected holding time at the Facility is stored in its second Parameter, Figure 7.16 shows a Block Diagram segment which implements this queue discipline. Transactions waiting for the Facility are put onto the User Chain QUE, ordered according to their P2 value. This means they are put onto the chain in order of "shortest imminent operation," with expected operation times increasing from the front of the User Chain toward the back. Furthermore, in event of ties, each most-recent arrival is placed *behind* earlier arrivals which have the same P2 value. In short, linking in Parameter mode results in direct implementation of the shortest imminent operation queue discipline (assuming, of course, that Transactions are later removed from the front of the User Chain). In the Figure 7.16 model segment, just before a Transaction releases the Facility, it moves into

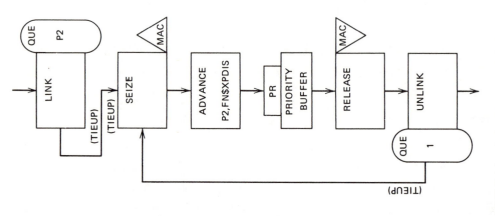

FIGURE 7.16   A fourth example of User Chain use

a "PRIORITY PR,BUFFER" Block. The Processor therefore repositions the Transaction on the Current Events Chain as the last member in its Priority Class, and restarts the scan. This guarantees that, in case of a time tie between the events "next arrival of a job" and "release of the Facility," the arriving job-Transaction is placed on the User-Chain before the next Transaction to capture the Facility is unlinked. (It is assumed that all Transactions which use the Facility have the same Priority Level.) The result is to insure that the arriving job-Transaction is included in the competition that takes place to see which waiting job has the shortest imminent operation. If this simultaneity-of-events situation arose and the PRIORITY Block were *not* included in the Figure 7.16 model segment, the shortest imminent operation queue discipline could be violated (see exercise 5, Section 7.11).

7.9 User Chain Standard Numerical Attributes

Each User Chain has five Standard Numerical Attributes associated with it. The predefined names of these attributes, and the significance of the corresponding values, are shown in Table 7.3.

When the Processor encounters a CLEAR card, the values of these Standard Numerical Attributes are set to zero, and any User Chain residents are removed and returned to the stack in the latent pool. The effect of the RESET card is to set the values of CA_j, CC_j, and CT_j to zero. The value of CH_j remains the same, and the value of CM_j is set to the current value of CH_j. Of course, any User Chain residents are left undisturbed during the resetting operation.

7.10 CASE STUDY 7A
A Second Tour Through Case Study 4D

(1) Statement of the Problem

Show how to modify the Case Study 4D models ("Comparison of Alternative Queuing Systems in a Bank") so that all customer-Transactions waiting for a teller are kept on a User Chain or Chains. Run the modified models under conditions identical to those used in Case Study 4D. Compare and contrast the CPU time requirements with and without use of User Chains.

(2) An Approach Leading to Solution

One-Line Model. In the one-line model, the tellers are simulated with a Storage. This means that the logic illustrated in Figure 7.11 can be applied directly to modify the one-line model as requested. All that is involved is addition of four Blocks (PRIORITY, GATE, LINK, and UN-LINK) to the one-line model as originally shown in Figure 4D.3(a).

Multiple-Line Model. In the multiple-line model, the tellers are simulated by parallel Facilities, with a separate Queue of customers forming ahead of each Facility. The basic teller-selection logic for the multiple-line model in Case Study 4D was (1) go to an available teller, if one is available; otherwise, (2) join the Queue with the least number of people in it. Part (1) of this logic was implemented by using the SELECT Block to scan for a Facility with an F_j value of zero; part (2) was implemented by using the MIN-mode SELECT Block to identify the Queue with the minimum current content. In fact, Queues 1 through 8 were provided ahead of teller-Facilities 1 through 8 just so the Q_j values would be available to support the MIN-mode SELECT Block logic.

In the modified model, part (1) of the logic will not be changed; part (2), however, is subject to considerable change. First of all, Queues 1 through 8 can be eliminated from the model. Their role is supplanted by the introduction of User Chains 1 through 8, corresponding to teller-Facilities 1 through 8, respectively. The User Chain Standard Numerical Attribute CH_j (current content of User Chain j) can be used to support the MIN-mode SELECT Block logic, which explains why the Q_j values are no longer needed. Of course, the Queue used in the multiple-line model to maintain aggregate waiting-line information (Queue 10) will still be included as part of the modified model; otherwise, the desired average waiting time information would not be available in the model output.

TABLE 7.3   Standard Numerical Attributes for User Chains

Predefined Name	Value
CA_j, or $CA\$sn$	Integer portion of the average number of Transactions on the chain
CC_j, or $CC\$sn$	The total number of Transactions placed on the chain during the course of the simulation
CH_j, or $CH\$sn$	The number of Transactions currently on the chain
CM_j, or $CM\$sn$	Maximum number of Transactions simultaneously resident on the chain during the simulation; the maximum value CH_j (or $CH\$sn$) has attained
CT_j, or $CT\$sn$	Integer portion of the average Transaction residence time on the chain

(3) Table of Definitions

Time Unit: 0.1 Seconds

TABLE 7A.1(a)   Table of Definitions for Case Study 7A: the One-Line Model

GPSS Entity	Interpretation
Transactions	
Model Segment 1	Customers P1: Service time required by the customer
Model Segment 2	A timer
Functions	
5	Function for sampling from the exponential distribution with a mean value of 1
MEAN	Function describing the mean service time required for various categories of business
Queues	
ONE	The Queue used to gather statistics for the one waiting line in the bank
Storages	
TELRS	Storage simulating the eight bank tellers
User Chains	
LINE	The User Chain on which customer-Transactions wait for a teller to become available

TABLE 7A.1(b)   Table of Definitions for Case Study 7A: the Multiple-Line Model

GPSS Entity	Interpretation
Transactions	
Model Segment 1	Customers P1: Service time required by the customer P2: The number of the User Chain on which the customer may be temporarily linked, and of the teller the customer uses
Facilities	
1, 2, 3, 4, 5, 6, 7, and 8	Facilities used to simulate the eight bank tellers
Queues	
10	The Queue used to gather aggregate waiting statistics for all customers moving through the bank
User Chains	
1, 2, 3, 4, 5, 6, 7, and 8	The User Chains on which customer-Transactions waiting for tellers 1 through 8 are kept, respectively

(4) Block Diagram

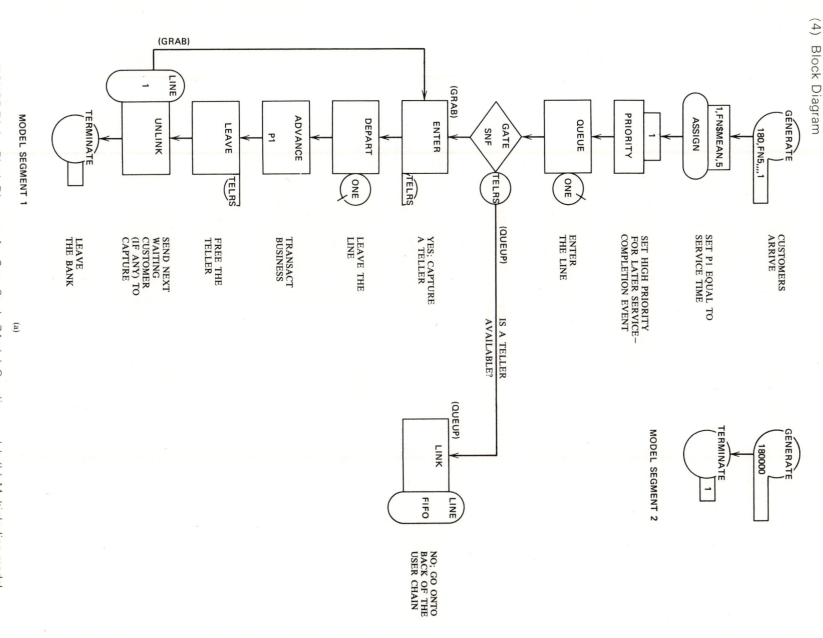

MODEL SEGMENT 1

MODEL SEGMENT 2

FIGURE 7A.1 Block Diagrams for Case Study 7A. (a) One-line model. (b) Multiple-line model.

(a)

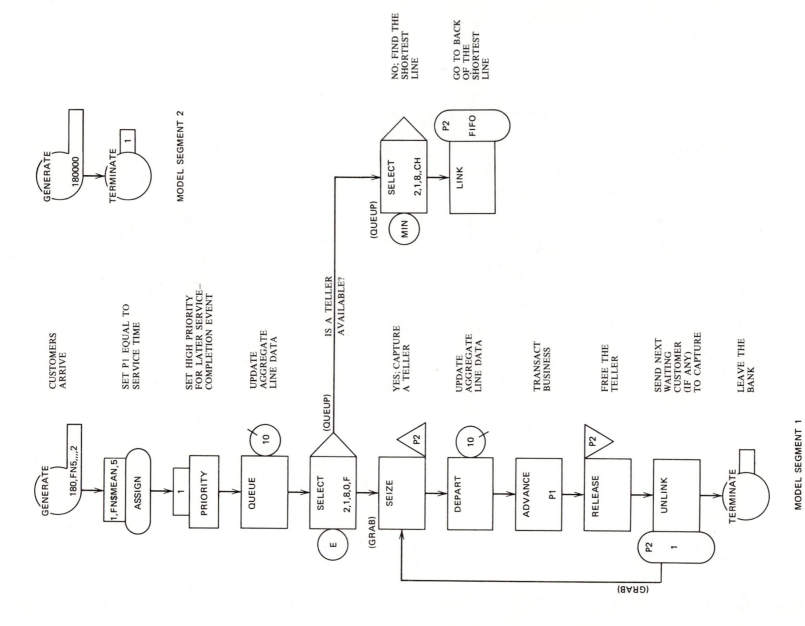

FIGURE 7A.1 (Continued)

(5) Extended Program Listings

BLOCK NUMBER	*LOC	OPERATION	A,B,C,D,E,F,G	COMMENTS	CARD NUMBER
		SIMULATE			1
		*			2
		*			3
		* FUNCTION DEFINITION(S)			4
	5	FUNCTION	RN1,C24	EXPONENTIAL DISTRIBUTION FUNCTION	5
		0,0/.1,.104/.2,.222/.3,.355/.4,.509/.5,.69/.6,.915/.7,1.2/.75,1.38			6
		.8,1.6/.84,1.83/.88,2.12/.9,2.3/.92,2.52/.94,2.81/.95,2.99/.96,3.2			7
		.97,3.5/.98,3.9/.99,4.6/.995,5.3/.998,6.2/.999,7/.9998,8			8
	MEAN	FUNCTION	RN1,D5	DISTRIBUTION OF MEAN SERVICE TIME	9
		1,450/.29,750/.61,1000/.85,1500/1,3000			10
		*			11
		* STORAGE CAPACITY DEFINITION(S)			12
		*			13
		STORAGE	S$TELRS,8	PROVIDE 8 TELLERS	14
		*			15
		* MODEL SEGMENT 1			16
		*			17
1		GENERATE	180,FN$5,,,1	CUSTOMERS ARRIVE	18
2		ASSIGN	1,FN$MEAN,5	SET P1 = SERVICE TIME	19
3		PRIORITY	1	SET HIGH PRIORITY FOR LATER	20
		*		SERVICE-COMPLETION EVENT	21
4		QUEUE	ONE	ENTER THE LINE	22
5		GATE SNF	TELRS,WAIT	IS A TELLER AVAILABLE?	23
6	GRAB	ENTER	TELRS	YES; CAPTURE A TELLER	24
7		DEPART	ONE	LEAVE THE LINE	25
8		ADVANCE	P1	TRANSACT BUSINESS	26
9		LEAVE	TELRS	FREE THE TELLER	27
10		UNLINK	LINE,GRAB,1	SEND NEXT WAITING CUSTOMER	28
		*		(IF ANY) TO CAPTURE	29
11		TERMINATE		LEAVE THE BANK	30
12	WAIT	LINK	LINE,FIFO	NO; GO ONTO BACK OF USER CHAIN	31
		*			32
		* MODEL SEGMENT 2			33
		*			34
13		GENERATE	18000	TIMER ARRIVES AFTER 5 HOURS	35
14		TERMINATE	1	SHUT OFF THE RUN	36
		*			37
		* CONTROL CARDS			38
		*			39
		START	1	START THE RUN FOR DAY 1	40
		CLEAR	1	CLEAR FOR DAY 2	41
		START	1	START THE RUN FOR DAY 2	42
		CLEAR	1	CLEAR FOR DAY 3	43
		START	1	START THE RUN FOR DAY 3	44
		CLEAR	1	CLEAR FOR DAY 4	45
		START	1	START THE RUN FOR DAY 4	46
		CLEAR	1	CLEAR FOR DAY 5	47
		START	1	START THE RUN FOR DAY 5	48
		END		RETURN CONTROL TO OPERATING SYSTEM	49

FIGURE 7A.2 Extended Program Listings for Case Study 7A (a) One-line model. (b) Multiple-line model.

(a)

```
BLOCK
NUMBER   *LOC    OPERATION  A,B,C,D,E,F,G              COMMENTS                        CARD
                                                                                       NUMBER

                 SIMULATE                                                               1
          *                                                                             2
          *                                                                             3
          *       FUNCTION DEFINITION(S)                                                4
          5       FUNCTION   RN1,C24     EXPONENTIAL DISTRIBUTION FUNCTION              5
 0.0/.1,.104/.2,.222/.3,.355/.4,.509/.5,.69/.6,.915/.7,1.2/.75,1.38                     6
 .8,1.6/.84,1.83/.88,2.12/.9,2.3/.92,2.52/.94,2.81/.95,2.99/.96,3.2                     7
 .97,3.5/.98,3.9/.99,4.6/.995,5.3/.998,6.2/.999,7/.9998,8                               8
 MEAN    FUNCTION   RN1,D5      DISTRIBUTION OF MEAN SERVICE TIME                       9
 .1,450/.29,750/.61,1000/.85,1500/1,3000                                               10
          *                                                                            11
          *       MODEL SEGMENT 1                                                      12
          *                                                                            13
                                                                                       14
  1              GENERATE   180,FN5,,,2   CUSTOMERS ARRIVE                             15
  2              ASSIGN     1,FN$MEAN,5   SET P1 = SERVICE TIME                        16
  3              PRIORITY   1             SET HIGH PRIORITY FOR LATER                  17
          *                              SERVICE-COMPLETION EVENT                      18
  4       LINE   QUEUE      10            UPDATE AGGREGATE LINE DATA                   19
  5              SELECT E   2,1,8,0,F,QUEUP  IS A TELLER AVAILABLE?                    20
  6       GRAB   SEIZE      P2            YES; CAPTURE A TELLER                        21
  7              DEPART     10            UPDATE AGGREGATE LINE DATA                   22
  8              ADVANCE    P1            TRANSACT BUSINESS                            23
  9              RELEASE    P2            FREE THE TELLER                              24
 10              UNLINK     P2,GRAB,1     SEND NEXT WAITING CUSTOMER                   25
          *                              (IF ANY) TO CAPTURE                           26
 11              TERMINATE                LEAVE THE BANK                               27
 12       QUEUP  SELECT MIN 2,1,8,,CH     NO; FIND THE SHORTEST LINE                   28
 13              LINK       P2,FIFO       GO TO BACK OF THE SHORTEST LINE              29
          *                                                                            30
          *       MODEL SEGMENT 2                                                      31
          *                                                                            32
 14              GENERATE   180000        TIMER ARRIVES AFTER 5 HOURS                  33
 15              TERMINATE  1             SHUT OFF THE RUN                             34
          *                                                                            35
          *       CONTROL CARDS                                                        36
          *                                                                            37
                 START      1             START THE RUN FOR DAY 1                      38
                 CLEAR                    CLEAR FOR DAY 2                              39
                 START      1             START THE RUN FOR DAY 2                      40
                 CLEAR                    CLEAR FOR DAY 3                              41
                 START      1             START THE RUN FOR DAY 3                      42
                 CLEAR                    CLEAR FOR DAY 4                              43
                 START      1             START THE RUN FOR DAY 4                      44
                 CLEAR                    CLEAR FOR DAY 5                              45
                 START      1             START THE RUN FOR DAY 5                      46
                 END                      RETURN CONTROL TO OPERATING SYSTEM          47
```

(b)

FIGURE 7A.2 (Continued)

(6) Program Output

(a)

STORAGE	CAPACITY	AVERAGE CONTENTS	AVERAGE UTILIZATION	ENTRIES	AVERAGE TIME/TRAN	CURRENT CONTENTS	MAXIMUM CONTENTS
TELRS	8	7.515	.939	1001	1351.355	4	8

(b)

QUEUE	MAXIMUM CONTENTS	AVERAGE CONTENTS	TOTAL ENTRIES	ZERO ENTRIES	PERCENT ZEROS	AVERAGE TIME/TRANS	$AVERAGE TIME/TRANS	TABLE NUMBER	CURRENT CONTENTS
ONE	51	14.138	1001	121	12.0	2542.459	2892.047		

$AVERAGE TIME/TRANS = AVERAGE TIME/TRANS EXCLUDING ZERO ENTRIES

(c)

USER CHAIN	TOTAL ENTRIES	AVERAGE TIME/TRANS	CURRENT CONTENTS	AVERAGE CONTENTS	MAXIMUM CONTENTS
LINE	880	2892.047		14.138	51

(d)

FACILITY	AVERAGE UTILIZATION	NUMBER ENTRIES	AVERAGE TIME/TRAN	SEIZING TRANS. NO.	PREEMPTING TRANS. NO.
1	.968	153	1139.274	50	
2	.966	116	1499.008	45	
3	.956	114	1510.280	28	
4	.943	98	1732.142	36	
5	.935	138	1220.536		
6	.925	107	1557.551		
7	.905	134	1216.500		
8	.913	141	1166.581		

(e)

QUEUE	MAXIMUM CONTENTS	AVERAGE CONTENTS	TOTAL ENTRIES	ZERO ENTRIES	PERCENT ZEROS	AVERAGE TIME/TRANS	$AVERAGE TIME/TRANS	TABLE NUMBER	CURRENT CONTENTS
10	45	15.152	1001	189	18.8	2724.756	3358.966		

$AVERAGE TIME/TRANS = AVERAGE TIME/TRANS EXCLUDING ZERO ENTRIES

(f)

USER CHAIN	TOTAL ENTRIES	AVERAGE TIME/TRANS	CURRENT CONTENTS	AVERAGE CONTENTS	MAXIMUM CONTENTS
1	126	3056.968		2.139	6
2	91	4357.656		2.203	6
3	95	3933.010		2.075	6
4	73	5205.875		2.111	6
5	116	2701.551		1.740	6
6	86	3818.918		1.824	5
7	108	2692.407		1.615	5
8	117	2217.982		1.441	5

FIGURE 7A.3 Selected Program Output for Case Study 7A. (a) Storage statistics (one-line model, day 1). (b) Queue statistics (one-line model, day 1). (c) User Chain statistics (one-line model, day 1). (d) Facility statistics (multiple-line model, day 1). (e) Queue statistics (multiple-line model, day 1). (f) User Chain statistics (multiple-line model, day 1).

(7) Discussion

Model Implementation. It was stated earlier that "use of the Link Indicator for look-ahead purposes is extremely restricted. In fact, it is really useful as a built-in look-ahead device only when the limited resource which might offer blockage is simulated with a Facility." In the multiple-line model, tellers are simulated with Facilities. Even so, the Link Indicator is not powerful enough to support use of these tellers in the model. As a result, the SELECT Block [Block 5, Figure 7A.2(b)] is used to determine whether a customer-Transaction should be placed on a User Chain or not. In the Figure 7.15(a) model in Section 7.8, where parallel servers were simulated with Facilities in parallel, it was also true that analyst-supplied look-ahead logic was required.

Program Output.[8] Selected output resulting from the first simulated day is shown in Figure 7A.3. Figures 7A.3(a), (b), and (c) show Storage statistics, Queue statistics, and User Chain statistics, respectively, for the one-line model. As would be expected, the Storage and Queue statistics in Figures 7A.3(a) and (b) are identical to the analogous Case Study 4D statistics [see Figure 4D.4(a) and (b)]. Note that the Queue statistics $AVERAGE TIME/TRANS in Figure 7A.3(b) is identical to the User Chain's AVERAGE TIME/TRANS statistic in Figure 7A.3(c). The reason for this is that there were no zero-residence-time entries to the User Chain in the one-line model. This is the case because the service-completion event always has higher priority in the model than the next-arrival event. (Compare this situation with that discussed in Section 7.6 for output from the Figure 7.7 model; also see exercise 10c, Section 7.11.)

Figures 7A.3(d), (e), and (f) show Facility statistics, Queue statistics, and User Chain statistics, respectively, for the multiple-line-model day 1 simulation. The Facility and Queue statistics in Figure 7A.3(d) and (e) are identical to the analogous Case Study 4D statistics [see Figure 4D.4(c) and (d)]. Also note that the various $AVERAGE TIME/TRANS Queue statistics in Figure 7A.3(e) are identical to the corresponding User Chain AVERAGE TIME/TRANS statistics in Figure 7A.3(f). As is true

for the one-line case, the reason for this is that if time ties occur, the service-completion event has priority over the next-arrival event; as a consequence, there are no "zero entries" to the User Chains in the multiple-line model.

Other pertinent results from the two simulations are not summarized here. All the results are identical, of course, to those shown in the Table 4D.4 summary in Case Study 4D.

The CPU times required for the modified one-line and multiple-line models are shown in Table 7A.2. For purposes of comparison, the CPU times required by the Case Study 4D models are also indicated in the table. Introduction of User Chains has led to some CPU time economy, but not much. Although blocked Transactions are kept off the Current Events Chain in Case Study 7A, a price must be paid for this benefit. In the one-line model, the price takes the form of having each customer-Transaction move through the PRIORITY, GATE, and UNLINK Blocks. (None of these blocks were required in Case Study 4D.) In addition, many of these customers (any who have to wait) cause the LINK Block to be executed. The resulting increase in the overall number of Block executions in the one-line model approximately counter-balances the more efficient Current Events Chain scan which results because blocked Transactions are kept on a User Chain.

In the multiple-line model, the price of introducing User Chains takes the form of having each customer-Transaction move through an UNLINK Block; furthermore, each customer-Transaction which cannot immediately capture a teller moves into a LINK Block. (Note that the PRIORITY Block in the Case Study 7A multiple-line model is not an "addition"; it was also present in the Case Study 4D multiple-line model, to control the event sequence whenever time-ties arose between service completion and next arrival events.) On the other hand, as already discussed in this case study, introduction of User Chains has permitted elimination of a QUEUE—DEPART Block pair in the multiple-line model. On balance, then, somewhat fewer

[8] Total CPU time for the one-line simulation on an IBM 360/67 computer was 34.9 seconds. For the multiple-line simulation, it was 43.2 seconds.

TABLE 7A.2 A Summary of the CPU Times Used in Case Studies 7A and 4D

	One-Line Model	Multiple-Line Model
Case Study 7A	34.9	43.2
Case Study 4D	35.3	48.7

Block executions are required in the Case Study 7A multiple-line model than in the equivalent Case Study 4D model. The combined effect of having somewhat fewer Block executions, and keeping blocked Transactions off the Current Events Chain, leads to about a 10 percent CPU time savings in Case Study 7A vs. Case Study 4D, as shown in Table 7A.2.

After all the elaboration on User Chains so far in this chapter, the modest CPU time differences in Table 7A.2 are probably disappointing. The User Chains do nothing to make the models more sophisticated; they reveal no insights about system behavior not already revealed by their Case Study 4D counterparts. The following points should be noted, however.

1. With User Chains, it *is* possible to build a more sophisticated multiple-line model, one in which line-switching is allowed. (See exercises 19 and 20, Section 7.11.) Without User Chains, this would not be possible.

2. In the system modeled in Case Studies 4D and 7A, all blocked Transactions are *uniquely* blocked. This means that the Scan Indicator concept is being taken advantage of in the Case Study 4D models; in turn, there is not as much *potential* CPU time economy to be realized by introduction of User Chains. In situations where *nonunique* blocking occurs, the potential CPU time economy is much greater. (See exercise 21, Section 7.11.)

7.11 Exercises

1. (a) Would the logic of the Figure 7.7 model be changed if the Location name GETEM were moved from the SEIZE Block to the DEPART Block, and the DEPART Block were moved ahead of the SEIZE Block?

   (b) Would the logic of the Figure 7.7 model be changed if the RELEASE and UNLINK Blocks were interchanged?

2. In Figure 7.7, Transactions are linked onto the *back* of the User Chain, and then are eventually unlinked from the *front* of the chain. This results in first-come, first-served queue discipline. The same queue discipline results if Transactions are linked onto the *front* of the User Chain, and then are eventually unlinked from the *back* of the chain. Show what changes to make in Figure 7.7 to implement this alternative approach.

3. Indicate where the QUEUE–DEPART Block pairs would be placed in the following figures if it were of interest to gather Queue statistics in the corresponding models.
   (a) Figure 7.9.
   (b) Figure 7.11.

4. These questions pertain to the Figure 7.11 model, and the corresponding discussion.
   (a) One of the conditions required for disruption of the first-come, first-served queue discipline (in the absence of use of the PRIORITY Block) is that the "leaving Transaction" be ahead of the "arriving Transaction" on the Current Events Chain. Explain how this relative ordering of the two Transactions on the Current Events Chain could come about.
   (b) Assume that the PRIORITY, GATE, LINK, and UNLINK Blocks are eliminated from the Figure 7.11 model, and that a QUEUE–DEPART Block pair is placed around the ENTER Block. Can the first-come, first-served queue discipline be disrupted by a simultaneity-of-events situation in this revised model? Explain exactly why, or why not.

5. (a) The model segment in Figure 7.16 shows how to employ a User Chain when implementing the "shortest imminent operation" queue discipline. In the discussion of that model segment, it is stated that if the "PRIORITY PR,BUFFER" Block were removed from that model segment, the desired queue discipline could be violated under a certain simultaneity-of-events situation. Completely describe the situation which would have to be in effect for this to happen.
   (b) The Figure 7.16 model segment assumes that all Transactions which use the Facility have the same Priority Level. Describe the circumstances under which the model logic would be invalid if this assumption were not in effect.

6. When a Transaction releases Facility 21, it is to send another Transaction from the front of User Chain 3 to capture that Facility. If there are no Transactions on User Chain 3, a Transaction from the back end of User Chain 5 is to be sent to capture the Facility. Show a Block Diagram segment which accomplishes this effect. Assume that the "SEIZE 21" Block is in the Location TAKEM.

7. Five Transactions in a group have Parameter 1 values of 1, 2, 3, 4, and 5, and Parameter 2 values of 8, 7, 10, 8, and 10, respectively. The five Transactions enter the Block "LINK PAUSE,P2" sequentially, in order of increasing Parameter 1 value. What are the Parameter 1 values at the front, middle, and back of the User Chain after the linking has taken place? Assume there are no other Transactions on the User Chain.

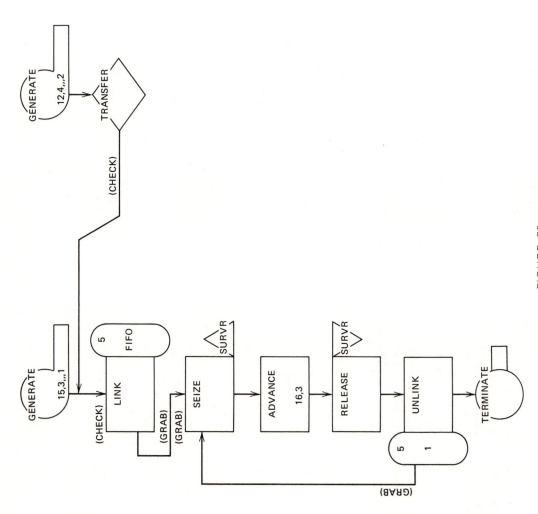

FIGURE E8

8. (a) Discuss the queue discipline practiced at the Facility SURVR in Figure E8. (Assume that there are no other references to the Facility in the model.)

   (b) Show what changes to make in Figure E8 if the queue discipline at the Facility SURVR is to be first-come, first-served, within Priority Class.

9. Disregard the GENERATE and PRIORITY Blocks in the Figure 7.11 model, and assume that Transactions arriving at the GATE Block to use the Storage have Priority Levels of 1, 2, and 3. Queue discipline at the Storage is to be first-come, first-served, within Priority Class. Show what changes must be made in the Figure 7.11 model to handle this situation.

10. (a) Given that there were three zero-residence-time entries to the User Chain HOLD, use the Figure 7.8(a) information to compute the

AVERAGE TIME/TRANS statistic for Transactions *which actually had to wait* on the User Chain. Compare your result with the SAVERAGE TIME/TRANS statistic in Figure 7.8(b). Are the two statistics identical, as would be expected?

   (b) Can there ever be zero-residence-time Transactions on the User Chains in the Figure 7.11 or 7.15 models? Explain why, or why not.

   (c) Show how to modify the Figure 7.7 model to make it unnecessary for Transactions to be put on the User Chain when their residence time there would turn out to be zero.

11. Show how a User Chain can be used to implement random queue discipline at the Facility JOE. That is, the server simulated with the Facility is to select his next customer at random from those who are waiting for him. (Hint: Determine some random integer in the range

between 0, and 1 less than the number of Trans- actions on the User Chain. Unlike this, many Transactions from the front of the User Chain, routing them to the back of the chain. When this has been done, send the Transaction now at the front of the chain to capture the server.)

12. If an odd number of Transactions are waiting at the Facility ODD, the Transaction in the middle of the waiting line is to receive service next. If an even number are waiting, the Transaction at the front of the line is to be served next. Transactions arriving at the Facility have the same Priority Level, and are put on the back of the User Chain. Show a Block Diagram segment with which this queue discipline can be implemented. Assume that, except for removing the Transaction to be served, ordering on the User Chain is to be pre- served.

13. (a) Show how to modify the Block Diagram for Case Study 2C (alternative queue disciplines in the one-line, one-server queuing system) so that only one SEIZE–RELEASE Block pair is used in the model, and all waiting mechanic-Transactions are kept on *one* User Chain.

   (b) Repeat (a), except that now the Category 1 and Category 2 mechanics are to be kept on separate User Chains.

14. In Case Study 4B (a grocery store model), there is only one checkout girl. Show how to modify the Block Diagram for the model to incorporate these changes.

   (a) A second girl is added to check people out at an express counter. Customers with three items or less (not counting the possible pur- chase of impulse items) use the express counter. All the other customers use the regular counter.

   (b) When the express-counter girl is idle, the customer at the front of the regular checkout line is permitted to check out at the express counter, and does so.

15. Show how to modify the Block Diagram for Case Study 5C (simulation of a production facility) so that all jobs waiting for availability of a machine in a given machine group are kept on a User Chain associated with that machine group.

16. Show how to change the model in Case Study 5E (the bus stop model) so that Transactions simulat- ing people waiting for a bus to come, or waiting their turn to try to board the bus, are kept on a User Chain.

17. Show what changes to make in the Block Diagram for Case Study 6A (oil tanker accommodation at a port) so that, when possible, tankers waiting to move into the port are kept on a User Chain.

18. At the Facility TOM, the queue discipline used is "longest time in the system." In this discipline, the server gives service next to the customer who has been in the *system* (that is, the Transaction which has been in the model) the greatest length of time. Suggest a method for implementing this queue discipline in GPSS. Explain the suggested method in detail.

19. The multiple-line bank model in Case Study 7A suffers from the same defect as the multiple-line model in Case Study 4D: no line-switching is permitted. This means that even if one of the tellers becomes available when other customers are waiting for *other* tellers, none of them move to capture the available teller. Suggest a method for rectifying this situation in the multiple-line model in Case Study 7A. Show all details of a GPSS model corresponding to your suggestion. How does your model behave if a customer leaves his line and moves to capture an available teller at precisely the same time that another customer is arriving at the bank?

20. In general, customers may switch lines under conditions other than the one described in exercise 19. For example, suppose that whenever a customer at the *back* of a waiting line containing three or more (including himself) sees another line containing only one person, he departs his line and goes to the back of the shorter one. Show what modifications to make in your solution to exercise 19 so that the line-switching criterion just described will also be implemented. How does your model behave if a customer decides to switch lines at precisely the same time that another customer is arriving at the bank?

21. If you have the time and interest, try this experi- ment to get a better feeling, albeit in a crude sense, for the potential CPU time economy which can be realized under some circumstances with User Chains.

   In the Figure 7.15 model, change the GENER- ATE Block from "GENERATE 7,3" to "GENER- ATE 100,,0", supply 1 as the A Operand at both TER- MINATE Blocks, and simulate with the resulting model, using "START 100" as the Start card. Then eliminate the User Chain from this modified model, and submit it for running again. How much difference is there in the CPU times required to run the two models? (When the User Chain is eliminated, the last 98 Transactions which are brought into the model at simulated time 1 encounter a nonunique blocking condition at the TEST Block. When the Processor scans the Cur- rent Events Chain at the next clock reading after time 1, then, it will encounter these 98 blocked Transactions before it reaches the "releasing" Transaction at the back of the Current Chain.

Then, because of the RELEASE Block execution, it will restart the scan, this time encountering 97 blocked Transactions. And so on.)

22. Case Study 5C presents a model in which a production shop is simulated. Three different types of jobs move through the shop, which consists of six different machine groups. The queue discipline practiced at each machine group is first-come, first served.

Consider this variation on that case study. For each job type, define a "due date" as being equal to some multiple of its "expected total operation time." For example, jobs of Type 1 have an expected total operation time of 240 minutes. If a multiple of 3 were used to convert this to a due date, then a job of Type 1 would be due out of the shop 720 minutes after it arrived. If the job is completed *before* 720 minutes after it arrived, it is early; if it is completed *after* 720 minutes have gone by, it is late. Modify the model in Case Study 5C to estimate the distribution of the random variable "job lateness time," which is to be measured independent of job type. (Define job lateness time as equal to the time out of the shop, minus the time *due* out of the shop. This random variable will then take on a negative value for jobs which leave the shop early.) Then experiment with the model to find what multiple of expected total operation time makes the average value of job lateness time be zero. Assume that the same multiple is to be used for each job type.

Now, using the multiple you have determined, try to find a queue discipline which, if practiced in the shop, will cause the distribution of job lateness time to shift so that its mean value becomes negative, or so that its standard deviation decreases, or both. With one or two exceptions, almost any queue discipline you might investigate will require User Chains for its implementation. Here are some queue disciplines you might consider.

(a) *Job Slack.* Job slack is defined as the time due, minus the current time, minus the total expected operation time remaining for the job. According to a job-slack queue discipline, that waiting job which has the least job slack gets the machine next.

(b) *Job Slack per Operation.* Job slack per operation is job slack, divided by the remaining number of operations for that job. According to this queue discipline, whichever waiting job has the least job slack per operation is the job which gets the machine next.

(c) *Job-Slack Ratio.* Job-slack ratio is the job slack divided by the time remaining until the job's time due. The waiting job with the smallest job-slack ratio is the job which gets the machine next.

(d) *Shortest Imminent Operation.* This queue discipline has been illustrated several times in the book. It first came up in Case Study 2C. Then it was used in Case Study 3C. User Chains are not needed here; by changing a job-Transaction's Priority Levels appropriately as the Transaction moves through the model, the shortest-imminent-operation effect can be achieved. When User Chains are used, however, it is not necessary to make such priority distinctions. The User Chain approach was shown earlier in this chapter.

Discuss the effect of these and other queue disciplines on the mean and standard deviation of the job-lateness-time random variable. If you compare and contrast the effect of different disciplines, the experimental conditions should be replicated in the simulations. This is especially true in the context of Case Study 5C, where the exponential distribution is used so frequently.

23. Consider exercise 7, Section 6.20, which involved modeling a trucking firm. The trucking firm picked up packages from store loading docks, and then delivered the packages to store customers. If Transactions are used in parts of that model to simulate packages, then there will very likely be a large number of blocked Transactions on the Current Events Chain, on average. Assuming that such an approach is taken to the problem, show how to incorporate User Chains into the solution to minimize the number of Transactions resident on the Current Events Chain. If possible, compare CPU times for two otherwise-identical solutions, one which uses User Chains, and one which doesn't. How much difference is there in CPU time for the two approaches?

7.12 Conditional Unlinking of Transactions from User Chains

In Section 7.5, use of the UNLINK Block D and E Operands to remove Transactions from (1) the front, or (2) the back of User Chains was introduced. In neither of these cases does a Transaction have to meet a particular condition, other than relative position on the chain, to qualify for unlinking. There are three other D and E Operand combinations which can be used to impose on potential Unlinkee Transactions the requirement that they satisfy a specified condition. These other three combinations are shown in Table 7.4.

For all three of the Table 7.4 combinations, the User Chain is scanned from front to back by the Processor until the Unlink Count has been satisfied, or the back of the chain has been

TABLE 7.4 Additional D and E Operand Combinations Possible for the UNLINK Block

Combination Number	D Operand	E Operand	Condition Required for Unlinking
1	Any Standard Numerical Attribute[a]	Not used	Let "j" represent the value of the D Operand; the User Chain Transaction qualifies for unlinking if its jth Parameter value equals the value of the Unlinker's jth Parameter
2	Any Standard Numerical Attribute[a]	Any Standard Numerical Attribute[a]	Let "j" represent the value of the D Operand; the potential Unlinkee qualifies if its jth Parameter value equals the value of the E Operand
3	BVj, or BV$$sn	Not used	The potential Unlinkee qualifies if the Boolean Variable numbered j (or symbolically named sn) is true when it is evaluated with that Transaction's Priority Level and Parameter values

[a]Remember that positive integer constants are included among the Standard Numerical Attributes.

reached, whichever occurs first. In *Combination 1*, the value of a specified Parameter of the potential Unlinkee must equal the value of the same Parameter of the Unlinker. The UNLINK Block's D Operand indicates the number of the applicable Parameter; the E Operand is not used. In *Combination 2*, the value of a specified Parameter of the potential Unlinkee must equal some other arbitrarily specified value. The UNLINK Block's D Operand again provides the number of the potential Unlinkee's applicable Parameter; the E Operand is the "match argument," i.e., provides the value which the Unlinkee's Parameter value must equal. In *Combination 3*, the D Operand references a Boolean Variable, and the E Operand is not used. For each Transaction on the User Chain, the Processor evaluates the Boolean Variable. Only if its value is *true* does the User Chain Transaction qualify for unlinking. The question naturally arises, how can the value of a Boolean Variable be made to depend on properties of a Transaction on a User Chain? The answer is that if numeric data references in the Boolean Variable include Priority and/or Parameter values, the *User Chain Transaction currently being examined* supplies these values, *not* the Transaction at the UNLINK Block.

An example will now be given to show use of a Boolean Variable with the UNLINK Block. Consider the shortest-imminent-operation queue discipline, as illustrated in Figure 7.16. A disadvantage of this queue discipline is that jobs with a large imminent operation time can be delayed for very long times waiting for the Facility. This happens if jobs with shorter opera-

tion times keep arriving at the Facility before the bigger jobs can capture it. The problem can be avoided by dividing all waiting jobs into two groups, as determined by how long they have been waiting. Highest priority is given to those jobs that have been waiting longer than some predetermined time, called the *critical threshold*. Jobs in this group are termed "critical." Within the set of critical jobs, queue discipline is shortest imminent operation. Queue discipline for the noncritical jobs is also shortest imminent operation. The overall queue discipline, then, is "serve critical jobs first, then serve noncritical jobs; in each of these two categories, select jobs according to shortest imminent operation."

A Block Diagram for this overall queue discipline is shown in Figure 7.17(a). When a job-Transaction is first marked in Parameter 3. The arrival is first marked in Parameter 3. The Transaction enters the segment, its time-of-Transaction then captures the Facility MAC immediately if possible, and otherwise goes onto the User Chain, ordered according to its imminent operation time as carried in Parameter 2. When a job-Transaction is finished using the Facility, it enters an UNLINK Block to request a Boolean-mode scan of the User Chain. The Chain is scanned from front-to-back in a search for the first job-Transaction, if any, for which the Boolean Variable CRJOB [defined in Figure 7.17(b)] is true, i.e., for which residence time on the User Chain exceeds the critical threshold, as held in the Savevalue CRTYM. If such a Transaction is found, it is unlinked and sent to capture; meantime, the Unlinker continues to the sequential Block. If there are no critical jobs, however, the Unlinker takes the nonsequential

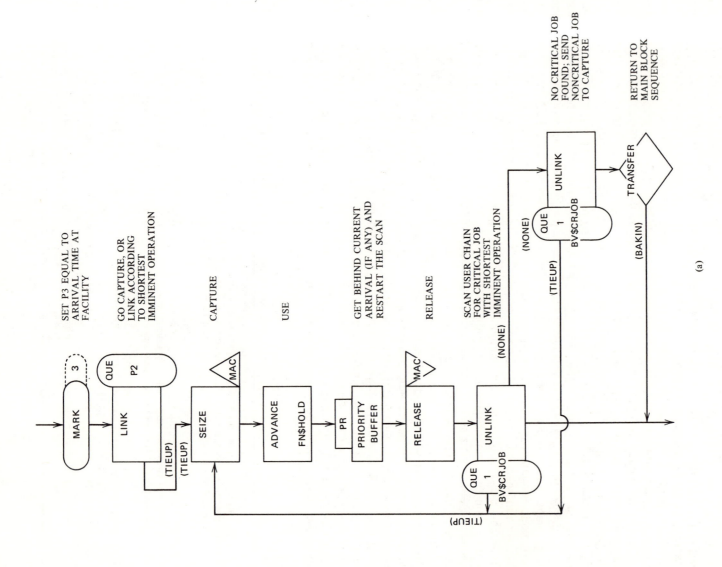

SET P3 EQUAL TO
ARRIVAL TIME AT
FACILITY

GO CAPTURE, OR
LINK ACCORDING
TO SHORTEST
IMMINENT OPERATION

CAPTURE

USE

GET BEHIND CURRENT
ARRIVAL (IF ANY) AND
RESTART THE SCAN

RELEASE

SCAN USER CHAIN
FOR CRITICAL JOB
WITH SHORTEST
IMMINENT OPERATION

NO CRITICAL JOB
FOUND; SEND
NONCRITICAL JOB
TO CAPTURE

RETURN TO
MAIN BLOCK
SEQUENCE

(a)

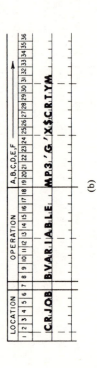

(b)

FIGURE 7.17   A fifth example of User Chain use. (a) Block Diagram segment. (b) Definition of the Boolean Variable CRJOB.

exit from the first UNLINK Block to a second UNLINK Block, where it unlinks the front-end Transaction from the User Chain and sends it to capture.

The Figure 7.17 model segment includes a "PRIORITY PR,BUFFER" Block for the same reason that such a Block is included in the Figure 7.16 model segment. As was the case in Figure 7.16, the Figure 7.17 model segment also assumes that Transactions moving through the model segment have the same Priority Level.

7.13 Exercises

1. For the logic shown in Figure 7.17, the queue discipline used for both critical and noncritical jobs is shortest imminent operation. Show what changes to make in the model so that a first-come, first-served criterion is used for *critical* jobs. As before, shortest imminent operation is to be used as the criterion for selecting the noncritical job to service next.

2. Show how User Chains can be used to solve exercise 7, Section 6.4.

3. At the Facility CHECK, service is provided first to customer-Transactions with a Parameter 5 value of 10 or more. Then service is provided to other Transactions. The queue discipline within each of these two categories is first-come, first-served. Show how a single User Chain can be used to implement this overall queue discipline.

4. At the Facility FLIP, service is provided first to customer-Transactions with a Parameter 7 value of 8 or less. Then service is provided to other Transactions. The queue discipline within each of these two categories is first-come, first-served. Show how a single User Chain can be used to implement this overall queue discipline.

5. Show how to change the model in Case Study 6B (checkout desk at a library) so that whenever people are waiting (either for their checkout slip to be picked up, or for the clerk to hand them the checked-out book), the corresponding Transactions are kept on a User Chain or Chains.

6. Consider using a Storage to simulate parallel servers under the following conditions. The number of servers required by a Transaction is recorded in Transaction Parameter 2, and in general varies from Transaction to Transaction. One Transaction may require 1 server, another may require 2 servers, another may require 3 servers, and so on. The queue discipline practiced at the Storage is essentially first-come, first-served. This queue discipline can be overridden, however, under some circumstances. Suppose, for example, that the following conditions are true.

1. The Storage is full.
2. Several Transactions are waiting on a User Chain to enter the Storage.
3. Proceeding from the front of the User Chain to enter the Storage, the first three Transactions require 3, 1, and 1 servers, respectively.

Now suppose that a Transaction leaves the Storage, thereby freeing one of the servers. The Transaction at the front of the User Chain cannot enter the Storage, because its needs cannot yet be satisfied. The User Chain is therefore polled from front to back in search for a Transaction whose needs can be satisfied. The first such Transaction found, if any, is to be permitted to enter the Storage immediately. In this example, then, the second Transaction is to be unlinked from the User Chain and sent to enter the Storage. This, of course, serves to override the first-come, first-served queue discipline.

Again suppose that conditions (1) through (3) above are in effect, but this time assume that a Transaction leaves the Storage and thereby frees two servers. It is again true that the Transaction at the front of the User Chain cannot yet have its needs satisfied. After the second Transaction is unlinked and sent to enter the Storage, however, there is *still* one available server. As a result, the *third* Transaction should also be unlinked and sent to enter the Storage.

There is, then, a large number of distinct circumstances under which one or more Transactions should be unlinked from the User Chain and permitted to enter the Storage for the problem as described. Nevertheless, it is a simple matter to model this queue discipline with User Chains. Show how to do so.

7. Suppose that Transactions waiting to enter the Storage in exercise 6 are *not* kept on a User Chain, but are simply left in blocked condition on the Current Events Chain. Explain in detail what kind of queue discipline is practiced at the Storage in this case.

8. A hospital blood bank uses a reorder-point, reorder-quantity system to maintain an inventory of whole blood for use during operations, etc. Whenever the inventory position of blood falls to ROP units *and* there is no replenishment order currently enroute from the blood supplier, an order is placed for ROQ units. Lead time for such orders is normally distributed, with mean and standard deviation of 30 and 3 hours, respectively.

The time between consecutive demands for blood is exponentially distributed, with 15 such demands occurring on average each 24-hour day. The number of units of blood required per person (i.e., per demand) is distributed as shown in Table E8. (A "unit" of blood is 450 cubic centimeters, or almost 1 pint.)

TABLE E8

Number of Units Required	Relative Frequency
1	.45
2	.25
3	.15
4	.10
5	.05

If there is a demand for blood which exceeds the number of blood units currently in inventory, an emergency results. What happens then is that all the blood in inventory, if any, is used to help meet the demand; and, in addition, the rest of the blood needed is acquired by a special procedure which will not be described here. Although an emergency does cause stock-on-hand to drop to zero (if it was not already zero), it otherwise has no effect on the hospital in terms of its en route replenishment order. That is, the hospital is not later required to make up the difference to some external agent because the emergency arose.

In addition to receiving blood through normal ordering procedures, the hospital receives blood via donations made by interested persons. The number of donations made each day is normally distributed, with mean and standard deviation of 5 and 1 units, respectively. Donated blood can be assumed to be added to the blood bank at 5 p.m. on the day it was given, and is not available before that time.

Unfortunately, blood deteriorates during storage. That is, blood has a maximum shelf life in inventory. If this shelf life is reached before the blood has been used, the blood must be discarded. Blood donated directly to the hospital has a shelf life of 25 days. Blood arriving via normal replenishment orders has an 18-day shelf life remaining after it arrives.

Because of these shelf-life considerations, demand for blood is met by taking from inventory that still-usable blood which has the shortest remaining lifetime.

Build a GPSS model to simulate this inventory situation. Design the model to estimate the distribution of these two random variables.

1. The number of emergencies which arise per 30-day period.

2. The number of units of blood which must be discarded per 30-day period.

Assume (realistically) that the hospital operates 24 hours per day, 7 days a week. Assume (unrealistically) that replenishment orders can arrive at any time (not just between 8 a.m. and 5 p.m., Monday through Friday), that blood donors give blood seven days a week (not just on certain selected days each week), and that the demand for blood is independent of the time of day. Initially, let there be ROP + ROQ/2 units of blood in inventory, each of these units having a remaining shelf-life of 15

days. When the model has been built, use it to estimate the duration of simulation required to reach an acceptable degree of stability in the mean values of the two random variables of interest. Then conduct additional experiments to determine the behavior of these mean values as a function of ROP and ROQ.

9. Make up clock conditions for exercise 8 which cause that problem to be more realistic. In particular, there should be clock-dependent conditions imposed on these features of the problem.

1. Feasible times of blood arrival via the normal ordering procedure.

2. Time between consecutive demands for blood.

3. Times when blood is donated to the hospital.

Then incorporate these conditions into your model for exercise 8, and repeat the experimentation suggested there.

7.14 The Concept of Facility Preemption

Transactions intending to capture a Facility usually have to wait their turn when they find it is already in use. Sometimes, however, systems are designed to permit a new arrival at an engaged Facility to *displace* the current user. This displacement involves taking the Facility away from the as-yet-unfinished user, in order to let the new arrival capture it immediately. Meantime, the displaced user may wait until the Facility again becomes available, and then re-capture it; or, he may choose to go elsewhere, with or without the intention of eventually coming back to the Facility from which he was displaced. (Synonyms for the term "displace" are "interrupt" and "preempt." The terms "interrupt" and "preempt" are the ones most frequently used in GPSS.)

Many questions immediately come to mind when the possibility of Facility preemption is allowed.[9] Here are some such questions.

1. Under what conditions is a preempt permitted?
2. What is the fate of the preempted Transaction?[10]

---

[9] The ability to preempt one or more servers simulated with the Storage entity is *not* available in GPSS. Hence, as pointed out in Chapter 2, one of the differences between a Facility and a Storage with a capacity of 1 is that the Facility can be preempted, whereas the Storage cannot.

[10] It is not actually a *Transaction* which is preempted; instead, what is pre-empted is the *Facility* which is held by the Transaction. For convenience in the discussion, however, such phrases as "the preempted Transaction" will be used. It should be understood that these phrases mean "the Transaction which was holding the Facility at the time the Facility was preempted."

3. When is a preempted Transaction made subject to its fate? Is it at the time the preempt occurs, or might it be at a later time, depending on the location and status of the Transaction when it was preempted?

In the next three subsections, some of the answers for these questions are provided at the conceptual level. Then, in Sections 7.15 and 7.16, some of the specific implementation details are taken up. Finally, after a case study, some additional features of preemption are considered, and an extended form of the earlier preemption case study is presented. Not all aspects of Facility preemption will be discussed in this book, however; the reader whose interest extends beyond the basics presented here is referred to the user's manual for his GPSS Processor for further details.

7.14.1 Conditions Required for Preemption to Occur

As to the conditions under which a preempt is permitted, there are two possibilities.

1. In the first possibility, a preempt occurs only if the current user is not himself a preempter. Note that a Transaction's Priority Level does not come into play here. Also note that this first possibility permits only "one level" of preemption. One level of preemption means that there can never be more than one interrupted Transaction waiting to recapture a given Facility.

2. In the second possibility, a preempt occurs if the Priority Level of the would-be preempter exceeds that of the current user. Whether the current user is himself a preempter does not matter. Because there are 128 Priority Levels in GPSS, this possibility then provides for up to 127 levels of preemption. That is, under the right circumstances there could be as many as 127 interrupted Transactions waiting to recapture a Facility.

Each of these two possibilities can be used relative to the same Facility in a given model. For example, at Point A in a model, a Transaction may be permitted to preempt Facility 5 only if the current user is not himself a preempter; at Point B, a Transaction may be able to preempt Facility 5 only if its Priority Level is higher than that of the current user.

7.14.2 Alternative Fates for Preempted Transactions

There are three alternative fates for preempted Transactions.

1. The preempted Transaction can simply wait until the Facility again becomes available to it.

2. The preempted Transaction can go elsewhere in the model, without remaining in contention for use of the Facility at which it was preempted.

3. The preempted Transaction can go elsewhere in the model, yet remain in contention for use of the Facility from which it was displaced.

Alternatives 2 and 3 are discussed briefly in Section 7.21. Alternative 1, which is the least complicated of the three possibilities, will be discussed now.

Under Alternative 1, consider first the case in which only one level of preemption is permitted. Suppose that a Transaction has captured a Facility and, while using it, is displaced from the Facility by another Transaction. Assume that at the time it is preempted, the Transaction is either (1) on the Future Events Chain, corresponding to being in an ADVANCE Block where Facility holding time is being simulated, or (2) on the Current Events Chain, scheduled to release the Facility at the simulated time in question. If the Transaction is on the Future Events Chain, the Processor removes it and puts it into inactive status by placing it on a special chain known as an Interrupt Chain. Before this is done, the Processor computes and saves the interrupted Transaction's "remaining holding time," i.e., determines how much longer the Transaction had been scheduled to hold the Facility before releasing it. As soon as the preempting Transaction finishes with the Facility, the Processor automatically causes the interrupted Transaction to recapture it. This involves removing the interrupted Transaction from the Interrupt Chain and placing it back on the Future Events Chain, where it will remain while its previously computed "remaining holding time" elapses.

When a given Transaction has been preempted and then later has the Facility restored to it, there is no reason why the Transaction cannot again be preempted. In fact, there is no limit to the number of times a Transaction can be preempted at a given Facility. This means, then, that the Transaction's overall Facility holding time may be composed of a series of discontinuous slices of time.

Now suppose that the Transaction subject to preemption is on the Current Events Chain, poised to release the Facility at which the preempt occurs. This means that the preemption event and the release event are scheduled to take place at the same time. In fact, if Transaction ordering on the Current Events Chain is such that the release event occurs first, then no displacement of the current user is required. Even if the event sequence is reversed, no displacement should take place either; by hypothesis, the Transaction which is a candidate for displacement is finished with the Facility anyway. In this case, the Processor does the only thing which it is logical to do. During the Current Events Chain scan, it permits the candidate for displacement to release the Facility, and simply continue its forward movement in the model. Consequently, the "candidate" is not put onto an Interrupt Chain in this circumstance.

During the remaining discussion of preemption in this book, this behavior of the Processor when faced with simultaneous preemption and release events should be kept in mind.

Assume now that multiple levels of preemption are possible, and that each preempted Transaction simply waits until the Facility again becomes available to it. As before, the preempted Transactions wait in inactive status on an Interrupt Chain. The ordering property used on the Interrupt Chain is last-in, first-out. In particular, each newcomer is placed on the front of the chain, with the possible exception of the back-end Transaction.[11] Then, when conditions permit an interrupted Transaction to recapture the Facility, the Processor removes the Transaction at the front of the Interrupt Chain for this purpose. Remember that multiple preempts are permitted only when each next preempter has a higher Priority Level than the Transaction being preempted. The "link onto the front of the Interrupt Chain" approach then guarantees that Priority Levels are in strictly descending order from the front of the chain toward the back, with the possible exception of the back-end Transaction.[11] By later removing Transactions from the front of the Interrupt Chain, the interrupted Transaction with the highest Priority Level is then the first to recapture the Facility.

Interrupt Chains are the fourth type of chain used by the GPSS Processor. Each Facility has an Interrupt Chain associated with it. Transaction movement to and from Interrupt Chains is accomplished automatically by the Processor.

[11] As pointed out above, under preemption condition (1), it is possible for a nonpreemptive user of a Facility to be preempted, without regard to its Priority Level. Furthermore, it is possible that preemption conditions (1) and (2) can both be in effect, in different parts of a model, for a given Facility. It is therefore conceivable that the Transaction at the *back* of an Interrupt Chain (i.e., the Transaction which was put onto the chain *first*) has a Priority Level equal to that of another Transaction on the chain, or possibly even higher than that of any other Transaction on the chain.

The only way a Transaction can become resident on such a chain is for it to be preempted while using the corresponding Facility. While a Transaction is on an Interrupt Chain, it does not contribute to the Current Count of any Block in the underlying GPSS model.

Unlike User Chains, but similar to the Current and Future Events Chains, there are no Standard Numerical Attributes for Interrupt Chains. Like the Current and Future Events Chains, nonempty Interrupt Chains are printed out by the Processor at the end of a simulation only if "1" is used as the D Operand on the START card.[12]

The PRINT Block can also be used to print out the Interrupt Chains. For this purpose, the Block's A and B Operands are not used; the field C mnemonic is the single character I. When a Transaction moves into the Block "PRINT ,,I", then, the Interrupt Chains are printed out as a result.

The other two alternative fates of preempted Transactions do not involve placing them in inactive status on an Interrupt Chain when they are preempted; instead, they are left in active status in the model. As indicated earlier, discussion of these other two alternatives will be deferred until Section 7.21.

7.14.3 Effect of a Transaction's Location and Status on the Timing of Its Preemption Fate

The preceding subsection assumed that when it was preempted, a Transaction was either on the Future Events Chain, or on the Current Events Chain. It was further assumed that when the Transaction was on the Current Events Chain, it was poised to release the Facility in question. In these two cases, the preempted Transaction is subjected to its fate at the same simulated time that the preempt occurs. Actually, in the Current Events Chain case, there is no "fate"; the Transaction simply releases the Facility, and goes on its way in the model.

More complicated cases can arise. For example, the Transaction may be on the Current Events Chain in a *blocked condition* when a preempt is put on a Facility it holds. Or, the Transaction might be on a User Chain when the preempt occurs. It is even possible that the preempted Transaction is on an Interrupt Chain

[12] In the printout for Interrupt Chains, it appears that there is only *one* such chain. Transactions on this "one" chain, however, are essentially segregated into subsets, one subset for each Facility involved. In Case Studies 7B and 7C, the Interrupt Chain will be printed out and its appearance will be discussed.

when the preempt takes place. The latter case implies that the Transaction has had two (or more) Facilities captured concurrently, and that it is already in a state of preemption at one Facility when a preempt is put on it at another Facility. Such states of "multi-Facility preemption" are permitted in GPSS. In fact, there is no limit to the number of different Facilities which a Transaction can concurrently hold in a state of capture; this implies that there is no limit to the number of different Facilities at which a Transaction can be preempted concurrently.

In these more complicated cases, the concept of "pending preempts" comes into play. In fact, if a Transaction is not on the Future Events Chain when it is preempted, the GPSS Processor simply "sets a flag" on that Transaction, indicating that a preempt is pending for it. The pending preemption is then implemented only when the Transaction moves into an ADVANCE Block where a positive holding time is computed.[13] Meantime, however, the preempter is permitted to take the Facility when the preempt occurs; it does not have to wait until the preemption which is pending for the as-yet-unfinished user takes place.

Except for the brief discussion above, these more complicated cases concerning the location and status of preempted Transactions will not be taken up in this book.

7.15 Making Preemptive Use of a Facility: The PREEMPT and RETURN Blocks

A Transaction can only preempt a Facility by moving into the PREEMPT Block. This Block, and its A and B Operands, are shown in Figure 7.18.[14] The A Operand indicates the Facility which is subject to possible preemption. The B Operand signals the condition under which a preempt is permitted to take place. When no B Operand is used, preemption occurs only if the current user is not himself a preempter. When the B Operand is used, it must be the two-character sequence PR. In this case, preemption is per-

[13]Under certain conditions, the pending preemption is also implemented when the preempted Transaction moves into an ASSEMBLE, GATHER, or MATCH Block. These three Blocks are discussed at the end of this chapter.

[14]The PREEMPT Block also has optional C, D, and E Operands associated with it. They are introduced in Section 7.21, where the other possible fates of the preempted Transaction are discussed.

mitted only if the would-be preempter has a higher Priority Level than the current user.

It is entirely possible that a Transaction may try to enter a PREEMPT Block when the referenced Facility is not in use. When this happens, the Transaction succeeds in entering the PREEMPT Block, thereby capturing the Facility. Even though no other Transaction has been displaced from the Facility in this case, the Processor still records the capturing Transaction as being a preemptive user of the Facility. In other words, any Transaction which captures a Facility by entering a PREEMPT Block is a preempter of that Facility, by definition.

When a preempt occurs at the PREEMPT Block as shown in Figure 7.18, the interrupted Transaction (if any) is transferred by the Processor from the Future Events Chain to the preceding section. This is true whether or not the PREEMPT Block's B Operand is used. The preempting Transaction then continues its forward movement in the model.

A Transaction which has preempted a Facility (that is,

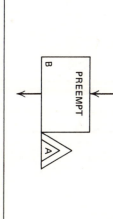

Operand	Significance	Default Value or Result
A	Name (numeric or symbolic) of the Facility to be preempted	Error
B	Optional Operand used to indicate the conditions under which preemption is to be permitted; there are two alternatives.	Explained Under "Significance"

B Operand	Preemption Condition
Not Used (Blank)	A preempt occurs only if the current user is not himself a preempter
PR	A preempt occurs only if the would-be preempter has a higher Priority Level than the current user

FIGURE 7.18 The PREEMPT Block and its A and B Operands

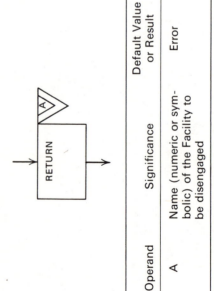

Operand	Significance	Default Value or Result
A	Name (numeric or symbolic) of the Facility to be disengaged	Error

FIGURE 7.19 The RETURN Block and its A Operand

"return" the Facility to the previously interrupted Transaction) by later moving into a RETURN Block. This Block, and its A Operand, are shown in Figure 7.19. The A Operand provides the name of the preempted Facility which is being returned to its displaced user (if any). Analogous to the SEIZE–RELEASE Block pair, only a Transaction which has preempted a Facility is permitted to RETURN it. An error message results if some Transaction other than the preempter itself attempts to execute the RETURN Block.

When the RETURN Block is executed, the Processor removes the Transaction (if any) from the front of the associated Interrupt Chain and restores it as the Facility's capturer of record. This involves linking the Transaction onto the Future Events Chain, scheduled to release (or return) the Facility after the previously computed "remaining holding time" has elapsed. When this restoration has been accomplished, the Processor continues the forward movement of the Transaction which entered the RETURN Block.

Blocking which occurs at a PREEMPT Block is *unique*. As described in Section 7.2, this means that the Processor turns on a Transaction's Scan Indicator when it is blocked while trying to move into a PREEMPT Block. This makes the Transaction scan-inactive. Later, when a RETURN Block is executed for the Facility in question, the Processor (1) turns off the Scan Indicator of all Transactions previously blocked because of the now changed condition, and (2) turns on the Status Change Flag.[15] Later,

when the RETURN-executing Transaction comes to rest, the Processor restarts its scan of the Current Events Chain. The previously blocked Transactions are then given an opportunity to resume their forward movement in the model.

7.16 A Summary of the Methods for Modeling the Use of Facilities

The analyst now has two types of complementary Block pairs at his disposal with which use of a given Facility can be modeled: SEIZE–RELEASE; and PREEMPT–RETURN. It is quite possible that, in a given model, one or more SEIZE–RELEASE Block pairs will be used to reference a given Facility, and that one or more PREEMPT–RETURN Block pairs will be used to reference the same Facility. A certain amount of care must be taken in deciding precisely how to exercise the several options available. The best way to approach the task of modeling the use of a Facility is to first resolve these two questions.

1. How many different Priority Classes do the users fall into.

2. How many levels of preemption (if any) are to be permitted.

Some of the simpler "Priority Class"–"preemption levels" combinations of possible interest are shown in Table 7.5. The feasible alternatives are designated as A, B, C, D, etc., in the table. The combinations which remain blank in the table are not feasible; it is impossible in GPSS to have the number of preemption levels at a Facility exceed the number of different Priority Classes into which users of the Facility fall.

For purposes of discussion, the feasible combinations in Table 7.5 will be divided into five categories. Some combinations fall into more

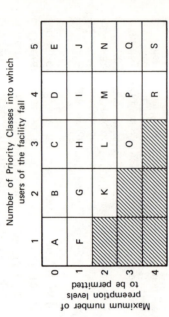

TABLE 7.5 Some Feasible and Infeasible "Priority Class"–"Preemption Levels" Combinations

Maximum number of preemption levels to be permitted	Number of Priority Classes into which users of the facility fall				
	1	2	3	4	5
0	A	B	C	D	E
1	F	G	H	I	J
2		K	L	M	N
3			O	P	Q
4				R	S

[15]The GPSS Processor also turns on the Status Change Flag whenever a PREEMPT Block is executed. The reason for this will be explained in Section 7.19.

than one of the five categories. Here are the categories.

1. Combinations in the "0" row.
2. Combinations in the "1" row.
3. Combinations on the A–G–L–P–S diagonal.
4. Combinations on the F–K–O–R diagonal.
5. Combinations above the A–G–L–P–S diagonal, but not in the "0" row.

The possible ways to model combinations in each of these categories will now be indicated.

Category 1 (Combinations in the "0" row). Combinations in the "0" row correspond to simple nonpreemptive use of a Facility. For such "first-come, first-served, within Priority Class" use of a Facility, the familiar application of the SEIZE–RELEASE Block pair is indicated. Alternatively, *all* the SEIZE–RELEASE Blocks for these cases could be replaced with PREEMPT–RETURN Blocks, assuming the default is taken on the PREEMPT Block's B Operand. Then, only a Facility not already in use could be captured, i.e., no preemption would be permitted.

Category 2 (Combinations in the "1" row). To permit up to one level of preemption (independent of Priority Level), one or more SEIZE–RELEASE Block pairs would be used in the model for the Facility of interest; *and* one or more PREEMPT–RETURN Block pairs would be used for the same Facility. Furthermore, the default would have to be taken on the PREEMPT Block's B Operand. (What could happen otherwise?)

Category 3 (Combinations on the A–G–L–P–S diagonal). These combinations are ones in which the number of preemption levels permitted is one less than the number of Priority Classes into which the users fall. The corresponding queue discipline is "first-come, first-served, within Priority Class, except that preemption is permitted whenever the would-be preempter has a higher Priority Level than the current user." It is almost trivial to model this queue discipline in GPSS. All references to the Facility are simply made with PREEMPT–RETURN Blocks, with PR used as the PREEMPT Block's B Operand.

Note that combination A falls into Category 1 as well as into Category 3. The Category 3 approach consequently offers yet another possibility for combination A. In summary, then, these are the three possibilities for combination A.

1. Make all references with SEIZE–RELEASE Blocks.
2. Make all references with PREEMPT–RETURN Blocks, defaulting on the PREEMPT Block's B Operand.
3. Make all references with PREEMPT–RETURN Blocks, using PR as the PREEMPT Block's B Operand.

Category 4 (Combinations on the F–K–O–R diagonal). For all combinations in this category, the number of preemption levels equals the number of Priority Classes into which users of the Facility fall. Such combinations can be modeled if references are made to the Facility via one or more SEIZE–RELEASE Block pairs, *and* two or more PREEMPT–RETURN Block pairs, at least one of which defaults on the PREEMPT's B Operand, and at least one of which uses PR as the PREEMPT's B Operand. To achieve the indicated level of preemptions, the following events would have to occur in the indicated sequence.

1. A Transaction having the lowest Priority Level involved first captures the Facility at a SEIZE Block.
2. Then, another Transaction also having the lowest Priority Level involved preempts the nonpreemptive user by entering a PREEMPT Block which defaults on the B Operand.
3. Finally, Transactions of increasingly higher Priority Level each preempt the current preempter by entering a PREEMPT Block with PR supplied as the B Operand.

The category 4 combinations admittedly appear to be of little interest. Nevertheless, to illustrate simultaneous use of "SEIZE," "PREEMPT," "PREEMPT with-out PR," and "PREEMPT with PR" Blocks in a single model, combination K in Table 7.5 is used in Case Study 7B (which is presented in the next section). Furthermore, the combination comes about quite naturally in the case study.

Category 5 (Combinations above the A–G–L–P–S diagonal, but not in the "0" row). For each of these combinations, the number of preemption levels is *less* than "one less than the number of Priority Levels involved." Before a preemption can be permitted when any one of these combinations is being modeled, the following two conditions must be true.

1. The number of preemption levels currently in effect must be less than the maximum number of levels permitted.
2. The Priority Level of the would-be preempter must exceed that of the current user of the Facility.

When the PR option is used with the PREEMPT Block, no preemption is permitted unless condition (2) above is satisfied. The PREEMPT Block has no feature, however, whereby preemption can be made to depend in general on the number of preemption levels currently in effect.[16] As a result, to model Category 5 combinations, the analyst must supply his own logic to determine that condition (1) is true. A suggested method for doing this is shown in the form of a Block Diagram segment in Figure 7.20,

Locations symbolically named GOIN and GO-OUT, respectively. The numeric difference between the Total Counts at these two Blocks is one *larger* than the number of Transactions currently preempted at the Facility. (When the current user has not preempted a Transaction, the difference in Block Counts is 1; when the current user preempted a Transaction which did not itself preempt some other Transaction, the difference in Block Counts is 2, and so on.) Suppose that the Variable named PLNOW (i.e., preemption levels _now_) is defined to equal N$GOIN−N$GOOUT−1. Then the value of the Variable equals the number of preemption levels now in effect. Also suppose that the maximum number of preemption levels to be permitted is stored in the Savevalue PLMAX (i.e., preemption levels maximum). Then, for condition (1) to be true, it must be true that V$PLNOW is less than X$PLMAX. This explains the role of the refusal-mode Block "TEST L V$PLNOW,X$PLMAX" in Figure 7.20. Before an oncoming Transaction can even *attempt* to enter the Figure 7.20 PREEMPT Block, the TEST Block must permit it to pass, i.e., condition (1) must be true.

Of course, movement through the Figure 7.20 TEST Block does not necessarily mean that a Transaction can preempt the Facility. For the preempt to occur, the Transaction must also be successful in entering the PREEMPT Block, i.e., condition (2) must be satisfied. Hence, the two conditions originally described must be satisfied before preemption occurs in the Figure 7.20 model segment.

When preemption is denied in the Figure 7.20 model segment, the blocked would-be preempters are held in either one of two Blocks. When condition (1) is true, but not condition (2), the would-be preempters are held *in* the TEST Block. (Note that, although they are *in* the TEST Block, their Next Block Attempted is the PREEMPT Block; in this sense, such blocked Transactions have succeeded in moving "through" the TEST Block.) When condition (1) is not true, the would-be preempters are held in whatever Block precedes the TEST Block. (Their Next Block Attempted is the TEST Block itself.) When there are blocked Transactions in both locations, it is quite possible that some Transactions in the TEST Block have a *lower* Priority Level than some of those in the Block preceding the TEST Block. That is, in terms of the Block they are in, lower priority Transactions can be "ahead of" higher priority Transactions in the

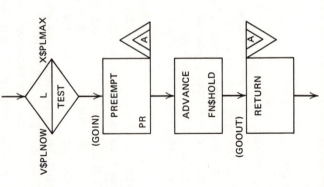

FIGURE 7.20 A Block Diagram segment showing the logic for the "Priority Class"—"preemption level" combinations in Category 5

where, for convenience, the name of the Facility of interest appears in the general form "A". The method is valid for all Category 5 combinations, but it does assume that all captures of the pertinent Facility occur in the Block Diagram segment shown. (This restriction can easily be relaxed. See exercise 8, Section 7.18.) The solution also assumes that use of the Facility involves a simple "PREEMPT–ADVANCE–RETURN" sequence. (This restriction can also be relaxed.)

Note how condition (1) is incorporated into the Figure 7.20 model segment. The PREEMPT and RETURN Blocks in the segment are in the

[16] It is true that when the PREEMPT Block is used *without* the PR option, a preempt takes place only if there are currently *no* levels of preemption in effect. More generality than this, however, is required to model the Category 5 combinations.

Figure 7.20 segment. This happens, for example, if low-priority Transactions arrive at the model segment while condition (1) is true, but not condition (2); and if higher-priority Transactions then arrive at the segment later, when condition (1) is no longer true. Despite this potential "Priority Level scrambling," however, these blocked Transactions of course are still arranged in "first-come, first-served, within Priority Class" fashion on the Current Events Chain. This guarantees that, when the next capture of the Facility occurs, the most highly qualified would-be preempter among the waiting Transactions will be the one to perform the capture. This will be true, independent of the location in which the most highly qualified Transaction is waiting.

Note that with the exception of combinations F and G, the entries in row "1" in Table 7.5 fall into Category 5. This means that the Figure 7.20 model segment applies to row "1" combinations H, I, and J. But, as previously discussed, the row "1" combinations constitute what has been termed Category 2. There are consequently *two* different ways to model the H, I, and J combinations. If the Category 2 approach is used, then one level of pre-emption is permitted, *independent of Priority Level.* If the Category 5 approach is used, then one level of preemption is permitted, but only when the Priority Level of the would-be preempter exceeds that of the current user. There is a nontrivial difference, then, in the two alternative approaches which can be used for combinations H, I, and J.

Finally, in concluding the discussion of the Category 5 combinations, note that entries in the "0" row in Table 7.5 have been *excluded* from the category. This is not *logically* necessary. That is, the Figure 7.20 model segment will work for combinations in row "0" if the Save-value PLMAX is set equal to 0. It would hardly make sense, however, to use the relatively complicated Figure 7.20 approach for the "0" row combinations; simple use of the SEIZE–RELEASE Block pair is indicated for these simple "no preemptions permitted" combinations.

7.17 CASE STUDY 7B
Model of a City's Vehicle-Maintenance Garage

(1) Statement of the Problem

A certain city owns and operates a garage in which maintenance and repair work is performed on city-owned vehicles. Included among these vehicles are motor-pool cars, heavy-duty trucks, and so on. The city is not large; as a result, the garage is equipped with only one service bay, and employs only one mechanic. This means that service can be performed on only one vehicle at a time.

All of the city-owned vehicles are regularly scheduled to come in to the garage for maintenance work. The number of vehicles coming in on a scheduled basis each day is uniformly distributed from 2 to 4. The time required to service one of these vehicles varies uniformly from 1.5 to 2.5 hours. Vehicles scheduled to come in on a given day are all left at the garage at the end of the preceding day. They are therefore already waiting at the garage when each work day begins. A work day itself consists of 8 hours.

Under certain conditions, regularly scheduled maintenance work which is in-progress can be interrupted, so that the service bay can be used for a more important purpose. In particular, the city attempts to keep a full fleet of police cars operating at all times. The police cars are in use 24 hours per day, under demanding conditions. Whenever there is a problem with one of these cars, the car is brought immediately to the garage for unscheduled service. If another vehicle is undergoing scheduled maintenance at the time, the just-arrived police car is permitted to preempt the service bay, so that its repair can begin without delay. However, a police car in need of unscheduled repair is not permitted to preempt another police car on which unscheduled repair is in progress.

Police cars arrive for unscheduled service in a Poisson stream with a mean interarrival time of 48 hours. Of course, if the garage is not open when they arrive, they must wait until 8 a.m. before servicing can begin. Their service time is exponentially distributed, averaging 2.5 hours.

Build a GPSS model with which to simulate the activities at the city's garage. Design the model to estimate the distribution of the random variable "number of police cars out of service for unscheduled repair." Simulate with the model for 25 days, producing snap-interval printout of all information, including the Current Event, Future Event, and Interrupt Chains, at the end of every fifth day. For simplicity, assume that the mechanic works his 8-hour day without taking breaks. Also neglect the "Saturdays and Sundays problem," i.e., neglect the problem of weekends. This is equivalent to assuming that the garage is open seven days a week (see exercise 3, Section 7.18).

(2) Approach Taken in Building the Model

Scheduled Maintenance Segment. Vehicle-Transactions arriving at the garage for scheduled maintenance are nonpreemptive users of the bay-Facility. These vehicle-Transactions move through a self-contained model segment. At 8 a.m. each day, a "master" vehicle-Transaction is brought into the segment. It then enters a SPLIT Block, bringing in the number of offspring-Transactions required to represent the other vehicles scheduled for maintenance that day. These vehicle-Transactions then proceed through a simple SEIZE–ADVANCE–RELEASE Block sequence, and leave the model.

Unscheduled Repair Segment. Police cars in need of unscheduled repair move through the model in their own self-contained segment. Their use of the bay-Facility is simulated with a simple PREEMPT–ADVANCE–RETURN Block sequence. PR is not required as the PREEMPT Block's B Operand; simply by virtue of trying to capture the bay by entering a PREEMPT Block, these Transactions succeed in displacing any nonpreemptive user of the bay. And, because the PR option is not used with the PREEMPT Block, they cannot succeed in displacing a preemptive user of the bay.

In Section 5.11, use of a weighted Table to estimate the distribution of waiting-line length was explained. The self-contained segment presented there for that purpose can be used in this model to estimate the requested distribution of "number of police cars out of service." This only requires that police-car Transactions enter a QUEUE Block when they arrive at the garage, and that they move through a DEPART Block just before they leave the garage. Being out of

service is therefore equivalent to being in the Queue. Then, as explained in Chapter 5, a separate model segment can be used to monitor the content of the Queue, and record appropriate observations in a weighted Table.

Closing and Opening the Garage. A self-contained model segment is used to arrange for closing up the garage at the end of each 8-hour work day, and opening it up again at 8 a.m. the next day. A "boss" Transaction enters the segment every 24 hours (beginning at the end of the first work day). This Transaction, given the highest priority in the model, then immediately moves into a PREEMPT Block which uses the PR option. The boss is consequently permitted to preempt the bay-Facility, independent of whether the current user (if any) is preemptive or nonpreemptive. Then, 16 hours later, the boss returns the bay-Facility, permitting the previously interrupted work (if any) to resume.

Data Gathering for "Out-of-Service" Police Cars. A self-contained model segment is used to gather data with which the distribution of the number of police cars out of service is estimated. The logic of this segment was discussed in Section 5.11, and will not be repeated here.

Snap-Interval Output. A GENERATE–TERMINATE Block sequence is used to produce the requested snap-interval output, and to shut off the simulation at the end of the twenty-fifth day.

Priority Level Considerations. There are several Priority Level considerations worth taking note of in the model. They will be discussed under Model Logic in the subsection at the end of the case study. Before turning to that subsection, the Block Diagram which follows should be reviewed with respect to the ideas which have just been presented.

(3) Table of Definitions

Time unit : 1 Minute

TABLE 7B.1 Table of Definitions for Case Study 7B

GPSS Entity	Interpretation
Transactions	
Model Segment 1	A vehicle scheduled for regular maintenance work
Model Segment 2	A police car in need of unscheduled repair
Model Segment 3	The "boss," who opens the garage each morning and closes it 8 hours later
Model Segment 4	The "observer" who monitors the content of the Queue TRUBL to estimate the distribution of out-of-service police cars
	P1 : Parameter in which clock readings are stored
	P2 : Parameter in which Queue content is stored
Model Segment 5	A snap-interval Transaction
Facilities	
BAY	The service bay in which maintenance and repair work is done
Functions	
JOBS	Describes the uniform distribution from 1 to 3 ; returns values interpretable as one less than the number of vehicles arriving each day for scheduled maintenance
XPDIS	Exponential distribution function
Queues	
TRUBL	The Queue in which police cars are resident while they are out of service
Tables	
LENTH	The Table in which observations on the number of out-of-service police cars are recorded

(4) Block Diagram

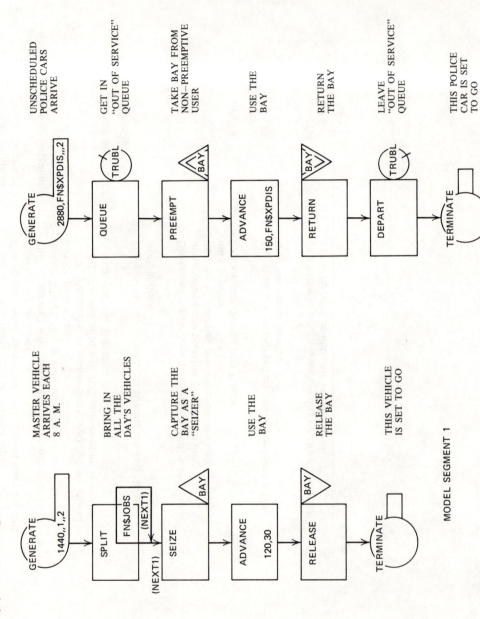

FIGURE 7B.1 Block Diagram for Case Study 7B

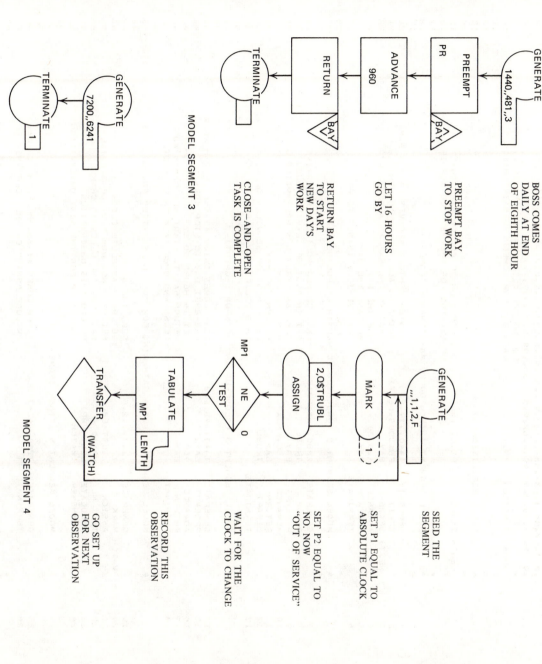

MODEL SEGMENT 3

GENERATE 1440,,481,,3 — BOSS COMES DAILY AT END OF EIGHTH HOUR

PREEMPT PR BAY — PREEMPT BAY TO STOP WORK

ADVANCE 960 — LET 16 HOURS GO BY

RETURN BAY — RETURN BAY TO START NEW DAY'S WORK

TERMINATE — CLOSE-AND-OPEN TASK IS COMPLETE

MODEL SEGMENT 4

GENERATE ,,,1,1,2,F — SEED THE SEGMENT

MARK 1 — SET P1 EQUAL TO ABSOLUTE CLOCK

ASSIGN 2,Q$TRUBL — SET P2 EQUAL TO NO. NOW "OUT OF SERVICE"

TEST NE 0 MP1 — WAIT FOR THE CLOCK TO CHANGE

TABULATE LENTH MP1 — RECORD THIS OBSERVATION

TRANSFER (WATCH) — GO SET UP FOR NEXT OBSERVATION

MODEL SEGMENT 5 (TIMER SEGMENT)

GENERATE 7200,,6241

TERMINATE 1

(5) Extended Program Listing

```
BLOCK
NUMBER   *LOC    OPERATION   A,B,C,D,E,F,G              COMMENTS                                          CARD NUMBER

                 SIMULATE                                                                                 1
                 *                                                                                        2
                 *         FUNCTION DEFINITION(S)                                                         3
                 *                                                                                        4
         XPDIS   FUNCTION    RN1,C24              EXPONENTIAL DISTRIBUTION FUNCTION                        5
         0.0/.1,.104/.2,.222/.3,.355/.4,.509/.5,.69/.6,.915/.7,1.2/.75,1.38                               6
         .8,1.6/.84,1.83/.88,2.12/.9,2.3/.92,2.52/.94,2.81/.95,2.99/.96,3.2                               7
         .97,3.5/.98,3.9/.99,4.6/.995,5.3/.998,6.2/.999,7/.9998,8                                         8
         JOBS    FUNCTION    RN1,C2               NO. OF VEHICLES, "MINUS 1", ARRIVING                     9
         0,1/1,4                                  EACH DAY FOR SCHEDULED MAINTENANCE                       10
                 *                                                                                        11
                 *         TABLE DEFINITION(S)                                                            12
                 *                                                                                        13
         LENTH   TABLE       P2,0,1,W6            DISTRIBUTION OF POLICE CARS OUT                          14
                 *                                 OF SERVICE FOR UNSCHEDULED REPAIR                       15
                 *                                                                                        16
                 *         MODEL SEGMENT 1 (SCHEDULED MAINTENANCE SEGMENT)                                17
                 *                                                                                        18
                 *                                                                                        19
 1               GENERATE    1440,,,2             MASTER VEHICLE ARRIVES EACH 8 A.M.                       20
 2               SPLIT       FN$JOBS,NEXT1        BRING IN ALL THE DAY'S VEHICLES                          21
 3       NEXT1   SEIZE       BAY                  CAPTURE THE BAY AS A "SEIZER"                            22
 4               ADVANCE     120,30               USE THE BAY                                              23
 5               RELEASE     BAY                  RELEASE THE BAY                                          24
 6               TERMINATE                        THIS VEHICLE IS SET TO GO                                25
                 *                                                                                        26
                 *         MODEL SEGMENT 2 (UNSCHEDULED REPAIR OF POLICE CARS)                            27
                 *                                                                                        28
 7               GENERATE    2880,FN$XPDIS,,,2    UNSCHEDULED POLICE CARS ARRIVE                           29
 8               QUEUE       TRUBL                GET IN "OUT OF SERVICE" QUEUE                            30
 9               PREEMPT     BAY                  TAKE BAY FROM NON-PREEMPTIVE USER                        31
10               ADVANCE     150,FN$XPDIS         USE THE BAY                                              32
11               RETURN      BAY                  RETURN THE BAY                                           33
12               DEPART      TRUBL                LEAVE "OUT OF SERVICE" QUEUE                             34
13               TERMINATE                        THIS POLICE CAR IS SET TO GO                             35
                 *                                                                                        36
                 *         MODEL SEGMENT 3 (CLOSE-UP AND OPEN-UP SEGMENT)                                 37
                 *                                                                                        38
14               GENERATE    1440,,481,,3         BOSS COMES DAILY AT END OF 8TH HOUR                      39
15               PREEMPT     BAY,PR               PRE-EMPT BAY TO STOP WORK                                40
16               ADVANCE     960                  LET 16 HOURS GO BY                                       41
17               RETURN      BAY                  RETURN BAY TO START NEW DAY'S WORK                       42
18               TERMINATE                        CLOSE-AND-OPEN TASK IS COMPLETE                          43
                 *                                                                                        44
                 *         MODEL SEGMENT 4 (DATA GATHERING FOR "OUT OF SERVICE" POLICE CARS)              45
                 *                                                                                        46
19               GENERATE    ,,,1,2,F             SEED THE SEGMENT                                         47
20       WATCH   MARK        1                    SET P1 = ABSOLUTE CLOCK                                  48
21               ASSIGN      2,Q$TRUBL            SET P2 = NO. NOW "OUT OF SERVICE"                        49
22               TEST NE     MP1,0                WAIT FOR THE CLOCK TO CHANGE                             50
23               TABULATE    LENTH,MP1            RECORD THIS OBSERVATION                                  51
24               TRANSFER    ,WATCH               GO SET UP FOR THE NEXT OBSERVATION                       52
                 *                                                                                        53
                 *         MODEL SEGMENT 5 (TIMER SEGMENT)                                                54
                 *                                                                                        55
25               GENERATE    7200,,6241           TIMER COMES AT END OF EACH 5TH DAY                       56
26               TERMINATE   1                    PRODUCE "SNAP" OR SHUT OFF THE RUN                       57
                 *                                                                                        58
                 *         CONTROL CARD(S)                                                                59
                 *                                                                                        60
                 START       5,,1,1                                                                       61
                 END                                                                                      62
```

FIGURE 7B.2 Extended Program Listing for Case Study 7B

(6) Program Output

CURRENT EVENTS CHAIN

TRANS	BDT	BLOCK	PR	SF	NBA	SET	MARK-TIME	P1	P2	P3	P4	SI	TI	DI	CI	MC	PC	PF
12		2	2		3	10	5761	0	0	0	0	1		1	2			
								0	0	0	0							
								0	0	0	0							
4	1	21	1		22	4	1	6241	1					1	2			

(a)

FUTURE EVENTS CHAIN

TRANS	BDT	BLOCK	PR	SF	NBA	SET	MARK-TIME	P1	P2	P3	P4	SI	TI	DI	CI	MC	PC	PF
2	7201		2		1	2	-5	0	0	0	0				4			
								0	0	0	0							
								0	0	0	0							
9	7201	16	3		17	9	6241	0	0	0	0				4			
								0	0	0	0							
								0	0	0	0							
8	7681		3		14	8	-5	0	0	0	0				4			
								0	0	0	0							
11	8912		2		7	11	-2	0	0	0	0				4			
								0	0	0	0							
								0	0	0	0							
3	13441				25	3	-1	0	0	0	0				4			
								0	0	0	0							
								0	0	0	0							

(b)

INTERRUPT CHAIN

TRANS	BDT	BLOCK	PR	SF	NBA	SET	MARK-TIME	P1	P2	P3	P4	SI	TI	DI	CI	MC	PC	PF
6	52		2		11	6	6230	0	0	0	0					1		1
								0	0	0	0							
								0	0	0	0							
10	81		2		5	12	5761	0	0	0	0			1	1			1
								0	0	0	0							
								0	0	0	0							

(c)

FIGURE 7B.3   Selected Program Output for Case Study 7B. (a) Current Events Chain (end of day 5). (b) Future Events Chain (end of day 5). (c) Interrupt Chain (end of day 5.

```
FACILITY        AVERAGE            NUMBER          AVERAGE          SEIZING       PREEMPTING
                UTILIZATION        ENTRIES         TIME/TRAN        TRANS. NO.    TRANS. NO.
    BAY           .975               115           297.130            11            10
```

(d)

```
QUEUE       MAXIMUM      AVERAGE     TOTAL     ZERO      PERCENT      AVERAGE      $AVERAGE     TABLE      CURRENT
            CONTENTS     CONTENTS    ENTRIES   ENTRIES   ZEROS        TIME/TRANS   TIME/TRANS   NUMBER     CONTENTS
  TRUBL        4           .221        13                  .0         595.769      595.769
 $AVERAGE TIME/TRANS = AVERAGE TIME/TRANS EXCLUDING ZERO ENTRIES
```

(e)

```
TABLE   LENTH
ENTRIES IN TABLE              MEAN ARGUMENT          STANDARD DEVIATION          SUM OF ARGUMENTS
        150                      .253                      .696                      38.000        NON-WEIGHTED
      35040                      .221                      .540                    7745.000        WEIGHTED

            UPPER       OBSERVED      PER CENT     CUMULATIVE      CUMULATIVE      MULTIPLE      DEVIATION
            LIMIT       FREQUENCY     OF TOTAL     PERCENTAGE      REMAINDER       OF MEAN       FROM MEAN
              0          29143         83.17         83.1            16.8           -.000          -.363
              1           4274         12.19         95.3             4.6           3.947          1.071
              2           1419          4.04         99.4              .5           7.894          2.506
              3            183           .52         99.9              .0          11.842          3.941
              4             21           .05        100.0              .0          15.789          5.377
REMAINING FREQUENCIES ARE ALL ZERO
```

(f)

FIGURE 7B.3   (d) Facility statistics (end of day 25). (e) Queue statistics (end of day 25). (f) Table statistics (end of day 25).

(7) Discussion

Model Logic. It is assumed in the model that a clock reading of "1" corresponds to 8 a.m. on the first day of the simulation. Note, then, that the master vehicle for scheduled maintenance comes into the model at time "1," via the Block "GENERATE 1440,,1,,2" (Block 1, Figure 7B.2). Thereafter, another master vehicle arrives every 24 hours (the A Operand on the GENERATE Block is 1440, which is the number of minutes contained in 24 hours).

The first appearance of a boss Transaction takes place at time 481, via the Block "GENER-ATE 1440,,481,,3" (Block 14, Figure 7B.2). This corresponds to the end of 8 hours on the first day. After that, another boss Transaction arrives every 24 hours.

The first appearance of a snap-interval Trans-action takes place at time 6241, via the Block "GENERATE 7200,,6241" (Block 25, Figure 7B.2). The Offset Interval of 6241 corresponds to the end of the 8th hour on the fifth day of the simulation. After arrival of the first snap-interval Transaction, a successor Transaction enters the model every 5 days.

Note that fullword Parameters are specified for the observer-Transaction in Model Segment 4 (see Block 19, Figure 7B.2). If halfword Parameters were used by default, an overflow error condition would very likely result. The reason is that the simulation does not shut off until time 35041 (corresponding to 25 days plus 8 hours, expressed in minutes). This means that the clock values saved in Parameter 1 of the observer-Transaction could eventually become larger than 32.767, which is the largest value that can be contained in a halfword Parameter.

Now consider the priority scheme used in the model. The various Priority Levels involved are summarized in Table 7B.2. Reading the table

TABLE 7B.2 Priority Level Assignments Used in Case Study 7B

Model Segment	Significance of Transactions	Level
3	The boss	3
1	Scheduled-maintenance vehicles	2
2	Unscheduled-repair police cars	2
4	The Queue-content observer	1
5	Snap-output Transactions	0

from top to bottom is equivalent to viewing the Current Events Chain from front to back. If there is a boss Transaction on the Current Chain, it is at the front of the chain; then come scheduled-maintenance Transactions (if any), and un-scheduled-repair Transactions (if any). These Priority Level 2 Transactions will, in general, be intermixed in terms of their chain positions rela-tive to each other. Finally come the queue-content observer (which is always on the Cur-rent Chain), and the snap-output Transaction (which is only on the chain at the end of each 5th day.)

The boss has the highest priority in the model simply because this is required if he is to suc-cessfully close up for the day by preempting the service bay. As for the scheduled-maintenance and unscheduled-repair Transactions, the only priority considerations are that they be (1) of lower priority than the boss, and (2) of higher priority than the snap-output Transactions. This latter condition guarantees that the model will be fully updated with respect to vehicle move-ment before each snap-output is produced.

There is an additional restriction on the pri-ority of unscheduled-repair Transactions. Their priority must be higher than that of the queue-content observer. Such an arrangement guar-antees that the queue content is completely up to date before the observation is made on it. This consideration explains why the priority of the queue-content observer is less than 2. The other consideration with respect to the observer is that he should be ahead of the snap-output Transaction on the Current Chain, so that the latest observation will be included in the Table when the snap-output is produced. The position of the observer behind police cars, but ahead of the snap-Transaction, is consequently explained.

Actually, whenever a snap-Transaction is put onto the Current Chain, the observer is already there (because it is always there). This means that the observer could have the same Priority Level as the snap-Transaction, and their relative ordering would still always be the one desired. The explicit priority distinction has been made in the model simply to emphasize the desired relative ordering of these Transactions.

As implied above, the snap-output Trans-action has the lowest priority of all to guarantee that output is not produced until the state of the system has been fully updated at the simulated time in question.

Program Output.[17]   In parts (a) and (b) of Figure 7B.3, the Current and Future Events Chains are shown as they appear at the end of the fifth day in the simulation. On the Current Events Chain, Transaction 12 is a scheduled-maintenance vehicle, waiting to capture the Facility BAY at the SEIZE Block in Location 3. (Its Next Block Attempted is Block 3. Figure 7B.2 indicates that this is the SEIZE Block in Model Segment 1.) Note that Transaction 12 is uniquely blocked (a "1" is entered in its Scan Indicator column.) Transaction 4 on the Current Events Chain is the observer-Transaction, which is blocked at the refusal-mode TEST Block in Model Segment 4 (Block 22, Figure 7B.2). Its Scan Indicator entry is "blank," meaning that its blocking condition is nonunique.

Transactions 2, 8, 11, and 3 on the Future Events Chain are incipient arrivals at the GEN-ERATE Blocks in Locations 1, 14, 7, and 25, respectively, in the model. This can be deter-mined from their Next Block Attempted informa-tion. Transaction 9 on the Future Events Chain is the boss Transaction which is the current user of the Facility BAY. Its Next Block Attempted is 17. As indicated in Figure 7B.2, Block 17 is the RETURN Block at which the boss will make the Facility BAY available for the next day's work.

The Interrupt Chain as it appears at the end of the fifth simulated day is shown in Figure 7B.3(c). There are two Transactions resident on the chain. Note that the various column labels for the Inter-rupt Chain are identical to those for the Current and Future Events Chain.

Transaction 10 on the Interrupt Chain is the nonpreemptive Facility user which is as yet un-finished with the Facility. It is known to be a nonpreemptive user because its Next Block At-tempted is Block 5, which is the RELEASE Block in Model Segment 1. The other Transaction on the Interrupt Chain, Transaction 6, is a pre-emptive Facility user which has itself been pre-empted. It is known to be a preemptive user of the Facility because its Next Block Attempted is Block 11, which is the RETURN Block in Model Segment 2.

The Interrupt Chain entries under the BLOCK column are blank. (Remember that the BLOCK column indicates which Block a Transaction is currently in.) When a Transaction is inactive status on an Interrupt Chain, it is not in any Block, which explains the blank BLOCK entries.

While on an Interrupt Chain, then, a Transaction does not contribute to the Current Count at any Block in a model.

The Interrupt Chain's BDT (Block Departure Time) column in Figure 7B.3(c) shows values of 52 and 81 for Transactions 6 and 10, respectively. *For each Transaction on an Interrupt Chain, the BDT entry can be interpreted as its remaining holding time at the Facility from which it has been displaced.* Hence, the preemptive Facility user has 52 time units to go before it will be done with the Facility. Similarly, the nonpreemptive Facility user has 81 time units to go before it will be done with the Facility.

The Interrupt Chain contains no information which tells directly which Facility it is from which the various chain residents have been displaced. Of course, there is only one Facility in the case study, so that the "which Facility" question is of little interest here. In general, the "which Facility" question can be answered by the analyst only by using the Interrupt Chain's Next Block Attempted information, in conjunc-tion with the model itself.

By coincidence, the ordering of Transactions in the Figure 7B.3(c) Interrupt Chain printout is identical to the internal ordering of the chain. That is, both in the printout and internally, Trans-action 6 is at the front of the Interrupt Chain, and Transaction 10 is at the back of the chain. In general, however, the ordering of Transactions in Interrupt Chain printout will *not* be identical to the internal chain ordering. The reason for this is that Interrupt Chain printout is always ordered from top to bottom according to *increas-ing Transaction number.* The probability is small that this ordering will match the internal ordering as well.

In chain printouts, the label CI appears over the fourth-to-last column. CI stands for "Chain Indicator." Values of blank or "1" in the CI column indicate that the corresponding Trans-actions are on a User Chain or an Interrupt Chain, respectively. Values of 2 or 4 indicate that the Transactions are on the Current or Future Events Chains, respectively. Except for User Chains, these statements can be verified in parts (a), (b), and (c) of Figure 7B.3.

The CI values are important only for internal purposes. They cannot be externally addressed by the analyst. Appearance of the CI values in chain printouts is actually redundant, because the various chains are otherwise labeled anyway.

The rightmost two columns in chain printouts

---

[17]Total CPU time for the simulation on an IBM 360/67 computer was 3.6 seconds.

are labeled PC and PF. PC stands for "Preempt Count." It is a count of the number of different Facilities from which the corresponding Transaction is currently displaced. This checks with the values of 1 entered under the PC column in part (c) of Figure 7B.3, and the "blank" (that is, zero) entries under the PC column for the Current and Future Events Chains in parts (a) and (b) of the figure.

PF stands for "Preempt Flag." A "1" in this column indicates that the corresponding Transaction has a preempt "pending" for it. When a Transaction's Preempt Flag is "on" (that is, has a value of 1), the preempt which is pending is carried out the next time the Transaction moves into an ADVANCE Block at which a nonzero holding time is specified. (Also see footnote 13 in Section 7.14.) If a Transaction is already in an ADVANCE Block when it is preempted (meaning it is on the Future Events Chain), then the concept of a "pending" preempt does not apply; in such a case, the Transaction is removed immediately from the Future Events Chain, and is subjected to whatever fate the analyst has specified for it.

Figure 7B.3(d) displays statistics for the Facility BAY at the end of the fifth simulated day. Note that values of 10 and 9 appear in the statistics under the SEIZING TRANS. NO. and PREMPTING TRANS. NO. columns, respectively. This is consistent with the Transaction information appearing in the Interrupt and Future Events Chain printouts. The Interrupt Chain shows that Transaction 10 is a displaced nonpreemptive user of the Facility, as discussed above; and the Future Events Chain shows that Transaction 9 is currently the user of the Facility, on a nonpreemptive basis. (Remember that the Next Block Attempted information on the chains had to be interpreted in terms of Block Location Numbers to determine whether the corresponding Transactions were preemptive or nonpreemptive users of the Facility.)

Parts (e) and (f) in Figure 7B.3 show Queue and Table statistics produced after 25 simulated days. The Queue statistics indicate that the average out-of-service time for a police car requiring unscheduled repair was 595 time units, or about 10 hours. The Queue statistics also show that on average, 0.221 police cars were out-of-service, and that as many as four were out-of-service concurrently. During the 25-day period, 13 police cars came in for unscheduled repair.

Statistics for the Table LENTH in part (f) of Figure 7B.3 provide more detailed information about out-of-service police cars than is provided in the Queue statistics. The mean weighted argument in the Table is 0.221. This statistic is interpretable as the average number of out-of-service police cars, which is consistent with the value in the Queue statistics. The Table information also shows that 83 percent of the time, no police cars were out-of-service for unscheduled repair. Twelve percent of the time, one car was out of service; 4 percent of the time, two cars were out of service; and only 0.52 and 0.5 percent of the time were three or four cars, respectively, concurrently out of service.

7.18 Exercises

1. (a) In Figure 2A.1 (the Block Diagram for Case Study 2A), what queue discipline does the barber practice if "SEIZE JOE" is replaced with "PREEMPT JOE", and "RELEASE JOE" is replaced with "RETURN JOE"?

   (b) Repeat (a), but assume "SEIZE JOE" is replaced with "PREEMPT JOE,PR".

   (c) Show four different ways to replace the SEIZE and RELEASE Blocks in Figure 2B.2 (the Block Diagram for Case Study 2B) with PREEMPT and RETURN Blocks without changing the first-come, first-served queue discipline practiced by the barber.

   (d) In Figure 2C.3 (the Block Diagram for Case Study 2C), the queue discipline practiced by the tool crib clerk is first-come, first-served, within Priority Class. What queue discipline will the clerk practice under each of the following alternative changes in the model?

   (i) Replace both "SEIZE CLERK" Blocks with "PREEMPT CLERK" Blocks, and replace both "RELEASE CLERK" Blocks with "RETURN CLERK" Blocks.

   (ii) In Model Segment 1, replace "SEIZE CLERK" and "RELEASE CLERK" Blocks with "PREEMPT CLERK" and "RETURN CLERK", respectively, but make no other changes.

   (iii) In Model Segment 1, replace "SEIZE CLERK" and "RELEASE CLERK" with "PREEMPT CLERK,PR" and "RETURN CLERK", respectively, but make no other changes.

   (iv) Replace both "SEIZE CLERK" Blocks with "PREEMPT CLERK,PR" Blocks, and replace both "RELEASE CLERK" Blocks with "RETURN CLERK" Blocks.

   (v) In Model Segment 2, replace "SEIZE CLERK" Blocks and "RELEASE CLERK" with

"PREEMPT CLERK" and "RETURN CLERK", respectively, but make no other changes.

(vi) In Model Segment 2, replace "SEIZE CLERK" and "RELEASE CLERK" with "PREEMPT CLERK,PR" and "RETURN CLERK,PR", respectively, but make no other changes.

2. These questions pertain to Case Study 7B.

(a) Show how to replace the Queue named TRUBL with a Savevalue. Discuss the differences in the information which would appear in the output if this were done.

(b) Would the logic of the model be changed if PR were supplied as the B Operand at the PREEMPT Block in Location 9 (see Figure 7B.2)?

(c) Show what changes to make in the model so that it is unnecessary to use the SEIZE–RELEASE Block pair.

(d) Would the logic of the model still be valid if Transactions simulating scheduled-maintenance vehicles were given a Priority Level of 1?

(e) Suppose that this sequence of events takes place. At the end of a given day, a vehicle is using the service bay on a scheduled-maintenance basis. Overnight, a police car is brought in for unscheduled repair. Describe what happens in the model when the garage opens at 8 a.m. the next day.

(f) Show what changes to make in the model so that it will estimate the distribution of the random variable "number of scheduled-maintenance vehicles which have not yet been serviced by the end of the day."

3. In its current form, the model in Case Study 7B behaves as though the garage is open 8 hours a day, 7 days a week. It would be more typical for the garage to be open only Monday through Friday. There would then be no maintenance scheduled for Saturdays or Sundays. The need for unscheduled repair of police cars would continue, however, 7 days a week; in particular, police cars would break down on Saturdays and Sundays as well as during the other days of the week. Any cars breaking down on the weekends would then stack up for Monday morning service. Furthermore, any unserviced police cars in the garage as of closeup time on Friday would remain unavailable throughout the weekend.

Show how to change the Case Study 7B model so that the garage is closed on Saturdays and Sundays. Assume that the simulation is to start on a Monday morning.

4. It is not clear in Case Study 7B how much is gained by letting police cars which come in for unscheduled repairs preempt the current user (if any) of the service bay. Change the model so that incoming police cars must wait their turn for service on a first-come, first-served basis. Then simulate with your model, and compare and contrast the results with those obtained when preempts are allowed. To make the comparisons as fair as possible, simulate with both alternatives under identical sets of circumstances. This means that the Case Study 7B model will have to be modified to permit strict control of experimental conditions.

5. Consider this variation on Case Study 7B. As in the case study, police cars brought in for unscheduled repair arrive in a Poisson stream at a mean rate of one car every 48 hours. The cars are classified into two categories, however, depending on the degree of repair they require. Repair time for category-1 cars is exponentially distributed, with a mean of 2 hours. Half the cars are in this category. The rest of the cars are in category 2, requiring a mean repair time of 4 hours, also exponentially distributed. If a category-2 car is using the service bay when a car in category-1 arrives, the category-1 car is permitted to preempt the bay. As before, independent of their category, cars brought in for unscheduled repair are permitted to preempt the bay if it is being used for scheduled maintenance.

Show how to modify the model for Case Study 7B to reflect these changes.

6. Exercise 6, Section 3.17, involves a work center in a job shop. Three different types of jobs move through the work center. It is of interest to model the center to estimate the expected waiting time (including service) for each of the three types of jobs when the queue discipline is (a) first-come, first-served, and (b) first-come, first-served, within priority class.

Build models for the exercise cited, but extend the problem so that the distribution of waiting time (including service) will be estimated, and so that these two additional queue disciplines will be considered: (1) one level of preempting is permitted, according to relative job importance; (2) two levels of preempting are permitted, according to relative job importance. Control experimental conditions, so that comparison of the alternative queue disciplines can be made in as fair a manner as possible.

7. Referring to the Block Diagram segment in Figure 7.20, suppose that an analyst decides to put the symbolic Location name users on the ADVANCE Block, and then interpret the value of W$USERS–1 as the number of preemption levels currently in effect. Why would this approach be in error?

8. At Facility 5 in a model, the queue discipline to be practiced corresponds to combination M in Table 7.5. Furthermore, PREEMPT–RETURN Block pairs must be used in two different segments of the model. Show what changes to make in the Figure 7.20 "restricted solution" for combination M so that the combination can be successfully modeled under these conditions.

9. In Table 7.5, combination J falls into Category 2 *and* into Category 5. When combination J is modeled, is there a difference in effect, depending on whether the Category 2 or the Category 5 approach is used? Explain.

10. As indicated in Section 7.2, blockage which occurs at a refusal-mode TEST Block is *nonunique*. This means that if many Transactions are delayed, on average, at the Figure 7.20 TEST Block, relatively high execution times may result. Show a Block Diagram segment which, while accomplishing the same purpose as the Figure 7.20 segment, keeps as many of the waiting Transactions as possible on a User Chain.

7.19 Testing the Logical Status of Facilities Subject to Preemption

When the SEIZE Block was introduced in Chapter 2, it was indicated that Transactions can test the logical status of a Facility "directly," simply by trying to move into a SEIZE Block. Then, with introduction of the GATE Block in Chapter 5, a method was provided whereby Transactions can "indirectly" test the logical status of Facilities. The type of test conducted at a GATE Block is indirect, because the test does not itself involve an actual attempt to capture a Facility. Next, with introduction of the logical-mode SELECT Block in Chapter 5, another method was made available for indirectly testing the logical status of Facilities. Finally, through introduction of Boolean Variables in Chapter 6, yet another method for indirectly examining Facility logical status was provided.

The various tests summarized above all have to do with whether a Facility is "in use" or not. But now, because of the preemption concept, there is not just a question of whether a Facility is in use; there is the additional question of whether it is being used by a preempter or not. That is, the *type* of user now becomes a consideration.

In GPSS, the analyst is provided with the ability to make distinctions among preemptive and nonpreemptive users of Facilities. This is done by supplying additional Logical Mne-

monics which can be used to test the status of Facilities at GATE and SELECT Blocks. Additional Logical Operators are provided, too, to expand the range of conditions which can be represented in Boolean Variables. In the following two subsections, these additional Logical Mnemonics and Logical Operators will be discussed.

7.19.1 Additional Logical Mnemonics for GATE and SELECT Blocks

In Sections 5.21 and 5.22, the Logical Mnemonics U and NU were introduced as Auxiliary Operators which could be used with GATE and SELECT Blocks to test the logical status of Facilities. U and NU represent "in use" and "not in use," respectively. If a Facility is in use, then the "in use" condition is true, *independent of whether the user is a preempter or not.* In some contexts, it may be important to know not just that a Facility is in use, but whether its user is a preempter or a "seizer," i.e., whether the capture was made at a PREEMPT Block or at a SEIZE Block. For this reason, the two additional Logical Mnemonics shown in Table 7.6 are supplied for use with the GATE and SELECT Blocks. The Logical Mnemonic "I" can be thought of as meaning "Interrupted"; similarly, the Logical Mnemonic "NI" can be thought of as meaning "Not Interrupted."

TABLE 7.6 Additional Logical Mnemonics for the GATE and SELECT Blocks

Logical Mnemonic	Meaning
I	Test for Facility in use by a preempter
NI	Test for Facility not in use by a preempter

The meaning of the Table 7.6 Logical Mnemonics should be considered carefully. For example, to say that a Facility is "not in use by a preempter" is not the same as saying it is "not in use at all." "Not in use by a preempter" can be *true* when, at the same time, "not in use" is *false.* Similarly, "in use by a preempter" can be *false* when, at the same time, "in use" is *true.*

Several examples for use of the Table 7.6 Logical Mnemonics are shown in Figure 7.21. When a Transaction arrives at the Figure 7.21(a) GATE Block, it moves through to the sequential Block if the Facility ALINE is being used by a preempter; otherwise, it moves to the nonse-

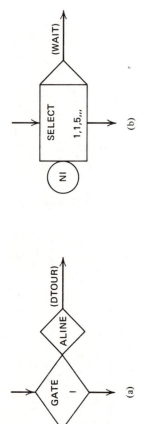

FIGURE 7.21   Examples for use of the Table 7.6 Logical Mnemonics. (a) A GATE Block example. (b) A SELECT Block example.

quential Block in the Location DTOUR. When a Transaction enters the Figure 7.21(b) SELECT Block, the Processor scans Facilities 1 through 5 in search for the first one (if any) which is not currently being used by a preempter. If such a Facility is found, its number is put into Parameter 1 of the selecting Transaction, which then moves to the sequential Block. If no such Facility is found, the selecting Transaction moves to the nonsequential Block in the Location WAIT.

Now consider the circumstances under which one or more Transactions might be blocked at a refusal-mode "GATE I" or "GATE NI" Block. These circumstances fall into a simple "cause and remedy" category, and therefore qualify for designation as unique blocking conditions, per the Section 7.2 discussion. Furthermore, as was already pointed out in Section 7.15, a Transaction blocked at a PREEMPT Block is undergoing a unique blocking condition. These several blocking conditions are summarized in Table 7.7, which is presented as an extension of Table 7.1. Note that the PREEMPT and GATE NI blocking conditions have a common remedy, execution of a corresponding RETURN Block. As a result, they constitute only one category of blocking condition.

As explained earlier, when a Transaction encounters a unique blocking condition, its Scan Indicator is turned on. This makes the Transaction scan-inactive, resulting in execution-time economies during subsequent scans of the Current Events Chain. Then, when a corresponding "remedy Block" is executed, the Processor (1) turns off the Scan Indicator of all pertinent blocked Transactions, thereby making them scan-active again, and (2) turns on the Status Change Flag. When the scan of the Current Events Chain is subsequently restarted, an attempt is then made to move the previously blocked Transactions forward in the model.

Table 7.7 makes it clear why the Status Change Flag is turned on when a PREEMPT Block is executed. The reason is that there may be Transactions blocked at a refusal-mode GATE, waiting for a Facility to be put into a state of preemption. To allow for this possibility, the Processor restarts the scan of the Current Events Chain whenever a preempt is put on a Facility.

7.19.2   Additional Logical Operators for Boolean Variables

Table 6.1 in Section 6.2 displays a list of Logical Operators which can be used in Boolean expressions to reference the logical status of Facilities, Storages, and Logic Switches. The Logical Operators presented there for Facilities are FU (or F) and FNU, for "Facility in Use" and "Facility Not in Use," respectively. Analogous to the situation with the GATE and SELECT Blocks, these operators do not distinguish between Facilities in use by a preempter, and those in use by a "seizer." For this reason, the two additional Logical Operators shown in Table 7.8 can be used to construct elements in Boolean expressions. As usual, when these operators are used, the number or symbolic name of the Facility in question must also be supplied. For example,

TABLE 7.7   Two Additional Unique Blocking Conditions, and Their Remedies

Blocking Condition Number	Block(s) Producing Blocking Condition	Block Which Must be Executed to Remove Blocking Condition[a]
10	{ PREEMPT GATE NI	RETURN
11	GATE I	PREEMPT

[a]Assuming the Facility referenced is the one responsible for the blockage.

TABLE 7.8 Additional Logical Operators for Facilities

Logical Operators	Entity Condition Referenced
FI	Facility in use by a preempter
FNI	Facility not in use by a preempter

FIGURE 7.22 An example of a Table 7.8 Logical Operator used in a Boolean Variable

suppose that a Boolean Variable is to be *true* only when the Facility LARRY is in use by a "seizer." Figure 7.22 shows a Boolean Variable which meets this requirement. Note that there is no *single* Logical Operator which can be used to convey the logic expressed by the Figure 7.22 Variable.

7.20 CASE STUDY 7C
A Second Tour Through Case Study 7B

(1) Statement of the Problem

Case Study 7B involved modeling a city's vehicle-maintenance garage. Because the city was small, there was only one service bay and one mechanic at the garage. City-owned vehicles used the garage principally on a scheduled-maintenance basis. If ever a police car required unscheduled repair, however, it was permitted to preempt the service bay if its current user was a scheduled-maintenance vehicle. The objective of such preemptive queue discipline was to minimize the number of police cars out of service because of the need for unscheduled repair.

Now model the same system on a scaled-up basis, in the simple sense of assuming that the city is large enough to have five service bays and five mechanics at its vehicle-maintenance garage. Let the number of vehicles coming in for scheduled maintenance each day be uniformly distributed between 12 and 18, instead of between 2 and 4. This is equivalent to multiplying the Case Study 7B average by 5, but multiplying the extremes by less than 5 because an attempt would presumably be made to even the work-load somewhat. Continue to let police cars arrive for unscheduled repair in a Poisson stream, but at a rate of five cars every 2 days, instead of one every 2 days. Use the same preemptive queue discipline that was used in Case Study 7B, and make the other assumptions made there.

That is, assume the mechanics work their 8-hour day without taking breaks, and neglect the "Saturdays and Sundays problem." Simulate for 25 days, then compare and contrast the distribution of out-of-service vehicles with that found in Case Study 7B. Also produce statistical print-out at the end of every fifth day, including print-out of the various chains used in the model.

(2) Approach Taken in Building the Model

The approach used in building the model parallels that used in Case Study 7B in the sense that five self-contained model segments are used. Several interesting variations on the Case Study 7B approach are required, however, in Model Segments 1, 2, and 3. The variations for these model segments will be discussed below.

But before discussing the model segments, note first of all from the problem statement that the service-bay/mechanic combinations are homogeneous. That is, they do not have individual characteristics which make it necessary to model them on an individual basis. Despite this fact, the Storage entity cannot be used to simulate these five combinations, because preemptive use of servers simulated with a GPSS Storage is not feasible. As a result, despite their homogeneity, the five service-bay/mechanic combinations must be modeled with five Facilities operating in parallel.

Given this parallel-Facility requirement, the individual model segments can now be discussed.

Model Segment 1 (Scheduled Maintenance Segment). Recall that, in Case Study 4D (Alternative Queuing Systems in a Bank), the multiple-line system made use of Facilities operating in parallel. When a customer arrived at the bank, he either captured an immediately available teller, or went to the back of the shortest waiting line. In that system, then, there were individual waiting lines which formed in front of each server.

The implication in the current system is that there is only one line of scheduled-maintenance vehicles at the garage. When the day begins at 8 a.m., the scheduled-maintenance vehicles do not commit themselves to a particular service bay if they find they must wait. They simply line up, one behind the other, in a single line. When they reach the front of the line, they go to whichever service bay next becomes available to vehicles of the scheduled-maintenance type.

The queuing system for scheduled-maintenance vehicles, then, can be described as a "one-line, multiple *individual servers*" system. There are two decision-making needs in such a system in the context of this case study.

1. At the beginning of the day, how does a scheduled-maintenance vehicle know whether there is still a service bay for it to capture, or whether it must get in line?

2. When the time comes for a previously waiting scheduled-maintenance vehicle to capture a service bay, how does it know which bay is available?

As was the case in the multiple-line banking model, use of the SELECT Block to answer these two questions is indicated. In fact, simply by entering the Block "SELECT NU 1,1,5,,,WAIT", a scheduled-maintenance Transaction can answer the above questions. But then the additional question comes up, what should scheduled-maintenance Transactions do when they take the nonsequential exit from the SELECT Block? In the multiple-line bank model, in equivalent circumstances they proceeded to *another* SELECT Block to find the shortest waiting line, then proceeded to wait in a unique blocking condition on the Current Events Chain. But in the present problem, with its one-line, individual-server feature, scheduled-maintenance Transactions which have to wait cannot yet make such a commitment to a particular service bay. There is no way, then, for them to proceed to wait in either a unique or a nonunique blocking condition on the Current Events Chain. Then where *can* they wait? There is really only one possibility. They must wait on a User Chain. That is, when scheduled-maintenance Transactions take the nonsequential exit from the Block "SELECT NU 1,1,5,,,WAIT", they must go into an unconditional-mode LINK Block. This causes such Transactions to wait in inactive status in the model. Later, when a scheduled-maintenance Transaction releases a service bay, it can unlink one of these waiting Transactions and send it back into the Block "SELECT NU 1,1,5,,,WAIT". On this reentry to the SELECT Block, the scheduled-maintenance Transaction will be able to make a commitment to a specific service bay; then, taking the sequential exit from the SELECT Block, it will move forward into a SEIZE Block to capture that particular bay as a nonpreemptive user.

Model Segment 2 (Unscheduled Repair of Police Cars). The pattern just described for Model Segment 1 can also be used for Model Segment 2. That is, unscheduled-repair police cars also go through a "one-line, multiple individual server" queuing system at the garage. At first, it might be thought that there would never be a line of unscheduled-repair cars in the system; after all, for such a line to form, all five service bays would have to be already in use by unscheduled-repair cars. But this is not true. Any unscheduled-repair cars which arrive at the garage during nonworking hours have no choice but to wait. Hence, for the system described, there will almost certainly be a line of unscheduled-repair police cars from time to time.

In Model Segment 2, however, there are two noticeable variations on Model Segment 1. First of all, Transactions moving through Model Segment 2 have the right to be preemptive users of a service bay. These Transactions consequently go through one or both of these decision-making steps.

1. Is there a bay not in use? If so, capture it. Otherwise, continue to the next decision step.

2. Is there a bay which, although in use, is not already preempted? If so, capture it. Otherwise, go to the back of a User Chain to wait for a bay to be returned by one of the current preempters.

The Blocks corresponding to decision steps 1 and 2 can be "SELECT NU 1,1,5,,,SCAN3", and "SCAN3 SELECT NI 1,1,5,,,NOLUK", respectively. The first SELECT Block is similar to the one in Model Segment 1. The principle feature of the second SELECT Block is that the Logical Mnemonic NI (instead of NU) is used. Police cars, then, scan first for not-in-use Facilities; if necessary, they go on to scan for noninterrupted Facilities. If they take the nonsequential exit from the second SELECT Block, they go to the Location NOLUK, where they are linked onto a User Chain via an unconditional-mode LINK Block.

The other variation required on Model Segment 1 involves the behavior of an unscheduled-repair Transaction after it has returned a service bay. Knowing that there is now a service bay available for preemption, the would-be unlinker-Transaction first attempts to unlink a Transaction from the unscheduled-repair User Chain and send it to preempt the bay. But it is possible that the User Chain containing these "special" (that is, unscheduled-repair) Transactions is empty. In this event, an attempt must then be made to un-link a Transaction from the "regular" User Chain (that is, the User Chain containing the scheduled-repair Transactions) and send it to capture the now-available Facility. In fact, if the "special" User Chain is empty, the unscheduled-repair Transaction can simply take the non-sequential exit from the UNLINK Block in Model Segment 2 and go to the Model Segment 1 UNLINK Block which references the "regular" User Chain.

Model Segment 3 (Close-up and Open-up Segment).

The boss Transactions which move through Model Segment 3 must be slightly more sophisticated than the equivalent boss Transactions in Case Study 7B. This reflects itself in two ways. First of all, instead of preempting just one Facility at the end of the day, a boss Transaction must preempt all five Facilities in the model. It can do this conveniently in a loop. Similarly, at the beginning of each day, the current boss Transaction can return all five Facilities by moving through a loop five times.

In Case Study 7B, the boss was done when it had returned the single Facility at the beginning of a day. In the present case study, however, the boss is not yet done when the Facilities have been returned. Consider the reason why. In Case Study 7B, any unscheduled-repair cars which had come in during the night were waiting on the Current Events Chain. As the Current Chain was scanned, then, at the beginning of a day, the corresponding Transactions were given a chance to preempt the service bay if conditions permitted it. In contrast to this, in the current case study any unscheduled-repair cars which come in during nonworking hours are doing their waiting on a User Chain, not on the Current Chain. The boss must unlink them before he leaves and put them on the Current Chain; otherwise, the GPSS Processor will not see them in its Current Chain scan at open-up time. If the Processor does not see them at open-up time, they are not given their rightful chance to preempt a service bay, and the logic of the model will be sour.

There is another feature of Model Segment 3 in this case study which makes it differ from that in Case Study 7B. It has to do with Priority Levels. Instead of now discussing the overall Priority Level scheme used in the model, however, the discussion will be deferred until the end of the case study. At this time, the best thing to do next is to study the Block Diagram, apart from Priority Level considerations, in terms of the discussion which has taken place so far.

Model Segments 4 and 5.

These two model segments correspond to the data-gathering segment and the timer segment, respectively. They can both be used in the present case study in their Case Study 7B form, without variation.

(3) Table of Definitions

TABLE 7C.1 Table of Definitions for Case Study 7C

Time Unit: 1 Minute

GPSS Entity	Interpretation
Transactions	
Model Segment 1	A vehicle scheduled for regular maintenance work
Model Segment 2	A police car in need of unscheduled repair
Model Segment 3	The "boss," who opens the garage each morning and closes it 8 hours later
Model Segment 4	The "observer" who monitors the content of the Queue TRUBL to estimate the distribution of out-of-service police cars
Model Segment 5	A snap-interval Transaction
P1:	Parameter in which clock readings are stored
P2:	Parameter in which Queue content is stored
Facilities	
1, 2, 3, 4, and 5	The five service bays in which maintenance and repair work are done
Functions	
JOBS	Describes the uniform distribution from 11 to 17; returns values interpretable as one less than the number of vehicles arriving each day for scheduled maintenance
XPDIS	Exponential distribution function
Queues	
TRUBL	The Queue in which police cars are resident while they are out of service
Tables	
LENTH	The Table in which observations on the number of out-of-service police cars are recorded
User Chains	
REG (for "regular")	The place where scheduled-maintenance vehicles wait their turn to go into a service bay.
SPEC (for "special")	The place where police cars coming in for unscheduled-repair wait their turn to go into a service bay

(4) Block Diagram*

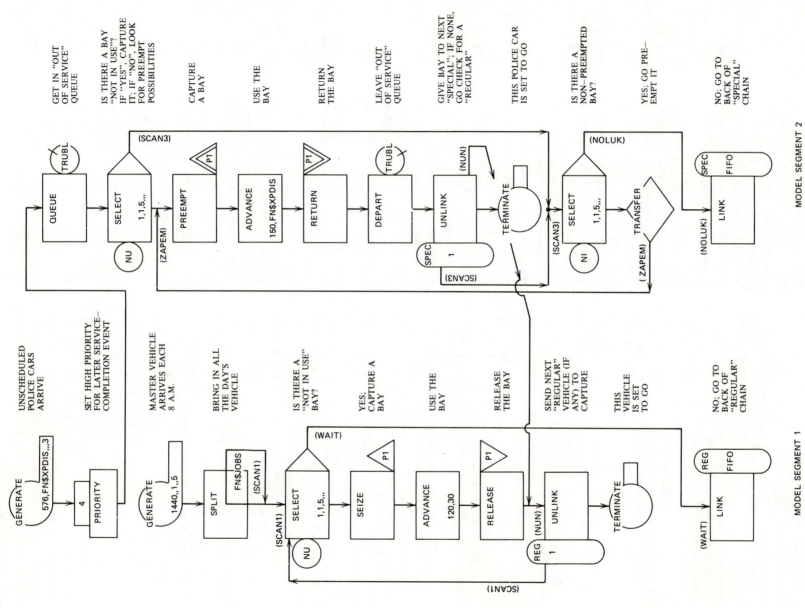

FIGURE 7C.1   Block Diagram for Case Study 7C.

*Model Segments 4 and 5 are identical to Model Segments 4 and 5 in Case Study 7B. They are not repeated here.

MODEL SEGMENT 3

GENERATE 1440,,481,,2 — BOSS COMES DAILY AT END OF EIGHTH HOUR

PRIORITY 6 — SET PRIORITY SO BOSS CAN PREEMPT

ASSIGN 1,5 — INITIALIZE LOOPING PARAMETER

PREEMPT PR (CLOSE) — PREEMPT BAY "P1" TO STOP WORK

LOOP 1 (CLOSE) P1 — GO PREEMPT NEXT BAY (IF ANY)

ADVANCE 960 — LET 16 HOURS GO BY

ASSIGN 1,5 — INITIALIZE LOOPING PARAMETER

RETURN (OPEN) P1 — RETURN BAY TO START NEW DAY'S WORK

LOOP 1 (OPEN) — GO RETURN NEXT BAY (IF ANY)

UNLINK SPEC ALL (SCAN3) — LET ALL CHAINED "SPECIALS" (IF ANY) TRY TO CAPTURE BAYS

TERMINATE — CLOSE-AND-OPEN TASK IS COMPLETE

(5) Extended Program Listings

```
BLOCK
NUMBER  *LOC    OPERATION  A,B,C,D,E,F,G              COMMENTS                              CARD NUMBER
                SIMULATE                                                                        1
        *                                                                                       2
        *       FUNCTION DEFINITION(S)                                                          3
        *                                                                                       4
        XPDIS   FUNCTION   RN1,C24           EXPONENTIAL DISTRIBUTION FUNCTION                  5
        0.0/.1,.104/.2,.222/.3,.355/.4,.509/.5,.69/.6,.915/.7,1.2/.75,1.38                      6
        .8,1.6/.84,1.83/.88,2.12/.9,2.3/.92,2.52/.94,2.81/.95,2.99/.96,3.2                      7
        .97,3.5/.98,3.9/.99,4.6/.995,5.3/.998,6.2/.999,7/.9998,8                                8
        *                                    NO. OF VEHICLES, "MINUS 1", ARRIVING              9
        JOBS    FUNCTION   RN1,C2            EACH DAY FOR SCHEDULED MAINTENANCE                10
        0,11/1,18                                                                              11
        *                                                                                      12
        *       TABLE DEFINITION(S)                                                            13
        *                                                                                      14
        LENTH   TABLE      P2,0,1,W10        DISTRIBUTION OF POLICE CARS OUT                   15
        *                                    OF SERVICE FOR UNSCHEDULED REPAIR                 16
        *                                                                                      17
        *       MODEL SEGMENT 1 (SCHEDULED MAINTENANCE SEGMENT)                                18
        *                                                                                      19
 1              GENERATE   1440,,1,,5        MASTER VEHICLE ARRIVES EACH 8 A.M.                20
 2              SPLIT      FN$JOBS,SCAN1      BRING IN ALL THE DAY'S VEHICLES                   21
 3      SCAN1   SELECT NU  1,1,5,,WAIT        IS THERE A "NOT IN USE" BAY?                      22
 4              SEIZE      P1                 YES; CAPTURE A BAY                                23
 5              ADVANCE    120,30             USE THE BAY                                       24
 6              RELEASE    P1                 RELEASE THE BAY                                   25
 7      NUN     UNLINK     REG,SCAN1,1        SEND NEXT "REGULAR" VEHICLE                       26
        *                                    (IF ANY) TO CAPTURE                               27
 8              TERMINATE                     THIS VEHICLE IS SET TO GO                         28
 9      WAIT    LINK       REG,FIFO           NO; GO TO BACK OF "REGULAR" CHAIN                 29
        *                                                                                      30
        *       MODEL SEGMENT 2 (UNSCHEDULED REPAIR OF POLICE CARS)                            31
        *                                                                                      32
10              GENERATE   576,FN$XPDIS,,,3   UNSCHEDULED POLICE CARS ARRIVE                    33
11              PRIORITY   4                  SET HIGH PRIORITY FOR LATER                       34
        *                                    SERVICE-COMPLETION EVENT                          35
12              QUEUE      TRUBL              GET IN "OUT OF SERVICE" QUEUE                     36
13              SELECT NU  1,1,5,,SCAN3       IS THERE A BAY NOT IN USE?                        37
        *                                    IF "YES", CAPTURE IT; IF "NO",                    38
        *                                    LOOK FOR PRE-EMPT POSSIBILITIES                   39
14      ZAPEM   PREEMPT    P1                 CAPTURE A BAY                                     40
15              ADVANCE    150,FN$XPDIS       USE THE BAY                                       41
16              RETURN     P1                 RETURN THE BAY                                    42
17              DEPART     TRUBL              LEAVE "OUT OF SERVICE" QUEUE                      43
18              UNLINK     SPEC,SCAN3,1,,,NUN IF NONE, GO CHECK FOR A "REGULAR"                 44
                                                                                               45
19      SCAN3   TERMINATE                     THIS POLICE CAR IS SET TO GO                      46
20              SELECT NI  1,1,5,,NOLUK       IS THERE A NON-PREEMPTED BAY?                     47
21              TRANSFER   ,ZAPEM             YES; GO PRE-EMPT IT                               48
22      NOLUK   LINK       SPEC,FIFO          NO; GO TO BACK OF "SPECIAL" CHAIN                 49
        *                                                                                      50
        *       MODEL SEGMENT 3 (CLOSE-UP AND OPEN-UP SEGMENT)                                 51
        *                                                                                      52
23              GENERATE   1440,,481,,2       BOSS COMES DAILY AT END OF 8TH HOUR               53
24              PRIORITY   6                  SET PRIORITY SO BOSS CAN PRE-EMPT                 54
25              ASSIGN     1,5                INITIALIZE LOOPING PARAMETER                      55
26      CLOSE   PREEMPT    P1,PR              PRE-EMPT BAY "P1" TO STOP WORK                    56
27              LOOP       1,CLOSE            GO PRE-EMPT NEXT BAY (IF ANY)                     57
28              ADVANCE    960                LET 16 HOURS GO BY                                58
29              ASSIGN     1,5                INITIALIZE LOOPING PARAMETER                      59
30      OPEN    RETURN     P1                 RETURN BAY TO START NEW DAY'S WORK                60
31              LOOP       1,OPEN             GO RETURN NEXT BAY (IF ANY)                       61
32              UNLINK     SPEC,SCAN3,ALL     LET ALL CHAINED "SPECIALS"                        62
        *                                    (IF ANY) TRY TO CAPTURE BAYS                      63
33              TERMINATE                     CLOSE-AND-OPEN TASK IS COMPLETE                   64
        *                                                                                      65
        *       MODEL SEGMENT 4 (DATA GATHERING FOR "OUT OF SERVICE" POLICE CARS)              66
        *                                                                                      67
34      WATCH   GENERATE   ,,,1,,2,F          SEED THE SEGMENT                                  68
35              MARK       1                  SET P1 = ABSOLUTE CLOCK                           69
36              ASSIGN     2,Q$TRUBL          SET P2 = NO. NOW "OUT OF SERVICE"                 70
37              TEST NE    MP1,0              WAIT FOR THE CLOCK TO CHANGE                      71
38              TABULATE   LENTH,MP1          RECORD THIS OBSERVATION                           72
39              TRANSFER   ,WATCH             GO SET UP FOR THE NEXT OBSERVATION                73
        *                                                                                      74
        *       MODEL SEGMENT 5 (TIMER SEGMENT)                                                75
        *                                                                                      76
40              GENERATE   7200,,6241         TIMER COMES AT END OF EACH 5TH DAY                77
41              TERMINATE  1                  PRODUCE "SNAP" OR SHUT OFF THE RUN                78
        *                                                                                      79
        *       CONTROL CARD(S)                                                                80
        *                                                                                      81
                START      5,,1,1                                                              82
                END                                                                            83
```

FIGURE 7C.2 Extended Program Listing for Case Study 7C.

(6) Program Output

INTERRUPT CHAIN

TRANS	BDT	BLOCK	PR	SF	NBA	SET	MARK-TIME	P1	P2	P3	P4	SI	TI	DI	CI	MC	PC	PF
8	132		5		6	15	34561	2	0	0	0					1		1
								0	0	0	0							
								0	0	0	0							
11	19		5		6	13	34561	4	0	0	0					1		1
								0	0	0	0							
								0	0	0	0							
13	44		5		6	2	34561	1	0	0	0					1		1
								0	0	0	0							
								0	0	0	0							
15	117		5		6	23	34561	3	0	0	0					1		1
								0	0	0	0							
								0	0	0	0							
23	130		5		6	11	34561	5	0	0	0					1		1
								0	0	0	0							
								0	0	0	0							

(a)

USER CHAIN	TOTAL ENTRIES	AVERAGE TIME/TRANS	CURRENT CONTENTS	AVERAGE CONTENTS	MAXIMUM CONTENTS
REG	331	283.184	5	2.674	25
SPEC	36	511.916		.525	6

(b)

FACILITY	AVERAGE UTILIZATION	NUMBER ENTRIES	AVERAGE TIME/TRAN	SEIZING TRANS. NO.	PREEMPTING TRANS. NO.
1	.958	105	320.038	13	27
2	.956	108	310.388	8	27
3	.953	109	306.687	15	27
4	.946	110	301.408	11	27
5	.949	109	305.247	23	27

(c)

TABLE LENTH ENTRIES IN TABLE	MEAN ARGUMENT	STANDARD DEVIATION	SUM OF ARGUMENTS	
499	.679	1.042	339.000	NON-WEIGHTED
35040	.855	1.203	29992.000	WEIGHTED

UPPER LIMIT	OBSERVED FREQUENCY	PER CENT OF TOTAL	CUMULATIVE PERCENTAGE	CUMULATIVE REMAINDER	MULTIPLE OF MEAN	DEVIATION FROM MEAN
0	17102	48.80	48.8	51.1	-.000	-.651
1	11319	32.30	81.1	18.8	1.471	.307
2	4104	11.71	92.8	7.1	2.943	1.266
3	1376	3.92	96.7	3.2	4.415	2.225
4	269	.76	97.5	2.4	5.887	3.183
5	99	.28	97.7	2.2	7.359	4.142
6	631	1.80	99.6	.3	8.831	5.101
7	140	.39	100.0	.0	10.303	6.060

REMAINING FREQUENCIES ARE ALL ZERO

(d)

FIGURE 7C.3   Selected Program Output produced at the end of day 25 in Case Study 7C. (a) Interrupt Chain(s). (b) User Chain statistics. (c) Facility statistics. (d) Table statistics.

Model Logic. It is assumed that the Block Diagram version of the model has now been studied and digested to a reasonable extent. Taking this as a given, the question of Priority Levels in the model will now be explored. Before starting a segment-by-segment commentary, however, note first of all that the Priority Levels with which Transactions *enter the model* in the various segments happen to form a decreasing sequence from Model Segment 1 through Model Segment 5. In particular, Transactions *enter* Model Segments 1 through 5 with Priority Levels of 5, 3, 2, 1, and 0, respectively.

The Priority Levels will first be discussed on a within-the-segment basis for each segment. Then, the manner in which interactions between segments bear on the choice of relative Priority Levels will be taken up.

Model Segment 1. Scheduled-maintenance Transactions come into their model segment with a Priority Level of 5, and retain this Priority Level throughout the model. This *should* seem strange, in terms of the potential "simultaneity of events" problem discussed earlier in this chapter with respect to User Chains. What if an arrival and a release were to occur simultaneously, with the release preceding the arrival? The Transaction unlinked after the release event would be put on the Current Chain *behind* the incipient arrival, given that they have the same Priority Level. The incipient arrival would then capture the just-released Facility, and the unlinked Transaction would have to go back onto the User Chain. In fact, to rub salt into the wound, he would have come off the *front* of the User Chain, and he would then return to the *back* of the User Chain, thereby violating the first-come, first-served concept for scheduled-maintenance Transactions.

What is wrong with the above critique of Model Segment 1? The discussion of what would happen if the indicated time tie occurred is accurate. But time ties don't occur in Model Segment 1. They can't. *All* incoming scheduled-maintenance Transactions arrive at 8 a.m. each day. It is impossible for a scheduled-maintenance vehicle to release its service bay at 8 a.m. If, at 5 p.m. on the preceding day, it had "1 minute to go" before releasing, then the release would take place at 8:01 a.m., not at 8:00 a.m. This is the reason why it isn't necessary in Model Segment 1 to defend against the simultaneity-of-events problem with respect to the User Chain.

Model Segment 2. Unscheduled-repair Transactions in Model Segment 2 arrive with a Priority Level of 3, and then immediately have their priority boosted to 4. This is done to defend against the simultaneity-of-events problem which can't arise in Model Segment 1. The simultaneity problem can arise in Model Segment 2, because with the random interarrival times in that segment, there is no reason why time ties cannot occur between incipient arrivals and Transactions poised to return the service bay.

Model Segment 3. The boss-Transaction enters the model with a Priority Level of 2. He then immediately has his priority boosted to 6, which enables him to carry out his intentions to preempt the service bays. The reason why he doesn't enter the model with a Priority Level of 6 in the first place is indicated below, under "interactions."

Model Segment 4. The data-gathering Transaction has a Priority Level of 1. This assures that when a line-length observation is made, the model will already be fully updated at that clock instant with respect to the status of police cars. Any Priority Level less than 3 would be fine for this purpose; that is, the data-gathering Transaction could have a Priority Level of 2, and the model would still be valid. If its Priority Level were 2, it would be ahead of the boss Transaction on the Current Chain at 5 p.m. But this wouldn't matter, because nothing the boss does affects the content of the Queue TRUBL anyway.

Model Segment 5. The snap-interval Transaction has the lowest Priority Level of all, 0. This guarantees that snap-output will be produced only after the model has been fully updated at 5 p.m. every fifth day.

Priority Interactions Between Model Segments. *Interaction Between Model Segments 1 and 2.* Scheduled-maintenance Transactions have a higher Priority Level than that of unscheduled-repair Transactions. This is done to defend against the simultaneity problem which would otherwise arise if the following conditions were in effect.

1. A scheduled-maintenance Transaction is poised to release a service bay.
2. There is an incipient arrival of an unscheduled-repair Transaction.
3. There is at least one scheduled-maintenance Transaction waiting on the User Chain REG (among other things, this means that all the bays are busy).
4. The release event precedes the arrival event.

Now, if Priority Levels were the same in Model Segments 1 and 2, the scheduled-maintenance Transaction unlinked after the release event would be put on the Current Chain behind the unscheduled-repair arrival. Next, the unscheduled-repair Transaction would proceed to capture the Facility. Then the just-unlinked Transaction, discovering that all the service bays are in use, would be linked back onto the User Chain REG. Unfortunately, whereas the Transaction had come off the *front* of the User Chain, its return would be to the *back* of the User Chain. This is a violation of first-come, first-served queue discipline for scheduled-maintenance Transactions.

How does the Priority Level distinction resolve this problem? With its higher Priority Level, the unlinked scheduled-maintenance Transaction goes onto the Current Chain ahead of the incipient arrival. It therefore captures the service bay before the arrival is processed. Granted, when the arrival is processed, it is permitted to preempt the service bay, thereby forcing the current user out onto an Interrupt Chain. Note that the service bay preempted may not be the same one which was just released-and-captured. (If some lower-numbered Facility is in use by a nonpreemptive user, the unscheduled-repair Transaction will take that Facility. This is a result of the SELECT Block scanning in order of increasing Facility number.) But that is neither here nor there. What matters is that by having higher Priority Levels in Model Segment 1 than in Model Segment 2, the first-come, first-served queue discipline for scheduled-maintenance vehicles is preserved.

Interaction Between Model Segments 2 and 3. The relationship between the boss and the unscheduled-repair Transactions is analogous to that between unscheduled-repair and scheduled maintenance Transactions. Discussion of the relationship is left to the exercises (see exercise 1b, Section 7.22).

Interaction Between Model Segment 3 and Model Segments 1 and 2. The curious thing about the boss Transaction is that it enters the model with a Priority Level lower than that of Transactions entering Model Segments 1 and 2, and then immediately has its priority boosted to 6. It is clear that the boss must have a Priority Level higher than 5 to be able to preempt the service bays, so the reason for the boost to 6 is evident. What might not be clear is why the boss didn't simply enter the model with a Priority Level of 6. There is presumably some reason why the boss must initially be on the Current Chain *in back of* the Model Segment 1 and 2 Transactions (if any). What is this reason? As usual, simultaneity-of-events is involved. Suppose there is a time tie between the boss's arrival, and either the release or the return of a service bay (or both). If the boss comes in with a Priority Level of 6, he is the Transaction processed first at close-up time, preempting all the service bays as a result. Then, when the release and/or return occurs, it (or they) are followed by the attempted unlinking of a Transaction which is to replace the departing Transaction in the service bay. If an unlink does take place, the Unlinkee finds that the bay it was supposed to get is not available, and goes back out onto the User Chain. This results in a disruption of first-come, first-served queue discipline. The Unlinkee came from the front of the User Chain, and then returns to the back of that chain.

The potential problem is resolved, of course, by having the boss hang back while other system events scheduled to take place at close-up time occur. *Then* the boss does his thing. If the conditions just described do come about, the Transaction (or Transactions) which just moved into the service bay is promptly put onto an Interrupt Chain. This is entirely acceptable, however, and the integrity of the desired queue discipline is preserved in the process.

Program Output.[18] Selected Program Output produced at the end of the twenty-fifth simulated day is shown in Figure 7C.3. The Interrupt "Chain" is shown in part (a). Note that there are really five Interrupt Chains, one for each of the five Facilities in the model. The Transactions resident on these five chains are printed out, however, in order of increasing Transaction number, as though they were on a single chain. The Transactions shown on the Interrupt Chain(s) were all nonpreemptive users of the service bays when the boss came. (Their Next Block Attempted is Block 6, which is the RELEASE Block in Model Segment 1.) Examination of their Parameter 1 values indicates which Transaction was at which Facility. Transaction 8 was at Facility 2, Transaction 11 was at Facility 4, and so on.

The User Chain statistics shown in part (b) indicate that as many as 25 scheduled-mainte-

[18]Total CPU time for the simulation on an IBM 360/67 computer was 7.4 seconds.

nance vehicles were in line at one time, waiting for a service bay (MAXIMUM CONTENTS equals 25). Similarly, as many as six police cars were concurrently waiting in line for unscheduled repair.

The Facility statistics in part (c) show that, at the end of the twenty-fifth day, each service bay was in a state of capture when the boss arrived (the SEIZING TRANS. NO. column contains a value for each Facility). The Facility information also shows that Transaction 27 is the boss. Note that the SEIZING TRANS. NO. information is consistent with the Interrupt Chain information commented on above. Also note that, based on Facility statistics alone, there is no way to tell whether the boss displaced nonpreemptive or preemptive users from the various Facilities. Such information would be available, however, from study of the Interrupt Chain.

The Table statistics in part (d) reveal that, on average, 0.855 police cars were out of service for unscheduled repair (WEIGHTED MEAN ARGUMENT equals 0.855). Less than half the time were all of the police cars in service (PERCENT OF TOTAL equals 48.8 percent for a Table UPPER LIMIT of 0). As many as seven cars were out of service simultaneously, but not for long (PERCENT OF TOTAL equals 0.39 percent for a Table UPPER LIMIT of 7).

The average number of out-of-service police cars, 0.855, is less than five times the average number out of service in Case Study 7B (0.221 percent). On the other hand, in queue information not shown, it turns out that there were only 52 unscheduled repairs in the five bay model. There were 13 unscheduled repairs in the 1-bay model. The number of such repairs in the five-bay case, then, was lower on a proportional basis than in the equivalent one-bay case. In fact, in the long run, there would be 62.5 unscheduled repairs during a 25-day period, so the experience here was atypically low.

7.21 Alternative Fates for Preempted Transactions

If a Transaction succeeds in moving into a PREEMPT Block when the referenced Facility is in use, it interrupts the current user. When only the A Operand, or the A and B Operands, are used at the PREEMPT Block, the interrupted Transaction is placed on the front of an Interrupt Chain.[19] It then remains there, on a last-in, first-out basis, until the Facility again becomes available to it. At that time, it regains control of the Facility, and is placed by the Processor on the Future Events Chain, where it stays while its remaining Facility holding time elapses.

The Transaction fate summarized above should be recognized as the one described in Section 7.14. That particular fate will be referred to here as Alternative 1. As indicated in Section 7.14, there are two other alternatives which can be specified for the preempted Transaction. These alternatives are modeled through use of the PREEMPT Block's C, D, and E Operands. Here are the two other alternatives, called Alternative 2, and Alternative 3.

Alternative 2. The interrupted Transaction is routed to some other Block in the model, and is removed from contention for use of the Facility. That is, it will not later be automatically reinstated by the Processor as the capturer of the Facility.

Alternative 3. The interrupted Transaction is routed to some other Block in the model, but is not removed from contention for later automatic reinstatement as the capturer of the Facility.

The role of the C, D, and E Operands in modeling these two alternatives is indicated in Table 7.9. The placement of these Operands in the PREEMPT Block itself is shown in Figure 7.23.

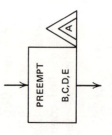

FIGURE 7.23 The PREEMPT Block and its A, B, C, D, and E Operands

As shown in Table 7.9, the PREEMPT Block's C Operand indicates the Location of the Next Block Attempted for the interrupted Transaction. The PREEMPT Block's D Operand is interpreted as the number of one of the interrupted Transaction's Parameters. When the D Operand is

[19] Remember that the preempted Transaction is placed on the Interrupt Chain immediately if it had been on the Future Events Chain; that it is not placed on the Interrupt Chain at all if it had been on the Current Events Chain, poised to release the Facility; and that under other circumstances, it goes onto the Interrupt Chain the next time the Processor moves it into an ADVANCE Block where a positive holding time is specified. (Also see footnote 13 in Section 7.14.)

TABLE 7.9   A Summary of the Role Played by the PREEMPT Block's Optional C, D, and E Operands

Operand	Significance
C	The C Operand supplies the name of the Block Location to which the interrupted Transaction will be sent.
D	The D-Operand's value is interpreted as the number of one of the interrupted Transaction's Parameters. The Processor places a copy of the Transaction's remaining Facility holding time into this Parameter.
E	The E Operand indicates whether or not the interrupted Transaction is to remain in contention for automatic reinstatement as the capturer of the Facility. When E is the two-character sequence RE (for remove), the Transaction is removed from contention. When the default is taken on the E Operand, the Transaction remains in contention.

used, the Processor places into the indicated Parameter a copy of the Transaction's remaining holding time at the Facility. This makes it possible for the analyst to subsequently take this remaining holding time into account in the logic of the model.

The PREEMPT Block's E Operand is used to specify whether or not the interrupted Transaction is to remain in contention for later reinstatement as the capturer of the Facility. If the analyst supplies the two characters RE (for remove) as the E Operand, the interrupted Transaction is removed from automatic contention for the Facility; that is, Alternative 2 is in effect.[20] If the analyst defaults on the E Operand, the interrupted Transaction remains in contention for the Facility; that is, Alternative 3 is in effect.

It is important to note the following three restrictions on use of the PREEMPT Block's C, D, and E Operands.

Restriction 1. If a default is taken on the PREEMPT Block's B Operand, then the Processor ignores the C, D, and E Operands.

Restriction 2. If a default is taken on the PREEMPT Block's C Operand, then the Processor ignores the D and E Operands.

[20]Of course, being removed from automatic contention does not mean that the Transaction cannot later attempt reuse of the Facility in the usual way, by entering a SEIZE or a PREEMPT Block.

Restriction 3. If the Transaction currently using the Facility is not on the Future Events Chain when the preempt occurs, then the C, D, and E Operands are ignored.

If the Processor ignores the C, D, and E Operands, even though they have been used, the fate of the preempted Transaction reverts to that described as Alternative 1.

In the following two subsections, the details of Alternatives 2 and 3 will be explored, and these alternatives will be illustrated with small examples.

7.21.1 Alternative 2: When the Preempted Transaction is Removed from Contention

When an interrupt specifying Alternative 2 occurs, the Processor removes the interrupted Transaction from the Future Events Chain, and places it on the Current Chain as the last member in its Priority Class. Because it is being removed from further contention for the Facility, the interrupted Transaction's Preempt Flag is not turned on; that is, there is no preemption pending for the Transaction. As a result of the PREEMPT Block execution, however, the Status Change Flag is turned on, meaning that the scan will be restarted as soon as the preempting Transaction comes to rest. When the interrupted Transaction is encountered in the restarted scan, the Processor simply attempts to move it into its Next Block Attempted, and so on. In other words, although the Transaction was interrupted, the fact that it was removed from contention means that it subsequently behaves like any other normal Transaction in the model.

Now consider Alternative 2 with respect to Block Counts. Before it is interrupted, a Transaction is contributing to the Current Count at its ADVANCE Block. Even at the time of interruption, when the Transaction is transferred from the Future to the Current Chain, it continues to remain in the ADVANCE Block, from the point of view of Current Block Counts. Only after the Transaction successfully enters its Next Block does it cease to contribute to the Current Count at its former ADVANCE Block.

For a small-scale example which uses Alternative 2, consider the simple case of a work station on a production line. Assume that work can be performed on only one part at a time at the work station. The machine used to do the work gets out of alignment occasionally, meaning that certain machine settings must be adjusted. The time that elapses between consecutive needs for adjustment varies at random. When adjustment is required, it must be done immediately; that is, it must be done not only before work on the next part begins, but even before work on the current part is finished. Furthermore, making the adjustment requires removing the current part from the machine. The removed part, instead of remaining in automatic contention for the machine, is simply sent to the back of the line of other parts waiting for the machine. The fact that work on the part was partially completed is of no consequence; when its turn comes again at the machine, the interrupted part must start over, as though it had never been on the machine in the first place.

Figure 7.24 shows parts of the Block Diagram for a GPSS model which might be used to simulate the work station. Model Segment 1 simulates the self-contained adjustment seg-

ment. A single Transaction circulates continuously throughout this segment. Transactions moving through Model Segment 2 simulate the parts on which processing is performed at the work station. The following assumptions are in effect.

1. The implicit time unit is 1 minute.
2. After it has just been adjusted, the machine will need adjusting again after another 960 ± 200 minutes.
3. The time required to process a part at the work station is 5 ± 1 minutes.
4. Transactions moving through Model Segment 2 have a Priority Level of 0.

The comments adjacent to the Blocks in Figure 7.24 make the logic involved largely self-explanatory. It is worth noting that PR has been used as the PREEMPT Block's B Operand in Model Segment 1. Recall that if this were not done, the Processor would ignore the Block's optional C and E Operands. But with use of the

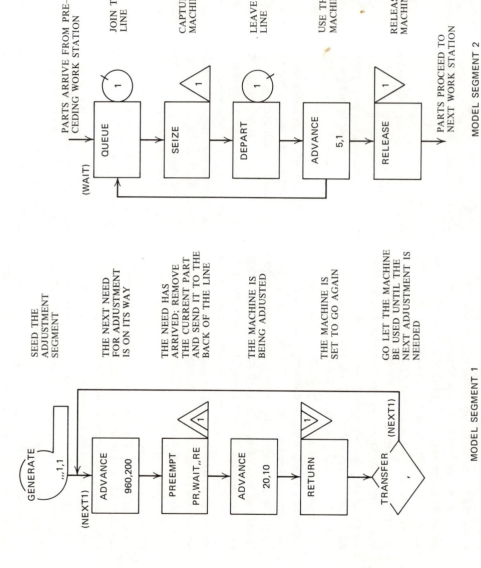

FIGURE 7.24   A first example of extended PREEMPT Block use

PR, preempts are permitted only when the would-be preempter has a higher Priority Level than that of the current user of the Facility. This explains why the Transaction which circulates in Model Segment 1 has a Priority Level of 1, whereas Transactions moving through Model Segment 2 are assumed to have a Priority Level of 0. Also note the return line between the ADVANCE and QUEUE Blocks in Model Segment 2. This line is included to suggest the path along which the preempted Transaction moves.

7.21.2 Alternative 3: When the Preempted Transaction Remains in Contention

When an interrupted Transaction's fate is Alternative 3, the Transaction goes to another Block in the model, but remains in contention for the Facility. As was pointed out earlier, Alternatives 2 and 3 take effect only if, at the time of preemption, the interrupted Transaction was on the Future Events Chain, i.e., was in an ADVANCE Block. When the interrupt occurs, the Processor transfers the Transaction from the Future to the Current Chain, where it becomes the last member in its Priority Class. In addition, its Preempt Flag is turned on, indicating there is a preemption pending for it. Then, when the interrupted Transaction is encountered during the rescan of the Current Chain, the Processor moves it forward until it enters an ADVANCE Block where a positive holding time is specified.[21] When this happens, the Transaction is put into inactive status at the front of the Interrupt Chain. Eventually, conditions permit the interrupted Transaction to be put back in control of the Facility. When these conditions come about, the Processor puts the Transaction back into the ADVANCE Block from which it was plucked *when it went onto the Interrupt Chain.* The Transaction then remains in that ADVANCE Block for whatever holding time had been computed when it entered that ADVANCE Block. (Note that *none* of this holding time had elapsed when the Transaction was put onto the Interrupt Chain.) When it leaves that ADVANCE Block, its Next Block Attempted will be whatever Block is sequential to the ADVANCE Block. Eventually, the Transaction will presumably move into a RELEASE or RETURN Block (depending

[21] It is quite possible that the interrupted Transaction will run into one or more blocking conditions before it finally finds its way into an ADVANCE Block. If this occurs, the eventual ADVANCE Block entry might not take place until some later simulated time.

on how it captured the Facility in the first place), thereby giving up control of the Facility.

It is important to realize that *two* potentially distinct ADVANCE Blocks have been included in the above discussion.

1. There is the ADVANCE Block the interrupted Transaction was in at the time of interruption. Call this the "primary" ADVANCE Block.

2. There is the ADVANCE Block the Transaction was just entering at the time it was put onto the Interrupt Chain. Call this the "secondary" ADVANCE Block.

The primary and secondary ADVANCE Blocks can be the same Block, but need not be. If they are not, the question naturally arises, "what about the primary ADVANCE Block, and the remaining holding time in effect at that Block when the preempt occurred?" The answer to this question is that the preempt simply forgets (deliberately) that the interrupted Transaction had been in the primary ADVANCE Block, and was scheduled to remain there for 1 or more additional time units. In fact, even if the primary and secondary ADVANCE Blocks are one and the same, the Processor forgets about the interrupted Transaction's remaining holding time at the Block. When the Transaction is next put back into that Block, the remaining holding time used will be that computed for the Transaction when it entered the ADVANCE Block on a secondary basis.

Now consider a small-scale example to illustrate Alternative 3 as a preemption fate. For this example, a Facility is used to simulate a professor who is holding office hours. Students come in during office hours to consult with the professor on a first-come, first-served basis. When there is a student in the office and the phone rings, however, the incoming phone call interrupts the student–professor conversation. Only after completing the phone conversation does the professor resume the discussion with the student. There is an overhead associated with such an interruption. When the in-office discussion starts again, some time is inevitably required to bring the discussion back to the point it had been at when the interrupt occurred. This time overhead must be added to what otherwise was the student's "remaining time in the office."

Figure 7.25 shows parts of the Block Diagram for a GPSS model which could be used to simulate this office situation. Model Segment 1

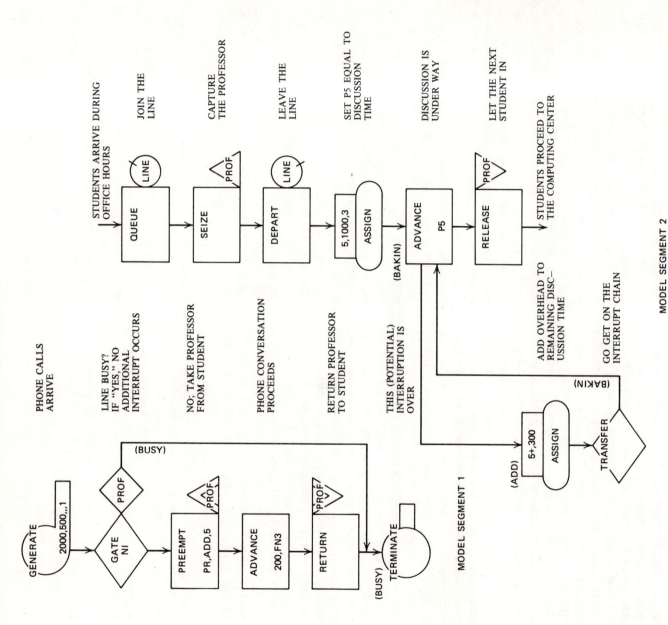

FIGURE 7.25 A second example of extended PREEMPT Block use

simulates the self-contained "incoming phone calls" segment. Transactions moving through Model Segment 2 simulate students coming in for office hours. The following assumptions are in effect.

1. The implicit time unit is 0.01 minutes.
2. Phone calls come in every 20 ± 5 minutes.
3. The duration of a phone conversation is exponentially distributed, with a mean of 2 minutes.

4. The duration of a discussion with a student is also exponentially distributed, with a mean of 10 minutes.
5. Function 3 is the 24-point Function used to sample from the exponential population.
6. There is a 3-minute overhead associated with having an in-office discussion interrupted.

Figure 7.25 is somewhat more complicated than was Figure 7.24. In Model Segment 1, when a phone-call-Transaction arrives, it first checks

secondary ADVANCE Blocks are distinctly different Blocks. Figure 7.26 repeats Model Segment 2 from Figure 7.25, showing how a secondary ADVANCE Block can be introduced into the model. As was the case in Figure 7.25, the interrupted Transaction's remaining holding time is copied into Parameter 5 at the time of interruption. Parameter 5 is then incremented at an ASSIGN Block, and the Transaction moves into an ADVANCE Block where the holding time is supplied via P5. Later, when the student transfers to free the professor, etc.

In comparing the models in Figures 7.25 and 7.26, it is easily seen that it is possible to be somewhat more specific with data references when the primary and secondary ADVANCE Blocks are distinct. In particular, in Figure 7.26,

to see if the line is already busy. If it is, the would-be caller simply leaves the model. (It would be more realistic to have such a caller try to call again later; but, for simplicity, no arrangement is made for this in the Figure 7.25 model.) Otherwise, the preempt occurs, and so on. Note the necessary use of PR at the PREEMPT Block in Model Segment 1, and the implied assumption that Transactions which move through Model Segment 2 have a Priority Level of 0.

In Model Segment 2, after capturing the professor, a student-Transaction pre-computes the in-office discussion time at an ASSIGN Block, saving the result in Parameter 5. The student then moves into an ADVANCE Block which specifies P5 as the holding time. Now suppose that a phone interruption occurs. Per the PREEMPT Block specifications in Model Segment 1, the interrupted student-Transaction is removed from the Future Chain and put on the Current Chain, scheduled to enter the Block in the Location ADD. At the same time, through use of the PREEMPT Block's D Operand, the student's remaining time-in-office is computed and placed in the student-Transaction's 5th Parameter. The "remaining time" therefore replaces that Parameter's previous "total discussion time" value. Then, during the rescan, the interrupted Transaction moves into the increment-mode ASSIGN Block in the Location ADD. There, 300 time units (i.e., 3 minutes) are added to Parameter 5. This amounts to taking into account the time overhead associated with the interruption. The student-Transaction is then routed into the ADVANCE Block in which it had just been. At that ADVANCE Block, of course, its P5 value is interpreted as its holding time. When the Transaction arrives at the ADVANCE Block, the Processor removes it from the Current Chain and puts it on the Interrupt Chain. Later, when the phone conversation ends, the Processor will remove the student-Transaction from the Interrupt Chain and cause it to resume doing what it was doing when it was put onto the Interrupt Chain. This means the Transaction is put back into the ADVANCE Block, where it will remain while P5 simulated time units elapse. Leaving the ADVANCE Block later, the student-Transaction will release the professor-Facility and go on its way.

The Figure 7.25 example is one in which the "primary" and "secondary" ADVANCE Blocks are one and the same Block. It is an easy matter to modify the model so that the primary and

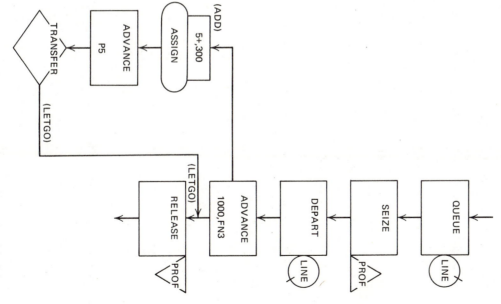

FIGURE 7.26 An alternative form for Model Segment 2 in Figure 7.25

there is no need to precompute the student's in-office discussion time. There is no reason why this computation cannot be performed at the primary ADVANCE Block itself, as shown. In the Figure 7.25 model, however, the indicated holding time at the ADVANCE Block has to depend on whether the entering Transaction is using the Block in a primary context, or in a secondary context. For this reason, the holding time specification at that ADVANCE Block has to be flexible enough to accommodate itself to both possibilities. This explains why holding time was provided in that instance through Parameter 5.

7.22 Exercises

1. Under certain conditions, the Case Study 7C model will fail to provide a FIFO queue discipline for scheduled-maintenance vehicles. (Fortunately, this small flaw in the model has no effect on the model's output.) Explain why this can come about in the model, and suggest a method for correcting the situation. (Hint: the flaw involves neither Priority Levels nor time ties.)

2. How would you answer the following criticism of the case study model? "From the UNLINK Block in Model Segment 2 (Block 18, Figure 7C.2), the Unlinkee should be sent first to Block 13 ("SELECT NU 1,1,5,,,SCAN3") to scan for a not-in-use Facility, instead of being sent directly to Block 20 ("SCAN3 SELECT NI 1,1,5,,,NOLUK") to scan for a non-interrupted Facility."

3. The Case Study 7C model employs a combination of User Chains and SELECT Blocks to control the way Transactions gain access to Facilities. Show how to build an alternative model for the problem without using User Chains. (Hint: as indicated on page 452, it is use of the optional F Operand at certain SELECT Blocks in the model which leads to use of User Chains.)

4. In exercise 5, Section 7.18, a distinction is made between two categories of unscheduled-repair police cars. Under the right conditions, cars in one category can preempt cars in the other category. Show what changes to make in the Case Study 7C model to incorporate these conditions into it.

5. In Case Study 7B, it is implicitly assumed that there is no time overhead involved in removing a scheduled-maintenance vehicle from the service bay to let an unscheduled-repair police car take its place. It is also assumed that there is no start-up time required when work finally begins again on the scheduled-repair vehicle. These assumptions are unrealistic. Show how to modify the model in Case Study 7B so that 10 ± 5 minutes are lost when a preempt occurs, and so that another 10 ± 5 minutes are lost when a previously interrupted scheduled-maintenance vehicle is returned to the service bay. Then, using this assumption, repeat the controlled-conditions comparison of alternatives requested in exercise 4, Section 7.18.

6. Repeat exercise 5 for the five-bay garage in the Case Study 7C problem.

7. Repeat exercise 4 under the assumption that the time overheads described in exercise 5 are in effect. Time overheads are to be assumed in effect whenever a preempt or a return occurs, independent of the types of vehicles involved.

7.23 The Concept of Assembly Sets

All Transactions in a model belong to groups known as *Assembly Sets*. There are usually many different Assembly Sets in a model. Each Transaction is a member of only one such set, however. A Transaction's Assembly Set membership is automatically assigned when the Transaction enters a model. The Transaction's membership in this set then continues until the Transaction is removed from the model, and returned to the top of the stack in the latent pool. If the Transaction later reenters the model, it will again be assigned membership in an Assembly Set (though not necessarily in the set to which it belonged previously). During any given "lifetime," then, a Transaction's Assembly Set membership does not change; from lifetime to lifetime, however, a Transaction may have membership in a number of different Assembly Sets.

The Assembly Set to which a Transaction belongs depends entirely on whether the Transaction enters the model through a GENERATE Block, or through a SPLIT Block. Each Transaction brought into a model through a GENERATE Block becomes the *first member* of a new Assembly Set. If this Transaction never moves through a SPLIT Block, then that Assembly Set never contains more than this one Transaction. (Such one-member Assembly Sets are of little or no interest.) If the Transaction enters a SPLIT Block, however, thereby becoming a parent, each of its offspring is assigned membership in the parent's Assembly Set. Furthermore, if any of these offspring later move through a SPLIT Block, thereby becoming parents themselves, then each of the resulting "second generation" Transactions also becomes a member of the original parent's Assembly Set, as transmitted through the "first generation." And so on.

In summary, the only way to have more than one member in an Assembly Set is for the first member to propagate itself by moving through a SPLIT Block. Note carefully, then, that Transactions which enter a model through a common GENERATE Block are *not* members of one and the same Assembly Set.

Although the various Assembly Sets are distinct from each other, they do not have names to which the analyst can make explicit reference as part of a model's logic. Nevertheless, there are several Blocks whose operation depends upon the property of Assembly Set membership. These are the ASSEMBLE, GATHER, and MATCH Blocks, and the GATE Block as used with appropriate Logical Mnemonics. These Blocks make it possible to control the movement of Transactions which are members of the same Assembly Set. The details of these Blocks, and illustration of their use in context, are considered in the following sections.

7.24 Removing One or More Assembly Set Members from a Model: The ASSEMBLE Block

The purpose of the ASSEMBLE Block is to remove one or more members of an Assembly Set from a model. This Block is shown with its A Operand in Figure 7.27. The Block's A Operand supplies a value which *exceeds by one* the number of Transactions which the Block is to eliminate from the model. The A Operand's value is termed the Assembly Count.

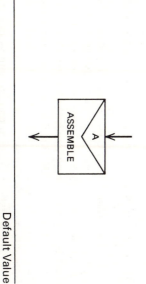

Operand	Significance	Default Value or Result
A	Assembly Count; indicates how many Assembly Set members are to be "combined" into a single Transaction	Error

FIGURE 7.27   The ASSEMBLE Block and its A Operand

The ASSEMBLE Block operates as follows. The first member of an Assembly Set to move into the Block is delayed there until the user-specified number of other members of that set have also entered the Block. As these other members arrive, they are removed from the model and returned to the top of the stack in the latent pool. Eventually, when the Assembly Count has been satisfied, the Transaction which was first to arrive at the ASSEMBLE Block is permitted to continue its forward movement in the model.

The ASSEMBLE Block, then, is complementary to the SPLIT Block. Whereas the SPLIT Block increases membership in an Assembly Set, the ASSEMBLE Block decreases the membership. (Of course, the membership can also be decreased at TERMINATE Blocks.) In effect, the Assembly Count indicates how many Assembly Set members are to be "combined" into a single Transaction. No true combining of Transactions occurs, however. The surviving Transaction has exactly whatever properties it had when it first arrived at the ASSEMBLE Block.

Here are some additional features of the ASSEMBLE Block, and of Assembly Sets, which are worth pointing out.

1. For a given Assembly Set at a given ASSEMBLE Block, only one assembly operation at a time can be in process.

2. For a given ASSEMBLE Block, assembly operations with respect to two or more Assembly Sets can be in process concurrently.

3. For a given Assembly Set, assembly operations can be in process concurrently at two or more ASSEMBLE Blocks.

4. After an assembly operation has been completed for a given Assembly Set and ASSEMBLE Block, another assembly operation can begin for that set, at that Block.

As for Block Counts, the surviving member of an Assembly Set contributes to the Current Count at the ASSEMBLE Block while an assembly operation is in process (and, later, until it succeeds in moving to the sequential Block). The surviving member also contributes to the Total Count at the ASSEMBLE Block. Of course, the eliminated Transactions do not contribute to the Current Count; nor do they contribute to the Total Count.

From the point of view of chains, the surviving member of an Assembly Set is removed from the Current Events Chain when it enters the ASSEMBLE Block, and is put on a *Matching Chain*. The Matching Chain can be thought of

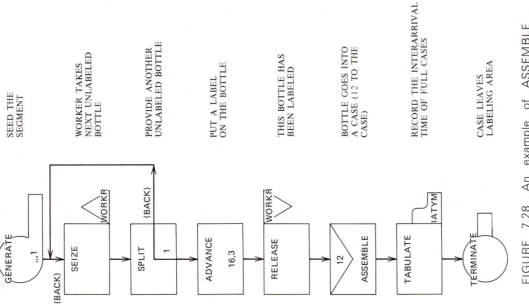

SEED THE
SEGMENT

WORKER TAKES
NEXT UNLABELED
BOTTLE

PROVIDE ANOTHER
UNLABELED BOTTLE

PUT A LABEL
ON THE BOTTLE

THIS BOTTLE HAS
BEEN LABELED

BOTTLE GOES INTO
A CASE (12 TO THE
CASE)

RECORD THE INTERARRIVAL
TIME OF FULL CASES

CASE LEAVES
LABELING AREA

FIGURE 7.28   An example of ASSEMBLE
Block use

as being unique to that Assembly Set *and* to that ASSEMBLE Block. Eventually, when the Assembly Count has been satisfied, the surviving Transaction is removed from the Matching Chain and returned to the Current Chain, as the last member in its Priority Class. The Processor then immediately restarts its scan of the Current Events Chain, insuring that the surviving Transaction will be processed at the current instant in simulated time.

For a simple example of ASSEMBLE Block use, consider part of the operation at a small winery in California. The winery was just started recently, and its production volume does not yet justify purchase of a machine which puts labels on bottles automatically. As a result, this operation is done by hand, by a single worker. It takes 16 ± 3 seconds to moisten a label, apply it to a bottle, straighten it, and then put the bottle into a case. (The bottles have been previously filled with wine, and corked.) Each case holds 12 bottles. The Figure 7.28 Block Diagram shows how the labeling operation can be modeled to estimate the interarrival times of filled cases as they move to the shipping room from the labeling area. (It is understood that the GPSS Table named IATYM has IA as its argument.) The features of the model are straightforward. It is of interest to note how the SPLIT Block has been used to guarantee an unlimited source of bottles which need labels, and to bring about the necessary condition that all pertinent Transactions are members of one and the same Assembly Set. (See exercise 7, Section 7.30.)

The Figure 7.28 model was run through one hour of simulated time. Selected output from the run is shown in Figure 7.29. Note these features of the output.

1. The Block Counts in part (a) (from which the timer-segment counts have been eliminated) clearly show that only the surviving member of an assembly operation contributes to the Total Count at an ASSEMBLE Block. The Total Count at Block 5 (the RELEASE Block) is 221, whereas the Total Count at Block 6 (the ASSEMBLE Block) is only 19. The difference of 1 in the Total Counts at the ASSEMBLE Block, and the Block sequential to it, reveals that an assembly operation was in progress when the simulation ended. The Current Count of 1 at the ASSEMBLE Block indicates that the surviving member of the Assembly Set does contribute to the Current Count at the Block while the assembly is taking place.

2. The Current Events Chain in part (b) indicates that Transaction 4 is currently in the SPLIT Block

(Block 3), waiting to capture the worker at the SEIZE Block (Block 2).

3. The Future Events Chain in part (c) shows that Transaction 3 is currently in the ADVANCE Block (Block 4), simulating the bottle of wine to which a label is currently being applied. (A Limit Count of 1 was used on the GENERATE Block in the timer segment. This explains why there is no incipient timer-Transaction on the Future Chain.)

4. The Matching Chain in part (d) shows that it is Transaction 1 which is the surviving member of the current assembly operation. Notice that the Next Block Attempted column on the Matching Chain is blank, even though it is known that the surviving member of an assembly operation moves sequentially from the ASSEMBLE Block when the assembly is complete. (There is no special explanation, then, for the blank entry in the NBA column on a Matching

```
RELATIVE CLOCK        3600  ABSOLUTE CLOCK         3600
BLOCK COUNTS
BLOCK CURRENT    TOTAL      BLOCK CURRENT    TOTAL     BLOCK CURRENT    TOTAL
  1      0           1
  2      0         222
  3      1         444
  4      1         222
  5      0         221
  6      1          19
  7      0          18
  8      0          18
  9      0           1
 10      0           1
```

(a)

```
CURRENT EVENTS CHAIN
TRANS         BDT BLOCK   PR  SF   NBA  SET   MARK-TIME        P1        P2        P3        P4   SI TI DI CI MC  PC PF
  4                  3             2    1          1            0         0         0         0    1    1  2
                                                                0         0         0         0
                                                                0         0         0         0
```

(b)

```
FUTURE EVENTS CHAIN
TRANS         BDT BLOCK   PR  SF   NBA  SET   MARK-TIME        P1        P2        P3        P4   SI TI DI CI MC  PC PF
  3         3601    4             5    4          1            0         0         0         0          1  4
                                                                0         0         0         0
                                                                0         0         0         0
```

(c)

```
TRANSACTIONS IN MATCHING STATUS
TRANS         BDT BLOCK   PR  SF   NBA  SET   MARK-TIME        P1        P2        P3        P4   SI TI DI CI MC  PC PF
  1         3517    6                  3          1            0         0         0         0              1
                                                                0         0         0         0
                                                                0         0         0         0
```

(d)

FIGURE 7.29   Selected Output produced when the Figure 7.28 model was run (simulated time: 3600 seconds). (a) Block counts. (b) Current Events Chain. (c) Future Events Chain. (d) Matching Chain.

Chain.) In the MC (Matching Condition) column on the Matching Chain (third column from the right), note the entry of 1. This indicates that the corresponding Transaction is "in matching condition." In Section 7.28, use of the GATE Block to test whether there is a Transaction in matching condition in a user-specified Block is described. For a Transaction to be in matching condition, it is both necessary and sufficient that the Transaction be resident on a Matching Chain. Note the blanks under the MC columns for the Current and Future Events Chains in Figure 7.29(b) and (c). These blanks indicate that the corresponding Transactions are not in matching condition.

Now consider the significance of the chain column labeled SET (seventh column from the left in the chain printouts). Entered in this column is the number of the *next* Transaction in the corresponding Transaction's Assembly Set. In other words, each member of an Assembly Set points to exactly one other member in the same set, thereby forming a one-way linked list. For example, if there are three Transactions in an Assembly Set, the first points to the second, the second points to the third, and the third points back to the first. In the Figure 7.29 chain printouts, then, note that Transaction 4 on the Current Chain points via the SET entry to Transaction 1; Transaction 1, in turn, happens to be on the Matching Chain, and via its SET entry points to Transaction 3; finally, Transaction 3 happens to be on the Future Chain, and via its SET entry points back to Transaction 4, which closes the one-way linked list.

When the membership of an Assembly Set is increased at a SPLIT Block, the first offspring is merged into the one-way linked list between the parent, and whichever other Assembly Set member the parent had been pointing to. The second offspring is then merged into the list between the parent and the first offspring, and so on, until finally the last offspring is merged into the list between the parent and the next-to-last offspring. As explained in Chapter 6, the offspring are fetched, one by one, from the top of the stack in the latent pool, and of course are not necessarily ordered by Transaction Number. There is clearly no implied ordering by Transaction Number within Assembly Set lists, either.

In the case of one-member Assembly Sets, the entries in the TRANS and SET columns are identical. In other words, the sole member of such an Assembly Set points to itself as the "next" member.

In the next section, use of the ASSEMBLE Block is further illustrated in the context of a case study.

7.25 CASE STUDY 7D
Impact of Limited Manpower on Completion Times in Precedence Networks

(1) Statement of the Problem

The network in Figure 7D.1 represents a series of subprojects which must be carried out to complete an overall project. A pair of circles (nodes) connected by a directed line segment is used to depict each particular subproject. For example, node 1 is connected to node 2, depicting what is called subproject 1-to-2. Each directed line segment is labeled to show how many men and how many time units are required to perform the corresponding subproject. Subproject 1-to-2 requires four men, then, and takes 14 ± 6 time units to complete.

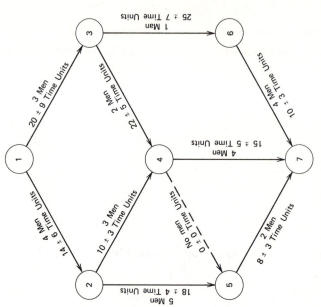

FIGURE 7D.1   Precedence Network for Case Study 7D

The Figure 7D.1 network also displays the precedence constraints on the various subprojects, indicating which subprojects must be completed before other subprojects can be started. For example, subprojects 2-to-4 and 3-to-4 must be completed before subproject 4-to-7 can be started. Similarly, subproject

5-to-7 cannot be initiated until subproject 2-to-5 is finished, and until the subprojects leading into node 4 have been completed. (Note that the dashed line leading from node 4 to node 5 represents a dummy subproject, requiring no men and no time. The dummy simply expresses a timing constraint with respect to initiation of subproject 5-to-7.)

In projects of the kind depicted in Figure 7D.1, it is of interest to know how much time is required to complete the overall project. More precisely, it is of interest to estimate the distribution of the "project completion time" random variable.[22] This distribution clearly depends on the subproject completion-time distributions, and on the precedence relations involved. Assuming a fixed number of men are assigned to work on the overall project, project completion time also depends on the available manpower. When economics are brought into the picture, a tradeoff may exist between project completion time, and overall manpower utilization.

Build a GPSS model to simulate the undertaking of the overall project shown in Figure 7D.1. Use the model to investigate behavior of the completion-time random variable, as a function of the number of men assigned to work on the overall project. Also estimate the distribution of the random variable "men-in-use" at each manpower level.

(2) Approach Taken in Building the Model

A Transaction is interpreted as a subproject foreman. Each subproject has its own foreman. The foreman does not come into the model, however, until precedence conditions permit the corresponding subproject to be initiated. (In some cases, a given foreman may remain in the model to handle two or more consecutive subprojects.) Of course, even when precedence conditions are satisfied, the foreman may have to wait for the needed manpower before he can initiate a subproject.

The following approach is taken to represent the various nodes in the network.

1. Whenever a node is the terminal point for two or more subprojects, an ASSEMBLE Block is used at the node. This guarantees that all subprojects leading into the node will be completed before an attempt is made to start subprojects originating at the node.

2. Whenever a node is the starting point for two or more subprojects, a SPLIT Block is used at the node. This provides the proper number of foremen to handle subprojects originating at the node.

Using these simple ideas, then, a SPLIT Block can be placed at node 1 in Figure 7D.1. Similarly, SPLIT Blocks (but no ASSEMBLE Blocks) can be used at nodes 2 and 3. At node 4, an ASSEMBLE-SPLIT sequence is indicated. At nodes 5 and 7, ASSEMBLE Blocks (but no SPLIT Blocks) are needed. Finally, neither an ASSEMBLE Block nor a SPLIT Block are needed at node 6. (Note that only 1 man is needed for subproject 3-to-6, whereas 4 men are needed for subproject 6-to-7. This explains why node 6 appears in the network in the first place.)

As for the manpower constraint, the manpower pool can be referenced by each subproject foreman from appropriately placed ENTER–LEAVE Blocks having the proper B-Operand values. In the simulation runs, the completion-time distribution can then be estimated when the capacity of the manpower Storage is 5 (the minimum number of men needed is 5, corresponding to subproject 6-to-7). Additional experiments can then be performed for increasingly larger Storage capacities. Eventually, the Storage capacity corresponding to essentially unlimited manpower will be found.

The distribution of the men-in-use random variable calls for use of a weighted Table, as discussed in Section 5.11. Instead of having the corresponding observer-Transaction be on the back of the Current Events Chain, however, it will be kept on the front of the Current Chain (see exercise 4 in Section 5.12). The disadvantage of doing this is that the observer-Transaction is virtually certain to be encountered by the Processor more than one time during each Scan Phase, with corresponding CPU-time implications. In this case, however, there is an offsetting reason for taking this approach (see exercise 3 in Section 7.30).

[22] Analytic techniques have been developed to estimate the distribution of project completion time in networks of the type shown in Figure 7D.1. Frequently, however, these techniques do not take the impact of limited manpower into account. Principal among these techniques are CPM (Critical Path Method), and PERT (Program Evaluation and Review Technique). For a brief introduction to these techniques, see chapter 13, "Management Planning Models", in reference A6, Section 1.7. Also see R. Van Slyke, "Monte Carlo Methods and the PERT Problem," Operations Research, Volume 11, No. 5 (September–October, 1963; pp. 839–860), and G. Ponce-Campos and T. J. Schriber, "Determination of Criticality Indices in the PERT Problem," Proceedings of the Third Conference on Applications of Simulation (AFIPS Press, Montvale, New Jersey; December, 1969, pp. 339–349).

(3) Table of Definitions

Time Unit : The time unit is implicit in the problem statement

TABLE 7D.1   Table of Definitions for Case Study 7D

GPSS Entity	Interpretation
Transactions	
Model Segment 1	Subproject foreman
Model Segment 2	Observer-Transaction
	P1 : Records the time an observation was most recently placed in the Table INUSE
Logic Switches	
NEXT1	Logic Switch used to prevent initiation of the next overall project simulation until the current iteration is finished
Storages	
MEN	Storage used to simulate the manpower constraint
Tables	
INUSE	Weighted Table in which the number of men-in-use is recorded
RTIME	Table in which project completion time is recorded

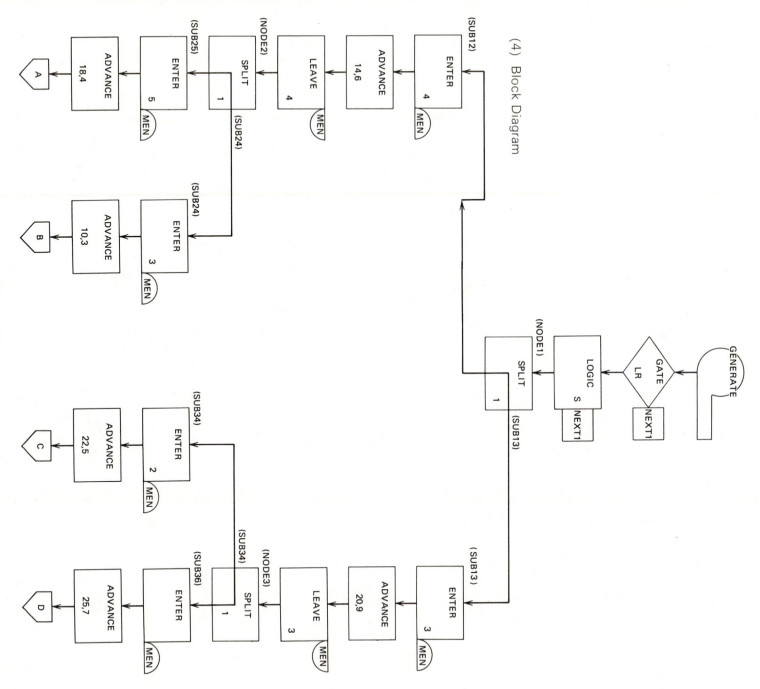

(4) Block Diagram

FIGURE 7D.2 Block Diagram for Case Study 7D

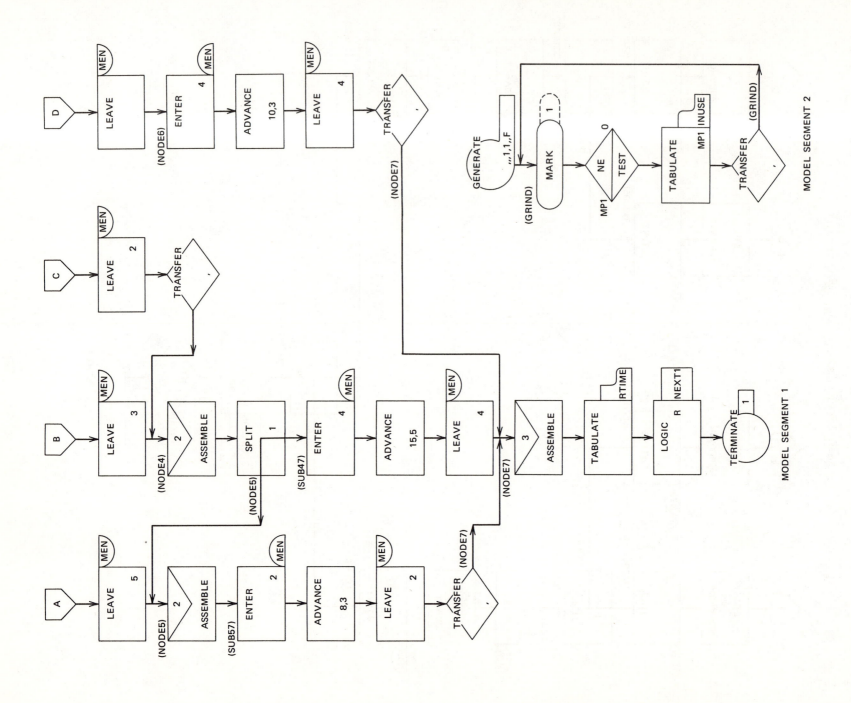

FIGURE 7D.2 (Continued)

(5) Extended Program Listing

BLOCK NUMBER	*LOC	OPERATION	A,B,C,D,E,F,G	COMMENTS	CARD NUMBER
		SIMULATE			1
	*				2
	*			STORAGE CAPACITY DEFINITION(S)	3
	*				4
		STORAGE	S$MEN,5	SUPPLY 5 MEN INITIALLY	5
	*				6
	*			TABLE DEFINITION(S)	7
	*				8
	INUSE	TABLE	S$MEN,0,1,W20	DISTRIBUTION OF MEN-IN-USE	9
	RTIME	TABLE	M1,25,25,20	TABLE FOR PROJECT COMPLETION TIMES	10
	*				11
	*				12
	*			MODEL SEGMENT 1	13
	*				14
1		GENERATE	NEXT1	PROVIDE A TRANSACTION WHENEVER NEEDED	15
2		GATE LR	NEXT1	WAIT UNTIL PRECEDING ITERATION IS FINISHED	16
3		LOGIC S	NEXT1	SHUT GATE ON FOLLOWING TRANSACTION	17
	*				18
4	NODE1	SPLIT	1,SUB13	SEND OFFSPRING TO HANDLE SUBPROJECT 1-TO-3	19
5	SUB12	ENTER	MEN,4	GET MEN FOR SUBPROJECT 1-TO-2	20
6		ADVANCE	14,6	DO THE SUBPROJECT	21
7		LEAVE	MEN,4	FREE THE MEN	22
	*				23
8	NODE2	SPLIT	1,SUB24	SEND OFFSPRING TO HANDLE SUBPROJECT 2-TO-4	24
9	SUB25	ENTER	MEN,5	GET MEN FOR SUBPROJECT 2-TO-5	25
10		ADVANCE	18,4	DO THE SUBPROJECT	26
11		LEAVE	MEN,5	FREE THE MEN	27
	*				28
12	NODE5	ASSEMBLE	2	WAIT FOR COMPLETION OF 2-TO-5 AND 4-TO-5	29
13	SUB57	ENTER	MEN,2	GET MEN FOR SUBPROJECT 5-TO-7	30
14		ADVANCE	8,3	DO THE SUBPROJECT	31
15		LEAVE	MEN,2	FREE THE MEN	32
16		TRANSFER	,NODE7	GO SIGNAL COMPLETION OF 5-TO-7	33
	*				34
17	SUB24	ENTER	MEN,3	GET MEN FOR SUBPROJECT 2-TO-4	35
18		ADVANCE	10,3	DO THE SUBPROJECT	36
19		LEAVE	MEN,3	FREE THE MEN	37
	*				38
20	NODE4	ASSEMBLE	2	WAIT FOR COMPLETION OF 2-TO-4 AND 3-TO-4	39
21		SPLIT	1,NODE5	SEND OFFSPRING TO SIGNAL NODE 4 COMPLETION	40
22	SUB47	ENTER	MEN,4	GET MEN FOR SUBPROJECT 4-TO-7	41
23		ADVANCE	15,5	DO THE SUBPROJECT	42
24		LEAVE	MEN,4	FREE THE MEN	43
	*				44
25	NODE7	ASSEMBLE	3	WAIT FOR COMPLETION OF FINAL SUBPROJECTS	45
26		TABULATE	RTIME	RECORD PROJECT TIME IN TABLE	46
27		LOGIC R	NEXT1	OPEN GATE FOR THE NEXT ITERATION	47
28		TERMINATE	1	CURRENT ITERATION IS FINISHED	48
	*				49
29	SUB13	ENTER	MEN,3	GET MEN FOR SUBPROJECT 1-TO-3	50
30		ADVANCE	20,9	DO THE SUBPROJECT	51
31		LEAVE	MEN,3	FREE THE MEN	52
	*				53
32	NODE3	SPLIT	1,SUB34	SEND OFFSPRING TO HANDLE SUBPROJECT 3-TO-4	54
33	SUB36	ENTER	MEN	GET A MAN FOR SUBPROJECT 3-TO-6	55
34		ADVANCE	25,7	DO THE SUBPROJECT	56
35		LEAVE	MEN	FREE THE MAN	57
	*				58
36	NODE6	ENTER	MEN,4	GET MEN FOR SUBPROJECT 6-TO-7	59
37		ADVANCE	10,3	DO THE SUBPROJECT	60
38		LEAVE	MEN,4	FREE THE MEN	61
39		TRANSFER	,NODE7	GO SIGNAL COMPLETION OF 3-TO-7	62
	*				63
40	SUB34	ENTER	MEN,2	GET MEN FOR SUBPROJECT 3-TO-4	64
41		ADVANCE	22,5	DO THE SUBPROJECT	65
42		LEAVE	MEN,2	FREE THE MEN	66
43		TRANSFER	,NODE4	GO SIGNAL COMPLETION OF 3-TO-4	67
	*				68
	*			MODEL SEGMENT 2	69
	*				70
44		GENERATE	,,1,1,,F	BRING IN ONE HIGH-PRIORITY OBSERVER	71
45	GRIND	MARK	1	SET P1 = ABSOLUTE CLOCK TIME	72
46		TEST NE	MP1,0	WAIT UNTIL THE CLOCK CHANGES	73
47		TABULATE	INUSE,MP1	RECORD CURRENT NUMBER OF MEN-IN-USE	74
48		TRANSFER	,GRIND	GO SET UP FOR THE NEXT CLOCK UPDATE	75

FIGURE 7D.3 Extended Program Listing for Case Study 7D

```
*
**     CONTROL CARDS AND STORAGE CAPACITY RE-DEFINITIONS

       STORAGE   CAPACITY
       MEN         11

          START    250                                                    76
          STORAGE  S$MEN,6   SIMULATE FOR A MANPOWER LEVEL OF  5           77
                             RECONFIGURE THE MANPOWER LEVEL                78
          CLEAR              CLEAR FOR THE NEW CONFIGURATION               79
          START    250       SIMULATE FOR A MANPOWER LEVEL OF  6           80
          STORAGE  S$MEN,7   RECONFIGURE THE MANPOWER LEVEL                81
                                                                          82
          CLEAR              CLEAR FOR THE NEW CONFIGURATION               83
          START    250       SIMULATE FOR A MANPOWER LEVEL OF  7           84
          STORAGE  S$MEN,8   RECONFIGURE THE MANPOWER LEVEL                85
          CLEAR              CLEAR FOR THE NEW CONFIGURATION               86
          START    250       SIMULATE FOR A MANPOWER LEVEL OF  8           87
          STORAGE  S$MEN,9   RECONFIGURE THE MANPOWER LEVEL                88
          CLEAR              CLEAR FOR THE NEW CONFIGURATION               89
          START    250       SIMULATE FOR A MANPOWER LEVEL OF  9           90
          STORAGE  S$MEN,10  RECONFIGURE THE MANPOWER LEVEL                91
          CLEAR              CLEAR FOR THE NEW CONFIGURATION               92
          START    250       SIMULATE FOR A MANPOWER LEVEL OF 10           93
          STORAGE  S$MEN,11  RECONFIGURE THE MANPOWER LEVEL                94
          CLEAR              CLEAR FOR THE NEW CONFIGURATION               95
          START    250       SIMULATE FOR A MANPOWER LEVEL OF 11           96
          STORAGE  S$MEN,12  RECONFIGURE THE MANPOWER LEVEL                97
          CLEAR              CLEAR FOR THE NEW CONFIGURATION               98
          START    250       SIMULATE FOR A MANPOWER LEVEL OF 12           99
          END                RETURN CONTROL TO THE OPERATING SYSTEM       100
```

FIGURE 7D.3 (Continued)

(6) Program Output

```
STORAGE   CAPACITY   AVERAGE    AVERAGE       ENTRIES   AVERAGE      CURRENT    MAXIMUM
                     CONTENTS   UTILIZATION             TIME/TRAN    CONTENTS   CONTENTS
MEN         11       7.136      .648          7000      15.067                  11
```

(a)

```
TABLE INUSE
ENTRIES IN TABLE      MEAN ARGUMENT     STANDARD DEVIATION   SUM OF ARGUMENTS
        2161          7.335             2.589                15853.000          NON-WEIGHTED
       14779          7.136             2.632               105476.000          WEIGHTED

UPPER       OBSERVED      PER CENT    CUMULATIVE    CUMULATIVE    MULTIPLE     DEVIATION
LIMIT       FREQUENCY     OF TOTAL    PERCENTAGE    REMAINDER     OF MEAN      FROM MEAN
   0            0           .00          .0           100.0        -.000        -2.832
   1           10           .06          .0            99.9         .136        -2.446
   2            2           .01          .0            99.9         .272        -2.060
   3         2425         16.40        16.4            83.5         .408        -1.674
   4         1156          7.82        24.3            75.6         .545        -1.288
   5          142           .96        25.2            74.7         .681         -.901
   6          381          2.57        27.8            72.1         .817         -.515
   7         4317         29.21        57.0            42.9         .954         -.129
   8         2804         18.97        76.0            23.9        1.090          .256
   9           25           .16        76.2            23.7        1.226          .642
  10          996          6.73        82.9            17.0        1.363         1.028
  11         2521         17.05       100.0             .0         1.499         1.414

REMAINING FREQUENCIES ARE ALL ZERO
```

(b)

```
TABLE RTIME
ENTRIES IN TABLE      MEAN ARGUMENT     STANDARD DEVIATION   SUM OF ARGUMENTS
         250          59.115            6.871                14779.000          NON-WEIGHTED

UPPER       OBSERVED      PER CENT    CUMULATIVE    CUMULATIVE    MULTIPLE     DEVIATION
LIMIT       FREQUENCY     OF TOTAL    PERCENTAGE    REMAINDER     OF MEAN      FROM MEAN
  25            0           .00          .0           100.0         .422        -4.965
  50           26         10.39        10.3            89.5         .845        -1.326
  75          224         89.59       100.0             .0         1.268         2.311

REMAINING FREQUENCIES ARE ALL ZERO
```

(c)

FIGURE 7D.4   Selected Program Output for Case Study 7D, corresponding to a manpower level of 11. (a) Storage statistics. (b) Tabulation of men-in-use. (c) Tabulation of project completion times.

(7) Discussion

Model Logic. In the Figure 7D.3 Extended Program Listing, Location names have been placed on some Blocks even though they are not needed. This has been done to make the Extended Program Listing correspond to the Figure 7D.2 Block Diagram. (For ease in studying the Block Diagram, these extra Location labels appear on key Blocks to assist in identifying the various network nodes and subprojects. To avoid clutter, there are no annotations on the Figure 7D.2 Block Diagram.)

Note how the GATE and Logic Switch have been used at the beginning of Model Segment 1 to prevent initiation of the next overall project simulation until the current iteration is finished. The initiating Transaction does not leave its GENERATE Block until it is time to begin the next iteration. Recall from Chapter 4 that a Transaction's Mark Time value is not assigned until it succeeds in leaving its GENERATE Block. Also recall from Chapter 6 that each offspring Transaction introduced at a SPLIT Block has the same Mark Time as its parent. This pair of facts explain why the M1 value of the surviving Transaction at the last ASSEMBLE Block (Block 25, Figure 7D.3) equals project completion time for the current simulation. (Note that M1 is the argument for the Table RTIME; see Card 10, Figure 7D.3.)

Model Segment 2 consists of the self-contained Block Diagram supplied to estimate the distribution of the men-in-use random variable. The logic of this segment is straightforward. Note the observer-Transaction's Priority Level of 1 (insuring that it will always be at the front of the Current Chain), and the fact that it has fullword Parameters (insuring there will not be overflow when the MARK Block is executed).

Model Implementation. As evident from the control-card sequence in Figure 7D.3, the simulation was performed sequentially for the cases of 5, 6, 7,..., 10, 11, and 12 men in a single batch session. (Preliminary work indicated there would never be more than 11 men in use concurrently.) Each estimate of project completion time is based on a sample of size 250 (250 project simulations at each manpower level).

Program Output.[23] Figure 7D.4 shows selected output from the simulation corresponding to a manpower level of 11. Parts (a), (b), and (c) show Storage statistics, and output for the Tables INUSE and RTIME, respectively. Note that the AVERAGE CONTENTS of the Storage and the weighted MEAN AVERAGE in the Table INUSE are identical, as expected.

A summary of the output produced by the Figure 7D.3 model appears in Table 7D.2. The table shows completion-time means and standard deviations. It also shows the utilization of manpower at each manpower level, and indicates the maximum number of men ever in use concurrently (as observed via the value of the last UPPER LIMIT statistic in the Table INUSE). At various times during one or more of the simulations, all men in the manpower pool were in use, providing the pool consisted of 11 men or less. As implied by the last row of information in Table 7D.2, 11 men corresponds to "unlimited manpower." (There were never 12 men in use concurrently. In spite of this, the statistics in the 12-man row do not exactly match those in the 11-man row. You are asked to explain why in exercise 6 in Section 7.30.) As for the manpower utilizations, they go through a maximum at a manpower level of 8, but do not increase

[23]Total CPU time for the simulation on an IBM 360/67 computer was 57.6 seconds.

TABLE 7D.2   Summary of Program Output for Case Study 7D

Number of Men Available	Project Completion Times		Manpower Utilization	Maximum Number of Men in Use Concurrently
	Mean	Standard Deviation		
5	118.1	9.1	.719	5
6	98.4	8.8	.715	6
7	81.4	6.9	.745	7
8	63.6	4.9	.835	8
9	66.0	6.1	.704	9
10	65.4	6.5	.646	10
11	59.1	6.9	.648	11
12	59.2	6.2	.592	11

consistently prior to that level, or decrease consistently beyond that level.

The decreasing trend shown by the completion-time mean and standard deviation in the first four rows of the Figure 7D.2 table is to be expected. With 9 or more men in the manpower pool, however, the trend is disrupted and the pattern becomes irregular. At first glance, this seems to be counter-intuitive. Could the average completion time possibly increase with increasing availability of manpower? The answer is, "under some circumstances, yes." Depending on the network involved, it is not always the best policy to initiate each next subproject as soon as possible. Doing so may delay the initiation of some other subproject longer than otherwise necessary. Depending on what lies beyond this other subproject in the network, the effect of its delay can be magnified as the overall project proceeds, resulting in an increase in project completion time. To make this point numerically, the holding times at the various ADVANCE Blocks in the Figure 7D.3 model were changed to their expected values, and the resulting deterministic model was run. (Each "START 250" card was also replaced with a "START 1" card for this run.) The resulting output is summarized in Table 7D.3. The irregular trend in project completion time is still present, even under these deterministic conditions. (In exercise 4, Section 7.30, you are asked to find the subproject whose early initiation actually increases project completion time when the manpower level is increased from 8 to 9 under these deterministic conditions.)

7.26 Accumulating Two or More Assembly Set Members at a Point: The GATHER Block

The purpose of the GATHER Block, shown in Figure 7.30, is to accumulate two or more mem-

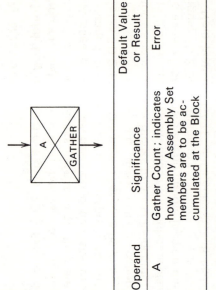

Operand	Significance	Default Value or Result
A	Gather Count; indicates how many Assembly Set members are to be accumulated at the Block	Error

FIGURE 7.30   The GATHER Block and its A Operand

bers of an Assembly Set at a point until a specified number of the set's members are present there. The specified number, termed the Gather Count, is supplied through the GATHER Block's A Operand. When the Gather Count has been reached, the accumulated members of the Assembly Set are permitted to leave the GATHER Block and resume their forward movement in the model.

Like the ASSEMBLE Block, the GATHER Block has the following features.

1. For a given Assembly Set at a given GATHER Block, only one gathering operation at a time can be in process.

2. For a given GATHER Block, gathering operations with respect to two or more Assembly Sets can be in process concurrently.

3. For a given Assembly Set, gathering operations can be in process concurrently at two or more GATHER Blocks.

4. After a gathering operation has been completed for a given Assembly Set and GATHER Block, another gathering operation can begin for that set, at that Block.

TABLE 7D.3   Output Produced for the Figure 7D.1 Network with Deterministic Subproject Completion Times

Number of Men Available	Project Completion Time	Manpower Utilization	Maximum Number of Men in Use Concurrently
5	117	.719	5
6	99	.708	6
7	85	.707	7
8	60	.876	8
9	67	.697	9
10	67	.628	10
11	58	.670	11
12	58	.615	11

As for Block Counts, each Transaction which enters a GATHER Block contributes both to the Total Count and, until it moves into the sequential Block, to the Current Count. From the point of view of chains, each Transaction which initiates a gathering operation is removed from the Current Events Chain when it enters the GATHER Block, and is put on a Matching Chain. As before, the Matching Chain can be thought of as being unique to both the Assembly Set *and* the GATHER Block involved. Each time another Transaction from that Assembly Set moves into that GATHER Block, it is removed from the Current Chain and placed on the back of the appropriate Matching Chain. Eventually, a Transaction arrives which satisfies the Gather Count. This Transaction, too, is removed from the Current Chain, and placed on the back of the Matching Chain. The Processor then transfers all the Transactions from the Matching Chain to the Current Chain, working from the front of the Matching Chain toward the back. Of course, as the Transactions are moved to the Current Chain, they are put down there as the last member in their Priority Class. This means that in event of Priority Level ties, the gathered Transactions are arranged first-come, first-served, on the Current Chain. After finishing the transfer operation, the Processor immediately restarts its scan of the Current Events Chain, insuring that the gathered Transactions will be processed at the current instant in simulated time.

As an example of GATHER Block use, consider this simple extension of the Figure 7.28 winery model. Before labeling the bottles of wine, the worker must cork the previously-filled bottles. Bottles are corked one at a time. The process requires that the worker position a bottle in an appropriate machine, which then automatically drives a cork into the neck of the bottle. The semi-automatic method takes 8 ± 3 seconds. The worker's procedure is to first cork two dozen bottles, then label them and put them into cases, then cork another two dozen bottles, etc.

A model for the corking-and-labeling operation is shown in Figure 7.31. The annotated model is self-explanatory. As in the Figure 7.28 model, the objective is to estimate the interarrival times of filled cases as they move to the shipping room from the corking-and-labeling area. Note the use of the PRIORITY Block to guarantee that after 24 bottles have been corked, the worker will next label the bottles before returning to the corking activity.

The Figure 7.31 model was run through 30 minutes of simulated time. Selected output from the model is shown in Figure 7.32. Note these features of the output.

1. The Block Counts in part (a) (from which the timer-segment counts have been eliminated) indicate that Transactions which are being gathered contribute to both the Current Count and the Total Count at the pertinent GATHER Block. At Block 7 (the GATHER Block), the Current Count is 6, and the Total Count is 78, whereas the Total Count at the preceding Block is also 78, but at the sequential Block is only 72.

2. The Future Events Chain in part (b) shows that Transaction 21 is currently in the ADVANCE Block (Block 3), simulating the bottle of wine which is currently being corked. (The Current Events Chain is empty. There was no blockage in the model at the time the simulation stopped, nor were there any incipient events to be performed.)

3. The Matching Chain in part (c) appears to contain only a single Transaction. This Transaction, number 14, is currently in the GATHER Block. From the Block Counts, we know there are 6 Transactions in the GATHER Block. From the logic of the model, we also know that each of these Transactions is on one and the same Matching Chain. Why, then, don't these 6 Transactions appear in the Matching Chain printout? Unfortunately, it turns out that only the Transaction at the *front* of each Matching Chain is printed out by the GPSS Processor. This explains why only one Transaction appears on the Matching Chain in part (c). As expected, Transaction 14 is in matching condition, i.e., its MC chain entry is 1. Also note, via the SET entries, how Transaction 21 points to Transaction 14 as the next member in its Assembly Set.

7.27 Coordinating Departure of Assembly Set Members from Two Points: The MATCH Block

Like the ASSEMBLE and GATHER Blocks, the MATCH Block, shown in Figure 7.33, has only an A Operand. The A Operand supplies the name of some Location in the model, and in this sense points to a Block. The Block pointed to is called the "conjugate Block." The operation of the MATCH Block is best explained in terms of this conjugate Block. When a Transaction enters a MATCH Block, the Processor follows one or the other of these two procedures.

Procedure 1. If the conjugate Block contains a member of the first Transaction's Assembly Set, and if that member is in matching condition (i.e., is on a Matching Chain), then "a match is found." When a match is found, the Processor (a) transfers the matching Transaction from its Matching Chain to the Current Events Chain, (b) turns the Status Change Flag on,

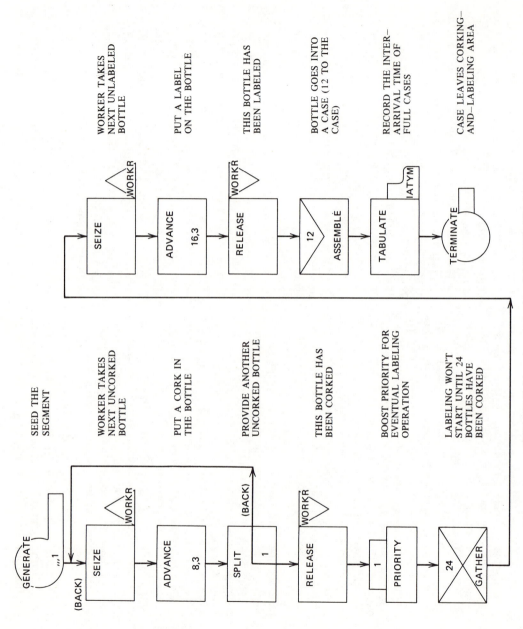

FIGURE 7.31   An example of GATHER Block use

and (c) continues to move the first Transaction forward in the model.

Procedure 2. If no match is found at the conjugate Block, the Processor removes the first Transaction from the Current Events Chain, and places it in matching condition on a Matching Chain. The Matching Chain is unique to that Assembly Set *and* to that MATCH Block.

Under Procedure 1, it is of interest to know what GPSS Blocks allow a Transaction to be in matching condition. In Sections 7.24 and 7.26, respectively, we saw that Transactions can be in matching condition at ASSEMBLE Blocks (while an assembly operation is in process), and at GATHER Blocks (while a gathering operation is in process). And, under Procedure 2 above, it is evident that Transactions can be put into matching condition at MATCH Blocks. The ASSEMBLE, GATHER, and MATCH Blocks are the only three types in which Transactions can be in a matching condition. Nevertheless, a MATCH Block does not have to have one of these three Block types as its conjugate. For example, a MATCH Block can point to an ADVANCE Block, or to a SEIZE Block, or whatever. If this is done, then Procedure 2 will always be invoked for a Transaction entering the MATCH Block in question, because for certain no match will be found.

Under Procedure 1, what happens if the conjugate Block is an ASSEMBLE Block (or a GATHER Block), and a match is found even though the assembly operation (or the gathering operation) is not yet complete? As indicated, the Processor removes the matched Transaction from its Matching Chain (and therefore from its matching condition), places it on the Current Events Chain, and so on. Although this may not appear to make sense logically (because the assembly or gathering operation is not yet complete, by hypothesis), this is what the GPSS

RELATIVE CLOCK   1800 ABSOLUTE CLOCK   1800

BLOCK COUNTS

BLOCK	CURRENT	TOTAL	BLOCK	CURRENT	TOTAL	BLOCK	CURRENT	TOTAL
1	0	1	11	0	6			
2	0	79	12	0	6			
3	1	79	13	0	6			
4	0	156						
5	0	78						
6	0	78						
7	6	78						
8	0	72						
9	0	72						
10	0	72						

(a)

FUTURE EVENTS CHAIN

TRANS	BDT	BLOCK	PR	SF	NBA	SET	MARK-TIME	P1	P2	P3	P4	SI	TI	DI	CI	MC	PC	PF
21	1804	3			4	14	1	0	0	0	0					4		
								0	0	0	0							
								0	0	0	0							

(b)

TRANSACTIONS IN MATCHING STATUS

TRANS	BDT	BLOCK	PR	SF	NBA	SET	MARK-TIME	P1	P2	P3	P4	SI	TI	DI	CI	MC	PC	PF
14	1755	7	1			1	1	0	0	0	0					1		
								0	0	0	0							
								0	0	0	0							

(c)

FIGURE 7.32   Selected Output produced when the Figure 7.31 model was run (simulated time : 1800 seconds). (a) Block counts. (b) Future Events Chain. (c) Matching Chain.

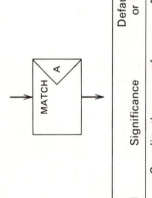

Operand	Significance	Default Value or Result
		Error
A	Supplies the name of the Location which the conjugate Block occupies	

FIGURE 7.33   The MATCH Block and its A Operand

Processor does. Fortunately, it is rarely of interest, if ever, to have a MATCH Block's conjugate be an ASSEMBLE or GATHER Block.

Now suppose that a Transaction moves into a MATCH Block, no match is found at the conjugate Block, and the Transaction is consequently put into matching condition on a Matching Chain. Under what conditions will this Transaction be taken off the Matching Chain, and be put back on the move? First of all, realize that while the Transaction is on the Matching Chain, it is totally inactive in the model. The Processor will not "test for a match" on behalf of this Transaction each time the Current Events Chain is scanned. There is no way, then, for this Transaction to help itself get back on the move. The Transaction will be put back on the move only if the MATCH Block in which it is resident is the conjugate of *some other MATCH Block*, called the "conjugate MATCH Block." Then, when a member of its Assembly Set moves into this other MATCH Block, the Processor follows Procedure 1, which has the effect of putting the detained Transaction back on the move.

The most frequent use of the MATCH Block by far is to have it point to another MATCH Block which, in turn, points back to the first MATCH Block. For an example of such MATCH-Block use, suppose that MATCH Blocks are placed at Locations LOCA and LOCB in a model, as suggested in Figure 7.34, each having the other as

its conjugate. Assume that a Transaction arrives at the LOCA MATCH Block, and finds no match. It is then put onto a Matching Chain, per Procedure 2 above. Later, when a member of the same Assembly Set moves into the LOCB MATCH Block, that Transaction finds a match. Procedure 1 is then invoked, with the effect that the two Assembly Set members leave their respective MATCH Blocks simultaneously (where the term "simultaneous" is subject to the usual interpretation). The overriding use of the MATCH Block is to bring about such coordinated departure of Assembly Set members from two distinct points in a model.

It is acceptable for a MATCH Block to have itself as its own conjugate. An example of such a Block would be "IAMIT MATCH IAMIT". This Block behaves exactly like a "GATHER 2" Block.

A more complete example of MATCH Block use is shown in the Figure 7.35 model. Units of work arrive at a point every 300 ± 200 time units. Each unit is split into two parts, Parts 1 and 2, with work being performed on the two parts in parallel by two different workers. The first worker (MAN1) works 100 ± 20 time units doing Step 1 on Part 1. The second worker (MAN2) works 110 ± 25 time units doing Step 1 on Part 2. Neither worker can begin Step 2 until the other has finished Step 1, because Parts 1 and 2 must be checked against each other at this intermediate point to determine that tolerance requirements are satisfied. (The Figure 7.35 model assumes that the time required to check tolerances is negligibly small. You are asked to relax this assumption in exercise 8, Section 7.30.) Eventually, after Step 2 is finished for each part, the first worker combines the two parts in what is called Step 3. Finally, the interarrival time of finished units is measured as they reach the end of the model.

Referring again to Figure 7.34, suppose that two (or more) members of an Assembly Set enter the LOCA MATCH Block, find no match, and consequently go onto a Matching Chain. Now suppose that another member of the Assembly Set enters the LOCB MATCH Block. Will both (or all) of the Transactions in the LOCA MATCH Block be returned to the Current Chain as a result, or only one? The answer is that only one Transaction will be removed from matching condition at the LOCA Block. Will this Transaction be the first of the two (or more) which entered the LOCA MATCH Block? Not except by coincidence. The Processor makes no attempt to follow first-in, first-out ordering under the circumstances

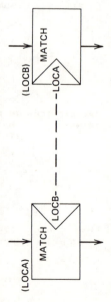

FIGURE 7.34   A first example of MATCH Block use

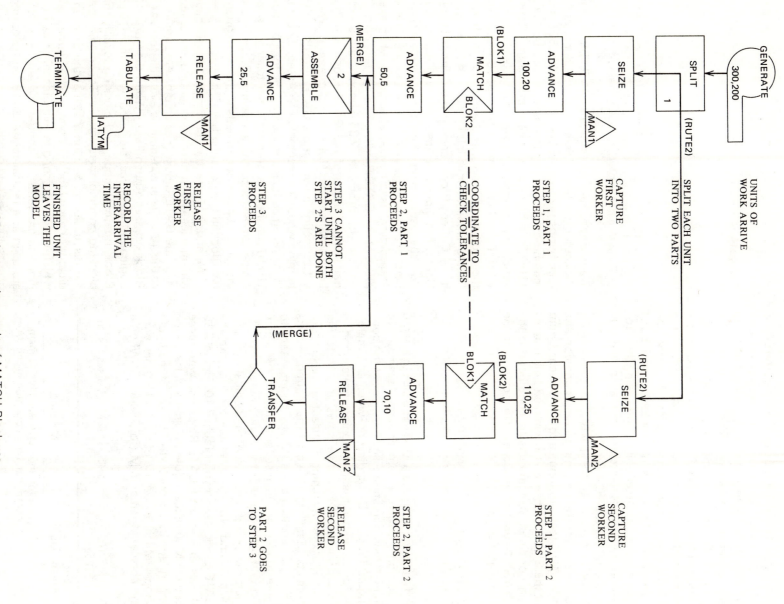

GENERATE
300,200

UNITS OF
WORK ARRIVE

SPLIT 1

SPLIT EACH UNIT
INTO TWO PARTS

(RUTE2)

SEIZE MAN1

CAPTURE
FIRST
WORKER

ADVANCE
100,20

STEP 1, PART 1
PROCEEDS

MATCH BLOK2 (BLOK1)

COORDINATE TO
CHECK TOLERANCES

ADVANCE
50,5

STEP 2, PART 1
PROCEEDS

(MERGE)

ASSEMBLE 2

STEP 3 CANNOT
START UNTIL BOTH
STEP 2'S ARE DONE

ADVANCE
25,5

STEP 3
PROCEEDS

RELEASE MAN1

RELEASE
FIRST
WORKER

TABULATE IATYM

RECORD THE
INTERARRIVAL
TIME

TERMINATE

FINISHED UNIT
LEAVES THE
MODEL

(RUTE2)

SEIZE MAN2

CAPTURE
SECOND
WORKER

ADVANCE
110,25

STEP 1, PART 2
PROCEEDS

MATCH BLOK1 (BLOK2)

ADVANCE
70,10

STEP 2, PART 2
PROCEEDS

RELEASE MAN2

RELEASE
SECOND
WORKER

TRANSFER

PART 2 GOES
TO STEP 3

(MERGE)

FIGURE 7.35   A second example of MATCH Block use

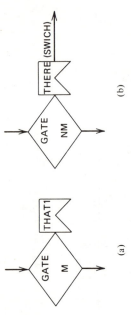

(a)

(b)

FIGURE 7.36   Examples of GATE Block use with the logical mnemonics M and NM. (a) Refusal mode. (b) Conditional transfer mode.

described. When the Transaction enters the LOCB MATCH Block, the Processor searches through its Assembly Set in a sequence corresponding to the underlying one-way linked list, looking for another Assembly Set member in matching condition at the conjugate Block. The first Assembly Set member checked is the one to which the LOCB Transaction points, via its SET entry; the second member checked is the one to which the first checked member points, and so on. This procedure clearly fails to provide for first-in, first-out, at the LOCA MATCH Block.

As is true with ASSEMBLE and GATHER Blocks, a Transaction in matching condition at a MATCH Block contributes to the Current Count at the Block. Even after it is removed from matching condition, it continues to contribute to the Current Count until it succeeds in moving into the sequential Block.

7.28 Testing for an Assembly Set Member in Matching Condition Elsewhere: The GATE Block

A Transaction can use a MATCH Block to ask the question, "is there a member of my Assembly Set in matching condition elsewhere, i.e., at the conjugate Block?" Depending on whether a match is found, either the questioning Transaction is placed into totally inactive status on a Matching Chain, or the "matching Transaction" is brought from its Matching Chain to the Current Events Chain. In some models, it may be important to have a Transaction test for a match elsewhere without having one or the other of these two effects occur. For this reason, the Logical Mnemonics M and NM are available for use with the GATE Block, as shown in Table 7.10. Figure 7.36 shows examples of GATE Block use with these Logical Mnemonics. (Note the shape of the Block appendage in this context.) Part (a) of the figure shows refusal-mode use of the GATE Block with the Logical Mnemonic M (for "match"). When a

Transaction tries to enter the GATE Block, the Processor will test to determine whether another member of the Transaction's Assembly Set is in matching condition in the Block in the Location THAT1. If there is a match, the testing Transaction is permitted to move into the GATE Block (and, from there, immediately tries to move into the sequential Block). If there is no match, the testing Transaction is left in a blocked condition in its Current Block, and on the Current Events Chain. The blocked Transaction will then reconduct the test each time the Current Chain is scanned. If and when a match is found, the "other Transaction" is in no way affected by what takes place at the GATE Block.

Part (b) of Figure 7.36 shows conditional-transfer-mode use of the GATE Block with the Logical Mnemonic NM (for "no match"). When a Transaction arrives at the GATE, it tests to determine whether a member of its Assembly Set is in matching condition in the Block in the Location THERE. If there is no match, the testing Transaction proceeds to the sequential Block in the model; otherwise, it proceeds to the nonsequential Block in the Location SWICH.

M and NM are the 11th and 12th Logical Mnemonics which have been introduced for use with the GATE Block. (For a complete summary of the 12 Logical Mnemonics available for GATE Block use, see Appendix J.) When the other 10 Logical Mnemonics are used with the GATE Block in refusal mode, and blocking results, the blocking conditions are *unique*. This means, per the discussion in Section 7.2, that the Scan Indicator of each blocked Transaction is turned on, which results in economy with respect to CPU-time requirements. In contrast, when M or NM are used at a refusal-mode GATE, and blocking occurs, the blocking condition is *nonunique*. The Scan Indicator on such blocked Transactions remains off, and the Processor tries anew, at each scan of the Current Chain, to move these blocked

TABLE 7.10   Additional Logical Mnemonics for the GATE Block

Logical Mnemonic	Meaning
M	Test for another Assembly Set member in matching condition in the "A-Block"
NM	Test for no other Assembly Set member in matching condition in the "A-Block"

Transactions into the "GATE M" or "GATE NM" Block. Hence, use of M or NM with the GATE Block is relatively inefficient with respect to CPU-time requirements.

7.29 Final Comments on Assembly Sets

7.29.1 Matching Chain(s): Singular or Plural?

Sections 7.24, 7.26, and 7.27, respectively indicate that each Assembly Set has a unique Matching Chain at each ASSEMBLE, GATHER, and MATCH Block in a model. This is true, internally. Nevertheless, in Matching Chain printout, the Processor makes no distinctions among these various Matching Chains. Matching Chain printout simply shows a single list of Transactions, arranged in order of increasing Transaction Number. These Transactions are not at all segregated in terms of the Matching Chains on which they are resident. (The situation here is analogous to the way Transactions appear in Interrupt Chain printout.) All Transactions which are in matching condition at ASSEMBLE Blocks appear in this list. For each gathering operation which is in process in the model, *one* Transaction appears in this list. (Remember from Section 7.26 that the Matching Chain printout for Transactions involved in a gathering operation is incomplete.) The Matching Chain does include each Transaction in matching condition at one or another of the various MATCH Blocks in the model. In particular, even when two or more members of a given Assembly Set are in matching condition at a given MATCH Block, they are all included in the Matching Chain printout.

As is true of the Current, Future, and Interrupt Chains, Matching Chain printout is produced by the Processor at the end of a simulation only if 1 is used as the D Operand on the START card. The PRINT Block can also be used to produce Matching Chain printout. For this purpose, the Block's A and B Operands are not used, and the field C mnemonic is MAT. Matching Chain printout occurs, then, when a Transaction moves into the Block "PRINT ,,MAT".

7.29.2 Implementation of Pending Preempts at ASSEMBLE, GATHER, and MATCH Blocks

What happens when a Transaction's Preempt Flag is on (indicating that a preemption is pending for the Transaction), and the Transaction moves into an ASSEMBLE, GATHER, or MATCH Block? If the Transaction happens to be the one which completes a gathering operation at a GATHER Block, or if it finds a match at the MATCH Block's conjugate, then the Transaction continues on the move, and the preempt continues to be pending. Otherwise, the Transaction goes into matching condition on a Matching Chain, as usual, *and* the preempt is implemented as well. (This statement assumes the analyst will avoid having a Transaction be removed from a model at an ASSEMBLE Block when that Transaction currently holds a Facility.) At this point, note that the Transaction is now experiencing delay for two different reasons: (a) It is waiting for completion of either an assembly or a gathering operation, or is waiting to be matched by another member of its Assembly Set, and (b) It is waiting for the return of the Facility at which it has been preempted. The delay of the Transaction will continue until neither of these reasons for delay is any longer in effect. At that time, the Transaction will be returned to the Current Chain, with its Next Block Attempted being sequential to the ASSEMBLE, GATHER, or MATCH Block at which the delay was originally initiated.

7.30 Exercises

1. In Figure 7D.4 (Case Study 7D), the MAXIMUM CONTENTS of the Storage MEN and the largest UPPER LIMIT value in the Table INUSE are equal. This need not always be the case. Explain how a certain type of time tie could result in the MAXIMUM CONTENTS statistic actually being *larger* than the true value for the maximum number of men in use concurrently.

2. Assume that in the Figure 7D.1 network (Case Study 7D), subproject 1-to-2 is completed at a time when exactly 1 man is available. Completion of subproject 1-to-2 makes another 4 men available, for a total of 5. In the Case Study 7D model, will subproject 2-to-5 or 2-to-4 be initiated next? Explain your reasoning. (Assume no other subprojects are waiting to be initiated at the simulated time in question.)

3. Show how to modify Model Segment 2 in Case Study 7D (designing it along the lines of Figure 5.21) so that the observer-Transaction will be last on the Current Events Chain, not first. There is a reason why this approach was not used in Case Study 7D. Can you determine the reason?

4. In the Figure 7D.1 network, set subproject completion times equal to their expected values. Then do a hand simulation of the overall project for a manpower level of 8. Now repeat the hand simulation for a manpower level of 9. Based on your project completion time

increases when the manpower level increases from 8 to 9, as shown in Table 7D.3.

5. Show how to modify the Case Study 7D model so that various manpower levels are investigated under otherwise-identical sets of experimental conditions. Simulate with the resulting model, and compare the mean completion times with those shown in Table 7D.2. Does the same irregular pattern evident in Table 7D.2 occur in your output?

6. Explain how it can be that the entries in the last row in Table 7D.2 can differ from the entries in the next-to-last row.

7. A small savings in CPU time would result if the SPLIT Block in Figure 7.28 were repositioned either between the ADVANCE and RELEASE Blocks, or between the RELEASE and ASSEMBLE Blocks. Explain why. (Note that in a similar situation in Figure 7.31, the SPLIT Block does appear between the ADVANCE and RELEASE Blocks.)

8. In the Figure 7.35 model, it is assumed that the time required for the two workers to check tolerances on Parts 1 and 2 is negligibly small. Show how to modify the model under the assumption that it requires 10 ± 4 time units to check tolerances.

9. In Figure 7.35, an error condition would eventually result if the offspring Transaction moved into the "ASSEMBLE 2" Block before its parent did. Reason: after completion of the assembly operation, the offspring would move into the "RELEASE MAN1" Block, thereby attempting to release a Facility not under its control. This would result in Execution Error 415, FACILITY RELEASED BY AN XACT WHICH DID NOT SEIZE IT.

  (a) Explain why this error condition cannot come about in the Figure 7.35 model.

  (b) Suppose that the Step 2, Part 2 ADVANCE Block in Figure 7.35 were changed from "ADVANCE 70,10" to "ADVANCE 60,10". The indicated error condition could then come about during a simulation performed with the modified model. Show how to restructure the model to make such an error impossible.

10. In a certain model, Assembly Set members arrive from time to time at Points A, B, and C. As soon as members have arrived at any two of these three points, the two members involved are to continue their forward motion in the model. Show how MATCH Blocks can be used to model this situation. (Hint: you may want to use one or more GATE Blocks as well.)

11. A certain manufactured product is assembled from 2, 5, and 3 parts of types A, B, and C, respectively. The interarrival times of these parts at the point of assembly are shown in Table E.11.

TABLE E11

Type of Part	Interarrival Time (minutes)
A	15 ± 5
B	6 ± 2
C	10 ± 3

The assembly operation involves the following steps.

  1. Combine 1 A and 2 B's. Call the result D. Time required: 15 ± 3 minutes.

  2. Combine 1 A, 1 B, and 1 C. Call the result E. Time required: 18 ± 3 minutes.

  3. Check tolerances between D and E. Time required: 5 ± 2 minutes.

  4. Combine the D from Step 1 with a B. Call the result F. Time required: 10 ± 2 minutes. (Step 4 cannot start until Step 3 is finished.)

  5. Combine the F from Step 4 with the E from Step 2. Call the result G. Time required: 15 ± 4 minutes.

  6. Combine the G from Step 5 with 1 B and 2 C's. This completes the assembly. Time required: 8 ± 3 minutes.

Assume that each of these steps can be carried out by one worker, and that workers are versatile enough to switch from step to step as needed. Model the manufacturing process to determine the minimum number of workers required to avoid irreversible buildup of A, B, and/or C parts at the point of assembly.

8

A Summary of Selected GPSS/360 Features Not Otherwise Covered in This Book

8.1 Introduction

The GPSS/360 Block vocabulary consists of more than 40 blocks. Over 35 of these Blocks have been considered in detail in this book. (Exact Block counts are subject to interpretation, depending for example on whether there is considered to be just one GATE Block, or four GATE Blocks [one each for Facilities, Storages, Logic Switches, and Transactions], etc.). Blocks not covered in this book, but contained in the GPSS/360 Block vocabulary, are briefly described in this chapter. Several other features of the language are also briefly indicated. For more specific details concerning the use of these Blocks and features, the pertinent user's manual should be consulted.

8.2 The HELP Block

When a Transaction enters a HELP Block, control is passed from the GPSS model to the user-supplied subroutine whose name appears as the HELP Block's A Operand. In GPSS/360, Version 1, the user can only supply subroutines written in System/360 assembler language. In GPSS/360, Version 2, GPSS models can also be interfaced with independently compiled subroutines written in FORTRAN. In GPSS V, the HELP Block interface has been extended to cover subroutines written in PL/1, as well as in FORTRAN and assembler language.

483

The Transaction which moves into a HELP Block parks there while the referenced subroutine is executed. Provisions are available for copying values from the parked Transaction's Parameter set, and from one- or two-dimensional halfword and fullword Savevalues, to the subroutine, and vice versa. When control is returned from the subroutine to the GPSS model, the GPSS Processor resumes its Scan Phase activity by moving the previously parked Transaction from the HELP Block and into the sequential Block, etc.

8.3 Blocks Supporting the Group Entity

The Group entity provides a means for having Transactions take up membership in clubs (that is, in Groups). A given Transaction can simultaneously belong to any number of different clubs. A Transaction joins a club by moving through a JOIN Block. It can later terminate its membership in the club (and, optionally, can selectively terminate the membership of other club members) by moving through a REMOVE Block. In addition, through use of the EXAMINE Block, a Transaction's Next Block Attempted can be made to depend on whether the Transaction belongs to a given club.

Club members can inspect the files of other club members (that is, examine the Priority Level and Parameter values of other Transactions in the club), searching for the first member which satisfies an equality condition imposed either on its Priority Level, or on the value of one of its Parameters. The SCAN Block is used for this purpose. In one use of the SCAN Block, the scanning Transaction's Next Block Attempted depends on whether the search produces a club member with an attribute satisfying the stated equality condition. In an alternative mode, the scanning Transaction fetches a copy of the Priority Level, or of a Parameter value, of the first club member found to satisfy the stated equality condition. The fetched copy is stored in one of the Parameters of the scanning Transaction.

Finally, club members can modify the files of other club members (that is, change their Priority Level, or the value of one of their Parameters). The ALTER Block supports this activity. The altering Transaction can unconditionally change the Priority Level of all members of a given club to a given value; or can unconditionally change a given Parameter of all club members to a given value. Alternatively, these changes can be imposed on only a subset of the club. Let the user-specified size of the subset be "n." Then the subset can consist of the n oldest club members; or it can consist of the first n club members whose Priority Level satisfies a stated equality condition, or which have a particular Parameter whose value satisfies a stated equality condition.

As implied above in part, the REMOVE, SCAN, and ALTER Blocks have optional nonsequential exits, which enhance the utility of the Group concept in GPSS modeling. As further implied, operations with respect to club members are independent of where those members happen to

be in a model. The member-Transactions can be on the Current or Future Events Chain, or on a User Chain, or on an Interrupt or Matching Chain, and will nonetheless be included in activities initiated at REMOVE, EXAMINE, SCAN, and ALTER Blocks.

The Group entity has no provision whereby one club member can directly dictate the planned movement of another club member. At the SCAN Block, for example, a club member *cannot* bring about the following action. "Find the first club member whose P5 value equals 21. Remove this member from the chain on which it is currently resident, and place it on the Current Events Chain, scheduled to move next into the Block in the Location TRUBL."

The above discussion pertains to clubs whose members are Transactions. The Group entity also supports the concept of clubs whose members are simply numbers. Of course, numbers do not have such attributes as "Priority Level," and "Parameter values." As a result, the SCAN and ALTER Blocks do not apply to clubs whose members are numbers. The JOIN, REMOVE, and EXAMINE Blocks, however, do apply to numeric clubs as well as to Transaction clubs.

8.4 The COUNT Block

The COUNT Block is identical to the SELECT Block, except in the following respects.

1. Recall that the SELECT Block scans a specified set of entity members to determine if at least one member currently satisfies a stated condition. In contrast, the COUNT Block counts the number of members in a specified set which currently satisfy an indicated condition.

2. If the SELECT Block's scan is successful, the number of a qualifying entity member is copied into a Parameter on the selecting Transaction. There is no question of whether the COUNT Block's scan will be "successful." The count resulting from the scan is copied into a Parameter on the counting Transaction.

3. For the reason implied under 2., the COUNT Block has no nonsequential exit.

4. The SELECT Block's Auxiliary Operator can be a relational operator, or a logical mnemonic, or MIN or MAX. The COUNT Block's Auxiliary Operator can be a relational operator, or a logical mnemonic, but cannot be either MIN or MAX.

The roles of Operands A through E for the COUNT Block, and for the SELECT Block, are identical.

8.5 The TRACE and UNTRACE Blocks

Each Transaction has a Trace Indicator. The Trace Indicator is either on or off. It is normally off. When a Transaction moves into a TRACE Block, its Trace Indicator is turned on. Then, each time the Transaction subsequently enters a Block, the Processor prints out the Transaction's Number, its Current Block, its Next Block Attempted, the Relative Clock value, and the value of the Termination Counter. In addition, standard chain printout is produced for the Transaction. These printouts at each subsequent Block entry continue, using much paper in the process, until the Transaction eventually moves into an UNTRACE Block. The on or off setting of the Trace Indicator appears in chain printouts, in the TI column (see Appendix D).

8.6 The INDEX Block

When a Transaction enters the INDEX Block, its old P1 value is replaced with a new value. The Block's A Operand supplies the number of a Parameter (any Parameter). The Block's B Operand supplies data. The A and B Operand values can be supplied directly, indirectly, or via indirect addressing. The new value of P1 is computed by adding the B-Operand data to a copy of the value of the A-Operand Parameter.

As an example of INDEX Block use, when a Transaction moves into the Block "INDEX 1,1", the effect is to increment its P1 value by 1. If Parameter 1 is being used as a counter, this is a convenient way to add one to the counter. Of course, the increment-mode ASSIGN Block could be used for the same purpose. The virtue of the INDEX Block is that it requires less CPU time than the ASSIGN Block.

8.7 Various TRANSFER Block Modes

The TRANSFER Block can be used in nine different modes in GPSS. Three of these modes (unconditional transfer, statistical transfer, and BOTH-mode transfer) have been discussed in this book. The other six modes will now be discussed briefly.

8.7.1 ALL Mode

The ALL-mode TRANSFER Block is the general case of the BOTH-mode Block. When a Transaction enters an ALL-mode TRANSFER Block, the Processor sequentially checks all Blocks in a specified set, searching for the first Block which will accept the Transaction. When the first such Block is found, the Transaction is moved into that Block, and continues on its way from there. If no such Block is found, the Transaction remains in the TRANSFER Block, and on the Current Events Chain. Each time the Transaction is subsequently encountered in the scan of the Current Chain, the Processor again tries to move the Transaction into one of the Blocks in the specified set. If the Blocks frequently all deny entry, the ALL-mode TRANSFER Block consumes telling amounts of CPU time.

8.7.2 PICK Mode

When a Transaction enters a PICK-mode TRANSFER Block, the Processor picks a Block at random from a specified set. The Block picked then becomes that Transaction's Next Block Attempted (whether or not the Transaction can immediately enter that Block). Each Block in the specified set has an equally likely chance of being picked as the Transaction's Next Block Attempted.

8.7.3 FN (Function) Mode

When a Transaction enters a FN-mode TRANSFER Block, the number of its Next Block Attempted is set equal to the value of the Function whose number is supplied as the Block's B Operand. If an optional C Operand is used, the Next Block Attempted is set equal to the sum of the Function's value, and the C-Operand data.

8.7.4 P (Parameter) Mode

When a Transaction enters a P-mode TRANSFER Block, the number of its Next Block Attempted is set equal to the value of the Parameter whose number is supplied as the Block's B Operand. If an optional C Operand is used, the Next Block Attempted is set equal to the sum of the Parameter's value, and the C-Operand data.

8.7.5 SBR (Subroutine) Mode

When a Transaction enters a SBR-mode TRANSFER Block, the number of its Next Block Attempted is set equal to the value of the Block's B Operand. Before the transfer takes place, however, the number of the TRANSFER Block itself is copied into that Parameter whose number is supplied through the C Operand. Hence, before the Transaction transfers to the subroutine, it picks up a copy of the Location from which the transfer was made. (The subroutine implied here is nothing other than some sequence of Blocks elsewhere in the model.) The last Block in the subroutine can then be a P-mode TRANSFER Block which routes the Transaction back to the point from which it originally transferred. (In practice, the analyst would supply 1 as the value of the optional C Operand on the P-mode TRANSFER Block. The effect would be to route the Transaction back to the Block sequential to the SBR-mode Block from which the transfer was originally made.)

8.7.6 SIM (Simultaneous) Mode

Through use of the SIM-mode TRANSFER Block, a Transaction's forward motion in a model can be delayed (albeit in relatively awkward fashion) until a number of conditions are simultaneously satisfied. This mode of TRANSFER Block use is a holdover from the days of GPSS III, when there was no Boolean Variable entity in the language. For the sake of upward compatibility, the Block remains in the language, even though its use has now been supplanted. As part of the SIM-mode TRANSFER Block concept, each Transaction has a Delay Indicator. The on or off setting of this indicator appears in chain printouts in the DI column (see Appendix D).

8.8 The CHANGE Block

With the CHANGE Block, the Block currently occupying a user-specified Location in a model can be *replaced* by some other Block. The "other Block" must already exist in the model. The CHANGE Block's A Operand supplies the number of the Location whose occupant is to become some new Block. The B Operand supplies the number of the Location currently occupied by what is to be the new Block. Call the Block to be replaced the "A Block," and the Block doing the replacing the "B Block." When the CHANGE Block is entered by a Transaction, a copy of the B Block replaces the A Block. Nothing happens to the original B Block itself. The Transaction then moves from the CHANGE Block to the sequential Block, and so on.

The CHANGE Block provides a dynamic capability, then, for modifying the Blocks occupying user-selected Locations. In the book, a static capability for producing such modifications is used from time to time in certain case studies. In the static approach, the definition of the new Location occupant is supplied somewhere between START cards in the program deck.

8.9 The EXECUTE Block

The EXECUTE Block's A Operand supplies the number of the Location occupied by some other Block. When a Transaction moves into the EXECUTE Block, the Block in that other Location is executed, just as though the Transaction had actually entered that Block. The Transaction remains in the EXECUTE Block, however, while the other Block is executed. The Transaction subsequently moves into the Block sequential to the EXECUTE Block.

8.10 The WRITE Block

When a Transaction enters a WRITE Block, the following information is written onto one of three magnetic tapes specified by the user.

1. Interarrival time, i.e., the amount of simulated time elapsed since the immediately preceding Transaction entered the WRITE Block. (For the first Transaction to enter the WRITE Block, a value of zero is used as the interarrival time.)

2. The Transaction's residence time in the model (that is, its M1 value).

3. The Transaction's Priority Level.

4. The Transaction's Parameter set (the numbers of its Parameters, and their corresponding values).

After this information has been written onto tape, the Transaction then proceeds to the sequential Block.

Using the WRITE Block, an exact history of the stream of Transaction traffic going past a point can be recorded. This history can then be played back, or recreated, in subsequent simulations. Such playbacks can obviously be useful in producing controlled experimental conditions, or in reproducing event sequences which actually took place when the behavior of a real system was observed. (Transaction tapes can also be created by non-GPSS programs, independent of WRITE Block use.)

8.11 STARTMACRO, ENDMACRO, and MACRO Cards

It sometimes happens that a given Block sequence is used in two or more places in a model. A certain amount of keypunching effort can be spared if the Block sequence is defined to be a macro. The Processor will then substitute these Blocks at various different points in a model, as specified by the analyst. A single card is used at each of these different points to indicate that the macro Block sequence is to be inserted there.

STARTMACRO and ENDMACRO are the control cards used to signal the starting and ending points, respectively, in a macro definition. After a macro has been defined, the MACRO card is used to request that the Blocks in the macro be inserted at that point.

Of course, a macro is not a subroutine. Transactions do not transfer to the first Block in a macro, and then later return to the point sequential to that from which the transfer was made. Instead, as indicated, the macro Block sequence is inserted in-line at the point in the model at which the MACRO card appears. Hence, the macro concept cannot be used to economize on the actual number of Blocks which appear in an *assembled* model; it can only be used to simplify the coding and keypunching of repetitive strings of Blocks.

The user can specify whatever Block sequence he chooses when he defines a macro (for example, QUEUE - SEIZE - DEPART - ADVANCE - RELEASE). After that, the Blocks in the macro sequence are fixed (for that macro, and in that model). The values of the Block's Operands, however, are not necessarily fixed. When the macro is defined, dummy variables can be supplied in the various Operand positions. When the macro is later inserted in place of the MACRO card, these dummy variables will then be replaced with actual variables (that is, Standard Numerical Attributes) as specified with the MACRO card.

8.12 The Output Editor

The GPSS Output Editor is referred to briefly in Section 4.23.3, where its use to produce a histogram is illustrated. In summary, the Output Editor can be used to do one or more of the following things.

1. Select and print only those output statistics which are of interest.
2. Supply titles and comments in various places within the output.
3. Print out selected statistics in both a format and an order specified by the user.
4. Exercise carriage control at the printer.
5. Display the values of various Standard Numerical Attributes in graphical form.

To accomplish objectives 1 through 4, the Output Editor provides nine different control cards (REPORT, TITLE, INCLUDE, FORMAT, TEXT, COMMENT, EJECT, SPACE, and OUTPUT). For purposes of displaying information in graphical form, six different control cards are available (GRAPH, ORIGIN, X, Y, STATEMENT, and ENDGRAPH).

8.13 *Fini*

If you've made it this far, a blessing on you. If you used a fixed page count of one in the process, a hundredfold blessing on you! Best of luck with GPSS.

Appendixes

APPENDIX A

Comparison and Contrast Between GPSS/360 and GPSS V[1]

General Purpose Simulation System V (GPSS V) is an IBM Corporation Program Product which is an enhancement of GPSS/360 Versions 1 and 2. Models developed and run under GPSS/360 can, with only relatively minor exceptions discussed subsequently, be run under GPSS V without modification.

GPSS V includes all of the features of GPSS/360 Versions 1 and 2 and the following new features :

1. Unavailable equipment entities, namely Storages and Facilities. Typically, the units or pools of equipment modeled by GPSS Storage and Facility entities are unavailable for periods of time for any one of a variety of reasons such as mechanical failure or employee absence.

To model this situation in GPSS/360, it is necessary to have a control Transaction enter a PREEMPT or an ENTER Block and occupy the Storage or Facility for the duration of the unavailable period. This technique prevents other Transactions from using the entity during the unavailable period ; however, this "artificial" usage is also reflected in the utilization statistics. To correct the utilization statistics as well as provide other processing options in the case of Facilities, Blocks which make one or more Storages or Facilities available or unavailable are provided as follows :

The availability status of these entities may be determined via a GATE Block :

"GATE SNV POOL"
"GATE FV MAN"

Entity	Unavailable	Available
Facility	FUNAVAIL	FAVAIL
Storage	SUNAVAIL	SAVAIL

Output statistics include both available and unavailable time statistics which make it possible to identify legitimate usage directly.

2. An interface capability between GPSS and user-written PL/1 routines. This capability is utilized via new modes of the HELP Block, namely HELPAPL1, HELPBPL1, and HELPCPL1 which provide various modes of one-way and two-way communication between PL/1 routines and GPSS. The PL/1 interface capability is similar to the FORTRAN interface capability now in GPSS/360 Version 2. The PL/1 F-level compiler as well as the Optimizing and the Checkout compilers are supported by this feature.

3. A maximum of 255 halfword, 255 fullword, 255 byte, and 255 single-precision floating point Transaction Parameters in any combination. Each Transaction can have as many as 1020 Parameters. Halfword, fullword, and byte Parameters can contain

[1] This appendix was written by Mary Jean Sorret, of the International Business Machines Corporation. Portions of the material in this appendix are taken from the *General Purpose Simulation System V Application Description Manual*, Form Number GH20–0825, pp. 9–11 [© (1970) by International Business Machines Corporation], and from the *General Purpose Simulation System V User's Manual*, Form Number SH20–0851, pp. 335–336 [© (1970, 1971) by International Business Machines Corporation]. These materials are reprinted here by permission of International Business Machines Corporation.

integer values in the range of $\pm 2^{15}-1$, $\pm 2^{31}-1$, and $\pm 2^7-1$, respectively. Floating point Parameters can contain integer and fractional values in the range of $\pm 2^{24}-1$ without loss of precision.

4. Byte and single-precision floating point Savevalues and Matrices. Each type has the same range of values as the respective Parameter type.

5. New Standard Numerical Attributes (SNA's) with which to reference the contents of the new entities.

	Parameters	Savevalues	Matrices
Fullword	PF	XF or X	MX
Halfword	PH	XH	MH
Byte	PB	XB	MB
Floating Point	PL	XL	ML

6. ASSIGN, SAVEVALUE, and MSAVEVALUE Block ranges. With one statement, it is possible to store the same value in multiple consecutive Parameters or Savevalues depending upon the Block type. For example, to store the value 25 in byte Parameters 1–9 inclusive, and halfword Savevalues 31–34 inclusive, the following statements may be coded:

```
"ASSIGN    1–9,25,PB"
"SAVEVALUE   31–34,25,XH"
```

In an MSAVEVALUE Block, the A, B, and C Operands may utilize the range notation. For example:

```
"MSAVEVALUE   1,1–2,4–5,26,MH"
"MSAVEVALUE   1–7,2,6,528,MH"
"MSAVEVALUE   1–4–,3,7–8,473,MH"
```

Under GPSS/360, one Block is needed for each Parameter or Savevalue to be altered.

7. Extended indirect addressing. In both versions of GPSS/360, the notation SNA*j is used to designate an Operand or element where the use of indirect addressing is allowed. The j is always assumed to be the number of a Parameter associated with the Transaction which triggers the evaluation of the Parameter. The indirect addressing notation in GPSS V is SNA*SNAj which means that the secondary SNA (to the right of the asterisk) may be any SNA. This eliminates the need to store the value which may already be in a Savevalue, for example, in a Parameter solely to facilitate indirect addressing. For example, in GPSS V the following is possible:

```
"ASSIGN    XH*FN$ADVTM"
```

Using GPSS/360, to perform the above, two Blocks are needed as follows:

```
"ASSIGN    1,FN$ADVTM"
"ADVANCE   XH*1"
```

8. Free-form statement coding which eliminates the need to start the statement Operation and Operands in positions 8 and 19 respectively. The Location entry or entity symbol (in a definition statement) must always start in position 1 in free-form coding. The Operation and Operands need only be separated by one blank position.

The statement Operands on the Input Phase or absolute listing (second statement listing) produced by GPSS V are not separated into columns of six positions each as they are under GPSS/360. The Location entry, Operation, and Operands of all statements are appropriately aligned. The Operands on the Input Phase listing are separated by commas. One of the byproducts of this change is that constants are no longer limited to six positions.

9. An optional cross-reference listing of all symbolically addressed entities.

10. Auxiliary Storage feature. This feature permits the user to place some or all of most entities on an auxiliary storage device to minimize memory utilization while at the same time increasing the capability to run very large models. A new AUXILIARY statement is the means by which the user specifies the split between main memory and a direct access device of the total allocation of an entity. There is a unique data set for each entity type residing on auxiliary storage.

When using this feature, some planning is recommended. For example, when placing GPSS Blocks on disk, it would be inadvisable to place the Blocks representing the most frequently referenced paths of logic on auxiliary storage while leaving the relatively infrequently traveled paths permanently resident in core. The number of direct accesses needed to run a model under these circumstances would needlessly increase model execution time.

11. Error messages that include the reason for the error as well as the error number. In many instances, error numbers have been changed for GPSS V error messages from those to which GPSS/360 users are accustomed for the same error condition. These changes are clerical in nature and have no bearing on the reasons for the errors.

12. A sequence number in positions 73 to 80 of each statement. This sequence number is printed on the Assembly Phase listing. No legality checking is performed on the sequence number which means that any combination of characters meaningful to the user is valid.

13. UNLINK, REMOVE, SCAN, and ALTER Block Transaction selection based on conditions greater than (G), greater than or equal (GE), less than (L), less than or equal (LE), equal (E) or not equal (NE).

14. Separate data sets for models being saved or read via the Read/Save feature. Under GPSS/360, models saved or read are written to or read from the same data set. GPSS/360 users taking advantage of this feature in GPSS V may find it necessary to revise READ/SAVE statements referencing models other than the first one in the data set.

In addition to the FORTRAN interface previously mentioned, the major GPSS/360 Version 2 features also included in GPSS V are:

1. Run Length feature. This capability prevents a model containing a modeling error, usually a modeling loop, from running indefinitely or until external operator intervention. After the run time specified has elapsed, the run is terminated after printing all statistics accumulated to that point. Under GPSS/360 Version 1, statistics are lost when run termination is initiated externally by an operator.

2. Load feature. This feature enables the user to specify that frequently entered GPSS modules, namely DAG06 (the output phase module) or user-written help routine modules, are to be permanently retained in core for the duration of the model run. Reasons for loading DAG06, for example, would be heavy use of PRINT or TRACE Blocks. The objective for loading these modules is to avoid the additional time to retrieve fresh copies of these modules from the program library each time they are to be entered.

Differences Between GPSS/360 and GPSS V

To specify the new Parameter types, the GENERATE Block has a new format and new Operands. It should be noted, however, that models with GENERATE Blocks coded the GPSS/360 way need not be changed before running the same model under GPSS V. A GPSS V GENERATE Block for creating Transactions having 10 byte and 25 fullword Parameters can be coded in either of the following ways:

"GENERATE 1,,,,,25PF,10PB"

or

"GENERATE 1,,,,10PB,25PF"

Note that Parameter specifications, if any, must begin in the F Operand and may be coded in any sequence ending with the I Operand, if necessary. The Parameter specifications cannot be coded PF25 and PB10 because such a notation means that an SNA is to be evaluated, and that is not what is intended here. Unless the user specifies otherwise, each Transaction will have twelve halfword Parameters as in GPSS/360.

Additional considerations resulting from the new Parameter types include the following:

1. ASSIGN Blocks should be coded with an additional Operand to designate Parameter type. To place the value 25 in halfword Parameter 8, either of the following is acceptable, provided there is no C Operand Function modifier:

"ASSIGN 8,25,PH"

or

"ASSIGN 8,25,,PH"

GPSS/360 users need not change ASSIGN Block statements in old models before running the same models under GPSS V. When creating new models, however, it is strongly recommended that the new format be adopted. Technically, the old format is acceptable as long as the Transactions entering the ASSIGN Block have only one Parameter type. The principal reason for adopting the new format is that, when the Parameter type is not specified, GPSS V first checks the entering Transaction to determine what type of Parameters it has. If, in the process of checking, it is determined that the Transaction really has more than one Parameter type, the simulation is terminated with an execution error.

The reason for this is that GPSS is unable to determine which Parameter the user intended to alter, and there is no default; that is, GPSS does not assume Parameter type when not specifically stated. For example:

"GENERATE 1,,,,10PB, 10PH, 16PB"

"ASSIGN 2,4" WHICH PARAMETER 2?

The sequence above results in an execution error because of the missing Parameter type Operand.

If, as a result of the Parameter type checking, it is determined that the entering Transaction has only one Parameter type, the appropriate routine for storing a value in a Parameter of that type can be entered. Had the Parameter type been specified, the appropriate storing routine could be entered directly without first performing the legality checking just described. In a long running model with many ASSIGN Blocks, this extra checking may needlessly extend running time.

2. Operand suffixes are utilized in GPSS V in conjunction with Operands specifically implying a Parameter. For example, the A Operand of a LOOP Block specifies a Parameter number.

In GPSS/360, the following is permissible:

```
        GENERATE  1
        ASSIGN    1,10
        .
        .
NEXT    .
        .
        .
LOOP    1,NEXT    REPEAT UNTIL P1=0
```

In GPSS V it is recommended that the sequence be coded:

```
        GENERATE    1
        ASSIGN      1,10,PH     HALFWORD PARAMETER 10
          .
NEXT
          .
        LOOP    1PH,NEXT
```

The reason for coding the suffix is to specify Parameter type and thereby save execution time by avoiding legality checking nearly identical to that described for the ASSIGN Block. Note that:

```
        "LOOP    PH1,NEXT"
```

has a very different meaning from:

```
        "LOOP    1PH,NEXT"
```

because PH1 is an SNA which specifies the value of halfword Parameter 1.

The first time through the following Block sequence the value of PH1 will be 10; consequently, in the LOOP Block, the value in halfword Parameter 10 is decremented by 1 and tested for zero to determine whether to enter the SAVEVALUE Block or the TEST Block next.

```
        GENERATE    1
        ASSIGN      1,10,PH
          .
NEXT    SAVEVALUE
          .
        LOOP    PH1,NEXT
        TEST        PH1 = 10 THE FIRST TIME
```

It is not necessary for GPSS/360 users to add suffixes where appropriate before running GPSS V; however, when constructing new models, use of suffixes, regardless of the number of Parameter types, is recommended to reduce execution time. Use of suffixes is mandatory if the entering Transaction has multiple Parameter types.

3. Because of the additional types and quantities of Parameters, jobtapes created either independently or by GPSS/360 must be created in the GPSS V format for use as input to GPSS V.

Users wishing to run GPSS/360 models under GPSS V should be aware that the notation, Pj, specified to reference the contents of Parameter j of the entering Transaction, is still allowed under GPSS V but principally for reasons of compatibility with GPSS/360. As new models are developed, the new notation, PHj, PFj, PBj, and PLj should be adopted to minimize execution time. The same type of legality checking described in relation to ASSIGN Block coding is performed when only Pj is specified.

GPSS/360 users should be aware that the Pj notation has been intentionally omitted from GPSS V documentation. The indirect addressing notation, *j, has also been omitted. This notation is processed correctly by GPSS V but is also subject to the additional legality checking already described when the Parameter type is not specified. Former GPSS/360 users should use the notation Pxj (where x is either H, F, B, or L representing halfword, fullword, byte, and floating point respectively) instead of *j when creating new models.

Models saved under GPSS/360 cannot be read and executed under GPSS V principally because of changes to the size of the basic areas for Tables as well as Storages and Facilities (to support the unavailable capabilities). Auxiliary Storage feature considerations also are part of the incompatibility, even though the feature is not being used in the model being saved.

When coding statements in ABS mode for input to GPSS V, instead of separating Operands into six-position fields as required by GPSS/360, Operands should start in position 19 and be separated by commas. ABS mode statements must be in the fixed format with the Location entry starting in position 2 and the Operation in position 8.

Users of GPSS V who formerly run under GPSS/360 Version 1, under GPSS V. These differences are the result of a change introduced in GPSS/360 Version 2 in the initial multiplier of each of the eight random number generators. Formerly, the initial multiplier of each random number generator was 1; it is now 37. The former sequences can be obtained, if necessary, via an RMULT statement.

Some SNA's which are truncated to integer values are maintained in floating point because of the new floating point entities. As a consequence, the result of evaluating these SNA's may be slightly different depending upon their use, principally as a Y-value of a Function, as an element of a floating point variable, or as a value to be stored in a floating point entity.

Users having Assembler Language HELP Block routines may need to revise them to some degree to reflect changes in the displacement of values accessible to the help routine.

Some of the normal output statistics have a slightly different format as a result of the new features. The biggest changes are in the Transaction chains. Matrices, regardless of type, have the same format with the contents of up to ten Matrix elements printing per line. Multiple consecutive rows of all zero values are indicated by an appropriate message to reduce the possibility of bulky printouts.

A slight modification has been made effective with GPSS V-OS Version 1 Modification Level 3 and GPSS V-DOS Version 1 Modification Level 2 to the rounding process of some statistical routines relating to Storages and Facilities. The objective for this change is to improve accuracy in the representation of values. This change exhibits itself generally in the thousandths position of fractional values. It is now possible to control the execution of models based on Facility and Storage utilization values (FR/ and SR/ respectively) in the range of 0 to 1000.

The GPSS V documentation has been completely rewritten and reorganized with the objective of presenting the material in a more logical order. The new manuals, like the GPSS/360 manuals, are intended primarily as reference manuals rather than student texts.

Significant additions to the GPSS V documentation are two fanfold reference cards containing the GPSS Blocks and their Operands, SNA's and related information, the standard entity allocations, and control statements and their contents.

APPENDIX B

Sources of Information About GPSS from IBM

Title of Publication[1]	Form Number	Price[2]
Simulation: Modeling Reality	G520–1542	
Capital Investment Studies Using GPSS—Bulk Material Movement Problems	GE20–0313	
An Introduction to Simulation by Computer—A Management Tool in Decision Making	GE20–0272	
360 GPSS Application Description Manual	GH20–0186	
360 GPSS Introductory User's Manual	GH20–0304	
360 GPSS Operator's Manual	GH20–0311	No Longer
360 GPSS User's Manual	GH20–0326	for Sale
360 OS GPSS Application Description Manual	GH20–0327	
360 OS GPSS Operator's Manual	GH20–0691	
360 OS GPSS Introductory User's Manual	SH20–0692	
360 OS GPSS Version 2 User's Manual	SH20–0693	
360 OS GPSS Version 2 Operations Manual	SH20–0694	
360 DOS GPSS Version 2 Operations Manual	SH20–0698	
GPSS V OS Application Description Manual	GH20–0825	
GPSS V DOS Application Description Manual	GH20–0826	
GPSS V Introductory User's Manual	SH20–0866	$5.70
GPSS V OS/DOS User's Manual	SH20–0851	$17.50
GPSS V OS Operations Manual	SH20–0867	$3.80
GPSS V DOS Operations Manual	SH20–0868	$3.00
GPSS V OS Program Product Specifications	GH20–4035	
GPSS V DOS Program Product Specification	GH20–4040	
GPSS V Reference Card (Block Statement Formats)	GX20–1828	
GPSS V Reference Card (Control Statement Formats; Standard Numerical Attributes; System Options)	GX20–1829	

[1] In March, 1973, IBM withdrew GPSS/360, Versions 1 and 2, from its program library. This means that IBM will no longer accept orders for manuals or for other documentation for these versions of GPSS. Nevertheless, the libraries in many computing centers have copies of the GPSS/360 manuals in their possession. The GPSS/360 entries in this list are provided, then, as a guide to what might be available in these libraries.

In general, copies of IBM publications still in print can be obtained through IBM offices. When these publications have Form Numbers beginning with GH, single copies may be available on a complimentary basis.

[2] When no price is shown, the cost is under $1.00.

496

APPENDIX C

GPSS Error Messages

There are five categories of "Error Messages" that can arise in GPSS. They are shown in Table C.1. Table C.1 also shows the range of Error Message numbers corresponding to each category, and indicates the pages in this appendix where interpretations are given for the various error message numbers.

TABLE C.1

Category	Designation	Range of Error Numbers	Pages Showing Interpretations
1	Assembly Program Errors	1–81	498–499
2	Input Errors	201–302	499–501
3	Execution Errors	401–699	501–502
4	Output Errors	702–769	503
5	Warning Messages	850–863	503

Assembly Program errors can arise when the Processor takes its first pass over the model, but before the Input Phase begins. The corresponding types of errors usually involve simple violations of GPSS syntax or entity range limitations. For example, error 43, ILLEGAL SYMBOL (TOO LONG), would occur if a Block's symbolic Location name consisted of more than five characters. Similarly, error 32, ILLEGAL FACILITY NUMBER, would arise if the model was being run at the 64K memory level and the analyst used a value of 36 or greater as a Facility number, but had not reallocated the maximum quantity of Facilities available. (The maximum quantity of Facilities under the indicated conditions is 35. The largest permissible Facility number equals the maximum number of different Facilities allowable in a model.)

Input errors can occur during the Input Phase when the Processor, among other things, schedules Transaction arrivals at GENERATE Blocks for the first time. A typical error condition that could come about in this category would be 216, MODIFIER EXCEEDS MEAN. This indicates that a GENERATE Block's Spread Modifier is larger that the mean interarrival time, which can cause a negative interarrival time to be computed.

Execution errors can arise while the simulation is proceeding, but before the Termination Counter has been decremented to zero. A typical message in this category is number 406, ILLEGAL PRIORITY COMPUTED FOR XACT BEING CREATED AT A 'GENERATE' BLOCK. (XACT is an abbreviation for Transaction.) This condition could occur if a GENERATE Block's E Operand were indirectly specified, and the value turned out to be less than 0, or larger than 127. (The only permissible Priority Levels are 0, 1, 2, 3, ..., 125, 126, and 127.)

Output errors can come about after the simulation has shut off, while the Processor is outputting the statistics developed during the simulation. If such an error arises, it is very likely because the Processor is attempting to output statistics for an entity which has an illegal number, i.e., is outside of the permissible range.

Finally, warning messages are printed out when circumstances come about which are not fatal (i.e., do not cause the run to be aborted), but nevertheless should probably be called to the analyst's attention. For example, warning message 850 is ATTEMPT TO STORE INTEGER OF MAGNITUDE GREATER THAN 32767 IN A HALFWORD PARAMETER. The largest value that can be held in a halfword Parameter is 32,767. If an attempt is made to store a value larger than this in such a Parameter, the value actually stored is: "MAINTAINED MODULO 2**15". Consequently, the stored value equals the remainder that would result if the too-large value were divided by 2**15 (i.e., divided by 32,768). This means, for example, that if the Block "ASSIGN 3, X$BIG" is executed, and the value of X$BIG is 43,562, the value stored in Parameter 3 will be 10,794, assuming the Transaction's Parameters are of the halfword type.

[1] The Error Messages contained in this appendix apply to GPSS/360. Users of GPSS V should be aware that for some error conditions, the Error Message number produced by the GPSS V Processor may differ from that which the GPSS/360 Processor produces. This is pointed out in Appendix A.

Assembly Program Errors

1 ILLEGAL SELECTION MODE SPECIFIED IN A-FIELD OF 'TRANSFER' BLOCK

2 ILLEGAL OPERATION FIELD

3 ENTITY NUMBER TO BE RESERVED BY AN 'EQU' CARD HAS BEEN RESERVED BY A PREVIOUS 'EQU' CARD

4 BLOCK SYMBOL HAS BEEN USED IN AN 'EQU' CARD

5 ILLEGAL TABLE ARGUMENT

6 FRACTIONAL SELECTION MODE IS MORE THAN A 3-DIGIT NUMBER

7 SYNTAX ERROR IN A 'MATRIX' OR 'EQU' CARD

8 ILLEGAL ENTITY INDICATOR.

9 A-FIELD OF 'ASSIGN' BLOCK IS GREATER THAN 100

10 FIRST OPERAND IN A 'MATRIX' CARD IS NOT 'X' OR 'H'

11 UNDEFINED BLOCK SYMBOL

12 ILLEGAL JOBTAPE SPECIFIED

13 THE NUMBER OF ROWS AND/OR COLUMNS SPECIFIED IN A 'MATRIX' CARD IS NOT CONSTANT

14 FIELD-E OF 'MSAVEVALUE' BLOCK IS ILLEGAL

15 'TRANSFER' BLOCK WITH 'ALL' OR 'PICK' SELECTION MODE CONTAINS C-FIELD WHOSE VALUE IS LESS THAN B-FIELD

16 'TRANSFER' BLOCK WITH 'ALL' SELECTION MODE HAS A B-FIELD TO C-FIELD RANGE WHICH IS NOT EVENLY DIVISIBLE BY THE D-FIELD

17 CARD WHICH MUST HAVE ENTRY IN LOCATION FIELD DOES NOT

18 ILLEGAL HALFWORD MATRIX SAVEVALUE

19 ILLEGAL MNEMONIC SPECIFIED IN OPERATION FIELD OF 'GATE', 'LOGIC', 'TEST', 'COUNT', OR 'SELECT' BLOCK

20 ILLEGAL B-FIELD IN 'PRIORITY' BLOCK

21 SYMBOL IN ENTITY FUNCTION FOLLOWER CARD HAS BEEN USED IN AN 'EQU' CARD OR HAS BEEN USED AS A BLOCK SYMBOL OR HAS BEEN USED IN A PREVIOUS ENTITY FUNCTION

22 ILLEGAL BOOLEAN VARIABLE NUMBER

23 ILLEGAL REPORT TYPE SPECIFIED IN 'REPORT' CARD

24 CARD TYPE IS NOT PERMITTED WITHIN THE REPORT TYPE SPECIFIED

25 STORAGE DEFINED WITH CAPACITY GREATER THAN THE MAXIMUM PERMISSIBLE VALUE

26 TABLE MUST BE SPECIFIED NUMERICALLY

27 ILLEGAL SYMBOL

28 ILLEGAL FUNCTION TYPE

29 MODIFIER OF 'GENERATE' OR 'ADVANCE' BLOCK EXCEEDS MEAN

30 A-FIELD OMITTED WHERE IT MUST BE SPECIFIED

31 B-FIELD OMITTED WHERE IT MUST BE SPECIFIED

32 ILLEGAL FACILITY NUMBER

33 ILLEGAL STORAGE NUMBER

34 ILLEGAL QUEUE NUMBER

35 ILLEGAL LOGIC SWITCH NUMBER

36 ILLEGAL CHAIN NUMBER

37 ILLEGAL TABLE NUMBER

38 ILLEGAL VARIABLE NUMBER

39 ILLEGAL SAVEVALUE NUMBER

40 ILLEGAL FUNCTION NUMBER

41 ILLEGAL SYMBOL IN LOCATION FIELD OR NO SYMBOL WHERE ONE IS REQUIRED

42 ILLEGAL GROUP NUMBER

43 ILLEGAL SYMBOL (TOO LONG)

44 SYNTAX ERROR IN CARD

45 ILLEGAL SNA

46 C-FIELD OMITTED WHERE IT MUST BE SPECIFIED

47 ILLEGAL MATRIX SAVEVALUE NUMBER

48 D-FIELD OMITTED WHERE IT MUST BE SPECIFIED

49 MAXIMUM NUMBER OF MACRO DEFINITIONS EXCEEDED

50 UNDEFINED MACRO

51 ILLEGAL MACRO ARGUMENT - ARGUMENT MUST BE ALPHABETIC A-J

52 MACRO CARD EXPANDED PAST COLUMN 72

53   MORE THAN 2 MACROS NESTED WITHIN A MACRO

54   MORE THAN 10 ARGUMENTS SPECIFIED IN ABOVE MACRO CARD

55   C-FIELD OF 'SAVEVALUE' BLOCK IS ILLEGAL

56   ILLEGAL HALFWORD SAVEVALUE

57   NO LEGAL ENTITY NUMBER LEFT TO BE ASSIGNED TO ENTITY SYMBOL

58   OPERAND FIELD EXTENDS INTO COLUMN 72

59   THERE ARE MORE RIGHT PARENS THAN LEFT PARENS IN A 'VARIABLE' CARD

60   THERE ARE MORE LEFT PARENS THAN RIGHT PARENS IN A 'VARIABLE'

61   IMPOSSIBLE MODULO DIVISION SPECIFIED IN A 'VARIABLE' CARD

62   E-FIELD OMITTED OR ILLEGAL WHERE IT MUST BE SPECIFIED

63   'EQU' CARD OR ENTITY FUNCTION SPECIFIES THAT ILLEGAL ENTITY NUMBER BE RESERVED

64   GRAPH CARDS OUT OF ORDER

65   ILLEGAL A-FIELD IN 'STATEMENT' CARD

66   ILLEGAL ROW REQUEST IN 'STATEMENT' CARD

67   ILLEGAL B-FIELD IN 'STATEMENT' CARD

68   TOO MANY COLUMNS REQUESTED IN 'STATEMENT' CARD

69   DECREASING ROW NUMBERS REQUESTED IN 'STATEMENT' CARD

70   ILLEGAL STARTING COLUMN FOR STATEMENT

71   ILLEGAL SNA REQUESTED IN 'GRAPH' CARD

72   ILLEGAL ENTITY RANGE IN 'GRAPH' CARD

73   ILLEGAL REQUEST IN 'ORIGIN' CARD

74   ILLEGAL ENTITY REQUESTED IN 'TITLE' CARD

75   ILLEGAL FIELD IN 'X' CARD

76   ILLEGAL NUMERIC FIELD IN 'X' OR 'Y' CARD

77   ILLEGAL REQUEST IN 'Y' CARD

78   NUMBER OF POINTS IN FUNCTIONS DOES NOT AGREE WITH NUMBER SPECIFIED ON FUNCTION HEADER CARD

79   CONSTANT WITH MORE THAN 6 DIGITS SPECIFIED WHERE NOT PERMITTED

81   SIGNED CONSTANT IN FIELD WHERE NOT PERMITTED

Input Errors

201   NUMBER OF TRANSACTIONS EXCEEDED

202   REFERENCED TRANSACTION NOT INACTIVE

203   PRIORITY EXCEEDS 127

205   NUMBER OF PARAMETERS EXCEEDS 100

206   'GENERATE' BLOCK : F-FIELD MUST BE 'F', 'H', OR BLANK

207   'PREEMPT' BLOCK : B-FIELD MUST BE 'PR'

208   'PREEMPT' BLOCK : E-FIELD MUST BE 'RE'

209   'PREEMPT' BLOCK : C-FIELD NOT SPECIFIED WITH D- AND/OR C-FIELDS

210   ILLEGAL MNEMONIC IN OPERATION FIELD

211   ILLEGAL STORAGE NUMBER

212   D-FIELD NOT NECESSARY IF 'MAX' OR 'MIN' MODE SPECIFIED

213   ILLEGAL MNEMONIC IN C-FIELD OF 'PRINT' BLOCK

214   ILLEGAL FORMAT IN LOGIC SWITCH 'INITIAL' CARD

215   AMOUNT OF GPSS/360 COMMON CORE EXCEEDED (See Section 4.16)

216   MODIFIER EXCEEDS MEAN

217   ACTION TIME NOT GREATER THAN OR EQUAL TO ZERO

218   ILLEGAL FULLWORD MATRIX NUMBER

219   ILLEGAL HALFWORD MATRIX NUMBER

220   ILLEGAL FORMAT FOR 'TRANSFER-ALL'

221   ILLEGAL TABLE NUMBER

222   ILLEGAL FUNCTION NUMBER

223   FUNCTION 'X' VALUES NOT IN ASCENDING ORDER

224   'UNLINK' BLOCK : E-FIELD MUST BE BLANK IF 'BACK' SPECIFIED

225   ILLEGAL FULLWORD SAVEVALUE NUMBER

226   ILLEGAL HALFWORD SAVEVALUE NUMBER

227   ILLEGAL FORMAT IN SAVEVALUE 'INITIAL' CARD

228   MNEMONIC OTHER THAN 'X' OR 'H' USED IN SAVEVALUE 'INITIAL' CARD

229	FIRST INDEX HIGHER THAN SECOND IN MULTI-INITIALLIZATION
230	ILLEGAL LOGIC SWITCH NUMBER
231	'VARIABLE' DEFINITION CARD : COLUMN 18 NOT BLANK
232	'VARIABLE' DEFINITION CARD : ILLEGAL VARIABLE NUMBER
233	'VARIABLE' DEFINITION CARD : NUMBER STATED INCORRECTLY
234	'VARIABLE' DEFINITION CARD : IMPROPER NUMBER OF PARENS
235	'VARIABLE' DEFINITION CARD : TOO MANY SETS OF PARENS
236	'VARIABLE' DEFINITION CARD : IMPOSSIBLE MODULO DIVISION
237	'VARIABLE' DEFINITION CARD : ILLEGAL BOOLEAN VARIABLE NUMBER
238	'VARIABLE' DEFINITION CARD : MODULO DIVISION IN FVARIABLE
239	NO COMMA IN 'MATRIX' STATEMENT
240	ILLEGAL BOOLEAN OPERATOR
241	ILLEGAL STATEMENT OF OPERATION IN VARIABLE
242	ILLEGAL SNA IN 'VARIABLE' STATEMENT
243	ILLEGAL MATRIX ROW NUMBER
244	ILLEGAL MATRIX COLUMN NUMBER
245	ILLEGAL MATRIX SAVEVALUE MNEMONIC
246	ILLEGAL FORMAT IN, MATRIX 'INITIAL' CARD
247	ILLEGAL FORMAT IN SAVEVALUE 'INITIAL' CARD
248	ILLEGAL HALFWORD SAVEVALUE
249	TOO MANY NUMERIC DIGITS IN A CONSTANT
250	ILLEGAL SNA MNEMONIC
251	MISSING OPERATOR IN VARIABLE
252	E-FIELD NOT BLANK WHEN 'BV' SPECIFIED IN 'UNLINK' BLOCK
253	ILLEGAL MNEMONIC IN A-FIELD OF 'TRANSFER' BLOCK
254	FRACTION IN 'TRANSFER' BLOCK A-FIELD NOT 3 DIGITS
255	MATRIX 'INITIAL' CARD : ILLEGAL INDEX FOR ROWS
256	MATRIX 'INITIAL' CARD : ILLEGAL INDEX FOR COLUMNS
257	ILLEGAL QUEUE NUMBER
258	ILLEGAL JOBTAPE NUMBER
259	CYCLIC (RECURSIVE) DEFINITION OF A VARIABLE
260	VARIABLE NOT DEFINED
261	ILLEGAL VARIABLE NUMBER
262	CYCLIC (RECURSIVE) DEFINITION OF A FUNCTION
263	ILLEGAL FUNCTION NUMBER
264	UNDEFINED FUNCTION
265	ILLEGAL FUNCTION TYPE
266	A FUNCTION MUST HAVE MORE THAN ONE POINT
267	ILLEGAL TYPE SPECIFIED IN B-FIELD OF A 'FUNCTION' CARD
270	NO C-FIELD IN 'EXAMINE' BLOCK
271	ILLEGAL ENTITY NUMBER IN 'RESET' CARD
272	ILLEGAL ENTITY TYPE REQUESTED ON 'RESET' CARD
273	SEQUENCE ERROR ON 'RESET' CARD
274	ILLEGAL REQUEST ON SELECTIVE 'CLEAR' CARD
275	ILLEGAL SAVEVALUE NUMBER ON 'CLEAR' CARD
276	ILLEGAL RANGE OF SAVEVALUES ON 'CLEAR' CARD
277	ILLEGAL HALFWORD SAVEVALUE ON 'CLEAR' CARD
278	ILLEGAL RANGE OF HALFWORD SAVEVALUES ON A 'CLEAR' CARD
279	'READ/SAVE' IDENTIFIER NOT FOUND ON SPECIFIED 'READ' DEVICE
280	ILLEGAL ALLOCATION OF ENTITIES ON 'READ' FILE OR DEVICE
282	ERROR IN BLOCK REDEFINITION
283	ILLEGAL BLOCK NUMBER
284	ILLEGAL XACT REFERENCED IN A CHAINING ROUTINE (PROBABLE SYSTEM BUG)
285	ILLEGAL FREQUENCY CLASS DESIGNATION ON 'TABLE' DEFINITION CARD
290	ILLEGAL REFERENCE TO GPSS/360 COMMON (PROBABLE SYSTEM BUG)
291	ILLEGAL SNA REFERENCED (PROBABLE SYSTEM BUG)
293	ILLEGAL SNA REFERENCED (PROBABLE SYSTEM BUG)

297   ILLEGAL RANDOM NUMBER GENERATOR REFERENCED

298   ATTEMPT TO READ PAST END-OF-FILE ON READ/SAVE FILE OR DEVICE

299   ILLEGAL 'RMULT' CARD SPECIFICATION

301   FUNCTION 'Y' VALUES ARE NOT CONSTANT

302   ILLEGAL TABLE ARGUMENT

Execution Errors

401   NO NEW EVENT IN THE SYSTEM

402   ILLEGAL XACT ON THE FUTURE EVENTS CHAIN (PROBABLE SYSTEM BUG)

403   ILLEGAL XACT IN THE FUTURE EVENTS CHAIN (PROBABLE SYSTEM BUG)

404   ILLEGAL XACT IN THE FUTURE EVENTS CHAIN (PROBABLE SYSTEM BUG)

405   NUMBER OF PARAMETERS EXCEEDED
       AN XACT CAN HAVE NO MORE THAN 100 PARAMETERS

406   ILLEGAL PRIORITY COMPUTED FOR XACT BEING CREATED AT A 'GENERATE'
       BLOCK
406   PRIORITIES MUST BE NON-NEGATIVE AND LESS THAN 128

413   ILLEGAL ENTRY TO A GENERATE BLOCK

415   FACILITY RELEASED BY AN XACT WHICH DID NOT SEIZE IT

416   FACILITY RELEASED BY AN XACT WHICH DID NOT SEIZE IT

417   INTERRUPT COUNT IS NEGATIVE (PROBABLE SYSTEM BUG)

421   FACILITY RETURNED BY AN XACT WHICH IS NOT PREEMPTING IT

425   XACT AT A 'LEAVE' BLOCK DECREMENTS STORAGE CONTENTS TO LESS THAN
       ZERO

428   XACT AT A 'DEPART' BLOCK DECREMENTS QUEUE CONTENTS TO LESS THAN
       ZERO

429   PARAMETER SPECIFIED IN A-FIELD OF A 'LOOP' BLOCK IS ZERO
       AS AN XACT ENTERS THE BLOCK

432   ILLEGAL HALFWORD SAVEVALUE NUMBER

433   ILLEGAL FULLWORD SAVEVALUE NUMBER

434   WEIGHTING NOT SPECIFIED IN D-FIELD OF 'TABLE' DEFINITION CARD
       FOR THE TABLE BEING REFERENCED IN THE CURRENT BLOCK

435   ILLEGAL 'TABLE' NUMBER

436   'TABLE' NOT DEFINED BY A 'TABLE' CARD

437   ILLEGAL XACT NUMBER REFERRED TO UNDER A BLOCKED CONDITION
       (PROBABLE SYSTEM BUG)

438   ATTEMPT TO PLACE AN XACT ON A DELAY CHAIN WHEN THE XACT IS
       ALREADY ON A DELAY CHAIN (PROBABLE SYSTEM BUG)

442   NO PREEMPT COUNT IN XACT RETURNED FROM PREEMPT CONDITION
       (PROBABLE SYSTEM BUG)

443   NUMBER OF XACTS EXCEEDED
       (See section 4.16)

453   ATTEMPT TO REMOVE XACT FROM ILLEGAL CHAIN (PROBABLE SYSTEM BUG)

463   ATTEMPT TO REMOVE XACT FROM ILLEGAL CHAIN (PROBABLE SYSTEM BUG)

466   ATTEMPT TO REMOVE XACT FROM ILLEGAL CHAIN (PROBABLE SYSTEM BUG)

467   ATTEMPT TO REMOVE XACT FROM ILLEGAL CHAIN (PROBABLE SYSTEM BUG)

468   NUMBER OF XACTS EXCEEDED
       (See Section 4.16)

469   NUMBER OF XACTS EXCEEDED
       (See Section 4.16)

470   ILLEGAL XACT NUMBER REFERENCED (PROBABLE SYSTEM BUG)

471   ILLEGAL XACT NUMBER REFERENCED (PROBABLE SYSTEM BUG)

472   ILLEGAL XACT NUMBER REFERENCED (PROBABLE SYSTEM BUG)

474   PREEMPT COUNT EXCEEDS 127

475   ILLEGAL XACT NUMBER REFERENCED (PROBABLE SYSTEM BUG)

476   ATTEMPT TO REMOVE AN INTERRUPT ON AN XACT WHICH HAS
       NOT BEEN INTERRUPTED (PROBABLE SYSTEM BUG)

477   ATTEMPT TO REMOVE AN INTERRUPT ON AN XACT WHICH HAS
       NOT BEEN INTERRUPTED (PROBABLE SYSTEM BUG)

478   AN XACT PREVIOUSLY TERMINATED WHILE SEIZING OR PREEMPTING
       A FACILITY REFERRED TO AT THE CURRENT BLOCK

479   AN XACT PREVIOUSLY TERMINATED WHILE SEIZING OR PREEMPTING
       A FACILITY REFERRED TO AT THE CURRENT BLOCK

480   ILLEGAL RANDOM NUMBER GENERATOR REFERENCED

Output Errors

702   ILLEGAL FACILITY NUMBER

704   ILLEGAL USER CHAIN NUMBER

708   ILLEGAL LOGIC SWITCH NUMBER

712   ILLEGAL FULLWORD SAVEVALUE NUMBER

713   ILLEGAL HALFWORD SAVEVALUE NUMBER

714   ILLEGAL FACILITY NUMBER

715   ILLEGAL STORAGE NUMBER

716   ILLEGAL QUEUE NUMBER

717   ILLEGAL GROUP NUMBER

718   ILLEGAL USER CHAIN NUMBER

722   ILLEGAL STORAGE NUMBER

723   ILLEGAL QUEUE NUMBER

724   ILLEGAL TABLE NUMBER

726   ERROR IN SQUARE ROOT ROUTINE

727   ILLEGAL HALFWORD MATRIX SAVEVALUE NUMBER

728   ILLEGAL FULLWORD MATRIX SAVEVALUE NUMBER

729   ILLEGAL ENTRY TO OUTPUT (DAG07 CONTROL SECTION)
(PROBABLE SYSTEM BUG)

769   ILLEGAL 'TITLE' CARD

Warning Messages

850   ****WARNING****
ATTEMPT TO STORE INTEGER OF MAGNITUDE GREATER THAN 32767
IN A HALFWORD PARAMETER.   CONTENT IS MAINTAINED MODULO 2**15

851   ****WARNING****
ATTEMPT TO STORE INTEGER OF MAGNITUDE GREATER THAN 32767
IN A HALFWORD SAVEVALUE.   CONTENT IS MAINTAINED MODULO 2**15

852   ****WARNING****
ATTEMPT TO STORE INTEGER OF MAGNITUDE GREATER THAN 32767
IN A HALFWORD MATRIX SAVEVALUE.   CONTENT MAINTAINED MODULO 2**15

853   ****WARNING****
XACT ATTEMPTING TO ENTER A 'QUEUE' BLOCK IS ALREADY A MEMBER OF
FIVE QUEUES. THE CONTENTS OF THE QUEUE SPECIFIED IN THE A-FIELD
WILL BE INCREMENTED BY THE AMOUNT SPECIFIED IN THE B-FIELD.
TESTING FOR MAXIMUM CONTENTS WILL BE MADE AND UPDATING DONE
ACCORDINGLY. STATISTICS ON AVERAGE TIME PER XACT, NUMBER OF ZERO
ENTRIES, PERCENT ZEROS, AND AVERAGE TIME PER XACT EXCLUDING ZERO
ENTRIES WILL BE IN ERROR.

854   ****WARNING****
XACT AT A 'DEPART' BLOCK IS NOT A MEMBER OF THE QUEUE SPECIFIED
IN THE A-FIELD. THE QUEUE CONTENTS ARE DECREMENTED BY THE
AMOUNT SPECIFIED IN THE B-FIELD AND THE XACT PROCEEDS
TO THE NEXT SEQUENTIAL BLOCK

861   ****WARNING****
END-OF-FILE REACHED ON JOBTAPE 1 (LOGICAL UNIT 1)
ALL XACTS ON THE CURRENT FILE HAVE ENTERED THE MODEL.

862   ****WARNING****
END-OF-FILE REACHED ON JOBTAPE 2 (LOGICAL UNIT 2)
ALL XACTS ON THE CURRENT FILE HAVE ENTERED THE MODEL.

863   ****WARNING****
END-OF-FILE REACHED ON JOBTAPE 3 (LOGICAL UNIT 3)
ALL XACTS ON THE CURRENT FILE HAVE ENTERED THE MODEL.

Explanation of Column Labels in GPSS Chain Printouts

TRANS   BDT   BLOCK   PR   SF   NBA   SET   MARK-TIME

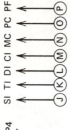

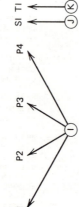

(A)   (B)   (C)   (D)   (E)   (F)   (G)   (H)

P1   P2   P3   P4

(I)

SI   TI   DI   CI   MC   PC   PF

(J)(K)(L)(M)(N)(O)(P)

A row of the column labels used by the GPSS Processor in producing printouts of the Current and Future Events Chains, and of User, Interrupt, and Matching Chains, appears above. The significance of the information contained in the various columns is briefly described below.

Column	Information
A[a]	TRANS indicates Transaction Number.
B[a]	BDT indicates Block Departure Time.
C[a]	BLOCK is the number of the Block which the Transaction is currently in, if any. If the Transaction is not in a Block, the BLOCK entry is blank.
D[a]	PR indicates a Transaction's Priority Level. A blank in this column means that the Transaction's Priority Level is 0.
E	SF stands for Selection Factor. If the SF entry is B, the Transaction is in a BOTH-mode TRANSFER Block. An SF entry of A indicates that the Transaction is in an ALL-mode TRANSFER Block. Except for B and A, the only other possible SF value is blank. The SF entry is probably of little interest.
F[a]	NBA indicates the Transaction's Next Block Attempted.
G	SET shows the number of the next Transaction in the subject Transaction's Assembly Set. For one-member Assembly Sets, the SET and TRANS entries are equal.
H	MARK-TIME is the time at which a Transaction moved out of its GENERATE Block into the model; if the Transaction entered the model as an "offspring" at a SPLIT Block, its MARK-TIME entry equals that of its parent. When a Transaction is on the Future Events Chain, still on its way to the model via a GENERATE Block, its MARK-TIME entry equals −1 times the number of Transactions which have already entered the model through that GENERATE Block.
I	These four columns display a Transaction's Parameter values. The P1 column displays the value of Parameter 1 in row 1, the value of Parameter 5 in row 2, the value of Parameter 9 in row 3, and so on for the other columns and rows.
J	SI stands for Scan Indicator. If the SI entry is 1, the Transaction is scan-inactive; that is, it is uniquely blocked on the Current Events Chain. A blank entry in this column indicates that the Transaction is not uniquely blocked.

Column	Information
K	TI stands for Trace Indicator. When a Transaction moves into a TRACE Block, its Trace Indicator is turned on, i.e., set to 1. Then, each time it subsequently moves into a Block, output describing its whereabouts is produced. The Trace Indicator can be turned off (i.e., set to 0, which prints as a blank in the TI column) by moving the Transaction through an UNTRACE Block.
L	DI stands for Delay Indicator. This indicator was of use in earlier versions of GPSS in which Boolean Variables had not yet been implemented. For the sake of upward compatibility, the Delay Indicator and the SIM-mode TRANSFER Block which uses it have been left in the later versions of GPSS. The DI concept is probably not of much use for those who have Boolean Variables at their disposal.
M	CI stands for Chain Indicator. The CI entry tells which chain a Transaction is on. The codes used are shown below.

CI Entry	Chain
"blank"	User Chain or Matching Chain
1	Interrupt Chain
2	Current Events Chain
4	Future Events Chain

Column	Information
N	MC stands for Matching Condition. A 1 in the MC column indicates that the Transaction is in matching condition, that is, is on a Matching Chain, and is in an ASSEMBLE, GATHER, or MATCH Block. (The MC column is otherwise blank.)
O	PC stands for Preempt Count. The preempt count is a count of the number of Facilities which the Transaction has had taken away from it by other Transactions, and for which it is remaining in contention.
P	PF stands for Preempt Flag. When the Preempt Flag is on (i.e., when the entry in the PF column is 1), there is a preempt pending for the corresponding Transaction. This means that the Transaction has had a Facility taken away from it, but has not yet been subjected to its preemption fate. It will be forced to submit to that fate the next time it enters an ADVANCE Block where a positive holding time is specified, or the next time it enters an ASSEMBLE, GATHER, or MATCH Block under the right conditions.

a See Sections 2.20 to 2.24 for a detailed discussion of Transaction Number, Move Time (i.e., Block Departure Time), Current Block, Priority Level, and Next Block Attempted.

APPENDIX E

Mnemonics for the PRINT Block

PRINT Block[1] mnemonics for the various GPSS entities discussed in this book are shown below.

Information to be Printed	Mnemonic
Block Counts[a]	
Current	W
Total	N
Current and Total	B
Chains[a]	
Current Events	MOV
Future Events	FUT
Interrupt	I
Matching	MAT
User	CHA
Clocks (Relative and Absolute)[a]	C
Logic Switches (Settings)[b]	LG
Matrix Savevalues[b]	
Halfword	MX
Fullword	MH
Savevalues[b]	
Halfword	XH
Fullword	X (or blank)
Statistics[b]	
Facilities	F
Queues	Q
Storages	S
Tables	T
User Chains	U

[a]To get this information, defaults must be taken on the PRINT Block's A and B Operands.

[b]The PRINT Block A and B Operands specify the inclusive lower and upper limits, respectively, of the range of entity numbers for which the information will be printed. In case of default, information for the entire range of the type of entity involved will be printed.

[1] For a discussion of PRINT Block use, see Section 2.42.

APPENDIX F[1]

Information Pertinent to the GPSS REALLOCATE Card

Entity Type[2]	Normally Available Quantities for Various Computer Memory Levels			Fixed Memory Requirement per Item (bytes)	Reallocation Mnemonic
	64K	128K	256K		
Transactions	200	600	1200	16[a]	XAC
Blocks	120	500	1000	12[b]	BLO
Facilities	35	150	1000	28	FAC
Functions	20	50	200	32[c]	FUN
Logic Switches	200	400	1000	6	LOG
Matrix Savevalues (fullword)	5	10	25	24[d]	FMS
Matrix Savevalues (halfword)	5	10	25	24[e]	HMS
Queues	70	150	300	32	QUE
Storages	35	150	300	40	STO
Savevalues (fullword)	100	400	1000	4	FSV
Savevalues (halfword)	50	200	500	2	HSV
Tables	50	200	500	48[f]	TAB
User Chains	15	30	100	24	CHA
Variables (Arithmetic)	20	40	100	48[g]	VAR
Variables (Boolean)	20	50	200	32[h]	BVR
COMMON (bytes)[i]	5600	14400	25600		COM

[a] Add 20 bytes of COMMON for every active Transaction, plus additional bytes for Parameters (2 bytes per halfword Parameter, 4 bytes per fullword Parameter).

[b] Add 4 bytes of COMMON for each Block with more than one Operand used. Add an additional 12 bytes of COMMON per Operand used if one or more of the Block Operands is indirectly specified through a Matrix Savevalue.

[c] Add 4 bytes of COMMON for each point of an L or M type Function.

[d] Add 8 bytes of COMMON for each pair of coordinates of a D or E type Function.

[e] Add 12 bytes of COMMON for each pair of coordinates of a C type Function.

[d] A 4 bytes of COMMON for each element in the Matrix.

[e] Add 2 bytes of COMMON for each element in the Matrix.

[f] Add 4 bytes of COMMON for each Table interval.

[g] Add 4 bytes of COMMON for each Standard Numerical Attribute in the defining expression.
Add 12 bytes of COMMON for each pair of parentheses used.
Add 20 bytes of COMMON for each pair of parentheses used.
Add 2 bytes of COMMON for each arithmetic operator used. (This is an approximation.)

[h] Add 12 bytes of COMMON for each Logical Operator used.
Add 24 bytes of COMMON for each pair of parentheses used. (This is an approximation.)
Add 8 bytes of COMMON for the first Boolean Operator used.
Add 4 bytes of COMMON for each Boolean Operator used after the first.
Add 16 bytes of COMMON for each Boolean Operator used.
Add 4 bytes of COMMON for each Relational Operator used.
Add 4 bytes of COMMON for each constant used.
Add 12 bytes of COMMON for each nonconstant Standard Numerical Attribute used.
Add 4 additional bytes of COMMON.

[i] COMMON is an otherwise-uncommitted pool of computer memory, portions of which can be used for such purposes as storing the pairs of points used to define Functions, providing the memory needed for Transaction Parameters, and so on.

[1] For a discussion of the significance and use of the information in Appendix F, and computational examples, see Section 4.16.

[2] Only those GPSS entities actually discussed in this book are included in this appendix.

APPENDIX G

Defining Contexts for Entity Numbers in GPSS

As discussed in Section 4.18, it is important to know which usage contexts are *defining* for the various GPSS entities when they are referred to by number. (Use of symbolic entity names is defining when the names appear in any context in a model.) The following table lists the Blocks whose A Operands provide defining contexts, and the definition cards whose Location fields provide defining contexts, for the GPSS entities discussed in this book.

Entity Type	Blocks[a,b] (If Any)	Definition Cards[a] (If Any)
Facilities	SEIZE RELEASE PREEMPT RETURN GATE[c]	
Functions		FUNCTION
Logic Switches	LOGIC GATE[d]	
Matrix Savevalues	MSAVEVALUE	MATRIX
Queues	QUEUE DEPART	
Savevalues	SAVEVALUE	
Storages	ENTER LEAVE GATE[f]	STORAGE[e]
Tables	TABULATE	TABLE QTABLE
User Chains	LINK UNLINK	
Variables Boolean Integer Real		BVARIABLE VARIABLE FVARIABLE

[a] Caution! When the form Kj is used to refer to an entity numerically, where j is the number itself, the Processor does *not* add the number j to the corresponding entity's numeric name-list. As a rule of thumb, avoid use of the form Kj. Otherwise, if symbolic names are used for the entity type in question, j may be made the numeric equivalent of a symbolic name.

[b] The A Operand on the EQU card also provides a defining context for each GPSS entity.

[c] When the Auxiliary Operator is U, NU, I, or NI.

[d] When the Auxiliary Operator is LR or LS.

[e] The Storage capacity definition card provides a defining context for Storages referenced numerically only when the number of the Storage *appears in the Location field*. Hence, the card "7 STORAGE 3" does cause 7 to be put on the numeric name-list for Storages, but the card "STORAGE S7,3" does not.

[f] When the Auxiliary Operator is SF, SE, SNF, or SNE.

APPENDIX H

Mnemonics for the Equivalence Declaration Card

Equivalence card[1] mnemonics for the various GPSS entities discussed in this book are shown below.

Entity Type	Mnemonic
Boolean Variables	B
Facilities	F
Functions	Z
Logic Switches	L
Matrix Savevalues	
Fullword	M
Halfword	Y
Queues	Q
Savevalues	
Fullword	X
Halfword	H
Storages	S
Tables	T
User Chains	C
Variables	V

[1] For a discussion of Equivalence card use, see Section 4.18.

509

APPENDIX I

Summary of GPSS Standard Numerical Attributes

The various GPSS Standard Numerical Attributes discussed in this book are summarized below, listed alphabetically under the various entity headings. The entities themselves are also listed alphabetically. Only a terse definition is given here for each SNA. Expanded definitions and discussion can be found in the book on the indicated page(s).

Entity	SNA[a]	Brief Description	Page Reference(s)
Blocks	N	Total Count	Page 188
	W	Current Count	
Clock	C1[a]	Value of Relative Clock	Page 188
Facilities	F	Facility status (1 = busy; 0 = available)	Page 186
	FC	Capture count	
	FR	Fractional utilization (parts per thousand)	
	FT	Average holding time per capture (integerized)	
Functions	FN	Current value of the Function	Page 158 (C: Continuous)
			Page 147 (D: Discrete)
			Page 362 (E: Attribute)
			Page 302 (L: List-Discrete)
			Page 363 (M: List-Attribute)
Matrix Savevalues	MH(a,b)[b]	Value of element in row a, column b, halfword Matrix	Page 292
	MX(a,b)[b]	Value of element in row a, column b, fullword Matrix	
Queues	Q	Current content	Page 186
	QA	Average content (integerized)	
	QC	Entry count (total entries)	
	QM	Maximum content	
	QT	Average residence time (based on QC) (integerized)	
	QX	Average residence time (based on QZ) (integerized)	
	QZ	Entry count (zero entries)	
Random Numbers	RN[c]	When used as a Function argument, a six-digit fraction between 0.000000 and 0.999999, inclusive; when used otherwise, a three-digit whole number between 000 and 999, inclusive	Page 144
Savevalues	X	Value of fullword Savevalue	Page 266
	XH	Value of halfword Savevalue	

510

Entity	SNA[a]	Brief Description	Page Reference(s)
Storages	R	Remaining capacity	Page 186
	S	Current content	
	SA	Average content (integerized)	
	SC	Entry count	
	SR	Fractional utilization (parts per thousand)	
	SM	Maximum content	
	ST	Average holding time per unit (integerized)	
Tables[d]	TB	Average value of nonweighted entries (integerized)	Page 285 (Weighted) Page 249 (Nonweighted)
	TC	Number of nonweighted entries (integerized)	
	TD	Standard deviation of nonweighted entries (integerized)	
Transactions	P	Parameter value	Page 195
	PR[a]	Priority Level	Page 207
	M1[a]	Residence time in model[e]	Page 241
	MP	Time since move into MARK Block	Page 242
User Chains	CA	Average content (integerized)	Page 411
	CC	Total entries	
	CH	Current content	
	CM	Maximum content	
	CT	Average time-on-chain per entry (integerized)	
Variables	BV	Current value of Boolean Variable	Page 326
	V	Current value of Arithmetic Variable	Page 258

[a] With the exception of C1, PR, and M1, each of these SNA "family names" must be followed by the directly or indirectly specified numeric name, or the directly specified symbolic name, of an entity member. [But see note (b).] When an entity member has been named symbolically, a dollar sign ($) must be placed between the family name and the symbolic name.

[b] For Matrix Savevalues, the name of the specific entity member must be placed between the MH (or MX) and the left parenthesis.

[c] The RN must be followed by a directly or indirectly specified numeric name, which in turn must be one of the integers 1, 2, 3, 4, 5, 6, 7, or 8.

[d] Each of the three Table Standard Numerical Attributes has its value computed based on the nonweighted Table entries; this is true even for a weighted Table.

[e] This assumes that whenever the MARK Block is used, an A Operand is supplied with it.

APPENDIX J

Summary of GPSS Relational Operators, Logical Mnemonics, and Logical Operators

Relational Operators

The Relational Operators take either one of two slightly differing forms, depending on the context in which they are used. The following table indicates these forms and contexts.

First Form[a]	Second Form[b]	Meaning
L	'L'	less than
LE	'LE'	less than or equal to
E	'E'	equal to
NE	'NE'	not equal to
GE	'GE'	greater than or equal to
G	'G'	greater than

[a]The first form is used when the Relational Operator appears as an Auxiliary Operator at SELECT and TEST Blocks. See the SELECT Block discussion in Section 4.14, and the TEST Block discussion in Section 5.8.
[b]The second form is used when the Relational Operator appears within expressions used to define Boolean Variables. For a discussion, see Section 6.2.2.

Logical Mnemonics

Logical Mnemonics are used as Auxiliary Operators at GATE and SELECT Blocks when a logical property of a Facility (GATE) or Facilities (SELECT), a Logic Switch (GATE) or Logic Switches (SELECT), a Storage (GATE) or Storages (SELECT), or a Transaction (GATE) is being examined. The following table summarizes the choices available.

Entity Type	Logical Mnemonic	Meaning
Facilities	U	Facility in Use
	NU	Facility Not in Use
	I	Facility Interrupted
	NI	Facility Not Interrupted
Logic Switches	LR	Logic Switch Reset
	LS	Logic Switch Set
Storages	SE	Storage Empty
	SNE	Storage Not Empty
	SF	Storage Full
	SNF	Storage Not Full
Transactions	M[a]	Match at A-Block
	NM[a]	No Match at A-Block

[a] M and NM can only be used as Auxiliary Operators at the GATE Block.

For a discussion of Logical Mnemonic use with the GATE Block, see Sections 5.20, 5.21, 7.19, and 7.28; for discussion pertaining to the SELECT Block, see Sections 5.22 and 7.19.

Logical Operators

Logical Operators are used in constructing elements which reference the logical status of a Facility, a Logic Switch, or a Storage. These logical elements, in turn, become part of expressions used to define Boolean Variables. The following table summarizes the available Logical Operators.

Entity Type	Logical Mnemonic	Meaning
Facilities	FU (or F)	Facility in Use
	FNU	Facility Not in Use
	FI	Facility Interrupted
	FNI	Facility Not Interrupted
Logic Switches	LR	Logic Switch Reset
	LS	Logic Switch Set
Storages	SE	Storage Empty
	SNE	Storage Not Empty
	SF	Storage Full
	SNF	Storage Not Full

Note that there are no Logical Operators for Transactions. Also note that the Logical Operators and Logical Mnemonics take identical forms for Logic Switches and Storages. The form of Facility Logical Operators can be arrived at by attaching a prefacing F to the form for Facility Logical Mnemonics. For a discussion of the use of Logical Operators in constructing Boolean Variables, see Section 6.2.3.

APPENDIX K

Summary of GPSS Non-Block Statements

Many of the GPSS statements which are discussed in this book do not correspond directly to Blocks in the language. Referring to such statements by their Operation word, statements like BVARIABLE, CLEAR, RMULT, and STORAGE fall into this non-Block statement category. Nineteen of these statements have been introduced in this book. Of the 19, 15 are summarized in this Appendix, on the following pages. The four non-Block statements excluded from the following pages are END, JOB, RESET, and SIMULATE. They are excluded simply because the entire statement consists only of the single word END, or JOB, etc., entered in the Operation field on a punch-card. The statements do not use the Location field or the Operations field.[1]

The 15 non-Block statements are listed alphabetically, according to their "Operation." In appendix columns corresponding to the Location and Operands fields, the following information appears.

1. The role of the field is briefly described.
2. The choices open to the analyst in supplying the information required in the various fields are then summarized.

The range of choices available in supplying entity names and numeric data, where either or both are needed, is indicated in this appendix with the notation *k*, sn, SNA*j*, and SNA**j*. For corresponding definitions, please turn to Table L.1 in Appendix L.

Whenever information *must* be provided, and options are available to the analyst, these options are listed within a pair of *braces*. Whenever it is *optional* whether certain information is provided, the choice or set of choices open to the analyst is listed within *square brackets*. Finally, when information *must* be supplied, and there are *no* options as to the form it takes, neither braces nor square brackets are used to enclose it.

For examples of the "braces" and "square brackets" notation, see Figures L.1 and L.2 in Appendix L. Observe that with respect to braces, square brackets, and the references *k*, sn, SNA, SNA*j*, and SNA**j*, the notation used throughout Appendix K is fully consistent with the notation used throughout Appendix L.

Three notational needs do arise in Appendix K, however, for which there are no corresponding needs in Appendix L. These occasions use specific instances of the general SNA*j* and SNA$sn forms. In particular, instead of *any* SNA being applicable, only a particular one or ones are applicable. The three occasions are cited below.

1. With respect to the CLEAR card, the specific forms are X*j*, X$sn, XH*j*, and XH$sn.
2. With respect to the INITIAL card, the specific forms are LS*j*, LS$sn, MX*j*, MX$sn, MH*j*, MH$sn, X*j*, X$sn, XH*j*, and XH$sn.
3. Finally, with respect to the STORAGE card as used for "multiple Storage capacity definition," the specific forms are S*j* and S$sn.

For the CLEAR, INITIAL, and STORAGE cards, then, the specific forms just cited are used in this appendix, instead of the general SNA*j* and SNA$sn forms.

Unlike the situation with statements for GPSS Blocks, the non-Block statements do not fit into a uniform

[1] As mentioned in the book, there is such a thing as a *selective* RESET card. This card does make use of the Operands field. But, because the selective RESET was not discussed in the book, it does not appear in this appendix.

514

scheme for summary purposes. Except for the common concept of "Location, Operation, and Operands" fields, there is wide potential variation in terms of the specifics for statements in the non-Block category. This appendix is provided, then, to draw all of these statements together in one place, as a convenience for the analyst who may need an occasional quick review of the composition of a particular type of non-Block statement. For those needing a more detailed discussion of the various statements, the rightmost column in the appendix indicates the page in the book at which discussion of the statement-type begins.

LOCATION	OPERATION	A	B	C	D	E	F,G,H →	Page Reference(s)
Name of Boolean Variable {k,sn}	BVARIABLE	Combination of numeric data specifications, relational operators, logical attributes, and Boolean operators						Page 326
		Numeric Data Specifications k,SNAj,SNA$sn,SNA*$j$	Delimiter if Multiple Entries [,]	Relational Operators 'G' 'GE' / 'L' 'LE' / 'E' 'NE'	Logical Attributes[a] FU (or F) LS SE / FNU LR SNE / FI SF / FNI SNF	Boolean Operators + (or) * (and)		

[a] Formed by appending j, $sn, or *$j$ to the above-listed Logical Operators

LOCATION	OPERATION	A	B	C	D	Page Reference(s)
	CLEAR	Savevalue(s) Not to be Cleared [Xj;Xsn, XHj$;XH$sn]	Delimiter if Multiple Entries [,]			Page 238
Symbolic Name of Entity sn	EQU	Numeric Equivalent of Symbolic Name k	Mnemonic for Entity Type {see Appendix H}			Pages 101 and 269
Name of Function {k,sn}	FUNCTION	Function Argument SNAj/SNA$sn, SNA*$j$, except MX, MH	Function Type and No. of Points C / D / E / L / M k			Page 158 / Page 147 / Page 362 / Page 302 / Page 363

Function Follow Card(s)

$X_1,Y_1/X_2,Y_2/X_3,Y_3,Y/$, etc. (X, must start in column 1; MX and MH are not allowed for Y values in E-type or M-type Functions.)

LOCATION	OPERATION	A	B	C	D	Page Reference(s)
	INITIAL	Logic Switch(s) to be Set {LSj;LS$sn}	Delimiter if Multiple Entries [/]			Page 305
		Savevalue(s) {Xj;Xsn, XHj$;XH$sn}	Initial Value [−] k	Delimiter if Multiple Entries [/]		Page 293
		Matrix Savevalue(s) {MXj;MX$sn, MH$j$;MH$sn}	Initial Value [−] k	Delimiter if Multiple Entries [/]		
Name of Matrix {k,sn}	MATRIX	Matrix Type {X,H}	Number of Rows k	Number of Columns k		Page 292
Name of Table {k,sn}	QTABLE	Name of Queue {sn k}	Inclusive Upper Limit of Lowest Frequency Class k	Width of Intermediate Frequency Classes k	Number of Frequency Classes k	Page 253

LOCATION	OPERATION	A	B	C	D	E	F,G,H →	Page Reference(s)
	REALLOCATE	Mnemonic for Entity Being Reallocated {see Appendix F}	Total Number of That Entity After Reallocation k	Delimiter if Multiple Entries [,]				Page 233
	RMULT	A positive *odd* integer constant can optionally be provided for one or more of Operands A through H, to specify a nonstandard initial multiplier for random number generators 1 through 8, respectively. The standard initial setting results when the Operand value is 1. In case of default, the current value of the multiplier is unaltered. A comma is the delimiter for multiple entries.						Page 172
	START	Initial Value of Termination Counter k	Printout Suppression [NP]	Initial Value of Snap Interval Counter [k]	Signal for Chain Printouts [1]			Pages 39, 74, 130, and 132
Name of Storage {k,sn}	STORAGE	Storage Capacity k						Page 109
	STORAGE	Reference to Storage {Sj; $S\$sn$}	Storage Capacity k	Delimiter if Multiple Entries [/]				Page 110
Name of Table {k,sn}	TABLE	Table Arguments {k,SNAj; SNA\$sn,SNA*j}	Inclusive Upper Limit of Lowest Frequency Class k	Width of Intermediate Frequency Classes k	Number of Frequency Classes [W]k	Time Interval for RT-Table [k]		Pages 244 and 285
Name of Variable {k,sn}	VARIABLE FVARIABLE	Combinations of numeric data specifications and arithmetic operators						Pages 259 and 261

Numeric Data Specifications	Arithmetic Operators
k,SNAj;SNA\$sn,SNA*j	+
	-
	/
	*
	@ (VARIABLE only)

APPENDIX L

Summary of the GPSS Blocks, and Significance of Their Operands

This appendix consists of a list of all the various GPSS Blocks discussed in this book, arranged in alphabetical order according to Block Operation. This information is provided for each Block.

1. In a BLOCK column, a picture of the Block is shown, with its Operands appearing in general form in their usual positions.
2. In an OPERATION column, the Block Operation is given. For those Blocks which use an Auxiliary Operator, the available choices of Auxiliary Operators are then listed beneath the Block Operation. (Auxiliary Operators are depicted in the BLOCK column with an X.)
3. In the next seven columns, the role of each of the Block's Operands is indicated. These columns also show, Operand-by-Operand, whether a default option is available, or whether the Operand must be explicitly provided. Finally, the range of choices in supplying Operand values is summarized.
4. The last of the seven Operand columns doubles for both the G Operand (if any), and a reference to the page or pages in the book where the Block is introduced and explained in detail.

The range of choices available in supplying Operand values is indicated in this appendix with the abbreviations shown in Table L.1.

TABLE L.1 Explanation of the Abbreviations Used in Appendix L

Abbreviation	Meaning
k	A nonnegative integer constant
sn	A symbolic name
SNA	Family Name of a Standard Numerical Attribute
SNAj	Family Name of a Standard Numerical Attribute, followed by a numeric entity name
SNA$sn	Family Name of a Standard Numerical Attribute, followed by a dollar sign ($) and a symbolic entity name
SNA*j	Family Name of a Standard Numerical Attribute, followed by an asterisk (*) and the number of a Parameter whose value is a (numeric) entity name

When a value *must* be provided explicitly for an Operand, the various available choices are listed within *braces*. For example, the notation shown in Figure L.1 applies to the ASSIGN Block's A Operand. It indicates that the

$$\begin{Bmatrix} k, \text{SNA}j, \\ \text{SNA\$sn}, \text{SNA}*j \end{Bmatrix}$$

FIGURE L.1 Notation Used When an Operand Value Must be Provided Explicitly

517

Operand can be a constant, or a data reference of the type SNA*j*, SNA$sn, or SNA**j*. Note that the abbreviation sn is not listed within the braces, indicating that it is invalid to use a symbolic name as an ASSIGN Block's A Operand.

When an Operand is *optional*. the available choices are enclosed within *square* brackets. An example appears in Figure L.2. The example applies to the ADVANCE Block's A Operand, which need not be provided explicitly at all, or can be provided as *k*, SNA*j*, SNA$sn, or SNA**j*.

$$\begin{bmatrix} k, \text{SNA}j, \\ \text{SNA}\$sn, \text{SNA}*j \end{bmatrix}$$

FIGURE L.2   Notation Used to Indicate that No Operand Value Need be Provided Explicitly

Finally, when an Operand must be supplied, and there are *no* options as to the form it takes, neither braces nor square brackets are used. An example of this situation arises with the BOTH-mode TRANSFER Block, where the word BOTH must be supplied as the Block's A Operand.

BLOCK	OPERATION	A	B	C	D	E	F	G and/or Page Reference(s)
ADVANCE A,B	ADVANCE	Mean Time $\begin{bmatrix} k,\text{SNA}j, \\ \text{SNA}\$sn,\text{SNA}*j \end{bmatrix}$	Spread Modifier $\begin{bmatrix} k,\text{SNA}j, \\ \text{SNA}\$sn,\text{SNA}*j \\ \text{but not} \\ \text{FN}j,\text{FN}\$sn,\text{FN}*j \end{bmatrix}$ or Function Modifier $[\text{FN}j,\text{FN}\$sn,\text{FN}*j]$					Pages 43, 149, and 167
A ASSEMBLE	ASSEMBLE	Assembly Count $\begin{Bmatrix} k,\text{SNA}j, \\ \text{SNA}\$sn,\text{SNA}*j \end{Bmatrix}$						Page 463
A,B,C ASSIGN	ASSIGN	Parameter No. $\begin{Bmatrix} k,\text{SNA}j, \\ \text{SNA}\$sn,\text{SNA}*j \end{Bmatrix} [\pm]$	Value to be Assigned $\begin{Bmatrix} k,\text{SNA}j, \\ \text{SNA}\$sn,\text{SNA}*j \end{Bmatrix}$	No. of Function Modifier $\begin{bmatrix} k,\text{SNA}j, \\ \text{SNA}\$sn,\text{SNA}*j \end{bmatrix}$				Page 197
BUFFER	BUFFER							Page 337
DEPART B A	DEPART	Queue Name $\begin{Bmatrix} sn,k,\text{SNA}j, \\ \text{SNA}\$sn,\text{SNA}*j \end{Bmatrix}$	No. of Units $\begin{Bmatrix} k,\ \text{SNA}j, \\ \text{SNA}\$sn,\text{SNA}*j \end{Bmatrix}$					Page 45

BLOCK	OPERATION	A	B	C	D	E	F	G and/or Page Reference(s)
ENTER	ENTER	Storage Name $\left\{\begin{array}{l} sn,k,SNAj, \\ SNA\$sn,SNA*j \end{array}\right\}$	No. of Units $\left[\begin{array}{l} k,SNAj, \\ SNA\$sn,SNA*j \end{array}\right]$					Page 106
GATE X	GATE $\left\{\begin{array}{l} LS \\ LR \end{array}\right\}$	Logic Switch Name $\left\{\begin{array}{l} sn,k,SNAj, \\ SNA\$sn,SNA*j \end{array}\right\}$	Next Block if Condition is False $\left[\begin{array}{l} sn,k,SNAj, \\ SNA\$sn,SNA*j \end{array}\right]$					Page 307
GATE X	GATE $\left\{\begin{array}{l} M \\ NM \end{array}\right\}$	Location of ASSEMBLE, GATHER, or MATCH Block $\left\{\begin{array}{l} sn,k,SNAj, \\ SNA\$sn,SNA*j \end{array}\right\}$	Next Block if Condition is False $\left[\begin{array}{l} sn,k,SNAj, \\ SNA\$sn,SNA*j \end{array}\right]$					Page 480
GATE X	GATE $\left\{\begin{array}{l} NI \\ I \\ NU \\ U \end{array}\right\}$	Facility Name $\left\{\begin{array}{l} sn,k,SNAj, \\ SNA\$sn,SNA*j \end{array}\right\}$	Next Block if Condition is False $\left[\begin{array}{l} sn,k,SNAj, \\ SNA\$sn,SNA*j \end{array}\right]$					Page 308
GATE X	GATE $\left\{\begin{array}{l} SE \\ SF \\ SNE \\ SNF \end{array}\right\}$	Storage Name $\left\{\begin{array}{l} sn,k,SNAj, \\ SNA\$sn,SNA*j \end{array}\right\}$	Next Block if Condition is False $\left[\begin{array}{l} sn,k,SNAj, \\ SNA\$sn,SNA*j \end{array}\right]$					Page 308
GATHER	GATHER	Gather Count $\left\{\begin{array}{l} k,SNAj, \\ SNA\$sn,SNA*j \end{array}\right\}$						Page 474

BLOCK	OPERATION	A	B	C	D	E	F	G and/or Page Reference(s)
GENERATE A,B,C,D,E,F,G	GENERATE	Mean Time [k,SNAj,SNA\$sn]	Spread Modifier [k,SNAj,SNA\$sn but not FNj,FN\$sn] or Function Modifier [FNj,FN\$sn]	Offset Interval [k,SNAj,SNA\$sn]	Limit Count [k,SNAj,SNA\$sn]	Priority Level [k,SNAj,SNA\$sn]	No. of Parameters [k,SNAj,SNA\$sn]	Type of Parameters [F] Pages 34, 149, and 165

Note: GENERATE Block Operands A through F are restricted to k and these SNA's: FN, V, X, XH, RN, N, and C1. Likewise, elements of Functions or Variables used for these Operands are restricted to these same SNA's.

BLOCK	OPERATION	A	B	C	D	E	F	G and/or Page Reference(s)
LEAVE A / B	LEAVE	Storage Name { sn,k,SNAj, SNA\$sn,SNA$*j$ }	No. of Units [k,SNAj, SNA\$sn,SNA$*j$]					Page 106
LINK A / B, (C)	LINK	Name of User Chain { sn,k,SNAj, SNA\$sn,SNA$*j$ }	Merge Criterion[a] { LIFO FIFO Pj }	Alternate Block [sn,k,SNAj, SNA\$sn,SNA$*j$]				Page 396
LOGIC X / A	LOGIC { I R S }	Logic Switch Name { sn,k,SNAj, SNA\$sn,SNA$*j$ }						Page 306
(B) A / LOOP	LOOP	Parameter No. { k,SNAj, SNA\$sn,SNA$*j$ }	Next Block if Parameter $\neq$ 0 { sn,k,SNAj, SNA\$sn,SNA$*j$ }					Page 302

[a]But see footnote 5 in Chapter 7 (page 397).

BLOCK	OPERATION	A	B	C	D	E	F	G and/or Page Reference(s)
MARK A	MARK	Parameter No.[a] $\begin{Bmatrix} k,\text{SNA}j, \\ \text{SNA\$sn,SNA}*j \end{Bmatrix}$						Page 242
MATCH A	MATCH	Location of Conjugate Match Block $\begin{Bmatrix} sn,k,\text{SNA}j, \\ \text{SNA\$sn,SNA}*j \end{Bmatrix}$						Page 475
MSAVEVALUE A,B,C,D,E	MSAVEVALUE	Matrix Name $\begin{Bmatrix} sn,k,\text{SNA}j, \\ \text{SNA\$sn,SNA}*j \end{Bmatrix}$ [±]	Row No. $\begin{Bmatrix} k,\text{SNA}j, \\ \text{SNA\$sn,SNA}*j \end{Bmatrix}$	Column No. $\begin{Bmatrix} k,\text{SNA}j, \\ \text{SNA\$sn,SNA}*j \end{Bmatrix}$	Value to be Saved $\begin{Bmatrix} k,\text{SNA}j, \\ \text{SNA\$sn,SNA}*j \end{Bmatrix}$	Matrix Type [H]		Page 294
PREEMPT B,C,D,E A	PREEMPT	Facility Name $\begin{Bmatrix} sn,k,\text{SNA}j, \\ \text{SNA\$sn,SNA}*j \end{Bmatrix}$	Priority Option [PR]	Next Block for Preempted Transaction $\begin{bmatrix} sn,k,\text{SNA}j, \\ \text{SNA\$sn,SNA}*j \end{bmatrix}$	Parameter No. of Preempted Transaction $\begin{bmatrix} k,\text{SNA}j, \\ \text{SNA\$sn,SNA}*j \end{bmatrix}$	Remove Option [RE]		Pages 429 and 456
A,B,D PRINT C	PRINT	Lower Limit $\begin{bmatrix} sn,k,\text{SNA}j, \\ \text{SNA\$sn,SNA}*j \end{bmatrix}$	Upper Limit $\begin{bmatrix} sn,k,\text{SNA}j, \\ \text{SNA\$sn,SNA}*j \end{bmatrix}$	Entity Mnemonic {See Appendix E}	Paging Indicator $\begin{bmatrix} \text{Any alpha} \\ \text{character} \end{bmatrix}$			Page 130

[a]But see the footnote to Figure 4.28 in Chapter 4 (page 243).

BLOCK	OPERATION	A	B	C	D	E	F	G and/or Page Reference(s)
PRIORITY	PRIORITY	New PR Value $\left\{\begin{array}{l}k,\text{SNA}j,\\ \text{SNA\$sn},\text{SNA}*j\end{array}\right\}$	Buffer Option [BUFFER]					Pages 207 and 408
QUEUE	QUEUE	Queue Name $\left\{\begin{array}{l}sn,k,\text{SNA}j,\\ \text{SNA\$sn},\text{SNA}*j\end{array}\right\}$	No. of Units $\left[\begin{array}{l}k,\text{SNA}j,\\ \text{SNA\$sn},\text{SNA}*j\end{array}\right]$					Page 45
RELEASE	RELEASE	Facility Name $\left\{\begin{array}{l}sn,k,\text{SNA}j,\\ \text{SNA\$sn},\text{SNA}*j\end{array}\right\}$						Page 41
RETURN	RETURN	Facility Name $\left\{\begin{array}{l}sn,k,\text{SNA}j,\\ \text{SNA\$sn},\text{SNA}*j\end{array}\right\}$						Page 429
SAVEVALUE A,B,C	SAVEVALUE	Savevalue Name $\left\{\begin{array}{l}sn,k,\text{SNA}j,\\ \text{SNA\$sn},\text{SNA}*j\end{array}\right\}$ [±]	Value to be Saved $\left\{\begin{array}{l}k,\text{SNA}j,\\ \text{SNA\$sn},\text{SNA}*j\end{array}\right\}$	Savevalue Type [H]				Page 268
SEIZE	SEIZE	Facility Name $\left\{\begin{array}{l}sn,k,\text{SNA}j,\\ \text{SNA\$sn},\text{SNA}*j\end{array}\right\}$						Page 41

BLOCK	OPERATION	A	B	C	D	E	F	G and/or Page Reference(s)
SELECT A,B,C,,, (F)	SELECT (Logical) {U,NU, I,NI, SE,SNE, SF,SNF, LR,LS}	Parameter in Which to Place Entity No. {k,SNAj, SNA$sn,SNA*j}	Lower Limit {sn,k,SNAj, SNA$sn,SNA*j}	Upper Limit {sn,k,SNAj, SNA$sn,SNA*j}	Not Used	Not Used	Alternate Exit [sn,k,SNAj, SNA$sn,SNA*j]	Pages 309 and 445
SELECT A,B,C,,E	SELECT (MIN or MAX) {MIN MAX}	Parameter in Which to Place Entity No. {k,SNAj, SNA$sn,SNA*j}	Lower Limit {sn,k,SNAj, SNA$sn,SNA*j}	Upper Limit {sn,k,SNAj, SNA$sn,SNA*j}	Not Used	Attribute To Examine {Any SNA except MX, MH}		Page 221
SELECT A,B,C,D,E (F)	SELECT (Relational) {G GE E NE LE L}	Parameter in Which to Place Entity No. {k,SNAj, SNA$sn,SNA*j}	Lower Limit {sn,k,SNAj, SNA$sn,SNA*j}	Upper Limit {sn,k,SNAj, SNA$sn,SNA*j}	Comparison Value {k,SNAj, SNA$sn,SNA*j}	Attribute To Examine {Any SNA except MX, MH}	Alternate Exit [sn,k,SNAj, SNA$sn,SNA*j]	Page 218
C SPLIT D (B) A	SPLIT	No. of Offspring {k,SNAj, SNA$sn,SNA*j}	Next Block for Offspring {sn,k,SNAj, SNA$sn,SNA*j}	Serialization Parameter [k,SNAj, SNA$sn,SNA*j]	No. of Parameters for Each Offspring [k,SNAj, SNA$sn,SNA*j]			Pages 350 and 373
TABULATE B A	TABULATE	Table Name {sn,k,SNAj, SNA$sn,SNA*j}	Weighting Factor [k,SNAj, SNA$sn,SNA*j]					Pages 244, 252, and 285
TERMINATE A	TERMINATE	Termination Counter Decrement [k,SNAj, SNA$sn,SNA*j]						Page 38

BLOCK	OPERATION	A	B	C	D	E	F	G and/or Page Reference(s)
	TEST $\left\{\begin{array}{l}G\\GE\\E\\NE\\LE\\L\end{array}\right.$	First Value $\left\{\begin{array}{l}k,\text{SNA}j,\\ \text{SNA\$sn},\text{SNA}*j\end{array}\right\}$	Second Value $\left\{\begin{array}{l}k,\text{SNA}j,\\ \text{SNA\$sn},\text{SNA}*j\end{array}\right\}$	Next Block if Condition is False $\left[\begin{array}{l}sn,k,\text{SNA}j,\\ \text{SNA\$sn},\text{SNA}*j\end{array}\right]$				Page 275
	TRANSFER (Conditional)	Selection Mode BOTH	First Block Examined $\left\{\begin{array}{l}sn,k,\text{SNA}j,\\ \text{SNA\$sn},\text{SNA}*j\end{array}\right\}$	Second Block Examined $\left\{\begin{array}{l}sn,k,\text{SNA}j,\\ \text{SNA\$sn},\text{SNA}*j\end{array}\right\}$				Page 139
	TRANSFER (Statistical)	Selection Mode $\left\{\begin{array}{l}.k,.\text{SNA}j\\ .\text{SNA\$sn},.\text{SNA}*j\end{array}\right\}$	First Block $\left[\begin{array}{l}sn,k,\text{SNA}j,\\ \text{SNA\$sn},\text{SNA}*j\end{array}\right]$	Second Block $\left\{\begin{array}{l}sn,k,\text{SNA}j,\\ \text{SNA\$sn},\text{SNA}*j\end{array}\right\}$				Page 132
	TRANSFER (Unconditional)	Selection Mode Not Used	Next Block Entered $\left\{\begin{array}{l}sn,k,\text{SNA}j,\\ \text{SNA\$sn},\text{SNA}*j\end{array}\right\}$					Page 97
	UNLINK	Name of User Chain $\left\{\begin{array}{l}sn,k,\text{SNA}j,\\ \text{SNA\$sn},\text{SNA}*j\end{array}\right\}$	Next Block for Unlinked Transactions $\left\{\begin{array}{l}sn,k,\text{SNA}j,\\ \text{SNA\$sn},\text{SNA}*j\end{array}\right\}$	Unlink Count $\left\{\begin{array}{l}k,\text{SNA}j,\\ \text{SNA\$sn},\text{SNA}*j\\ \text{ALL}\end{array}\right\}$	Parameter No. $\left[\begin{array}{l}k,\text{SNA}j,\\ \text{SNA\$sn},\text{SNA}*j\end{array}\right]$ or [BACK]	Match Argument $\left[\begin{array}{l}k,\text{SNA}j,\\ \text{SNA\$sn},\text{SNA}*j\end{array}\right]$	Alternate Exit $\left[\begin{array}{l}sn,k,\text{SNA}j,\\ \text{SNA\$sn},\text{SNA}*j\end{array}\right]$	Pages 396 and 422

Index

(These references pertain throughout the
index.)
[a] Also see Appendix L, page 517.
[b] Also see the Index for Case Study use
of Various GPSS Features, page 533.

527

Index for case study use of various GPSS features

GPSS Features		2A	2B	2C	2D	2E	2F	3A	3B	3C	4A	4B	4C	4D	5A	5B	5C	5D	5E	6A	6B	6C	6D	6E	7A	7B	7C	7D
Entities[a]																												
	Facilities	•	•	•			•	•			•	•	•	•		•	•	•	•	•	•	•	•	•	•	•	•	•
Functions	C-type								•			•																
	D-type						•	•																				
	L-type																											
	M-type																											
Logic Switches													•															•
Queues		•	•	•			•			•	•	•						•		•		•		•	•	•	•	
Savevalues	Matrix type																•											
Storages				•	•	•		•			•	•	•			•	•	•	•	•	•	•	•	•		•	•	•
Vector type																•												
Tables	Unweighted															•	•	•		•	•	•	•	•	•		•	•
	Weighted																											
User Chains																				•	•		•					
Variables	Boolean																•	•		•	•		•				•	•
	Integer														•			•		•	•	•		•			•	•
	Real														•	•		•			•				•			
Blocks[b]																												
	ASSEMBLE											•				•	•	•			•	•	•	•	•	•	•	•
	ASSIGN								•	•										•	•		•					
	BUFFER																				•		•					
	GATE																				•	•					•	
	MARK																	•		•	•	•		•	•			
	PRIORITY													•						•			•		•		•	
	SELECT													•								•	•				•	
	SPLIT																					•	•				•	•
	TEST								•					•	•	•	•		•	•	•	•		•		•	•	•
TRANSFER	BOTH mode									•																		
	Statistical						•					•																
	Unconditional				•	•	•	•	•	•		•	•	•	•			•			•							•
Control Cards[c]																												
	CLEAR							•	•	•											•							•
	EQU															•												
	RESET																					•		•	•			
	RMULT														•	•		•			•	•	•	•	•			

Case Studies

533

[a] Blocks corresponding to Entities are not shown. For example, because Queues appears as an entry under "Entities", the Blocks QUEUE and DEPART are not shown under "Blocks". The Blocks GENERATE, ADVANCE, and TERMINATE are used in each case study, therefore they have also been deleted from the "Blocks" list.

[b] Use of the ASSIGN Block implies use of Transaction Parameters in the same case study.

[c] The control cards SIMULATE, START, and END are used in each case study, therefore they have been deleted from the "Control Cards" list. REALLOCATE and JOB have not been used in any of the case studies.